The Oxford Handbook of Justice in the Workplace

OXFORD LIBRARY OF PSYCHOLOGY

Editor in Chief PETER E. NATHAN

The Oxford Handbook of Justice in the Workplace

Edited by

Russell S. Cropanzano and

Maureen L. Ambrose

OXFORD
UNIVERSITY PRESS

OXFORD
UNIVERSITY PRESS

Oxford University Press is a department of the University of Oxford. It furthers the University's objective of excellence in research, scholarship, and education by publishing worldwide.

Oxford New York
Auckland Cape Town Dar es Salaam Hong Kong Karachi
Kuala Lumpur Madrid Melbourne Mexico City Nairobi
New Delhi Shanghai Taipei Toronto

With offices in
Argentina Austria Brazil Chile Czech Republic France Greece
Guatemala Hungary Italy Japan Poland Portugal Singapore
South Korea Switzerland Thailand Turkey Ukraine Vietnam

Oxford is a registered trademark of Oxford University Press in the UK and certain other countries.

Published in the United States of America by
Oxford University Press
198 Madison Avenue, New York, NY 10016

Library of Congress Cataloging-in-Publication Data
The Oxford handbook of justice in the workplace / edited by Russell S. Cropanzano and Maureen L. Ambrose.
pages cm. — (Oxford library of psychology)
Includes bibliographical references and index.
ISBN 978–0–19–998141–0
1. Organizational justice. 2. Employee rights. I. Cropanzano, Russell. II. Ambrose, Maureen L.
HD6971.3.O94 2015
331.01′1—dc23
2014037128

9 8 7 6 5 4 3 2 1
Printed in the United States of America
on acid-free paper

To Carol

—R.C.

To Marshall, the perfect husband and my favorite co-author

—M.L.A.

SHORT CONTENTS

OXFORD LIBRARY OF PSYCHOLOGY

The *Oxford Library of Psychology*, a landmark series of handbooks, is published by Oxford University Press, one of the world's oldest and most highly respected publishers, with a tradition of publishing significant books in psychology. The ambitious goal of the *Oxford Library of Psychology* is nothing less than to span a vibrant, wide-ranging field and, in so doing, to fill a clear market need.

Encompassing a comprehensive set of handbooks, organized hierarchically, the *Library* incorporates volumes at different levels, each designed to meet a distinct need. At one level are a set of handbooks designed broadly to survey the major subfields of psychology; at another are numerous handbooks that cover important current focal research and scholarly areas of psychology in depth and detail. Planned as a reflection of the dynamism of psychology, the *Library* will grow and expand as psychology itself develops, thereby highlighting significant new research that will impact on the field. Adding to its accessibility and ease of use, the *Library* will be published in print and, later on, electronically.

The *Library* surveys psychology's principal subfields with a set of handbooks that capture the current status and future prospects of those major subdisciplines. This initial set includes handbooks of social and personality psychology, clinical psychology, counseling psychology, school psychology, educational psychology, industrial and organizational psychology, cognitive psychology, cognitive neuroscience, methods and measurements, history, neuropsychology, personality assessment, developmental psychology, and more. Each handbook undertakes to review one of psychology's major subdisciplines with breadth, comprehensiveness, and exemplary scholarship. In addition to these broadly conceived volumes, the *Library* also includes a large number of handbooks designed to explore in depth more specialized areas of scholarship and research, such as stress, health and coping, anxiety and related disorders, cognitive development, or child and adolescent assessment. In contrast to the broad coverage of the subfield handbooks, each of these latter volumes focuses on an especially productive, more highly focused line of scholarship and research. Whether at the broadest or most specific level, however, all of the *Library* handbooks offer synthetic coverage that reviews and evaluates the relevant past and present research and anticipates research in the future. Each handbook in the *Library* includes introductory and concluding chapters written by its editor to provide a roadmap to the handbook's table of contents and to offer informed anticipations of significant future developments in that field.

An undertaking of this scope calls for handbook editors and chapter authors who are established scholars in the areas about which they write. Many of the nation's and world's most productive and best-respected psychologists have agreed to edit *Library* handbooks or write authoritative chapters in their areas of expertise.

For whom has the *Oxford Library of Psychology* been written? Because of its breadth, depth, and accessibility, the *Library* serves a diverse audience, including graduate students in psychology and their faculty mentors, scholars, researchers, and practitioners in psychology and related fields. Each will find in the *Library* the information they seek on the subfield or focal area of psychology in which they work or are interested.

Befitting its commitment to accessibility, each handbook includes a comprehensive index, as well as extensive references to help guide research. And because the *Library* was designed from its inception as an online as well as a print resource, its structure and contents will be readily and rationally searchable online. Further, once the *Library* is released online, the handbooks will be regularly and thoroughly updated.

In summary, the *Oxford Library of Psychology* will grow organically to provide a thoroughly informed perspective on the field of psychology, one that reflects both psychology's dynamism and its increasing interdisciplinarity. Once published electronically, the *Library* is also destined to become a uniquely valuable interactive tool, with extended search and browsing capabilities. As you begin to consult this handbook, we sincerely hope you will share our enthusiasm for the more than 500-year tradition of Oxford University Press for excellence, innovation, and quality, as exemplified by the *Oxford Library of Psychology*.

Peter E. Nathan
Editor-in-Chief
Oxford Library of Psychology

ABOUT THE EDITORS

Dr. Russell Cropanzano

Dr. Russell Cropanzano is a professor of management and entrepreneurship at the Leeds School of Business. Dr. Cropanzano's primary research explores workplace justice and behavioral ethics. He has edited four books and published over 120 scholarly articles and chapters. Dr. Cropanzano has also authored two books. The first, *Organizational Justice and Human Resources Management,* won the 1998 Book Award from the International Association of Conflict Management. The second, *Social Justice and the Experience of Emotion,* was released in November of 2011. Dr. Cropanzano was also a winner of the 2000 Outstanding Paper Award from the *Consulting Psychology Journal,* the 2007 Best Paper Award from *Academy of Management Perspectives,* and the 2010 Best Paper Award from the *Journal of Management.* He is a past editor of the *Journal of Management* and a fellow in the Academy of Management, the Society for Industrial/Organizational Psychology, the Southern Management Association, and the Association for Psychological Science.

Maureen L. Ambrose

Maureen L. Ambrose is the Gordon J. Barnett Professor of Business Ethics in the College of Business at the University of Central Florida. Her research interests include organizational fairness, workplace deviance, and ethics. Her work has appeared in the *Academy of Management Journal, Academy of Management Review, Administrative Sciences Quarterly, Journal of Applied Psychology, Journal of Management,* and *Organizational Behavior and Human Decision Processes.* She has served as associate editor for the *Academy of Management Journal* and on editorial boards for the *Academy of Management Journal, Human Resource Management Review, Journal of Applied Psychology, Journal of Organizational Behavior, Journal of Management, Journal of Managerial Issues,* and *Organizational Behavior and Human Decision Processes.* She is an Academy of Management fellow as well as a fellow of the Society for Industrial and Organizational Psychology and the Association for Psychological Science.

ACKNOWLEDGMENTS

Support for this project was provided by the Gordon J. Barnett Memorial Foundation through the Gordon J. Barnett Professorship in Business Ethics.

CONTRIBUTORS

Maureen L. Ambrose
Department of Management
College of Business Administration
University of Central Florida
Orlando, FL

Laurie J. Barclay
School of Business and Economics
Wilfrid Laurier University
Waterloo, CA

Talya N. Bauer
School of Business Administration
Portland State University
Portland, OR

Robert J. Bies
McDonough School of Business
Georgetown University
Washington, DC

Steven L. Blader
Stern School of Business
New York University
New York, NY

D. Ramona Bobocel
Department of Psychology
University of Waterloo
Waterloo, CA

Lauren A. Borden
The University of Akron
Department of Psychology
Akron, OH

Kenneth D. Butterfield
Carson College of Business
Washington State University
Pullman, WA

Matthew L. Call
Moore School of Business
University of South Carolina
Columbia, SC

Caitlin M. Cavanaugh
The University of Akron
Department of Psychology
Akron, OH

Irina Cojuharenco
Católica Lisbon School of Business and Economics
Portuguese Catholic University, Palma de Cima
Lisbon, PT

Jason A. Colquitt
Terry College of Business
University of Georgia
Athens, GA

Russell S. Cropanzano
Management and Entrepreneurship Division
Leeds School of Business
University of Colorado at Boulder
Boulder, CO

Robert Folger
Department of Management
College of Business Administration
University of Central Florida
Orlando, FL

Marion Fortin
Center for Research in Management
University of Toulouse 1 Capitole
France

Noelle B. Frantz
The University of Akron
Department of Psychology
Akron, OH

David R. Glerum
Industrial/Organizational Psychology
University of Central Florida
Orlando, FL

Barry Goldman
Eller College of Business
University of Arizona
Tucson, AZ
Jerry Goodstein
Carson College of Business
Washington State University
Vancouver, WA
Leanne Gosse
Department of Psychology
University of Waterloo
Waterloo, CA
Matthew D. Griffith
Department of Management
College of Business Administration
University of Central Florida
Orlando, FL
Ronald L. Hess, Jr.
School of Business Administration
The College of William & Mary
Williamsburg, VA
Keith James
Department of Psychology
Portland State University
Portland, OR
Michael A. Johnson
Department of Management
College of Business Administration
University of Central Florida
Orlando, FL
Ali Kazemi
School of Health and Education
University of Skövde
Skövde, Sweden
M. Audrey Korsgaard
Moore School of Business
University of South Carolina
Columbia, SC
Carol T. Kulik
School of Management
University of South Australia
Adelaide, AU
James J. Lavelle
Department of Management
College of Business
University of Texas
Arlington, TX
Melvin J. Lerner
Distinguished Professor Emeritus
Department of Psychology
University of Waterloo
Waterloo, CA
Paul E. Levy
The University of Akron
Department of Psychology
Akron, OH
Andrew Li
Department of Management
College of Business
West Texas A & M University
Canyon, TX
Yiqiong Li
UQ Business School
University of Queensland
Brisbane, AU
E. Allan Lind
Fuqua School of Business
Duke University
Durham, NC
Jennifer Manegold
Department of Management
College of Business
University of Texas
Arlington, TX
Suzanne S. Masterson
Department of Management
Carl H. Lindner College of Business
University of Cincinnati
Cincinnati, OH
Julie M. McCarthy
Department of Management
University of Toronto
Toronto, CA
Bruce M. Meglino
Moore School of Business
University of South Carolina
Columbia, SC
Agustin Molina
Department of Personnel & Employment Relations
Kemmy Business School
University of Limerick
Limerick, IE

Elizabeth Mullen
Department of Management
George Washington University School of Business
Washington, DC
Tyler G. Okimoto
Department of Management
University of Queensland Business School
Brisbane, AU
Dr. James Olver
School of Business Administration
The College of William & Mary
Williamsburg, VA
Jane O'Reilly
Telfer School of Management
University of Ottawa
Ottawa, CA
David Patient
Católica Lisbon School of Business and Economics
Portuguese Catholic University, Palma de Cima
Lisbon, PT
Devon Proudfoot
Fuqua School of Business
Duke University
Durham, NC
Darryl Rice
Department of Management
Farmer School of Business
Miami University
Oxford, OH
Jessica B. Rodell
Department of Management
Terry College of Business
University of Georgia
Athens, GA
Deborah E. Rupp
Department of Psychological Sciences
College of Health and Human Sciences/
Krannert School of Management
Purdue University
West Lafayette, IN
Maria Francisca Saldanha
School of Business and Economics
Wilfrid Laurier University
Waterloo, CA
Marshall Schminke
Department of Management
College of Business Administration
University of Central Florida
Orlando, FL
Debra L. Shapiro
Department of Management and Organization
University of Maryland
College Park, MD
Elad N. Sherf
Department of Management and Organization
University of Maryland
College Park, MD
Daniel P. Skarlicki
Sauder School of Business
University of British Columbia
Vancouver, CA
M. Susan Taylor
Department of Human Resources and Organizational Change
Robert H. Smith School of Business
University of Maryland
College Park, MD
Meghan A. Thornton
Department of Psychological Sciences
College of Health and Human Sciences
Purdue University
West Lafayette, IN
Nathan Tong
Department of Management
Carl H. Linder College of Business
University of Cincinnati
Cincinnati, OH
Kjell Törnblom
ETH Zurich
Department of Environmental Systems Science
USYS TdLab, CH
Thomas M. Tripp
Department of Management, Information Systems, and Entrepreneurship
Washington State University
Vancouver, WA

Donald M. Truxillo
Department of Psychology
Portland State University
Portland, OR

Tom R. Tyler
Yale Law School
New Haven, CT

Kees van den Bos
Department of Social Psychology
Utrecht University
Utrecht, The Netherlands

Sara L. Wheeler-Smith
Department of Management
Warrington College of Business Administration
University of Florida
Gainesville, FL

Batia M. Wiesenfeld
Stern School of Business
New York University
New York, NY

David X. H. Wo
Department of Management
College of Business Administration
University of Central Florida
Orlando, FL

CONTENTS

PART 1

Structure of Justice

CHAPTER

1 Organizational Justice: Where We Have Been and Where We Are Going

Russell S. Cropanzano *and* Maureen L. Ambrose

Abstract

This chapter provides an introduction to the *Handbook of Justice in the Workplace*. It begins with a brief review of the foundation of organizational justice and the organizational justice paradigm. Next, we provide an overview of the *Handbook*. We identify areas of growth and change in the organizational justice literature and describe the structure of the volume. Specifically, the *Handbook* is organized into four sections: the structure of justice, perspectives on justice, justice and conflict, and applications of justice. We provide a brief description of the contents of the *Handbook* for each section. We invite scholars to delve into some or all the chapters, because each provides new insights about organizational justice.

Key Words: organizational justice, workplace fairness, review of justice, organizational fairness, workplace justice

This is a book about "justice," an elusive noun that is seldom easy to define. Confronting a review of this daunting topic, it is perhaps most manageable to begin this volume by simply listing a few attributes of this old idea. We can begin with the sorts of characteristics that everyone could agree on and then build upward from there. For one thing, we know that justice is a broadly applicable quality. Much as salt can be used to enhance the flavor of many different foods, justice can be widely applied to a wide variety of outcomes, processes, and behaviors. Beyond its breadth, we also know that the word *justice* suggests or connotes a kind of moral correctness or ethical appropriateness. In particular, justice is present when people have what they deserve or have been treated as they deserve to be treated. For instance, it is rather easy to imagine situations in which people receive favorable outcomes that they do not deserve (e.g., Price, 2010) or unfavorable outcomes that they do deserve (e.g., Treviño & Weaver, 2010). This insinuation of morality tells us that justice is not economic favorability, though sometimes people are prone to egocentrically confuse the two (Cropanzano & Moliner, 2013).

The concept of justice, therefore, tells us something about how the normal human mind operates. The yardstick of economic value is not the only measure that human beings employ (Appiah, 2008; Fiske, 1991). Most of us are also concerned with "right" and "wrong" (Greene, 2013). We would not automatically designate an outcome as *just* if the only thing that it did was to provide something favorable. Rather, we reserve *justice* for those situations in which people get what they deserve (Folger & Salvador, 2008), not necessarily (or at least not only) for whether things turn out to be good or bad. Justice implies that normatively correct outcomes have been assigned in a morally appropriate way. It involves what people receive (distributive justice), the allocation process (procedural justice), and the interpersonal treatment along the way (interactional justice). There could be other things as well, but we'll save those for later chapters. For the moment, let us consider matters in a general way.

In order to behave justly, people need to at least be able to evaluate outcomes, procedures, and interpersonal behavior. This brings us to a central theme in the justice literature, for individuals need some sort of guidelines or standards for making these judgments. Speaking broadly, appraising an event requires a set of normative standards. These are presumably stored in memory and capable of activation for use (Cugeró-Escofet & Rosanas, 2013). These rules or criteria can then be compared to actual or potential events in the real world. If there is a mismatch between what should have been done (specified by the normative standards) and what has been done (specified by the actual behavior), then fairness is likely to be called into question (van der Toorn, Berkics, & Jost, 2010). Batson (1999, p. 303) and Blader and Tyler (2001, p. 235) refer to this process as "principlism."

These observations are important, as they allow us to place boundaries around the broad notions we have been discussing. Though the word justice is broadly applicable, it also has its limits. While just behaviors are moral behaviors, all moral behaviors are not necessarily just (Blader & Tyler, 2001; Cropanzano & Stein, 2009). You can do a morally good thing without doing a fair one. For example, everyone would agree that compassion is a laudable ethical quality. However, compassion, which suggest sympathy and a desire to provide assistance, can lead one to provide preferential advantage to some people at the expense of others (Batson, Klein, Highberger, & Shaw, 1995; Blader & Rothman, 2014). Justice is an aspect of morality or a way of being moral, but there are other ways.

Our picture is becoming a bit clearer. Justice is not necessarily economic benefit, nor does it necessarily involve compassion, though it may be correlated with each. Rather, justice is the application and use of a set of moral principles for guiding the manner in which one behaves toward other people, at least with respect to outcome distributions, decision processes, and interpersonal treatment (Fortin & Fellenz, 2008). These principles can be applied carefully and deliberately or else they can be applied automatically and heuristically (Bobocel, McCline, & Folger, 1997; Goldman & Thatcher, 2002). Although having an emotional connection to another person appears to enhance justice (Patient & Skarlicki, 2010), justice principles might be workable even without this emotional tie (Blader & Tyler, 2001).

It is because of these unique properties that justice is able to meet two major challenges of social life, including work life. First, many important activities are performed most effectively when people work collaboratively toward common goals. These include everything from big game hunting with spears (Boehm, 2012) to operating large and diversified organizations (Connolly, Conlon, & Deutsch, 1980). Cooperation is facilitated to the extent that people are valued by the group (Tyler & Blader, 2000) and that their interests—at least over the long run—will be taken into account. Justice signals that people are viewed as worthwhile and important (Smith, Tyler, Huo, Ortiz, & Lind, 1998). Second, when working as part of an organization or community, low-power individuals are at risk of exploitation from others. Lind (1995, p. 86) refers to this as the "fundamental organizational dilemma." Not only is exploitation personally painful it could also be very costly to the individual. Justice obviates this concern, by demonstrating that those with power are making decisions with some moral grounding. As such, employees are at less risk and can be more trusting (e.g., van den Bos, Wilke, & Lind, 1998). For these reasons, considerations of justice will almost always be important when individuals are thrust into the give-and-take of cooperation and sharing.

The Organizational Justice Paradigm

Given the central place of justice in group life, it should come as no surprise to discover that considerable scholarly effort has gone into understanding justice. Each of these approaches brings its own paradigm. For example, philosophers generally take a normative approach to fairness (though for an exception, see Appiah, 2008). They seek underlying principles that make some things just and other things unjust (Bird, 1967). For this reason, the philosophical agenda is prescriptive (Blackburn, 2001). It strives to advise people as to how others should be treated (Allen, 2004) and how public policy should be formulated (Sandel, 2009). This is an important approach to fairness, but it is not the only one.

A somewhat different approach is taken by legal studies. Legal justice has a number of characteristics that distinguish it from both philosophical justice and organizational justice. Legal justice pays close attention to substantive due process. This involves rules that are rationally based on the characteristics of the case at hand, rather than being coercive and unpredictable (Abadinsky, 2003). Among other things, these rules are enacted by legitimate authorities (Skogan & Frydl, 2004) and applied to individuals in a disinterested manner (Sadurski, 1985). The legal approach is partly prescriptive (it seeks to determine what is just) and partly descriptive (it provides guiding principles). Clearly, the legal and the organizational justice tradition share important elements in common, but although one can inform the other (e.g., Thibaut & Walker, 1975; 1978), there remains more to the story.

Within the domain of organizational justice, the topic of this book, justice is approached as an empirical and subjective concept. Management scholars, like many other behavioral scientists, treat justice as an evaluation or perception that pertains to some outcome, interpersonal interaction, and so forth. These judgments can be empirically assessed, such as through a survey, but they are also subjective. That is, organizational scientists tend to emphasize individual and group perceptions of justice. The research agenda is also descriptive, because it explores the antecedents and consequences of justice judgments. Consequently, the topics in this book will draw on legal and philosophical studies, but they are not isomorphic with those older branches of knowledge. The collected papers included in this volume will, instead, emphasize empirical investigations regarding the structure of fairness perceptions, their antecedents, their impact on organizations, and methods for increasing justice.

Overview of the Present Handbook

Our goal for this *Handbook* was both modest and ambitious. We sought to compile a set of comprehensive reviews of research on justice in the workplace. All our authors have provided such reviews, although many have gone beyond and provided new models, identified new challenges raised by existing work, and provided thoughts for future research. We enthusiastically embrace these additions. We believe they serve readers well and reflect the dynamic nature of the field of organizational justice—a field with a strong history and a strong future.

One issue we considered in undertaking this project was the need for such a book. The first handbook that addressed organizational justice was published slightly less than a decade ago (Greenberg & Colquitt, 2005). Has the field of justice changed substantially since that time to warrant another handbook? We believe the answer to that question is a resounding "Yes!" Indeed, a quick review of the table of contents for the two volumes provides some insight to the development of the field. Although certain topics are represented in both (distributive justice, procedural justice, interactional justice, the fair process effect, justice and morality), the content of these chapters shows that these fundamental areas of justice continue to evolve. In addition to these chapters, a variety of new topics appear in the current volume. These chapters reflect emerging areas in justice research—overall justice, justice climate, third-party justice, justice and time, justice and emotion—areas that had received scant attention ten years ago. The current handbook also includes chapters on areas of justice that have received some attention over the years and warrant a forum in which this research can be brought together in a meaningful way (e.g., justice and culture, justice and structure, justice and organizational change). Finally, there are chapters that provide new perspectives on workplace fairness by integrating work from other areas (e.g., justice recovery, the social construction of justice, justice and complaint handling, workplace justice and legal justice).

In all, we commend the contributors to this handbook. They have exceeded our expectations. We have each been studying organizational justice for over 30 years and are deeply embedded in the literature—both classic work (much of which was "new research" when we first read it!) and current research. Yet, as we read each chapter, we learned something new. This new insight sometime came from recent research, sometimes from work we had forgotten, and often from the connections and analysis the author provided for research we know well. Thus, we are confident that each of these chapters will be of interest to readers—whether they are exploring justice for the first time, or are, as we are, seasoned veterans of justice research.

Below we provide a brief description of the handbook sections and a brief summary of each of the chapters. We hope this will serve as a guide for readers as they explore this volume. Whether you read one chapter or all the chapters, we know you will come away with both a clear overview of the state of research in that area and some interesting new insights. This *Handbook* provides not only a review of where we have been but also a roadmap of where we might go.

Part I: Structure of Justice

Following this present introductory chapter, we turn to the substantive topics. We begin with chapters providing reviews of the building blocks of organizational justice research and address the structure of organizational fairness. These chapters include the standard facet approach to fairness—distributive, procedural, and interactional—as well as more recent developments in how we might conceptualize and study organizational fairness. Specifically, the chapters consider overall justice, multifoci justice, unit-level justice, and the measurement fairness perceptions.

Chapter 2: *Distributive Justice: Revisiting Past Statements and Reflecting on Future Prospects.* Törnblom and Kazemi begin with a historical review of distributive justice. They note the importance of knowing the past if we are to make new discoveries in the future. Törnblom and Kazemi provide a comprehensive review of models of justice relevant to the allocation of resources. They also describe both the nuance and complexity typically overlooked by researchers in their discussions of the three dominant allocation rules (equity, equality, and need). Further, they focus our attention on allocation principles beyond these standards. Törnblom and Kazemi utilize Social Resource Theory (Foa, 1971; Foa & Foa, 1974) to highlight the breadth of resources that are relevant in allocation decision. They discuss the importance of the nature of the resource allocated and raise question about the role of the means of production in the evaluation of the fairness of the resource allocation decision. Törnblom and Kazemi address the role of the situation and the context in affecting the perceived fairness of allocation rules, including the consideration of the conditions under which injustice goes unnoticed and when injustice is seen as just.

Chapter 3: *Procedural Justice in Work Organizations: An Historical Review.* The second chapter in this section, authored by Bobocel and Grosse, traces the development of procedural justice conceptually, theoretically, and empirically. The chapter is organized into four parts. Bobocel and Grosse begin with the emergence and early development of procedural justice, including theoretical and empirical work addressing the relationship between procedural and interactional justice. The second part of the chapter examines procedural justice in the workplace. Bobocel and Grosse describe research examining the differential effects of procedural and distributive justice, procedural and interactional justice, and interactions among the types of fairness. In the third part of the chapter, Bobocel and Grosse review the theoretical perspectives used to explain why people care about procedural justice. Finally, they explore recent research that examines limitations to the "fair process effect." Specifically, they describe research that asks the question, "is procedural justice is always beneficial?" In all, Bobocel and Grosse's chapter is a tour de force on procedural justice, balancing both breadth and depth and provides insights both for newcomers to justice research and for justice veterans.

Chapter 4: *Interactional Justice: Looking Backward, Looking Forward.* Bies begins his chapter on interactional justice with an insider's view of the evolution of the construct. He describes his early interest in justice and interpersonal treatment and how that interest evolved into the study of interactional justice. Bies summarizes the research on interactional justice, noting the strength of the effects and the broad range of organizational processes and outcomes in which it has been studied. Utilizing Feinberg's (1974) framework that distinguishes between comparative and noncomparative principles of justice, Bies suggests interactional justice is fundamentally different than procedural and distributive justice. Specifically, he argues that noncomparative principles, truth and human dignity, underlie interactional justice. Finally, considering attributes of truth and human dignitiy, Bies suggests implications of these principles for organizational encounters. Bies ends his chapter with three questions to provoke readers into thought and into action.

Chapter 5: *Overall Justice: Past, Present, and Future.* In the fourth chapter, Ambrose, Wo, and Griffith address the issue of overall justice. Although the concept of overall justice can be found in early justice literature, interest in overall justice and its relationship to justice facets are relatively recent. Ambrose et al. review the early work on overall justice as well as the burgeoning empirical research in this area. Ambrose et al. structure their review by the conceptual role overall justice plays in the research (e.g., as an independent variable, mediator, dependent variable, and moderator). Ambrose et al. conclude their chapter with an identification of trends in the existing research and areas in need of additional study.

Chapter 6: *Fairness at the Unit Level: Justice Climate, Justice Climate Strength, and Peer Justice.* The chapter by Li, Cropanzano, and Molina also explores an emerging area in organizational justice—fairness at the unit level. Justice research has typically focused on individual-level perceptions. Li et al. identify and review recent research that considers justice at the group level as a shared perception. Li et al. distinguish between two types of group-level perceptions: justice climate and peer justice. Justice climate research examines group members' shared perceptions of how the group is treated by authorities. Peer justice is group members' shared perceptions of how group members treat each other. The chapter provides reviews of the climate emergence process, empirical work examining justice climate level, justice climate strength literature, and a review of the peer justice literature. Li et al. conclude with a discussion of future directions in justice climate research, including issues reflected elsewhere in this section of the *Handbook*—overall justice climate, the measurement of justice climate, and multiple sources relevant to the emergence of justice climate.

Chapter 7: *Multifoci Justice and Target Similarity: Emerging Research and Extensions.* Lavelle, Rupp, Manegold, and Thorton review research on the multifoci perspective and its successor, the target similarity perspective to organizational justice. In contrast to traditional justice research that has focused on types of justice (i.e., distributive, procedural, interactional), the multifoci perspective focuses on the different sources or parties that employees see as accountable for fairness (or unfairness) at work. The multifoci perspective suggests employees experience fairness from a range of sources (e.g., the organization, coworkers, customers) and are likely to have unique experiences with each of these different parties. The target similarity perspective extends the multifoci perspective by suggesting employees react to each source of fairness, such that behavior is targeted at the source of (un)fairness. Lavelle et al. review research on these perspectives and contrast a type versus source conceptualization of organizational fairness. Lavelle et al. suggest a source-based approach to justice provides a more nuanced understanding of how employees experience and react to fairness in the workplace. In considering future directions, they suggest researchers examine a broader range of justice sources (e.g., co-workers, customers, clients, unions) and examine the interactive influence of different sources of fairness. Finally, they identify novel outcomes, new contexts, and the consideration of fairness targeted at external constituents as areas that arise from a multifoci/target similarity perspective.

Chapter 8: *Measuring Justice and Fairness.* Colquitt and Rodell tackle the important topic of measuring justice. Not surprisingly, their chapter addresses many of the issues raised in the other chapters in the *Handbook*: facet versus global, types versus sources, experience bracketing, and context. Contrary to the common interchangability of the terms *justice* and *fairness,* Colquitt and Rodell use the term *justice* to refer to "the perceived adherence to rules that reflect the appropriateness in decision contexts" and provide a list of such rules for procedural, distributive, interpersonal, and informational concepts. Measures of justice, therefore, are similar to what have previously been referred to as *indirect* measures (Colquitt & Shaw, 2005). In contrast, Colquitt and Rodell use the term *fairness* to refer to "a global perception of appropriateness." Thus, "fairness is theoretically 'downstream' from justice" (p. 188). Measures of fairness are similar to what has previously been referred to as *direct* measures. Colquitt and Rodell introduce a 2 x 2 taxonomy that distinguishes between an emphasis on justice and fairness and the emphasis on dimensional distinctions. Colquitt and Rodell also address measurement issues associated with emerging conversations in the justice literature. Specifically, they consider the measurement of anticipations and expectations, within person assessments of justice/fairness, supervisors' perceptions of their justice/fairness behaviors, and the conceptual distinctiveness of injustice. The chapter reminds us that organizational justice is a dynamic field. As research in justice evolves, the measurement of justice must similarly evolve. Advancement in the field requires measures capable of tapping our constructs of interest.

Part II: Perspectives on Justice

The second section of the *Handbook* provides a set of chapters that raise the issue of perspective and justice. Each chapter demonstrates how perspective influences reactions to fairness—both for participants in justice events and for researchers who choose to study fairness.

Chapter 9: *Understanding How the Justice Motive Shapes Our Lives and Treatment of One Another: Exciting Contributions and Misleading Claims.* Lerner explores the development and influence of the justice motive. Lerner is critical of current justice research, raising questions about its abilities to distinguish justice motives from other motives. Lerner reviews research suggesting the Personal Contract Theory provides an explanation for the origins of the justice motive. Further, he suggests preconscious scripts and controlled norm-based conventions determine the justice motives influence on social behavior. Finally, Lerner takes researchers to task. He suggests researchers confuse preconscious beliefs that "I am better" with self-interested motives and suggests that "the basic research underlying the emphasis and importance of procedural versus distributive justice has been deeply flawed in both theory and methods almost from its inception" (p. 228). His review requires organizational justice researchers to rethink their assumptions and broaden their perspective.

Chapter 10: ***The Third Party Perspective of (In)justice***. In their chapter on third-party perspective of justice, Skarlicki, O'Reilly, and Kulik structure their review around the model of third-party justice presented by Skarlicki and Kulik (2005). They then note three recent developments in the third-party literature and discuss evolutionary mechanisms that incorporate both moral and self-interested motives for third-party reactions, third-party reactions aimed at helping the victim of injustice (rather than punishing the transgressor), and the role of "hot" versus "cold" emotional processes in third-party reactions. These recent developments are incorporated into a revised and extended model of third-party reactions.

Chapter 11: ***Organizational Justice and Legal Justice: How Are They Related?*** Goldman takes on the challenge of bridging the worlds of organizational justice and legal justice. As Goldman notes, "even a casual reading of the scholarship and application of 'justice,' in these disciplines indicates that the two set of scholars are not speaking the same language" (p. 257). Thus, Goldman provides a rosetta stone for organizational scholars to help them understand, appreciate, and benefit from the different perspective provided from the legal view of justice. Goldman identifies differences in the underlying assumptions of legal and organizational justice. He notes that early interest in organizational justice was often associated with issues relevant to the legal systems. This included (Thibaut & Walker, 1975; 1978; Lind et al., 1990; Lind, Kulik, Ambrose & deVera, 1993), and police (Tyler, 1987; Tyler & Folger, 1980), Goldman notes organizational researchers' interests in outcomes relevant to the legal system (e.g., litigation, legal claiming), and identifies areas for future research that may benefit both organizational and legal scholars.

Chapter 12: ***Culture and Organizational Justice: State of the Literature and Suggestions for Future Directions***. James examines the relationship between justice and culture and how culture may shape individuals' perspective on justice. James notes the increased interest in recent years in the relationship between justice and culture. Yet, he proposes most previous research has not fully considered the complexity and nuance of the integration of culture as a multilevel construct and justice as a multilevel construct or adequately integrated the interrelationships between justice and culture with other organizational constructs. Based on his review, James identifies current gaps in current culture and justice research and develops a model that incorporates leadership, teams, identity, justice, and culture and provides a guide for future research in the area.

Chapter 13: ***Justice Perception Formation in Social Settings***. In the fifth chapter in this section, Masterson and Tong examine the social construction of justice perceptions. Masterson and Tong note that most justice research ignores the influence of the social setting on individuals' assessments of justice. Yet, a careful review of the literature reveals a body of research that demonstrates how social context influences justice formation. Masterson and Tong examine three processes by which the social context affects perceptions of justice: social comparisons, social information processing, and sense-making. Further, the authors go beyond the traditional focus on targets. They examine not only the influence of social context on employees' perceptions, but also how actors (e.g., managers) may use social information to shape subordinates' perceptions of fairness. They describe work that demonstrate the influence of social networks, organizational culture, and organizational climate on justice perceptions, and they conclude the review section with a discussion of justice contagion. Finally, they pose a set of research questions as a starting point for future investigation.

Chapter 14: ***The "When" of Justice Events and Why It Matters***. Patient, Cojuharenco, and Fortin take a temporal perspective on justice. In their chapter, they review the influence of temporal characteristics on perceptions of and reactions to organizational justice. Patient et al. find that despite repeated calls for longitudinal research, the vast amount of research on organizational justice is cross-sectional. Yet, a small, but important body of theoretical and empirical justice work has begun to directly address the influence of time-relevant dimensions on justice perceptions and reactions to justice. Patient et al. focus on three aspects of temporal justice research: (1) justice theorizing in relation to time, (2) temporal dynamics of justice events (the timing of events, the frequency of events, and duration and trajectory of events), and (3) temporal perspective of justice events (anticipations of future justice events, a focus on past or future events, recency/distance of the event, length of the episode considered). Patient et al. demonstrate that this small, but growing area holds substantial promise for enhancing our understanding of justice by explicitly incorporating time into the study of organizational justice.

Part III: Psychological Processes and Motivation

As we have already seen, the organization justice perspective is descriptive and empirical. It does not necessary tell us what *is* fair, but rather focuses on what people believe to be fair (and unfair). Broadly speaking, this paradigm requires that researchers address two closely related issues. Content approaches emphasize the underlying concerns that animate justice, such as social standing (the relational model) and moral principles (the deontic model). Process approaches emphasize the manner in which fairness judgments are made, such as though the use of fairness heuristics, as well as psychological influences on these judgments, such as emotion. All these matters are discussed in the six chapters that comprise this section.

Chapter 15: ***Justice and Deonance: "You Ought to be Fair."*** Folger and Glerum discuss the deontic model of justice, reviewing considerable evidence consistent with it. The theory argues that many people possess internalized moral duties. These duties oblige individuals to behalf fairly and also to enforce norms of justice. Folger and Glerum review related conceptual framework, which make similar observations about justice. They also review empirical work. Finding, for example, that individuals will forgo economic gains in order to punish an individual that has putatively behaved unjustly.

Chapter 16: ***The Relational Model of Justice.*** Tyler and Blader discuss the influential relational model of justice. According to the relational model, justice—especially formal and informal procedures—signals that an individual is valued by a desirable social group. For this reason, fair process helps authority members to establish legitimacy and promote voluntary sacrifices that benefit the group. Unjust treatment, with its signal of poor social standing, lowers social self-esteem and reduces cooperation within the group.

Chapter 17: ***Fairness Heuristic Theory, the Uncertainty Management Model, and Fairness at Work.*** According to Proudfoot and Lind, members of groups face a "fundamental social dilemma." Although there are many advantages of being part of a group, there are also risks of exploitation and exclusion. Fair treatment from authors, including those in authority, signals that one is a respected and value member. For this reason, people are attentive to justice in their work environments. In order to make fairness evaluations efficiently, individuals employ fairness heuristics. The heuristics are useful, though they are prone to many of the biases that affect other human decisions. Proudfoot and Lind conclude their chapter with a consideration of System Justification Theory and suggest how the System Justification Theory might be integrated with Fairness Heuristic Theory and Uncertainty Management Theory to provide a more complete understanding of fairness.

Chapter 18: ***The Role of Concern for Others in Reactions to Justice: Integrating the Theory of Other Orientation with Organizational Justice.*** Korsgaard, Meglino, and Call discuss other orientation and its implications for organizational justice. According to Korsgaard and her colleagues, individuals high on other orientation, as compared to their counterparts who are lower, are less focused on their personal economic self-interest or on deontic concerns. Other orientation has trait-like qualities, as it exists as a stable individual difference. However, there are also aspects of the situation that make others more or less salient.

Chapter 19: ***Humans Making Sense of Alarming Conditions: Psychological Insight into the Fair Process Effect.*** In this chapter van den Bos explores the "fair process effect." As van den Bos observes, individuals care about how they are treated; we are mindful of more than outcomes. Van den Bos suggests that considerations of process help us to understand potentially troublesome situations. Notably, van den Bos suggests it is more appropriate to discuss a "fair treatement effect." He argues that the term *process* refers not only to the perceived fairness of formal procedures, but also to the fairness people experience in interactions with other. He argues the perceived fairness of interpersonal treatment is an essential part of what has become known in the literature as the fair process effect. Finally, van den Bos introduces research on the human alarm system. He suggests when something alarming transpires people seek information as to its causes and consequences. Formal and informal processes tell individuals a great deal about what happened to them and what is likely to occur in the future.

Chapter 20: ***Justice and Affect: A Dimensional Approach.*** In this important chapter, Fortin, Blader, Wiesenfeld, and Wheeler-Smith review theory and research pertaining to justice and affect. Fortin and her colleagues consider the principle dimensions of affect, such as valance (good/bad), focus (inward/outward), and arousal (high/low). They then review and integrate a number of theories of justice from the perspective of these affective dimensions. The authors find that each theory of justice is especially pertinent to a different dimension of affect.

Part IV: Justice and Conflict

Ever since French (1964) coined the term *organizational justice,* conflict has been a central topic for researchers. Our present book is no exception. We present five chapters. The first two emphasizing the causes of conflict, the latter three emphasizing solutions for resolving these conflicts.

Chapter 21: ***The Role of Conflict in Managing Injustice.*** Shapiro and Sherf provide the reader with an overview of the literature on organizational conflict, though told from the perspective of workplace fairness. Toward this end, the authors discuss different types of conflict, especially task, process, and relationship. They further observe that conflict, broadly defined, involves some type of goal blockage. When this goal blockage violates a social norm, then a sense of injustice is likely to result. Shapiro and Sherf also consider the conflict management literature, thereby analyzing a number of potential tactics for resolving conflict.

Chapter 22: ***"Doing Justice": The Role of Motives for Revenge in the Workplace.*** Tripp and Bies provide a thorough review of the literature on revenge. A key insight from their work is that people who engage in retaliatory behavior often view themselves as doing justice. Their seemingly antisocial acts are undertaken to restore a sense of fairness. Though revenge-seeking can sometimes create problems for organizations, Bies and Tripp demonstrate that there can be beneficial consequences as well. In particular, workplace revenge can sometimes prompt positive social change, especially when other opportunities have been closed off.

Chapter 23: ***Compensatory Justice.*** Mullen and Okimoto consider how injustice can be alleviated once a transgression has occurred. To do so, they build a comprehensive model of compensatory justice. Mullen and Okimoto observe that different types of transgressions activate different types of concerns. Thus, a suitable solution for one problem may be less appropriate for another. For instance, instrumental concerns could be address through equitable compensation. Apologies are expedient for addressing relational concerns. The authors also discuss a number of individual differences that determine the effectiveness of various forms of compensation.

Chapter 24: ***Recovery from Organizational Injustice: New Directions in Theory and Research.*** Injustice can take a terrible toll on people. Barclay and Saldanha argue that there are ways to recover from injustice that need not involve "dark side" behaviors, such as revenge seeking. They review research that takes the employee's perspective, understanding how an individual heals him or herself after a serious experience of injustice. Toward this end, they consider the effectiveness of such things as emotional expression, forgiveness, trust repair, and a number of psychological interventions.

Chapter 25: ***Restorative Justice.*** According to Goodstein and Butterfield, restorative justice is a "dialogue between stakeholders." Restorative justice seeks to repair the harm that injustice does to people and relationships. It is a vital tool, allowing organizations and communities to grow and learn. Goodstein and Butterfield discuss the key features of restorative justice, such as making amends and forgiveness. They further review the research evidence attesting to its effectiveness.

Part VI: Applications of Justice

The final section of the *Handbook* examines applications of justice. The chapters in this section reflect the broadening of justice. Early justice research focused on narrow applications of justice theory, such as advance notice in drug testing and voice in performance appraisal (for an review of this initial work, see Cropanzano & Greenberg, 1997). Current research on justice applications has moved beyond these narrow questions and focuses on how to build justice into the fabric of organizations, their structures, their climates, their policies, and their procedures. Each of these chapters provides a comprehensive review of justice relevant to a particular aspect of organizations. As a whole, the set of chapters demonstrates the relevance of justice to organizational life and provide guidance for going beyond fair policies and procedures to developing fair organizations.

Chapter 26: ***Justice and Organizational Structure.*** Schminke, Johnson, and Rice provide the most macro-examination of justice. Schminke et al. review 30 years of empirical research linking justice and structure. Specifically, they review the relationship between justice and bureaucracy, organic-mechanistic structure, formalization, centralization, formal power and authority, size and complexity, task interdependence, communication systems, structure as a form of leadership and hierarchical level. Schminke et al.'s review illustrates "structure is tightly interwoven with the emergence and impact of justice judgments" (p. 556). Structure plays a direct, mediating, and moderating role in the relationship between justice perceptions and justice-relevant outcomes. And, as Schminke et al. note, structure is a resource managers and organizations can use to promote fairness and alleviate the negative consequences of unfairness. The work on structure provides guidance for building fairness into the very bones of the organization.

Chapter 27: *The Fork in the Road: Diversity Management and Organizational Justice.* Kulik and Li review research on diversity management and organizational justice. Kulik and Li identify two primary approaches to diversity management: identity blind and identity conscious. Drawing on Cropanzano, Rupp, Mohler, & Schminke's (1999) three roads to justice, Kulik and Li analyze each of these approaches. Next, Kulik and Li address two aspects of diversity management research—work on diversity climate and work on affirmative action—to illustrate how research on justice might help inform work in these areas. They suggest ways diversity management researchers might incorporate justice constructs into their theory building and theory testing and gain greater insight into diversity-management practices that create and sustain employees' perceptions of fairness.

Chapter 28: *The Role of Work Place Justice in the Midst of Organizational Change.* Taylor reviews the literature on justice and organizational change. In the chapter, Taylor categorizes articles according to the type of change pursued and by the role that workplace justice plays in the article. For each section, she highlights one article that exemplifies research in the area and identifies commonalities—and lack of commonality—in the findings of the research. Taylor provides an integrative section centered on five research questions addressing (1) the frequency and influence of types of justice examined in the organizational change literature; (2) theories and conceptual frameworks utilized in the change literature; (3) the influence of perceived justice on the overall effectiveness and success of organizational change; (4) the major theoretical and practical contributions provided by the current research; and (5) future research that would enable a better understanding of the role that workplace justice plays in the processes of organizational change. In all, Taylor provides not only a comprehensive review of the justice and organizational change literature but also a synthesis and analysis of this work that increases our understanding and provides researchers a roadmap for extending our understanding of how justice can be a driver of successful change.

Chapter 29: *The Role of Due Process in Performance Appraisal: A 20 Year Retrospective.* Levy, Cavanaugh, Frantz, and Borden provide a review of justice and performance appraisal. First, using the due process metaphor introduced by Folger, Konovsky, and Cropanzano (1992), Levy et al. provide a review of empirical work that has examined the due process approach to performance appraisal. Specifically, Levy et al. review research that has investigated the three elements of due process: adequate notice, a fair hearing, and judgment based on evidence. Second, Levy et al. describe systemic (e.g., communication, training) and interpersonal (e.g., rater and rate characteristics) characteristics that influence the success of the due process approach to performance appraisal. Third, Levy et al. identify applications of the due process approach in non-Western contexts—and describe the (generally successful) results of these applications. However, they suggest researcher and practitioners should carefully consider if the due process approach should be applied in other cultural contexts. Finally, Levy et al., identify paths for future research.

Chapter 30: *Applicant Fairness Reactions to the Selection Process*. Truxillo, Bauer, and McCarthy review research on fairness and applicant reactions to selection systems. Whereas early work on selection focused on the employers' perspective, the advent of research on organizational justice led to a shift in focus toward applicant reactions. Truxillo et al. identify three dominant model of selection fairness and describe both attributes of fair selection processes and the effects of selection fairness on applicants' attitudes and behaviors. Truxillo et al. discuss how changes in personnel selection suggest changes in these models may be warranted. Truxillo et al. then consider applicant reactions in different cultures. They conclude with a discussion challenge remaining and avenues for future research.

Chapter 31: *Failure and Complaint Handling in Marketing: An Organizational Justice Inquiry*. The final chapter in this section moves justice from within the organization and considers how fairness influences customer attitude and behaviors. Hess and Olver structure their review around a model of fairness and complaint handling. Specifically, they identify four antecedents of perceived fairness (characteristics of the failure event, chatacteristics of the complaint handling, characteristics of the organization, and characteristics of the industry) as well as event-related outcomes of the perceived fairness (satisfaction with complaint handling/recovery and emotions) and system-related outcomes (overall satisfaction, repurchase intentions, commitment/loyalty, trust with the organization, word-of-mouth, overall perceived fairness). Hess and Olver conclude with some trends that create both challenges and opportunities for organizations and researchers (e.g., customers' use of social media for complaints, organizations' reluctance to treat complaints as learning/opportunities). Although these issues are framed in terms of customers, they are applicable to employee-related events as well.

Concluding Thoughts

Organizational justice has grown into a capacious domain of scholarly inquiry. It touches on fundamental human concerns—social standing, legitimacy of authority, fear of exploitation, and moral principles. The chapters in this handbook testify to how much scholars have learned in only a few decades. But perhaps the greatest strength of justice research is in its potential for improving the effectiveness of work organizations while simultaneously improving the lives of employees. For that reason, justice is both a challenge and an opportunity for all of us.

References

Abadinsky, H. (2003). Law and justice: An introduction to the American legal system (5th ed.), Upper Saddle, NJ: Pearson.

Allen, A. L. (2004). The new ethics: A guided tour of the twenty-first century moral landscape. New York, NY: Miramax Books.

Appiah, K. A. (2008). *Experiments in ethics*. Boston, MA: Harvard University Press.

Batson, C. D. (1999). Altruism and prosocial behavior. In D. T. Gilbert, S. T. Fiske, & G. Lindzey (Eds.), *Handbook of social psychology* (Vol. 2, pp. 333–381). Boston, MA: McGraw-Hill.

Batson, C. D., Klein, T. R., Highberger, L., & Shaw, L. L. (1995). Immorality from empathy-inducted altruism: When compassion and justice conflict. *Journal of Personality and Social Psychology, 68*, 1042–1054.

Bird, O. (1967). *The idea of justice*. New York, NY: Praeger.

Blackburn, S. (2001). *Being good: A short introduction to ethics*. Oxford, UK: Oxford University Press.

Blader, S. L., & Rothman, N. B. (2014). Paving the road to preferential treatment with good intentions: Empathy, accountability and fairness. *Journal of Experimental Social Psychology, 50*, 65–81.

Blader, S. L., & Tyler, T. R. (2001). Justice and empathy: What motivates people to help others? In M. Ross & D. T. Miller (Eds.), *The justice motive in everyday life* (pp. 226–250). New York, NY: Cambridge University Press.

Bobocel, D. R., McCline, R. L., & Folger, R. (1997). Letting them down gently: Conceptual advances in explaining controversial organizational policies. In C. L. Cooper & D. M. Rousseau (Eds.), *Trends in organizational behavior* (Vol. 4, pp. 73–88). New York, NY: Wiley.

Boehm, C. (2012). Moral origins: The evolution of virtue, altruism, and shame. New York, NY: Basic Books.

Colquitt, J. A., & Shaw, J. C. (2005). How Should Organizational Justice Be Measured?. In J. Greenberg, J. A. Colquitt (Eds.), *Handbook of organizational justice* (pp. 113–152). Mahwah, NJ, US: Lawrence Erlbaum Associates Publishers.

Connolly, T., Conlon, E. J., & Deutsch, S. J. (1980). Organizational effectiveness: A multiple-constituency approach. *Academy of Management Review, 5*, 211–217.

Cropanzano, R., & Moliner, C. (2013). Hazards of justice: Egocentric bias, moral judgments, and revenge-seeking. In S. M. Elias (Ed.), *Deviant and criminal behavior in the workplace* (pp. 155–177). New York, NY: New York University Press.

Cropanzano, R., & Greenberg, J. (1997). Progress in organizational justice: Tunneling through the maze. In C. L. Cooper & I. T. Robertson (Eds.), *International review of industrial and organizational psychology* (pp. 317–372). New York, NY: Wiley.

Cropanzano, R., Rupp, D. E., Mohler, C. J., & Schminke, M. (2001). Three roads to organizational justice. In G. R. Ferris (Ed.), *Research in personnel and human resources management* (Vol 20, pp. 1–123). US: Elsevier Science/ JAI Press.

Cropanzano, R., & Stein, J. H. (2009). Organizational justice and behavioral ethics: Promises and prospects. *Behavioral Ethics Quarterly, 19*, 193–233.

Cugueró-Escofet, N., & Rosanas, J. M. (2013). The just design and use of management control systems as requirements for goal congruence. *Management Accounting Research, 24*, 23–40.

Feinberg, J. (1974). Noncomparative justice. *The Philosophical Review, 83*, 297–338.

Fiske, A. P. (1991). Structures of social life: The four elementary forms of human relations. New York, NY: The Free Press.

Foa, U. G. (1971). Interpersonal and economic resources. *Science, 71*, 345–351.

Foa, U. G., & Foa, E. B. (1974). *Societal Structures of the Mind*. Springfield, IL: Charles C. Thomas Publisher.

Folger, R., Konovsky, M. A., & Cropanzano, R. (1992). A due process metaphor for performance appraisal. *Research in organizational behavior, 14*, 129–129.

Folger, R., & Salvador, R. (2008). Is management theory too "self-ish"? *Journal of Management, 34*, 1127–1151.

Fortin, M., & Fellenz, M. R. (2008). Hypocrisies of fairness: Towards a more reflexive ethical base in organizational justice research. *Journal of Business Ethics, 78*, 415–433.

French, W. (1964). The personnel management process: Human resources administration. New York, NY: Houghton Mifflin.

Goldman, B. M., & Thatcher, S. M. B. (2002). A social information processing view of organizational justice. In S. W. Gilliland, D. D. Steiner, & D. P. Skarlicki (Eds.), *Emerging perspectives on managing organizational justice* (pp. 103–130). Greenwich, CT: Information Age Publishing.

Greenberg, J., & Colquitt, J. A. (2005). *Handbook of organizational justice.* Mahwah, NJ: Lawrence Erlbaum Associates.

Greene, J. (2013). Moral tribes: Emotion, reason, and the gap between us and them. New York, NY: Penguin Press.

Lind, E. A. (1995). Justice and authority relations in organizations. In R. S. Cropanzano & K. M. Kacmar (Eds.), *Organizational politics, justice, and support: Managing the social climate of the workplace* (pp. 83–96). Westport, CT: Quorum Books.

Lind, E. A., Kulik, C. T., Ambrose, M.L., & deVera, M.V. (1993). Individual and corporate dispute resolution: Using procedural fairness as a decision heuristic. *Administrative Science Quarterly, 38*, 224–251.

Lind, E. A., MacCoun, R. J., Ebner, J. P. A., Felstiner, W. L. F., Hensler, D. R., Resnik, J., & Tyler, T. R. (1990). In the eye of the beholder: Tort litigants' evaluations of their experiences in the civil justice system. *Law and Society Review, 24*, 953–996.

Patient, D. L., & Skarlicki, D. P. (2010). Increasing interpersonal and informational justice when communicating negative news: The role of the manager's empathic concern and moral development. *Journal of Management, 36*, 555–578.

Price, M. E. (2010). Free riders as a blind spot of equity theory: An evolutionary correction. In M. Schminke (Ed.), *Managerial ethics: Managing the psychology of morality* (pp. 235–256). New York, NY: Routledge.

Sadurski, W. (1985). *Giving desert its due: Social justice and legal theory.* Boston, MA: D. Reidel.

Sandel, M. J. (2009). *Justice: What is the right thing to do?* New York, NY: Farrar, Straus and Giroux.

Skarlicki, D. P., & Kulik, C. T. (2005). Third-party reactions to employee (mis)treatment: A justice perspective. In B. M. Staw, R. M. Kramer (Eds.), *Research in organizational behavior: An annual series of analytical essays and critical reviews* (Vol 26, pp. 183–229). US: Elsevier Science/JAI Press.

Skogan, W., & Frydl, K. (Eds.) (2004). *Fairness and effectiveness in policing: The evidence.* Washington, DC: National Academies Press.

Smith, H. J., Tyler, T. R., Huo, Y. J., Ortiz, D. J., & Lind, E. A. (1998). The self-relevant implications of the group-value model: Group membership, self-worth, and treatment quality. *Journal of Personality and Social Psychology, 34*, 470–493.

Thibaut, J. W., & Walker, L. (1975). *Procedural justice: A psychological analysis.* Hillsdale, NJ: Erlbaum.

Thibaut, J. W., & Walker, L. (1978). A theory of procedure. *California Law Review, 66*, 541–566.

Treviño, L. K., & Weaver, G. R. (2010). Advances in research on punishment in organizations: Descriptive and normative perspectives. In M. Schminke (Ed.), *Managerial ethics: Managing the psychology of morality* (pp. 177–204). New York, NY: Routledge.

Tyler, T. R. (1987). Conditions leading to value expressive effects in judgments of procedural justice: A test of four models. *Journal of Personality and Social Psychology, 52*, 333–344.

Tyler, T. R., & Blader, S. L. (2000). Cooperation in groups: Procedural justice, social identity, and behavioral engagement. Washington, DC: Psychology Press.

Tyler, T. R., & Folger, R. (1980). Distributional and procedural aspects of satisfaction with citizen-police encounters. *Basic and Applied Social Psychology, 1*, 281–292.

Van den Bos, K., Wilke, H. A. M., & Lind, E. A. (1998). When do we need justice? The role of trust in authority. *Journal of Personality and Social Psychology, 75*, 1449–1458.

Van der Toorn, J., Berkics, M., & Jost, J. T. (2010). System justification, satisfaction, and perceptions of fairness and typicality at work: A cross-system comparison involving the U.S. and Hungary. *Social Justice Research, 23*, 189–210.

CHAPTER

2

Distributive Justice: Revisiting Past Statements and Reflecting on Future Prospects

Kjell Törnblom *and* Ali Kazemi

Abstract

This chapter starts with brief discussions of the whens and whys of justice reasoning and acting, after which descriptions of several distributive justice theories are provided. These are analyzed on the basis of four dimensions: type of justice motivation, orientation of justice behavior, the source of justice behavior initiation, and the source of justice behavior direction. We suggest that the overemphasis in the distributive justice literature on the three principles of equity, equality, and need, ought to be tempered by finer distinctions among the varieties of each and increased attention to additional principles and combinations of principles. The chapter ends by outlining suggestions for future research. Four issues are featured: the nature of the object (social resource) that is distributed and the focus of justice judgments, how the way the resource was produced may affect its allocation and justice judgment, how justice relates to various types of conflict, and why people sometimes do not react to perceived injustices.

Key Words: justice models, distributive justice, justice principles, justice conflict, (non)reactions to injustice, resource allocation, resource production

> "... justice is seen as such a basic component of any human society that it does not have to appear as an explicit postulate for an ideal social order. This implies that perceived injustice will readily provoke strong protest and demands for the reestablishment of justice. How can we explain the existence of such a powerful need for perceived justice in human social life?"
>
> —*Scherer*, 1992, p. 3

> "... the quest for justice takes its place beside the quest for God, philosophical knowledge, beauty—neither answered nor abandoned, but pursued without cease in spite of its apparent futility."
>
> —*Morgenthau*, 1974, pp. 174–175

This chapter will provide neither an overview nor an integrative review of recent social psychological research on social justice in general or of the subarea of distributive justice in particular, or even as it specifically pertains to the organizational context. Several reviews covering distributive justice theory and research already exist, e.g., Cook and Hegtvedt (1983), Hegtvedt (2006), Hegtvedt and Cook, (2001), Hegtvedt and Markovsky (1995), Jost and Kay (2010), Kazemi and Törnblom (2008), Törnblom (1992), and Tyler and Smith (1998). An additional review similar to those seems superfluous at this point in time. Therefore, to avoid redundancy, our focus is a bit unorthodox as compared to a typical review chapter.

Frequently, younger generations studying distributive justice may not be fully familiar with its theoretical origins and its relevance and importance to the organizational/industrial context. This is understandable, since the rate at which new knowledge is produced is constantly increasing, resulting in a very large volume of literature that present day generations must plow through in preparation for their own contributions to the field. And lacking a historical perspective, what is believed to be a novel contribution may actually turn out to be not so novel or new, if previous work had been known and acknowledged. Shapiro (2001) put it this way: "... if justice theory is to escape death (i.e., a lack of meaningfulness to its readers) ..." (p. 236), then justice researchers and theorists need "... to stop neglecting theories that are already in existence. This neglect can occur in two ways: either by reinventing what is already known or by ignoring it (i.e., not citing it)" (p. 236). She very correctly concludes that the "reinvention routine" gives rise to "a plethora of theories" that take us nowhere. And, to quote Greenberg (1990, p. 424): "Although some facets of some findings may be unique, it is currently at least as important for researchers to thoroughly compare and explain the connections between their own findings and earlier work as it is to announce a novel result." Unfortunately, available time and publish-or-perish pressures will frequently make it very difficult for scholars new to a field to acquire a rigorous historical perspective.

We have tried to meet two major objectives with this chapter, specifically with those researchers in mind that are relatively new to this area. First, subsequent to brief discussions of the whys and whens of justice, we provide brief descriptions of several distributive justice theories of the past. Hopefully, this may serve to accentuate the importance of relating own contributions to the works of predecessors and facilitate the accumulation of knowledge about justice issues. Second, and in order to counteract the prevailing tendency to favor a disproportionate focus on the three allocation principles of equity, equality, and need, we present a reminder that several other principles have been discussed by various scholars. These principles may be relevant and considered just or unjust at different occasions and in different contexts. The chapter is concluded with a few suggestions for future lines of research.

Why People Distribute Social Resources Justly and Why They Don't

> "The distribution of resources among persons or social units poses a fundamental problem, the solution to which determines the degree of social order and cohesion that will prevail. This is termed the *distributive problem* and is involved whenever resources are to be allocated between person and other, as well as between groups within a society or between nation-states."
>
> —*Sampson*, 1976, p. 47

Justice or Other Interests?

The problems related to the inference of covert phenomena (e.g., a justice motive) from the observation of overt behavior (e.g., resource allocation) or verbal statements is certainly not unique to the area of distributive justice (see, for example, the huge amount of literature on the relationship between attitudes and behavior). In general, one must proceed with great caution before accepting conclusions based on empirical studies that (what is designated as) just behavior was exclusively, or at least primarily, prompted by a desire or intention to act justly. "Such an assumption may obfuscate the actual motives underlying behavior in that situation" (Reis, 1984, p. 28). Further, it is likely that "... when the justice motive is operative, its actual impact is modified by integration with other relevant motives" (Reis, 1986, p. 198). The results of even those studies in which the participants have been explicitly instructed to distribute outcomes fairly or justly are not free from interpretive problems of this and other kinds. "Goethe went so far as to say that he who acts is always unjust and that nobody has justice but the observer, that is, the one whose interests are not involved" (Morgenthau, 1974, p. 164).

The potential collision between justice and self-interest has been the focus of many discussions (see a recent monograph by Lerner & Clayton, 2011). There are several additional motives that may either conflict with the justice motive (e.g., efficiency, or empathy that may reduce the amount of punishment justice would demand) or be mutually compatible (as when a justice outcome is also favorable to the recipient). Another type of clash may occur when one's preferences are at odds with what is considered just (see Messick & Sentis, 1983); it is quite conceivable that justice is not always preferred, or even that injustice is preferred. Greenberg and Cohen (1982) discuss how concerns with justice interact with efficiency, power, and productivity. See also Törnblom and Kazemi's (2007) resource production theory of distributive justice.

When and Why Justice: Thinking About Justice and Acting Justly

Leventhal (1976b, p. 225) suggested that people make justice evaluations of a recipient's outcomes (a) when the person "... occupies a social role whose primary function is to evaluate ... [a recipient's] ... deservingness or to adjudicate conflict and disagreement," (b) "... when there is reason to believe that applicable justice rules are being violated," (c) "... when there has been a large or sudden change in their outcomes," and (d) "... when not preoccupied with activities of greater importance." Adding to this, justice considerations are obviously crucial (e) in times of scarcity (Greenberg, 1981).

Even though we might be able to accurately determine that an individual's just behavior was, indeed, motivated by a desire to act justly, another difficult question arises: *Why* do people want to act justly? Perhaps the most obvious and appealing reply to that question is that people are moral beings (nature and/or nurture). Justice is "conceived as a norm, a value, a virtue, a standard of evaluation of almost any aspect of life and living together, and as a human motive affecting thoughts, emotions, and actions" (Kals & Maes, 2012, p. v). Presumably, moral conduct (of which just behavior is an important aspect) is intrinsically satisfying, that is, a goal in its own right. However, it is possible to have different conceptions of human nature. The most frequent assumption in social psychological theories of distributive justice is that people behave justly for instrumental extrinsic and self-interested rather than intrinsic moral reasons. Lerner and Clayton (2011) recently analyzed existing research relevant to the two motivational forces of justice and self-interest and proposed a model that seeks to integrate the two.

Instrumental models of *procedural justice* focus on the expected and actual outcomes that people receive (e.g., Thibaut & Walker, 1975). The relational or group-value model of procedural justice (Lind & Tyler, 1988, Tyler & Lind, 1992) provides an alternative perspective. According to this view, people are concerned about their position in groups, and justice is, similar to the instrumental variety, a means rather than as an end itself. Thus, both models consider justice to be a means rather than an end in itself, that is, the relational model focuses on obtaining status in the group, whereas the instrumental model has control as an end. In this respect, they merely differ in terms of the social resource they see as an outcome. In that sense, these models are equally valid for distributive justice conceptions. These models do not address justice as a moral ought or virtue, as an end in itself, conditions under which people are motivated intrinsically and morally to behave justly. People do sometimes act in ways that are irrelevant or even detrimental to self-interest and maximization of own outcomes.

The following list outlines a number of reasons suggested by various theorists about why people may prefer just conduct. For most of the reasons we have provided references to relevant works, but we have been unable to do so in a couple of cases.

1. People have a need to maintain cognitive consistency (Adams, 1963, 1965). Inequity constitutes a particular case of cognitive dissonance (i.e., when inputs are not proportional to outcomes). Because this is often an aversive state, people will want to avoid it by acting justly and being justly treated themselves.
2. Others reward just behavior (Walster, Berscheid, & Walster, 1973) via, for example, approval and cooperation (Blau, 1964; Homans, 1961; Thibaut & Faucheux, 1965).
3. A need to maintain a belief in a just world (BJW), that is, a conviction that people receive what they deserve regarding positive and negative outcomes (Lerner, 1970, 1974, 1980; Long & Lerner, 1974; for more details, see the description of Lerner's justice motive theory later).
4. It is morally right to act justly. In general, conformity to shared values and ethical standards is expected and often taken for granted, and these ideals are reinforced by religious beliefs and imperatives (Cropanzano & Rupp, 2002).
5. It benefits the collective (e.g., Walster et al., 1973). Norms prescribing how valuable social resources should be distributed among members of the collective (e.g., a small group, an organization, a society) may help guide behavior, minimize disagreements, prevent conflict, and maintain social order. Just treatment also tends to encourage productivity.
6. A desire to avoid injustice as it might cause harm to self or others (cf. Gouldner's 1960 formulation of the norm of reciprocity: people should help those who have helped them, and people should not injure those who have helped them).
7. It serves (material) self-interest (Cropanzano & Rupp, 2002). Just behavior may conceal one's true intentions, namely to gain benefits for oneself (cf. Walster, Walster & Berscheid, 1978).
8. People maintain a positive self-concept by acting justly (Lerner, 1974; Walster et al., 1973; Walster & Piliavin, 1972); they take pride in having moral principles and integrity.
9. It fulfills four different types of identity maintenance needs: instrumental (material

identity needs; Skitka, 2003; Thibaut & Walker, 1975), relational (social identity needs; Lind & Tyler, 1988; Tyler & Lind, 1992), protective (certainty or predictability needs; Lind & Van den Bos, 2002; and moral (personal identity needs; Skitka & Mullen, 2002).

10. It provides control over outcomes in the sense of reducing uncertainty in social relationships (Kayser, Köhler, Mikula, & Schwinger, 1980; Lerner, 1980). This view appears in the notion of a belief in a just world (e.g., Lerner, 1970), Cohens' (1974) discussion of mastery and justice, and Lind and van den Bos (2002) uncertainty management theory.

11. The law, but only when the laws prescribe or proscribe just behavior. Thus, and in line with Martin Luther King's standpoint, people are obligated to obey just laws and to disobey unjust laws.

12. Out of habit, tradition (we've always acted this way) but not for reasons of justice with which it coincides).

13. Because of empathy and sympathy for other people.

Theories and Models of Justice

Justice Model Dimensions

Despite the considerable problems associated with empirical attempts to assess whether (and under what circumstances) just behavior is motivated by a justice motive, per se, or by something else, social psychologists have produced a variety of theoretical models intended to explain why people act fairly. Some of these models are here described in the following subsections in terms of their assumptions about (a) the type of justice motivation, (b) the orientation of justice behavior, (c) the source of justice behavior initiation, and (d) the source of justice behavior direction.

Type of justice motivation refers to whether just behavior is assumed to be an ultimate end in itself (i.e., the morally right thing to do, justice is rewarding in itself), in which case the *consummatory* quality of just behavior is stressed, or whether it is intended as a vehicle for attaining other goals than justice, whereby the *instrumental* quality of just behavior takes priority (cf. Greenberg & Cohen, 1982, Ch. 12; Van Avermaet, McClintock, & Moskowitz, 1978). In the latter case I act justly only because such behavior will provide opportunities to reach other goals, not because it is morally right. Some goals may be sought in order to benefit others, and other goals will be directly advantageous to oneself. In line with a suggestion by Walster, Walster and Berscheid (1978), perhaps the most acceptable way to be selfish is via just behavior. Greenberg and Cohen (1982) note, that the consummatory and instrumental alternatives are not independent of one another, and that they are not the only motives behind just behavior. Some theories seem to include both alternatives, and for others their assumptions are not unambiguously obvious.

Orientation of justice behavior refers to whether people are believed to act in a *reactive* or *proactive* manner in their approach to justice (see Greenberg, 1987). A *reactive* orientation involves behaviors seeking to redress an already existing injustice (i.e., the ways in which individuals respond to injustice). A *proactive* approach refers to behaviors intended to create justice (or avoiding behavior that may result in injustices) (cf. Greenberg, 1982; Syroit, 1991; Van Avermaet, McClintock, & Moskowitz, 1978). Theories viewing justice motivation as proactive are more useful, if one is interested in knowing how and why people *control* their environment and select actions that produce just outcomes. If the objective is to understand how actors behave *reactively* to perceived inequity, then Adams' equity theory (see later) seems appropriate since actors are focused upon escaping from a negatively valenced state of injustice.

Source of justice behavior initiation and *source of justice behavior direction* (both of which may involve the resource provider, the victim, or the observer/third party) may be located on the *intrapersonal* or *interpersonal* level (cf. Reis, 1984; Syroit, 1991). Theories positing intrapersonal and interpersonal loci for the initiation and direction of just behavior (regardless of whether justice is viewed as a goal in itself or as a means to other ends) imply different strategies for the encouragement and guidance of just behavior or for attempts to understand, explain, and predict the occurrence of unjust behavior. Theories that posit an *intrapersonal* locus implicate the individual as the major subject of attention, whereas the external environment would be emphasized in theories stressing the *interpersonal* aspect of the initiation and direction of behavior.

Justice Models

The following justice models and theories of the past are described and analyzed in terms of the aforementioned dimensions that are (or at least appear to be) part of each model. The selection below is confined to theories presented during the pioneering first two decades of the social psychological study of distributive justice, that is, from the mid-1960s up to the mid-1980s. However, we make no claim of being exhaustive, and all aspects of the focalized theories are not summarized. Finally, the term *theory* is used in a very general sense. If strict definitional criteria for theory were applied, many of the "theories" that follow would rather more legitimately be called models.

The preceding qualifications notwithstanding, theoretical, empirical, and applied research on distributive justice may stand on firmer ground by acknowledging and assimilating previous theoretical developments. This is possible only via the incorporation of a historical perspective which we hope the following overview may encourage.

EQUITY THEORY

In Adams' (1963, 1965) influential equity theory [building on the seminal formulations of social exchange by Homans (1958, 1961, 1974), and Blau (1964), as well as Festinger's (1954, 1957) social comparison and cognitive dissonance theories] the individual is assumed to experience injustice (inequity) if she perceives discrepancy between her and another person's outcome/input ratios. As the experience of inequity (a special case of cognitive dissonance) is psychologically distressing, the individual is motivated to reduce or eliminate it (especially when facing unfavorable/disadvantageous inequity). Thus, the individual *reacts* to (i.e., justice-seeking behavior is *initiated* by) a state of felt injustice, experiencing a desire to escape from this *intra-personally* unpleasant state (Adams, 1965; Sayles, 1958).

The direction of justice restoring behavior is determined by the outcome of *interpersonal* comparisons, resulting in a definition of the unjust situation as either favorably or unfavorably inequitable (i.e., as over- or under-reward). Equity is desired as an end state; thus the perceived value of justice is perhaps best viewed as *consummatory* in nature. However, although justice is a desired end state and is not used strategically to reach other goals, the basic underlying motivational factor of equity-restoring behavior is a desire to avoid or getting away from the psychological distress resulting from inequity. This seems to be the main reason for desiring justice. Thus, behavior is motivated by a "negative" (reactive) rather than a "positive" (proactive) concern for equity.

INTERNAL STANDARD

It may also be noted that psychological distress derives from interpersonal comparisons in Adams' model. In contrast, Pritchard's (1969) "internal standard" version of equity theory—a concept adopted from Weick (1966) and similar to notions found in the theories of Helson (1964), Thibaut and Kelley (1959), and Upshaw (1969)—posits that feelings of inequity primarily results from a lack of correspondence between the focal *person's own* inputs and outcomes (i.e., distress results from *intra-personal social comparisons*, that is, intra-personal comparisons do not occur in a vacuum but are anchored socially).

This view seems to be challenged by empirical results (Austin, McGinn, & Susmilch, 1980) indicating that activation of the internal standard affects *satisfaction* with outcomes, whereas interpersonal social comparisons determine *justice* judgments. Another objection is conceptual and concerns the nature of the internal standard: if it is based on previous experiences in exchange relationships and on knowledge about the market value of different inputs, as Pritchard (1969, pp. 205–206) argues, then the internal standard is likely to derive from interpersonal social comparisons at earlier points in time (see Törnblom, 1977a).

STATUS VALUE THEORY OF DISTRIBUTIVE JUSTICE

Berger, Zelditch, Anderson and Cohen's (1972) status value theory of distributive justice was formulated as a competing and improved framework to that of Adams' (1965). For Berger et al. (1972) injustice occurs when actual rewards are lesser or greater than expected rewards. This model accounts not only for states of (in)justice for Person (P) visavi Other (O) in a dyadic exchange relationship, which is the focus of Adams' equity theory, Status value theory also incorporates predictions about phenomena covered inadequately by Adams' equity formulation, especially regarding states of collective (in)justice, thereby avoiding misclassifications of just and unjust states.

This and other extensions were possible due to a distinction between "local" and "referential" comparisons. The former refers to comparisons with the actual rewards of a specific similar individual (P compares herself with O). The latter refers to comparisons with a "generalized other," that is, a category of people to which the comparer belongs (P compares her own and O's situation to that of a reference group of similar others on the basis of which expectations about rewards are formed). The type of justice motivation involved appears to be *reactive* as the theory focuses on responses to injustice, that is, violations of normative expectations (see also Anderson, Berger, Zelditch, & Cohen, 1969).

Justice is viewed as *consummatory*, that is, a desirable state in its own right rather than as a means to other ends. *Intrapersonal* processes seem to explain the *initiation* of just behavior, whereas the source of *direction* of such behavior appears to be *interpersonal* (i.e., direction is determined by the particular type of injustice at hand, as defined by means of social comparisons).

EQUITY AND STATUS VALUE THEORY INTEGRATION

Törnblom (1977a) extended Berger et al.'s (1968) status value theory of distributive justice by juxtaposing local and referential comparisons on which justice evaluations are based. Adams (1963) derived 16 situations of justice and injustice based on local comparisons on the basis of a dichotomization of two exchange partners' inputs and outcomes. Berger et al. (1968) arrived at a corresponding typology based on referential comparisons. These typologies were elaborated and extended by specifying P's and O's relative to each other's as well as to those of the members of the referential group. These additions revealed that each one of the 16 original situations consists of several variations (main types, subtypes, and minor types), and that they must be clearly specified before meaningful comparisons can be made between the results of different studies concerned with magnitude of reactions to experienced injustice.

A set of seven propositions permitted a rank ordering among the various types of inequity in terms of magnitude of justice motivation that they are likely to generate. Like the theories described earlier, Törnblom viewed justice as *consummatory* (an end in itself) and focused on *reactive* responses to perceived inequity. People react to inequity because it is both *intrapersonally* and *interpersonally* an unpleasant state and the direction of equity-restoring responses is a result of *interpersonal* comparisons. Considerations of the combined effects of the perceived magnitude of injustice, type of injustice, and the identity of the victim (and perpetrator) of injustice (P, O, or both) generate new and more precise predictions than previously.

EQUITY THEORY AS A GENERAL SOCIAL PSYCHOLOGICAL THEORY

Walster, Berscheid, and Walster (1973) extended Adams' (1965) equity theory into a more general social psychological theory. These authors suggested two explanations about why people behave justly. In short, (1) Propositions III and IV state that inequity, distress, and equity-restoring attempts are positively and linearly related, whereas (2) Propositions I, II, and Corollary I.1 suggest that equitable behavior is not only contingent on its instrumentality for the goal of maximizing one's own outcomes, but also upon the group's attempts at inducing equitable behavior through the use of rewards and punishments. Thus, the locus of justice motivation with regard to its behavior *initiating* element is *intrapersonal* in the first instance, and *interpersonal* in the second.

The *direction* of behavior appears to be provided by *interpersonal* comparisons in both cases. Curiously, justice (or rather, as in Adams' model, inequity avoidance to escape distress) appears to be the *ultimate goal* only in the first case, whereas equity is used *strategically* to reach other ends (one's own outcome-maximization) when justice is viewed as interpersonally motivated. Further, when conceived as triggered by internal mechanisms, just behavior is *reactive* in orientation, but *proactive* when externally induced (i.e., in order to attain a given goal without being exposed to punishment, the individual must conform to the group's demands to behave justly).

MULTIPRINCIPLE JUSTICE

Deutsch (1975) suggested that a different justice principle is linked to each of three kinds of cooperative group orientation. Groups are assumed to be concerned with justice because it is *instrumental* to reaching various group goals (economic productivity, solidarity, personal development and welfare) (see Kazemi & Eek, 2007, 2008). As the analytic focus is placed on the rational tendencies of groups (rather than on the individual), the motivational locus of just behavior with regard to its *initiation* as well as its *direction* is *interpersonal* in nature.

Under what circumstances, then, will one group orientation or goal dominate over others? To answer this question Deutsch offers the hypothesis (his "Crude Law of Social Relations"—that "... the typical consequences of a given type of social relation tend to elicit that relation" (p. 147, original italics omitted). That is, certain characteristics of a given social situation (e.g., competition) are conducive to the development of a particular group orientation (e.g., economic) and to the application of a specific justice principle (e.g., equity). Thus, the justice orientation of the group appears to be *proactive.*

JUSTICE MOTIVE THEORY

Lerner's (1975, 1977, 1981) justice motive theory emphasizes the individual's need to create and maintain an organized structure of the environment. The child invents a "personal contract" with the self, that is, learns to defer immediate and modest satisfactions in favor of delayed greater gratifications. Because the child is willing to make this temporary sacrifice, s/he will come to consider future compensations as deserved. As a person's deserts are contingent upon the cooperation of others, who should also receive what they are entitled to, the personal contract gets linked to the notion of justice. Thus, the environment is perceived as controllable; people are believed to obtain what they deserve, and others are believed to think and act accordingly.

Lerner assumes that the child's "... outcome-maximizing self-interested motivations are radically altered very early in the developmental process," and that the "... central motivational force probably stems from the need to protect the integrity of this organizational structure" (Lerner, 1981, p. 27). The nature of people's orientation toward justice is clearly *proactive* in Lerner's model.

The locus of justice motivation with regard to its behavior *direction* component is embedded within *interpersonal* relationships. Rewards or deserts are understood to be contingent upon whether the individual orients his/her behavior to conform to the perceived expectations of others. Thus, the individual must realize that it is in everybody's interest to act in such ways as to maintain the organized construction of "reality" and to maintain the character of the social relationship in which the individual participates. However, and similar to the interpersonal reactive theories discussed earlier, the behavior *initiation* component of justice motivation appear to operate on the *intrapersonal* level: "The resultant organized construction is experienced as a demand, an impulse to act and feel in a particular way" (Lerner, 1981, p. 27). Just behavior is seen both as an end in itself (i.e., *consummatory*) and as a means (i.e., *instrumental*) to gaining control over the environment and over the causal connection between own behavior and intended outcomes.

A person's organized structure of the environment includes his/her perceived *relation* to others (P views herself as "same," "similar" to, or "different" than O) as well as the nature of the resource-acquisition *process* ("vicarious dependency," "convergent goals," or "divergent goals"). Both elements enter into the construction of an event, and either relation or process may become salient ("figure") while the other become "ground" in a given situation, resulting in a typology of 3x3x2 "emergent activities." To each of the 18 activities is linked a (presumed) matching distribution rule that is perceived as just.

Some years later, Lerner (1987) hypothesized that people acquire two bases for evaluating their own and others' entitlements: (1) people incorporate within their psychological structure and "... reflect in their conscious thought processes the publicly available normative systems located in the social structure" (p. 113), and (2) by means of "... unconscious processes originating in the earliest and most primitive stages of cognitive organization" (p. 111) "... people develop a construction of their world that includes personally compelling imperatives concerning the entitlements of kinds of people, outcomes, and acts" (p. 113). These entitlements follow rules that typically contradict those emanating from the social structure. Lerner advances three propositions about when each of these two bases is activated in the evaluation of entitlements. First, people are assumed to automatically, and most of the time, follow social-structural prescriptions. However, when required to make a conscious decision, they rationally make a choice among alternatives and select the option most conducive to their "enlightened self-interest." Further, when the personally compelling imperatives are threatened or violated, the individual becomes affectively engaged and the unconscious rules of entitlement are activated. Finally, the existence of a psychological process or structure is assumed "... that performs a gatekeeping or integrating function, determining when and how the consequences of the information processed at these two levels appear in the person's reactions" (p. 114). Within this framework, people are assumed to be both *reactively* and *proactively* motivated to accomplish justice. They are concerned with justice for *consummatory* as well as *instrumental* reasons. The *initiation* of just behavior appears to have an *intrapersonal* locus, whereas the directive element is *interpersonal* in nature.

JUSTICE PRINCIPLE COMBINATION

Leventhal (1976a) assumes that several allocation principles are often simultaneously salient. Therefore, ". . . an allocator must decide which allocation norm or combination of norms to follow" (p. 129). Further, an allocator's choice of distribution principles is not only determined by his/her desire to treat others justly, per se. S/he frequently applies those principles that are approved and accepted by others. However, his/her decisions are also, and primarily, influenced by the *benefits* resulting from the application of each principle. Hence, justice motivation is clearly *proactive* in nature. If a particular distribution is perceived to be just by recipients, they are more likely to contribute to the solution of group problems.

Different norms are associated with different instrumental benefits. For example, an allocator may decide to use the *equity* principle because s/he desires to maximize productivity among group members. However, negative results may also result from the application of a given principle. Equitable allocations might, for instance, sabotage group solidarity. Thus, both the *initiation* and *direction* of just behavior appear to be *interpersonally* motivated.

JUSTICE AS GOAL AND STRATEGY

In a paper on alternative approaches to equity, Van Avermaet, McClintock, and Moskowitz (1978) proposed that the function of justice (equity) may be *consummatory* as well as *instrumental*, that is, both an intrinsically valued goal and a strategy for the attainment of other ends. The formulation of Van Avermaet et al. (1978) is an elaboration of McClintock's (1972) social motivation model within both of which justice motivation is *proactive*, emphasizing the predecisional attractiveness of equitable outcomes (Greenberg, 1982). Whether equitable behavior is viewed as a socially valued goal in itself or as a strategy that, when adopted under appropriate circumstances, renders social legitimacy to the achievement of other goals (or both, as in Walster et al., 1973), it appears that the *initiating* as well as the *directing* behavioral elements of justice motivation are assumed to be *interpersonal* in origin.

JUSTICE AS A MEANS FOR CONTROL

Within the framework of various "contract" theories (inspired by Lerner's conception of the "personal contract") just behavior is conceived by Kayser and associates, Mikula, and Reis as a manifestation of the individual's desire to exert *control* over his/her environment, in particular the outcomes of his/her own actions as well as of those of other people (Kayser, Köhler, Mikula, & Schwinger, 1980; Kayser & Schwinger, 1982; Kayser, Schwinger, & Cohen, 1984; Mikula, 1982, 1984; Reis, 1984). During the course of socialization experiences, the individual acquires skills at identifying causal connections between his/her behavior and environmental events, thereby enabling him/her to explain and predict these events. The person comes to believe that pleasurable consequences (e.g., satisfaction of needs) may be achieved by means of his/her behavior. Subsequently, a sense of personal control over outcomes is gained; some means are socially defined as just, a value that encompasses several different principles and that may guide and legitimize social behavior.

As just behavior frequently results in desired consequences and unjust actions in undesired consequences, the individual will try to secure positive behavioral outcomes by *justifying* his/her actions. This is accomplished by making reference to some justice principle that is considered appropriate under the prevailing circumstances and to which the person's actions correspond (Mikula, 1984, p. 209). Thus, the individual's justice behavior is clearly *proactively* oriented, although his/her primary goal may not be to accomplish justice, per se.

Instead, justice serves an *instrumental* function in that the notion is used to legitimize and justify behavior by means of which other (or, at least, additional) goals are sought (e.g., harmonious social relationships, productivity, positive self-presentation, optimal self-rewards, etc.). Mikula assumes that the primary concern with justice is not to accomplish justice, per se, but stems from a wish ". . . to avoid the negative consequences which are usually associated with events that are considered to be unjust by the social environment" (p. 209). When the individual experiences a loss of control or a loss of outcomes, s/he is likely to make appeals for justice (Reis, 1984, p. 36). There seems to be only minor differences among the three frameworks, and they contain similar assumptions about both the *initiating* and the *directive* elements of motivation as being *interpersonal* in nature.

NEGOTIATED JUSTICE

Inspired by the works of Mead (1934), Vygotsky (1978), Mills (1975), and Sullivan (1953, 1954), Sampson (1983) stresses the negotiated quality of justice. Rather than viewing justice motivation as an intrapersonal force, he conceives of it in terms of an *interpersonally* derived "address frame": "An address frame grounds action in the social process; it makes people's acts intelligible to others and to themselves. In this view, justice becomes part of a conversation taking place between people" (p. 107). In line with traditional symbolic interactionist thinking Sampson emphasizes the *interpersonal* nature of the individual's mind.

The outcome of a person's cognitive activity is assumed to emerge out of a process in which the person addresses himself in response to the real or imagined attitudes of others. It is through this conversation a particular act is given meaning, that is, defined as just or unjust. This approach clearly views justice motivation as *proactive* in nature. Although Sampson does not appear to address the issue of whether the concern for justice is of consummatory or instrumental value to the individual, it seems that his formulation might encompass both possibilities.

JUSTICE VERSUS PREFERENCE

Messick and Sentis (1983) argue that both *preferences* and beliefs about the *justness* of outcomes (two different notions that are frequently in conflict with each other) influence a person's behavior. As people are assumed to have better knowledge of their preferences than of what is just, these authors consider preferences to be the more immediate influence on behavior of the two. Once a preference order among possible outcomes has been established, the individual decides whether justice considerations are relevant to the choice of outcomes. If this is the case, the individual will try to justify the more preferred outcomes as the most just ones. As the reactions of real or imagined others will affect the legitimacy of a person's claims, it is important that their justice conceptions agree with those of the person. "The result of this process is a type of constrained optimization of preference in which the various ways of interpreting "fair" or "equal" determine the subset of outcomes that are feasible" (p. 90). This compromise of motives assures considerate behavior toward others (but also creates ambiguity in the interpretation of the intentions guiding behavior). The model proposed by Messik and Sentis (1983) clearly assumes a *proactive* orientation toward justice. *Preferences* are seen as the prime *motivators* of behavior which, in turn, is tempered or provided *direction* by justice considerations (i.e., by what is socially defined as right). The demand or *need* to consider justice, as well as the form (*direction*) it takes, appear to be externally (*interpersonally*) determined.

EQUITY AND SOCIAL COMPETITION INTEGRATION

Syroit (1991) attempts to integrate major concepts of Adams' (1965) equity and Rijsman's (1983) social competition theories into a model of "interpersonal (rather than intrapersonal) justice." Inequity is viewed as "... the perception and experience of a conflict between the person who evaluates the exchange and his exchange partner" (p. 47), that is, a discrepancy between P's and O's evaluations of P's worth, as inferred from his inputs and outcomes. Even though inequity emanates from an interpersonal conflict, this conflict is assumed to eventually be internalized and cause emotional *reactions* likely to motivate justice restoring attempts.

Thus, it appears that this theory is very similar to that of Adams' in that both (a) view inequity to be interpersonally (externally) derived (i.e., P perceives discrepancies between his/her inputs and/or outcomes and those of O's), and (b) posit an intrapersonal (internal) locus of justice motivation (i.e., emotional arousal that triggers justice-restoring behavior). Even though the reduction of injustice (i.e., the *direction* of justice behavior) is seen as interactive or *interpersonal* (i.e., a negotiation between the exchange partners) in Syroit's model, it appears to be more accurately classified as an intrapersonal model due to the *intrapsychic* locus of the behavior initiation element of justice motivation. Just behavior is assumed to be *instrumentally* oriented with an emphasis on its conflict resolution function.

Resource Allocation and Distributive Justice Principles

> "What is to be considered a truly fair principle for distributing benefits and burdens and why? This question has ... been addressed by some of the greatest minds in Western civilization, including Plato, Aristotle, Hobbes, Locke, Hume, Rousseau, Kant, Hegel, Marx, Mill, and Rawls."
>
> —*Jost & Kay*, 2010, p. 1123

The concept *allocation* principle (rule, norm) is often used synonymously with *distributive justice* principle (rule, norm). Leventhal (1976a, p. 94) defined allocation norm as "a social rule which specifies criteria that define certain distributions of rewards and resources as fair and just." However, a given allocation principle may, at times, be considered irrelevant to or not evaluated in terms of justice. Thus, it is only when an allocation principle is evaluated in terms of justice (rather than efficiency, pleasantness, appropriateness, etc.) that the term *distributive justice* applies. However, in this chapter, the two terms (labels) are used interchangeably for the simple reason that theoretical discussions and empirical research reported by many of the scholars we refer to have often neglected to make note of this distinction. It is important to be aware not only of the distinction between an allocation or distributive principle and a distributive *justice* principle (i.e., a justice-evaluated allocation principle) but also of distinctions among types of evaluations other than justice evaluations, which have received inadequate attention in the justice literature). When overlooked, justice evaluations may not be properly operationalized in empirical studies. Let us explain more clearly (see also Jonsson & Törnblom, 1984, for a more detailed discussion).

For the sake of conceptual clarity, it is useful to distinguish among three categories of *evaluations* (moral evaluations, justice evaluations, and all other types of evaluations) and two categories of *referents*, that is, "targets" of evaluation (justice referents and all other types of referents). A *referent* is an entity that may be evaluated in terms of a wide variety of characteristics. A *justice referent* is an entity that may be evaluated in terms of how just or unjust it is. Most referents surrounding us are not justice referents (e.g., languages, planets, car brands, earth worms, etc.); they are neither just nor unjust. Unfortunately, no classification or inventory exists that provide information regarding what phenomena *are* justice referents. Minimally, they include how something is distributed and the rules according to which distribution is effectuated, behaviors and decisions that result in rewards or punishments, and persons making such decisions.

A *moral evaluation* is a judgment of what is morally right or wrong, what ought to be, whereas a *justice evaluation* involves the assertion that X is just or unjust. Justice evaluations are always moral evaluations of justice referents (for example, the size of my salary is exactly what I deserve)—see (5) in Figure 2.1—but moral evaluations are not always evaluations of justice referents (for example, cheating is unethical)—see (2) in Figure 2.1.

Justice referents may be subject to other evaluations than justice as well—(for example, the size of my salary corresponds to what I prefer or my salary is an insult)—see (3) and (4), respectively, in Figure 2.1. Moral evaluations (judgments regarding what is ethical or unethical) are made via the use of *moral principles*. Justice evaluations are made via the use

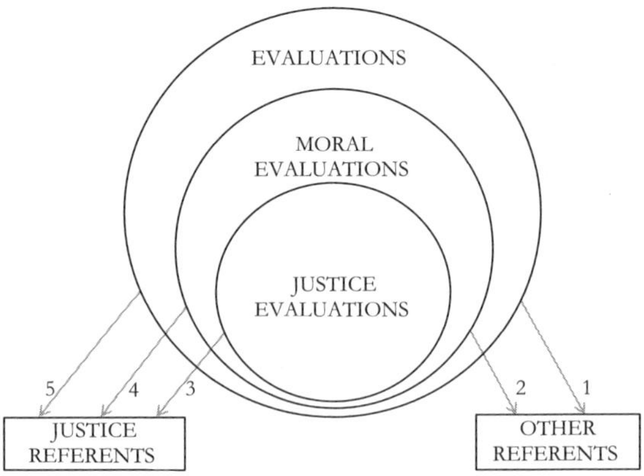

Fig. 2.1 Different types of evaluation.

of (distributive, procedural, and/or interactional) *justice principles*.

Finally, allocation behavior and principles may be influenced by other types of evaluations than moral and justice evaluations (for example, social competence is valuable)—see (1) in Figure 2.1—e.g., favorability, efficiency, profitability, appropriateness, preference, and so forth.

The conceptual distinctions among the different types of evaluations do not imply that they are empirically unrelated. On the contrary, they generate research questions about the empirical relationships among such evaluations. As a final observation, it is prudent to note the relationship between moral and justice principles. As we have seen, justice evaluations are always moral evaluations—see (5) in Figure 2.1. But moral evaluations are more inclusive than justice evaluations, something which is evident from various lists of moral principles or norms, most of which include justice as one of the moral precepts. Consider for example the following set of eight moral principles presented by Resnik (1998):

- *Nonmaleficence*: Do not harm yourself or other people.
- *Beneficence*: Help yourself and other people.
- *Autonomy:* Allow rational individuals to make free and informed choices.
- *Justice*: Treat people fairly: treat equals equally, unequals unequally.
- *Utility*: Maximize the ratio of benefits to harms for all people.
- *Fidelity*: Keep your promises and agreements.
- *Honesty*: Do not lie, defraud, deceive, or mislead.
- *Privacy*: Respect personal privacy and confidentiality.

Another scholar who offered a list of moral principles is Schumann (2001) who provided the following framework for human resource management ethics consisting of five complementary moral principles:

- *Utilitarian Principle:* an action should result in maximal good and minimal harm.
- *Rights Principle:* the actor should have a moral right to act.
- *Distributive Justice Principle:* the results of the distribution of goods and bads should be fair.
- *Caring Principle:* care and nurture of relationships among persons affected by an act.
- *Virtue Principle:* actions should represent virtue rather than vice.

Again, justice is included as a moral principle, but whereas Resnick's justice principle is wider than Schumann's in that it may include distributive, procedural, as well as interactional justice, Schumann specifically choses to include only its distributive aspect.

Having placed justice within a framework of other moral principles, we now turn to the criteria on the basis of which justice is differentiated into several distributive justice principles. Indeed, "our strong emotional belief in morality impels us to search for justice and gives us the motive to do the right thing for its own sake, but it does not supply the explicit principles of justice that we need" (Halliday, 2012, p. 19).

Cohen and Greenberg (1982, p. 31) posed the question of how many principles of justice there are, and which one of the various principles is more fundamental. They concluded that these questions seem unanswerable. However, the latter question is probably easier to handle than the first, as we now know that the evaluation and choice/application of justice principles is context specific or context dependable. This led Blalock and Wilken (1979, p. 229) to ask "Under what conditions are which distribution rules applied?" We can rephrase this question in more specific terms: Within which contexts, under what conditions, and from whose viewpoints should which social resources be allocated to whom according to which distributive (as well as procedural and interactional) principles or a combination of some of them? For example, in impersonal organizational and market settings, both superordinates and subordinates commonly agree that a just allocation of wages is accomplished if they are calculated on the basis of contributions (according to the equity principle), mutually determined (procedurally), and respectfully executed (interactionally). In other settings and contexts, different principles may be more fundamental and considered the most just ones. In a family situation, for example, the need or equality distributive principle (and the representativeness procedural principle and the respect interactional principle) are often considered the fairest ones.

Although the first question (i.e., how many principles of justice there are) may be unanswerable, we might benefit from a reminder that there are other distributive justice principles than the commonly focused equity, equality, and need. Unless at least some of these other principles are spelled out and made explicit as reminders of their (at least conceptual) existence, theory and research may be constrained and oversimplified. Further, we need to know under what conditions these principles are relevant and applicable (see later), as well as what the consequences are when they are applied.

Social psychologists typically want to explore people's actual evaluations and applications of allocation principles, that is, to identify the *conditions* under which a given allocation principle is applied and considered just, and to examine what *consequences* the application of a given principle may have for different types of social relationships, a task group's productivity, group members' satisfaction, and so forth. Given this focus on the personal sense (i.e., the subjective aspects) of distributive justice and injustice, a fruitful starting point is trying to assess just how differentiated and complex people's justice conceptions are. Are people able to, and do people generally, conceive of distributive justice in terms of many or in terms of a limited few principles, singly or in combinations?

Discussions of other allocation principles are certainly not lacking. There is a rich tradition within philosophy of treatises on different principles in search of the "true" nature of justice or the ideal nature of society (e.g., Nozick, 1974; Rawls, 1971; Rescher, 1966). Besides the normative approach of philosophy, social psychological approaches are *descriptive* and *explanatory*. Researchers within the approach, variously called the contingency (e.g., Lansberg, 1984), classification (e.g., Lamm et al., 1981), or multiprinciple approach (e.g., Lerner, 1975; Leventhal, 1976a, 1976b; Mikula, 1980; Mikula & Schwinger, 1978; Schwinger, 1980; Törnblom, 1977b; Törnblom & Foa, 1983; Törnblom & Jonsson, 1985; Törnblom, Jonsson, & Foa, 1985), agree that a variety of additional principles (qualitatively different from equity) are perceived as appropriate and just in different situations.

This insight resulted in conceptual and theoretical refinements in social psychological analyses of distributive justice issues. However, there still exists a knowledge gap with regard to what and how many different principles (beyond the contribution, equality, and need principles) in terms of which different categories of people understand, define, and implement justice in various contexts. Common research strategies are to present fictitious positive or negative outcomes to subjects and observe their reactions, or to describe resource allocations resulting from the application of different allocation principles, and ask subjects to evaluate their justness. In other types of studies, subjects are asked to actually allocate (or state how they intend to allocate) outcomes in various contexts and situations.

Gaining information about people's naive conceptions of justice may very well extend current (and tentative) accounts of "important" justice principles. Although there is a lack of empirical studies with this focus (for exceptions, see for example Mikula, Petri, & Tanzer, 1989; Mikula, Schoebi, Jagoditsch, & Macher, 2009), a number of justice theorists have discussed allocation and justice principles other than the contribution, equality, and need principles.

A selection of theorists and the various distributive justice principles they have discussed appear in Box 2.1. The designations within parentheses indicate the subrule in terms of which a principle may be specified, categorized, and grouped (see further details later and Figure 2.2, as well as Törnblom, 1977b, 1992; Törnblom & Jonsson, 1985). It is not obvious whether some of the principles can be categorized as a particular subrule. The contribution, equality, and needs principles may be operationalized into at least three subrules each:

1. Cp, Ce, and Ca = Contribution of productivity, effort, and ability rules, respectively (see, for example, Rescher, 1966).

2. Et, Er, and Eo = Equality of treatment, results, and opportunity rules, respectively (Et refers to identical treatment at every occasion, Er to equality in the long run even if treatment at each occasion may be unequal, and Eo to same chance to receive rewards or punishments).

3. Nbi, Nba, and Nf = Biological, basic, and functional need rules, respectively (see Benn & Peters, 1959, pp. 144–147). Biological needs are those that concern survival; basic needs refer to those that allow a "decent" life in parity with the 'normal' standard of living in the person's society; and functional needs are those that enable a person to do his/her job).

Principles Versus Subrules

Several studies indicate that subjects distinguish and differentially evaluate subrules of the equality as well as the contribution principle (e.g., Brickman, 1977; Brickman, Folger, Goode, & Schul, 1981; Kayser & Lamm, 1980; Lamm & Kayser, 1978a, 1978b; Lamm, Kayser, & Schanz, 1983; Schmitt & Montada, 1982—see review in Törnblom and Jonsson, 1985). Thus, although a given equality subrule may be perceived as just in a given situation, another subrule of the equality principle may be viewed as unjust. Stated in other words, a situation defined as equal and just on the basis of a particular subrule (e.g., equality of treatment) may be perceived as unjust if a different subrule is applied to represent equality (e.g., equality of results). To take another example, an outcome allocation meant to accomplish equality of results may have to be generated via the application of *in*equality of treatment.

The need for conceptual clarity when communicating about justice is obvious, as the term *justice* may mean different things to different people. Even if the particular justice principle (e.g., equality) one has in mind is made explicit and named, it may still be unclear which one of its component subprinciples the person refers to (e.g., equality of opportunity). To further complicate the task of clear communication, the subprinciple may, for example, be interpreted and realized in more than one way (e.g., equality of opportunity may be realized via a lottery, by providing a common starting point, etc.). "No matter how much agreement there is among nations as to the desirability of distributive justice, conflicts will always occur in the absence of shared consensus about the general principle which best represents justice or . . . [in the absence of] . . . shared consensus about which subrule should be the legitimate representative of the principle in question)" (Törnblom, 1992, p. 196). Figure 2.2 (the "distributive justice tree") illustrates many of the distinctions that must be made in order promote communication clarity and avoid the many possible traps that threaten the accomplishment of a "common universe of discourse."

Box 2.1 Allocation Principles Discussed By Various Scholars

Lenski (1966)

1. Needs rule—(N).
2. Power rule—(Ca—acquired ability; or Cp).

Rescher (1966)

". . . distributive justice has been held to consist, wholly or primarily, in the treatment of all people:

1. as equals (except possibly in the case of certain "negative" distributions such as punishments) (Et)
2. according to their needs (N)
3. according to their ability or merit or achievements (Ca, Ce, or Cp)
4. according to their efforts and sacrifices (Ce)
5. according to their actual productive contribution (Cp)
6. according to the requirements of the common good, or the public interest, or the welfare of mankind, or the greater good of a greater number
7. according to a valuation of their socially useful services in terms of their scarcity in the essentially economic terms of supply and demand." (p. 73, abbreviations added)

Eckhoff (1974)

1. Objectively equal amounts to each—(Et).
2. Subjective equality—(Er) (need, desert).
3. Relative equality—(Cp) (fitness—ability to use/preserve, bear the burdens of the received outcome).
4. Rank order equality—(Cp, Ce, Ca) (status, position in a queue, rank, worthiness, seniority, etc.).
5. Equal opportunity—(Eo).

Deutsch (1985)

"Justice has been viewed as consisting in the treatment of all people:

1. so that all receive outcomes proportional to their inputs (Cp, Ce, Ca)
2. as equals (E)
3. according to their needs (N)
4. according to their ability (Ca)
5. according to their efforts (Ce)
6. according to their accomplishments (Cp)
7. So that they have equal opportunity to compete without external favoritism or discrimination (Eo)
8. according to the supply and demand of the market place
9. according to the requirements of the common good
10. according to the principle of reciprocity
11. so that none falls below a specified minimum."

Deutsch (1975)

1. Equality—(E).
2. Need—(N).
3. Equity—(Ca). The usual equity formulation is turned upside down: ". . . in pure cooperative systems a person's share of economic goods should be determined by his relative skill in using such goods for the common weal and that he should share in the consumer goods with others

Box 2.1 (Continued)

according to need (from each according to his ability, to each according to his need)." (p. 144) ". . . a person who can more effectively utilize a given scarce resource as a means of production than another person should have greater claim to its use." (pp. 143–144)

Lerner (1975)

1. Needs—(N).
2. Parity—(Eo, Et, Er).
3. Law, Darwinian justice.
4. Entitlement, social obligations.
5. Equity—(Ca, Ce, Cp).
6. Justified self-interest.

Leventhal (1976b)

1. Adhering to commitments (allocation acc to prior agreements).
2. Equity (acc. to how resources will be used, preserved, increased)—(Ca).
3. Equality—(Eo, Et, Et).
4. Reciprocity.
5. Need—(N).

Leventhal (1980)

1. The rule of justified self-interest.
2. The rule of adhering to commitments.
3. The ownership rule (i.e., continue possessing what's already owned).
4. The legality rule (distribution must be consistent with existing laws and regulations).
5. The status rule (high status persons should have higher outcomes than low status).

Brickman, Folger, Goode and Schul (1981)

1. Microjustice principles.
2. Need (N).
3. Effort (Ce).
4. Ability (Ca).
5. Macrojustice principles.
6. Minimum principle.
7. Subgroup principle.
8. Average or total principle.

Greenberg and Cohen (1982)

1. Own desires.
2. Self-interested justice.
3. Equality—(Er, Et, Eo).
4. Mutual need—(N).

Messick and Sentis (1983)

1. Equality of outcome per unit input—(Cp, Ce, Ca).
2. Equality of outcome—(Er).
3. Equal excess—equality above a minimum level—(Er).
4. Equality in psychic profit—(Er).
5. Procedural equality—equality in the application of rules and procedures rules (Thibaut & Walker, 1975)—(Er, Et, Eo).
6. Equality of opportunity—(Eo).

Box 2.1 (Continued)

Kayser, Schwinger, and Cohen (1984)

1. Need—(N).
2. Equality—(Et, Er, Eo).
3. Contribution—(Cp, Ce, Ca).
4. Maximal difference.
5. Maximal harm.

Reis (1984)

13 out of 17 principles can be categorized as

1. Justified self-interest (A*, B, D, L & N).
2. Reciprocity (G).
3. Altruism (K).
4. Need (C, P & Q)—(N).
5. Contributions (F & O)—(Cp & Cp, Ce and Ca).
6. Equality (I)—(Et, Er, Eo).

* Letters refer to Reis' original list of principles, some of which don't seem to be distributive principles (i.e., E, H, J, and M).

Sabbagh, Dar, and Resh (1994)

1. Arithmethic equality (Et).
2. Equality of results (Er).
3. Equality of opportunities (Eo).
4. Primary needs—survival and normal physical functioning—(Nbi).
5. Secondary needs—higher needs and emotional development—(Nba, Nf).
6. Effort (Ce).
7. Contribution (Cp).
8. Ability (Ca).

Conlon, Porter, and Parks (2004)

1. Contribution-of-past performance—(Cp).
2. Contribution-of-future/potential performance—(Cp).
3. Contribution-of-rank—(Cp).
4. Equality-of-opportunity (random draw)—(Eo).
5. Equality-of-chance meetings (first person run into)—(Eo).
6. Business need—(N).
7. Personal need—(N).
8. Political reasons (i.e., influence tactic of reciprocity for own benefit). This does not appear to be an allocation principle, per se, as reciprocity obligations may be created via the application of several different principles.

These insights may have theoretical and practical implications. Stating that distributive justice has been accomplished by applying *the* equality (or *the* contribution) principle is not very informative, unless the specific subrule that was applied to represent the principle is specified. Comparing the results from two studies reporting the impact of resource allocation according to the equality principle, for instance, may result in erroneous conclusions unless equality was operationalized into the same subrule in both studies.

Politically, it is quite possible to create social arrangements compatible with one principle by using the vocabulary of another as a disguise. For example, the application of the equality of opportunity subrule may serve conservative motives in that it tends to justify and maintain existing social inequalities (or create new ones), whereas

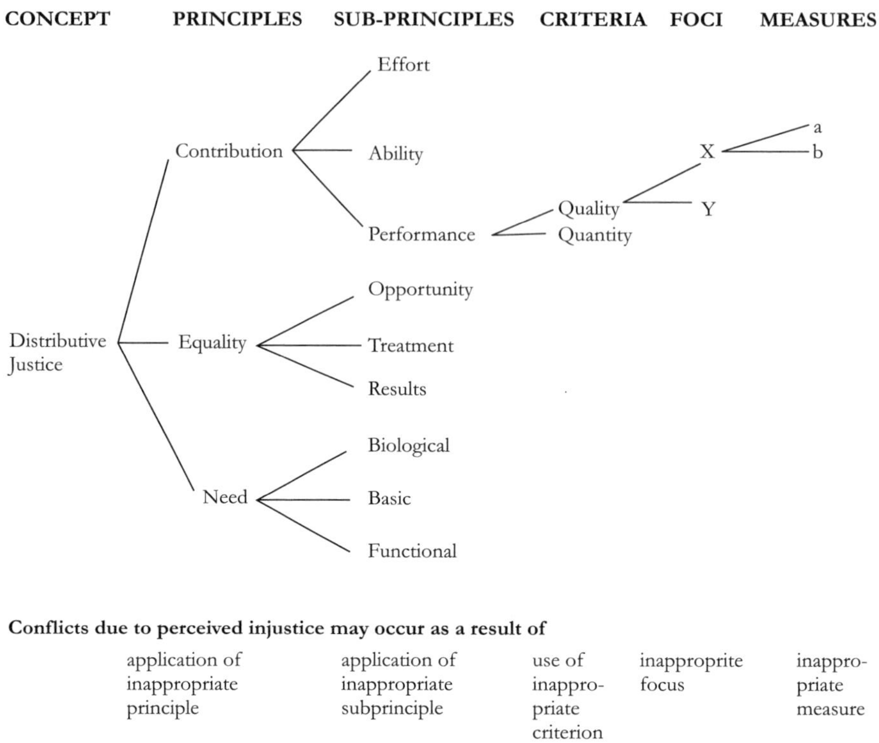

Fig. 2.2 The distributive justice tree.

(Reprinted with kind permission from Springer: Törnblom, K., & Kazemi, A. (2012). Advances in justice conflict conceptualization: A new integrative framework. In E. Kals & J. Maes (Eds.), *Justice and conflicts* (pp. 21–52).

the equality-of-results subrule may serve radical purposes in that it focuses on a redistribution of given resources (e.g., wealth and/or power) such that everyone will end up with equal amounts in the long run. Similar deceptions and/or misunderstandings may result when stipulations that salaries are based on the contribution principle are interpreted in terms of contributed efforts or productivity by factory workers and ability (in the shape of power and position in the company hierarchy) by managers. Thus, subordinates may easily be led into an erroneous assumption that the party they vote for, or the company they work for, is endorsing the version of the equality or the contribution principle that they favor and consider just.

We have sorted the principles discussed by the earlier listed scholars into four categories: equality, contribution, need, and other principles (see Boxes 2.2, 2.3, 2.4, and 2.5, respectively). Subsequent to the next section, we discuss the fact that sometimes combinations of allocation principles are applied. Finally, before we turn to some thoughts on future developments, we put the spotlight on macrojustice principles and sociopolitical perspectives. We have not identified or given credit to the scholar(s), for each principle in Boxes 2.2, who have attended to them theoretically and/or empirically. Due to the large number of social scientists in whose work the principles appear, such a task would be huge and unlikely to serve any significant purpose.

Varieties of the Equality, Contribution, Need, and Other Principles

> "... equality is at the heart of the concept of fairness. The issue is not whether equality is important but on what dimension the equality should be established. The problem of finding fair arrangements is not one of equality versus inequality but one of equality with regard to what."
>
> —Messick & Sentis, 1983, p. 68

Thus, as equality may be conceptualized in a variety of ways, it is important to avoid miscommunication by being explicit about the specific (sub)type of equality at hand, rather than using the vague term *equality*. Furthermore, some of those subtypes (e.g., equality of opportunity) may be incompatible with and conflict with others (e.g., equality of results). Examples of different types of principles designated as equality are listed in Box 2.2.

Box 2.2 Varieties of the Equality Principle

1. Objectively equal amounts to each (Et)—preserves existing inequalities.
2. Subjective equality (Er)—outcomes according to subjectively experienced needs)
3. Relative equality (C) (re: fitness—ability to use/preserve, bear the burdens of the received outcome)—better conceived as a contribution principle.
4. Rank-order equality (C) (status, position in a queue, rank, worthiness, seniority, etc.)—better conceived as a contribution principle.
5. Equal opportunity—equality of potential outcomes (Eo)—e.g., lottery.
6. Equality of outcome per unit input (C)—better conceived as a contribution principle.

(Principles 1–5 are discussed by Eckhoff, 1974, pp. 35–39.)

7. Equality of outcome (Et)—e.g., same wages to all, regardless of recipient characteristics.
8. Equal excess—equality above a minimum level (N + E)—a compound principle.
9. Equality in psychic profit from an exchange (Er)—a distinction based on the distributed type of outcome.
10. Procedural equality—equality in the application of rules and procedures (Et)

(Principles 1 and 6–10 are mentioned by Messick & Sentis, 1983, p. 68.)

11. Treating equals as equals (Cr, Ce and/or Ca)—Aristotle's proportional justice definition: treating equals equally and unequals unequally (Aristotle, 2002).
12. Arithmetic equality (Et).

Please note that some of the equality principles listed in Box 2.2 are often identified by different labels than equality in the behavioral-science literatures (especially by psychologists and social psychologists). Most theorists would call principles 3, 4, 6, and 11 contribution (equity, merit, or proportionality) principles rather than equality, as they refer to proportionality between outcomes and some differentiating criterion like "input" (rather than the same outcome to all, irrespective of individual differences regarding inputs). Further, the equal excess principle (8) is likely a combination of equality and some other principle(s), for example, need or contributions/equity (see later for other examples of "compounded principles").

If each equality principle is specified in terms of the *subprinciple* it is represented by, and they are sorted accordingly, principles 1, 7, and 10 are examples of the *equality of treatment* (Et) subprinciple, that is, each recipient receives equal amounts/values at each allocation event. Principles 2 and 9 are examples of the *equality of results* (Er) subprinciple, that is, each recipient receives equal amounts/values in the long run, even though they may receive unequal amounts at each allocation event. Equal final outcomes (Er) are often implemented to accomplish a fulfillment of needs. It should be noted that this is not an allocation principle, per se, because equal total outcomes can be accomplished by applying several allocation rules, singly or in combination. Thus, the means (principles) by which equality of results is accomplished must be specified. Principle 5 exemplifies an *equality of opportunity* (Eo) subprinciple, that is, recipients have the same opportunity to obtain a potential outcome via lottery or chance, for example. Equality in psychic profit (principle 9, discussed by Cook & Emerson, 1978) may perhaps represent either one of the equality subprinciples, as it is specified in terms of the type of outcome involved (i.e., psychic profit). Of course, all principles (not only equality) may be characterized according to the social resources (the various kinds of goods and bads, benefits and liabilities) that are allocated or exchanged.

Apart from the group of principles defined as *equality*, two other groups of principles are defined in terms of (a) *proportionality*, that is, the fit between outcomes and some criterion, such as various kinds of inputs or contributions (effort, power, ability, contributions to the group's welfare, etc.; see Box 2.3), and (b) between outcomes and needs (see Box 2.4). In addition, some principles that do not seem to be definable as varieties of the equality, contribution/equity, and need principles are featured in Box 2.5.

Box 2.3 Varieties of the Contribution (Equity, Merit) Principle

Contribution-of-performance subprinciple (Cp)

Several forms distinguished on the basis of outcomes according to inputs of:

1. Past performance, achievements, accomplishments, and actual productive contribution.
2. Future/potential performance.
3. The way resources will be used, preserved, increased, or delegated.
4. The social usefulness of contributions.

Contribution-of-effort and sacrifices (Ce)

Contribution-of-ability (Ca)

Less specific contribution/equity terms

1. Equity.
2. Outcomes proportional to inputs.
3. According to merit.
4. According to a valuation of socially useful services in terms of their scarcity in the essentially economic terms of supply and demand.
5. Darwinian justice.
6. Entitlement.
7. Social obligations.
8. Status rule.
9. Power principle.

Combinations of Allocation Principles

The recognition that justice may be conceptualized in terms of several criteria or allocation principles (rather than in terms of a single equity/contribution/merit/proportionality principle) led to the question "Under what conditions is a particular principle considered to yield a just resource allocation?" This multiprinciple approach is often based on the assumption that just resource distributions are typically guided by a single dominating principle that differs from situation to situation (e.g., Deutsch, 1975; Greenberg & Cohen, 1982; Kayser & Schwinger 1982; Kayser, Schwinger & Cohen, 1984; Lerner, 1975; Mikula & Schwinger, 1978; Törnblom & Jonsson, 1985).

Box 2.4 Varieties of the Needs Principle

1. Business need (Nf).
2. Personal need.
3. Biological (Nbi).
4. Basic (Nba).
5. Functional (Nf).
6. From each according to ability to each according to needs (Nba).

However, although the application of one single principle may be perceived as appropriate and just in some contexts, a *combination of two or more principles* may be viewed as most fair and beneficial in other contexts. For example, some political theorists (e.g., Raphael, 1970) have argued that the Welfare State combines the need and contribution principles. When basic needs are met, people may compete for additional rewards. Democratic socialist distributive justice is characterized by combining a system of social insurance to aid the disadvantaged with opportunities to secure rewards in some proportion to investments based on performance, effort, abilities, power, and so forth.

A more recent and complex exemplification of the need for a combination of principles is an interesting attempt at formulating a morally acceptable allocation system intended for application in contexts of scarce medical interventions, such as access to organs and vaccines (Persad, Wertheimer, & Emanuel, 2009). Their focus on a multiprinciple allocation system was necessitated by the realization that no single principle can cover all morally relevant issues that must be considered in a context where lives are at stake. As this might be equally true for most less-serious real-life situations in which resource allocations are at issue, increased

Box 2.5 Principles Other Than Contribution, Equality, and Need

1. Reciprocity.
2. The rule of justified self-interest (typically applied within a bargaining relationship).
3. Own desires.
4. The rule of adhering to commitments.
5. The ownership rule (continue possessing what's already owned).According to Nozick (1974) entitlement to a holding requires that the holding was acquired in two ways: (1)". . . in accordance with the principle of justice in acquisition," (2) ". . . in accordance with the principle of justice in transfer, from someone else entitled to the holding," and that "No one is entitled to a holding except by (repeated) applications of 1 and 2" (p. 151).
6. The legality rule (distribution consistent with laws and regulations).
7. Subgroup principle (i.e., ". . . an appropriate balance kept between the average allocations to two different subgroups of the total population"; Brickman et al., 1981, p. 190).
8. Minimum principle (i.e., ". . . the smallest allocation [should] be not too much less favorable than the largest allocation"; Brickman et al., 1981, p. 190).
9. Average or total principle (i.e., ". . . the average or the total allocation within the particular domain in question take into account constraints placed by requirements of other domains or other systems; Brickman et al., 1981, p. 190).
10. So that nobody falls below a specified minimum (Brickman et al., 1981).
11. Social utility rule (according to the requirements of the common good, or the public interest, or the welfare of mankind, or the greater good of a greater number, or supply and demand of the marketplace).
12. Maximal difference.
13. Maximal harm.
14. Altruism.
15. Compassion.

research efforts seems prudent here. Toward that end, an inventory of clearly distinguished and well formulated allocation principle candidates seems crucial. This is one of the reasons for the inventory of principles that we have provided in this chapter. The multiprinciple allocation system ("the complete lives system") advocated by Persad et al. (2009) as the most morally defensible for the allocation of organs and vaccines consists of a six-principle combination: lottery, youngest first, number of lives saved, life-years saved, instrumental value (i.e., social usefulness; to be included only in some public health emergencies), and reciprocity (to be included only for irreplaceable people who have suffered serious losses). The authors summarize their recommended complete-lives system as follows: it ". . . prioritizes younger people who have not yet lived a complete life, and also incorporates prognosis, save the most lives, lottery, and instrumental value principles" (p. 423).

A second approach to principle combination is when outcome justice is determined by arriving at an *overall estimate* via a calculation of the total amount (and kind) of rewards deserved on the basis of each relevant justice principle. In this respect, Leventhal's (1976b) "theory of justice judgment" is different from those that assume that a single principle governs resource distribution at any particular occasion. To arrive at a final assessment of deserved outcomes the individual is assumed to go through a four-phased justice judgment sequence: a *weighting phase*, during which the individual ". . . must decide which justice rules to use and how much weight to give them" (p. 215); a *preliminary estimation phase*, during which ". . . the amount and type of outcomes the receiver deserves on the basis of each applicable justice rule" is assessed (p. 215); a *rule combination phase*, during which an equation is used ". . . to obtain a final overall estimate of the amounts and types of outcomes deserved by the receiver" (p. 215); and an *outcome evaluation phase*, during which the justice of the actual outcome is assessed by comparing it to the deserved outcome.

A third, less common but perhaps equally plausible assumption is that people make *compromises* between two or more justice principles. Debusschere and Van Avermaet (1984) found that compromises occurred between the equality and contribution principles. However, with increased computational complexity, the amount of compromising decreased in favor of the equality principle. A re-examination of research (Griffith, 1989) suggested that compromise solutions may be more common than previously recognized, probably because allocations satisfying an *ordinal* conception of the contribution are frequently and erroneously regarded as an allocation "in the spirit of" equity (cf. Elliott & Meeker, 1984). In the context of a developmental study Damon (1977) outlined six age-related levels of justice reasoning in children. During the fifth level (Level 2-A) the child tries to compromise between competing and legitimate allocation claims. Other theorists (e.g., Deutsch, 1975; Leventhal, 1976b) agree that compromises among allocation principles are often necessary and not uncommon, a conclusion that is supported by a number of empirical studies (e.g., Greenberg, 1978a, 1978b; Leventhal, Michaels, & Sanford, 1972).

A different slant on the issue of compromise between justice principles was suggested by Sampson (1976). He focused on the equality and contribution principles and argued that we might miss the point by asking whether people are motivated by one or the other of the two conceptions of justice. Instead, he proposed that it is a balancing between them that yields justice, and that a too heavy emphasis on one of the principles may constitute a violation of justice. Sampson's hypothesis was that ". . . as either the differentiating tendencies of equity or the homogenizing tendencies of equality were to become excessive, the opposing process would enter as a kind of self-protective feedback circuit" (p. 470).

Macrojustice Principles and Socio-Political Justice Perspectives

We previously mentioned the distinction between micro- and macrojustice principles (Brickman et al., 1981), and up to this point we have primarily focused our attention to microjustice principles. Macrojustice refers to "the aggregate fairness of reward in a society," and microjustice is "the fairness of rewards to individual recipients" (Brickman et al., 1981, p. 173). Macrojustice concerns the fairness of the overall distribution of positive and negative outcomes across an aggregate, rather than how fair the distribution is for the individual members or the various subgroups of the larger aggregate entity. The authors discuss three macrojustice principles: the minimum, subgroup, and average or total macrojustice principles. According to the *minimum principle*, the smallest allocation should not be much smaller than the largest; the subgroup principle states that ". . . there should be an appropriate balance kept between the average allocations to two different *subgroups* of the total population" (p. 190); and the *average or total principle* prescribes that the total allocation should honor the requirements of other domains or systems.

Thus, macro-level justice principles are deindividuating and concern distributive justice assessments of the collectivity as a whole, as a unit of analysis. This distinction is important, because it calls for a focus on actual or potential conflicts between the individual's personal situation of justice and that of his membership group (see Jasso, 1983). For example, the reactions to and consequences of injustice will certainly differ (qualitatively as well as quantitatively) when both the individual and his group experience injustice as compared to when only the individual experiences injustice or when one of the two perceives injustice while the other does not (see Törnblom, 1995). Brickman et al. (1981, p. 180) argue that ". . . some version of microjustice principles and some version of macrojustice principles are present in every group and every culture. The main difference is how important the one set of principles is relative to the other."

From the perspectives of moral and political philosophers as well as political economists justice is conceived as one of several political ideals (e.g., liberty, fraternity, freedom). Schumann (2001), for instance, suggested that at least five different perspectives guide people's justice evaluations of positive and negative resource distributions:

1. Egalitarianism (i.e., the equality principle).
2. Capitalism (i.e., the equity, contribution principle).
3. Socialism (i.e., the need principle, Marx's principle "from each according to ability, to each according to needs").
4. Libertarianism (encompasses free choice, agreements, justified self-interest).
5. Rawls' (1971) principles of distributive justice, that is, behind the "veil of ignorance" people will choose two principles—the equal liberty principle (i.e., equality of treatment) and the difference principle: "The first

statement of the two principles reads as follows. First: each person is to have an equal right to the most extensive scheme of equal basic liberties compatible with a similar scheme of liberties for others. Second: social and economic inequalities are to be arranged so that they are both (a) reasonably expected to be to everyone's advantage, and (b) attached to positions and offices open to all." (Schumann, 2001, p. 53)

These listed principles reflect political ideologies that may characterize more than one level of social organization, from whole societies to smaller entities like work organizations. Of course, all these principles are not relevant to or meaningful for the distribution of all kinds of social resources. Indeed, most of the principles do target economic resources like money, goods and services. Thus, by considering the nature of the social resource at hand, some principles may need to be rephrased or even considered irrelevant.

The nature of the resources also has important implications in the context of a number of additional issues, and we now turn to some of those in the next section.

New Questions and Future Research Directions

In the following subsections, we provide some suggestions for future research. We specifically target some issues pertaining to (a) the object of distributive justice judgments, because these judgments concern not only the allocated amount or the application of certain allocation principles but also the type and production of allocated resources; (b) how justice relates to conflict and its various types; and (c) why people sometimes do not react to perceived injustices. Addressing these issues is relevant to general theorizing in the field of distributive justice and may also serve theory development in the domain of organizational justice.

Highlighting the Object of Distributive Justice Judgments

> "... the notion of Justice always involves allotment of something considered as advantageous: whether it be money or other material means of happiness; or praise, or affection, or other immaterial good, or some merited pain or loss."
>
> —*Henry Sidgwick*, 1893, p. 193, Chapter V of Book III

THE NATURE OF SOCIAL RESOURCE

Although the particular allocated or transacted resource is at the heart of any allocation event, surprisingly little research has been devoted to exploring the role of *the nature of the resource* in understanding justice phenomena (e.g., justice conceptions and evaluations as well as emotional and behavioral reactions to injustice). In addition to (social) resources, procedures are distributed as well (Cropanzano & Ambrose, 2001). For example, the procedural justice criterion "voice" (e.g., the opportunity to make one's standpoint known) may be allocated equitably (more opportunities to an expert than to a lay person), equally to all, or according to needs (see for example Greenberg & Cropanzano, 2001). It should be noted, however, that in the context of Foa's (1971) *social resource theory* (SRT), voice would be conceived as a "status" resource (because it indicates respectful treatment, that the person's views are valued and worth considering).

Recently SRT was presented and discussed in a special section of *Journal of Occupational and Organizational Psychology* aiming at "expanding the boundaries of resource theories in occupational and organizational psychology" (Gorgievsky, Halbesleben, & Bakker, 2011). The *Handbook of Social Resource Theory* (edited by Törnblom and Kazemi, 2012a) featured several chapters dealing with applications of resource theory in understanding organizational processes (Chiaburu, Byrne, & Weidert, 2012; Kazemi, Gholamzadehmir, & Törnblom, 2012; Kraemer & Chen, 2012; Mitchell, Cropanzano, & Quisenberry, 2012). This recent research attests to a revived interest in applying resource theories to understand distributive justice processes in general, as well as within the subfield of organizational justice in particular. For our present purposes we confine our discussions of resource theory to the original formulation by Foa (1971) and Foa and Foa (1974).

A large proportion of managerial decisions concerns resource allocation. There is, however, an unbalanced emphasis in the organizational justice literature on decisions regarding monetary allocation and the subsequent consequences for job performance, productivity, job satisfaction, commitment. As allocation and exchange processes encompass a variety of different kinds of resources (e.g., money, status, and information), a restricted focus on economic resources is too limited. A *social resource* is defined within SRT as "any commodity—material or symbolic—which is transmitted through interpersonal behavior" (Foa & Foa, 1974, p. 36), or "any item, concrete or symbolic, which can become the object of exchange among people" (Foa & Foa, 1980, p. 78).

SRT classifies interpersonal behavior in terms of six distinct resource categories: Love (an expression of affect, warmth, comfort, caring and support), status (judgments and expressions conveying high or low prestige, esteem, respect, acknowledgment and appreciation), information (advice, opinions, or instruction), money (currency with a standard unit of exchange value), goods (tangible products), and services (include activities on the body or belongings of an individual which involves labor for the person performing the service).

The six resource categories are circularly arranged along two orthogonal dimensions of particularism–universalism and concreteness–abstractness. Particularism is defined as the extent to which the value of a given resource is influenced by the identity of the provider or the relationship between provider and recipient. Thus, love or affection is the most particularistic resource category, whereas money is the least particularistic (i.e., most universalistic) resource. The value of money is little, or not at all, dependent on the identity of the provider. Concreteness refers to the form of the exchange, how it is expressed or the degree of tangibility of the resource (e.g., exchange of goods and services include concrete activities, whereas the exchange of status information occurs through more symbolic and abstract behaviors).

The particularism and concreteness dimensions define the attributes of the six resource categories and allow the generation of new rules of exchange of which our focus is on those relevant to distributive (and exchange) justice. One such rule stipulates that the resources provided and received in return should match; for example, the more particularistic a resource, the greater the likelihood that the behavior will be reciprocated with the same or similar type of resource. If this does not happen, people tend to perceive the exchange as unfair (Foa & Stein, 1980). According to this line of reasoning, justice prevails not only when the quantities of the invested and reciprocated resource match but also, and more importantly, when the kinds of exchanged resources match.

Research also indicates a relationship between allocation preferences and resource type: most people choose equality for the allocation of love, equity for status and money, and equality and need for information (e.g., Martin & Harder, 1994; Törnblom & Foa, 1983).

Beside their type, resources have two other features or attributes that are relevant to our discussion and which also impact allocation preferences and justice conceptions: *quantity* and *valence*. Research suggests that scarce resources are allocated according to the merit or need justice principles. On the other hand, when resources are abundant, distributive justice either becomes irrelevant or is established by applying an equal distribution (see Greenberg, 1981). A notion related to quantity is *resource priority*. Realizing that policy decisions in resource allocation very often entail a tension between achieving equality and efficiency, Matania and Yaniv (2007) proposed that resource priority or the degree of importance of resources impacts how much weight people gave to efficiency (operationalized in terms of equity: more to those who would benefit most from receiving the resource at hand) and equality concerns, respectively. Specifically, these researchers contrasted nonbasic (higher-level growth resources, e.g., education facilitating self-actualization) with basic (lower-level deficiency resources) resources and found that efficiency was conceived as weightier than equality in allocation of nonbasic resources.

Under what conditions do people prefer positive and negative resources to be allocated according to same or different justice principles? Research results do not provide us with unequivocal answers. Some studies found that subjects preferred both gains and losses to be allocated according to the same principle and that equality was generally considered more just than the equity principle (e.g., Griffith, 1989; Utz & Sassenberg, 2002). Other studies found that that profit/surplus was distributed equally and a loss/deficit equitably (e.g., Mannix, Neale, & Northcraft, 1995; Törnblom & Ahlin, 1998). This latter line of research suggests that people pursue different goals when allocating positive (i.e., achieving enjoyable social relationships) and negative outcomes (i.e., punishment), which may affect the choice of allocation principle in these contexts (cf. Kazemi & Eek, 2007).

There are other resource characteristics than type, quantity, and valence discussed here. Blalock (1991) identified a number of resource properties of relevance for allocation processes: divisibility, re-tractability, generalized value, depletion and replenishment, the degree to which they are subject to devaluation, the degree to which recipients share future power with allocators, and valence. Bothner, Godart, and Lee (2010) argued that resources differ in their stickiness, that is, the speed by which they fluctuate or how long they stick to a person. Galvin & Lockhart (1990) suggested a two-dimensional arrangement of resources based on their divisibility and fungibility (a resource is fungible when its value is not dependent on the identity of its possessor).

RESOURCE PRODUCTION AND ACQUISITION

> "If it matters how current holdings arose, then justice is to that extent historical, in which case questions arise about how to rectify past injustice. When it is too late to punish wrongdoers or make victims whole, rectification has to be about something other than undoing wrongs"
>
> —*Schmidtz*, 2006, p. 208.

As implied by this citation, the way social resources are produced or acquired will have consequences for justice-related issues. Nevertheless, most empirical and theoretical analyses of distributive justice have been confined to the nature and sufficiency of the resources of consumption that were awarded on the basis of some allocation principle. Very little attention has been given to the production of resources and the allocation of means of production, despite the fact that production normally precedes distribution. Perhaps the restriction of the analysis of distributive justice to consumption was a result of the longstanding instrumental view of work in Western industrialized societies. Labor was mainly viewed as a means to securing the financial means (monetary outcomes) that may be spent toward gratifying consumer needs such as food, shelter, education, health care, and various commodities. Nowadays, when labor is also conceived as an end in itself (e.g., a creative activity, self-actualization), the producer rather than the consumer perspective should be emphasized. Thus, issues pertaining to the aspect of production merit more research attention in studying justice judgments.

Previous research on justice and resource allocation has been criticized for a one-sided focus on the allocation of resources, as if it were separate from the process of production of those resources. Deutsch (1975) suggested that "... a person who can more effectively utilize a given scarce resource as a means of production than another person should have greater claim to its use" (pp. 143–144). Is the critique concerning the neglect of production-related issues pertinent to all types of resources?

Törnblom and Kazemi (2007) suggested that the relevance to justice conceptions of mode of resource production depends (at least partly) on the nature of the resource at hand. They concluded that the process of production is likely to be more relevant to the distribution of universalistic resources (i.e., goods, money, and information) than to particularistic resources (e.g., affect, status, services). For instance, the way retirement funds are generated (produced—via taxes or via private savings) will quite likely affect employees' views about the fairest way to allocate pensions. However, it seems a bit farfetched to assume that the fairness of the amount of concern a supervisor shows an employee is affected by the way the concern was generated. Furthermore, it seems reasonable to assume that the impact of mode of production on justice conceptions will be strongest within formal/impersonal/distant/economic social relationships and weakest within informal/personal/close/non-economic relationships (Törnblom & Kazemi, 2007, p. 54).

Törnblom and Kazemi (2007) posed two basic questions: (1) According to what distributive justice criteria should the means of production (rather than the resources of consumption) be distributed?, and (2) Does the manner in which a resource is produced affect people's conceptions about justice in resource distribution? For instance, do people allocate resources jointly produced by all group members differently as compared to resources produced by a single group member or just a few of them? What happens when outcomes are produced by means of positive or negative commission (i.e., doing good or doing bad, respectively) or through positive or negative omission (i.e., not doing bad or not doing good, respectively)? It should be noted that as different types of social resources may be produced in different ways, and as a given resource can be produced in more than one way, answering the second question is a complex undertaking.

To make the notion of process of production amenable to empirical research Törnblom and Kazemi (2007) proposed a conceptualization that included: (a) how the resource was produced, for example, how are abstract resources like services and information produced as compared to material goods? In what ways may different kinds of resources be produced? (b) the type of resource that was produced, (c) its valence, (d) the kind of required investment, (e) the amount of investment, (f) the purpose for which the resource was produced, (g) by whom it was produced, (h) for whom it was intended, (i) when and (j) within what social context it was produced. Some of the implications of this line of work are briefly mentioned later in this section where a number of work-related issues are discussed.

Other aspects in the context of resource production and its implications for justice cognitions and behavior concern certain "resource transformations" that may occur because of some rather nonobvious linkages among the production, possession, and provision of social resources (see Törnblom & Kazemi, 2007). Insights along these lines may generate a number of new research tasks that seem potentially fruitful for the study of organizational justice. At their present stage of elaboration, however, the practical implications of the three distinctions described below await future exploration.

1. *Resource-of-origin and resource-of-possession linkage.* A resource possessed by a person may have been acquired via an identical, similar, or dissimilar type of resource. For example, the code for a safety box (i.e., information) may be obtained via written instructions in the manual (i.e., information) published by the manufacturer, "purchased" (via monetary bribes), or it may be acquired by inflicting pain on the owner until s/he reveals the correct code (negative service in Foa's (1971) resource classification scheme). As far as we know, existing literature provides no clues about whether/how the impact of the mode of production on justice conceptions is moderated by the degree of correspondence between the resource-of-origin and the resource-of-possession.

2. *Resource-of-possession and resource-of-distribution linkage.* A resource of possession may be allocated not only as an identical but also in the form of a different kind of resource. Thus, a resource possessed by a person may be transformed into another when provided to others. For example, a plumber's know-how (i.e., information) about how to fix a leaking faucet may be written down and handed to a tenant to fix it on her own, or it may be "transformed" into the act of carrying out the repair on behalf of the tenant (i.e., service). Again, we have found no theoretical or empirical attention to this type of "linkage" in the literature.

3. *Resource production and its distribution may coincide.* The two stages or processes of production and distribution/provision of a resource may coincide in that its production and distribution are one and the same process. For instance, material goods have to be produced and possessed before they can be provided to somebody. But this is not the case when it comes to services; a service (e.g., on-the-job training) does not exist and cannot be possessed before it is materialized (via energy, money, effort, know-how and time expenditure) and given to a recipient. Only a prepotent resource, for example, information (or money), which allows the performance of a service, exists. Thus, the production of a resource is sometimes identical with its distribution.

To sum up our discussion regarding SRT, we may ask what implications these insights have for theory development and research in organizational justice and how they may guide practice in this field? Our present aim is to facilitate theoretical progress and the development of novel research questions for the study of organizational justice rather than formulating propositions or providing specific directions for research.

SRT (or resource theory of social exchange) is a development and refinement of theories within the social exchange orientation, the major statements of which were formulated by Thibaut and Kelley (1959), Homans (1958, 1961) and Blau (1964). According to Mitchell, Cropanzano, and Quisenberry (2012), "social exchange theory has provided organizational researchers with an influential framework for explaining work behavior" (p. 99). Some social-exchange-theory inspired justice research acknowledges the importance of socio-emotional resources and distinguishes these from economic resources (e.g., Chen, 1995; Cropanzano & Schminke, 2001; Martin & Harder, 1994). However, this simple distinction does not fully capture the complex nature of social exchange. Foa's (1971) resource theory is an important development in its analysis of the attributes and nature of the exchanged resources, as well as the resulting generation of new principles of exchange (see Törnblom & Kazemi, 2012a, Chapter 3 for a critical examination of the rules of exchange). Surprisingly, SRT has not, for some reason, been part of the social exchange approaches that have been adopted in analyses of organizational behavior.

SHEDDING NEW LIGHT ON JUSTICE-RELATED WORK ISSUES VIA SRT

We now turn our attention to some organizational justice related issues in the context of which SRT may inspire and contribute to theoretical developments and practical applications: health and stress, organizational support, leader-member-exchange theory, on-the-job professional training, and service-profit-chain.

Demand-control model. Demand-control model in its original formulation (Karasek, 1979) posits that factors enabling the employee to exert job control reduce the adverse effects of organizational demands. Organizational demands (stressors) vary in their nature—an issue that is not addressed by this model—and are evaluated in terms of justice (Vermunt, 2002; Vermunt & Steensma, 2005). Organizational demands may be imposed on employees by delivering negative or withholding positive resources. Occupational stress is assessed on the bases of how demanding a job is and how much control (or decision latitude) the employee has over his/her work tasks. A fit between the number and nature of demands and the employee's level of decision-making authority positively affects health.

According to the Person-Environment fit model (French, 1973), healthy jobs are characterized by a fit between the employees' resources (i.e., abilities and skills) and the demands of their job. Thus, organizations should pay attention to the needs of their employees for resources. Apparently, even though organization stress-strain models focus on resource exchanges and the match between the exchanged resources, they do not acknowledge or distinguish between different types of resources in terms of which strain of different kinds may occur.

Looking at the demand-control model through the lens of SRT reveals that whether and to what extent stressors cause strain and negative outcomes depends on the nature of control factors (e.g., information given to employees) and whether these match the nature of the organizational demands (e.g., uncertainty related to a re-organization). Specifically, SRT predicts that exchanges between compatible (or similar) resources are more likely to reduce negative stress effects, provided organizational demands (i.e., imposed re-organization) are accompanied by the provision of matching control resources (e.g., information about and in relation to the specific demand). In sum, as the demand-control model provides little guidance concerning the specific nature of demands and control resources, SRT may be a fruitful complement. SRT provides conceptual clarity, which is crucial for making more precise predictions about how different types of demands and control resources interact in affecting health related issues, productivity, coping, and so forth.

Perceived organizational support. Organizational demands, stress, and perceptions of justice are related to what has been called perceived organizational support (POS) (e.g., Eisenberger, Huntington, Hutchison, & Sowa, 1986; Shore & Shore, 1995). Eisenberger et al., define POS as employees' "global beliefs concerning the extent to which the organization values their contributions and cares about their well-being" (1986, p. 501). A scrutinization of their questionnaire shows that it only taps what is called particularistic resources (i.e., love, status, and services). However, the way POS conceptually is defined also suggests receiving support also in terms of universalistic resources (e.g., financial support or being provided with information in the form of feedback). Thus, the notion of POS may be re-conceptualized and re-operationalized by specifying the kind of support that the organization is providing to its employees and extending the support to include universalistic resources.

Instead of combining all items (related to different types of support resources) and treating POS as a one-dimensional concept, future research should examine the differential effects of various support sources on a number of organizational outcomes. More specifically, an interesting question awaiting future research is the relative weight of each resource in terms of which support can be provided (or withheld). For instance, is a lack of organizational support and the strains this places on the employee more related to particularistic (i.e., love, status, and services) or universalistic (i.e., money, goods, and information) resources? And which resource of organizational support is more strongly related to other important outcomes such as employee performance and turnover?

Leader-member exchange. Another specific workplace issue is the quality of relationships between the leader and co-workers. "Leader-Member Exchange (LMX) theory suggests that leaders do not use the same style in dealing with all subordinates, but rather develop a different type of relationship or exchange with each subordinate" (Liden & Maslyn, 1998, p. 43). LMX focuses on resource exchanges between the leader/manager and the co-workers (Graen & Uhl-Bien, 1995). Fundamental to the quality of these relationships is exchanges of various kinds (e.g., appreciation, monetary rewards, support, and loyalty).

Implicit contracts determine in several ways how leaders and employees act toward each other. High-quality occupational relationships positively affect employee qualities such as responsibility, commitment, creativity, etc. (Gerstner & Day, 1997). LMX theory reminds us of the fact that leaders develop several relationships with members of their work group, and that the nature of the various exchanges between the leader and the employee result from the nature of the various kinds of relationships between them.

Cross-fertilization between LMX and SRT would most likely be fruitful, because LMX and the scales used to assess the leader-follower relationship quality do not specify leader-member exchanges in terms of the nature of resources being transacted and thus fail to tap relationship quality as a multifaceted concept. Future research may want to integrate these two theories to enhance the predictive and explanatory power of LMX concerning various organizational outcomes (e.g., justice perceptions and work behavior resulting from these). A scale could also be constructed that tap leader-member relationship quality in terms of resource exchange profiles that describe the perceived access to, lack and importance of different types of social resources.

On-the-job professional training. The basic idea behind all personnel training is to provide resources to the participants who will eventually reciprocate with increased productivity, higher sale rates, and knowledge transfer to the organization. By designing resource-conscious training programs (making inputs and outcomes explicit in terms of the resources provided and received), the employer organization can to some extent affect the kind of culture and workplace climate that it wishes to maintain or create. Training as such can be conceived as a service to the employees. At the same time, providing training signals that the employer cares about its personnel (i.e., love). Moreover, trainees acquire technical skills (i.e., information) which in turn increase their status due to their better mastery of their tasks which, in turn, frequently results in a higher salary (i.e., money). Using SRT reveals that on-the-job training provides employees with multiple resources and is, therefore, a good investment on the part of the organization. Training also has a bearing on the resources the trainees bring back to and invest in the organization (cf. de Grip & Sauermann, 2012; Minhong & Jae-Sung, 2012).

Service-profit chain. Service-profit chain (SPC) is a conceptual framework linking employee satisfaction and loyalty to customer satisfaction, customer loyalty, and financial performance (Heskett, Jones, Loveman, Sasser, & Schlesinger, 1994; Heskett, Sasser, & Schlesinger, 1997). SPC starts with the overall question of what makes some companies sustainably more profitable than other companies. When Heskett and his colleagues (1994) investigated that overall question, they soon found a series of interlinked activities between customers, employees serving those customers and the interaction between employees and their managers. Good service quality starts with the service providing company's internal way of organizing work—called the internal service quality—which is assumed to lead to a certain degree of perceived quality by the customer (called the external service quality) via employee satisfaction and loyalty. The internal service quality or leadership practices is to a great extent about allocating resources, and this shows a promising (but hitherto missing) link between justice theory, social resource theory, and SPC.

If the external service quality is perceived by the customer to be good enough, the customers feel satisfied with and continue being loyal toward the company, which in turn results in company profitability and growth. One of us has reported a partial test of the SPC-model focusing on the relationship between leadership practices and employee engagement and loyalty (Andersson, Kazemi, Tengblad, & Wickelgren, 2011). The results indicated that giving employees the opportunities to improve their work performance by helping them grow in their jobs through employee development practices (training, see our previous discussion of training in terms of social resources) was positively associated with the way they judged their work satisfaction in a more general sense and how engaged they were. Retail worker loyalty and engagement was furthermore positively associated with employee LMX and how retail workers judged managerial capacities of the retail manager, indicating that leader-member exchanges are of importance for the level of engagement and loyalty among retail workers.

All these links in the SPC-framework can be re-conceptualized and conceived of in terms of different social resources being exchanged between the organization (via the manager) and the employees on one hand, and between the employees and their customers/clients on the other hand. To the best of our knowledge, no research has investigated how exchanges in one relationship spill over and affect exchanges in other relationships (cf. research on transrelational justice, Moschetti & Kues, 1978). SRT may extend and deepen our understanding of the processes involved in these kinds of multirelational activities and chain processes as proposed by the SPC-framework.

To conclude, we have briefly given some hints at the utility of social resource theory in shedding new light on some areas and theories in organizational research. We have also shown that SRT may generate re-conceptualizations and re-interpretations of some previous findings in the field of (organizational) distributive justice.

Justice Conflicts

A fair amount of theory and research has been devoted to justice conflict (e.g., Deutsch, 1986; Hegtvedt, 1992; Hegtvedt & Cook, 1987; Jasso, 1993; Lamm, 1986; Mikula & Korytko, 1990; Mikula & Wenzel, 2000; Montada, 2007; Törnblom, 1988, 1995). Within organizational settings, justice issues typically become salient in the context of organizational changes. Reorganizations typically involve changes in the way resource allocations are calculated and carried out. When previously accepted and applied-allocation principles are replaced, feelings of injustice frequently emerge. When the rules of the game are altered by changing how inputs are valued, or by changing the criteria specifying what inputs are required to obtain certain outcomes, it is likely that employees perceive that current agreements guiding resource allocation are violated, and that the new situation is, therefore, unjust. Such violations may be viewed as potential (or "conceptual") conflicts, i.e., "discord, incongruence, inconsistency, incompatibility, divergence, discrepancy . . . between concepts/phenomena such as values, norms, and rules, and . . . between concepts like these and behavior" (Törnblom & Kazemi, 2012b, p. 24).

Unfortunately, the meaning of conflict is most often taken for granted by justice researchers and seldom spelled out. It is implicitly equated with the general and unspecific notion of social conflict, the definition of which lack consensus among scholars concerned with the analysis of social conflict phenomena (see Törnblom & Kazemi, 2012b). Even though, as Montada (2007) points out, "All social conflicts may be interpreted as justice conflicts" (p. 256), the progress of justice-conflict theorizing and relevant empirical research are contingent on clear conceptual distinctions among and definitions of different types of such conflicts. Remedying the conceptual confusion in the justice literature has important implications for theory development and the analysis of intrapersonal, interpersonal, intragroup, and intergroup justice conflicts (e.g., Jasso, 1993) as well as for the planning of conflict resolution strategies at societal, organizational, and interpersonal levels.

Törnblom and Kazemi (2012b) defined and distinguished among three major kinds of distributive justice conflicts. *Conceptual (potential) distributive justice conflict*, is "a situation in which different and incompatible allocation principles or subprinciples are perceived as equally just and legitimate for a particular resource allocation event" (p. 25). Conceptual conflicts are potential conflicts that can be managed before they evolve into a social conflict. *Social distributive justice conflict*, is "a situation in which two or more parties struggle against each other for (scarce) resources that each party feel entitled to, each party defining just entitlement in terms of the same allocation principle" (p. 25). *Conceptual-social distributive justice conflict* is a mixture of both kinds, that is, "two or more parties who struggle against each other for resources that each party feel entitled to, each party defining just entitlement in terms of different and incompatible allocation principles" (p. 25).

Each of these types of conflict were further specified into a total of 13 subtypes (e.g., Conceptual distributive justice conflict subtypes: justice principle determinant conflict, justice principle conflict, justice subprinciple conflict, violation of a justice principle by means of other conflicting justice principles, and conflicts between justice and other goals [e.g., sympathy, efficiency, self-interest]. Social distributive justice subtypes: perspective conflict [e.g., allocator, recipient], interpersonal justice conflict, individual–group justice conflict, intergroup justice conflict, and individual/group–intergroup justice conflict).

The nature of workplace (justice) conflicts may certainly differ, in terms of these (and other) distinctions and may not be effectively managed if lumped together and exposed to identical resolution strategies. Törnblom and Kazemi's typology may serve as a framework within which previous and future theoretical and empirical studies of justice conflict issues may be located and compared.

Reactions, and Lack Thereof, to Injustice

People frequently do not think in terms of justice until it is violated. Previous justice research has focused on reactions to perceived injustice. On the individual level, common reactions are self-centered, e.g., stress, dissatisfaction, depression, self-depreciation, feeling of guilt, loss of motivation, and apathy. There are also other-centered reactions toward sources of injustice include disobedience, anger, theft, sabotage, violence, murder, and sick leave. Some reactions are transrelational, that is, manifested in some relationship other than the one within which the injustice occurred. Although research has convincingly demonstrated the importance of justice in a wide variety of contexts, the fact that people sometimes do not react to injustice has not elicited matching interest by social scientists.

We have identified and listed a number of reasons in the following paragraphs about why people do not always react to acts of injustice (see Box 2.6) . In some cases, we have given references to relevant work; in other cases, we have not been able to do so. Because some of the reasons behind nonreactions are self-explanatory, we only comment on those that are not.

"*Forgiveness* [italics added] means deciding not to punish a perceived injustice, taking action on that decision, and experiencing the emotional relief that follows" (Affinito, 1999, p. 11). Estrada-Hollenbeck (1996) found that forgiveness had a great impact on victims' emotions but also on how they assessed the quality of their relationship with the perpetrator, suggesting that victims may forgive because it is instrumental in giving them a sense of inner peace.

Justice trap refers to a situation in which the victim strategically instigates unjust behavior from another person and deliberately chooses not to react in order to parade his/her own virtuous behavior and expose the perpetrator's moral deficiencies.

Nonreactions to injustice may also be culturally determined. We have not been able to locate any studies that specifically have investigated nonreactions to injustice in different national cultures. But there is an interesting observation called the *generosity effect* reported in Leung and Bond (1984) that may be relevant to our discussion here. These researchers found that both Chinese and American participants used the equity principle with out-group members in a joint task. However, with in-group members, Chinese participants—in contrast to American participants—allocated equally when the fellow group member had contributed less than the participant, but they opted for the equity principle when the other member had contributed more than the participant. Leung and Bond called this the generosity effect, a behavior consistent with the concern for harmony in the Chinese culture. This study illustrates that the greater preference for the equality or need principles in collectivist cultures depends on who the recipient is. This evidence is also consistent with the contention that people from collectivist cultures are more responsive to group and group membership than people from more individualistic cultures. This may imply that people from collectivistic cultures may choose not to react to injustices (i.e., that an in-group member who does not deserve to receive a share from a collective good actually receives a share) due to a norm of generosity conducive to the maintenance of harmony in close social relationships. The generosity effect may explain why people refrain from reacting to injustice in some cultures.

According to the "*hurdle model*," people will not act on the basis of their attitude until its magnitude exceeds a certain level (cf. Campbell's 1963 discussion of attitude-behavior inconsistency). Verbal expression of an attitude has a lower threshold than overt behavior (a response that must "jump over the highest hurdle") that is consistent with the attitude, especially in the case of negative attitudes. In other words, people are less ready to overtly act on the basis of an attitude than to announce their feelings verbally, unless its intensity exceeds a certain level. And if the intensity of the attitude is very low, it may not even be expressed verbally (i.e., pass the verbal hurdle). In line with this reasoning, if the magnitude of perceived injustice is low, verbal or overt reactions may not occur (we usually don't bother to make ourselves upset about small injustices that are part of everybody's daily experiences).

Equalization effect is related to what has been discussed as *equity with the world* (Austin & Walster, 1974b). Equity with the world is defined as "the degree of equity present in the *totality* of a person's relationships" (p. 531). Thus, an employee may refrain from reacting to an unjust salary because supplementary income is derived via yields from his shares in the company.

Individual difference factors may affect our propensity to react to acts of injustice. Schmitt, Neumann, and Montada (1995) proposed that the *dispositional sensitivity to befallen injustice* consists of the dimensions of *frequency* (of experiencing yourself as a victim of injustice), *intensity of anger* (subsequent to unfair distribution or treatment), *intrusiveness of thoughts* (moral mental load, how much the person dwells on an unfair event), and *punitivity* (to what extent and in what way a person thinks that an agent of injustice should be forced to restore justice). These researchers found that this disposition predicted cognitive, emotional, and behavioral reactions to injustices in both laboratory and field settings. It is also reasonable that the four aspects of the dispositional sensitivity to befallen injustice also explain nonreactions to acts of injustice. More specifically, a person who subjectively perceives herself/himself to be a victim of injustice only occasionally may not get angry in the face of injustice, think intensely on unjust events, or show strong tendencies to punish the source of injustice, and thus may not react to the injustice.

Whether the injustice is expected or unexpected has also been shown to be related to whether and how people react to injustice: "expectancy ameliorates distress, even when a person clearly realizes that the expected event is inequitable.. . . A warning should dampen his affective and physiological response, thus damping his motivation to combat the injustice" (Austin & Walster, 1974a, pp. 208–209).

False consciousness is an attitude held by members of a class that does not accurately reflect their objective position; thus, they are unable to recognize inequality, oppression, and exploitation. This phenomenon was discussed by Marx and Engels. Thus, sometimes people do not react to injustice simply because they are unaware that injustice has occurred.

Due to the so called *trickle-down effect* (cf. Rawls, 1971, 1985) "underdogs" may choose not to react, not because they are unaware of inequalities, but because they assume that if the "upperdogs" get richer, this will have a positive effect on their situation as well. The situation may still be perceived as unfair, and the gap between them and the well-to-do may have grown wider but the less well-off are better off, and, therefore, they neither protest nor react to injustice.

System justification theory (e.g., Jost & Banaji, 1994; Jost, Banaji, & Nosek, 2004) states that people have a general tendency to defend and justify the status quo even in the face of disadvantageous inequality on the part of some groups. The motivation to preserve stability may be characterized as a fear of change and, thus, prevent observers and even victims from reacting to injustice.

There is a considerable potential for theory development in this subject area. The reasons listed in Box 2.1 are not categorized. However, at least three criteria might provide a basis for classification into categories of reasons, active–passive, victim–perpetrator perspective, and justice for self-justice for others. An interesting line of inquiry would focus on the conditions under which certain ways of nonreaction are more likely than others and whether they are mediated by different psychological processes. For instance, is it reasonable to assume that people low on justice sensitivity or belief-in-a-just-world would have higher thresholds and that these people use other "strategies" than people high on justice sensitivity and/or belief-in-a-just-world? Is it reasonable to assume that people high on justice sensitivity always react to injustices, and if not when do they tend to refrain from reacting to injustices? And what about "viewing injustice as just," under what conditions do people view an injustice as just?

Kazemi and Törnblom (2010) proposed a number of circumstances under which *unfairness/injustice may be seen as fair/just*, for example, (a) when the victim is blamed (the victim deserves his fate, Lerner, 1980); (b) when unfairness is advantageous; (c) when legal and subjective perceptions of justice collide; (d) when multiple types of resources are considered; (e) when another justice principle is salient or appropriate; (f) when fair procedures overshadow distributive unfairness; (g) when the moral community is redefined (Deutsch, 1985); and (h) when rationalizing and redefining the situation makes us feel better.

To sum up, two questions were posed here: (a) Under what conditions may people refrain from reacting to injustices?, and (b) Under what conditions may injustices be defined as just? These questions seem worthy of attention as they serve theoretical as well as practical interests. Why is closer attention to what appears to be indifference to injustice important? First of all, it is important for political-ideological reasons. Specifically, indifference to injustice is a threat to democracy and its core values, or as Martin Luther King Jr. put it: "Injustice anywhere is a threat to justice everywhere." The question is also relevant from a humanitarian perspective. Again, Martin Luther King Jr. said: "The ultimate tragedy is not the oppression and cruelty by the bad people but the silence over that by the good people." Nonreaction to injustice may breed injustice and undermine the courage to defend humanitarian values in the workplace and society. Appropriate and timely reactions to injustice may result in just (or at least less unjust) outcomes (particularly on the part of those who for various reasons are incapable to act on behalf of themselves). Finally, explanations for lack of responses to injustice need to be considered in the context of research studies that did not observe any reactions to injustice by victims (or perpetrators or observers) of injustice.

Concluding Remarks

As we mentioned in the opening of this chapter, our objective was not to provide overviews of recent theory and research of social justice in general, the area of distributive justice, or organizational justice

Box 2.6 Why Don't People React To Injustice?

1. *Intra-psychic revenge* (e.g., fantasies about inflicting pain on the source of injustice).
2. Victim of injustice *forgives* the perpetrator (cf. Estrada-Hollenbeck, 1996).
3. *Attribution of intention* (e.g., s/he didn't mean to be unjust, it just happened; cf. Mikula, 2003).
4. *Transrelational redress* (the victim targets a person other than the source of injustice; Moschetti & Kues, 1978).
5. *Justice trap.*
6. *Fear of negative consequences* (e.g., humiliation or harm if one acts favorable toward the victim, see Deutsch, 1985).
7. Trickle-down effect (cf. Rawls, 1971, 1985).
8. *Sin punishes itself.*
9. Feeling *powerless*; lack *of means to act.*
10. *Expected future payoff* (e.g., strategic use of fairness, see van Dijk, De Cremer, & Handgraaf, 2004).
11. *Victim's incapability of translating feelings of injustice into appropriate actions* (e.g., due to physical disabilities, imprisonment, long distance from the source of injustice).
12. *Source of injustice* is unknown, ambiguous, or unavailable.
13. Belief that *one's own and the victim's personal interests are opposed* (Deutsch, 1985).
14. Belief that the *victim's situation is improving* and justice will soon be established (Lerner, 1980).
15. *Victimizer is ignorant of the victim's experience* of injustice due to lack of contact (Deutsch, 1985).
16. Belief that the *situation is hopeless* so that all attempts to redress will be inadequate (Deutsch, 1985).
17. *Culturally determined* (e.g., Leung & Bond, 1984).
18. *"Hurdle model"* (cf. Campbell's 1963 discussion of attitude-behavior inconsistency)
19. *Equalization effect* (cf. equity with the world, Austin & Walster, 1974b).
20. *Individual difference factors* (Dalbert, 2001; Huseman, Hatfield & Miles, 1987; Schmitt, Neumann, & Montada, 1995; e.g., belief that man is inherently amoral and that the world is not just, Deutsch, 1985).
21. *Expected vs. unexpected injustice* (Austin & Walster, 1974a).
22. *Change of perspective* (e.g., from victim to perpetrator or outside observer) (cf. Deutsch, 1985; Lerner, 1980).
23. *False consciousness* (see Lukács, 1972; Marx, 1977).
24. *System justification* (e.g., Jost & Banaji, 1994; Jost, Banaji, & Nosek, 2004).
25. Viewing *injustice as just* (Kazemi & Törnblom, 2010).

specifically. Also, there are several types or dimensions of social justice that we have not discussed in this chapter, for example, retributive or restorative justice, transitional or redistributive justice. The interested reader may consult several already existing excellent reviews. Instead, we chose to put special foci on descriptions and analyses of some selected distributive justice theoretical statements of the past, and several distributive justice principles and their combinations—in addition to various forms of the equity, equality, and need principles—that have been discussed in the psychological, social psychological, and sociological literatures but very seldom appear in empirical research. We based our descriptions of the selected theoretical statements on four dimensions or criteria. However, we have not engaged in "theoretical analysis" to determine which of the theoretical statements qualify as models or as theories. Thus, the terms *model* and *theory* are used loosely. With regard to distributive justice principles we have been careful to warn against assuming that an allocation principle and a distributive justice principle are the same thing.

Another objective with this chapter was to encourage research targeting the significance of the nature of the exchanged or distributed object (social resource) for justice evaluations and processes. The nature of a resource may be described in terms of several dimensions or properties (e.g., valence, divisibility, particularism, and concreteness) in addition to prevailing "external conditions" like its available amount, importance, production, fungibility, and acquisition. In this context, we provided several examples regarding how several areas of organizational justice may benefit by incorporating resource-related insights. Another area that has been combined with distributive justice for mutual fertilization resulting in further elaboration and development is social conflict. We concluded the chapter with a discussion about why injustices may pass unnoticed or even be considered just by victims, perpetrators, and observers.

Our vision for the next generation of justice researchers is that past theoretical statements and research findings will form a rigorous foundation on which the evaluation of new ideas, the formulation of more sophisticated theories, and empirical research progress will stand. This foundation will benefit efforts to apply knowledge within the area to alleviate pressing problems in work organizations.

References

Adams, J. S. (1963). Toward an understanding of inequity. *Journal of Abnormal and Social Psychology, 67*, 422–436.

Adams, J. S. (1965). Inequity in social exchange. In L. Berkowitz (Ed.), *Advances in experimental social psychology* (pp. 267–299). New York, NY: Academic Press.

Affinito, M. G. (1999). *When to forgive: a healing guide to help you come to terms with your emotions and values, make the tough choices, and put your decision into action.* Oakland, CA: New Harbinger.

Anderson, B., Berger, J., Zelditch, M. Jr., & Cohen, B. P. (1969). Reactions to inequity. *Acta Sociologica, 12*, 1–12.

Andersson, T., Kazemi, A., Tengblad, S., & Wickelgren, M. (2011). Not the inevitable bleak house? The positive experiences of workers and managers in retail employment in Sweden. In I. Grugulis & Ö. Bozkurt (Eds.), *Retail work* (pp. 253–276). London, UK: Palgrave Macmillan.

Aristotle (2002). Nichomachean ethics (S. Broadie & C. Rowe [Eds.], Trans.). New York, NY: Oxford University Press. (Originally published 384-322 BCE).

Austin, W. N., McGinn, C., & Susmilch C. (1980). Internal standards revisited: Effects of social comparisons and expectancies on judgments of fairness and satisfaction. *Journal of Experimental Social Psychology, 16*, 426–441.

Austin, W., & Walster, E. (1974a). Reactions to confirmations and disconfirmations of expectancies of equity and inequity. *Journal of Personality and Social Psychology, 30*, 208–216.

Austin, W., & Walster, E. (1974b). Participants' reactions to "equity with the world." *Journal of Experimental Social Psychology, 10*, 528–548.

Benn, S. I., & Peters, R. S. (1959). *Social principles and the democratic state.* London, UK: George Allen and Unwin.

Berger, J., Zelditch, M, Jr., Anderson, B., & Cohen, B. P. (1972). Structural aspects of distributive justice: A status value formulation. In J. Berger, M. Zelditch, & B. Anderson (Eds.), *Sociological theories in progress* (Vol. 2, pp.119–246). Boston, MA: Houghton-Mifflin.

Blalock, H. M., Jr. (1991). *Understanding social inequality. Modeling allocation processes.* Newbury Park, CA: SAGE Publications.

Blalock, H. M., Jr., & Wilken, P. H. (1979). *Intergroup processes. A micro-macro perspective.* New York, NY: The Free Press.

Blau, P. M. (1964). *Exchange and power in social life.* New York, NY: Wiley.

Bothner, M. S., Godart, F. C., & Lee, W. (2010). *What is social status? Comparisons and contrasts with cognate concepts.* Working Paper, European School of Management and Technology, Berlin, Germany.

Brickman, P. (1977). Preference for inequality. *Sociometry, 40*, 303–310.

Brickman, P., Folger, R., Goode, E., & Schul, Y. (1981). Microjustice and macrojustice. In M. J. Lerner & S. C. Lerner (Eds.), *The justice motive in social behavior: Adapting to times of scarcity and change* (pp. 173–204). New York, NY: Plenum Press.

Campbell, D. T. (1963). Social attitudes and other acquired behavioral dispositions. In S. Koch (Ed.), *Psychology: A study of a science* (pp. 94–172). New York, NY: McGraw-Hill.

Chen, C. C. (1995). New trends in rewards allocation preferences: A Sino-U.S. comparison. *Academy of Management Journal, 38*, 408–428.

Chiaburu, D. S., Byrne, Z. S., & Weidert, J. (2012). Resources and transactions in the organization's underworld: Exchange content and consequences. In K. Y. Törnblom & A. Kazemi (Eds.), *Handbook of social resource theory. Theoretical extensions, empirical insights, and social applications* (pp. 333–348). New York, NY: Springer.

Cohen, R. L. (1974). Mastery and justice in laboratory dyads: A revision and extension of equity theory. *Journal of Personality and Social Psychology, 29*, 464–474.

Cohen, R. L., & Greenberg, J. (1982). The justice concept in social psychology. In J. Greenberg & R. L. Cohen (Eds.), *Equity and justice in social behavior* (pp. 1–41). New York, NY: Academic Press.

Conlon, D. E., Porter, C. O. L. H., & McLean Parks, J. (2004). The fairness of decision rules. *Journal of Management, 30*, 329–349.

Cook, K. S., & Emerson, R. M. (1978). Power, equity, and commitment in exchange networks. *American Sociological Review, 43*, 721–739.

Cook, K. S., & Hegtvedt, K. A. (1983). Distributive justice, equity, and equality. *Annual Review of Sociology, 9*, 217–241.

Cropanzano, R., & Ambrose, M. L. (2001). Procedural and distributive justice are more similar than you think: A monistic perspective and a research agenda. In J. Greenberg & R. Cropanzano (Eds.), *Advances in organizational justice* (pp. 119–151). Stanford, CA: Stanford University Press.

Cropanzano, R., & Rupp, D. E. (2002). Some reflections on the morality of organizational justice. In S. W. Gilliland, D. D. Steiner, & D. P. Skarlicki (Eds.), *Emerging perspectives on managing organizational justice* (pp. 225–278). Greenwich, CT: Information Age Publishing.

Cropanzano, R., & Schminke, M. (2001). Using social justice to build effective work groups. In M. Turner (Ed.), *Groups at work: Advances in theory and research* (pp.143–171). Hillsdale, NJ: Erlbaum.

Dalbert, C. (2001). *The justice motive as a personal resource: Dealing with challenges and critical life events.* New York, NY: Plenum Press.

Damon, W. (1977). *The social world of the child.* San Fransisco, CA: Josey-Bass.

Debusschere, M., & Van Avermaet, E. (1984). Compromising between equity and equality: The effects of situational ambiguity and computational complexity. *European Journal of Social Psychology, 14*, 323–333.

De Grip, A., & Sauermann, J. (2012). The effects of training on own and co-worker productivity: Evidence from a field experiment. *Economic Journal, Royal Economic Society, 122*, 376–399.

Deutsch, M. (1975). Equity, equality, and need: What determines which value will be used as the basis of distributive justice? *Journal of Social Issues, 31*, 137–149.

Deutsch, M. (1985). *Distributive justice: A social-psychological perspective.* New Haven, CT: Yale University Press.

Deutsch, M. (1986). Cooperation, conflict, and justice. In H. W. Bierhoff, R. L. Cohen, & J. Greenberg (Eds.), *Justice in social relations* (pp. 3–18). New York, NY: Plenum Press.

Eckhoff, T. (1974). *Justice: Its determinants in social interaction.* Rotterdam, Netherlands: Rotterdam University Press.

Eisenberger, R., Huntington, R., Hutchison, S., & Sowa, D. (1986). Perceived organizational support. *Journal of Applied Psychology, 71*, 500–507.

Elliot, G. C., & Meeker, B. F. (1984). Modifiers of the equity effect: Group outcome and causes for individual performance. *Journal of Personality and Social Psychology, 46*, 586–597.

Estrada-Hollenbeck, M. (1996). *Forgiving in the face of injustice: Victims' and perpetrators' perspectives.* In B. Galaway & J. Hudson (Eds.), *Restorative justice: International perspectives* (pp. 303–314). Monsey, NY: Criminal Justice Press.

Festinger, L. (1954). A theory of social comparison processes. *Human Relations, 7*, 117–140.

Festinger, L. (1957). *A theory of cognitive dissonance.* Evanston, IL: Row, Peterson.

Foa, U. G. (1971). Interpersonal and economic resources. *Science, 71*, 345–351.

Foa, U. G., & Foa, E. B. (1974). *Societal Structures of the Mind.* Springfield, IL: Charles C. Thomas Publisher.

Foa, E. B., & Foa, U. G. (1980). Resource theory: Interpersonal behavior as exchange. In K. J. Gergen, M. S. Greenberg, & R. H. Willis (Eds.), *Social exchange: Advances in theory and research* (pp. 77–94). New York, NY: Plenum Press.

Foa, U. G., & Stein, G. (1980). Rules of distributive justice: Institution and resource influences. *Academic Psychology Bulletin, 2*, 89–94.

French, J. R. P., Jr. (1973). Person role fit. *Occupational Mental Health, 3*, 15–20.

Galvin, R. F., & Lockhart, C. (1990). Discrete idiosyncratic goods and structural principles of distributive justice. *The Journal of Politics, 52*, 1182–1204.

Gerstner, C. R., & Day, D. V. (1997). Meta-analytic review of leader-member exchange theory: Correlates and construct issues. *Journal of Applied Psychology, 82*, 827–844.

Gorgievsky, M. J., Halbesleben, J. R. B., & Bakker, A. B. (2011). Expanding the boundaries of psychological resource theories. *Journal of Occupational and Organizational Psychology, 84*, 1–7.

Gouldner, A. W. (1960). The norm of reciprocity: A preliminary statement. *American Sociological Review, 25*, 161–178.

Graen, G. B., & Uhl-Bien, M. (1995). Relationship-based approach to leadership: Development of leader-member exchange (LMX) theory of leadership over 25 years: Applying a multi-level multi-domain perspective. *Leadership Quarterly, 6*, 219–247.

Greenberg, J. (1978a). Equity, motivation, and effects of past rewards on allocation decisions. *Personality and Social Psychology Bulletin, 4*, 131–134.

Greenberg, J. (1978b). Effects of reward value and retaliative power on allocation decisions: Justice, generosity, or greed? *Journal of Personality and Social Psychology, 36*, 367–379.

Greenberg, J. (1981). The justice of distributing scarce and abundant resources. In M. J. Lerner & S. C. Lerner (Eds.), *The justice motive in social behavior: Adapting to times of scarcity and change* (pp. 289–316). New York, NY: Plenum Press.

Greenberg, J. (1982). Approaching equity and avoiding inequity in groups and organizations. In J. Greenberg & R. L. Cohen (Eds.), *Equality and justice in social behavior* (pp. 389–435). New York, NY: Academic Press.

Greenberg, J. (1987). A taxonomy of organizational justice theories. *Academy of Management Review, 12*, 9–22.

Greenberg, J. (1990). Organizational justice: Yesterday, today, and tomorrow. *Journal of Management, 16*, 399–432.

Greenberg, J., & Cohen R. L. (1982). Why justice? Normative and instrumental interpretations. In J. Greenberg and R.L. Cohen (Eds.), *Equity and justice in social behavior* (pp. 437–469). New York, NY: Academic Press.

Greenberg, J., & Cropanzano, R. (Eds.) (2001). *Advances in organizational justice.* Stanford, CA: Stanford University Press.

Griffith, W. I. (1989). The allocation of negative outcomes: Examining the issue. In E. E. Lawler & B. Markovsky (Eds.), *Advances in group processes* (Vol. 6, pp. 107–137). Greenwich, CT: JAI Press.

Halliday, R. (2012). Enforceable rights. A libertarian theory of justice. Retrieved from http://royhalliday.home.mindspring.com/c2.htm#2.3.5.

Hegtvedt, K. A. (1992). Bargaining for justice: A means to resolve competing justice claims. *Social Justice Research, 5*, 155–172.

Hegtvedt, K. A. (2006). Justice frameworks. In P. Burke (Ed.), *Contemporary social psychological theories* (pp. 46–69). Stanford: Stanford University Press.

Hegtvedt, K. A., & Cook, K. S. (1987). The role of justice in conflict situations. In E. Lawler & B. Markovsky (Eds.), *Advances in group processes* (Vol. 4, pp. 109–136). Greenwich, CT: JAI Press.

Hegtvedt, K. A., & Cook, K. S. (2001). Distributive justice: Recent theoretical developments and applications. In J. Sanders & V. L. Hamilton (Eds.), *Handbook of justice research in law* (pp. 93–132). New York, NY: Kluwer Academic.

Hegtvedt, K. A., & Markovsky, B. (1995). Justice and injustice. In K. S. Cook, A. Fine, & J. House (Eds.), *Sociological perspectives on social psychology* (pp. 257–280). Boston, MA: Allyn & Bacon.

Helson, H. (1964). *Adaptation-level theory.* New York, NY: Harper & Row.

Heskett, J. L., Jones, T. O., Loveman, G. W., Sasser, W. E., Jr Schlesinger, L. A. (1994). Putting the service profit chain to work. *Harvard Business Review, 72*, 164–174.

Heskett, J., Sasser, E., & Schlesinger, L. (1997). *The service profit chain: how leading companies link profit and growth to loyalty, satisfaction, and value.* New York, NY: The Free Press.

Homans, G. (1961). *Social behavior: Its elementary forms.* New York, NY: Harcourt, Brace & World.

Homans, G. C. (1958). Social behavior as exchange. *American Journal of Sociology, 63,* 447–458.

Homans, G. C. (1961). *Social behavior: Its elementary forms.* New York, NY: Harcourt, Brace.

Homans, G. C. (1974). *Social behavior: Its elementary forms.* New York, NY: Harcourt, Brace.

Huseman, R. C., Hatfield, J. D., & Miles, E. W. (1987). A new perspective on equity theory: The equity sensitivity construct. *Academy of Management Review, 12,* 222–234.

Jasso, G. (1983). Fairness of individual rewards and fairness of the reward distribution: Specifying the inconsistency between micro and macro principles of justice. *Social Psychology Quarterly, 46,* 185–199.

Jasso, G. (1993). Analyzing conflict severity: Predictions of distributive justice theory for the two-subgroup case. *Social Justice Research, 6,* 357–382.

Jonsson, D., & Törnblom, K. Y. (1984). The conception of justice: Towards a coherent analytical framework. *Resources and Relations,* Report no. 14. Göteborg University, Sweden.

Jost, J. T., & Banaji, M. R. (1994). The role of stereotyping in system-justification and the production of false consciousness. *British Journal of Social Psychology, 33,* 1–27.

Jost, J. T., Banaji, M. R., & Nosek, B. A. (2004). A decade of system justification theory: Accumulated evidence of conscious and unconscious bolstering of the status quo. *Political Psychology, 25,* 881–919.

Jost, J. T., & Kay, A. C. (2010). Social justice. History, theory, and research. In S. T. Fiske, D. T. Gilbert & G. Lindzey (Eds.), *Handbook of social psychology* (5th ed.). (Vol. 2, pp. 1122–1165). Hoboken, NJ: Wiley.

Kals, E., & Maes, J. (2012). Preface. In E. Kals & J. Maes (Eds.), *Justice and conflicts. Theoretical and empirical contributions* (pp. v–xi). New York, NY: Springer.

Karasek, R. A. (1979). Job demands, job decision latitude, and mental strain: Implications for job redesign. *Administrative Science Quarterly, 24,* 285–308.

Kayser, E., Köhler, B., Mikula, G., & Schwinger, T. (1980). *Intrapersonale kontrakte und gerechtigkeit: Entwurf einer theorie.* Bericht aus dem Sonderforschungsbereich 24, Universität Mannheim.

Kayser, E., & Lamm, H. (1980). Input integration and input weighting in decisions on allocations of gains and losses. *European Journal of Social Psychology, 10,* 1–15.

Kayser, E., & Schwinger, T. (1982). A theoretical analysis of the relationship among individual justice concepts, layman psychology and distribution decisions. *Journal for the Theory of Social Behavior, 12,* 47–51.

Kayser, E., Schwinger, T., & Cohen, R. L. (1984). Laypersons' conceptions of social relationships: A test of contract theory. *Journal of Social and Personal Relationships, 1,* 433–548.

Kazemi, A., & Eek, D. (2007). Effects of group goal and resource valence on allocation preferences in public good dilemmas. *Social Behavior and Personality, 35,* 803–818.

Kazemi, A., & Eek, D. (2008). Promoting cooperation in social dilemmas via fairness norms and group goals. In A. Biel, D. Eek, T. Gärling, & M. Gustafsson (Eds.), *New issues and paradigms in research on social Dilemmas* (pp. 72–92). New York, NY: Springer.

Kazemi, A., Gholamzadehmir, M., & Törnblom, K. Y. (2012). Predicting reactions to procedural injustice via insights from resource theory. In K. Y. Törnblom & A. Kazemi (Eds.), *Handbook of social resource theory. Theoretical extensions, empirical insights, and social applications* (pp. 373–381). New York, NY: Springer.

Kazemi, A., & Törnblom, K. (2008). Social psychology of justice: Origins, central issues, recent developments, and future directions. *Nordic Psychology, 60,* 209–234.

Kazemi, A., & Törnblom, K. (2010). *Is it fair that unfairness is perceived as fair?* Paper presented at the 7th Nordic Conference on Group and Social Psychology, Gothenburg, Sweden.

Kraemer, J., & Chen, C. C. (2012). Cultural differences in social exchange at the workplace: A Sino-US comparison. In K. Y. Törnblom & A. Kazemi (Eds.), *Handbook of social resource theory. Theoretical extensions, empirical insights, and social applications)* (pp. 283–300). New York, NY: Springer.

Lamm, H. (1986). Justice considerations in interpersonal conflict. In H. W. Bierhoff, R. L. Cohen & J. Greenberg (Eds.), *Justice in social relations* (pp. 43–63). New York, NY: Plenum Press.

Lamm, H., & Kayser, E. (1978a). The allocation of monetary gain and loss following dyadic performance: the weight given to effort and ability under conditions of low and high intra-dyadic attraction. *European Journal of Social Psychology, 8,* 275–278.

Lamm, H., & Kayser, E. (1978b). An analysis of negotiation concerning the allocation of jointly produced profit or loss: The roles of justice norms, politeness, profit maximization, and tactics. *International Journal of Group Tensions, 8,* 64–80.

Lamm, H., Kayser, E., & Schanz, V. (1983). An attributional analysis of interperpersonal justice: Ability and effort as inputs in the allocation of gain and loss. *The Journal of Social Psychology, 119,* 269–281.

Lamm, H., Kayser, E., & Schwinger, T. (1981). Justice norms and other determinants of allocation and negotiation behavior. In M. Irle (Ed.), *Decision making: Social-psychological and socio-economic analyses* (pp. 359–410). Berlin, Germany/New York, NY: de Gruyter.

Lansberg, I. (1984). Hierarchy as a mediator of fairness: A contingency approach to distributive justice in organizations. *Journal of Applied Social Psychology, 14,* 124–135.

Lenski, G. (1966). *Power and privilege: A theory of social stratification.* New York, NY: McGraw-Hill.

Lerner, M. J. (1970). The desire for justice and reactions to victims. In J. Hacaulay & L. Berkowitz (Eds.), *Altruism and helping behavior.* New York, NY: Academic Press.

Lerner, M. J. (1974). The justice motive: "Equity" and "parity" among children. *Journal of Personality and Social Psychology, 29,* 538–550.

Lerner, M. J. (1975). The justice motive in social behavior: Introduction. *Journal of Social Issues, 31,* 1–19.

Lerner, M. J. (1977). The justice motive: Some hypotheses as to its origins and forms. *Journal of Personality, 45,* 1–52.

Lerner, M. J. (1980). *The belief in a just world: A fundamental delusion.* New York, NY: Plenum Press.

Lerner, M. J. (1981). The justice motive in human relations. Some thoughts on what we know and need to know about justice. In M. J. Lerner & S. C. Lerner (Eds.), *The justice motive in social behavior. Adapting to times of scarcity and change* (pp. 11–35). New York, NY: Plenum Press.

Lerner, M. J. (1987). Integrating societal and psychological rules of entitlement: The basic task of each social actor and fundamental problem for the social sciences. *Social Justice Research, 1*, 107–125.

Lerner, M. J., & Clayton, S. (2011). *Justice and self-interest. Two fundamental motives.* New York, NY: Cambridge University Press.

Leung, K., & Bond, M. H. (1984). The impact of cultural collectivism on reward allocation. *Journal of Personality and Social Psychology, 47*, 739–804.

Leventhal, G. S. (1976a). The distribution of rewards and resources in groups and organizations. In L. Berkowitz and E. Walster (Eds.), *Advances in experimental social psychology* (Vol. 9, pp. 91–131). New York, NY: Academic Press.

Leventhal, G. S. (1976b). Fairness in social relationships. In J. W. Thibaut, J. T. Spence, & R. C. Carson (Eds.), *Contemporary topics in social psychology* (pp. 211–239). Morristown, NJ: General Learning Press.

Leventhal, G. S. (1980). What should be done with equity theory? In K. Gergen & R. Willis (Eds.), *Social exchange theory.* New York, NY: Plenum Press.

Leventhal, G. S., Michaels, J. W., & Sanford, C. (1972). Inequity and interpersonal conflict: Reward allocation and secrecy about reward as methods of preventing conflict. *Journal of Personality and Social Psychology, 23*, 88–102.

Liden, R. C., & Maslyn, J. M. (1998). Multidimensionality of leader-member exchange: An empirical assessment through scale development. *Journal of Management, 24*, 43–73.

Lind, E. A., & Tyler, T. R. (1988). *The social psychology of procedural justice.* New York, NY: Plenum.

Lind, E. A., & Van den Bos, K. (2002). When fairness works: Toward a general theory of uncertainty management. In B. M. Staw & R. M. Kramer (Eds.), *Research in organizational behavior* (Vol. 24, pp. 181–223). Boston, MA: Elsevier.

Long, G. T., & Lerner, M. J. (1974). Deserving, the "personal contract," and altruistic behavior by children. *Journal of Personality and Social Psychology, 29*, 551–556.

Lukács, G. (1972). *History and class* consciousness. Cambridge, MA: MIT Press.

Mannix, E. A., Neale, M. A., & Northcraft, G. B. (1995). Equity, equality, or need? The effects of organizational culture on the allocation of benefits and burdens. *Organizational Behavior and Human Decision Processes, 63*, 276–286.

Martin, J., & Harder, J. W. (1994). Bread and roses: Justice and the distribution of financial and socioemotional rewards in organizations. *Social Justice Research, 7*, 241–264.

Marx, K. (1977—originally published 1875) Critique of the Gotha Program. In D. McLellan (Ed.), *Karl Marx: Selected writings.* Oxford, UK: Oxford University Press.

Matania, E., & Yaniv, I. (2007). Resource priority, fairness, and equality-efficiency compromises. *Social Justice Research, 20*, 497–510.

McClintock, C. G. (1972). Social motivation—a set of propositions. *Behavioral Science, 17*, 438–454.

Mead, G. H. (1934). *Mind, self and society.* Chicago, IL: Unversity of Chicago Press.

Messick, D. M., & Sentis, K. (1983). Fairness, preference, and fairness biases. In D. M. Messick & K. S. Cook (Eds.), *Equity theory: Psychological and sociological perspectives* (pp. 61–94). New York, NY: Praeger Publishers.

Mikula, G. (1980). On the role of justice in allocation decisions. In G. Mikula (Ed.), *Justice and social interaction. Experimental and theoretical contributions from psychological research* (pp. 127–166). New York, NY: Springer-Verlag.

Mikula, G. (1982). *Concerns with justice and motivation for control.* Graz Universitaet, Institut fur Psychologie.

Mikula, G. (1984). Justice and fairness in interpersonal relations: Thoughts and suggestions. In H. Tajfel (Ed.), *The social dimension: European developments in social psychology* (pp. 204–227). Cambridge, UK: Cambridge University Press.

Mikula, G. (2003). Testing an attribution-of-blame model of judgments of injustice. *European Journal of Social Psychology, 33*, 793–811.

Mikula, G., & Korytko, E. (1990). Just as you like it: How allocators decide in cases of conflict between own and recipients' views of justice. *Social Justice Research, 4*, 133–151.

Mikula, G., Petri, B., & Tanzer, N. K. (1989). What people regard as unjust: Types and structures of everyday experiences of injustice. *European Journal of Social Psychology, 20*, 133–149.

Mikula, G., Schoebi, D., Jagoditsch, S., & Macher, S. (2009). Roots and correlates of perceived injustice in the division of family work. *Personal Relationships, 16*, 553–674.

Mikula, G., & Schwinger, T. (1978). Intermember relations and reward allocation. In H. Brandstätter, J. H. Davis & H. Schuler (Eds.), *Dynamics of group decisions* (pp. 229–250). Beverly Hills, CA: Sage.

Mikula, G., & Wenzel, M. (2000). Justice and social conflict. *International Journal of Psychology, 35*, 126–135.

Mills, C. W. (1975). Situated actions and vocabularies of motive. In D. Brissett & C. Edgley (Eds.), *Life as theater* (pp. 162–170). Chicago, IL: Aldine.

Minhong, L., & Jae-Sung, C. (2012). Positive side effects of a job-related training program for older adults in South Korea. *Educational Gerontology, 38*, 1–9.

Mitchell, M. S., Cropanzano, R. S., & Quisenberry, D. M. (2012). Social exchange theory, exchange resources, and interpersonal relationships: A modest resolution to theoretical difficulties. In K. Y. Törnblom & A. Kazemi (Eds.), *Handbook of social resource theory. Theoretical extensions, empirical insights, and social applications* (pp. 99–118). New York, NY: Springer.

Montada, L. (2007). Justice conflicts and the justice of conflict resolution. In K. Y. Törnblom & R. Vermunt (Eds.), *Distributive and procedural justice: Research and social applications* (pp. 255–268). Hampshire, UK: Ashgate.

Morgenthau, H. J. (1974). Justice and power. *Social Research, 41*, 161–175.

Moschetti, G. J., & Kues, J. R. (1978). Transrelational equity comparisons: Extensions to the third partner relationship and a decision-making model. *Journal of Personality and Social Psychology, 36*, 1107–1117.

Nozick, R. (1974). *Anarchy, state and utopia.* New York, NY: Basic Books.

Persad, G., Wertheimer, A., & Emanuel, E. (2009). Principles for allocation of scarce medical interventions. *Lancet, 373*, 423–431.

Pritchard, R. A. (1969). Equity theory: A review and critique. *Organizational Behavior and Human Performance, 4*, 176–211.

Raphael, D. D. (1970). *Problems of political philosophy.* New York, NY: Praeger Publishers.

Rawls, J. (1971). *A theory of justice*. Cambridge, MA: Harvard University Press.

Rawls, J. (1985). Justice as fairness: Political not metaphysical. *Philosophy and Public Affairs, 14*, 223–251.

Reis, H. T. (1984). The multidimensionality of justice. In R. Folger (Ed.), *The sense of injustice: Social psychological perspectives* (pp. 26–61). New York, NY: Plenum Press.

Reis, H. T. (1986). Levels of interest in the study of interpersonal justice. In H. W. Bierhoff, R. L. Cohen, & J. Greenberg (Eds.), *Justice in social relations* (pp. 187–225). New York, NY: Plenum Press.

Rescher, N. (1966). *Distributive justice. A constructive critique of the utilitarian theory of distribution*. New York, NY: Bobbs-Merrill.

Resnik, D. B. (1998). *The ethics of science: An introduction*. New York, NY: Routledge.

Rijsman, J. (1983). The dynamics of social competition in personal and categorical comparison situations. In W. Doise & S. Moscovici (Eds.), *Current issues in European social psychology*, (Vol. 1, pp. 279–312). Cambridge, UK: Cambridge University Press.

Sabbagh, C., Dar, Y., & Resh, N. (1994). The structure of social justice judgments: A facet approach. *Social Psychology Quarterly, 57*, 244–261.

Sampson, E. E. (1976). *Social psychology and contemporary society*. New York, NY: Wiley.

Sampson, E. E. (1983). *Justice and the critique of pure psychology*. New York, NY: Plenum Press.

Sayles, L. R. (1958). *Behavior of industrial work groups: prediction and control*. New York, NY: Wiley.

Scherer, K. R. (1992). Issues in the study of justice. In K. R. Scherer (Ed.), *Justice: Interdisciplinary perspectives* (pp. 1–14). Cambridge, UK: Cambridge University Press.

Schmidtz, D. (2006). *Elements of justice*. New York, NY: Cambridge University Press.

Schmitt, M., & Montada, L. (1982). Determinanten erlebter Gerechtigkeit. *Zeitschrift für Sozialpsychologie, 13*, 32–44.

Schmitt M., Neumann R., & Montada L. (1995). Dispositional sensitivity to befallen injustice. *Social Justice Research, 8*, 385–407.

Schumann, P. L. (2001). A moral principles framework for human resource management ethics. *Human Resource Management Review, 11*, 93–111.

Schwinger, T. (1980). Just allocations of goods: Decisions among three principles. In G. Mikula (Ed.), *Justice and social interaction. Experimental and theoretical contributions from psychological research* (pp. 95–125). New York, NY: Springer-Verlag.

Shapiro, D. L. (2001). The death of justice theory is likely if theorists neglect the "wheels" already invented and the voices of the injustice victims. *Journal of Vocational behavior, 58*, 235–242.

Shore, L. M., & Shore, T. H. (1995). Perceived organizational support and organizational justice. In R. S. Cropanzano & K. M. Kacmar (Eds.), *Organizational politics, justice, and support: Managing the social climate of the workplace* (pp. 149–164). Westport, CT: Quorum.

Sidgwick, H. (1893). *The methods of ethics* (5th ed.). London: Macmillan.

Skitka, L. J. (2003). Of different minds: An accessible identity model of justice reasoning. *Personality and Social Psychology Review, 7*, 286–297.

Skitka, L. J., & Mullen, E. (2002). Understanding judgments of fairness in a real-world political context: A test of the value protection model of justice reasoning. *Personality and Social Psychology Bulletin, 28*, 1419–1429.

Sullivan, H. S. (1953). *The interpersonal theory of psychiatry*. New York, NY: Norton.

Sullivan, H. S. (1954). *The psychiatric interview*. New York, NY: Norton.

Syroit, J. E. M. M. (1991). Interpersonal and intergroup injustice: Some theoretical considerations. In R. Vermunt & H. Steensma (Eds.), *Social justice in human relations: Societal and psychological origins of justice*; (Vol. 1, pp. 259–277). New York, NY: Plenum Press.

Thibaut, J. W., & Faucheux, C. (1965). The development of contractual norms in a bargaining situation under two types of stress. *Journal of Experimental Social Psychology, 1*, 89–102.

Thibaut, J. W., & Kelley, H. H. (1959). *The social psychology of groups*. New York, NY: Wiley.

Thibaut, J. W., & Walker, L. (1975). *Procedural justice*. Hillsdale, New Jersey: Erlbaum.

Törnblom, K. Y. (1977a). Distributive justice: Typology and propositions. *Human Relations, 30*, 1–24.

Törnblom, K. Y. (1977b). *The psycho-sociological and behavioral definitions of equity and their extension to social dimensions*. Reports/Studies EQU.2. Paris, France: Unesco.

Törnblom, K. Y. (1988). Positive and negative allocations: A typology and a model for conflicting justice principles. In E. Lawler & B. Markovsky (Eds.), *Advances in group processes* (pp. 141–168). Greenwich, CT: JAI Press.

Törnblom, K. Y. (1992). The social psychology of distributive justice. In K. R. Scherer (Ed.), *Justice: Interdisciplinary perspectives* (pp. 177–284). Cambridge, UK: Cambridge University Press.

Törnblom, K. Y. (1995). Individual and collective justice and injustice: Implications for intergroup conflict. *Social Justice Research, 8*, 91–101.

Törnblom, K. Y., & Ahlin, E. (1998). Mode of accomplishing positive and negative outcomes: Its effect on fairness evaluations. *Social Justice Research, 11*, 425–444.

Törnblom, K. Y., & Foa, U. G. (1983). Choice of a distribution principle: Crosscultural evidence on the effects of resources. *Acta Sociologica, 26*, 161–173.

Törnblom, K. Y., & Jonsson, D. R. (1985). Subrules of the equality and contribution principles: Their perceived fairness in distribution and retribution. *Social Psychology Quarterly, 48*, 249–261.

Törnblom, K. Y., Jonsson, D. R., & Foa, U. G. (1985). Nationality, resource class, and preference among three allocation rules: Sweden vs. USA. *International Journal of Intercultural Relations, 9*, 51–77.

Törnblom, K. Y., & Kazemi, A. (2007). Toward a resource production theory of distributive justice. In K. Y. Törnblom & R. Vermunt (Eds.), *Distributive and procedural justice. Research and social applications* (pp. 39–66). Burlington, VT: Ashgate.

Törnblom, K. Y., & Kazemi, A. (Eds.) (2012a). *Handbook of social resource theory. Theoretical extensions, empirical insights, and social applications*. New York, NY: Springer.

Törnblom, K. Y., & Kazemi, A. (2012b). Advances in justice conflict conceptualization: A new integrative framework. In E. Kals & J. Maes (Eds.), *Justice and conflict: Theoretical and empirical contributions* (pp. 21–51). New York, NY: Springer.

Tyler, T. R., & Lind, E. A. (1992). A relational model of authority in groups. In M. Zanna (Ed.), *Advances in experimental social psychology* (Vol. 25, pp. 115–191). New York, NY: Academic Press.

Tyler, T. R., & Smith, H. J. (1998). Social justice and social movements. In D. T. Gilbert, S. T. Fiske, & G. Lindzey (Eds.), *The handbook of social psychology* (Vol. 2, pp. 595–629). Boston, MA: McGraw-Hill.

Upshaw, H. S. (1969). The personal reference scale: An approach to social judgment. In L. Berkowitz (Ed.), *Advances in experimental social psychology* (Vol. 4, pp. 315–371). New York, NY: Academic Press.

Utz, S., & Sassenberg, K. (2002). Distributive justice in common-bond and common-identity groups. *Group Processes and Intergroup Relations, 5*, 151–162.

Van Avermaet, E. McClintock, C., & Moskowitz, J. (1978). Alternative approaches to equity: pro-social motivation, strategic accommodation and dissonance reduction. *European Journal of Social Psychology, 8*, 419–437.

Van Dijk, E., De Cremer, D., & Handgraaf, M. J. J. (2004). Social value orientations and the strategic use of fairness in ultimatum bargaining. *Journal of Experimental Social Psychology, 40*, 697–707.

Vermunt, R. (2002). Employee stress, injustice, and the dual position of the boss. In S. Gilliland, D. Steiner, & D. Skarlicki (Eds.), *Emerging perspectives on managing organizational justice* (pp. 159–176). Greenwich, CT: IAP.

Vermunt, R., & Steensma, H. (2005). How can justice be used to manage stress in organizations? In J. Greenberg & J. A. Colquitt (Eds.), *Handbook of organizational justice* (pp. 383–410). Mahwah, NJ: Erlbaum.

Vygotsky, L. S. (1978). *Mind in society.* Cambridge, MA: Harvard University Press.

Walster, E., Berscheid, E., & Walster, G. W. (1973). New directions in equity research. *Journal of Personality and Social Psychology, 25*, 151–176.

Walster, E., Walster, G. W., & Berscheid, E. (1978). *Equity: Theory and research.* Boston, MA: Allyn & Bacon.

Walster, E., & Piliavin, J. A. (1972). Equity and the innocent bystander. *Journal of Social Issues, 28*, 165–189.

Weick, K. E. (1966). The concept of equity in the perception of pay. *Administrative Science Quarterly, 11*, 414–439.

CHAPTER

3 Procedural Justice: A Historical Review and Critical Analysis

D. Ramona Bobocel *and* Leanne Gosse

Abstract

People are fundamentally concerned with *fair process* in many social contexts. The work organization has offered fertile ground for the study of procedural justice. In this chapter, we provide readers with a broad foundation for understanding the literature on procedural justice in the workplace. We first review the origins of the concept in psychology in the 1970s and the early theoretical accounts. Next we discuss and critique research that has examined the effects of procedural justice perceptions in the workplace. In the third part, we build on our discussion of the early theories by reviewing contemporary revisions, and we present newer theoretical models that have emerged to explain why people care about process fairness. In the final section, we review recent research that challenges a fundamental assumption in the study of procedural justice—that procedural justice is always beneficial.

Key Words: procedural justice, fair process, procedural fairness, organizational justice, justice in the workplace

The study of social justice has been a central theme in psychology for over half a century. As with other social scientists and philosophers, psychologists have long recognized that, to function effectively, all social systems must deal with the problem of how to distribute or allocate resources fairly. As reviewed in Chapter 2 of this volume, the earliest psychological research on justice took a *distributive justice* orientation. Inspired originally by the work of social exchange theorists (e.g., Blau, 1964; Homans, 1974; Thibaut & Kelley, 1959), research on distributive justice focused on the question of how people judge the fairness of the outcomes of a social exchange. In the 1970s, it was becoming evident to many social scientists that people were concerned not only with the outcomes of a social exchange but also with the fairness of the procedures by which allocation decisions are made. The concept of procedural justice was born. Initially investigated within the context of legal dispute resolution, researchers soon saw its relevance to the workplace (e.g., Lind & Lissak, 1985; Sheppard & Lewicki, 1987).

In the 1980s, the concept of procedural justice was formally introduced to the organizational sciences in two book chapters by Jerald Greenberg and Robert Folger (Folger & Greenberg, 1985; Greenberg & Folger, 1983) and in a chapter by Allan Lind and Tom Tyler (Lind & Tyler, 1988) in their book on the social psychology of procedural justice. These scholars reviewed what was known about procedural justice in other social domains and argued for the relevance of the concept to understanding many important workplace phenomena. As they pointed out, many organizational practices—such as performance evaluation and compensation—implicitly recognized employees' procedural concerns. Moreover, at that time, there was a growing trend in organizations toward participatory work practices such as participative management and flexible work schedules, which were based on the premise that employees respond better when they are involved in decision-making procedures than when they are left out.

As these founders forecasted, the study of procedural justice in the workplace would prove to be highly productive in two ways. First, it would advance researchers' understanding of many organizational phenomena. Over the past decades, investigators have demonstrated the relevance of procedural justice for almost every organizational procedure, such as performance appraisal (Greenberg, 1986; Korsgaard & Roberson, 1995), employee selection and hiring (Gilliland, 1993, 1994), layoffs and terminations (Brockner et al., 1994), affirmative action (Bobocel, Son Hing, Davey, Stanley, & Zanna, 1998; Cropanzano, Slaughter, & Bachiochi, 2005), conflict resolution (Shapiro & Brett, 1995; Sheppard, 1984), drug testing (e.g., Cropanzano & Konovsky, 1995), and grievance systems (Gordon & Fryxell, 1993).

Moreover, procedural justice predicts many employee reactions, including emotions (Barclay, Skarlicki, & Pugh, 2005), self-evaluations (Gilliland, 1994; Ployhart, Ryan, & Bennett, 1999; Schroth & Shah, 2000), stress (Vermunt & Steensma, 2005), work attitudes such as organizational commitment (Korsgaard, Schweiger, & Sapienza, 1995), trust (Aryee, Budhwar, & Chen, 2002; Colquitt & Rodell, 2011; Kernan & Hanges, 2002), leader-member exchange and perceived organizational support (Tekleab, Takeuchi, & Taylor, 2005).

Finally, it is associated with, and work behaviors such as organizational citizenship behavior (Moorman, 1991, Konovsky & Pugh, 1994), job performance (Aryee, Chen, & Budhwar, 2004; Williams, 1999; Zapata-Phelan, Colquitt, Scott, & Livingston, 2009), cooperation (Tyler, Degoey & Smith, 1996; Tyler & Blader, 2000), forgiveness, revenge, and retaliation (Aquino, Tripp, & Bies, 2006; Bies & Tripp, 2001; Skarlicki & Folger, 1997), turnover (Posthuma, Maertz, & Dworkin, 2007), theft (Greenberg, 1993a), sabotage (Ambrose, Seabright, & Schminke, 2002) counterproductive work behavior (Dalal, 2005; Hershcovis et al., 2007), and legal claiming (Goldman, 2003; Lind, Greenberg, Scott, & Whelchans, 2000). In fact, only a few years after the concept of procedural justice was introduced to organizational scholars, Sheppard, Lewicki, and Minton (1992) published a book on the topic of justice in work organizations in which they reviewed what was an already large literature.

The founders' second prediction was that the workplace context would provide fertile ground to better understand the procedural justice concept itself. As we aim to illustrate in the present chapter, it is clear that collectively we now have a far greater understanding of what procedural justice is and why it matters, deriving from the decades of research examining procedural justice as it pertains to work-related phenomena. Given the vast size of the research literature on procedural justice, it is beyond the scope of the present chapter to review the research findings comprehensively. Instead, our goal is to provide a broad historical review of the procedural justice literature, which will serve as a foundation on which the subsequent chapters will build.

This chapter comprises four main parts. In the first part, we discuss the emergence of the construct in psychology and early ideas about the theoretical underpinnings of procedural justice. In this part, we also examine the breadth of the procedural justice construct, an issue that was brought to the fore with the introduction of the concept of interactional justice. In the second part of the chapter, we focus on how researchers have traditionally examined procedural justice effects in the workplace. We first review "differential effects" models in which researchers sought to demonstrate the relevance of the concept by examining attitudes and behaviors that are uniquely associated with procedural justice perceptions, rather than with other justice perceptions. Although the differential effects paradigm has been useful, we also highlight several limitations. We then review "interaction effects" models in which the goal was to examine the joint effects of procedural justice and other justice constructs. As research proliferated, justice scholars elaborated on early theories and developed new models. Thus, in the third part of the chapter, we provide an overview of the main theoretical accounts offered to explain why people care about procedural justice. Finally, in the fourth part, we highlight recent research that questions a fundamental assumption in the procedural justice literature—that procedural justice is always beneficial.

What Is Procedural Justice?

Origins of the Concept and Early Theoretical Accounts

Although several researchers contributed to the emergence of the procedural justice construct in the psychological literature, three lines of research are considered especially groundbreaking. In this section, we highlight these contributions, with an emphasis on how each group of researchers defined and conceptualized procedural justice.

THIBAUT AND WALKER'S (1975, 1978) THEORY OF PROCEDURE

Social psychologist, John Thibaut, and law professor, Laurens Walker, and their colleagues typically are credited with providing the earliest systematic study of procedural justice in their program of research on legal dispute resolution in the early 1970s. In addition to publishing numerous empirical articles (e.g., LaTour, 1978; Thibaut, Walker, LaTour, & Holden, 1974; Walker, LaTour, Lind, & Thibaut, 1974), they summarized their program of research in a monograph entitled *Procedural Justice: A Psychological Analysis* (Thibaut & Walker, 1975), and presented a more extensive account of their theoretical work in an article (Thibaut & Walker, 1978) entitled *"A Theory of Procedure."*

For our purpose, the key contribution of their empirical work was the demonstration in experimental simulations that variation in dispute resolution *procedures* affected disputants' subjective perceptions of the fairness of those procedures, as well as their satisfaction with the resulting verdicts. Thibaut and Walker (1978) distinguished legal dispute resolution procedures in terms of the degree to which they vested control in disputants versus in a third party (e.g., a judge). Control could be distributed between disputants and a third party in two key phases of the resolution: a process phase during which evidence is presented, and an outcome phase during which a verdict is rendered. One of their most significant findings as it pertains to this chapter was that disputants *preferred procedures that allowed them to present evidence for their case*—thereby retaining control over the process (process control)—even when they did not retain control over the final verdict (outcome control).

Critically, Thibaut and Walker demonstrated that disputant preference for *process control* was due to perceived *procedural fairness*. That is, resolution procedures that afforded disputants process control were perceived as more fair than were procedures that did not, and this was true even when outcome control was vested in the third party (e.g., Lind, Kurtz, Musante, Walker, & Thibaut, 1980; Walker, Lind, & Thibaut, 1979). Thus, for example, the researchers found that disputants prefer the adversary courtroom procedure of the American legal system to the inquisitorial procedure of the European legal system because disputants perceive the adversary procedure as more fair. Both procedures vest outcome control in the third party, but disputants retain process control in the adversary procedure. From this perspective, then, having input into decisions was a cornerstone of procedural justice perceptions.

Over the next decade (and still to the present day), researchers repeatedly replicated the finding that allowing people to provide input into decisions that affect them enhances their perceptions of procedural fairness and increases outcome acceptance, even when the outcomes are undesirable. Folger (1977) labeled process control as "voice" in his formative research on reward allocation, and later he and colleagues coined the term the "*fair process effect*" to refer to "cases in which greater satisfaction results from giving people a voice in decisions" (Folger, Rosenfield, Grove, & Corkran, 1979, p. 2254).[1] Although the voice effect would prove to be very robust, there would be considerable debate among scholars over the years about why the effect occurs (see Chapter 19; for other reviews, see Shapiro & Brett, 2005; Van den Bos, 2005).

Thibaut and Walker's conceptualization of procedural justice drew on existing theories of justice such as equity theory (Adams, 1965), which emanated from broader theories of social exchange (Blau, 1964; Thibaut & Kelley, 1959). Fundamentally, these theories claimed that outcomes are the major determinant of people's satisfaction and perceived fairness. Accordingly, Thibaut and Walker argued that disputants want process control as a means by which they may achieve equitable outcomes; in other words, process control is desired because it gives disputants indirect control over the outcome.

LEVENTHAL'S (1980) JUSTICE JUDGMENT MODEL

Around the same time that Thibaut and Walker were studying procedural justice in the context of legal dispute resolution, there was a growing recognition among social psychologists who were studying resource allocation that people's experience of fairness derives not solely from consideration of the distribution of outcomes. Although several scholars were recognizing the importance of procedural justice (e.g., Deutsch, 1975; Folger, 1977; Lerner & Whitehead, 1980), social psychologist Gerald Leventhal published several book chapters that highlighted in detail the concept of procedural justice in resource allocation (Leventhal, 1976, 1980; Leventhal, Karuza, & Fry, 1980). Like

Thibaut and Walker's research, these chapters had a lasting impact on theory and research on procedural justice in the workplace. In his 1980 chapter, Leventhal presented what he labeled a "justice judgment model"—his conceptualization of the cognitive process by which people form justice judgments. Although included in his analysis were his ideas about how people form distributive justice judgments, Leventhal paid particular attention to the more novel question of how people might form procedural justice judgments. Given that there was little prior systematic study of procedural justice in reward allocation, most of Leventhal's ideas were speculative rather than empirically grounded, but they were nonetheless influential.

One aspect of the justice judgment model that has had lasting impact on procedural justice research is Leventhal's (1980) specification of the procedural rules, or "criteria," by which he thought people may evaluate whether an allocation procedure is fair or unfair. In short, he speculated that allocation procedures will be perceived as more fair if they (a) are applied consistently across people and over time (consistency rule), (b) prevent personal self-interest and "blind allegiance to narrow preconceptions" (bias suppression rule), (c) ensure that decisions are based on as much good information and informed opinion as possible (accuracy rule), (d) provide opportunities to modify and reverse incorrect decisions (correctability rule), (e) reflect the concerns of all subgroups and individuals who may be affected (representativeness rule), and (f) are "compatible with prevailing moral and ethical values accepted by the individual" (ethicality rule) (see pp. 41–46). It is noteworthy that Leventhal also outlined different phases of the allocation sequence at which these criteria might be applied. Similarly, he argued that the procedural rules are not necessarily weighted equally in people's assessments but will vary as a function of the context.

Over the years, evidence has accrued that supports the validity of Leventhal's procedural justice criteria in resource allocation decisions in general (e.g., Barrett-Howard & Tyler, 1986), and in decision-making in the workplace (e.g., Folger & Konovsky, 1989; Greenberg, 1986; Sheppard & Lewicki, 1987). For example, Greenberg (1986) conducted a qualitative study of managers who described the determinants of what they perceived were fair and unfair performance evaluations that they had received. He found evidence for both distributive and procedural determinants. Several of the latter concurred with Leventhal's criteria (e.g., ability to appeal evaluations, consistent application of standards), but others were identified (e.g., two-way communication). It is interesting to note that an early study by Barrett-Howard and Tyler (1986) confirmed Leventhal's idea that the relevance of the criteria will depend on the nature of the interpersonal relationship involved in the allocation, although this theme has not been picked up to a great extent in contemporary research. Support for the validity of Leventhal's criteria has also been demonstrated in experimental studies in which the manipulation of procedural justice is operationalized as one of Leventhal's criteria, and the manipulation is shown to affect procedural justice perceptions. As noted earlier, although the vast majority of experimental studies have operationalized procedural justice by manipulating voice (which most researchers consider to be subsumed by Leventhal's representativeness criteria), other criteria such as accuracy and consistency have been manipulated as well (e.g., Van den Bos, 2001).

Leventhal's analysis of procedural justice was similar to Thibaut and Walker's approach in two key ways. First, Thibaut and Walker (1975) and Leventhal (1976, 1980; Leventhal et al., 1980) agreed on the important role of process control in people's evaluations of outcomes. Second, both frameworks assumed that people care about fair procedures because they increase the likelihood of receiving fair outcomes. The models differed somewhat on specifying the elements of procedures that give people process control, which may be attributable to the contexts (legal dispute resolution versus resource allocation) in which they were studying procedural justice. As noted earlier, Thibaut and Walker's model conceptualized process control as having the opportunity to present evidence relevant to one's case; Leventhal's work expanded the criteria by which people can gain control over decision procedures.

It is noteworthy that the models also differed in how they conceptualized the relation between procedural justice perceptions and distributive justice perceptions. Leventhal (1976, 1980) argued that the two perceptions are related; in fact, he argued that perceptions of distributive justice depend on perceived procedural justice. In contrast, Thibaut and Walker (1975, 1978) argued that procedural justice and distributive justice are objectively independent, likely because this is possible in the context of the courtroom (i.e., a guilty person can be found guilty even if the procedures are flawed). Nevertheless, although they argued for objective independence, Thibaut and Walker (1975) recognized that the concepts may overlap perceptually, as borne out in their findings that disputants perceived verdicts to be more fair when they arose from procedures that were perceived to be more fair (for more details, see Folger & Greenberg, 1985; Lind & Tyler, 1988).

GROUP-VALUE MODEL OF PROCEDURAL JUSTICE (1988) AND RELATIONAL MODEL OF AUTHORITY (1992)

In 1988, social psychologists Allan Lind and Tom Tyler published a book entitled, *The Social Psychology of Procedural Justice*. Their book was a vast undertaking and one of the most influential early contributions to the field. In addition to providing a thorough review and analysis of Thibaut and Walker's research program, Lind and Tyler presented an in-depth review of the empirical literature on procedural justice from the early 1970s, which had quickly expanded from the context of legal-dispute resolution, to dispute resolution in nonlegal contexts, to resource allocation more generally, to the political arena, and to the context of the work organization.

In one chapter, devoted to a conceptual synthesis of the research findings and theory to date, Lind and Tyler introduced their group-value model of procedural justice. They argued that the previous models of procedural justice (e.g., Leventhal, 1976, 1980; Thibaut & Walker, 1975) were rooted in a view of the person as "self-interested"—that is, as primarily concerned with maximizing the material outcomes that they receive in their interactions with others (p. 222). Under this view, people are concerned with procedures because of their *instrumental value* in obtaining beneficial outcomes. Lind and Tyler argued that such instrumental motivation could not adequately capture the range of procedural justice findings.

Instead, they argued that decision-making procedures convey information to people about their standing (status) within social groups, and, therefore, that procedural justice has implications for people's social identity, and ultimately their sense of self-worth. The group-value model was rooted in social identity theory (Tajfel & Turner, 1979, 1986), which argued that people's views of themselves are shaped by their experiences in the groups to which they belong. Thus, for Lind and Tyler, rather than functioning as a means to a particular end (e.g., winning a dispute or obtaining a favorable outcome), decision-making procedures carry symbolic meaning, and can themselves serve as an end.

Lind and Tyler's (1988) group-value model was highly influential in procedural justice research, expanding the existing conceptualizations in several important ways. First, as noted earlier, the group-value model argued that fair procedures (e.g., those that offer voice) have instrumental value to recipients, as well as noninstrumental value in that they convey identity–related information to people. They rejected the traditional outcome-oriented conceptualization of procedural justice in which the person is viewed as primarily motivated by immediate self-interest. Rather, they argued that people want something different from their membership in groups: Namely, people gain identity from their associations with others. Of note, Lind and Tyler recognized that neither the outcome-oriented (self-interest) nor the group-value (identity) models of procedural justice alone can explain all the prior research findings. Thus, they suggested that both processes likely operate simultaneously or "side-by-side" in the same situations (Lind & Tyler, 1988, p. 241).

Following from their reasoning about the psychological function of fair procedures, Lind and Tyler (1988) argued that procedural justice perceptions should be most relevant in the formation of people's general attitudes toward the groups or relationships to which they belong, whereas distributive justice judgments should be more relevant predictors of people's reactions to a specific outcome. They stated that "when people are evaluating the extent to which they will be loyal to a group or relationship, people focus on the manner in which group decisions are made. If they believe that such decisions are made fairly, then group members are more inclined to accept a long-term commitment to the group" (pp. 225–226). Thus, Lind and Tyler predicted that, "In making leadership or institutional evaluations people are taking a long-term perspective on membership within a group. With personal satisfaction, they are reacting to a single decision" (p. 224). These ideas were supported by early research outside the workplace context, which demonstrated that people's procedural justice perceptions contributed unique variance to their endorsement of police, government leaders, and teachers more strongly than did factors related to the outcome (e.g., outcome level, outcome satisfaction, distributive justice) (e.g., Tyler & Caine, 1981; Tyler & Folger, 1980; Tyler, Rasinski, & Spodick, 1985). Moreover, in other research, distributive justice perceptions were found to predict outcome satisfaction more strongly than did procedural justice perceptions (e.g., Tyler, Rasinski, & McGraw, 1985).

Tyler and Lind (1992) elaborated on the group-value model in a chapter in which they articulated their relational model of authority. Whereas the group-value model focused primarily on demonstrating the role of noninstrumental factors involved in procedural justice judgments, the relational model built on the earlier work in an effort to understand how authorities gain legitimacy in hierarchical groups. As with the group-value model, the relational model argues that procedures in organizations or other institutions are interpreted as reflecting basic values of the group; thus procedures convey information to people regarding their relationship with the group and the authority enacting the procedure, which fosters authority legitimacy. The theoretical core of the relational and group-value models is the same (in fact the labels are often used interchangeably); in short, both models argue that people are concerned with *relational* aspects of procedures, which are different from—and indeed often more important than—their concerns with short-term material resources (Tyler, 1994).

Given the premise that people gain identity from their association with others, the group-value and relational models also diverged from the previous procedural justice models in terms of the criteria by which people evaluate procedural fairness. These newer models argued that people evaluate procedural fairness by the presence or absence of relational criteria, whereas the older models focused more on how procedures should be structured (although this is not entirely true in Leventhal's model). For example, in early research, Tyler and Folger (1980) demonstrated that a key predictor of citizens' satisfaction with their encounters with police was the recognition of their "rights to call upon the police and to be taken seriously in that request" (p. 292) regardless of the outcome of the encounter, such as whether they received a citation for violating the law. Later research defined three relational criteria (e.g., Tyler, 1989, 1994), namely the neutrality of the decision-making procedure (operationalized as lack of bias, propriety of behavior, quality of questions), trust in (or benevolence of) the authorities' intentions, and standing/status recognition, an index of quality of treatment (operationalized as polite treatment and respect for one's rights). Several studies have demonstrated the contribution of such relational concerns to procedural justice perceptions and evaluations of authorities (police, political leaders) over and above effects of perceived distributive justice, process control, and outcome control (see Tyler, 1991; Tyler & Caine, 1981).

How Broad Is the Procedural Justice Concept?

In the mid-1980s, Bies and Moag (1986) published a chapter in which they coined a new justice concept: interactional justice. Bies and Moag argued that resource allocation decisions comprise a "sequence of events in which a procedure generates a process of interaction and decision making through which an outcome is allocated to someone" (p. 45). Accordingly, they suggested that the *structure* of decision procedures, the *enactment* of those procedures, and the *outcomes* can each be conceptualized as separate aspects of an allocation sequence and, therefore, that all three are potentially subject to fairness considerations. Bies and Moag argued that much of the prior procedural justice research either had neglected the interpersonal element or had confounded the two elements of process.

Bies and Moag (1986) conceived the concept of interactional justice to encompass people's concerns about the "quality of interpersonal treatment exhibited by leaders during the enactment or implementation of decision procedures" (p. 44). Initially derived from content analyses of MBA students' job search experiences, Bies and Moag focused on the fairness of the communication aspect of interpersonal treatment, and identified four criteria that people use to evaluate fairness: truthfulness, respect, propriety of questions, and justification. In the early research, the four criteria set out by Bies and Moag were typically summarized into two broader classes that appear to cover the initial content domain. In brief, interactional justice was conceptualized as deriving from (a) clear and adequate explanations of, or justifications for, allocation decisions, and (b) treatment of recipients with dignity and respect during the implementation of procedures (e.g., Tyler & Bies, 1990; also see Bies, 2005, Chapter 4).

The idea that authorities' behavior during the enactment of decision procedures could influence employees' fairness perceptions was supported in early studies conducted by Bies and his colleagues on managerial justifications (e.g., Bies & Shapiro, 1987, 1988; Bies, Shapiro, & Cummings, 1988). These studies demonstrated that justifications offered by managers for unfavorable decisions had the effect of enhancing recipients' perceptions of fairness and their outcome acceptance. For example, Bies and Shapiro (1987) asked MBA students to evaluate several cases describing a manager's questionable conduct. Half the participants were provided with an excuse for the manager's conduct; the other half received no such information. Participants perceived the manager as more fair and endorsed him more strongly in the presence of the excuse than in its absence. In a follow-up study, Bies and Shapiro asked MBA students to recount a time when a request was denied by their boss and to respond to a set of questions with the event in mind. Again, participants perceived their boss as more fair, and reported less anger and resentment, the more they rated their boss's explanation for the refusal to be adequate (for reviews, see Bobocel & Zdaniuk, 2005; Shaw, Wild, & Colquitt, 2003).

Not surprisingly, debate soon emerged in the literature about whether interactional justice is distinguishable from procedural justice. Much of the conceptual confusion in the literature arose because many procedural justice studies had operationalized the concept in ways that included the enactment of procedures. In other words, many of the interactional justice criteria were being examined under the rubric of the procedural justice construct. For example, in experimental research to examine the conditions that arouse resentment, Folger and his colleagues demonstrated that participants were less angry about receiving a negative outcome in the presence of procedural justification, that is, when the experimenter provided a credible justification for the decision procedures that led to the outcome (e.g., Folger & Martin, 1986; Folger, Rosenfield, & Robinson, 1983).

Similarly, research leading to the group-value model had adopted a broader definition of procedural justice. For example, in the study by Tyler and Folger (1980) discussed earlier, procedural justice was operationalized by relational criteria, the core of which involved judgments regarding the respectful treatment that people received from the police. In their review, Lind and Tyler (1988) stated that "procedural justice involves more than questions of how decisions are made. It also involves questions of how people are treated by authorities and other parties" (p. 214). Thus, Lind and Tyler (1988) suggested that both the structure of decision procedures and their enactment are integral "process fairness" considerations (also see Folger & Bies, 1989; Tyler & Bies, 1990).

In contrast, Bies and Moag (1986) suggested that the concept of procedural justice should be defined as people's perceptions of the fairness of the formal structure of decision procedures, which they suggested was in line with early conceptions of procedural justice (e.g., Leventhal, 1980; Thibaut & Walker, 1975), and that interactional justice should be defined in terms of the "propriety of the decision maker's behavior during the enactment of procedures" (Bies & Shapiro, 1988, p. 201). Thus, Bies and Moag (1986) acknowledged that it might be best to consider interactional justice as part of a broader conceptualization of procedural justice because people may only come to know procedures through their enactment; therefore the two elements will be highly interrelated perceptually (also see Tyler & Bies, 1990). But they maintained that "interactional fairness will generalize to the procedure itself only when a person attributes responsibility for the action to the organization, a systemic attribution, rather than the decision maker. On the other hand, if a person attributes the deception and rudeness solely to the decision maker and not the organization, then there should be less implications for the procedure itself" (p. 52).

Following Bies and Moag's (1986) analysis, Greenberg (1993b) offered another model. Greenberg argued that the differentiation between social and nonsocial elements of the procedures can also apply to the outcomes of decisions. That is, he contended that people are concerned about fair interpersonal treatment not only during the implementation of decision procedures but also during the distribution phase of an allocation sequence. Thus, Greenberg suggested that we may conceptualize social and nonsocial elements of both procedures and distributions, resulting in a four-component model of fairness perceptions. He used the labels *procedural and distributive justice* to refer to the nonsocial *mechanisms* by which decisions are made and outcomes are allocated. He used the labels *informational and interpersonal* justice to refer to the *interpersonal behaviors* of those implementing procedures and outcome distributions, or in other words to the *social enactment* of the rules of procedures and outcome allocations.

The issue of whether procedural justice should be conceptualized broadly or more narrowly became a topic of much discussion in the literature over the next 15 years (e.g., see Bies, 2001, 2005; Bobocel & Holmvall, 2001; Cropanzano & Greenberg, 1997; Folger & Bies, 1989; Greenberg, 1990; Tyler &

Bies, 1990), and captured considerable research attention, as we will review in the next part of the chapter. Despite the debate over construct labels, the research on interactional justice would serve to highlight the central role of how authorities implement decision procedures in determining employees' experience of fairness and their downstream reactions.

It is important to note that researchers have highlighted other procedural justice criteria that are pertinent in specific organizational contexts. For example, in the context of performance evaluation, several researchers remarked on the importance of adequate notice, fair hearing, and judgments based on evidence (e.g., Folger, Konovsky, & Cropanzano, 1992; Greenberg, 1986; Taylor, Tracy, Renard, Harrison, & Carroll, 1995). In the context of personnel selection, Gilliland (1993) identified 10 procedural rules that should improve applicant reactions to employment selection systems, including job relatedness, the opportunity to perform, propriety of questions, honesty, and feedback. Interestingly, Gilliland also identified rules that may be important within this context, but which have not previously been considered explicitly, such as the ease of faking answers and the invasiveness of questions. In most cases, however, the criteria that researchers have identified within a particular organizational context have turned out to be consistent with those identified by the early theorists. Thus, there appear to be some general considerations that people take into account when evaluating procedural justice that are relatively universal (see Cropanzano & Greenberg, 1997).

Summary

It is clear that the organizational context has provided a fertile ground in which researchers have been able to deepen their understanding of the criteria by which people evaluate procedural justice. Researchers have learned a tremendous amount about what comprises people's evaluations of "fair process." Moreover, as researchers came to further understand the criteria that influence procedural justice perceptions, they illuminated the motives underlying people's concerns with procedures. In the early history of the literature, the group-value/relational models were especially influential in this regard, as they highlighted the notion that people's desire for procedural justice derives from more than their concern with the fair distribution of outcomes, which was the dominant perspective of the day. Instead, it became evident that people use procedural justice to gauge their social identity, and ultimately their sense of self-worth.

Examining the Effects of Procedural Justice in the Workplace

As we noted at the outset of this chapter, it was not long after the concept of procedural justice first emerged in the psychological literature that researchers began to study procedural justice in the workplace (e.g., Folger & Greenberg, 1985; Greenberg & Folger, 1983; Lind & Lissak, 1985; see for review, Lind & Tyler, 1988). Although early research had a number of goals, an obvious agenda was to demonstrate that procedural justice perceptions in fact matter in the workplace. Thus, much research examined the role of procedural justice perceptions in predicting employee attitudes and behaviors. In this section, we provide an overview of the research paradigms used to examine the effects of procedural justice in the workplace.

Differential Effects Models

One way that researchers attempted to demonstrate that procedural justice is relevant in the workplace was to examine attitudes and behaviors that might be uniquely associated with employees' perceptions of procedural justice, initially in relation to distributive justice and later in relation to interactional justice. Researchers have referred to this approach as the "differential effects" framework because the goal was to demonstrate, for example, that procedural justice and distributive justice predict different employee attitudes and behaviors.

PROCEDURAL VERSUS DISTRIBUTIVE JUSTICE: THE TWO-FACTOR MODEL

In an early study, Alexander and Ruderman (1987) examined the relative contributions of procedural and distributive justice perceptions for predicting employee evaluations of their supervisors and their trust in management. This study drew on previous research conducted by Tyler and Caine (1981), which demonstrated across four studies in two contexts (student evaluations of teachers in a laboratory context and citizen evaluations of political leaders in natural settings) that people's endorsement of leaders is influenced by their assessment of the leaders' procedural fairness, over and above any effects of outcome fairness or the level of outcomes received. From these findings, Alexander and Ruderman predicted that procedural justice should have a stronger effect than distributive justice on employees' evaluations of their supervisor and on their trust in management. Using an existing large-scale survey of US federal government employees, the researchers created predictor measures to represent the procedural and distributive justice constructs and demonstrated that procedural justice perceptions indeed accounted for significantly greater variance in the criteria than did distributive justice perceptions.

These results were soon clarified and extended in a landmark study conducted by Folger and Konovsky (1989) in which they examined employee reactions to a recent pay raise. Drawing on Lind and Tyler's (1988) group-value model, Folger and Konovsky argued that procedural and distributive justice should have *differential* effects on employee reactions. As discussed earlier, Lind and Tyler suggested that people attend to procedural fairness when taking a long-term perspective on their membership in groups, and they focus on distributive fairness when responding to a single decision. Thus, Folger and Konovsky (1989) predicted that employees' satisfaction with the pay raise should be more strongly predicted by their perceptions of distributive justice relative to procedural justice. In contrast, employees' commitment to the organization and its authorities should be more strongly predicted by their perceptions of procedural justice relative to distributive justice. In line with these hypotheses, Folger and Konovsky (1989) found that distributive justice accounted for more unique variance in employees' satisfaction with their pay raise, whereas procedural justice accounted for more unique variance in employees' trust in supervisor and organizational commitment. These findings were important because they demonstrated the generalizability of earlier research findings on procedural justice which had been seen outside of the workplace context, and they further supported the predictions of the group-value model.

Subsequent research replicated the dissociation observed by Folger and Konovsky (1989). For example, several researchers found that employees' distributive justice perceptions were strongly associated with pay satisfaction (e.g., Harder, 1992; Summers & Hendrix, 1991), whereas procedural justice perceptions were strongly associated with trust in management and institutional commitment (e.g., Konovsky & Pugh, 1994; Korsgaard, Schweiger, & Sapienza, 1995; Tyler & Degoey, 1995). Similarly, McFarlin and Sweeney (1992) found that distributive justice was a stronger predictor of pay satisfaction and job satisfaction, whereas procedural justice was a stronger predictor of organizational commitment and employees' evaluations of their supervisors.

In another article, Sweeney and McFarlin (1993) put forth the two-factor model of justice, which specified that distributive justice perceptions are expected to have stronger effects than procedural justice perceptions on *person-referenced* variables, such as pay satisfaction and job satisfaction. In contrast, procedural justice perceptions are expected to have stronger effects than distributive justice perceptions on *system-referenced* variables, such as organizational commitment, trust in management, and subordinates' evaluations of organizational agents. In their study, Sweeney and McFarlin (1993) compared the validity of the two-factor model against three alternative models (procedural primacy model, distributive halo model, additive model) and concluded that the two-factor model received the most support.

This dissociation paradigm was highly influential because it provided researchers with a useful framework for examining the differential effects of procedural and distributive justice perceptions. This line of research not only confirmed the idea that employees form both distributive and procedural justice judgments, but also established that both justice judgments are important in the workplace. Moreover, to many, the research suggested that procedural justice perceptions were comparatively more important than distributive justice perceptions given the wider range and nature of organizational variables associated with the former than with the latter. Procedural justice was said to be more important than distributive justice for fostering variables reflecting long-term commitment and loyalty to the system and its authorities, variables that are critical for the survival of organizations (e.g., for reviews, see Cropanzano & Greenberg, 1997; Tyler & Lind, 1992). This view has been echoed more recently in a meta-analytic study of the relations between procedural and distributive justice and work attitudes (Viswesvaran & Ones, 2002). Later in this part of the chapter, however, we will discuss research that challenges the validity of the two-factor model.

PROCEDURAL VERSUS INTERACTIONAL JUSTICE: THE AGENT-SYSTEM MODEL

Following the introduction of the concept of interactional justice, the 1990s also saw a marked increase in studies that attempted to distinguish the effects of the structure of decision procedures from the social enactment of procedures. In an initial study, Moorman (1991) used causal modeling techniques to assess the associations between employees' perceptions of fairness and their tendency to engage in organizational citizenship behaviors (OCB) as rated by their supervisor. Moorman created measures to assess perceptions of procedural justice (operationalized as employee ratings of their organizations' adherence to the criteria specified by Leventhal) and interactional justice (operationalized as employee ratings of their supervisors' adherence to the criteria specified by Bies & Moag, 1986). He assessed distributive justice perceptions using a scale previously developed by Price and Mueller (1986). In brief, Moorman found that employees' perceptions of interactional justice, but not of procedural or distributive justice, were significantly associated with supervisor-rated citizenship behaviors. Moorman's findings were consistent with the idea that the role of decision-maker conduct may have been underemphasized in prior research on procedural justice (but see Lind & Tyler, 1988).

As with the two-factor model, researchers soon assessed the distinction between social (decision-maker conduct) and structural aspects of procedures by examining differential effects on attitudes and behaviors. In their original analysis, Bies and Moag (1986) argued that people may draw on their procedural justice perceptions (defined in terms of the structural elements of procedures) when deciding how to react to the overall organization, whereas they use interactional justice perception (defined in terms of the enactment of procedures) when deciding how to react to the agents who are enacting the procedures, such as supervisors. This theme became known as the "agent-system model," which proposed that interactional justice elements are stronger predictors than structural elements of agent-referenced outcomes—such as supervisor trust, and supervisor-directed deviance—because the source of justice is presumed to be the agent. In contrast, perceptions that the organization adheres to procedural rules of fairness are a stronger predictor than social enactment of system-referenced outcomes—such as organizational affective commitment and organization-directed deviance—because adherence to procedural rules is attributed to the organization.

Malatesta and Byrne (1997) used structural equation modeling to test this idea in a survey of employee-supervisor dyads. They found that employees' perceptions of procedural justice related to their level of affective organizational commitment. In contrast, employees' perceptions of interactional justice influenced their self-reported supervisory commitment and supervisor-reported organizational citizenship behavior. Masterson, Lewis, Goldman, & Tayler (2000) replicated and extended these findings by examining the mediating mechanism through which the justice concepts could relate to different organizational variables. Consistent with the notion that a social exchange process develops between employees and the source to which they attribute justice (i.e., the organization or the supervisor), the researchers found that the relations between procedural justice and organization-directed outcomes were mediated by perceived organizational support. In contrast, the relations between interactional justice perceptions and supervisor-directed outcomes were mediated by the quality of leader-member exchange. If people's concerns about the structure of procedures and about interpersonal treatment do represent separate constructs, then one might expect this disjunctive pattern of results. In contrast, job satisfaction was predicted similarly by the two justice perceptions, presumably because it is influenced by justice perceptions derived from both sources (also see Cropanzano, Prehar, & Chen, 2002; Cropanzano, Rupp, Mohler, & Schminke, 2001).

Two influential events that occurred around this time reinforced the distinction between procedural and interactional justice. In an effort to bring consensus and clarification regarding construct definitions and, therefore, regarding the measurement of justice perceptions in field research, Colquitt (2001) developed and validated the first standardized measure in which the structural and enactment components of procedures were conceptualized as distinct dimensions. To index procedural justice perceptions, respondents indicate the degree to which the criteria identified by Thibaut and Walker and by Leventhal are upheld. The enactment of procedures (interactional justice) is further distinguished into the two components discussed by Bies and Moag (1986): (1) the criteria of truthfulness and justification, and (2) the criteria of respect and propriety of questions. Colquitt labeled the former informational justice, and the latter interpersonal justice, drawing on Greenberg (1993b), noted earlier. Of note, Colquitt suggested that the relational criteria identified by the group-value and relational models of procedural justice (e.g., Lind & Tyler, 1988; Tyler & Lind, 1992) are subsumed either under items that index procedural justice (e.g., neutrality is indexed by bias suppression) or under those that index interpersonal justice (e.g., standing, status recognition are indexed by respect). Finally, distributive justice perceptions are indexed by adherence to the norm of equity (e.g., Leventhal, 1976; Deutsch, 1975). As noted earlier, the measure assesses justice perceptions indirectly rather than directly (see Lind & Tyler, 1988) by assessing the degree to which respondents perceive that specific justice rules (e.g., consistency in procedures, respectful treatment) are upheld. Importantly, the measure can be tailored to specific contexts (for discussion of measurement issues, see Chapter 8; Colquitt & Shaw, 2005).

As more researchers used Colquitt's measure after its publication, the majority of contemporary studies that measure justice perceptions in the workplace have come to separate the structural and enactment components. Clearly, this must be recognized when comparing findings from more recent research on procedural justice in which the construct is assessed more narrowly to earlier procedural justice research in which the concept was assessed more broadly. For example, given the central role of respectful treatment in the group-value/relational models of procedural justice, it should not be surprising to find stronger effects for interactional justice than for procedural justice in contemporary research in which procedural justice is defined more narrowly than in earlier research where it was defined more broadly.

The second influential event that reinforced the distinction between procedural and interactional justice occurred in the same year as Colquitt's measure appeared: Two meta-analytic studies involving the three justice concepts were published (Colquitt, Conlon, Wesson, Porter, & Ng, 2001; Cohen-Charash & Spector, 2001; a third meta-analysis appeared in the same year on the relation between procedural and distributive justice, see Hauenstein, McGonigle, & Flinder, 2001). Although the structure of the meta-analyses differed somewhat, both bolstered the distinctions among the three (or four) justice constructs. For example, Cohen-Charash and Spector (2001) meta-analyzed the results of 190 study samples and concluded that the three constructs are related yet distinct, and are associated with different organizational outcomes. In particular, procedural justice was more strongly related than distributive justice or interactional justice to job performance and counterproductive work behavior. Other dissociations were not as clear; for example, procedural justice was primarily related to organizational commitment and trust, although distributive and interactional justice were also substantially related to these variables. Both procedural and distributive justice predicted organizational citizenship behavior, and all three constructs were related to satisfaction measures.

Colquitt and his colleagues (2001) meta-analyzed 183 studies and examined the distinction between distributive and procedural justice, and the two social enactment components of interactional justice. Although the constructs were moderately to highly related, Colquitt et al. demonstrated that they contribute unique variance explained in fairness perceptions. Moreover, their analysis demonstrated support for differential relations among the constructs and several organizational variables. To guide their predictions, the researchers drew on the two-factor and agent-system models. As discussed earlier, according to the two-factor model, procedural justice is expected to have stronger effects than distributive justice on system-referenced variables, but weaker effects than distributive justice on person-referenced variables. The results revealed some support for the two-factor model for attitudinal variables (organizational commitment, system-referenced evaluation of authority *vs* outcome satisfaction and job satisfaction, respectively) but not for most of the behavioral variables examined (organizational citizenship behavior, withdrawal, and negative reactions). Job performance was an exception, if it is conceptualized as a system-referenced variable.

From the agent-system model, the researchers expected informational or interpersonal justice to have stronger effects than procedural justice on agent-referenced variables but weaker effects than procedural justice on system-referenced variables. The results again revealed some support for the model (OCB-toward supervisor, evaluation of the authority *vs* job satisfaction, organizational commitment, and job performance). However, some results were contrary to the agent-system model in that stronger relations than expected were found between informational or interpersonal justice and OCB-toward organization, withdrawal, and negative reactions. Colquitt et al. suggested that the agent-system model may underestimate the importance of the social enactment of justice for predicting behavioral variables, a point echoed subsequently (e.g., Ambrose, Seabright, & Schminke, 2002; Rupp & Cropanzano, 2002).

Like the justice measure, the meta-analytic studies had substantial impact on the literature. The majority of studies assessing procedural justice in the workplace over the next 15 years would adopt the distinction between procedural and interactional justice, and often use the two-factor and agent-system models to guide predictions. Indeed, from this period right up to the present day, justice researchers have heavily emphasized examination of differential effects of the three (or four) justice components and their mediation (see for review, Colquitt et al., 2013).

SOME LIMITATIONS OF THE DIFFERENTIAL EFFECTS PARADIGM

Although the two-factor framework was especially prominent in early years, it continues to guide justice research to the present day (e.g., Colquitt, 2001; Colquitt et al., 2001; Reithel, Baltes, & Buddhavarapu, 2007; Pillai, Williams, & Tan, 2001; Viswesvaran & Ones, 2002). Nevertheless, researchers have highlighted several limitations of the model. For example, Skitka, Winquist, and Hutchinson (2003) pointed out that in early procedural justice studies, researchers often treated outcome valence/favorability and outcome fairness (distributive justice) interchangeably, or they confounded these constructs. Although related, these constructs are not identical. An outcome is unfavorable to the extent that it does not benefit the recipient, whereas an outcome is unfair to the extent that it violates a referent normative standard (Skikta et al., 2003, also see Kulik & Ambrose, 1992). Skitka and her colleagues thus questioned whether previous research demonstrating the relative effects of procedures and outcomes (and their interactive effects, to follow) in fact informs us about the relative power of procedural justice and *outcome favorability*, rather than of procedural justice and *distributive justice.* If so, then conclusions regarding the relative effects of procedural and distributive justice may be misleading, and indeed researchers may have tended to underestimate the importance of distributive justice relative to procedural justice.

To examine this question, Skitka and her colleagues (2003) conducted a meta-analytic review of 89 independent samples, teasing apart the outcome favorability and outcome fairness constructs. Importantly, they found that procedural justice perceptions have *less* impact when the criterion is outcome fairness as opposed to outcome favorability. In addition, the researchers demonstrated that the effects of outcome fairness on system-referenced variables were stronger than the effects of outcome favorability, and outcome fairness effects were as strong as, or stronger than, the effects of procedural fairness perceptions. Together, these findings question the validity of the two-factor framework in which procedural justice is said to relate to system-referenced outcomes and distributive justice is said to relate to person-referenced outcomes.

Skitka et al.'s (2003) findings also revealed that experimental manipulations of outcome fairness and outcome favorability have *stronger* effects on procedural fairness perceptions than the converse. This finding is important because it runs in opposition to the dominant view that procedures shape outcome judgments, rather than the reverse (e.g., Greenberg, 1987; Leventhal, 1980; Lind & Tyler, 1988). It is interesting to note a related finding in the meta-analysis of the effects of procedural and distributive justice mentioned earlier. Viswevaran and Ones (2002) found that the relations between distributive justice and work attitudes were in most cases mediated by procedural justice perceptions.

Other research findings suggest that the two-factor model is likely to be an oversimplification of the interplay between procedural and distributive justice perceptions. Although the model has been supported in some research, other research has failed to support its predictions (e.g., Clemmer, 1993; Smith, Bolton, & Wagner, 1999; for review see Conlon, Meyer, & Nowakowski, 2005). In addition, researchers have demonstrated support for alternative hypotheses. For example, in one of the first longitudinal investigations, Ambrose and Cropanzano (2003) examined the relations between faculty members' perceptions of procedural and distributive justice and their reactions to promotion and tenure decisions. The researchers argued that, due to changes in information acquired over the course of time, perceptions of procedural and distributive justice may be differentially influential as predictors of attitudes *over time.* As expected, they demonstrated that faculty member's perceptions of procedural justice were more influential prior to and soon after the decisions were made, but that distributive justice perceptions were more important one year later. These results imply that procedural and distributive justice may relate to similar attitudes, but that their influence may be more potent at different points in time (also see Cropanzano & Ambrose, 2001). Fortunately, over the last decade, more researchers have examined justice processes longitudinally (e.g., Holtz & Harold, 2009), and the study of time in justice processes has drawn greater systematic attention (see Chapter 14).

In the late 1999s, researchers similarly noted difficulties in drawing clear conclusions from research examining the agent-system model. For one, the early research generally confounded the *source* of the justice (organization vs agent) with the "*content*" of justice (procedural vs interactional). Within the agent-system model, procedural justice was assumed to emanate from the organization, and interactional justice (informational, interpersonal) was assumed to emanate from the supervisor. Thus, as noted earlier, procedural justice was assumed to predict system-referenced variables (e.g., organizational commitment) through a social exchange process that develops between employees and the organization as a whole. Correspondingly, interactional justice was assumed to predict agent-referenced variables (e.g., supervisor legitimacy) through a social exchange process that develops between employees and the agents of decisions. Researchers wondered whether the more fundamental distinction between measures of procedural and interactional justice was one of source (organization, supervisor) rather than of justice content.

To examine this possible problem, Byrne (1999) suggested that "justice source" and "justice content" can be fully crossed such that employees can experience several sources of justice or injustice, two of the most obvious being their immediate supervisors or managers and their employing organizations as a whole. Thus, Byrne argued that both procedural and interactional justice can emanate from both sources (organization and supervisor). She further suggested that employees' responses could be source-directed due to the formation of social exchange relationships that develop between employees and the sources of justice.

Rupp and Cropanzano (2002) examined a social exchange model of these hypothesized "multifoci justice effects" in a survey of employee-supervisor dyads. As predicted, they found that organization-emanating justice (procedural justice and interactional) was significantly related to organization-relevant variables (e.g., job performance, organizational citizenship behavior directed toward organization). In contrast, supervisor-emanating justice (procedural and interactional) was significantly related to supervisory-relevant variables (organizational citizenship behavior directed toward supervisor). Moreover, the researchers demonstrated that these effects were mediated, respectively, by organizationally focused relational exchange and supervisory-focused relational exchange. Of note, Rupp and Cropanzano argued for (and observed) an interesting "cross-foci" effect, in which supervisory-emanating justice would impact organizational-focused variables as well as supervisory-focused variables (also see Ambrose, Seabright, & Schminke, 2002), a finding similar to that noted earlier in the meta-analysis by Colquitt et al. (2001). In general, the data supported the researchers' model, although the results were not as strong for procedural justice as for interactional justice.

In an independent line of research, Blader and Tyler (2003a, 2003b) similarly argued that both the quality of decision procedures (captured by the procedural justice construct in the preceding research) and their enactment (captured by the interactional justice construct earlier) can emanate both from formal rules of the group, such as the organization, and informally through actions of individual agents, such as one's supervisor (also see Tyler & Blader, 2000). Thus, Blader and Tyler argued for a broader conceptualization of procedural justice that derives from fully crossing people's concerns regarding the structure and social enactment of decisions with the formal or informal source of justice. The results of a workplace survey and laboratory experiment (Blader & Tyler, 2003a) demonstrated support for their idea that all four procedural components contribute to people's overall evaluation of the fairness of group procedures.

Both sets of preceding studies question the validity of the traditional agent-system model in which procedural justice is said to be more strongly associated with system-referenced reactions than is interactional justice, whereas the converse should hold for agent-referenced reactions. It is worth noting that, since these initial studies, researchers have continued to demonstrate the existence of additional sources of justice (beyond the organization and supervisors), such as co-workers (e.g., Donovan, Drasgow, & Munson, 1998), customers (e.g., Wang, Liao, Zhan, & Shi, 2011), and one's workgroup (Lavelle et al., 2009). Moreover, researchers have demonstrated "target similarity" effects (Lavelle, Rupp, & Brockner, 2007) in which justice source is aligned with response target (e.g., Horvath & Andrews, 2007; Karriker, &

Williams, 2009; Lavelle et al., 2009; Liao & Rupp, 2005). Indeed, the results of a recent meta-analysis of multifoci justice effects revealed that *source-based* justice perceptions have greater predictive validity than *type-based* justice perceptions (Rupp, Shao, Jones, & Liao, 2014; also see Chapter 7; cf. Colquitt et al., 2013).

Ambrose and Arnaud (2005) pointed out another important limitation of the differential effects paradigms, which is that they fail to recognize the relationships among criterion variables. Thus, the differential effects frameworks do not allow for the possibility of indirect effects of the justice components on attitudes and behaviors. Ambrose, Hess, and Ganesan (2007) discuss this issue in greater detail, and examine the possibility that, for example, distributive justice can affect system-level attitudes indirectly via reactions to events (Cropanzano et al., 2001). Consistent with their reasoning, Ambrose and her colleagues found that all three components of justice (distributive, procedural, and interactional) relate to overall attitudes toward the organization indirectly through their direct relation to attitudes about specific events.

Interaction Effect Models

Another way that researchers have historically attempted to demonstrate the importance of procedural justice in the workplace has been to examine how people combine information about the process and the outcomes. Thus, rather than examining the separate effects (i.e., statistical main effects) of procedural justice and distributive justice perceptions, researchers have examined their joint effects (i.e., statistical interactions). We will first review the early research examining the question of how people combine information about process fairness (structural elements and social enactment elements) with information about outcomes. Then we will review more recent research that separates the two elements of process fairness. Therefore, for the early research, we are discussing the two-way statistical interaction effect, and for the more recent research, the three-way interaction.

OUTCOME X PROCESS INTERACTION EFFECTS

As noted earlier, many researchers have examined the differential effects of procedural and distributive justice perceptions, an approach that grew out of the instrumental and group-value/relational models of procedural justice. Those models were initially derived to explain the overall beneficial effects of people's preference for procedural justice, independent of distributive justice perceptions. To complement these approaches, justice scholars called for research and theory that *integrated* people's concerns about outcomes and procedures (Folger & Cropanzano, 1998; Greenberg, 1990). It is important to realize that, over the years, researchers have come to refer to this interaction as one between *outcome favorability* and procedural justice (or process fairness). This is because, as noted earlier (e.g., Skitka et al., 2003), researchers often measured or manipulated outcome valence rather than outcome fairness in early research to examine the statistical interaction effect.[2]

In the mid-1980s, Folger had developed a justice framework in his research on reward allocation that he labelled referent cognitions theory (RCT). This explanation explicitly considered how people combine information about outcomes and procedures (Folger, 1986, 1987). As originally specified, Folger sought to explain the conditions that created negative reactions, such as resentment, moral outrage, and perceived injustice, in response to negative outcomes. Drawing on social cognitive research in psychology (e.g., Kahneman & Tversky, 1982), Folger argued that when people are faced with negative events, they engage in "referent cognitions"—that is, they think about "what if" or "what might have been." Thus, in the context of resource allocation decisions, Folger predicted that people would experience the most resentment under two conditions: when they can easily imagine that they *would* have received a better outcome (high versus low referent outcome conditions) had a different allocation procedure been used, and when they believe that the alternative procedure *could* have been used (low versus high procedural justification conditions).

From this logic, Folger predicted a two-way interaction between procedural and distributive aspects of an exchange, such that the most negative reactions to a resource allocation decision that recipients can easily imagine having been better will occur when people perceive the procedures associated with the decision to be unfair (e.g., unjustified). Stated differently, when decisions are procedurally fair (for example, recipients have input into the decision, or an adequate justification is provided) rather than unfair, procedural information should mitigate negative reactions to high referent outcomes (those one can easily imagine being better). Several early studies by

Folger and his colleagues confirmed the predicted outcome x procedure interaction in the context of reward allocation in the laboratory (Folger, 1977; Folger, Rosenfield, Rheume, & Martin 1983; Folger, Rosenfield, Hayes, & Grove, 1978; Folger, Rosenfield, & Robinson, 1983). As we will see next, the outcome x procedure interaction has also been demonstrated repeatedly in the organizational context.

To better integrate research findings on interactional justice, Folger (1993) explicitly defined the "procedure" component of RCT theory more broadly to encompass both structural and enactment elements of procedures. He suggested that decision makers have moral obligations to recipients not only to structure procedures fairly, but also to treat recipients respectfully when implementing procedures (see p. 174). Thus, he suggested that resentment to high referent outcomes can occur as a function of two elements of decision-maker conduct: the implementation of unfair procedures (attributes of process which may have a causal influence on outcome) and inappropriate treatment when implementing the decision (attributes of process that are not necessarily causally related to the outcome, but which may signal disrespect). According to the revised theory, then, in the case of high referent outcomes, decision-maker conduct can be exonerated by behaviors that have no causal association with outcome (e.g., apologies, polite treatment) in addition to behaviors that are causally associated (e.g., unbiased procedures).

Note that RCT differed from the instrumental and relational models of procedural justice in two ways. First, as noted earlier, RCT was designed to explicitly consider how people integrate their concerns with both outcomes and procedures, whereas the instrumental and group-value models were initially postulated to account for the overall beneficial effects of procedures (although they too can account for the interaction, see Brockner & Wiesenfeld, 1996). Second, RCT was concerned with predicting *how* people form judgments of injustice by integrating information about outcomes and procedures, whereas the instrumental and group-value models are fundamentally concerned with explaining *why* procedural justice influences people's assessments of outcomes, and other attitudes and behaviors.

Following from Folger's early work on RCT, many researchers examined the joint effects of procedures and outcomes in laboratory simulations (e.g., Cropanzano & Folger, 1989), as well as within the organizational context. In the organizational context, researchers have examined joint effects on employees' reactions to a wide variety of workplace decisions, including layoffs (e.g., Brockner, DeWitt, Grover, & Reed, 1990), pay freezes (Schaubroeck, May, & Brown, 1994), institution of a smoking ban (Greenberg, 1994), and implementation of drug-testing policies (Cropanzano & Konovsky, 1995). For example, Brockner and colleagues (1994) demonstrated across three studies that when procedural justice in the context of layoffs was perceived to be low, employees were less trusting and supportive of the organization than when the layoff outcomes were perceived to be negative (e.g., low severance pay). In contrast, when individuals perceived procedural justice to be high, perceived layoff negativity was unrelated to employees' reactions. Thus, perceptions of procedural justice mitigated the effects of outcome negativity on employees' reactions to the layoff. Put differently, the interaction effect suggested that procedural justice perceptions have particularly strong beneficial effects on employees' evaluations of the organization when outcomes are unfavorable. The results were the same whether for layoff victims (Study 1), layoff survivors (Study 2), and employees soon to be laid off (Study 3). These results are in line with RCT predictions.

In an influential review, Brockner and Wiesenfeld (1996) meta-analyzed the outcome x process interaction across 45 independent samples and demonstrated its robust nature. In general, the pattern of the interaction was the same across a number of settings (legal arena, work organizations, laboratory), across a number of contexts within the organizational setting as noted earlier, across a number of operationalizations of the procedure and outcome, and across a number of dependent/criterion work-related reactions (e.g., organizational commitment, trust, turnover intentions, job performance, fairness perceptions, theft, task performance).

In keeping with their broad approach, Brockner and Wiesenfeld (1996) did not distinguish between the structural and enactment elements of process fairness. Although they recognized these aspects as conceptually different, Brockner and Wiesenfeld suggested that they should (and do) have similar patterns in moderating the effects of outcome favorability on work-related reactions (e.g., see Greenberg, 1990, 1993a, 1994). Similarly, the researchers combined studies that assessed or manipulated outcome fairness and those that assessed or manipulated outcome valence on the argument that outcome fairness and outcome favorability are conceptually related and typically highly empirically related.

In addition to demonstrating the robust nature of the outcome x process interaction on a variety of work-related reactions, Brockner and Wiesenfeld (1996) provided a detailed theoretical account for *why* it occurs. In particular, they set out an integrative explanation by drawing on common elements of prior theories. Brockner and Wiesenfeld suggested that the interaction between procedures and outcomes can be understood as the product of a broader behavioral self-regulation process, which is threatened by events that are experienced as unexpected, negative, or both. They suggested that such events initiate information search, and that this serves to increase peoples' sensitivity to salient external cues. Thus, they argued that unfavorable outcomes, which are generally perceived as both negative and unexpected, serve to heighten people's sensitivity to procedural information. Similarly, they argued that unfair procedures and disrespectful treatment (process elements) are experienced negatively, and they are also unexpected, in that they violate normative standards regarding how decisions should be made and how people should be treated. As a consequence, the authors argued that unfair procedure serves to heighten people's sensitivity to outcome information. Under this *sense-making* account, procedures can heighten people's concerns with outcomes, and outcomes can heighten their concerns with procedures.

The Brockner and Wiesenfeld (1996) review contributed to the literature in another important way. Whereas they found that the outcome x process interaction was robust across many criterion variables that gauge work-related reactions, a different pattern emerged in four independent samples from two studies in which self-evaluations were the criteria (Gilliland, 1994; Schroth & Shah, 1993/2000).[3] People had more favorable self-evaluations, such as higher state self-esteem, when they received positive feedback about their performance relative to negative feedback, but this effect was more pronounced when procedural fairness was relatively high. In other words, on self-evaluations, procedural fairness was found to *heighten* (rather than reduce) the adverse effects of negative outcome feedback. Thus, in the context of receiving an unfavorable outcome, fairer procedures can have a negative impact on recipients. This observation has been replicated and followed up in more recent research, and has led to important insights regarding procedural justice, as we will discuss in the fourth part of the chapter. In general, research on the outcome x process interaction has remained popular over the years (e.g., Brockner & Wiesenfeld, 2005; De Cremer & Sedikides, 2005; De Cremer & Van Knippenberg, 2003; Hakonen & Lipponen, 2008). In a recent book, Joel Brocker (2010) provides a comprehensive and engaging review of this vast body of research and suggests new lines of research on procedural justice.

OUTCOME X PROCEDURES X ENACTMENT INTERACTION EFFECTS

Relatively less research has examined the joint effects of procedures, enactment, and outcomes compared to differential (main) effects of each construct on organizational variables, but several studies have examined this possibility (also see for review, Brockner, 2010). In the first study of this kind, Skarlicki and Folger (1997) examined how employees' perceptions of interactional, procedural, and distributive justice combine to predict their retaliation behaviors (as rated by coworkers). To formulate their hypotheses, the researchers drew on RCT (Folger, 1986, 1993). As noted earlier, employees should be more likely to retaliate following the receipt of unfair outcomes, when the conduct of decision-making agents is judged to be inappropriate. Inappropriate conduct can be determined by perceptions of procedural and interactional justice. If recipients believe that conduct was inappropriate (e.g., different procedures "could" and "should" have been used), then they are more likely to blame the agent for the outcomes.

Given this, Skarlicki and Folger (1997) predicted that either fair decision procedures or fair interpersonal conduct may mitigate the negative impact of receiving less than is expected, because both minimize the agent's accountability (Folger & Cropanzano, 1998). Put another way, both procedures and interactions convey information about intentionality, and as such both should mitigate the otherwise negative effect of unfair outcomes on retaliatory behavior. This theorizing would suggest that procedural justice and interactional justice perceptions will separately interact with distributive justice perceptions (two 2-way interactions) in predicting retaliation.

In addition, Skarlicki and Folger (1997) predicted that the two-way interactions should be qualified by a higher-order, three-way interaction among the justice constructs, on the theory that procedural and interaction justice are "substitutable." If it is true that procedural justice and interactional justice perceptions are substitutable, then the relation between outcome fairness and retaliation (such that increasing outcome fairness is associated with greater retaliation) should be most pronounced when a low amount of one construct is not "offset" by a high amount of the other. Thus, the effect of low interactional justice should be offset by high procedural justice, and vice versa. In contrast, when either procedural justice is high, or interactional justice is high, then the effect of outcome unfairness on retaliation will be mitigated. From this logic, Skarlicki and Folger predicted a three-way interaction in which the effect of distributive justice on retaliation (such that increasing outcome unfairness is associated with greater retaliation) should be strongest when procedural justice is relatively low and interactional justice is relatively low.

As predicted, Skarlicki and Folger observed a three-way interaction among the justice measures, such that procedural and interactional justice perceptions had substitutable effects, in which either was sufficient to mitigate the effect of low distributive justice perceptions on retaliation behavior. That is, when employees perceived poor interpersonal treatment, the relation between distributive unfairness and retaliation was mitigated by procedural justice. Similarly, when procedural justice was low, the relation between distributive injustice and retaliation was mitigated by interactional justice. These results are consistent with the idea that procedural and interactional justice perceptions are substitutable (also see Folger & Skarlicki, 1999; Skarlicki, Folger, & Tesluk, 1999).

These findings have been replicated and extended in several later studies. For example, Goldman (2003) examined the interaction among distributive, procedural, and interactional justice in predicting discrimination legal claims filed by terminated workers. Consistent with Skarlicki and Folger's findings and predictions from RCT, Goldman demonstrated that the effect of distributive justice on legal claiming (such that unfair termination predicted greater legal claiming) was significant only when both procedural justice and interactional justice were low. Again, procedural justice and interaction justice served as substitutes for each other, in that each mitigated the effect of distributive justice on legal claiming when the other was low. Goldman also demonstrated that state anger partially mediates the interaction effect, and that trait anger moderates the relation between the three-way justice interaction and legal claiming.

Cropanzano, Slaughter, and Bachiochi (2005) examined the three-way interaction among distributive, procedural, and interactional justice from the same theoretical framework but in yet another context. They explored the effect of a variety of affirmative action programs on Black respondents' perceptions of distributive, procedural, and interactional justice, and predicted a three-way interaction on attractiveness of organizations using affirmative action and intentions to apply for a job with the organization. Consistent with the other studies, respondents perceived the organization as least attractive when all three justice perceptions were low. Moreover, again, the relation between distributive justice and organization attractiveness was mitigated by procedural justice (when interactional justice was low) and by interactional justice (when procedural justice was low). The findings on intentions to apply were generally similar. This study is important not only for replicating the earlier findings in a new context, but also because it sought to rule out the possible confounding role of outcome favorability in analyses involving distributive justice (following Skikta et al., 2003). Cropanzano et al. demonstrated that the three-way interaction was significant beyond any confounding effects of outcome favorability (also see Bauer, Maetz, Dolen, & Campion, 1998).

Two other studies in this vein are worthy of consideration for different reasons. Barclay, Skarlicki, and Pugh (2005) conducted a study of layoff victims to examine the role of emotions in injustice perceptions and retaliation. Although they did not examine the three-way interaction, they predicted and found that outcome favorability interacted separately with both procedural justice and interactional justice on emotions categorized as inward focused (such as guilt) and outward focused (such as anger). For example, participants experienced greater anger (outward focused emotion) the less favorable the outcomes of the layoff were perceived, and this effect was attenuated by either fair procedures or fair interactional justice. Similarly, participants experienced greater guilt (inward focused emotion) the less favorable the outcomes of the layoff, and this effect was exacerbated by either fair procedures or fair interactional justice.

Barclay et al.'s findings can be related to Brockner and Wiesenfeld's (1996) meta-analytic findings in two ways. One, as noted earlier,

Brockner and Wiesenfeld examined the interactive effects of outcome favorability and process fairness, but they did not distinguish the operationalization of process fairness in terms of the structural and enactment components because they suggested that the two process fairness components should have similar interactive effects. The Barclay et al. findings support this view. Second, the Barclay et al. findings support Brockner and Weisenfeld's observation that the pattern of interaction between outcome favorability and process-related judgments will differ depending on whether the dependent variable gauges other-focused reactions or self-focused reactions. In particular, high process fairness appears to *attenuate* the relation between outcome favorability and reactions toward others (anger in this case); in contrast, high process fairness appears to *intensify* the relation between outcome favorability and self-focused reactions (guilt in this case).

Finally, at least one study of which we are aware has failed to find support for the predicted three-way interaction effect. Rahim, Magner, and Shapiro (2000) examined the joint effects of the three justice perceptions on conflict resolution styles used by student employees when managing conflict with their supervisors. Although the predicted three-way interaction was not evident, the researchers found a two-way interaction between interactional and distributive justice on students' use of an integrating (cooperative) style, in line with RCT. Contrary to RCT predictions, however, they found an interaction between procedural and interactional justice suggesting that interactional justice predicted greater integrating style but only when procedural justice was also high.

Despite the latter study, the weight of the evidence thus far suggests that the interaction among the three justice constructs may be quite robust, particularly given the different contexts in which the research has been conducted. It appears that both the structure of procedures and their social implementation can moderate the effects of distributive justice perceptions, and that the two elements of process are substitutable.

Summary

Undoubtedly, procedural justice matters in the workplace. Employee perceptions of procedural justice are associated with many important work attitudes and behaviors, and this is true across many decision contexts. The two-factor and agent-system frameworks have been useful in guiding predictions about the differential effects of procedural justice relative to distributive justice and interactional justice, although limitations to the differential effects paradigm should be kept in mind. Another approach has been to examine how people combine information about procedures and outcomes by testing statistical interaction effects. As much of the research demonstrates, the beneficial effects of procedural justice on work-related variables are often most pronounced in the context of receiving outcomes that are less than expected. These findings in the workplace context are, of course, consistent with the early research findings in research on legal dispute resolution in the context of the courtroom, in field research on citizen reactions to police and political leaders, and in research on resource allocation more generally, all of which attests to the generalizability of procedural justice phenomena.

Why Do People Care About Procedural Justice?

In the preceding sections, we described several of the early theoretical accounts offered to explain why people attend to and care about procedural justice. As researchers continued to investigate the conceptual and empirical distinctions between distributive, procedural, and interactional justice, they expanded early theories, or offered new accounts to integrate new research findings. In this section, we highlight the dominant explanations that have been developed over the ensuing years to account for why procedural justice matters.

Given that many of these theories are discussed in detail in other chapters in this volume, our coverage here will be brief and more focused. In particular, we will review the main theories in the context of one guiding question: Why do people attend to the fairness of procedures and why are they affected by procedural justice? Asked another way, what is the psychological function of procedural justice? As we will see, different theories offer different answers to this question.

Instrumental/Control Models

As described in the first part of the chapter, Thibaut and Walker (1975, 1978) argued that disputants want process control in legal conflict resolution procedures as a way to indirectly influence the outcome of the conflict. To these theorists, the paramount goal for disputants was to achieve distributive justice. They argued that disputants are the people who know best their own inputs and contributions, thus the most equitable outcome would be achieved when individuals are allowed to participate and to present evidence on their own behalf (Thibaut & Walker, 1978). Leventhal had a similar view of the function of procedures, and thus conceptualized procedural justice as an instrument for achieving fair outcomes. Both models, therefore, viewed procedures as means to an end, with the end being the fair distribution of outcomes. Of note, in these models, outcomes typically referred to material or economic outcomes, which may not be surprising given the legal dispute resolution and reward allocation contexts in which the models were developed.

Given these features, these models are referred to interchangeably by contemporary justice researchers as "control" or "instrumental" models of procedural justice. Implicit in these labels is the recognition that (a) people care about procedures because of their causal connection to the resulting outcomes, and, therefore, that (b) people are ultimately motivated by the outcomes of an allocation sequence. As we will discuss more, researchers have long debated the degree to which procedural-justice phenomena can be explained by people's instrumental concerns (or by other outcome-related considerations) as opposed to by noninstrumental information (e.g., respect) conveyed by the procedures (e.g., Giacobbe-Miller, 1995; Lind, Kanfer, & Earley, 1990; Shapiro & Brett, 2005; Tyler, 1989, 1994). At this point in the development of the field, it seems clear that people's concerns for procedural justice can at times be motivated by their desire to influence their material outcomes, but this is equally clearly not the only reason why people attend to and care about procedural justice, as we will see next.

Identity/Relational Value Models

As discussed earlier, another explanation for why people care about procedural justice was brought to light by the group-value and relational models of procedural justice (Lind & Tyler, 1988; Tyler & Lind, 1992). These researchers argued that people care about their long-term relationships with groups that employ procedures, and this is one reason why they react so strongly to procedural fairness. Procedural treatment conveys to people how they are viewed by the group—when an authority uses fair procedures and treats a recipient respectfully, this sends the message that recipients are valued by the group that the authority represents. This, in turn, enhances people's feelings of belonging and self-worth. Thus, rather than functioning as a means to a particular end, such as winning a dispute or obtaining a desired reward, Lind and Tyler suggested that decision-making procedures carry symbolic meaning regarding people's social identity and self-worth. In essence, they claimed that fair procedures have both instrumental and non-instrumental value to recipients. Much early evidence was generated in support of the predictions emanating from these relational models (e.g., Lind, Kanfer, & Earley, 1990; Smith, Tyler, Huo, Ortiz, & Lind, 1998; Tyler, 1990, 1991, 1994, 1997; Tyler, Degoey, & Smith, 1996; also see Chapter 16 in this volume).

Tests of the relational models have continued at a steady pace over the years. Whereas many of the early studies examined noninstrumental main effects of procedural justice, contemporary research often provides evidence for the relational models by testing theoretically derived moderation effects (e.g., Brockner, De Cremer, Van den Bos, & Chen, 2005; De Cremer & Blader, 2006; Van Prooijen, Van den Bos, & Wilke, 2005; Van Prooijen & Zwenk, 2009). So, for example, De Cremer and Blader (2006) demonstrated that voice effects were more pronounced for individuals with high belongingness needs than for those with low belongingness needs, a prediction that follows from the relational models. Similarly, Brockner et al. (2005) found that the effects of procedural justice on cooperation and positive affect were strengthened among people with stronger interdependent self-construals.

As noted earlier, the relational model of authority (Tyler & Lind, 1992) built on the group-value model in an effort to explain how authorities gain legitimacy in hierarchical groups. Contemporary justice researchers typically refer to both the group-value model and the relational model of authority as "relational models" of procedural justice. In more recent years, Tyler and Blader advanced another relational framework, the group-engagement model, in a monograph on cooperation in groups (Tyler & Blader, 2000; also see Tyler & Blader, 2003). This model differs from the earlier models in scope and thus offers a more general account of the relationship between people and groups.

The core idea is that procedural justice of a group shapes people's identity judgments, and identity judgments are the primary determinant of people's engagement and cooperation with the group. There are some key differences between the group-engagement model and previous relational models; in particular, the group-engagement model predicts that social identity judgments mediate the relation between procedural justice judgments and cooperation. Furthermore, resource judgments (e.g., outcome favorability, distributive justice) are predicted to exert an indirect rather than a direct influence on cooperative behavior through their influence on social identity judgments (see Chapter 16 for more details on the roles of pride, respect, and identification in the formation of social-identity judgments). Although there are important differences between the group engagement model and previous relational models, a core similarity lies in the fundamental assumptions concerning people's essential motivation for involving themselves in groups.

Following initial evidence to support the group engagement model (e.g., Blader & Tyler, 2003b; Tyler & Blader, 2000), researchers have continued to examine the role of social identity in mediating procedural justice effects on group-oriented behaviors. For example, research has demonstrated that employees' social identity mediated the relations between procedural justice and support for union formation (Blader, 2007) and between procedural justice and citizenship behavior (Blader & Tyler, 2009). The findings are consistent with the idea that people use procedural justice information to evaluate their standing within the group, which ultimately affects the strength of their social identity. This, in turn, drives cooperative behavior. In another set of studies, De Cremer, Tyler, and den Ouden (2005) proposed that respectful treatment should increase "self–other" merging (in which people define themselves in terms of their group), which in turn should increase group-oriented behaviours. The findings supported these propositions.

It is important to note that relational model theorists recognize that the structure of procedures and the interpersonal enactment of procedures are distinct elements, but they do not treat these elements as fundamentally different justice *constructs* (e.g., procedural versus interactional justice). Instead, within the framework of relational models, procedural justice refers to both how procedures are structured and how they are enacted or implemented by decision makers (e.g., see Blader & Tyler, 2003a, 2003b). Thus, in research deriving predictions from relational models, procedural justice is typically operationalized broadly, involving structural aspects of procedures (e.g., voice, consistency) and aspects of interpersonal treatment (e.g., respect).

Fairness Heuristic Theory/Uncertainty Management Model

Another account of why people are concerned with procedural justice appeared in the 1990s by Lind and Van den Bos (e.g., Lind, Kulik, Ambrose, & de Vera Park, 1993; Van den Bos, Lind, Vermunt, & Wilke, 1997) and was further developed around the new millennium. In brief, Lind and Van den Bos proposed that procedural justice has such pervasive influence because it helps people to reduce uncertainty. In an initial theory, which they labeled fairness heuristic theory, these theorists maintained that people are motivated to form fairness judgments quickly in social interactions to reduce uncertainty about whether their interacting party can be trusted not to exploit or exclude them (for reviews, see Lind, 2001, 2002; Van den Bos, 2001).

For example, Lind and Van den Bos argued that very often in social situations people do not have the information to determine whether their outcomes are fair (e.g., the social comparison information needed to judge whether their outcomes are equitable is lacking). As a consequence, people use procedural fairness as a heuristic substitute to assess outcome fairness (e.g., Van den Bos et al., 1997; Van den Bos, Vermunt, & Wilke, 1997). Similarly, when people are uncertain about whether they can trust authorities, they are most strongly affected by procedural justice (Van den Bos, Wilke, & Lind, 1998; Van den Bos, Van Schie, & Colenberg, 2002). Importantly, in line with fairness heuristic theory, the evidence also demonstrates that people are more strongly influenced by distributive justice information in the absence (vs. presence) of procedural justice information (Van den Bos, Vermunt, & Wilke, 1997). These studies indicate that (a) people will use whatever fairness information is available to determine whether they are being treated fairly, and (b) they do so in an effort to reduce uncertainty regarding whether they can trust their interaction partner (also see Jones & Skarlicki, 2005; Lind, Kray, & Thompson, 2001).

Around the millennium, Van den Bos and Lind expanded fairness heuristic theory to a broader theory, which they labeled uncertainty management theory (e.g., Lind & Van den Bos, 2002; Van den Bos, 2001; Van den Bos & Lind, 2002). Under this account, people use fairness information to resolve uncertainty more generally, not only with respect to reducing uncertainty pertaining to trust in authorities. An impressive body of research has supported this idea, demonstrating that procedural justice effects are strongest when people are reminded about aspects of their lives that make them feel uncertain (e.g., Van den Bos, 2001), or when general self-uncertainty is salient (Van den Bos & Miedema, 2000).

Since 2001, numerous studies have examined the implications of both uncertainty management theory and fairness heuristic theory for understanding a range of organizational phenomena. For example, researchers have found that cognitive-based trust (Colquitt, LePine, Piccolo, Zapata, & Rich, 2012) mediates the relation between procedural justice and job performance. Specifically, greater procedural justice was associated with increased cognitive-based trust and reduced uncertainty, which, in turn, improved job performance. Other research has examined contextual factors that raise uncertainty in a situation, and which therefore should moderate procedural justice effects. For example, Hakonen and Lipponen (2008) argued that lack of face-to-face contact and greater geographical dispersion among virtual work teams creates higher uncertainty and ambiguity. Thus, they reasoned that these factors should moderate procedural justice effects. As predicted, they found that people rely more strongly on procedural justice information in developing their team identity when teams have little face-to-face contact due to geographical dispersion.

Common to these variables is that they arouse uncertainty. This line of this research thus not only supports the theory, but the findings also elucidate the conditions under which procedural justice is most beneficial. Although many of the studies have examined the interaction between uncertainty-arousing variables and procedural justice, the predictions from the theories should not be specific to procedural justice per se. Theoretically, similar effects should be found for any experience of justice (whether interpersonal or distributive) because under this theoretical account people are said to consider justice holistically rather than making distinctions between the fairness of procedures, treatment, and outcomes (in a way, taking the field full circle to early theorizing about justice; see Chapter 5).

Fairness Theory

In 1998, Robert Folger and Russell Cropanzano published a book summarizing the organizational justice literature and its application to human resource management. In the last two chapters, they present fairness theory, with the goal of integrating earlier theoretical frameworks (in particular, control theories, group-value/relational models, and referent cognitions theory). The main goal of fairness theory was to explain how people judge an agent's accountability for events that harm one's material or psychological well-being (also see Folger & Cropanzano, 2001).

Like RCT, fairness theory argued that when people experience a negative event, this gives rise to counterfactual thinking about three issues: (1) alternate states of well-being, that is, what they "would" have experienced had the event been different, (2) considerations of causal responsibility for the event, that is whether the event "could" have been different, and (3) considerations of the moral obligation of those involved, that is whether the event "should" have been different. However, there are several differences between fairness theory and RCT. For example, whereas RCT argued that less than expected outcomes serve to elicit "would" thinking, fairness theory holds that considerations about the structure of procedures or interpersonal treatment can also generate such counterfactual thinking. Thus, within fairness theory, outcomes, procedures, and interactions each can serve as the "negative event impact" variable which generates "would" thinking. If the recipient then determines that the event could have been different and should have been different, then they will judge the agent involved as accountable for the harm.

Accordingly, Folger and Cropanzano reconceptualized the statistical interaction effect between outcomes and procedures, which we discussed earlier (Brockner & Wiesenfeld, 1996), in more fundamental terms. In other words, the original interaction, which stated that procedural justice mitigates the adverse effect of unfavorable outcomes on work-related variables, is recast as a negative impact x accountability interaction. Related to this, whereas RCT originally assumed a particular order among the counterfactuals ("would" counterfactuals precede "could" and "should" counterfactuals), fairness theory posited no such causal ordering. Finally, fairness theory explicitly recognized that counterfactual thinking does not necessarily involve conscious deliberation but instead can occur at an automatic cognitive level. Predictions from fairness theory have been well supported in research, as illustrated in the previous section on interaction effects (e.g., Cropanzano et al., 2005; Goldman, 2003; Skarlicki & Folger, 1997; also see Gilliland, Groth et al., 2001).

As noted earlier, according to fairness theory, either fair decision procedures or fair interpersonal treatment can mitigate the negative impact of receiving less than is expected, because both minimize the agent's accountability. Interestingly, Folger and Cropanzano (1998) suggest that poor enactment of procedures (interactional injustice) may have more impact on accountability judgments than do the structural elements of procedures because the former are likely to be seen as more discretionary. According to fairness theory then, both structural and enactment components of process fairness can inform recipients about an agent's accountability, but the enactment component may be especially potent in this regard. What is critical to fairness theory in terms of predicting reactions is the *attribution of responsibility* for the negative impact, rather than the particular normative rules that are violated (e.g., procedural versus enactment).

There is an interesting possible extension of fairness theory. If recipients determine that the agent is *not* accountable for a negative event, then recipients may be more likely to judge *themselves* as responsible for it. This could explain why, as noted earlier, the pattern of the outcome x process interaction on self-evaluations is reversed. We will return to research on self-evaluations in the fourth part of the chapter, but it is worth noting here that contemporary justice researchers recognize both that (a) recipients use procedural fairness information to judge an *agent's accountability* for negative events, and (b) recipients use procedural fairness information to determine *personal responsibility* for their outcomes (Brockner, 2002, 2010). Typically, this latter function of procedural justice is interpreted with the framework of attribution theory (Weiner, 1985; see Brockner & Wiesenfeld, 1996; Brockner, 2002). In summary, although fairness theory was not originally designed to explain the joint effects of procedures, interactions, and outcomes on *self-evaluations*, it may be possible to understand these effects using the framework of fairness theory.

Moral Virtues Model

Folger (1994, 1998, 2001) offered another account for why people care about and attend to matters of justice, which Cropanzano et al. (2001) referred to as the moral virtues model and Folger (2001) referred to as deontic justice (see also Cropanzano, Goldman, & Folger, 2003). Folger suggested that both the instrumental and relational models of procedural justice are fundamentally "self-interest" models because they argue that people care about procedural justice for reasons that pertain to personal gain, whether the gain is material (instrumental models) or socio-emotional (relational models) (e.g., Turrillo, Folger, Lavelle, Umphress, & Gee, 2002). Thus, Folger argued that the existing models do not take into account the possibility that people care about justice even when it has no implications for material outcomes or relational value (cf. Gillespie & Greenberg, 2005).

Instead, Folger argued that people care about justice because of a basic human drive to respect human dignity and worth. This, he maintained, helps to understand why individuals who are not directly affected by injustice can nevertheless experience strong negative emotions and retributive motivations when they observe injustice (for reviews of third-party reactions to injustice, see Chapter 10; also Skarlicki & Kulik, 2005). The deontic model proposes that such reactions are a result of a collection of evolutionarily based reactions to violations of normative standards of moral and social conduct that are automatic and visceral (see Folger & Skarlicki, 2008).

As noted in the previous section, fairness theory predicts that, in general, interactional justice may be viewed as especially discretionary given that the source of the injustice is quite clear; thus, all else being equal, deontic reactions may be elicited especially strongly by perceived violations of interactional justice. Consistent with these ideas, in research that examines the predictions of the deontic model, researchers often manipulate or measure aspects of interactional injustice (e.g., Skarlicki & Rupp, 2010; Skarlicki, Ellard, & Kelln, 1998; Turillo et al., 2002; Umphress, Simmons, Folger, Ren, & Bobocel, 2013). Deontic reactions can also be triggered, however, by agents' use of unfair procedures (e.g., Skarlicki et al., 1998) and by unfair outcome distributions (Turillo et al., 2002).

In whatever way that deontic emotions and reactions are aroused, the central point for present purposes is that the deontic model suggests that people can react to injustice because of a commitment to ethical and moral standards of social conduct, rather than because of the loss of control over material outcomes, or the loss of identity. Also as with fairness theory, under the deontic model, the critical driver of individuals' reactions is not the particular normative standard that is violated; rather, it is individuals' judgments of the agent's moral accountability.

Summary

Over the years since the concept of procedural justice was introduced, researchers have articulated several answers to the question of why people attend to procedural justice. Many of the theories are, of course, broader than this, attempting to explain how people integrate information about distributions, procedures, and interpersonal treatment. Given the volume of research that supports each of the theoretical perspectives, it seems reasonable to think of the theories as complementary rather than as strictly competing explanations. Moreover, given that many of the models have grown out of previous versions, they are inherently related to each other. Overall, it appears that there are multiple reasons why people are concerned with how decision-making procedures are structured and implemented. Thus, it is most likely that procedural justice has multiple, albeit possibly related, psychological functions, which may be differentially relevant depending on the circumstances. For example, in some situations, people may be especially concerned with the outcome of a procedure, in which case they may be instrumentally motivated; in other situations, they may be more concerned about their sense of belonging, in which case relational motivation may be salient. Of course, it is also likely that several processes operate simultaneously in a particular situation, with the context determining the weighting of each process.

One other point is important. One way that researchers have distinguished between the concepts of procedural and interactional justice is to recognize that decision procedures and outcomes are causally connected; whereas interactional justice *accompanies* the distribution of outcomes (see Bies & Moag, 1986; Brockner & Wiesenfeld, 1996). In view of this, researchers who assess procedural justice and interactional justice with Colquitt's (2001) measure often assume that observed effects of procedural justice perceptions on work-related variables are due to instrumental motivation, whereas observed effects of interactional justice perceptions are due to relational (or noninstrumental) motivation.

This logic is, however, problematic because there is not a 1:1 correspondence between construct and mechanism. As research has demonstrated, people value voice—which is considered to be an indicator of procedural justice perceptions in Colquitt's 2001 measure—for both instrumental and noninstrumental reasons. Similarly, receiving a complete and adequate explanation for a decision—which is considered to be an indicator of interactional justice perceptions in the 2001 measure—can conceivably be valued for both instrumental and noninstrumental reasons. This is because, although objectively there is no causal connection between explanation and outcome, it is very likely that people infer a fair decision structure from fair interpersonal treatment. As noted earlier, research on fairness heuristic theory has demonstrated that people substitute information from one domain (procedural justice) to make inferences in another domain (distributive justice) when direct information is lacking (e.g., Van den Bos et al., 1997). Similarly, people are likely to make inferences about the decision structure from the quality of interpersonal conduct received when direct information about the structure is lacking. This latter proposition is indeed borne out in correlational and experimental research that has demonstrated an effect of criteria subsumed under the interactional justice construct in the 2001 measure (e.g., justification) on procedural justice perceptions (e.g., Bies & Shapiro, 1987, Study 3; Bies & Shapiro, 1988; Bies, Shapiro, & Cummings, 1988; Blader & Tyler, 2003a; Bobocel, Agar, Meyer, & Irving, 1998; Heuer, Blumenthal, Douglas, & Weinblatt, 1999). In light of evidence for the substitutability of justice information from different domains (e.g., procedures, interactions), several of the justice theories described in this section emphasize *conceptual similarities* among the justice constructs rather than distinctions.

Is Procedural Justice Always Beneficial?

As illustrated in the preceding sections of this chapter, decades of research have demonstrated positive effects of procedural justice on a host of work attitudes and behaviors, effects which are especially strong when outcome distributions are unfavorable. Thus, a central tenet in the justice literature has rightly been that procedural justice is beneficial and desired by employees. Despite this large body of research findings, researchers have also begun to investigate when, and for whom, fair procedures might fail to elicit the "typical" benefits. In one of the earliest studies on procedural justice in the context of resource allocation, Folger (1977) demonstrated that under certain conditions the manipulation of voice (process control) had a negative effect on outcome satisfaction, which he referred to as a "frustration effect" (Folger et al., 1979). Similarly, in their review of the literature on the interaction between outcomes and process, Brockner and Weisenfeld (1996) noted the likelihood of boundary conditions of their interactive effect. Only more recently, however, have investigators begun to examine more systematically when and why the usual beneficial effects of procedural justice might be attenuated, eliminated, or reversed (see Brockner, 2010; Brockner, Wiesenfeld, & Diekman, 2009). By investigating conditions under which procedural justice *fails* to have the usual beneficial effects, researchers are at once uncovering boundary conditions on the role of procedural justice and advancing theory regarding its psychological functions. Thus, research in this vein promises to move the literature on procedural justice forward considerably.

It should be noted that many studies have been conducted to identify variables that *strengthen* the usual beneficial effects of procedural justice. In fact, it is beyond the scope of this chapter to review the numerous studies of this type. We noted some of these studies in the previous third part of the chapter because often the goal of this research is to test the validity of a particular theoretical framework. For example, early research on the relational models demonstrated that the effects of procedural justice on endorsement of authorities are stronger among people who are more highly identified with the group compared to those who are less highly identified (e.g., Tyler & Degoey, 1995). By definition in this line of research, procedural justice has weaker effects in some conditions (e.g., among people who are less identified) but the latter effects are not of primary interest. In this final section, we focus on research that explicitly seeks to understand factors that weaken, eliminate, or reverse the usual beneficial effects of procedural justice.

Outcome x Process Interaction on Self-Evaluations

In the second part of the chapter, we noted that Brockner and Wiesenfeld (1996) observed in their meta-analysis a "contrary" pattern of interaction between outcome and process on recipient self-evaluations in two separate studies (Gilliland, 1994; Schroth & Shah, 1993/2000). When decision procedures lead to an unfavorable rather than favorable outcome, there is a negative association between procedural justice and self-evaluations. Stated differently, procedural justice *heightens* the relation between outcome favorability and self-evaluations (in which less favorable outcomes lead to lower self-evaluations). As noted earlier, this finding demonstrated that, in the context of receiving an unfavorable outcome, fairer procedures can have a negative impact on recipients. Moreover, it ran against most of the theoretical frameworks outlined earlier. For example, relational models suggest that fair procedures are beneficial because they lead people to feel valued and respected by others, which in turn bolsters their feelings of positive self-regard. These models leave no room for a negative influence of fair procedure.

By and large, researchers turned to attribution theory (e.g., Weiner, 1985) to explain the *reversal* of the usual effect of procedural justice on self-evaluations. For example, Brockner and Weisenfeld (1996) speculated that unfavorable outcomes received via fair procedures (relative to unfair procedures) may be threatening to the self because procedural justice affects the *internality* of individuals' outcome attributions. That is, when people receive outcomes via what they perceive to be fair procedures, they may be more likely to judge *themselves to be responsible* (e.g., their ability or effort) for the outcome. When the outcome for which they feel responsible is negative, this diminishes positive self-regard, whereas when the outcome is positive, self-regard in enhanced. In contrast, when people receive outcomes via what they perceive to be *unfair* procedures, they are less likely to judge themselves as responsible for the outcomes. Thus, when people receive negative outcomes via unfair procedures, they are less likely to blame themselves relative to when the procedures are fair. As a consequence of these processes, procedural fairness *heightens* the adverse effect of receiving unfavorable outcomes on self-evaluations.

Following the initial demonstrations (e.g., Gilliland, 1994; Schroth & Shah, 1993/2000) researchers have replicated the reverse effect of procedural fairness on self-evaluations. For example, Ployhart, Ryan, and Bennett (1999) conducted two studies to examine student applicants' reactions to informational and sensitivity features of explanations on rejected and selected applicants. They examined how these process features influenced ratings of the system (process fairness, evaluations of the organization) and self-evaluations (self-efficacy). Importantly, they demonstrated that procedural explanations had the predicted trade-offs among rejected applicants. Informational and sensitivity features enhanced perceived process fairness and organizational perceptions. However, these features diminished applicants' sense of self-efficacy.

In another series of studies, Van den Bos, Bruins, Wilke, and Dronker (1999) demonstrated initial support for the attribution interpretation. In particular, Van den Bos et al. found that, relative to fair procedures, unfair procedures allowed recipients to make external attributions for unfavorable events (e.g., improper procedures), which protect feelings of positive self-regard (also see Brockner, 2002).[4] Brockner et al. (2003) replicated and extended these earlier findings to the workplace context. In addition, in a more direct test of the attributional mechanism, they demonstrated that it is people's tendency to consider themselves responsible for the outcome when procedures are fair and the outcome is unfavorable that accounts for the reverse effect of procedural fairness on self-evaluations. Importantly, they also demonstrated that both forms of the outcome x process interaction—the usual interaction on appraisals of the system and the contrary interaction on self-evaluations—can occur simultaneously (also see Ployhart et al., 1999).

Thus, Brockner et al.'s findings support the idea that procedural fairness can have a "dual function" via attribution processes. The fairer the procedures, the less likely people are to see the other party as responsible for the outcomes received, which *reduces* negative reactions toward the system in the face of unfavorable outcomes. At the same time, the fairer the procedures, the more likely people are to see themselves as responsible for the outcomes received, which *heightens* negative self-evaluations in the face of unfavorable outcomes (also see Brockner, 2002; Brockner & Weisenfeld, 2005).

More recently, Brockner and colleagues (2008) noted that research on self-evaluations reveals an inconsistency. In some studies, researchers have demonstrated an *inverse* relation between procedural fairness and self-evaluations in the context of receiving unfavorable outcomes; in other studies, researchers have found that the usual beneficial effect of procedural fairness (on work-related reactions) is *attenuated* on self-evaluations. In an effort to understand these inconsistencies, the researchers proposed that the psychological relevance of the outcome may moderate this relation, such that when the outcome carries greater psychological relevance, the inverse relation between procedural fairness and self-evaluations will be more likely to occur.

To investigate this idea, Brockner and colleagues (2008) examined prevention focus as a moderator of the relation between procedural fairness and self-evaluations. According to theory and research on regulatory focus (e.g., Idson, Liberman, & Higgins, 2004), individuals who are more prevention focused tend to place greater psychological significance on unfavorable outcomes, whereas those who are more promotion focused place greater significance on positive outcomes. Following this logic, Brockner and colleagues predicted that the inverse relation sometimes demonstrated between procedural fairness and self-evaluations in the case of unfavorable outcomes will be more likely to occur in individuals who are higher in prevention focus. Across a series of three studies, they found support for their hypothesis, providing further evidence of boundary conditions of procedural justice effects.

Taken together, the research on people's self-evaluations following the receipt of unfavorable outcomes highlights one condition in which the usual beneficial effect of fairer procedures may be attenuated or even reversed. It is interesting to note that, whereas most of the research in this vein has operationalized procedural justice in terms of what would be labeled a structural feature (e.g., voice), similar effects on self-evaluations have been observed in studies that have varied social enactment features. Namely, in addition to the research by Ployhart et al. (1999) reviewed earlier, Leung, Su, and Morris (2001) found similar effects on self-evaluations when participants were given negative performance feedback in an interpersonally respectful manner (versus disrespectfully). These findings are important because, as we noted in the preceding third part of the chapter, they suggest that, all else equal, people infer that decision structure is fair when they are treated fairly interpersonally. Thus, criteria often subsumed under the interactional justice construct can be perceived as having a causal connection to outcomes, even though objectively they do not. These findings are consistent with research on fairness heuristic theory discussed earlier, in which people use fairness information from one domain (procedures) to infer fairness in another domain (outcomes) (e.g., see Van den Bos, Vermunt, et al., 1997; Van den Bos, Lind, et al., 1997). We will revisit this point later in this part of the chapter.

The body of research on the two forms of the outcome x process interaction has highlighted serious potential trade-off effects of procedural justice. When delivering unfavorable outcomes, managers who use fairer decision procedures can improve recipient reactions toward the organization and enhance outcome acceptance. However, they do so at the risk of diminishing employees' feelings of positive self-regard. Clearly, research is needed to determine how managers can avoid these detrimental effects on employees' self-evaluations. Moreover, these findings should remind investigators more generally that there may be situations in which employee attitudes and behaviors that benefit the organization (e.g., commitment, trust, authority legitimacy), may not necessarily benefit employees themselves. For example, in some cases, it may not be in employees' best interests to remain committed to an organization or leader, despite procedural justice (Cohen, 1985).

Brockner and colleagues have highlighted the need to examine dependent variables other than self-evaluations to more fully explore the conditions under which the usual beneficial effects of procedural justice are altered, whether attenuated, eliminated, or reversed (e.g., Brockner, 2010; Brockner et al., 2009). Fortunately, as we will illustrate next, as researchers have continued to explore boundary conditions of procedural justice effects, they have examined additional dependent variables.

Identity Processes that Alter the Fair Process Effect

In a different line of research in the early 2000s, Skitka and her colleagues argued that there will be times when the nature of the outcomes in question will render procedural fairness ineffective in shaping people's perceptions of distributive justice perceptions. In what they labeled the moral mandate effect (MME), Skitka and her colleagues demonstrated that when people have a strong *a priori* conviction that a given outcome is right or wrong—when they have a strong moral mandate—people are less sensitive to procedural justice compared to when they do not have strong moral convictions about the outcome (see Skitka, 2002; Skitka & Houston, 2001; Skitka & Mullen, 2002). In other words, contrary to conventional wisdom that "the means justify the ends," Skitka and colleagues found that when people have strong moral convictions about the outcome, evaluations of outcome fairness will be influenced less by the fairness of the procedures or the interpersonal treatment that one receives, and more by whether the procedures yield an outcome that affirms or threatens their moral mandate.

In two later laboratory studies, Mullen and Skitka (2006) replicated the moral mandate effect and tested three explanations for why people are less sensitive to procedural information when they have strong moral conviction regarding an outcome (motivated reasoning, in-group biases, moral outrage/anger). Mullen and Skitka asked participants to read a newspaper article about a defendant's trail. The researchers varied the outcome such that it supported, opposed, or was unrelated to participants' moral mandate. Their results demonstrated that when people had moral mandates regarding the outcome, they suspended their judgments of fairness until they were made aware of the outcome. When the outcome supported their moral mandates, people judged both the procedure and outcome to be fairer. However, when the outcome went against their moral mandates, they judged the procedures and outcomes to be less fair. Furthermore, the researchers demonstrated that this effect was mediated by anger that occurs as a result of receiving an outcome that is against one's moral mandate.

In an important extension, Mayer, Greenbaum, Kuenzi, and Shteynberg (2009) examined whether the effect demonstrated by Skitka and her colleagues would generalize to outcomes that violate identity more generally, rather than moral mandates in particular. Mayer et al. argued that moral mandates may be too narrow a test of the effect and, based on social identity theory (Tajfel & Turner, 1979), one could argue that an outcome that violates an individual's identity will render procedural fairness ineffective in shaping outcome evaluations. Building on the accessible identity model (Skitka, 2003) and the writings of James (1890/1950), Mayer et al. reasoned that both personal and social identities are important and can lead to effects similar to those of moral mandates. Although one's personal identity relates to morality, and morality can, in turn, influence justice judgments, as demonstrated by Mullen and Skitka, Mayer et al. argued that people also value their social identity. They suggested that, through the process of depersonalization, an outcome that violates one's social identity can also wipe out the usual effect of fair procedures on outcome evaluations.

Similar to Mullen and Skitka, Mayer and colleagues (2009) proposed that the effect of an identity violation on distributive justice judgments will occur via motivated reasoning processes, which would cause participants to cognitively re-evaluate the fairness of the procedures post hoc. In other words, Mayer et al. predicted that when an outcome violates people's personal or social identity, people will be motivated to find flaws in the procedures after the fact. For example, one way in which employees might easily do this in the workplace context is to question whether management actually considered their input, after an identity-violating decision has been made via procedures that had solicited employee voice.

In two laboratory studies, participants read a letter regarding an issue they held strong opinions about (Study 1) or recalled a decision at work that impacted them strongly (Study 2). In both cases, the fairness of procedures and the outcome favourability were manipulated (information in the letter in Study 1, and recalling different events in Study 2), and personal and social identification were measured. Further, Mayer et al. (2009) asked participants the extent to which they thought their opinions were considered by management (Study 2) as a test of the mediator (i.e., participant's tendency to find a procedural flaw). Results of the two studies supported the authors' predictions, demonstrating that the manipulation of procedures had nonsignificant effects on both procedural and distributive judgments when the outcomes violated participants' personal or social identities. Mayer et al. also demonstrated that the interactive effects of voice and identity violation on distributive and procedural justice perceptions were fully mediated by participants' doubts that their opinions were considered by management. These findings suggest that participants evaluated the procedures in light of the outcomes, providing good support for the motivated reasoning hypothesis.

The findings of Mayer et al. converge on those of Skitka and colleagues. It is interesting to note, however, that these two groups of researchers revealed different mediators of the effects, namely motivated re-evaluation of the procedure and anger, respectively. It is possible that this is due to methodological differences between the studies (e.g., vignettes used by Mayer et al. may not elicit anger to the same degree as outcomes that violate moral mandates). However, it is also possible that outcomes that are related to people's morals elicit anger, whereas those that violate people's identity do not. This implies that multiple mediators may be at play, and suggests an area for future research.

At a broader level, the findings of Skitka and colleagues and those of Mayer et al. are consistent with research noted earlier on fairness heuristic theory, in which Van den Bos and colleagues demonstrated other conditions that lead to nonsignificant effects of procedural justice on outcome fairness. For example, when people have information by which to judge outcome fairness directly (e.g., social comparison information), procedural justice has little impact on outcome fairness ratings (e.g., Van den Bos, Vermunt, et al. 1997). Different psychological processes drive these different lines of research, but they converge on their demonstration of conditions that attenuate or eliminate the usual effects of procedural justice on outcome judgments.

In other research drawing on the accessible identity model (Skitka, 2003), Holmvall and Bobocel (2008) argued that it may help to understand how people will respond to unfavorable outcomes received via fair procedures—that is, positively or negatively—by considering the aspects of people's identity that are activated in a particular situation. Building on the research of Brockner and others reported earlier in this section, Holmvall and Bobocel noted that in the context of receiving unfavorable outcomes via fair decision-making procedures, people can exhibit as least two reactions. They may react positively because procedural fairness communicates to them that they are valued and respected by their interaction partner (in line with relational models). Alternatively, they may react negatively because procedural fairness implies that they are personally responsible for the unfavorable outcomes, which diminishes feelings of positive self-regard (in line with attribution models).

Holmvall and Bobocel (2008) argued that people's self-identity should moderate the psychological function of procedural fairness. When *interdependent* or social aspects of the self are activated, then people should focus on the relational information conveyed by fair procedures, and thus procedural fairness should enhance outcome acceptance. In contrast, when *independent* or achievement-related aspects of the self are activated, people should focus on the attribution information conveyed by fair procedures, and therefore they should experience greater self-esteem threat. To protect the self, these latter individuals should be more likely to reject the outcome and to view it as unfair when it follows from fair rather than unfair procedures. In a series of three laboratory studies, the researchers found support for their predictions. Moreover, in one study they demonstrated evidence for the attribution framework used to explain the reverse effect of fair procedures: Self-esteem was lower among participants whose independent self-identity was salient when they received the unfavorable outcome via fair procedures, compared to unfair procedures.

These findings are important because they demonstrate that people can interpret procedural fairness information differently as a function of other factors (in this case, self-identity), and this can explain why fair procedures sometimes can have a beneficial effect but other times can have the reverse effect. Moreover, the findings reveal the relevance of the attribution framework for explaining the reverse effects of procedural justice on reactions other than self-evaluations (also see Jones & Skarlicki, 2003; Van den Bos et al., 1999). Finally, it is worth noting that Holmvall and Bobocel (2008) operationalized procedures by varying the interpersonal sensitivity by which the unfavorable outcome was delivered (high vs. low), which they presumed would lead participants to perceive the decision-making procedures as structurally fair versus unfair, respectively. Thus, like the other findings noted earlier in this section (e.g., Ployhart et al., 1999; Leung et al., 2001; Van den Bos, Lind, et al., 1997), the Holmvall and Bobocel findings suggest that people may infer a causal connection between treatment and outcomes when information about the decision structure is lacking.

As a whole, each of the sets of studies reviewed in this section speaks to the important role of *identity* in altering the usual manner in which procedural justice affects outcome evaluations. When outcomes violate a moral mandate, or when outcomes violate one's personal or social identity, procedures fail to influence outcome fairness. Put differently, in these cases, the means do not justify the ends. The studies by Holmvall and Bobocel demonstrate a different function of identity in the context of unfavorable outcomes: When people's social identity is salient, procedural fairness leads to outcome acceptance, but it has the reverse effect when personal identity is salient.

Paradoxical Effects on Work Attitudes and Behaviors

We began this fourth part of the chapter by discussing variables that reverse the pattern of interaction between procedures and outcomes on self-evaluations. Then we discussed the role of identity in attenuating, eliminating, or reversing the effect of procedural justice on outcome fairness. In both cases, we thus considered the interplay between procedures and outcomes. Researchers have also begun to examine variables that attenuate, eliminate, or reverse the typical overall (i.e., main) beneficial effects of procedural justice on work attitudes and behavior.

For example, Desai, Sondak, and Diekmann (2011) examined the effects of procedural justice on job performance and satisfaction, moderated by risk aversion. Whereas uncertainty management theory argues that procedural justice relates positively to work attitudes because it reduces employees' uncertainty, Desai et al. challenged the view that *certainty* is necessarily desirable. The authors suggested that for some employees, such as those high in risk-seeking, uncertainty may be desirable. Theoretically, individuals who are higher risk-seekers might prefer the lack of predictability offered by unfair procedures relative to fair procedures, and therefore prefer the latter over the former (Desai et al., 2011). In this case, the researchers suggested that procedural fairness would be inversely related to work attitudes. In two field studies and one laboratory study, Desai and colleagues tested their reasoning, and demonstrated that risk seeking moderated the relation between procedural fairness and job satisfaction and performance, such that high risk-seeking individuals revealed decreased job satisfaction and performance in response to fairer procedures. Desai and colleagues further demonstrated that this interaction was due to the greater perceived certainty elicited by fair procedures relative to unfair procedures.

In another series of field and laboratory studies, Wiesenfeld, Swann, Brockner, and Bartel (2007) examined the role of self-esteem in moderating the relation between procedural justice and organizational commitment. According to Wiesenfeld and colleagues, self-verification theory specifies that individuals who suffer from low self-regard may become uncomfortable if they learn that others view them positively. Moreover, under certain circumstances, the need to be viewed accurately is more important than the need to be viewed positively. Taken together, these tenets of self-verification theory would predict that individuals with low self-esteem, who doubt that they are worthy of fair treatment, will be ambivalent to the positive message that fair treatment gives about themselves, and may be more comfortable with unfair procedures because they verify people's self-views. This should be true in particular where self-verification strivings are made salient. Importantly, the researchers pointed out that the predictions from self-verification theory are opposite to those from the dominant justice theories which we discussed in the third part of the chapter.

As predicted, the results demonstrated that the positive effect of procedural justice on organizational commitment was eliminated for individuals with low self-esteem, compared to individuals with high self-esteem. Furthermore, this interaction between procedural justice and self-esteem was found only when self-verification goals were made salient (Wiesenfeld et al., 2007).

Summary

The research reviewed in this part of the chapter challenges a central assumption in the literature, which is that procedural justice is necessarily beneficial to employees, and therefore always desired by them. Although decades of research have demonstrated that procedural justice has many beneficial effects, the research described in this section indicates that there are boundary conditions. Procedural justice effects can indeed be attenuated, eliminated, and even reversed (Brockner, 2010; Brockner, et al., 2009). Research in this vein has elucidated a number of novel findings, and as a result has provided a deeper understanding of the psychological mechanisms underlying procedural justice phenomena. Importantly, this research often draws on broader theories and novel literatures (e.g., self-verification theory), and as such provides key bridges between procedural justice and other literatures. Therefore, future research on the boundary conditions of procedural justice promises to advance the literature considerably.

Summary and Conclusion

From the early 1970s to the present day, procedural justice has remained a topic of great interest in psychology and the organizational sciences. As predicted in the 1980s, the work organization has proved to be a rich social context for the study of procedural justice. As in other social contexts, in the workplace people attend to how decisions are made and implemented by organizational leaders. Overall, this body of research has helped investigators and practitioners better understand an array of organizational practices and employee attitudes and behaviors. It has also contributed greatly to our collective understanding of what procedural justice is, why it matters, and how it affects members of work organizations. In fact, we wonder if the scholars who argued early on for the relevance of procedural justice in the workplace could have anticipated just how productive research on this topic would be.

Our goal in this chapter has been to provide a broad historical overview of the study of procedural justice in the workplace. We discussed the origins of the concept and early theoretical accounts of procedural justice. Beginning with the notion that having input into decisions alters people's subjective perceptions of the fairness of procedures, researchers have uncovered a broad array of additional criteria by which people evaluate procedural justice. People evaluate two components of process—the procedural mechanisms by which decisions are made and the quality of treatment during the implementation of procedures (interactional justice).

We next reviewed the primary paradigms that researchers have used to study the effects of procedural justice in the workplace. The differential effects paradigm attempted to demonstrate dissociations, initially between procedural and distributive justice perceptions, and later between procedural and interactional justice perceptions. The interaction effects paradigm examined the joint effects of these justice perceptions. Research from both paradigms has uncovered myriad ways in which organizational members are affected by the structure of decision procedures and their implementation, well beyond the initial demonstrations of outcome acceptance.

Important for both theory and practice, over the last four decades investigators have learned a great deal about the psychological processes underlying people's concerns with procedural justice. Thus, in the third part of the chapter, we built on our discussion of the early theories of procedural justice by reviewing more contemporary revisions and new models that have emerged. Initially viewed as an instrument for obtaining fair outcomes, researchers have demonstrated that people are affected by procedural justice for a number of other reasons. Decision-making procedures communicate information about whether people are valued by the organization and its authorities and whether they can trust these social entities. Procedures help to reduce uncertainty. They help people to judge accountability for harm, and to gauge one's personal responsibility for outcomes. People also use the quality of decision procedures and their implementation to make inferences regarding whether the organization and its leaders are committed to upholding normative standards of moral conduct.

Finally, in the fourth part of the chapter, we reviewed research that has challenged the most fundamental assumption in the study of procedural justice—that procedural justice is always beneficial and desired. Research in this vein has demonstrated several boundary conditions of procedural justice, as well as factors that may lead to paradoxical effects. This newest domain of research not only has uncovered novel findings but also provided a deeper theoretical understanding of procedural justice phenomena.

Clearly, procedural justice research has come a long way from the early years. The concept is being continually enriched. No review could cover every branch of research on procedural justice in the workplace or cite every relevant study, but we have aimed to provide readers with a foundation for understanding where the literature started and where it has been since then. We look forward to witnessing the development of procedural justice research in the future, confident that there is much valuable knowledge yet to be gleaned, at both the practical and the theoretical levels.

Acknowledgments

We thank Colin MacLeod, Maureen Ambrose, and Russell Cropanzano for comments on an earlier version. A special thanks to Colin, Nate, and Elisha—they'll know why. Preparation of this chapter was supported by research funds award to the first author from the Social Sciences and Humanities Research Council of Canada.

Notes

1. Note that researchers often define the fair process effect as the effect of procedural justice *perceptions* on recipient reactions, but we use the original definition here (cf. Van den Bos, 2005).
2. In contemporary research, there continues to be inconsistency in whether people measure/manipulate outcome fairness or outcome valence.
3. The Schroth & Shah 1993 paper was published in 2000; both references are provided to avoid confusion.
4. Although few studies report an effect of procedural justice when procedures lead to *favorable* outcomes, it is interesting to note that in an earlier study of applicant reactions, Ployhart and Ryan (1997) demonstrated that being selected (favorable outcome) under unfair procedures damaged participants' self-evaluations relative to fair procedures. This finding is consistent with the idea that, under unfair procedures, recipients cannot make an internal attribution for the outcome (being selected, in this case), and thus they feel less deserving of the positive outcome.

References

Adams, J. S. (1965). Inequity in social exchange. In L. Berkowitz (Ed.), *Advances in experimental social psychology* (Vol. 2, pp. 267–299). New York, NY: Academic Press.

Alexander, S. & Ruderman, M. (1987). The role of procedural and distributive justice in organizational behavior. *Social Justice Research, 1*, 177–198.

Ambrose, M. L., & Arnaud, A. (2005). Are procedural justice and distributive justice conceptually distinct? In J. Greenberg & J. A. Colquitt (Eds.), *Handbook of organizational justice* (pp. 59–84). Mahwah, NJ: Erlbaum.

Ambrose, M. L., & Cropanzano, R. (2003). A longitudinal analysis of organizational fairness: An examination of reactions to tenure and promotion decisions. *Journal of Applied Psychology, 88*(2), 266–275. doi:10.1037/0021-9010.88.2.266

Ambrose, M., Hess, R. L., & Ganesan, S. (2007). The relationship between justice and attitudes: An examination of justice effects on event and system-related attitudes. *Organizational Behavior and Human Decision Processes, 103*, 21–36. doi:10.1016/j.obhdp.2007.01.001

Ambrose, M. L., Seabright, M. A., & Schminke, M. (2002). Sabotage in the workplace: The role of organizational injustice. *Organizational Behavior and Human Decision Processes, 89*, 947–965. doi:10.1016/S0749-5978(02)00037-7

Aquino, K., Tripp, T.M., & Bies, R.J. (2006). Getting even or moving on? Power, procedural justice, and types of offense as predictors of revenge, forgiveness, reconciliation, and avoidance in organizations. *Journal of Applied Psychology, 91*, 653–658.

Aryee, S., Budhwar, P. S., & Chen, Z. X. Trust as a mediator of the relationship between organizational justice and work outcomes: Test of a social exchange model. *Journal of Organizational Behavior, 23*, 267–285. doi:10.1002/job.138

Aryee, S., Chen, Z. X., & Budhwar, P. S. (2004). Exchange fairness and employee performance: An examination of the relationship between organizational politics and procedural justice. *Organizational Behavior and Human Decision Processes, 94*, 1–14. doi:10.1016/j.obhdp.2004.03.002

Barclay, L. J., Skarlicki, D. P., & Pugh, S.D. (2005). Exploring the role of emotions in injustice perceptions and retaliation. *Journal of Applied Psychology, 90*, 629–643. doi:10.1037/0021-9010.90.4.629

Barrett-Howard, E. & Tyler, T. (1986). Procedural justice s a criterion in allocation decisions. *Journal of Personality and Social Psychology, 50*, 296–304.

Bauer, T. N., Maertz, C. P., Jr., Dolen, M. R., & Campion, M. A. (1998). Longitudinal assessment of applicant reactions to employment testing and test outcome feedback. *Journal of Applied Psychology, 83*, 892–903. doi:10.1037/0021-9010.83.6.892

Bies, R. J. (2001). Interactional (in)justice: The sacred and the profane. In J. Greenberg & R. Cropanzano (Eds.), *Advances in organizational justice* (pp. 89–118). Stanford, CA: Stanford University Press.

Bies, R. J. (2005). Are procedural justice and interactional justice conceptually distinct? In J.Greenberg & J. A. Colquitt (Eds.), *Handbook of organizational justice* (pp. 85–112). Mahwah, NJ: Erlbaum.

Bies, R. J., & Moag, J. F. (1986). Interactional justice: Communication criteria of fairness. In R. J. Lewicki, B. H. Sheppard, & M. H. Bazerman (Eds.), *Research on negotiations in organizations* (Vol. 1, pp. 43–55). Greenwich, CT: JAI Press.

Bies, R. J., & Shapiro, D. L (1987). Interactional fairness judgements: The influence of causal accounts. *Social Justice Research, 1*, 199–218.

Bies, R. J., & Shapiro, D. L. (1988). Voice and justification: Their influence on procedural fairness judgments. *Academy of Management Journal, 31*, 676–685. doi:10.2307/256465

Bies, R. J., Shapiro, D. L., & Cummings, L. L. (1988). Causal accounts and managing organizational conflict: Is it enough to say it's not my fault? *Communication Research, 15*, 381–399. doi:10.1177/009365088015004003

Bies, R. J., & Tripp, T. M. (2001). A passion for justice: The rationality and morality of revenge. In R. Cropanzano (Ed.), *Series in applied psychology. Justice in the workplace: From theory to practice* (Vol. 2, pp. 197–208). Mahwah, NJ: Erlbaum.

Blader, S. L. (2007). What determines people's fairness judgments? Identification and outcomes influence procedural justice evaluations under uncertainty. *Journal of Experimental Social Psychology, 43*, 986–994. doi:10.1016/j.jesp.2006.10.022

Blader, S. L., & Tyler, T. R. (2003a). A four-component model of procedural justice: Defining the meaning of a "fair" process. *Personality and Social Psychology Bulletin, 29*, 747–758. doi:10.1177/0146167203029006007

Blader, S. L., & Tyler, T. R. (2003b). What constitutes fairness in work settings? A four component model of procedural justice. *Human Resource Management Review, 13*, 107–126. doi:10.1016/S1053-4822(02)00101-8

Blader, S. L., & Tyler, T. R. (2009). Testing and extending the group engagement model: Linkages between social identity, procedural justice, economic outcomes, and extrarole behavior. *Journal of Applied Psychology, 94*, 445–464. doi:10.1037/a0013935

Blau, P. M. (1964). *Exchange and power in social life*. New York, NY: Wiley.

Bobocel, D. R., Agar, S. E., Meyer, J. P., & Irving, P. G. (1998). Managerial accounts and fairness perceptions in conflict resolution: Differentiating the effects of minimizing responsibility and providing justification. *Basic and Applied Social Psychology, 20*, 133–143.

Bobocel, D. R., Son Hing, L. S., Davey, L. M., Stanley, D. J., Zanna, M. P. (1998). Justice-based opposition to social policies: Is it genuine? *Journal of Personality and Social Psychology, 3*, 653–669.

Bobocel, D. R., & Holmvall, C. M. (2001). Are interactional justice and procedural justice different? Framing the debate. In S. Gilliland, D. Steiner, & D. Skarlicki (Eds.), *Theoretical and cultural perspectives on organizational justice* (pp. 85–110). Greenwich, CT: Information Age Publishing.

Bobocel, D. R., & Zdaniuk, A. (2005). How can explanations be used to foster organizational justice? In J. Greenberg & J. A. Colquitt (Eds.), *Handbook of organizational justice* (pp. 469–498). Mahwah, NJ: Erlbaum.

Brockner, J. (2002). Making sense of procedural fairness: How high procedural fairness can reduce or heighten the influence of outcome favorability. *Academy of Management Review, 27*, 58–76.

Brockner, J. (2010). *A contemporary look at organizational justice: Multiplying insult times injury. Organization and management series*. New York, NY: Routledge/Taylor & Francis Group.

Brockner, J., De Cremer, D., Fishman, A. Y., & Spiegel, S. (2008). When does high procedural fairness reduce self-evaluations following unfavorable outcomes?: The moderating effect of prevention focus. *Journal of Experimental Social Psychology, 44*, 187–200. doi:10.1016/j.jesp.2007.03.00

Brockner, J., De Cremer, D., Van den Bos, K., & Chen, Y.-R. (2005). The influence of interdependent self-construal on procedural fairness effects. *Organizational Behavior and Human Decision Processes, 96*, 155–167. doi:10.1016/j.obhdp.2004.11.001

Brockner, J., DeWitt, R. L., Grover, S., & Reed, T. (1990). When it is especially important to explain why: Factors affecting the relationship between managers' explanations of a layoff and survivors' reactions to the layoff. *Journal of Experimental Social Psychology, 26*, 389–407. doi:10.1016/0022-1031(90)90065-T

Brockner, J., Heuer, L., Magner, N., Folger, R., Umphress, E., Van den Bos, K., Magner, M., Siegel, P. (2003). High procedural fairness heightens the effect of outcome favorability on self-evaluations: An attributional analysis. *Organizational Behavior and Human Decision Processes, 91*, 51–68. doi:10.1016/S0749-5978(02)00531-9

Brockner, J., Konovsky, M., Cooper-Schneider, R., Folger, R., Martin, C., & Bies, R. J. The interactive effects of procedural justice and outcome negativity on the victims and survivors of job loss. *Academy of Management Journal, 37*, 397–409.

Brockner, J., & Wiesenfeld, B. M. (1996). An integrative framework for explaining reactions to decisions: Interactive effects of outcomes and procedures. *Psychological Bulletin, 120*, 189–208.

Brockner, J., & Wiesenfeld, B. (2005). How generalizable is the interactive relationship between outcome favorability and procedural fairness? In J. Greenberg & J. Colquitt (Eds.), *Handbook of organizational justice: Fundamental questions about fairness in the workplace* (pp. 525–553). Hillsdale, N.J.: Erlbaum.

Brockner, J., Wiesenfeld, B. M., & Diekmann, K. A. (2009). Towards a "fairer" conception of process fairness: Why, when and how more may not always be better than less. *The Academy of Management Annals, 3*, 183–216. doi:10.1080/19416520903047228

Byrne, Z. S. (1999). *How do procedural and interactional justice influence multiple levels of organizational outcomes?* Paper presented at the annual meeting of the Society for Industrial and Organizational Psychology, Atlanta, GA.

Clemmer, E. C. (1993). An investigation into the relationship of fairness and customer satisfaction with services. In R. Cropanzano (Ed.), *Justice in the workplace: Approaching fairness in human resource management* (pp. 193–207). Hillsdale, NJ: Erlbaum.

Cohen, R. L. (1985). Procedural justice and participation. *Human Relations, 38*, 643–663. doi:10.1177/001872678503800703

Cohen-Charash, Y., & Spector, P. E. (2001). The role of justice in organizations: A meta analysis. *Organizational Behavior and Human Decision Processes, 86*, 278–321. doi:10.1006/obhd.2001.2958

Colquitt, J. A. (2001). On the dimensionality of organizational justice: A construct validation of a measure. *Journal of Applied Psychology, 86*, 386–400.

Colquitt, J. A., Conlon, D. E., Wesson, M. J., Porter, C. O. L. H., & Ng, K. Y. (2001). Justice at the millennium: A meta-analytic review of 25 years of organizational justice research. *Journal of Applied Psychology, 86*, 425–445. doi:10.1037/0021-9010.86.3.425

Colquitt, J. A., LePine, J. A., Piccolo, R. F., Zapata, C. P., & Rich, B. L. (2012). Explaining the justice–performance relationship: Trust as exchange deepener or trust as uncertainty reducer? *Journal of Applied Psychology, 97,* 1–15. doi:10.1037/a0025208

Colquitt, J. R. & Rodell, J. B. (2011). Justice, trust, and trustworthiness: A longitudinal analysis integrating three theoretical perspectives. *Academy of Management Journal, 54,* 1183 1206. http://dx.doi.org/10.5465/amj.2007.0572

Colquitt, J. A., Scott, B. A., Rodell, J. B., Long, D. M., Zapata, C. P., Conlon, D. E., & Wesson, M. J. (2013). Justice at the millennium, a decade later: A meta-analytic test of social exchange and affect-based perspectives. *Journal of Applied Psychology, 98,* 199–236. doi:10.1037/a0031757

Colquitt, J. A., & Shaw, J. C. (2005). How should organizational justice be measured? In J. Greenberg & J. A. Colquitt (Eds.), *Handbook of organizational justice* (pp. 113–152). Mahwah, NJ: Erlbaum.

Conlon, D. E., Meyer, C. J., & Nowakowski, J. M. (2005). How does organizational justice affect performance, withdrawal, and counterproductive behavior? In J. Greenberg & J. A. Colquitt (Eds.), *Handbook of organizational justice* (pp. 301–327). Mahwah, NJ: Erlbaum.

Cropanzano, R., & Ambrose, M. L. (2001). Procedural and distributive justice are more similar than you think: A monistic perspective and a research agenda. In J. Greenberg & R. Cropanzano (Eds.), *Advances in organizational justice.* Lexington, MA: The New Lexington Press.

Cropanzano, R., & Folger, R. (1989). Referent cognitions and task decision autonomy: Beyond equity theory. *Journal of Applied Psychology, 74,* 293–299. doi:10.1037/0021-9010.74.2.293

Cropanzano, R., & Greenberg, J. (1997). Progress in organizational justice: Tunneling through the maze. In L. T. Robertson & C. L. Cooper (Eds.), *International review of industrial and organizational psychology.* New York, NY: Wiley.

Cropanzano, R., Goldman, B., & Folger, R. (2003). Deontic justice: The role of moral principles in workplace fairness. *Journal of Organizational Behavior, 24,* 1019–1024. doi:10.1002/job.228

Cropanzano, R., & Konovsky, M. A. (1995). Resolving the justice delimma by improving the outcomes: The case of employee drug screening. *Journal of Business and Psychology, 10,* 221–243. doi:10.1007/BF02249581

Cropanzano, R., Prehar, C. A., & Chen, P. Y. (2002). Using social exchange theory to distinguish procedural from interactional justice. *Group & Organization Management, 27,* 324–351. doi:10.1177/1059601102027003002

Cropanzano, R., Rupp, D. E., Mohler, C. J., & Schminke, M. (2001). Three roads to organizational justice. In G. R. Ferris (Ed.), *Research in personnel and human resources management* (Vol. 20, pp. 1–123). doi:10.1016/S0742-7301(01)20001-2

Cropanzano, R., Slaughter, J. E., & Bachiochi, P. D. (2005). Organizational justice and Black applicants' reactions to affirmative action. *Journal of Applied Psychology, 90,* 1168 1184. doi:10.1037/0021 -9010.90.6.1168

Dalal, R. S. (2005). A meta-analysis of the relationship between organizational citizenship behavior and counterproductive work behavior. *Journal of Applied Psychology, 90,* 1241–1255. doi:10.1037/0021-9010.90.6.1241

De Cremer, D., & Blader, S. L. (2006). Why do people care about procedural fairness? The importance of belongingness in responding and attending to procedures. *European Journal of Social Psychology, 36,* 211–228. doi:10.1002/ejsp.290

De Cremer, D., & Sedikides, C. (2005). Self-uncertainty and responsiveness to procedural justice. *Journal of Experimental Social Psychology, 41,* 157–173. doi:10.1016/j.jesp.2004.06.010

De Cremer, D., Tyler, T. R., & den Ouden, N. (2005). Managing cooperation via procedural fairness: The mediating influence of self-other merging. *Journal of Economic Psychology, 26,* 393–406. doi:10.1016/j.joep.2004.12.004

De Cremer, D., & van Knippenberg, D. (2003). Cooperation with leaders in social dilemmas: On the effects of procedural fairness and outcome favorability in structural cooperation. *Organizational Behavior and Human Decision Processes, 91,* 1–11. doi:10.1016/S0749-5978(02)00539-3

Desai, S. D., Sondak, H., & Diekmann, K. A. (2011). When fairness neither satisfies nor motivates: The role of risk aversion and uncertainty reduction in attenuating and reversing the fair process effect. *Organizational Behavior and Human Decision Processes, 116,* 32–45. doi:10.1016/j.obhdp.2011.06.004

Deutsch, M. (1975). Equity, equality, and need: What determines which value will be used as the basis for distributive justice? *Journal of Social Issues, 31,* 137–149.

Donovan, M. A., Drasgow, F., & Munson, L. J. (1998). The Perceptions of Fair Interpersonal Treatment scale: Development and validation of a measure of interpersonal treatment in the workplace. *Journal of Applied Psychology, 83,* 683–692. doi:10.1037/0021-9010.83.5.683

Folger, R. (1977). Distributive and procedural justice: Combined impact of "voice" and improvement on experienced inequity. *Journal of Personality and Social Psychology, 35,* 108–119.

Folger, R. (1986). A referent cognitions theory of relative deprivation. In J. M. Olson, C. P. Herman, & M. P. Zanna (Eds.), Social comparison and relative deprivation: The Ontario symposium (Vol. 4, pp. 33–55). Hillsdale, NJ: Erlbaum.

Folger, R. (1987). Reformulating the preconditions of resentment: A referent cognitions model. In J. C. Masters & W. P. Smith (Eds.), *Social comparison, social justice, and relative deprivation: Theoretical, empirical, and policy perspectives* (pp. 183–215). Hillsdale, NJ: Erlbaum.

Folger, R. (1993). Justice, motivation, and performance beyond role requirements. *Employee Responsibilities and Rights Journal, 6,* 239–248. doi:10.1007/BF01419447

Folger, R. (1994). Workplace justice and employee worth. *Social Justice Research, 7,* 225–241.

Folger, R. (1998). Fairness as moral virtue. In M. Schminke (Ed.), *Managerial ethics: Moral management of people and processes* (pp. 13–34). Mahwah, NJ: Erlbaum.

Folger, R. (2001). Fairness as deonance. In S. W. Gilliand, D. D. Steiner, & D. P. Skarlicki (Eds.), Research in social issues in management (Vol.1, pp. 3–33). New York, NY: Information Age.

Folger, R., & Bies, R. J. (1989). Managerial responsibilities and procedural justice. *Employee Responsibilities and Rights Journal, 2,* 79–90. doi:10.1007/BF01384939

Folger, R., & Cropanzano, R. (1998). *Organizational justice and human resource management: Foundations for organizational science.* Thousand Oaks, CA: Sage Publications.

Folger, R., & Cropanzano, R. (2001). Fairness theory: Justice as accountability. In J. Greenberg & R. Cropanzano (Eds.), *Advances in organization justice* (pp. 1–55). Stanford University Press.

Folger, R., & Greenberg, J. (1985). Procedural justice: An interpretive analysis of personnel systems. In K. Rowland & G. Ferris (Eds.), *Research in personnel and human resources management* (Vol. 3, pp. 141–183). Greenwich, CT: JAI Press.

Folger, R., & Konovsky, M. A. (1989). Effects of procedural and distributive justice on reactions to pay raise decisions. *Academy of Management Journal, 32*, 115–130.

Folger, R., Konovsky, M. A., & Cropanzano, R. (1992). A due process metaphor for performance appraisal. In B. M. Staw & L. L. Cummings (Eds.), *Research in organizational behavior* (Vol. 14, pp. 129–177). Greenwich, CT: JAI.

Folger, R., & Martin, C. (1986). Relative deprivation and referent cognitions: Distributive and procedural justice effects. *Journal of Experimental Social Psychology, 22*, 531–546. doi:10.1016/0022-1031(86)90049-1

Folger, R., Rosenfield, D., Hays, R., & Grove, R. (1978). Justice *vs* justification effects on productivity: Reconciling equity and dissonance findings. *Organizational Behavior & Human Performance, 22*, 465–473. doi:10.1016/0030-5073(78)90028-4

Folger, R., Rosenfield, D., Grove, J., & Corkran, L. (1979). Effects of "voice" and peer opinions and responses to inequity. *Journal of Personality and Social Psychology, 37*, 2253–2261.

Folger, R., Rosenfield, D. D., & Robinson, T. (1983). Relative deprivation and procedural justifications. *Journal of Personality and Social Psychology, 45*, 268–273. doi:10.1037/0022-3514.45.2.268

Folger, R., Rosenfield, D., Rheaume, K., & Martin, C. (1983). Relative deprivation and referent cognitions. *Journal of Experimental Social Psychology, 19*, 172–184. doi:10.1016/0022-1031(83)90036-7

Folger, R., & Skarlicki, D. P. (1999). Unfairness and resistance to change: Hardship as mistreatment. *Journal of Organizational Change Management, 12*, 35–50. doi:10.1108/09534819910255306

Folger, R., & Skarlicki, D. P. (2008). The evolutionary basis of deontic justice. In S. Gilliland, D. Steiner, & D. Skarlicki (Eds.), *Research in social issues in management: Justice, morality, and social responsibility* (pp. 29–62). Greenwich CT: Information Age Publishing.

Giacobbe-Miller, J. K. (1995). A test of the group values and control models of procedural justice from the competing perspectives of labor and management. *Personnel Psychology, 48*, 115–142. doi:10.1111/j.1744-6570.1995.tb01749.x

Gillespie, J. Z., & Greenberg, J. (2005). Are the goals of organizational justice self-interested? In J. Greenberg & J. A. Colquitt (Eds.), *Handbook of organizational justice* (pp. 179–213). Mahwah, NJ: Erlbaum.

Gilliland, S. W. (1993). The perceived fairness of selection systems: An organizational justice perspective. *Academy of Management Review, 18*, 694–734.

Gilliland, S. W. (1994). Effects of procedural and distributive justice on reactions to a selection system. *Journal of Applied Psychology, 79*, 691–701.

Gilliland, S. W., Groth, M., Baker, R. C. IV, Dew, A. F., Polly, L. M., & Langdon, J. C. (2001). Improving applicants' reactions to rejection letters: An application of fairness theory. *Personnel Psychology, 54*, 669–703. doi:10.1111/j.1744-6570.2001.tb00227.x

Goldman, B. (2003). An application of referent cognitions theory to legal-claiming by terminated workers: The role of organizational justice and anger. *Journal of Management*, 29, 705–728.

Goldman, B. M. (2003). The application of referent cognitions theory to legal-claiming by terminated workers: The role of organizational justice and anger. *Journal of Management, 29*, 705–728. doi:10.1016/S0149-2063(03)00032-1

Gordon, M. E., & Fryxell, G. E. (1993). The role of interpersonal justice in organizational grievance systems. In R. Cropanzano (Ed.), *Justice in the workplace: Approaching fairness in human resources management* (pp. 231–255). Hillsdale: NJ: Erlbaum.

Greenberg, J. (1986). Determinants of perceived fairness of performance evaluations. *Journal of Applied Psychology, 71*, 340–342. doi:10.1037/0021-9010.71.2.340

Greenberg, J. (1987). Reactions to procedural injustice in payment distributions: Do the means justify the ends? *Journal of Applied Psychology, 72*(1), 55–61. doi:10.1037/0021-9010.72.1.55

Greenberg, J. (1990). Organizational justice: Yesterday, today, and tomorrow. *Journal of Management, 16*, 399–432.

Greenberg, J. (1993a). Stealing in the name of justice: Informational and interpersonal moderators of theft reactions to underpayment inequity. *Organizational Behavior and Human Decision Processes, 54*, 81–103.

Greenberg, J. (1993b). The social side of fairness: Interpersonal and informational classes of organizational justice. In R. Cropanzano (Ed.), *Justice in the workplace: Approaching fairness in human resource management* (pp. 79–103). Hillsdale, NJ: Erlbaum.

Greenberg, J. (1994). Using socially fair treatment to promote acceptance of a work site smoking ban. *Journal of Applied Psychology, 79*, 288–297.

Greenberg, J., & Folger, R. (1983). Procedural justice, participation, and the fair process effect in groups and organizations. In P. Paulus (Ed.), *Basic group processes* (pp. 235–256). New York, NY: Springer-Verlag.

Hakonen, M., & Lipponen, J. (2008). Procedural justice and identification with virtual teams: The moderating role of face-to-face meetings and geographical dispersion. *Social Justice Research, 21*, 164–178. doi:10.1007/s11211-008-0070-3

Harder, J. W. (1992). Play for pay: Effects of inequity in a pay-for-performance context. *Administrative Science Quarterly, 37*, 321–335. doi:10.2307/2393227

Hauenstein, N. M. A., McGonigle, T., & Flinder, S. W. (2001). A meta-analysis of the relationship between procedural justice and distributive justice: Implications for justice research. *Employee Responsibilities and Rights Journal, 13*, 39–56. doi:10.1023/A:1014482124497

Hershcovis, M. S., Turner, N., Barling, J., Arnold, K. A., Dupré, K. E., Inness, M., Inness, M., Sivanathan, N. (2007). Predicting workplace aggression: A meta-analysis. *Journal of Applied Psychology, 92*, 228–238.

Heuer, L., Blumenthal, E., Douglas, A., & Weinblatt, T. (1999). A deservingness approach to respect as a relationally based fairness judgment. *Personality and Social Psychology Bulletin, 25*, 1279–1292. doi:10.1177/0146167299258009

Holtz, B. C., & Harold, C. M. (2009). Fair today, fair tomorrow? A longitudinal investigation of overall justice perceptions. *Journal of Applied Psychology, 94*, 1185–1199. doi:10.1037/a0015900

Homans, G. C. (1974). Social behavior: Its elementary forms. (Revised ed.). Oxford, UK: Harcourt Brace Jovanovich.

Holmvall, C. M., & Bobocel, D. R. (2008). What fair procedures say about me: Self-construals and reactions to procedural fairness. *Organizational Behavior and Human Decision Processes, 105*, 147–168. doi:10.1016/j.obhdp.2007.09.001

Horvath, M., & Andrews, S. B. (2007). The role of fairness perceptions and accountability attributions in predicting reactions to organizational events. *Journal of Psychology: Interdisciplinary and Applied, 141*, 203–222. doi:10.3200/JRLP.141.2.203-223

Idson, L. C. Liberman, N., & Higgins, E. T. (2004). Imagining how you'd feel: The role of motivational experiences from regulatory fit. *Personality and Social Psychology Bulletin, 30*, 926–937. doi:10.1177/0146167204264334

James, W. (1950). *The principles of psychology*. New York, NY: Dover. (Original work published 1890).

Jones, D. A., & Skarlicki, D. P. (2003). The relationship between perceptions of fairness and voluntary turnover among retail employees. *Journal of Applied Social Psychology, 33*, 1226–1243.

Jones, D. A., & Skarlicki, D. P. (2005). The effects of overhearing peers discuss an authority's fairness reputation on reactions to subsequent treatment. *Journal of Applied Psychology, 90*, 363–372. doi:10.1037/0021-9010.90.2.363

Kahneman, D., & Tversky, A. (1982). The simulation heuristic. In D. Kahneman, P. Slovic, & A. Tversky, (Eds.), *Judgement under uncertainty: Heuristics and biases*. Cambridge, UK: Cambridge University Press.

Karriker, J. H., & Williams, M. L. (2009). Organizational justice and organizational citizenship behavior: A mediated multifoci model. *Journal of Management, 35*, 112–135. doi:10.1177/0149206307309265

Kernan, M. C. & Hanges, P. J. (2002). Survivor reactions to reorganization: Antecedents and consequences of procedural, interpersonal, and informational justice. *Journal of Applied Psychology, 87*, 916–928. doi:10.1037//0021-9010.87.5.916

Konovsky, M. A., & Pugh, S. D. (1994). Citizenship behavior and social exchange. *Academy of Management Journal, 37*, 656–669. doi:10.2307/256704

Korsgaard, M. A., & Roberson, L. (1995). Procedural justice in performance evaluation: The role of instrumental and non-instrumental voice in performance appraisal discussions. *Journal of Management, 21*, 657–669.

Korsgaard, M., Schweiger, D., & Sapienza, H. (1995). Building commitment, attachment, and trust in strategic decision-making teams: The role of procedural justice. *Academy of Management Journal, 38*, 60–84.

Kulik, C. T., & Ambrose, M. L. (1992). Personal and situational determinants of referent choice. *Academy of Management Review, 17*, 212–237. doi:10.2307/258771

LaTour, S. (1978).Determinants of participants and observer satisfaction with adversary and inquisitorial modes of modes of adjudication. *Journal of Personality and Social Psychology, 12*, 1531–1545.

Lavelle, J. J., Brockner, J., Konovsky, M. A., Price, K. H., Henley, A. B., Taneja, A., & Vinekar, V. (2009). Commitment, procedural fairness, and organizational citizenship behavior: A multifoci analysis. *Journal of Organizational Behavior, 30*, 337–357. doi:10.1002/job.518

Lavelle, J. J., Rupp, D. E., & Brockner, J. (2007). Taking a multifoci approach to the study of justice, social exchange, and citizenship behavior: The target similarity model. *Journal of Management, 33*, 841–866. doi:10.1177/0149206307307635

Lerner, M. & Whitehead, L. A. (1980). Procedural justice viewed in the context of justice motive theory. In G. Mikula (Ed.), *Justice in social interaction* (pp. 216–256). New York, NY: Springer-Verlag.

Leung, K., Su, S., & Morris, M. W. (2001). When is criticism not constructive? The roles of fairness perceptions and dispositional attributions in employee acceptance of critical supervisory feedback. *Human Relations, 54*, 1155–1187. doi:10.1177/0018726701549002

Leventhal, G. S. (1976). The distribution of rewards and resources in groups and organizations. In L. Berkowitz & W. Walster (Eds.), *Advances in experimental social psychology* (Vol. 9, pp. 91–131). New York, NY: Academic Press.

Leventhal, G. S. (1980). What should be done with equity theory? New approaches to the study of fairness in social relationships. In K. Gergen, M. Greenberg, and R. Willis (Eds.), *Social exchange: Advances in theory and research* (pp. 27–55). New York, NY: Plenum Press.

Leventhal, G. S., Karuza, J., & Fry, W. R. (1980). Beyond fairness: A theory of allocation preferences. In G. Mikula (Ed.), *Justice and social interaction* (pp. 167–218). New York, NY: Springer-Verlag.

Liao, H., & Rupp, D. E. (2005). The impact of justice climate and justice orientation on work outcomes: A cross-level multifoci framework. *Journal of Applied Psychology, 90*, 242–256. doi:10.1037/0021-9010.90.2.242

Lind, E. A. (2001). Fairness heuristic theory: Justice judgments as pivotal cognitions in organizational relations. In J. Greenberg & R. Cropanzano (Eds.), *Advances in organization justice* (pp. 56–88). Stanford, CA: Stanford University Press.

Lind, E. A. (2002). Fairness judgments as cognitions. In M. Ross & D. T. Miller (Eds.), *The justice motive in everyday life* (pp. 416–431). doi:10.1017/CBO9780511499975.023

Lind, E. A., Greenberg, J., Scott, K. S. & Welchans, T. D. (2000). The winding road from employee to complainant: Situational and psychological determinants of wrongful-termination claims. *Administrative Science Quarterly, 45*, 557–590. doi:10.2307/2667109

Lind, E. A., Kanfer, R., & Earley, P. C. (1990). Voice, control, and procedural justice: Instrumental and non-instrumental concerns in fairness judgments. *Journal of Personality and Social Psychology, 59*, 952–959. doi:10.1037/0022-3514.59.5.952

Lind, E. A., Kray, L., & Thompson, L. (2001). Primacy effects in justice judgments: Testing predictions from fairness heuristic theory. *Organizational Behavior and Human Decision Processes, 85*, 189–210. doi:10.1006/obhd.2000.2937

Lind, E. A., Kulik, C. T., Ambrose, M., & de Vera Park, M. V. (1993). Individual and corporate dispute resolution: Using procedural fairness as a decision heuristic. *Administrative Science Quarterly, 38*, 224–251. doi:10.2307/2393412

Lind, E. A., Kurtz, S., Musante, L., Walker, L., & Thibaut, J. W. (1980). Procedure and outcome effects on reactions to adjudicated resolution of conflicts of interests. *Journal of Personality and Social Psychology, 39*, 643–653.

Lind, A., & Lissak, R. I. (1985). Apparent impropriety and procedural fairness judgments. *Journal of Experimental Social Psychology, 21*, 19–29.

Lind, E. A., & Tyler, T. R. (1988). *The social psychology of procedural justice*. New York, NY: Plenum Press.

Lind, E. A., & Van den Bos, K. (2002). When fairness works: Toward a general theory of uncertainty management. In B. M. Staw & R. M. Kramer (Eds.), *Research in organizational behavior: An annual series of analytical essays and critical reviews* (Vol. 24, pp. 181–223). US: Elsevier Science/JAI Press.

Malatesta, R. M., & Byrne, Z. S. (1997). *The impact of formal and interactional justice on organizational outcomes*. Paper presented at the annual meeting of the Society for Industrial and Organizational Psychology, St. Louis, MO.

Masterson, S. S., Lewis, K., Goldman, B. M., & Taylor, M. S. (2000). Integrating justice and social exchange: The differing effects of fair procedures and treatment on work relationships. *Academy of Management Journal, 43*, 738–748. doi:10.2307/1556364

Mayer, D. M., Greenbaum, R. L., Kuenzi, M., & Shteynberg, G. (2009). When do fair procedures not matter? A test of the identity violation effect. *Journal of Applied Psychology, 94*, 142–161. doi:10.1037/a0013108

McFarlin, D. B., & Sweeney, P. D. (1992). Distributive and procedural justice as predictors of satisfaction with personal and organizational outcomes. *Academy of Management Journal, 35*, 626–637. doi:10.2307/256489

Moorman, R. H. (1991). Relationship between organizational justice and organizational citizenship behaviors: Do fairness perceptions influence employee citizenship? *Journal of Applied Psychology, 76*, 845–855.

Mullen, E., & Skitka, L. J. (2006). Exploring the psychological underpinnings of the moral mandate effect: Motivated reasoning, group differentiation, or anger? *Journal of Personality and Social Psychology, 90*(4), 629–643. doi:10.1037/0022-3514.90.4.629

Pillai, R., Williams, E. S., & Tan, J. J. (2001). Are the scales tipped in favor of procedural or distributive justice?: An investigation of the US, India, Germany, and Hong Kong (China). *International Journal of Conflict Management, 12*, 312–332. doi:10.1108/eb022861

Ployhart, R. E., & Ryan, A. M. (1997). Toward and explanation of applicant reactions: An examination of organizational justice and attribution frameworks. *Organizational Behavior and Human Decision Processes, 72*, 308–335. doi:10.1006/obhd.1997.2742

Ployhart, R. E., Ryan, A. M., & Bennett, M. (1999). Explanations for selection decisions: Applicants' reactions to informational and sensitivity features of explanations. *Journal of Applied Psychology, 84*, 87–106. doi:10.1037/0021-9010.84.1.87

Posthuma, R. A., Maertz, C. P., Jr., &Dworkin, J. B. (2007). Procedural justice's relationship with turnover: Explaining past inconsistent findings. *Journal of Organizational Behavior, 28*, 381–398. doi:10.1002/job.427

Price, J. L., & Mueller, C. W. (1986). *Handbook of organizational measurement*. Marshfield, MA: Pitman.

Rahim, M. A., Magner, N. R., & Shapiro, D. L. (2000). Do justice perceptions influence styles of handling conflict with supervisor?: What justice perceptions, precisely? *International Journal of Conflict Management, 11*, 9–31. doi:10.1108/eb022833

Reithel, S. M., Baltes, B. B., & Buddhavarapu, S. (2007). Cultural differences in distributive and procedural justice: Does a two-factor model fit for Hong Kong employees? *International Journal of Cross Cultural Management, 7*, 62–76. doi:10.1177/1470595807075172

Rupp, D. E., & Cropanzano, R. (2002). The mediating effects of social exchange relationships in predicting workplace outcomes from multifoci organizational justice. *Organizational Behavior and Human Decision Processes, 89*, 925–946. doi:10.1016/S0749-5978(02)00036-5

Rupp, D. E., Shao, R., Jones, K. S., Liao, H. (2014). The utility of a multifoci approach to the study of organizational justice: A meta-analytic investigation into the consideration of normative rules, moral accountability, bandwidth-fidelity, and social exchange. *Organizational Behavior and Human Decision Processes, 123*, 159–185. doi:10.1016/j.obhdp.2013.10.011

Schaubroeck, J., May, D. R., & Brown, F. W. (1994). Procedural justice explanations and employee reactions to economic hardship: A field experiment. *Journal of Applied Psychology, 79*, 455–460. doi:10.1037/0021-9010.79.3.455

Schroth, H. A., & Shah, P. P. (2000). Procedures: Do we really want to know them? An examination of the effects of procedural justice on self-esteem. *Journal of Applied Psychology, 85*, 462–471. doi:10.1037/0021-9010.85.3.462

Shapiro, D. L., & Brett, J. M. (2005). What is the role of control in organizational justice? In J. Greenberg & J. A. Colquitt (Eds.), *Handbook of organizational justice* (pp. 155–177). Mahwah, NJ: Erlbaum.

Shaw, J. C., Wild, E., & Colquitt, J. A. (2003). To justify or excuse?: A meta-analytic review of the effects of explanations. *Journal of Applied Psychology, 88*, 444–458. doi:10.1037/0021-9010.88.3.444

Sheppard, B. H. (1984). Third party conflict intervention: A procedural framework. In B.M. Staw & L.L. Cummings (eds.) *Research in Organizational Behavior* (Vol VI, pp. 141–190). Greenwich, CT: JAI Press.

Sheppard, B. H. & Lewicki, R. J. (1987). Toward general principles of managerial fairness. *Social Justice Research, 1*, 161–176.

Sheppard, B. H., Lewicki, R. J. & Minton, J. (1992). *Organizational justice*. Lexington, Mass: Lexington Books.

Skarlicki, D. P., Ellard, J. H., & Kelln, B. R. C. (1998). Third-party perceptions of a layoff: Procedural, derogation, and retributive aspects of justice. *Journal of Applied Psychology, 83*, 119–127. doi:10.1037/0021-9010.83.1.119

Skarlicki, D. P., & Folger, R. (1997). Retaliation in the workplace: The roles of distributive, procedural, and interpersonal justice. *Journal of Applied Psychology, 82*, 434–443.

Skarlicki, D. P., Folger, R., & Tesluk, P. (1999). Personality as a moderator in the relationship between fairness and retaliation. *Academy of Management Journal, 42*, 100–108. doi:10.2307/256877

Skarlicki, D. P., & Kulik, C. T. (2005). Third-party reactions to employee (mis)treatment: A justice perspective. In B. M. Staw & R. M. Kramer (Eds.), *Research in organizational behavior: An annual series of analytical essays and critical reviews* (Vol. 26, pp. 183–229). US: Elsevier Science/JAI Press.

Skarlicki, D. P., & Rupp, D. E. (2010). Dual processing and organizational justice: The role of rational versus experiential processing in third-party reactions to workplace mistreatment. *Journal of Applied Psychology, 95*, 944–952. doi:10.1037/a0020468

Skitka, L. J. (2002). Do the means always justify the ends, or do the ends sometimes justify the means? A value model of justice reasoning. *Personality and Social Psychology Bulletin, 28*, 588–597. doi:10.1177/0146167202288003

Skitka, L. J. (2003). Of different minds: An accessible identity model of justice reasoning. *Personality and Social Psychology Review, 7*, 286–297. doi:10.1207/S15327957PSPR0704_02

Skitka, L. J., & Houston, D. A. (2001). When due process is of no consequence: Moral mandates and presumed defendant guilt or innocence. *Social Justice Research, 14*, 305–326. doi:10.1023/A:1014372008257

Skitka, L. J., & Mullen, E. (2002). Understanding judgments of fairness in a real-world political context: A test of the Value Protection Model of Justice Reasoning. *Personality and Social Psychology Bulletin, 28*, 1419–1429. doi:10.1177/014616702236873

Skitka, L. J., Winquist, J., & Hutchinson, S. (2003). Are outcome fairness and outcome favorability distinguishable psychological constructs? A meta-analytic review. *Social Justice Research, 16*, 309–341. doi:10.1023/A:1026336131206

Smith, A. K., Bolton, R. N., & Wagner, J. (1999). A model of customer satisfaction with service encounters involving failure and recovery. *Journal of Marketing Research, 36*, 356–372. doi:10.2307/3152082

Smith, H. J., Tyler, T. R., Huo, Y. J., Ortiz, D. J., & Lind, E. A. (1998). The self-relevant implications of the group-value model: Group membership, self-worth, and treatment quality. *Journal of Experimental Social Psychology, 34*, 470–493. doi:10.1006/jesp.1998.1360

Summers, T. P., & Hendrix, W. H. (1991). Modelling the role of pay equity perceptions: A field study. *Journal of Occupational Psychology, 64*, 145–157. doi:10.1111/j.2044-8325.1991.tb00549.x

Sweeney, P. D., & McFarlin, D. B. (1993). Workers' evaluations of the "ends" and the "means": An examination of four models of distributive and procedural justice. *Organizational Behavior and Human Decision Processes, 55*, 23–40. doi:10.1006/obhd.1993.1022

Tajfel, H., & Turner, J. C. (1979). An integrative theory of intergroup conflict. *Social Psychology of Intergroup Relations, 33*, 47.

Tajfel, H. & Turner, J. C. (1986). The social identity theory of inter-group behavior. In S. Worchel & L. W. Austin (Eds.), *Psychology of Intergroup Relations*. Chicago, IL: Nelson-Hall.

Taylor, M. S., Tracy, K. B., Renard, M. K., Harrison, J. K., & Carroll, S. J. (1995). Due process in performance appraisal: A quasi-experiment in procedural justice. *Administrative Science Quarterly, 40*, 495–523. doi:10.2307/2393795

Tekleab, A. G., Takeuchi, R., & Taylor, S. M. (2005). Extending the chain of relationships among organizational justice, social exchange and employee reactions: The role of contract violations. *Academy of Management Journal, 48*, 146–157. doi:10.5465/AMJ.2005.15993162

Thibaut, J. W. & Kelley, H. H. (1959). *The social psychology of groups*. New York, NY: Wiley.

Thibaut, J., & Walker, L. (1975). *Procedural justice: A psychological analysis*. Hillsdale, NJ: Erlbaum.

Thibaut, J., & Walker, L. (1978). A theory of procedure. *California Law Review, 66*, 541–559.

Thibaut, J., Walker, L., LaTour, S. & Houlden, P. (1974). Procedural justice as fairness. *Stanford Law Review, 26*, 1271–1289.

Turillo, C. J., Folger, R., Lavelle, J. J., Umphress, E. E., & Gee, J. O. (2002). Is virtue its own reward? Self-sacrificial decisions for the sake of fairness. *Organizational Behavior and Human Decision Processes, 89(1)*, 839–865. doi:10.1016/S0749-5978(02)00032-8 (Erratum, 2003, doi:10.1016/S0749-5978(03)00065-7)

Tyler, T. R. (1989). The psychology of procedural justice: A test of the group-value model. *Journal of Personality and Social Psychology, 57*, 830–838.

Tyler, T. R. (1990). Justice, self-interest, and the legitimacy of legal and political authority. In J. J. Mansbridge (Ed.), *Beyond self-interest* (pp. 171–179). Chicago, IL: University of Chicago Press.

Tyler, T. R. (1991). Using procedures to justify outcomes: Testing the viability of a procedural justice strategy for managing conflict and allocating resources in work organizations. *Basic and Applied Social Psychology, 12*, 259–279. doi:10.1207/s15324834basp1203_2

Tyler, T. R. (1994). Psychological models of the justice motive: Antecedents of distributive and procedural justice. *Journal of Personality and Social Psychology, 67*, 850863.

Tyler, T. R. (1997). The psychology of legitimacy: A relational perspective on voluntary deference to authorities. *Personality and Social Psychology Review, 1*, 323–345. doi:10.1207/s15327957pspr0104_4

Tyler, T. R, & Bies, R. J. (1990). Beyond formal procedures: The interpersonal context of procedural justice. In J. Carroll (Ed.), *Applied social psychology and organizational settings* (pp. 77–98). Hillsdale, NJ: Erlbaum.

Tyler, T. R., & Blader, S. (2000). *Cooperation in groups: Procedural justice, social identity, and behavioral engagement*. Philadelphia, PA.: Psychology Press.

Tyler, T. R., & Blader, S. L. (2003). The group engagement model: Procedural justice, social identity, and cooperative behavior. *Personality and Social Psychology Review, 7*, 349–361. doi:10.1207/S15327957PSPR0704_07

Tyler, T. R. & Caine, A. (1981). The influence of outcomes and procedures on satisfaction with formal leaders. *Journal of Personality and Social Psychology, 41*, 642–655. doi:10.1037/0022-3514.41.4.642

Tyler, T. R., & Degoey, P. (1995). Collective restraint in social dilemmas: Procedural justice and social identification effects on support for authorities. *Journal of Personality and Social Psychology, 69*, 482–497. doi:10.1037/0022-3514.69.3.482

Tyler, T. R., Degoey, P., & Smith, H. J. (1996). Understanding why the justice of group procedures matters: A test of the psychological dynamics of the group-value model. *Journal of Personality and Social Psychology, 70*, 913–930.

Tyler, T. R., & Folger, R. (1980). Distributional and procedural aspects of satisfaction with citizen-police encounters. *Basic and Applied Social Psychology, 1*, 281–292.

Tyler, T. R., & Lind, E. A. (1992). A relational model of authority in groups. In M. P. Zanna (Ed.), *Advances in experimental social psychology* (Vol. 25, pp. 115–1919). San Diego, CA: Academic Press. doi:10.1016/S0065-2601(08)60283-X

Tyler, T. R., Rasinski, K. A., & McGraw, K. M. (1985). The influence of perceived injustice on the endorsement of political leaders. *Journal of Applied Social Psychology, 15*, 700–725. doi:10.1111/j.1559-1816.1985.tb02269.x

Tyler, T. R., Rasinski, K. A., & Spodick, N. (1985). Influence of voice on satisfaction with leaders: Exploring the meaning of process control. *Journal of Personality and Social Psychology, 48*, 72–81. doi:10.1037/0022-3514.48.1.72

Umphress, E. E., Simmons, A. L., Folger, R., Ren, R., & Bobocel, R. (2013). Observer reactions to interpersonal injustice: The roles of perpetrator intent and victim perception. *Journal of Organizational Behavior, 34*, 327–349. doi:10.1002/job.1801

Van den Bos, K. (2001). Uncertainty management: The influence of uncertainty salience on reactions to perceived procedural fairness. *Journal of Personality and Social Psychology, 80*, 931–941. doi:10.1037/0022-3514.80.6.931

Van den Bos, K. (2001). Fairness heuristic theory: Assessing the information to which people are reacting has a pivotal role in understanding organizational justice. In S. Gilliland, D. Steiner, & D. Skarlicki (Eds.), *Theoretical and cultural perspectives on organizational justice* (pp. 63–84). Greenwich, CT: Information Age Publishing.

Van den Bos, K. (2005). What is responsible for the fair process effect? In J. Greenberg & J. A. Colquitt (Eds.), *Handbook of organizational justice* (pp. 273–300). Mahwah, NJ: Erlbaum.

Van den Bos, K., Bruins, J., Wilke, H. A. M., & Dronkert, E. (1999). Sometimes unfair procedures have nice aspects: On the psychology of the fair process effect. *Journal of Personality and Social Psychology, 77*, 324–336. doi:10.1037/0022-3514.77.2.324

Van den Bos, K., & Lind, E. A. (2002). Uncertainty management by means of fairness judgments. In M. P. Zanna (Ed.), *Advances in experimental social psychology* (Vol. 34, pp. 1–60). San Diego, CA: Academic Press.

Van den Bos, K., Lind, E. A., Vermunt, R., & Wilke, H. A. M. (1997). How do I judge my outcome when I do not know the outcome of others? The psychology of the fair process effect. *Journal of Personality and Social Psychology, 72*, 1034–1046. doi:10.1037/0022-3514.72.5.1034

Van den Bos, K., & Miedema, J. (2000). Toward understanding why fairness matters: The influence of mortality salience on reactions to procedural fairness. *Journal of Personality and Social Psychology, 79*, 355–366. doi:10.1037/0022-3514.79.3.355

Van den Bos, K., Van Schie, E. C. M., & Colenberg, S. E. (2002). Parents' reactions to child day care organizations: The influence of perceptions of procedures and the role of organizations' trustworthiness. *Social Justice Research, 15*, 53–62. doi:10.1023/A:1016097715802

Van den Bos, K., Vermunt, R., & Wilke, H. A. M. (1997). Procedural and distributive justice: What is fair depends more on what comes first than on what comes next. *Journal of Personality and Social Psychology, 72*, 95–104. doi:10.1037/0022-3514.72.1.95

Van den Bos, K., Wilke, H. A. M., & Lind, E. A. (1998). When do we need procedural fairness? The role of trust in authority. *Journal of Personality and Social Psychology, 75*, 1449–1458.

Van Prooijen, J.-W., Van den Bos, K., & Wilke, H. A. M. (2005). Procedural justice and intragroup status: Knowing where we stand in a group enhances reactions to procedures. *Journal of Experimental Social Psychology, 41*, 664–676. doi:10.1016/j.jesp.2004.12.003

Van Prooijen, J.-W., & Zwenk, F. (2009). Self-construal level and voice procedures: The individual self as psychological basis for procedural fairness effects. *Journal of Experimental Social Psychology, 45(2)*, 392–397. doi:10.1016/j.jesp.2008.10.008

Vermunt, R., & Steensma, H. (2005). How can justice be used to manage stress in organizations? In J. Greenberg & J. A. Colquitt (Eds.), *Handbook of organizational justice* (pp. 113–152). Mahwah, NJ: Erlbaum.

Viswesvaran, C., & Ones, D. S. (2002). Agreements and disagreements on the role of general mental ability (GMA) in industrial, work, and organizational psychology. *Human Performance, 15*, 212–231. doi:10.1207/S15327043HUP1501&02_13

Walker, L., LaTour, S., Lind, E. A. & Thibaut, J. (1974). Reactions of participants and observers to modes of adjudication. *Journal of Applied Social Psychology, 4*, 295–310.

Walker, L., Lind, E. A., and Thibaut, J. (1979). The relation between procedural and distributive justice. *Virginia Law Review, 65*, 1401–1420.

Wang, M., Liao, H., Zhan, Y., & Shi, J. (2011). Daily customer mistreatment and employee sabotage against customers: Examining emotion and resource perspectives. *Academy of Management Journal, 54*, 312–334. doi:10.5465/AMJ.2011.60263093

Weiner, B. (1985). An attributional theory of achievement motivation and emotion. *Psychological Review, 92*, 548–573. doi:10.1037/0033-295X.92.4.548

Wiesenfeld, B. M., Swann, W. B., Jr., Brockner, J., & Bartel, C. A. (2007). Is more fairness always preferred? Self-esteem moderates reactions to procedural justice. *Academy of Management Journal, 50*, 1235–1253. doi:10.2307/20159922

Williams, S. (1999). The effects of distributive and procedural justice on performance. *Journal of Psychology: Interdisciplinary and Applied, 133*, 183–193. doi:10.1080/00223989909599732

Zapara-Phelan, C. P., Colquitt, J. A., Scott, B. A., & Linvingston, B. (2009). Procedural justice, interactional justice, and task performance: The mediating role of intrinsic motivation. *Organizational Behavior and Human Decision Processes, 108*, 93–105. doi:10.1016/j.obhdp.2008.08.001

CHAPTER 4

Interactional Justice: Looking Backward, Looking Forward

Robert J. Bies

Abstract

Over the past 25 years, interactional justice has captured the imagination and energy of scholars from many different fields of study. In this chapter, I look backward, presenting an overview of research findings on interactional justice. This review demonstrates its power of interactional justice as a construct, one which adds additional insight and explanation into organizational justice dynamics across a wide variety of organizational processes and outcomes. In addition, I will argue that truth and human dignity are the two core principles underlying interactional justice, which enables me to "look forward," identifying new directions and empirical questions for research for interactional justice.

Key Words: justice, fairness, respect, truth, human dignity, trust, leadership

> "In matters of truth and justice, there is no difference between large and small problems, for issues concerning the treatment of people are all the same."
>
> —*Albert Einstein*

Since my undergraduate years at the University of Washington, I had always been interested in the study of justice in the workplace, a passion first encouraged by one of my professors, Vern Buck, and then nurtured by another of my professors, Bill Scott. Working with my advisor at Stanford, Joanne Martin, only deepened my interest and passion in the study of justice.

In the Fall of 1980, after I had just successfully completed my field exams at Stanford University, I developed a dissertation proposal on justice that, in my dreams (or fantasies), would shift the paradigm of study of justice in organizations. In part, the proposal would center on the justice of interpersonal treatment, a fairness concern absent from the paradigm of organizational justice at that time.

In 1980, the paradigm of organizational justice was firmly grounded in two types of justice. First, there was research on *distributive justice*—or the fairness of outcomes distributed or allocated. Adams equity theory (1965), along with the work of Homans on social exchange (1958), and research on relative deprivation (Crosby, 1984; Stouffer, Suchman, DeVinney, Star, & Williams, 1949; Martin, 1981) are exemplars of this approach.

However, a growing number of empirical studies created anomalies that could not be handled by the distributive justice framework, leading to a broadening of the organizational justice paradigm (Kuhn, 1970). Research began to demonstrate that it was not just the outcome that mattered to people; in addition, they also focused on the procedures used to distribute or allocate the outcomes—or, what is referred to as *procedural justice*. The groundbreaking theory and research on procedural justice, done by Thibaut and Walker (1975), identified process control and decision control as two key dimensions of procedures that would influence people's judgments of procedural justice.

Following an inductive approach, Leventhal (1980) developed an alternative theory of procedural justice. In his theory, Leventhal identified six procedural rules that people used to assess the fairness of procedures. These rules are the consistency rule, the bias-suppression rule, the accuracy rule, the correctability rule, the representativeness rule, and the ethicality rule. Building on Thibaut and Walker, and Leventhal, Lind and Tyler (1988) advanced a new theory of procedural justice which they referred to as the *group values model*, which they later refined in their *relational model of authority* (Tyler & Lind, 1992). Lind and Tyler argued that procedures are valued, in part, because they communicate status and inclusion in groups, which introduced relational motivations in assessing procedural justice.

But I believed in my core idea that people were not just concerned about outcomes and procedures; in addition, based on observations and interviews with managers and staff employees while conducting research at Stanford, it was "obvious" to me that they were also concerned about the quality of interpersonal treatment they received from others in organizations. So, with great passion, I developed my ideas and presented my proposal to my dissertation committee. But the proposal was rejected by all three members of my committee, and I was devastated.

But, as one door closed, another opened. One of my dissertation committee members, Gene Webb, suggested to me that, if I could design five experiments that demonstrate how to effectively and humanely "fire" employees, I would become rich and famous (or something like that). Out of rejection, I developed a second dissertation proposal on the delivery of bad news, one that focused on the explanations and justifications given for bad news and how social information shaped people's reactions to bad news.

Both the first proposal, which was rejected, and the second proposal, which was accepted, became the foundation for the study of interpersonal treatment as a key aspect of organizational justice. In 1985, at the *Research on Negotiations Conference,* I presented empirical findings from my research on individual reactions to corporate recruitment practices. My findings suggested that people were quite concerned with the fairness of the interpersonal treatment they received from corporate recruiters, concerns that I referred to as *interactional justice* (Bies & Moag, 1986). I was told by a senior faculty member at the conference that "there is no third type of justice." But, I was not discouraged, for now I was "armed" with data to support my ideas.

I further elaborated on interactional justice in my chapter in the *Research in Organizational Behavior* series (Bies, 1987). In that chapter, I presented a typology of social accounts—that is, explanations and justifications—that I conceptualized as important to people's concerns about interactional justice. The work on social accounts grew out of my dissertation. Together, these two chapters became the conceptual "sparks" that have generated growing scholarly interest in interactional justice for almost 30 years now.

In writing this chapter, I have two primary objectives. First, I will look backward, examining the past and present of interactional justice. I will present an overview of research findings on interactional justice, demonstrating its power of explanation of and impact on a growing number and wide variety of organizational processes and outcomes. Second, utilizing Feinberg's (1974) framework that distinguishes between comparative and noncomparative principles of justice, I will argue that truth and human dignity are the core noncomparative principles underlying interactional justice. This analysis will enable me to look forward, identifying new directions for research for interactional justice. I close the chapter with a call to justice researchers to broaden their conceptual mindsets to analyze justice and injustice more broadly—in terms of good and evil in organizations (Bies & Fox, 2013). In so doing, new empirical questions will emerge for justice researchers (e.g., Why do people treat others unjustly? Why do people tolerate or condone the unjust treatment of others?).

Looking Backward: The Past and Present of Interactional Justice

Over the past 25 years, interactional justice has captured the imagination and energy of scholars, which has resulted in many publications, and generated some controversy. All the while, though, there has been widespread agreement that interactional justice matters to people. Let me provide an overview of the conceptual status of interactional justice. That discussion will be followed by an overview of the empirical research demonstrating that interactional justice matters, including new domains and processes illustrating the explanatory power of the construct.

Interactional Justice Matters: The Conceptual Status of a Construct

Over the past two decades, there has been a debate among organizational justice researchers about whether organizational justice is best conceptualized as one, two, three, or four factors. The traditional view over the years had been that of a "two-factor" theory of organizational justice—distributive justice and procedural justice (Sweeney & McFarlin, 1993). With the introduction of interactional justice, we had the emergence of a three-factor theory (Bies, 1987; Bies & Moag, 1986). Greenberg (1993b) introduced a four-factor theory in which he argued that interactional justice should be separated into two separate constructs that he labeled as *informational justice* and *interpersonal justice*, a conceptualization validated empirically by Colquitt (2001). Finally, in what they refer to as a "monistic" perspective, Cropanzano and Ambrose (2001) argue that justice is all about expectations with respect to two kinds of outcomes: economic and socio-emotional. Distributive, procedural, and interactional factors each provide information about the two kinds of outcomes, which is the core judgment with respect to evaluating justice. This is the one-factor theory.

Although some justice researchers have questioned whether interactional justice is a separate factor, or just an interpersonal component of procedural justice (see Bies, 2005, for a summary of this controversy), this controversy has been resolved. Indeed, three different meta-analytic reviews of research have demonstrated that interactional justice is separate from the other dimensions of organizational justice and predicts different outcomes (Cohen-Charash, & Spector, 2001; Colquitt, Conlon, Wesson, Porter, & Ng, 2001; Colquitt, Scott, et al., 2013). In their meta-analysis, Cohen-Charash and Spector (2001) examined three different factors of organizational justice (distributive, procedural, interactional). Although all three factors were strongly related, they were found to be distinct constructs.

Colquitt et al. (2001) conducted a meta-analytic review of 25 years of organizational justice research, examining the four factors of organizational justice, and followed up that meta-analytic review a decade later (Colquitt et al., 2013). Each meta-analysis yielded several conclusions that converged. First, in both reviews, distributive, procedural, interpersonal, and informational justice emerged as distinct constructs, empirically distinguishable from each other. Second, the analysis demonstrated that distributive, procedural justice, interpersonal justice, and informational justice have different correlates. Although procedural justice, along with distributive justice, was the strongest or second strongest predictor of many key outcomes (e.g., job satisfaction, organizational commitment), informational and interpersonal justice were the strongest contributors to predicting other important outcomes. (e.g., trust, organizational commitment, organizational citizenship behaviors—individual referenced, withdrawal, negative reactions).

However, despite Greenberg's (1993b) conceptualization, and Colquitt's (2001) subsequent construct validation studies, most organizational scholars do not measure informational and interpersonal justice separately. Most scholars still measure interactional justice as one construct, and that global construct predicts very well. An overview of research on interactional justice is presented next.

Interactional Justice Matters: An Overview of the Research

That interactional justice matters is not in question; the question is when, where, and why does interactional justice have an impact? Stimulated by Bies (1987), there has been one stream of research that has focused on social accounts—explanations and justifications—as a key element of interactional justice. Interactional justice, in the form of social accounts, has been found to be an important variable for understanding individual reactions to a variety of decisions across different organizational processes including: (a) *organizational entry*—corporate recruitment practices (Bies & Moag, 1986; Bies & Shapiro, 1987) and employee selection (Gilliland, 1994; Gilliland et al., 2001; Ployhart, Ryan, & Bennett, 1999); (b) *resource allocation*—the refusal of requests (Bies, Shapiro, & Cummings, 1988; Izraeli & Jick, 1986) and budget decisions (Bies & Shapiro, 1987, 1988; Bies et al., 1988); (c) *feedback and evaluation*—giving criticism (Baron, 1990), performance appraisals (Greenberg, 1991), and evaluation procedures (Cobb, Vest, & Hills, 1997); (d) *negotiation and conflict*—negotiation tactics (Daly, 1991; Shapiro & Bies, 1994), deceptive actions (Shapiro, 1991), conflict management (Bobocel, Agar, Meyer, & Irving, 1998; Sitkin & Bies, 1993), and rebuilding cooperation after opportunistic behavior (Bottom, Gibson, Daniels, & Murnighan, 2002); (d) *counterproductive work behaviors*—employee theft (Greenberg 1993a) and revenge (Bies & Tripp, 1996); (e) *change and bad news*—worksite smoking bans (Greenberg, 1994), pay cuts (Greenberg, 1990), company relocations (Daly & Geyer, 1994), organizational change (Cobb, Wooten & Folger, 1995; Daly, 1995), job layoffs (Brockner, DeWitt, Grover, & Reed, 1990; Konovsky & Folger, 1991; Wanberg, Gavin, & Bunce, 1999), and the delivery of bad news (Bies, 2013a); and (f) *corporate actions*—market exploitation practices (Bies, Tripp, & Neale, 1993) and corporate responses to consumer product complaints (Conlon & Murray, 1996).

Stimulated by Bies and Moag (1986), another stream of research has focused on interactional justice in the form of respectful and socially sensitive treatment. Scholars have found interactional justice to be an important variable explaining a variety of individual affects, judgments, and behaviors—and individual reactions to organizational processes and new workplace arrangements. In addition, several variables that act as moderators on the impact of interactional justice have been identified by researchers. An overview of these research findings is presented next.

AFFECTS, JUDGMENTS, AND BEHAVIORS

Interactional justice has been associated with a variety of individual affects including emotional arousal (Stecher & Rosse, 2005); anger (Bies & Tripp, 1996), psychological distress (Tepper, 2000), occupational stress (Elovainio, Kivimäki, & Helkama, 2001), and workplace stress-induced insomnia (Greenberg, 2006). Interactional justice has also been associated with a variety of judgments including job satisfaction (Laschinger, 2004), trust in leadership and management (Barling & Phillips, 1993; Cropanzano, Bowen, & Gilliland, 2007; Dirks & Ferrin, 2002; Aryee, Budhwar, & Chen, 2002), supervisor legitimacy (Masterson, Lewis-McClear, Goldman, & Taylor, 2000), social exchange satisfaction (Hui, Au, & Zhao, 2007; Tekleab, Takenchi, & Taylor, 2005), reactions to drug testing (Konovsky & Cropanzano, 1991), acceptance of a work site smoking ban (Greenberg, 1994), organizational commitment (Barling & Phillips, 1993), and perceptions of systemic justice (Beugre & Baron, 2001).

Interactional justice has been associated with a variety of behaviors including organizational citizenship behaviors (Maletesta & Byrne, 1997; Moorman, 1991; Rupp & Cropanzano, 2002; Skarlicki & Latham, 1996; Williams, Pitre, & Zainuba, 2002), job performance (Cropanzano, Prehar, & Chen, 2002), quality of care in hospitals (Laschinger, 2004), union participation (Fuller & Hester, 2001), teamwork quality (Dayan & Di Benedetto, 2008), and voluntary turnover (Tepper, 2000). Interactional justice has also been associated with a variety of counterproductive work behaviors including workplace revenge (Bies & Tripp, 1996; McLean Parks, 1997; Miller, 2001; Tripp & Bies, 1997, 2009), workplace incivility (Andersson & Pearson, 1999; Cortina, Magley, Williams, & Langhout, 2001), workplace sabotage (Ambrose, Seabright, & Schminke, 2002), workplace deviance (Aquino, Galperin, & Bennett, 2004; Aquino, Lewis, Bradfield, 1999; Henle, 2005), organizational retaliatory behaviors (Skarlicki & Folger, 1997; Skarlicki, Folger, & Tesluk, 1999), supervisor-targeted aggression (Hershcovis, Turner, Barling, Arnold, Dupré, Innis, LeBlanc, & Sivanathan, 2007), teacher-targeted aggression by students (Chory-Assad & Paulsel, 2004), employee theft (Greenberg, 1990, 1993a), cyberloafing (Lim, 2002; De Lara, 2006), employee litigation behavior (Bies & Tripp, 1993; Bies & Tyler, 1993), and organizational silence (Tulubas & Celep, 2012).

ORGANIZATIONAL PROCESSES AND NEW WORKPLACE ARRANGEMENTS

Interactional justice has shaped individual reactions to different organizational processes including performance feedback (Baron, 1988), corporate recruitment practices (Bies & Moag, 1986), negotiation (Leung, Tong, & Ho, 2004; Shapiro & Bies, 1994), conflict resolution (Rahim, Magner, & Shapiro, 2000), and abusive bosses (Bies & Tripp, 1999; Hornstein, 1996; Tepper, 2000).

Interactional justice has been found to be a useful construct for analyzing individual reactions to boundary-spanning processes including customer service (Clemmer, 1993; Rupp & Spencer, 2006), consumer complaint behavior (Blodgett, Hill, & Tax, 1997), and invasions of consumer privacy (Culnan & Bies, 2003; Son & Kim, 2008). Consistently, interactional justice has been found to shape the customer experience. For example, when hotel guests witness mistreatment of hotel staff, it leads to dysfunctional guest behavior and reduced guest loyalty to the hotel (Zoghbi-Maurique-de-Lana, Aguiar-Quintara, & Suarez-Acota, 2012). Similarly, customer satisfaction is related to interactional justice (Martínez-Tur, Peiro, Ramos, & Moliner, 2006; Simons & Roberson, 2003). Finally, failures of service recovery efforts are often connected to customers experiencing interactional *in*justice (Blodgett & Tax, 1993; Chebat & Slusarczyk, 2005; Collie, Bradley, & Sparks, 2002; Collie, Sparks, & Bradley, 2000; del Río-Lanza, Vazquez-Carielles, & Díaz- Martín, 2009; Kuo & Wu, 2012; Maxham & Netermeyer, 2002).

Interactional justice has also shaped reactions to new workplace arrangements created by telecommuting (Kurland & Egan, 1999), radical organizational change (Kickul, Lester, & Finkl, 2002), workplace reconfigurations (Kernan & Hanages, 2002), job layoffs (Bennett, Martin, Bies, & Brockner, 1995; Bies, Martin, & Brockner, 1993; Naumann, Bennett, Bies, & Martin, 1998), and technological advances in monitoring workplace behavior (Alder & Ambrose, 2005b; Alge, 2001; Ambrose & Alder, 2000; Bies, 1993, 1996). Interactional justice has also been useful in explaining inter-organizational relationships such as strategic alliances (Ariño & Ring, 2010; Luo, 2007), cross-cultural joint ventures (Lu, 2006), and marketing channel dynamics (Sindhav, 2001).

MODERATOR VARIABLES

Several studies have identified variables that moderate the influence and impact of interactional justice. Individual difference variables such as aggressiveness (Aquino et al., 2004), impulsivity and sensitivity to interpersonal interactions (Henle, 2005), self-esteem (De Cremer, Van Knippenberg, van Dijke, & Bos, 2004), and gender (Tata & Bowes-Sperry, 1996) have been found to moderate the effects of interactional justice. Situational variables such as social status (Aquino et al., 2004), and organizational variables such as organizational structure (Ambrose & Schminke, 2003) have also been found to moderate the effects of interactional justice.

Summary

In looking back, there is converging evidence that interactional justice is a separate factor of organizational justice. Further, it is clear that interactional justice matters to people, and it matters in a wide variety of contexts. In the next section, I will examine interactional justice and its core properties.

Getting to the Core of Interactional Justice: Truth and Human Dignity

In this section, I will identify the core properties of the psychological phenomenon of interactional justice (cf. Lewin, 1935). I will argue that the core properties of interactional justice are truth and human dignity (Bies, 2001). Each of those properties parallels the Colquitt's (2001) dimensions of interactional justice: informational justice and interpersonal justice. A review of empirical evidence will illustrate how different aspects of truth and human dignity—and violations of them—are related to interactional justice, which will identify new directions for theory and research on interactional justice.

Given that truth and human dignity are relevant variables for explaining interactional justice dynamics (Bies, 1987, 2001), why aren't they more figural in our models and study of organizational justice? One answer to that question can be found in the underlying principles of fairness that are the foundation of the paradigm of organizational justice (Bies, 1987, 2001). Specifically, our models of organizational justice are grounded primarily in principles of comparative justice, whereas truth and human dignity are noncomparative principles of justice (Feinberg, 1974).

In the next section of the chapter, I reexamine the foundations of fairness and demonstrate how comparative and noncomparative principles underlie all of our current theories and research on organizational justice—but we often confound the two sets of principles. This analysis will be guided by Feinberg's (1974) framework of justice principles that distinguishes between comparative and noncomparative principles of justice. I will follow this analysis with a review of empirical evidence regarding two noncomparative principles of interactional justice: truth and human dignity.

Rethinking Organizational Justice: Comparative and Noncomparative Principles

Although the identification of different types of justice has advanced our understanding of organizational justice and its dynamics, very little attention has been given to the justice principles underlying the different types of justice. Our theories of organizational justice are grounded in two different principles of justice that need to be identified and disentangled conceptually (Bies, 1987). These two principles are *comparative justice* and *noncomparative justice* (Feinberg, 1974).

What justice fundamentally means is to give a person *his or her due* (Feinberg, 1974). But how that due is determined may vary. Feinberg (1974) argues that "in some cases one's due is determined independently of that of other people, while in other cases, a person's due is determinable *only* by reference to his relations to other persons . . . the contexts, criteria, and principles of the former kind (are referred to) as *noncomparative*, and those of the latter sort as *comparative*" (p. 297). This distinction between comparative and noncomparative principles represents an alternative, yet potentially useful, approach for exploring organizational justice.

Further, identifying the underlying principles of justice (comparative, noncomparative) in contrast to types of justice (distributive, procedural, interactional) is consistent with Lewin's (1935) important distinction between genotypes (akin to principles of justice—comparative, noncomparative) and phenotypes (akin to different types of justice—distributive, procedural, interactional).

Following Feinberg (1974), our theories of distributive justice are based primarily on Aristotelian notions of *comparative justice.* By comparative justice, it is meant that a person assesses whether he or she has been fairly treated by reference to the outcome or treatment of other people. For example, research inspired by equity theory (e.g., Adams, 1965; Walster, Walster, & Berscheid, 1978), and relative deprivation theory (e.g., Crosby, 1976; Martin, 1981), explicitly assume that justice is determined through comparison with others. In other words, fairness judgments are relative.

But, as Feinberg (1974) demonstrates, there is another class of principles, those that are noncomparative in nature, that can form and shape perceptions of justice and injustice. As Feinberg notes: "When our problem is to make assignments, ascriptions, or awards in accordance with noncomparative justice, what is 'due' the other person is not a share or portion of some divisible benefit or burden; hence it is not necessary for us to know what is due other in order to know what is due the person with whom we are dealing. *His* rights-or-deserts alone determine what is due him; and once we have come to a judgment of *his* due, that judgment cannot be logically affected by subsequent knowledge of the condition of other parties. . . . When our task is to do noncomparative justice to each of a large number of individuals, we do not compare them with each other, but rather we compare each in turn with an objective standard and judge each (as we say) 'on his merits'" (p. 282).

Noncomparative principles of justice are central to theories of procedural justice, except for one notable exception that will be discussed later. For example, the opportunity for voice or process control (Thibaut & Walker, 1975), neutrality and standing in the group value and relational models of procedural justice (Lind & Tyler, 1988; Tyler & Lind, 1992), and many of the different procedural rules identified by Leventhal (1980), such as bias suppression, accuracy, correctability, representativeness, and ethicality, are noncomparative in nature.

But the consistency rule identified by Leventhal is clearly a comparative principle of justice, because the consistency rule requires equal treatment for all affected by the procedure (Leventhal, 1980). Any deviation from equality of opportunity or the equality of administration of the rules forms the basis for claims of procedural *in*justice.

Noncomparative principles of justice are at the core of theories of interactional justice. Examples of such objective and absolute standards might include truth, freedom, and human dignity, concerns that are highlighted by my conceptualization of interactional justice (Bies, 2001; Bies & Moag, 1986). Related conceptualizations of informational justice and interpersonal justice are based on noncomparative principles of justice (Colquitt, 2001; Greenberg, 1993b). Models of deontic justice (Cropanzano, Goldman, & Folger, 2003; Rupp & Bell, 2003) are also grounded in noncomparative principles of justice.

To further illustrate the importance of distinguishing between comparative and noncomparative principles, consider the following example taken from Bies (1987). Let us assume there is a "rude and abusive" journal reviewer who makes caustic and derogatory remarks to five different authors about their manuscripts. Let us further assume that each of the manuscripts was of equal quality. Given that the manuscript "inputs" were the same, the outcomes were the same, and each author was treated "equally." Applying principles of comparative justice would suggest there should be no sense of injustice aroused as the result of this process.

Yet, for most of us, there would be some residual resentment or anger as the target of such treatment. The principles that would explain our sense of injustice would be noncomparative in nature. For example, we might have some conception that we have a *right* to be treated with respect, and that no one deserves to be the target of such mean-spirited comments or insults (Folger & Bies, 1989). Further, if the reviewer made derogatory and false accusations about the work, one would feel unjustly treated because they had not been "done justice" (Feinberg, 1974). Regardless that everyone else was treated in the same manner, it would not totally mitigate the sense of injustice aroused by the violation of noncomparative principles.

By making the distinction between comparative and noncomparative principles of justice, it provides a new insight into a consistent finding from my research on the delivery of bad news (Bies, 2010). That finding is this: *People want to be treated equally, but uniquely.* I call this finding one of the *paradoxes of justice* (Bies, 2013b). But this paradox makes sense conceptually, if we follow the insight of Feinberg (1974): any action or outcome may be evaluated by comparative and noncomparative principles simultaneously.

The distinction between comparative and noncomparative principles of justice is important conceptually, as distributive and procedural justice theories have confounded the two principles in their formulations. Take the case of equity theory, for example. Following Adams (1965) formulation of equity theory, it is argued that people will judge the fairness of rewards and punishments based on a social comparison of their inputs or contributions. Clearly there are comparative principles operative in that people compare their outcomes as a function of their inputs. But to "do justice" to the person being evaluated, the assessment of inputs or contributions must be based on an accurate or truthful representation of one's contributions, which involves noncomparative principles.

Procedural justice theory also confounds comparative and noncomparative principles of justice. For example, in Leventhal's (1980) seminal theory of procedural justice, the consistency rule is comparative in nature, as discussed earlier. Yet, other Leventhal rules, such as the accuracy rule and the correctability rule, focus on the noncomparative principles of making sure that one gets what one is due. The issue of truth, as a noncomparative principle, may be central to understanding reactions to different procedures.

Why is making this distinction between comparative and noncomparative justice important? One reason is that we may be confounding comparative and noncomparative principles of justice in our study and analysis of organizational justice. This confounding not only muddies the conceptual waters surrounding the concept of organizational justice, but it may also lead to misinterpreting findings about justice dynamics (Bies, 1987).

Second, by highlighting the importance and relevance of noncomparative principles of justice, it will generate new theory, thus opening new directions for research on organizational justice. In the next section, I review research that illustrates two noncomparative principles that are at the core of interactional justice: truth and human dignity.

Truth and Human Dignity: Noncomparative Principles of Justice

In this section of the chapter, I review the empirical evidence on truth and human dignity and their relationship to interactional justice. A review of the empirical evidence finds *deception* and *derogatory judgments* to be two key violations of truth. In addition, the empirical evidence finds that *disrespect, invasion of privacy*, and *exposure to personal danger* are three key violations of human dignity. This literature review will suggest a richer analysis of interactional justice and identify new directions for research and theory building, thus demonstrating the usefulness noncomparative justice as a framework for analysis

—Lakatos, 1971.

TRUTH AND INTERACTIONAL JUSTICE

"All I want is the truth. Just gimme some truth."

—*John Lennon*

Across my almost three-decade journey in the study of interactional justice in the workplace, one of the interesting findings that popped up first unexpectedly, and then, consistently, was the concept of truth as a variable that played a supporting, if not leading, role in the drama of interactional (in)justice in the workplace. For example, in my first study on interactional justice (Bies & Moag, 1986), truthfulness and candor were important criteria that job candidates used to judge the fairness of their treatment by corporate recruiters; similarly, the job candidates claimed unfair treatment when they felt deceived or lied to by corporate recruiters.

Truth and interactional justice also emerged together in my chapter in *Research in Organizational Behavior*, entitled The Predicament of Injustice: The Management of Moral Outrage (Bies, 1987). In that chapter, I outlined a framework of social accounts that managers might use to lessen the anger and increase the sense of fairness when employees received unfavorable outcomes or bad news. The perceived sincerity and truthfulness of the account-giver was a key criterion for people in assessing the adequacy of the social account; similarly, the adequacy of the account was also filtered through the facts presented in the account, which is a dimension of truth. Sincerity and truthfulness have been key truth-related variables in account-giving, as found in empirical studies (Bies et al., 1988; Shapiro, 1991; Shapiro & Bies, 1994).

Truth and interactional justice were found connected in my research on revenge with Tom Tripp (Bies & Tripp, 1996; for a comprehensive review of the empirical findings, see Tripp & Bies, 2009). Across 15 years of research on revenge, we found violations of truth often cited as "triggers" of revenge. Being the victim of lying or deception was a quick trigger for the revenge motive. Violations of truth also aroused the sense of injustice when people claimed that they were wrongfully accused or blamed for some behavior or outcome, or when someone took credit for or stole their ideas, or when they were the victim of "bad-mouthing" to impugn their character or performance.

DECEPTION

The first category of actions violating truth involves *deception* or *lying* (Grover, 1993, 1997), which refers to the lack of correspondence between one's words and actions. As an example, when people feel "lied" to, it makes them angry and resentful (Bies, 2001). For example, in a review of research on the delivery of bad news (Bies, 2013a), it was found that, when people feel lied to or intentionally deceived, it elicits the most anger and rage in people's responses (Bies, 2001; Shapiro, 1991). Whether it be corporate recruitment practices (Bies & Moag, 1986) or negotiator tactics (Shapiro & Bies, 1994), lying to others creates intense feelings of distrust (Lewicki, McAllister, & Bies, 1998) and outrage (Bies & Tripp, 1996), particularly when people feel "used" by the person who was doing the lying (Bies, 2001).

But within the context of lying, Anton (1990) discovered some intriguing findings about people's reactions to being deceived. In a negotiation study, Anton compared four categories of deception commonly used in a negotiation: bluffing, misrepresentation of position, deception, and falsification. He found that the misrepresentation of position was perceived as most ethical. Bluffing was viewed as morally neutral by participants while deception and falsification were viewed as the least ethical. In other words, people appear to "draw the line" between different levels of deception or lying. Lying may not be perceived as wrong or unjust, depending on the normative context in which the lying occurs. Indeed, in the case of a negotiation, it is often "expected" that some deception will occur, and that is just part of the ground rules of the game. In other words, the normative context of negotiation "allows" for some deception as a legitimate strategy of bargaining—and both parties should know that and expect it (Bies & Tripp, 2012).

Managing the line between telling the truth and lying raises a related issue facing leaders every day: managing the tension between honesty versus disclosure (Bies, 2013a). For example, one can be honest and tell the truth, but not disclose all the facts, as a strategy for blame management (Bies, 2013b). Yet, for those receiving bad news, the failure to disclose all the facts may be viewed as deception, once the truth comes to light, incurring greater anger and a sense of injustice on the part of receivers relative to telling the truth in the first place (Bies, 2010). Or, one can disclose all the facts, be blamed, incur the anger and wrath of those receiving the news, and lose legitimacy, if not one's job (Bies, 2013b). This example highlights one of the political dilemmas central to justice and leadership (Bies, 2013a).

DEROGATORY JUDGMENTS

A category of violations of the truth is *derogatory judgments* made about people by others, which refers to the lack of truthfulness and accuracy of statements and judgments about a person (Bies & Tripp, 1993), or what Feinberg (1974) refers to as *the justice of judgments*. In the legal environment, this would be called libel or slander. Let me provide illustrative examples of this category. Wrongful accusation as when one accuses another of "stealing ideas," when, in fact, that was not true, would be an example of a derogatory statement (Bies & Tripp, 1996). Similarly, a manager blaming the team for a performance failure, when it was really due to a bad decision by the manager, would be another example of a derogatory statement (Bies & Tripp, 1996). Finally, "bad-mouthing" another person to create an unfavorable image of that person, a common occurrence in organizations (Bies & Tripp, 1996), can violate one's sense of interpersonal justice (Mikula, Petri, & Tanzer, 1990). The damage created to one's reputation by a judgmental injustice creates a specific problem for the victim. Specifically, people may believe the derogatory allegations about the victim are true, when, *in fact,* they are false.

Derogatory judgments as a form of interactional injustice raises the issue of its similarity to a related behavior, *social undermining* (Duffy, Ganster, & Pagon, 2002). In their groundbreaking study, Duffy et al. (2002) define social undermining as "behavior to hinder, over time, the ability to establish and maintain positive interpersonal relationships, work-related success, and favorable reputations" (p. 332). Given that definition, a derogatory judgment that impacts one's social standing or reputation is clearly a form of social undermining—or alternatively, some social undermining behaviors are acts of interactional injustice. Although a derogatory judgment can be a one-time action, not sustaining across time, interactional justice and social undermining are conceptually related. Yet, Duffy et al. (2002), and more recent analyses (e.g., Herschovis, 2011), never make the conceptual linkage between interactional justice and social undermining, even though interactional justice perceptions have been found to mediate the impact of reactions to social undermining behavior (Duffy, Ganster, Shaw, Johnson, & Pagon, 2006).

HUMAN DIGNITY AND INTERACTIONAL JUSTICE

"R-E-S-P-E-C-T."

—*Aretha Franklin*

In the case of interactional justice, people possess a view of the self as "sacred," and a violation of that sacred self is personal and painful, resulting in an emotionally intense experience (Bies & Tripp, 2002). This sense of sacredness is at the core of human dignity (Bies, 2001; Miller, 2001). Indeed, writing about privacy, Bloustein (1964) argued that the concern for privacy follows from the assumption that an individual has an "inviolate personality . . . [and] the individual's independence, dignity and integrity" (p. 971).

As it was with truth, human dignity has been a core element for the experience of interactional (in)justice since the beginning (Bies, 2001; Bies & Moag, 1986). In this section, three violations of human dignity are identified: *disrespect, invasion of privacy*, and *exposure to personal danger*.

DISRESPECT

As the first category of violations, people are concerned about a variety of forms of *disrespect*, which are actions that demean or devalue the worth of an individual. Respect refers to the signs and symbols conveying respect for the intrinsic value or worth of the individual, or what Grover (2014) refers to as *recognition respect*. At a fundamental level, the quality of the interpersonal treatment accorded by one person to another can have an impact on one's self-identity (Steele, 1988) and self-esteem (Grover,2014).

When interpersonal treatment conveys disrespect, it should arouse the sense of injustice (Bies & Moag, 1986; Lind & Tyler, 1988; Tyler & Lind, 1992). Several studies support this line of reasoning and identify a variety of forms of disrespect: *inconsiderate actions* and *abusive words or actions*.

INCONSIDERATE ACTIONS

On a fundamental level, people have minimal expectations for considerate treatment as core to their concerns of interactional justice (Bies & Moag, 1986; Tyler & Bies, 1990). In a work setting, one important sign of respect to the dignity of the person is *timely feedback* (Bies & Moag, 1986). When people have to wait an undue amount of time for a response, they feel unfairly treated (Bies, 2013b). Similarly, people expect to *receive an explanation or account* of decisions made that affect them, and, when they fail to receive such information, they feel unfairly treated (Bies, 1987; Bies & Moag, 1986).

ABUSIVE WORDS OR ACTIONS

What people say or do, and the manner in which they do it (e.g., abusively), can signal disrespect, thus arousing the sense of injustice (Bies & Tripp, 1996, 1999; Mikula et al., 1990). One example of such disrespect is *rudeness* (Bies & Moag, 1986; Katz, Gutek, Kahn & Barton, 1975; Mikula et al., 1990). For example, Bies and Moag (1986) found job candidates angry and resentful at interviewers who would interrupt their answers to questions or take phone calls in the middle of the interview. Similarly, in a study of service agency clients, Katz et al. (1975) found that clients were angry and resentful at bureaucratic officials who were impolite and rude.

Rudeness as a form of interactional injustice raises the issue of its similarity to a related behavior, *workplace incivility* (Anderssen & Pearson, 1999). Anderssen and Peasrson (1999) define workplace incivility as "low-intensity deviant behavior with ambiguous intent to harm the target, in violation of workplace norms for mutual respect. Uncivil behaviors are characteristically rude and discourteous, displaying a lack of regard for others" (p. 457). That definition is very similar to my analysis of respect and rudeness in Bies and Moag (1986). Yet, Anderssen and Pearson never compare or distinguish workplace incivility from interactional justice, even though they conceptualize interactional justice as a starting point in the incivility spiral (Anderssen & Pearson, 1999, p. 458). More recently, however, Caza and Cortina (2007) found justice perceptions to be a key mediator variable on the impact of workplace incivility. In addition, Cortina (2008) has conceptualized workplace incivility in justice terms.

Public criticism and beratment have also been identified as forms of abusive words and actions that can arouse the sense of injustice (Baron, 1988; Bies & Tripp, 1996, 1999; Hornstein, 1996). This is particularly true in the case of the boss-subordinate relationship. For example, in a study of abusive bosses (Bies & Tripp, 1999), one manager reported that his boss had a "Dr. Jeckyll and Mr. Hyde" personality. This meant that in one moment the boss could be very calm, peaceful, and satisfied; but then, without any warning, the boss would erupt into a loud, angry, temper tantrum, a public tirade directed at one or all employees.

Related to public criticism and beratement, abusive treatment may take the form of *actions intended to embarrass and humiliate a person publicly* (Bies & Tripp, 1996, 1999; Glass & Singer 1972; Mikula et al., 1990). For example, Glass and Singer (1972) reported the results of a laboratory study in which people felt unfairly treated when they were unduly embarrassed or humiliated by a "bureaucratic administrator" who acted in an arrogant manner. Bies and Tripp (1999) report about one boss who brought the whole department together and singled out one employee for poor performance in "harsh" and "angry" terms, even making "fun" of the employee's lack of skills and abilities. According to the employee, he felt he had "lost face," and felt "belittled and degraded" and "emotionally scarred" as a result of this attack.

Public criticism, beratement, and humiliation as forms of interactional injustice raise the issue of the similarity of interactional justice to a related construct, *abusive supervision* (Tepper, 2000). Previously, I have argued that acts of abusive supervision are, in fact, acts of interactional injustice (Bies, 2001). Tepper and others are now aligning with that view in varying degrees. For example, in Tepper's (2007) emergent model of abusive supervision, subordinate perceptions of injustice play a key moderator role in reactions to abusive supervision. Further, Ayree, Chen, Sun, and Debrah (2007) found subordinates' perceptions of interactional injustice fully mediate the relationship between abusive supervision and work outcomes.

Prejudicial statements, as in racist and sexist statements, convey disrespect, arousing the sense of injustice (Bies & Moag, 1986). Similarly, being the target of *insults* can arouse the sense of injustice (Bies & Tripp, 1996, 1999). Insults on a personal level typically involved name-calling, as in questioning the person's intellectual capacities by referring to the employee as a moron, or in challenging a male employee's lack of assertiveness by stating that he was a "wimp, probably had no balls." Insults also included sexist and racist remarks targeted at women and African-Americans (Bies & Tripp, 1996).

INVASION OF PRIVACY

A second category of actions involves *invasion of privacy*, which refers to the unwarranted disclosure of personal information about one person to another. Research on privacy (Stone & Stone, 1990) and self-disclosure (Derlega & Berg, 1987; Jourard, 1966) make it clear that people have a part of their selves that they want kept hidden or private from others. When the "hidden self" (Bies, 1996) is invaded, the violation should arouse the sense of injustice. Several studies support this line of reasoning.

The *disclosure of confidences and secrets* is a common form of invasion of privacy in organizations (Bies & Tripp, 1996; Morrill, 1995) and everyday life (Mikula, 1986; Mikula et al., 1990). Bies and Tripp (1996) report that regardless of whether it be disclosing a subordinate's private matter that was supposed to be held in confidence by the boss—or a co-worker who received secret information disclosed by another, but used it to his own advantage—such an action was viewed as a "fundamental betrayal" and "a knife in the back," resulting in what one person described as "not just a splintering, but a shattering of trust." (p. 251)

Research on privacy suggests a similar response to the unwarranted disclosure of personal information (Bies, 1993, 1996). For example, Woodman et al. (1982) and Tolchinsky et al. (1981) found that employees were much more concerned about the disclosure of personal information to parties outside the organization than about disclosure of the same information for internal uses of the organization. However, when people give permission for disclosure of information, then the sense of injustice is less likely aroused (Fusiler & Hoyer, 1980; Tolchinsky et al., 1981).

The *asking of improper questions* is also viewed as an invasion of privacy. For example, in a study of corporate recruiting practices, Bies and Moag (1986) found that respondents were very upset with questions about marital status or whether the job candidate was thinking about having children.

The view of privacy as information control is not just limited to the relevancy of information for a specific decision or whether the individual authorized the disclosure of information. In addition, as Schein (1977) argues, one must consider the psychological impact of information-gathering procedures on the individual. That is, if the procedure is too psychologically *intrusive* or *invasive* to the individual, such information gathering may be perceived as invasion of privacy.

Two studies support this line of reasoning. Stone, O'Brien, & Bommer (1989) found individuals were more likely to accept a job offer if job applicants were not directly monitored when providing a urine sample for drug testing. In a survey of private and public sector employees by Le Roy (1990), over 75% of respondents reported acceptance of drug testing in the work place "*under controlled conditions where the individual's privacy is protected*" (p. 167, emphasis added).

The relationship between intrusiveness and invasion of privacy has also been studied in the context of computer monitoring and electronic workplace surveillance. For example, Alder and Ambrose (2005b) propose a model identifying interpersonal justice and procedural justice as key factors shaping individual reactions to computer monitoring. Alder and Ambrose (2005a) provide empirical corroboration of that model. In another empirical study, Alge (2001) found that employee participation reduced the perceived invasion of electronic workplace surveillance and enhanced perceptions of procedural justice. Alge, Greenberg, and Brinsfield (2006) present a model that integrates organizational justice, information privacy, and social identity as variables that can explain individual reactions to organizational monitoring.

EXPOSURE TO PERSONAL DANGER

A third category of actions that people are concerned about involves exposure to personal danger, which refers to violations of one's psychological and/or physical safety (Kahn, 1990). Research suggests that when management practices impose undue psychological or physical pain, such actions are viewed as unjust. For example, job candidates in the Bies and Moag (1986) study viewed "*stress interviews*" as unfair because of the psychological pain and physiological stress they experienced during those types of interactions with recruiters.

Bies and Tripp (1999) reported about people expressing fear of working for "petty tyrants" and abusive bosses. They couldn't sleep at night. They felt terrorized. They were afraid of physical violence from their bosses. Abusive bosses create psychological and physical consequences for people (Tepper, 2000).

Recent examples from Bangladesh and China suggest that exposure to personal danger can often result in the loss of lives. Poor working conditions in factories in Bangladesh and China expose people to real danger. It raises the interactional justice issues of human dignity and human rights (Bies & Greenberg, 2001). Working conditions that create exposure to personal danger adds another dimension to psychological safety (Kahn, 1990), and it represents another new direction for research on interactional justice.

Summary and Implications

In this section, I have argued that the core properties of interactional justice are truth and human dignity. From these two properties, I identified a broader array of interactional justice violations that justice researchers should think about. In the case of truth, the focus of analysis for interactional justice violations was broadened to include deception and derogatory judgments. In the case of human dignity, the focus of analysis of interactional justice violations was broadened to include disrespect, invasion of privacy, and exposure to personal danger. I summarized empirical research findings that support this broader focus of analysis for researchers to consider and study empirically in the future.

For justice researchers, this broader focus of analysis raises new empirical questions about the relationship of these new interactional justice violations and their relationships to procedural justice and distributive justice factors, which should also stimulate new empirical studies. For example, procedural and distributive justice variables surround such violations as derogatory judgments, invasion of privacy, and exposure to personal danger. In addition, interactional justice violations such as deception, disrespect, and invasion of privacy may grow in frequency and importance in the 21st-century workplace, one in which virtual teams, cross-cultural work teams, and electronic-mediated communication have become the "new normal" (Bies & Tripp, 2012).

But there is a more fundamental implication that follows from the present analysis. That being, the analysis of interactional justice cannot be limited only to the *exchange* context with specific organizational decision-making procedures and outcomes in a hierarchical boss-subordinate relationship. What the present analysis clearly illustrates is that interactional justice concerns are raised by people in their everyday *encounters* in organizations (Bies, 2001). Interactional justice should be analyzed and studied in the encounter, not just the exchange.

Indeed, as the evidence reviewed in this chapter suggests, people raise interactional justice concerns about bad-mouthing, disclosure of confidences and secrets, and exposure to personal danger—and such concerns often have nothing to do with a specific decision or resource allocation

(Bies, 2001). Similarly, interactional justice concerns are raised in the use of insults (Cropanzano & Ambrose, 2001; Miller, 2001) and working environments that are oppressive and inhumane (Bies & Greenberg, 2001). In the eyes of the victim, all these interpersonal actions are viewed as *harmful* and *wrong*, the bases for feeling unjustly treated (Bies, 2001, 2005).

The argument for the encounter perspective is not new (Bies, 2001; see also Cropanzano, Byrne, Bobocel, & Rupp, 2001). Over 15 years ago, Mikula et al. (1990) advanced a similar argument when they analyzed the controversy over status of interactional justice relative to procedural justice. From that analysis, Mikula et al. (1990) concluded that "the results of the present and the Messick et al. (1985) studies suggest a broader concept of interpersonal treatment which goes beyond situations of judgement and decision-making includes all kinds of interactions and encounters. (p. 143)." Similarly, in their groundbreaking theory of procedural justice, Lind and Tyler (1988, p. 214) proposed that procedural justice effects might also occur in *routine social interaction* (emphasis added), thus linking procedural justice concerns to encounters.

In sum, going forward, justice researchers should broaden the focus of analysis to include everyday encounters, not just more formal exchange and decision-making processes in organizations. This means that interactional justice is not limited to the boss-subordinate relationship (Bies, 2001); indeed, it may involve a peer-to-peer interaction or an employee–customer encounter (Tripp & Bies, this volume). To fully embrace the encounter perspective will lead justice researchers to more fully realize the richness of interactional justice as a construct.

The Future of Interactional Justice: Concluding Thoughts and Questions

If past is prologue, then the future of interactional justice is, indeed, quite bright. As this chapter reveals, over 25 years of empirical studies and conceptual refinement has resulted in a burgeoning volume of research that demonstrates the uniqueness and importance of interactional justice as a construct. Interactional justice has proved to be a useful construct for understanding and analyzing justice dynamics in a variety of organizational domains and processes.

To close, I want to pose three questions that came to me in my writing of this chapter. I will not attempt to fully answer these questions, because that is outside of the scope of this chapter, as I understand it. Rather, my intent is to provoke with these questions, to provoke others—and myself—to reflection and action. What follows are the three questions, and my initial "answers" for each of the queries.

Question 1: What are the similarities and differences between interactional justice and related constructs?

Throughout the chapter, I raised the issue about the similarities between interactional justice and related constructs such as workplace incivility, social undermining, and abusive supervision. And at each time I raised this issue, I noted that acts of interactional injustice were also examples of behaviors associated with each of those constructs (or, should I say, examples of behaviors associated with workplace incivility, social undermining, and abusive supervision are acts of interactional injustice?). One need only look at Table 1 in the analysis by Hershcovis (2011, p. 502) in which she describes related constructs such as workplace incivility, social undermining, and abusive supervision with sample items used to measure each construct. Even a cursory review reveals that many, if not most, of those items are acts of interactional justice. Yet, neither the Herschcovis analysis, or Tepper's (2007) comparative analysis of the same constructs, includes interactional justice as a relevant construct for comparison. Such an analysis seems warranted and important for the field.

Question 2: What are the emotions of injustice, and how do they shape justice dynamics?

Emotions are at the heart of the experience of injustice (Bies, 2001), and, indeed, all injustice is painful (Bies & Tripp, 2002). Yet, for the most part, our understanding and analysis of the emotions of injustice begin and end with anger (Tripp & Bies, this volume). Clearly, more sophisticated modeling of the emotions of injustice is warranted (Cropanzano, Stein, & Nadisic, 2010).

Such modeling can begin with a qualitative analysis of "narratives of injustice" (Shreve & Shreve, 1997), an approach that has led Tom Tripp and me to conduct several qualitative studies of narrative of injustice. What we find is that the emotions of injustice have a variety of facets including intensity, tyrannical quality, and enduring in nature (see Tripp & Bies, 2009, for a summary of these findings).

More recent analyses hold great promise for the study of emotions. For example, Barclay and Whiteside (2011) provide a useful conceptual map to analyze the experience and intensity of the emotions of injustice. I have great excitement for the neuroscience approaches and models to analyze the emotions of injustice (Becker, Cropanzano, & Sanfey, 2011). I would urge other scholars follow the guidance provided in each of those analyses.

Question 3: Why do people treat others unfairly?

A question that has always fascinated me is why to do people treat others unfairly? This question was "top of mind" for me while writing this chapter. Yet, as a field, we really have not come to terms with answering that question, which raises the question about why?

True, there are those who have addressed this question in the positive form—why people behave and treat others fairly. In other words, let's examine "justice as a dependent variable" (Folger & Skarlicki, 2001). A good starting point for this analysis is a chapter by Ambrose and Schminke (2009) on a model of fair behavior in organizations. As further guidance in answering why people behave and treat others in an interactionally fair manner, I direct you to the work done by a handful of researchers (Korsgaard, Roberson, & Rymph, 1998; Masterson, Byrne, & Mao, 2005; Patient & Skarlicki, 2005, 2010; Scott, Colquitt, & Zapata-Phelan, 2007).

But my third question is a different one than that addressed by the researchers just named. I am interested in why people treat others *badly*, and often so intentionally (Tripp & Bies, 2009). Intentionally harming another person is an act of aggression (Anderson & Bushman, 2002), and an act of injustice is construed as an act of aggression or emotional violence (Bies, 2001).

The conceptualization of an act of injustice as an act of aggression may be new to the organizational justice literature, but it is not new to social and legal analyses of justice. For example, the influential legal theorist, Edmond Cahn (1949), articulates this perspective more eloquently in his seminal book, *The Sense of Injustice*. In the book, Cahn poses the question: "Why do we speak of the 'sense of injustice' rather than the 'sense of justice'?" (p. 13). He responds with the answer: "Because 'justice' has been so beclouded by natural-law writings that is almost inevitably brings to mind some ideal relation or static condition or set of perceptual standards, while we are concerned, on the contrary, with what is active, vital, and experiential in the reactions of human beings." (p. 13). Cahn (1949) defines the sense of injustice as "the sympathetic reaction of outrage, horror, shock, resentment, and anger, those affections of the viscera and abnormal secretions of the adrenals that prepare the human animal to resist attack. Nature has thus equipped all men to regard injustice to another as personal aggression" (p. 24).

Note the similarity of Cahn's conceptualization of injustice as an act of aggression with the basic definition of human aggression found in the psychology literature. For example, in their chapter in the *Annual Review of Psychology*, Anderson and Bushman (2002) define human aggression as "any behavior directed toward another individual that is carried out with the *proximate* (immediate) intent to cause harm. In addition, the perpetrator must believe that the behavior will harm the target, and that the target is motivated to avoid the behavior" (p. 28).

To view an act of injustice as an act of aggression opens up new theoretical and empirical questions. For example, what is the psychological profile of those who perpetrate acts of injustice, and do so consistently (Bies & Whiteside, 2013)? People who engage in acts of injustice consistently, often done in an organization structure and culture that either ignores or condones such behavior (Scott, 1988; Scott & Hart, 1979, 1989), raises a larger question for the field: should we not view injustice as part of evil in organizations (Bies & Fox, 2013; Fox & Bies, 2013)? Reframing injustice as part of evil in organizations may be unsettling for many; but, such a reconceptualization of injustice will raise new questions for justice scholars, which is the primary objective of good theory building (Lakatos, 1971).

Final Thought

This chapter is grounded in the fundamental belief and value that individuals possess certain innate and inalienable rights that we ascribe them because they are human beings. For those of us who adopt this view, our role will be that of a social critic: on the margin, not in the mainstream, motivated by what Beaney (1966) calls "a never-ending quest to increase the respect of all . . . for the essential values of human life" (p. 271). It is to this quest, that I invite one and all.

References

Adams, J. S. (1965). Inequity in social exchange. In L. Berkowitz (Ed.), *Advances in experimental social psychology* (Vol. 2, pp. 267–299). New York, NY: Academic Press.

Alder, G. S., & Ambrose, M. L. (2005a). An examination of the effect of computerized performance monitoring feedback on monitoring fairness, performance, and satisfaction. *Organizational Behavior and Human Decision Processes, 97,* 161–177.

Alder, G. S., & Ambrose, M. L. (2005b). Towards understanding fairness judgments associated with computer performance monitoring: An integration of the feedback, justice, and monitoring research. *Human Resource Management Review, 15,* 43–67.

Alge, B. J. (2001). Effects of computer surveillance on perceptions of privacy and procedural justice. *Journal of Applied Psychology, 86,* 797.

Alge, B. J., Greenberg, J., & Brinsfield, C. T. (2006). An identity-based model of organizational monitoring: Integrating information privacy and organizational justice. *Research in Personnel and Human Resources Management, 25,* 71–135.

Ambrose, M. L., & Alder, G. S. (2000). Designing, implementing, and utilizing computerized performance monitoring: Enhancing organizational justice. *Research in personnel and human resources management, 18,* 187–220.

Ambrose, M. L., & Schminke, M. (2003). Organization structure as a moderator of the relationship between procedural justice, interactional justice, perceived organizational support, and supervisory trust. *Journal of Applied Psychology, 88,* 295–305.

Ambrose, M. L., & Schminke, M. (2009). Assessing roadblocks to justice: A model of fair behavior in organizations. *Research in personnel and human resources management, 28,* 219–263.

Ambrose, M. L., Seabright, M. A., & Schminke, M. (2002). Sabotage in the workplace: The role of organizational injustice. *Organizational Behavior and Human Decision Processes, 89,* 947–965.

Anderson, C. A., & Bushman, B. J. (2002). Human aggression. *Annual Review of Psychology, 53,* 27–51.

Andersson, L. M., & Pearson, C. M. (1999). Tit for tat? The spiraling effect of incivility in the workplace. *Academy of Management Review, 24,* 452–471.

Anton, R. J. (1990). Drawing the line: An exploratory test of ethical behavior in negotiations. *International Journal of Conflict Management, 1,* 265–280.

Aquino, K., Galperin, B. L. and Bennett, R. J. (2004). Social status and aggressiveness as moderators of the relationship between interactional justice and workplace deviance. *Journal of Applied Social Psychology, 34,* 1001–1029.

Aquino, K., Lewis, M. U., & Bradfield, M. (1999). Justice constructs, negative affectivity, and employee deviance: A proposed model and empirical test. *Journal of Organizational Behavior, 20,* 1073–1091.

Ariño, A., & Ring, P. S. (2010). The role of fairness in alliance formation. *Strategic Management Journal, 31,* 1054–1087.

Aryee, S., Budhwar, P. S., & Chen, Z. X. (2002). Trust as a mediator of the relationship between organizational justice and work outcomes: Test of a social exchange model. *Journal of organizational Behavior, 23,* 267–285.

Aryee, S., Chen, Z. X., Sun, L. Y., & Debrah, Y. A. (2007). Antecedents and outcomes of abusive supervision: Test of a trickle-down model. *Journal of Applied Psychology, 92,* 191.

Barclay, L. J., & Whiteside, D. B. (2011). Moving beyond justice perceptions: The role of experience and intensity. In S. W. Gilliland, D. D. Steiner, & D. P. Skarlicki (Eds.), *Research in social issues in management, Volume 7: Emerging perspectives on organizational justice and ethics* (pp. 49–74). Greenwich, CT: Information Age Publishing.

Baron, R. A. (1990). Countering the effects of destructive criticism: The relative efficacy of four interventions. *Journal of Applied Psychology, 75,* 235–245.

Baron, R. A. (1988). Negative effects of destructive criticism: Impact on conflict, self-efficacy, and task performance. *Journal of Applied Psychology, 73,* 199–207.

Barling, J., & Phillips, M. (1993). Interactional, formal, and distributive justice in the workplace: An exploratory study. *Journal of Psychology, 127,* 649–656.

Beaney, W. M. (1966). The right to privacy and American Law. *Law and Contemporary Problems, 31,* 253–271.

Becker, W. J., Cropanzano, R., & Sanfey, A. G. (2011). Organizational neuroscience: Taking organizational theory inside the neural black box. *Journal of Management, 37,* 933–961.

Bennett, N., Martin, C. L., Bies, R. J., & Brockner, J. (1995). Coping with a layoff: A longitudinal study of victims. *Journal of Management, 21,* 1025–1040.

Beugre, C. D., & Baron, R. A. (2001). Perceptions of systemic justice: The effects of distributive, procedural, and interactional justice. *Journal of Applied Social Psychology, 31,* 324–339.

Bies, R. J. (1987). The predicament of injustice: The management of moral outrage. In L. L. Cummings & B. M. Staw (Eds.), *Research in organizational behavior* (Vol. 9, pp. 289–319). Greenwich, CT: JAI Press.

Bies, R. J. (1993). Privacy and procedural justice in organizations. *Social Justice Research, 6,* 69–86.

Bies, R. J. (1996). Beyond the hidden self: Psychological and ethical aspects of privacy in organizations. In D. Messick & A. Tenbrunsel (Ed.), *Codes of conduct: Behavioral research into business ethics* (pp. 104–116). New York, NY: Russell Sage Foundation.

Bies, R. J. (2001). Interactional (in)justice: The sacred and the profane. In J. Greenberg & R. Cropanzano (Eds.), *Advances in organizational justice* (pp. 89–118). Palo Alto: Stanford University Press.

Bies, R. J. (2005). Are procedural justice and interactional justice conceptually distinct? In J. Greenberg & J. A. Colquitt (Eds.), *Handbook of organizational justice* (pp. 85–112). Mahwah, NJ: Erlbaum.

Bies, R. J. (2010, April). Leading change in the era of bad news: Dealing with anger, distrust, and revenge in the workplace. Paper presented at the ProSci Global Conference, Las Vegas, NV.

Bies, R. J. (2013a). The delivery of bad news in organizations: A framework for analysis. *Journal of Management, 39,* 136–162.

Bies, R. J. (2013b). The manager as intuitive politician: Blame management in the delivery of bad news. Working paper no. 10–108, Georgetown University, McDonough School of Business, Washington, D.C.

Bies, R. J., & Fox, M. (2013). On the nature of evil in organizations. Unpublished manuscript.

Bies, R. J., & Greenberg, J. (2001). Justice, culture, and corporate image: The swoosh, the sweatshops, and the sway of public opinion. In M. Gannon & K. Newman (Eds.),

Handbook of cross-cultural management (pp. 320–334). Oxford, UK: Blackwell.

Bies, R. J., Martin, C. L., & Brockner, J. (1993). Just laid off, but still a "good citizen"? Only if the process is fair. *Employee Responsibilities and Rights Journal, 6*, 227–238.

Bies, R. J., & Moag, J. S. (1986). Interactional justice: Communication criteria of fairness. In R. J. Lewicki, B. H. Sheppard, & M. H. Bazerman (Eds.), *Research on negotiation in organizations* (pp. 43–55). Greenwich, CT: JAI Press.

Bies, R. J., & Shapiro, D. L. (1987). Interactional fairness judgments: The influence of causal accounts. *Social Justice Research, 1*, 199–218.

Bies, R. J., & Shapiro, D. L. (1988). Voice and justification: Their influence on procedural fairness judgments. *Academy of Management Journal, 31*, 676–685.

Bies, R. J., Shapiro, D. L., & Cummings, L. L. (1988). Causal accounts and managing organizational conflict: Is it enough to say it's not my fault? *Communication Research, 15*, 381–399.

Bies, R. J., & Tripp, T. M. (1993). Employee-initiated defamation lawsuits: Organizational responses and dilemmas. *Employee Responsibilities and Rights Journal, 6*, 313–324.

Bies, R. J., & Tripp, T. M. (1996). Beyond distrust: "Getting even" and the need for revenge. In R. M. Kramer and T. Tyler (Eds.), *Trust in organizations* (pp. 246–260). Newbury Park, CA: Sage Publications.

Bies, R. J., & Tripp, T. M. (1999). Two faces of the powerless: Coping with tyranny. In R. M. Kramer & M. A. Neale (Eds.), *Power and influence in organizations.* Thousand Oaks, CA: Sage Publications.

Bies, R. J., & Tripp, T. M. (2002). Hot flashes, open wounds: Injustice and the tyranny of its emotions. In S. Gilliland, D. Steiner, and D Skarlicki (Eds.), *Emerging perspectives on managing organizational justice* (pp. 203–223). Greenwich, CT: IAP Press.

Bies, R. J., & Tripp, T. M. (2012). Negotiating the peace in the face of modern distrust: Dealing with anger and revenge in the 21st century workplace. In B. Goldman & D. L. Shapiro (Eds.), *The psychology of negotiation in the 21st century workplace* (pp. 181–210). New York, NY: Psychology Press/ Routledge.

Bies, R. J., Tripp, T. M., & Neale, M. A. (1993). Procedural fairness and profit seeking: The perceived legitimacy of market exploitation. *Journal of Behavioral Decision Making, 6*, 243–256.

Bies, R. J., & Tyler, T. (1993). The "litigation mentality" in organizations: A test of alternative psychological explanations. *Organization Science, 4*, 352–366.

Bies, R. J., & Whiteside, D. B. (2013). Addicted to injustice: The psychological DNA of abusive bosses. Unpublished manuscript.

Blodgett, J. G., Hill, D. J., & Tax, S. S. (1997). The effects of distributive, procedural, and interactional justice on postcomplaint behavior. *Journal of Retailing, 73*, 185–210.

Blodgett, J. G., & Tax, S. S. (1993). The effects of distributive and interactional justice on complainants' repatronage intentions and negative word-of-mouth intentions. *Journal of Consumer Satisfaction, Dissatisfaction and Complaining Behavior, 6*, 100–110.

Bloustein, E. J. (1964). Privacy as an aspect of human dignity: An answer to Dean Prosser. *New York University Law Review, 39*, 962–1007.

Bobocel, D. R., Agar, S. E., Meyer, J. P., & Irving, P. G. (1998). Managerial accounts and fairness perceptions in conflict resolution: Differentiating the effects of minimizing responsibility and providing justification. *Basic and Applied Social Psychology, 20*, 133–143.

Bottom, W. P., Gibson, K., Daniels, S. E., & Murnighan, J. K. (2002). When talk is not cheap: Substantive penance and expressions of intent in rebuilding cooperation. *Organization Science, 13*, 497–513.

Brockner, J., DeWitt, R. L., Grover, S., & Reed, T. (1990). When is it especially important to explain why: Factors affecting the relationship between managers' explanations of a layoff and survivors' reactions to the layoff. *Journal of Experimental Social Psychology, 26*, 389–407.

Cahn, E. (1949). *The sense of injustice.* New York: New York University Press.

Caza, B. B., & Cortina, L. M. (2007). From insult to injury: Explaining the impact of incivility. *Basic and Applied Social Psychology, 29*, 335–350.

Chebat, J. C., & Slusarczyk, W. (2005). How emotions mediate the effects of perceived justice on loyalty in service recovery situations: an empirical study. *Journal of Business Research, 58*, 664–673.

Chory-Assad, R. M., & Paulsel, M. L. (2004). Antisocial classroom communication: Instructor influence and interactional justice as predictors of student aggression. *Communication Quarterly, 52*, 98–114.

Clemmer, E. C. (1993). An investigation into the relationship of fairness and customer satisfaction with services. In R. Cropanzano (Ed.), *Justice in the workplace: Approaching fairness in human resource management* (pp. 193–207). Hillsdale, NJ: Erlbaum.

Cobb, A. T., Wooten, K. C., & Folger, R. (1995). Justice in the making: Toward understanding the theory and practice of justice in organizational change and development. In W. A. Pasmore & R. W. Woodman (Eds.), *Research in organizational change and development* (pp. 243–295). Greenwich, CT: JAI Press.

Cobb, A. T., Vest, M., & Hills, F. (1997). Who delivers justice? Source perceptions of procedural fairness. *Journal of Applied Social Psychology, 27*, 1021–1040.

Cohen-Charash, Y., & Spector, P. E. (2001). The role of justice in organizations: A meta-analysis. *Organizational Behavior and Human Decision Processes, 86*, 278–324.

Collie, T. T., Bradley, G., & Sparks, B. A. (2002). Fair process revisited: Differential effects of interactional and procedural justice in the presence of social comparison information. *Journal of Experimental Social Psychology, 38*, 545–555.

Collie, T. A., Sparks, B., & Bradley, G. (2000). Investing in interactional justice: A study of the fair process effect within a hospitality failure context. *Journal of Hospitality & Tourism Research, 24*, 448–472

Colquitt, J. A. (2001). On the dimensionality of organizational justice: A construct validation of a measure. *Journal of Applied Psychology, 86*, 386–400.

Colquitt, J. A., Conlon, D. E., Wesson, M. J., Porter, C., & Ng, K. Y. (2001). Justice at the millennium: A meta-analytic review of 25 years of organizational justice research. *Journal of Applied Psychology, 86*, 425–445.

Colquitt, J. A., Scott, B. A., Rodell, J. B., Long, D. M., Zapata, C. P., Conlon, D. E., & Wesson, M. J. (2013). Justice at the millennium, a decade later: A meta-analytic test of social

exchange and affect-based perspectives. *Journal of Applied Psychology, 98*, 199–236.
Conlon, D. E., & Murray, N. M. (1996). Customer perceptions of corporate responses to product complaints. *Academy of Management Journal, 39*, 1040–1056.
Cortina, L. M. (2008). Unseen injustice: Incivility as modern discrimination in organizations. *Academy of Management Review, 33*, 55–75.
Cortina, L. M., Magley, V. J., Williams, J. H., & Langhout, R. D. (2001). Incivility in the workplace: Incidence and impact. *Journal of Occupational Health Psychology, 6*, 64–80.
Cropanzano, R., & Ambrose, M. L. (2001). Procedural and distributive justice are more similar than you think: A monistic perspective and a research agenda. In J. Greenberg & R. Cropanzano (Eds.), *Advances in organizational justice* (pp. 119–151). Palo Alto: Stanford University Press.
Cropanzano, R., Bowen, D. E., & Gilliland, S. W. (2007). The management of organizational justice. *The Academy of Management Perspectives, 21*, 34–48.
Cropanzano, R., Byrne, Z. S., Bobocel, D. R., & Rupp, D. E. (2001). Moral virtues, fairness heuristics, social entities, and other denizens of organizational justice. *Journal of Vocational Behavior, 58*, 164–209.
Cropanzano, R., Goldman, B., & Folger, R. (2003). Deontic justice: The role of moral principles in workplace fairness. *Journal of Organizational Behavior, 24*, 1019–1024.
Cropanzano, R., Prehar, C. A., & Chen, P. Y. (2002). Using social exchange theory to distinguish procedural from interactional justice. *Group & Organization Management, 27*, 324–351.
Cropanzano, R., Stein, J. H., & Nadisic, T. (2010). *Social justice and the experience of emotion*. New York, NY: Routledge.
Crosby, F. (1976). A model of egoistic relative deprivation. *Psychological Review, 83*, 85–113.
Crosby, F. (1984). Relative deprivation in organizational settings. In B. M. Staw & L. L. Cummings (Eds.), *Research in organizational behavior* (Vol. 6, pp. 51–93). Greenwich, CT: JAI Press.
Culnan, M. J., & Bies, R. J. (2003). Consumer privacy: Balancing economic and justice considerations. *Journal of Social Issues, 59*, 323–342.
Daly, J. P. (1991). The effects of anger on negotiation in mergers and acquisitions. *Negotiation Journal, 7*, 31–39.
Daly, J. P. (1995). Explaining changes to employees: The influence of justifications and change outcomes on employees' fairness judgments. *Journal of Applied Behavioral Science, 31*, 415–428.
Daly, J. P., & Geyer, P. D. (1994). The role of fairness in implementing large-scale change: Employee evaluations of process and outcome in seven facility relocations. *Journal of Organizational Behavior, 1*, 623–638.
Dayan, M., & Di Benedetto, A. (2008). Procedural and interactional justice perceptions and teamwork quality. *Journal of Business & Industrial Marketing, 23*, 566–576.
De Cremer, D., van Knippenberg, D., van Dijke, M., & Bos, A. E. (2004). How self-relevant is fair treatment? Social self-esteem moderates interactional justice effects. *Social Justice Research, 17*, 407–419.
De Lara, P. Z. M. (2006). Fear in organizations: does intimidation by formal punishment mediate the relationship between interactional justice and workplace internet deviance?. *Journal of Managerial Psychology, 21*(6), 580–592.
del Río-Lanza, A. B., Vázquez-Casielles, R., & Díaz-Martín, A. M. (2009). Satisfaction with service recovery: Perceived justice and emotional responses. *Journal of Business Research, 62*, 775–781.
Derlega, V. J., & Berg, J. H. (Eds.) (1987). *Self-disclosure: Theory, research, and therapy*. New York, NY: Plenum Press.
Dirks, K. T., & Ferrin, D. L. (2002). Trust in leadership: meta-analytic findings and implications for research and practice. *Journal of Applied Psychology, 87*, 611.
Duffy, M. K., Ganster, D. C., & Pagon, M. (2002). Social undermining in the workplace. *Academy of Management Journal, 45*, 331–351.
Duffy, M. K., Ganster, D. C., Shaw, J. D., Johnson, J. L., & Pagon, M. (2006). The social context of undermining behavior at work. *Organizational Behavior and Human Decision Processes, 101*, 105–126.
Elovainio, M., Kivimäki, M., & Helkama, K. (2001). Organizational justice evaluations, job control, and occupational strain. *Journal of Applied Psychology, 86*, 418–424.
Feinberg, J. (1974). Noncomparative justice. *The Philosophical Review, 83*, 297–338.
Folger, R., & Bies, R. J. (1989). Managerial responsibilities and procedural justice. *Employee Responsibilities and Rights Journal, 2*, 79–90.
Folger, R., & Skarlicki, D. P. (2001). Fairness as a dependent variable: Why tough times can lead to bad management. *Justice in the workplace: From theory to practice, 2*, 97–118.
Fox, M., & Bies, R. J. 2013. The greatest trick the devil ever pulled: Evil in organizational settings. Unpublished manuscript.
Fuller, J. B., & Hester, K. (2001). A closer look at the relationship between justice perceptions and union participation. *Journal of Applied Psychology, 86*, 1096–1105.
Fusilier, M. R., & Hoyer, W. D. (1980). Variables affecting perceptions of invasion of privacy in a personnel selection situation. *Journal of Applied Psychology, 65*, 623–626.
Gilliland, S. W. (1994). Effects of procedural and distributive justice on reactions to a selection system. *Journal of Applied Psychology, 79*, 691–701.
Gilliland, S. W., Groth, M., Baker, B., Dew, A. F., Polly, L., & Langdon, J. (2001). Improving applicants' reactions to rejection letters: An application of fairness theory. *Personnel Psychology, 54*, 669–703.
Glass, D. C., & Singer, J. E. (1972). Behavioral aftereffects of unpredictable and uncontrollable aversive events. *American Scientist, 60*, 457–465.
Greenberg, J. (1990). Employee theft as a reaction to underpayment: The hidden cost of pay cuts. *Journal of Applied Psychology, 75*, 561–568.
Greenberg, J. (1991). Using explanations to manage impressions for performance appraisal fairness. *Employee Responsibilities and Rights Journal, 4*, 51–60.
Greenberg, J. (1993a). Stealing in the name of justice: Informational and interpersonal moderators of theft reactions to underpayment inequity. *Organizational Behavior and Human Decision Processes, 54*, 81–103.
Greenberg, J. (1993b). The social side of fairness: Interpersonal and informational classes of organizational justice. In R. Cropanzano (Ed.), *Justice in the workplace: Approaching*

fairness in human resource management (pp. 79–103). Hillsdale, NJ: Erlbaum.
Greenberg, J. (1994). Using socially fair treatment to promote acceptance of a work site smoking ban. *Journal of Applied Psychology, 79*, 288.
Greenberg, J. (2006). Losing sleep over organizational injustice: Attenuating insomniac reactions to underpayment inequity with supervisory training in interactional justice. *Journal of Applied Psychology, 91*, 58–69.
Grover, S. L. (1993). Lying, deceit, and subterfuge: A model of dishonesty in the workplace. *Organization Science, 4*, 478–495.
Grover, S. L. (1997). Lying in organizations. In R. A. Giacalone & J. Greenberg (Eds.), *Anti-social behavior in organizations* (pp. 68–84). Thousand Oaks, CA: Sage.
Grover, S. L. (2014). Unraveling respect in organization studies. *Human Relations, 67*, 27–52.
Henle, C. A. (2005). Predicting workplace deviance from the interaction between organizational justice and personality. *Journal of Managerial Issues, 17*, 247–263.
Hershcovis, M. S. (2011). "Incivility, social undermining, bullying . . . oh my!": A call to reconcile constructs within workplace aggression research. *Journal of Organizational Behavior, 32*, 499–519.
Hershcovis, M. S., Turner, N., Barling, J., Arnold, K. A., Dupré, K. E., Inness, M., LeBlanc, M. M., & Sivanathan, N. (2007). Predicting workplace aggression: A meta-analysis. *Journal of Applied Psychology, 92*, 228.
Homans, G. C. (1958). Social behavior as exchange. *American Journal of Sociology, 63*, 597–606.
Hornstein, H. A. (1996). *Brutal bosses and their prey*. New York, NY: Riverhead Books.
Hui, M. K., Au, K., & Zhao, X. (2007). Interactional justice and the fair process effect: The role of outcome uncertainty. *Journal of Experimental Social Psychology, 43*, 210–220.
Izraeli, D. M., & Jick, T. D. (1986). The art of saying no: Linking power to culture. *Organization Studies, 7*, 171–192.
Jourard, S. M. (1966). Some psychological aspects of privacy. *Law and Contemporary Problems, 31*, 307–318.
Kahn, W. A. (1990). Psychological conditions of personal engagement and disengagement at work. *Academy of Management Journal, 33*, 692–724.
Katz, D., Gutek, B. A., Kahn, R. L., & Barton, E. (1975). *Bureaucratic encounters*. Ann Arbor, MI: Institute for Social Research.
Kernan, M. C., & Hanges, P. J. (2002). Survivor reactions to reorganization: Antecedents and consequences of procedural, interpersonal, and informational justice. *Journal of Applied Psychology, 87*, 916–928.
Kickul, J., Lester, S. W., & Finkl, J. (2002), Promise breaking during radical organizational change: do justice interventions make a difference? *Journal of Organizational Behavior, 23*, 469–488.
Konovsky, M. A., & Cropanzano, R. (1991). The perceived fairness of employee drug testing as a predictor of employee attitudes and job performance. *Journal of Applied Psychology, 76*, 698–707.
Konovsky, M. A., & Folger, R. (1991). The effects of procedures, social accounts, and benefits level on victims' layoff reactions. *Journal of Applied Social Psychology, 21*, 630–650.
Korsgaard, M. A., Roberson, L., & Rymph, R. D. (1998). What motivates fairness? The role of subordinate assertive behavior on manager's interactional fairness. *Journal of Applied Psychology, 83*, 731–744.
Kuo, Y. F., & Wu, C. M. (2012). Satisfaction and post-purchase intentions with service recovery of online shopping websites: Perspectives on perceived justice and emotions. *International Journal of Information Management, 32*, 127–138.
Kuhn, T. (1970). *The structure of scientific revolutions* (2d ed.). Chicago, IL: University of Chicago Press.
Kurland, N. B., & Egan, T. D. (1999). Telecommuting: Justice and control in the virtual organization. *Organization Science, 10*, 500–513.
Lakatos, I. (1971). Falsification and the methodology of scientific research programmes. In I. Lakatos & A. Musgrove (Eds.), *Criticism and the growth of knowledge* (pp. 91–196). Cambridge, UK: Cambridge University Press.
Laschinger, H. K. S. (2004). Hospital nurses' perceptions of respect and organizational justice. *Journal of Nursing Administration, 34*, 354–364.
LeRoy, M. H. (1990). Drug testing in the public sector: Union member attitudes. *Journal of Collective Negotiations in the Public Sector, 19*, 165–173.
Leung, K., Tong, K. K., & Ho, S. S. Y. (2004). Effects of interactional justice on egocentric bias in resource allocation decisions. *Journal of Applied Psychology, 89*, 405–415.
Leventhal, G. S. (1980). What should be done with equity theory? New approaches to the study of fairness in social relationships. In K. Gergen, M. Greenberg, & R. Willis (Eds.), *Social exchange: Advances in theory and research* (pp. 27–55). New York, NY: Plenum Press.
Lewicki, R. J., McAllister, D. M., & Bies, R. J. (1998). Trust and distrust: New relationships and realities. *Academy of Management Review, 23*, 438–458.
Lewin, K. (1935). *A dynamic theory of personality*. New York, NY: McGraw-Hill.
Lim, V. K. (2002). The IT way of loafing on the job: cyberloafing, neutralizing and organizational justice. *Journal of Organizational Behavior, 23*, 675–694.
Lind, E. A., & Tyler, T. R. (1988). *The social psychology of procedural justice*. New York, NY: Plenum.
Lu, Y. (2006). Toward the micro and macro-level consequences of interactional justice in cross-cultural joint ventures. *Human Relations, 59*, 1019–1047.
Luo, Y. (2007). The independent and interactive roles of procedural, distributive, and interactional justice in strategic alliances. *Academy of Management Journal, 50*, 644–664.
Malatesta, R. M., & Byrne, Z. S. (1997). The impact of formal and interactional procedures on organizational outcomes. In *12th Annual Conference of the Society for Industrial and Organizational Psychology*, St. Louis, MO.
Martin, J. (1981). Relative deprivation: A theory of distributive injustice for an era of shrinking resources. In L. L. Cummings & B. M. Staw (Eds.), *Research in organizational behavior* (Vol. 3, pp. 53–107). Greenwich, CT: JAI Press.
Martínez-Tur, V., Peiró, J. M., Ramos, J. and Moliner, C. (2006), Justice perceptions as predictors of customer satisfaction: The impact of distributive, procedural, and interactional justice. *Journal of Applied Social Psychology, 36*, 100–119.
Masterson, S., Byrne, Z., & Mao, H. (2005). Interpersonal and informational justice. Identifying the differential antecedents of interactional justice behaviors. In S. W. Gilliland, D. D. Steiner, D. P. Skarlicki, & K. van den Bos (Eds.),

What motivates fairness in organizations? (pp. 79–103). Charlotte, NC: Information Age Publishing.

Masterson, S. S., Lewis-McClear, K., Goldman, B. M., & Taylor, M. S. (2000). Integrating justice and social exchange: The differing effects of fair procedures and treatment on work relationships. *Academy of Management Journal, 43*, 738–748.

Maxham, J. G., III & Netemeyer, R. G. (2002). Modeling customer perceptions of complaint handling over time: the effects of perceived justice on satisfaction and intent. *Journal of Retailing, 78*, 239–252.

McLean Parks, J. (1997). The fourth arm of justice: The art and science of revenge. In R. J. Lewicki, R. J. Bies, & B. H. Sheppard (Eds.), *Research on negotiation in organizations* (Vol. 6, pp. 113–144). Greenwich, CT: JAI Press.

Messick, D. M., Bloom, S., Boldizar, J. P., Samuelson, C. D. (1985). Why we are fairer than others. *Journal of Experimental Social Psychology*, 21, 480–500.

Mikula, G. (1986). The experience of injustice: Toward a better understanding of its phenomenology. In H. W. Bierhoff, R. L. Cohen, & J. Greenberg (Eds.), *Justice in interpersonal relations* (pp. 103–123). New York, NY: Plenum Press.

Mikula, G., Petri, B., & Tanzer, N. (1990). What people regard as just and unjust: Types and structures of everyday experiences of injustice. *European Journal of Social Psychology, 20*, 133–149.

Miller, D. T. (2001). Disrespect and the experience of injustice. *Annual Review of Psychology, 52*, 527–553.

Moorman, R. H. (1991). Relationship between organizational justice and organizational citizenship behaviors: Do fairness perceptions influence employee citizenship? *Journal of Applied Psychology, 76*, 845–855.

Morrill, C. (1995). *The executive way: Conflict management in corporations*. University of Chicago Press.

Naumann, S. E., Bennett, N., Bies, R. J., & Martin, C. (1998). Laid off, but still loyal: The influence of perceived justice and organizational support. *International Journal of Conflict Management, 9*, 356–368.

Patient, D. L., & Skarlicki, D. P. (2005). Why managers don't always do the right thing when delivering bad news: The role of empathy, self-esteem, and moral development on interactional fairness. In S. W. Gilliland, D. D. Steiner, D. P. Skarlicki, & K. van den Bos (Eds.), *What motivates fairness in organizations?* (pp. 149–178). Charlotte, NC: Information Age Publishing.

Patient, D. L., & Skarlicki, D. P. (2010). Increasing interpersonal and informational justice when communicating negative news: The role of the manager's empathic concern and moral development. *Journal of Management, 36*, 555–578.

Ployhart, R. E., Ryan, A. M., & Bennett, M. (1999). Explanations for selection decisions: Applicants' reactions to informational and sensitivity features of explanations. *Journal of Applied Psychology*, 84, 87–106.

Rahim, M. A., Magner, N. R., & Shapiro, D. L. (2000). Do justice perceptions influence styles of handling conflict with the supervisor? What justice perceptions, precisely? *International Journal of Conflict Management, 11*, 9–31.

Rupp, D. E., & Bell, C. M. (2009). Extending the deontic model of justice. *Business Ethics Quarterly, 20*, 89–106.

Rupp, D. E., & Cropanzano, R. (2002). The mediating effects of social exchange relationships in predicting workplace outcomes from multifoci organizational justice. *Organizational Behavior and Human Decision Processes, 89*(1), 925–946.

Rupp, D. E., & Spencer, S. (2006). When customers lash out: the effects of customer interactional injustice on emotional labor and the mediating role of discrete emotions. *Journal of Applied Psychology, 91*, 971–978.

Schein, V. E. (1977). Individual privacy and personnel psychology: The need for a broader perspective. *Journal of Social Issues, 33*, 154–167.

Scott, B. A., Colquitt, J. A., & Zapata-Phelan, C. P. (2007). Justice as a dependent variable: Subordinate charisma as a predictor of interpersonal and informational justice perceptions. *Journal of Applied Psychology, 92*, 1597–1609.

Scott, W. G. (1988). Management governance theories of justice and liberty. *Journal of Management, 14*, 277–298.

Scott, W. G., & Hart, D. K. (1979). *Organizational America: Can individual freedom survive within the security it promises?* Boston, MA: Houghton Mifflin.

Scott, W. G., & Hart, D. K. (1989). *Organizational values in America*. New Brunswick, NJ: Transaction Publishers.

Shapiro, D. L. (1991). The effect of explanations on negative reactions to deceit. *Administrative Science Quarterly, 36*, 614–630.

Shapiro, D. L., & Bies, R. J. (1994). Threats, bluffs, and disclaimers in negotiations. *Organizational Behavior and Human Decision Processes, 60*, 14–35.

Shreve, S. R., & Shreve, P. (Eds.) (1997). *Outside the law: Narratives on justice in America*. Boston, MA: Beacon Press.

Simons, T., & Roberson, Q. (2003). Why managers should care about fairness: the effects of aggregate justice perceptions on organizational outcomes. *Journal of Applied Psychology, 88*, 432.

Sindhav, B. (2001). The role of organizational justice in managing change within marketing channels. *Journal of Marketing Channels, 9*, 65–91.

Sitkin, S. B., & Bies, R. J. (1993). Social accounts in conflict situations: On using explanations to manage conflict. *Human Relations, 46*, 349–370.

Skarlicki, D. P., & Folger, R. (1997). Retaliation in the workplace: The roles of distributive, procedural, and interactional justice. *Journal of Applied Psychology, 82*, 434–443.

Skarlicki, D. P., Folger, R., & Tesluk, P. (1999). Personality as a moderator in the relationship between fairness and retaliation. *Academy of Management Journal, 42*, 100–108.

Skarlicki, D. P., & Latham, G. P. (1996). Increasing citizenship behavior within a labor union: A test of organizational justice theory. *Journal of Applied Psychology, 81*, 161–169.

Son, J. Y., & Kim, S. S. (2008). Internet users' information privacy-protective responses: A taxonomy and a nomological model. *MIS Quarterly, 32*, 503–529.

Stecher, M. D., & Rosse, J. G. (2005). The distributive side of interactional justice: The effects of interpersonal treatment on emotional arousal. *Journal of Managerial Issues, 17*, 229–246.

Steele, C. M. (1988). The psychology of self-affirmation: Sustaining the integrity of the self. In L. Berkowitz (Ed.), *Advances in experimental social psychology* (Vol. 21, pp. 261–302). New York, NY: Academic Press.

Stone, D. L., O'Brien, J. E., & Bommer, W. (1989, June). Individuals' reactions to job applicant drug testing practices. Paper presented at the Annual Conference of the American Psychological Society, Washington, D.C.

Stone, E. F., & Stone, D. L. (1990). Privacy in organizations: Theoretical issues, research findings, and protection mechanisms. In K. M. Rowland & G. R. Ferris (Eds.), *Research in personnel and human resources management*, (Vol. 8, pp. 349–411). Greenwich, CT: JAI Press.

Sweeney, P. D., & McFarlin, D. B. (1993). Workers' evaluations of the "ends"and the "means": An examination of four models of distributive and procedural justice. *Organizational Behavior and Human Decision Processes, 55*, 23–40.

Tata, J., & Bowes-Sperry, L. (1996). Emphasis on distributive, procedural, and interactional justice: Differential perceptions of men and women. *Psychological Reports, 79*, 1327–1330.

Tepper, B. J. (2000). Consequences of abusive supervision. *Academy of Management Journal, 43*, 178–190.

Tepper, B. J. (2007). Abusive supervision in work organizations: Review, synthesis, and research agenda. *Journal of Management, 33*, 261–289.

Tekleab, A. G., Takeuchi, R., & Taylor, M. S. (2005). Extending the chain of relationships among organizational justice, social exchange, and employee reactions: The role of contract violations. *Academy of Management Journal, 48*, 146–157.

Thibaut, J. W., & Walker, L. (1975). *Procedural justice*. Hillsdale, NJ: Erlbaum.

Tolchinsky, P. D., McCuddy, M., Adams, J., Ganster, D. C., Woodman, R., & Fromkin, H. L. (1981). Employee perceptions of invasion of privacy: A field simulation experiment. *Journal of Applied Psychology, 66*, 308–313.

Tripp, T. M., & Bies, R. J. (1997). What's good about revenge? The avenger's perspective. In R. J. Lewicki, R. J. Bies, & B. H. Sheppard (Eds.), *Research on negotiation in organizations* (Vol. 6, pp. 145–160). Greenwich, CT: JAI Press.

Tripp, T. M., & Bies, R. J. (2009). *Getting even: The truth about workplace revenge—and how to stop it*. San Francisco, CA: Jossey-Bass.

Tulubas, T., & Celep, C. (2012). Effect of perceived procedural justice on faculty members' silence: The mediating role of trust in supervisor. *Procedia-Social and Behavioral Sciences, 47*, 1221–1231.

Tyler, T. R., & Bies, R. J. (1990). Beyond formal procedures: The interpersonal context of procedural justice. In J. S. Carroll (Ed.), *Applied social psychology and organizational settings* (pp. 77–98). Hillsdale, NJ: Lawrence Erlbaum Associates.

Tyler, T. R., & Lind, E. A. (1992). *A relational model of authority in groups. In* M. P. Zanna *(Ed.), Advances in experimental social psychology* (Vol. 25, pp. 115–191). New York, NY: Academic Press.

Wanberg, C. R., Gavin, M. B., & Bunce, L. W. (1999). Perceived fairness of layoffs among individuals who have been laid off: A longitudinal study. *Personnel Psychology, 52*, 59–84.

Walster, E., Walster, G., & Berscheid, E. (1978). *Equity: Theory and research*. Boston, MA: Allyn & Bacon.

Williams, S., Pitre, R., & Zainuba, M. (2002). Justice and organizational citizenship behavior intentions: Fair rewards versus fair treatment. *Journal of Social Psychology, 142*, 33–44.

Woodman, R. W., Ganster, D. C., Adams, J., McCuddy, M. C., Tolchinsky, P. D., & Fromkin, H. (1982). A survey of employee perceptions of information privacy in organizations. *Academy of Management Journal, 25*, 647–663.

Zoghbi-Manrique-de-Lara, P., Aguiar-Quintana, T., & Suárez-Acosta, M. A. (2013). A justice framework for understanding how guests react to hotel employee (mis) treatment. *Tourism Management, 36*, 143–152.

CHAPTER

5 Overall Justice: Past, Present, and Future

Maureen L. Ambrose, David X. H. Wo, *and* Matthew D. Griffith

Abstract

Although there has been some interest in overall justice for about 15 years, it is only in the last five years that scholars have begun systematic, empirical research on the construct. In this chapter, we review both theoretical and empirical work on overall justice. We begin with a review of conceptual work on overall justice and address similarities and differences in the conceptualization of the construct. Next we summarize empirical work on overall justice. We categorize this research based on its treatment of overall justice (i.e., as an antecedent, a consequence, a mediator, a moderator, and as a group-level construct). Finally, we identify strengths and weaknesses of the current research, and suggest directions for future study.

Key Words: overall justice, justice facets, overall fairness, fairness facets, overall justice climate

For the last 50 years, justice researchers have been interested in justice facets—attributes of justice that relate to the fairness of the distribution of outcomes, the procedures by which the outcomes are determined, and the fairness of the treatment individuals receive during the enactment of procedures. Indeed, as research on justice has evolved, it has been characterized by identifying and highlighting distinctions between different types of fairness (Colquitt, Zapata-Phelan, & Greenberg, 2005). This research has proven fruitful, and we have learned much about fairness in organizations and its impact on employees. Yet, after 50 years of making distinctions between justice types, the value of a more holistic approach to justice has gained a foothold in the literature. Indeed, in the last five years, researchers have begun to embrace the idea that overall justice is an important and useful construct—one that warrants attention in parallel to the vast research on justice facets.

In this chapter, we review research on overall justice.[1] We begin by addressing the arguments for examining overall justice. Next, we describe conceptual work that has suggested a more holistic approach to justice. Following the conceptual summary, we examine the empirical work on overall fairness. Specifically, we examine the role overall justice has played in the study of fairness. We examine overall justice as an antecedent, a consequence, a mediator, a moderator, and at the group-level. We conclude with some observations about current research on overall justice and thoughts for future investigations.

Why Overall Justice?

As noted earlier, research on organizational justice has been dominated by a focus on facet-specific justice judgments (distributive, procedural, interactional, interpersonal, informational). Although this research has been crucial to understanding justice in organizations, research suggests it does not fully capture the justice phenomenon (Ambrose & Schminke, 2009a; Greenberg, 2001; Lind, 2001a; Shapiro, 2001). These gaps have led to the interest in investigating overall justice.

There are several arguments for examining overall justice. First, research suggests that although individuals can distinguish between the different facets of justice when asked, they experience justice in a more holistic, Gestalt-like manner (Ambrose & Schminke, 2009a; Jones & Martens, 2009). Thus, overall justice is a better phenomenological representation of individuals' justice experience (Ambrose & Schminke, 2009a; Lind, 2001a). Second, focusing on justice facets leads to a focus on unique variance, which may underrepresent the total influence of justice in a situation (Ambrose & Arnaud, 2005; Ambrose & Schminke, 2009a). Thus, when researchers are interested in the influence of fairness in organizations, they are better served by examining overall fairness (Hauenstein, McGonigle, & Flinder, 2001). Third, researchers often make the same predictions for different justice facets (e.g., Andrews, Baker, & Hunt; 2008; DeConinck; 2010; Frazier, Johnson, Gavin, Gooty, & Snow, 2010; Holtz & Harold, 2013; Hulland, Nenkov, & Barclay, 2012). This suggests they are likely more interested in a general sense of fairness than in specific facets of fairness. That is, overall justice better represents their interests. Fourth, overall justice accounts for variance in outcomes above and beyond that accounted for by justice facets and, thus, increases predictability (Ambrose & Schminke, 2009a; Jones & Martens, 2009). Finally, as Leventhal (1980; Leventhal, Karuza, & Fry, 1980) and others (Ambrose & Schminke, 2009b; Greenberg, 2001; Lind, 2001a) indicate, justice is only one of many motivational forces that influence behavior. Studying overall justice facilitates the examination of the influence of justice relative to other motivational forces. These potential benefits have given rise to an interest in overall justice.

Overall Justice: Conceptual Research

Although empirical interest in overall justice has increased only in the last five years, the concept of overall justice has been part of the organizational fairness literature since the introduction of the construct of procedural justice. Indeed, early work on procedural justice conceptualized procedural and distributive justice as components of overall fairness. For example, Leventhal's (1980) article, "What Should Be Done with Equity Theory?," although viewed as a seminal work on procedural justice, focused on both distributive allocation rules and procedural allocation rules. This dual focus was associated with Leventhal's observation that "the perception of fairness is governed by two types of rules—distribution rules and procedural rules" (p. 53). Indeed, the Justice Judgment Model described by Leventhal and his colleagues (Leventhal, 1980; Leventhal, Karuza, & Fry, 1980) incorporated both distributive and procedural rules in the assessment of fairness. Similarly, in their seminal book on procedural justice, Lind and Tyler (1988) indicated procedural fairness "plays at least as large a role as distributive fairness in determining overall justice judgments" (p. 135). Further, in work focused on demonstrating the importance of procedural fairness, Tyler and his colleagues (Barrett-Howard & Tyler, 1986; Tyler, 1989; Tyler & Caine, 1981), referred to the relative importance of procedural fairness in predicting respondents' perceptions of the general fairness of authorities.

Although early research on procedural fairness acknowledged the construct as part of a more general fairness judgment, almost no research in more than 20 years following Thibaut and Walker's (1975) publication of *Procedural Justice: A Psychological Analysis* explicitly examined the relationship between distributive fairness, procedural fairness, and overall fairness. However, around 2000, an interest in overall justice began to emerge. Some of this interest came from researchers who noted deficiencies in the traditional justice facet approach. For example, Lind (2001b) argued "although people can certainly distinguish between different types of justice . . . the real impact of justice depends on a more overall perception of the fairness of a given relationship" (p.221). Greenberg (2001) suggested the distinction between procedural and interactional justice did not really matter. Rather, he suggests impressions of justice are likely to be "holistic," based on whatever information is available and salient. Similarly, Shapiro (2001) suggested victims of injustice are likely to be reacting to their general experience of injustice, rather than worrying if there are one, two, three, or four types of justice. In addition to these general acknowledgments of the relevance of overall justice, several researchers provided a more thorough consideration of a general fairness construct and its relationship to facet judgments (Ambrose & Arnaud, 2005; Colquitt & Shaw, 2005; Hauenstein et al., 2001; Lind, 2001a; Törnblom & Vermunt, 1999). Below we describe these conceptualizations.

Conceptualizations of Overall Justice

TOTAL FAIRNESS

The first contemporary article to explicitly address the relationship between distributive justice, procedural justice, and an overall justice judgment was Törnblom and Vermunt (1999). Törnblom and Vermunt's goal was to construct "an integrated approach to justice, wherein both the distribution of outcome and the procedure would enter as two indispensable terms in accounting for people's conceptions and experiences of justice and injustice" (p. 40). Thus, Törnblom and Vermunt developed the Total Fairness Model. Notable about the Total Fairness Model is the inclusion not only of justice facets (procedural and distributive justice—interactional justice had yet to emerge as an independent facet), but also outcome favorability. Specifically, Törnblom and Vermunt conceptualize overall justice evaluations as a function of individuals' "experiences with both distributive and procedural aspects, tempered by the valence of the outcome" (p. 43). Although some scholars have equated outcome favorability and outcome fairness (e.g., Brockner & Wiesenfeld, 1996), Törnblom and Vermunt indicate the distinction between the two constructs is important. An outcome can be fair and unfavorable (e.g., losing a promotion to a more qualified candidate), unfair and favorable (receiving an undeserved promotion), fair and favorable (receiving a deserved promotion), or unfair and unfavorable (losing a promotion to a less qualified candidate).

Törnblom and Vermunt (1999) developed a series of propositions based on the possible combinations of positive and negative assessments of procedural fairness, distributive fairness, and of the outcome. Several of these propositions warrant attention. First, Törnblom and Vermunt suggest total fairness mediates the relationship between the components of total fairness (procedural justice, distributive justice, and outcome favorability) and employee outcomes. Second, they propose eight configurations of the components that are associated with higher to lower levels of total fairness. Notable in this ranking of configurations is that fair distributions are predicted to be more strongly related to total fairness than fair procedures. Third, consistent with Fairness Heuristic Theory (described later), Törnblom and Vermunt suggest when full information is not available, people infer what is missing from the information that is available. Thus, outcome favorability may substitute for distributive or procedural fairness information. Procedural fairness information may substitute for distributive fairness information, and so on. In all, Törnblom and Vermunt conclude, "people conceive of the fairness of a situation as a Gestalt … the components of fairness—distributive fairness (DF), procedural fairness (PF), and the valence of the outcome (OV) to be allocated—are meaningful only in relation to the overall fairness of the situation" (p. 51).

FAIRNESS HEURISTIC THEORY

The most well-known conceptual treatment of overall justice comes from Fairness Heuristic Theory (Lind, 2001a; Lind, Kulik, Ambrose & de Vera Park, 1993; van den Bos, Wilke, Lind, & Vermunt, 1998). Fairness Heuristic Theory suggests individuals' fairness judgments are a proxy for interpersonal trust and serve as a heuristic to guide decisions about cooperation. In the exposition of the theory, Lind (2001a) noted:

> it is important to point out one way that my theorizing here differs both from my own previous work on justice judgments and from the conventional wisdom in social and organizational psychology about the distinctiveness of various types of justice judgments. I would argue that the fairness judgment that is used as a heuristic to decide involvement and investments in groups or organizations is an overall judgment of how fairly one has been (and will be) treated in the social context in question. (p. 68)

Lind (2001a) identified two phases relevant to the general justice judgment. In the judgmental phase, individuals rely on information from the justice facets to form the general fairness judgment. In the use phase, the general fairness judgment guides individuals' attitudes and behaviors—as well as their subsequent assessments of the justice facets.

There are several implications from Fairness Heuristic Theory for the relationship between justice facet judgments and general fairness judgments. First, as with Törnblom and Vermunt (1999), Lind (2001a) proposed missing information about one justice facet will be "filled-in" by available information about other justice facets. However, for Lind, this *substitutability effect* is the result of the general fairness judgment. Specifically, individuals form the general fairness judgment quickly, based on available information (e.g., procedural fairness). The general fairness judgment then guides subsequent assessments of justice facets for which information is missing (e.g., distributive justice). Thus, procedural fairness substitutes for distributive fairness only because it influences individuals' assessment of authorities' overall fairness. Second, Lind proposed, once formed, the general fairness judgment is assumed to be accurate and typically stable. The general fairness judgment will serve as a lens for interpreting subsequent information. Thus, information relevant to fair treatment will be interpreted in light of the existing general fairness judgment and assimilated into the existing judgment.

FACET COMPOSITE APPROACH

Hauenstein et al. (2001) provides the third article explicitly addressing the relationship between justice facets and overall justice. Hauenstein et al. conducted a meta-analysis to assess the relationship between procedural justice and distributive justice. Examining 94 correlations from 63 studies that fit their criteria, they found an estimated population correlation of 0.64 between the two constructs. Noting previous work that suggested the utility of a "simpler view" of justice (Cropanzano & Ambrose, 2001; Lind, 2001a), Hauenstein et al. concluded, "when the goal of research is to examine the variance explained by a justice construct, it appears the predictive research may be better served by using overall perceptions of organizational justice (i.e., a composite of the subcomponents of justice) as the predictor variable" (p. 49). Further, they stated, "researchers should give greater consideration to models of justice that consider general fairness perceptions to be the central causal mechanism, instead of models that focus on specific subcomponents of justice" (p. 51) and "research using justice constructs as predictors should consider using overall justice as the predictor rather than interpreting the relationship between individual components of justice and the criterion" (p. 52). Finally, it deserves mention that Hauenstein et al. are not clear on the relationship between justice facets and overall justice. Whereas they suggest assessing overall justice as a composite of the justice facets, they also state, "specific forms of justice may emanate from a perception of more general justice" (p. 51). Thus, Hauenstein et al., suggested both that facet judgments determine overall justice and that overall justice judgments determine facet judgments, a position that is implicitly consistent with Fairness Heuristic Theory.

Other Conceptualizations of Overall Fairness

EVENT JUDGMENTS AND ENTITY JUDGMENTS

Cropanzano, Byrne, Bobocel, and Rupp (2001) provided a comprehensive review of the organizational justice literature in which they identified and attempted to integrate multiple justice perspectives. In so doing, Cropanzano et al. distinguished between two types of justice judgments that had emerged in the literature: event judgments and entity judgments. As the name suggests, event judgments are fairness evaluations associated with a single event or closely related set of events (e.g., an employee's most recent performance appraisal). Entity judgments reflect fairness appraisals of social entities—a person, group, or organization. Entity judgments are reflected by assessments such as "my supervisor is fair" and "in my organization, all job decisions are applied consistently across all affected employees." That is, the assessment refers to the social entities' behavior in general.

Cropanzano et al. (2001) suggest event judgments may form the basis for entity judgments. That is, as individuals accumulate event information, they come to form an impression of the overall fairness of the entity. Notably, in their figure depicting this process (p. 191), entity judgments are specified at the level of the specific facet (e.g., social entity distributive fairness, social entity procedural fairness, social entity interactional fairness). Further, these three facet-based entity judgments predict individuals' reactions. However, in their descriptions of social entities in the text, it is clear their conceptualization of entity judgments reflects global (overall) evaluations (e.g., my supervisor is a fair person), rather than assessments of the entities fairness on a particular justice facet (e.g., my supervisor is procedurally fair).

Cropanzano et al. (2001) primarily discuss social entity judgments arising from individuals' assessments of events—a bottom-up conceptualization. However, they also note entity judgments might drive the assessment of events. Thus, like Fairness Heuristic Theory, they recognize that once individuals have an impression of an entity as fair or unfair, that impression may influence the interpretation of events.

Finally, Cropanzano et al. (2001) suggest overall fairness judgments may exist for multiple entities. Individuals may make judgments about the overall fairness of their organization, their supervisor, or their co-workers. In the Observations and Future Research section later in this chapter, we discuss the issue of multiple social entity judgments.

HANDBOOK OF ORGANIZATIONAL JUSTICE

With the publication of Greenberg and Colquitt's (2005) *Handbook of Organizational Justice*, two additional conceptualizations of overall justice emerged. In their chapter on the conceptual distinctiveness of procedural and distributive justice, Ambrose and Arnaud (2005) devoted the final section to an argument for the importance and benefit of examining overall justice. Ambrose and Arnaud noted the call from other scholars (Greenberg, 2001; Hauenstein et al., 2001; Lind, 2001a, b; Shapiro, 2001; Törnblom and Vermunt, 1999) for a consideration of a more holistic approach to fairness judgments. Observing that other literatures had balanced the interest in facets and overall judgments (e.g., job satisfaction), they argued that justice researchers' fascination with justice facets stemmed from two aspects of the literature: (1) a focus on unique (rather than total) variance, and (2) the focus on differential effects.

Ambrose and Arnaud (2005) suggested justice research would benefit from considering the total variance accounted for by justice constructs, rather than focusing on the unique variance accounted for by specific facets. Specifically, Ambrose and Arnaud argued justice research often underestimates the total impact of justice because, by focusing on unique variance, the impact of shared variance on outcomes is overlooked. The facet approach provides information about the unique impact of specific justice facets. However, given the typically high correlations between facets, it ignores the shared influence of the facets. This position is consistent with Hauenstein et al. (2001) who suggested an overall justice construct is preferable when variance explained is the goal of the research.

Ambrose and Arnaud (2005) also suggested the differential effects approach (in which different justice facets are predicted to affect different types of outcomes) was flawed as it failed to consider the relationship between justice facets as well as the relationship among the differentiated outcomes. They concluded, "there is much to be gained by focusing less on the differences between justice types, more on how these conceptually distinct forms of justice contribute to an employee's overall sense of organizational fairness, and how this overall sense of fairness 'stacks up' to other motivational forces in organizations" (p. 79).

The second chapter in the *Handbook of Organizational Justice* to address overall justice was Colquitt and Shaw's (2005) discussion of justice measurement. Colquitt and Shaw suggested two conceptualizations of overall justice: (1) as a latent construct, and (2) as a global perception. Colquitt and Shaw analyzed data from 16 independent samples that used Colquitt's (2001) measure. Colquitt and Shaw combined the four justice facet scale scores to create an overall organizational justice score. The coefficient alpha for the overall justice "scale" was 0.80. Colquitt and Shaw provided this test as an indicator of the latent construct conceptualization. However, this approach might be better described as a composite approach to overall justice. That is, the facet measures are combined to form a measure of overall justice.

Colquitt and Shaw (2005) also provided a more direct test of the latent factor conceptualization. By conducting a second-order confirmatory factor analysis based on the data from the 16 independent samples, they found a reasonable fit for the model with overall justice as a higher order latent factor. They conclude, "These kinds of results suggest that overall justice could be modeled as a higher order latent variable that drives responses to the more specific justice factors" (p.139). However, they note modeling justice as a second-order latent factor is most likely appropriate for field studies in which researchers are examining multiple events or assessing entity (i.e., supervisor, organization, co-worker) judgments.

The second approach suggested by Colquitt and Shaw (2005) characterizes most of the subsequent empirical work on overall justice. This approach is a direct assessment of overall fairness (e.g., my supervisor is a fair person; my organization is a fair one). Colquitt and Shaw indicate this direct approach reflects the general fairness perceptions discussed by Lind (2001a). Colquitt and Shaw suggest this approach is most appropriate when justice is an endogenous variable. They conclude such a direct approach, "could be used in the laboratory to assess the effects of manipulations or multiple justice dimensions on overall fairness, or could be used in the field as mediators of the relationship between indirect assessments and attitudinal and behavioral reactions" (p. 141). Further, they indicate the use of a direct measure of overall justice addresses the concerns raised by Ambrose and Arnaud (2005) regarding the shared variance of facet measures.

We should note that the conceptualizations Colquitt and Shaw (2005) provide for the relationship between overall justice and justice facets differs between their description of the latent construct and the direct measure. When discussing overall justice as a second-order latent construct, overall justice is conceptualized as Lind (2001a) does during the use phase—as driving perceptions of justice facets. Yet, when discussing a direct measure of overall justice, Colquitt and Shaw suggests it may mediate between facet measures and outcomes. This latter conceptualization is consistent with Törnblom and Vermunt (1999) as well as the judgmental phase of Fairness Heuristic Theory (Lind, 2001a).

SUMMARY

The conceptual work on overall fairness suggests different relationships between the justice facets and overall fairness. However, these different conceptualizations fall into two general categories—those that suggest the fairness components are the foundation for the general justice judgment (Ambrose & Arnaud, 2005; Colquitt & Shaw, 2005 (direct measure); Leventhal, 1980; Leventhal, Karuza, & Fry, 1980; Lind, 2001a (judgmental stage); Törnblom & Vermunt, 1999) and those that suggest general fairness judgments are the foundation for facet judgments (Lind, 2001a (use phase); Colquitt & Shaw, 2005 (second-order latent factor)). Empirical work that examines both facets and overall justice (described in the next section) typically has adopted the former conceptualization. We know of only one study (Rodell & Colquit, 2009) that has examined the latter. Thus, although Fairness Heuristic Theory remains one of the most commonly used theories to explain the influence of fairness—and general fairness judgments are central to the theory—there have been few tests of the proposed relationship between general fairness judgments and facet judgments. Rather, empirical work that positions facet judgments as antecedents of overall justice dominates the empirical literature.

Overall Justice: Empirical Work

In the remainder of this chapter, we review the empirical work on overall fairness. (Table 5.1 provides a list of the operationalizations of overall justice for the empirical articles reviewed in this chapter.) Specifically, we examine research in which overall justice is an antecedent, a consequence, a mediator, a moderator, and a group-level construct. Of course, there is overlap between examining overall justice as an antecedent and a consequence and examining it as a mediator. Conceptualizing overall justice as a mediator requires overall justice to be both an antecedent of the focal outcomes and a consequence of the focal antecedents. However, the interest in these mediation studies is of overall justice as the transmitter of influence; the mechanism by which the antecedents influence the outcomes. Thus, in this review, research summarized in the "Overall Justice as an Antecedent" section includes studies in which overall justice is the first variable in the causal chain. Research summarized in the Overall Justice as a Consequence section includes work in which overall justice is the focal outcome. In the section on Overall Justice as a Mediator, our primary focus is on the mediating role of overall justice. We will address the relationship between overall justice and outcomes as well as between predictors overall justice. These findings are relevant to both the overall justice as an antecedent and overall justice as a consequence conceptualizations. However, research in the Overall Justice as a Mediator section is primarily concerned with the mediating effect of overall justice. We begin with research on overall justice as an antecedent.

Overall Justice as an Antecedent

Most of the empirical work on overall justice conceptualizes it as an antecedent—as the first variable in a causal chain. This research includes several types of studies: research examining direct effects of overall fairness on outcomes, research examining the indirect effect of overall justice on outcomes, and research examining moderators of the relationship between overall justice and outcomes. Next we review the 14 articles that examine overall fairness as an antecedent. We begin with a review of research examining the direct effect of overall justice on outcomes. This is followed by a review of research examining the indirect effect of overall justice on outcomes and research that examines moderators of the relationship between overall justice and outcomes.

DIRECT EFFECTS OF OVERALL JUSTICE

In the first empirical examination of overall justice as an antecedent, Tansky (1993) examined the relationship between employees' perceptions of overall justice, organizational citizenship behavior (OCB), job satisfaction, and commitment. Drawing on social exchange theory, Tansky predicted a positive relationship between overall justice and OCB, job satisfaction, and commitment.

Tansky (1993) collected data from 75 supervisor/subordinate dyads employed by a Fortune 100 company. Tansky created a three-item measure of overall fairness ("management in my organization treats me honestly and ethically," "overall my organization is fair," "the programs and policies in my organization are fair"). The results demonstrated employee perceptions of overall fairness predicted altruism behavior, job satisfaction, and organizational commitment.

Table 5.1 Operationalizations of Overall Justice

Article	Year	Measure of Overall Justice
Konovsky & Folger	1991	Created a two-item measure
Tansky	1993	Created a three-item measure
Beugre & Baron	2001	Created 12-item measure (systemic justice)
Trevino & Weaver	2001	Composite 9-item measure of general fairness items and facet items
Colquitt, Scott, Judge, & Shaw	2006	Manipulation check used 4-item global fairness measure
Kim	2007	Composite of organizational procedural justice items and organizational interactional justice items from Rupp and Cropanzano (2002)
Kim & Leung	2007	Utilized three-item developed by Kim (2004)
Choi	2008	Created a 3-item of overall supervisory entity justice perceptions
Mayer, Bardes, & Piccolo	2008	Used Ambrose & Schminke's (2009) 6-item measure of POJ
Ambrose & Schminke	2009	Developed a 6-item Perceived Overall Justice (POJ) measure
Holtz & Harold	2009	Used Ambrose & Schminke's (2009) 6-item POJ measure
Johnson, Truxillo, Erdogan, Bauer, & Hammer	2009	Used Beugre & Baron's (2001) 12-item measure
Jones & Martens	2009	Used a 3-item short version of Ambrose & Schminke's (2009) POJ measure
Rodell & Colquitt	2009	Created a 3-item measure of global supervisory fairness
Rosen, Chang, Johnson, & Levy	2009	Latent overall unfairness; three indicators: perceived politics, procedural justice, psychological contract breach
Johnson & Lord	2010	Manipulated justice in experiment by violating DJ, PJ and IPJ simultaneously; manipulation check used a composite of facets on Colquitt's (2001) measure
Johnson, Chang, & Rosen	2010	Used the same manipulation as Johnson & Lord (2010)
Tremblay	2010	Used Ambrose & Schminke's (2009) 6-item POJ measure
De Backer et al.	2011	Latent OJ; 16-items assessing individual and team PJ and DJ, and team IFJ (Colquitt, 2001)
Herda & Lavelle	2011	Used 3 personal-experience items of Ambrose & Schminke's (2009) POJ measure
Nicklin, Greenbaum, McNall, Folger, & Williams	2011	Used Ambrose & Schminke's (2009) 6-item POJ measure
Christian, Christian, Garza, & Ellis	2012	Manipulated justice in experiment by using a "global justice violation" that violated three types of justice (DJ, PJ, IJ).
Cojuharenco, Shteynberg, Gelfand, & Schminke	2012	Used a 3-item short version of Ambrose & Schminke's (2009) POJ measure

(continued)

Table 5.1 (Continued)

Article	Year	Measure of Overall Justice
Herda & Lavelle	2012	Used 3 personal-experience items of Ambrose & Schminke's (2009) POJ measure
Patel, Budhwar, & Varma	2012	Adapted Ambrose & Schminke's 6-item POJ measure to assess overall *supervisory* justice
Sharoni, Tziner, Fein, Shultz, Shaul, & Zilberman	2012	Used a composite of Niehoff & Moorman's (1993) 20-item facet measure (DJ, PJ, and IJ)
Tang & Tang	2012	Used a 3-item short version of Ambrose & Schminke's (2009) POJ measure
Bobocel	2013	Used Ambrose & Schminke's (2009) 6-item POJ measure
Whiteside & Barclay	2013	Used a 3-item short version of Ambrose & Schminke's (2009) POJ measure
Barclay & Kiefer	2014	Latent OJ; Used Colquitt's (2001) 20-item measure of three facets (DJ, PJ, IJ)

Note: DJ=distributive justice; PJ=procedural justice; IFJ=informational justice; IJ=interactional justice; IPJ=interpersonal justice.

Several aspects of Tansky's (1993) study deserve attention. First, long before most researchers were interested in perceptions of overall fairness, Tansky argued for shifting from facet perceptions to a more global assessment of fairness. Second, Tansky saw overall fairness as an indicator of a culture of fairness, or what scholars would now refer to as justice climate. Third, although social exchange theory is now commonly used to explain the relationship between justice and outcomes, Tansky provided an early description of this relationship. In all, Tansky's work was ahead of its time.

INDIRECT EFFECTS OF OVERALL JUSTICE ON OUTCOMES

In all, eight studies examine the indirect effect of overall justice on outcomes. Two studies address the mediating role of emotion in the relationship between overall justice and outcomes. Barclay and Kiefer (2014) examined the relationship between overall justice, positive and negative emotions, and performance, psychological withdrawal, and helping. Barclay and Kiefer used a latent variable approach with Colquitt's (2001) measures of procedural, distributive, and interactional justice as indicators of overall justice. In two field studies, Barclay and Kiefer found overall justice predicted both positive and negative emotions. Further, both positive and negative emotions mediated the relationship between overall justice and performance. Negative emotions mediated the relationship between overall justice and withdrawal behavior, whereas positive emotions mediated the relationship between overall justice and helping.

In a study examining self-construal and unethical behavior, Cojuharenco, Shteynberg, Gelfand, and Schminke (2012) examined overall justice as a control variable. Consistent with Barclay and Kiefer (2014), they found overall justice significantly predicted self-reported unethical organizational behavior and a direct measure of cheating. However, when positive and negative emotions were included in the regression model with overall justice, the effect of overall justice on outcomes became insignificant.

De Backer et al. (2011) examined the relationship between overall justice, leader need-supportive behavior (i.e., support of the players' autonomy, competence, and belongingness needs), identification with the team, and team task cohesion and social cohesion. De Backer et al. were interested in the relative influences of overall fairness and a well-known sport psychological variable—the supportive behavior of the coach.

De Backer et al. (2011) assessed overall justice as a latent factor composed of 16 items assessing individual and team procedural justice and distributive justice, and team informational justice. In a survey of top-level female volleyball players and male handball players, De Backer et al. found identification with the team fully mediated the relationship between overall justice and team task cohesion and team social cohesion. Further, the influence of overall justice was comparable to that of the coach's need-supportive behavior. De Backer et al.'s research addresses the issue raised by Leventhal (1980) and the call by Ambrose and Arnaud (2005) for research examining the influence of overall justice relative to other motivational forces.

Two studies examine the relationship between overall justice, social exchange, and auditor behavior (Herda & Lavelle, 2011, 2012). The first study examines the relationship between overall justice and auditor's behavior toward their former firm. The second examines overall justice and auditor burnout and turnover.

Herda and Lavelle (2011) surveyed auditors who had left one of the Big 4 accounting firms. They examined the perceived overall fairness of the former firm as a predictor of previous perceived firm support and previous commitment to the firm and postemployment citizenship behavior (behavior aimed at helping the firm). To assess perceived overall fairness, Herda and Lavelle adapted the three personal experience items from the overall justice scale developed by Ambrose and Schminke (2009a). Using structural equation modeling, they found a direct effect of overall fairness on perceived organizational support and postemployment citizenship. Additionally, perceived organizational support mediated the relationship between overall justice and organizational commitment, which further mediated the relationship between overall justice and postemployment citizenship.

In the second study, Herda and Lavelle were interested in the behavior of current employees. Herda and Lavelle (2012) surveyed 204 auditors at two accounting firms. Using a direct measure of overall fairness based on the three personal experience items from the Ambrose and Schminke (2009a) scale, Herda and Lavelle found auditors' perceptions of their firm's overall fairness predicted perceived firm support, burnout, and turnover intentions. Further, although Herda and Lavelle do not provide explicit tests for mediation, it appears there was an indirect effect of overall fairness on auditors' commitment to the firm and indirect effects (as well as the previously mentioned direct effects) for burnout and turnover intentions. These indirect effects are consistent with the results of the first study.

Two studies examine the mediating effect of self-identity on the relationship between overall justice and outcomes. In a lab study, Johnson and Lord (2010) examined the relationship between overall justice, identity, trust, cooperation and theft. Johnson and Lord based their hypotheses on research that demonstrates the self can be represented at multiple levels (e.g., individual and interdependent), each of which has distinct motivational consequences (Brewer & Gardner, 1996). The individual level is associated with self-definitions based on being unique compared with others. At the individual level, behavior is driven by personal attitudes and concern for one's own welfare. In contrast, interdependent identities are associated with self-definitions based on the relationship with others (either dyads or groups). At the interdependent level, behavior is motivated by the role expectations of these others and the welfare of these others. Drawing on Fairness Heuristic Theory and the group engagement model, Johnson and Lord (2010) hypothesized overall fairness would activate interdependent identity and overall unfairness would activate self-identity. Thus, for participants who were treated fairly, relationships would be salient, increasing trust and cooperation. For participants who were treated unfairly, self-concerns would be salient, increasing theft behavior.

Johnson and Lord (2010) manipulated overall perceptions of justice by creating a situation in which procedural, distributive, and interactional justice principles were violated simultaneously. Their manipulation check of this overall justice manipulation was a composite scale of the 20 items from Colquitt (2001). Using both implicit and explicit measures of identity, Johnson and Lord found support for their hypotheses. Fairness activated interdependent identity. Additionally, interdependent identity mediated the relationship between fairness and trust and cooperation. Also, as predicted, unfairness elicited self-identity, and self-identity mediated the relationship between unfairness and theft. Finally, results suggested the effects of implicit measures of identity were stronger than the effects of explicit identity measures.

Johnson, Chang, and Rosen (2010) also examined the influence of fairness on individuals' identity. Additionally, they assessed individuals' regulatory focus and affect. Drawing primarily on Fairness Heuristic Theory and Uncertainty Management Theory, Johnson et al. predicted fairness would elicit relational and collective (interdependent) identities, promotion-focus, and happy affect. In contrast, they predicted unfairness would elicit individual identity, prevention-focus, and anxious affect. Further in a second study (described later in the section on Moderating Effects of the Relationship between Overall Justice and Outcomes), they examined sensitivity to injustice and locus of control as moderators of the relationship between overall justice and their outcome variables. In the first lab study using the same manipulation as Johnson and Lord (2010), Johnson et al. found support for the hypothesized effect of overall justice on identity, regulatory focus, and affect (although the effect of unfairness on prevention-focus was not significant).

Finally, Whiteside and Barclay (2013) examined overall justice as an antecedent of two types of silence: acquiescent (silence motivated by futility) and quiescent (silence motivated by fear). In two scenario-based lab studies, they found overall justice was negatively associated with silence. In a third study utilizing a field survey, Whiteside and Barclay demonstrated acquiescent and quiescent silence mediated the relationship between overall justice and psychological withdrawal, physical withdrawal, and emotional exhaustion. Further, acquiescent silence also mediated the relationship between overall justice and performance.

MODERATING EFFECTS OF THE RELATIONSHIP BETWEEN OVERALL JUSTICE AND OUTCOMES

Five studies conceptualize overall justice as an antecedent of a relationship that is moderated. First, Rodell and Colquitt (2009) examined the relationship between overall judgments of supervisory fairness in the context of the introduction of a smoking ban. Rodell and Colquitt were interested in the relationship between supervisors' overall fairness and employees' anticipatory justice perceptions (i.e., individuals' expectations about future fairness; Time 1) and experienced justice (Time 2). Additionally, they examined the moderating effect of uncertainty and outcome favorability on the relationship between overall supervisory justice and experienced justice.

Rodell and Colquitt (2009) based their predictions on Fairness Heuristic Theory. Specifically, consistent with the conceptualization of the influence of overall justice judgments during the use phase, Rodell and Colquitt predicted overall supervisory fairness would predict both anticipatory justice facets (procedural, interpersonal, and informational) at Time 1, and experienced justice facets (procedural, interpersonal, and informational) at Time 2. They also hypothesized that the anticipatory justice facets would mediate the relationship between overall justice judgments and experienced justice. Finally, they suggested higher levels of uncertainty and lower levels of outcome favorability would lead employees to rely less heavily on the existing global (heuristic) fairness judgment. Thus, uncertainty and outcome favorability were predicted to moderate the relationship between supervisor overall justice and experienced justice.

The results generally supported Rodell and Colquitt's (2009) predictions. First, overall judgments of supervisor fairness (assessed by a three-item measure developed for the study) predicted the anticipatory facets as well as experienced interpersonal justice and experienced informational justice. Second, anticipatory justice facets mediated the relationship between supervisor overall justice and the experienced justice facets. Finally, uncertainty moderated the relationship between supervisor overall justice and experienced interpersonal justice and experienced informational justice. However, outcome favorability did not moderate the relationship.

Rodell and Colquitt's (2009) results support a key tenant of Fairness Heuristic Theory. Consistent with Fairness Heuristic Theory existing evaluations of overall fairness influence individuals' expectations about events and their interpretation of subsequent fairness experiences.

The second study examining moderators of the relationship between overall justice and outcomes was conducted by Johnson, Truxillo, Erdogan, Bauer, and Hammer (2009). Johnson et al. examined the relationship between organizational overall fairness and departmental overall fairness on employees' organizational citizenship behavior directed toward the organization (OCBO), organizational citizenship behavior directed toward individuals (OCBI), and task performance. Further, they examined the moderating effect of leader-member exchange (LMX). Because fairness serves as a proxy for trust (consistent with Fairness Heuristic Theory), Johnson et al. proposed the relationship between overall fairness and outcomes would be most pronounced when information about trust was lacking. However, if employees had information that an authority figure (e.g., their supervisor) was trustworthy, fairness information would be less important. Johnson et al. utilized the quality of the subordinates' relationship with their supervisor (LMX) as an indicator of trust.

Johnson et al. (2009) surveyed subordinates and supervisors in a large healthcare organization. Johnson et al. assessed overall justice with a 12-item measure of overall justice created by Beugre and Baron (2001). Their results revealed subordinates' perceptions of departmental overall fairness were a significant predictor of task performance and OCBO. However, organizational overall fairness was not a significant predictor of outcomes when departmental fairness was included in the regression. The tests for moderation showed a significant interaction for organizational overall fairness and LMX for task performance. Similarly, LMX moderated the relationship between departmental overall fairness and task performance and OCBO. In all cases, the form of the interaction was as predicted—the relationship between overall fairness and outcomes was stronger when LMX was low.

Two aspects of Johnson et al.'s (2009) analyses deserve mention. First, Johnson et al. test the main effect of organizational overall justice and departmental overall justice in the same regression equation. However, this equation does not include the interaction terms. Therefore, it is an underspecified model (Echambadi, Arroniz, Reinartz, & Lee, 2006; Echambadi, Campbell, & Agarwal, 2006; Edwards, 2009; Stone-Romero & Liakhovitski, 2002). Second, when they test the interactions, each interaction is tested separately; again underspecifying the model. That is, although they predict both forms of justice interact with LMX, they do not test a fully specified model (i.e., one that includes both main effects and both interactions). It is impossible to know what the results of the fully specified model are. Yet, it is notable that when examining the main effects with either of the interactions included, the effect of departmental overall fairness on task performance is no longer significant. Only the interaction of the included Overall Fairness X LMX is significant.

Johnson et al. (2010), Study 2, examined sensitivity to injustice and locus of control as moderators of the relationship between overall justice and identity, promotion-focus, and affect. Consistent with the results of Study 1 (described earlier), Johnson et al. found fairness elicited relational and collective identities and happy affect. Unfairness elicited individual identity, prevention-focus, and anxious affect. Additionally, consistent with their hypotheses, but not supported in Study 1, in Study 2 overall fairness elicited promotion-focus. Finally, the hypothesized moderating effects of sensitivity to injustice and locus of control were also significant. Specifically, insensitivity to injustice and locus of control strengthened the relationship between fairness (and unfairness) and the outcomes.

The fourth examination of moderators was conducted by Christian, Christian, Garza, and Ellis (2012). Christian et al. examined the influence of justice violation and justice recovery in teams. Christian et al. were interested in how justice violations of one team member influenced that member's behavior as well as the behavior of the team. Furthermore, Christian et al. examined the moderating influence of the violated team member's core role in the team. Christian et al. manipulated global (overall) justice violations by creating a situation in which distributive, procedural, and interactional justice were simultaneously violated. Similarly, they examined global (overall) justice recovery—recovery that addressed procedural, distributive, and interactional components of fairness.

Consistent with their predictions, Christian et al. (2012) found violated team members and their teammates engaged in fewer experimenter-directed OCBs, and this pattern was more pronounced when a core member was subjected to overall unfairness than when a non-core member was the recipient of unfair behavior. Furthermore, overall justice recovery efforts led to higher levels of OCBs for the violated team member and his/her teammates, relative to violated team members for whom there was no recovery effort. Again, as with the overall justice violation results, the positive response to overall justice recovery was greater for core team members and their teammates than for non-core members. Finally, although Christian et al. also examined the influence of overall justice violations and overall justice recovery on team members' evaluations of the experimenter, significant effects were generally not found.

Finally, Bobocel (2013) considered the relationship between overall justice, self and other orientation, and outcomes. Bobocel drew on tenets of Fairness Heuristic Theory to suggest the relationship between overall justice and reactions to an unfair event (forgiveness or revenge) is moderated by individuals' chronic orientation toward self or others. The distinction between chronic self-orientation and chronic other-orientation is similar to the distinction made between individual identity and relational/collective identity in the self-construal literature (Johnson, Selenta, & Lord, 2006). Individuals who are chronically self-concerned focus their attention on cues in the environment that are self-related: personal attributes, personal preference, individual outcomes, and individual achievements. Individuals who are chronically other-oriented focus their attention on information in the environment that is other-related: group characteristics, collaborative inputs and outcomes, and joint achievements.

Bobocel (2013) argued overall fairness would be related to forgiveness following an unfair event because overall fairness signals that, in general, the target of the unfair behavior is valued and included and the relationship is a cooperative one. Thus, the interpretation of the unfair event would be influenced by the positive, supportive overall fair relationship. Individuals who believe their organization is generally fair will be more forgiving of an unfair event than those who believe their organization is generally unfair. Further, this influence will be greater for individuals with a chronic other-orientation, those for whom relational concerns are particularly important. Bobocel also argued overall justice perceptions would have a tempering effect on revenge. As overall justice perceptions drive the interpretation of unfair events, employees who perceive their organization as generally fair, would feel confident in their standing in the group and with their inclusion. However, if the organization is perceived as generally unfair, employees would be concerned about exploitation and social exclusion. These concerns are likely to increase employees' willingness to disengage from the organization and to engage in retaliatory, vengeful behavior. Further, this tendency will be greater for employees with strong chronic self-orientation, as these individuals are particularly attentive to self-relevant cues such as inclusion/exclusion and exploitation.

Bobocel (2013) tested her predictions in a study of 153 employees surveyed at two points in time. Participants provided an assessment of the overall fairness of their organization. They also recalled a recent unfair event at work and responded to questions about their reactions (forgiveness and revenge) associated with that event. Consistent with predictions, overall justice was positively related to forgiveness and negatively related to revenge. Additionally, the predicted interactions were significant. The positive influence of overall fairness on forgiveness was stronger for individuals with a stronger chronic other-orientation. However, for individuals with a chronic self-orientation, there was not a relationship between overall fairness and forgiveness. In contrast, there was a negative relationship between overall justice and revenge, but only for individuals with stronger chronic self-orientation. For individuals with a chronic other-orientation, there was no significant relationship between overall justice and revenge.

Bobocel's (2013) research provides support for the tenants of Fairness Heuristic Theory. General fairness judgments influence individuals' interpretation of subsequent events. Additionally, her research supports the relational explanation for fairness effects by demonstrating the moderating effect of self- and other-orientation. Finally, Bobocel's study demonstrates reactions to specific fairness events is a function of the context (e.g., overall organizational fairness) and the individual.

SUMMARY

Most of the research on overall justice as an antecedent explores the mechanism by which and the conditions under which overall justice influences outcomes. This research provides insight into why fairness affects attitudes and behaviors and when that influence is most/least pronounced. However, most of this research has examined either a single mediator or a single moderator. As Johnson and Lord (2010) state, it is likely justice influences outcomes through multiple channels. Consequently, the simultaneous examination of multiple mediators would be useful. Additionally, research examining conditional indirect effects (i.e., both mediators and moderators) is undoubtedly warranted. The examination of more complex models will likely enhance our understanding of the influence of overall justice on outcomes.

Overall Justice as a Consequence

Several studies have conceptualized overall justice as a consequence (i.e., as the focal outcome variable). A review of the extant literature identified nine such studies as well as two additional studies that included overall justice measures to establish validity or as a manipulation check. Much of this research examines one or more of the justice facets as an antecedent of overall justice. However, only a few studies examine a complete set of justice facets. Additionally, other antecedents are frequently included. Consequently, rather than discuss the facet-based studies together (as we do in the Overall Justice as a Mediator section later), we examine the studies chronologically.

Early work by Tyler and his colleagues (Tyler, 1989; Tyler & Caine, 1981) examined the effect of procedural fairness and outcomes on overall fairness. Tyler and Caine (1981) used both experiments and surveys to test the hypothesis that procedures used by leaders to allocate outcomes influence leadership satisfaction independent of outcome fairness. Relevant to this chapter regarding overall justice are Studies 1 and 2, which tested the hypothesis in the context of student evaluation of teachers, in both a hypothetical, experimental setting and in a naturally occurring setting. One of the dependent variables in the studies was overall teacher fairness. The results suggest when students assess their teachers, they focus on procedures, not outcomes. Of the four predictor variables (outcome level, outcome satisfaction, outcome fairness, and procedural fairness) only procedural fairness significantly predicted overall teacher fairness.

Tyler (1989) tested Lind and Tyler's (1988) group-value model of procedural justice. Tyler contrasts the group-value model with what he labels Thibaut and Walker's (1975) control model. Tyler notes that Thibaut and Walker's research suggests people prefer fair procedures because controlling the process eventually leads to favorable outcomes. In contrast, the group-value model proposes people value membership in social groups and are concerned with their long-term relationships with authorities or institutions (Lind & Tyler, 1988). Specifically, Lind and Tyler propose people are concerned with three (noncontrol) issues: neutrality of decision maker, trust of authorities, and respect for their social standing in the group.

Tyler (1989) tested what effect these group-value variables (neutrality, trust, and standing), control, and outcome favorability had on beliefs about the overall fairness of the authorities. He found the group-value variables accounted for 8% of unique variance of the overall beliefs about the fairness of authorities. Outcome favorability accounted for an additional 3% of the variance, whereas control did not explain any unique variance. Of the group-value variables, trust and group standing were found to be the best predictors of overall justice beliefs, whereas neutrality had little influence. Tyler (1989) suggested Thibaut and Walker's (1975) control model was unique to the setting they studied (court trials), and that control is less important in most other situations.

Konovsky and Folger (1991) included a global measure of fairness in their study of the victims of layoffs. Their rationale for including this variable was strictly to provide convergent validity evidence for their predictor variables. Their predictors included three measures of layoff practices: procedures, social accounts, and severance benefits. These predictors relate to procedural justice, informational justice, and outcome favorability, respectively. For social accounts, they examined both causal accounts (accounts that mitigate the harmdoer's responsibility for the harm) and referential accounts (accounts that minimize the unfavorableness of the outcome by comparing it to a less desirable referent outcome). They found significant positive correlations between each of their predictors and overall fairness perceptions. The authors concluded that this was enough to establish convergent validity for their constructs and, therefore, did not include overall fairness perceptions in any further analysis.

In addition to the relationships described earlier in the section Overall Justice as an Antecedent, Tansky (1993) also examined the relationship between overall justice and supervisor relationship quality (assessed by LMX). Although in her hypothesis, Tansky predicted only that relationship quality would be positively associated with overall fairness, her subsequent analyses and discussion conceptualize LMX as a predictor of overall justice and the results support this relationship.

Beugre and Baron (2001) provided a direct assessment of the relationship between justice facet perceptions and overall fairness. Beugre and Baron drew on Fairness Heuristic Theory by arguing that because employees have a difficult time gathering information about the overall fairness of an organization, they will rely on their perceptions of the three traditional facets of justice: distributive, procedural, and interactional. Specifically, the authors hypothesized that each facet would positively influence perceptions of overall justice (which they also refer to as systemic justice).

To assess overall justice, Beugre and Baron (2001) developed a 12-item measure that included both overall fairness items (e.g., "Fairness is an important objective in this company") and general facet items (e.g., "In this company, job decisions are made in an unbiased manner"). Beugre and Baron found procedural and interactional justice to be significant predictors of the perceptions of overall justice, but did not find support for distributive justice as an independent predictor. They suggested a fair process and a fair interpersonal treatment effect exist, noting procedural and interactional justice both have a positive influence on subsequent evaluations about the overall fairness of the organization. Further, the authors explained the unexpected finding that distributive justice was not a significant predictor by drawing on previous research (e.g., Folger & Konovsky, 1989) that suggested the effects of distributive justice may only impact specific attitudes (e.g., satisfaction with outcomes), and therefore did not serve as a decision heuristic for overall justice.

Colquitt, Scott, Judge, and Shaw (2006) did not set out to test overall justice in their study. However, they did examine the influence of each of the justice dimensions on global fairness perceptions as part of their manipulation checks for their experiment. They found all three manipulations had a significant effect on global justice perceptions and explained 17% of the total variance. Further, distributive justice was most strongly related to overall justice, followed by interpersonal justice and procedural justice.

Hollensbe, Khazanchi, and Masterson (2008) conducted a qualitative study designed to examine the justice rules underlying entity-based judgments. Hollensbe et al. argued researchers have assumed event-based rules that serve as the indicators of facet judgments (e.g., consistency, bias suppression, equity, explanations, respect) also serve as the foundation for entity-based judgments. Hollensbe et al. argue overall fairness assessments of entities may be influenced by other factors. Analyzing interview data from 33 participants at their entry into new jobs, Hollensbe et al. found that, in addition to the traditional justice rules (i.e., justice facets), overall organizational fairness judgments were influenced by factors such as organizational support, organizational flexibility, organizational diversity, supervisor fairness, the stability of the workforce, and affect. Similarly, in addition to traditional justice rules, overall supervisory fairness judgments were influenced by supervisor support, supervisor characteristics, supervisor flexibility, and organizational fairness. Both types of overall judgments were influenced by how others in the workplace were treated and how others viewed the organization and supervisor. Notably, Hollensbe et al. found the nontraditional justice rules were used by more respondents—and used more frequently—than the traditional facet-based justice rules.

Holtz and Harold (2009) tested the effects of the four justice facets (distributive, procedural, interpersonal, and informational) on overall justice. In addition, they added organizational trust and supervisory trust as predictor variables. Holtz and Harold were primarily interested in employees' within-person change over time. They also tested two different types of "overall" justice: overall organizational justice and overall supervisory justice. The authors found employees' overall justice perceptions changed over time and about a quarter of the total variance in overall justice perceptions was within-person variance.

Holtz and Harold (2009) also found overall organizational justice was predicted by (in descending order of contribution) organizational trust, interpersonal justice, distributive justice, and procedural justice. Overall supervisory justice perceptions were best predicted by supervisor trust and interpersonal justice. The results also showed employees with higher levels of trust had more stable overall justice perceptions over time.

Rosen, Chang, Johnson, and Levy (2009) examined the relationship between organizational politics, psychological contract breach, and procedural fairness and attitudes and behaviors. Rosen et al. examined four different models presenting different relationships among these variables. The fourth model conceptualized organizational politics, psychological contract breach, and procedural fairness as indicators of a higher-order latent general (un)fairness factor. Attitudes then mediated the relationship between the latent (un)fairness factor and OCB. Across three studies, Rosen et al. found support for this model. Notably, organizational politics, psychological contract breach, and procedural justice were equally influential in determining the global (un)fairness factor.

It is important to note that although there was support for the latent unfairness model, the fit was comparable to the "environmental responsiveness model" in which procedural justice and organizational politics predicted psychological contract breach and the effect of psychological contract breach on OCB was then mediated by attitudes. Further, as Rosen et al. (2009) only considered one of the justice facets (procedural justice), it is unclear how inclusion of the other facets would influence the relationships they report.

In a recent study, Nicklin, Greenbaum, McNall, Folger, and Williams (2011) used three experimental studies to examine the relationship between context, counterfactual thoughts, and perceptions of overall fairness. They found perceptions of overall justice—measured using Ambrose and Schminke's (2009a) scale—were lower when a knowledgeable person (expert) made a mistake (because they should have been able to prevent it). They found that experts are held more accountable than nonexperts for misfortune and the perceptions of overall justice decrease as the severity of the misfortune increases. Nicklin et al. also found counterfactual thoughts were related to perceived overall justice. The authors called for future research to examine counterfactual thoughts as a mediator based on preliminary evidence in their studies, though their research was more exploratory in nature.

Finally, prior to testing their hypothesized model, Barclay and Kiefer (2014; described earlier) tested a model that predicted procedural and interactional justice would be more influential on overall justice than distributive justice. Drawing on Lind and Tyler (1988), they argued relational models of justice suggest individuals are particularly sensitive to fair procedures and interpersonal treatment because of the conveyance of value and standing within a group. Indeed, across two studies, the authors found both procedural and interactional justice were better predictors of overall justice than distributive justice. However, they also found procedural justice was significantly more predictive of overall justice than interactional justice. They draw on instrumental models of procedural justice (e.g., Thibaut & Walker, 1975) to explain this finding. Barclay and Kiefer argue people have a long-term perspective of fairness and prefer fair procedures that will be beneficial over time (e.g., Greenberg, 1990).

SUMMARY

All of the research focusing on overall justice as a consequence has included at least one justice facet as a predictor. In all, the results from these studies demonstrate justice facets contribute to an overall justice perception. The research also shows perceived politics (Rosen et al., 2009), psychological contract breach (Rosen et al., 2009), trust (Holtz & Harold, 2009), and relationships with authorities (Tyler, 1989) and supervisors (e.g., Holtz, & Harold, 2009), and organizational and supervisory characteristics such as support and flexibility (Hollensbe et al., 2008) also influence overall justice perceptions. Thus, the research reviewed here suggests a broad range of antecedents for overall justice. However, it is notable that much of this research fails to control for justice facets while exploring new antecedents of overall fairness. Clearly, it will be important in the future to further examine the relative impact of justice facet judgments and other antecedents. Such examinations will enhance our understanding of overall fairness.

Overall Justice as a Mediator

An increasing amount of evidence in recent justice literature suggests overall justice plays an important mediating role in influencing employees' attitudes and behavior. Below we review this research. We begin with research examining overall justice as a mediator between the justice facets and outcomes. We then review research that has considered overall justice as a mediator of the relationship between other antecedents (e.g., leadership style, organization structure) and outcomes.

JUSTICE FACETS, OVERALL JUSTICE, AND OUTCOMES

Kim and Leung (2007) provided the first examination of overall justice as a mediator of the relationship between justice facets and outcomes. Kim and Leung's primary focus was on the influence of culture on the relationship between justice facets and overall justice and on the relationship between overall justice and employee attitudes (job satisfaction and turnover intentions). Kim and Leung (2007) examined how respondents from four cultures (U.S., China, Japan, and Korea) form and react to overall justice perceptions. The authors predicted individuals from countries with higher materialism (Chinese and Koreans) weigh distributive justice more highly when forming overall fairness judgments. They also predicted individuals from countries with lower materialism (Japanese and Americans) weigh procedural and interactional justice more highly.

Consistent with their predictions, Kim and Leung (2007) found the effect of distributive justice on overall justice perceptions was significantly stronger for Chinese and Koreans than for Japanese or Americans. They also found the effect of interactional justice was stronger for Japanese and Americans than for Chinese or Koreans. However, they did not find any difference between countries regarding the effect of procedural justice on overall justice. In fact, procedural justice had very weak effect sizes (explaining less than one percent of the variance) in all countries. Kim and Leung (2007) were also interested in cultural differences in the relationship between overall justice and attitudes. Their results revealed the relationship between overall justice and attitudes was stronger for U.S. respondents than for Chinese, Japanese, or Korean respondents.

In supplementary analyses (footnote 1, p. 90), Kim and Leung use structural equation modeling to examine overall justice as a mediator between the justice facets and outcomes. The results were consistent with what can be extrapolated from their regressions (i.e., the facets predicted overall justice and overall justice predicted attitudes). That is, overall justice mediated the relationship between the facets and attitudes and this relationship was affected by culture.

Ambrose and Schminke (2009a) provided the first empirical test focused exclusively on examining if overall justice judgments mediated the effects of specific justice facets (distributive, procedural, and interactional) on employees' attitudes and behavior. Ambrose and Schminke examined this relationship in two studies. In Study 1, based on the data of 330 employees from 54 organizations, the authors found overall justice fully mediated the effect of distributive justice, procedural justice, and interactional justice on job satisfaction, commitment, and turnover intentions. In Study 2, based on 137 supervisor-subordinate dyad data from 58 organizations, they demonstrated overall justice fully mediated the effects of procedural justice and interactional justice on task performance, OCB, and organizational deviance.

In order to empirically test the mediating role that overall justice plays between specific justice facets and employees' attitude and behavior, Ambrose and Schminke (2009a) developed a new scale—Perceived Overall Justice (POJ). This scale incorporated new developments in the justice literature that suggested a person's justice perception may be based on a general evaluation of his or her justice experiences (Lind, 2001a) or on his or her consideration of the general fairness of the organization (Colquitt & Shaw, 2005). Accordingly, the POJ scale includes items measuring individual's personal overall justice experiences (e.g., " Overall, I'm treated fairly by my organization," "In general, I can count on this organization to be fair," and "In general, the treatment I receive around here is fair.") and items measuring overall organizational justice in general (e.g., "Usually, the way things work in this organization are not fair," "For the most part, this organization treats its employees fairly," and "Most of the people who work here would say they are often treated unfairly"). This new POJ scale laid an important foundation for the overall justice literature and facilitated future empirical testing centered around this construct.

Following Ambrose and Schminke's (2009a) work on overall justice, other researchers provided additional evidence that overall justice serves as a mediating factor in the effects of specific justice types. For example, Jones and Martens (2009) were interested in whether employees' overall fairness perceptions of a senior management team mediated the relationship between justice facets and workplace outcomes (e.g., affective commitment, perceived managerial support, job satisfaction, turnover intentions, and trust in leaders). Based on Fairness Heuristic Theory and adapting the POJ scale developed by Ambrose and Schminke (2009a), in two studies, the authors found different justice facets affected employee attitudes through overall justice perceptions of the senior management team. Specifically, in Study 1, with data from 1,340 members of an international transportation organization, they showed overall justice perceptions of the senior management team fully mediated the effect of distributive justice on perceived managerial support and the effect of informational justice on job satisfaction. Overall justice perceptions also partially mediated the effect of distributive justice on affective commitment and job satisfaction, the effect of informational justice on perceived managerial support, and the effects of interpersonal justice on perceived managerial support and affective commitment. Overall justice fully mediated the relationship between interpersonal justice and job satisfaction.

In the second study, Jones and Martens (2009) sought to extend their findings from Study 1 by examining the moderating effect of trust uncertainty. Specifically, with data from 881 members of a different unit of the same international transportation company, the authors replicated the mediating effects in Study 1 and also found distributive justice and interpersonal justice exerted more influence on overall justice than procedural justice and informational justice. Additionally, they found the effect of overall justice on trust was moderated by trust certainty.

Patel, Budhwar, and Varma (2012) showed a similar mediating role of overall justice using a sample of Indian call-center employees. Specifically, Patel et al. were interested in exploring the mechanism underlying the relationship between specific justice facets and counterproductive work behaviors. They modified the POJ scale (Ambrose & Schminke, 2009a) to measure overall supervisory justice perceptions. Building on the group engagement model and social identity theory, they found the effect of the justice facets on group identification was fully mediated by overall supervisory justice perceptions. In addition, group identification was related to the counterproductive work behaviors of presenteeism (i.e. being physically present but functionally absent) and social loafing (i.e., reduced effort when working in groups).

OTHER ANTECEDENTS, OVERALL JUSTICE, AND OUTCOMES

Whereas Kim and Leung (2007), Ambrose and Schminke (2009a), Jones and Martens (2009), and

Patel et al. (2012) empirically examined how overall justice mediates the effects of specific justice facets, Kim (2007), Mayer, Bardes, and Piccolo (2008), Tremblay (2010), and Tang and Tang (2012) investigated the mediating role of overall justice using other variables as antecedents.

Kim (2007) examined the relationship between organizational structure, internal communication, overall justice, and employee exchange beliefs and attitudes. In a study of 31 organizations and 1191 employees, Kim found overall justice partially mediated the relationship between internal communication and exchange beliefs and attitudes as well as between organizational structure and exchange beliefs and attitudes.

Mayer et al. (2008) and Tremblay (2010) examined the mediating role of overall justice on the effects of leadership. Mayer et al. were interested in exploring the relationship between servant-leadership, overall justice, employees' need satisfaction and job satisfaction. In a survey study of 187 business undergraduates, the authors found the effect of servant-leadership on employees' overall need satisfaction was partially mediated by employees' overall organizational justice perceptions. Additionally, employees' overall need satisfaction fully mediated the relationship between employees' overall organizational justice perceptions and employees' job satisfaction.

Tremblay (2010) tested the relationship between transformational leadership, transactional leadership, overall justice, trust in leader, group commitment, and turnover intentions. In a field study of 1,443 Canadian Forces personnel from five different army units, the author showed individuals' overall justice perceptions fully mediated the relationship between transactional leadership and trust in leader, and partially mediated the relationship between transformational leadership and trust in leader. Further, trust in leader mediated the relationship between overall justice perceptions and group commitment and turnover intentions.

Tang and Tang (2012) were interested in how human resource (HR) practices affect employees' organizational citizenship behavior and tested the mediating role of overall justice in the relationship. The authors adopted Ambrose and Schminke's (2009a) POJ scale and conceptualized overall justice as an indicator climate. Building on social exchange theory and information processing theory, they examined the effect of high-performance HR practices on service-oriented OCB. In a field study of 1,133 employee and 119 human resource managers, they found the relationship between high-performance HR practices and service-oriented OCBs was mediated by both overall justice and service climate. Additionally, Tang and Tang found the influence of service climate on service-oriented OCBs was over twice that of overall justice.

SUMMARY

In the last five years there has been a growing body of research examining the mediating role of overall justice in organizational settings. Half of the studies examined the mediation of overall justice between justice facets and employee outcomes (Ambrose & Schminke, 2009a; Jones & Martens, 2009; Kim & Leung, 2007; Patel et al., 2012). Overall, findings from these studies consistently show distributive justice, procedural justice, and interactional justice (informational justice and interpersonal justice) predict overall justice perceptions, although the magnitudes of the effects of different justice facets on overall justice vary. (See Table 5.2 for a summary of these effects.)

The review of overall justice as a mediator also demonstrates overall justice may play a broader role in explaining individuals' reactions to their workplace. Overall justice also mediates the relationship between outcomes and variables such as leadership style (Mayer et al., 2008; Tremblay, 2010), human resource practices (Tang & Tang, 2012), and organization characteristics (communication, structure; Kim, 2007). The results suggest overall justice perceptions may be formed independent of specific justice facets, and based on non-justice antecedents, an idea we return to later in this chapter.

Overall Justice as a Moderator

Four studies have examined the moderating effect of overall justice. The first (Treviño & Weaver, 2001) examined overall justice in the context of employees' responses to organizational ethics programs. Specifically, Treviño and Weaver examined the influence of overall justice and ethics program follow-through on employees' unethical behavior and their willingness to report wrongdoing.

Treviño and Weaver (2001) surveyed nearly 1,000 employees in four large companies. Based on Fairness Heuristic Theory and equity theory, they predicted general fairness judgments would be negatively related to unethical behavior. Additionally, utilizing Fairness Heuristic Theory, social exchange theory, and social learning theory, they predicted a positive relationship between overall justice and

Table 5.2 The Effects of Justice Facets on Overall Justice Across Studies

Article	Year	Distributive Justice	Procedural Justice	Interactional Justice	Rank Ordering	Focus of Overall Justice Measure
Konovsky & Folger	1991	r = .14**	r = .88***	Causal accounts, r = .52*** Referential accounts, r = .34***	PJ > IJ > OF	Organization
Beugre & Baron	2001	–.09 n.s.	.44**	.26**	PJ > IJ	Organization
Colquitt, Scott, Judge, & Shaw	2006	.67***	.28*	.54***	DJ > IJ > PJ	Organization
Kim & Leung	2007	China, .69** Japan, .23** Korea, .56** U.S., .39**	.12* .11 n.s. .19** .15*	.15** .65** .24** .47**	DJ > IJ > PJ IJ > DJ DJ > IJ > PJ IJ > DJ > PJ	Organization
Ambrose & Schminke	2009	Study 1, .25** Study 2, .08 n.s.	.43** .58**	.14** .24**	PJ > DJ > IJ PJ > IJ	Organization
Holtz & Harold	2009	H2(a), .15*** H2(b), .06 n.s.	.37*** .14*	Informational justice, .04 n.s. Interpersonal justice, .30*** Informational justice, .23*** Interpersonal justice, .46***	PJ > IPJ > DJ IPJ > INJ > PJ	Organization Supervisor
Jones & Martens	2009	Study 1, .08** Study 2, .21***	.01, n.s. n.s.	Informational justice, .25*** Interpersonal justice, .33*** Informational justice, .16*** Interpersonal justice, .35***	IPJ > INJ > DJ IPJ > DJ > INJ	Supervisor
Rosen, Chang, Johnson, & Levy	2009		Study 1, .82* Study 3, .89*			Organization
Patel, Budhwar, & Varma	2012	.24***	.22***	Informational justice, .32*** Interpersonal justice, .42***	IPJ > INJ > DJ > PJ	Supervisor
Barclay & Kiefer	2014	Study 1, .40* Study 2, .59*	.89* .87*	.78* .75*	PJ > DJ⁺; IJ > DJ⁺; PJ > IJ⁺ PJ > DJ⁺; IJ > DJ⁺; PJ > IJ⁺	Organization

*$p < .05$, **$p < .01$, ***$p < .001$

Notes: DJ = distributive justice; PJ = procedural justice; IFJ = informational justice; IJ = interactional justice; IPJ = interpersonal justice. Barclay and Kiefer (2014) was the only article to perform statistical tests of the differences between the facets. ⁺indicates difference tests were significant. Konovsky and Folger's (1991) measured level of benefits received (outcome favorability (OF)) rather than distributive justice.

reporting of unethical behavior (which they viewed as discretionary behavior). They also expected a similar pattern of relationships between ethics program follow-through and unethical behavior and reporting. Finally, they predicted overall justice would moderate the relationship between ethics program follow-through and outcomes.

The results generally supported Treviño and Weaver's (2001) predictions. Overall justice (assessed by a composite of general fairness items and facet items) and ethics program follow-through significantly predicted unethical behavior and reporting behavior. Additionally, overall justice moderated the relationship between ethics program follow-through and unethical behavior. However, the predicted interaction was not significant for reporting behavior. Treviño and Weaver concluded that the results demonstrate the importance of context on employee responses to ethics programs. Notable, like Tansky (1993), in their discussion of overall fairness, Treviño and Weaver equate individual-level perceptions of overall fairness with "perceptions of the overall fairness climate in the organization" (p. 666). Also worth noting, although Treviño and Weaver describe ethics program follow-through as an antecedent of overall fairness, they do not test this relationship. Consistent with Cropanzano et al.'s (2001) discussion of the relationship between event judgments and entity judgments, Treviño and Weaver suggest lack of ethics' program follow-through negatively influences perceptions of procedural justice and retributive justice and overall fairness.

Sharoni et al. (2012) examined the moderating effect of overall justice on the relationship between OCB and turnover intentions. Sharoni et al. assessed overall justice by creating a composite of the procedural, distributive, and interactional items from the Niehoff and Moorman (1993) scale. They found a significant negative relationship between overall justice and turnover intentions. Furthermore, overall justice moderated the relationship between self-reported OCB and turnover intentions. However, contrary to expectations, for low overall justice, there was a positive relationship between OCB and turnover intentions—a finding they did not address in their discussion.

Choi (2008) investigated the influence of entity judgments and event judgments on employees' organization-directed outcomes and supervisor-directed outcomes. Based on Fairness Heuristic Theory, Choi hypothesized employees' overall fairness judgments would influence employee reactions to the fairness of a specific event. Furthermore, he predicted overall judgments of supervisor fairness would moderate the relationship between event facet fairness and supervisor-directed outcomes (trust in manager and supervisor-directed OCB), whereas overall judgments of organizational fairness would moderate the relationship between event facet fairness judgments and organization-directed outcomes (organizational commitment and organization-directed OCB).

In a field study of 265 subordinates and 74 supervisors, Choi (2008) found some support for his hypotheses. Specifically, the relationships between distributive event fairness and procedural event fairness and organizational commitment were moderated by overall organizational fairness. Additionally, the procedural event justice × overall organizational justice interaction and the interpersonal event justice × overall organizational justice interactions were significant for organization-directed OCB. For supervisor-directed outcomes, the relationships between interpersonal event justice and trust in supervisor was moderated by supervisor overall fairness judgments. Similarly, the interpersonal event justice × supervisor overall justice and the informational event justice × supervisor overall justice interactions were significant for supervisor-directed OCB. Finally, an examination of the main effects revealed the overall justice judgments were stronger predictors of employee attitudes and behaviors than the justice facet event judgments.

Finally, Sora, Caballer, Peiró, Silla, and Gracia (2010) examined overall justice at the individual-level (described here) and group-level (described in the next section) on the relationship between job insecurity and outcomes. Sora et al. gathered data from 942 employees from 47 Spanish organizations. Using a four-item measure that assessed each of the justice facets, Sora et al. found overall justice moderated the relationship between job insecurity and job satisfaction and turnover intentions. The negative effects of job insecurity were buffered by overall organizational fairness.

SUMMARY

There is not a common theme to the research examining overall justice as a moderator. Further, only the Choi (2008) article has a strong theoretical foundation for the proposed moderating effect of overall justice. Still, the research suggests overall justice influences the relationship between antecedents and outcomes either by influencing how the antecedents are viewed or by augmenting the positive benefits of the antecedent or compensating for its deficiencies.

Overall Justice at the Group Level: Overall Justice Climate

Although most research on organizational justice has examined perceptions of justice at the individual level, there is also a body of research examining justice climate. Justice climate is defined as "a distinct unit-level cognition regarding shared perceptions of treatment by organizational authorities" (Whitman, Caleo, Carpenter, Horner, & Bernerth, 2012). Justice climate research has been traditionally characterized by a focus on facet-specific climates. Most research examines procedural justice climate, although interactional justice climate (Ambrose, Schminke, & Mayer, 2013; Dayan, Di Benedetto, & Colak, 2009; Griffin, 2010; Liao & Rupp, 2005; Simons & Roberson, 2003) and distributive justice climate (Erdogan & Bauer, 2010; Hammer, Bayazit, & Wazeter, 2009; Spell & Arnold, 2007) have also been explored.

Ambrose and Schminke (2007) were the first to introduce the construct of overall justice climate. They argue many of the benefits that are derived from examining overall justice at the individual-level can be obtained at the climate level as well. For example, consistent with their work on overall justice at the individual-level, Ambrose and Schminke argue for "a path for justice climate research based on greater simplification, not increased complexity" (p. 403). Specifically, they suggest individuals may be able to distinguish between different types of justice climate, but "they are likely to respond to an overarching justice climate" (p. 406). They argue an examination of overall justice climate would be productive for the field. This argument is supported by Whitman et al. (2012), who conclude that results from their meta-analysis of justice climate provides some evidence (e.g., high intercorrelations among facet-specific justice climates) that the examination of overall justice climate is warranted.

Only a few scholars have explored the overall justice climate construct. In conceptual work, Rupp and Paddock (2010) proposed a temporal model in which individuals' justice experiences and judgments lead to the development of overall justice climate. Specifically, Rupp and Paddock suggested information is aggregated about justice-relevant events to form impressions of the fairness of different sources of justice (i.e., entity judgments about supervisors, co-workers, customers, organizations). These individual-level perceptions evolve through shared experiences, sensemaking, socialization, and attraction-selection-attrition mechanisms to become source specific fairness climate perceptions (e.g., supervisory justice climate, intragroup justice climate). Finally, these source specific justice climates become aggregated to form overall justice climate. Overall justice climate then "exerts a strong force on the culture of workgroups and is stable, long-lasting, and relatively impervious to change" (p. 249). Further, if both individual and collective information processing have occurred, Rupp and Paddock suggested "overall justice climate will serve as the most proximal antecedent of individual and organizational outcomes" (p. 261).

Empirically, we found only three published articles that examine overall justice climate.[2] In addition to the individual-level analysis described above, Sora et al. (2010) also examined the moderating effect of overall justice climate on the relationship between job insecurity and employee reactions. They expected fair overall justice climate to weaken the negative relationship between job insecurity and employee reactions. Sora et al. used a direct consensus approach to assessing overall justice climate. That is, they aggregated respondents' personal overall justice judgments to form an indicator of overall justice climate. As with the individual-level data, overall justice climate moderated the relationship between job insecurity and job satisfaction and turnover intentions.

Priesemuth, Arnaud, and Schminke (2013) examined the influence of contextual variables on employee deviance and political behavior. Specifically, they examined the relationship between overall justice climate, functional dependence (i.e., task interdependence), and deviant and political behavior. They suggested overall justice climate will be significantly related to deviant and political behavior, and this relationship would be stronger when task interdependence was low.

Priesemuth et al. (2013) collected data from supervisors and multiple subordinates from 113 work units. To assess overall justice climate, they used a referent-shift adaptation of the three-item Ambrose and Schminke (2009a) POJ scale. Consistent with their predictions, overall justice climate was negatively related to employee deviance and political behavior, and this relationship was stronger when functional dependence was low. Their study is the first to demonstrate the influence of overall justice climate on employee behavior.

Li, Cropanzano, and Bagger (2013) operationalized overall justice climate as a higher-order factor of distributive justice climate, procedural justice climate, and interpersonal justice climate. Li et al. found the higher-order model provided an acceptable fit to the data. However, contrary to their expectations, overall justice climate was not related to team cooperative behavior, team satisfaction, or team performance.

Although Sora et al. (2010), Priesemuth et al. (2013) and Li et al. (2013) provide the only published empirical work on overall justice climate, several conference presentations have also examined this construct. Ambrose and Mayer (2013) examined the influence of overall justice climate on the fair behavior of co-workers and workgroup outcomes. In two studies, they found co-worker fair behavior mediated the relationship between overall justice climate and workgroup cooperation, workgroup OCB, workgroup deviance, and workgroup performance. Additionally, in Study 2 they found support for a moderated mediation model, in which the influence of overall justice climate on co-worker fair behavior is moderated by workgroup structure.

Kwon and Rupp (2013; Kwon, Rupp & Young, 2008) examined overall justice climate as a mediator. They predicted overall justice climate would partially mediate the relationship between high-performance work systems (HPWS) and individual and organizational outcomes. Kwon and Rupp argue HPWS, which are characterized by high levels of interaction and interdependence, create an environment in which information and experiences are likely to be shared. Furthermore, HPWS typically incorporate components that are strongly related to fairness perceptions (e.g., voice, participation, transparency). Consequently, shared perceptions (i.e., climate) of fairness are likely to emerge. Kwon and Rupp found overall justice climate partially mediated the relationship between HPWS and firm performance and fully mediated the relationship between HPWS and job satisfaction. Kwon and Rupp's research is the first to examine antecedents of overall justice climate and to demonstrate a relationship between overall justice climate and firm performance.

Cropanzano, Walumbwa, and Ayree (2013) examined the relationship between leadership, overall justice climate, group ethical behavior and group-learning behavior. Cropanzano et al. surveyed employees and supervisors for 95 workgroups in two large banks. Cropanzano et al. assessed overall justice climate by using a referent-shift adaptation of the three item version of Ambrose and Schminke's (2009a) overall justice measure that focused on the supervisor rather than the organization. Consistent with their expectations, they found ethical leadership mediated the relationship between transformational leadership and overall justice climate. Further, overall justice climate predicted group ethical behavior, but not group learning behavior. Overall justice climate also mediated the effect of ethical leadership on group ethical behavior and the effect of overall justice climate on group learning behavior was mediated by group ethical behavior. Finally, Cropanzano et al. examined the relationship between overall justice climate and overall peer justice (shared perceptions of how co-workers treat each other). Consistent with expectations, overall justice climate predicted peer justice and partially mediated the effect of leadership on peer justice. Further, peer justice partially mediated the effect of overall justice climate on group outcomes.

SUMMARY

There is limited research on overall justice climate. However, the existing research suggests overall justice climate plays an important role in organizations. Overall justice climate has been shown to predict individual-level behavior and attitudes, group-level behavior, and firm performance. Furthermore, research has cast overall justice climate as an antecedent, a mediator, and a moderator, highlighting its potential in explaining employee reactions.

Observations and Future Research

In the past five years, overall justice has gone from a construct that received a passing mention in commentaries about organizational fairness to one that is fully embedded in the field. The acceptance of overall justice as an important construct is reflected in a number of ways. Most obvious is the amount of empirical work on the topic (reviewed in this chapter) that has emerged in the last five years. However, there are additional indicators as well. For example, in methodological work discussing multidimensional constructs, overall justice is now included as an exemplar along with well-established multidimensional constructs such as job satisfaction and organizational commitment (Johnson, Rosen, Chang, Djurdjevic, & Taing, 2012; Williams, Vandenberg, & Edwards, 2009). In recent reviews of the justice literature, overall justice is included

(Coyle-Shapiro & Dhensa, 2011). Overall justice is also now included as a control variable in empirical research (Cojuharenco, Patient, & Bashshur, 2011; Cojuharenco et al., 2012). Finally, it has become common for justice researchers who have examined justice facets to suggest that future research on overall justice is also warranted (Erdogan & Bauer, 2010; Heslin & VandeWalle, 2011; See, 2009). In all, after years on the fringe, overall justice has joined the mainstream.

Our review of the existing overall justice literature identifies areas in which research insights have been made. However, it also identifies areas in need of future research. For example, most research has examined overall justice as an antecedent of individual and organizational outcomes. Further, this antecedent research typically examines factors that mediate the relationship between overall justice and outcomes. Yet, as we indicated in our summary of the "Overall Justice as an Antecedent" section, the existing research takes a single mediator perspective. This research would benefit from a multiple mediator approach in which the mechanisms identified by theory and previous empirical research could be examined simultaneously. The simultaneous consideration of multiple mediators would provide information about the relative importance of emotions, identity, social exchange, and so forth, in transmitting the influence of fairness to employees' attitudinal and behavioral reactions. This allows researchers to assess which theory most adequately explains the phenomenon or effect (Cooper & Richardson, 1986) and to enhance precision of theoretical predictions (Edwards & Berry, 2010). Further, such an understanding facilitates the development of a research area (Colquitt & Zapata-Phelan, 2007; Kenny, 2008).

Second, research on both overall justice as a consequence and overall justice as a mediator has examined justice facets as antecedents of overall justice. However, these studies do not provide a strong and consistent pattern in terms of which of the justice facets are most influential in predicting overall justice. (See Table 5.2.) In the 15 samples examining facets and overall justice, procedural justice is the strongest predictor of overall justice for six, interactional justice (or its subdimensions interpersonal justice and informational justice) is the strongest predictor for six, and distributive justice is the strongest predictor for three. However, procedural justice was also found not to be significantly related to overall justice in three samples and distributive justice was not significantly related in two samples.

Fairness Heuristic Theory suggests procedural justice will have the greatest impact on overall justice, given the primacy of procedural information (Lind, 2001a; van den Bos et al., 1998). However, empirical findings seem to suggest otherwise. The inconsistent pattern of results suggests the impact of the justice facets may vary from one situation to another and it may be fruitful for future research to further examine the moderators (e.g., individual characteristics, situational factors) that alter the relative importance of specific justice facets on overall justice. However, it is worth nothing that one pattern that does emerge is that interactional justice is the strongest predictor of overall justice in the three studies that examine overall *supervisory* justice.

In terms of moderators of the relationship between justice facets and overall justice, some likely constructs have emerged. Lind (2001a) suggests salience and relevance of justice facet information influences overall justice judgments. Ambrose and Schminke (2009a) suggest contextual variables such as organizational structure and climate may influence the relationship. Kim and Leung (2007) examined culture as a moderator. Clearly, individual difference variables, such as equity sensitivity or self-construal, may also have an impact. Future research exploring moderators would increase our understanding of the relationship between justice facets and overall justice judgments.

Third, research on the relationship between the specific justice facets and overall justice demonstrates that, on average, the facets account for less than half of the variance in overall justice judgments. This raises the question, "What else accounts for individuals' perceptions of overall justice?" Ambrose and Schminke (2006) suggest part of the unaccounted variance may reflect the fact that when researchers sum the justice facets, they implicitly weight each facet equally in the prediction of overall justice. Yet individuals may not do so as they form their overall justice judgments. Some facets may be more important for some individuals—and in some contexts—yet these idiosyncratic differences are not captured by current research.

Additionally, the existing research suggests there may be aspects of fairness not captured by the three or four specific facets justice researchers typically examine. For example, the research reviewed above suggests trust in and the quality of relationship with the source of fairness predict overall justice. Further, overall justice judgments may capture affective components of fairness not captured by the primarily cognitive assessments of justice facets that dominate current research. Rodell, Colquitt, and Baer (2012) examined supervisor's humor, similarity to subordinate, and physical attractiveness as antecedents of perceptions of supervisor's overall fairness. They argued these factors would influence overall justice indirectly, through their influence on positive affect. Rodell et al. found support for the indirect effect of supervisor's humor and similarity on perceptions of supervisor's overall justice. Additionally, these effects were stronger when the supervisor made more frequent justice-related decisions. Similarly, Rosen et al. (2009, described previously) demonstrated perceptions of politics and psychological contract breach were indicators of a latent overall fairness factor. Finally, as reviewed earlier, Hollensbe et al. (2008) identify a broad range of factors that appear to influence judgments of overall fairness. This research suggests understanding overall fairness judgments will require looking beyond justice facets.

Finally, there may be methodological reasons for the limited amount of variance justice facet judgments predict in overall justice judgments. Much of the empirical work that examines justice facets as predictors of overall justice uses indirect measures at the facet level and a direct measure at the overall justice level. The difference in the type of measure used may be responsible for the difference. Clearly, more research that examines antecedents of overall justice as well as these measurement issues is warranted.

The entity approach to overall fairness deserves some further consideration on several fronts. First, how do entity judgments for supervisors relate to overall (organizational) justice? Our belief is overall organizational justice judgments are broader than judgments for specific entities in the organization (e.g., supervisors, co-workers). For example, because supervisors are agents of the organization, their behavior is likely to be seen as indicative of the organization's overall fairness. Similarly, co-workers' behavior is likely to be seen as indicative of the organization's acceptance (or disapproval) of behavior. We suggest the fairness of supervisors and co-workers will influence employees' overall organizational fairness judgments. This belief is reflected in the Ambrose and Schminke (2009a) POJ items, some of which are worded broadly ("In general people are treated fairly in my organization").

Second, just as there are times when an examination of facets is important, there are undoubtedly times when an examination of specific entities is important. For example, when researchers are interested in employees' supervisor-directed attitudes and behavior (e.g., Johnson et al., 2009) an examination of supervisory fairness is appropriate. Finally, it is possible that entity judgments will predict some unique variance in outcomes. Supervisors may represent the organization, but they are independent of it as well. Indeed, research on supervisor organizational embodiment (Eisenberger et al., 2010) suggests individuals differ in the extent to which they see the supervisor as representing the organization. This is an area that clearly warrants empirical investigation.

Finally, let us address an area of research we find particularly lacking in the current empirical literature. Ambrose and her colleagues (Ambrose & Arnaud, 2005; Ambrose & Schminke, 2007, 2009a) suggest one of the benefits of examining overall justice is its ability to allow researchers to more easily examine the influence of fairness relative to other motivational forces (e.g., personality, leadership). One of the characteristics that led to the explosion of interest in justice was its ability to be relevant to a broad range of organizational topics. As fields evolve, researchers tend to look more inward, to ask more "within" field questions. The work on organizational justice is consistent with this evolution. Yet, a focus on within-field questions runs the risk of making justice research too insular. Overall justice provides a mechanism for integrating justice into the broader organizational literature and allowing for the examination of when justice is influential and when it is not. Only two studies in our review considered the influence of justice relative to other forces (De Backer et al., 2011; Tang & Tang, 2012). We believe there is much to be gained by examining how employees' overall sense of fairness "stacks up" against other constructs that influence employee behavior and encourage researchers to more vigorously pursue this type of research.

Conclusion

The first author of this chapter had a rocky start with her research on overall justice. In 2000, Ambrose and Schminke submitted an early article examining the relationship between justice facets and overall justice. It was not well-received. Comments included, "It is not clear that overall fairness judgments make a meaningful theoretical contribution to an already voluminous literature. What is gained by adding yet another justice concept?" (Associate Editor, *Journal of Applied Psychology*); "I think this paper should be rejected. There's just not much here." (Reviewer 1, *Journal of Applied Psychology*)[3]; "I question the value of your study's dependent variable, namely, overall fairness perceptions. In particular, why is it an important outcome variable in its right?" (Associate Editor, *Academy of Management Journal*). The manuscript was not successful, in part, because Ambrose and Schminke naively assumed: (a) everyone recognized justice facets "combined" to form overall justice perceptions, and (b) given the importance of fairness in organizations, overall justice would be acknowledged as important. Thus, their arguments were not as thorough and as carefully crafted as they needed to be. However, the manuscript also failed because at that time the field was not interested in an integrated, global evaluation of fairness. Indeed, in 2000, the field was in the midst of debate about whether interactional justice was distinct from procedural justice (Bobocel & Holmvall, 2001; Colquitt, 2001). Nearly 15 years later, it is gratifying to see the acceptance of overall justice. Current research demonstrates the usefulness of overall fairness. Moreover, it is theoretically interesting. Additionally, the current research provides a path for future investigation. We look forward to future research on this topic that will enhance our understanding not only of overall fairness, specifically, but of organizational fairness in general.

Acknowledgments

This research was supported by the Gordon J. Barnett Memorial Foundation.

Notes

1. We focus our review on research that examines overall fairness generally. There is some research (cf. Cropanzano & Konovsky, 1995; Evans & McShane, 1988; Gilliland, 1993) that examines the overall fairness of a particular event or system (e.g., drug testing, performance appraisal, selection) or of a particular facet (e.g., overall procedural justice; Folger & Konovsky, 1989; Lind et al., 1993; Madera, 2012). We do not include this work in our review.
2. Three other studies refer to "overall justice climate," but do not assess employees' shared perceptions. As noted in the text, Tansky (1993) and Treviño and Weaver (2001) refer to overall justice perceptions as reflecting overall justice climate. Tang and Tang (2012) purport to study justice climate, but they rely on the report of a single informant for their assessment. Thus, their measure might be better conceptualized as psychological climate.
3. Seriously, this was the entire review!

References

Ambrose, M. L., & Arnaud, A. (2005). Distributive and procedural justice: Construct distinctiveness, construct interdependence, and overall justice. In J. Greenberg & J. A. Colquitt (Eds.), *The handbook of organizational justice* (pp. 59–84). Mahwah, NJ: Erlbaum.

Ambrose, M. L., & Mayer, D. M. (2013). Justice climate and workgroup outcomes: The role of coworker fair behavior and workgroup structure. Unpublished manuscript.

Ambrose, M. L., & Schminke, M. (2006, April).An examination of overall justice. Paper presented at the annual meeting of the Society of Industrial and Organizational Psychology, Dallas, TX.

Ambrose, M. L., & Schminke, M. (2007).Examining justice climate: Issues of fit, simplicity, and content. In F. Dansereau, & F. J. Yammarino (Eds.), *Research in multi-level issues* (Vol. 6, pp. 397–413). New York, NY: Elsevier.

Ambrose, M. L., & Schminke, M. (2009a). The role of overall justice judgments in organizational justice research: A test of mediation. *Journal of Applied Psychology, 94*, 491–500.

Ambrose, M. L., & Schminke, M. (2009b). Assessing roadblocks to justice: A model of fair behavior in organizations. *Research in Personnel and Human Resource Management, 28*, 219–263.

Ambrose, M. L., Schminke, M., & Mayer, D. M. (2013). Trickle-down effects of supervisor perceptions of interactional justice: A moderated mediation approach. *Journal of Applied Psychology, 98*, 678–689.

Andrews, M. C., Baker, T. L., & Hunt, T. G. (2008). The interactive effects of centralization on the relationship between justice and satisfaction. *Journal of Leadership & Organizational Studies, 15*, 135–144.

Barclay, L. J., & Kiefer, T. (2014). Approach or avoid? Exploring overall justice and the differential effects of positive and negative emotions. *Journal of Management, 40*, 1857–1898.

Barrett-Howard, E., & Tyler, T. R. (1986). Procedural justice as a criterion in allocation decisions. *Journal of Personality and Social Psychology, 50*, 296–304.

Beugre, C. D., & Baron, R. A. (2001). Perceptions of systemic justice: The effects of distributive, procedural, and interactional justice. *Journal of Applied Social Psychology, 31*, 324–339.

Bobocel, D. R. (2013). Coping with unfair events constructively or destructively: The effects of overall justice and self-other orientation. *Journal of Applied Psychology, 98*, 720–731.

Bobocel, D. R., & Holmvall, C. M. (2001). Are interactional justice and procedural justice different? Framing the debate. In S. Gilliland, D. Steiner, & D. Skarlicki (Eds.), *Theoretical and cultural perspectives on organizational justice* (pp. 85–108). Greenwich, CT: Information Age.

Brewer, M. B., & Gardner, W. (1996). Who is this "We"? Levels of collective identity and self representations. *Journal of Personality and Social Psychology, 71*, 83–93.

Brockner, J., & Wiesenfeld, B. M. (1996). An integrative framework for explaining reactions to decisions: Interactive effects of outcomes and procedures. *Psychological Bulletin, 120*, 189–208.

Choi, J. (2008). Event justice perceptions and employees' reactions: Perceptions of social entity justice as a moderator. *Journal of Applied Psychology, 93*, 513–528.

Christian, J. S., Christian, M. S., Garza, A. S., & Ellis, A. P. J. (2012). Examining retaliatory responses to justice violations and recovery attempts in teams. *Journal of Applied Psychology, 97*, 1218–1232.

Cojuharenco, I., Patient, D., & Bashshur, M. R. (2011). Seeing the "forest" or the "trees" of organizational justice: Effects of temporal perspective on employee concerns about unfair treatment at work. *Organizational Behavior and Human Decision Processes, 116*, 17–31.

Cojuharenco, I., Shteynberg, G., Gelfand, M., & Schminke, M. (2012). Self-construal and unethical behavior. *Journal of Business Ethics, 109*, 447–461.

Colquitt, J. A. (2001). On the dimensionality of organizational justice: A construct validation of a measure. *Journal of Applied Psychology, 86*, 386–400.

Colquitt, J. A., Scott, B. A., Judge, T. A., & Shaw, J. C. (2006). Justice and personality: Using integrative theories to derive moderators of justice effects. *Organizational Behavior and Human Decision Processes, 100*, 110–127.

Colquitt, J. A., & Shaw, J. C. (2005). How organizational justice should be measured. In J. Greenberg & J. A. Colquitt (Eds.), *Handbook of organizational justice* (pp.113–154). Mahwah, NJ: Erlbaum.

Colquitt, J. A., & Zapata-Phelan, C. P. (2007). Trends in theory building and theory testing: A five-decade study of the Academy of Management Journal. *Academy of Management Journal*, 50, 1281–1303.

Colquitt, J. A., Zapata-Phelan, C. P., & Greenberg, J. (2005). What is organizational justice? A historical overview. In J. Greenberg & J. A. Colquitt (Eds.), *Handbook of organizational justice* (pp. 3–58). Mahwah, NJ: Erlbaum.

Cooper, W. H., & Richardson, A. J. (1986). Unfair comparisons. *Journal of Applied Psychology, 71*, 179–184.

Coyle-Shapiro, J., & Dhensa, R. K. (2011). Justice in the twenty-first-century organization. In K. Townsend & A. Wilinson (Eds.), *Research Handbook on the Future of Work and Employment Relations* (pp. 385–404). Northampton, MA: Edward Elgar.

Cropanzano, R., & Ambrose, M. L. (2001). Procedural and distributive justice are more similar than you think: A monistic perspective and a research agenda. In J. Greenberg & R. Cropanzano (Eds.), *Advances in organizational justice* (pp. 119–151). Stanford, CA: Stanford University Press.

Cropanzano, R., Byrne, Z. S., Bobocel, D. R., & Rupp, D. E. (2001). Moral virtues, fairness heuristics, social entities, and other denizens of organizational justice. *Journal of Vocational Behavior, 58*, 164–209.

Cropanzano, R., & Konovsky, M. A. (1995). Resolving the justice dilemma by improving the outcomes: The case of employee drug screening. *Journal of Business and Psychology, 11*, 239–263.

Cropanzano, R., Walumbwa, F. O., & Aryee, S. (2013, April). *The creation and consequences of work unit fairness*. Paper presented at the Annual Meeting of the Society for Industrial and Organizational Psychology. Houston, TX.

Dayan, M., Di Benedetto, C. A., & Colak, M. (2009). Managerial trust in new product development projects: Its antecedents and consequences. *R&D Management, 39*, 21–37.

De Backer, M., Boen, F., Ceux, T., De Cuyper, B., Hoigaard, R., Callens, F. . . . & Vande Broek, G. (2011). Do perceived justice and need support of the coach predict team identification and cohesion? Testing their relative importance among top volleyball and handball players in Belgium and Norway. *Psychology of Sport and Exercise, 12*, 192–201.

DeConinck, J. B. (2010). The effect of organizational justice, perceived organizational support, and perceived supervisor support on marketing employees' level of trust. *Journal of Business Research, 63*, 1349–1355.

Echambadi, R., Arroniz, I., Reinartz, W., & Lee, J. (2006). Empirical generalizations from brand extension research: How sure are we? *International Journal of Research in Marketing, 23*, 253–261.

Echambadi, R., Campbell, B. A., & Agarwal, R. (2006). Encouraging best practice in quantitative management research: An incomplete list of opportunities. *Journal of Management Studies, 43*, 1801–1820.

Edwards, J. R. (2009). Seven deadly myths of testing moderation in organizational research. In R.J. Vandenberg (Ed.), *Statistical and methodological myths and urban legends: Doctrine, verity and fable in the organizational and social sciences* (pp. 143–164). New York, NY: Routledge/ Taylor & Francis Group.

Edwards, J. R., & Berry, J. W. (2010). The presence of something or the absence of nothing: Increasing theoretical precision in management research. *Organizational Research Methods, 13*, 668–689.

Eisenberger, R., Karagonlar, G., Stinglhamber, F., Neves, P., Becker, T. E., Gonzalez-Morales, M. G., & Steiger-Mueller, M. (2010). Leader-member exchange and affective organizational commitment: The contribution of supervisor's organizational embodiment. *Journal of Applied Psychology, 95*, 1085–1103.

Erdogan, B., & Bauer, T. N. (2010). Differentiated leader–member exchanges: The buffering role of justice climate. *Journal of Applied Psychology, 95*, 1104–1120.

Evans, E. M., & McShane, S. L. (1988). Employee perceptions of performance appraisal fairness in 2 organizations. *Canadian Journal of Behavioural Science-Revue Canadienne Des Sciences Du Comportement, 20*, 177–191.

Folger, R., & Konovsky, M. A. (1989). Effects of procedural and distributive justice on reactions to pay raise decisions. *Academy of Management Journal, 32*, 115–130.

Frazier, M. L., Johnson, P. D., Gavin, M., Gooty, J., & Snow, D. B. (2010). Organizational justice, trustworthiness, and trust: A multifoci examination. *Group & Organization Management, 35*, 39–76.

Gilliland, S. W. (1993). The perceived fairness of selection systems: An organizational justice perspective. *Academy of Management Review, 18*, 694–734.

Greenberg, J. (1990). Organizational justice: Yesterday, today, and tomorrow. *Journal of Management, 16*, 399–432.

Greenberg, J. (2001). Setting the justice agenda: Seven unanswered questions about "what, why, and how." *Journal of Vocational Behavior, 58*, 210–219.

Greenberg, J., & Colquitt, J. A. (2005). *Handbook of organizational justice*. Mahwah, NJ: Erlbaum.

Griffin, B. (2010). Multilevel relationships between organizational-level incivility, justice and intention to stay. *Work and Stress, 24*, 309–323.

Hammer, T. H., Bayazit, M., & Wazeter, D. L. (2009). Union leadership and member attitudes: A multi-level analysis. *Journal of Applied Psychology, 94*, 392–410.

Hauenstein, N. M. A., McGonigle, T., & Flinder, S. W. (2001). A meta-analysis of the relationship between procedural justice and distributive justice: Implications for justice research. *Employee Responsibilities and Rights Journal, 13*, 39–56.

Herda, D. N., & Lavelle, J. J. (2011). The effects of organizational fairness and commitment on the extent of benefits big four alumni provide their former firm. *Accounting Organizations and Society, 36*, 156–166.

Herda, D. N., & Lavelle, J. J. (2012). The auditor-audit firm relationship and its effect on burnout and turnover intention. *Accounting Horizons, 26*, 707–723.

Heslin, P. A., & VandeWalle, D. (2011). Performance appraisal procedural justice: The role of a manager's implicit person theory. *Journal of Management, 37*, 1694–1718.

Hollensbe, E. C., Khazanchi, S., & Masterson, S. S. (2008). How do I assess if my supervisor and organization are fair? Identifying the rules underlying entity-based justice perceptions. *Academy of Management Journal, 51*, 1099–1116.

Holtz, B. C., & Harold, C. M. (2009). Fair today, fair tomorrow? A longitudinal investigation of overall justice perceptions. *Journal of Applied Psychology, 94*, 1185–1199.

Holtz, B. C., & Harold, C. M. (2013). Effects of leadership consideration and structure on employee perceptions of justice and counterproductive work behavior. *Journal of Organizational Behavior, 34*, 492–519.

Hulland, J., Nenkov, G. Y., & Barclay, D. W. (2012). Perceived marketing-sales relationship effectiveness: a matter of justice. *Journal of the Academy of Marketing Science, 40*, 450–467.

Johnson, J., Truxillo, D. M., Erdogan, B., Bauer, T. N., & Hammer, L. (2009). Perceptions of overall fairness: Are effects on job performance moderated by leader-member exchange? *Human Performance, 22*, 432–449.

Johnson, R. E., Chang, C. H., & Rosen, C. C. (2010). "Who I am depends on how fairly I'm treated": Effects of justice on self-identity and regulatory focus. *Journal of Applied Social Psychology, 40*, 3020–3058.

Johnson, R. E., & Lord, R. G. (2010). Implicit effects of justice on self-identity. *Journal of Applied Psychology, 95*, 681–695.

Johnson, R. E., Rosen, C. C., Chang, C. H., Djurdjevic, E., & Taing, M. U. (2012). Recommendations for improving the construct clarity of higher-order multidimensional constructs. *Human Resource Management Review, 22*, 62–72.

Johnson, R. E., Selenta, C., & Lord, R. G. (2006). When organizational justice and the self-concept meet: Consequences for the organization and its members. *Organizational Behavior and Human Decision Processes, 99*, 175–201.

Jones, D. A., & Martens, M. L. (2009). The mediating role of overall fairness and the moderating role of trust certainty in justice-criteria relationships: The formation and use of fairness heuristics in the workplace. *Journal of Organizational Behavior, 30*, 1025–1051.

Kenny, D. A. (2008). Reflections on mediation. *Organizational Research Methods, 11*, 353–358.

Kim, H.-S. (2007). A multilevel study of antecedents and a mediator of employee-organization relationships. *Journal of Public Relations Research, 19*(2), 167–197.

Kim, T.-Y. (2004). The effects of cognitive appraisal on justice judgments: How and why do Asians differ from United States Americans? *Dissertation Abstracts International, 65*, 2671.

Kim, T.-Y., & Leung, K. (2007). Forming and reacting to overall fairness: A cross-cultural comparison. *Organizational Behavior and Human Decision Processes, 104*, 83–95.

Konovsky, M. A., & Folger, R. (1991). The effects of procedures, social accounts, and benefits level on victims layoff reactions. *Journal of Applied Social Psychology, 21*, 630–650.

Kwon, K., & Rupp, D. E. (2013). Overall justice climate partially mediates the relationship between high performance work systems and multilevel outcomes. Unpublished manuscript.

Kwon, K., Rupp, D. E., & Young E. (2008, August). HPWS, justice climate, and organizational effectiveness: A multilevel investigation. Paper presented at the 68th annual meeting of the Academy of Management, Anaheim, CA.

Leventhal, G. S. (1980). What should be done with equity theory? New approaches to the study of fairness in social relationships. In K. Gergen, M. Greenberg, & R. Willis (Eds.), *Social exchange: Advances in theory and research* (pp. 27–55). New York, NY: Plenum Press.

Leventhal, G. S., Karuza, J., & Fry, W. R. (1980). Beyond fairness: A theory of allocation preferences. In G. Mikula (Ed.), *Justice and social interaction* (pp. 167–218). New York, NY: Springer-Verlag.

Li, A., Cropanzano, R., & Bagger, J. (2013). Justice climate and peer justice climate. *Small Groups Research*.

Liao, H., & Rupp, D. E. (2005). The impact of justice climate and justice orientation on work outcomes: A cross level multifoci framework. *Journal of Applied Psychology, 90*, 242–256.

Lind, E. A. (2001a). Fairness Heuristic Theory: Justice judgments as pivotal cognitions in organizational relations. In J. Greenberg, & R. Cropanzano (Eds.), *Advances in organizational justice* (pp. 56–88). Stanford, CA: Stanford University Press.

Lind, E. A. (2001b). Thinking critically about justice judgments. *Journal of Vocational Behavior, 58*, 220–226.

Lind, E. A., Kulik, C. T., Ambrose, M. L., & deVera Park, M. V. (1993). Individual and corporate dispute resolution: Using procedural fairness as a decision heuristic. *Administrative Science Quarterly, 38*, 224–251.

Lind, E. A., & Tyler, T. R. (1988). *The social psychology of procedural justice*. New York, NY: Plenum Press.

Madera, J. M. (2012). Using social networking websites as a selection tool: The role of selection process fairness and job pursuit intentions. *International Journal of Hospitality Management, 31*, 1276–1282.

Mayer, D. M., Bardes, M., & Piccolo, R. F. (2008). Do servant-leaders help satisfy follower needs? An organizational justice perspective. *European Journal of Work and Organizational Psychology, 17*, 180–197.

Nicklin, J. M., Greenbaum, R., McNall, L. A., Folger, R., & Williams, K. J. (2011). The importance of contextual variables when judging fairness: An examination of counterfactual thoughts and fairness theory. *Organizational Behavior and Human Decision Processes, 114*, 127–141.

Niehoff, B. P., & Moorman, R. H. (1993). Justice as a mediator of the relationship between methods of monitoring and organizational citizenship behavior. *Academy of Management Journal, 36*, 527–556.

Patel, C., Budhwar, P., & Varma, A. (2012). Overall justice, work group identification and work outcomes: Test of moderated mediation process. *Journal of World Business, 47*, 213–222.

Priesemuth, M., Arnaud, A., & Schminke, M. (2013). Bad behavior in groups: The impact of overall justice climate and functional dependence on counterproductive work behavior in work units. *Group & Organizational Management, 38*, 230–257.

Rodell, J. B., & Colquitt, J. A. (2009). Looking ahead in times of uncertainty: The role of anticipatory justice in an organizational change context. *Journal of Applied Psychology, 94*, 989–1002.

Rodell, J. B., Colquitt, J. A., & Baer, M. D. (2012, April). From justice to injustice to ajustice: What else explains fairness? Paper presented at the annual meeting of the Society for Industrial and Organizational Psychology, San Diego, CA.

Rosen, C. C., Chang, C. H., Johnson, R. E., & Levy, P. E. (2009). Perceptions of the organizational context and psychological contract breach: Assessing competing perspectives. *Organizational Behavior and Human Decision Processes, 108*, 202–217.

Rupp, D. E., & Cropanzano, R. (2002). The mediating effects of social exchange relationships in predicting workplace outcomes from multifoci organizational justice. *Organizational Behavior and Human Decision Processes, 89*, 925–946.

Rupp, D. E., & Paddock, E. L. (2010). From justice events to justice climate: A multi-level temporal model of information aggregation and judgment, in E. A. Mannix, M. A. Neale, & E. Mullen (Eds.), *Research on managing groups and teams: Fairness and groups* (Vol. 13, pp. 245–273). Bingley, UK: Emerald Group Publishing.

Shapiro, D. L. (2001). The death of justice theory is likely if theorists neglect the "wheels" already invented and the voices of the injustice victims. *Journal of Vocational Behavior, 58*, 235–242.

See, K. E. (2009). Reactions to decisions with uncertain consequences: Reliance on perceived fairness versus predicted outcomes depends on knowledge. *Journal of Personality and Social Psychology, 96*, 104–118.

Sharoni, G., Tziner, A., Fein, E. C., Shultz, T., Shaul, K., & Zilberman, L. (2012). Organizational citizenship behavior and turnover intentions: Do organizational culture and justice moderate their relationship? *Journal of Applied Social Psychology, 42*(S1), E267–E294.

Simons, T., & Roberson, Q. (2003). Why managers should care about fairness: The effects of aggregate justice perceptions on organizational outcomes. *Journal of Applied Psychology, 88*, 432–443.

Sora, B., Caballer, A., Peiro, J. M., Silla, I., & Gracia, F. J. (2010). Moderating influence of organizational justice on the relationship between job insecurity and its outcomes: A multilevel analysis. *Economic and Industrial Democracy, 31*, 613–637.

Spell, C. S., & Arnold, T. J. (2007). A multi-level analysis of organizational justice climate, structure, and employee mental health. *Journal of Management, 33*, 724–751.

Stone-Romero, E. F., & Liakhovitski, D. (2002). Strategies for detecting moderator variables: A review of conceptual and empirical issues. *Research in Personnel and Human Resources Management, 21*, 333–372.

Tang, T.-W., & Tang, Y.-Y. (2012). Promoting service-oriented organizational citizenship behaviors in hotels: The role of high-performance human resource practices and organizational social climates. *International Journal of Hospitality Management, 31*, 885–895.

Tansky, J. W. (1993). Justice and organizational citizenship behavior: What is the relationship? *Employee Responsibilities and Rights Journal, 6*, 195–207.

Thibaut, J. & Walker, L. (1975). *Procedural justice: A psychological analysis*. Hillsdale, NJ: Erlbaum.

Törnblom, K. Y., & Vermunt, R. (1999). An integrative perspective on social justice: Distributive and procedural fairness evaluations of positive and negative outcome allocations. *Social Justice Research, 12*, 39–64.

Tremblay, M. A. (2010). Fairness perceptions and trust as mediators on the relationship between leadership style, unit commitment, and turnover intentions of Canadian Forces Personnel. *Military Psychology, 22*, 510–523.

Treviño, L. K., & Weaver, G. R. (2001). Organizational justice and ethics program "follow-through": Influences on employees' harmful and helpful behavior. *Business Ethics Quarterly, 11*, 651–671.

Tyler, T. R. (1989). The psychology of procedural justice: A test of the group-value model. *Journal of Personality and Social Psychology, 57*, 830–838.

Tyler, T. R., & Caine, A. (1981).The influence of outcomes and procedures on satisfaction with formal leaders. *Journal of Personality and Social Psychology, 41*, 642–655.

van den Bos, K., Wilke, H. A. M., Lind, E. A., & Vermunt, R. (1998). Evaluating outcomes by means of the fair process effect: Evidence for different processes in fairness and satisfaction judgments. *Journal of Personality and Social Psychology, 74*, 1493–1503.

Whiteside, D. B., & Barclay, L. J. (2013). Echoes of silence: Employee silence as a mediator between overall justice and employee outcomes. *Journal of Business Ethics, 116*, 251–266.

Whitman, D. S., Caleo, S., Carpenter, N. C., Horner, M. T., & Bernerth, J. B. (2012). Fairness at the collective level: A meta-analytic examination of the consequences and boundary conditions of organizational justice climate. *Journal of Applied Psychology, 97*, 776–791.

Williams, L. J., Vandenberg, R. J., & Edwards, J. R. (2009). Structural equation modeling in management research: A guide for improved analysis. *Academy of Management Annals, 3*, 543–604.

CHAPTER

6 Fairness at the Unit Level: Justice Climate, Justice Climate Strength, and Peer Justice

Andrew Li, Russell S. Cropanzano, *and* Agustin Molina

Abstract

Historically, organizational justice research has been studied at the individual level of analysis. Although this perspective remains important, fairness can also be studied at the collective or unit level. In this chapter we review research on justice climate, defined as the extent to which work group members form shared judgments regarding how they have been treated by authority figures. We also discuss related concepts. These include justice climate strength, defined as the extent to which teammates agree in their fairness perceptions, and peer justice climate, defined as the collective perceptions regarding how coworkers treat one another. We find that unit level fairness has main and interactive effects on important criterion variables, such as performance, worker mental health, and citizenship behaviors.

Key Words: justice climate, peer justice, justice climate strength, justice climate level, overall justice climate

Originally grounded in philosophy (e.g., Rawls, 1971; Sandel, 2009), the concept of justice has been introduced into organizational settings in order to explain individuals' experiences with resource distributions, policies, and interpersonal treatment (Cohen-Charash & Spector, 2001; Colquitt, Conlon, Wesson, Porter, & Ng, 2001). The scholarly interest in workplace justice has spawned a large body of literature addressing its implications for a number of organizational practices, including such things as staffing (Cropanzano & Wright, 2003), performance evaluation (Levy & Williams, 2004), compensation (Greenberg, 1990, 2006), negotiation (Giacobbe-Miller, 1995; Porter, Conlon, & Barber, 2004), layoffs (Brockner, Konovsky, Cooper-Schneider, Folger, Martin, & Bies, 1994; Skarlicki, Barclay, & Douglas Pugh, 2008), sexual harassment (Elkins, Phillips, & Ward, 2008; Krings & Facchin, 2009), affirmative actions (Cropanzano, Slaughter, Bachiochi, 2005; Parker, Baltes, & Christiansen, 1997), and work/life balance (Judge & Colquitt, 2004), among others.

One theme emerging from this work is that employee perceptions of justice matter. Specifically, research has suggested that when employees believe that they have been subjected to fair treatment, they tend to show a higher level of work performance, have a greater tendency to go beyond job requirements by performing more citizenship behaviors, have better attitudes toward work and their employment, and enjoy better psychological and physical health (Cohen-Charash & Spector, 2001; Colquitt et al., 2001; Fassina, Jones, & Uggerslev, 2008; Hausknecht, Day, & Thomas, 2004; Li & Cropanzano, 2009a; Shaw, Wild, & Colquitt, 2003).

Historically, justice research has been conducted at the individual level. As Konovsky (2000, p. 504) noted over a decade ago, "almost wholly absent from consideration has been the influence of higher-order factors on procedural justice including culture and organization or group-level procedural justice antecedents and consequences." The same sentiment was echoed by Lind, Kray, and Thompson (1998, p. 19) who noted that "most of the potential information about the fairness of any given authority or institution lies in collective, not personal, experience." Responding to these calls, in the last 15 years, justice scholars have elevated justice research from the individual level to the unit level (for qualitative reviews, see Colquitt, Zapata-Phelan, & Roberson, 2005; Li & Cropanzano, 2009b; Rupp, Bashshur, & Liao, 2007, and for a quantitative review, see Whitman, Caleo, Carpenter, Horner, & Bernerth, 2012). An important construct emerging from these studies is justice climate (Naumann & Bennett, 2000), defined as the shared perceptions of how fairly a unit has been treated (usually by an authority figure). As our review in this chapter will reveal, this line of scholarly investigations holds significant promises in advancing justice research and enhancing our understanding of how individuals form their justice perceptions within the context of groups/teams/organizations. As we shall discuss, these collective experiences of justice may translate into meaningful actions and attitudes targeting those who are responsible for these experiences.

Despite these encouraging developments, this body of literature has also evidenced a number of limitations, such as the lack of longitudinal studies to benchmark the emergence of justice climate in a unit, the need for additional theories to guide the understanding of the differential effects of the different types and sources of justice climate, and lingering issues related to the operationalization of justice climate. To address these limitations, we will provide a comprehensive review of the empirical work related to justice climate in the literature. Our review begins with some brief comments on earlier work, which treated justice at the individual level of analysis. With this foundation behind us, we then explore the theoretical positions underlying justice climate research, subsequently following this with a detailed review of the empirical evidence. Afterwards, we consider the related concept of justice climate strength, which pertains to the level of agreement among teammates. We then turn to peer justice climate, the general manner in which group members treat one another. Finally, we conclude with a discussion of future research needs. The articles included in our review are presented in Table 6.1 in chronological order.

Justice at the Individual Level

Historically, justice scholars have emphasized three types of justice. Distributive justice pertains to the fairness of the allocation or outcomes received. Procedural justice pertains to the decision-making policies or processes. Interactional justice pertains to the interpersonal treatment that one receives from others. Interactional justice is sometimes subdivided into two parts. Informational justice refers to the availability of explanations when something questionable occurs, whereas interpersonal justice refers to the dignity and respect with which one is treated (Colquitt, 2001). We discuss each of these in more detail below.

Distributive Justice

Distributive justice refers to the perceptions of fairness of the distribution of valuable resources in organizations, such as compensation, benefits, and promotions. Historically, three rules of distributive justice have received the most research attention. Equality is the rule by which everyone gets the same amount. The rule of need stipulates that allocations are based upon necessity. The rule of equity dictates that people are compensated based upon the size of their contribution (Leung & Bond, 1984).

Among these three rules, equity has been the most influential (Adams, 1965). Equity theory posits that individuals compare the ratio of their own input (such as the number of work hours, education, skills) and output (such as their salary, ranking, and the size of their office) with the same ratio of a reference other. Individuals experience a state of equity when the two ratios are equivalent. In contrast, individuals tend to believe that they have been treated inequitably if the ratios are not equivalent, although past research has suggested that they tend to respond more negatively when their own input/output ratio compares unfavorably to the same ratio of others (as when they are underpaid, Walster, Berscheid, & Walster, 1973). Equity theory predicts that individuals who experience inequity may be motivated to restore the equity by withholding efforts to contribute to the success of the organization. Direct tests of the theory have provided supportive evidence. For example, Greenberg (1990) found that employee theft rate went up dramatically when they received a dramatic pay cut. Greenberg (1990) argued that a substantial pay cut reduces employees' perceptions of fairness. They may even steal from the company in order to restore equity (because doing so increases the output obtained through theft).

Table 6.1 **Justice Climate Measures and Sample**

Author	Year	Justice Constructs	Justice Measures	Sample
Mossholder et al.	1998	PJC	4-item scale constructed for the study	323 employees working in 53 locations of a company
Naumann et al.	2000	PJ	9-item scale by Moorman (1991)	220 employees working in 34 bank branches
Naumann et al.	2002	PJ	9-item scale by Naumann and Bennett (2000)	220 employees working in 34 bank branches
Colquitt et al.	2002	PJ	7-item scale by Colquitt (2001)	1,747 employees nested in 88 teams
Johnson et al.	2002	PJ	6-item scale developed by Kim and Mauborgne (1991)	51 International Joint Ventures
Dietz et al.	2003	PJ	4-item scale consistent with past PJ climate research	250 plants of a large public service organization
Simons et al.	2003	PJ, IPJ	PJ (3 items) and IPJ (4 items) were based on Niehoff and Moorman (1993)	8,832 employees working in 111 hotels
Ehrhart	2004	PJ	4-item scale by Colquitt (2001)	249 departments
Caldwell et al.	2004	PJ*	3-item scale consistent with Leventhal et al. (1980)	299 employees in 34 work units
Chen et al.	2005	PJ	9-item scale by Naumann and Bennett (2000)	743 employees nested in 148 work groups
Moliner et al.	2005	PJ, IJ, DJ	DJ (4 items), PJ (3 items), and IJ (4 items) scales were created based on the definitions of these constructs	324 employees nested in 108 work units
Liao et al.	2005	PJ, IFJ, IPJ	PJ (3 items), IFJ (5 items), and IPJ (3 items) were based on Byrne (1999)	231 employees nested in 44 groups
Brown et al.	2005	IJ	2-item measure of interactional fairness	485 employees in 183 groups
Deery et al.	2005	PJ	4-item scale based on Moorman (1991)	990 employees nested in 305 bank branches
Roberson	2006a	PJ, DJ	4-item PJ scale was adapted from Kanfer, Sawyer, Early, & Lind (1987). Three-item DJ scale was adapted from Tyler (1994)	372 students in 124 3-person teams
Fedor, et al.	2006	PJ*	4-item scale based on Caldwell et al. (2004)	806 employees in 34 organizations
Roberson	2006b	PJ, DJ	4-item PJ scale was adapted from Kanfer et al. (1987). Three-item DJ scale was adapted from Tyler (1994)	372 students in 124 3-person teams
Spell & Arnold	2007	PJ, IJ, DJ	PJ (7 items), DJ (4 items), and IJ (9 items) by Colquitt (2001)	677 responses from 72 groups
Yang et al.	2007	PJ	7-item scale by Moorman (1991)	280 employees nested in 56 groups

(continued)

Table 6.1 (Continued)

Author	Year	Justice Constructs	Justice Measures	Sample
Herold et al.	2007	PJ*	3-item scale based on Caldwell et al. (2004)	266 employees in 25 work units
Mayer et al.	2007	PJ, IFJ, IPJ	PJ (4 items), IFJ (3 items), and IPJ (3 items) were based on Colquitt (2001)	3445 employees working in 383 departments
Lin et al.	2007	PJ	6-item scale by Niehoff and Moorman (1993)	135 employees nested in 45 teams
Wallace et al.	2008	PJ	6-item scale based on Leventhal (1980)	54 district facilities of a large Fortune 500 company
Walumbwa et al.	2008	PJ	7-item scale by Colquitt (2001)	212 employees from 42 work units
Tangirala et al.	2008	PJ	6-item scale by Niehoff and Moorman (1993)	606 nurses nested within 30 nursing departments
Hakonen et al.	2008	PJ	5-item scale based on Moorman (1991) and Tyler and Blader (2000)	293 people embedded in 39 virtual teams
Luo	2008	PJ	11-item measure created for the study	168 strategic alliances
Luria et al.	2008	PJ	5-item scale based on Folger and Konovsky (1989)	171 employees in 20 restaurants
Trevor et al.	2008	PJ	3-item scale consistent with Moorman (1991)	267 company-years
Dayan et al.	2009	PJ, IJ, DJ	PJ (5 items) scale was based on Colquitt (2001), IJ (3 items) scale was based on Moorman (1991). DJ (6 items) scale was based on Price and Mueller (1986)	228 team members working in 107 teams
Caldwell et al.	2009	PJ*	4-item scale by Fedor et al. (2004)	431 employees working in 33 organizations
Griffin	2010	IJ	4-item scale that is similar in content to Bies and Moag (1986)	34209 employees from 179 organizations
Cho et al.	2010	PJ	4-item scale by Colquitt (2001)	119 employees from 40 groups
Walumbwa et al.	2010	PJ	7-item scale by Colquitt (2001)	815 employees from 123 groups
Li et al.	2010	PJ	7-item scale by Farh et al. (1997)	200 employees from 54 work groups
Erdogan et al.	2010	PJ, DJ	PJ (6 items) and DJ (5 items) scales were based on Niehoff and Moorman (1993)	276 employees nested in 25 stores
Lipponen et al.	2010	PJ, IJ, DJ	PJ (7 items), IJ (unclear), and DJ (unclear) scales were based on Moorman (1991)	441 employees from 59 academic departments

(continued)

Table 6.1 (Continued)

Author	Year	Justice Constructs	Justice Measures	Sample
Sora et al.	2010	OJC	4-item scale from Guest and Conway (2002)	597 employees from 29 organizations
Cropanzano et al.	2011	PPJ, PIJ	PPJ (5 items) scale was based on Li and Cropanzano (2009b). PIJ (4 items) scale was based on Donovan, Drasgow, & Munson (1998)	625 members embedded in 170 teams
Hsiung	2012	PJ	Six-item scale by Niehoff and Moorman (1993)	404 salespersons embedded in 70 work groups
Priesemuth et al.	2013	OJC	Three-item scale from Ambrose and Schminke (2009)	539 employees working in 113 units
Zhang et al.	2013	IFJ, IPJ	IFJ (5 items) and IPJ (4 items) were based on Colquitt (2001)	351 employees working in 117 departments
Cropanzano et al.	2013	OPJ, OJC	OPJ was a three-item scale, OJC was a three-item scale based on Ambrose and Schminke (2009)	323 employees in 95 work units
Oc et al.	2013	OJC	Three-item scale constructed for the study	312 students embedded in 109 groups
Ogunfowora	2013	IPJ	Four-item scale from Colquitt (2001)	297 employees nested in 58 work groups
Li et al.	2013	PPJ, PIJ, PDJ, PJ, IJ, DJ	PDJ (5 items) scale was based on Li and Cropanzano (2009b). PPJ (5 items) and PIJ (4 items) scales were based on Cropanzano et al. (2011). DJ (3 items) scale was based on Colquitt (2001). PJ (6 items) and IJ (4 items) scales were based on Masterson (2001)	175 members embedded in 47 teams

Note: DJ: Distributive Justice; IFJ: Informational Justice; IJ: Interactional Justice; IPJ: Interpersonal Justice; OJC: Overall Justice Climate; OPJ: Overall Peer Justice; PDJ: Peer Distributive Justice; PIJ: Peer Interpersonal Justice; PJ: Procedural Justice; PJ*: Change Process Fairness; PJC: Procedural Justice Context; PPJ: Peer Procedural Justice.

Procedural Justice

Procedural justice refers to the extent to which decision makers use a fair procedure to make decisions in organizations. Thibaut and Walker (1975) distinguished decision control from process control in the litigation process. Specifically, they argued that when litigants are given process control (for example, by being allowed to voice their opinion), they tend to view the system more favorably even if they encounter negative outcomes, compared to a system that denies them any process control. Since Thibaut and Walker's seminal work, process control has been incorporated into standards used to gauge the level of procedural justice. Leventhal (1976, 1980) identified six rules of process fairness. Specifically, he argued that organizations can enhance employees' perceptions of procedural fairness by (1) applying policies and standards consistently across all those affected by them (the consistency rule), (2) using accurate information for decision-making to enhance the quality of the decision made (the accuracy rule), (3) resisting the influence of personal bias in the decision-making process (the bias suppression rule), (4) creating a mechanism that allows mistakes to be corrected once identified (the error correctability rule), (5) ensuring that decisions are made in an ethical manner (the ethicality rule), and (6) providing a channel that allows every group of employees to have a voice in the decision-making process (the representativeness rule). These six rules have been incorporated into subsequent procedural justice measures (e.g., Colquitt, 2001; Niehoff & Moorman, 1993). A substantial body of research has attested to the effects of fair procedures in the workplace, especially when the outcomes that employees receive are negative and unexpected (see Brockner & Wiesenfeld, 1996, for an extensive review of the literature).

Interactional Justice

Bies and colleagues (Bies, 2001; Bies & Moag, 1986) suggested that employees not only attend to decision outcomes and process, they also attend to the interpersonal treatment they receive, which they termed interactional justice. According to Bies (2001), employees experience a high level of interactional justice when they are treated with respect and dignity and when they are provided with timely justifications for decisions. Subsequent research has split interactional justice into two subtypes. Interpersonal justice focuses on the level of warmth, trust, and respect. Informational justice focuses on the degree of accuracy and timeliness in information provision (Colquitt, 2001; Greenberg, 1993). Available evidence suggests that interactional justice softens the blow of negative outcomes. For example, Li, Evans, Christian, Gilliland, Kausel, and Stein (2011) found that when there was a match between the regulatory priming of the study participants and the framing of the explanation given to them for a negative event, these participants tended to perceive a higher level of interactional justice.

Closing Thoughts Regarding the Types of Justice

Past research has linked all three (or four) types of justice perceptions to important criterion variables, at least at the individual level of analysis. In a meta-analysis, Colquitt and colleagues (2001) found that justice is related to performance, organizational citizenship behaviors (OCB), job satisfaction, organizational commitment, withdrawal behaviors, and counterproductive behaviors, among others. In addition, they found that these different types of justice accounted for incremental variance over each other. This is important for justice climate research, which is conducted at the unit level. In general, most of the available evidence has emphasized procedural justice climate, with less work focusing on distributive or interactional justice (Li & Cropanzano, 2009b). However, there are a number of exceptions to this generality. This work suggests that distinct dimensions of unit level justice can be identified, and these roughly parallel their counterparts at the individual level of analysis.

The Emergence of Justice Climate

The review thus far has focused on justice perceptions at the individual level. In recent years, justice researchers have expressed significant interest in studying justice as a unit-level construct. Naumann and Bennett (2000) were among the first to examine this construct, which they termed "justice climate." They defined justice climate as "group-level cognition about how a work group as a whole is treated" (p. 882). The scholarly interest in justice climate is propelled by organizations' increasing reliance on the use of teams to organize the workforce and the perceived inadequacy of the single-level method of analyses to examine complex phenomena in organizations where it's not uncommon for individuals to be embedded in teams that are, in turn, embedded in even higher-level organizational units. In addition, recent research on the third-party justice effects demonstrates that individuals not only respond to the fairness that they experience personally, but also care about the extent to which others in their social network are treated fairly and react accordingly (Rupp et al., 2007). Two theoretical perspectives have been proposed to account for the emergence of justice climate. These are the social information processing theory (SIP, Salancik & Pfeffer, 1978) and the attraction-selection-attrition model (ASA, Schneider, 1987). A brief discussion of these two theories and their implications for justice climate is presented next.

Social Information Processing Theory

According to SIP (Salancik & Pfeffer, 1978), employees do not operate in an organizational vacuum. Instead, they are constantly influenced by others who exist in their social space, such as their supervisors and co-workers. Since most members of the same unit tend to receive the same organizational outcome and are subjected to the same (or similar) company procedures/policies, they are apt to come to a similar evaluation of justice. However, there is more to the story. When employees encounter ambiguous information pertaining to the distribution of outcomes, company policies and practices, and interpersonal treatment, they tend to rely on their co-workers to help them make sense of their experience.

Degoey (2000) proposed the idea of justice contagion in the workplace, arguing that the sharing of justice experience operates in a manner akin to the spread of contagious diseases. Degoey (2000) distinguished two types of justice contagion, cognitive and emotional contagion. Cognitive contagion refers to the sharing of information and opinion about events that have justice implications. For example, members of the same unit may rely on each other to fill in the gap in their interpretation of justice-related information (for example, they may discuss with each other whether a particular event is fair or not, whether an explanation provided by the management may satisfactorily ameliorate a negative event, or what standards or criteria should be employed to evaluate the fairness of certain company polices). Evidence supports this possibility (Hollensbe, Khazanchi, & Masterson, 2008; Kray & Lind, 2002).

Emotional contagion refers to the extent to which members within the same unit are influenced by each other's emotional response to justice-related events. In other words, justice violation may instigate emotional reactions (such as anger and distress, Rupp & Spencer, 2006; Weiss, Suckow, & Cropanzano, 1999), and such affective responses to justice may trigger the same emotions on others who experience the same justice event or validate the feelings that they experience as a result of being exposed to the event. Overtime, social and emotional construction and interpretation of justice may lead to somewhat similar justice evaluations of the same target by individuals within the same unit.

There is some evidence for SIP in the context of justice climate. Drawing on SIP, Roberson (2006a) argued that individuals who encounter justice-related events may seek out each other to make sense of their experience. Greater sense making, defined as "an attentional process through which individuals interpret their environment and subsequently, come to assign and share subjective meanings of past events" (p. 178), may allow members of the same unit to converge on their perspective of justice. Roberson (2006a) found substantial support for her prediction.

Attraction-Selection-Attrition Model

The ASA model (Schneider, Goldstein, & Smith, 1995; Schneider, Smith, Taylor, & Fleenor, 1998) posits that individuals are attracted to those who are similar to themselves (in terms of, for example, personality, disposition, education, and physical features), job applicants and organization select each other on the basis of their similarities, and finally individuals who do not fit in are more likely to leave compared to those who do. The ASA model predicts that, over time, organizations become increasingly homogeneous as individuals are less likely to apply for positions in organizations with employees that are deemed to be dissimilar to themselves, and even if they do, they may decide to leave due to incompatibility with others in the organization.

There are three reasons to believe that this process may promote the emergence of justice climate. First, individuals who are similar to each other are apt to respond in a similar manner to events or information that has justice implications. They may use similar standards to evaluate whether a certain outcome is fair or whether an explanation is sufficiently convincing, which may allow them to come to similar judgments on justice. Second, Degoey (2000) argued that individuals are more likely to seek out those who are similar to themselves to share their experience and emotional response to justice-related information, which may reinforce each other's opinion and lead to a similar perspective on justice. Third, socialization is defined as the process through which individuals are indoctrinated by the unique culture or norm in a unit. Socialization facilitates the development of a mental model shared by individuals within the same unit, which they rely on to interpret ambiguous or emotionally charged situations, such as justice violations (Rupp et al., 2007). This ASA model has been explicitly applied to justice climate research. Colquitt, Noe, and Jackson (2002) drew on the ASA model to predict a relationship between demographic diversity within a team and the level of agreement among team members on procedural justice (termed as justice climate strength, which we discuss later).

SIP theory and the ASA model do more than provide a framework for understanding the emergence of justice climate. They also help us understand the emergence of additional constructs pertaining to unit level fairness (Rupp & Paddock, 2010). These other climates may emerge from sources of justice different from those related to authority figures. One example that we will discuss in a later section has to do with the general manner in which group members treat one another—peer justice.

Reviewing the Justice Climate Level Literature

Having considered the theoretical issues pertaining to the emergence of justice climate, we shift our attention in the next section to the empirical literature on justice climate. Justice climate researchers sometimes make a distinction between climate *strength* and justice climate *level* (Colquitt et al., 2002; Naumann & Bennett, 2000). Justice climate level refers to the extent to which members of the same unit believe that their unit as a whole has been treated fairly. Operationally, justice scholars tend to derive climate level based on the average score of the justice perceptions reported by members within the same unit, with a higher average score representing a more favorable climate. Justice climate strength, in contrast, refers to the degree of agreement among members of the same unit on whether the unit has been treated fairly. Two units may have similar levels of justice climate but have varying levels of agreement among members of the team. For example, one team may include all members who report similar levels of justice whereas the other one may include some members who report extremely high levels of justice and others who report extremely low levels of justice. In this section, we review studies that focus primarily on climate level, and we will review studies focusing on climate strength in the following section.

Our review is structured as follows. First, we examine studies that treat justice climate as the predictor of outcome variables, both at the group level and at the individual level. Second, we consider a series of three applications of justice climate—organizational change, managing strategic relationships, and leadership. Third, we discuss how justice climate interacts with other variables to predict employee and organizational outcomes. Finally, we conclude with a discussion of Whitman et al.'s (2012) meta-analysis. In each of these subsections, we review the relevant literature in chronological order.

Justice Climate as an Antecedent Variable

MOSSHOLDER, BENNETT, AND MARTIN (1998)

The first investigation of justice at the unit level is the study by Mossholder and colleagues (1998). Lamenting the exclusive focus on justice as an individual phenomenon, Mossholder and colleagues (1998) argued that being subjected to similar treatments (such as company policies that are applied to everyone in the same unit) may promote discussion of the level of fairness among members of the same unit. The discussion may lead to social influence and comparison, a process that may eventually give rise to unit-level justice perceptions that they termed "procedural justice context." Mossholder and colleagues (1998) found that procedural justice context was related to employees' job satisfaction but not their organizational commitment. In addition, they found that the unit-level construct explained variance above and beyond the variance explained by its individual-level counterpart.

NAUMANN AND BENNETT (2000)

Naumann and Bennett (2000) replicated and extended the work by Mossholder and colleagues (1998) in two important ways. First, they provided a theoretical justification for why (procedural) justice climate may predict outcome variables even when the effects of its individual-level counterpart are controlled for. Specifically, Naumann and Bennett (2000) argued that individuals determine their attitudes and behaviors not only on the basis of the treatment that they personally receive from the management, but also on the basis of the experience of the entire group as a whole. In other words, individuals are influenced by the justice experienced by their co-workers and take that into account when they respond to justice in the workplace. These arguments suggest that both individual-level justice and unit-level justice should uniquely explain variance on employees' attitudes and behaviors. Second, Naumann and Bennett (2000) examined employee behavior (helping behavior) reported by supervisors as a function of justice, in addition to their attitude (organizational commitment). Naumann and Bennett (2000) found that justice climate was uniquely related to employees' helping behaviors, even when the effects of procedural justice at the individual level were controlled for. However, they found no support for the effects of justice climate on organizational commitment, a finding similar to those reported by Mossholder and colleagues (1998). In addition to these important findings, Naumann and Bennett (2000) also evaluated factors predictive of the strength of justice climate within a unit. We will present these findings in a later section of this review.

NAUMANN AND BENNETT (2002)

Naumann and Bennett (2002) examined whether justice climate may impact unit-level performance, and the mechanisms through which these effects are realized. Unlike their earlier work (Naumann & Bennett, 2000), helping behavior was conceptualized as a group-level construct, representing the mean amount of helping behaviors exhibited by a group. Naumann and Bennett (2002) distinguished two types of unit-level performance, perceived group performance rated by supervisors and financial performance that was based on quantitative measures of profitability. Naumann and Bennett (2002) found that the level of procedural justice climate was positively related to the level of helping behaviors within the group (or branch). More importantly, helping behaviors mediated the relationship between procedural justice climate and perceived group performance but not to the financial performance of the group.

SIMONS AND ROBERSON (2003)

Simons and Roberson (2003) examined the relationships between two facets of justice climate (procedural and interpersonal) and unit-level outcomes and the process through which these effects occur. Simons and Roberson (2003) found that procedural justice climate and interpersonal justice climate were both related to guest service satisfaction aggregated to the hotel level. These effects were mediated by employee commitment and discretionary service behavior. Although they found that the link between interpersonal justice climate and employee commitment was mediated by satisfaction with supervision, the link between procedural justice climate and employee commitment was not. They also found that procedural and interpersonal justice climates were related to hotel-level employee turnover; these relationships were mediated by satisfaction with supervision, employee commitment, and intent to remain with their organization.

DIETZ, ROBINSON, FOLGER, BARON, AND SCHULZ (2003)

Dietz et al. (2003) studied factors leading to aggression in the workplace. One of the factors that they identified was the level of procedural justice climate in the organization. These authors argued that a low level of procedural justice climate may promote aggression for two reasons. First, organizational injustice may create an environment characterized by a negative affective tone that may elicit aggressive behaviors. Second, a low level of procedural justice climate may also create the norm encouraging and condoning disrespectful behaviors and the use of aggression to resolve differences at work. However, their prediction was not supported. Dietz and colleagues speculated that their procedural justice climate measure, which had not been validated psychometrically, might have contributed to these findings, or the lack thereof. We will discuss the measurement issue in a later section of the review.

CHEN, LAM, NAUMANN, AND SCHAUBROECK (2005)

Chen and his colleagues (2005) identified procedural justice climate as one of the predictors of group citizenship behaviors (GCB), defined as the extent to which groups engage in behaviors to support other groups and the entire organization. Chen et al. argued that a high level of procedural justice climate may create a pleasant work environment, which may motivate group members to engage in extra-role behaviors to assist other groups. Results of their study conducted in Hong Kong provided substantial support for their prediction.

LIN, TANG, LI, WU, AND LIN (2007)

Another study that also examines the mechanism through which justice climate influences outcome variables is the one by Lin and colleagues (2007). These authors found that procedural justice climate was related to employees' helping behavior, and this relationship was mediated by the cooperative norm within the group. Very few studies have investigated mediating mechanisms linking justice climate to outcome variables at the unit level. Although much research has been conducted to understand the situations under which justice climate may influence outcome variables (we will review these studies in a later section), much less is known about how these effects unfold, and this is certainly an important area for future research.

DEERY AND IVERSON (2005)

Deery and Iverson (2005) examined the relationship between procedural justice climate and labor relations. These authors argued that a high level of procedural justice climate may create the incentives for labor unions to work with the management, thus promoting a cooperative relationship. These authors found that procedural justice climate was positively related to cooperative labor relations. In addition, they also found that procedural justice climate was significantly related to employees' organizational commitment, productivity, and quality of service.

LURIA AND YAGIL (2008)

Luria and Yagil (2008) examined the relationship between two facets of organizational climate: ethical climate and procedural justice climate. Ethical climate refers to "the prevailing perception of typical organizational practices and procedures that have ethical content" (p. 277). Luria and Yagil (2008) found that ethical and procedural climates were related to each other, suggesting that organizational leadership that uses fair processes to make decisions tends to be viewed as moral models by employees.

DAYAN, BENEDETTO, AND COLAK (2009)

These scholars investigated justice climate as an antecedent of managerial trust in new product development project teams. These authors reasoned that since justice treatment conveys the message that employees are valued members of the community and assures a favorable outcome in the long term (cf., Tyler & Dawes, 1993; Tyler & Lind, 1992), employees should respond positively by having more trust in their managers. Dayan and colleagues examined all three types of justice climate, finding that all were related to managerial trust. However, when all of them were included in the same equation, the effects of interactional justice climate on managerial trust became nonsignificant.

LIPPONEN AND WISSE (2010)

These investigators focused on justice climate as the predictors of academic performance at the department level in a large university. Drawing on the group engagement model (e.g., Tyler & Blader, 2000), Lipponen and Wisse (2010) argued that justice climate may enhance employees' identification with their unit, which may in turn increase their motivation to perform at a higher level. They found support for the links between distributive and procedural justice climates and performance but not the link between interactional justice climate and performance. These findings paralleled those of Dayan et al. (2009).

GRIFFIN (2010)

Griffin (2010) examined the role of justice climate in attenuating the relationship between unit-level incivility, defined as the extent to which group members engage in behaviors that violate the norm for mutual respect and harm the well-being of others in the group, and employees' intention to stay. Griffin (2010) argued that a high level of interactional justice climate may reduce the negative effects of unit-level incivility because the negative effects of uncivil behaviors exhibited by their co-workers are offset by the respectful and supportive behaviors demonstrated by organizational leadership. The moderating role of interactional justice climate was not supported in her study. Instead, Griffin (2010) found that interactional justice climate mediated the relationship between unit-level incivility and individuals' intention to remain in the organization. Griffin (2010) argued that a high level of unit-level incivility may create an environment that reduces individuals' perceptions of interpersonal fairness characterizing the workplace.

Justice Climate and Organizational Change

One specific application of justice climate has been the study of organizational change. Based on individual-level research stressing the importance of change participants' perceptions of procedural justice (e.g., Brockner et al., 1994), four studies examined the role of "change process fairness," a group-level construct designed to assess the fairness associated with the implementation of change processes. Following Leventhal's rules of process fairness (1976, 1980), change process fairness climate covers facets of procedural justice but it does so while considering specific organizational changes. Examples of such facets include participation, well-informed communication, rationale for change, and advance notice. As depicted in these four studies, a given organizational change can be viewed and interpreted differently, depending on the level of unit-level fairness.

CALDWELL, HEROLD, AND FEDOR (2004)

Caldwell et al. (2004) examined the cross-level effect of change process fairness climate on individuals' perceptions of changes in predicting person–job fit and person–organization fit. Caldwell and colleagues argued that a change process climate that is fair may increase individuals' person–job and person–organization fit because it provides them with a sense of control resulting from involvement with decision-making. Although the direct effect of change process fairness climate on person–job and person–organization fit was not supported, Caldwell et al. (2004) did find a significant positive relationship between change process fairness climate and person–organization fit when additional interaction terms were considered. Caldwell et al. (2004) found that the positive relationship between change process fairness climate and person–organization fit was moderated by the extent of change. Specifically, the relationship between change process fairness climate and person–organization fit became stronger as the extent of the change became smaller. The authors found a similar interaction between change process fairness climate and the age of individuals. Once again, the relationship between change process fairness climate and person-organization fit became stronger when age was low rather than high. Lastly, Caldwell and colleagues (2004) reported an interaction between change process fairness climate and individuals' mastery orientation such that the relationship between change process fairness climate and person-job fit became negative when mastery was low rather than high.

FEDOR, CALDWELL, AND HEROLD (2006)

Fedor et al. (2006) investigated the effect of change process fairness climate on individuals' commitment to a specific change and commitment to the organization. Based on a significant amount of research suggesting that when change is handled in a fair manner individuals' reactions are more favorable (e.g., Novelli, Kirkman, & Shapiro, 1995), Fedor and colleagues (2006) hypothesized that change process fairness climate would be positively related to change commitment and organizational commitment. Even though Fedors' hypotheses were not supported, they did find that change process fairness climate interacted with the extent of the change at the unit level when predicting organizational commitment. Specifically, Fedor and colleagues (2006) observed that the effect of the extent of change occurring at the unit level on organizational commitment was negative when change process fairness climate was low, but it was positive when fairness was high. In other words, relatively extensive changes promote commitment when they are implemented fairly, but relatively extensive changes work against commitment when they are implemented unfairly.

HEROLD, FEDOR, AND CALDWELL (2007)

In a similar study to the one conducted by Fedor et al. (2006), Herold and colleagues (2007) examined the effect of change self-efficacy (personal confidence about the ability to handle a specific change) and change turbulence (changes that represent additional distractions and adaptation demands and thus form an important part of the context for individuals' reactions to the focal change) on commitment to a specific change. Since change process fairness climate seems to be an important aspect of any given change, Herold et al. (2007) controlled for the effect of this variable. Similar to Fedor et al. (2006), Herold and colleagues (2007) did not find a significant relationship between change process fairness climate and employees commitment to change. However, they did observe an interesting relationship. Herold et al. (2007) reported a negative correlation between change process fairness climate and change turbulence. This inverse relationship suggests that the more changes that have been implemented, the less attention is paid to developing a fair procedural climate.

CALDWELL, LIU, FEDOR, AND HEROLD (2009)

Caldwell and colleagues (2009) attempted to understand why actions generally considered fair by management may be interpreted differently depending on the "eye of the beholder." In their study, Caldwell et al. (2009) referred to change process fairness climate as "procedural justice context," though they did not alter the definition. As part of their study, Caldwell and colleagues (2009) examined the role of procedural justice context on individuals' formations of procedural justice judgments associated with organizational change, and tested the moderating effects of job-level change and age dissimilarity. In addition to finding a positive main effect of procedural justice context, Caldwell et al. (2009) observed that unit-level procedural justice was positively related to individual-level procedural justice only when job-level change was low. Furthermore, Caldwell et al. (2009) reported that age dissimilarity interacted with procedural justice context to predict individual-level procedural justice judgment, such that the relationship between procedural justice context and individual-level procedural justice judgment was greater when employees were similar to others in age than when they were dissimilar.

Justice Climate and Strategic Relationships

Two studies examined the role of justice climate in managing strategic partnerships. Both are reviewed here, though they did so from different perspectives.

JOHNSON, KORSGAARD, AND SAPIENZA (2002)

Johnson et al. (2002) focused on the role of procedural justice climate in international joint venture management teams. International joint ventures are defined as legal entities "created by two or more organizations (the 'parent'), at least one of which is headquartered in another country" (p. 1141). Johnson and colleagues (2002) found that procedural justice climate was related to management teams' commitment toward the joint ventures and commitment toward parent companies (both foreign and local), suggesting that a high level of procedural justice climate may provide the assurance that the interest of the team will be protected, thereby increasing their identification with and commitment toward the parent company. They also found that the relationship between commitment toward the local parent company and procedural justice climate was stronger when decision control was low rather than high. In other words, when these teams did not have control over the decision-making process, they were more likely to become sensitive to justice climate and to respond strongly to justice violations. Finally, they also found that in the event of a high level of justice climate, individuals did not differentiate their level of commitment toward the joint venture, the local parent company, and the foreign parent company.

LUO (2008)

Luo (2008) investigated the role of procedural justice climate in managing interpartner relationships in strategic alliances. Luo (2008) found that procedural justice climate was related to the financial and operational outcomes of the strategic alliances. Trust mediated the relationship between procedural justice climate and financial outcomes, but not the relationship between procedural justice climate and operational outcomes. He also found that the relationship between procedural justice climate and cooperation outcomes was moderated by governance form, such that the relationship became stronger when the strategic alliances were equity joint ventures than when they were contractual agreements. Luo (2008) argued that equity-based alliances create a hostage situation with more stake on the line for alliance partners, thereby increasing the importance of procedural justice climate in influencing the outcome of the relationship.

Justice Climate and Leadership

A few studies examine leadership as the antecedent of justice climate. The general framework is to explore some dimension or dimensions of leadership that impact justice climate. Justice climate, in turn, is treated as a partial mediator, which intervenes between leadership and some work-relevant criterion variables.

SERVANT LEADERSHIP: EHRHART (2004) AND WALUMBWA, HARTNELL, AND OKE (2010)

Probably the first study on leadership and justice climate was conducted by Ehrhart (2004). He examined the role of procedural justice climate in linking servant leadership to group-level OCB. Servant leadership is defined as "an understanding and practice of leadership that places the good of those led over the self-interest of the leader, emphasizing leader behaviors that focus on follower development, and de-emphasizing glorification of the leader" (Hale & Fields, 2007, p. 397). Ehrhart found support for the mediating model for OCB rated by employees, suggesting that procedural justice climate channels the effects of servant leadership on employees' self-reported tendency to engage in OCB. However, there was much weaker support for the mediating model when OCB was reported by managers.

Building on these ideas, Walumbwa et al. (2010) also investigated how justice climate mediates the effects of servant leadership. These scholars posited a relationship between servant leadership and procedural justice climate, arguing that servant leaders tend to promote a high level of ethical conducts, treat their followers with respect, encourage their followers to express their views, thus enhancing the level of procedural justice climate within the unit that they lead. Consistent with their prediction, they found that the relationship between servant leadership and employees' OCB was mediated by the level of procedural justice climate within the group.

In addition to examining the role of procedural justice climate in mediating the relationship between servant leadership and employees' OCB, Walumbwa and his coauthors (2010) also examined a potential moderating effect. Specifically, they focused on whether procedural justice climate moderated the relationships between employees' self-efficacy and their OCB level and between commitment to their supervisor and OCB. They predicted that procedural justice climate enhances the relationships between employee's commitment to their supervisor and their self-efficacy and OCB, such that the relationships will become stronger when procedural justice climate is high than when it is low. Walumbwa and colleagues (2010) argued that a high level of procedural justice climate sets the tone for the group and reinforces employees' commitment towards their leaders and their self-efficacy, manifested in a higher level of OCB. Although they found support for the moderating role of procedural justice climate on the relationship between commitment and OCB, they failed to find the same effects on the relationship between employees' self-efficacy and OCB.

ETHICAL LEADERSHIP: BROWN, TREVINO, AND HARRISON (2005)

Brown and his colleagues (2005) examined the relationship between ethical leadership and interactional justice climate. These authors found ethical leadership was related to the level of interactional justice climate in the organization. These results suggest that ethical leaders tend to care about the well-being of their followers. As such, they are more likely to treat their followers with respect, thereby creating a high level of interactional justice climate within the organization. Generally similar findings were later reported by Cropanzano, Walumbwa, and Aryee (2013). We will review this study later.

TRANSFORMATIONAL LEADERSHIP: CHO AND DANSEREAU (2010)

Cho and Dansereau (2010) focused on two dimensions of transformational leadership—individualized consideration and charisma—and their relationship with justice climate. Using a sample of employees working in various branches in South Korea, they found that individualized consideration, defined as leaders' tendency to attend to the specific needs of each of their followers, was related to followers' OCB directed toward the leaders. This relationship was mediated by interpersonal justice at the individual level. In contrast, they found that leaders' charisma, defined as leaders' abilities to inspire their followers to contribute to the mission of the organization, was related to followers' OCB directed toward the group. This relationship was mediated by the level of procedural justice climate within the unit.

Interactive Effects of Justice Climate

In recent years, researchers have explored the interaction between justice climate and other variables. These studies are important, because they indicate that the effects of justice climate may be best understood through its joint effects with various features of the work environment and employee personality.

LIAO AND RUPP (2005)

Liao and Rupp (2005) conducted one of the most ambitious studies of justice climate. They focused on justice climate coming from two different sources: supervisor and organization. They found that these two sources crossed with the three types of justice to create six justice climate variables: supervisor-focused procedural justice climate, supervisor-focused informational justice climate, supervisor-focused interpersonal justice climate, organization-focused procedural justice climate, organization-focused informational justice climate, and organization-focused interpersonal justice climate. This six-factor structure of these justice variables was superior to other structures that either combine the sources (a three-factor structure distinguishing the justice variables by type) or combine the types (a two-factor structure distinguishing the justice variables by source) of justice.

In addition, Liao and Rupp (2005) tested the notion that justice will have greater impact when the source of justice matches the outcome variables directed to the same source. They found mixed support for this prediction. For example, although they found that supervisor-focused procedural and interpersonal justice climate predicted the outcome variables directed at supervisors (commitment and satisfaction), supervisor-focused informational justice climate did not. Similarly, although organization-focused procedural justice climate predicted commitment and citizenship behaviors directed toward the organization, its interpersonal justice climate counterpart did not. One interesting finding based on their research is that individual-level justice and justice climate appeared to have different relationships with outcome variables, suggesting that the construct of justice may not be functionally isomorphic.

Finally, Liao and Rupp (2005) also examined whether the effects of justice climate on outcome variables depend on each individual's justice orientation, defined as the extent to which individuals internalize justice as one of the most important values that they hold. They found that supervisor-focused procedural justice climate interacted with justice orientation to predict commitment and satisfaction directed at the supervisor, such that the effects were stronger when orientation was high rather than low.

MAYER, NISHII, SCHNEIDER, AND GOLDSTEIN (2007)

These authors examined the antecedents of justice climate and how justice climate moderates the effects of justice at the individual level. They found that leader agreeableness was positively related to the level of interpersonal and information justice climate, suggesting that leaders who are trusting, cooperative, and affable are more likely to treat their followers with respect and dignity and share information with them in a timely manner. They also found that leader neuroticism was negatively related to the level of procedural, interpersonal, and informational justice climate, suggesting that leaders who are emotionally unstable are less likely to treat their followers consistently, treat them in an interpersonally decent manner, and provide justifications for their decision. Leader conscientiousness was positively related to the level of procedural justice climate, but not interpersonal or informational justice climate. Conscientious leaders tend to be more precise, allowing them to apply standards in a consistent manner. Extraversion was not related to any of the justice climate dimensions. They also found interactive effects between justice at the individual level and justice at the unit level. Specifically, they found the interactive effects of individual-level justice and justice climate on job satisfaction for interpersonal and informational justice but not for procedural justice. They also found the interactive effects of individual-level justice and justice climate on organizational commitment for interpersonal and informational justice but not for procedural justice. On the whole, the relationships between individual-level justice and outcome variables became stronger when justice climate was also high compared to when justice climate was low.

SPELL AND ARNOLD (2007)

Spell and Arnold (2007) examined how the various types of justice climate interact with each other to predict outcome variables. These authors found that distributive and procedural justice climate interacted to predict employees' mental health (anxiety and depression), even when their direct effects at the individual level were controlled for. Specifically, they found that a high level of procedural justice climate buffered the effects of distributive justice climate. They did not find an interaction between interactional and distributive justice. These investigations are important because they show that different types of justice perceptions may interact with each other, both at the individual level and at the unit level. Spell and Arnold (2007) also examined whether organizational structure (mechanistic versus organic) moderates the effects of justice climate. However, they found that the effects of procedural and interactional justice climate did not vary as a function of the structure of the organization.

YANG, MOSSHOLDER, AND PENG (2007)

Yang and his colleagues (2007) focused on whether the effects of procedural justice climate may depend on the level of power distance orientation in a group. Power distance orientation is defined as "the extent to which people expect and accept the unequal distribution of power between superiors and subordinates in institutions" (p. 683). These authors found that although procedural justice climate was related to organizational commitment and OCB, these relationships were also moderated by the level of power distance in the group, such that the relationships were stronger when power distance was lower rather than higher. One explanation for these findings is that when group power distance is high, group members are more likely to defer to those in power in the group; therefore, they are less likely to respond positively to a high level of procedural justice climate in the group (in other words, procedural fairness, such as the use of due process and the ability to voice their opinion, may matter less to them). Conversely, individuals are also less apt to respond negatively to procedural injustice climate when they believe that the authority figure has the prerogative to treat them badly due to their positional power.

HAKONEN AND LIPPONEN (2008)

Hakonen and Lipponen (2008) examined the relationship between procedural justice climate and identification with the team in virtual teams and whether the relationship is moderated by the frequency of face-to-face meetings and the level of geographical dispersion among members of the team. They found that the relationships between procedural justice climate and identification were stronger when the frequency of face-to-face meetings was low and when the amount of dispersion was high. These authors argued that individuals use justice to reduce the uncertainties that they experience. The fewer face-to-face meetings that these teams have and the more dispersedly team members are geographically located, the more they rely on procedural justice climate to make sense of their experience. As such, they tend to respond more strongly to a lower level of procedural justice climate within the team when they meet infrequently face-to-face and when they are not geographically co-located.

TREVOR AND NYBERG (2008)

These authors explored the role of procedural justice climate in moderating the effects of downsizing on employees' voluntary turnover. Trevor and Nyberg (2008) found that there was a positive relationship between downsizing and turnover, suggesting that downsizing may have eroded the trust employee have in their management, prompting them to look for alternative employment opportunities. However, they also found that the relationship between downsizing and turnover was higher when procedural justice climate was low. These authors argued that a low level of procedural justice climate may create the fear of more negative outcomes down the road, thus increasing employees' tendency to quit in response to downsizing.

TANGIRALA AND RAMANUJAM (2008)

Tangirala and Ramanujam (2008) found that procedural justice climate had powerful impact on whether employees choose to stay silent at work. Specifically, they found that employee's identification with their work group and their professional commitment were negatively related to employee silence only when procedural justice climate was high. In contrast, these effects were not significant when procedural justice climate was low. The reasoning behind their findings is that speaking out about problems at work (the opposite of employee silence) can be precarious as it may put employees and their co-workers at risk of management retaliation. A high level of procedural justice climate provides the assurance that employees who speak out will not suffer adverse consequences for their behaviors, thereby increasing the tendency of those who strongly identify with their group and who have strong professional commitment to express their opinions or views (rather than remaining silent). Contrary to their expectation, procedural justice climate did not interact with supervisory status and individual procedural justice to predict employee silence.

WALLACE, EDWARDS, MONDORE, AND FINCH (2008)

Wallace et al. (2008) investigated the role of procedural justice climate in ameliorating discrimination claimants' tendency to file lawsuits against their organization. These authors argued that a low level of procedural justice climate may increase the motivation of employees who were victims of discriminations to file litigations because they did not expect favorable outcomes from an unfair process. Consistent with their prediction, they found that the number of discrimination claims in a district was positively related to the number of lawsuits only when the level of procedural justice climate was low, attesting to the ability of justice climate to reduce discrimination victims' intention to pursue lawsuits against their employers.

ERDOGAN AND BAUER (2010)

Erdogan and Bauer (2010) examined whether justice climate may buffer the negative effects of leader-member exchange (LMX) differentiation on employee attitudes and behaviors. LMX differentiation refers to the existence of different levels of LMX such that a supervisor may enjoy high-quality relationships with some followers but low-quality relationships with others in the same unit. Erdogan and Bauer (2010) argued that a high level of justice climate sends a signal to employees that even if they are not within the inner circle of the leader, they will not necessarily suffer from negative employment outcomes because decisions that affect them will be made in a bias-free and consistent manner and the rewards they receive will be commensurate with their effort. Erdogan and Bauer (2010) found that the relationships between LMX differentiation and employee organizational commitment, their satisfaction with co-workers, and withdrawal behaviors were moderated by procedural and distributive justice climate, such that these relationships were weaker when justice climate was high. However, they failed to find the interactive effects with job satisfaction and helping behaviors towards co-workers.

SORA, CABALLER, PEIRO, SILLA, AND GRACIA (2010)

Sora and colleagues (2010) also examined the role of justice climate in softening the blow of job insecurity on employees' attitudes. They reasoned that justice climate may serve to reduce the stress of job insecurity, thereby reducing its effects on employees' attitudes and well-being. Consistent with their expectations, these authors found that the relationships between job insecurity and job satisfaction and turnover intentions were weaker in the presence of a high level of justice climate. It is important to note that Sora and colleagues employed a scale of overall justice climate (rather than one that distinguishes the various dimensions of justice), an issue that we will revisit subsequently in our review.

LI, LIANG, AND CRANT (2010)

Li et al. (2010) investigated the relationship between proactive personality and employees' job satisfaction and OCB. Proactive personality means an individual's tendency to take initiatives to bring positive changes to the work environment. Li and colleagues (2010) argued that employees' proactive personality may be positively linked to their level of job satisfaction and OCB, because individuals who are proactive are more likely to go above and beyond to enhance the work experience for themselves and others. However, they found that the relationship between proactive personality and OCB (but not job satisfaction) was moderated by procedural justice climate, such that the relationship was positive only when justice climate was high. These authors reasoned that a high level of procedural justice climate sends the signal that employee input and initiatives are welcome, thereby increasing proactive employees' tendency to engage in OCB.

HSIUNG (2012)

Hsiung (2012) was interested in predicting employees' tendency to express their opinion at work (voice behavior). To do so, he examined two moderated relationships—(a) the interaction between employee mood and procedural justice climate and (b) the interaction between LMX and procedural justice climate. Hsiung reported evidence in favor of both relationships. The author suggested that a high level of procedural justice climate facilitates the creation of a safe environment, which may increase the tendency of individuals who experience positive moods and who enjoy a special relationship with their leaders to speak out.

PRIESEMUTH, ARNAUD, AND SCHMINKE (2013)

Priesemuth and her colleagues (2013) investigated the role of overall justice climate in predicting counterproductive work behaviors. Priesemuth et al. reasoned that the effect of justice climate would be moderated by the functional dependence of team members. Functional dependence refers to the level of interdependence among co-workers when performing their job duties. As predicted, justice climate interacted with functional dependence to predict two types of counterproductive work behaviors—general political behavior and interpersonal deviance. Specifically, overall justice climate was only weakly related to these two criterion variables when functional dependence was low. However, as functional dependence became higher, the relationship of justice climate to each type of deviance became stronger.

ZHANG AND JIA (2013)

Zhang and Jia (2013) investigated the role of justice climate in moderating the negative effects of stretch goals in organizations. Stretch goals are defined as goals that are extremely difficult to accomplish. These authors argued that stretch goals may have unintended consequences because they may fuel unethical behaviors and create relationship conflict in organizations. However, they argued that these effects may be potentially mitigated by a high level of informational and interpersonal justice climate because the favorable climate condition may create a more positive environment, thereby reducing the relationship between stretched goals and the negative outcomes. These authors found that informational justice climate reduced the relationship between stretch goals and unethical behavior, whereas interpersonal justice climate attenuated the relationship between stretch goals and relationship conflict.

Whitman, Caleo, Carpenter, Horner, and Bernerth's (2012) Meta-Analysis and Summary of the Findings

Whitman and colleagues (2012) conducted a meta-analysis of the justice climate literature. A total of 37 studies were included in their meta-analytic review. Their review focuses on four research questions: (1) Are the three types of justice climate—distributive, procedural, and interactional—related to team effectiveness? In addition, does the magnitude of these relationships vary depending on the specific index of team effectiveness? (2) Does justice climate strength moderate the relationship between justice climate level and team effectiveness? (3) Does the magnitude of the relationships between justice climate and team effectiveness depend on the reference of the measure? (4) Does the magnitude of the relationships between justice climate and team effectiveness depend on the level of analysis? We will focus on research questions 1, 3, and 4 in this section, and come back to 2 in the next section.

The first research question focuses on the relationship between justice climate and indicators of team effectiveness. Whitman and colleagues (2012) grouped the outcome variables into four categories: attitudes, processes, withdrawal, and performance. They found that the three types of justice climate were related to most of these outcome variables. The one exception was withdrawal, though these null findings may have been an artifact of the data. The database for this outcome variable only included procedural justice and not the other two types of fairness climate. Whitman et al. also investigated whether the three types of justice climate may have differential effects depending on the category of outcome variables. Their meta-analysis revealed that distributive justice climate was more strongly related to team performance than were procedural justice climate and interactional justice climate. Procedural justice climate had a much weaker relationship with attitudinal variables than did distributive justice climate and interactional justice climate. Interactional justice climate was also found to have a stronger effect on process-related variables than did procedural justice climate and distributive justice climate.

The third research question pertains to whether the magnitude of the relationships between justice climate and team effectiveness depends on the reference of the measure. Historically, climate researchers in general and justice climate scholars in particular tend to use two different referents in their climate measures. Some scholars use the individual referent in their climate measure (e.g., "I have received rewards consistent with the amount of efforts I put into my work"), whereas others use a unit referent (e.g., "Our team has received rewards consistent with the amount of efforts we put into our work"). These two measurement methods are consistent with the two process composition models proposed by Chan (1998). Specifically, the use of the individual as the target of reference is consistent with the direct-consensus model whereby a minimum level of agreement among members of the same unit has to be ensured before aggregation. The use of the unit as the target of reference is consistent with the referent-shift model which focuses on individuals' perceptions of their external environment (see Li and Cropanzano, 2009b, for a more detailed review of these two methods in justice climate research). Whitman and colleagues (2012) predicted and found in their meta-analysis that the magnitude of the relationships between justice climate and team effectiveness was greater when a unit referent was used compared to when an individual referent was used.

In the fourth research question, these authors address the issue of whether the magnitude of the relationships between justice climate and team effectiveness depends on the level of analysis. Whitman and colleagues (2012) predicted that the relationships would be stronger at lower levels of analysis (such as the team/group levels) compared to higher levels of analysis (such as the branch and the organizational levels). They argued that lower-level units provide a more optimal environment for members of the same unit to interact with each other and to exchange justice perceptions, thereby potentially enhancing the effects of justice climate on unit-level outcomes. They found substantial support for their predictions in the meta-analysis.

Some Closing Thoughts Regarding Climate Level

In general, results of this meta-analysis are consistent with our review this far. The past decade has produced an exciting body of literature on justice climate. These studies, taken together, demonstrate that justice climate level predicts important outcome variables, provides an explanatory mechanism for why certain variables (such as leadership) demonstrate their effects, and renders the effects of some other variables (such as LMX differentiation and downsizing) less pernicious.

Justice Climate Strength

The previous section is devoted to the review of empirical studies focusing on justice climate level. There is also a concurrent research stream that focuses on justice climate strength. Justice climate strength, as you may recall, refers to the level of agreement on justice among members of the same unit. We will review the relevant literature in this section.

Measurement of Justice Climate Strength

Operationally, some scholars use the standard deviation (or the variance) of members' justice perceptions within a unit to represent justice climate strength (Roberson, 2006a). Others, however, use more sophisticated analytic approaches. For example, Colquitt and colleagues (2002) computed justice climate strength by dividing the standard deviation of unit members' justice perception by the mean level of the unit. The ratio was then standardized and reversed in sign so that a higher value represents a higher level of justice strength. This approach was also adopted by Cropanzano, Li, and Benson (2011) and Walumbwa, Wu, and Orwa (2008). Similarly, Naumann and Bennett (2000) used interrater agreement index (r_{wg}) to define justice climate strength.

Research on Justice Climate Strength

Climate research, in general, has demonstrated that justice strength is an important construct in its own right, and a number of studies have shown that climate level has a greater effect when it's accompanied by a high level of agreement (high climate strength) by all members within the same unit (Colquitt et al., 2002; Moliner, Martinez-Tur, Peiro, Ramos, & Cropanzano, 2005).

NAUMANN AND BENNETT (2000)

As stated previously, Naumann and Bennett (2000) should be given the credit for introducing the term "justice climate" to the justice lexicon, but they also introduced the concept of justice climate strength. Naumann and Bennett (2000) examined factors antecedent to justice climate strength. They found that the level of cohesion in a group and the visibility of the supervisor helped promote a high level of justice climate strength. Contrary to their prediction, they did not find a significant relationship between justice climate strength and diversity within a unit.

COLQUITT, NOE, AND JACKSON (2002)

Colquitt et al. (2002) also explored the antecedents of justice climate strength. They argued that demographic diversity may reduce the level of similarity among members of the same team, which may potentially reduce the likelihood that they discuss justice-related information and the development of similar perspectives and standards to interpret the information, a process that may eventually lead to less agreement in justice within the team. They found substantial support for their argument (although it's worth noting that Naumann and Bennett, 2000, did not find similar results in their study of the relationship between diversity and justice climate strength). Interestingly, Colquitt et al. (2002) also determined that while procedural justice climate level was predicted by the size of the team and the level of collectivism of team members (but not team diversity), climate strength was predicted by team size and team diversity (but not team collectivism).

In addition to exploring the antecedents of justice climate strength and justice climate level, Colquitt and colleagues' (2002) study was also the first to examine the interaction between the two. Colquitt and colleagues (2002) found that although procedural justice climate level was positively related to team performance and absenteeism, climate strength was not. However, they also found that procedural justice climate level and strength interacted with each other to predict these two outcome variables. Specifically, the relationships between climate level and the outcome variables were higher when there was a high level of agreement on justice within the team (high justice climate strength).

These authors accounted for these findings based on fairness heuristic theory (Lind, 2001). According to the theory, the formation of justice judgment goes through a two-stage process. At the first stage, termed as the "judgment phase," individuals form an overall fairness evaluation of a target. At the second stage, termed as the "use phase," individuals rely on the justice judgment to interpret new information and to guide their attitudes and behaviors. In other words, the response to justice violations occurs primarily at the second stage. In a team context, a high level of justice climate strength may allow individuals to move relatively quickly from the judgment phase to the use phase, thereby enhancing the relationship between climate level and outcome variables. In contrast, when the level of justice climate strength is low, members of the same unit may continue to engage in sense-making activities to reconcile their different evaluations of justice climate within the unit, consequently prolonging the duration of the judgment phase and reducing the effects of justice climate level on outcome variables.

MOLINER, MARTINEZ-TUR, PEIRO, RAMOS, AND CROPANZANO (2005)

Moliner et al. (2005) examined the relationship between justice climate and unit-level burnout. Their study was the first to examine all three types of justice climate (distributive, procedural, and interactional). Another notable feature of their study is that they used a sample from Spain, providing converging evidence that justice climate research is relevant in areas outside North America. Moliner and her colleagues (2005) found that interactional justice climate level was negatively related to the level of burnout. They also found an interaction between interactional justice climate level and strength on the level of burnout, such that the relationship between justice climate level and burnout was stronger when justice climate strength was high. Finally, they also found that interactional justice climate strength was positively related to the level of agreement on burnout within the unit. Although the authors found very promising results with interactional justice climate, they did not find significant results with either distributive or procedural justice climate.

Roberson (2006a; 2006b)

Roberson (2006b) examined factors leading to a high level of agreement on justice within a group. The one factor identified in her study was the level of interdependence in the group. Roberson (2006b) argued that groups that are high in interdependence tend to have more opportunities to share information with each other and create the motivation to observe the treatment of other members in the team by organizational authorities, thereby potentially leading to more agreement on justice. Roberson (2006b) found support for the effects of interdependence on the strength of procedural and distributive justice climate. In addition, Roberson (2006b) found that the relationship between interdependence and procedural justice climate strength was mediated by team identification (but not the relationship between interdependence and distributive justice climate strength). In other words, a higher level of interdependence increased team members' identification with the team, which increased the level of agreement on procedural justice with other members of the team.

In another study, Roberson (2006a) examined the role of sense-making in promoting the level of agreement on justice in a team. She found that more sense-making activities in a team were related to a higher level of procedural and distributive justice climate strength. She also found an interaction between procedural fairness and outcome favorability on sense making in their experimental study. Specifically, teams that were exposed to fair procedural treatment in combination with unfavorable outcomes were more likely to engage in sense making relative to other conditions. Teams that were exposed to unfavorable outcomes and unfair procedural treatment were more likely to engage in sense making relative to those who experienced favorable outcomes and fair procedural treatment.

Walumbwa, Wu, and Orwa (2008)

Walumbwa et al. (2008) investigated the role of procedural justice climate level and procedural justice climate strength in mediating the effects of contingent reward leadership on work attitudes and behaviors. Contingent reward leadership refers to the tendency of leaders to reward their followers based on their performance and the extent to which their followers have met the predefined performance expectations. Walumbwa and colleagues (2008) found that procedural justice climate level and strength were related to employees' OCB, organizational commitment, and satisfaction with supervisors. In addition, they found that procedural justice climate level and strength simultaneously mediated the relationship between contingent reward leadership and these outcome variables. These findings suggest that contingent reward leaders define performance expectations, emphasize the link between performance and rewards to their employees, and consistently apply these standards to all their followers, thereby fostering a strong and high level of procedural justice climate, which, in turn, motivates employees to exhibit positive work attitudes and behaviors to maintain the favorable work environment.

Oc, Bashshur, and Paddock (2013)

Oc and colleagues (2013) examined the relationship between leader behaviors and the level and strength of overall justice climate over time. They focused on two aspects of leader behaviors: Allocation (whether leaders assign more rewards to themselves or they assign rewards equally/equitably) and their reaction to follower voice (whether they respond to the voice of their follower or they simply ignore their voice). They found that both aspects of leader behaviors were significantly related to the level and strength of justice climate. Specifically, justice climate level was higher over time when leaders acted equally and justice climate level was lower when leaders were not responsive to the voice of their employees. In addition, justice climate strength was weaker when leaders distributed rewards equally than when leaders acted selfishly by allocating more rewards to themselves. Finally, they also found that justice climate strength was stronger when leaders were consistent in their allocation compared to when leaders were inconsistent or reactive in their allocation pattern.

OGUNFOWORA (2013)

Ogunfowora (2013) examined the role of interpersonal justice climate strength in mediating the effects of abusive supervision variability on group- and individual-level outcomes. Abusive supervision variability refers to the different levels of abusive treatments that members in the same unit receive from a supervisor. Ogunfowora (2013) found that abusive supervision variability was related to ethics-related outcomes (for example, individual perceptions of leader ethicality) and nonethics-related outcomes (such as leader satisfaction), and these effects were mediated by interpersonal justice climate strength.

Whitman, Caleo, Carpenter, Horner, and Bernerth's (2012) Meta-Analysis

As we alluded to in the previous section of this review, Whitman and colleagues' meta-analysis (2012) also examined whether justice climate strength moderates the relationship between justice climate level and team effectiveness. They argued that a low level of justice climate strength will introduce ambiguity in terms of how unit members interpret events with justice implications, thereby reducing the effects of justice climate level on team effectiveness. Consistent with their prediction, they found bigger effect sizes for justice climate level in the presence of greater justice climate strength.

Some Closing Thoughts Regarding Climate Strength

Research on justice climate strength can be divided into three families—consequences, antecedents, and moderating impact. Of these three sets, the first is in need of the greatest research attention. Although the relationship between justice climate strength and outcome variables has been investigated, the results so far have been inconclusive, and more evidence is needed to ascertain whether justice climate strength has main effects on outcome variables (Colquitt et al., 2002; Moliner et al., 2005).

Relative to the lack of studies examining the consequences of justice climate strength, there has been a large body of literature focusing on its antecedents. Specifically, past research has found that predictors of justice climate strength include team size (Colquitt et al., 2002), team diversity (Colquitt et al., 2002), team cohesion (Naumann & Bennett, 2000), supervisor visibility (Naumann & Bennett, 2000), sense-making activities among team members (Roberson, 2006a), the level of interdependence among team members (Roberson, 2006b), among others.

Finally, findings for the moderating effect of justice climate strength are promising. In their meta-analysis, Whitman et al. (2012) found that justice climate level had a greater effect when it was accompanied by a high level of climate strength. These findings suggest that future research should include justice climate strength in order to fully appreciate the effects of justice climate level.

Peer Justice Climate

As we have seen, justice climate is generally defined as the manner in which the group as a whole is treated by some outside figure (Colquitt et al., 2005). Although this perspective has proven fruitful, other sources of fair and unfair treatment exist (Rupp et al., 2007). With this possibility in mind, scholars have come to investigate how teammates treat one another. For example, Branscombe, Spears, Ellemers, and Doosje (2002) found that individuals who belonged to a low-status group were more motivated to perform group-serving activities only when they received respectful treatment from others in their own group (high interactional justice from teammates). These authors argued that respectful treatment by teammates communicates the message that they are valued members of the group, which increases their identification with the group and the desire to contribute to its success. Likewise, Lavelle and colleagues (2009) found that work group commitment mediated the relationship between perceived fairness of the decision-making process and their reported commitment to the group (see also, Lavelle, Rupp, & Brockner 2007). Although the work of Branscombe et al. and of Lavelle et al. was conducted at the individual level of analysis, it seems likely that work groups form unit-level evaluations of themselves. Addressing this issue is the construct of *peer justice climate.* Peer justice climate, or simply peer justice, is defined as the collective perception that individuals, who work together within the same unit and who do not have formal authority over each other, judge the extent to which they treat one another fairly (Cropanzano et al., 2011). This concept has also been referred to as "intraunit justice climate" (e.g., by Cropanzano, Li, & James, 2007; Li & Cropanzano, 2009b).

CROPANZANO, LI, AND BENSON (2011)

The first published study on peer justice climate was conducted by Cropanzano and colleagues (2011). Cropanzano et al. focused on only two dimensions of peer justice: Procedural and interactional peer justice. Procedural peer justice refers to the extent to which group members use a fair process to make important decisions in the group. Interactional peer justice refers to the extent to which group members treat each other with respect and dignity. These authors found that these two dimensions of peer justice were distinct from each other, evidenced by the results of their confirmatory factor analysis showing that a two-factor structure that separates these two dimensions was superior in fit to a one-factor structure that merges them together. Additionally, Cropanzano and colleagues (2011) also found that both procedural and interactional peer justice explained incremental variance beyond the effects of their counterpart at the individual level. These findings suggest that, in the team context, it's important to examine peer justice at both levels in order to fully appreciate the effects of justice from co-workers on employees' attitudes and behavior. Apart from these validation findings, a few other aspects of their findings are noteworthy.

First, Cropanzano and colleagues (2011) found that peer justice climate (both procedural and interactional) was related to team citizenship behaviors via the effects of interpersonal teamwork process (which signals the level of cohesion, effort, and interpersonal support in the team). Peer justice climate (both procedural and interactional) was also related to team performance, but through a different mediating mechanism, namely task teamwork process (which signals the level of communication, coordination, and contribution of team members in the team) mediated the impact of peer justice.

Second, these authors also examined the effects of peer justice strength, defined as the level of agreement among teammates in terms of the level of fairness with which they treat each other. They found that peer procedural justice strength was related to team performance through the effects of task teamwork process and to team helping behaviors through the effects of interpersonal teamwork process. No such effects were observed on peer interactional justice climate strength.

LI, CROPANZANO, AND BAGGER (2013)

In a follow-up study, Li, Cropanzano, and Bagger (2013) simultaneously explored the effects of three types of peer justice climate—distributive, procedural, and interpersonal. In this study, the authors also compared these three dimensions of peer justice to the corresponding three dimensions of justice climate. One noteworthy finding from this study was structural. Li and his colleagues found that both peer justice and justice climate were best represented by a hierarchical two-level model. In each case, the first-order factors were the three types of justice, whereas the second-order factors were overall peer justice and overall justice climate. Neither peer justice nor justice climate predicted team performance. However, the effects of peer justice on team satisfaction were mediated by teamwork process.

CROPANZANO, WALUMBWA, AND ARYEE (2013)

Cropanzano et al. (2013) conducted a field study of overall peer justice and overall justice climate. The authors found that transformational leaders tended to become more ethical leaders. This ethical leadership, in turn, increased both peer justice and justice climate. Finally, teams benefited from these two types of collective fairness by becoming more ethical and engaging in more learning behavior. Notably, both peer justice and justice climate predicted group ethical behavior beyond the other.

New Research Directions

In this section, we focus on some opportunities to advance the justice climate literature. Based on our review, we consider the following topics: measurement of justice climate, structure of justice climate, the multiple sources of fair and unfair treatment, and the development of justice climate over time.

The Measurement of Justice Climate

Li and Cropanzano (2009b), in their initial review of the justice climate literature, raised serious concerns with the scales used to operationalize the construct of justice climate. Specifically, they raised three issues in their review. First, a large number of justice climate measures have been used in the empirical literature. Table 6.1 provides information about the justice climate measures used in prior research. Although the measures developed by Colquitt (2001) and Niehoff and Moorman (1993) were used in many of these studies, other measures were also employed to measure justice climate. Second, some justice researchers also use measures that are the abbreviated forms of established measures. Alternatively, others use measures that have not been validated in the empirical literature. This practice raises significant concerns with the validity of the findings based on justice climate measures that may have questionable psychometric properties. Third, as Li and Cropanzano (2009b) stated in their review, there is still considerable debate on whether justice should be operationalized similarly across different levels.

Moving forward, we implore justice scholars to adopt one justice climate measure to be used in their research. Doing so may facilitate replication and combination of studies for additional meta-analytic efforts in the future. In other words, it's less likely that the difference in results can be attributed to the use of different justice climate measures in different studies. At the individual level, the measure developed by Colquitt (2001) has been used extensively in the literature. Moving to the unit-level, many studies have also used the Colquitt (2001) measure to operationalize justice climate (see Table 6.1).

In addition, although past research has used either the individual or the unit as the targets of reference in their justice climate measure, there have been some speculations on whether empirical results may be impacted by these different operationalizations of justice climate (e.g., Tangirala & Ramanujam, 2008). Recent meta-analytic findings have demonstrated that effect sizes tend to be greater when a unit-referent (rather than an individual-referent) is employed (Whitman et al., 2012). Henceforth, we suggest that researchers should use the unit as the referent of their justice climate measure in order to more accurately capture its effects.

Finally, it's also important to examine whether justice should be operationalized equivalently across levels and foci. For example, Li and colleagues (2013) used different scales to measure peer justice and justice climate, citing the difference in how these two constructs are theorized. In particular, since teammates do not determine each other's pay directly in most teams, distributive peer justice cannot be assessed based on the extent to which teammates allocate fair rewards (as this is a task typically performed by supervisors). Instead, distributive peer justice should be conceptualized as the extent to which teammates' rewards are appropriate based on the contributions that they make to the team. Similarly, past research has used different measures to operationalize justice at different levels (Mossholder et al., 1998), affirming climate scholars' premonition that the structure and function of unit-level constructs should be explicitly tested rather than assumed (that they will take the same structural form and have the same effects on outcome variables as their counterparts at the individual level; Kozlowski & Klein, 2000).

Overall Justice Climate

A related issue is the structure of justice climate. Justice research at the individual level tends to eschew a one-factor conceptualization of justice in favor of distinguishing the various types of justice (Colquitt et al., 2001). This argument is supported by the literature showing that the different types of justice may have differential effects on different outcome variables. However, other approaches are available.

Some justice scholars have advanced the construct of overall justice. Ambrose and Schminke (2007) articulated three benefits that an overall justice construct offers over specific justice types. First, overall justice provides a more accurate representation of individuals' justice experience relative to discrete justice types. Second, a focus on overall justice allows researchers to evaluate the total impact that justice has relative to other variables (such as service climate and personality) that may also impact work attitudes and behaviors. In other words, the use of specific justice types offers a piecemeal and incomplete view of the effect of an individual's overall justice judgment. Third, the use of an overall justice construct offers a more parsimonious approach to theorize the effects of justice at work. That is because researchers tend to make identical predictions on the effects of the three types of justice. Empirical evidence supports this view. At the individual level of analysis, Ambrose and Schminke (2009) found that overall justice mediated the relationship between the three dimensions of justice perceptions and outcome variables (for similar findings see Jones & Martens, 2009). Ambrose and Schminke (2007) call for more research on the construct of overall justice at the unit level, stating that "organizational justice climate research could benefit from a contemporaneous line of research that focuses on overall justice climate . . . a balance between focusing on finer distinction within the justice climate construct and seeking a more holistic justice climate construct might prove productive as well" (p. 407).

In a direct response to this call, the Li et al. (2013) study discussed earlier conceptualized unit-level fairness as a hierarchical construct. The three types of justice were measured separately. Thus, the first-order factors represented the separate dimensions of distributive, procedural, and interactional fairness. These dimensions were then combined into a single second-order construct. The results of this study were supportive of the hierarchical model for both peer justice and justice climate. However, it bears mention that Li and colleagues (2013) used a sample of student teams for their study. For this reason the external validity of their findings has yet to be determined.

Another approach to assess overall justice was taken by Priesemuth and her colleagues (2013). Following Ambrose and Schminke's (2009) recommendation, these investigators measured overall justice climate with a single, global scale. When using this method, there is only a single dimension of overall justice, rather than a composite of different justice types. This approach was found to be effective. The Priesemuth et al. measurement strategy was also employed by Cropanzano and his colleagues (2013). Cropanzano et al. successfully replicated the findings for overall justice climate, and also extended them by treating peer justice as a single dimension. These findings are promising, and should be examined further in future research. It would be useful to determine which approach to operationalizing overall justice yields the most valid results at the group level of analysis. Li and colleagues (2013) suggested two criteria to guide the choice between the two approaches. First, researchers should rely on theory to determine their operationalization of overall justice climate. For example, if they have sufficient reasons to believe that overall justice perceptions may be formed independent of each of the justice dimensions, then they should follow the lead of Priesemuth and her colleagues (2013) and operationalize justice climate as a single-level variable (rather than creating a composite variable of overall justice as Li and colleagues did in their study). Second, the choice should also be determined by pragmatic reasons, such as whether the measure of overall justice predicts important outcome variables. We are unaware of any empirical studies that compare these two approaches to assess overall justice climate, which is certainly an important avenue for future scholarly investigations.

More Research into Justice from Other Sources

One important extension of the justice literature is multifoci justice, which posits that individuals are able to distinguish the various sources of justice perceptions and respond to them accordingly. Empirical research on multifoci justice has flourished, showing that justice perceptions tend to have greater effects when the source of the justice perceptions matches the target of the outcome variables (Lavelle et al., 2007). Other studies have shown that the relationship between justice and outcome variables is mediated by the social exchange relationship that employees establish with the source of justice (Rupp & Cropanzano, 2002). However, it's important to note that this body of research has primarily been conducted at the individual level. Rupp and colleagues (2007) cogently plead that "more research is needed that explores justice climate from a multifoci perspective" (p. 371). The few empirical studies of multifoci justice at the unit level have focused on supervisors or organizational authority as the source of justice (e.g., Liao & Rupp, 2005). One exception is the study of peer justice climate, described previously, which shows that perceptions of co-worker justice can be generalized to the unit level and that these perceptions have significant impact on team outcomes (Cropanzano et al., 2011; Li et al., 2013). Recent work by Li et al. (2013) and Cropanzano et al. (2013) has found that respondents can reliably distinguish peer justice from justice climate. This supports the multi-foci model.

Future research should also examine customers as the source of unit-level justice. Past research at the individual level has demonstrated that being treated poorly by customers may reduce employees' interactional justice (Rupp & Spencer, 2006). We are not aware of any studies that treat customer justice as a unit-level construct, although it's not inconceivable that employees within the same unit may develop similar perceptions of how fairly they have been treated by customers, particularly when they experience the same level of treatment by their customers. Employees may also develop similar distributive justice perceptions based on the tips that are left to them by their customers (e.g., most of the customers consistently tip them at a level not commensurate with their effort). Of course, customer justice may be more relevant to interactional justice and less so to the other types of justice.

In sum, unit-level justice research should keep abreast with the development of multifoci justice research at the individual level. Investigating justice perceptions both at multiple levels and from different sources will enable justice scholars to have a better understanding of employees' justice experience in the workplace.

The Longitudinal Development of Justice Climate

Although a number of theoretical perspectives have been proposed to account for the development of justice climate in a unit, such as the SIP theory and the ASA model described previously, we are not aware of any studies that test these theories in a longitudinal manner. Granted, past research has shown that sense making (Roberson, 2006a), level of interdependence (Roberson, 2006b), and the level of diversity (Colquitt et al., 2002) may all lead to more or less agreement on justice by members of the same unit, lending tentative support to these theories.

Drawing on research in network analysis, Roberson and Colquitt (2005) proposed a social network model of justice. Their model stipulates that individuals share information with each other in a network that may facilitate the convergence of justice evaluations. One benefit of viewing justice from a network perspective is that structural variables in networking research can be brought to bear in explaining the similarity of views on justice among members of the same network. For example, Roberson and Colquitt (2005) suggested that structural equivalence, defined as "the extent to which people occupy similar positions in a network and are therefore influenced by those with whom they have similar patterns of interaction" (p. 597), may potentially enhance the similarity of justice perceptions. Umphress, Labianca, Brass, Kass, and Scholten (2003) distinguished two types of network ties: expressive ties, which refer to the emotional connections established among network contacts, and instrumental ties, which refer to the information and resource sharing among network contacts. They found that strong expressive ties were related to greater similarity in interactional justice, suggesting that individuals who communicate with each other emotionally are more likely to influence each other, thereby leading to more agreement on their justice perceptions.

The combination of longitudinal research with the use of network analyses may unlock the black box of how members of the same unit come to resemble each other in their justice perceptions. This line of research is particularly beneficial with newly formed teams that include members who have never worked with each other before and who have to rely on each other in order to complete task requirements. A longitudinal design may allow researchers to track the similarity of justice perceptions over time. The use of network analysis may allow researchers to establish the amount and nature of contact among team members and their network positions in relation to the similarity of justice perceptions. A design like this will provide definitive empirical support to the notion that justice spreads in a unit like a contagious disease and network properties of a network may serve to expedite or slow the transmission of justice.

Conclusion

The increasing reliance on teams and groups in modern organizations has propelled justice scholars to expand their research span to include organizational justice as a unit-level phenomenon. As presented in the present chapter, justice climate has been found to be an important construct that predicts individual and group-level outcomes, even when its counterpart at the individual level has been accounted for. Not only has justice climate research enriched the justice literature but it has also proliferated to other research areas such as leadership, organizational change, and strategic relationships. Despite the encouraging and exciting progress in justice climate research over the last two decades, there remains much more to know about justice at the unit level. Our review provides theoretical insights and sets the agenda for future research, urging scholars to pay greater attention to unit-level justice from multiple sources and how they interact with each other to predict individual and unit outcomes. We also believe that the literature may benefit from a more precise conceptualization and measurement of justice at the unit level and greater understanding of the development of justice as a group phenomenon through the lens of longitudinal studies. Pursuing these avenues will not only enhance our understanding of how justice operates at the unit level but also provide prescriptions for managers as they seek to create a fairer and more humanized work environment.

References

Adams, J. S. (1965). Inequity in social exchange. In L. Berkowitz (Ed.), *Advances in experimental social psychology* (pp. 267–299). New York, NY: Academic Press.

Ambrose, M. L., & Schminke, M. (2007). Examining justice climate: Issues of fit, simplicity, and content. In F. Dansereau & F. J. Yammarino (Eds.), *Multi-level issues in organizations and time* (Vol. 6, pp. 397–413). Oxford, UK: Elsevier.

Ambrose, M. L., & Schminke, M. (2009). The role of overall justice judgments in organizational justice research: A test of mediation. *Journal of Applied Psychology, 94*, 491–500.

Bies, R. J. (2001). Interactional (in)justice: The sacred and the profane. In J. Greenberg & R. Cropanzano (Eds.), *Advances in organizational justice* (pp. 89–118). Stanford, CA: Stanford University Press.

Bies, R. J., & Moag, J. S. (1986). Interactional justice: Communication criteria of fairness. In R. J. Lewicki, B. H. Sheppard, & M. H. Bazerman (Eds.), *Research on negotiation in organizations* (pp. 43–55). Greenwich, CT: JAI Press.

Branscombe, N. R., Spears, R., Ellemers, N., & Doosje, B. (2002). Intragroup and intergroup evaluation effects on group behavior. *Personality and Social Psychology Bulletin, 28*, 744–753.

Brockner, J., & Wiesenfeld, B. M. (1996). An integrative framework for explaining reactions to decisions: interactive effects of outcomes and procedures. *Psychological Bulletin, 120*, 189–208.

Brockner, J., Konovsky, M., Cooper-Schneider, R., Folger, R., Martin, C., & Bies, R. (1994). Interactive effects of procedural justice and outcome negativity on victims and survivors of job loss. *Academy of Management Journal, 37*, 397–409.

Brown, M. E., Trevino, L. K., & Harrison, D. A. (2005). Ethical leadership: A social learning perspective for construct development and testing. *Organizational Behavior and Human Decision Processes, 97*, 117–134.

Byrne, Z. S. (1999). *How do procedural and interactional justice influence multiple levels of organizational outcomes?* Paper presented at the 14th Annual Conference of the Society for Industrial and Organizational Psychology, Atlanta, GA.

Caldwell S. D., Herold D. M., & Fedor D. B. (2004). Towards an understanding of the relationships among organizational change, individual differences, and changes in person-environment fit: A cross-level study. *Journal of Applied Psychology, 89*, 868–882.

Caldwell, S., Liu, Y., Fedor, D. B., & Herold, D. M. (2009). Why are perceptions of change in the "eye of the beholder"? The role of age, sex, and tenure in procedural justice judgments. *Journal of Applied Behavioral Science, 45*, 437–459.

Chan, D. (1998). Functional relations among constructs in the same content domain at different levels of analysis: A typology of composition models. *Journal of Applied Psychology, 83*, 234–246.

Chen, X. P., Lam, S. S. K., Naumann, S. E., & Schaubroeck, J. (2005). Group citizenship behavior: Conceptualization and preliminary tests of its antecedents and consequences. *Group and Organization Review, 1*, 273–300.

Cho, J., & Dansereau, F. (2010). Are transformational leadership fair? A multi-level study of transformational leadership, justice perceptions, and organizational citizenship behaviors. *The Leadership Quarterly, 21*, 409–421.

Cohen-Charash, Y., & Spector, P. E. (2001). The role of justice in organizations: A meta-analysis. *Organizational Behavior and Human Decision Processes, 86*, 278–321.

Colquitt, J. A. (2001). On the dimensionality of organizational justice: A construct validation of a measure. *Journal of Applied Psychology, 86*, 386–400.

Colquitt, J. A., Conlon, D. E., Wesson, M. J., Porter, C. O. L. H., & Ng, K. Y. (2001). Justice at the millennium: A meta-analytic review of 25 years of organizational justice research. *Journal of Applied Psychology, 86*, 425–445.

Colquitt, J. A., Noe, R. A., & Jackson, C. L. (2002). Justice in teams: Antecedents and consequences of procedural justice climate. *Personnel Psychology, 55*, 83–109.

Colquitt, J. A., Zapata-Phelan, C. P., & Roberson, Q. M. (2005). Justice in teams: A review of fairness effects in collective contexts. In J. J. Martocchio (Ed.), *Research in personnel and human resources management* (Vol. 24, pp. 53–94). Oxford, UK: Elsevier.

Cropanzano, R., Li, A., & Benson, L. (2011). Peer justice and teamwork process. *Group and Organization Management, 36*, 567–596.

Cropanzano, R., Li, A., & James, K. (2007). Intraunit justice and interunit justice and the people who experience them. In F. Dansereau & F. J. Yammarino (Eds.), *Research in multi-level issues* (Vol. 6, pp. 415–437). Oxford, UK: Elsevier.

Cropanzano, R., Slaughter, J. E., & Bachiochi, P. D. (2005). Organizational justice and black applicants' reactions to affirmative action. *Journal of Applied Psychology, 90*, 1168–1184.

Cropanzano, R., Walumbwa, F. O., & Aryee, S. (2013, April). *The creation and consequences of work unit fairness.* Paper presented at the Annual Meeting of the Society for Industrial and Organizational Psychology. Houston, TX.

Cropanzano, R., & Wright, T. A. (2003). Procedural justice and organizational staffing: A tale of two paradigms. *Human Resource Management Review, 13*, 7–39.

Dayan, M., Benedetto, C. A. D., & Colak, M. (2009). Managerial trust in new product development projects: Its antecedents and consequences. *R&D Management, 39*, 21–37.

Deery, S. J., & Iverson, R. D. (2005). Labor-management cooperation: Antecedents and impact on organizational performance. *Industrial and Labor Relations Review, 58*, 588–609.

Degoey, P. (2000). Contagious justice: Exploring the social construction of justice in organizations. *Research in Organizational Behavior, 22*, 51–102.

Dietz, J., Robinson, S. L., Folger, R., Baron, R. A., & Schulz, M. (2003). The impact of community violence and an organization's procedural justice climate on workplace aggression. *Academy of Management Journal, 46*, 317–326.

Donovan, M. A., Drasgow, F., & Munson, L. J. (1998). The perceptions of fair interpersonal treatment scale: Development and validation of a measure of interpersonal treatment in the workplace. *Journal of Applied Psychology, 83*, 683–692.

Ehrhart, M. G. (2004). Leadership and procedural justice climate as antecedents of unit-level organizational citizenship behavior. *Personnel Psychology, 57*, 61–94.

Elkins, T. J., Phillips, J. S., & Ward, S. G. (2008). Organizational sexual harassment investigations: Observers' perceptions of fairness. *Journal of Managerial Issues, 20*, 88–108.

Erdogan, B., & Bauer, T. N. (2010). Differentiated leader-member exchanges: The buffering role of justice climate. *Journal of Applied Psychology, 95*, 1104–1120.

Farh, J. L., Earley, P. C., & Lin, S. C. (1997). Impetus for action: A cultural analysis of justice and organizational citizenship behavior in Chinese Society. *Administrative Science Quarterly, 42*, 421–444.

Fassina, N. E., Jones, D. A., & Uggerslev, K. L. (2008). Meta-analytic tests of relationships between organizational justice and citizenship behavior: Testing agent-system and shared-variance models. *Journal of Organizational Behavior, 29*, 805–828.

Fedor, D. B., Caldwell, S., & Herold, D. M. (2006). The effects of organizational changes on employee commitment: A multilevel investigation. *Personnel Psychology, 59*, 1–29.

Folger, R., & Konovsky, M. A. (1989). Effects of procedural and distributive justice on reactions to pay raise decisions. *Academy of Management Journal, 32*, 115–130.

Giacobbe-Miller, J. (1995). A test of the group values and control models of procedural justice from the competing perspectives of labor and management. *Personnel Psychology, 48*, 115–142.

Greenberg, J. (1990). Employee theft as a reaction to underpayment inequity: The hidden cost of pay cuts. *Journal of Applied Psychology, 75*, 561–568.

Greenberg, J. (1993). The social side of fairness: Interpersonal and informational classes of organizational justice. In R. Cropanzano (Ed.), *Justice in the workplace: Approaching fairness in human resource management* (pp. 79–103). Hillsdale, NJ: Erlbaum.

Greenberg, J. (2006). Losing sleep over organizational injustice: Attenuating insomniac reactions to underpayment inequity with supervisory training in interactional justice. *Journal of Applied Psychology, 91*, 58–69.

Griffin, B. (2010). Multilevel relationships between organizational-level incivility, justice and intention to stay. *Work and Stress, 24*, 309–323.

Guest, D., & Conway, N. (2002). Communicating the psychological contract: An employer perspective. *Human Resource Management Journal, 12*, 22–38.

Hakonen, M., & Lipponen, J. (2008). Procedural justice and identification with virtual teams: The moderating role of face-to-face meetings and geographical dispersion. *Social Justice Research, 21*, 164–178.

Hale, J. R., & Fields, D. L. (2007). Exploring servant leadership across cultures: A study of followers in Ghana and the USA. *Leadership, 3*, 397–417.

Hausknecht, J. P., Day, D. V., & Thomas, S. C. (2004). Applicant reactions to selection procedures: An updated model and meta-analysis. *Personnel Psychology, 57*, 639–683.

Herold, D. M., Fedor, D. B., & Caldwell, S. D. (2007). Beyond change management: A multilevel investigation of contextual and personal influences on employees' commitment to change. *Journal of Applied Psychology, 92*, 942–951.

Hollensbe, E. C., Khazanchi, S. & Masterson, S. S. (2008). How do I assess if my supervisor and organization are fair? Identifying the rules underlying entity-based justice perceptions. *Academy of Management Journal, 51*, 1099–1116.

Hsiung, H. H. (2012). Authentic leadership and employee voice behavior: A multi-level psychological process. *Journal of Business Ethics, 107*, 349–361.

Johnson, J. P., Korsgaard, M. A., & Sapienza, H. J. (2002). Perceived fairness, decision control, and commitment in international joint venture management teams. *Strategic Management Journal, 23*, 1141–1160.

Jones, D. A., & Martens, M. L. (2009). The mediating role of overall fairness and the moderating role of trust certainty in justice-criteria relationships: The formation and use of fairness heuristics in the workplace. *Journal of Organizational Behavior, 30*, 1025–1051.

Judge, T. A., & Colquitt, J. A. (2004). Organizational justice and stress: The mediating role of work-family conflict. *Journal of Applied Psychology, 89*, 395–404.

Kanfer, R., Sawyer, J., Earley, P. C., & Lind, E. A (1987). Participation in task evaluation procedures: The effects of influential option expression and knowledge of evaluative criteria on attitudes and performance. *Social Justice Research, 1*, 235–249.

Kim, W. C., & Mauborgne, R. A. (1991). Implementing global strategies: The role of procedural justice. *Strategic Management Journal, 12*, 125–143.

Konovsky, M. A. (2000). Understanding procedural justice and its impact on business organizations. *Journal of Management, 26*, 489–511.

Kozlowski, S. W. J., & Klein, K. J. (2000). A multilevel approach to theory and research in organizations: Contextual, temporal, and emergent processes. In K. J. Klein & S. W. J. Kozlowski (Eds.), *Multilevel theory, research, and methods in organizations: Foundations, extensions, and new directions* (pp. 3–90). San Francisco, CA: Jossey-Bass.

Kray, L. J., & Lind, E. A. (2002). The injustices of others: Social reports and the integration of others' experiences in organizational justice judgments. *Organizational Behavior and Human Decision Processes, 89*, 906–924.

Krings, F., & Facchin, S. (2009). Organizational justice and men's likelihood to sexually harass: The moderating role of sexism and personality. *Journal of Applied Psychology, 94*, 501–510.

Lavelle, J. J., Brockner, J., Konovsky, M. A., Price, K. H., Henley, A. B., Taneja, A., & Vinekar, V. (2009). Commitment, procedural fairness, and organizational citizenship behavior: A multifoci analysis. *Journal of Organizational Behavior, 30*, 337–357.

Lavelle, J. J., Rupp, D. E., & Brockner, J. (2007). Taking a multifoci approach to the study of justice, social exchange, and citizenship behavior: The target similarity model. *Journal of Management, 33*, 841–866.

Leung, K., & Bond, M. H. (1984). The impact of cultural collectivism on reward allocation. *Journal of Personality and Social Psychology, 47*, 793–804.

Leventhal, G. S. (1976). The distribution of rewards and resources in groups and organizations. In L. Berkowitz & E. Walster (Eds.), *Advances in experimental social psychology* (vol. 9, pp. 91–131). New York, NY: Academic Press.

Leventhal, G. S. (1980). What should be done with equity theory? New approaches to the study of fairness in social relationships. In K. Gergen, M. Greenberg, & R. Willis (Eds.), *Social exchange: Advances in theory and research* (pp. 27–55). New York, NY: Plenum.

Levy, P. E., & Williams, J. R. (2004). The social context of performance appraisal: A review and framework for the future. *Journal of Management, 30*, 881–905.

Li, A., & Cropanzano, R. (2009a). Do East Asians respond more/less strongly to organizational justice than North Americans? A meta-analysis. *Journal of Management Studies, 46*, 787–805.

Li, A., & Cropanzano, R. (2009b). Fairness at the group level: Justice climate and intraunit justice climate. *Journal of Management, 35*, 564–599.

Li, A., Cropanzano, R., & Bagger, J. (2013). Justice climate and peer justice climate. *Small Groups Research, 44*, 563–592.

Li, A., Evans, J., Christian, M. S., Gilliland, S. W., Kausel, E. E., & Stein, J. H. (2011). The effects of managerial regulatory fit priming on reactions to explanations. *Organizational Behavior and Human Decision Processes, 115*, 268–282.

Li, N., Liang, J., & Crant, J. M. (2010). The role of proactive personality in job satisfaction and organizational citizenship behavior: A relational perspective. *Journal of Applied Psychology, 95*, 395–404.

Liao, H., & Rupp, D. (2005). The impact of justice climate and justice orientation on work outcomes: A cross-level multi-foci framework. *Journal of Applied Psychology, 90*, 242–256.

Lin, S., Tang, T., Li, C., Wu, C., & Lin, H. (2007). Mediating effect of cooperative norm in predicting organizational citizenship behaviors from procedural justice climate. *Psychological Reports, 101*, 67–78.

Lind, E. A. (2001). Fairness heuristic theory: Justice judgments as pivotal cognitions in organizational relations. In J. Greenberg & R. Cropanzano (Eds.), *Advances in organizational justice* (pp. 56–88). Stanford, CA: Stanford University Press.

Lind, E. A., Kray, L., & Thompson, L. (1998). The social construction of injustice: Fairness judgments in response to own and others' unfair treatment by authorities. *Organizational Behavior and Human Decision Processes, 75*, 1–22.

Lipponen, J., & Wisse, B. (2010). Shared perceptions of perceived justice as a predictor of externally rated departmental level academic performance. *Journal of Occupational and Organizational Psychology, 83*, 1065–1074.

Luo, Y. (2008). Procedural fairness and interfirm cooperation in strategic alliances. *Strategic Management Journal, 29*, 27–46.

Luria, G., & Yagil, D. (2008). Procedural justice, ethical climate and service outcomes in restaurants. *International Journal of Hospitality Management, 27*, 276–283.

Masterson, S. S. (2001). A trickle-down model of organizational justice: Relating employees' and customers' perceptions of and reactions to fairness. *Journal of Applied Psychology, 86*, 594–604.

Mayer, D., Nishii, L., Schneider, B., & Goldstein, H. (2007). The precursors and products of justice climates: Group leader antecedents and employee attitudinal consequences. *Personnel Psychology, 60*, 929–963.

Moliner, C., Martinez-Tur, V., Peiro, J., Ramos, J., & Cropanzano, R. (2005). Relationships between organizational justice and burnout at the work-unit level. *International Journal of Conflict Management, 12*, 99–106.

Moorman, R. R. (1991). Relationship between organizational justice and organizational citizenship behaviors: Do fairness perceptions influence employee citizenship? *Journal of Applied Psychology, 76*, 845–855.

Mossholder, K. W., Bennett, N., & Martin, C. L. (1998). A multilevel analysis of procedural justice context. *Journal of Organizational Behavior, 19*, 131–141.

Naumann, S. E., & Bennett, N. (2000). A case for procedural justice climate: Development and test of a multilevel model. *Academy of Management Journal, 43*, 881–889.

Naumann, S. E., & Bennett, N. (2002). The effects of procedural justice climate on work group performance. *Small Group Research, 33*, 361–377.

Niehoff, B. P., & Moorman, R. H. (1993). Justice as a mediator of the relationship between methods of monitoring and organizational citizenship behavior. *Academy of Management Journal, 36*, 527–556.

Novelli, L. Jr., Kirkman B. L., Shapiro D. L. (1995). Effective implementation of organizational change: An organizational justice perspective. In C. L. Cooper & D. M. Rousseau (Eds.), *Trends in organizational behavior* (Vol. 2, pp. 15–36). Chichester, UK: Wiley.

Oc, B., Bashshur, M. R., & Paddock, E. L. (2013). Consistency and reactivity: Leader behavior and follower reactions in the formation of group fairness climate perceptions. Working paper.

Ogunfowora, B. (2013). When the abuse is unevenly distributed: The effects of abusive supervision variability on work attitudes and behaviors. *Journal of Organizational Behavior, 34*, 1105–1123.

Price, J. L., & Mueller, C. W. (1986). *Handbook of organizational measurement.* Marshfield, MA: Pittman.

Parker, C. P., Baltes, B. B., & Christiansen, N. D. (1997). Support for affirmative action, justice perceptions, and work attitudes: A study of gender and racial-ethnic group differences. *Journal of Applied Psychology, 82*, 376–389.

Porter, C. O. L. H., Conlon, D. E., & Barber, A. E. (2004). The dynamics of salary negotiations: Effects of applicant's justice perceptions and recruitment decisions. *International Journal of Conflict Management, 15*, 273–303.

Priesemuth, M., Arnaud, A., & Schminke, M. (2013). Bad behavior in groups: The impact of overall justice climate and functional dependence on counterproductive work behavior in work units. *Group and Organization Management, 38*, 230–257.

Rawls, J. (1971). *A theory of justice.* Cambridge, MA: Harvard University Press.

Roberson, Q. M. (2006a). Justice in teams: The activation and role of sensemaking in the emergence of justice climates. *Organizational Behavior and Human Decision Processes, 100*, 177–192.

Roberson, Q. M. (2006b). Justice in teams: The effects of interdependence and identification on referent choice and justice climate strength. *Social Justice Research, 19*, 323–344.

Roberson, Q. M., & Colquitt, J. A. (2005). Shared and configural justice: A social network model of justice in teams. *Academy of Management Review, 30*, 595–607.

Rupp, D. E., Bashshur, M., & Liao, H. (2007). Justice climate past, present, and future: Models of structure and emergence. In F. Dansereau & F. J. Yammarino (Eds.), *Multi-level issues in organizations and time* (Vol. 6, pp. 357–396). Oxford, UK: Elsevier.

Rupp, D. E., & Cropanzano, R. (2002). The mediating effects of social exchange relationships in predicting workplace outcomes from multifoci organizational justice. *Organizational Behavior and Human Decision Processes, 89*, 925–946.

Rupp, D. E., & Paddock, E. L. (2010). From justice events to justice climate: A multilevel temporal model of information aggregation and judgment. In B. Mannix, M. Neal, & E. Mullen (Eds.), *Research on managing groups and teams: Fairness and groups* (pp. 239–267). Bingley, UK: JAI Emerald.

Rupp, D. E., & Spencer, S. (2006). When customers lash out: The effects of customer interactional justice on emotional labor and the mediating role of discrete emotions. *Journal of Applied Psychology, 91*, 971–978.

Salancik, G. R., & Pfeffer, J. (1978). A social information processing approach to job attitude and task design. *Administrative Science Quarterly, 23*, 224–253.

Sandel, M. J. (2009). *Justice: What's the right thing to do?* New York, NY: Farrar, Straus, and Giroux.

Schneider, B. (1987). The people make the place. *Personnel Psychology, 40*, 437–453.
Schneider, B., Goldstein, H., & Smith, D. B. (1995). The ASA framework: An update. *Personnel Psychology, 48*, 747–773.
Schneider, B., Smith, D. B., Taylor, S., & Fleenor, J. (1998). Personality and organizations: A test of the homogeneity of personality hypothesis. *Journal of Applied Psychology, 83*, 462–470.
Shaw, J. C., Wild, E., & Colquitt, J. A. (2003). To justify or excuse? A meta-analytic review of the effects of explanation. *Journal of Applied Psychology, 88*, 444–458.
Simons, T., & Roberson, Q. (2003). Why managers should care about fairness: The effects of aggregate justice perceptions on organizational outcomes. *Journal of Applied Psychology, 88*, 432–443.
Skarlicki, D. P., Barclay, L. J., & Pugh, S. D. (2008). When explanations for layoffs are not enough: Employers' integrity as a moderator of the relationship between informational justice and retaliation. *Journal of Occupational and Organizational Psychology, 81*, 123–146.
Sora, B., Caballer, A., Peiro, J. M., Silla, I., & Gracia, F. J. (2010). Moderating influence of organizational justice on the relationship between job insecurity and its outcomes: A multilevel analysis. *Economic and Industrial Democracy, 31*, 613–637.
Spell, C. S., & Arnold, T. J. (2007). A multi-level analysis of organizational justice climate, structure, and employee mental health. *Journal of Management, 33*, 724–751.
Tangirala, S., & Ramanujam, R. (2008). Employee silence on critical work issues: The cross level effects of procedural justice climate. *Personnel Psychology, 61*, 37–68.
Thibaut, J., & Walker, L. (1975). *Procedural justice: A psychological analysis*. Hillsdale, NJ: Erlbaum.
Trevor, C. O., & Nyberg, A. J. (2008). Keeping your headcount when all about you are losing theirs: Downsizing, voluntary turnover rates, and the moderating role of HR practices. *Academy of Management Journal, 51*, 259–276.
Tyler, T. R. (1994). Psychological models of the justice motive: Antecedents of distributive and procedural justice. *Journal of Personality and Social Psychology, 67*, 850–863.
Tyler, T. R., & Blader, S. (2000). *Cooperation in groups: Procedural justice, social identity, and behavioral engagement*. Philadelphia, PA: Psychology Press.
Tyler, T. R., & Dawes, R. M. (1993). Fairness in groups: Comparing the self-interest and social identity perspectives. In B. A. Mellers & J. Baron (Eds.), *Psychological perspectives on justice: Theory and applications* (pp. 87–108). New York, NY: Cambridge University Press.
Tyler, T. R., & Lind, E. A. (1992). A relational model of authority in groups. In M. P. Zanna (Ed.), *Advances in experimental social psychology* (Vol. 25, pp. 115–191). New York, NY: Academic Press.
Umphress, E. E., Labianca, G., Brass, D. J., Kass, E., & Scholten, L. (2003). The role of instrumental and expressive social ties in employees' perceptions of organizational justice. *Organizational Science, 14*, 738–753.
Wallace, J. C., Edwards, B. D., Mondore, S. P., & Finch, D. M. (2008). Employee discrimination claims and employee-initiated lawsuits: Does procedural justice climate moderate the claims—disputes relationship? *Journal of Managerial Issues, 20*, 313–326.
Walster, E., Berscheid, E., & Walster, G. W. (1973). New directions in equity research. *Journal of Personality and Social Psychology, 25*, 151–176.
Walumbwa, F. O., Hartnell, C. A., & Oke, A. (2010). Servant leadership, procedural justice climate, service climate, employee attitudes, and organizational citizenship behavior: A cross-level investigation. *Journal of Applied Psychology, 95*, 517–529.
Walumbwa, F. O., Wu, C., & Orwa, B. (2008). Contingent reward transactional leadership, work attitudes, and organizational citizenship behavior: The role of procedural justice climate perceptions and strength. *The leadership Quarterly, 19*, 251–265.
Weiss, H. H., Suckow, K., & Cropanzano, R. (1999). Effects of justice conditions on discrete emotions. *Journal of Applied Psychology, 84*, 786–794.
Whitman, D. S., Caleo, S., Carpenter, N. C., Horner, M. T., & Bernerth, J. B. (2012). Fairness at the collective level: A meta-analytic examination of the consequences and boundary conditions of organizational justice climate. *Journal of Applied Psychology, 97*, 776–791.
Yang, J., Mossholder, K. W., & Peng, T. K. (2007). Procedural justice climate and group power distance: An examination of cross-level interaction effects. *Journal of Applied Psychology, 92*, 681–692.
Zhang, Z., & Jia, M. (2013). How can companies decrease the disruptive effects of stretch goals? The moderating role of interpersonal- and informational- justice climate. *Human Relations, 66*, 993–1020.

CHAPTER

7 Multifoci Justice and Target Similarity: Emerging Research and Extensions

James J. Lavelle, Deborah E. Rupp, Jennifer Manegold, *and* Meghan A. Thornton

Abstract

This chapter addresses progress within the emergent area of multifoci organizational justice and identifies promising avenues for future multifoci research. First, the origins of the multifoci perspective and its successor, the target similarity model, are discussed. Empirical support for the model is reviewed, including meta-analytic investigations. Next, the newest wave of multifoci research is explored, emphasizing the role of important, yet under examined sources of justice, such as co-workers, customers, and clients, in gaining a more complete understanding of the effects of justice on employee attitudes and behaviors in the workplace. Further, we point to promising avenues for future research that include the study of interactive effects between justice sources, as well as the extension of multifoci research to cross-cultural justice and corporate social responsibility.

Key Words: multifoci justice, target similarity model, organizational justice, sources of justice, workplace fairness

Organizational justice research demonstrates that perceptions of fairness in the workplace exert a powerful influence on employee attitudes and behaviors. Perceptions of fairness have been found to predict positive attitudes such as affective commitment and trust and behaviors such as organizational citizenship and other cooperative behaviors (e.g., Cohen-Charash & Spector, 2001; Colquitt, Conlon, Wesson, Porter, & Ng, 2001; Konovsky, 2000). Alternatively, perceptions of unfairness have been associated with employee withdrawal such as turnover and negative workplace behaviors including deviance, sabotage, and other forms of counterproductive work behaviors (Colquitt et al., 2001; Cropanzano, Byrne, Bobocel, & Rupp, 2001). Such findings highlight the important role of workplace justice research in the organizational sciences and inform effective management practices (Brockner, 2006; Rupp & Aquino, 2009).

Our chapter addresses an emerging trend in the organizational justice literature referred to as the multifoci perspective (cf., Lavelle, Rupp, & Brockner, 2007; Rupp & Cropanzano, 2002). This perspective focuses attention on explicitly identifying the many different sources or parties that employees may deem as accountable for treating them in a fair or unfair manner at work. In addition to the broader organization itself, these sources may include entities internal to the organization (such as supervisors and co-workers) and external to the organization (such as customers and clients). As employees are likely to have unique experiences with each of these different parties, employees may come to view one source (e.g., the supervisor) as unfair and at the same time, perceive another source (e.g., co-workers) as fair.

In contrast to traditional conceptualizations of justice structured according to sets of normative rules (procedural, distributive, and interactional), the multifoci perspective adds emphasis by explicitly incorporating the actor held responsible for the violation of such rules. This brings the socio-relational aspects of justice to the forefront, and returns the study of justice to its roots in accountability (Cropanzano, Chrobot-Mason, Rupp, & Prehar, 2004; Felstiner, Abel, & Sarat, 1980-1981; Folger & Cropanzano, 2001; Weiner, 1995). First, to provide relevant background, we briefly review historical approaches to studying justice (i.e., justice types, overall justice, and the agent-system model). We then elaborate the multifoci model of justice and its successor, the target similarity model, selectively reviewing relevant empirical research. Following this, we discuss what we see as the next "wave" of target similarity research, which emphasizes the importance of considering co-workers, customers, and clients as sources of justice. Extensions of the multifoci perspective to the prediction of effective employee behaviors such as learning and creativity are then discussed. The final sections of our chapter discuss additional avenues for extending multifoci research including implications for cross-cultural justice and corporate social responsibility.

Background

Types of Justice as Normative Criteria for Fairness

Traditionally, researchers have conceptualized justice according to sets of rules used by perceivers to assess fairness of a focal party (e.g., those in positions of authority over the perceiver). *Distributive justice* grew out of social psychology, and considered the rules applied by employees to determine the fairness of outcomes such as personnel-related decisions (e.g., pay). This included rules of equity (Adams, 1965), equality, and need (Deutsch, 1975; Leventhal, 1976). *Procedural justice* grew out of research largely concerning the psychology of legal phenomena, and considered process control (Thibaut & Walker, 1975), consistency, bias-suppression, accuracy, correctability, representativeness, and ethicality (Leventhal, 1980) as rules for evaluating the fairness of procedures. *Interactional justice* was later proposed within organizational behavior as an additional set of rules governing the acceptability of how procedures were implemented in organizations (Bies & Moag, 1986; Greenberg, 1993). Interactional justice criteria included politeness, dignity, respect, and thorough explanations for decisions (delivered by the party accountable for carrying out the procedure). Since its introduction, researchers have further broken out interactional justice criteria into two dimensions. The first dimension, referred to as *interpersonal justice*, concerns normative rules of politeness, dignity, and respect. The second, referred to as *informational justice*, includes the criterion that explanations for decisions are thorough, sincere, and accurate.

Empirical evidence indicates that employees distinguish among these classes of judgments. For example, Colquitt and colleagues (Colquitt, 2001; Colquitt et al., 2001) found support for a four-component (distributive, procedural, informational, and interpersonal) model, whereas Cohen-Charash & Spector (2001) found support for a three-component (distributive, procedural, interactional) model. Although these factors represent different sets of normative rules, which are theoretically considered to be criteria that are applied as one forms a justice judgment (and hence, theoretically, antecedents to justice perceptions; Ambrose & Arnaud, 2005), as described earlier, the zeitgeist in the literature has been to refer to these as *types* of justice perceptions. Thus throughout this chapter, we refer to distributive, procedural, interactional, interpersonal, and informational as "types" of justice perceptions, and demarcate them from "sources" of justice perceptions. A point we will expand upon in this chapter is that, despite this loose terminology, a comprehensive review of the literature points to justice perceptions as being the product of holding an identifiable party accountable for the violation of normative justice rules (i.e., both "type" and "source"; Rupp, Shao, Jones, & Liao, 2014). Before we do, however, it is also relevant to highlight the research that has explored how these more specific perceptions contribute to employee perceptions of how fairly they are treated in a more global sense, which has been termed overall justice perceptions.

Overall Justice

The identification and examination of different types of justice has been important to the development and study of organizational justice. Researchers have suggested, however, that an exclusive focus on the types of justice may not provide a complete picture of how employees make and respond to assessments of fairness (Rupp, 2011). For example, scholars have argued that it is important to consider when employees are asked about fairness (e.g., in the judgment or use phase; Lind, 2001a) and how broad vs. specific the outcomes theorized to be predicted are relative to the specificity of the justice construct being used to predict outcomes (Ambrose & Arnaud, 2005; Colquitt &

Shaw, 2005). In the words of Lind (2001b, p. 225), "Justice types, although distinct, may not in the final analysis be very different in either their dynamics or their consequences."

This led Ambrose and Schminke (2009) to predict a model whereby global perceptions of justice are the most proximal predictors of global organizational outcomes (e.g., job attitudes, citizenship behaviors), and, therefore, mediate the effect of the justice types. They defined "overall justice" as an employee's global perception of how fairly both the employee and others within the organization are treated. In a first study, they showed that procedural, distributive, and interactional justice each predicted overall justice. Further, as hypothesized, overall justice fully mediated the relationship between justice types and global employee attitudes including job satisfaction, affective commitment, and turnover intentions. A second study sought to replicate these findings using task performance, organizational citizenship behavior, and organizational deviance as outcome variables. Results were largely replicated, with the exception that distributive justice did not significantly predict overall justice. Jones and Martens (2009) revealed similar findings. They too found overall justice to mediate the effects of justice types on outcomes, but they found the relative salience of the various types of justice to depend on the organizational context. Another line of research, which takes into account the organizational context when considering the differential role played by different types of justice is the agent-system model.

Agent-System Model

According to the theorizing of Bies and Moag (1986), procedural justice perceptions should be associated with organizationally-directed outcomes because procedures may be viewed as institutionalized. That is, policies and procedures are an inherent part of the organizational system and thus, the organization is the implied source of procedural justice. Alternatively, Bies and Moag suggested that perceptions of interactional justice should be linked to the agent enacting the procedures because the agent has discretion over the degree of interpersonal sensitivity demonstrated toward employees.

The view that procedural justice relates to the organization and interactional justice to organizational agents has since been referred to as the agent-system model of organizational justice (Tyler & Bies, 1990). Research examining the effects of procedural and interactional justice offers support for this perspective. For example, Masterson, Lewis, Goldman, and Taylor (2000) examined the effects of procedural and interactional justice on organizational citizenship behavior directed toward the organization (OCB-O) and directed toward the supervisor (OCB-S). Drawing from social exchange theory and an agent-system perspective of justice, Masterson and colleagues hypothesized and found that perceived organizational support mediated the relationship between procedural justice and OCB-O, whereas leader-member exchange mediated the relationship between interactional justice and OCB-S.

The findings of Masterson et al. (2000) are consistent with an agent-system perspective. Colquitt et al.'s (2001) meta-analysis, however, reports mixed support for this perspective. Integrating meta-analytic and multiple regression techniques, Colquitt and colleagues simultaneously examined the unique effects of procedural, interpersonal, informational, as well as distributive justice on system-referenced and agent-referenced outcome variables. Consistent with Bies and Moag (1986), Colquitt and colleagues argued that the agent-system model would predict "higher unique effects of interpersonal or informational justice for agent-referenced outcomes and higher unique effects of procedural justice for system-referenced outcomes" (Colquitt et al., 2001: 435). Support for this prediction was found for five dependent variables including organizational commitment, agent-referenced evaluations of authority, and individually-directed citizenship behaviors (OCB-I). For example, procedural justice was found to account for 9% of the unique variance in organizational commitment whereas the unique variance explained by interpersonal justice and informational justice was 2% and less than 1%, respectively.

No support was found however, when predicting five other dependent variables including organizationally-directed citizenship behaviors (OCB-O), trust, system-referenced evaluation of authority, withdrawal, and negative behaviors. For example, procedural and informational justice each accounted for the same amount of unique variance (1%) in OCB-O. Furthermore, in the case of withdrawal behaviors (argued to be an organizational outcome), interpersonal and informational justice actually accounted for more unique variance (2% each) than did procedural justice (1%). Taken together, the mixed pattern of results found by Colquitt et al. (2001) suggests that employees may not exclusively link interactional fairness to supervisors and procedural fairness to organizations.

Summary

Our brief review of overall justice and the agent-system model suggests a few potential nuances of each perspective. First, in terms of outcomes, overall justice focuses on the prediction of global employee attitudes and behaviors. Thus, researchers need to take a different perspective when predicting more specifically targeted attitudes and behaviors such as those directed toward a supervisor. In this regard, the agent-system model suggests that interactional justice should best predict employee responses toward supervisors, whereas procedural justice should best predict responses toward the organization. The mixed meta-analytic support for the agent-system model found by Colquitt and colleagues (2001) suggests that an expanded, more flexible approach to linking justice type and source may be useful to researchers. In this regard, the multifoci model of justice offers such a framework and further argues that a number of different sources of fairness are relevant to employees.

Multifoci Justice

As described earlier, the agent-system perspective suggests that employees hold different parties (either the organization or the supervisor) accountable for procedural and interactional forms of justice. Consistent with this perspective, the multifoci model of organizational justice argues that accountability for injustice plays a critical role in employee reactions. The multifoci perspective, however, goes further and argues that employees can assess the procedural, interactional, *and* distributive fairness of any relevant party as long as the party is viewed as accountable for the unfairness received (Cropanzano et al., 2001). Indeed, justice research and theory over the years demonstrates the importance of accountability in the formation of justice perceptions, especially when a negative or unfavorable event occurs (cf. Aquino, Tripp, & Bies, 2001; Bradfield & Aquino, 1999; Cropanzano et al., 2004; Felstiner, et al., 1980-1981; Ferguson & Rule, 1983; Folger & Cropanzano, 1998, 2001; Weiner, 1995). Thus, the multifoci perspective asserts that perceptions of unfairness can be attributed to a number of different sources, including not only organizations and supervisors, but also co-workers, workgroup members, customers, clients and other potential entities an employee may encounter during working hours. However, given the historical roots of this perspective, initial research seeking to empirically differentiate sources of justice began with a focus on the organization and the supervisor.

Organizations and Supervisors as Unique Sources of Procedural Justice and Interactional Justice

Although many have assumed that interactional justice items conjure memories and perceptions related to one's supervisor, whereas procedural justice measures largely get at organizationally-focused perceptions, recent analysis of the justice measures and items used throughout history suggest this has not been the case. Measures of justice types often reference multiple sources or no source at all (Rupp et al., 2014). In fact, the focus of early multifoci justice research was concerned with differentiating the organization and the supervisor as unique sources of *both* procedural and interactional justice. For example, Byrne (1999) argued that supervisors can often develop their own procedures for decision-making and thus can be perceived by employees as a unique source of procedural justice. Further, organizations as "juristic persons" (Coleman, 1974, 1982; Cropanzano et al., 2004) have been argued to be a unique source of justice, whose actions are evaluated by employees, and with whom employees perceive having a relationship. In contrast to the agent-system perspective, supervisors and organizations may both be held accountable for procedural as well as interactional injustice. Byrne's work offered initial support for such a four-factor model of justice including organizational procedural justice, organizational interactional justice, supervisory procedural justice, and supervisory interactional justice—a model further confirmed by Rupp and Cropanzano (2002) via a sample of employees working in a variety of different organizations and industries.

OVERALL ORGANIZATIONAL AND OVERALL SUPERVISORY JUSTICE

Holtz and Harold (2009) examined how types of justice associated with the organization and types of justice associated with the supervisor may differentially predict employee perceptions of overall organization-focused justice and overall supervisor-focused justice, respectively. The overall organization-focused justice construct refers to a holistic judgment of an employee's general experience of fairness from the organization, whereas overall supervisor-focused justice refers to a holistic judgment of an employee's experience of fairness from the supervisor. Extending research by Ambrose and Schminke (2009) on overall justice, Holtz and Harold found that employees viewed overall organizationally-referenced justice (assessed by general justice items pertaining to the organization such as, "For the most part, my organization treats its employees fairly") and overall supervisory-referenced justice (assessed by general justice items pertaining to the supervisor such as, "For the most part, my supervisor treats his/her employees fairly") as unique constructs.

Further, Holtz and Harold (2009) hypothesized and found that perceptions of organization-referenced procedural and distributive justice were more strongly related to perceptions of overall organizational justice than to perceptions of overall supervisory justice. A consistent pattern was found for the prediction of overall supervisory justice. Specifically, they found that informational and interpersonal justice from the supervisor was a better predictor of overall supervisory justice than of overall organizational justice. This pattern of results is consistent with a multifoci perspective of justice and suggests that in addition to differentiating types of justice according to a specific source (the approach most often taken by prior multifoci research) employees can also distinguish between overall perceptions of fairness by source—in this case, overall organizational and overall supervisory fairness.

Target Similarity Model

Lavelle and colleagues' (2007) target similarity model integrates multifoci perspectives of justice, social exchange, and organizational citizenship behavior in an attempt to provide a more complete conceptualization of the employee experience at work and to better predict employee attitudes and behaviors. Their model argues that, based on assessments of accountability, a number of different parties internal and external to the organization may be held responsible for distributive, procedural, and interactional justice. In addition to emphasizing that multiple sources of justice are relevant to employees, the model argues that employees may also hold multiple, unique social exchange relationships with these sources (e.g., the organization, supervisors, co-workers, clients, and others). In contrast to economic exchange, which reflects short-term, quid pro quo exchanges, social exchange relationships are long-term in focus and convey mutual support, trust and commitment (Cropanzano & Mitchell, 2005; Lavelle et al., 2007). Consistent with this definition of social exchange, Lavelle and colleagues suggest that a number of constructs such as commitment, support, identification, and trust can be viewed as proxies for multifoci social exchange relationships.

The target similarity model argues that, when treated fairly by a particular party, a social exchange relationship may develop between the employee and that party. Further, when employees are in a high-quality social exchange relationship with a specific party, the employee feels a relational obligation to the party and thus is motivated to engage in behaviors, such as citizenship behavior, intended to directly benefit the particular party. For example, Lavelle, McMahan, and Harris (2009) simultaneously examined the effects of three target-specific support variables (social exchange indicators) on multifoci citizenship behavior. As hypothesized, they found that perceived organizational support uniquely predicted citizenship toward the organization, perceived supervisor support uniquely predicted citizenship toward the supervisor, and that perceived workgroup support uniquely predicted citizenship toward the workgroup.

As the preceding findings suggest, employees can selectively direct their citizenship behavior toward certain parties and not others based upon the quality of their social exchange relationships. In this regard, the target similarity model emphasizes the unique predictability of both source-based justice perceptions and target-specific social exchange relationships. Consequently, in order to enhance predictive ability, the target similarity model "encourages researchers to hypothesize links between key employee perceptions (e.g., justice), relationships (e.g., social exchange), and behaviors (e.g., citizenship) with more precision than ever before—by specifying foci at all stages of the psychological processes being investigated" (Lavelle et al., 2007: 841).

Although the target similarity model recognizes that multiple sources of justice and social exchange partners are relevant to the employee work experience, the majority of existing empirical research tends to focus only on the organization and the supervisor as foci. The results of research examining the independent effects of these two justice sources are largely consistent with the target similarity model, finding differential effects of justice by source. For example, Masterson and colleagues

(2000) found that leader-member exchange mediated the relationship between supervisory-focused justice and supervisor-directed citizenship, whereas perceived organizational support was found to mediate the relationship between organizational justice and citizenship behaviors directed toward the organization. Olkkonen and Lipponen's (2006) research found a similar pattern of results. Specifically, they found that procedural justice from the organization predicted employee identification with the organization whereas interactional justice from the supervisor predicted employee identification with their work unit. Moreover, identification with the organization predicted OCB-O, whereas identification with the supervisor predicted citizenship toward the work unit.

The findings just described are consistent with what Lavelle and colleagues (2007) refer to as a target-similarity effect. That is, when simultaneously examining the effects of multiple justice sources, fairness stemming from a particular source should best predict employee attitudes and behaviors directed toward that particular party. It should be noted that the target similarity model also speaks to the possibility of "spillover" or carry-over effects from one source to another. That is, although target-similar relationships are expected to be larger in magnitude, it is possible that smaller effects may occur between dissimilar targets. In developing their target similarity model, Lavelle and colleagues reviewed a number of empirical studies reporting results consistent with a target-similarity prediction when relationships among two or three different sources of justice, social exchange partners, or beneficiaries of citizenship behaviors were examined simultaneously. We now turn to a recent meta-analysis that further examines evidence for the target similarity effect and sheds light on the implications of structuring justice according to the source or according to the type.

Meta-Analysis of Justice Sources, Types, and Target Similarity

As noted earlier, many empirical studies of organizational justice have adopted the traditional type-based approach consisting of distributive, procedural, interpersonal and informational justice (e.g., Colquitt et al., 2001). Alternatively, the target similarity model suggests that structuring justice according to the source may provide more precision in predicting employee attitudes and behaviors directed toward the source. In a recent meta-analysis, Rupp and colleagues (2014) sought to establish evidence for the target similarity model by combining meta-analysis and path analysis techniques in an effort to demonstrate that target-specific social exchange mediates relationships between the corresponding sources of justice and target-specific citizenship behaviors. Notably, their analyses were conducted using 647 distinct samples containing over 12,236 correlation coefficients among justice and outcomes, comprising a sample size of over 235,000.

In setting up their hypotheses, Rupp et al. (2014) articulated what the literature has argued are the fundamental components of a justice perception; namely, that an identifiable party is held accountable for the violation of normative standards for justice and fairness (Folger & Cropanzano, 2001). This operationalization, which is one of the few universally agreed upon tenants within the justice community, suggests that the justice types (i.e., the normative rule sets) are only one component to justice perception formation—that the violation of such rules must be connected with an accountable party, and therefore, optimal prediction of outcomes will result when, as the target similarity model argues, the party deemed accountable for justice rule violations is aligned with the party to whom subsequent attitudes and behaviors are targeted. Whereas some of the utility gained by the precision of specification may be simply due to the fact that this allows for predictor and criterion variables to be aligned according to their breadth or generality (also known as bandwidth, see Cronbach, 1970; Cronbach & Gleser, 1957), multifoci and target similarity researchers argue that it is the impact of source-specific justice perceptions on source-specific social exchange that truly drives these relationships.

This led Rupp and colleagues (2014) to predict that multifoci justice perceptions (i.e., supervisor and organizational justice perceptions, which may include reference to distributive, procedural, and interactional justice rules) would show incremental variance in predicting source-specific outcomes, over and above the effects of type-based justice perceptions (which only sometimes make mention of a specific source). They further predicted that target similarity effects would be mediated by source-specific social exchange relationships (which if confirmed, would evidence the phenomenon being more than bandwidth-fidelity in that the effects are attenuated when social exchange is present in the theoretical model).

To provide evidence for these arguments, Rupp et al. (2014) coded all of the justice measures used in all prior empirical organizational justice research according to type (distributive, procedural, and interactional) and source (the supervisor or the organization).[1] The authors coded both social exchange and other outcome variables according to source. Supervisor-focused exchange variables included supervisory trust, supervisory identification, supervisory commitment, and leader-member exchange. Organization-focused social exchange variables included organizational trust, organizational identification, organizational commitment, and perceived organizational support. Outcome variables included job performance, job satisfaction, target-specific citizenship (directed toward the organization or toward the supervisor), and target-specific counterproductive behaviors (directed toward the organization or toward the supervisor).

Combining meta-analysis and regression techniques, the unique effects of justice from the organization, justice from the supervisor, and three types of justice (procedural justice, distributive justice, and interactional justice) on 18 outcome variables were estimated. The results offered support for the hypothesis that structuring justice by source more strongly predicts employee attitudes and behaviors toward that source than does structuring justice by type. Further, Rupp et al. (2014) found solid support for the target similarity effect. Specifically, justice from the organization better predicted outcomes targeting the organization than did justice perceptions stemming from the supervisor. Moreover, justice from the supervisor better predicted outcomes targeting the supervisor than did justice stemming from the organization. In sum, the results pertaining to 16 of the 18 criterion variables offered support for the target similarity effect and for the hypothesis that justice source is a stronger predictor of employee reactions toward the source than justice type.

Employing path analysis techniques, Rupp et al. (2014) further found that target-specific proxies for social exchange (support, trust, identification, LMX, and commitment) mediated the relationships between source-specific justice perceptions and employee citizenship toward the focal party. Specifically, the relationship between supervisory justice and OCB-S was mediated by supervisory trust and leader-member exchange with the supervisor. Further, the relationship between justice from the organization and OCB-O was mediated by organizational support, organizational trust, organizational affective commitment and organizational identification.

Finally, Rupp and colleagues (2014) took the additional step of comparing models that mismatched the source of justice and social exchange proxies with a nonmatched beneficiary of citizenship behavior. Consistent with the target similarity model, they found that the indirect effect of perceived organizational support, organizational affective commitment, organizational trust, and organizational identification on the relationship between justice from the organization and OCB-S was significantly weaker than the indirect effect of these social exchange proxies when justice from the organization predicted OCB-O. Moreover, the indirect effect of supervisor-related leader-member exchange and supervisory trust in the relationship between justice from the supervisor and OCB-O was substantially weaker than the indirect effect when justice from supervisor predicted OCB-S.

Although the findings of Rupp et al. (2014) are quite supportive of target similarity predictions, another recent meta-analysis by Colquitt et al. (2013), which was broader in nature and sought to update the Colquitt et al. (2001) meta-analysis, reached a somewhat different conclusion. Below, we describe key elements of Colquitt et al.'s (2013) meta-analysis as it pertains to target similarity predictions, primarily referred to by these authors as "focus-matching." We then compare certain aspects of the research conducted by Rupp et al. and Colquitt et al. (2013) that may contribute to the different conclusions drawn in each study.

Colquitt and colleagues (2013) tested focus-matching hypotheses by examining the bivariate, meta-analytic correlations among two sources of justice (the organization and the supervisor) and nine focus-specific (organization-directed and supervisor-directed) employee attitudes and behaviors. In their coding of prior studies, sources of justice were delineated according to each of the four types of justice when possible. For example, procedural justice was broken out into organization-focused procedural justice and supervisor-focused procedural justice. Interpersonal justice was broken out into organization-focused interpersonal justice and supervisor-focused interpersonal justice. The same approach was applied to denote organization and supervisor-focused forms of informational and distributive justice. The focus-specific outcomes examined were similar to those included in Rupp et al.'s (2014) study and included perceived organizational support, leader-member exchange, trust in the organization, trust in the supervisor, commitment to the organization, organization-directed citizenship behavior, supervisor-directed citizenship, counterproductive work behavior toward the organization and toward the supervisor.

In their analyses, Colquitt et al. (2013) examined the bivariate meta-analytic correlations and confidence intervals when the focus of justice (according to type) matched the focus of the outcome compared to when the focus of justice (according to type) did not match that outcome. For example, the bivariate relationship between organization-focused procedural justice and trust in the organization was compared to the bivariate relationship between supervisor-focused procedural justice and trust in the organization. As a final example, the bivariate relationship between supervisor-focused interpersonal justice and supervisor-directed citizenship behavior was compared to the bivariate relationship between organization-focused interpersonal justice and supervisor-directed citizenship behavior. Among 36 possible justice-outcome comparisons of this type, only three were found to significantly support a focus-matching perspective. Consequently, Colquitt and colleagues concluded there was little support for taking a focus-matching approach when the organization and the supervisor are examined as foci.

There are important differences between the meta-analyses conducted by Rupp et al. (2014) and Colquitt et al. (2013) that should be noted when attempting to make sense of these seemingly different conclusions. Procedurally, the sample of studies used across these two meta-analyses was different. There were 647 prior empirical papers analyzed in Rupp et al.'s meta-analysis, and 493 were analyzed by Colquitt and colleagues. Of those, 213 papers were the same across the two investigations. Operationally, the "multifoci" justice variables were conceptualized differently across the two studies. Colquitt et al. took an approach similar to earlier multifoci studies, employing fully-crossed multifoci variables (e.g., organization-focused distributive justice, supervisor-focused procedural justice, etc.). In contrast, Rupp et al. applied more recent theorizing (which is reviewed later) that, although these specific fully crossed variables can be distinguished from one another, they are more potent in the aggregate as broader perceptions of multifoci justice (e.g., overall supervisory- and organizationally-focused justice; see Holtz & Harold, 2009; Rupp, 2011; Rupp & Paddock, 2010).

In terms of their analytic approach, Colquitt et al. (2013) examined bivariate meta-analytic correlations. As such, this approach does not readily capture the unique, independent effects of justice sources on target-specific outcomes in the presence of (or above and beyond) the main effects of justice types. In comparison, Rupp and colleagues (2014) integrated hierarchical multiple regression and meta-analytic techniques in order to examine the unique contributions made by justice sources and justice types (in the same regression model) on each target-specific outcome. As such, this analytic approach more readily captures the unique effects of justice sources on target-specific outcomes above and beyond the main effects of the justice types and is consistent with prior multifoci research that contributed to the development of the target similarity model. As the Colquitt et al. meta-analysis was designed to test a broader set of research questions, including the role of affect and social exchange (both of which received support), we conclude that Rupp et al.'s meta-analysis comprised a more in-depth and sophisticated approach for isolating the unique and incremental contribution made by a multifoci approach (which was the sole focus of their investigation).

That said, Colquitt et al.'s (2013) work certainly reinforces the importance of normative justice rules for understanding how employees respond to work events. The multifoci perspective amplifies our understanding by connecting this notion with another fundamental aspect of justice perception formation—that of accountability. Next, we turn to a recently articulated temporal model that may serve to bridge these two perspectives.

A Temporal Model of Justice Type and Source

Rupp and colleagues (Rupp, 2011; Rupp & Paddock, 2010) have recently argued for a temporal approach to understanding how time may affect employee responses to injustice. This work compliments that of Lind (2001a), which discusses the relative importance of justice rules at different stages of the justice process (e.g., the judgment and use phases). Rupp and Paddock (2010) suggest that justice "type" (i.e., the application of normative criteria for assessing the fairness of a situation) is especially relevant at the level of the event. That is, it is when a particular event or interaction occurs, that employees are likely to apply distributive, procedural, and/or interactional justice criteria. Drawing from Folger and Cropanzano's (1998) fairness theory, this model argues that employees will quickly seek to make an assessment of accountability for the negative event. Once accountability has been determined, perceptions of unfairness are thought to be encoded and categorized in memory according to the responsible party or *source* of injustice.

As time progresses, employees are expected to form general judgments of fairness for each party. That is, distributive, procedural, and international information pertaining to a particular source become aggregated into a more holistic view of source-based overall fairness. It is argued that it is this overall or general assessment of source fairness that becomes stored in memory. Consequently, Rupp and colleagues' (Rupp, 2011; Rupp & Paddock, 2010) temporal model suggests that justice type is most salient at the time an event occurs, whereas the source of justice becomes increasingly salient over time.

One question that emerges from the preceding discussion pertains to the measurement of justice constructs. One could measure distributive, procedural, and interactional justice in the traditional way, not specifying source (we do not recommend this, however). One could measure source-based judgments, asking employees to rate the fairness of supervisors, co-workers, and so forth. One could create separate distributive, procedural, and interactional justice scales for their various sources of interest (e.g., creating multiple versions of the Colquitt (2001) scale for each relevant source/type combination), and either aggregate the types of justice within a source, or create "fully crossed" models with a scale score for each type/source combination (e.g., supervisor procedural justice, supervisor interactional justice, organizational procedural justice, organizational interactional justice, etc.). Adding even further complexity to this mix is recent research that has been advocating for the study of overall justice, which, as explained earlier, refers to an employee's holistic judgment of how they are treated, overall, across sources and types (Ambrose & Schminke, 2009). This has been measured both using more fine-grained facets as indicators of a latent overall justice construct (Fassina et al., 2008; Jones & Martens, 2009), and as a separate construct with a separate measure (i.e., questions inquiring about generalized, overall treatment, see Ambrose & Schminke, 2009; Holtz & Harold, 2009). Indeed, such a large number of facets and approaches is potentially dizzying.

What Rupp and Paddock's (2010) model implies is that how we choose to measure justice should largely depend on *when* we measure it. In other words, measuring justice as facets, as foci, and as an overall construct, might all be an appropriate approach, depending on when in the judgment process the researcher focuses his/her attention. This is an extremely ripe area for future research, and we hope the justice community can work together to further sort out these issues.

Summary

Empirical evidence demonstrates that employees perceive organizations and supervisors as unique sources of justice. Further, a recent meta-analysis (Rupp et al., 2014) concludes that structuring justice by source (the organization and the supervisor) can explain more variance in employee attitudes and behaviors directed toward the source than does structuring justice by type. Moreover, the target similarity model has garnered support via meta-analytic evidence showing that social exchange with a source (supervisor or organization) mediates multifoci effects.

The target similarity model suggests that a number of different parties internal and external to the organization may be relevant sources of justice that affect the work lives of employees. The vast majority of justice research to date, however, focuses on only supervisors or organizations as sources of fairness. A handful of recent empirical studies have incorporated additional sources of justice both internal and external to the organization. We discuss these studies next.

New Sources of Justice

Researchers have recently extended the multifoci perspective by examining the effects of notable, yet understudied sources of justice in the workplace, including internal organizational sources (e.g., workgroup members and co-workers) and external organizational sources (e.g., customers and clients). Given empirical research on these sources is relatively rare, we view these studies as the starting point for the next wave of multifoci justice research. Below, we begin by discussing the important and growing role of co-workers in the workplace and then turn to recent empirical studies examining the effects of justice stemming from co-workers on focal employees. We then review findings from research establishing customers and clients as external sources of justice that can impact a range of employee attitudes and behaviors. We conclude this section with a discussion of multifoci justice in union contexts.

Co-workers

Organizations are becoming less hierarchical, and consequently, employees are working and interacting more closely with peers than ever before (Chiaburu & Harrison, 2008). Co-workers can be defined as fellow employees with whom individuals work and interact on a regular, perhaps daily basis, who are of roughly equal status within the organizational hierarchy. As organizations continue to flatten their hierarchies and create team-based work structures, the influence of co-workers on each other will continue to grow (Harrison, Johns, & Martocchio, 2000). Meta-analytic evidence supports this notion. For example, Chiaburu and Harrison (2008) found that perceptions of co-worker support positively contribute to focal employee job satisfaction, job involvement, and performance. Further, perceived co-worker support was found to have a negative impact on turnover intentions, absenteeism, role conflict, and role ambiguity. Importantly, this study found the effect of co-worker support to be over and above the contribution of leader support. Consequently, these results suggest that co-worker support is uniquely important to predicting and understanding key employee attitudes and behaviors in the workplace.

As the target similarity model makes explicit, co-workers are likely to be relevant sources of justice in the workplace (Lavelle et al., 2007). For example, self-managing work teams often develop and apply their own decision-making procedures to allocate job responsibilities and determine work schedules for the team members. Further, given employees are likely to interact with their team members and other co-workers on a daily basis, employees are likely to form judgments and perceptions according to the normative criteria specific to interpersonal justice. That is, employees are likely to assess whether they were treated in a polite manner and shown dignity and respect by their co-workers during these interactions. In fact, in a scale development effort pertaining to fair interpersonal treatment (e.g., treating others with respect and akin to interpersonal justice), Donovan, Drasgow, and Munson (1998) demonstrated that employees differentiate between co-workers and supervisors as sources of fair interpersonal treatment.

CO-WORKER INTERPERSONAL JUSTICE, SUPPORT, AND CITIZENSHIP

Informed by the target similarity model, Lavelle, McMahan, et al. (2009) simultaneously examined relationships among three different sources of justice (the organization, supervisors, and the workgroup), social exchange partners (as assessed by perceived workgroup support, perceived supervisor support, and perceived organizational support) and target-specific forms of citizenship behavior (citizenship directed toward the workgroup, toward the supervisor, and toward the organization) as rated by supervisors. Using a sample of nurses, the authors confirmed that employees perceived each source of justice and each social exchange relationship as unique and that supervisors were able to differentiate employee citizenship behavior according to the intended beneficiary (the workgroup, supervisor, and organization). In support of the target similarity perspective, workgroup justice (operationalized as interpersonal workgroup justice) positively predicted perceived workgroup support whereas supervisor and organizational justice did not. Moreover, perceived workgroup support predicted supervisor ratings of employee citizenship toward the workgroup, whereas perceived supervisor support and perceived organizational support did not.

These findings indicate that employees view their workgroup members as a unique source of justice and also offer support for the multifoci linkages of the target similarity model when assessing the three sources of justice simultaneously. That is, perceived workgroup support, perceived supervisor support, and perceived organizational support were differentially and positively predicted by workgroup fairness, supervisor fairness, and organizational fairness, respectively. In addition, the link between multifoci support and citizenship behavior was also supported in that perceived workgroup support, perceived supervisor support, and perceived organizational support differentially and positively predicted citizenship toward the workgroup, the supervisor, and the organization, respectively.

CO-WORKER PROCEDURAL JUSTICE, COMMITMENT, AND CITIZENSHIP

Whereas Lavelle, McMahan, et al. (2009) considered the effects of interpersonal workgroup justice, Lavelle, Brockner, et al. (2009) identified and examined workgroups as a source of procedural justice. Specifically, using a sample of students working in course project teams over the course of a semester, Lavelle and colleagues hypothesized and found that commitment to the workgroup mediated the effects of perceived workgroup justice on individuals' citizenship toward the workgroup (operationalized as the extent to which the group member volunteered extra-time to help group members, going above and beyond the call of duty as rated by fellow workgroup members). These findings further support the target similarity model in that perceived co-worker justice led to commitment to the workgroup, which, in turn, led to citizenship behavior toward the workgroup.

Customers

Researchers have become increasingly interested in employee interactions with customers, especially in the area of customer service. Customer service employees can have a number of interactions with different customers on a daily basis (Groth, Hennig-Thurau, & Wang, 2013). Although a number of organizations emphasize the importance of treating customers well, recent research turns the tables so to speak and treats the customer as a source of fairness that may impact a range of customer-service employee attitudes and behaviors. Next, we discuss recent studies in both experimental and field research demonstrating that customers are indeed an important source of justice in the workplace.

CUSTOMER INJUSTICE AND EMOTIONAL LABOR

Rupp, McCance, and Grandey (2007) argued that unfair treatment by customers can affect the employee's ability to comply with emotional display rules (Ashforth & Humphrey, 1993). Display rules refer to emotional displays that are stationed by the organization as being required within service encounters (e.g., exhibiting courtesy and friendliness). Adhering to these display rules is important because they can affect customer perceptions of service quality (Schneider & Bowen, 1985). However, when an employee is treated in an unfair manner by a customer, it may elicit negative emotions in the employee, making it more difficult to comply with such display rules. In this regard, emotional labor refers to the extent that complying with these display rules requires effortful emotion regulation.

Rupp and Spencer's (2006) laboratory experiment simulated a customer service call center and manipulated the levels of interactional fairness coming from customers (confederates) during interactions with the call center employees (participants). They found that when customers treated participants in an interpersonally just manner, participants reported it was easier to comply with display rules compared to those who were treated unfairly by their customers. Thus, participants' emotional labor was higher for those who were treated unfairly by customers.

Spencer and Rupp (2009) extended this line of inquiry to the consideration of face-to-face (as opposed to telephone) interactions in a simulated customer service department. In this experiment, subjects experienced either fair or unfair treatment from customers (confederates) and observed their co-workers being treated either fairly or unfairly by customers. Fair interpersonal treatment was represented by polite interactions whereas unfair treatment was represented by undeserved verbal attacks and the withholding of information (i.e., violation of the normative justice rules of interactional justice). In addition to examining the effects of customer injustice on emotional labor, they also considered how observing another co-worker being treated unfairly by a customer affected participants' emotional labor (measured with items assessing the extent to which participants tried hard to suppress anger and distress and tried hard to display enthusiasm and be cheerful). These authors found that customer injustice led to higher levels of emotional labor. Further, they found this relationship to be mediated by counterfactual thinking as elaborated in Folger and Cropanzano's (1998) accountability-based fairness theory. Counterfactual thinking was assessed by measuring the extent to which participants felt customers *could* have and *should* have behaved differently as well as the extent to which participants *would* have felt better if treated differently by customers.

In support of affective events theory (Weiss & Cropanzano, 1996), Spencer and Rupp (2009) found that discrete emotions (anger and guilt) partially mediated the relationship between customer justice and emotional labor. Participants' affect and emotional labor was also impacted by simply observing their co-workers being treated unfairly by customers. Taken together, these findings suggest that experiencing and observing injustice from customers can lead to emotional labor through the mechanisms of counterfactual thinking and discrete emotions.

Extending this laboratory research to a field setting, Rupp, McCance, Spencer, and Sonntag (2008) examined customer justice and its influence on surface acting in a field study of bank tellers in Germany. Surface acting occurs when an employee modifies his or her outwardly displayed emotions to hide true feelings. Rupp and colleagues found that greater levels of customer unfairness led to higher levels of surface acting by employees. Taken together, the results of these studies suggest that employee perceptions of unfair treatment from customers can lead to higher levels of emotional labor and surface acting, potentially making it more difficult for employees to deliver high levels of service quality to those customers. We now turn to recent research that further examines the effects of customer injustice on employee sabotage toward customers—a dependent variable almost certain to reduce customer perceptions of service quality.

CUSTOMER INJUSTICE AND CUSTOMER-DIRECTED SABOTAGE

Skarlicki, Van Jaarsveld, and Walker (2008) examined the relationship between employee perceptions of customer fairness and employee sabotage toward customers using a sample of call-center employees. In the context of call centers, customer-service employees tend to have episodic interactions with customers over the phone (for further elaboration of the call center context, see Van Jaarsveld & Poster, 2013). Skarlicki and colleagues drew from a moral perspective of unfairness to argue that even though employers may espouse the motto that the "customer is always right," employees may desire to hold customers accountable when they exhibit unfair behavior. For example, interpersonal mistreatment by customers is likely to be viewed as violating moral norms of conduct, thus motivating employees to seek ways to punish customers (e.g., sabotage) who treat them unfairly. Customer interpersonal unfairness reflects customer behaviors such as yelling, being condescending, and speaking aggressively to call-center employees during telephone conversations. Customer-directed sabotage includes employee behaviors such as intentionally putting customers on hold for a long period of time, purposefully transferring the customer to the wrong department, and purposefully disconnecting the call (Skarlicki et al., 2008).

As hypothesized, Skarlicki and colleagues (2008) found a positive relationship between perceptions of customer injustice and employee sabotage toward customers. Moreover, consistent with a target similarity perspective, they found that customer injustice predicted variance in customer-directed sabotage above and beyond the four components of organizational justice (i.e., procedural, distributive, informational, and interpersonal). That is, customer-directed sabotage was better predicted by injustice from customers than by types of justice stemming from the organization or its agents. As such, Skarlicki and colleagues conclude that "customers warrant attention in the organizational justice research as a distinct source of workplace unfairness."

Additional support for this conclusion is provided by Wang, Liao, Zhan, and Shi (2011), who examined the daily relationship between customers' mistreatment of employees and employee sabotage toward customers. Their sample consisted of call-center employees providing customer-service support for phone products in China. On average, these employees responded to 60 to 90 customer calls per day. Consistent with Skarlicki and colleagues (2008), Wang et al. argued that mistreatment from customers may anger employees and motivate them to reciprocate with sabotage. Drawing from Skarlicki and colleagues measures of customer interpersonal injustice and customer-directed sabotage, Wang et al. found support for their hypothesis that daily customer injustice predicted daily customer-directed sabotage. Further, Wang and colleagues found that employee negative affectivity strengthened this relationship.

Clients

As demonstrated earlier, much of the research examining the effects of customer injustice on employee responses has taken place in the context of call centers or in situations where employees are likely to have limited interactions with customers. In these situations, employee interactions with customers tend to be episodic, with a short-term focus, involving relatively few interactions with the same customers over time (Skarlicki et al., 2008). In contrast, interactions between employees of professional services firms (such as those in public accounting or consulting) and their clients often take on longer-term relationships with more frequent interactions (e.g., Herda & Lavelle, 2013). Such a relational focus is also evident in provider-client relationships in human services such as healthcare and education (Buunk & Schaufeli, 1993). Next, we discuss research conducted in the context of professional services firms followed by a brief review of relevant research in human services.

PROFESSIONAL SERVICE FIRMS

Integrating research on the effects of customer injustice and the social exchange-based mechanisms of the target similarity model, Herda and Lavelle (2013) examined the effects of public accountants' perceptions of how fairly they are treated by clients to whom they provide general business and tax advice. In this study, auditor-client relationships spanned four years or more, constituting a much longer service relationship than those reviewed earlier. The authors found that accountants' perceptions of client fairness significantly impacted their service quality, and that this relationship was mediated by social exchange. Providing additional support for a target similarity perspective, the results were found to hold even when accountants' commitment to their firm was controlled. This pattern of results highlights the role of client fairness in engendering social exchange relationships between professional service providers and their clients. Such high-quality relationships motivate professionals to provide higher levels of client service. More generally, these findings suggest that clients of professional services firms are a relevant, unique source of fairness that can affect the attitudes and behaviors of employees working in a wide variety of areas.

HUMAN SERVICES

A related stream of research in the context of human services demonstrates that perceived inequity (or distributive injustice) in provider-client relationships can produce unfavorable consequences for providers (e.g., Cropanzano & Wright, 2011; Schaufeli, 2006). This stream of research points to reciprocity norms associated with social exchange, as drivers of expected rewards (such as gratitude for the care and attention they afford their clients). However, in human service professions such as healthcare and education, these expectations are often left unfulfilled (Buunk & Schaufeli, 1993). As such, perceived inequity fosters stress, which in turn may lead to burnout in providers. Indicators of burnout include emotional exhaustion, depersonalization, and reduced feelings of personal accomplishment (Maslach, 1982).

Empirical research demonstrates support for the effects of distributive injustice on providers. In a sample of medical doctors, van Dierendonck, Schaufeli, and Sixma (1994) demonstrated that doctors' perceptions of inequity in their relationships with patients were related to higher levels of emotional exhaustion. Schaufeli and Janczur (1994) extended this research using a sample of Dutch and Polish nurses, showing that feelings of inequity in provider-client relationships were predictive of burnout in nurses above and beyond other stressors, such as a perception of control and the number of hours worked per week. Similarly, Bakker, Schaufeli, Sixma, Bosveld, and van Dierendonck (2000) tested a process model of burnout based on social exchange and equity theory. Surveying Dutch general practitioners over a five-year period, they found that perceived inequity in the provider-client relationship triggered emotional exhaustion, which led to negative attitudes toward the client and self. As a final example, Van Horn, Schaufeli, and Taris (2001) found that perceived inequity in the teacher-student relationship was more predictive of teacher burnout than was inequity in teacher-colleague or teacher-organization relationships.

In sum, we note that, in contrast to the short-term, episodic nature of interactions between employees in lower-level service positions (e.g., call center and service desk employees) and customers, the longer-term focus inherent to the relationships between professional service providers and their clients seems to be an appropriate context for understanding the effects of client justice from a relational, social exchange perspective. For example, employees of professional services firms can develop unique social-exchange relationships with their clients that can motivate these professionals to provide higher levels of client service. Further, perceptions of inequity in provider-client relationships have been found to trigger undesirable outcomes, such as feelings of provider burnout. In brief, the findings of recent research indicate that both customers and clients are important sources of justice in the workplace.

Unions

In unionized contexts, injustice may differ phenomenologically from how it is understood to function within the typical work contexts studied in nonunionized work contexts. The union and the organization, although technically separate organizations, simultaneously affect and influence one another. The behaviors of supervisors affect union leadership and members (e.g., filing of grievances) and the behaviors of union leadership and members affect the organization (e.g., engaging in bargaining). Further, union members and leaders exist as employees and work for employers, blurring the distinction between union locals and organizations as two completely separate entities. Thus, exploring the (in)justice experienced by unionized workers from union leaders and unions is critical to understanding the full milieu of unionized workers' justice-related experiences.

As previously argued for organization- and supervisor-based perceptions of fairness, one would expect that union-based perceptions of fairness should affect outcomes directed toward the union. Fair treatment from union leaders would engender social exchange with union members, such that union members would be motivated to engage in behaviors that benefit the union in reciprocation for their fair treatment. This could be manifested in OCBs directed toward the union, more engagement in union activities, and satisfaction with union leadership.

Research has shown that union leader behaviors can affect perceptions of fairness. Studies by Skarlicki and Latham (1996, 1997) examined the effect of union-leader justice training on union members' fairness perceptions as well as citizenship behaviors. After union leaders were trained on justice principles (namely procedural and interpersonal justice criteria), union member perceptions of fairness and union member citizenship behaviors within the union were assessed. Across both studies, Skarlicki and Latham found that perceptions of fairness were affected by training such that perceptions of fairness were higher among union members whose leaders had undergone training than among those whose leaders had not. Further, the findings supported the target similarity model, showing that OCB directed at the union and OCBs directed at union members were also higher among union members whose leaders had been trained.

Although these studies indicate that union leader justice affects employee behaviors within union contexts, very few studies have examined union contexts as unique sources of justice and their effects on behaviors other than OCBs (for a recent exception examining strike votes, see Cloutier, Denis, & Bilodeau, 2013). Based on the previously discussed theories, we would expect that union-based justice would affect outcomes such as engagement within the union, satisfaction with union leadership, and performance within the union. Further, we would expect that the effects of union leader fairness would uniquely affect these outcomes above and beyond the influence of fairness from organizations and supervisors. However, it still remains for researchers to address and to test these expectations comparing different sources of justice that include unions.

Summary

The studies described above point to the importance of incorporating sources of justice beyond the traditional emphasis on the organization and the supervisor in order to provide a more complete picture of the employee justice experience. In particular, we see that external sources of justice, such as customers and clients, as well as internal sources of justice, such as co-workers, impact employee attitudes and behaviors in a target-specific manner.

Other recent studies have examined the effects of multifoci justice on important dependent variables that do not necessarily or obviously reflect attitudes or behaviors directed toward a specific source. These studies do suggest however, that justice from different sources can have unique effects on the outcome variables of interest. Thus, in order to extend the implications of assessing fairness from multiple sources, we now discuss recent multifoci justice research that does not necessarily invoke target similarity predictions.

Effects of Justice Sources: Beyond a Target Similarity Perspective

The importance of considering multiple sources of justice simultaneously may go beyond the explicit incorporation of a target similarity perspective. That is, different sources of justice can help explain variance in outcome variables that may not have a clear or obvious matching referent. In this section we review a few recent studies taking a multifoci justice approach when predicting employee learning behavior and forms of creativity.

Voluntary Learning Behavior

Drawing from a multifoci perspective of justice and social exchange, Walumbwa, Cropanzano, and Hartnell (2009) examined the effects of procedural and distributive justice from the organization, and informational and interpersonal justice from the supervisor, on voluntary learning behavior among employees of a car dealership. Voluntary learning refers to proactive behaviors undertaken when an employee seeks to increase job knowledge and skills that will help enhance performance in his or her current role or in future work roles (Edmondson, 1999; Maurer & Tarulli, 1994). Walumbwa and colleagues argue that, in contrast to citizenship behaviors that are directed toward and primarily intended to benefit other individuals or the organization, the most direct beneficiary of learning behavior is the employee in the form of "self-development or self-improvement." Drawing from the target similarity model, Walumbwa et al. found support for their hypotheses that organizational procedural and distributive justice would engender a social exchange relationship with the organization (as measured by organizational identification) whereas supervisory interpersonal and informational justice would lead to a social exchange relationship with the supervisor (as measured by LMX).

Going beyond a target similarity perspective, Walumbwa and colleagues (2009) argued that social exchange relationships with the organization and the supervisor would each contribute uniquely to the prediction of employee learning behavior. Thus, they hypothesized that organizational identification would mediate the relationship between organizational justice (procedural and distributive) and voluntary learning behavior, whereas LMX would mediate the relationship between supervisory justice (interpersonal and informational) and learning behavior. Walumbwa and colleagues found support for these hypotheses suggesting the importance of simultaneously considering multiple sources of justice and social exchange relationships in the prediction of voluntary learning behavior. As expected, they further found that voluntary learning behavior predicted employee performance as rated by supervisors. Overall, Walumbwa and colleagues suggest that fairness from multiple sources can enhance the overall work context and consequently motivate employees to engage in desirable work behaviors (such as self-improvement), which, in turn, can enhance their job performance.

Creativity-Related Behaviors: Idea Promotion and Idea Generation

Khazanchi and Masterson (2011) examined the relationship between employee perceptions of organization fairness, supervisor fairness, and supervisor ratings of employee idea promotion and idea generation behaviors relevant to creativity. The researchers used survey data to test these relationships using a sample of employees and their supervisors in a chemical engineering plant in India. The fairness measures assessed employee perceptions of the informational and interpersonal fairness of the organization and the informational and interpersonal fairness of the supervisor.

Results indicated that organizational informational justice (the extent to which employees perceived that the organization provided complete explanations for decisions) was positively related to the upward appeal component of idea promotion behaviors (whereas perceptions of supervisor informational and interpersonal justice were not so related), and this effect was mediated by the organizationally-focused social exchange indicators of organizational trust and perceived organizational support. In contrast, supervisory informational and interpersonal justices were each positively related to the information sharing component of idea generation behaviors (whereas the organizational fairness variables were not related) through the supervisory-focused social-exchange mediators of supervisor trust and LMX.

The pattern of results found by Khazanchi and Masterson (2011) further support the importance of taking a multifoci perspective. Specifically, by simultaneously examining the effects of supervisor and organizational fairness, the researchers found that each source uniquely predicted idea generation and promotion behaviors, respectively. Further, we note that the relationships between fairness and the mediator variables were consistent with the target similarity model. That is, fairness from the organization predicted a social exchange relationship with the organization, whereas fairness from the supervisor predicted a social-exchange relationship with the supervisor. Finally, this pattern of results suggests that employee relationships with the organization are central to idea promotion (i.e., upward appeals), whereas, employee relationships with supervisors are central to idea generation.

Interaction Effects between Different Sources

As we have seen, multifoci research and theory tends to focus on main and mediating effects of different sources of justice on employee attitudes and behaviors. As such, we know little about the potential for joint effects of different sources on employee reactions. In fact, we are aware of only a handful of recent studies at the individual level that explicitly examine such interactions. Next, we discuss two studies that hypothesized interaction effects between different sources of justice. The first used an experimental methodology in a laboratory setting and the other employed a cross-sectional survey design of employees and their supervisors in the field.

INTERDEPENDENT STAGES OF DECISION-MAKING AND VOICE

Organizations of all types often use task forces or advisory committees in the decision- making process pertaining to a variety of different issues and decisions. In these situations, members of a task force or committee may meet and arrive at a recommendation, which is then presented to decision makers at the next level of the process. When multistage decision-making processes are used, the ultimate decision outcome is often dependent upon the events that occur at each stage. Notably, the perceived fairness of the procedures used by the different parties (or sources of justice) at each stage can vary.

Price, Lavelle, Henley, Cocchiara, and Buchanan (2006) modeled such a multistage decision-making process using a scenario-based (Study 1) and laboratory (Study 2) experiment. The results were consistent across both of these studies; therefore, we describe the laboratory study here only. The participants were assigned to a committee (chaired by a confederate) that ostensibly was in place to develop recommendations to address the student parking problems on campus. Those recommendations were then to be presented to an organizational authority (another confederate) at the next stage in the process.

Voice was manipulated at each stage of the process. At the first stage, the committee chair either allowed or denied the participants voice. At the second stage, the participants observed the organizational authority either allowing or denying voice to the committee. The dependent variables of interest included the perceived *overall* procedural fairness of the decision making process and participants' intent to volunteer for similar committee work in the future. The authors found that the Stage 1 and Stage 2 voice manipulations interacted such that participants judged the overall decision-making procedures as fairest and intent to volunteer was greatest when voice was allowed by both authorities (i.e., the committee chair and the organizational authority both allowed voice). When voice was denied at both stages or at any one stage, judgments of overall fairness and intentions to volunteer were depressed and did not significantly differ from each other. Price et al. argued that this pattern of results indicates that participants thought conjunctively about the decision-making process, taking into account events that occurred at each stage. Further, they suggest the findings are supportive of the counterfactual reasoning process described by fairness theory (Folger & Cropanzano, 1998). That is, participants likely thought that a different decision outcome *would* have been possible if one or both authorities used a different procedure (allowed voice), and that this *could* have and *should* have been allowed in the process.

The interaction effect found in these studies indicates that when just one party behaves unfairly in an interdependent decision-making context, employees are likely to judge the whole process as unfair. We now turn to a field study examining the interaction between different sources in day-to-day encounters. In particular, this research examines how employee perceptions of unfair treatment from an external party may attenuate the positive effects of fairness by an internal party.

MODERATING EFFECTS OF EXTERNAL PARTY UNFAIRNESS ON INTERNAL SOURCE-OUTCOME RELATIONSHIPS

Lavelle, McMahan, and Harris (2011) addressed the question of whether unfairness from one source may moderate target similarity effects of fairness from a different source. In developing their hypotheses, Lavelle and colleagues integrated insights from conservation of resources theory (COR) with the injustice-as-stressor perspective. According to COR (Hobfoll, 1989), people have a certain number of valued psychological and energy-relevant resources that they strive to protect (such as emotional energy, time, and self-esteem). Thus, when workplace stressors drain these resources, employees may respond by trying to conserve their remaining resources.

According to recent research, perceptions of injustice can be considered as a workplace stressor resulting in stress-related consequences for employees (Tepper, 2001). In support of this perspective, Judge and Colquitt (2004) found that both procedural and interpersonal injustice were positively related to employee self-reports of feeling nervous and stressed. Further, Tepper (2001) found that both procedural and distributive injustice predicted emotional exhaustion and depression. Consequently, Lavelle and colleagues (2011) argued that when employees experience an injustice from one source it can deplete resources and reduce the energy available to employees for engaging in extra-effort (such as citizenship behavior) on behalf of their other relationship partners. In this regard, Edwards and Rothbard (2000) argued that personal resources such as time, attention, and energy may be finite, and those resources used up in one domain may not be available for use in another domain.

Lavelle and colleagues (2011) conducted their research in a senior-care healthcare organization providing care to patients with serious illnesses. The external source of interpersonal injustice was the patients' family (somewhat akin to customers), the internal source of justice was the employee's workgroup, and the dependent variable of interest was employee citizenship behavior toward the workgroup as rated by the supervisor. Consistent with predictions, results indicated that injustice from the external source weakened the positive relationship between workgroup justice and employee citizenship behavior toward the workgroup. Although Lavelle and colleagues did not measure any form of stress or resource drain, their findings suggest the potential applicability of a COR and injustice-as-stressor framework for understanding the interactive effects of different sources of justice on employee attitudes and behaviors. Taken together, the results of Price et al. (2006) and Lavelle et al. (2011) suggest that different sources of justice may jointly affect employee reactions in multistage decision-making and in day-to-day encounters.

Cross-Cultural Implications of Multifoci Justice

As noted at the outset, research has supported the positive effects of justice on employee behaviors and outcomes (e.g., Cohen-Charash & Spector, 2001; Colquitt et al., 2001). However, other researchers have suggested and demonstrated that justice effects may not generalize across cultural contexts (e.g., Leung, 2005; Shao, Rupp, Skarlicki, & Jones, 2013). According to Leung (2005), different cultural norms and values influence justice rules, criteria, and actions, such that the way in which justice perceptions are formed and reacted to may vary based on culture. Most of the empirical research to date exploring cross-cultural differences, however, has taken a type-based approach (i.e., focusing on the effect of different types rather than sources) to examining cross-cultural differences in justice. For example, Kim and Leung (2007) demonstrated that different justice facets contribute more strongly to overall perceptions of fairness dependent on the cultural context in which the employees work (Kim & Leung, 2007). Other studies have approximated a multifoci approach, by examining specific sources of justice or source-specific mediators. For example, Ertürk (2007) explored the mediating role of supervisor trust in the relationship between justice and OCBs in a Turkish context. However, neither the source of justice nor the target of the citizenship behaviors was specified, making the study only partially target-specific. Finally, Rego, Ribeiro, and Cunha (2010) also discussed the role of supervisors as mediators between the organization and employees in Portuguese contexts. Once again, this study was only partially multifoci in nature because the theoretical underpinnings only touched on the role of supervisors rather than testing their direct effect.

Only one study to date has explicitly explored source-specific justice across cultural contexts. Shao and colleagues (2013) suggested that the strength of well-established justice relationships and source-specific effects may be diminished based on cultural values. Using a multifoci perspective, Shao and colleagues meta-analyzed studies to ascertain the moderating effects of individualism, masculinity, uncertainty avoidance, and power distance on the effects of supervisor- and organizational-justice on source-specific outcomes such as OCB-S, OCB-O, supervisor trust, and organizational trust.

They found that justice effects were stronger in individualistic cultures, arguing that in highly individualistic cultures, employees will react more strongly to injustice as it directly affects outcomes that are related to their personal gain or self-interest. Collectivistic cultures, however, are better characterized by subservience to group harmony, such that the injustice experienced by one may not have a strong effect on individual reactions, so long as the group outcomes are maximized. Related to multifoci justice, this suggests that source-specific effects may not be strong in collectivistic cultures on individual outcomes. However, these findings might suggest that justice or justice climate might have a stronger effect on group-level outcomes in highly collectivistic societies than individualistic societies.

Shao and colleagues' (2013) also found that femininity related to stronger justice effects. Taking social-exchange into account, feminine values should predict stronger justice effects, as femininity reflects values placed on relationships and cultivating them. Applied to source-specific justice, social exchange acts as a mechanism for the effect of fairness on citizenship, performance, and other outcomes. As such, source-specific effects should be especially strong in feminine cultures where relationships are of great importance. Finally, power distance moderated the effect of justice such that when power distance was lower, the effect of justice was stronger. In low power distance cultures, individuals have more leeway to question authority. In high power distance cultures, employees do not often question authority and thus, responses to the decisions or actions of their supervisor or organization may be muted.

Looking Out: Fair Treatment of External Stakeholders

Recent research and theory expands the multifoci justice framework by looking outward from the organization and incorporating external stakeholders as targets of organizational injustice (Rupp, 2011). In this regard, the question faced by employees now becomes, "How fairly does my organization treat external stakeholders such as customers, communities, unions, and the natural environment?" Research on third-party observers is germane to this question and indicates that employee attitudes and behaviors can be influenced by justice perceptions even when the employee is not the recipient of the (un)fair treatment (e.g., Turillo, Folger, Lavelle, Umphress, & Gee, 2002).

Whereas much of the justice literature focuses on victims' reactions to unfair treatment, third-party justice is concerned with how and why observers may react when others are treated unfairly. The deontic model of justice (Folger, 2001) is particularly relevant to understanding why observers might respond to the unfair treatment of others. From this perspective, fairness matters as an end in and of itself. That is, people are concerned with and respond to unfair treatment based upon a desire to uphold moral standards and principles (Cropanzano, Goldman, & Folger, 2003). A series of experiments by Turillo and colleagues (2002) offer support for this perspective demonstrating that participants desired to punish perpetrators and were willing to sacrifice personal economic gain even when they had no relationship with the victim. Thus, the deontic perspective suggests that employees are likely to pay attention and react to perceptions of how fairly the organization treats its external stakeholders.

Recent empirical findings support the rationale that employees may react to their organization's corporate social responsibility (CSR) initiatives via third-party justice judgments. For example, Turker (2008) found that employee organizational commitment was positively influenced by CSR efforts. Hansen et al. (2011) showed that employees with positive perceptions of organizational CSR activities were less likely to leave the organization and more likely to engage in citizenship behaviors, with these relationships being partially mediated by employee trust. These results demonstrate the utility of studying employees' third-party reactions to their organization's treatment of external constituents.

Rupp, Shao, Thornton, & Skarlicki (2013) extend this line of research by investigating a multimotive framework that simultaneously assesses reactions to both first-party (i.e., self-focused) and third-party (i.e., other-focused) perceptions of justice. These researchers found that both job applicants and employees react negatively toward organizations that they perceive to be socially irresponsible. First, through a scenario-based experiment, the authors demonstrated that the positive relationship between CSR perceptions and applicants' job pursuit intentions was strengthened by the applicants' moral identity. A second study replicated these interactive effects by showing that the relationship between employees' CSR perceptions and their organizational citizenship behavior was stronger for employees who were high in moral identity. Across both studies, the effects of CSR perceptions were also found to be stronger the less individuals perceived that they themselves were treated in a fair manner. Based on this intriguing pattern of results, Rupp et al. suggest that the strength of deontic concerns may vary across individuals, and that self-focused fairness perceptions may alert individuals to the unfair treatment of others.

Overall, research that considers the psychology of CSR perceptions is only just beginning to accumulate (Greening & Turban, 2000; Gully, Phillips, Castellano, Han, & Kim, 2013; Jones, 2010; Jones, Willness, & Madey, 2013; Turban & Greening, 1997), making this area ripe for future contributions. In particular, the multifoci perspective of justice is amenable to future research on the micro-foundations of CSR through the study of justice perceptions and reactions of various sources (e.g., job applicants, employees, customers, etc.). In brief, by shifting the focus of multifoci justice to external targets of organizational justice, researchers may develop a more complete understanding of the far-reaching effects of justice on employee reactions and behavior.

Conclusion

The goal of this chapter has been to discuss emerging research pertaining to the multifoci perspective of justice including sources both internal and external to the organization. Although much of the extant organizational justice literature has recognized the consequences of differing types of justice, our chapter suggests there is much to be gained by emphasizing the source of justice. Recently, scholars have stressed the importance of a target similarity approach to the study of organizational justice by highlighting the significance of the source of justice to a more nuanced understanding of target-specific employee attitudes and behaviors. In particular, there is a need for additional research that focuses on the interpersonal dynamics between employees and their co-workers, customers, and clients.

Throughout the chapter, we emphasize the utility of a multifoci perspective to justice, highlighting novel avenues for future research development. For example, more studies are needed to gain an understanding of the interactive effects between different sources on employee attitudes and behaviors and the impact of time on both justice type and source. Promising extensions of the multifoci perspective include the study of unique outcome variables such as employee learning, creativity, and the application of multifoci research to cross-cultural justice and corporate social responsibility. Overall, it is our hope that this review will motivate future application and exploration of the multifoci perspective to organizational justice research.

Note

1. Although the target similarity model argues that additional sources of justice are also relevant to employees such as co-workers and customers, there was not enough empirical research including such sources to warrant inclusion in their meta-analysis. We discuss this point in a future section on the next "wave" of multifoci justice research.

References

Adams, J. S. (1965). Inequity in social exchange. In L. Berkowitz (Ed.), *Advances in experimental social psychology, Vol. 2* (pp. 267–299). New York, NY: Academic Press.

Ambrose, M. L., & Arnaud, A. (2005). Distributive and procedural justice: Construct distinctiveness, construct interdependence, and overall justice. In J. Greenberg & J. Colquitt (Eds.), *The handbook of organizational justice* (pp. 59–84). Mahwah, NJ: Erlbaum.

Ambrose, M. L., & Schminke, M. (2009). The role of overall justice judgments in organizational justice research: a test of mediation. *Journal of Applied Psychology, 94*, 491–500.

Aquino, K., Tripp, T. M., & Bies, R. J. (2001). How employees respond to personal offense: The effects of blame attribution, victim status, and offender status on revenge and reconciliation in the workplace. *Journal of Applied Psychology, 86*, 52–59.

Ashforth, B. E., & Humphrey, R. H. (1993). Emotional labor in service roles: The influence of identity. *Academy of Management Review, 18*, 88–115.

Bakker, A. B., Schaufeli, W. B., Sixma, H. J., Bosveld, W., & van Dierendocnck, D. (2000). Patient demands, lack of reciprocity, and burnout: A five year longitudinal study among general practitioners. *Journal of Organizational Behavior, 21*, 425–441.

Bies, R. J., & Moag, J. F. (1986). Interactional justice: The communication criteria of fairness. In R. J. Lewicki, B. H. Sheppard, & M. H. Bazerman (Eds.), *Research on negotiation in organizations, Vol. 1* (pp. 43–55). Greenwich, CT: JAI Press.

Bradfield, M., & Aquino, K. (1999). The effects of blame attributions and offender likableness on forgiveness and revenge in the workplace. *Journal of Management, 25*, 607–631.

Brockner, J. (2006). Why it's so hard to be fair. *Harvard Business Review, 84*(3), 122–129.

Buunk, B. P., & Schaufeli, W. B. (1993). Burnout: A perspective from social comparison theory. In W. B. Schaufeli, C. Maslach, & T. Marek (Eds.), *Professional burnout: Recent developments in theory and research* (pp. 53–69). New York, NY: Hemisphere.

Byrne, Z. (1999). April-May. How do procedural and interactional justice influence multiple levels of organizational outcomes? Paper presented at the *Annual Meeting of the Society for Industrial and Organizational Psychology*, Atlanta, GA.

Chiaburu, D. S., & Harrison, D. A. (2008). Do peers make the place? Conceptual synthesis and meta-analysis of coworker effects on perceptions, attitudes, OCBs, and performance. *Journal of Applied Psychology, 93*, 1082–1103.

Cloutier, J., Denis, P. E., & Bilodeau, H. (2013). The dynamics of strike votes: Perceived justice during collective bargaining. *Journal of Organizational Behavior, 34*(7), 1016–1038.

Cohen-Charash, Y., & Spector, P. E. (2001). The role of justice in organizations: A meta-analysis. *Organizational Behavior and Human Decision Processes, 86*, 278–321.

Coleman, J. S. (1974). *Power and the structure of society.* New York, NY: W. W. Norton.

Coleman, J. S. (1982). *The asymmetric society.* Syracuse, NY: Syracuse University Press.

Colquitt, J. A. (2001). On the dimensionality of organizational justice: A construct validation of a measure. *Journal of Applied Psychology, 86*, 356–400.

Colquitt, J. A., Conlon, D. E., Wesson, M. J., Porter, C. O. L. H., & Ng, K. Y. (2001). Justice at the millennium: A meta-analytic review of 25 years of organizational justice research. *Journal of Applied Psychology, 86*, 425–445.

Colquitt, J. A., Scott, B. A., Rodell, J. B., Long, D. M., Zapata, C. P., Conlon, D. E., & Wesson, M. J. (2013). Justice at the millennium, a decade later: A meta-analytic test of social exchange and affect-based perceptions. *Journal of Applied Psychology, 98*, 199–236.

Colquitt, J. A., & Shaw, J. C. (2005). Measuring organizational justice. In J. Greenberg & J. A. Colquitt (Eds.), *The handbook of organizational justice* (pp. 113–152). Mahwah, NJ: Erlbaum.

Cronbach, L. J. (1970). *Essentials of psychological testing.* (3rd Ed.). New York: Harper and Row.

Cronbach, L. J., & Gleser, G. (1957). *Psychological tests and personnel decisions.* Urbana: University of Illinois Press.

Cropanzano, R., Byrne, Z. S., Bobocel, D. R., & Rupp, D. E. (2001). Moral virtues, fairness heuristics, social entities, and other denizens of organizational justice. *Journal of Vocational Behavior, 58*, 164–209.

Cropanzano, R., Goldman, B., & Folger, R. (2003). Deontic justice: The role of moral principles in workplace fairness. *Journal of Organizational Behavior, 24*, 1019–1024.

Cropanzano, R., & Mitchell, M. (2005). Social exchange theory: An interdisciplinary review. *Journal of Management, 31*, 874–900.

Cropanzano, R., Chrobot-Mason, D., Rupp, D. E., & Prehar, C. (2004). Accounting for corporate injustice. *Human Resource Management Review, 14*, 107–133.

Cropanzano, R., & Wright, T. A. (2011). The impact of organizational justice on occupational health. In J. C. Quick & L. E. Tetrick (Eds.) *Handbook of occupational health psychology* (2nd ed., pp. 205–219). Washington, DC: American Psychological Association.

Donovan, M. A., Drasgow, F., & Munson, L. J. (1998). The perceptions of fair interpersonal treatment scale: Development and validation of a measure of interpersonal treatment in the workplace. *Journal of Applied Psychology, 83*, 683–692.

Deutsch, M. (1975). Equity, equality and need: What determines which value will be used as the basis for distributive justice? *Journal of Social Issues, 31*, 137–149.

Edmondson, A. (1999). Psychological safety and learning behavior in work teams. *Administrative Science Quarterly, 44*, 350–383.

Edwards, J. R., & Rothbard, N. P. (2000). Mechanisms linking work and family: Clarifying the relationship between work and family constructs. *Academy of Management Review, 25*, 178–199.

Ertürk, A. (2007). Increasing organizational citizenship behaviors of Turkish academicians: Mediating role of trust in supervisor on the relationship between organizational justice and citizenship behaviors. *Journal of Managerial Psychology, 22*, 257–270.

Fassina, N. E., Jones, D. A., & Uggerslev, K. L. (2008). Meta-analytic tests of relationships between organizational justice and citizenship behavior: Testing agent-system and shared variance models. *Journal of Organizational Behavior, 29*, 805–828.

Felstiner, W. L. F, Abel, R. L., Sarat, A. (1980-1981). The emergence and transformation of disputes. *Law and Society Review, 15*, 631–654.

Ferguson, T. J., & Rule, B. G. (1983). An attributional perspective on anger and aggression. In R. G. Green & E. Donnerstein (Eds.), *Aggression: Theoretical and empirical perspectives: Vol. 1. Theoretical and methodological issues* (pp. 41–74). New York, NY: Academic Press.

Folger, R. (2001). Fairness as deonance. In S. W. Gilliland, D. D. Steiner, & D. P. Skarlicki (Eds.), *Theoretical and cultural perspectives on organizational justice* (pp. 3–34). Greenwich, CT: Information Age.

Folger, R., & Cropanzano, R. (1998). *Organizational justice and human resource management.* Thousand Oaks, CA: Sage.

Folger, R., & Cropanzano, R. (2001). Fairness theory: Justice as accountability. In J. Greenberg & R. Cropanzano (Eds.), *Advances in organizational justice* (pp. 89–118). Stanford, CA: Stanford University Press.

Greenberg, J. (1993). The social side of fairness: Interpersonal and informational classes of organizational justice. In R. Cropanzano (Ed.), *Justice in the workplace: Approaching fairness in human resource management* (pp. 79–103). Hillsdale, NJ: Erlbaum.

Greening, D. W., & Turban. D. B. (2000). Corporate social performance as a competitive advantage in attracting a quality workforce. *Business & Society, 39*, 254–280.

Groth, M., Hennig-Thurau, T., Wang, K. (2013). The customer experience of emotional labor. In A. A. Grandey, J. M. Diefendorff & D. E. Rupp (Eds.), *Emotional labor in the 21st century: Diverse perspectives on the psychology of emotion regulation at work* (pp. 127–151). New York, NY: Routledge.

Gully, S. M., Phillips, J. M., Castellano, W. G., Han, K., Kim, A. (2013). A mediated moderation model of recruiting socially and environmentally responsible job applicants. *Personnel Psychology, 66*(4), 935–973.

Hansen, S. D., Dunford, B. B., Boss, A. D., Boss, R. W., & Angermeier, I. (2011). Corporate social responsibility and the benefits of employee trust: A cross disciplinary perspective. *Journal of Business Ethics, 102*, 29–25.

Harrison, D. A., Johns, G., & Martocchio, J. J. (2000). Changes in technology, teamwork, and diversity: New directions for a new century of absenteeism research. *Research in Personnel and Human Resources Management, 18*, 43–92.

Herda, D. N., & Lavelle, J. J. (2013). Auditor Commitment to Privately-Held Clients and its Effect on Value-Added Audit Service. *Auditing: A Journal of Practice & Theory, 32*(1), 113–137.

Hobfoll, S. E. (1989). Conservation of resources: A new attempt at conceptualizing stress. *American Psychologist, 44*, 513–524.

Holtz, B. C., & Harold, C. M. (2009). Fair today, fair tomorrow? A longitudinal investigation of overall justice perceptions. *Journal of Applied Psychology, 94*, 1185–1199.

Jones, D. A. (2010). Does serving the community also serve the company? Using organizational identification and social exchange theories to understand employee responses to a volunteerism programme. *Journal of Occupational and Organizational Psychology, 83*, 857–878.

Jones, D. A., Willness, C., & Madey, S. (2013). Why are job seekers attracted by corporate social performance? Experimental and field tests of three signal-based mechanisms. *Academy of Management Journal.* doi:10.5465/amj.2011.0848.

Jones, D. A., & Martens, M. L. (2009). The mediating role of overall fairness and the moderating role of trust certainty in justice–criteria relationships: the formation and use of fairness heuristics in the workplace. *Journal of Organizational Behavior, 30*, 1025–1051.

Judge, T. A., & Colquitt, J. A. (2004). Organizational justice and stress: the mediating role of work-family conflict. *Journal of Applied Psychology, 89*, 395–404.

Khazanchi, S., & Masterson, S. S. (2011). Who and what is fair matters: A multi-foci social exchange model of creativity. *Journal of Organizational Behavior, 32*, 86–106.

Kim, T. Y., & Leung, K. (2007). Forming and reacting to overall fairness: A cross-cultural comparison. *Organizational Behavior and Human Decision Processes, 104*, 83–95.

Konovsky, M. A. (2000). Understanding procedural justice and its impact on business organizations. *Journal of Management, 26*, 489–511.

Lavelle, J. J., Brockner, J., Konovsky, M. A., Price, K., Henley, A., Taneja, A., & Vinekar, V. (2009). Commitment, Procedural Fairness, and Organizational Citizenship Behavior: A Multifoci Analysis. *Journal of Organizational Behavior, 30*, 337–357.

Lavelle, J. J., McMahan, G. C., & Harris, C. M. (2009). Fairness in human resource management, social exchange relationships, and citizenship behavior: Testing linkages of the target similarity model among nurses in the United States. *The International Journal of Human Resource Management, 20*, 2419–2434.

Lavelle, J. J., McMahan, G. C., & Harris, C. (2011). Patients and workgroups as beneficiaries of organizational citizenship behavior: A multifoci justice and resource depletion perspective. Paper presented at the *Southern Management Association Conference*, Savannah, GA.

Lavelle, J. J., Rupp, D. E., & Brockner, J. (2007). Taking a multifoci approach to the study of justice, social exchange, and citizenship behavior: The target similarity model. *Journal of Management, 3*, 841–866.

Leung, K. (2005). How generalizable are justice effects across cultures? In J. Greenberg, & J. A. Colquitt (Eds.), *Handbook of Organizational Justice* (pp. 555–586). Mahwah, NJ: Erlbaum.

Leventhal, G. S. (1976). The distribution of rewards and resources in groups and organizations. In L. Berkowitz & E. Walster (Eds.), *Advances in experimental social psychology, Vol. 9* (pp. 91–131). New York, NY: Academic Press.

Leventhal, G. S. (1980). What should be done with equity theory? In K. J. Gergen, M. S. Greenberg, & R. H. Willis (Eds.), *Social exchange: Advances in theory and research* (pp. 27–55). New York, NY: Plenum.

Lind, A. (2001a). Fairness heuristic theory: justice judgments as pivotal cognitions in organizational relations. In J. Greenberg, & R. Cropanzano (Eds.), *Advances in organizational justice* (pp. 56–88).

Lind, A. (2001b). Thinking critically about justice judgments. *Journal of Vocational Behavior, 58*, 220–226.

Maslach, C. (1982). *Burnout: The cost of caring.* Englewood Cliffs, NJ: Erlbaum.

Masterson, S. S., Lewis, K., Goldman, B. M., & Taylor, M. S. (2000). Integrating justice and social exchange: The differing effects of fair procedures and treatment on work relationships. *Academy of Management Journal, 43*, 738–748.

Maurer, T. J., & Tarulli, B. A. (1994). Investigation of perceived environment, perceived outcome, and person variables in relationship to voluntary development activity by employees. *Journal of Applied Psychology, 79*, 3–14.

Olkkonen, M., & Lipponen, J. (2006). Relationships between organizational justice, identification with organization and work-unit, and group related outcomes. *Organizational Behavior and Human Decision Processes, 100*, 202–215.

Price, K., Lavelle, J. J., Henley, A. B., Cocchiara, F., & Buchanan, R. (2006). Judging the fairness of voice-based participation across multiple and interrelated stages of decision making. *Organizational Behavior and Human Decision Processes, 99*, 212–226.

Rego, A., Ribeiro, N., & Cunha, M. P. (2010). Perceptions of organizational virtuousness and happiness as predictors of organizational citizenship behaviors. *Journal of Business Ethics, 93*, 215–235.

Rupp, D. E. (2011). An employee-centered model of organizational justice and social responsibility. *Organizational Psychology Review, 1*, 72–94.

Rupp, D. E., & Aquino, K. F. (2009). Nothing so practical as a good justice theory. *Industrial and Organizational Psychology, 2*, 205–210

Rupp, D. E., & Cropanzano, R. (2002). Multifoci justice and social exchange relationships. *Organizational Behavior and Human Decision Processes, 89*, 925–946.

Rupp, D. E., Ganapathi, J., Aguilera, R. V., & Williams, C. A. (2006). Employee reactions to corporate social responsibility: An organizational justice framework. *Journal of Organizational Behavior, 27*, 537–543.

Rupp, D. E., McCance, A. S., & Grandey, A. (2007). A cognitive-emotional theory of customer injustice and emotional labor. In D. De Cremer (Ed.) *Advances in the psychology of justice and affect* (pp.199–226). Charlotte, NC: Information Age.

Rupp, D. E., McCance, A. S., Spencer, S., & Sonntag, K. (2008). Customer (in)justice and emotional labor: The role of perspective taking, anger, and emotional regulation. *Journal of Management, 34*, 903–924.

Rupp, D. E., & Paddock, E. L. (2010). From justice events to justice climate: A multilevel temporal model of information aggregation and judgment. *Research on Managing Groups and Teams, 13*, 239–267.

Rupp, D. E., Shao, R., Jones, K. S., & Liao, H. (2014). The utility of a multifoci approach to the study of organizational justice: A meta-analytic investigation into the consideration of normative rules, moral accountability, bandwidth-fidelity, and social exchange. *Organizational Behavior and Human Decision Processes, 123*, 159–185.

Rupp, D. E., Shao, R., Thornton, M. A., & Skarlicki, D. P. (2013). Applicants' and employees' reactions to corporate social responsibility: The moderating effects of first-party justice perceptions and moral identity. *Personnel Psychology, 66*(4), 895–933. doi:10.1111/peps.12030.

Rupp, D. E., & Spencer, S. (2006). When customers lash out: The effect of customer interactional injustice on emotional labor and the mediating role of discrete emotions. *Journal of Applied Psychology, 91*, 971–978.

Schneider, B., & Bowen, D. E. (1985). Employee and customer perceptions of service in banks: Replication and extension. *Journal of Applied Psychology, 70*, 423–433.

Shao, R., Rupp, D. E., Skarlicki, D. P., & Jones, K. S. (2013). Employee justice across cultures: A meta-analytic review. *Journal of Management, 39*, 263–301.

Schaufeli, W. B. (2006). The balance of give and take: Toward a social exchange model of burnout. *Revue Internationale de Psychologie Sociale, 19*(1), 87–131.

Schaufeli, W. B., & Janczur, B. (1994). Burnout among nurses: A Polish-Dutch comparison. *Journal of Cross-Cultural Psychology, 25*, 95–113.

Skarlicki, D. P., & Latham, G. P. (1996). Increasing citizenship behavior within a labor union: A test of organizational justice theory. *Journal of Applied Psychology, 81*, 161–169.

Skarlicki, D. P., & Latham, G. P. (1997). Leadership training in organizational justice to increase citizenship behavior within a labor union. *Personnel Psychology, 50*, 617–633.

Skarlicki, D. P., Van Jaarsveld, D. D., & Walker, D. D. (2008). Getting even for customer mistreatment: The role of moral identity in the relationship between customer interpersonal injustice and employee sabotage. *Journal of Applied Psychology, 93*, 1335–1347.

Spencer, S., & Rupp, D. E. (2009). Angry, guilty, and conflicted: Injustice toward co-workers heightens emotional labor through cognitive and emotional mechanisms. *Journal of Applied Psychology, 94*, 429–444.

Tepper, B. J. (2001). Health consequences of organizational injustice: Tests of main and interactive effects. *Organizational Behavior and Human Decision Processes, 86*, 197–215.

Thibaut, J., & Walker, L. (1975). *Procedural justice: A psychologicala*. Hillsdale, NJ: Erlbaum.

Turban, D. B., & Greening, D. W. (1997). Corporate social performance and organizational attractiveness to prospective employees. *Academy of Management Journal, 40*, 658–672.

Turillo, C. J., Folger, R., Lavelle, J. J., Umphress, E. E., Gee, J. O. (2002). Is virtue its own reward? Self-sacrificial decisions for the sake of fairness. *Organizational Behavior and Human Decision Processes, 89*, 839–865.

Turker, D. (2008). How corporate social responsibility influences organizational commitment. *Journal of Business Ethics, 89*, 189–204.

Tyler, T. R., & Bies, R. J. (1990). Beyond formal procedures: The interpersonal context of procedural justice. In J. Carroll (Ed.), *Advances in Applied Social Psychology: Business Settings* (pp. 77–98). Hillsdale, NJ: Erlbaum.

Van Dierendonck, D., Schaufeli, W. B., & Sixma, H. J. (1994). Burnout among general practitioners: A perspective from equity theory. *Journal of Social and Clinical Psychology, 13*, 86–100.

Van Horn, J. E., Schaufeli, W. B., Taris, T. W. (2001). Lack of reciprocity among Dutch teachers: Validation of reciprocity indices and their relation to stress and well-being. *Work & Stress, 15*(3), 191–213.

Van Jaarsveld, D., & Poster, W. R. (2013). Call centers: Emotional labor over the phone. In A. A. Grandey, J. M. Diefendorff & D. E. Rupp (Eds.), *Emotional labor in the 21st century: Diverse perspectives on the psychology of emotion regulation at work* (pp. 153–173). New York, NY: Routledge.

Walumbwa, F. O., Cropanzano, R., & Hartnell, C. A. (2009). Organizational justice, voluntary learning behavior, and job performance: A test of the mediating effects of identification and leader-member exchange. *Journal of Organizational Behavior, 30*, 1103–1126.

Wang, M., Liao, H., Zhan, Y., & Shi, J. (2011). Daily customer mistreatment and employee sabotage against customers: Examining emotion and resource perspectives. *Academy of Management Journal, 54*, 312–334.

Weiner, B. (1995). *Judgments and responsibility*. New York, NY: Guilford Press.

Weiss, H. M., & Cropanzano, R. (1996). Affective events theory: A theoretical discussion of the structure, causes and consequences of affective experiences at work. In B. M. Staw, & L. L. Cummings (Eds.), *Research in organizational behavior: An annual series of analytical essays and critical reviews, Vol. 18* (pp. 1–74). US: Elsevier Science/JAI Press.

CHAPTER

8 Measuring Justice and Fairness

Jason A. Colquitt *and* Jessica B. Rodell

Abstract

This chapter reviews the measurement approaches used in the justice literature. We begin by describing fundamental issues involved in constructing measures, such as item content, focus, context, and experience bracketing. We then introduce a 2 x 2 taxonomy wherein measurement approaches are distinguished by (a) whether they emphasize more descriptive perceptions of justice rule adherence or more evaluative perceptions of fairness, and (b) whether they distinguish among particular justice dimensions. The chapter concludes by reviewing a number of emerging measurement issues, including anticipations and expectations, within-person methodologies, the use of multiple sources, and the explicit operationalization of injustice.

Key Words: justice, fairness, measurement, construct validity, time

> "I often say that when you can measure what you are speaking about, and express it in numbers, you know something about it; but when you cannot measure it, when you cannot express it in numbers, your knowledge is of a meagre and unsatisfactory kind: it may be the beginning of knowledge, but you have scarcely, in your thoughts, advanced to the stage of science whatever the matter might be."
>
> —*William Thomson* [Lord Kelvin], 1891, p. 80.

A number of scholars have theorized about why employees care about justice (Folger, 2001; Lind, 2001; Tyler & Lind, 1992), how cognitions and emotions shape justice perceptions (Barsky & Kaplan, 2007; Folger & Cropanzano, 2001; Lind, 2001), and how those perceptions impact subsequent attitudes and behaviors (Lind, 2001; Tyler & Blader, 2003). Without measurement, such theorizing remains just that: theoretical. Measuring justice by expressing it in numbers allows scholars to conduct empirical tests of conceptual propositions, thereby advancing our knowledge of the justice landscape.

If the ability to measure something does reflect what is known about a phenomenon, then scholars have increased their knowledge of justice across the decades. Early studies tended to use ad hoc scales with a handful of items (e.g., Earley & Lind, 1987; Folger, Rosenfield, Grove, & Corkran, 1979; Tyler, Rasinski & Spodick, 1985). Subsequent studies introduced more comprehensive measures that began to be widely used by other scholars (Moorman, 1991; Sweeney & McFarlin, 1993). More recently, scholars introduced additional scales that kept pace with conceptual developments and trends in the literature (Ambrose & Schminke, 2009; Blader & Tyler, 2003; Colquitt, 2001; Rupp & Cropanzano, 2002).

The purpose of this chapter is to review the measurement approaches used in the justice literature (see Colquitt & Shaw, 2005, for an earlier review). We begin by describing some of the fundamental issues involved in justice measurement, including item content, focus, context, and experience bracketing. Next, we introduce a taxonomy that distinguishes whether measures emphasize descriptive perceptions of justice rule adherence or evaluative perceptions of fairness, and whether measures distinguish between multiple dimensions. Finally, we conclude by reviewing emerging issues that affect the measurement of justice, including anticipations and expectations, within-person methodologies, the use of multiple sources, and the explicit operationalization of injustice.

Fundamental Issues in Measuring Justice

As with other constructs, measuring justice requires an understanding of construct definitions. Construct validity reflects the correspondence between a definition and a measure (Schwab, 1980), and a construct's definition can form the foundation for the generation of survey items (Hinkin, 1995, 1998). Reviews of the literature have tended to describe justice as the perceived fairness of decision events (e.g., Colquitt, 2012; Cropanzano & Greenberg, 1997; Greenberg, 2010). That definitional tradition illustrates that the terms *justice* and *fairness* tend to be used interchangeably in the literature. Thus, one measure may reference a condition assumed to evoke fairness (e.g., consistency, equity, respect, truthfulness), whereas another references perceptions of fairness themselves (Colquitt & Shaw, 2005). This same operational flexibility can be seen in the job satisfaction literature, where one measure may reference a condition that gives rise to satisfaction (e.g., interesting work, smart coworkers, knowledgeable supervisors, high pay) whereas another references satisfaction directly (Ironson, Smith, Brannick, Gibson, & Paul, 1989; Smith, Kendall, & Hulin, 1969).

Although the interchangeability of justice and fairness has served the literature well in many respects, we see value in distinguishing them definitionally in this chapter. After all, more and more scholars are operationalizing justice and fairness as separate constructs in their models (Ambrose & Schminke, 2009; Choi, 2008; Kim & Leung, 2007; Rodell & Colquitt, 2009). Thus, we define justice as the perceived adherence to rules that reflect appropriateness in decision contexts. Those rules are summarized in Table 8.1 and reflect procedural (Leventhal, 1980; Thibaut & Walker, 1975), distributive (Adams, 1965; Leventhal, 1976), interpersonal (Bies & Moag, 1986; Greenberg, 1993), and informational concepts (Bies & Moag, 1986; Greenberg, 1993). Fairness, in turn, is defined here as a global perception of appropriateness. In this formulation, fairness is theoretically "downstream" from justice (Ambrose & Schminke, 2009; Kim & Leung, 2007).

Regardless of whether scholars focus on justice or fairness, a certain degree of "convertibility" is often needed when constructing measures (Greenberg, 2010). Such conversions ensure that the measure matches the research question and the operative theoretical lens. The first conversion decision concerns the focus of the measure. Just as attitudes like commitment, perceived support, trust, obligation, and identification can be referenced to either an organization or a supervisor, so too can justice and fairness (Blader & Tyler, 2003; Colquitt, 2001; Rupp & Cropanzano, 2002). Thus, organization-focused justice reflects the degree to which one's company or top management is perceived to act consistently, equitably, respectfully, and truthfully in decision contexts. In contrast, supervisor-focused fairness reflects the degree to which one's manager is perceived to be fair.

How are such focus decisions made, in practice? Sometimes the focus is dictated by the research question. For example, a study on the effects of large scale organizational changes on justice might focus measures on the organization (e.g., Brockner et al., 2007; Brockner, Wiesenfeld, & Martin, 1995; Daly & Geyer, 1994). A study on training managers to be more just would, instead, focus measures on the supervisor (Skarlicki & Latham, 1996, 1997). Sometimes the focus is dictated by the theoretical lens. For example, social exchange theory argues that beneficial treatment from one exchange partner will result in reciprocation on the part of the other exchange partner (Blau, 1964). That theoretical logic functions more seamlessly when the focus of the benefit matches the target of the reciprocation. Thus, organization-focused justice might be used to predict organization-targeted citizenship behavior, with supervisor-focused justice predicting supervisor-targeted citizenship behavior (Horvath & Andrews, 2007; Karriker & Williams, 2009; Lavelle et al., 2009; Liao & Rupp, 2005; Rupp & Cropanzano, 2002).

Although the practice of matching the focus of the justice to the target of the reciprocation is logical and attractive conceptually (Lavelle, Rupp, & Brockner, 2007), a recent meta-analysis suggests that it makes little difference empirically (Colquitt et al., 2013). Colquitt et al.'s (2013) review examined 36 justice-outcome relationships to see if "focus matching" correlations (e.g., supervisor-focused procedural justice and supervisor-targeted citizenship) were statistically significantly higher than non-focus-matching correlations (e.g., supervisor-focused procedural justice and organization-targeted citizenship). Only 3 of the 36 correlations revealed stronger effect sizes for "focus matching." Instead, the results suggested that supervisor-focused justice tends to be associated with stronger effects in general, regardless of whether the reciprocation is targeted at supervisors or organizations. Colquitt et al. (2013) speculated that supervisor-focused justice may simply be more salient, observable, and interpretable than the actions of the broader company or top management. Thus, when it comes to converting the source of a measure, the bottom line is that matching one's outcome has conceptual benefits that may not be realized empirically.

The second conversion decision concerns the context of the measure. In general, the rules summarized in Table 8.1 govern actions in some resource allocation or conflict resolution environment (Adams, 1965; Bies & Moag, 1986; Leventhal, 1976, 1980; Thibaut & Walker, 1975). Over the years, justice scholars have applied those rules in a number of specific contexts, including selection, performance evaluation, training, compensation, dispute, separation, and change contexts (Colquitt & Greenberg, 2003). In most cases, existing justice and fairness scales can be easily tailored to the context in question. Occasionally, however, the context introduces a new rule that captures some unique aspect of appropriateness. For example, Gilliland (1993) argued that selection tests were procedurally just not only when they were administered consistently and without bias but also when their content was job relevant. Subsequently, Bauer et al. (2001) introduced a measure of "selection procedural justice" that incorporated context-specific rules. Such context tailoring is similar to the emic (as opposed to etic) distinction in cross-cultural research, where some constructs wind up possessing different facets in non-U.S. cultures (e.g., Farh, Earley, & Lin, 1997).

The third conversion decision centers on the experience bracketing of the measure. In their discussion of time in theorizing, George and Jones (2000) noted that constructs are given meaning by a bracketing process wherein specific episodes

Table 8.1 Justice Rules

Type	Name	Description
Procedural[a]	Process Control	Procedures provide opportunities for voice
	Decision Control	Procedures provide influence over outcomes
	Consistency	Procedures are consistent across persons and time
	Bias Suppression	Procedures are neutral and unbiased
	Accuracy	Procedures are based on accurate information
	Correctability	Procedures offer opportunities for appeals of outcomes
	Representativeness	Procedures take into account concerns of subgroups
	Ethicality	Procedures uphold standards of morality
Distributive[b]	Equity	Outcomes are allocated according to contributions
	Equality	Outcomes are allocated equally
	Need	Outcomes are allocated according to need
Interpersonal[c]	Respect	Enactment of procedures are sincere and polite
	Propriety	Enactment of procedures refrain from improper remarks
Informational[c]	Truthfulness	Explanations about procedures are honest
	Justification	Explanations about procedures are thorough

[a] Rules taken from Thibaut and Walker (1975) and Leventhal (1980).
[b] Rules taken from Adams (1965) and Leventhal (1976).
[c] Rules taken from Bies and Moag (1986) and Greenberg (1993).

are aggregated into some time period that warrants reflection and exploration. Cropanzano, Byrne, Bobocel, and Rupp (2001) articulated a similar process with respect to justice, noting that measures can assess one-time events or a more extensive bracketing of multiple events. For example, a study might ask respondents to evaluate their most recent performance appraisal event, their most recent compensation event, or their most recent dispute resolution event. Alternatively, a study might ask respondents to evaluate performance appraisals in general, compensation in general, or dispute resolutions in general. As a third alternative, a study might ask respondents to consider decision-making about performance evaluations, compensation, and dispute resolution in aggregate. Here the employee would presumably be drawing on a very extensive bracketing of multiple events when assessing justice or fairness.

At some point, the bracketing of events becomes so extensive that measures begin assessing entities rather than events (Cropanzano et al., 2001). For example, a measure might ask about a supervisor's or organization's decision-making in general, without even evoking particular decision contexts. Alternatively, a measure might simply refer to the supervisor him/herself, or the organization itself, with no mentioning of decision-making at all. Here the focus is squarely on the supervisor and organization as beings or objects. To varying degrees, such entity approaches move the focus from the justice or fairness of "trees" to the justice or fairness of "forests." As with the other conversion decisions, the guiding question should be whether the experience bracketing matches the research question and the operative theoretical lens.

A Taxonomy of Measurement Approaches in the Justice Literature

Having described the fundamental issues involved in structuring and converting measures, we turn our attention to reviewing the most common approaches used in the literature. As shown in Table 8.2, those approaches can be contrasted by (a) whether they emphasize justice versus fairness, and (b) whether they distinguish between procedural, distributive, interpersonal, and informational dimensions.

Faceted Justice

The first justice measure that wound up being widely used by other scholars was introduced by Moorman (1991) in his study of justice and citizenship behavior. Moorman's (1991) work occurred

Table 8.2 A Taxonomy of Measurement Approaches

	Assessing Justice	Assessing Fairness
Emphasizing Dimensional Distinctions	*Faceted Justice*	*Faceted Fairness*
Deemphasizing Dimensional Distinctions	*Latent Justice*	*Overall Fairness*

at a time in the literature when the distinctions in Table 8.1 were in a state of flux. Bies and Moag (1986) had introduced their "interactional justice" rules of respect, propriety, truthfulness, and justification, arguing that they stood apart from the procedural rules expressed by Thibaut and Walker (1975) and Leventhal (1980). However, Bies's subsequent work described respect, propriety, truthfulness, and justification as capturing the "interpersonal context of procedural justice" (Tyler & Bies, 1990; see also Folger & Bies, 1989; Greenberg, Bies, & Eskew, 1991).

Against this backdrop, Moorman (1991) introduced a "procedural justice" scale with two dimensions: formal procedures and interactional justice. As was common for the time, the latter focused on the organization with the former focused on the supervisor. The formal procedures scale assessed—for the most part—Leventhal's (1980) rules. The interactional justice scale assessed—for the most part—Bies and Moag's (1986) rules. Unfortunately, the formal procedures scale also assessed Bies and Moag's (1986) justification rule, with the interactional justice scale also assessing Thibaut and Walker's (1975) process control rule and Leventhal's (1980) bias suppression rule.

The "cross pollination" present in Moorman's (1991) formal and interactional dimensions would not have been problematic had the boundary between procedural and interactional justice remained soft. However, subsequent chapters offered compelling arguments for separating the two dimensions (Bies, 2001; Bobocel & Holmvall, 2001). Empirical studies also increasingly attempted to separate the dimensions. Unfortunately, the overlapping item content in Moorman's (1991) scales seemed to inflate the procedural-interactional correlations, with scholars sometimes forced to combine the dimensions in their modeling (e.g., Mansour-Cole & Scott, 1998; Skarlicki & Latham, 1997).

Colquitt (2001) introduced a new measure of faceted justice while attempting to bring some clarity to these issues. An adaptation of this measure—converted to be supervisor-focused and based in multiple contexts and events, is shown in Box 8.1. The procedural justice items focused solely on Thibaut and Walker's (1975) and Leventhal's (1980) rules. The interactional justice items focused solely on Bies and Moag's (1986) rules. A comparison of alternative measurement models supported the distinctiveness of procedural and interactional justice in two separate studies. In addition,

Box 8.1 A Supervisor-Focused, Multiple Event-Based Adaptation of Colquitt's (2001) Measure

Procedural Justice

The questions below refer to the procedures your **supervisor** uses to make decisions about *pay, rewards, evaluations, promotions, assignments, etc.* To what extent:

1. Are you able to express your views during those procedures?
2. Can you influence the decisions arrived at by those procedures?
3. Are those procedures applied consistently?
4. Are those procedures free of bias?
5. Are those procedures based on accurate information?
6. Are you able to appeal the decisions arrived at by those procedures?
7. Do those procedures uphold ethical and moral standards?

Distributive Justice

The questions below refer to the outcomes you receive from your **supervisor**, such as *pay, rewards, evaluations, promotions, assignments, etc.* To what extent:

1. Do those outcomes reflect the effort you have put into your work?
2. Are those outcomes appropriate for the work you have completed?
3. Do those outcomes reflect what you have contributed to your work?
4. Are those outcomes justified, given your performance?

Interpersonal Justice

The questions below refer to the interactions you have with your **supervisor** as decision-making procedures (about *pay, rewards, evaluations, promotions, assignments, etc.*) are implemented. To what extent:

1. Does he/she treat you in a polite manner?
2. Does he/she treat you with dignity?
3. Does he/she treat you with respect?
4. Does he/she refrain from improper remarks or comments?

Informational Justice

The questions below refer to the explanations your **supervisor** offers as decision-making procedures (about *pay, rewards, evaluations, promotions, assignments, etc.*) are implemented. To what extent:

1. Is he/she candid when communicating with you?
2. Does he/she explain decision-making procedures thoroughly?
3. Are his/her explanations regarding procedures reasonable?
4. Does he/she communicate details in a timely manner?
5. Does he/she tailor communications to meet individuals' needs?

Note. All items utilize a five point scale where 1 = *To a Very Small Extent*, 2 = *To a Small Extent*, 3 = *To a Moderate Extent*, 4 = *To a Large Extent*, 5 = *To a Very Large Extent*. The **boldfaced** portion is where conversions for focus are made. The *italicized* portion is where conversions for context and experience bracketing are made.

Colquitt (2001) tested a structure suggested by Greenberg (1993) wherein interactional justice was separated into its interpersonal (respect and propriety) and informational (truthfulness and justification) facets. Measurement model comparisons provided empirical support for that distinction as well, creating the four-dimensional structure shown in Table 8.1.

Subsequent studies using Colquitt's (2001) measure have provided factor-analytic support for the distinctiveness of interpersonal and informational justice (e.g., Ambrose, Hess, & Ganesan, 2007; Bell, Wiechmann, & Ryan, 2006; Camerman, Cropanzano, & Vandenberghe, 2007; Choi, 2008; Cole, Bernerth, Walter, & Holt, 2010; Colquitt & Rodell, 2011; El Akremi, Vandenberghe, & Camerman, 2010; Hausknecht, Sturman, & Roberson, 2011; Jawahar, 2007; Jones & Martens, 2009; Judge & Colquitt, 2004; Liao & Rupp, 2005; Mayer, Nishii, Schneider, & Goldstein, 2007; Rodell & Colquitt, 2009; Scott, Colquitt, & Zapata-Phelan, 2007; Streicher et al., 2008). Such studies illustrate that authorities can be respectful when communicating about decision events but not be truthful and candid, or vice-versa. Indeed, that distinction is foundational in the literature on explanations and causal accounts (Bobocel, Agar, Meyer, & Irving, 1998; Gilliland & Beckstein, 1996; Greenberg, 1994; Ployhart, Ryan, & Bennett, 1999). Ultimately, however, the handling of interpersonal and informational justice should be dictated by one's research question and operative theoretical lens. Thus, some studies have included only interpersonal justice or informational justice (e.g., Johnson, Selenta, & Lord, 2006; Judge, Scott, & Ilies, 2006; Karriker & Williams, 2009; Roberson & Stewart, 2006) whereas others have combined the two into a broader interactional variable (e.g., Ambrose & Schminke, 2003, 2009; Chiaburu, 2007; DeConinck, 2010; Klendauer & Deller, 2009; Neubert, Carlson, Kacmar, Roberts, & Chonko, 2009; Spell & Arnold, 2007).

Regardless of the particular measure and the particular dimensionality, a strength of the faceted justice approach is that it grounds the phenomenon in a set of specific and actionable principles. If procedural justice is linked to lower turnover in a field study, and if an organization wants to become more procedurally just, the items in the scale embody the action steps: provide more control, be more consistent, use more accurate information, reduce sources of bias, and offer mechanisms for correction (Colquitt, 2001; Moorman, 1991). That grounding removes some of the mystery and ambiguity from the phenomenon. It also facilitates interventions, which are an important piece of the literature's DNA. Indeed, in his discussion of the "top ten reasons everyone should study justice," Greenberg (2006, pp. 323, 333) listed "justice concepts can be applied" as reason three. Studies illustrating that supervisors can be trained to be more just are one example of those applications (Skarlicki & Latham, 1996, 1997), as are field experiments that demonstrate the effects of justice concepts on key organizational outcomes (Greenberg, 1990; Schaubroeck, May, & Brown, 1994).

Latent Justice

The use of faceted justice measures has allowed the literature to explore a number of important questions. For example, scholars have been able to explore the conceptual distinctions among the rules and dimensions in Table 8.1. Scholars have argued that procedural justice is especially relevant to employees because systems stay in place, even as outcomes ebb and flow (Lind & Tyler, 1988). For their part, interpersonal and informational justice may be especially mutable because of the increased discretion authorities have over them, relative to procedures and outcomes (Scott, Colquitt, & Paddock, 2009). As another example, scholars have been able to compare the relative effects of the justice dimensions on attitudinal and behavioral outcomes. Those findings show that the various dimensions are often differentially predictive of key outcomes (Colquitt, Conlon, Wesson, Porter, & Ng, 2001). Finally, scholars have been able to investigate potential interaction effects among dimensions. Several studies have uncovered interactions between procedural justice and distributive justice, with appropriate procedures becoming more or less important depending on the outcomes (Brockner, 2002; Brockner & Wiesenfeld, 1996).

Although these studies represent a sizable portion of the justice literature—and will continue to do so—the faceted approach does come with some drawbacks. Statistically speaking, the justice dimensions are very highly correlated, potentially creating problematic levels of multicollinearity in structural models. Colquitt et al.'s (2013) meta-analytic review revealed correlations among the four dimensions ranging from 0.37 to 0.64, with an average of 0.49. Such correlations may be higher when all four dimensions focus on the same source and are bound in the same time frame and experience bracketing. As Ambrose and Arnaud (2005) noted, multicollinearity often causes scholars to focus on narrow slices of incremental variance-explained, taking the focus off of the total variance explained by justice, in general (see also Fassino, Jones, & Uggerslev, 2008). Multicollinearity also inflates the standard errors associated with path coefficients, potentially resulting in "bouncing betas" from one study to the next (Cohen, Cohen, West, & Aiken, 2003; Schwab, 2005). Conceptually speaking, many studies do not draw distinctions between justice dimensions in their hypothesis development, focusing their theorizing, instead, on a more overarching level of abstraction. If studies expect the same pattern of findings for procedural, distributive, interpersonal, and informational justice, what becomes the reason for the separate operationalization?

One solution to these issues is to model justice as a second-order latent variable, with procedural, distributive, interpersonal, and informational justice as lower-order indicators. Colquitt and Shaw (2005) demonstrated this approach with 16 samples utilizing Colquitt's (2001) scales. The second-order structure fit the data well, with the loadings of the dimensions onto the latent justice factor ranging from 0.64 to 0.86. This conceptualization is consistent with the "latent model" formulation in Law, Wong, and Mobley's (1998) discussion of multidimensional constructs (see also Wong, Law, & Huang, 2008). The latent model formulation is appropriate when the construct can be defined by the common variance shared by the multiple dimensions, when the dimensions are highly correlated, and when the dimensions are functionally similar and more or less substitutable. As noted by Colquitt (2012), exchange-based explanations for justice effects do tend to view the dimensions as functionally similar in their ability to breed reciprocation. Moreover, cognitive models of the formation of justice perceptions do view dimensions as substitutable, with the emphasis being on rule-relevant data that can be easily encountered and interpreted (Lind, 2001).

Put simply, if faceted justice represents the stable portion of a "measurement approach portfolio," latent justice promises to be a "growth stock" down the road. One example of this approach is Liao's (2007) study of the perceived justice of customer service employees as they handled customer complaints about service failures. Liao (2007) modeled procedural, distributive, interpersonal, and informational justice as indicators of a latent justice variable, with the factor loadings ranging from 0.76 to 0.95 and the measurement model providing an adequate fit to the data. This measurement approach was appropriate because none of the hypotheses referenced specific justice dimensions (or unique aspects of the justice dimensions). Moreover, the correlations among the four justice dimensions and the outcome variables were consistent, suggesting that the aggregation to latent justice did not collapse across important nuances.

Overall Fairness

Like latent justice, overall fairness does not consider the distinctions among procedural, distributive, interpersonal, and informational facets. Unlike latent justice, however, overall fairness does so with a single scale that focuses on a global perception of appropriateness (Ambrose & Schminke, 2009; Choi, 2008; Colquitt, Long, Rodell, & Halvorsen-Ganepola, in press; Kim & Leung, 2007; Masterson, 2001; Rodell & Colquitt, 2009; Zapata-Phelan, Colquitt, Scott, & Livingston, 2009). For example, overall fairness scales include items like, "Overall, I'm treated fairly by my organization" (Ambrose & Schminke, 2009), "My supervisor is a fair person" (Choi, 2008), and "Does your supervisor behave like a fair person would?" (Colquitt et al., in press).

If latent justice has the potential to be a growth stock in a measurement approach portfolio down the road, overall fairness is realizing that growth already. A number of recent studies have included overall fairness, often in tandem with measures of the justice dimensions (Bobocel, 2013; Holtz & Harold, 2009; Jones & Martens, 2009). Overall fairness is the subject of another chapter in this volume (by Ambrose, Wo, & Griffith), so we will devote little discussion to it here. However, we should note that many overall fairness scales are easily convertible between supervisor and organizational foci, as the sample items in the previous paragraph illustrate. In terms of context and experience bracketing, overall fairness scales tend to be structured as "entity" measures that transcend particular contexts or events (Cropanzano et al., 2001). That need not be the case if the research question demands a different structure, however. One could envision items like "Overall, I was treated fairly by my organization during my last performance evaluation" (Ambrose & Schminke, 2009) or "Does your supervisor behave like a fair person would during performance evaluations?" (Colquitt et al., in press). Both items embed overall fairness in a performance evaluation context while varying the experience bracketing.

Faceted Fairness

The final cell in our taxonomy of measurement approaches is faceted fairness, where dimensional distinctions are examined but items focus on global perceptions of appropriateness rather than specific justice rules. The first scale in this category that became widely used by other scholars is Price and Mueller's (1986) measure of distributive fairness. This measure opens with the following instructions: "Fairness in the following questions means the extent to which a person's contributions to the hospital are related to the rewards received. Money, recognition, and physical facilities are examples of rewards." The measure then includes six items, including "To what extent are you fairly rewarded considering the *responsibilities* that you have?" and "To what extent are you fairly rewarded for the *amount of effort* that you have put forth?" (1 = *rewards are not distributed at all fairly* to 5 = *rewards are very fairly distributed*). Although the items implicitly evoke the equity rule from Table 8.1 (Adams, 1965; Leventhal, 1976), both the items and the anchors explicitly refer to fairness. Not surprisingly, the items are bounded in a compensation context, with extensive experience bracketing being used as opposed to one event.

Price and Mueller's (1986) index wound up inspiring and/or being incorporated into other widely used measures (Colquitt, 2001; McFarlin & Sweeney, 1992; Moorman, 1991; Sweeney & McFarlin, 1993). One of those was used in two field studies by Sweeney and McFarlin that sought to differentiate the effects of procedural and distributive fairness on outcomes like job satisfaction and organizational commitment (McFarlin & Sweeney, 1992; Sweeney & McFarlin, 1993). The authors crafted four procedural fairness items that mimicked some aspects of Price and Mueller's (1986) formatting. Specifically, respondents were asked "How fair or unfair are the *procedures* used to evaluate performance?" "How fair or unfair are the *procedures* used to communicate performance feedback?" "How fair or unfair are the *procedures* used to determine promotions?" and "How fair or unfair are the *procedures* used to determine salary increases?" (1 = *very unfair* to 5 = *very fair*). Thus, the items assessed multiple contexts with extensive experience bracketing. It should be noted that the "communicate performance feedback" item could evoke the interpersonal and informational rules in Table 8.1 (Bies & Moag, 1986; Greenberg, 1993). The studies occurred at a time when interactional concepts were often subsumed under the procedural umbrella (Folger & Bies, 1989; Greenberg et al., 1991; Tyler & Bies, 1990), making such cross-pollination unproblematic for the times.

As the distinctiveness of procedural and interactional concepts began to be sorted out, subsequent studies introduced additional measures of procedural and distributive fairness. For example, Rupp and Cropanzano (2002) reported a measure of procedural fairness that could be easily converted between supervisor and organization foci. Items included "I can count on [my supervisor] to have fair policies," and "[The organization's] procedures and guidelines are fair." As another example, Blader and Tyler (2003) introduced a measure of distributive fairness that asked "How fairly are resources (e.g., salary, bonuses, etc.) allocated among employees where you work?" and "Overall, how fair is the salary you receive at work?" Blader and Tyler (2003) also introduced procedural scales, but they included both fairness items ("The rules and procedures are equally fair to everyone") and justice items ("The rules ensure that decisions are based on facts, not personal biases and opinions"). Relative to the structure shown in Table 8.2, such scales represent hybrids that cross the justice-fairness cells.

What is noteworthy about these subsequent scales is that they did not attempt to measure interactional concepts using fairness items. Rupp and Cropanzano (2002) included interactional justice items like "[My supervisor] keeps me informed of why things happen in the way they do," and "[The organization] treats me with dignity and respect." Blader and Tyler's (2003) interactional justice items included "I am treated with dignity by [this organization]," and "[My supervisor] respects my rights as a person." Why is there a general absence of interactional fairness items, relative to procedural and distributive fairness items? One reason is that the border between interactional/interpersonal fairness and overall fairness can be quite blurry. Consider the following three items:

> "Overall, I'm treated fairly by [my supervisor]."
> "In general, I don't think [my supervisor] treats me fairly."
> "All in all, [my supervisor] treats me fairly."

The first item is an overall fairness item from Ambrose and Schminke's (2009) scale; the third item is an overall fairness item from Kim and Leung's (2007) work. In contrast, the middle item is from Aquino (1995) and was used to measure interpersonal fairness. The blurriness between interpersonal fairness and overall fairness results from the multiple meanings of the word *treat.* The *Oxford English Dictionary*'s definitions for *treat* include "To deal kindly with; to show kindness or respect to . . ." That usage supplies the sentiments that Aquino (1995) was seeking to assess with interpersonal fairness. However, the dictionary also includes definitions like "To deal with, behave or act towards in some specified way . . ." and "To manage, rule, govern; to lead, induce; to conduct oneself, behave." Those usages match the sentiments that Ambrose and Schminke (2009) and Kim and Leung (2007) were seeking to assess with overall fairness, given that they can embody all the concepts in Table 8.1. That blurriness seems to have stalled momentum for faceted fairness approaches, especially given the increasing visibility of overall fairness in the literature. Thus, of the four approaches in Table 8.2, faceted fairness seems to have the most limited "growth potential."

Summary

Having reviewed all the measurement approaches, the operative question becomes "when should each of them be used?" Colquitt and Shaw (2005) offered some discussion of these issues already, and many of the same decision rules apply. First and foremost, faceted justice and latent justice are more appropriate as independent variables than as mediators or outcomes, with some exceptions. Consider a study arguing that idealized influence on the part of a leader (Bass & Avolio, 1995) results in citizenship behavior because it makes employees perceive higher levels of justice/fairness. Leaders who exhibit idealized influence talk about important values, emphasize the collective, and consider the ethical consequences of their actions (Bass & Avolio, 1995). There are good reasons to expect those behaviors to trigger a global sense of appropriateness, making fairness scales a logical choice. In contrast, there are many rules in Table 8.1 that should be unaffected by those behaviors, making justice approaches less optimal. Just as importantly, the "considering ethical consequences" aspect of idealized influence itself taps some of the same content as the ethicality and truthfulness rules in Table 8.1. It might, therefore, be more appropriate to label idealized influence and justice as exogenous covarying predictors than to label one an independent variable and the other a dependent variable.

Thus, in field studies, fairness approaches could often be used as mediators of some independent variable's effects, whether justice or otherwise. In this way, fairness could be acting as one of the sentiments that encourages reciprocation in exchange-based theorizing (Blau, 1964). Similarly, fairness approaches would represent appropriate manipulation checks in laboratory work. Most laboratory studies in the justice domain manipulate one or more of the rules in Table 8.1, most commonly process control, accuracy, consistency, equity, respect, or justification. Such studies might utilize one justice item as a manipulation check, to ensure—for example—that a manipulation of consistency did register as a difference in perceived consistency. However, such studies should also use measures of fairness to ensure that the manipulation of consistency also triggered differential fairness perceptions (see Zapata-Phelan et al., 2009, for an example of this dual approach for manipulation checks).

The exception to the independent-variable rule for faceted and latent justice is when a study is explicitly focused on predicting adherence to the rules in Table 8.1. A number of scholars have turned their attention to predicting justice rule adherence in recent years, using organization, supervisor, and employee-centered predictors (Gilliland & Schepers, 2003; Korsgaard, Roberson, & Rymph, 1998; Mayer et al., 2007; Patient & Skarlicki, 2010; Schminke, Ambrose, & Cropanzano, 2000; Scott, Garza, Conlon, & Kim, in press; Scott et al., 2009; Scott, Colquitt, & Zapata-Phelan, 2007; Zapata, Olsen, & Martins, 2013). For example, Zapata et al. (2013) linked a supervisor's assessment of employee trustworthiness to increased adherence to interpersonal and informational justice rules. The authors were focused on predicting the act of being respectful, proper, truthful, and candid, making a justice-based measurement approach the appropriate choice, even as a dependent variable.

Emerging Measurement Issues

A handful of emerging topics in the justice literature have implications for the measurement of justice and fairness. In this section, we review recents trends of justice scholars to consider anticipations and expectations, within-person methodologies, the use of multiple sources to assess justice, and the operationalization of injustice. In addition to providing novel insights into the theoretical and practical importance of justice and fairness, these emerging issues represent refinements in the way scholars measure the constructs.

Anticipations and Expectations

Regardless of whether they emphasize single events, multiple events, or entities, the measurement approaches in the justice literature have one thing in common: they assess the past. That is, the research questions in justice studies focus on some past experience or the accumulation of experiences with a supervisor or organization. As important as such "experienced" justice has been shown to be when predicting attitudes and behaviors (Colquitt et al., 2013), Shapiro and Kirkman (1999; 2001) pointed out that employees may consider the justice or fairness of events before they actually occur. For example, with an impending merger looming in the future, employees may wonder if there will be layoffs and begin to make conclusions about how their supervisor will make such decisions.

This concept, labeled either "anticipatory justice" (Shapiro & Kirkman, 1999, 2001) or "justice expectations" (Bell, Ryan, & Wiechmann, 2004; Bell, Wiechmann, & Ryan, 2006), captures the extent to which employees believe that they will or will not experience justice in some future situation. Much like experienced justice, justice anticipations can be of a distributive, procedural, interpersonal, or informational nature. Given that employees do not have full information about future situations, justice scholars have theorized that employees create justice anticipations from information that they already possess (Shapiro & Kirkman, 2001). Drawing from the literature on expectations, this information may include personal experiences, vicarious experiences, and relevant individual differences (Bell et al., 2004). Empirical research has supported this theorizing by demonstrating that preexisting perceptions (i.e., prior experiences) and employee race (relevant individual differences) predict anticipations of justice (Bell et al., 2006; Ritter, Fischbein, & Lord, 2005; Rodell & Colquitt, 2009).

Once formed, anticipations about justice and fairness may be especially powerful. As Shapiro and Kirkman (2001) pointed out in their seminal theorizing, employees are likely to experience whatever it is that they expect, regardless of the eventual reality of a situation. Indeed, anticipatory justice tends to be moderately positively correlated with experienced justice (Bell et al., 2006; Rodell & Colquitt, 2009). Anticipatory justice also predicts a variety of employee attitudes and behaviors, including self-esteem, acceptance of change, and commitment (Bell et al., 2006; Ritter et al., 2005; Rodell & Colquitt, 2009; Shapiro & Kirkman, 1999). Such work illustrates that justice or fairness measures can be converted in yet another way: to capture future time horizons rather than past events and experiences.

Within-Person Methodologies

Traditionally, scholars have examined justice and fairness on a between-individuals basis, linking variations to between-person differences in job attitudes and behaviors. Such studies are, in the end, based on averages. That is, employees who feel more justly treated are, on average, more likely to engage in, say, citizenship behavior. Although such findings are robust and practically significant, between-individual conclusions do not tell the entire story. What this focus specifically overlooks is the dynamic nature of justice. Not only do some employees have meaningfully different perceptions of justice than others (between-individual variation), their own perceptions of justice may vary from day to day or week to week (within-individual variation). How likely is it that employees think that their supervisor is open to input, consistent, accurate, equitable, and respectful with *every* decision event? Employing within-person methodologies (as in experience sampling studies) enables scholars to capture variations in justice and fairness within individuals over time.

The appropriate time frame to explore within-individual variation in justice and fairness may depend on the relevant dimensions or foci. Greenberg (1993) classified the justice dimensions according to their structural and social natures—suggesting that the more structural dimensions should be more stable over time and the more social dimensions should be more variable over time. Thus, procedural and distributive justice should be more stable over time, especially when focused on the organization. Although perceptions of these dimensions may oscillate over time, they seem likely to evolve less frequently and at a slower pace. Recent examinations of within-individual procedural and distributive justice demonstrated significant variance over periods of four weeks (Holtz & Harold, 2009) and three months (Hausknecht et al., 2011). In contrast, interpersonal and informational justice are considered social in nature, especially when focused on supervisors. They should, therefore, evolve more frequently and at a faster rate. Indeed, aside from evidence of weekly and monthly variation in interpersonal and information justice (Hausknecht et al., 2011; Holtz &

Harold, 2009), these dimensions have also been shown to vary from day-to-day (Judge, Scott, & Ilies, 2006; Loi, Yang, & Diefendorff, 2009).

Within-individual methodologies also allow scholars to capture different experience bracketing for justice and fairness. Adopting a within-individual methodology allows for perceptions of events and entities to be examined simultaneously, and provides insights into the relationship between justice as experienced in a particular event and more general perceptions of an entity. For example, Loi et al. (2009) demonstrated the impact of procedural and distributive justice perceptions about the organization (between-individual) on employees' reactions to day-to-day perceptions of interpersonal and informational justice (within-individual). This methodology also affords scholars the opportunity to examine the hierarchical structure of experience bracketing. That is, do a series of justice events "add up" to create some overall perception of an entity as suggested in the literature (Cropanzano et al., 2001)? In conducting this research, scholars should be careful to keep the contexts consistent. If events reference a compensation context, then measures of entity perceptions might also reference that same context so as to not confound context with bracketing.

Multiple Sources

The modal field study in the justice literature has tended to utilize two sources. Employees rate either justice or fairness while also reporting on relevant mediators. Supervisors, in turn, rate outcome variables such as citizenship behavior, task performance, or counterproductive behavior. Although a widely utilized design in a number of literatures, that homogeneity of method has impacted the literature in at least two ways. First, we know surprisingly little about whether employee perceptions of justice and fairness match the views of their supervisors. Second, justice → mediator linkages in most field studies may be subject to dispositional sources of common method bias, such as trait affectivity (Podsakoff, MacKenzie, Lee, & Podsakoff, 2003).

Zapata et al.'s (2013) study of employee trustworthiness and supervisor justice rule adherence offers data on the first question. The authors included typical measures of interpersonal and informational justice by asking employees to respond to Colquitt's (2001) scales. However, they also asked supervisors to rate their own adherence to interpersonal and informational justice rules, again using Colquitt's (2001) scales. That is, supervisors were asked, "Do you treat this subordinate in a polite manner?" and "Are you candid when communicating with this subordinate?" Notably, employee and supervisor ratings of interpersonal justice were correlated at 0.26, with the corresponding informational justice correlation being 0.46. Such convergent validities reveal some correspondence but more slippage when it comes to adhering to justice rules. That slippage represents an important area for future research, especially given that supervisors' understanding of their own justice reputations is likely relevant to their motivations to improve their rule adherence (Skarlicki & Latham, 1996; 1997).

If employees and supervisors disagree about justice levels, how then could justice → mediator linkages be tested in a way that is not source bound? One promising direction would be to rely on co-worker reports of justice. Research on justice climate has revealed that co-worker assessments of a supervisor or organization's justice rule adherence can converge enough to justify aggregation (Colquitt, Noe, & Jackson, 2002; Ehrhart, 2004; Moon, Kamdar, Mayer, & Takeuchi, 2008; Mossholder, Bennett, & Martin, 1998; Naumann & Bennett, 2000; Roberson, 2006; Simons & Roberson, 2003). That convergence points to the possibility of asking co-workers to supply ratings of justice in a study in which the focal employee reports the mediators and the supervisors report the outcomes. This strategy could be especially effective if co-workers are asked to focus on a supervisor's or organization's treatment of the focal employee, as opposed to the co-worker's own treatment. This strategy may be less appropriate with fairness measures, as fairness is more evaluative than descriptive, with "the beholder" looming larger.

Operationalizing Injustice

Despite the fact that the literature is most typically described by the "organizational justice" moniker, a number of scholars have argued that it is actually *injustice* that "moves the needle" on relevant attitudes and behaviors (Bies, 2001; Cropanzano, Stein, & Nadisic, 2011; Gilliland, 2008; Organ, 1990; Rupp & Spencer, 2006). For example, Rupp and Spencer (2006) speculated that "In the absence of injustice, fairness becomes a camouflaged phenomenon . . . Fairness often implies simple adherence to expected norms, which observers tend to take for granted and hence fail to notice . . . Thus, a study in justice must use injustice as the dominant theme because it is more salient to those who experience it or observe it" (p. 972). Although such speculations are intuitive, they remain largely untested. One exception is work by Gilliland, Benson, and Schepers (1998), who conducted three studies where students were asked to react to a layoff scenario. The studies varied both justice (termed "nonviolations," and indicated by the provision of a severance package) and injustice (termed "violations," and indicated by the absence of advance notice), with one of the outcomes being whether the students would recommend the company for an ethics-based award. Their results showed that violations were a stronger predictor of recommendation intentions than nonviolations.

Unfortunately, it becomes difficult to follow up on Gilliland et al.'s (1998) results in the field because most measures of justice reflect the degree of adherence to the rules in Table 8.1. Colquitt's (2001) items ask about the extent to which authorities are consistent, accurate, unbiased, equitable, respectful, and truthful using a scale from 1 = *To a Very Small Extent* to 5 = *To a Very Large Extent.* Similarly, Moorman's (1991) items ask whether authorities have all sides represented, hear concerns, provide feedback, and show kindness using a scale from 1 = *Strongly Disagree* to 5 = *Strongly Agree.* That emphasis on the degree or extent of rule adherence creates a certain "continuum truncation," with measures sampling only a portion of the full range of experiences associated with justice (and sometimes the less relevant portion).

Colquitt, Long, Rodell, and Halvorsen-Ganepola (in press) examined this issue by supplementing Colquitt's (2001) original items with items focused on justice rule violations. Those new items included "Are those procedures based on faulty information?" (procedural justice), "Are those outcomes inconsistent with the effort you have put into your work?" (distributive justice), "Does he/she treat you in a rude manner?" (interpersonal justice) and "Is he/she secretive about decision-making procedures?" (informational justice). A field study then revealed that an "untruncated" or "full-range" measure (i.e., one using Colquitt's original items alongside reversed versions of the new items) explained more variance in state affect, trust, focus of attention, self-esteem, social exchange perceptions, and counterproductive behavior. Thus, a more frequent operationalization of rule violation may prove to be valuable in future work, especially when predicting deviant or counterproductive outcomes.

Conclusion

If being able to express justice and fairness in numbers shows that scholars know something about them, then it is safe to say that the literature has amassed significant knowledge about the phenomena. The fundamental issues involved in constructing and tailoring measures are well-understood, and four approaches for operationalizing justice and fairness have emerged. Those approaches give scholars choices as they seek to match their measures to their research questions and to their operative theoretical lens. Of course, measurement in any literature remains a living, dynamic, and fluid enterprise. As questions, theories, and points of emphasis change, so, too, will measures of justice and fairness. The studies on anticipations, within-person methodologies, multiple sources, and injustice represent some examples of that fluidity, and the years to come will certainly bring additional examples.

References

Adams, J. S. (1965). Inequity in social exchange. In L. Berkowitz (Ed.), *Advances in experimental social psychology* (Vol. 2, pp. 267–299). New York, NY: Academic Press.

Ambrose, M., & Arnaud, A. (2005). Are procedural justice and distributive justice conceptually distinct? In J. Greenberg & J. A. Colquitt (Eds.), *The handbook of organizational justice* (pp. 59–84). Mahwah, NJ: Erlbaum.

Ambrose, M., Hess, R. L., & Ganesan, S. (2007). The relationship between justice and attitudes: An examination of justice effects on event and system-related attitudes. *Organizational Behavior and Human Decision Processes, 103*, 21–36.

Ambrose, M. L., & Schminke, M. (2003). Organization structure as a moderator of the relationship between procedural justice, interactional justice, perceived organizational support, and supervisory trust. *Journal of Applied Psychology, 88*, 295–305.

Ambrose, M. L., & Schminke, M. (2009). The role of overall justice judgments in organizational justice research: A test of mediation. *Journal of Applied Psychology, 94*, 491–500.

Aquino, K. (1995). Relationships among pay inequity, perceptions of procedural justice, and organizational citizenship. *Employee Responsibilities and Rights Journal, 8*, 21–33.

Barsky, A., & Kaplan, S. A. (2007). If you feel bad, it's unfair: A quantitative synthesis of affect and organizational justice perceptions. *Journal of Applied Psychology, 92*, 286–295.

Bass, B. M., & Avolio, B. J. (1995). *MLQ Multifactor Leadership Questionnaire for research.* Redwood City, CA: Mind Garden.

Bauer, T. N., Truxillo, D. M., Sanchez, R. J., Craig, J. M., Ferrara, P., & Campion, M. A. (2001). Applicant reactions to selection: Development of the selection procedural justice scale (SPJS). *Personnel Psychology, 54*, 387–419.

Bell, B. S., Ryan, A. M., & Wiechmann, D. (2004). Justice expectations and applicant perceptions. *International Journal of Selection and Assessment, 12*, 24–38.

Bell, B. S., Wiechmann, D., & Ryan, A. M. (2006). Consequences of organizational justice expectations in a selection system. *Journal of Applied Psychology, 91*, 455–466.

Bies, R. J. (2001). Interactional (in)justice: The sacred and the profane. In J. Greenberg & R. Cropanzano (Eds.), *Advances in organizational justice* (pp. 89–118). Stanford, CA: Stanford University Press.

Bies, R. J., & Moag, J. F. (1986). Interactional justice: Communication criteria of fairness. In R. J. Lewicki, B. H. Sheppard, & M. H. Bazerman (Eds.), *Research on negotiations in organizations* (Vol. 1, pp. 43–55). Greenwich, CT: JAI Press.

Blader, S. L., & Tyler, T. R. (2003). What constitutes fairness in work settings? A four-component model of procedural justice. *Human Resource Management Review, 13*, 107–126.

Blau, P. (1964). *Exchange and power in social life*. New York, NY: Wiley.

Bobocel, D. R. (2013). Coping with unfair events constructively or destructively: The effects of overall justice and self-other orientation. *Journal of Applied Psychology, 98*, 720–731.

Bobocel, D. R., Agar, S. E., Meyer, J. P., & Irving, P. G. (1998). Managerial accounts and fairness perceptions in conflict resolution: Differentiating the effects of minimizing responsibility and providing justification. *Basic and Applied Psychology, 20*, 133–143.

Bobocel, D. R., & Holmvall, C. M. (2001). Are interactional justice and procedural justice different? Framing the debate. In S. Gilliland, D. Steiner, & D. Skarlicki (Eds.), *Theoretical and cultural perspectives on organizational justice* (pp. 85–110). Greenwich, CT: Information Age.

Brockner, J. (2002). Making sense of procedural fairness: How high procedural fairness can reduce or heighten the influence of outcome favorability. *Academy of Management Review, 27*, 58–76.

Brockner, J., Fishman, A. Y., Reb, J., Goldman, B., Spiegel, S. & Garden, C. (2007). Procedural fairness, outcome favorability, and judgments of an authority's responsibility. *Journal of Applied Psychology, 92*, 1657–1671.

Brockner, J., & Wiesenfeld, B. M. (1996). An integrative framework for explaining reactions to decisions: Interactive effects of outcomes and procedures. *Psychological Bulletin, 120*, 189–208.

Brockner, J., Wiesenfeld, B. M., & Martin, C. L. (1995). Decision frame, procedural justice, and survivors' reactions to job layoffs. *Organizational Behavior and Human Decision Processes, 63*, 59–68.

Camerman, J., Cropanzano, R., & Vandenberghe, C. (2007). The benefits of justice for temporary workers. *Group and Organization Management, 32*, 176–207.

Chiaburu, D. S. (2007). From interactional justice to citizenship behaviors: Role enlargement or role discretion. *Social Justice Research, 20*, 207–227.

Choi, J. (2008). Event justice perceptions and employees' reactions: Perceptions of social entity justice as a moderator. *Journal of Applied Psychology, 93*, 513–528.

Cohen, J., Cohen, P., West, S. G., & Aiken, L. S. (2003). *Applied multiple regression/correlation analysis for the behavioral sciences*. Mahwah, NJ: Erlbaum.

Cole, M. S., Bernerth, J. B., Walter, F., & Holt, D. T. (2010). Organizational justice and individuals' withdrawal: Unlocking the influence of emotional exhaustion. *Journal of Management Studies, 47*, 367–390.

Colquitt, J. A. (2001). On the dimensionality of organizational justice: A construct validation of a measure. *Journal of Applied Psychology, 86*, 386–400.

Colquitt, J. A. (2012). Organizational justice. In S. W. J. Kozlowski (Ed.), *The Oxford handbook of organizational psychology* (Vol. 1, pp. 526–547). New York, NY: Oxford University Press.

Colquitt, J. A., Conlon, D. E., Wesson, M. J., Porter, C. O. L. H., & Ng, K. Y. (2001). Justice at the millennium: A meta-analytic review of 25 years of organizational justice research. *Journal of Applied Psychology, 86*, 425–445.

Colquitt, J. A., & Greenberg, J. (2003). Organizational justice: A fair assessment of the state of the literature. In J. Greenberg (Ed.), *Organizational behavior: The state of the science* (pp. 165–210). Mahwah, NJ: Erlbaum.

Colquitt, J. A., Long, D. M., Rodell, J. B., & Halvorsen-Ganepola, M. D. K. (in press). Adding the "in" to justice: A qualitative and quantitative investigation of the differential effects of justice rule adherence and violation. *Journal of Applied Psychology*.

Colquitt, J. A., Noe, R. A., & Jackson, C. L. (2002). Justice in teams: Antecedents and consequences of procedural justice climate. *Personnel Psychology, 55*, 83–109.

Colquitt, J. A., & Rodell, J. B. (2011). Justice, trust, and trustworthiness: A longitudinal analysis integrating three theoretical perspectives. *Academy of Management Journal, 54*, 1183–1206.

Colquitt, J. A., Scott, B. A., Rodell, J. B., Long, D. M., Zapata, C. P., Conlon, D. E., & Wesson, M. J. (2013). Justice at the millennium, a decade later: A meta-analytic test of social exchange and affect-based perspectives. *Journal of Applied Psychology, 98*, 199–236.

Colquitt, J. A., & Shaw, J. C. (2005). How should organizational justice be measured? In J. Greenberg & J. A. Colquitt (Eds.), *The handbook of organizational justice* (pp. 113–152). Mahwah, NJ: Erlbaum.

Cropanzano, R., Byrne, Z. S., Bobocel, D. R., & Rupp, D. E. (2001). Moral virtues, fairness heuristics, social entities, and other denizens of organizational justice. *Journal of Vocational Behavior, 58*, 164–209.

Cropanzano, R., & Greenberg, J. (1997). Progress in organizational justice: Tunneling through the maze. In C. L. Cooper & I. T. Robertson (Eds.), International review of industrial and organizational psychology (pp. 317–372). New York, NY: Wiley.

Cropanzano, R., Stein, J. H., & Nadisic, T. (2011). *Social justice and the experience of emotion*. New York, NY: Routledge.

Daly, J. P., & Geyer, P. D. (1994). The role of fairness in implementing large-scale change: Employee evaluations of process and outcome in seven facility locations. *Journal of Organizational Behavior, 15*, 623–638.

DeConinck, J. B. (2010). The effect of organizational justice, perceived organizational support, and perceived supervisor support on marketing employees' level of trust. *Journal of Business Research, 63*, 1349–1355.

Earley, P. C., & Lind, E. A. (1987). Procedural justice and participation in task selection: The role of control in mediating justice judgments. *Journal of Personality and Social Psychology, 52*, 1148–1160.

Ehrhart, M. G. (2004). Leadership and procedural justice climate as antecedents of unit-level organizational citizenship behavior. *Personnel Psychology, 57*, 61–94.

El Akremi, A., Vandenberghe, C., & Camerman, J. (2010). The role of justice and social exchange relationships in workplace deviance: Test of a mediated model. *Human Relations, 63*, 1687–1717.

Farh, J.-L., Earley, P. C., & Lind, S.-C. (1997). Impetus for action: A cultural analysis of justice and organizational citizenship behavior in Chinese society. *Administrative Science Quarterly, 42*, 421–444.

Fassina, N. E., Jones, D. A., & Uggerslev, K. L. (2008). Meta-analytic tests of relationships between organizational justice and citizenship behavior: Testing agent-system and shared-variance models. *Journal of Organizational Behavior, 29*, 805–828.

Folger, R. (2001). Fairness as deonance. In S. W. Gilliland, D. D. Steiner, & D. P. Skarlicki (Eds.), *Theoretical and cultural perspectives on organizational justice* (pp. 3–34). Greenwich, CT: Information Age.

Folger, R., & Bies, R. J. (1989). Managerial responsibilities and procedural justice. *Responsibilities and Rights Journal, 2*, 79–89.

Folger, R., & Cropanzano, R. (2001). Fairness theory: Justice as accountability. In J. Greenberg & R. Cropanzano (Eds.), *Advances in organizational justice* (pp. 89–118). Stanford, CA: Stanford University Press.

Folger, R., Rosenfield, D., Grove, J., & Corkran, L. (1979). Effects of "voice" and peer opinions on responses to inequity. *Journal of Personality and Social Psychology, 37*, 2253–2261.

George, J. M., & Jones, G. R. (2000). The role of time in theory and theory building. *Journal of Management, 26*, 657–684.

Gilliland, S. W. (1993). The perceived fairness of selection systems: An organizational justice perspective. *Academy of Management Review, 18*, 694–734.

Gilliland, S. (2008). The tails of justice: A critical examination of the dimensionality of organizational justice constructs. *Human Resource Management Review, 18*, 271–281.

Gilliland, S. W., & Beckstein, B. A. (1996). Procedural and distributive justice in the editorial review process. *Personnel Psychology, 49*, 669–691.

Gilliland, S. W., Benson, L. III, & Schepers, D. H. (1998). A rejection threshold in justice evaluations: Effects on judgment and decision-making. *Organizational Behavior and Human Decision Processes, 76*, 113–131.

Gilliland, S. W., & Schepers, D. H. (2003). Why we do the things we do: A discussion and analysis of determinants of just treatment in layoff implementation decisions. *Human Resource Management Review, 13*, 59–83.

Greenberg, J. (1990). Employee theft as a reaction to underpayment inequity: The hidden cost of paycuts. *Journal of Applied Psychology, 75*, 561–568.

Greenberg, J. (1993). The social side of fairness: Interpersonal and informational classes of organizational justice. In R. Cropanzano (Ed.), *Justice in the workplace: Approaching fairness in human resource management* (pp. 79–103). Hillsdale, NJ: Erlbaum.

Greenberg, J. (1994). Using socially fair treatment to promote acceptance of a work site smoking ban. *Journal of Applied Psychology, 79*, 288–297.

Greenberg, J. (2006). The top ten reasons why everyone should know about—and study—organisational justice. In A. I. Glendon, B. M. Thompson, & B. Myors (Eds.), *Advances in Organisational Psychology*. Bowen Hills, Queensland: Australian Academic Press.

Greenberg, J. (2010). Organizational justice: The dynamics of fairness in the workplace. In S. Zedeck (Ed.), *APA handbook of industrial and organizational psychology* (Vol. 3, pp. 271–327). Washington, D.C.: American Psychological Association.

Greenberg, J., Bies, R. J., & Eskew, D. E. (1991). Establishing fairness in the eye of the beholder: Managing impressions of organizational justice. In R. Giacalone & P. Rosenfeld (Eds.), *Applied impression management: How image making affects managerial decisions* (pp. 111–132). Newbury Park, CA: Sage.

Hausknecht, J. P., Sturman, M. C., & Roberson, Q. M. (2011). Justice as a dynamic construct: Effects of individual trajectories on distal work outcomes. *Journal of Applied Psychology, 96*, 872–880.

Hinkin, T. R. (1995). A review of scale development practices in the study of organizations. *Journal of Management, 21*, 967–988.

Hinkin, T. R. (1998). A brief tutorial on the development of measures for use in survey questionnaires. *Organizational Research Methods, 1*, 104–121.

Holtz, B. C., & Harold, C. M. (2009). Fair today, fair tomorrow? A longitudinal investigation of overall justice perceptions. *Journal of Applied Psychology, 94*, 1185–1199.

Horvath, M., & Andrews, S. B. (2007). The role of fairness perceptions and accountability attributions in predicting reactions to organizational events. *Journal of Psychology, 141*, 203–222.

Ironson, G. H., Smith, P. C., Brannick, M. T., Gibson, W. M., & Paul, K. B. (1989). Construction of a job in general scale: A comparison of global, composite, and specific measures. *Journal of Applied Psychology, 74*, 193–200.

Jawahar, I. M. (2007). The influence of perceptions of fairness on performance appraisal reactions. *Journal of Labor Research, 28*, 735–754.

Johnson, R. E., Selenta, C., & Lord, R. G. (2006). When organizational justice and the self-concept meet: Consequences for the organization and its members. *Organizational Behavior and Human Decision Processes, 99*, 175–201.

Jones, D. A., & Martens, M. L. (2009). The mediating role of overall fairness and the moderating role of trust certainty in justice-criteria relationships: The formation and use of fairness heuristics in the workplace. *Journal of Organizational Behavior, 30*, 1025–1051.

Judge, T. A., & Colquitt, J. A. (2004). Organizational justice and stress: The mediating role of work-family conflict. *Journal of Applied Psychology, 89*, 395–404.

Judge, T. A., Scott, B. A., & Ilies, R. (2006). Hostility, job attitudes, and workplace deviance: Test of a multilevel model. *Journal of Applied Psychology, 91*, 126–138.

Karriker, J. H., & Williams, M. L. (2009). Organizational justice and organizational citizenship behavior: A mediated multifoci model. *Journal of Management, 35*, 112–135.

Klendauer, R., & Deller, J. (2009). Organizational justice and managerial commitment in corporate mergers. *Journal of Managerial Psychology, 24*, 29–45.

Kim, T. Y., & Leung, K. (2007). Forming and reacting to overall fairness: A cross-cultural comparison. *Organizational Behavior and Human Decision Processes, 104*, 83–95.

Korsgaard, M. A., Roberson, L., & Rymph, R. D. (1998). What motivates fairness? The role of subordinate assertive behavior on managers' interactional fairness. *Journal of Applied Psychology, 83*, 731–744.

Lavelle, J. J., Brockner, J., Konovsky, M. A., Price, K. H., Henley, A. B., Taneja, A., & Vinekar, V. (2009). Commitment, procedural fairness, and organizational citizenship behavior: A multifoci analysis. *Journal of Organizational Behavior, 30*, 337–357.

Lavelle, J. J., Rupp, D. E., & Brockner, J. (2007). Taking a multifoci approach to the study of justice, social exchange, and citizenship behavior: The target similarity model. *Journal of Management, 33*, 841–866.

Law, K. S., Wong, C. S., & Mobley, W. H. (1998). Toward a taxonomy of multidimensional constructs. *Academy of Management Review, 23*, 741–755.

Leventhal, G. S. (1976). The distribution of rewards and resources in groups and organizations. In L. Berkowitz & W. Walster (Eds.), *Advances in experimental social psychology* (Vol. 9, pp. 91–131). New York, NY: Academic Press.

Leventhal, G. S. (1980). What should be done with equity theory? New approaches to the study of fairness in social relationships. In K. Gergen, M. Greenberg, and R. Willis (Eds.), *Social exchange: Advances in theory and research* (pp. 27–55). New York, NY: Plenum Press.

Liao, H. (2007). Do it right this time: The role of employee service recovery performance in customer-perceived justice and customer loyalty after service failures. *Journal of Applied Psychology, 92*, 475–489.

Liao, H., & Rupp, D. E. (2005). The impact of justice climate and justice orientation on work outcomes: A cross-level multifoci framework. *Journal of Applied Psychology, 90*, 242–256.

Lind, E. A. (2001). Fairness heuristic theory: Justice judgments as pivotal cognitions in organizational relations. In J. Greenberg & R. Cropanzano (Eds.), *Advances in organizational justice* (pp. 56–88). Stanford, CA: Stanford University Press.

Lind, E. A., & Tyler, T. R. (1988). *The social psychology of procedural justice.* New York, NY: Plenum Press.

Loi, R., Yang, J. & Diefendorff, J. M. (2009). Four-factor justice and daily job satisfaction: A multilevel investigation. *Journal of Applied Psychology, 94*, 770–781.

Mansour-Cole, D. M., & Scott, S. G. (1998). Hearing it through the grapevine: The influence of source, leader-relations, and legitimacy on survivors' fairness perceptions. *Personnel Psychology, 51*, 25–54.

Masterson, S. S. (2001). A trickle-down model of organizational justice: Relating employees' and customers' perceptions of and reactions to fairness. *Journal of Applied Psychology, 86*, 594–604.

Mayer, D., Nishii, L., Schneider, B., & Goldstein, H. (2007). The precursors and products of justice climates: Group leader antecedents and employee attitudinal consequences. *Personnel Psychology, 60*, 929–963.

McFarlin, D. B., & Sweeney, P. D. (1992). Distributive and procedural justice as predictors of satisfaction with personal and organizational outcomes. *Academy of Management Journal, 35*, 626–637.

Moon, H., Kamdar, D., Mayer, D. M., & Takeuchi, R. (2008). Me or we? The role of personality and justice as other-centered antecedents to innovative citizenship behaviors within organizations. *Journal of Applied Psychology, 93*, 84–94.

Moorman, R. H. (1991). Relationship between organizational justice and organizational citizenship behaviors: Do fairness perceptions influence employee citizenship? *Journal of Applied Psychology, 76*, 845–855.

Mossholder, K. W., Bennett, N., & Martin, C. L. (1998). A multilevel analysis of procedural justice context. *Journal of Organizational Behavior, 19*, 131–141.

Naumann, S. E., & Bennett, N. (2000). A case for procedural justice climate: Development and test of a multilevel model. *Academy of Management Journal, 43*, 881–889.

Neubert, M. J., Carlson, D. S., Kacmar, K. M., Roberts, J. A., Chonko, L. B. (2009). The virtuous influence of ethical leadership behavior: Evidence from the field. *Journal of Business Ethics, 90*, 157–170.

Organ, D. W. (1990). The motivational basis of organizational citizenship behavior. In L. L. Cummings & B. M. Staw (Eds.), *Research in organizational behavior* (pp. 43–72). Greenwich, CT: JAI.

Patient, D. L., & Skarlicki, D. P. (2010). Increasing interpersonal and informational justice when communicating negative news: The role of manager's empathic concern and moral development. *Journal of Management, 36*, 555–578.

Ployhart, R. E., Ryan, A. M., & Bennett, M. (1999). Explanations for selection decisions: Applicants' reactions to informational and sensitivity features of explanations. *Journal of Applied Psychology, 84*, 87–106.

Podsakoff, P. M., MacKenzie, S. B., Lee, J., & Podsakoff, N. P. (2003). Common method bias in behavioral research: A critical review of the literature and recommended remedies. *Journal of Applied Psychology, 88*, 879–903.

Price, J. L., & Mueller, C. W. (1986). *Handbook of organizational measurement.* Marshfield, MA: Pitman.

Ritter, B. A., Fischbein, R. L., & Lord, R. G. (2005). Implicit and explicit expectations of justice as a function of manager and subordinate race. *Human Relations, 58*, 1501–1521.

Roberson, Q. M. (2006). Justice in teams: The activation and role of sensemaking in the emergence of justice climates. *Organizational Behavior and Human Decision Processes, 100*, 177–192.

Roberson, Q. M., & Stewart, M. M. (2006). Understanding the motivational effects of procedural and informational justice in feedback processes. *British Journal of Psychology, 97*, 281–298.

Rodell, J. B., & Colquitt, J. A. (2009). Looking ahead in times of uncertainty: The role of anticipatory justice in an organizational change context. *Journal of Applied Psychology, 94*, 989–1002.

Rupp, D. E., & Cropanzano, R. (2002). The mediating effects of social exchange relationships in predicting workplace outcomes from multifoci organizational justice. *Organizational Behavior and Human Decision Processes, 89*, 925–946.

Rupp, D. E., & Spencer, S. (2006). When customers lash out: The effects of customer interactional injustice on emotional labor and the mediating role of discrete emotions. *Journal of Applied Psychology, 91*, 971–978.

Schaubroeck, J., May, D. R., & Brown, F. W. (1994). Procedural justice explanations and employee reactions to economic hardship: A field experiment. *Journal of Applied Psychology, 79*, 455–460.

Schminke, M., Ambrose, M. L., & Cropanzano, R. S. (2000). The effect of organizational structure on perceptions of procedural fairness. *Journal of Applied Psychology, 85*, 294–304.

Schwab, D. P. (1980). Construct validity in organizational behavior. In L. L. Cummings & B. M. Staw (Eds.), *Research in organizational behavior* (Vol. 2, pp. 3–43). Greenwich, CT: JAI Press.

Schwab, D. P. (2005). *Research methods for organizational studies.* Mahwah, NJ: Erlbaum.

Scott, B. A., Colquitt, J. A., & Paddock, E. L. (2009). An actor-focused model of justice rule adherence and violation: The role of managerial motives and discretion. *Journal of Applied Psychology, 94,* 756–769.

Scott, B. A., Colquitt, J. A., & Zapata-Phelan, C. P. (2007). Justice as a dependent variable: Subordinate charisma as a predictor of interpersonal and informational justice perceptions. *Journal of Applied Psychology, 92,* 1597–1609.

Scott, B. A., Garza, A., Conlon, D. E., & Kim, Y. J. (in press). Why do managers act fairly in the first place? A daily investigation of "hot" and "cold" motives and discretion. *Academy of Management Journal.*

Shapiro, D. L., & Kirkman, B. L. (1999). Employees' reaction to the change to work teams: The influence of "anticipatory" injustice. *Journal of Organizational Change Management, 12,* 51–66.

Shapiro, D. L., & Kirkman, B. L. (2001). Anticipatory injustice: The consequences of expecting injustice in the workplace. In J. Greenberg & R. Cropanzano (Eds.), *Advances in organizational justice* (pp. 152–178). Lexington, MA: New Lexington.

Simons, T., & Roberson, Q. (2003). Why managers should care about fairness: The effects of aggregate justice perceptions on organizational outcomes. *Journal of Applied Psychology, 88,* 432–443.

Skarlicki, D. P., & Latham, G. P. (1996). Increasing citizenship behavior within a labor union: A test of organizational justice theory. *Journal of Applied Psychology, 81,* 161–169.

Skarlicki, D. P., & Latham, G. P. (1997). Leadership training in organizational justice to increase citizenship behavior within a labor union: A replication. *Personnel Psychology, 50,* 617–633.

Smith, P. C., Kendall, L. M., & Hulin, C. L. (1969). *The measurement of satisfaction in work and retirement.* Chicago, IL: Rand McNally.

Spell, C. S., & Arnold, T. J. (2007). A multi-level analysis of organizational justice climate, structure, and employee mental health. *Journal of Management, 33,* 724–751.

Streicher, B., Jonas, E., Maier, G. W., Frey, D., Woschée, & Waßmer, B. (2008). Test of the construct and criteria validity of a German measure of organizational justice. *European Journal of Psychological Assessment, 24,* 131–139.

Sweeney, P. D., & McFarlin, D. B. (1993). Workers' evaluation of the "ends" and the "means": An examination of four models of distributive and procedural justice. *Organizational Behavior and Human Decision Processes, 55,* 23–40.

Thibaut, J., & Walker, L. (1975). *Procedural justice: A psychological analysis.* Hillsdale, NJ: Erlbaum.

Thomson, W. (Lord Kelvin). (1891). *Popular lectures and addresses.* London, UK: Macmillan.

Tyler, T. R., & Bies, R. J. (1990). Beyond formal procedures: The interpersonal context of procedural justice. In J. Carroll (Ed.), *Applied social psychology and organizational settings* (pp. 77–98). Hillsdale, NJ: Erlbaum.

Tyler, T. R., & Blader, S. L. (2003). The group engagement model: Procedural justice, social identity, and cooperative behavior. *Personality and Social psychology Review, 7,* 349–361.

Tyler, T. R., & Lind, E. A. (1992). A relational model of authority in groups. In M. P. Zanna (Ed.), *Advances in experimental social psychology* (Vol. 25, pp. 115–191). San Diego, CA: Academic Press.

Tyler, T. R., Rasinski, K. A., & Spodick, N. (1985). Influence of voice on satisfaction with leaders: Exploring the meaning of process control. *Journal of Personality and Social Psychology, 48,* 72–81.

Wong, C. S., Law, K. S., & Huang, G. (2008). On the importance of conducting construct-level analysis for multidimensional constructs in theory development and testing. *Journal of Management, 34,* 744–764.

Zapata, C. P., Olsen, J. E., & Martins, L. L. (2013). Social exchange from the supervisor's perspective: Employee trustworthiness as a predictor of interpersonal and informational justice. *Organizational Behavior and Human Decision Processes, 121,* 1–12.

Zapata-Phelan, C. P., Colquitt, J. A., Scott, B. A., & Livingston, B. (2009). Procedural justice, interactional justice, and task performance: The mediating role of intrinsic motivation. *Organizational Behavior and Human Decision Processes, 108,* 93–105.

PART 2

Perspectives on Justice

CHAPTER

9

Understanding How the Justice Motive Shapes Our Lives and Treatment of One Another: Exciting Contributions and Misleading Claims

Melvin J. Lerner

Abstract

This chapter begins with a review of the evidence for the personal contract theory of the social psychological origins of the justice motive. It then considers how, in the normal course of events, justice appears in two cognitive-affective processes: first, in preconscious scripts and then in controlled norm-based conventions, to determine its various forms in social behavior. This is followed by illustrations of justice considerations in the workplace, and critical analyses of the theoretical and empirical bases of procedural justice as a distinct form of the justice motive. The analyses reveal two important findings: (I) The failure to recognize the appearance of different forms of the Justice Motive leads to over-estimating the importance and prevalence of self-interest, and (2) the only meaningful distinction among procedural, distributive and interactional justice involves the appearance of symbolic versus concrete resources in arriving at justice judgments.

Key Words: personal contract, justice motive, preconscious justice scripts, procedural justice

In this chapter I will present what I believe are some basic truths concerning the social psychology of justice that emerged out of approximately 50 years of research. They are not meant to provide the complete story of justice in the workplace, but, rather, they should be read as tentatively held propositions to be elaborated and built upon. Hopefully, they will provide guidelines for distinguishing between valid and helpful contributions and misleading or confusing errors concerning how justice appears in the workplace, or anywhere else for that matter.

So, what have we learned about how justice appears in people's lives? To flesh all this out, I will begin with two seemingly imposing complexities that upon further analysis actually enabled me to understand and reinterpret many reported findings. The first, and possibly most commonly recognized, is that in the natural course of human encounters justice imperatives can appear in several different forms, but with common unifying elements. Though commonly understood, as we will see in later discussions, it is amazing how frequently that has been forgotten or ignored by highly sophisticated investigators when it comes to deriving inferences about the motives underlying their research participants' behavior.

Secondly, two quite distinct sets of cognitive processes: those that occur in the preconscious and those that appear under conscious cognitive control, typically influence evaluative social judgments: good–bad, fair–unfair, desirable–undesirable. Considerably before the psychoanalytic efforts of Freud (1953), investigators suspected that people process and retain information without their conscious awareness. It is only relatively recently, however, that investigators employing rather ingenious techniques have systematically examined how pre-consciously processed information influences people's behavior. (see, e.g., Aguiar et al., 2008; Correia et al., 2007;

Hafer, 2000a). Their findings are particularly important for the study of justice.

They reveal, for example, that preconscious processes, automatically elicited by familiar cues, often include simple scripted evaluations and associations between actors and outcomes, e.g., "good things belong to good people," and "bad outcomes happen to bad people" (Callan et al., 2006). These preconscious scripts may generate an associated emotion that is experienced as the imperative to restore justice: punish bad guys and rescue victims (Lerner, 1975; Lerner & Clayton, 2011). The more elaborate consciously controlled cognitive processes are somewhat slower to appear. They introduce familiar conventional rules of thought in arriving at attributions and moral blame, as well as the planful search for an appropriate course of action: usually guided by social conventions defining "rational" cost-benefit considerations (Shaver, 1985; Weiner, 1993). The person will exhibit more or less impulsive or thoughtfully directed behaviors depending upon the relative strengths of the initial emotion-driven imperatives and the cognitive resources available for the subsequent more controlled "sensible" considerations.

The extent to which the person's behavior reflects conventional norms rather than simpler rules of association linking the value of outcomes, actors, and acts (see Heider, 1958) is a rough indicator of whether the automatically generated or thoughtful processes were more influential. Also, the more time that elapses between the instigating event and the person's reaction the greater the probability that thoughtfully controlled processes played a primary, though not necessarily exclusive, role in shaping the response.

Recent findings also suggest that, even when the person's reactions appear rational and conventionally appropriate, the initial emotion automatically elicited by preconscious justice imperatives may persist and without the person's awareness measurably influence their reactions in the next situation (see, e.g., Goldberg, Lerner, & Tetlock, 1999; Lerner, Goldberg, & Tetlock, 1998). For present purposes, it is important to note that if investigators were to ask or even prompt their participants to provide the reasons for their subsequent reactions, since that information is not consciously available or retrievable, they will often cooperate by resorting to best guesses, usually based upon conventional norms (see Haidt, 2001, 2012). As a consequence, directly asking participants in those experiments who were previously aroused by justice imperatives what motivated their subsequent behavior or how much they care about justice, although an increasingly common procedure, will often elicit conventionally acceptable but misleading responses.

With these complexities in mind, there is yet one more task before describing different forms of justice and their distinct justice rules. Given these complexities, how can you reliably know when you are observing the influence of justice on someone's reaction? Are there distinguishing, defining features, signs of a justice-motivated reaction?

I have the impression that the failure to recognize or misidentifications of justice-based reactions are among the most frequent sources of error in the study of how justice appears in people's lives. Some investigators fail to recognize justice-based responses when they appear, at least to me, screamingly evident; whereas, at other times they claim they were studying justice motivated acts when they had merely elicited norm compliant reactions from cooperative participants. Hopefully, those errors can be minimized by providing a more complete description of the social psychological events—indicators—and properties that characterize justice and some of the intrinsically associated experiences, for example, deserving, entitlement, fairness. The importance of this will be more apparent in deciding whether someone's reaction reflects a justice imperative or is actually better understood as the manifestation of some other process (e.g., a self-interested or altruistically motivated act).

How, then, can we recognize justice-based judgments, experiences, reactions? How do they differ from other psychological events, especially other moral imperatives? What are some identifiable rudimentary elements to the social psychology of justice: within the boundaries of the dictionary-based guides, what do justice-injustice based reactions look, act, feel like? Of course, those markers may vary to some extent across different social contexts. Nevertheless, it is worth noting, as a beginning, some of the more pervasive and central ones.

For example, justice judgments and their consequences are identified by the person experiencing a particular kind of imperative: the experience of "ought" linking people and their outcomes including a cognitive-affectively guided obligation, an imperative to maintain or restore justice, where everyone gets what they each deserve and no one is treated unjustly. Although tacitly present in their preconscious, people become aware of the consequences of this imperative only when confronted with the need to make a decision about a course of action. At that point they may experience the imperative to act in a way that does not violate a rule of justice, as well as an imperative, affect-driven obligation, to re-establish justice.

The experienced imperatives, often based upon the assessments of who deserves what from whom in terms of treatment or desired resources, emerge from the overlearned rules of entitlement elicited by the situational context and relevant cues including the personal attributes, and actions of the participants and their relations to one another. Terribly complex? Not really, given the guides derived from culturally imparted and highly assimilated rules as well as scripts derived from familiar forms of early and repeated experiences.

What Characteristics Distinguish Justice Imperatives from Other Moral Imperatives?

There are several recognizable aspects of the justice imperative. In spite of the celebrated scene where everyone cheers when the good-guy finally guns down the bad-guy, under normal circumstances, complying with justice imperatives, including correcting injustices, in the normal course of events, is not considered especially meritorious. Maintaining the rules of justice is expected of everyone: nothing to cheer about! Meeting one's obligations, although typically judged to be appropriate and desirable, does not incur enhanced personal evaluations or special social credit.

The failure to act justly, or correct an injustice, however, will elicit negative evaluations and sanctions. No cheers, if you do, but "boos" or "shame on you," if you don't. Unlike justice imperatives, moral supererogatory injunctions to be virtuous offer the promise of gaining praise and admiration and can be ignored without incurring negative reactions. Although people admire heroes and acts of generosity they do not condemn someone for avoiding obviously costly heroic acts "above and beyond the call of duty" as they pursue more rationally self-interested alternatives (Miller, 1999; Dols et al., 2010).

These differences between the social psychology of justice imperatives and moral supererogatory injunctions, that is, beyond that which is required in our culture, are illustrated in easily available observations. For example, parents who voluntarily allocate the necessary resources to meet their children's needs do not expect praise or admiration. They are doing nothing more than meeting their parental obligations. Failure to do so, however, would invite public condemnations and possibly sanctions. If, however, the parents voluntarily provide the same resources to care for other people's children, that might well be considered a virtuous and praiseworthy act of charity. They would not be condemned, however, if they chose to avoid taking on those additional obligations while caring for their own families. For most people, moral imperatives to be virtuous, generous, and love thy neighbor are experienced as moral ideals, whereas justice imperatives are obligatory.

Other unique aspects of justice imperatives are indirectly recognizable in the ways they appear in Western societies and can provide valuable guides in searching for answers to central questions. A theory of the origins or motivational underpinnings of justice imperatives must be able to account for the fact that no other value, or moral imperative, is as pervasive in people's lives. The imperatives to preserve and restore deserving and entitlements appear as the motivating force in virtually all organized social activities. The status-roles inherent in each social institution specify more or less explicitly the obligations each of the participants must meet, as well as everyone's privileges. Anyone who is culturally conversant recognizes them and enforces their performance with the threat of negative sanctions. All know to a greater or lesser detail the essential obligations, experienced as imperatives—entitlements—of parents—children, husband–wife, brother–sister, teacher–pupil, drivers on the road, manager–employee. In the normal course of events people automatically meet those obligations and expect everyone else to be as compliant and socially responsible. Our society contains extensive formal as well as informal social institutions for detecting and punishing those who fail to meet their obligations or exceed their privileges.

Other more generic statuses and social categories include justice imperatives as obligations and privileges. For example, most people who are culturally conversant can complete the assertions that very human, citizen, man, woman, child is entitled to, deserves, can expect to be treated with roughly the same statements. Some social psychologists distinguish between those justice imperatives associated with how people are obligated to treat one another, for example, with respect, dignity, contempt, from those imperatives concerning the distribution of concrete desired resources. It would seem at first look that there is a natural and easily identifiable distinction between those obligations defining how someone must treat another person, especially how they speak to them, and the allocation of typically desired resources, what they actually take or give them. Recent research however, supporting the insights of earlier exchange theorists, suggests that these are relatively superficial rather than meaningful psychological differences that refer mainly to the acquisition and allocation of symbolic rather than concrete desired resources.

Generally desired concrete (e.g., money), and symbolic resources (e.g., public and self-esteem), are differently packaged but typically substitutable kinds of outcomes that are gained and distributed by following salient rules of deserving (see, esp. Greenberg, 1993). The evidence indicates that people experience and react in the same manner to "procedural" as well as distributive justice imperatives. Although they appear in different forms, procedural as well as distributive justice judgments follow the same rules of deserving and justice: People must get what they are entitled to have, what they deserve (Brockner et al., 1998; Heuer, Blumenthal, Douglas, & Weinblatt, 1999; Sunshine & Heuer, 2002).

Appropriately respectful treatment and social status on the one hand and more concrete resources on the other, symbolic and concrete resources, are equally fungible and interchangeable in arriving at judgments of critical events—undesirable outcomes, injustices. That equivalence is captured in the prototypical experience of an employee's excellent performance being rewarded with a raise in status—a title attached to your name on the door—or public gratitude, rather than with a raise in salary. Similarly, upon receipt of a gift, one is supposed to reciprocate by enhancing the donor's status: "You are so generous and much too kind."

Possibly the least appreciated by social psychologists but most commonly experienced characteristic of justice is its unique status as the dominant value in our secular society. It is the only value that can require the sacrifice of all others. Justice can and all too frequently requires that designated people are deprived of their liberty, pursuit of happiness, even their lives, all in the pursuit and name of justice. Although virtually all societies have sacred values that reign supreme, in our essentially secular society governed by the rule of law, what is deemed to be just cannot be contravened by a religious or sacred mandate.

Rules of justice in the form of justice imperatives also include the power to set limits on and thus modify the cultural truism that people prefer pleasure to pain, and more of a good thing rather than less. The findings generated from the study of relative deprivation suggest that regardless of the magnitude of their share of desired resources people will not be satisfied if they believe they actually "deserve" more, and people can endure and accept the most miserable of circumstances if they believe that is no less than they deserve (see, e.g., Crosby, 1976). A well-documented variant of this phenomenon can be seen in the research showing that getting more than one deserves reliably elicits a measurable degree of discomfort, upset (Adams, 1963; Walster, Walster, & Berscheid, 1978). In one experiment (Markovsky, 1988) the participants' GSR autonomic responses clearly confirmed they were just as distressed by receiving more payment when they were getting less than they deserved, and were most satisfied with the pay they deserved. Not surprisingly, upon questioning, their verbal reports did not reflect their emotional arousal, but, rather followed conventional normative expectations (Miller, 1999): The more money they were given, the greater their reported pleasure. After all, isn't that just common sense: what everyone knows? That is how I am supposed to react?

But now, with these rudimentary guides in mind let's take a closer look at the earlier described complexities and review what we know about the various rules of deserving and entitlement. Up to this point the essence of justice has been defined as people getting what they deserve. So, the next important question becomes: How do people know who deserves what from whom?

Some investigators are impressed by the large number of identifiable rules and the common observation that people often select or even invent a justice rule to justify and support getting what they want. Those observations led them, or possibly appeared to confirm, the commonly held assumption that everyone at all times is trying to maximize their outcomes. From this perspective they reason that justice rules gained social currency as a cultural form because they promised greater benefits for the collectivity (Walster et al, 1978). But given people's basic self-maximizing motivation, they continually need to be controlled by the anticipation of external punishment for violations of the commonly accepted rules and arrangements for them to internalize self-punitive reactions for noncompliance. This might explain why people try to justify their self-benefiting acts by reference to a rule of justice. Given the extent to which the fundamental assumptions underlying these self-maximizing theories of human motivation are supported in our culture they are probably irrefutable, but not unassailable (Miller,1999; Ratner & Miller, 2001).

More elaborate versions of this model propose that rules of justice are derived from people acting rationally to select the most functional rules for generating and allocating particular desired resources (Deutsch, 1975). For example, allocating resources according to performance and merit would encourage effort and productivity and thus would be considered appropriate to economic institutions; whereas, if the goal is to maintain friendly personal relationships it would be better to distribute desired resources equally. And, of course, when valued members are undeveloped or unable to care for themselves it would be most sensible to follow a justice based on meeting needs rather than allocating according to performance or equality. There is even a well-recognized and often employed rule of justice that appears under conditions of scarce or indivisible but highly desired resources. Under those circumstances, since no one has a greater prior claim, it makes sense for all eligible members to act on behalf of their own justified self-interest. As long as they do not harm the other participants and they are entitled to any acquired benefits (Lerner, Miller, & Holmes, 1976).

A more recent effort emphasizes the importance of the resources at issue and tries to derive the applicable justice rules from the nature of those resources (Skitka, Aramavitch, Lytle, & Sargis, 2009). For example, the importance of interpersonal relationships among a collection of highly interdependent people would seem to enhance everyone's concern with status and reputation. Their interdependence would lead to their focusing upon rules of treatment, that is, procedures that protect or enhance one's status. Institutionalized rules governing the exchange of concrete resources, money, and tangible goods would represent the activities involved in the production of those resources. As a consequence, the relative value of the members' efforts and investments would determine a fair exchange, with less concern for the interpersonal treatment and social status. And some justice rules appear as "moral" mandates governing both interpersonal treatment and resources.

In essence, however, all these theories and many similar others are based upon a fundamental error: They portray justice rules as instrumental devices generated by collective wisdom to meet some common goal. Even though they each offer an intuitively appealing explanation, they do not recognize nor can they account for the unique characteristics of justice imperatives. Contrary to viewing justice motivation as a social or personal device to meet some other goal, a compelling theory must encompass or at least appear compatible with justice imperative's functional role in all social institutions and as the supreme secular value.

In addition, but not nearly as critical, attempts to generate additional supporting evidence have been relatively unpersuasive. For example, it is one thing to point to the relative prevalence of equity- and merit-based norms governing many commercial encounters, but the recognition that equal allocation of jointly produced outcomes can be effective in some circumstances raises serious questions about the assumed instrumental causal processes. Similarly, although allocating resources to meet someone's needs rather than merit is common among family members, it also appears in the way people automatically empathize with and commonly react to a stranger's suffering or deprivation.

Origins of Justice Motivation: Plausible and Falsifiable Theories?

If we recognize that justice has a uniquely important and pervasive presence in human affairs, where does it come from? What are its social psychological origins including the various ways it appears in people's lives? An adequate explanation, of course, must be consistent with its pervasiveness and unique importance. Although they make for intriguing stories and speculation, I am convinced it is not necessary or even helpful to look for usable answers in the studies of infra-human behavior (see, e.g., Brosnan & De Waal, 2003), or informed and elaborate speculations about human social and biological evolution (Haidt, 2012). I believe evolution has occurred and we all are born with the resultant evolution-shaped genetically programmed determinants of behavior. Having said that, I find no less need for, nor theory-informed short-cuts to, a satisfactory description of the developmental origins and consequences of contemporary human motivation to seek and maintain justice.

Of course, evolutionary processes generated human concerns with justice, but what does that tell us about how those concerns emerge in the human developmental processes and what forms they take in the process? Evidence that baboons may appear to be disturbed by another baboon not getting what would appear to be its fair share, helps me understand what about how humans develop a commitment to justice? That there is a genetic component in justice motivation, some of which is shared with infra human organisms, is neither surprising nor illuminating.

Fortunately, it is possible to extrapolate from what we already know about human development and cognitive processes to generate compelling answers to those questions. The explanation offered here begins with the development of the "personal contract," and includes the conversion of familiar repeated earlier experiences into preconscious imperatives.

These answers, unlike the evolutionary explanations, are amenable to further elaboration and test by additional research with contemporary humans.

The Emergence of the Personal Contract

Human behavior appears to be driven initially by direct attempts at immediate gratifications, attributable to biological needs, with little if any planned efforts at impulse-control. Those impulses become transformed in to a personal contract by the inherited rapidly developing abilities to perceive similarities and differences, remember sequences of acts and outcomes, and to recall and represent multiple sequences. If they live in a relatively stable benign environment, children will develop a commitment to deserving and justice. Here is more about how that occurs.

Beginning at an early stage of development, children gain the cognitive skills to recognize the availability of alternative courses of action to replace impulsive efforts at direct gratification and evaluate the relative desirability of their outcomes. That recognition emerging from rapidly developing cognitive resources enables gratification seeking children to recognize and choose among alternative ways of satisfying their salient wants. Some available courses of action require greater efforts with longer periods of self-deprivation. Typically those alternatives promise commensurately greater rewards. Initially, instinctively, however, the child wants immediate gratification.

The crucial developmental task, then, for the gratification and pain-avoidant dominated child is to control those initial impulses and accept self-imposed deprivation in order to pursue the behavioral alternative that promises the larger rewards. The child's early cognitive executive functions (reflection, evaluation, choice) emerge out of the memory and evaluative comparison of alternative act-outcome sequences, with greater costs typically required for more desirable outcomes. The implementation of the alternative that promises the most gratifying outcomes is dependent upon the child's ability to control the inherited impulses for immediate gratification and accept the self-imposed periods of relatively painful deprivation.

Considerable research has examined the determinants as well as interesting short- and long-term consequences of young chldren's ability or willingness to delay gratification (see, e.g., Mischel, 1961; Mischel, Shoda, & Peake, 1988). That research fits very nicely with the theory of the personal contract: an essentially metaphorical description of how children are able and willing to delay and replace immediately gratifying their desires with goal-directed activities. Children's commitment to deserving and justice begins when they develop the cognitive abilities that enable them to engage in the relatively complex process of decision-making.

The emerging executive cognitive processes enable children to accomplish the crucial task of quieting, if not entirely controlling, their initial impulses for immediate gratification, which can hypothetically be represented as an internal dialogue: Children promise themselves that the self-deprivation and relatively costly efforts will ultimately lead to greater gratification. It is as if children generate a contract between the part of themselves that wants immediate gratification and the more rational but equally gratification-seeking parts; the terms of that personal contract promise that the greater desirability of the ultimate outcomes will be worth the required self-deprivation and relatively costly efforts.

Do most children actually develop something like a personal contract? Certainly, when describing their feelings about their outcomes, their complaints or satisfactions will often refer to what most adults would describe as deserving or their specific entitlements. The degree and kind of expressed affect appears to roughly correspond to their evaluation of the outcomes involved: A comparison of the promised and the actual: "That's not fair!!"

Early on, children recognize the crucial importance of the value of the attained outcome being commensurate with the prior self-imposed deprivation and costs. By virtue of their self-denial and efforts they feel they deserve and are entitled to the promised outcomes. If, whenever, that fails to occur, it threatens the viability of the personal contract and jeopardizes their ability to engage in future activities that require a delay of gratification.

There are good reasons to believe that the impulses for immediate gratification among humans are never fully eliminated or even tamed; nevertheless, children increasingly recognize the greater value of long-term goals. Initially, then, a major task of the developing executive processes consists of controlling and possibly guiding those impulses by sufficient successful completions of personal contracts. Eventually most people appear persuaded that "most of the time, and in most part, I can and will get what I deserve." How does this happen?

Because children, as well as adults, are inevitably confronted with failures and disappointments, if possible, most find ways to frame those experiences so that they retain sufficient confidence in the success and resultant value of planned long-term efforts. Nevertheless, in the normal course of their arriving at adulthood, children have had to engage in increasingly longer periods of delayed gratification and more costly long-term efforts in their pursuit of greater outcomes, and inevitably, at times, to greater failed expectations. As a consequence, most people must reinforce their valuable personal contracts with a binding virtually inviolable commitment to the process and consequences of deserving. That commitment guides how they pursue and evaluate their desired outcomes as well as structure their relations with one another. The emotional vulnerability to other people not getting what they deserve may be attributed to an automatic empathic attachment: They vicariously share the other's experiences. And their concern for justice for others may be the result of experiences reinforced by the assumption that their ability to gain deserved outcomes is dependent upon the shared social and physical environments. I am vulnerable to the same injustices as others in my world.

Although the commitment to deserving and justice becomes the central theme in their lives, for understandable reasons, it does not become an unassailable assumption. As a consequence most people develop habitual ways of deflecting or neutralizing information that threat the viability of their commitment. The evidence presented in subsequent sections will illustrate some of those defensive reactions (see also, Lerner, 1980).

Research Linking the Presence and Function of the Personal Contract to Justice Motivation

I realize that given the clumsy writing and the reliance on imprecise metaphorical concepts, the theory presented here, at best, may seem to be somewhat plausible conjectures. However, before rejecting it entirely, consider some of the available evidence. If not fully persuaded, you should be impressed with the creativity and ingenuity of the young investigators' experiments concerning the appearance and consequences of the "personal contract" in people's lives. I will go into considerable detail in describing the earliest experiments that examined the personal contract origins of the commitment to deserving and justice.

One investigator adapted an easily administered instrument that appeared to generate a reliable measure of the extent to which a child was willing to delay immediate gratification (DG) for a larger, greater payoff. The design of the experiment assumed, with some supporting evidence, that children's willingness to DG increased with age but with considerable variation among children of roughly the same age, depending upon their differing developmental history. Also, if, as the theory proposes, children need to be willing to DG in order to deserve their desired outcomes, then it should be possible to demonstrate that proposed connection between their measured DG and commitment to deserving. Assuming that there is a way of measuring the extent of that commitment, along with the child's level of DG, the operative hypothesis becomes more interesting, even brave. Previous investigations with the measure of DG had concluded that greater DG was associated with a willingness to engage in socially approved even altruistic behaviors (Mischel, 1961). Fortunately, as illustrated in some of the experiments, deserving-guided behaviors in some instances can be distinguished, for example, from altruistic acts.

Gary Long (Long & Lerner, 1974) generated the rather elaborate procedure and conducted the experiment to test the hypothesis: the greater children's DG, the greater their responsiveness to issues of deserving. That was a brave decision, given that the major investigator of children's delay of gratification had emphasized the role of situational factors as the major determinant of whether a child chose a prize of lesser value rather than wait for the considerably more valuable prize to be delivered later (Mischel, 1961). In fact, at that time, those investigators greatly doubted whether the willingness to delay gratification was transferrable across situations. But, the personal contract theory promised otherwise, and so he designed an experiment requiring two purportedly unrelated sessions that seemed appropriate for fourth-grade children.

In the first session, the children were recruited to test a toy that was to be marketed. They were each brought to a trailer where they played and evaluated the desirability of a rather enjoyable bowling game, after which, all the children were given a packet containing 70 cents (7 dimes). The experimenter, however, instructed half the children that the money in their pay packet had been prepackaged payment for older more qualified children. Those instructions mimicked a procedure that, in previous research, had effectively led adult employees to feel undeserving of their overpayment (Adams, 1963). The other half was led to believe that the 70 cents in their envelope was the appropriate pay for testing the game: They deserved the 70 cents.

After the children received their envelopes they were told of the opportunity to donate any part of their pay to a charity that buys toys for poor orphan children, and shown a box with an opening for any donations. Some children were led to believe that there was an audience, (e.g., experimenter and/or teacher) who would become aware of whether and how much they donated. Other children believed that no one could know if or how much, they donated: The experimenter left the room and instructed the children to return to their classrooms on their own.

So what influenced the children's donations: Whether or not they were assured of their donation was a private or public act; or, when they believe they had been properly paid or overpaid and thus did not deserve their pay? Before answering, there is another factor you might want to consider. Several weeks subsequent to the first task, a different, actually female, experimenter conducted a procedure to measure each child's willingness to delay gratification for later greater rewards in their classrooms. She offered all the children a series of things that children like. She gave them a series of choices between a smaller prize that they could keep and a similar but much more valuable one to be delivered next week or, at least, so promised. To add credibility to the task, although they were required to make several choices, they actually could and did get one that they chose. For the purpose of analysis, the children were subsequently classified as either high or low DG, depending on whether they were above or below the median on the proportion of their long-term versus immediate choices.

Now, what is your guess concerning the factors that influenced the children's donations? Did they depend on whether an audience was salient versus their acting privately; or, whether they had been properly or overpaid (i.e., they did or did not deserve all their pay). Or, were the sizes of their donations to the charity in the first situation predictable from their classification in a completely different context, as either relatively high or low in choices to delayed gratification versus immediate gratification?

The results (see Long & Lerner, 1974) revealed that the children who believed they had been overpaid, and in a separate session had exhibited greater preference for the larger but delayed rewards, donated much more to the poor orphan children than the other children. The children who believed they deserved all their pay kept most of it for themselves, regardless of whether they believed it was a private or public act or they had been classified as high or low DG. Mainly, the pay was the fulfillment of a personal contract with themselves. They deserved it. Similarly confirming the role of deserving, the appropriately paid high DG children who believed they deserved all their pay actually donated relatively little regardless of whether others would know how much they had donated: They had earned, deserved, that pay and they intended to keep it.

To a remarkable extent, the findings fit nicely with the personal contract theory of how and why people care about deserving and justice, especially how the willingness to DG allows the commitment to deserving to emerge. The children who exhibited greater willingness to delay gratifying their desires were also more likely keep pay they deserved and donate pay they did not deserve to deprived children, regardless of whether they believed authority figures would know of their behavior. That is exactly what the personal contract theory predicts: their willingness to delay gratification was associated with their sensitivity to and responsiveness to deserving their desired outcomes.

But does that mean that high DG children are not responsive to maintaining justice-what other people deserve? Shortly after that encouraging experiment, Janine Braband (Braband & Lerner, 1975) conducted an experiment with similarly aged children and the same measure of children's willingness to delay gratification. She examined the children's reaction to the deservingness of others as a function of their own willingness to delay gratification. Would children's willingness to delay gratification predict their responsiveness to the deservingness of another child's request for help?

Her participants were performing a moderately pleasant task for a teacher when they were confronted with the opportunity to help a student, not from their class, who desperately needed help making sufficient copies of an important exam. All the children were told that the student needed help making copies because his copy machine had been broken. Half of them were led to believe that the breakage was the result of an unavoidable accident (an innocent victim). The other half learned that the student's carelessness had broken the machine (a culpable victim). The main dependent variable was how much work the children volunteered to help the student in need.

The main finding of interest supported the theory's predicted relationship between the willingness to delay gratification with their commitment to deserving and justice. In this experiment the critical event was whether the student needing the help was an innocent victim of circumstances beyond his control and thus deserved help. Overall, as expected, the children offered considerably less help to the victim of his own carelessness. However, the children designated as high DG, by virtue of their having previously scored above the median for the class on the measure of DG, did remarkably more work for the innocent victim. Their behavior reflected the judgment that he deserved their help.

These two experiments increased our confidence in the important, if not crucial, role of children's personal contract on their commitment to deserving in their own lives and justice for others. It was not until many years later that equally persuasive evidence appeared.

More Recent Research on the Dynamics Associated with Personal Contracts

Carolyn Hafer (2000b) designed an experiment to address the important hypothesis that people's ability to maintain their personal contracts required their confidence in the greater profitability of giving up immediate gratifications (deferring gratification) in order to pursue and acquire later greater outcomes, that is, confidence that they could and would get what they deserved. In other words, the extent of their commitment to and concern with deserving and justice at any given time is dependent on their confidence in the promised fulfillment of their costly investments in future outcomes. If that is true, then witnessing other people similar to them fail to get what they deserve, especially when inflicted with undeserved suffering, could pose a threat to their confidence in the value and thus viability of their own personal contracts. Their subsequent attempts to reduce or counter that threat could appear as measurable increases in their efforts to generate or find evidence that victims, especially those similar to themselves, actually do get what they deserve.

She designed several experiments to gather evidence that could speak to those predictions. One creatively constructed experiment relied on the reasonable assumption that most university students were required to give up considerable immediately gratifying activities as well as invest considerable and ongoing financial costs and efforts in order to arrive at their highly desired future goals. Also, in the normal course of events for most students, all those incurred costs, invested efforts, and promised outcomes, were tucked away in their preconscious as they met the immediately compelling demands of their studies and daily activities. But, presumably, they could be reactivated and made salient by the right cues.

That expectation led her to design a simple procedure that required some participants to recall and think about the futures they were anticipating what they expected their lives would be like after graduation as well as 1, 5, and 10 years later. She hoped this procedure would make the terms of their personal contract salient, that is, that they would recognize that they had promised themselves certain more desirable outcomes that would compensate them for the current costs as well as the past and future investments they were making. Those students as well as others who, instead, had been asked to describe some of their daily activities with no mention of their future expectations, then became participants in a study of counselor client relations.

That was the context in which they were shown a videotape of a highly distressed female student describing her terrible fate to a counselor: her suffering was elicited by a recently acquired STD (sexually transmitted disease). The extent of the victim's apparent deserving of her fate was varied by having some of the participants believe that she had acquired the STD after having unprotected sex with a relative stranger. The other participants learned that a condom had accidentally broken while she was having sex with someone with whom she had a close relationship. Subsequently, all the participants as part of the client-counselor study completed measures of their evaluation of the victim, the extent of her blame and responsibility for her present condition, as well the extent they felt similar to and empathically involved with her.

The ratings of the students, whose long-term investments had not been made salient, followed conventional moral norms. They rated the innocent victim in much more positive sympathetic terms than the victim whose own carelessness caused her to suffer.

Those participants whose costs and long-term investments had been made salient for them, however, portrayed the relatively innocent victim as negatively and blameworthy as the careless victim, while psychologically distancing of themselves from her. That was the pattern of responses that would be expected, if the innocent victim's undeserved suffering had threatened the students' confidence in their own now salient important future investments. Consistent with the personal contract theory, both the salience of the students' future investments and the victim's relative innocence were critical to the students' reactions to the innocent victim closely resembling the clearly more culpable victim of her own carelessness. As expected, the threat to their personal contract caused by the innocent students' undeserved suffering led them to search for or invent ways of perceiving the victim and their relation to her. They saw her as a rather undesirable person, more blameworthy, and thus deserving of her suffering. And besides, "I am not vulnerable to the same kind of undeserved suffering: we are rather different people living in a different world."

Mitch Callan and his colleagues (Callan et al., 2013b) further explored the role of the personal contract in experiments where they varied the salience of the person's investment in future outcomes. They examined the role of investing in long-term goals on participants' motivation to find a correspondence between someone's merit and the desirability of their outcomes, what they deserve. In one experiment, they elicited script-based automatic associations between people's merit and their outcomes, and then demonstrated how those associations would be enhanced by activating the salience of their own personal contracts.

The participants reacted to an apparently real news story involving the victim of a freak accident, a tree falling on his automobile. The story also portrayed the victim as having committed either a relatively immoral (cheating on his wife) or moral act prior to the accident. As in earlier research, the participants rated the immoral victim's prior acts as making a greater contribution to their accident and their greater deserving of their suffering, than to the moral victim's prior acts. Of greater theoretical importance, the linking of the victim's suffering to his prior immoral act, was greatly enhanced when the participants had just previously focused on their own long term plans, the next 1–15 years.

Callan, Kay, Davidenko, & Ellard (2009) generated additional evidence linking the willingness to delay gratification and the person's commitment to deserving and justice. In one experiment with adults they employed the procedure that previous research had shown to persuasively elicit the perception of an innocent suffering victim or an equally suffering but personally culpable victim of an HIV infection (e.g., see Hafer, 2000b, earlier).

Adult participants who had been previously exposed to the suffering innocent victim were subsequently less willing to defer the opportunity for an immediate reward in order to receive a much larger one in 90 days than those participants who believed the victim had caused her own suffering. Apparently, not only is the willingness to delay gratification essential to the development of a commitment to deserving and justice, but compelling evidence of this process is revealed in the finding that the awareness of an injustice can temporarily, at least, reduce the person's willingness to delay immediate gratifications, at least in the next immediate situation. Confidence in that important finding was enhanced by additional analyses that ruled out the possibility that the reduced willingness to delay gratification effects elicited by the awareness of the innocent victims' continued suffering could not be attributed to a simple change in mood rather than the greater injustice.

Although fully committed to deserving and justice, it is not entirely surprising that adults continue to be vulnerable, at times, to the discouraging effects of failing to get what they believe they deserve, or the awareness of terrible injustices inflicted on others. If sufficiently intense or chronic, those experiences can lead to at least temporarily debilitating demoralization. Typically, however, they are relatively transient effects, but when people can not restore sufficient confidence in their personal contracts, they may become demoralized to the point where they act upon the conclusion, "It is not worth it," and, at least, fantasize about giving it all up to go off to Tahiti. Sociologists (e.g., Robert Merton, 1957) have described the ways Americans react in those times when it becomes apparent that the culturally prescribed means and activities do not reliably eventuate in the promised culturally desired outcomes.

The Justice Motive in People's Lives: A Tentative Statement and Some Evidence of the Preconscious Processes

What we can say, at this point, is that most people, most of the time, develop a commitment to living by deserving and justice. Fortunately, the theoretical conjectures about the origins and consequences of that commitment generated eminently testable hypotheses concerning how they influence people's lives.

1. The association of the value of peoples outcomes with the what they deserve, beginning in early childhood, becomes a preconscious assumption reinforced by their motivational commitment, which automatically influences the way they perceive, evaluate, and remember events.
2. People are motivated to believe that everyone's outcomes reflect the value of their efforts and/or personal qualities. Eventually this motivation yields automatic linking of people's outcomes and their merit, so that good (bad) things should (and do) happen to good(bad) people; bad (good) outcomes are caused by bad(good) people, acts.
3. In addition and typically in conjunction with those automatic associations, people experience and are strongly influenced by emotion-directed imperatives to maintain and re-establish justice: Everyone gets what they are entitled to.

Mitch Callan and his colleagues (Callan, Ellard, & Nicol, 2006; Callan, Kay, Davidenko, & Ellard, 2009; Callan, Shead, & Olson, 2009; Callan, Sutton, & Dovale, 2010; Callan, Harvey, Dawtry, & Sutton, 2013b) conducted a series of experiments to examine the automatic and motivated preconscious processes linking people's deserving and their fates. Knowing either the person's merit or fate leads people to assume and create the deserving link to the other: the more aroused their commitment to deserving and justice, and the less the intrusion of conscious controlled processes, the stronger the association. In several experiments, Callan et al. presented participants with news articles that described a victim of an automobile accident, or the winner of a lottery together with information that portrayed the target person (victim or winner) as either a morally desirable or rather reprehensible person. Participants' ratings of what they had read indicated that they thought the victim's prior moral transgressions contributed to the accident and their judgments of his deserving of the accident mediated their attributions of responsibility. The lottery winner's personal worth influenced the participants subsequent memory of the size of their winnings: The more morally desirable the person, the larger the amount they recalled.

These and similar effects were enhanced among the participants who had previously watched a video of a young relatively innocent victim of an STD whose suffering would continue versus the same victim whose suffering had ended and who had recovered. Prior research had demonstrated that the victim of continuing suffering elicited a preconscious but measurable concern with issues of deserving and justice.

In an ingenious experiment using eye-tracking methodology Callan, Ferguson, & Bindemann (2013a) showed that when participants were confronted with someone who had behaved either badly or in morally desirable ways, their eye movements showed that they were expecting further information to reveal a corresponding either bad or good outcome (i.e., what the target person deserved).

These findings were not limited to the influence of deserving on the way people perceive and remember what happens to others. Participants in one experiment (Callan et al., 2009a) by chance either won or lost a desirable outcome and then they were asked to recall the good and bad deeds they had done in the recent past. The accidental winners tended to remember more good outcomes than bad and the reverse was true for the accidental losers; that is, they tended to construe their present (good/bad) fate as relatively appropriate for their past (good/bad) behavior. Similarly, those who were randomly assigned to remember recent past good deeds or bad past deeds were influenced in how they subsequently evaluated the fairness of being assigned an undesirable outcome. Those whose recent past deeds were salient judged their present undesirable fate to be more fairly determined. They deserved the bad luck. In yet another experiment (Callan, under review), employing a different accident victim who had been previously engaged in moral or immoral behavior, the participants attributed greater responsibility for the accident to the immoral victim's prior acts. That effect was measurably reduced if the participants also learned that the immoral victim had been additionally victimized prior to her accident. In yet another experiment (Callan et al., 2009b) these effects were enhanced by the participants prior focusing on their long-term goals, thus increasing their motivation to believe that people get what they deserve.

Callan, Sutton, & Dovale (2010) also show that, consistent with an automatic preconscious process, reducing the opportunity for participants to consciously reflect on their reaction increases their association of victim's personal worth with their prior immoral behavior.

Additional, somewhat-enduring effects can be attributable to the influence of the preconscious processing of the theme of injustice–justice. Goldberg, Lerner, & Tetlock (1999) employed a very arousing videotape of an adult bully humiliating and beating up a vulnerable teenager. Their findings confirmed earlier evidence indicating that the videotape elicited considerable anger among the viewers (J. Lerner et al, 1998; Gross & Levenson, 1995). In this experiment, some of the viewers were led to believe prior to viewing the tape that the bully had been caught and severely punished by the courts—justice had been done—whereas others were led to believe he got off with no punishment. Subsequently, all participants were asked to recommend the punishment of someone who had, through greater or lesser degrees of negligence, caused harm to others.

As expected, from previous research (Lerner, J. et al., 1998) there were no differences in the amount of anger reported by the participants in the two previous conditions. If, however, the participants' believed the bully in the videotape had been released with no punishment, their initial anger determined the degree of punishment they recommended for the negligent harm-doers. That was not the case, however, among those participants who believed justice, at least relatively speaking, had been done to the bully. Their previously aroused anger did not lead to more severe punishment for the "next" harm-doers. Instead their recommendations seemed to follow from conventional rules for assigning culpability for harm.

In addition to the justice-related scripts and processes, what can we conjecture, about additional scripted processes in the preconscious that may be elicited, automatically? There are probably many of varied complexity derived from overlearned representations of the cultural norms, values, and mores including moral evaluations of relative good–bad, right–wrong, and desirability often linking categories of people, behavior sequences, interactions, and outcomes. They appear in probably more complex forms in the subsequent conscious-controlled processing of information that with some notable exceptions (e.g., heuristics) follow conventional norms. These include information processing, social preferences, causal inferences and evaluations as well as morality, from which some of the automatic scripted responses were derived (Shaver, 1985; Weiner, 1993).

Confusing the Preconscious Assumption that I Am/We Are Better More Worthy with Evidence of Self-Serving Motives

In addition to the scripted contents of the automatic preconscious that elicit justice imperatives, it is possible to detect the influence of at least one other rather ubiquitous script that has been misunderstood as motivated efforts to engage in self-enhancing or self-serving behavior.

It is most evident when people's reactions seem to reveal the assumption that they and people like them are more worthy of merit, more moral than others: "I/we, are the good guys." It is as if they have the unrecognized or at least unarticulated sense of being relatively superior, a kind of conceit. When that assumption becomes salient, it influences the attention to and processing of new information in a thematically consistent, that is, conceited, manner. As a consequence of this biased processing of information, their subsequent behavior may at times appear to be self-enhancing or self-serving, but, in actuality, the consequences are just as often self-defeating or deflating. Their subsequent reactions, however, were not designed nor intended to accomplish any self-enhancing instrumental goals, but rather were based upon unintentionally biased automatic assessments of their relative merit (Lerner & Clayton, 2011).

Several well-cited experiments provide examples where the effects of this self-conceited script had been misattributed to self-serving or self-enhancing motives. Stilwell and Baumeister (1997) had their participants read a rather detailed description of someone exploiting and harming another person of the same age. Prior to reading the story, they were told to imagine they were either the person who inflicted the harm or the victim. Subsequently, after a brief interlude, they were asked to describe the details of what they had read, and then rate both the harmful behaviors and the victim's reactions.

As expected, their prior instructions had rather remarkable dramatic effects on what the participants recalled. Depending upon whom they were told to identity with they reported more or fewer incidents of harm, some of which were invented, whereas others were forgotten, and the ratings of greater or lesser severity of the harm inflicted were tailored to be more or less flattering to either the inflictor or victim. Did Stilwell and Baumeister (1997) demonstrate systematically biased portrayals of the harm-doer and victims? Yes, of course, but did those biased portrayals reveal self-serving, self-enhancing motives? Their responses added up to more or less flattering portrayals, but what did those biased portrayals actually enhance, and what ends did they serve?

In answering that, consider that neither the participants nor the actors were identifiable or accountable to the experimenters, nor anyone else, so what could the participants have possibly had to gain or protect by systematically distorting their portrayals? And, in fact, when their experimenters reminded and explicitly requested some participants to be as accurate as possible in their responses, their "accurate" recall did not eliminate the biased representations. Rather, it would appear that the participants did not realize that their immediate recall had been previously biased in their preconscious, encoding of what they were reading.

A similar analysis and questions apply to the research described by Messick and Sentis (1983). In a carefully constructed set of conditions, they asked their respondents several questions about the hypothetical allocations of pay to themselves and another worker who provided various amounts of work and productivity. Of most importance is their repeated finding that the participants' ratings of fair pay allocated considerably more to themselves than to a comparably contributing other worker. These allocations were systematically biased in favor of the self, but, as in the previous research, there appears to be no self-serving or enhancing effects involved. Since these were essentially anonymous responses to explicitly brief simulations, vignettes, with no implicit or explicit consequences, the most likely explanation for those biased allocations is that the participants were expressing their objective opinions based on their accurate assessments of the workers' relative merits. Their preconscious assessments of contributions included the biased assessments of their relative contributions, effort, productivity, and so forth, thus generating the biased allocations of their relative fair pay.

I first became aware of the possible ubiquitous existence of conceited scripts after reading another report by Messick and Sentis (1983). Using their procedure in several classroom demonstrations I would ask the students to take out a blank sheet of paper and write down all the things that people do that are fair (or unfair). If you do them more than others, begin the sentence with "I," if others do them more than you begin the sentence with "They." After the allotted period of time, I would ask them to stop and simply add up the number of I's and they's on their pages. I would then go around the room and write the numbers reported by each of the students on the blackboard.

Much to the students' surprise when describing fair things, the number of I's was remarkably larger than the they's; however an equally great discrepancy between I's and they's was reversed when they listed all the unfair things they could recall. It is possible to speculate about the possible causes of those reported great discrepancies, but a few inferences are fairly clear: they could reflect the preconscious assessments of their own moral worth versus the moral worth of other persons There is recently reported evidence suggesting that people do not have self-flattering scripts concerning all socially desired abilities and behaviors; rather, they appear with reference to more common social behaviors, especially those involving morality (Moore, 2007).

What about the evidence of people engaging in self-serving or self-enhancing behaviors? Even more to the point: Is there any evidence confirming the distinction between automatic preconscious script-based (conceit) biasing of information rather than a self-serving motivated distortion and biasing? An experiment by Babcock, and her colleagues (Babcock, Loewenstein, Issacharoff, & Camerer, 1995) most clearly addressed the hypothesis that automatic preconscious biasing of information to be consistent with an "I am/we are better, more moral" script leads to behavior that may appear self-serving, self-enhancing.

They assigned participants to the role of attorneys for either the plaintiff or defendant in actual damages for negligence suit that had been previously adjudicated and an award allocated. The participants were given a rather complete description of the evidence presented to the court, and then asked to evaluate the importance of the various details each side presented to support its case, and also provide an estimate of the amount the judge awarded the plaintiff. Obviously, those ratings described their assessments of the relative merits of the case for the plaintiff and the defendant.

The participants then engaged in up to five controlled brief "negotiations" (exchange of settlement offers) with the participant-attorney for the other side in order to arrive at an agreed upon settlement. Prior to the negotiations they learned that their pay for participating would be greater or lesser depending on the value of the settlement for their "clients," but mainly the number of sessions it took to reach an agreement including an added penalty if they failed to agree after the allotted five tries.

The most important feature of this experiment for our purposes is the time when the participants were given the detailed description of the evidence presented during the actual trial. *Did they familiarize themselves with this evidence before or after they learned whom they would be representing in the negotiations: the plaintiff or the defendant?* That difference in timing generated rather dramatic differences in their prenegotiation ratings of the evidence and their estimates of what the previous judge had actually awarded, as well as the success of their subsequent negotiations.

You may have guessed that the participants who knew which side they would represent prior to reading the detailed description gave systematically biased assessments of the value of the evidence for their side, and similarly self-favoring assessments of what the judge's actual award had been. Not surprisingly, then, with opposing attorneys having more extreme self-favoring views of the merits of their cases, their negotiations went much worse: with each side seemingly having more extreme demands resulting in greater losses of money for both. Those losses were predictable from the size of their previously assessed biased ratings of the evidence. The participant-attorneys who learned of their assignments after reading and forming their views of the evidence in the case, although similarly motivated to gain the most for their clients and themselves, approached the negotiations with a much more realistic view of the merits of their cases, and this was reflected in their subsequent relatively successful negotiations.

It is important to note that all the participants had equally good reason to arrive at a realistic assessment of the evidence in the case in order to engage in the most effective and efficient and thus self-profiting negotiations. Since the participants who had read the evidence prior to learning whether they would be advocating for the plaintiff or defendant did in fact arrive at relatively objective evaluations of the evidence, including the judge's award, the systematic biasing of the evidence must have occurred while the participants, who knew which side they would be representing, were reading the details of the case. And, it must have occurred without their awareness; otherwise, they would have adjusted their assessments to arrive at negotiations that were no less successful than the relatively unbiased participants who had read the details of the case without knowing whom they would represent.

What seems to have been the operative influence shaping the biased assessments was the biased processing of what they were reading to be consistent with the assumption that they and their clients were better, more worthy, than their opposition. That automatic processing resulted in their becoming convinced of the greater merits of their case and thus the likelihood of prevailing in the negotiations. The authors concluded that the reason the biased participants could not arrive at agreements is because they each believed their own demands were just and should prevail, *not* because of their desire to maximize their outcomes.

Everyone who has taken a course in social psychology almost certainly was exposed to the classic study by Hastorf and Cantril (1954), "They saw a game." In that study, though responding to the same game, students' gave symmetrically biased reports of the fouls committed by their own or the opposing team in a hotly contested and penalty-ridden football game. It has been commonly recognized that these biased reports enabled the students' to maintain the image of their team as relatively moral and the opposing team as evil. Whatever led to those systematically biased reports of the same game, it is quite conceivable that the students would deny both having any self-serving motivation or a biased image of what had occurred. They would probably claim they were honestly reporting the objective facts concerning what had happened in that game. The previously cited research suggests that although their portrayal of what they observed clearly reflects a self-serving bias, they were unaware aware that their assessment of the relevant facts had been biased. The biasing may have occurred in their preconscious processing of the information to comply with their unrecognized assumption that they and their team were better and thus more worthy than others. Is this always the case when people appear to be self-serving? Possibly not, but it is certainly more frequent among research participants and in the normal course of events than has been recognized.

The Appearance and Integration of Justice Motivation in Our Two Rather Distinct Cognitive-Affective Processes

Having laid out a rudimentary description of what happens in their preconscious when people are confronted with a consequential event, it is time to consider how those automatic initial reactions interact with their subsequent conventional norms and controlled thought processes (Lerner, 2001).

There is one set of experiments that illustrates the importance of distinguishing between those processes that are automatically initiated in the preconscious before being expressed in behavior, and the subsequent influence, often over-riding, of consciously controlled essentially norm-driven considerations. Bazerman, White, & Loewenstein (1995) provided clear comparisons of the relatively direct expression of the initial automatic processes and the influence of subsequent controlled processing.

Using very simple vignettes, their participants, for example, rated their satisfaction with a fair distribution (hypothetically) $400 for self and $400 for the other party greater than their satisfaction with $500 for the self and $700 for the other party. However, when they asked their participants to simultaneously consider both possibilities and choose the one they preferred, the preferences were reversed. In their comparative judgments contrary to their singular statements of satisfaction, significantly more chose the 500–700 alternatives over the 400–400. Apparently, when considering both sets of alternatives they were more influenced by the greater pay for themselves than the fairness of the distribution. What might account for that shift in preference?

When they asked graduate students to rate their satisfaction with a job offer after their MBA of $75,000 when the usual offer was $75,000 and, similarly, their satisfaction with an offer of $85,000 while others were offered $95,000. When rated separately, the fairer but lesser offer elicited greater satisfaction ratings. However, given a choice between the former option or the latter, that is, the greater though less-fair pay, again, the preferences were reversed. In arriving at a choice upon direct comparison, the second offer was preferred to the fairer but lesser offer.

Moving beyond the hypothetical, they demonstrated similar effects by offering students $7 to participate in an experiment while paying others $7; or $8 while paying others $10. The lesser but fair pay elicited significantly greater acceptance than the greater but unfair pay. When, however, given simultaneous choice between the two alternatives, their preferences were reversed, reflecting greater preference for the unfair but larger pay.

Apparently, the more complex task of choosing between two sets of alternatives required more thoughtful processing. To make a decision they had to reflect on and weigh the relative benefits and costs of both sets of alternatives. In this manner, the initial more automatic fairness-based response was replaced with the more thoughtfully arrived at norm-appropriate response of enlightened self-interest (see Miller, 1999; Ratner & Miller, 2001). Thoughtful controlled processing typically reflects conventional norms.

We have seen considerable evidence that individuals' reactions to important events are automatically generated by the scripts in our preconscious that are vigilant to signs of justice and injustice (Aguiar et al., 2008; Correia et al., 2007; Hafer, 2000a). However, prior to their expression, those reactions are often modified by more thoughtful controlled processing to be consistent with conventional norms (see, e.g., Markovsky,1988). Armed with that information, it is possible to understand two rather prevalent kinds of errors that have appeared in contemporary investigations.

We can now better understand, for example, how the research methods commonly employed by contemporary investigators may generate erroneous inferences about the influence of self-interest and justice imperatives. In the normal courses of events, people's reactions are often generated by their automatic preconscious scripts and emotions with minimal influence of the conventional norms introduced by the requirement to engage in more thoughtful controlled processing and decision-making. The research cited earlier demonstrates the importance of those justice-based scripts and motives in people's automatic reactions.

The prototypical investigation, however, involves assessing participants' reactions while role-playing in a simulation or to hypothetical events and/or vignettes. They all require participants to engage, primarily, in thoughtful controlled processes to generate their reactions As a result, their participants' reactions reflect the dominance of conventional norms, especially those involved in the pursuit of enlightened self-interest (Bazerman et al., 1995; Miller, 1999; Ratner & Miller, 2001).

A second source of errors can be traced to the fact that although the normative system recognizes the values of justice and fairness, they are embedded in a complex and, at times, conflicting array of obligations to various participants. For most people, most of the time, the controlled processing manages those potential conflicts by using social contexts to recognize and highlight or silence various obligations—to one's family, neighbors, co-workers, supervisors, employees, and so forth, including, and especially for some, the obligation to be rationally self-benefiting. Without recognizing the presence and importance of justice-imperatives in the various obligations, it is natural to assume, instead, the influence of the norm of self-interest.

In the two examples of this problem that come most readily to mind, the experienced investigators' found evidence confirming the influence of self-serving motives, when the more plausible interpretations were that the participants' reactions reflected their recognizing and responding to the appropriate, norms-based expectations.

Rusbult and her colleagues (Rusbult, Lowery, Hubbard, Maravankin, & Neises, 1988) pursued reports of an undesirable practice in some corporations where financial compensation is influenced and even limited by factors extraneous to the normally appropriate criteria of performance and loyalty. In one set of studies, to test their hypotheses concerning the self-serving denial of fair bonuses, they asked participants to play the role of a manager who was awarding bonuses to excellent performing employees. In the critical conditions, they described employees who were roughly equal in merit and performance, but some of whom were known to have external constraints that would make them less likely to be attracted away from the company (e.g., they had compelling family obligations in the community). As expected, their role-playing participant-supervisors offered measurably smaller bonuses to employees who were thus constrained than to the other employees of no greater merit but who were more amenable or at least vulnerable to being lured away.

According to the investigators, those substantial differences in bonuses their manager-participants awarded to equally high-performing workers were self-serving violations of the rules of equity and fairness. Or, were they?

To be sure, the bonuses did not comply with the application of a justice of fairness or equity, but does that necessarily indicate that the supervisors' awards were influenced by self-serving rather than justice maintaining motivations? Is it not possible that the supervisors were complying with a different set of justice-motivated rules that were normatively appropriate to that situation?

Set aside the question of how role-playing participants responding to vignettes could have possibly been engaged in self-serving behaviors of any kind, maybe other than sneaking out before the time was up or demanding more credits or money for their participation or they would tear up their ratings? Let's say, though, that the participants were able to channel the prototypical manager and their discrepant assigned bonuses were accurate representations of what does occur in the real world between employees and management. In order to describe those unequal allocations to employees of equally good performance as a self-serving violation of equity or fairness, it would be necessary to consider the position of the prototypical good manager in these instances.

First, it is important to recognize that managers typically do not use their own funds to provide substantial bonuses with the understanding that they could keep whatever was saved for themselves. Rather, it is safe to assume that, in awarding bonuses, they are fulfilling their fundamental and over-riding obligation to their superiors and ultimately the company stakeholders: Increase productivity and reduce costs in order to increase corporate profits. If the manager had adequate reason to believe that a smaller bonus to an employee was sufficient to accomplish those goals, awarding a larger bonus would violate the manager's obligations. And, since bonus amounts are typically not considered part of the employees explicit or implicit contract for payment, to award a greater amount simply to make it equal to the bonus offered an equally performing but more mobile employee would violate the managers' commitments to the company. Awarding a considerably greater bonus to the equally high-performing—i.e., profit-generating but potentially mobile employee—would be consistent with those commitments and is usually described as a wise decision.

This analysis is illustrated in a familiar comparable situation in academia. It is fairly common knowledge that more than a few highly productive faculty members have confronted their administrators with a higher-paying offer from another university with the intention, explicit to all concerned, of eliciting a competing offer. My understanding is, or at least according to the common myth, that strategy often succeeds in gaining the potentially mobile excellent faculty member a larger salary from the university, and with no expectation that the successfully extorted higher pay would also be offered to all other equally performing faculty—unless, of course, they too threatened to leave for a better offer.

It is not the case that participants in economic transactions have no sense of, much less allegiance to, justice. Rather, it is that the prevailing norms in Western economies are based on the assumption that all social actors are expected to do whatever possible to advance their own interests and meet their obligations, while not violating prior obligations or well-understood rules of fair competition, such as being devious, dishonest, deceptive, and so forth. There is considerable evidence that these norms of justified or enlightened self-interest have permeated many of the interactions that occur in the normal course of events to the point where they become the prevalent social norms in virtually all but the most intimate encounters (see especially Miller, 1999). And, as will be described in the next section, that norm is particularly relevant and easily recognized when an encounter involves participants who have no compelling prior claim to an indivisible and or highly desired resource (Dols et al., 2010; Lerner & Lichtman, 1968; Lerner & Miller, 1978).

Another highly regarded series of experiments provides an important illustration of how the failure to recognize the influence of the norm of justified self-interest can lead to inadvertent but clearly mistaken attributions of self-interested violations of justice. Dan Batson and his colleagues appear to have failed to recognize the norm of justified self-interest in a series of experiments they conducted that focused on "hypocrisy," that is, people portraying their self-serving acts as relatively moral (Batson, Kobrynowicz, Dinnerstein, Kampf, & Wilson, 1997; Batson, Thompson, Seuferling, Whitney, & Strongman, 1999; Batson, Thompson, & Chen, 2002). The important question is whether Batson and his colleagues validly portrayed their participants' behaviors as examples of "hypocrisy." To answer that, it is first necessary to consider what events led up to the behaviors they described as hypocritical, especially what the experimenters told their participants and how they then responded to the experimenters' instructions.

In their basic hypocrisy-inducing situation, they first confronted their participants with the opportunity to choose between assigning either themselves or another participant (fictitious) to the considerably more desirable of two alternative conditions, with the other participant relegated to the remaining clearly undesirable condition. They told the participants they could make the assignments as they wished. Then prior to being left alone to make the assignments, the experimenters informed them that most participants thought the most fair way to make the assignments was to flip a coin, and some of them were shown a coin they could use. In yet other conditions, they were told that most participants chose to assign the other participant to the desirable condition, and in some conditions they were told nothing about what other participants had done Subsequently, and just prior to leaving the participants alone, they reminded the participants that they could make the assignments any way they wished, and the (fictitious) other participant would be told—given the misinformation—that the conditions were assigned randomly.

The participants were left alone to make the assignments, and then, when returning, the experimenters gave them a questionnaire that essentially allowed them to describe their choice in relatively moral terms, which they often did. Unbeknownst to the participants in many experiments the experimenters actually knew how the participants had arrived at their assignments (e.g., flip a coin or not) and were thus able, to compare the "morality" of the participants decisions: self-interested (e.g., ignoring the coin flip), fair, or altruistic, with the description offered by the participants of the morality of their choices.

Upon reading the published description of these instructions, several of us with a history of studying social norms and justice-motivated behavior came to the conclusion that the architecture of that experimental situation placed the participants in a situation of having to deal with their experimenters' contradictory and barely implicit demands: not a conflict between self-interest and moral behaviors. The experimenters initially supported the participants' right to select the desirable condition for themselves. They even notified the participants of their willingness to deceive the possibly jealous or resentful other participants. However, between the initial and final legitimizing instructions, the experimenter inserted a barely disguised, "most prior participants," recommendation concerning how a moral participant would make the assignments.

The findings revealed that the participants' subsequent ratings mimicked the experimenter's instructions in their ratings of the most moral way to make the assignments. Parenthetically, it is worth noting that the instructions referring to what most prior participants thought was in itself deceptive since their own reported evidence revealed that the majority of participants, without explicit prior instructions from their experimenters, did not believe there was one most moral way to make the assignments.

In a subsequent experiment (Dols et al., 2010) employing Batson et al.'s experimental situation, the participants revealed little reluctance to take the desirable condition for themselves when the experimenter either gave no instructions concerning what prior participants had done, or gave the accurate instructions: they were told that some had flipped a coin, some had assigned themselves to the desirable condition, and some had given the desirable condition to the other participant. In other words, as suspected, when allowed to make the assignments as they chose, the majority of participants elected the normatively appropriate alternative of taking the desirable condition for themselves (Lerner & Lichtman, 1968). On the other hand, to answer their experimenters' queries concerning the most moral way to make the assignments, they simply repeated whatever their experimenter had previously claimed was the most moral way.

Was this evidence of participants engaging in self-serving acts and hypocritical attempts to portray their selfish behaviors as moral? More probably, the participants' reactions, both the assignments and responses to the questionnaire, revealed rather cooperative participants who complied with the justice-motivated norm of justified self-interest and attempted not to explicitly contradict their experimenters' preferences. It is not at all clear how anyone who recognized the operative justice norm could derive evidence of hypocrisy from the participants' decisions and ratings.

These experiments were selected to provide examples of the serious consequences that follow from experienced investigators' failing to recognize when people are responding to their justice imperatives. How is it possible to avoid such important errors? Conceivably, one rather obvious answer to that question points to the need for a better, more complete, understanding of how justice appears in people's lives: what forms does it takes, and what "cues" elicit those forms in a particular context? This, then, is a good time to try to provide a more complete understanding of how justice imperatives appear in people's lives.

What Determines the Individual's Assessment of an Injustice or Just Event?

Since most of us walk around with many rules of justice and deserving in both our preconscious and accessible memories, what determines which of them influences our reactions at any given time and place, in a particular interaction? The answer, for those rules that are accessible to conscious retrieval, is relatively familiar to anyone who is culturally conversant: the societal norms and conventions that describe who is entitled to what from whom are elicited in particular social contexts: status-role relations, both institutionalized and informal. That is the easy part, but what about the justice imperatives that automatically appear in the preconscious and often influence people's reactions? As it happens, there is evidence that we know something about when and how they appear, as well as how they influence the individuals' decisions and reactions.

We can begin with the relatively obvious and simplest determinants. Most people walk around with many rules denoting who deserves what from whom, that are directly traceable to the culture in which they were socialized. These include rules that apply to members of relatively general categories where the who and whom would be any human being, or citizen, or man, woman, child, someone in desperate need, or someone who just gave you a gift.

More specific justice imperatives apply to anyone who occupies a particular status in a social institution: each status-role entails obligations, that is, with reference to occupants of other positions in the institutions (e.g., teacher–pupil; father–child, etc). In addition, there are commonly understood privileges accorded to occupants of each position. The status-role imperatives with minor variations are understood by everyone who has become reasonably culturally conversant. As a result, they function as the "glue" enabling the social system to provide the stability and predictability required for effective social coordination and cooperation. Although essential to how they go about their daily activities, most people function very nicely including appropriate changes in status-roles without conscious articulation of the imperatives that are regulating their own and other's activities. People, however, remain highly attentive to any behavioral signs of an actor's failure to fulfill an obligation, and, typically, are willing to enforce corrective sanctions.

Some theorists, complying with current trends, refer to biological and social-evolution-based functions to explain why a particular rule of justice (e.g., reciprocity, fairness) appears in our culture. I find myself nodding in agreement when I read their descriptions of how primitive cultures eventually developed and then follow, for example, the moral rule of "reciprocity." that was passed on to subsequent cultures via the gene pool and social evolution. After finishing the charming evolutionary narrative, if I then put on my scientist cap to decide how to use the information, I realize that

I was reading untestable speculations rather than verifiable or refutable findings. An author of a recent article in the New Yorker magazine, pointed out that, in order to decide which if any evolutionary theories apply to contemporary social psychological events, we must first provide a complete description of those events: how they occur and unfold. And, of course, once having completed that description, there will be neither need for, nor explanatory value, in the evolutionary history. But they can make for enjoyable reading, not unlike science fiction. In truth, however, I must confess I find them no less informative or valuable than the recent articles appearing in prestigious scientific journals describing how infrahuman species (apes, etc.) manifest justice-mimicking behaviors.

In the spirit of generating a description of how justice imperatives appear in people's lives, rather than look for historical antecedents in earlier cultures or among the apes, I will offer a verifiable descriptive composite of the experiences children in contemporary society encounter and how they interact with developing cognitive abilities to generate various justice imperatives.

Previously, I briefly described the "easy stuff": The commonly understood and accepted entitlements, obligations, and privileges extant in the culture that we incorporate into our private lives and interactions with others and which appear in two forms: as publicly available rules and as privately experienced imperatives denoting who deserves what from whom.

Virtually everyone, with some minor subcultural variations, is able to verbalize the content of those culturally pre and proscribed rules. It is also commonly recognized, however, that there are individual differences in compliance and adherence, especially when other incentives are salient. In situations containing salient highly valued resources, the anticipation of public sanctions as well as those that are self-administered are often the critical determinants of whether the person complies or defects. The important defining characteristic of these justice imperatives is their common recognition and participation in conscious internal and interpersonal dialogues.

Preconscious Scripts

Another set of important imperatives appears in the preconscious automatic reactions to critical cues as scripted links among a particular category of person, action, and outcome. Although the elements in these scripts can have conscious manifestations, and have their origins in commonly experienced familiar early patterns of social interactions, the cognitions in both the automatic preconscious and conscious deliberations are linked by simple rules of association. Knowing the origins and content of these scripts, however, the observer can recognize their important influence on the appearance and influence of a particular justice imperative. In many encounters these prior scripted links are the tacit power behind-the-scenes creating emotion-driven imperatives. They influence by blending with or dominating the person's conscious decision-making.

Three fundamental scripts emerged out of repeated associations among particular categories of people, interactions, and outcomes in children's earliest and continued social encounters. The scripts were the products of children's cognitive efforts to create a stable and manageable representation of their world. By recognizing repeated occurrences in their experiences, children generate discrete images (categories) of people, kinds of people, objects, and ways of locomoting: ways to get from here to there. If sufficiently repeated, these cognitive elements, may become objectified and imbued with stable characteristics, most typically, desirable–undesirable, positive–negative. When linked together, they may participate as "scripts" in children's preconscious assumptive world and influence their reactions to new experiences.

The earliest of these scripts is produced by the neonates' interactions with their mothers. At the outset, the infant's experiences are so intimately tied to their mother that their identities are merged. To infants, cognitively and affectively, they and their mothers are one. The mothers' emotions are immediately transferred to the infants so that their mothers' sadness, happiness are experienced by their infants. The perception of distress, such as crying among other infants, in the infant's world may elicit a similar reaction. It is as if any perceived event in their world is happening to them, and in the world of adults we would recognize these reactions as expressions of identification-based empathy (Aron, Aron, & Smollan, 1992; Hoffman, 1970).

Conceivably, the infant's dependency on the mother for gratifying virtually all needs reinforces this sense of identity. The merging of identities creates a prototypical pattern of interaction involving cognitive representations of both direct and vicarious need gratification. The elements in the derived script include perception of *kinds of people*: "same," "mine," a sense of empathy with;

prototypical interactions, include responding to one another's needs promoting their welfare; the *associated outcome* is vicarious gratification. Once established in the preconscious, the automatic dynamic process can be described as: *if cues in the situation elicit any of the elements of the script that will automatically regenerate the other elements, as well.*

Eventually, as children mature and accrue additional experiences, they recognize that even though they may, at times, share experiences and outcomes with particular others, they often recognize themselves as self-contained independent identities. Though still vulnerable on occasion to the automatic initial script-generated reactions of sympathy and identity, they recognize they can have some degree of control over their own pains and pleasures, as well as need gratifications, and goal acquisitions. With this separation, they begin to adjust to the fact that people, generally, not just their mothers, are the most important powerful forces in their lives especially for gratifying their newly acquired wants.

As a consequence, most children generate additional scripts out of two important repeated and common co-occurrences in their interactions with other people. They learn that with "similar" others, "we–us," they typically experience relatively cooperative amicable interactions leading to equally shared outcomes, whereas, the typical pattern when interacting with culturally or situationally defined "different" others, "they–them," includes goal-inhibiting interactions that eventuate in different, greater–lesser outcomes.

When children recognize they are relatively separate identifiable individuals and learn from their repeated early experiences that it is possible to predict, roughly, the way other children as well as adults generally react to them and one another. As a consequence, they develop scripted associations linking kinds of people, with typical interactions, and outcomes. They share an identity with or are similar to, or they are different from.

Of course, it begins with adults in their world who in very important ways react to children according to whether they belong to a particular category based on, for example age, gender, neighborhood, You are treated just like everyone else in that category and differently from those in another category. As a result, other children, recognizing you belong together and are "similar" to one another, will be relatively friendly and willing to cooperate, leading to similar outcomes, whereas when they perceive an important difference—you are not one of, are different from them—the interactions are typically competitive or inhibiting leading to commensurately different, better/worse outcomes. Although the resultant scripts were generated out of early and repeated co-occurrences, once established they become part of the person's preconscious assumptive world *where the salience of any element in the script will elicit the imperative to regenerate all three: type of person, interaction, and outcome.*

Even if one is willing to at least tentatively accept, as plausible, these conjectures about the origins and contents and dynamics of these preconscious scripts, there are some remaining important questions For example, it is not entirely clear how the "is" co-occurrences and associations in the scripts become imbued with the experienced requirement of an "ought" imperative. Conceivably, the *valence and affect associated with each of the elements (e.g., desirable, "good" outcomes) is eventually generalized to the other elements; similar people are good, desirable. Some of the associations among the elements may be supported by familiar social norms (e.g., "team members are expected to share and share alike"). Also, the motivating force underlying the script-based "ought" experience in the justice imperative may arise from or be reinforced by the developing personal contract.* In the process of children developing their commitment to their personal contract they will be motivated to believe, as previously cited research demonstrated, that valued outcomes come from good people whose good efforts and self-deprivations yield good outcomes: people who have "good" outcomes should be good people, similar to me; whereas different "bad, people deserve, should have, bad outcomes (Olson, Banaji, Dweck, & Spelke, 2006; Olson, Dunham, Dweck, Spelke, & Banaji, 2008). In any case, although how it happens has yet to be verified, there is ample evidence that *justice imperatives are elicited by the elements in the scripts.*

Having provided brief descriptions of the origins, nature, and dynamics of the three fundamental scripts that form the way people automatically respond to compelling cues, I should point out that three earlier publications offer fuller descriptions of how these scripts influence people's judgments and behavior. The first two appeared in 1975 (Lerner, 1975; Lerner, Miller & Holmes, 1975), the third somewhat modified and elaborated version, my favorite by far, was published in 1981 (Lerner, 1981). In any case, the next step is to consider some of the supporting evidence.

What Are Those Scripts and How Do They Influence Individual's Reactions?

Rather than a complete systematic review of the available literature, I think brief descriptions of the relevant evidence that most easily comes to mind will be sufficient to provide a persuasive answer for all but the most acutely skeptical readers. For them, I acknowledge in advance my inability to provide the required instantaneous religious conversion.

The Identity Script

Dan Batson (1991, 1998) over the past several years has published an enormous amount of experimentally generated evidence to demonstrate that eliciting empathy in an observer for someone in serious need will reliably elicit measurable degrees of altruistic behavior. Over the years, he has successfully generated evidence to refute most attempts to reduce the elicited altruism to the observers' self-interested motivation to reduce their own pain. One set of experiments, however, particularly relevant to the theory presented here, has not been refuted. For example Maner, et al. (2002) persuasively demonstrated that the success of Batson's method of eliciting empathy-based altruism is mediated by the empathic observers' graphically describable merging of the victims and their own identities (see Aron et al., 1992). Absent that merging of identities, the empathy-altruism link is disrupted. That, of course, nicely confirms the presence and predicted relations among the three elements in the identity script described here. The observer's awareness of the victim's needs elicits an identity relation impelling the empathic observer to meet those needs. As Maner et al. (2002) demonstrated, absent the perceived merging of their identity with the victim, the observer will not act altruistically. It is worth noting at this point that Batson's (1991; 1998) typical procedure for generating a control or contrasting response of failure to provide help, explicitly instructs the observer to remain psychologically detached from the victim.

Similarly, several investigators (e.g., Buunk et al., 1983) have shown that people who experience a "communal" relationship with another (e.g., in romantic involvement, as initially described by Clark and Mills; 1979), are motivated to meet that person's needs and wants without expecting or even be accepting of any efforts to reciprocate in kind. That is, consistent with the link between the perception of merged identities, altruistic acts, and vicarious gratification, rather than cooperation for equal outcome as in perceived unit relations.

Unit and Nonunit Scripts

Most of us can recognize the difference between the Identity merging of selves as in the romantic phase of a relationship and being friends, or partners. Among the latter the dominant expectation is not having needs or wants gratified but rather cooperation and equal sharing of outcomes. If a relationship goes sour when, for example, there is a shortage of commonly desired or needed resources, the relationship often then becomes relatively competitive, even antagonistic in the participants' efforts to maximize their own individual outcomes (see Lerner, et al., 1989).

As it happens, most of the evidence that readily comes to mind includes both unit and nonunit relations. For example, an early experiment (Lerner & Becker, 1962) involved university students reading a case history of a young delinquent. They were to select an alternative ranging from severe punishment to benevolent therapeutic interventions. The vast majority of these students, as expected, elected a benevolent treatment for the delinquent. After making their ratings they were told they would be asked to make a final recommendation after a period of discussion with another student who had, as they learned, elected a very punitive alternative. They were given the choice between two students, both of whom elected roughly equally punitive alternatives. They also learned that one of them had the same major as theirs whereas the other had a different major. A second factor in the design varied the seriousness of the consequences

Table 9.1 Preconscious Scripts

	Perception of other	Interaction	Outcomes
Identity	me, mine	meet needs, welfare	vicarious shared outcome
Unit	similar/us	cooperate	equal outcomes
Nonunit	different, them	compete–antagonism	more–less

associated with their recommendations. Half of all participants were led to believe that the judge in this case was willing to consider the students' recommendations in the sentencing of the delinquent, and for the other half there was no mention of any consequences.

The findings confirmed the reasoning based on the expectation that although the participants were more surprised by the punitive choice of someone relatively "similar" to them than from someone with a "different" major, they could expect more friendly cooperative interaction with the similar rather than different other. However, when they realized the final choice had potentially significant consequences they expected the interaction to be rather contentious if not antagonistic. In this situation they preferred to fight with the different student.

A considerably later experiment provided an interesting elaboration on those findings (Lerner, Dillehay & Sherer, 1967). The theory predicts that activating any of the elements in a script would automatically activate the others. Supporting evidence for this predication came from an experiment in which the participants expecting to compete or cooperate with another participant for desired outcomes were given the opportunity to gain an impression of the other participant by listening to their rather banal interview with one of the experimenters. Of course, all participants heard the same taped interview. Following that, they described their impressions of the other participant in terms of personal attributes as well as similarity and difference on various dimensions. It was not surprising to find that, by comparison to participants in a control condition (i.e., no anticipated further interaction), the participants who expected cooperative interaction and equal sharing of the outcomes found the other participant to be a relatively desirable person. The participants who anticipated competitive interaction with unequal outcomes, however, did not describe the other participant in relatively negative terms, but they did describe the competitor to be remarkably different from themselves. Making salient different outcomes and competitive interaction elicited the perception of the competitor as a different person, one of "them."

In one early experiment (Lerner, 1974) first-grade children were given the opportunity to perform a simple task as part of testing a new game. It consisted of their attempting to paste as many stars on designated places as they could during a specific time period: the more stars they pasted, the more prize stickers they could take home. Half of them were led to believe they had completed five stars and the other half 15 stars before their time was up. As an additional factor, half were led to believe they were paired with another child in another room who was a teammate, whereas the other half were told simply there was another child in the other room working on the same task. At the end of the time period, they were shown that the other child had pasted either many more than they, 15 versus 5, or many fewer, 5 versus 15. Finally they were shown 20 prize stickers as rewards and asked to take their share and leave the rest for the other child.

The results were nicely supportive of the hypotheses. The children who believed the other child was a "teammate" stayed relatively close to an equal division by taking almost half when they produced considerably less, but also equally close to only half when they had been much more productive: teammates share and share alike. When the other child had been referred to as simply another child, the children kept much more than half when they had been the more productive, but even more interesting was the fact that those children who were less productive than the other child kept considerably less than half of the rewards for themselves.

The distinction between a justice of equality and a justice of equity, based on relative merit, seems to apply, respectively, here to the allocation behavior of 6-year-old children's decisions concerning what they and a "teammate" deserve versus what they and "another child" deserve. That is consistent with the hypothesis that the former were perceived to be in a unit relation, whereas the latter were in a nonunit relation. It is also worth noting that there was remarkably little evidence of children's dominant self-interested desire to maximize their own outcomes. Overall, their self-allocations revealed no difference between the amount they kept for themselves that was greater than half or than the amount that was less than half. Clearly, if self- interested motivation had been a significant influence, the amount greater than an even division would have been remarkably larger.

Additional research with third-grade students, when allocating rewards, revealed their preference for equal outcomes between two members of the same "team," even though their relative performances were widely discrepant, whereas the same discrepancy between two members of different or competing teams elicited their preference for relative performance-based allocations (Towson et al., 1981; Lerner & Grant, 1990).

As for adults, Tajfel and Turner (1996) have published a vast array of evidence that adult participants exhibit referential treatment for someone who was similar to them in almost any respect over someone who was "different." Those findings are probably "overdetermined" in the sense of reflecting the influence of more than one motivation and process, including the observation that people have a natural preference for others who are similar in virtually any respect; however, they are also consistent with the predicted influence of unit and nonunit scripts. The key finding distinguishing the two theories is the co-occurrence of perceived difference and competitive interactions, without negative evaluation of "different," but rule-following competitors (see, e.g., Lerner, Dillehay, & Sherer, 1967; Lerner & Lichtman,1978).

Lowenstein, Thompson, and Bazerman (1989) systematically assessed their participants' anticipated level of satisfaction with various amounts of desirable–undesirable outcomes in comparison with the outcomes awarded to a cooperative versus antagonistic or altruistic other participant in various contexts as portrayed in hypothetical situations. By and large, the less the participants' comparative under-reward, the greater their anticipated satisfaction, whereas, comparable levels of relatively greater outcomes (i.e., over-reward) did not reveal a symmetrical pattern. Although the levels of predicted satisfaction of the over-rewarded participants tended to remain relatively close to the high level reached with equal outcomes, the major deviation from that occurred when they had a positive relationship: they became increasingly less satisfied with greater amounts of over-reward, and with a negative prior relationship their satisfaction increased with greater rewards. In addition, they anticipated being considerably less satisfied with an equal outcome when they had an antagonistic relationship with the other participant than when the prior relationship had been cooperative.

Again, although these findings and others reported in the article may reflect the influence of several factors, including impression management, they are, for the most part, remarkably consistent with the predicted influence of unit (positive relationship) and nonunit (antagonistic relationship) scripts. Having described, in the main, what I have learned about the social psychology of justice, it is time to turn more directly to issues specifically related to justice in the workplace.

Justice in the Workplace: Some Illuminating Examples

The previously described norm of justified self-interest probably is the most prevalent form of justice that is operative in workplace interactions, whether they occur among employees or management or corporate stakeholders or between different categories of participants. Everyone is allowed and is expected to do whatever they can to maximize their outcomes, as long as they do not violate fairly well-understood rules of fair competition: no cheating, lying, deception, coercion, and so forth. Some notable exceptions include the application of norms of equity in allocating desired outcomes (e.g., relative merit, productivity, costs, investments). A common blending of these two norms involves participants legitimately preferring and also promoting the particular contribution that is most self-profiting in determining what is "equitable," "fair" (Walster et al., 1978). Although the participants' obvious self-profiting efforts can be vigorous and extensive, they are typically couched in justice promoting terms—fair, equitable, deserving, entitlement, and must not violate the recognized rules of fair competition.

Although not as prevalent, in the service of profit-seeking, both management and labor have at times resorted to the justice of unit-relations—team membership—with shared outcomes, and even identity-based justice of meeting one another's needs and welfare. A familiar example of unit-relations appears in the efforts of employees to organize as teams with common membership (e.g., unions) in order to effectively negotiate with management for greater shared outcomes. Managements' introduction of quality circles among employees, for example, is an attempt to use the early scripted identity relations to generate imperatives among their employees to voluntarily promote, in every way possible, the welfare of their company, their "family" (see, e.g., Blader & Tyler, 2003).

It is also true that along with the predominant well-recognized influence of these norms, it is not possible for the participants in workplace encounters to completely ignore and thus rule out the effects of justice imperatives that automatically emanate from their preconscious scripts. A rather dramatic example of the unexpected intrusion of their preconscious scripts appeared in the lives of managers who were performing their duties that were sanctioned and morally justified by the operative norms of rational, justified self-interest (Smith, 1994). These managers were experiencing strong, certainly painful, guilt feelings as a consequence of their fulfilling their obligations to their employer and the stakeholders. It was well recognized that those obligations had been completely and thoughtfully legitimized by the unavoidable need to cope with market demands.

The unanticipated influence of automatically elicited preconscious justice scripts appeared among several members of management when they instituted downsizing in their companies. Managers complained of seriously lowered morale consequent to having to fire employees "not for cause, but because their skills were no longer needed" (Smith, 1994, p. 2). Given the typical procedures that companies go through before downsizing and actually dismissing some employees, the managers had no discernible "rational" reason to feel any guilt or blame. Prior to downsizing, management at all levels is made aware of the unavoidable, typically market-induced requirement that they let some employees go or the entire company will have to close with much greater loss of jobs. Once that reality is recognized, the companies engage in thorough analyses, often together with expert consultants, to determine which employees will be let go and with what compensation. That decision is recognized by all involved as eminently justifiable in terms of being the most rational and fair solution to the unavoidable market-imposed realities.

As a consequence, according to societal norms and conventional morality the managers, in implementing that solution, have no reason to feel either guilt or shame. And yet, in his invited address to the American Psychological Association, a management consulting psychologist stated: "The conscious guilt any manager of conscience has about terminating someone without cause is compounded by the unconscious guilt that arises from the sense that he or she is destroying the other" (Levinson, 1994, p. 429).

I do not agree with this analysis of the cause, but I am willing to believe that the managers in the process of implementing the downsizing often do experience considerable guilt, and that must be demoralizing especially since it was not anticipated and there is no normatively legitimate cause for it. When the suffering among the dismissed employees becomes salient, that automatically elicits scripts that define the manager as an evil harm doer: bad things are caused by bad people. Because those scripts are preconscious and contrary to the accepted rules of conventional morality and culpability, the possibility of their inducing guilt among the management did not enter into their plans for downsizing.

It is conceivable, however, that with sufficient repeated and common experiences, these "irrational" but predictably unavoidable guilt feelings can lead to preventive measures in the form of institutionalized practices. Some firms, faced with the necessity of downsizing, decide to hire "outside" management groups to actually institute the required procedures including dismissing the unfortunate employees.

Another possible candidate for that would be the rituals and practices in the military that serve to distinguish officers from enlisted men. The former, in performing their duty are required to make the most "rational" decisions that may lead to harm, suffering, even death among the latter. The distinguishing and separating rituals reduce the visibility and salience of the enlisted men's suffering and deprivation to those who are required to make and live with the consequences of their "rational" decisions.

The Unique Importance of Procedural Justice: Myth or Reality?

Arguably, the most active justice-related research in the context of a workplace, has appeared under the rubric of procedural justice or "fair process" effects. The focus on the justice of procedures as distinct from and often more important than distributive justice has been prominent in various content areas including conflict resolution and social dilemmas, as well as plant closures and downsizing. Unfortunately, although demonstrably copious, there are good reasons to believe that the basic research underlying the emphasis and importance of procedural versus distributive justice has been deeply flawed in both theory and methods almost from its inception. Since these issues have been discussed in considerable detail in relatively recent sources (Lerner, 2003; Lerner & Clayton, 2011), I will present here rather brief descriptions of the major points together with some new material.

Various definition(s) of procedural or fair-process justice have appeared in the literature. As far as I can tell, however, they all boil down to how people are treated by others: whether they are accorded the normatively required degrees of respect (Miller, 2001), as distinct from the required allocation of desired resources. That distinction is not substantively different from the early exchange theorists' categories of symbolic and concrete resources (Blau, 1964).

Exchange theorists, however, demonstrated that both kinds of resources, though morphologically distinguishable were often indistinguishable and in fact interchangeable and similarly occurring in social psychological processes. The famous "potlatch" ritual among some Northwest Coastal Native peoples, is a familiar example of exchanging concrete resources for social status (Boas, 1966; Mauss,1990), and fits nicely with the fabled practice of awarding symbols of higher status (key to the executive wash room, title on the door) as a legitimate substitute for higher pay.

More recent, carefully conducted research has shown that procedural fairness, or courtesies (giving voice) involve the same psychological processes as distributive justice. They are acquired and allocated according to well-recognized rules of deserving and entitlement (Brockner et al., 1998; Heuer et al., 1999; Sunshine & Heuer, 2002). As a consequence the attempt to maintain the false essentially meaningless distinction between procedural and distributive justice promises to be more misleading than constructive. The perpetuation, even growth, of procedural and fair-process justice publications may be traced, at least in part, to highly cited research confirming the uniquely important influence of procedural justice on how people react to important events.

For example, Tyler (1994), in a most noteworthy example, claimed to have documented the important differences between procedural and distributive justice. His demonstration (Tyler, 1994) relied upon sophisticated statistical analyses (modeling) of participants' responses to telephone surveys. For those analyses, their responses to questions with regard to a self-selected recent experience with either law enforcement or a supervisor were categorized as measuring either independent or mediating variables that elicited their present emotional reactions to the incident, positive-negative: the dependent variable. Taken at face value as published, the statistical analyses of the responses to the interviews clearly confirmed the distinctiveness and relative importance of the fairness of how they were treated in comparison with the rated fairness of the outcome.

The subsequent examination of the procedure employed in generating the interviews, however, revealed an equally if not more plausible interpretation of the participants responses (see Lerner, 2003). Although not described in the published article, fuller details of the procedure as well as the actual questions appeared in another publication (Lind & Tyler, 1988). The important fact uncovered in that publication is what happened prior to the interviewer asking the respondents to select an incident and then answer questions concerning the fairness of how they were treated, the fairness of the outcomes, and how they felt about it all.

Before selecting an incident and answering those questions, the respondents had been asked a series of questions about their reactions to and feelings about the law enforcement and judicial authorities. Inevitably, responding to those earlier questions primed the respondents' current attitudes toward the authorities prior to their responses that were used in the analyses. In their second study, as revealed in a footnote (Tyler, 1994), the investigators sought additional respondents who reported having clearly negative attitudes toward their supervisors. As a consequence, in both studies their participants' salient current attitudes were, in all probability, the true "independent variable" influencing the incident they selected and all their answers—relatively positive to negative—to the questions concerning what had transpired and how they now felt about the incident.

Pursuing that hypothesis, it was not surprising to find that their participants' responses to virtually all the questions used to generate the variables in the statistical analyses fell easily along a positive–negative dimension. A factor analysis of the intercorrelations among all the measures revealed essentially one positive-to negative attitude factor accounting for virtually all their respondents' answers to the questions of what had transpired and their present emotions.

There were additional confounding issues, but one highly respected colleague claimed to be most impressed by the simple correlation of 0.77 between the supposedly independent measures of procedural and distributive justice. In any case, that promising investigation and reinterpretation of Tyler's research provided sufficient reason to continue my examination of the evidence underpinning the procedural justice movement.

I searched for additional research that did not rely on the analyses of cross-sectional data hoping to turn up clearer evidence of the important influence of procedural rather than distributive justice. I found another highly cited article (Brockner, Tyler, & Cooper-Schneider, 1992) based on the results of two-stage panel studies intended, again, to illustrate the importance of how one is treated (procedural fairness) as distinct from the fairness of the outcome (distributive justice).

In one of the reported studies, the participants' in one session (not quite the traditional panel design) responded to questions that assessed their present attitudes toward and commitment to their company and the fairness of a previous layoff and their memory of how they felt about the company a month prior to the layoffs. Their main independent variables were based on their reported "prior commitments" (low–high) and their reported "fairness" of the layoff process (low–high). The dependent variables were assessed by their reported present commitment, work effort, and turnover intention: presumably the consequences of the interactions of prior commitment and fairness. They portrayed their main hypothesis as: "the higher they are the harder they fall." Their analyses offered some support for the anticipated interaction, especially with the measure of subsequent organizational commitment: the higher their initial commitment, the lower their reported resultant commitment when they claimed the layoffs had been relatively unfair.

I realized that those findings were based upon self-reports of present attitudes and their recall of what they felt and thought a month before the layoff. Those reactions do make good sense, but to what extent were they influenced or constructed by accurate reports versus present attitudes, for example, what someone who is presently very upset about the layoffs would report about his prior commitments to the company and the fairness of the layoffs: "Before they screwed us, I was highly committed to the company. That's why I am really pissed-off now"

They reported a second study that, ostensibly, was not vulnerable to that kind of plausible alternative explanation. They analyzed their respondents' answers to telephone surveys conducted at two separate times, one year apart, concerning their self-selected experiences with police officers or judges. Both interviews were part of the same project. (However, as you might have guessed, data from the first interviews were employed in the first Tyler, 1994, study described earlier.)

In their second study, measures of the important variables at both times were derived from the respondents' answers to the same questions concerning their commitment to (respect for) the law, as well as their reports of the fairness of procedures. Again, the expectation was for a cross-over interaction of the effects of prior commitment and procedural fairness on the respondents' subsequent commitment. The authors concluded that the statistically significant interaction term (between prior commitment and fairness of procedures) on the second measure of commitment (respect for) authorities had confirmed their hypothesis: "Negative change in the respondents' institutional commitment after experiencing unfairness was significantly greater for those whose prior commitment was high" (Brockner et al., 1992, p. 256.)

Unless I am mistaken, the authors had no way of knowing what their respondents' commitments to the authorities had been prior to the actual critical contact they selected for their interviews. Nevertheless, before concluding that their data confirm the expected importance of fair procedures, it is necessary to examine the means involved in the interaction term (see Brockner et al., 1992, p. 256).

Contrary to the predictions, there was no predicted crossover. At time 2, the initially high-committed respondents (time 1) were still more committed than the initially low-committed respondents; also, among those who reported relatively fair treatment, the initially high committed also remained more committed than the initially less committed. Although the greatest drop in commitment occurred among the initially unfairly treated but highly committed, inconsistent with the expectations, the next largest drop occurred among those who reported having been fairly treated. Actually, a case could be made that the reported fairness of the procedures had relatively little consistent effect on the participants' levels of subsequent commitment. That may not be so surprising, because the reported experiences occurred prior to, not between, the two measurement periods. I can't imagine how one would conclude that either of the efforts described here provides persuasive evidence for the influence, much less distinctiveness, of procedural justice.

My search for clear confirming evidence of the important influence of procedural justice, however, finally led to a well-cited report of a true experiment using random assignment, to examine the hypotheses. One of the most eminent procedural justice advocates did an experiment to supplement his observations in a real-world setting where unfair treatment seemed to cause some employees to steal from the company. Rather than relying on observations or self-reports to questionnaires, his participants experienced a compelling violation of a procedure and then had the opportunity to steal money from the experimenter (Greenberg, 1993).

The participants were recruited with the offer of a payment of $5.00 for their participation. After performing the tasks for the required period of time, some were told that they would receive $3.00—considerably less than the promised amount. That was clearly a violation of fair procedures. Then, after performing the required task, a relatively large amount of money ($5.00) was put out before them in coins of various denominations, and they were instructed to take their pay and leave. Then the experimenter left the room. While the experimenter was gone, as expected, some participants took—"stole"—money, up to approximately the initial promise for their participation. Was that really stealing?

If, however, their experimenter had also given them various more or less good reasons why he could not pay the full promised amount (e.g., the grant funds had been inadvertently exceeded and the experimenter had not been informed, and/or the experimenter took time to apologize and express "sincere" regrets and sorrow for the unfortunate turn of events over which he had no control), the participants, when given the opportunity, stole predictably lesser amounts. Thus, clear evidence of the important influence of procedural justice?

That would be the case, if employing familiar rituals for denying culpability for an immoral act, and/or displaying esteem and respect for one's victim were examples of procedural rather than distributive justice of symbolic resources. And, the dependent variable, the taking, the stealing, of promised payments when given the opportunity had nothing to do with the influence of distributive justice. Actually, it seems more appropriate to describe these findings as demonstrating the substitutability of symbolic and concrete resources—status and money—in the way people calculate and define justice.

I was very surprised when an eminent social psychologist in response to my complaints about what I thought were the deeply flawed theoretical and empirical bases of the procedural justice movement justified it all by the vast amount of research it has generated. The crucial question then became: what advances in the study of justice can we point to that has come from this flood of published "research"?

In response to that question, let us look at the investigation the authors offered as an important representative of such advances. They (Blader & Tyler, 2003; Tyler & Blader, 2003) proposed and then claimed to have empirically confirmed that treating employees with fair procedures will lead them to identify with their supervisors and organization. Their identifications then will generate voluntary, even personally costly efforts to promote the welfare of the company. That, of course, is a truly remarkable discovery.

Prior to this innovative contribution, considerable evidence indicated that treating employees fairly, that is, not treating them unfairly, was merely managements' fulfilling their recognized contractual obligations: giving their employees "A fair day's pay for a fair day's work" with, of course, no degrading additional treatment. Although treating employees disrespectfully or unfairly would certainly preclude their possibly identifying with the company, it was well understood that meeting one's obligations under normal circumstances would not elicit identification in the recipient. That would happen if and only when management went above and beyond the contracted obligations to benefit their employees, obviously promote their welfare beyond what is required, that is, treat them like "family." To be sure, the employees would then be inclined to reciprocate and identify with and voluntarily benefit management. Clearly, however, treating employees fairly will elicit a "fair day's work." The employees will reciprocate the fairness, but it was commonly understood that is all anyone would expect them to do.

If that is true, how was it possible for Blader and Tyler (2003) to suggest and then demonstrate otherwise: that procedural fairness is the key and sufficient to generate employees' identification with the company? I am not certain, but one possible explanation readily emerged from examining the instrument—questionnaire items—Blader and Tyler (2003) used to assess the employees perceptions of being treated with procedural fairness.

Along with familiar measures of perceived fair–unfair treatment, their questionnaire included the following items:

> I trust (the organization) to do what is best for me.
>
> (The organization) really cares about my well being.
>
> (The organization) cares about my satisfaction.
>
> My supervisor takes account of my needs when making decisions.
>
> My supervisor really cares about my well-being.
>
> My supervisor cares about my satisfaction.

I doubt that we could find a handful of employees or managers who would recognize such treatment—cares about my well being, does what is best for me—as even implicit considerations in an organization's fair treatment of their employees. Even if I had not grown up in a blue-collar city with a steel plant, shipyard, and many smaller enterprises, and lived among various blue and white-collar workers, I could not imagine what employees would take those questions seriously rather than as a silly joke, similar to asking them, with a straight face, if they were working for Santa Claus and their supervisor was actually the tooth fairy. As I recall, there have been some, but relatively few, well-recognized companies that attempted to treat their employees as "family," whose employees would be able to treat those questions seriously and reciprocate their treatment by more or less identification with the company. The operative factor, however, would not be fair treatment or procedural fairness in any recognizable form.

Obviously, the authors were able to affirm their innovative hypothesis only after re-defining fair procedures to include well-documented extra, generous, caring behaviors above and beyond fairness or justice (Blader & Tyler, 2003).

After parts of two summers working as a bartender in a well-frequented bar close to a shipyard and many other companies, I can't recall hearing any utterances of any kind that would indicate a company might treat their employees as "family"—not even as distant relatives. All these employees expected, all they wanted and worked for, was a fair day's pay for a fair day's work. From what I could tell, for that, they were willing to take their pay and shrug or laugh off the occasional "stupid shit" they got from their supervisors. I don't think anyone would describe these employees as identified with their companies. As I now recall, in an entirely different context, a genius IQ middle-class employee whom I knew very well, actually an ex-student, proudly told me how he would occasionally retaliate, symbollically re-establish equity(?), by spitting in his supervisor's coffee. I know it sounds childish, but it is a true story and does make a point.

In retrospect, as well as looking forward, I can't imagine what would slow, much less lead to a theoretical reinterpretation, of the increasingly flourishing literature on procedural justice, especially as it appears in the workplace. I will pretend, however, that the evidence and ideas presented here may lead some editors to require investigators to raise and address the next necessary questions. We know a great deal more than we did 50 years ago about how justice considerations influence people's lives, but it is still only a promising beginning.

In the meantime, while waiting to see what happens next, I hope none of the authors whose work I cited to present my arguments here have the opportunity to offer me a cup of coffee.

References

Adams, J. S. (1963). Toward an understanding of inequity. *Journal of Abnormal and Social Psychology, 67*, 422–436.

Aguiar, P., Vala, J., Correis, I., & Pereira, C. (2008). Justice in our world and in that of others: Belief in a just world and reactions to victims. *Social Justice Research, 21*, 50–68.

Aron, A., Aron, E. N., & Smollan, D. (1992).Inclusion of the other in the self scale and the structure of interpersonal closeness. *Journal of Personality and Social Psychology, 63, 596–612.*

Babcock, L., Loewenstein, G., Issacharoff, S., & Camerer, C. (1995). Biased judgments for fairness in bargaining. *American Economic Review, 85*, 1337–1343.

Batson, C. D. (1991). *The altruism question: Toward a social-psychological answer*. Hillsdale, NJ: Erlbaum.

Batson, C. D. (1998). Altruism and prosocial behavior. In D. Gilbert, S. Fiske, & G. Lindzey (Eds.) *Handbook of Social Psychology* (pp. 282–316). New York, NY: McGraw-Hill.

Batson, C. D., Kobrynowicz, D., Dinnerstein, J. L., Kampf, H. C., & Wilson, A. D. (1997). In a very different voice: Unmasking moral hypocrisy. *Journal of Personality and Social Psychology, 72*, 1335–1348.

Batson, C. D., Thompson, E. R., & Chen, H. (2002). Moral hypocrisy: Addressing some alternatives. *Journal of Personality and Social Psychology, 83*, 330–339.

Batson, C. D., Thompson, E. R., Seuferling, G., Whitney, H., & Strongman, J. A. (1999). Moral hypocrisy: Appearing moral to oneself without being so. *Journal of Personality and Social Psychology, 77*, 525–537.

Bazerman, M. H., White, S. B., & Loewenstein, G. F. (1995). Perceptions of fairness in interpersonal and individual choice situations. *Current Directions in Psychological Science, 4*, 39–42.

Blader, S. L., & Tyler, T. R. (2003). A Four-component model of procedural justice: Defining the meaning of a "fair" process. *Personality and Social Psychology Bulletin, 29*, 747–758.

Blau, P. M.(1964). *Exchange and Power in Social Life*. New York, NY: Wiley.

Boas, Franz (1966). *Kwakiutl ethnography*. Helen Codere (Ed.). Chicago, IL: University of Chicago Press.

Braband, J., & Lerner, M. J. (1975). "A little time and effort" . . . Who deserves what from whom? *Personality and Social Psychology Bulletin, 1*, 177–180.

Brockner, J., Heuer, L., Siegel, P., Wiesenfeld, B., Martin, C., Grover, S., . . . Bjorgvinsson, S. (1998). The moderating effect of self-esteem: Converging evidence from four studies. *Journal of Personality and Social Psychology, 75*, 394–407.

Brockner, J., Tyler, T. R., & Cooperr-Schneider R. (1992).The influence of prior commitment to an institution on reactions to perceived unfairness: The higher they are the harder they fall. *The Administrative Science Quarterly, 37*, 241–261.

Brosnan, S., & De Waal, F. (2003). Monkeys reject unequal pay. *Nature, 425*(6955), 297–299.

Buunk, B. P., Doosje, B. J. Jans, L. G. J. M., & Hopstaken, L. E. M. (1993). Perceived reciprocity, social support, and stress at work: The role of exchange and communal orientation. *Journal of Personality and Social Psychology, 65*, 801–811.

Callan, M. J. (Under Review) Immanent justice reasoning: Heightened when justice is frustrated, diminished when it is satisfied. *Social Psychological and Personality Sciences.*

Callan, M. J., Ellard, J. H. and Nicol, J. E. (2006). Belief in a just world and immanent justice reasoning. *Personality and Social Psychology Bulletin, 32*, 1–13.

Callan, M. J., Ferguson, H. J., & Bindemann, M. (2013a). Eye Movements to Audio-Visual Scenes Reveal Expectations of a Just-World. *Journal of Experimental Psychology: General, 142*, 34–40.

Callan, M. J., Harvey, A. J., Dawtry, R. J., & Sutton, R. J. (2013b). Focusing on long term goals increases immanent justice reasoning. *British Journal of Social Psychology, 52*, 377–385.

Callan, M., Kay, A., Davidenko, N., & Ellard, J. H. (2009a). The effects of justice motivation on memory for self- and other-relevant events. *Journal of Experimental Social Psychology, 46*, 614–623,

Callan, M. J., Shead, N. W., & Olson, J. M. (2009b). Foregoing the labor for the fruits: The effect of just world threat on the desire for immediate monetary rewards, *Journal of Experimental Social Psychology, 45*, 246–249.

Callan, M. J., Sutton, R. M., & Dovale, C. (2010). When deserving translates into causing: The effect of cognitive load on imminent justice. *Journal of Experimental Social Psychology, 46*, 1097–1100.

Clark, M. S., & Mills, J. (1979). Interpersonal attraction in exchange and communal relationships. *Journal of Personality and Social Psychology, 37*, 12–24.

Correia, I., Vala, J., & Aguiar, P. (2007). Victim's innocence, social categorization, and the threat to the belief in a just world. *Journal of Experimental Social Psychology, 43*, 31–38.

Crosby, F. (1976). A model of egoistical relative deprivation. *Psychological Review, 83*, 85–113.

Deutsch, M. (1975). Equity, equality, and need: What determines which value will be used as the basis of distributive justice? *Journal of Social Issues, 31*, 137–150.

Dols, J. F., Aguilar, P., Campo, S., Vallacher, R., Janowsky, A., Rabbia, H., ... Lerner, M. J. (2010). Moral hypocrisy or legitimate self interest? Normative conflict and decision-making in zero-sum situations. *Journal of Experimental Social Psychology, 46*, 525–530.

Freud, Sigmund (1953). *The standard edition of the complete psychological works of Sigmund Freud* (James Strachey, Trans.). London UK: Hogarth.

Goldberg, J., Lerner, J., & Tetlock, P. (1999). Rage and reason: The psychology of the intuitive prosecutor. *The European Journal of Social Psychology, 29*, 781–795.

Greenberg, J. (1993). Stealing in the name of justice: information and interpersonal moderators of theft reactions to underpayment inequity. *Organizational Behavior and Human Decision Processes, 54*, 81–103

Hafer, C. L. (2000a). Do innocent victims threaten the belief in a just world? Evidence from a modified Stroop task. *Journal of Personality and Social Psychology, 79*, 165–173.

Hafer, C. L. (2000b). Investment in long term goals and commitment to just means drive the need to believe in a just world. *Personality and Social Psychology Bulletin, 26*, 1059–1073.

Haidt, J. (2001). The emotional dog and its rational tail: A social intuitionist approach to moral judgment. *Psychological Review, 108*, 814–834.

Haidt, J.(2012). *Righteous Mind: Why good people are divided by politics and religion.* New York, NY: Random House.

Hastorf, A. H., & Cantril, H. (1954). They saw a game: A case study. *Journal of Abnormal and Social, 49*, 129–134.

Heider, F. (1958). *The psychology of interpersonal relations.* New York, NY: Wiley.

Heuer, L., Blumenthal, E., Douglas, A., & Weinblatt, T. (1999). A deservingness approach to respect as a relationally based fairness judgment. *Personality and Social Psychology Bulletin, 25*(10), 1279–1292.

Hoffman, M. (1970). Moral development. In P. Mussen (Ed.), *Carmichael's manual of child psychology* (pp. 261–359). New York, NY: Wiley.

Lerner, J., Goldberg, J., & Tetlock, P. (1998). Sober second thoughts: The effects of accountability, anger, and authoritarianism on attributions of responsibility. *Personality and Social Psychology Bulletin, 24*, 563–574.

Lerner, M. J. (1974). The justice motive: "Equity" and "parity" among children. *Journal of Personality and Social Psychology, 29*, 539–550.

Lerner, M. J. (1975). The justice motive in social behavior: Introduction. *Journal of Social Issues, 31*, 1–20.

Lerner, M. J. (1980). *The belief in a just world: A fundamental delusion.* New York, NY: Plenum.

Lerner, M. J. (1981). The justice motive in human relations: Some thoughts on what we know and need to know about justice. In M. J. Lerner & S. C. Lerner (Eds.), *The justice motive in social behavior: Adapting to times of scarcity and change* (pp. 11–35). New York, NY: Plenum.

Lerner, M. J. (2003). The justice motive: Where social psychologists found it, how they lost it, and why they may not find it again. *Personality and Social Psychology Review, 7*, 388–409.

Lerner, M. J. (2001). The "Normative" and "Intuitive" senses of justice., ISJR-Newsletter—1st Issue; June 2001,

Lerner, M. J., & Becker, S. W. (1996). Managers at risk: The hidden costs of normatively justified harm doing. *Quality Management Journal, 3*, 23–35.

Lerner, M. J., & Clayton, S. (2011). Justice & Self Interesst: Two fundamental motives. New York, NY: Cambridge University Press.

Lerner, M. J., Dillehay, R. C., & Sherer, W. C. (1967). Similarity and attraction in social contexts. *Journal of Personality and Social Psychology, 5*, 481–486.

Lerner, M. J., & Grant, P. R. (1990). The influence of commitment to justice and ethnocentrism on children's allocations of pay. *Social Psychology Quarterly, 53*, 229–238.

Lerner, M. J. *and* Lichtman, R. R. (1968). Effects of perceived norms on attitudes and altruistic behavior toward a dependent other. *Journal of Personality and Social Psychology, 9*, 226–232.

Lerner, M. J., & Miller, D. T. (1978) "Just World" research and the attribution process: Looking back and ahead. *Psychological Bulletin, 85*, 1030–1051.

Lerner, M. J., Miller, D. T., & Holmes, J. G. (1976). Deserving and the emergence of forms of justice. In L. Berkowitz

(Ed.), *Advances in experimental social psychology*, Vol. 9 (pp 134–162). New York, NY: Academic Press.

Lerner, M. J., Somers, D., Reid, D., & Tierney, M. (1989). Sibling Conflicts induced by dependent elderly parents: The social psychology of individual and social dilemmas in Spacapan, S., & S. Oskamp (Eds.). *The social psychology of aging: Claremont Symposium on Applied Social Psychology* Newbury Park, CA: Sage.

Levinson, H. (1994). Why the behemoths fell: Psychological roots of corporate failure. *American Psychologist, 49*, 428–436.

Lind, E. A. and Tyler, T. R. (1988). *The social psychology of procedural justice*. New York, NY: Plenum.

Long, G. T., & Lerner, M. J. (1974). Deserving, the "Personal Contract," and altruistic behavior by children. *Journal of Personality and Social Psychology, 29*, 551–556.

Loewenstein, G., Thompson, L., & Bazerman, M. H. (1989). Social utility and decision making interpersonal contexts. *Journal of Personality and Social Psychology, 57*, 426–441.

Maner, J. K., Luce, C. L., Neuberg, S. L., Cialdini, R. B., Brown, S., & Sagarin, B. J. (2002). The *Personality and Social Psychology Bulletin, 28*,1601–1610.

Markovsky. B. (1988). Injustice and arousal. *Social Justice Research, 2*, 223–233.

Mauss, Marcel (1990). *The Gift*. London, UK: Routledge.

Merton, R. K. (1957). *Social theory and social structure*. Glencoe, IL: Free Press.

Messick, D. M., & Sentis K. (1983). Fairness preference and fairness biases. In D. M. Messick, and K. S. Cook (Eds.), *Equity theory: Psychological and sociological perspectives* (pp. 61–94). New York: Praeger.

Miller, D. T. (1999). The norm of self-interest. *American Psychologist, 54*, 1053–1060.

Miller, D. T. (2001). Disrespect and the experience of injustice. *Annual Review of Psychology, 52*, 527–553.

Mischel, W. (1961). Preference for delayed reinforcement and social responsibility. *Journal of Abnormal and Social Psychology, 62*, 1–7.

Mischel, W., Shoda, Y & Peake, P. K. (1988); the nature of adolescent competencies predicted by preschool delay of gratification. *Journal of Personality and Social Psychology, 54*(4), 687–696.

Moore, D. A. (2007). Not so above average afer all: When people believe they are worse than average and its implications for theories of bias construction. *Organizational Behavior and Human Decision Processes, 102*, 42–58.

Olson, K. R., Banaji, M. R., Dweck, C. S., & Spelke, E. S. (2006). Children's bias against lucky vs. unlucky people and their social groups. *Psychological Science, 17*, 845–846.

Olson, K. R., Dunham, Y., Dweck, C. S., Spelke, E. S., and Banaji, M. R. (2008). Judgments of the lucky across development and culture. *Journal of Personality and Social Psychology, 94*, 757–776.

Ratner, R. K., & Miller, D. T. (2001). The norm of self-interest and its effects on social action. *Journal of Personality and Social Psychology, 81*, 5–16.

Rusbult, C. E., Lowery, D., Hubbard, M. L., Maravankin, O. J. and Neises, M. (1988). Impact of employee mobility and employee performance on the allocation of rewards under conditions of constraint. *Journal of Personality and Social Psychology, 54*, 605–615.

Shaver, K. G. (1985). *The attribution of blame: Causality, responsibility, and blameworthiness*. New York, NY: Springer-Verlag.

Skitka, L., Aramavitch, L. P., Lytle, B. L., & Sargis, E. G. (2009). Knitting together an elephant: An integrative approach to understanding the psychology of justice reasoning. In D. R. Bobocel, A. C. Kay, M. P. Zanna, & J. M. Olson (Eds.), *The psychology of justice and legitimacy: The Ontario symposium, Vol. 11* (pp. 1–26). Philadelphia, PA: Psychology Press.

Smith, L. (1994). Burned out Bosses. *Fortune, 25*, 44–52.

Stillwell, A. M., & Baumeister, R. F. (1997). The construction of victim and perpetrator memories: Accuracy and distortion in role-based accounts. *Personality and Social Psychology Bulletin, 23*, 1157–1172.

Sunshine, J., & Heuer, L. (2002). Deservingness and perceptions of procedural justice in citizen encounters with the police. In M. Ross, & D. T. Miller (Eds.), *The justice motive in everyday life*. Cambridge, UK: Cambridge University Press.

Tajfel, H., & Turner, J. C. (1986). The social identity theory of intergroup behavior. In S. Worchel & W. G. Austin (Eds.), *Psychology of intergroup relations* (pp. 7–24). Chicago, IL: Nelson-Hall.

Towson, S., Lerner, M. J., & de Carufel, A. (1981). Justice rules or ingroup loyalties: The effects of competition on children's allocation behavior. *Personality and Social Psychology Bulletin, 7*, 696–674.

Tyler, T. R. (1994). Psychological models of the justice motive: Antecedents of distributive and procedural justice. *Journal of Personality and Social Psychology, 67*, 850–863.

Tyler, T. R., & Blader, S. L. (2003). The group engagement model: Procedural justice, social identity, and cooperative behavior. *Personality and Social Psychology Review, 7*, 349–361.

Walster, E., Walster, G. W., & Berscheid, E. (1978). *Equity theory and research*. New York, NY: Allyn Bacon.

Weiner, B. (1993). On sin versus sickness: A theory of perceived responsibility and social motivation. *American Psychologist, 48*, 957–965.

CHAPTER

10

The Third-Party Perspective of (In)justice

Daniel P. Skarlicki, Jane O'Reilly, *and* Carol T. Kulik

Abstract

For every victim unfairly treated by an organization or its agents, there are many third parties who can witness or learn about the mistreatment. Skarlicki and Kulik (2005) presented a model of third-party reactions to injustice, describing the attributional and perceptual processes that operate between learning about an injustice and acting on that injustice. In this chapter, we review the literature on third-party responses to injustice and note three post-2005 developments. First, drawing from research on the adaptationist perspective, we discuss the evolutionary mechanisms that incorporate both moral and self-interest motives for third-party reactions. Second, we review research that has moved beyond a focus on punishing the transgressor to third parties helping the victim. Third, we highlight research that examines the role of "hot" versus "cold" emotional processes in third-party reactions. We incorporate these developments into a revised model of third-party behavior.

Key Words: third parties, moral motives, self-interest, cold versus hot reactions, punishment, helping

"Justice will not be served until those who are unaffected are as outraged as those who are."

—*Benjamin Franklin*

This chapter is about the third party's perspective on workplace (mis)treatment. Third parties are defined as individuals who are not the direct recipients of a given treatment, but who can react nonetheless. Their perspective is important because, for every victim, multiple third parties exist, including those occupying informal (friends, co-workers, customers) and formal (managers, judges, mediators) roles. Third-party reactions to unfair treatment can range from a sympathetic (e.g., providing aid to the victim; punishing the transgressor) to an unsympathetic (e.g., siding with the transgressor; victim blaming) response to the victim, which can have important consequences for the transgressor, the victim, and other third parties. On occasion, individuals can occupy a dual role as a first person (e.g., a victim) and third party (e.g., observing co-workers' treatment) to workplace (mis)treatment. Research shows that the first- and third-party justice perceptions combined to predict eight times more variance in employee behavior than did first person perceptions alone (Colquitt, 2004). Although most often studied at the individual level of analysis, the third-party perspective of mistreatment also has important group and firm level effects. For example, if a supervisor mistreats one member of a group, team members can band together as a collective to retaliate (Christian, Christian, Garza, & Ellis, 2012). Bosse, Phillips, and Harrison (2009) proposed that (*ceteris paribus)* firms that are viewed by their stakeholders as fair generate higher firm performance than firms viewed as unfair.

Drawing from research on a broad set of disciplines, Skarlicki and Kulik (2005) developed a model of third parties' reactions to others' mistreatment. Since that time, considerable research has amassed on this topic. Studies have found, for instance, that observing mistreatment can negatively impact third parties' cooperation and citizenship behaviors (De Cremer & Van Hiel, 2006) and performance on both routine and creative tasks (Porath & Erez, 2009). The way hotel management treats its staff significantly predicts guests' loyalty and dysfunctional behavior (Zoghbi-Manrique-de-Lara, Aguiar-Quintana, & Suárez-Acosta, 2013). Furthermore, when employees treat one another in an uncivil manner, bystander customers make negative inferences about the entire company and its other employees (Porath, MacInnis, & Folkes, 2010). Research has identified important biases (Blader, Weiesenfeld, Fortin, & Wheeler-Smith, 2013) and nonconscious processes (Zdaniuk & Bobocel, 2013) that impact third-party responses. Studies have also examined how social media can engage third parties to respond to organizational wrongdoing (Kulik, Pepper, Shapiro, & Cregan, 2012).

Our objective in this chapter is to integrate the key features of Skarlicki and Kulik's (2005) model with recent theory and empirical research. First, we address the key question: Why do people care about others' (mis)treatment in the first place? Skarlicki and Kulik (2005) focused on two key reasons: self-interest and moral, which are described briefly in the following subsection. In moving the field forward, however, we explain how the adaptationist perspective can advance understanding of third-party reactions. Second, we explain how research appears to be moving beyond a focus on transgressor punishment toward helping the victim. Third, we review the new empirical research within the Skarlicki and Kulik (2005) framework, with particular emphasis on the third party's decision to act. Last, we offer suggestions for future research.

Why Do Third Parties Care about Others' Mistreatment?

Third parties can care about another's mistreatment for a host of reasons. Skarlicki and Kulik (2005) defined third-party motives in terms of two general orientations: self-interest and justice as a moral imperative.

SELF-INTEREST PERSPECTIVE

Self-interest theories are based on the assumption that people are motivated by rational self-interest in their dealings with others (c.f. Miller, 1999). Instrumental models of justice suggest that injustice imposes a "cost," either tangible (e.g., money, resources, time) or intangible (e.g., threat to self-esteem), and that individuals respond negatively to injustice in order to protect or restore their interests. In line with the self-interest view, equity theory (Adams, 1965) recognizes that people often compare their outcomes-to-inputs ratio with that of others, and they become upset when the relative ratios do not match. Social exchange theories (Blau, 1964) suggest that it is personally beneficial to abide by normative exchange rules. The relational model of justice (Lind & Taylor, 1988) posits that justice concerns are also associated with concerns about one's own social standing in a group (Lind & Tyler, 1988). Instrumental models of procedural justice (Thibaut & Walker, 1975) propose that people care about fair procedures in order to ensure more control over the decision-making process and maximize their own benefits. Finally, the uncertainty model (formerly the fairness heuristic model) proposes that individuals strive to reduce the uncertainty in their lives, and fair treatment of others can contribute to one's own feelings of certainty (Lind & van den Bos, 2002). Put simply, third parties sometimes care about others' mistreatment because it arouses self-concerns. Third parties might be disturbed by injustice because they are worried about similar mistreatment befalling them or because they internalize the harm caused to someone else, such as a close friend or kin.

THE MORAL PERSPECTIVE

The moral perspective presents an alternative to pure self-interest explanations. Third parties sometimes respond to the mistreatment of others because it is the "right thing to do." The third party's concern is an end in itself, not solely a means to attaining self-interest goals (Cropanzano, Goldman, & Folger, 2005). Folger (2001) coined the term *deontic justice* to reference an evolutionary-based psychological state producing emotionally charged reactions to events seen as violating or infringing on moral norms about social conduct. Deontic emotional experiences are derived from individuals' moral assumptions regarding how human beings *should* be treated and motivate third parties to punish rule-breakers (Folger, 2001).

The moral perspective opens up the possibility that third parties can become upset and react negatively even when they have no apparent self-interest in the situation and no relevant relationship with a victim of mistreatment. When consumers become outraged by workers toiling in dangerous conditions in third-world countries, or when citizens condemn a business executive's sex scandal even when they have no direct stake in the company, they are likely motivated by a moral imperative (Nowak & Sigmund, 2005). Furthermore, third-party behavior can explicitly contradict self-interest motives when third parties are willing to accept a personal cost to protest mistreatment, stand up for a victim, or punish a transgressor (Adams & Mullen, 2012). Whistle-blowing research, for example, has documented the severe backlash and life-changing repercussions whistle-blowers face when they attempt to expose unethical behavior to public scrutiny (Rehg, Miceli, Near, & Van Scotter, 2008).

Integrating Self-Interest and Moral Motives: The Adaptationist Perspective

Although scholars have argued over the relative importance of self-interest versus moral motives in explaining third-party reactions (see Cropanzano et al., 2005), we propose that these two motives can be complementary and operate simultaneously. Several scholars have adopted an adaptationist perspective to explain people's reactions to unfairness (e.g., Darwin, 1871; Fehr & Gächter, 2000, 2002; Folger & Skarlicki, 2008; Haidt, 2007; Kesebir, 2012; Trivers, 1971).

The adaptationist perspective describes individuals' psychological responses to unfairness as mechanisms that evolved from efforts to solve ancestral problems (Cosmides & Tooby, 1987). A key feature of the adaptationist perspective is that it explains third-party responses by emphasizing *ultimate* (i.e., the evolutionary history) rather than *proximate* (i.e., psychological, emotional, and cognitive) mechanisms of human behavior (Barclay, 2012). This perspective integrates moral and self-interest explanations: third parties' reactions to injustice can be innate and evolutionary-based psychological responses centered on feelings and cognitions of right and wrong, but these reactions serve a self-interest function, even if this function is not consciously acknowledged by the individual.

The adaptationist perspective suggests that sensitivity to others' mistreatment has positive implications for group functioning and individual success. This literature highlights the evolutionary foundation of *reciprocity*, the near universal human propensity to respond with hostility (kindness) to hostility (to kindness) (Dunfee, 2006; Gouldner, 1960). Reciprocity can promote and sustain cooperation over time; cooperative individuals experience more success than uncooperative individuals because their cooperative behavior is reciprocated within their exchange relationships (Axelrod, 1984).

The adaptationist perspective emphasizes the evolutionary role of social sanctioning in maintaining cooperative behavior. Punishment discourages uncooperative behavior—including unfair behavior. Experiments using economic distribution-game paradigms show that people are willing to accept a cost to punish players who take more than their fair share of resources, even when the punishers are third parties to the injustice (Fehr & Gächter, 2002; Fehr & Fischbacher, 2004; Henrich et al., 2006; Turillo, Folger, Lavelle, Umphress, & Gee, 2002). Furthermore, when the game makes it possible to punish unfair players, players engage in less unfair behavior, and act more cooperatively after they have been punished for a transgression (Boyd & Richerson, 1992; Fehr & Gächter, 2002). Punishment puts a cost on behaving unfairly, and can discourage unfair behavior so that more positive exchanges can benefit the entire group.

To date, little research has directly tested whether social punishment in organizations has benefits that parallel those observed in economic game contexts. However, research on workplace gossip suggests that social punishment does encourage cooperation. Gossip enables people to show contempt and ridicule wrongdoers. It has been described as a mechanism for the "unpowerful" to rein in abusive power (Keltner, Van Kleef, Chen, & Kraus, 2008). Gossip can also create incentives for people to modify their behavior, because negative gossip can adversely affect one's reputation and social standing (Beersma & van Kleef, 2012). Workplace ostracism can also be wielded as an informal tool to punish co-workers who violate social norms (Robinson, O'Reilly, & Wang, 2013). An individual will conform (either consciously or unconsciously) to protect his or her own interpersonal success and social integration, and the group benefits from the cooperative behavior of its members.

The link between third-party retribution and positive outcomes can also be observed at the macro level, where organizations are concerned with their corporate reputation and brand image. Bosse et al. (2009) noted that broader societal norms of fairness can rein in organizations' otherwise selfish utility-maximizing behavior. Drawing from stakeholder theory, they argued that firms that act in accordance with fairness norms generate economic value and those that do not can face retribution from their stakeholders.

DeScioli and Kurzban (2009) proposed that third-party contempt and punishment have also played an evolutionary role in developing a moral conscience. When third parties who care about norm violations are present in a social system, and are willing to sanction norm violators, individuals feel greater responsibility to act in socially acceptable ways (Sommerfeld, Krambeck, Semmann, & Milinski, 2007). Third-party punishment promotes cooperation because it imposes external costs to engaging in counter-normative behavior, but it also encourages internal costs. When one treats another unfairly, or violates norms of ethical conduct, these costs are experienced as guilt and shame.

How Will Third Parties Respond?

When third parties recognize others' injustice, they can react in a number of ways. Lerner's (1980) research on belief in a just world suggests that most people need to believe that they live in a world where people, including themselves, get what they deserve and conversely, deserve what they get. Becoming aware of others' experience of injustice, either in the form of deprivation and suffering (Lerner & Simmons, 1966) or privilege (Lerner, 1980), poses a threat to the just world belief that, in turn, motivates the third party to restore justice. But justice can be restored cognitively as well as behaviorally, and observers can derogate innocent victims as a way of maintaining their belief in a just world (see Lerner, 1980, for a review). Triana, Kim, and Garcia (2011) found a negative relationship between third-party perceptions of discrimination against minorities at work and their own citizenship behavior toward minorities. Just-world beliefs can be maintained in the presence of observed discrimination by blaming victims for the discrimination—and if the victims are deemed somehow responsible for the discrimination, they don't deserve to be helped. In some cases, third parties can instead punish an otherwise innocent mistreatment victim. Skarlicki and Turner (2013) showed that the victim derogation process can infiltrate human-resource decisions. Specifically, they found that managers provide lower ratings to a job applicant, and peers provide a lower performance rating to a co-worker, who was previously unfairly treated as compared to an identical employee who was treated fairly. Loseman and van den Bos (2012) provide evidence that the tendency to blame an innocent victim is exacerbated under conditions of ego-depletion, and lessened when third parties experience self-affirmation.

Much of the recent research on third-party reactions in an organizational context has focused on third-party punishment (e.g., Christian et al., 2012; Folger, 2001; Porath, MacInnis, & Folkes, 2011; Skarlicki & Rupp, 2010). Consistent with predictions based on the deontic and adaptationist perspectives, the urge to punish transgressors can be so great that third parties are sometimes willing to accept a considerable cost to punish (Adams & Mullen, 2012). For example, in protest against the United States' former military policy of "Don't Ask, Don't Tell," which prevents openly gay, lesbian, and bisexual individuals from joining the military, the Vermont Law School refused to allow military recruiters to recruit on campus—forfeiting nearly $500,000 in federal funding as a result (Sanchez, 2005).

However, not all third parties will engage in costly punishment. Guala (2012) documented group-based strategies that offer less costly ways for people to punish transgressors, including gossip, social ridicule, and ostracism. Third parties might withdraw support of a transgressor rather than actively punishing him or her. Christian and colleagues (2012) found that employees will indirectly retaliate against abusive supervision directed toward one of their co-workers by reducing organizational citizenship behaviors that aid their supervisor. Third parties' contempt for unfairness can also be displayed in reduced commitment toward the transgressor (Lambert, Hogan, & Griffen, 2007). Hotel customers are less likely to return to hotels that treat their staff unfairly (Zoghbi-Manrique-de-Lara et al., 2013), and employees will quit as a means of resistance to bullying (Lutgen-Sanvik, 2005).

Rather than attempt to get back at the transgressor, a third party might try to mediate or solve the conflict. In a qualitative study, Ryan and Wessel (2012) found that when third parties witnessed sexual orientation harassment directed toward co-workers, the most likely intervention strategy (beyond doing nothing) was to try to defuse the situation by steering the conversation to a different subject. Third parties might also help the victim. In a recent survey, the Workplace Bullying Institute found that 30% of those who felt mistreated at work indicated that at least one bystander offered them socio-emotional support or helped them directly. Helping the victim is a relatively low-cost strategy, and one that third parties can implement without engaging other people. For example, Nadisic (2008) proposed that managers can engage in Robin Hoodism—providing unfairly treated employees with an "unauthorized" benefit as a way to restore their employees' and their own fairness perceptions. Third parties can also show their support for a labor strike by refusing to cross a picket line, writing supportive letters, and directly encouraging union members (Kelloway, Francis, Catano, & Dupré, 2008).

Researchers have suggested that punishing a transgressor and helping a victim of injustice are complementary third-party reactions (Darley & Pitman, 2003; Leliveld, van Dijk, & van Beest, 2012; Lotz, Baumert, Schlösser, Gresser, & Fetchenhauer, 2011; Lotz, Okimoto, Schlössera, & Fetchenhauer, 2011; O'Reilly & Aquino, 2011; Okimoto, Wenzel, & Feather, 2012; van Prooijen, 2009). This research has focused on explaining why and when a third party will either punish a transgressor or help a victim of unfairness (or engage in both forms of recourse). Some scholars have argued for "punishment primacy" suggesting that third parties will punish rather than help if this course of action is available to them. For example, in an economic game paradigm, van Prooijen (2009) found that when a third party is more socially distant from a victim, s/he prefers to punish a transgressor (impose a fine) rather than support the victim (offer financial compensation). Other scholars have noted, however, that how a third party responds to injustice ultimately depends on the context, and the third party's relationships with the other people involved (O'Reilly & Aquino, 2011). Third parties can both punish the transgressor and help the victim if both strategies are available. Evidence that third parties use a "mixed-strategy" approach is found in a series of economic distribution game experiments (Leliveld et al., 2012; Lotz, Okimoto, et al., 2011). Charness, Cobo-Reyes, and Jiménez (2008) reported that when third parties were able to both help a victim (through monetary compensation) and punish the transgressor (through fines), they devoted less money to punishing as opposed to when they were only given the option to punish. However, third parties spent more on both compensation and punishment combined when this option was available than the amount spent on punishment in the "punishment-only" condition. Similarly, in a policy-capturing study of labor disputes, Mahony and Klaas (2008) found that arbitration experts and jurors endorse punitive damages, over and above victim compensation awards, when a victim is seen as less deserving of unfair treatment.

Some scholars have explored why helping the victim, instead of punishing a transgressor, can help to satisfy a third party's need for justice. Darley and Pittman (2003), for example, discuss how both the retributive and compensatory arms of the justice system can help restore justice. In social-justice research, compensatory justice refers to restoring a victim to a position that is similar to the position they had before the injustice occurred, usually in an economic sense. In the social-sphere, providing the victims of injustice with comfort and support can help restore their otherwise threatened relational needs. From a psychological perspective, injustice, whether it is directed at one's self or another, disrupts one's sense of balance (Zhu, Martens, & Aquino, 2012), and helping the victim is another strategy (beyond punishment) a third party can use to restore their own sense of balance.

In summary, third parties' behavioral reactions can take a variety of forms. In the following section, expanding on Skarlicki and Kulik (2005), we describe a model that aims to describe the process underlying third parties' decision to act.

An Integrated Model of Third-Party Reactions

Drawing upon previous work (Skarlicki & Kulik, 2005), we present a model of third-party reactions to employee (mis)treatment in Figure 10.1. Bold text indicates those areas where the most research attention has been directed since 2005. The model begins at the point where third parties gain information about an exchange between an organizational member (including bosses, co-workers, or customers) and an employee. Judgments are made regarding whether the potential "victim" has been negatively impacted and whether his or her entitlements regarding distributive (i.e., outcomes), procedural (i.e., procedures used to derive one's outcomes), informational (i.e., explanations by an authority figure) or interpersonal (i.e., lacking dignity and respect) treatment have been neglected or violated.

Once negative impact has been established, third parties are motivated to locate blame. As noted earlier, once a third party decides to act, their responses

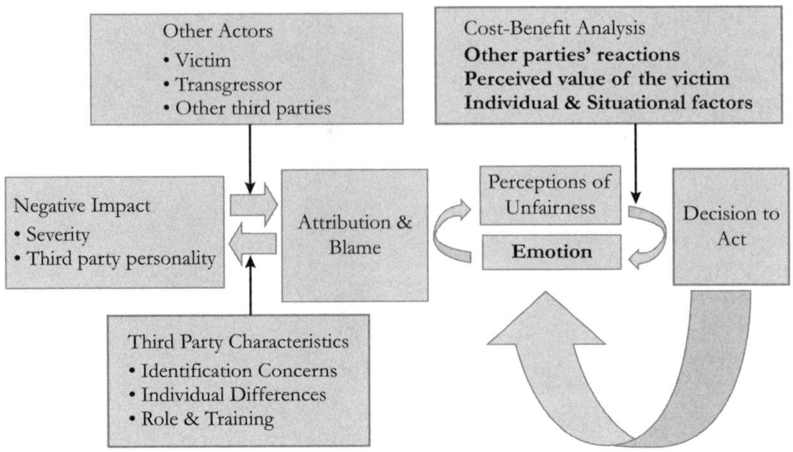

Fig. 10.1 Model of Third-Party Reactions.

can range from sympathetic (e.g., acknowledging the victim's dilemma, blaming the organization and/or its agent, taking action to restore the injustice, distancing oneself from or punishing the organization or its agent) to unsympathetic responses (e.g., denying that an injustice has occurred, blaming the victim for his or her own plight, ignoring or distancing oneself from the victim, aligning oneself with the organization or its agent) (Batson, Fultz, & Schoenrade, 1987; Brockner & Greenberg, 1990; Hoffman, 1989; Stotland, 1969).

Establishing Negative Treatment

As a general principle, the more severe the mistreatment, the greater the perceived unfairness. The more severe the mistreatment, the easier it is for third parties to imagine an alternative state that would have occurred had the transgressor treated the victim fairly (Folger & Cropanzano, 1998). Violations of distributive (outcome fairness), procedural (process fairness), informational (explanations for decisions), and interpersonal (dignity and respect) justice can all trigger perceptions of negative treatment. When assessing (un)fairness, the third party can consider multiple distribution rules: the equality principle (everyone should be treated the same), the need principle (those who are most in need should benefit), or the equity principle (rewards should be based on one's contributions) (Deutsch, 1975). Generally, individuals prefer the decision rule that best aligns with their predominant value system or provides them with the most favorable outcomes. If the third party has a strong preference for a different decision rule than the one that the organization or its agent applied to the victim, and can imagine that the victim would have received a more favorable outcome had the preferred rule been applied, then the third party is likely to deem the victim's outcome to be unfair. Moreover, the greater the severity, the more information processing is activated (Langer, 1989).

Although outcome negativity can be objectively determined (e.g., a larger versus smaller financial loss), it is also socially constructed, and the victim and other actors (e.g., other third parties or the organizational agent) in the broader context can influence the third party's perceptions about how much negative impact has occurred. Further, some third parties are predisposed to view a victim's outcomes as particularly negative. Individuals who score high on negative affectivity (NA), for instance, experience greater distress and dissatisfaction over life events and lower assessments of others (Watson & Clark, 1984). Negative affectivity tends to increase one's susceptibility or responsiveness to negative emotion-generating stimuli (Larsen & Ketelaar, 1991; Miceli, Van Scotter, Near & Rehg, 2001). Based on this research, third parties with high NA are more likely to be sensitive to the negative impact of someone else's mistreatment and perceive greater injustice as a result, compared to those with low NA. However, as we will detail next, how and whether high NA third parties respond ultimately depends on their interpretations of the situation, the emotions they experience, and their relationships with the parties involved.

Attributions and Blame

If the third party concludes that the victim has suffered negative impact, the next step is to allocate blame for the outcome, and decide who should be held accountable. Bell and Main (2011), for example, found that third parties were motivated to seek information about agents who had behaved unethically, even if the agent and available information were irrelevant to the third parties' goals and interests. This information seeking took place even when third parties could disengage from and were not vulnerable to the agent. In short, third parties can act on an innate motivation to gain information about justice violations, particularly when they perceive the transgressor has violated a moral and social norm.

In order for the third party to conclude that the victim was unfairly treated, the third party must hold the organization or its agent(s) responsible for the victim's outcomes. Negative outcomes that were unavoidable, or negative outcomes that were brought about by the victim's own behavior, are not deemed to be mistreatment. If unfavorable outcomes are seen as being self-inflicted—as though the victim behaved carelessly or "brought it on him- or herself"—justice concerns are often allayed (Ryan, 1971).

Outcome negativity and attributions of blame can have a reciprocal impact on one another, as indicated by the parallel arrows in the figure. Studies of whistle-blowing show that the more severe the wrongdoing, the more that third parties will be motivated to determine its source and what should be done about it (Miceli & Near, 1992). Moreover, the greater the harm experienced by a victim, the more likely it is that a third party will ascribe intention and responsibility to the transgressor (Lerner & Miller, 1978; Shaver, 1970; Walster, 1966). But once an attribution of responsibility is made, the attribution itself can impact the perceived negativity of the victim's outcomes.

When one person intentionally harms another, far more is involved than the resulting physical or material hurt. The intentional offender can be seen as demonstrating contempt for the victim or the victim's social group, as though asserting superiority over the victim's beliefs or value system (Miller & Vidmar, 1981). Intentional wrongdoing is seen as more severe and unfair than unintentional mistreatment because the former threatens the social order and can predict future offenses (Heider, 1958; Miller & Vidmar, 1981). Umphress, Simmons, Folger, Ren, and Bobocel (2012), for example, found that third parties reacted more negatively to another's mistreatment when a transgressor indicated intent to cause harm. Interestingly, the mere intent to cause injustice generated negative reactions even in the absence of a true victim (Zoghbi-Manrique-de-Lara & Suárez-Acosta, 2013) suggesting that third parties are especially reactant to violations of interpersonal justice because the transgressor is deemed to be personally responsible for his or her actions.

Once a third party concludes that the organization or its agents intended to harm the victim, these social wrongs are included in the third party's assessment and add to the third party's impressions of the severity of the victim's negative outcomes. As the perceived severity of the victim's outcomes grows, the more intensely the third party searches for a responsible agent, and sees the organization or transgressor as firmly "on the hook" and accountable for the victim's negative experience.

This reciprocal relationship between negative impact and attributions of responsibility (Miller, 2001) suggests that third parties are likely to deem some types of fairness rule violations as more offensive than others. For instance, whereas third parties can view distributive and procedural justice violations as unfair (Brockner, 1990; Skarlicki, Ellard, & Kelln, 1998), interpersonal injustices are likely to loom especially large. This is because, whereas the responsibility associated with distributive and procedural justice violations can be hard to pinpoint, there is less ambiguity when locating blame for interpersonal mistreatment. A manager who fires an employee with no advance notice and no severance pay might not be seen as responsible for the employee's job loss if other parties (e.g., the President who failed to revive a sagging economy, the profit-seeking shareholders, or the bullies in corporate headquarters) are viable causal agents. However, that manager will be seen as highly responsible for mistreatment if the news of the firing is communicated insensitively or rudely to the employee. Moreover, interpersonal violations can lead the victim to experience social or psychological harm. Such violations are deemed more severe and unfair than violations of material harm (Alicke, 1992). Interpersonal justice violations signal that the transgressor not only lacks concern for the justice rule, but also that he or she is not concerned about preserving the other person's "face" (Goffman, 1952). In turn, intentionality has the greatest impact on judgments of causality and responsibility (Shultz, Schleifer, & Altman, 1981) because intentional mistreatment is viewed as predictive of subsequent wrongdoing by the offender (Miller & Vidmar, 1981).

Factors Moderating the Relationship Between (Mis)treatment and Blame

The interplay between outcome negativity, attributions of responsibility, and unfairness perceptions occurs as a function of numerous third-party factors, such as their identity concerns, individual differences, and their training and background, as well as a function of other actors' reactions.

Third-Party Characteristics

Identity concerns. A primary factor for attributing blame for mistreatment concerns the third party's identification with the victim and/or the transgressor. The more a third party identifies with the transgressor, the less likely he or she will attribute responsibility for a negative outcome (Abrams & Hogg, 1990; Kramer, 1993; Tajfel, 1982; Turner, 1987). The more a third party identifies with the victim, the more unfair the mistreatment will be perceived. Factors in this category can include affect (i.e., liking the victim), personal similarities (e.g., similar traits or experiences), and group similarities (e.g., similar work roles; Brockner & Greenberg, 1990). For example, Blader and colleagues (2013) found that the congruence of a social emotion (i.e., the extent to which a third party's emotion reflected a subjective alignment with the target of the emotion) can influence third-party evaluations of recipients' decision outcomes. Incongruent emotions toward a victim (feelings of jealousy, resentment, schadenfreude, and the like) can lead third parties to perceive objectively unfair outcomes as fair. Finally, third parties are more likely to locate blame when an injustice threatens their own outcomes (Chaiken & Darley, 1973).

INDIVIDUAL DIFFERENCES

Another aspect of the third party's identity concerns their scope of justice (Opotow, 1990; 2012). Victims who fall outside a third party's scope of justice are outside the boundary within which the third party perceives his or her moral values, rules, and considerations of fairness to apply (Staub, 1989). Mitchell, Vogel, and Folger (2012) proposed that third parties' perceptions of injustice and subsequent reactions to abusive supervision depend on the extent to which both the victim and the transgressor are included in or excluded from their scope of justice. A third party is likely to perceive the most injustice when a victim of injustice is included in their scope of justice, and the transgressor is not. Mild instances of exclusion include not recognizing undeserved suffering and mistreatment; severe instances can include being blind to violations of human rights, political repression, slavery, and genocide (Opotow, 1990). When resources are abundant, one's scope of justice is generally broad (Hogan & Emler, 1981). As resources become scarce, however, conflict between groups increases, cohesion within groups increases (Elster, 1993), and fairness concerns across groups decrease (Opotow, 2012).

Using a similar concept to scope of justice, O'Reilly and Aquino (2011) proposed that the size of third parties' "circle of moral regard" was positively related to one's moral identity, defined as the degree to which moral concerns are salient in one's identity. Skarlicki and Rupp (2010) found that managers who scored higher on moral identity saw greater unfairness and punished the transgressor more strongly for subordinate mistreatment than managers lower on moral identity.

Third parties high (versus low) on belief in a just world (BJW) (e.g., Lerner, 1980) tend to experience greater discomfort when confronted with mistreatment of innocent victims because of a greater discrepancy between their beliefs and their observations. As a result, high BJW individuals can react more strongly to injustice, but can alternatively engage in victim blaming, even without any objective evidence regarding blameworthiness (Skarlicki et al., 1998).

Individuals who see themselves as being in control of their own environment can project this perspective on others and, as a result, are more likely to assign blame for a mistreatment to a victim. Examples include authoritarianism (Adorno, Frenkel-Brunswik, Levinson, & Sanford, 1950), self-esteem (e.g., Spencer, Josephs, & Steele, 1993), illusions of control (e.g., Langer, 1975), and illusions of invulnerability (e.g., Perloff, 1983). Certain cross-cultural variables, such as power distance—the degree to which unequal distributions of power are accepted or rejected within a given society (Hofstede, 1980)—could also moderate the relationship between outcome negativity and attributions of blame among third parties. One reason for these effects are that when inequalities are powerfully justified (e.g., by political leaders), individuals in high power distance cultures are more likely to suspend or suppress their judgment of the leader's culpability for a wrongdoing.

ROLE AND TRAINING

Some third parties (e.g., arbitrators and judges) have been trained to "weigh the evidence" when judging blame (Elkouri & Elkouri, 1985). Lay observers, in contrast, are more likely to pay attention to hearsay and tend to be impacted by emotional reactions, resulting in differences in blame (Skarlicki, Brown, & Bemmels, 2012).

Other Actors

THE VICTIM

In general, the greater the victim's perceived suffering (Geer & Jarmecky, 1973) and emotional distress (Skarlicki et al., 2013), the more the third party will deem the event unfair. Whether outcome negativity relates to perceived responsibility depends on whether the third party believes that the victim deserved the treatment. Choosing to disregard rules, for instance, suggests a lack of commitment to or a lack of respect for authority. Third parties are more likely to blame a poor-performing victim for eliciting a transgressor's behavior (Niehoff, Paul, & Bunch, 1998). The victim's reaction to the transgressor's treatment can also serve as an important cue for the third party. For example, victims who respond negatively to a sexual advance (by disagreeing, frowning, or speaking in an angry tone) are more likely to be perceived by third parties as victims of sexual harassment (Summers, 1996; York, 1989). Further, federal judges are more likely to decide cases in favor of a victim of sexual harassment if the evidence indicates that the victim had subsequently utilized internal organizational grievance channels (Perry, Kulik, & Bourhis, 2004; Terpstra & Baker, 1992). Diekmann, Walker, Galinsky, and Tenbrunsel (2013) found that third parties' condemnation of passive victims of sexual harassment is in part explained by errors in third parties' affective forecasting. The more third parties believed they (themselves) would confront their own hypothetical harasser, the more they blamed passive victims for their predicament.

THE TRANSGRESSOR

The transgressor's behavior and perceived character provides information about the transgressor's intent and are used in deciding where responsibility for a negative outcome should be assigned (Landy & Aronson, 1969). A wrongdoer who has a history of rule violations is more likely to be perceived as a potential recidivist than a first-time offender. Prior offenses signal that the offender does not share a commitment to fairness rules, which threatens a third party's need for stability and control. Although mistreatment arising out of a transgressor's negligence is likely to contribute to unfairness perceptions, their behavior is not as likely to be judged as negative as when the treatment was intentional (Carroll & Payne, 1977). Similarly, if a rule-breaker expresses pleasure, a third party will attribute greater responsibility to the transgressor, deem the mistreatment more unfair, and hold the transgressor as more responsible than when pleasure is not evident (Schwartz, Kane, Joseph, & Tedeschi, 1978). Third parties attribute greater intentionality to actions of high (versus low) status transgressors because high status wrongdoers are deemed to be more self-interested than concerned about others (Fragale, Rosen, Xu, & Merideth, 2009).

Third parties' attribution of blame for a negative outcome can be affected by the use of social accounts (Bies & Moag, 1986). Providing a rationale for the mistreatment or expressing remorse can affect a third party's attributions and subsequent fairness perceptions of a mistreatment (Montada, 1998; Skarlicki et al., 1998). Social accounts can also have a direct impact on outcome negativity. Referential accounts (i.e., "the outcome could have been worse") can reduce third parties' perception of outcome negativity. Multiple causes for unfavorable outcomes can lead to a diffusion of responsibility either to other actors or to mitigating factors (Shaver, 1985). Penitential accounts (i.e., apologies) can convey a transgressor's responsibility for the wrongdoing, but suggest that the event is not representative of the transgressor's character (Schlenker, 1980). Remorse can be interpreted as an indicator of regret and suffering on the part of the transgressor, which can also reduce perceptions that the mistreatment was purposeful and intentional (Austin, Walster, & Utne, 1976; Schwartz et al., 1978). Apologies are important not only because they help determine attributions of responsibility but also because of the societal implications of mistreatment. A nonremorseful rule-breaker is more likely to be viewed as a potential recidivist than an offender who expresses remorse (Sykes & Matza, 1957). The more contrite the transgressor, the greater the third party's confidence that the individual will not violate the rule again. If the transgressor indicates respect for a fairness rule or at least acknowledges that a fairness rule has been broken, the violation is seen as less purposeful and less threatening to social order. From an equity perspective, expressing remorse or providing an explanation can serve as a means of restoring equity to the injured party.

Moreover, there are better and worse reasons for intentionally breaking a fairness rule. Transgressions committed to avoid loss are less disturbing to third parties than those committed for the purposes of gain (Kelley, 1971). Third parties who believe that an individual or organization was motivated to unfairness by greed and selfishness are particularly likely to trigger unfairness perceptions (Blount, 1995).

The transgressor's credibility can also moderate the effect of unfairness on attributions of blame (Gundlach, Douglas, & Martinko, 2003). People are more likely to infer intent and take action when the transgressor has a poor reputation or is not well liked (Robertson, Stefaniak, & Curtis, 2011).

OTHER THIRD PARTIES' REACTIONS

Third parties in a person's social environment—family, friends, neighbors, colleagues—can play a key role in defining the experience. Social information theories (e.g., Cialdini, 1993; Festinger, 1957; Salancik & Pfeffer, 1978) and fairness research (e.g., Lerner & Simmons, 1966) suggest that other third parties can influence both perceptions of outcome negativity and perceived blameworthiness (Latane & Darley, 1970). Lind, Kray, and Thompson (1998) proposed that the most powerful socially mediated injustice judgments involve shared and mutually reinforced experiences. This shared injustice reaction is generated by public discussion and consensus judgment (Degoey, 2000).

"Hot" versus "Cold" Third-Party Reactions

How a third party determines blame and subsequently responds to others' mistreatment can occur through a "cold," deliberate thought process, or a "hot," reflexive emotional process (Edwards, Ashkanasy, & Gardner, 2009: Henik, 2008; O'Reilly & Aquino, 2011; Sekerka & Bagozzi, 2007; Skarlicki & Rupp, 2010). This same distinction is found in broader theories of dual-process models of information processing, which describe two processes through which individuals form judgments: an automatic, reflexive process versus a rational, reflective process (Chaiken & Trope, 1999; Epstein, 1990; Sloman, 1996).

Early work by Folger (Folger, Cropanzano, & Goldman, 2005) on the moral perspective described deontic reactions as relatively rapid and automatic—third parties need not engage in complex cognitive analysis in order to assess a moral violation. Furthermore, more recent views of justice have begun to recognize the role of affective components in influencing individuals' justice perceptions and reactions more broadly. For example, Barsky, Kaplan, and Beal (2011) described three channels through which affect can influence justice perceptions: affect can influence one's justice appraisal; affect in the form of both discrete emotions and mood can influence the justice event itself; and finally affective components can influence the perceptions of justice across time and groups' collective experiences. These views contrast traditional perspectives of justice reasoning in which justice appraisals are described more akin to that of an impartial judge, who carefully weighs the facts of the situation against objective standards of right and wrong. Affect-based views of justice are also consistent with evolutionary views of moral reasoning as an intuitive process (Haidt, 2007), and neuroscience evidence, which shows that making attributional inferences about others' misbehavior can be an instantaneous process in the brain (Lieberman, 2007).

Considerable evidence shows that third parties can experience emotion in response to others' mistreatment (De Cremer & Van Hiel, 2006, 2010). Spencer and Rupp (2009), for instance, showed in a laboratory study that participants' emotional labor increased in response to customer mistreatment directed toward themselves and in response to customer mistreatment directed toward their co-workers. Emotional labor was triggered by customer mistreatment even when the participants themselves had been treated fairly. Specifically, the participants experienced guilt emotions when their co-worker was treated unfairly and they were treated fairly, resulting in higher levels of emotional labor. These studies are important because they document that emotions such as anger and guilt can result from merely witnessing unfair events (see also Cropanzano, Stein, & Goldman, 2007).

The affect associated with intuitive or reflexive reactions is usually a good predictor of subsequent reasoning and behavior (Damasio, 1994; Hoffman, 1982). In an experiment by Skarlicki and Rupp (2010), managers took the role of a third-party observer of workplace interpersonal injustice. Managers primed to make quick, intuitive judgments showed stronger retributive tendencies compared to those primed to put more cognitive effort into their assessment of right or wrong. However, third parties who reported a higher level of moral identity exhibited strong retributive desires regardless of whether they were asked to use a more experiential versus deliberative thought process.

In "hot" theories of third parties' behavior, moral emotions play a central role in motivating actions. Scholars have alluded to feelings of anger, contempt, indignation, disgust, and outrage in response to injustice (Bies, 2001; Folger, 1998, 2001; Haidt, 2003; Henik, 2008). O'Reilly and Aquino (2011) referred to these emotions as *moral anger*, a series of discrete but related emotions sparked by a perceived violation of moral standards that does not directly affect one's material interests but, rather, is linked to the interests or welfare of others. Haidt (2003) classified these emotions within a broader "family" that he refers to as other-condemning emotions. Moral anger is associated with the desire to attack or retaliate (Haidt, 2003). More broadly, Sekerka and Bagozzi (2007) argued that moral emotions are an important ingredient in producing morally courageous actions, defined as doing what one feels is morally right even in the face of severe personal repercussions for doing so. Support that these emotions are innate comes from Skarlicki, Hoegg, Aquino, and Nadisic (2013), who found that observing an injustice triggered third parties' disgust (Studies 2 & 3), which was positively associated with self-reported heightened sense of taste and smell. The findings suggest that violations of dignity and respect can trigger an evolutionary-based reaction that activates a human alarm system, warning individuals of impending threats even when no physical threat is imminent.

Moral anger is not the only emotional reaction third parties can experience. Scholars have recognized that witnessing or learning about someone's experience of injustice can spark fear as well, and fear can prevent third parties from getting involved in a situation even when they are strongly motivated to do so (Edwards et al., 2009; Henik, 2008). The experience of fear is a prevalent theme within the whistle-blowing literature more broadly and has direct relevance for third parties' reactions to others' mistreatment specifically (e.g., Gundlach et al., 2003).

Integrating the "Hot" and "Cold" Perspectives

Despite the evidence supporting the role of third parties' automatic psychological reactions, scholars have also acknowledged that third parties do not always show emotional, kneejerk reactions following injustice (e.g., Miceli & Near, 1988). In an integration of these two perspectives, O'Reilly and Aquino (2011) propose that third parties' first reactions to injustice are sparked by an intuitive recognition that someone has acted in a way that violates moral norms of behavior. This intuition is almost immediately accompanied by the experience of moral anger. However, they also propose that an intuition of wrong in and of itself will not motivate a third-party behavioral response. Third parties will strive to understand *why* an act violated moral standards before they become sufficiently motivated to intervene. The process through which third parties make sense of injustice need not be a conscious deliberative process (but it could be). However, it must confirm third parties' intuitive conclusions in order for them to want to respond. In effect, both emotions and cognitions are important in producing a third party intervention. See Henik (2008) for a discussion of "hot cognitions" as a motivating factor behind whistle-blowing for a similar perspective.

Whereas "hot" theories of third-party reactions focus heavily on the role of moral emotion, particularly in the form of moral anger in promoting an intervention, "cold" theories of third-party reactions are not completely devoid of emotions. Less theoretical and empirical attention has been devoted to understanding how self-focused moral emotions can influence third-party reactions (see Spencer & Rupp, 2009 for one exception). Self-focused moral emotions refer to the guilt or shame a third party might feel as a result of not speaking up on behalf of or helping victims of mistreatment (Haidt, 2003). These emotions are also likely to factor into third parties' reactions. Third parties might act because they anticipate guilt if they do not act, and the guilt associated with inaction might accumulate over time (Lutgen-Sanvik, 2005).

Factors Moderating the Relationship between Perceptual/Emotional Reactions and Action

As noted earlier, once a third party perceives that a transgressor's behavior was unfair, their response can take a variety of forms, including punishing the transgressor, mediating the situation, standing up or protecting the victim from future mistreatment, or helping the victim by providing social or emotional support. However, fairness perceptions do not always translate into action. Numerous factors can moderate the relationship between unfairness and action, including a cost-benefit analysis, other parties' reactions, the perceived value of the victim, and individual and situational determinants.

Cost-Benefit Analysis

Third parties are likely to assess their own resources (e.g., time) available to react to their (un) fairness perceptions. Possessing particular skills, knowledge, expertise, a supportive network, and having certainty about how best to help (Schwartz, 1975; Vadera, Aguilera, & Caza, 2009; Wortman & Lehman, 1985) increases the likelihood that a third party will take action, whereas a sense of helplessness reduces the likelihood of action (Notarious & Herrick, 1988). Providing organizational policies and training on how to blow the whistle promotes whistle-blowing behavior (Miceli, Near, & Dworkin, 2009; Vadera et al., 2009). Walster, Berscheid, and Walster (1976) found that if the resources available to a third party would only be partially effective in eliminating the victim's deprivation, then the act of helping was entirely avoided. Third parties are more likely to intervene when they perceive that they can do something for a victim that the victim cannot do on his or her own (Utne & Kidd, 1980).

The cost-benefit analysis is also likely to include a review of the resources available to the third party to protect him or her against subsequent retaliation from the wrongdoer or the organization (Henik, 2008). Third parties who have observed that other people's proactive behavior to correct injustice is punished will expect similar outcomes in the future (Trevino & Ball, 1992). Third parties inside the organization might be more willing to take action against perceived injustice if they have higher position power (e.g., critical job knowledge, high organizational status) or believe that their actions will be supported by senior executives. These resources are likely to provide some protection, since they give the third party some power to defend themselves within the organization (O'Reilly & Aquino, 2011).

However, low-status third parties can still garner resources that offer protection against organizational retaliation. For example, an employee with a sufficiently high balance of idiosyncrasy credits may be able to defend a victim without experiencing personal penalties. Third parties who are outside the organization could feel particularly free to act on perceived injustice because they are beyond the reach of organizational counter-retaliation efforts (Shapiro & Kulik, 2004). News reporters, customers, concerned citizens, or equal opportunity representatives, for example, can feel protected because they might not depend on the wrongdoing organization's goodwill or support.

Third parties are also likely to assess their own personal vulnerability to future mistreatment. Personal vulnerability can motivate action in order to prevent his or her own unjust treatment in the future (Trevino, 1992). Third parties' vulnerability to mistreatment can also affect their motivation to help others in the future. Having narrowly escaped a similar fate, the third party may be motivated to help someone who is in a similar predicament. Furthermore, research has shown that those who have recently experienced social mistreatment, compared to those who have little past experience with firsthand mistreatment, tend to be more understanding and empathetic toward other victims of mistreatment (Nordgren, Banas, & MacDonald, 2011). On the other hand, it is worth noting that third parties who fear retribution or mistreatment for helping a victim might avoid intervening (O'Reilly & Aquino, 2011).

The cost benefit analysis is likely to include an assessment of the organization's policies (Perry, Davis-Blake, & Kulik, 1994), grievance procedures (Wittenberg, Mackenzie, Shaw, & Ross, 1997), and climate (Miceli et al., 2009). Some professions or organizations have explicit codes of conduct that emphasize an individual's responsibility to respond to wrongdoing; these codes can encourage third parties to act on perceived injustice (McLain & Keenan, 1999). However, the mere presence of a policy or a grievance procedure is unlikely to be sufficient to prompt third-party action. Perry, Kulik, and Schmidtke (1997), for example, found that an organizational grievance system had to be perceived as responsive to employee complaints before individuals were likely to bring forward harassment claims.

Third parties whose cost–benefit analysis is positive are more likely to take action against the injustice than third parties whose analysis is negative. Third parties whose cost–benefit analysis is negative are unlikely to engage in behaviors that are sympathetic to the victim. Their reluctance to take action against organizations or their agents can occur due to the perception that the risk of physical harm, embarrassment, or other negative outcomes outweighs potential gains (Baker, 1974; Bar-Tal, 1976; Schwartz, 1975). Co-workers, for example, can be highly motivated to reestablish justice for the victim but may be unwilling to risk their own job security for an uncertain outcome (Gundlach et al., 2003; Trevino, 1992; Utne & Kidd, 1980).

Other Third Parties' Reactions

Darley and Latane's (1968) classic study on the bystander effect suggests that a third party is less likely to act in the presence of others. They found that when confronted with someone in need of help, 70% of study participants who were alone would act to help a victim within four minutes of learning about the incident, whereas when other onlookers were present, this proportion dropped to 12%. Recent research on whistle-blowing, however, has indicated that when other bystanders also perceive injustice, a third party might be more likely to act. For example, Robinson, Robertson, and Curtis (2012) found that managers indicated they would be more likely to report unethical behavior in their firm if they knew that their colleagues agreed that the behavior was unethical. Similarly, Mayer and colleagues (Mayer, Nurmohamed, Treviño, Shapiro, & Schminke, 2013) found that employees are more likely to report unethical behavior if others in their environment generally model ethical behavior.

If the injustice has been widely reported (e.g., if the incident has appeared in a newspaper account), a third party can also feel more anonymous and less responsible for responding to the injustice (LePine & Van Dyne, 1998). Finally, third parties might decide not to react when they observe another third party adequately addressing injustice. For example, Lin, Dahl and Argo (2012) found that when an experimenter punished a confederate for ostensibly violating a social norm rather than ignoring the violation, bystander participants were less likely to punish the confederate themselves. Lin et al. (2012) suggest that, once a third party perceives that justice has been served, they will be less likely to intervene.

The Perceived Value of the Victim

Christian et al. (2012) showed that, in a team setting, who is violated also matters; the more that a violation affects a core person (i.e., a person who is tightly linked to the overall performance of the group), the more likely it is that other group members will engage in retribution. Also, the transgressor's attempts to repair an injustice were more effective when they were directed toward the core (versus noncore) person.

Individual Differences

Colquitt (2004) reported that differences in social self-construal (e.g., collectivism) can make a third party more sensitive to someone else's experience of injustice, increasing his or her likelihood of responding on behalf of the victim. Miceli, Near, Rehg, and Van Scotter (2012) found that those with a more proactive personality are more likely to blow the whistle on unethical behavior (see Bjørkelo, Einarsen, & Matthiesen, 2010, for a similar finding).

Third parties' ability to self-regulate can also diminish the strength of the relationship between fairness perceptions and action. Rupp and Bell (2010), for example, found that third parties will self-regulate their behavior and can suppress urges to punish transgressors even when they believe such reactions are wrong. Related, Greenbaum, Mawritz, Mayer, and Priesemuth (2013) found that third parties with a strong moral identity were less likely to act out against transgressors of workplace mistreatment in ways that could be construed as morally reprehensible (e.g., deviance) but were more likely to act out in ways that could be construed as potentially productive (e.g., constructive retaliation, quitting in protest). Finally, Barclay, Whiteside, and Aquino (2013) found that third parties with both a strong moral identity and who strongly support the negative reciprocity norm are more likely to punish individuals who treat another person unfairly.

Situational Factors

The link between unfairness and action can depend on work context. The effects appear to be larger in a context of high interdependency (Colquitt, 2004) and high group cohesion (Ferguson & Barry, 2011). De Cremer and Van Hiel (2006), for instance, reported that another person's mistreatment affected the participants' own emotions and behavior (cooperation, organizational citizenship behavior (OCB), exit), but only when the other person demonstrated a willingness to provide support or help the participant. Porath and Erez (2009) found that individuals lowered their own performance as a result of observing another's mistreatment. This reaction was lessened, however, when the third party was in direct competition with the victim over scarce resources. De Cremer and Van Hiel (2010) similarly found that in a competitive interdependent context (positive performance on a task would lead to negative effects for one's partner and vice versa), unfairly treated individuals reported stronger negative emotions and were more likely to exhibit antisocial behaviors when the other was treated fairly (versus unfairly). The opposite pattern of results emerged in a cooperative interdependence condition (positive performance on a task would lead to positive effects for one's partner and vice versa). Thus, third-party reactions can be especially prominent in situations where cooperation is important.

Consequences of Third Parties' Reactions

Finally, a third party's decision whether to ignore or intervene can affect their subsequent perceptions of injustice as well as their postdecision emotions. If a third party perceives injustice but decides not to respond, it can instill a sense of guilt or distress (Baumeister, Stillwell, & Heatherton, 1994). Furthermore, to cope with this sense of guilt or in an attempt to preempt it entirely, a third party might change his or her perception of the situation. This could include blaming the victim instead of the transgressor, aligning oneself with the transgressor, or reassessing the situation to support a new belief that no injustice actually occurred (e.g., Batson et al., 1987; Brockner & Greenberg, 1990; Hoffman, 1989; Stotland, 1969). These strategies help third parties maintain a positive self-view (e.g., Ashforth & Anand, 2003) and sustain a belief in a just and balanced world (e.g., Lerner, 1980; Lerner & Simmons, 1966).

When third parties decide to punish a perceived transgressor, their actions can allay feelings of anger and contempt and offer a sense of satisfaction (Feather, 1999; Miller, 1998; Solomon, 1999; Tripp & Bies, 1997). In fact, research on the neural basis for altruistic punishment (i.e., costly punishment directed toward a transgressor) has shown that punishing those who violate moral norms activates parts of the brain associated with pleasure (de Quervain et al., 2004). Finally, helping the victims of injustice can bestow particularly emotional benefits to third parties. Research has found that when we voluntarily help others, it can satisfy important psychological individual needs (e.g., Weinstein & Ryan, 2010) and showing compassion and providing social support toward others in need can elevate our psychological well-being (e.g., Post, 2005).

Future Research Directions

Despite the accumulating research on third-party perceptions, opportunities for future research are vast. In this section, we illustrate but a few directions that we believe have considerable potential to contribute to this research literature.

Nonconscious Factors

Emerging research has highlighted the nonconscious impact of injustice. In an interesting link of deontic and fairness heuristic theories, Zdaniuk and Bobocel (2013) showed that third-party reactions can be influenced via automatic, nonconscious cognitive processes. Participants completed an impression formation task by reading descriptions of a fair or unfair leader. The description included photographs of the leader. In an ostensibly different study, participants were then subliminally shown the photographs of the fair or unfair manager or a neutral face, and asked to assume the role of a manager and write a letter communicating a dismissal decision to a subordinate. Participants' written responses were coded in terms of interactional justice. The results showed that participants were significantly less interactionally fair when communicating the dismissal decision after being subliminally exposed to the face of a leader whom they had mentally associated with unfairness, as compared to either the face of a leader they associated with fairness or the neutral face. Future research should continue this line of research to understand how witnessing injustice in daily life can impact how people subsequently react to injustice, and how they treat others as a result.

Broadening the Third-Party Lens to Corporate Social Responsibility

Researchers have utilized the third-party lens to explain how individuals react to corporate social responsibility (CSR). Evidence is mounting that a variety of stakeholders, including current and perspective employees, customers, and shareholders, respond favorably to CSR (Jones, 2010; Jones, Willness, & Madey, 2014). Based on the third-party perspective—that individuals care about how *others* are treated—Rupp, Gulpathi, Aguilera and Williams (2006) conceptualized CSR as multistakeholder third-party justice. Specifically, they argued that a variety of third parties can judge the actions of the firm and subsequently retaliate (or support) perceived acts of social irresponsibility (or responsibility). This perspective proposes that stakeholder groups evaluate organizations based on the practices that support or threaten the best interest of their own group, but also on how the firm treats *other* stakeholder groups. From this perspective, potential and current employees are third parties responding to the way a firm treats other stakeholders.

In a test of this perspective, Rupp, Shao, Thornton, and Skarlicki (2013) found that a company's CSR positively impacted job applicant intentions (Study 1) and employee OCB (Study 2). These effects, however, were moderated by first-party justice such that the effects were stronger among individuals who reported low first-person justice. Thus, individuals who are unfairly treated appear to "have their antennae up" for the way their company treats its other stakeholders (i.e., CSR). The relationship between CSR and OCB was more pronounced among individuals who were high on moral identity. The fact that moral identity amplified CSR effects provides evidence that moral concerns can underlie individuals' responses to perceived CSR. We believe that the third-party perspective of injustice can provide considerable insight into how different organizational stakeholders respond to a company's CSR efforts and hope more research continues down this path.

The Role of Social Media and Third-Party Reactions

The Internet and information technology in general has enhanced the opportunity for aggrieved employees to share their stories publicly, increasing the likelihood that third parties will become aware of injustices. Kulik and colleagues (2012) found that third parties can impact the tone of the conversation differently than employees. They studied discussion board threads on Vault.com, focusing on threads initiated by postings containing organizational justice content and authored by an organizational insider or outsider. Insiders capitalized on anonymity to post messages that were significantly more negative in both cognitive content (describing organizations as less fair) and emotional tone (using more negative emotional language) than organizational outsiders. Cognitive content (the extent to which the initial poster described the organization as fair or unfair) had a significant downstream effect on the emotional tone of replies—but only when the initial posting had been authored by an organizational outsider. The authors concluded that the power of the outsider lies in his or her perceived objective description of the organization as fair or unfair. Discussion-board participants responded to the cognitive content of the outsider's message, not the outsider's emotional tone. In short, cognitive content appears to sway public opinion far more than emotional content. Given the growing prevalence and diverse uses of social media, we suspect that the role it plays in influencing third parties' and victims' experiences of mistreatment will only become more salient. Social media also offers a unique and relatively public outlet to study third-party phenomena.

Conclusion

In this chapter, we used Skarlicki and Kulik's (2005) model to organize a review of the third-party literature. Based on our review, we make three observations about how the "state of the science" has advanced since 2005. First, the literature reflects a more sophisticated understanding of third-party motives. Skarlicki and Kulik's (2005) model was based on two primary motivations: self-interest formulations and justice as a moral imperative. However, these two motives are likely to operate simultaneously, even if they operate without conscious awareness. Second, the literature demonstrates a greater appreciation of the role emotions play in third-party behavior. Skarlicki and Kulik (2005, p. 188) positioned perceptions of unfairness at the heart of the model. In our revised model, perceptions share this space with emotions. We acknowledge that third-party reactions involve both "cold" rational processes and "hot" affective ones. Third, although the pre-2005 literature emphasized the severity-attribution link in the model, the post-2005 literature has emphasized the perception/emotion-action link (see bold text in Figure 10.1). Moreover, we present a broader array of the many different ways that third parties can respond to injustice, beyond the sole focus of punishing the transgressor. These responses encompass cognitive and behavioral reactions, and they can be directed toward either the transgressor (e.g., punishing), the victim (e.g., helping or denigrating), or both. At the same time, we have developed a greater awareness of the many individual and situational factors that facilitate or constrain a third party's response options.

Where do we go from here? We encourage researchers to continue to develop the "back end" of our model, so that we can better predict not just *if* a third party will react to injustice, but *when* and *how*. Indeed, factors such as technology are likely to increase the third party's perspective more and more prominent. This attention would enable us to develop organizational procedures and societal policies that, as Benjamin Franklin suggests in the opening quote, encourage third parties to act on perceived injustice as if it was their own.

References

Abrams, D., & Hogg, M. A. (1990). Social identification, self categorization and social influence. *European Review of Social Psychology, 1*, 195–228.

Adams, J. S. (1965). Inequity in social exchange. *Advances in Experimental Social Psychology, 62*, 335–343.

Adams, G. S., & Mullen, E. (2012). The social and psychological costs of punishing. *Behavioral and Brain Sciences, 35*, 15–16.

Adorno, T. W., Frenkel-Brunswik, E., Levinson, D. J., & Sanford, R. N. (1950). *The authoritarian personality.* New York, NY: Harper and Row.

Alicke, M. D. (1992). Culpable causation. *Journal of Personality and Social Psychology, 63*, 368–378.

Ashforth, B. E., & Anand, V. (2003). The normalization of corruption in organizations. *Research in Organizational Behavior, 25*, 1–52.

Austin, W., Walster, E., & Utne, M. K. (1976). Equity and the law: The effect of a harmdoer's "suffering in the act" on liking and assigned punishment. In L. Berkowitz (Ed.), *Advances in Experimental Social Psychology*, (Vol. 9., pp. 163–190). New York, NY: Academic Press.

Axelrod, R. (1984). *The evolution of cooperation.* New York, NY: Basic Books.

Baker, K. (1974). Experimental analysis of third-party justice behavior. *Journal of Personality and Social Psychology, 30*, 307–316.

Barclay, L. J., Whiteside, D. B., & Aquino, K. (2013). To avenge or not to avenge? Exploring the interactive effects of moral identity and the negative reciprocity norm. *Journal of Business Ethics, 121*(1), 15–28.

Barclay, P. (2012). Proximate and ultimate causes of punishment and strong reciprocity. *Behavioral and Brain Sciences, 35*, 16–17.

Barsky, A., Kaplan, S., & Beal, D. (2011). Just feelings? The role of affect in the formation of organizational fairness judgments. *Journal of Management, 37*(1), 248–279.

Bar-Tal, D. (1976). *Prosocial behavior: Theory and research.* New York, NY: Halsted Press.

Batson, C. D., Fultz, J., & Schoenrade, P. A. (1987). Distress and empathy: Two qualitatively distinct vicarious emotions with different motivational consequences. *Journal of Personality, 55*(1), 19–39.

Baumeister, R. F., Stillwell, A. M., & Heatherton, T. F. (1994). Guilt: an interpersonal approach. *Psychological bulletin, 115*(2), 243–267.

Beersma, B., & van Kleef, G. A. (2012). Why people gossip: An empirical analysis of social motives, antecedents, and consequences. *Journal of Applied Social Psychology, 42*, 2640–2670.

Bell, C. M., & Main, K. J. (2011). Deonance and distrust: Motivated third party information seeking following disclosure of an agent's unethical behavior. *Journal of Business Ethics, 102*(1), 77–96.

Bies, R. J. (2001). International (in)justice: The sacred and the profane. In J. Greenberg & R. Cropanzano (Eds.), *Advances in organization justice* (pp. 89–118). Palo Alto, CA: Stanford University Press.

Bies, R. J., & Moag, J. F. (1986). Interactional justice: Communication criteria of fairness. In R. J. Lewicki, B. H. Sheppard, & M. H. Bazerman (Eds.), *Research on negotiations in organizations* (Vol. 1, pp. 43–55). Greenwich, CT: JAI Press.

Bjørkelo, B., Einarsen, S., & Matthiesen, S. B. (2010). Predicting proactive behaviour at work: Exploring the role of personality as an antecedent of whistleblowing behaviour. *Journal of Occupational and Organizational Psychology, 83*(2), 371–394.

Blader, S. L., Wiesenfeld, B. M., Fortin, M., & Wheeler-Smith, S. L. (2013). Fairness lies in the heart of the beholder: How the social emotions of third parties influence reactions to injustice. *Organizational Behavior and Human Decision Processes, 121(1)*, 62–80.

Blau, P. M. (1964). Justice in social exchange. *Sociological Inquiry, 34*(2), 193–206.

Blount, S. (1995). When social outcomes aren't fair—the effect of causal attributions on preferences. *Organizational Behavior and Human Decision Processes, 63*(2), 131–144.

Bosse, D. A., Phillips, R. A., & Harrison, J. S. (2009). Stakeholders, reciprocity, and firm performance. *Strategic Management Journal, 30*, 447–456.

Boyd, R., & Richerson, P. J. (1992). Punishment allows the evolution of cooperation (or anything else) in sizable groups. *Ethology and Sociobiology, 13*, 171–195.

Brockner, J. (1990). Scope of justice in the workplace: How survivors react to co-worker layoffs. *Journal of Social Issues, 46*, 95–106.

Brockner, J., & Greenberg, J. (1990) *The impact of layoffs on survivors: an organizational justice perspective*, In J. S. Carrol (Ed.), *Applied social psychology and organizational settings* (pp. 45–75). Hillsdale, NJ: Erlbaum.

Carroll, J. S., & Payne, J. W. (1977). Crime, seriousness, recidivism risk, and causal attributions in judgments of prison term by students and experts. *Journal of Applied Psychology, 72*, 595–602.

Chaiken, A. L., & Darley, J. M. (1973). Victim or perpetrator? Defensive attribution of responsibility and the need for order and justice. *Journal of Personality and Social Psychology, 25*, 268–275.

Chaiken, S., & Trope, Y. (1999). *Dual-process theories in social psychology.* New York, NY: Guilford Press.

Charness, G., Cobo-Reyes, R., & Jiménez, N. (2008). An investment game with third-party intervention. *Journal of Economic Behavior & Organization, 68*(1), 18–28.

Christian, S. J., Christian, M. S., Garza, A. S., & Ellis, A. P. J. (2012). Examining retaliatory responses to justice violations and recovery attempts in teams. *Journal of Applied Psychology, 97*(6), 1218–1232.

Cialdini, R. B. (1993). *Influence: Science and practice.* New York, NY: Harper Collins College Publishers.

Cosmides, L., & Tooby, J. (1987). From evolution to behavior: Evolutionary psychology as the missing link. In J. Dupre, (Ed.), *The latest on the best: Essays on evolution and optimality* (pp. 277–306). Cambridge, MA: MIT Press.

Colquitt, J. A. (2004). Does the justice of the one interact with the justice of the many? reactions to procedural justice in teams. *Journal of Applied Psychology, 89*, 633–646.

Cropanzano, R., Goldman, B., & Folger, R. (2005). Self-interest: Defining and understanding a human motive. *Journal of Organizational Behavior, 26*, 985–991.

Cropanzano, R., Stein, J., & Goldman, B. M. (2007). Self-interest. In E. H. Kessler & J. Bailey (Eds.), *Handbook of organizational and managerial wisdom* (pp. 181–221). Thousand Oaks, CA: Sage Publications.

Damasio, A. R. (1994). *Descartes' error: Emotion, reason, and the human brain.* New York, NY: Putnam.

Darley, J. M., & Latané, B. (1968). Group inhibition of bystander intervention in emergencies. *Journal of Personality and Social Psychology, 10*(3), 215–221.

Darley, J. M., & Pittman, T. S. (2003). The psychology of compensatory and retributive justice. *Personality and Social Psychology Review, 7*, 324–336.

Darwin, C. (1871). *The descent of man, and selection in relation to sex*. London, UK: John Murray.

De Cremer, D., & Van Hiel, A. (2006). Effects of another person's fair treatment on one's own emotions and behaviors: The moderating role of how much the other cares for you. *Organizational Behavior and Human Decision Processes, 100*(2), 231–249.

De Cremer, D., & Van Hiel, A. (2010). Becoming angry when other is treated fairly: On understanding when own and other's fair treatment influences negative reactions. *British Journal of Management, 21*(2), 280–298.

de Quervain, D. J. F., Fischbacher, U., Treyer, V., Schellhammer, M., Schnyder, U., Buck, A., & Fehr, E. (2004). The neural basis of altruistic punishment. *Science*, 305 (5688), 1254–1258.

Degoey, P. (2000). Contagious justice: Exploring the social construction of justice in organizations. *Research in Organizational Behavior, 22*, 51–102.

DeScioli, P., & Kurzban, R. (2009). Mysteries of morality. *Cognition, 112*, 281–299.

Deutsch, M. (1975). Equity, equality, and need: What determines which value will be used as the basis of distributive justice? *Journal of Social Issues, 31*(3), 137–149.

Diekmann, K. A., Walker, S. D. S., Galinsky, A. D., & Tenbrunsel, A. E. (2013). Double victimization in the workplace: Why observers condemn passive victims of sexual harassment. *Organization Science, 24*, 614–628.

Dunfee, T. W. (2006). A critical perspective of integrative social contracts theory: Recurring criticisms and next generation research topics. *Journal of Business Ethics, 68*, 303–328.

Edwards, M., Ashkanasy, N. M., & Gardner, J. (2009). Deciding to speak up or to remain silent following observed wrongdoing: The role of discrete emotions and climate of silence. In J. Greenberg and M. Edwards (Ed.), *Voice and silence in organizations* (pp. 83–109). Bingley, UK: Emerald Group.

Elkouri, F., & Elkouri, E. A. (1985). *How arbitration works*. Washington, DC: Bureau of National Affairs.

Elster, J. (1993). Ethical individualism and presentism. *Monist, 76*(3), 333–348.

Epstein, S. (1990). Cognitive-experiential self-theory. In L. A. Pervin (Ed.), *Handbook of personality: Theory and research* (pp. 165–192). New York, NY: Guilford Press.

Feather, N. T. (1999). *Values, achievement, and justice: Studies in the psychology of deservingness*. New York, NY: Kluwer Academic/Plenum.

Fehr, E., & Fischbacher, U. (2004). Third-party punishment and social norms. *Evolution and Human Behavior, 25*, 63–87.

Fehr, E., & Gächter, S. (2000). Fairness and retaliation: The economics of reciprocity. *Journal of Economic Perspectives, 14*, 159–181.

Fehr, E., & Gächter, S. (2002). Altruistic punishment in humans. *Nature, 415*, 137–140.

Ferguson, M., & Barry, B. (2011). I know what you did: The effects of interpersonal deviance on bystanders. *Journal of Occupational Health Psychology, 16*(1), 80–94.

Festinger, L. (1957). *A theory of cognitive dissonance*. Evanston, Ill: Row, Peterson.

Folger, R. (1998). Fairness as a moral virtue. In M. Schminke (Ed.), *Managerial ethics: Morally managing people and processes* (pp. 13–34). Mahwah, NJ: Erlbaum.

Folger, R. (2001). Fairness as deonance. In S. W. Gilliland, D. D. Steiner, & D. P. Skarlicki (Eds.), *Theoretical and cultural perspectives on organizational justice* (pp. 3–34). Greenwich, CT: Information Age.

Folger, R., & Cropanzano, R. (1998). *Organizational justice and human resource management*. Thousand Oaks, CA: Sage Publications.

Folger, R., Cropanzano, R., & Goldman, B. (2005). What is the relationship between justice and morality. In J. Greenberg & J. A. Colquitt (Eds.), *Handbook of organizational justice* (pp. 215–245). Mahwah, NJ: Erlbaum.

Folger, R., & Skarlicki, D. P. (2008). The evolutionary basis of deontic justice. In S. Gilliland, D. Steiner, & D. Skarlicki (Eds.) *Research in social issues in management: Justice, morality, and social responsibility* (pp. 29–62). Greenwich CT: Information Age.

Fragale, A. R., Rosen, B., Xu, C., & Merideth, I. (2009). The higher they are, the harder they fall: The effects of wrongdoer status on observer punishment recommendations and intentionality attributions. *Organizational Behavior and Human Decision Processes, 108*(1), 53–65.

Greenbaum, R. L., Mawritz, M. B., Mayer, D. M., & Priesemuth, M. (2013). To act out, to withdraw, or to constructively resist? Employee reactions to supervisor abuse of customers. *Human Relations. (Special issue on Organizational Justice and Behavioral Ethics)*, 66(7), 925–950. doi:10.1177/0018726713482992

Geer, J. H., & Jarmecky, L. (1973). The effect of being responsible for reducing another's pain on subjects' response and arousal. *Journal of Personality and Social Psychology, 26*, 232–237.

Goffman, R. (1952). On cooling the mark out: Some aspects of adaptation to failure. *Psychiatry, 15*, 451–463.

Gouldner, A. W. (1960). The norm of reciprocity: A preliminary statement. *American Sociological Review*, 161–178.

Guala, F. (2012). Reciprocity: Weak or strong? What punishment experiments do (and do not) demonstrate. *Behavioral and Brain Sciences, 35(1)*, 1–59.

Gundlach, M. J., Douglas, S. C., & Martinko, M. J. (2003). The decision to blow the whistle: A social information processing framework. *Academy of Management Review, 28*(1), 107–123.

Haidt, J. (2003). The moral emotions. In R. J. Davidson, K. R. Scherer, & H. H. Goldsmith (Eds.), *Handbook of affective sciences* (pp. 852–870). Oxford, UK: Oxford University Press.

Haidt, J. (2007). The new synthesis in moral psychology. *Science, 316*, 998–1002.

Heider, F. (1958). *The psychology of interpersonal relations*. New York, NY: Wiley.

Henik, E. (2008). Mad as hell or scared stiff? The effects of value conflict and emotions on potential whistle-blowers. *Journal of Business Ethics, 80*(1), 111–119.

Henrich, J., McElreath, R., Barr, A., Ensminger, J., Barrett, C., Bolyanatz, A., ... & Ziker, J. (2006). Costly punishment across human societies. *Science, 312*, 1767–1770.

Hoffman, M. L. (1982). Development of prosocial motivation: Empathy and guilt. In N. Eisenberg-Berg, (Ed.),

Development of prosocial behavior (pp. 281–313). New York, NY: Academic Press.

Hoffman, M. L. (1989). Empathic emotions and justice in society. *Social Justice Research, 4*, 283–311.

Hofstede, G. (1980). *Culture's Consequences: International differences in work related values.* Beverly Hill, CA, Sage.

Hogan, R., & Emler, N. (1981). Retributive justice. In M. J. Lerner & S. Lerner (Eds.), *The justice motive in social behavior* (pp. 125–144). New York, NY: Plenum.

Jones, D. (2010). Does serving the community also serve the company? Using organizational identification and social exchange theories to understand employee responses to a volunteerism program. *Journal of Occupational and Organizational Psychology, 83*(4), 857–878.

Jones, D. A., Willness, C. R., & Madey, S. (2014). Why are job seekers attracted by corporate social performance? Experimental and field tests of three signal-based mechanisms. *Academy of Management Journal.* 57 (2), 383–404.

Kelley, H. H. (1971). Moral evaluation. *American Psychologist, 26*(3), 293–300.

Kelloway, E. K., Francis, L., Catano, V. M., & Dupré, K. (2008). Third party support for strike action. *Journal of Applied Psychology, 93*, 806–817.

Keltner, D., Van Kleef, G. A., Chen, S., & Kraus, M. W. (2008). A reciprocal influence model of social power: Emerging principles and lines of inquiry. *Advances in experimental social psychology, 40*, 151–192.

Kesebir, S. (2012). The super-organism account of human sociality how and when human Groups are like beehives. *Personality and Social Psychology Review, 16*, 233–261.

Kramer, R. M. (1993). Cooperation and organizational identification. In J. K. Murnighan (Ed.), *Social Psychology in Organizations* (pp. 244–268). Englewood Cliffs, NJ: Prentice-Hall.

Kulik, C., Pepper, M., Shapiro, D., & Cregan C. (2012). The electronic water cooler: Insiders and outsiders talk about organizational justice on the internet. *Communication Research, 39* (5), 565–591.

Lambert, E. G., Hogan, N. L., & Griffin, M. L. (2007). The impact of distributive and procedural justice on correctional staff job stress, job satisfaction, and organizational commitment. *Journal of Criminal Justice, 35*(6), 644–656.

Landy, D., & Aronson, E. (1969) The influence of the character of the criminal and his victim on the decisions of simulated jurors. *Journal of Experimental Social Psychology, 5*, 141–152.

Langer, E. J. (1975). The Illusion of Control. *Journal of Personality and Social Psychology 32*(2), 311–328.

Langer, E. J. (1989). *Mindfulness.* Reading, MA: Addison Wesley.

Larsen, R. J., & Ketelaar, T. (1991). Personality and susceptibility to positive and negative emotional states. *Journal of Personality and Social Psychology, 61*, 132–140.

Latané, B., & Darley, J. M. (1970). *The unresponsive bystander: Why doesn't he help?* New York, NY: Appleton-Century Crofts.

Leliveld, M. C., van Dijk, E., & van Beest, I. (2012). Punishing and compensating others at your own expense: The role of empathic concern on reactions to distributive injustice. *European Journal of Social Psychology, 42*, 135–140.

LePine, J. A., & Van Dyne, L. (1998). Predicting voice behaviour in work groups. *Journal of Applied Psychology, 83*, 853–868.

Lerner, M. J. (1980). *The belief in a just world: A fundamental delusion.* New York, NY: Plenum.

Lerner, M. J., & Miller, D. T. (1978). Just world research and the attribution process: Looking back and ahead. *Psychological Bulletin, 85*(5), 1030–1051.

Lerner, M. J., & Simmons, C. H. (1966). Observer's reaction to the "innocent victim": Compassion or rejection? *Journal of Personality and Social Psychology, 4*(2), 203–210.

Lieberman, P. B. (2007). Knowing without reasons. *Philosophy, Psychiatry & Psychology, 14*(1), 23–24.

Lin, L., Dahl, D. W., & Argo, J. J. (2012). Do the crime, always do the time? Insights into consumer-to-consumer punishment decisions. *Journal of Consumer Research, 40*, 64–77.

Lind, E. A., Kray, L., & Thompson, L. (1998). The social construction of injustice: Fairness judgments in response to own and others' unfair treatment by authorities. *Organizational Behavior and Human Decision Processes, 75*, 1–22.

Lind, E. A., & Tyler, T. R. (1988). *The social psychology of procedural justice.* New York, NY: Plenum.

Lind, E. A., & Van den Bos, K. (2002). When fairness works: Toward a general theory of uncertainty management. *Research in Organizational Behavior, 24*, 181–223.

Loseman, A., & van den Bos, K. (2012). A self-regulation hypothesis of coping with an unjust world: Ego-depletion and self-affirmation as underlying aspects of blaming an innocent victim. *Social Justice Research, 25*, 1–13. doi:10.1007/s11211-012-0152-0

Lotz, S., Baumert, A., Schlösser, T., Gresser, F., & Fetchenhauer, D. (2011a). Individual differences in third-party interventions: How justice sensitivity shapes altruistic punishment. *Negotiation and Conflict Management Research, 4*, 297–313.

Lotz, S., Okimoto, T. G., Schlösser, T., & Fetchenhauer, D. (2011b). Punitive versus compensatory reactions to injustice: Emotional antecedents to third-party interventions. *Journal of Experimental Social Psychology, 47*(2), 477–480.

Lutgen-Sandvik, P. (2005). *Water smoothing stones: Subordinate resistance to workplace bullying.* Unpublished doctoral dissertation, Arizona State University, Tempe, Arizona.

Mahony, D., & Klaas, B. S. (2008). Comparative dispute resolution in the workplace. *Journal of Labor Research, 29*, 251–271.

Mayer, D. M., Nurmohamed, S., Treviño, L., Shapiro, D. L., Schminke, M. (2013). Encouraging employees to report unethical conduct internally: It takes a village. *Organizational Behavior and Human Decision Processes, 121*, 89–103.

McLain, D., & Keenan, J. (1999). Risk, information, and the decision about response to wrongdoing in an organization. *Journal of Business Ethics, 19*, 255–271.

Miceli, M. P., & Near, J. P. (1988). Individual and situational correlates of whistle-blowing. *Personnel Psychology, 41*, 267–282.

Miceli, M. P., & Near, J. P. (1992). *Blowing the whistle: The organizational and legal implications for companies and employees.* New York, NY: Maxwell Macmillan International.

Miceli, M. P., Near, J. P., & Dworkin, T. M. (2009). A word to the wise: How managers and policy-makers can encourage employees to report wrongdoing. *Journal of Business Ethics, 86*(3), 379–396.

Miceli, M. P., Near, J. P., Rehg, M. T., & Van Scotter, J. R. (2012). Predicting employee reactions to perceived organizational wrongdoing: Demoralization, justice, proactive personality, and whistle-blowing. *Human Relations, 65*(8), 923–954.

Miceli, M. P., Van Scotter, J. R., Near, J. P., & Rehg, M. T. (2001). Individual differences and whistle-blowing. In *Academy of Management Proceedings* (Vol. 2001, pp. C1–C6). Academy of Management Annual Meeting, Washington, DC.

Miller, D. T. (1999). The norm of self-interest. *American Psychologist, 54*(12), 1053–1060.

Miller, D. T. (2001). Disrespect and the psychology of injustice. *Annual Review of Psychology, 52*, 527–553. Palo Alto, CA: Annual Reviews Inc.

Miller, D. T., & Vidmar, N. (1981). The social psychology of punishment reactions. In M. J. Lerner & S. C. Lerner (Eds.), *The Justice Motive in Social Behavior* (pp. 145–172). New York, NY: Plenum.

Miller, W. I. (1998). Clint Eastwood and equity: Popular culture's theory of revenge. In A. Sarat, & T. R. Kearns (Eds.), *Law in the domains of culture* (pp. 161–202). Ann Arbor, MI: University of Michigan Press.

Mitchell, M. S., Vogel, R. M., & Folger, R. (2012). Beyond the consequences to the victim: The impact of abusive supervision on third-party observers. In R. A. Giacalone & M. D. Promislo (Eds.), *Handbook of unethical work behavior: Implications for well-being* (pp. 21–43). Armonk, NY: M. E. Sharpe.

Montada, L. (1998). Justice: Just a rational choice? *Social Justice Research, 11*(2), 81–101.

Nadisic, T. (2008). The Robin Hood effect: Antecedents and consequences of managers using invisible remedies to correct workplace injustice. In S. W. Gilliland, D. Skarlicki, & D. Steiner (eds.), *Justice, morality and social responsibility.* Charlotte, NC: IAP

Niehoff, B. P., Paul, R. J., & Bunch, J. F. S. (1998). The social effects of punishment events: The influence of violator past performance record and severity of the punishment on observers' justice perceptions and attitudes. *Journal of Organizational Behavior, 19*(6), 589–602.

Nordgren, L. F., Banas, K., & MacDonald, G. (2011). Empathy gaps for social pain: why people underestimate the pain of social suffering. *Journal of Personality and Social Psychology, 100*(1), 120–128.

Notarius, C. I., & Herrick, L. R. (1988). Listener response strategies to a distressed other. *Journal of Social and Personal Relationships, 5*, 97–108.

Nowak, M. A., & Sigmund, K. (2005). Evolution of indirect reciprocity. *Nature, 437*, 1291–1298.

Okimoto, T. G., Wenzel, M., & Feather, N. T. (2012). Retribution and restoration as general orientations towards justice. *European Journal of Personality, 26*(3), 255–275.

Opotow, S. (1990). Moral execution and injustice: An introduction. *Journal of Social Issues, 26*(1), 1–20.

Opotow, S. (2012). The scope of justice, intergroup conflict, and peace. In L. R. Tropp (Ed.), *Oxford handbook of intergroup conflict and peace* (pp. 72–86). Oxford, UK: Oxford Library of Psychology.

O'Reilly, J., & Aquino, K. (2011). A model of third parties' morally motivated responses to mistreatment in organizations. *Academy of Management Review, 36*(3), 526–543.

Perloff, L. S. (1983). Perceptions of vulnerability to victimisation. *Journal of Social Issues, 39*, 41–61.

Perry, E. L., Davis-Blake, A., & Kulik, C. T. (1994). Explaining gender-based selection decisions - A synthesis of contextual and cognitive approaches. *Academy of Management Review, 19*(4), 786–820.

Perry, E. L., Kulik, C. T., & Bourhis, A. C. (2004). The reasonable woman standard: Effects on sexual harassment court decisions. *Law and Human Behavior, 28*, 9–27.

Perry, E. L., Kulik, C. T., & Schmidtke, J. M. (1997). Blowing the whistle: Determinants of responses to sexual harassment. *Basic and Applied Social Psychology, 19*, 457–482.

Porath, C. L., & Erez, A. (2009). Overlooked but not untouched: How rudeness reduces onlookers' performance on routine and creative tasks. *Organizational Behavior and Human Decision Processes, 109*(1), 29–44.

Porath, C. L., Macinnis, D., & Folkes, V. (2010). Witnessing incivility among employees: Effects on consumer anger and negative inferences about companies. *Journal of Consumer Research, 37*(2), 292–303.

Porath, C. L., MacInnis, D., & Folkes, V. S. (2011). It's Unfair Why Customers Who Merely Observe an Uncivil Employee Abandon the Company. *Journal of Service Research, 14*(3), 302–317.

Post, S. G. (2005). Altruism, happiness, and health: It's good to be good. International journal of behavioral medicine, 12(2), 66–77.

Rehg, M. T., Miceli, M. P., Near, J. P., & Van Scotter, J. R. (2008). Antecedents and outcomes of retaliation against whistleblowers: Gender differences and power relationships. *Organization Science, 19*(2), 221–240.

Robertson, J. C., Stefaniak, C. M., & Curtis, M. B. (2011). Does Wrongdoer Reputation Matter? Impact of Auditor-Wrongdoer Performance and Likeability Reputations on Fellow Auditors' Intention to Take Action and Choice of Reporting Outlet. *Behavioral Research in Accounting, 23*(2), 207–234.

Robinson, S. L., O'Reilly, J., & Wang, W. (2013). Invisible at work an integrated model of workplace ostracism. *Journal of Management, 39*(1), 203–231.

Robinson, S. N., Robertson, J. C., & Curtis, M. B. (2012). The effects of contextual and wrongdoing attributes on organizational employees' whistleblowing intentions following fraud. *Journal of Business Ethics, 106*, 213–227.

Rupp, D. E., & Bell, C. M. (2010). Extending the deontic model of justice: Moral self-regulation in third-party responses to injustice. *Business Ethics Quarterly, 20*, 89–106.

Rupp, D. E., Ganapathi, J., Aguilera, R. V., & Williams, C. A. (2006). Employee reactions to corporate social responsibility: An organizational justice framework. *Journal of Organizational Behavior, 27*, 537–543.

Rupp, D. E., Shao, R., Thornton, M., & Skarlicki, D. P. (2013). Applicants' and employees' reactions to corporate social responsibility: The moderating effects of first-party justice perceptions and moral identity. *Personnel Psychology, 66*(4), 895–933.

Ryan, W. (1971). *Blaming the victim*. New York, NY: Vintage.

Ryan, A. M., & Wessel, J. L. (2012). Sexual orientation harassment in the workplace: When do observers intervene? *Journal of Organizational Behavior, 33*(4), 488–509.

Salancik, G., & Pfeffer, J. (1978). A social information processing approach to job attitudes and task design. *Administrative Science Quarterly, 23*, 224–253.

Sanchez, C. (2005) U.S. Government punishes schools that ban military recruiting. NPR News (Online), June 1, 2005. http://www.npr.org/templates/story/story.php?storyId=4675926.

Schlenker, Barry R. (1980). *Impression Management: The self-concept, social identity, and interpersonal relations.* Monterey, CA: Brooks/Cole.

Schwartz, B. (1975). *Queuing and waiting: Studies in the social organization of access and delay.* Chicago: University of Chicago Press.

Schwartz, G. S., Kane, T. R., Joseph, J. M., & Tedeschi, J. T. (1978). The effects of post-transgression remorse on perceived aggression, attributions of intent, and level of punishment. *British Journal of Social and Clinical Psychology,* 17, 293–297.

Sekerka, L. E., & Bagozzi, R. P. (2007). Moral courage in the workplace: Moving to and from the desire and decision to act. *Business Ethics: A European Review, 16*(2), 132–142.

Shapiro, D. L., & Kulik, C. T. (2004). Disputing with faceless opponents: New challenges for conflict management research. In M. J. Gelfand & J. M. Brett (Eds.), *Handbook of negotiation and culture:* (pp.177–192). Palo Alto, CA: Stanford University Press.

Shaver, K. G. (1985). *The attribution of blame: Causality, responsibility, and blameworthiness.* New York, NY: Springer-Verlag.

Shaver, K. (1970). Redress and conscientiousness in the attribution of responsibility for accidents. *Journal of Experimental Social Psychology, 6*(1), 100–110.

Shultz, T. R., Schleifer, M., & Altman, I. (1981). Judgments of causation, responsibility, and punishment in cases of harm-doing. *Canadian Journal of Behavioral Science, 13,* 238–253.

Skarlicki, D. P., Brown, G., & Bemmels, B. (2012). The impact of a victim's reaction to unfair treatment on third parties' emotion and retribution: A moral perspective. In L. Neider and C. Schriesheim (Eds), *Research in management: Perspectives on justice and trust in organizations* (vol. 9, pp. 77–106). Greenwich CT: Information Age.

Skarlicki, D., Ellard, J., & Kelln, B. (1998) Third-party perceptions of a layoff: Procedural derogation and retributive aspects of justice. *Journal of Applied Psychology, 83,* 119–127.

Skarlicki, D. P., Hoegg, J., Aquino, K., & Nadisic, T (2013). Does employee mistreatment affect your sense of taste and smell? The mediating role of moral disgust. *Journal of Experimental and Social Psychology, 49(5),* 852–859.

Skarlicki, D. P., & Kulik, C. (2005). Third-party reactions to employee (mis)treatment: A justice perspective. *Research in Organizational Behavior, 26,* 183–229.

Skarlicki, D. P., & Rupp, D. E. (2010). Dual processing and organizational justice: The role of rational versus experiential processing in third-party reactions to workplace mistreatment. *Journal of Applied Psychology, 95*(5), 944–952.

Skarlicki, D. P., & Turner, A., (2013). Unfairness begets unfairness: Victim derogation and moral identity in human resource decision making. Manuscript under review.

Sloman, S. A. (1996). The empirical case for two systems of reasoning. *Psychological Bulletin, 119*(1), 3–22.

Solomon, R. C. (1999). Justice v. vengeance: On law and the satisfaction of emotion. In S. A. Bandes (Ed.), *The passions of law* (pp. 123–148). New York, NY: New York University Press.

Sommerfeld, R. D., Krambeck, H. J., Semmann, D., & Milinski, M. (2007). Gossip as an alternative for direct observation in games of indirect reciprocity. *Proceedings of the National Academy of Sciences, 104*(44), 17435–17440.

Spencer, S. J., Josephs, R. A., & Steele, C. M. (1993). Low self-esteem: The uphill struggle for self-integrity. In R. Baumeister (Ed.), *Self-esteem; The puzzle of low self-regard* (pp. 201–218). New York, NY: Plenum.

Spencer, S., & Rupp, D. E. (2009). Angry, guilty, and conflicted: Injustice toward coworkers heightens emotional labor through cognitive and emotional mechanisms. *Journal of Applied Psychology, 94*(2), 429–444.

Staub, E. (1989). The evolution of bystanders, German psychoanalysts, and lessons for today. *Political Psychology, 10*(1), 39–52.

Stotland, E. (1969). *The psychology of hope.* San Francisco, CA: Jossey-Bass.

Summers, R. J. (1996). The effect of harasser performance status and complainant tolerance on reactions to a complaint of sexual harassment. *Journal of Vocational Behavior, 49*(1), 53–53.

Sykes, G. M., & Matza, D. (1957). Techniques of neutralization: A theory of delinquency. *American Sociological Review, 22*(6), 664–670.

Tajfel, H. (1982). Social psychology of intergroup relations. *Annual Review of Psychology, 33,* 1–59.

Terpstra, D. E., & Baker, D. D. (1992). Outcomes of federal court decisions on sexual harassment. *The Academy of Management Journal, 35*(1), 181–190.

Thibaut, J. W., & Walker, L. (1975). *Procedural justice: A psychological analysis.* Mahwah, NJ: Erlbaum.

Trevino, L. K. (1992). Moral reasoning and business ethics: Implications for research, education, and management. *Journal of Business Ethics, 11,* 445–459.

Trevino, L. K., & Ball, G. A. (1992). The social implications of punishing unethical behavior: Observers' cognitive and affective reactions. *Journal of Management, 18,* 751–768.

Triana, M., Kim, K., and Gracia M. (2011). To help or not to help? Personal value for diversity moderates the relationship between discrimination against minorities and citizenship behavior toward minorities. *Journal of Business Ethics, 102,* 33–342.

Tripp, M., & Bies, R. J. (1997). What's good about revenge? The avenger's perspective. In R. J. Lewicki, R. J. Bies, & B. H. Sheppard (Eds.), *Research on negotiation in organizations* (Vol. 6, pp. 145–160). Greenwich, CT: JAI.

Trivers, R. L. (1971). The evolution of reciprocal altruism. *Quarterly Review of Biology, 46*(1), 35–57.

Turillo, C. J., Folger, R., Lavelle, J. J., Umphress, E. E., & Gee, J. O. (2002). Is virtue its own reward? Self-sacrificial decisions for the sake of fairness. *Organizational Behavior and Human Decision Processes, 89,* 839–865.

Turner, J. C. (1987). *Rediscovering the social group: A self-categorization theory.* Oxford, UK: Blackwell.

Umphress, E. E., Simmons, A. L., Folger, R., Ren, R., & Bobocel, R. (2012). Observer reactions to interpersonal injustice: The roles of perpetrator intent and victim perception. *Journal of Organizational Behavior, 34*(3), 327–349.

Utne, M. K., & Kidd, R. F. (1980). Attribution and equity. In G. Mikula (Ed.), *Justice and social interaction* (pp. 69–93). New York, NY: Springer-Verlag.

Vadera, A. K., Aguilera, R. V., & Caza, B. B. (2009). Making Sense of Whistle-Blowing's Antecedents. *Business Ethics Quarterly, 19*(4), 553–586.

van Prooijen, J. W. (2009). Retributive versus compensatory justice: Observers' preference for punishing in response to criminal offenses. *European Journal of Social Psychology, 40,* 72–85.

Walster, E. (1966). Assignment of responsibility for an accident. *Journal of Personality and Social Psychology, 3*(1), 73–79.

Walster, E., Berscheid, E., & Walster, G. W. (1976). New directions in equity research. In L. Berkowitz & E. Walster (Eds), *Advances in experimental social psychology* (Vol. 9, pp. 1–42). New York, NY: Academic Press.

Watson, D., & Clark, L. A. (1984). Negative affectivity: The disposition to experience aversive emotional states. *Psychological Bulletin, 96*(3), 465–490.

Weinstein, N., & Ryan, R. M. (2010). When helping helps: autonomous motivation for prosocial behavior and its influence on well-being for the helper and recipient. *Journal of Personality and Social Psychology, 98*(2), 222.

Wittenberg, C., Mackenzie, S., Shaw, M., & Ross, D. (1997). And justice for all. *HR Magazine, 42*(9), 131.

Wortman, C. B., & Lehman, D. R. (1985). Reactions to victims of life crises: Support attempts that fail. In I. G. Samson & B. R. Sarason (Eds.), *Social support: Theory, research and applications* (pp. 463–489). Dordrect, The Netherlands: Martinus Nijhoff.

York, K. M. (1989). Defining sexual harassment in workplaces: A policy-capturing study. *Academy of Management Journal, 32*(4), 830–850.

Zdaniuk, A., & Bobocel, D. R. (2013). The automatic activation of (un)fairness behavior in organizations. *Human Resources Management Review, 23*(3), 254–265.

Zhu, L. L., Martens, J. P., & Aquino, K. (2012). Third party responses to justice failure: An identity-based meaning maintenance model. *Organizational Psychology Review, 2*, 129–151.

Zoghbi-Manrique-de-Lara, P., Aguiar-Quintana, T., & Suárez-Acosta, M. A. (2013). A justice framework for understanding how guests react to hotel employee (mis) treatment. *Tourism Management, 36*, 143–152.

Zoghbi-Manrique-de-Lara, P., & Suárez-Acosta, M. A. (2013). Employees' reactions to peers' unfair treatment by supervisors: The role of ethical leadership. *Journal of Business Ethics*. doi 10.1007/s10551-013-1778-z

CHAPTER

11

Organizational Justice and Legal Justice: How Are They Related?

Barry Goldman

Abstract

Even though scholars in the disciplines of legal justice and organizational justice both maintain that they investigate justice, even a casual reading of the scholarship and application of "justice," in these disciplines indicates that the two set of scholars are not speaking the same language. The purpose of the paper is to expose the backgrounds, development, assumptions, and approaches of each of legal and organizational justice. Moreover, the chapter provides guidance for organizational justice scholars and researchers to better use, develop, and integrate legal justice into their research. Finally, it provides insights for future research integrating both areas of justice scholarship.

Key Words: legal justice, justice, natural law, legal assumptions, legitimacy, justice types, justice as fairness, expert witnesses

This chapter will examine the relationship between organizational justice and legal justice. Since organizational justice and legal justice each deal with "justice," it may seem at first blush that they should be essentially the same—or at least very similar—based on the similarity of names alone. However, it does not take long before even a casual reader realizes that they are very different—although the precise differences often seem elusive. Generally speaking, legal justice amounts to justice in following rules; organizational justice involves justice in the rules themselves. For purposes of typology, it is important to note that organizational justice, although it is a discipline of social science, it is also a subcategory of social justice insofar as the latter is concerned with the moral quality of rules in society. Therefore, organizational justice is focused on the moral quality of rules in organizations (Greenberg & Colquitt, 2005; Sadurski, 1985). Each of these will be discussed in this chapter.

Scholars in each of legal and social justice seem somewhat puzzled by the goals of the other. On the one hand, social justice scholars are frequently of the opinion that there is "too much law, there are too many lawyers, and there is too much litigation.... [which] produces economic waste [and] perverts justice." (Friedman, 1994, p. 23). But, on the other hand, legal scholars often believe that social justice scholars and social scientists allow personal bias and values to masquerade as truth, have a tendency to ignore individual-level factors that are often at the core of legal justice, and frequently are unable to admit opposing points of view (Chesler, Kalmuss, & Sanders, 1984). How can these opposing views be reconciled? Is this a situation where one side is right, or more right, than the other? Or, is this, to paraphrase George Bernard Shaw, simply a situation in which we are two academic fields separated by a common language?[1] What is apparent, after a careful reading of the literatures relating to justice is that we do not follow a shared linguistic criteria for deciding whether a situation is just or unjust. The most intense disputes societal members have about justice (e.g., affirmative action, tax, voting—where the question is whether the facts conform with some agreed upon test in a particular situation) often involve implicitly differing standards.

Yet, the present balkanization is regrettable in light of the promise of joint scholarship that existed in the 1970s. During that time, for example, John Thibaut, a social psychologist, and Laurens Walker, a law professor, co-authored *Procedural Justice: A Psychological Analysis* (1975). The first line of the book is revealing in its intent: "This book represents a fully interdisciplinary enterprise in which we have attempted to integrate some small part of the wisdom of the fields of law and social psychology." (p. vii). Moreover, other joint research involving legal scholars and social psychologists investigated the relationship between procedural and distributive justice (Walker, Lind, & Thibaut, 1979). Some of this early, integrated scholarship involved assisting the judicial system in understanding the work and development of social scientists, including paradigmatic development. This scholarship facilitated the use of social science research in the courtroom, in drafting legislation, and in providing social frameworks for larger societal issues (Walker & Monahan, 1987). Moreover, Tom Tyler investigated a number of issues relating to how these topics overlapped in the 1980s (see, e.g., Tyler, 1988a, 1988b, 1990). However, for reasons not entirely clear, there has been little integrated work in recent decades involving both groups of scholars.

The following parable from the New Testament may be helpful to illustrate the differences in approach between organizational justice and legal justice.

> A landowner went out early in the morning to hire workers for his vineyard. He agreed to pay them a denarius [the normal daily wage] for the day and sent them into his vineyard. About nine in the morning he went out and saw others standing in the marketplace doing nothing. He told them, "You also go and work in my vineyard, and I will pay you whatever is right." So they went. He went out again about noon and about three in the afternoon and did the same thing. About five in the afternoon he went out and found still others standing around. He asked them, "Why have you been standing here all day long doing nothing?" "Because no one has hired us," they answered. He said to them, "You also go and work in my vineyard." When evening came, the owner of the vineyard said to his foreman, "Call the workers and pay them their wages, beginning with the last ones hired and going on to the first." The workers who were hired about five in the afternoon came and each received a denarius. So when those came who were hired first, they expected to receive more. But each one of them also received a denarius. When they received it, they began to grumble against the landowner. "These who were hired last worked only one hour," they said, "and you have made them equal to us who have borne the burden of the work and the heat of the day." But he answered one of them, "I am not being unfair to you, friend. Didn't you agree to work for a denarius? Take your pay and go. I want to give the one who was hired last the same as I gave you. Don't I have the right to do what I want with my own money? Or are you envious because I am generous?" "So the last will be first, and the first will be last." (Matthew 20: 1–16).

The parable illustrates the difference between legal justice and organizational justice. From the perspective of legal justice, there was no injustice: the landowner was *more* generous than the law (as is typified by the normal daily wage) required. However, to the workers hired first, this behavior violated principles of equity important to organizational justice.

The following recent court case illustrates some of the significant differences in approach between organizational justice and legal justice: In 2012 (later reaffirmed in 2013), the Supreme Court of Iowa held that a male employer may terminate a female employee without legal liability because the employer's wife—due to no fault of the employee (she did not, according to the court, engage in flirtatious behavior)—was concerned about the nature of the relationship between the employer and employee. The boss admitted that he was afraid he would try to engage in an affair with the employee. Moreover, the employee was by all accounts an exemplary worker. In essence, the court admitted that there was no liability for the firing of an irresistible worker. In that case, Nelson vs. Knight the court held that the employer's, a dentist, conduct against his employee, a dental assistant, did not amount to illegal sex discrimination under the Iowa Civil Rights Act. In a significant portion of the legal opinion, the court wryly observed:

> ... It seems odd at first glance to have the question of whether the *employer* engaged in unlawful discrimination turn on the *employee's* conduct, assuming that such conduct (whatever it is) would not typically be a firing offense. Usually our legal focus is on the employer's motivation, not on whether the discharge in a broader sense is *fair* (emphasis added) because the employee did

something to "deserve it." Title VII [the federal antidiscrimination law] and the Iowa Civil Rights Act are *not general fairness laws, and an employer does not violate them by treating an employee unfairly so long as the employer does not engage in discrimination based upon the employee's protected status.*

This parable and recent court case both illustrate the major differences between legal justice and organizational justice: legal justice involves conforming to the rules whatever they may be; organizational justice involves the moral quality of the rules, that is, whether the treatment of the individual is as it should be compared to similarly situated others. Implied in this distinction is another important difference: legal justice at its core involves individual justice; whereas, organizational justice involves societal-level or social justice (Sadurski, 1985).

The purpose of this chapter is to investigate the key distinctions between organizational and legal justice, including an analysis of the underlying assumptions for each, and the overlapping areas of research affecting each. Finally, we discuss some potential new areas of research affecting both of these disciplines.

What Is to Be Gained from Investigating Legal and Organizational Justice?

Justice, in both conceptions, is different from many other political and moral virtues (e.g., moderation, industry, charity, mercy) because, as conceptualized by modern scholars, it is a matter of entitlement—a belief that those affected individuals have a right to expect certain treatment from institutions or institutional actors (Dworkin, 1986). Notwithstanding the evolution of organizational justice from legal justice, there remains confusion and misunderstanding between the two concepts. Moreover, this confusion can lead to differences in research and practice. For example, social scientists may scoff at the Iowa Supreme Court's conclusions in the "irresistible worker" case, (indeed, some attorney's may also scoff at it) previously cited. However, it would be wrong for social scientists to base their objections on their collective views of social justice: That would not be the appropriate criteria to evaluate a legal case. Moreover, legal scholars, judges, or lawmakers may dismiss research on organizational justice as naïve and inappropriate without fully understanding the implications of its descriptive approach to the modern workplace (Greenberg & Colquitt, 2005). Yet, a more complete understanding of each type of justice would likely benefit each group by providing context and nuance to each. For example, organizational justice scholars have occasionally approached legal problems with a set of assumptions that only properly apply to organizational justice issues (e.g., such as assuming guidelines issues by a federal agency, such as the Equal Employment Opportunity Commission, are inviolable). Moreover, legal scholars have sometimes dismissed the aggregated effects of organizational justice (e.g., Mitchell, Monahan, & Walker, 2011).

Types of Justice

Legal Justice

Ironically, the term *law* has defied authoritative definition. Even lawyers and judges have no agreed-upon definition for it: "For them it is simply what they practice and what courts do" (Loh, 1984, p. 23). Kant condemned lawyers for failing to define the subject matter of their profession and then proceeded to define the term *law*, but it received no more universal acceptance than any other definition (Berman & Greiner, 1980). Zane (1998: p. 2) observed: "no jurist has yet achieved a definition of law that does not require the use of the idea of law, either implied or expressed, as part of the definition." Justice, as conceived by western legal systems appears to have four fundamental aspects to it: (1) norms, (2) regularly enforced by coercion, (3) by persons authorized by society, (4) as applied by courts of law (Abadinsky, 2003). The following section will further examine some of the fundamental concepts that assist in understanding and defining the law.

DEFINING THE LAW

Law is sometimes viewed as a set of authoritative and prescriptive rules for conduct (e.g., pay taxes, do not segregate public school pupils on the basis of race, or instruct persons on how to do what they want in a way that makes them legally enforceable, as in the case of contracts). This is known as *positive law*, and refers to the rules set forth by human society. It is often viewed as amoral (e.g., the laws of Nazi Germany or the Fugitive Slave Law of the United States) (Abadinsky, 2003). However, before there was positive law, there was *natural law* or the "law of nature" (Rommen, 1998). It is this aspect of law, natural law, with which the concept of morality in law is associated. It holds that law necessarily has a moral basis and "its criteria are grounded in something more than ordinary experience—in nature. It assumes the quest for an absolute ideal of justice" (Levy, 1988: p. 3). It presupposes that humans have an inborn notion of right and wrong and, therefore, the essence of rules for human behavior does not rest upon the arbitrary will of a ruler or views of the multitude (Rommen, 1998). It does not require a belief in a deity but does refer to a higher law, primordial or law of nature, that is consistent across all societies. Some well-known proponents of natural law include Aristotle, the Greek Stoics, and Thomas Aquinas. We see it in the law in such notable documents as the Declaration of Independence ("We hold these Truths to be self-evident, that all Men are created equal, that they are endowed by their Creator with certain inalienable Rights....") and the United States Constitution ("Congress shall make no law ... prohibiting the freedom of speech."). Moreover, it has frequently been employed by the courts to guard against overzealous government by acknowledging "natural rights," "fundamental principles of civilized society," and "immutable principles of justice" (Abadinsky, 2003, p. 9).

The courts and legal scholars have various levels of agreement on the types of legal justice. *Substantive law* is statutory or written law, as opposed to common, or court-made, law. It defines rights and duties, such as criminal or contract law. This stands in contrast to *procedural law*, the rules by which a court hears and determines what happens in a civil or criminal lawsuit (e.g., notice of hearing, rules of evidence). Among other reasons, these rules are in place to ensure *due process*, which ensures three types of rights for the individual over government: (1) criminal procedural protections (e.g., against unreasonable search and seizure, see, Burnham, 2011, pps. 283–323); (2) procedural protections against government actions (e.g., rules applicable to eminent domain actions, see Burnham, 2011, pp. 205–209); and (3) "substantive" due process rights, which seem to have little to do with "process," and much to do with substance. For example, although the due process clause of the U. S. Constitution states that the government shall not "deprive any person of life, liberty or property without due process of law," substantive due process states that there are certain rights encompassed within the term *liberty* that the state cannot infringe upon no matter how protective its "process" is (e.g., the right to privacy, used by the U.S. Supreme Court in *Roe v. Wade*).

Some legal scholars recognize other types of justice, such as restorative justice, which emphasizes reparation to the victim or the community by a criminal offender. Or, retributive justice, that considers when—and to what degree—punishment of a harm-doer is appropriate (e.g., Feinberg, 1984; Nozick, 1981).

What is apparent—especially with respect to a type of justice such as substantive due process, is that the line between these types of legal justice can get pretty murky at times. However, in the legal world, the precise antecedent to justice matters less than whether, in the end, legal justice is applied (Dworkin, 1986).

ASSUMPTIONS OF LEGAL JUSTICE

Western legal systems—and exceptions abound, as in any man-made aspirational system—generally operate with the following set of assumptions, which we will discuss: (a) rational, (b) objective in application, (c) individually applied, and (d) legitimacy.

Rational

A rational legal order is generally regarded as one where general norms are applied to specific cases. Weber (1967: p. 63) describes irrational legal systems in which decisions are "influenced by concrete factors of the particular case as evaluated upon an ethical, emotional, or political basis rather than by general norms." For example, Weber uses the example of Islamic *kadi (qadi)* justice as a contrast to rational-based systems of legal justice. Under this system, decisions are made by a religious judge—without referring to generalized principles of law—but, rather, according to what the individual judge determines to be morally correct in the particular situation.

This type of system can work very well in a close-knit, relatively homogenous, and small population. It is designed to customize legal justice when the judge has access to a rich set of circumstances affecting the litigants. However, "that pastoral model cannot serve an ethnically and ideologically diverse nation where litigants are strangers to the judge and often each other. The liberties and fortunes of citizens cannot be left at the mercy of each judge's personal sense of what procedures are fair, what outcome is just, who needs protection, and who deserves compassion" (Glendon, 1994, p. 164). Moreover, an irrational legal system tends to be more unpredictable than a rational one, impeding a modern capitalist economy, which requires rational rules, predictability, and coercive power (Abadinsky, 2003; Weber, 1967).

Objective

The second assumption of legal justice is that it is objective in application. For the most part, this assumption is manifested in the "reasonable person" standard. This standard is a "wholly impersonal fiction where no special characteristic of the accused should be attributed" (*Bedder v. Director of Public Prosecutions*, 1954). This standard is found in both criminal and civil law (e.g., negligence) and is used to assess standards of care owed from one person to another. It is the basis on which the fact-finder (typically, juries) determine whether one person violated a duty to another. It is not necessarily an average person but a composite of the relevant community's standard of how one member of the community should act toward another in situations where there is a threat of harm (through action or inaction) toward the public. Although there is a loose consensus in common law on the meaning, there is no agreed upon technical definition. For example, "an ordinary person, of either sex, not exceptionally excitable or pugnacious, but possessed of such powers of self-control as everyone is entitled to expect that his fellow citizens will exercise in society as it is today" (*R v Camplin*, A. C. 705, 1978). American jurist Oliver Wendell Holmes explained the theory of the standard to allow society to function: "a certain average of conduct, a sacrifice of individual peculiarities going beyond a certain point, is necessary to the general welfare" (Holmes, 1909, p. 108). The effect is to occasionally punish individuals who harm society (or individuals in society), even though they had no intent to do so, because they did not conform in their personal behavior to this fictitious reasonable-person (initially, it was a reasonable man) standard. The reasonable person has been specifically distinguished from the average person, who is not always reasonable (*The T. J. Hooper*, 1932). Such a person is assumed to be aware of the law, adequately informed, capable, and fair-minded, and has been referred to as an "excellent but odious character" (Herbert, 1989, p. 12):

"He is an ideal, a standard, the embodiment of all those qualities which we demand of the good citizen . . . [he] invariably looks where he is going, . . . is careful to examine the immediate foreground before he executes a leap or bound; . . . neither stargazes nor is lost in meditation when approaching trapdoors or the margins of a dock; . . . never mounts a moving [bus] and does not alight from any car while the train is in motion, . . . uses nothing except in moderation, and even flogs his child in meditating only on the golden mean" (Herbert, 1989, pps. 9-11). In sum, he (or she) is not necessarily (or even desirably) an actual average person but an aspirational one. As we will see, this is a noteworthy difference in standards from that of organizational justice.

Individually Applied

The third assumption is that legal justice is individually applied. Although, as noted earlier, the law assumes the fiction of a reasonable person to assess objective standards of behavior, all legal determinations are applied to an individual (as opposed to groups of people) (Sadurski, 1985, p. 2). This concept is so embedded in our culture that we take it for granted. It is operationalized in a number of ways through legal justice. One prominent way is through guaranteed rights of notice of any proceeding against the individual and an opportunity to be heard. Another prominent way this standard is manifested in legal justice is through the Bill of Rights to the United States Constitution, which is a list of individual rights against government encroachment. What each of these rights mean in application is that societal standards of legal justice must, barring extraordinarily unusual circumstances, be proved to have been satisfied for each and every affected individual. So, for example, there must be proof in a legal proceeding that an individual defendant has received a written notice of the charges against him or her. This individual application can also be in contrast to how organizational scholars approach justice, as we will also discuss later in this chapter.

Legitimacy

The final legal assumption applies to legitimacy. Once a governmental entity enacts a law, the degree of compliance with it is generally a function of the costs associated with its violation (e.g., prison sentence, fines, penalties), an instrumental perspective, and also by the moral legitimacy of the law (a normative perspective) (Tyler, 1990). Moral legitimacy refers to a belief "that the authorities, and their political and legal framework, are legitimate. As long as that belief is widespread, people will largely regulate their own behavior by reference to internalized values that correspond with the law and its underlying principles, and force need only occasionally when people get out of line" (Skogan & Frydl, 2004). Those entities having an interest in enforcing the law would, all things being equal, rather have the legal actors and legal system be perceived as morally legitimate by the population subject to it for several reasons; chief among them is that it facilitates enforcement of these laws. All laws are violated by a certain proportion of the affected population over time; moral legitimacy keeps noncompliance to a relatively low level.

A recent study examined this question from an unusual perspective, asking why do criminals obey the law? As the authors observed, even convicted felons comply with the law more than they do not comply. Using a survey methodology of active criminal offenders, the authors reported that although criminals, as a whole, have a low opinion of the law and its enforcement agents, they are more likely to comply with the law when they believed in its substance and in the moral legitimacy of its enforcement agents, the police (Papachristos, Meares, & Fagan, 2012). One of the important determinants of legitimacy in their study was procedural justice, for which they relied on a measure of organizational justice familiar to organizational justice researchers (Tyler & Huo, 2002).

With reliance on moral legitimacy as a means of compliance, it is clear that legal justice relies on at least one important foundational element in common with organizational justice. This is important to help harmonize the two areas, although important differences in assumptions remain. Moreover, this reliance on the legitimacy of process (e.g, procedural justice) becomes even more important in a heterogeneous and large population where many differences in values and points of view arise. Perceived legitimacy of process may pacify those on the losing end of legal disputes, notably in the civil judgments where disagreements about numerous disputes between individuals or entities (e.g., businesses) often leave little agreement about the substance of the dispute (Lind, Greenberg, Scott, & Welchans, 2000; Lind, Kurtz, Musante, Walker, & Thibaut, 1980; Lind et al., 1990). However, collective belief in the moral legitimacy of the legal system (more or less) allows virtually all these disputes to be resolved peacefully (see also, Feldman & Levy, 1994).

Organizational Justice

Organizational justice has much of its foundation in social justice but with a focus on the workplace (Greenberg & Colquitt, 2005; Lind & Tyler, 1988). Social justice tends to focus on justice with a society, as a whole. Moreover, both organizational and social justice share a number of qualities that distinguish them from legal justice but perhaps none more so than this: legal justice is essentially about conforming to the rules whatever they may be; social (and organizational justice) is about justice in the substance of the rules themselves (Sadurski, (1985). For these reasons, it is best to first examine some of the essential assumptions underlying social justice before moving on to organizational justice.

SOCIAL JUSTICE BACKGROUND

Hayek (1976, p. 97) maintained that social justice was "intellectually disreputable, the mark of demagogy or cheap journalism" because he believed justice was an attribute of individual, and not collective, action. Notwithstanding Hayek's position, concerns regarding social justice have probably increased since his statements. As the world has increased in growing economic affluence and education, concerns with inequalities in social distribution of good and opportunities have risen. With the growing realization that the benefits and burdens of society are not impersonally and incomprehensibly distributed by unapproachable forces but, rather, as the consequence of rational and conscious actors, injustices previously assumed as natural fail to be justified (Sadurski, 1985). In turn, this led in the 1960s and 1970s to a growing interest in distributive justice (e.g., Homans, 1961). However, legal theory was largely unaffected by this research.

This is not to say that legal scholars have not contributed to the ideas behind social justice. Indeed, some of the most provocative scholarship in the area of social justice has been done by legal scholars (see Dworkin, 1986). However, legal doctrine has usually been a laggard in adopting the prevailing standards of social justice. This is largely explained by the assumption (referred to earlier) that the operation of law has little to do with social (as opposed to individual) justice. Moreover, it is also explained by the view that any attempt to use the law as a mechanism to adjust the distributive qualities of justice degrade the assumption of legitimacy on which the law relies. Hence, with respect to social justice, the law generally moves very slowly, allowing for a broad consensus on new standards or values to emerge.

One of the areas in which legal justice and social justice are often in direct conflict is in the area of "equality under the law." There can never, in fact, be any objective or neutral standard of legal equality because no law can do so without classification (some groups are in; others are out, e.g, blacks, women, gays—all at different points of time have been excluded from the promises of equality). Moreover, classification becomes discrimination or favoritism—another form of discrimination—depending on substantive moral views.

Although concerns with justice, per se, go back to Plato's *Republic*, the bible, and perhaps earlier, many early writers concerned with issues of justice (e.g., Adam Smith, Immanuel Kant) had not established a set of principles from which the distribution of benefits and burdens could be institutionalized until the 19th century (e.g., Herbert Spencer, Karl Marx) (Johnston, 2011). With this emphasis on the appropriate distribution of the benefits and burdens of society, it is not surprising that early scholarship on social justice emphasized distributive justice (e.g., Johnston, 2011).

ASSUMPTIONS OF ORGANIZATIONAL JUSTICE

In the previous section, assumptions relating to legal justice were discussed. In this section, several important assumptions relating to organizational justice, particularly as they relate to legal justice are discussed: (a) there are different and distinct types of organizational justice, (b) they are subjectively perceived, and (c) justice is assumed to be the same as fairness.

Different Types of Organizational Justice

As noted numerous times in this volume, the field of organizational justice is assumed to contain within it several different types of justice. According to most scholars, at least three (distributive, procedural, and interactional, see, e.g., Bies & Moag, 1986; Bies, 2001; Bobocel & Holmvall, 2001; Cropanzano, Rupp, Mohler, & Schminke, 2001) but, according to some, four types (adding informational justice, Colquitt, 2001), and, to others, additional types of justice (e.g., Shapiro & Kirkman, 1999). The fact that the discipline of organizational justice is not monolithic but, rather, has within it various types of organizational justice does not, by itself, distinguish it from legal justice. Within legal justice, scholars argue, are various types of legal justice (e.g. substantive, procedural, restorative, retributive). However, what is different between legal and organizational justice in this regard is the emphasis by organizational scholars in arguing for and empirically verifying conceptual distinctiveness among the subcategories of justice (see, Colquitt, 2001; Colquitt, Conlon, Wesson, Porter, & Ng, 2001; Greenberg & Colquitt, 2005). Indeed, as is appropriate in social science, much attention is devoted to construct validity by organizational justice scholars (Colquitt, 2001).

Subjectively Perceived

Organizational justice is based on the assumption that justice is subjectively perceived. For example, it is common in organizational justice research for individuals to be asked various questions relating to either "direct" or "indirect" measures of justice. With direct measures, the respondent is asked to comment on the fairness of the outcome, process, or interpersonal treatment; whereas, in indirect measures, the respondent is asked to comment on the rules that relate to the various types of organizational justice (see Colquitt & Shaw, 2005: Lind & Tyler, 1988). This has been described as a descriptive approach to justice, which is consistent with social science as a field (Cohen, 1986). It is based upon the idea that social science can best advance human understanding and knowledge with respect to organizational justice by advancing two chief aims: (1) addressing concerns about justice in organizational settings, and (2) investigating the consequences of following (or not) these rules in these organizations (Greenberg & Bies, 1992). Thus, organizational justice adopted a descriptive (aimed at describing the attitudes and behaviors of people toward justice) approach to justice as opposed to the prescriptive (aimed at determining what should be done to achieve justice) approach of philosophers and foundational social justice scholars (e.g., Nozick, 1974, 1981; Rawls, 1971). Nevertheless, by adopting this descriptive and subjective approach, organizational justice scholars necessarily focus on a "bottom up" assessment of justice, whereby justice is assessed as consisting of what the aggregate set of individuals in an organization determine what it is (and not—as in legal justice—a "top down" approach of what it should be).

Justice as Fairness

Organizational justice is assumed to be synonymous with fairness (see, e.g, Cropanzano, Stein, & Nadisic, 2011; Greenberg & Bies, 1992; Greenberg & Colquitt, 2005, p. 4: ". . . justice and fairness (terms that tend to be used interchangeably)"). However, generally speaking, justice is a broader concept than fairness. Or, to put in another way: fairness is one possible conception of justice (see, Johnston, 2011; Rawls, 1958,1971). The two concepts can be thought of as having subtle but important differences. As noted earlier, *justice* is the concept having to do with what members of a society expect to receive from social institutions, including organizations (e.g., Rawls, 1958, p. 164: "... I consider justice only as a virtue of social institutions, or what I shall call practices."). The basis for this expectation is derived from the responsibilities of individuals toward each other. It is concerned with what is morally required as opposed to what is morally praiseworthy. For example, the concept of charitable giving assumes it is not a requirement of justice. Rawls (1958; p. 164) explained it thusly: "It might seem at first sight that the concepts of justice and fairness are the same, and that there is no reason to distinguish them, or to say that one is more fundamental than the other. I think that this impression is mistaken."

There are two principles to Rawls's view of justice as fairness. The first argues for equal basic liberties for all members of a society and are intended to apply to the design of political systems. The second one applies primarily to economic institutions. It consists of two parts: The first part involves fair equality of opportunity, and argues that citizens with the same talents and will to use them have the same educational and economic opportunities regardless of background. The second part, the difference principle, regulates the distribution of wealth and income. It recognizes that there will be inequalities in wealth and income but that these should be arranged so that the least-advantaged group does best (relative to what it may do in other distributions) (Rawls, 1958).

Distinguished from the concept of justice, Rawls (1958, p. 178) defines the "concept of fairness which relates to right dealing between persons who are cooperating with or competing against one another.. . ." From this perspective, it is at least arguable that the discipline of organizational justice is more often concerned with fairness than justice because it more often nowadays is focused on relations between and among individual persons than between individuals and the state. However, earlier justice researchers did seem to investigate more situations involving state action than present researchers (e.g., Lind & Tyler, 1988; Tyler, 1990). Parenthetically, Rawls's (1971) focus was on the structure of society as a whole. As a consequence of this, he was unconcerned with the kinds of rules that regulate transactions between private persons, such as contracts and many other legal relationships between individuals. His view was that these rules may be just or unjust, but they were not the subject of his theory.

Although organizational justice scholars tend to assume the two terms are the same, that is generally not the case with legal scholars who view them as different. For example, Dworkin (1986; p. 374) illustrated the differences between the terms as follows:

> We recognize different political virtues, which may compete with one another, in deciding which interpretation of the equal protection or due process clause [of the U. S. Constitution], for example, would make them better in political morality. Justice is one of these virtues: an interpretation of equal protection is better . . . if it comes closer to realizing what justice actually requires. But fairness is another: an interpretation is also better . . . if it reflects convictions that are dominant or at least popular in the community as a whole than if it expresses convictions unpopular or rejected there.

Early researchers in organizational justice may have contributed to the use of *justice* and *fairness* as synonyms in an attempt to establish construct validity. As part of the process to establish measurement repetition for a direct measure of justice, synonyms or substitutes for the same concept were used (e.g., Earley & Lind, 1987, used a two-item measure with the words *fair* and *just;* see also, Tyler, 1984; Lind & Tyler, 1988, especially their Table A-1 and p. 3, n. 1 ["we will use the terms procedural *justice* and procedural *fairness* interchangeably"]). As noted earlier, there are reasons to believe organizational scholars are fundamentally researching fairness—as the type of justice Rawls envisioned—rather than justice, at least as used by a number of other scholars. In any event, use of the term *organizational fairness* may help to distinguish the field from broader legal conceptualizations of justice.

Differences Between Legal and Organizational Justice as They Affect Research

The purposes of organizational justice and legal justice are largely distinct from each other. Broadly speaking, organizational justice is concerned with ways to foster cooperation (or, conversely, ways to decrease conflict) in groups or organizations (see, e.g., Blader & Tyler, 2005), particularly as they relate to group identification or interpersonal relationships (Cropanzano et al., 2001). It is generally descriptive in nature. To do this, it tends to focus on perceptions by individual workers (Greenberg & Colquitt, 2005). A consequence of the measurement of individual perceptions is that the measure of some aspects of organizational justice, such as procedural or interactional justice, can be affected by social comparisons and knowledge of outcomes, the so-called "self-serving bias" (van den Bos, Lind, & Wilke, 2001; Schmitt, Oswald, Kim, Gillespie, Ramsay, 2004). For example, Tyler (1984b) reported that favorability of outcomes received and fairness judgments were found to be distinguishable but not totally independent (r = .39). However, there is little evidence that this is a significant problem in the measure of organizational justice.

By contrast, as noted briefly earlier, and at the risk of some simplification, legal justice focuses on conforming to the rules *whatever those rules may be* (fair or unfair, despised or loved). It invokes the principle that we should treat people according to their rights but it does not determine any requirements or conditions of the moral quality of those rights (Sadurski, 1985). Assessments of legal justice generally involve consistency with legal rules (Hart, 1961, 2012b); they confirm that a general rule is properly applied to a particular case. Judgments about organizational justice have, as their object, the content of those rules or procedures or interactions; they confirm that the burdens or benefits of these are distributed justly (or fairly). Organizational and legal justice are neither mutually exclusive nor necessarily correlated. They apply to different aspects of the social process. Organizational justice applies to interactions, typically between an authority figure and a worker, done within the organization; legal justice applies to work done by a judge (or any other agent acting authoritatively on behalf of the government in applying legal rules). (Parenthetically, social justice applies to work done by a legislator or other policy maker, Sadurski, 1985). Legal justice is a process intended to arrive at normative standards; organizational justice is a process intended to describe reactions to those perceived standards.

However, a more nuanced view of the relationship between legal and organizational justice adds complexity. Although, a number of legal scholars describe legal justice as "conformity to rules" (Honore, 1962, p. 82.) there is necessarily a moral component to the law. Some prominent legal scholars, such as Ronald Dworkin (1986) argue that a judge always has a duty to search for the morally justifiable decision. Organizational justice is, then, a form of ideal standard of justice within organizations; legal justice is the standard of assessment of law enforcement within the structural values of a given legal system. This is why legal justice is sometimes described as "static" or "conservative" justice (Sadurski, 1985) and organizational justice can be thought of as a dynamic, reformative, or ideal form of justice.

Nevertheless, it would be wrong to view organizational justice as necessarily involving moral actions. For example, take one common metric for procedural justice, consistency. It has long been held to be a key component of procedural justice, going back to Leventhal (1980), and seemingly adopted henceforth as an appropriate and desirable aspect of procedural justice. Indeed, Rawls (1971, p. 59) commented that: "even where laws and institutions are unjust, it is often better that they should be consistently applied." For example, a consistent—but morally corrupt—performance evaluation system (e.g., one that is based on racial criteria or sexual preferences) may lead to more moral outcomes if it were inconsistently applied. Moreover, the self-serving bias raises the possibility that a significant portion of respondents in organizational justice studies are responding to self-centered interests with some frequency, rather than pure morally correct choices. Nevertheless, as a general rule, the component constructs of organizational justice have long-established construct validity (Greenberg & Colquitt, 2005). Moreover, the study of deontic justice makes a valid case for the inherent morality of organizational justice, see Cropanzano, Goldman, & Folger, 2005; Cropanzano, Goldman, & Folger, 2003; Johnston, 2011).

Organizational Justice Involving Legal Issues or Legal Justice

Approaches to the Study of Legal Justice

In the following two subsections, we will examine how organizational justice scholars have approached the study of legal issues. Organizational justice scholars have generally taken one of two approaches to the study of legal issues, a direct approach and an indirect approach.

DIRECT STUDY OF LEGAL ISSUES

The direct study of legal issues involves the study of justice involving legal procedures or mechanisms in a legal context. Much of this work occurred in the 1970s and 1980s and involved considerable investigation of procedural justice in legal settings. For example, Thibaut (a social psychologist) and Walker (a law professor) are generally credited with initiating the psychological investigation of procedural justice in 1975 (Thibaut & Walker, 1975, 1978). In this work, they focused on third-party dispute-resolution procedures (e.g., mediation, arbitration, litigation) to better understand decision-making in legal contexts. Primarily, the legal context involved a trial that moved through two stages: a *process* stage where evidence was presented, and a *decision* stage where a judgment was reached (see Cropanzano et al., 2001, for a good review of this research). In one study, Thibaut and Walker (1975) investigated the effectiveness of mediation in disputes in which the degree of disagreement between the parties was either great or small. In this laboratory study involving young law school graduates taking a bar review course, they reported that mediation was significantly more likely to settle a dispute when the reported difference in outcomes was only slight (minor noncorrespondent) as opposed to when it was great (major noncorrespondent). In this situation, they theorized, a great difference in outcome expectation was likely to require more intrusive third-party intervention (e.g., arbitration, litigation) to resolve the differences. Their hypotheses were generally supported. This study was important to demonstrate that there are limits on the social exchange explanation that we want to maximize our gain in interactions with others by maintaining control over decisions that affect outcomes. In particular, people will relinquish some of this control to a third-party in certain circumstances, and the method for third-party resolution depends on the degree of outcome expectation differences. Furthermore, early procedural justice researchers also investigated biases relating to the accuracy of evidence and legal decisions (see, Lind & Tyler, 1988, pps. 112–121).

Moreover, Tyler, Lind, and colleagues have devoted considerable thought and attention to the investigation of legal issues (Lind & Tyler, 1988; Tyler, 1990, Tyler & Huo, 2002; Huo & Tyler, 2000). Several studies investigated individual experiences with the court system, such as judges and police (e.g., Casper, Tyler, & Fisher, 1988; Tyler, 1984; Tyler, Casper, & Fisher, 1989). These studies report significant relationships between the individual respondents' experiences and distributive and procedural justice. Another study investigated respondent reactions to the level of benefits they received from the federal government compared to the taxes they paid (Tyler, Rasinski, & McGraw, 1985a; Tyler, Raskinki, & Spodick, 1985b). They were asked about the fairness of the benefits and taxes, as well as the fairness of the procedures used to allocate benefits and tax rates. The study found relationships between both types of justice and evaluations of government benefits and taxation, but the relationship was stronger for procedural justice. Another study reported that procedural justice had more of an effect on respondent perceptions when they were stopped by the police than when they had called the police (Tyler & Folger, 1980).

A recent study in this area deserves mention. Stein, Steinley, and Cropanzano (2011) primarily relied upon terror management theory (Greenberg, Pyszczynski, & Solomon, 1986) to test the sentencing decisions of the entire population of U.S. federal judges. The database created exceeded 950,000 cases. They investigated whether the sentencing deviated from consistency before or after the events of September 11, 2001. The authors reported that the most morally severe crimes were punished more severely after 9/11 than before in violation of the consistency rule of procedural justice.

INDIRECT STUDY OF LEGAL ISSUES

The other approach to legal issues taken by organizational justice researchers involves indirect study of legal issues. These investigations do not involve an evaluation of direct legal procedures or mechanisms in a legal context but are grounded in organizational aspects of justice that have significant legal implications (e.g. litigation or legal claiming behavior). Typically, these studies involve legal consequences of injustice. A number of these arise in the context of the investigation of human resource issues and revolve around litigation or fear of litigation (see, Folger & Cropanzano, 1998; Sitkin & Bies, 1993). For example, Wallace, Page, and Lippstreu (2006) report that legally problematic job application blanks are associated with lower perceptions of organizational justice and higher litigation intentions. Moreover, Gillespie and Parry (2006) state a model that, in part, proposes that multisource performance feedback leads to lower procedural injustice which, in turn, leads to lower intentions to litigate.

A substantial amount of research reports that low distributive and low procedural justice are both associated with litigation-related attitudes and behaviors (see Goldman, 2001). Some of this work relates to employee attitudes toward litigation, i.e., when will employees consider suing their employers, and some relates to actual litigation behavior (i.e., when will employees take tangible steps to engage in actual litigation against their employer). One of the earliest examples of the former is Bies and Tyler (1993) where the authors report that employees were more likely to consider litigation against their employer after perceiving negative experiences at work. The authors do not report a relationship between these considerations and actual litigation behavior (see also, Gillespie & Parry, 2006). An example of the latter is Goldman (2001) where the author reported that both distributive and procedural justice were associated with decisions to file employment discrimination suits by terminated workers. Another study reported that procedural, distributive, and interactional justice all interacted to predict actual legal claiming by terminated workers (Goldman, 2003).

Several explanations have been offered about why employees use litigation as a response to injustice. With respect to distributive injustice, it has been suggested that litigation may be an attempt to restore perceived inequity (Walster, Walster, & Berscheid, 1978). As for procedural injustice, several explanations have been provided for why it may lead to litigation among aggrieved workers, among them: (a) that employees value procedural justice as a social norm, violation of which threatens important social standards, (b) the "voice effect," which argues that employees value the opportunity to have their opinions heard in the organization, and (c) that it provides evidence of social standing (see Goldman, 2006).

However, because organizational justice is a perceptual measure, it cannot be concluded that individual's expressing litigation attitudes or behaviors are likely to prevail on these claims. In other words, no third party has evaluated the merits of the claims in much of this research. Nevertheless, a number of organizational harms (e.g., loss to reputation, morale of employees, uncertainty) have been associated with the mere act of employees filing litigation grievances that go beyond the threatened or actual legal claim filed by the individual employee (Goldman, 2006: Groth, Goldman, Gilliland, & Bies, 2002). Interestingly, research suggests that the courts tend to be more aligned with the instrumental approach to organizational justice, which emphasizes economic gains and losses, than with either the interpersonal or moral principles approach (see Cropanzano et al., 2001; Grant, 2010). This makes sense given the courts' historical deference to economics (Posner, 1977). However, as noted earlier, there are significant groups of legal scholars arguing that other perspectives should be taken into account as well (e.g., Dworkin, 1986).

Considerations for Organizational Justice Scholars Studying Legal Issues

HISTORICAL TRADITION

Legal justice and organizational justice are different and distinct fields. Each has its own vocabulary and historical tradition. Moreover, in the case of legal justice, the historical tradition has a palpable affect on the interpretation and accretion of knowledge in the field. This relates to the concept of "precedent" in the common-law system. This concept is based on the idea that consistency in legal application is a good thing. In application, this means that courts (and their agents, legal counsel) each assume that a case like the case immediately before the court, has come before a similar court at an earlier time and, if so, should be decided similarly. If the circumstances of a particular case are unique, the common law resorts to analogy from previous cases that have some similarities. To be sure, the law changes; it is intended to change, to evolve and adapt to society (Corbin, 1954). However, it is by nature a late adapter, forced to sift changes through the filter of the past. This has implications for organizational justice researchers.

FUTURE RESEARCH

When important variables, particularly dependent variables, involve litigation or legal-claiming, or similar variables, researchers may be able to create more realistic models of legal-claiming if they consider some attitudinal, behaviorial, and contextual variables that have, to date, received little attention. For example, there are distinct differences in outcomes (and perhaps antecedents) of attitudes toward litigation and actual litigation behaviors that should be further explored. It is possible, for example, that there is little or no relationship between these two, that is, it is not clear that expressing a willingness to consider litigation against one's employer (Bies & Tyler, 1993) is related to the slew of behaviors that lead to litigation. One possibility is that the social support that has been reported to be related to legal claiming by friends, family, or co-workers when litigation attitudes are engaged is, instead, provided by an attorney when actual litigation arises.

Moreover, when organizational justice has been reported in several studies to lead to litigation-related behavior, particularly in the context of employment discrimination claims, there is a common moment when an unjust or other injurious event in the workplace is transformed from a "bad" event to a discriminatory event (e.g. Goldman, 2001). Although, several field studies are suggestive of the importance of organizational justice in this context, causality has not been firmly established.

Furthermore, there are a number of third-party dispute-resolution procedures that could benefit from new research involving various aspects of organizational justice. In addition to mediation, which has received some attention, there are a number of alternative dispute resolution techniques that have been largely overlooked by justice researchers, such as arbitration, med-arb (mediation followed by arbitration), arb-med (the reverse), conciliation, collaborative law, lawyer supported mediation, party-directed mediation, mock juries, and restorative justice (see Goldman, Cropanzano, Stein, & Benson, 2008; Tesler, 2008).

POTENTIAL CONTRIBUTION OF ORGANIZATIONAL JUSTICE RESEARCHERS TO LEGAL SCHOLARSHIP

Organizational justice researchers also have much they can contribute to legal scholars in this area. For example, there has lately been some call from legal scholars for an increase in empirical research in the law. Hence, journals such as the *Journal for Empirical Research* have arisen to respond to this demand. More collaborative research between the two fields can produce innovative solutions to problems involving the machinery of justice (e.g. how to make judicial systems both more efficient and more fair, resulting in mechanisms to improve the distribution of resources as well as the satisfaction with judicial procedures as well as interactions). As noted, early justice researchers began much of their work directly involved with investigating various aspects of the court system and its agents (e.g., police). Perhaps it is time to return to these areas since we now have another 25 years of knowledge of justice content and methods.

Moreover, it is, perhaps, surprising that the organizational justice researchers have not been more involved in the legislative advocacy. There have been occasional calls for the use of justice research to change legislation (e.g., Stone-Romero & Stone, 2005) but, by and large, legislative change has often not been the goal of organizational justice scholars. This is where legal scholars, working collaboratively, can help make an effective partnership. In turn, this could aid organizations more by ensuring that the fruits of this research make more effective organizations.

CAUTIONARY NOTE FOR ORGANIZATIONAL JUSTICE SCHOLARS INTERACTING WITH LEGAL SYSTEM

An area where justice researchers (and social scientists generally) should be cautious is when interacting with the court system as an expert witness or as a party to an amicus curiae brief (which is a brief to a court written by a nonparty to litigation ostensibly to support the position of one of the parties but really advocating its own views). Both of these situations amount to traps for the unwary. The problem being that, as social scientists, research is based on aggregated data. However, this can often be a problem for the courts (as often pointed out by opposing counsel) because, as noted earlier, the legal system hesitates to take general patterns of human behavior and apply them to individual cases. For example, if a justice researcher were an expert witness in a legal case and noted what most people find to be unfair behavior in certain situations, it may be difficult to argue that the parties in a particular lawsuit found that same behavior to be unfair in a particular case. Recently, an impressive group of legal scholars including Laurens Walker (from Thibaut & Walker, 1975) faulted a social scientist for this very thing in a case involving Walmart: "Dr. _____ failed to explain how much of the research he relied on was based on aggregated data and how findings from aggregated data cannot be assumed to hold for any individual entity or person" (Mitchell, Monahan, & Walker, 2011, p. 4; see also, Monahan & Walker, 2011).

Conclusion

This chapter briefly outlined the development and differences between legal justice and organizational justice. It did this by providing some historical perspective but by also examining, at a deeper level, some of the major assumptions behind each of the fields. It then provided a historical overview of areas relating to legal justice that organizational justice researchers have explored. Finally, it offers some cautionary notes for organizational scholars choosing to involve themselves in the legal process as well as suggestions for future research including some suggestions for collaborative research between both groups of scholars

Note

1. The original quote attributed to Shaw is that (in referring to cultural differences between the English and Americans is: "The United States and Great Britain are two countries separated by a common language."

References

Abadinsky, H. (2003). *Law and justice: An introduction to the American legal system* (5th ed.), Upper Saddle, NJ: Pearson.

Beddier v. Director of Public Prosecutions (1954), 1 WLR 1119.

Berman, H. J. & Greiner, W. R. (1980). *The nature and functions of law* (4th ed.). Mineola, NY: Foundation Press.

Bies, R. J. (2001). Interactional (in)justice: The sacred and the profane. In J. Greenberg & R. Cropanzano (Eds.), *Advances in organizational justice* (pp. 85–108). Stanford, CA: Stanford University Press.

Bies, R. J., & Moag, J. F. (1986). Interactional justice: Communication criteria of fairness. In R. J. Lewicki, B. H. Sheppard, & M. H. Bazerman (Eds.), *Research on negotiations in organizations* (pp. 43–55). Greenwich, CT: JAI Press.

Bies, R. J., & Tyler, T. R. (1993). The "litigation mentality" in organizations: A test of alternative psychological explanations. *Organization Science*, *4*, 352–366.

Blader, S. L. & Tyler, T. R. (2005). How can theories of organizational justice explain the effects of fairness? In Greenberg, J., & Colquitt, J. (2005). *Handbook of organizational justice*. (pp. 329–354). Mahwah, NJ: Erlbaum.

Bobocel, D. R., & Holmvall, C. M. (2001). Are interactional justice and procedural justice different? Framing the debate. In S. Gilliland, D. Steiner, & D. Skarlicki (Eds.), *Theoretical and cultural perspectives on organizational justice* (pp. 85–108). Greenwich, CT: Information Age.

Burnham, W. (2011). *Introduction to the law and legal system of the United States* (5th ed.). St. Paul, MN: West.

Casper, J. D., Tyler, T. R. & Fisher, B. (1988). Procedural justice in felony cases. *Law and Society Review*, *22*, 483–507.

Chesler, M., Kalmuss, D., & Sanders, J. (1984). *Strategies for cross-examining expert witnesses: Social scientists encounters with attorneys in the school desegregation cases.* Working Paper 310, Center for Research on Social Organization, University of Michigan. http://deepblue.lib.umich.edu/bitstream/handle/2027.42/51078/310.pdf?sequence=1

Cohen, R. L. (1986). *Justice: Views from the social sciences.* New York, NY: Plenum.

Colquitt, J. A. (2001). On the dimensionality of organizational justice: A construct validation of a measure. *Journal of Applied Psychology*, *86*, 386–400.

Colquitt, J. A., Conlon, D. E., Wesson, M. J., Porter, C., & Ng, K. Y. (2001). Justice at the millennium: A meta-analytic review of 25 years of organizational justice research. *Journal of Applied Psychology*, *86*, 425–445.

Colquitt, J. A., & Shaw, J. C. (2005). How should organizational justice be measured? Chapter 4 In Greenberg, J., & Colquitt, J. (2005). *Handbook of organizational justice.* (pp. 113–152). Mahwah, NJ: Erlbaum.

Corbin, A. (1954). Principles of law and their evolution. *Yale Faculty Scholarship Series*. Paper 2898.

Cropanzano, R., Goldman, B., & Folger, R. (2003). Deontic justice: The role of moral principles in workplace fairness. *Journal of Organizational Behavior*, *24*, 1019–1024.

Cropanzano, R, Goldman, B, & Folger, R. (2005). What is self-interest? *Journal of Organizational Behavior*, *26*, 985–991.

Cropanzano, R., Rupp, D., Mohler, C., & Schminke, M. (2001). Three roads to organizational justice. In G. R. Ferris (ed.), *Research in personnel and human resources management.* (pp. 1–113). Amsterdam: JAI.

Cropanzano, R., Stein, J., & Nadisic, T. (2011). *Social justice and the experience of emotion*. New York, NY: Routledge.

Dworkin, R. (1986). *Law's Empire*. Cambridge, MA: Harvard University Press.

Feinberg, J. (1984). *Harm to others*. New York, NY: Oxford University Press.

Feldman, M. S., & A. J. Levy (1994). Effects of legal context on decision making under ambiguity. In S. B. Sitkin & R. J. Bies (Eds.), *The legalistic organization*. (pp. 109–136). Thousand Oaks, CA: Sage Publications.

Folger, R., & Cropanzano, R. (1998). *Organizational justice and human resource management*. Thousand Oaks, CA: Sage.

Friedman, L. M. (1994). *Total justice*. New York, NY: Russell Sage Foundation.

Gillespie, T. L., & Parry, R. O. (2006). Fuel for litigation? Links between procedural justice and multisource feedback, *Journal of Managerial Issues*, *4*, 530–546.

Glendon, M. A. (1994). *A nation under lawyers*. Cambridge, MA: Harvard University Press.

Goldman, B. M. (2001). Toward an understanding of employment discrimination claiming: An integration of organizational justice and social information processing theories. *Personnel Psychology*, *54*, 361–386.

Goldman, B. M. (2003). The application of referent cognitions theory to legal-claiming by terminated workers: The role of organizational justice and anger. *Journal of Management*, *29*, 705–728.

Goldman, B. M. (2006). Employment discrimination in organizations: Antecedents and consequences. *Journal of Management*, *32*, 786–830.

Goldman, B. M., Cropanzano, R., Stein, J., & Benson, L. III (2008). The role of third parties/mediation in managing conflict in organizations. In De Dreu, C. K. W., & Gelfand, M. (Eds.), *The psychology of conflict and conflict management in organizations*. Mahwah, NJ: Lawrence Erlbaum.

Grant, J. D. (2010). Workplace justice: An examination of employee dismissal in the views of the courts and human resource practitioners. *Dissertation Abstracts International Section A: Humanities and Social Sciences*, *70*(8-A), pp. 3081–3114.

Greenberg, J. & Bies, R. (1992). Establishing the role of empirical studies of organizational justice into philosophical inquiries into business ethics. *Journal of Business Ethics*, *11*, 433–444.

Greenberg, J., & Colquitt, J. (Eds.) (2005). *Handbook of organizational justice*. Mahwah, NJ: Erlbaum.

Greenberg., J., Pyszczynski, T., & Solomon, S. (1986). The causes and consequences of a need for self-esteem: A terror management theory. In R. F. Baumeister (Ed.), *Public and private self* (pp. 189–212). New York, NY: Springer-Verlag.

Groth, M., Goldman, B. M., Gilliland, S. W., & Bies, R. J. (2002). Commitment to legal claiming: Influences of attributions, social guidance, and organizational tenure. *Journal of Applied Psychology, 87*, 781–788.

Hart, H. L. A. (1961, 2012). *The concept of law*. (3rd ed.). Oxford, UK: Oxford University Press.

Hayek, F. A. (1976). *Law, legislation, and liberty, Vol. 2*. London, UK: Routledge and Kegan Paul.

Herbert, A. P., Sir (1989). *Misleading cases in the common law* (4th ed.). Buffalo, NY: William S. Hein.

Holmes, Oliver Wendell, Jr. (1909). *The common law* (2nd ed.). Little, Brown.

Homans, G. C. (1961). *Social behavior: Its elementary forms*. New York, NY: Harcourt Brace & World.

Honore, A. M. (1962). Social justice. *McGill Law Journal, 8*, 77–105.

Huo, Y. J. & Tyler, T. R. (2000). *How different ethnic groups react to legal authority*. San Francisco, CA: Public Policy Institute of California.

Johnston, D. (2011). *A brief history of justice*. UK: Wiley-Blackwell.

Leventhal, G. S. (1980). What should be done with equity theory? New approaches to the study of fairness in social relationships. In K. Gergen, M. Greenberg, & R. Willis (Eds.), *Social exchange: Advances in theory and research* (pp. 27–55). New York, NY: Plenum Press.

Levy, L. W. (1988). *Original intent and the framers' constitution*. New York, NY: Macmillan.

Lind, E. A., Greenberg, J., Scott, K. S., & Welchans, T. D. (2000). The winding road from employee to complainant: Situational and psychological determinants of wrongful termination claims. *Administrative Science Quarterly, 45*, 557–590.

Lind, E. A., Kurtz, S., Musante, L., Walker, L., & Thibaut, J. (1980). Procedure and outcome effects on reactions to adjudicated resolutions of conflicts of interest. *Journal of Personality and Social Psychology, 39*, 338–350.

Lind, E. A., MacCoun, R. J., Ebener, P. A., Felstiner, W. L. F., Hensler, D. R., Resnik, J., & Tyler, T. R. (1990). In the eye of the beholder: Tort litigants' evaluations of their experiences in the civil justice system. *Law and Society Review, 24*, 953–996.

Lind, E. A., & Tyler, T. R. (1988). *The social psychology of procedural justice*. New York, NY: Plenum.

Loh, W. D. (1984). *Social research in the judicial process: Cases, readings, and text*. New York, NY: Russell Sage Foundation.

Mitchell, G., Monahan, J., & Walker, L. (2011). The ASA's missed opportunity to promote sound science in court. *Sociological Methods and Research, 40*, 605–620.

Monahan, J., & Walker, L. (2011). Twenty-five years of social science in law. *Law and Human Behavior, 35*, 72–82.

Nelson v. Knight, Supreme Court of Iowa (Dec. 21, 2012, & July 12, 2013, No. 11-1857)

Nozick, R. (1974). *Anarchy, state, and utopia*. New York, NY: Basic Books.

Nozick, R. (1981). *Philosophical explanations*. Cambridge, MA: Harvard University Press.

Papachristos, A., Meares, T., & Fagan, J. (2012). Why do criminals obey the law? The influence of legitimacy and social networks on active gun offenders. *Journal of Criminal Law and Criminology, 102*, 397–440.

Posner, R. A. (1977). *The economic analysis of law* (2nd ed.). Boston, MA:Little Brown.

Rawls, J. (1958). Justice as fairness. *Philosophical Review, 67*, 164–194.

Rawls, J. (1971). *A theory of justice*. Cambridge, MA: Belknap.

Roe v. Wade, U. S. Supreme Court, 410 U. S. 113.

Rommen, H. A. (1998). *The natural law: A study in legal and social history and philosophy*. Indianapolis, IN: Liberty Fund.

Sadurski, W. (1985). *Giving desert its due: Social justice and legal theory*. Boston, MA: D. Reidel.

Schmitt, N., Oswald, F. L., Kim, B. H., Gillespie, M. A., & Ramsay, L. J. (2004). The impact of justice and self-serving bias explanations of the perceived fairness of different types of selection tests. *International Journal of Selection and Assessment, 12*, 160–171.

Shapiro, D. L. & Kirkman, B. L. 1999. Employees' reaction to the change in work teams: The influence of "anticipatory" injustice. *Journal of Organizational Change Management, 12*, 51–66.

Sitkin, S. B., & Bies, R. J. (1993). The legalistic organization: Definitions, dimensions, and dilemmas. *Organization Science, 4*, 345–351.

Skogan, W., & Frydl, K. (Eds.) (2004). *Fairness and effectiveness in policing: The evidence*. Washington, DC: National Academies Press.

Stein, J., Steinley, D., & Cropanzano, R. (2011). Death awareness and organizational behavior, *Journal of Organizational Behavior, 32*, 984–1007.

Stone-Romero, E. F., & Stone, D. (2005). How do organizational justice concepts relate to discrimination and prejudice? In Greenberg, J., & Colquitt, J. (2005). *Handbook of organizational justice* (pp. 439–467). Mahwah, NJ: Erlbaum.

Tesler, P. H. (2008). *Collaborative law: Achieving effective resolution in divorce without litigation*. Chicago, IL: American Bar Association.

Thibaut, J., & Walker, W. L. (1975). *Procedural justice: A psychological analysis*. Hillsdale, NJ: Erlbaum.

Thibaut, J., & Walker, W. L. (1978). *A theory of procedure, California Law Review, 66*, 541–566.

The T. J. Hooper (1932). 60 F.2d. 737 (2d. Cir.)

Tyler, T. R. (1984a). Public support for increases in police authority. *Law and Policy, 6*, 329–338.

Tyler, T. R. (1984b). The role of perceived injustice in defendant's evaluations of their courtroom experience. *Law and Society Review, 18*, 51–74.

Tyler, T. R. (1988a). What is procedural justice? Criteria used by citizens to assess the fairness of legal procedures. *Law and Society Review, 22*, 103–135.

Tyler, T. R. (1988b). Client perceptions of litigation. *Trial, 24*, 40–45.

Tyler, T. R. (1990). *Why people obey the law: Procedural justice, legitimacy, and compliance*. New Haven, CT: Yale University Press.

Tyler, T. R., Casper, J. D. & Fisher, B. (1989). Maintaining allegiance toward political authorities: The role of prior attitudes and the use of fair procedures. *American Journal of Political Science, 33*, 629–652.

Tyler, T. R. & Folger, R. (1980). Distributional and procedural aspects of satisfaction with citizen-police encounters. *Basic and Applied Social Psychology, 1*, 281–292.

Tyler, T. R. & Huo, Y. J. (2002). *Trust in the law; Encouraging public cooperation with the police and courts*. New York, NY. Russell Sage Foundation.

Tyler, T. R., Rasinski, K., & McGraw, K. (1985a). The influence of perceived injustice on the endorsement of political leaders. *Journal of Applied Social Psychology, 15*, 700–725.

Tyler, T. R., Rasinski, K. & Spodick, N. (1985b). The influence of voice on satisfaction with leaders: Exploring the meaning of process control. *Journal of Personality and Social Psychology, 48*, 72–81.

van den Bos, K., Lind, E. A., & Wilke, H. A. M. (2001). The psychology of procedural and distributive justice viewed from the perspective of fairness heuristic theory. In R. Cropanzano (Ed.), *Justice in the workplace: From theory to practice* (pp. 49–66) Mahwah, NJ: Erlbaum.

Wallace, J. C., Page, E. E., Lippstreu, M. (2006). Applicant reactions to pre-employment application blanks: A legal and procedural justice perspective. *Journal of Business and Psychology, 20*, 467–488.

Walker, L., Lind, E. A., Thibaut, J. (1979). The relation between procedural and distributive justice. *Virginia Law Review, 65*, 1401–1420.

Walker, L., & Monahan, J. (1987). Social frameworks: A new use of social science in law. *Virginia Law Review, 73*, 559–598.

Walster, E., Walster, G., & Berscheid, E. (1978). *Equity: Theory and research*. Boston, MA: Allyn & Bacon.

Weber. M. (1925/1967). On law in economy and society. Max Rheinstein (Ed.). New York, NY: Simon and Schuster. [Translated from the 1925 German edition.]

Zane, J. M. (1927/1998). The story of law (2nd ed.). Indianapolis, IN: Liberty Fund.

CHAPTER

12 Culture and Organizational Justice: State of the Literature and Suggestions for Future Directions

Keith James

Abstract

In the current chapter, I review findings from existing scholarship on the intersection of culture with organizational justice. Major levels and components of organizational justice, and major levels and components of culture are outlined and examined for relationships. A unified nomological network is developed for how justice and culture may tie together with other major constructs from organizational science. Multiple levels of leadership, employee affect, and identification with both the organization and one's work team are included in the network with justice and culture as suggested predictors of multiple types of employee and organizational outcomes. Implications for are outlined for both research and practice on culture's relation to organizational-justice.

Key Words: culture, organizational justice, multilevel justice, multilevel culture, workplace identity

Implications and mechanisms of both organizational justice and of culture have been substantially elaborated in the last 50 years. Research has shown that organizational justice is associated with, among other things, affect (e.g., Barsky & Kaplan, 2007; Weiss, Sukow & Cropanzano, 1999), leadership (Hammer, Bayazit & Wazeter, 2009), identity (e.g., James, Hiza, Hall & Doppelt, 2008; Opotow, 1995; Tyler, 1999), performance (e.g., Ellemers, De Gilder & Haslam, 2004), and organizational citizenship behaviors (e.g., Fassina, Jones & Uggerslev, 2008; Ilies, Nahrgang & Morgeson, 2007). Culture has also been shown empirically to be associated with, among other things, affect (e.g., Hofstede & McCrae, 2004) leadership (House, Hanges, Javidan, Dorfman, and Gupta, 2004; Schein, 2004), identity (Haslam, Powell & Turner, 2000; Lord, Brown & Freiberg, 1999), performance (Schein, 2004; Simonton & Ting, 2010), and OCB's (Erkutu, 2011).

Not surprisingly given the prominence of each construct, recent decades have seen an increase in the number of works that focus on how culture and organizational justice are associated with each other (e.g., Brockner et al. 2001; Erkutlu, 2011; Li & Cropanzano, 2009). As both justice and culture are multifaceted constructs, however, and as the examination of their intersection is still in its early stages, there is still substantial need to incorporate the relation between the two into a pattern of interrelationships with other key organizational constructs. In this chapter, existing research of culture and organizational justice is reviewed and, based on results, gaps and extrapolations, a model for future systematic exploration of the relation of the two is developed.

Culture

Culture was defined by Hofstede (2001) as the shared mental programming of a group of people, and that definition is followed here. That definition is complicated by the fact that "shared mental programming" covers a multitude of individual constructs and, potentially, even multiple subtypes of individual constructs (e.g., power/distance and individualism/collectivism both within the construct of "cultural values"). In organizational science, cultural values are most frequently discussed and empirically analyzed. The cultural value of individualism/collectivism is the cultural component that has been the subject of the most theory and research. Individualism/collectivism (I/C) is, however, only one value polarity that can affect justice perceptions and behaviors.

Hofstede (1980; 2001) described five core values (or value polarities) (I/C; power/distance; masculinity/femininity; uncertainty avoidance; and time orientation) that underlay differences in preferences and judgments in the workplace across cultures. The first four have been widely employed in cross-cultural studies of organizational justice. Shao, Rupp, Skarlicki and Jones (2013), for instance, used those four in a meta-analysis of justice outcomes. They did not, though, use time orientation because, they argue, it has a somewhat muddled definition that is reflected in unreliable results from Hoftstede's measure of it. Other individual cultural values (e.g., Triandis, 1989) and taxonomies of cultural values (e.g., Russo, 2000; Schwartz, 1992; Schwartz, et al., 2001) have been developed and are important, but have generally been employed less in the study of justice.

Cultures also include many other elements in addition to values such as symbols, knowledge, schemas, technology, and tools (e.g., Chick, 1997; Hofstede & McCrae, 2004; Kluckhohn & Strodbeck, 1961; Mor-Barak, 2013). Culture has also been tied to affect (Hofstede, 2001; James, 1993; Schwartz & Boehnke, 2004). Crucially for the purposes of the current chapter, cultures also provide norms for various behaviors—rules for members about how to behave with given people and in particular circumstances—including justice behaviors (Chick, 1997; Hofstede, 2001; Hofstede & McCrae, 2004; Triandis & Suh, 2002). Instead of culture as a single construct, then, it seems more useful to discuss cultural syndromes, and that is the approach taken here.

Cultural syndromes are defined as multiple shared elements of a culture (e.g., attitudes, culture-specific symbols, behavioral norms, values) that come together to create a theme that a group of people use to organize their experience and behavior (Coopey, 1995; Gupta, Hanges, & Dorfman, 2002; Kristof-Brown, Zimmerman & Johnson, 2005; Triandis, 1995a; Triandis & Suh, 2002). The group of people involved can range from small in number (often called a "cult" when its culture is very strong) to very large in number (McCauley & Segal, 1987). Relatively strong and active collective cultures, then, promote particular patterns of justice perceptions and action; such justice patterns may, in fact, be a major defining element of culture (Chick, 1997; James, 1993, James et al., 2008; Opotow, 1995).

Organizational Justice

Organizational justice is generally defined as employee *perceptions* of how they are treated by the organization they work for (Colquitt, Conlon, Wesson, Porter, & Ng, 2001). Studies of perceived organizational justice have typical involved both perceptions of fairness of outcomes (distributive justice), and perceptions of fairness of organizational processes and procedures (procedural justice). More recently, interactional justice has been added and subdivided into interpersonal fairness, and informational fairness perceptions by employees (Colquitt, 2001). Overall (summary) organizational justice perceptions have also been found to be important predictors of individual and organizational outcomes, and there is some indication that overall justice perceptions vary across cultures (T-Y. Kim & Leung, 2007; Sarlicki, 2001).

There are, then four key questions about the intersection of organizational justice types and culture: (1) Do people from all cultures value justice equally? (2) Are people from different cultures influenced equally or differently by their perceptions of the different justice subtypes? (3) Does culture moderate the *outcomes* experienced as a result of organizational justice by individual workers, individual supervisors, teams (or other suborganizational units), or organizations? (4) If either the general import of organizational justice, perception of its subtypes, or the impact of justice dimension on various outcomes vary with culture, what are the mechanisms through which culture creates such impacts?

One potential answer to questions 1, 3, and 4 is given by James (1993; see also Opotow, 1995), who discusses how the justice-triggered emotional reactions and behaviors may differ because of culturally specified variations in the circumstances under which justice norms are seen as relevant. A partial answer to question 2 comes from Opotow (1995; see also James et al., 2008), who develops the idea that culture impacts the *scope of justice*, or the extent to which different individuals and groups are viewed as deserving of application of the rules of justice. A potential answer to all four questions may lie in the construct of *justice motives*, which are viewed as driving both perceptions of justice *from* other entities (including corporate ones), and justice behaviors directed *toward* other entities (including collective ones) (e.g., Cropanzano, Rupp, Mohler & Schminke, 2001; Deutsch, 1985; Opotow, 1996).

Organizational justice perceptions and behaviors seem to be substantially driven by internalized justice motives (Cropanzano et al., 2001; Folger, 2001; Folger, Cropanzano, & Goldman, 2005; Lind & Tyler, 1988; Lind & van den Bos, 2002; Shao et al., 2013). There are four primary justice motives: instrumental, relational (Lind & Tyler, 1988—or interpersonal), uncertainty-reducing (Lind & van den Bos, 2002; Shao et al., 2013), and deontic (or "deonantic"—Folger, 2001). Justice is instrumentally driven when it is directed primarily toward efforts to personally desired ends or goals. Justice, in this case, serves as a means to an end. Relational justice motives, on the other hand, derive from importance of perceiving that one is valued by others who are important to oneself. Perceiving fair treatment from important others promotes, along the lines of Social Identity Theory (SIT—Tajfel & Turner, 1979) a sense of identity and self-esteem (Lind & Tyler, 1988). Treating important others fairly, then, also becomes a motive for individuals because it is seen as likely to yield reciprocal fair treatment and, in turn, positive affective and cognitive consequences. Uncertainty-reduction is a rather self-explanatory justice motive; it is the desire for fairness (in, e.g., information access and procedural approaches) because it promotes a sense of control and understanding of how things operate. Deontic motives for justice are those driven by internalized moral precepts for "good" behavior (Folger, 1998; 2001). Adherence to justice standards, in this case, leads to perceptions of morality. Similarly, being treated fairly by others reinforces one's sense of morality, whereas being treated unfairly offends one's sense of morality, so the former is experienced positively and the latter negatively.

Multiple justice motives can be active at the same time, and each may be differentially related to different important workplace outcomes (Shao et al., 2013). For instance, Tyler (1991) provides some evidence that relatively high procedural justice aids in-group cohesiveness and conflict resolution across cultures but that, at the same time, use of equity distributive allocations promotes task performance.

Note how three of the four core justice motives that have been outlined substantially correspond to the core cultural values from Hofstede's taxonomy: instrumental (individualistic); relational (collectivism and/or femininity); and uncertainty-reducing (uncertainty avoidance) (James et al. 2008; Shao et al., 2013; see also Triandis, 1995b and Triandis, Leung, Villareal & Clack, 1985 on the utility of treating individualism and collectivism as two constructs rather than a single polarity). Deonance as a justice motive does not have a corresponding value in Hofstede's scheme and, because it was proposed more recently, it has also been tested substantially less than the other justice motives as a potential mediator of justice effects on workplace outcomes. However, posited effects of three (of four) of Hofstede's national cultural values have been tested relatively frequently for effects on individual workers' justice motives (three of four), justice perceptions, and justice-based behaviors. Shao et al. (2013) review the evidence of those studies, and those results are summarized following the introduction of concepts of *levels of culture* and *levels of justice* immediately following.

MULTILEVEL CULTURE

Culture is a multilevel construct—we can speak of the shared mental programming of all humans compared, say, to the shared programming of dolphins. More typically, national cultures (or groups of national cultures thought to share major elements and history (see, e.g., Li & Cropanzano, 2009) are contrasted against each other to illustrate the similarities and differences of citizens of different countries.

However, there is often also recognition that major subgroups *within* a nation can share things in common internally, and differ substantially enough from other subgroups, for it to sometimes make sense to talk about subnational cultural groups (McCauley & Segal, 1987). In organizational science, of course, we add the *organizational* culture level of analysis (e.g., House, Hanges, Javidan, Dorfman, & Gupta, 2004; Schien, 2004). Organizational cultures, like national ones, are multifaceted, but values again seem the construct most frequently used to assess them (Katz & Kahn, 1978; Schien, 2004). *Sub*cultures within organizations have also, though, received attention from scholars (Kramer, 1991; Martin & Siehl, 1983).

That means, of course, that to study the influence of culture on justice perceptions, we must be careful which level of culture to consider. In fact, we may need to assess multiple levels of culture at once. A major premise of this chapter, then, is that each of those levels of culture is potentially relevant to some aspects of justice in the workplace. Evidence supporting that view is accumulating (e.g., Elovainio, Kivimaeki, Steen & Vahtera, 2004; Erkutlu, 2011; Cropanzano, Li, & James, 2007).

MULTILEVEL JUSTICE

Organizational justice is also multilevel. Most studies have focused on individual-level perceptions of justice and interpersonal-interaction fairness inputs, even when distributive or procedural (rather than interpersonal) justice is the type examined (Rupp, Bashshur & Liao, 2007). Rupp et al. (2007) argue, however, that unit- (i.e., team) level justice perceptions exhibit stability, as well as impact important outcomes such that unit-level justice perceptions also need to be incorporated into theory and research. Existing data supports the potential importance of unit-level justice variables for important individual and organizational outcomes (e.g., Moliner, Martínez-Tur, Peiró, Ramos, & Cropanzano, 2005; Simons & Roberson, 2003; Whitman, Caleo, Carpenter, Horner, & Bernerth, 2012).

Whitman et al. (2012) performed a meta-analytic review of the unit (or team) level of justice climate. They found that collective unit-level justice perceptions, when actually assessed (and sometimes they were not) at the collective level, had an average correlation with unit effectiveness of 0.40. Distributive justice climate was more strongly related to unit performance, whereas procedure justice climate was most strongly related to unit procedural effectiveness. Moderators, such as the hierarchic level of the unit, and justice climate strength were observed to cross with those effects. Overall, it seems clear that there is a unit or team level of collective justice perceptions that has potentially important implications for organizational outcomes.

Cropanzano, et al., (2007) and James (2006), on the other hand, are among those who make the case for *inter*group justice as an important, but understudied, aspect of fairness in the workplace (see also Azzi, 1992; and Elovainio, Kivimaeki, & Vahtera, 2002). They argue that distributive, procedural, and interactional justice are all shaped by intergroup relations in addition to interpersonal and intragroup processes, as well as that intergroup justice has important implications for both individual-level and organizational-level outcomes.

Recent works have even begun to examine the *interorganizational* level of justice as a construct. For instance, Provan, Lamb, and Doyle (2004) provide evidence that the stability and effectiveness of inter-organizational networks is facilitated by fairness in the relationships among the organizations. Luo (2005), in a study of 124 cross-national alliances in China, similarly found that higher perceived procedural justice from organizational partners was associated with higher levels of profitability by alliances.

Finally, some works (e.g., James et al., 2008; Opotow, 1996) extend the examination of organizational justice to perceptions of how fair the organization, as an entity, is to society, to social groups within society, and to the environment. This line of work also focuses on how norms for justice behaviors influence the actions of organizational members toward outside entities (Clayton & Opotow, 2003; James et al., 2008; cf., Rupp, Ganapathi, Aguilera, & Williams, 2006).

Recent Research on Culture and Organizational Justice

An early (James, 1993) review of substantially cultural influences on organizational justice was based largely on extrapolations of studies of justice outside the workplace to organizational justice, as well as from examinations of organizational justice relationships to constructs closely related to culture. Since that time, a number of direct studies of culture and organizational justice have been executed. Given the range of cultures, cultural constructs, justice constructs, levels, and outcomes that need to be examined, though, the available studies of culture and justice are still too limited.

The four main subtypes of justice (and western-derived measures of them) seem to largely hold up cross-culturally. The published studies of organizational justice in nonwestern setting generally produce relatively good (>0.70) reliability scores for measures of distributive, procedural and interactional justice. The subset of studies that include confirmatory factor analyses tests of measurement models on data sets that include organizational justice measures also generally support the posited structure of justice and the distinctiveness of organizational justice scores from scores for nonjustice constructs (e.g., Dbaibo, Harb, & van Meurs, 2010; Erkutu, 2011).

Next, some existing individual studies indicate general associations—or so the authors argue—between organizational justice perceptions and cultural dimensions such as power/distance (e.g., Brockner et al., 2002; see also Fischer & Smith, 2003), culturally based identity (e.g., James et al., 2008; Li & Cropanzano, 2009); masculinity/femininity (Rego & Cunha, 2010); and collectivism (Erkutlu, 2011; Fassina et al., 2008; Finkelstein, Minibas-Poussard, & Bastounis, 2009).

Lam, Schaubroeck and Aryee (2002), for instance, provide data from a comparison of workers in Hong Kong and the US that showed that cultural power/distance scores both differed between the two nationalities of workers, and moderated the relationship of perceived justice to satisfaction, performance, and absenteeism. Similarly, it has been argued that interpersonal justice may be particularly important in forming Chinese employee reactions to performance appraisal events because of a general cultural emphasis on the importance of quality of relationship with supervisor (Tata, Fu, & Wu, 2003).

Li and Cropanzano (2009) did a related meta-analysis. It compared, between North American and East Asian workers, organizational-justice score impacts on individual (e.g., job satisfaction) and organizational (e.g., turnover intentions) outcomes. The results indicated a generally lower importance of justice perceptions among East Asians than among North Americans. Li and Cropanzano (2009) interpreted this as indicating that East Asian culture de-emphasizes, relative to mainstream North American ones, concern over personal (i.e., instrumentally motivated) fair treatment on the job. On the other hand, East Asians, Li and Cropanzano (2009) conclude, are vested more in collectivistic identities that make the relational justice motive primary for them.

Shao et al.'s (2013) recent meta-analysis yielded related results. They aimed to detail the evidence regarding the effects of all four (I/C, power/distance, masculinity/femininity, and uncertainty avoidance) of Hofstede's (2001) primary cultural values on justice perceptions, and the latter's relations to employees', supervisors', and organizations' outcomes. The results indicated that higher cultural individualism, femininity, and uncertainty avoidance, as well as lower cultural power/distance, were associated with greater justice effects on work outcomes. Shao et al. (2013) conclude that the cultural-value effects observed in their meta-analysis substantially support cultural effects on inclination toward instrumental (individualism; low power/distance) versus relational (femininity; high power/distance) justice motives.

Results that point away from general national-culture effects on justice perceptions are, though, found in studies of interactional (interpersonal+informational) justice elements in performance appraisals that yield similar justice perceptions and appraisal reactions among Chinese and western workers (Child & Markoczy, 1993; Chow, 1995; Dessler & Tan, 2006; Fisher & Yuan, 1998). In a related effect, Zhao, Wu, Jian- Sun and Chen (2012) developed evidence, through confirmatory factor analysis, that two supposedly emic (i.e., culturally distinct—see Farh, Earley, & Lin, 1997) subscales of organizational citizenship in China, which were also correlated by organizational justice, were actually dimensions of a different and etic (i.e., extent cross-culturally) construct, organizational deviance. When defined as deviance, their relationships to organization justice were the same for both western and Chinese workers. A discussion later in this chapter of how (especially East Asian) *organizational* cultures may sometimes differ from *national* cultures relative to organizational justice will elaborate somewhat on the foregoing.

On tests of the taxonomy of justice *motives* across cultures, the results are mixed. Deutsch (1985) describes variations across cultures in which norm—equity versus equality versus need—is generally endorsed as the appropriate guide for both distributive justice behaviors, as well as for organizing one's own justice perceptions (see also James et al. 2008; and Miles & Greenberg, 1993). According to this view, the individualist values (relative to organizational justice) *equity* justice distributions, along with relatively high interactional and procedural justice (with the latter showing that the organization values and honors individual rights). Collectivists, on the other hand, supposedly value *equality* or *need* distributions to in-group members, procedures that support group-level identities, and group-level rights (e.g., James, 1993; K. I. Kim, Park, & Suzuki, 1990; van Olffen & de Cremer, 2007). James et al. (2008) extended that model by linking cultural individualism and collectivism to, respectively, the instrumental and the relational justice motives, and by reviewing evidence that other cultural values (e.g., time orientation) also help to shape the justice motives that dominate the perceptions and behaviors of individuals with different cultural programming.

One meta-analysis (Sama & Papamarcos, 2000) supported the view that equity (i.e., instrumental) norms dominate in individualistic cultures, whereas the equality (i.e., relational) norm dominates in collectivistic cultures. A second meta-analysis by Fischer and Smith (2003), though, yielded results indicating that national-culture individualism/collectivism is *not* related to norms for distributive justice.

Gelfand, Erez, and Aycan (2007) argue the difference in the results of those two meta-analyses derive from the role of the reward-allocator (i.e., the individual making the distributions) in the two meta-analyses. In Sama and Papamarcos' (2000) meta-analysis, the allocator was also part of the group among whom rewards were being distributed. When the allocator is a member of the group being allocated to, relational motives drive behavior, according to Gelfand et al. (2007). In the studies reviewed by Fischer and Smith (2003), however, the allocator was *not* part of the group receiving the distribution. In the latter circumstance, according to Gelfand et al. (2007; see also James, 1993, James et al., 2008; Opotow, 1995), justice norms for *out*-groups, not for *in*-groups, tend to be employed by members of both individualistic and collectivistic (national) cultures, yielding an (instrumental) equity justice motive regardless of culture. Here we have a situational influence (allocator also a part of the recipient group? Yes or no?) on justice behavior.

There is also some evidence (e.g., Fodchuk & Sherman, 2008; James et al., 2008; Shao et al., 2013) that multiple cultural values may work together to influence justice motives and, through them, justice actions and perceptions. For instance, Fodchuk and Sherman (2008) produced data indicating that individualism/collectivism (I/C) and power/distance combined to produce differences between French- and US-born workers in their reactions to performance evaluations. French workers were relatively high in both I/C and power/distance, and were characterized by Fodchuk and Sherman (2008) as "pseudo-instrumental" in their orientation: they reacted to both the relational (e.g., group identity) information conveyed by performance evaluations, and the instrumental (voice) opportunities provided by procedural justice. The US workers, on the other hand, were relatively high in I/C but relatively *low* in power/distance. According to Fodchuk and Sherman (2008), the U.S. workers in their study were genuinely and largely driven by instrumental motives. Therefore, voice (within procedural justice) was the major influence on their reactions to their performance evaluations.

Along the same lines, Shao et al. (2013) found, in their meta-analysis, that the effects of the uncertainty avoidance and masculinity/femininity on organizational justice effects varied depending on whether the (frequently statistically significant) moderating effects of either individualism/collectivism, or of power/distance, was extracted. They also supported the importance of considering levels of effects by showing that some cultural interaction patterns have greater implications for organizational outcomes, and others greater implications for the outcomes of supervisory leaders (Shao et al. did not look at the employee or team levels of outcomes). The latter aspect of Shao et al.'s (2013) results is elaborated on in the Levels sub-section, next.

Culture x Justice x Levels

Culture at levels other than the national as an influence on organizational justice and its effects has been the focus of some studies (e.g., Erkutlu, 2011; Haslam et al., 2000; He, Chen & Zhang, 2004; Sharoni et al., 2012; Zhao et al., 2012). For instance, Sharoni et al. (2012) present data indicating that organizational culture contents moderate the impact of justice perceptions on both OCB's, and on turnover intentions. St-Pierre and Holmes (2010), on the other hand, used archival data to support a *mediating* role of organizational justice between organizational culture and workplace aggression.

Higher levels of culture and of justice should, of course, also influence lower levels of each (see, e.g., Kristof-Brown, et al.'s, 2005; and Lindsley, Brass, & Thomas, 1995; and meta-analysis of P-E fit across organizational levels). Some evidence supports the existence and mechanisms of such cross-level cascades specific to organizational justice (James, Burlacu & Drown, 2011). For instance, House, et al. (2004) concluded that national cultural influences tend to guide the development of organizational cultures for leadership. St-Pierre and Holmes (2010) indicate that national culture norms regarding aggressive behavior both guide the development of, and are moderated by, organizational-culture norms for justice.

Shao et al. (2013) also incorporate the supervisory versus organizational *outcome* levels in their meta-analysis of culture and organizational justice. They show that cultural values differentially moderate the subtypes of organizational justice such that organizational outcomes versus supervisory outcomes are differentially affected. For instance, they found that individualism moderated (negatively) effects of supervisor-level justice behavior on citizenship directed at supervisor, but it did not moderate effects of organizational-level justice (OJ) behaviors on citizenship directed toward the organization (OJ did, though, have a positive main effect on organizational citizenship). The pattern of difference across supervisor outcomes versus organization outcomes is noted by Shao et al. (2013), but largely not interpreted—probably because of the complexity of the results.

Cultural components have also been related to inter-organizational justice patterns and outcomes. Beugre and Acar (2008), for instance, proposed a model of cultural influences on interorganizational justice perceptions and outcomes (see also James, et al 2011). It indicates that cultural similarity among boundary-spanning individuals who link the organizations into a network promotes relatively positive perceptions of distributive, procedural, and interactional justice among them, whereas cultural difference promotes negative justice perceptions. Positive interorganizational justice perceptions are, then, in Beugre and Acar's (2008) model, a driver of commitment by individual organizations to the network, as well as a driver of positive performance by the network as a whole in its collaborative efforts.

Although national cultural norms for justice, or national cultural-value influences on justice perceptions, may shape the averages of those things at lower levels, the evidence (e.g., Ashkanasy, Trevor-Roberts and Earnshaw, 2002; Zhao et al., 2012) indicates that organizational cultures, for instance, can still deviate significantly from the national culture that hosts the organization.

Studies have also indicated that organizational justice effects sometimes vary systemically with organizational culture, but not with societal (national) culture. Chen, Meindl and Hui (1998), for instance, found that both US and Hong Kong workers were influenced in their preferences for justice rules (e.g., equity versus equality) significantly by organizational goals and the extent to which tasks are organized interdependently. *National culture* individualism/collectivism scores across the workers from the two countries were, though, unrelated (as either main effects or in interaction with organizational conditions) to their organizational justice preferences (Chen et al. 1998). Similarly, there is evidence that both distributive and procedural justice predict job satisfaction equally among Chinese employees and western workers (Chun & Giacobbe-Miller, 2012; Leung, Smith, Wang, & Sun, 1996; More & Tzafrir, 2009).

Zhao et al. (2012) argue that many Chinese organizations, in their efforts to compete in the globalized economy, have adopted managerial values, norms, and procedures—in other words, the organizational culture—that was developed in and that largely characterize "western" organizations. Many Chinese organizations, in this formulation, essentially have a westernized organizational culture even though the organization, itself, resides in a national culture that differs significantly from those in nations outside of East Asia. This fits, to some extent, with Ashkanasy et al.'s (2002) report out of the Globe study of leadership that indicates that even members of the "Anglo" national-culture cluster show relatively high *familial* collectivism and moderate levels of *institutional* collectivism, even though the national cultures in that cluster are relatively low in *societal* (national) collectivism. Culture apparently occurs at multiple major levels, and a strong organizational culture can potentially outweigh national culture in impacts on certain behaviors, in some circumstances.

Team-level perceptions and shared affective tendencies (i.e., team climate or culture) have also been implicated in moderating some types of justice perceptions and some justice-related outcomes. For instance, Brass and Labianca (1999) indicated that work units that view themselves as organizational outgroups are less likely to internalized organizational-culture level norms for justice behaviors.

The major types of organizational justice perceptions have also been differentially linked to the level from which the justice behavior originates. Whitman et al. (2012), for instance, did a meta-analysis of studies of the relationship between collective fairness perceptions and unit-level effectiveness, and found that distributive justice had the strongest relationship to unit performance. Interactional justice, on the other hand, had the stronger relationship to unit-level *process* effectiveness. Similarly, Zacharatos, Hershcovis, Turner and Barling's (2007) meta-analysis of the impacts of major categories of human-resource management practices on organizational-level justice perceptions found that the latter were influenced mainly by work systems and human-resource policies, and less so by employees' views of leadership. Organizational-level justice was, in turn, more strongly associated with job performance, turnover, and absenteeism than with job satisfaction, perceived social support at work, or employee health. The latter three, though, were significantly associated with leaders' behaviors.

Fassina et al. (2008) did meta-analysis and path analysis to develop evidence for the hypothesis that effects of perceived justice effects on organizational citizenship behaviors (OCB's) would be independent of (i.e., neither mediating nor were mediated by) of job-satisfaction relationship to OCB's. The results, however, indicated that each different major types of justice (e.g., procedural versus distributive) had different relationships with each major type of OCB's (e.g., altruistic versus conscientious). Fassina et al (2008) concluded that their pattern of justice-type to OCB results supported the theory that procedural justice is seen as driven mainly by upper-level organizational leadership and organizational culture and systems. Those organization-level associations, then. supposedly lead organization-level justice perceptions to implicate organizational identity, and organization-directed OCB's (see also Masterson, Lewis, Goldman, & Taylor, 2000). Interpersonal justice, on the other hand is seen, according to Fassina et al. (2008 and Masterson et al, 2000), as deriving mainly from immediate supervisor. Because of that source link, it implicates mainly team-level (or within-team in-group and out-group) and/or personal identity, such that supervisor- and team-directed OCB's are affected.

Stress as an outcome also seems to be influenced by multiple levels of culture and multiple types of organizational justice. Finkelstein et al. (2009), for instance, found that only procedural and interpersonal justice, not distributive or informational justice, were associated with multiple types of stress coping among Turkish workers. French workers in the same study, though, exhibited significant relationships between distributive, procedural, and interactional justice (but not informational justice) to emotional coping but not to other stress-coping strategies.

Although there have been recent increases in attention to both multiple levels of culture and multiple levels of justice, few studies directly examine culture-to-justice links from a multilevel perspective. Thus, the remainder of this chapter is targeted toward elaborating the pattern of multiple levels of culture and multiple levels of organizational justice within the context of outcomes of importance in organizational science.

Integrated Nomological Networks for Organizational Justice and for Culture

As was outlined earlier, various partial conceptual integrations of culture and organizational justice have been articulated and tested. Better theoretical guidance is needed, though, for empirical tests of culture (its contents and discontents) to justice (and its contents and discontents) influences and justice outcomes. The constructs of identity, leadership, and affect may be well suited to provide conceptual binders to the culture, justice, and levels literatures, and they are employed as such in the conceptual model that follows. Figure 12.1 shows the integrative model among multilevel culture, multilevel justice, leadership, organizational identity, workplace affect, and justice outcomes (at various levels and of various sorts).

Identity

Identities have been tied to both individuals' justice behaviors and their justice perceptions (e.g., Clayton & Opotow, 2003; Cropanzano et al., 2007; James et al. 2008; Opotow, 1995; Semmer, Jacobshagen, Meier, & Elfering, 2007; Wegner, 1982). Clayton and Opotow (2003) review evidence that the major justice conceptions all implicitly invoke identity as a key underlying construct, but that few studies have directly examined that relationship. Clayton and Opotow (2003) also give evidence that identity-based justice problems are more likely to trigger strong emotions than will justice issues that are not identity driven. Kepes, Delery and Gupta (2009) report converging data indicating that justice outcomes are most stressful and have their greatest negative impact on health when they are seen as driven by social factors.

Figure 12.1 indicates that, in the workplace, at least three levels of identity are relevant: identity as an individual (employee affect and perceptions), team identity with regular immediate co-workers and immediate supervisor (team affect and shared perceptions), and identity with the organization (organizational goals, norms, and values). An example of cultural impacts by way of identity impacts is found in Li and Cropanzano (2009), who interpreted the results of the meta-analysis of differential effects of justice perceptions on outcomes among East Asians relative to North Americans as reflecting personal-identity driven (e.g., instrumental; uncertainty reduction) mechanisms, which may generally be more accessible in individualistic cultures (such as the mainstream cultures of Canada and the United States) than in collectivistic cultures (such as those in East Asia). Of course, only quantitative assessments of national cultural values, of identities, of organizational justice perceptions, and of outcomes together can really test that claim (James et al., 2008; Opotow, 1995; Semmer, et al., 2007).

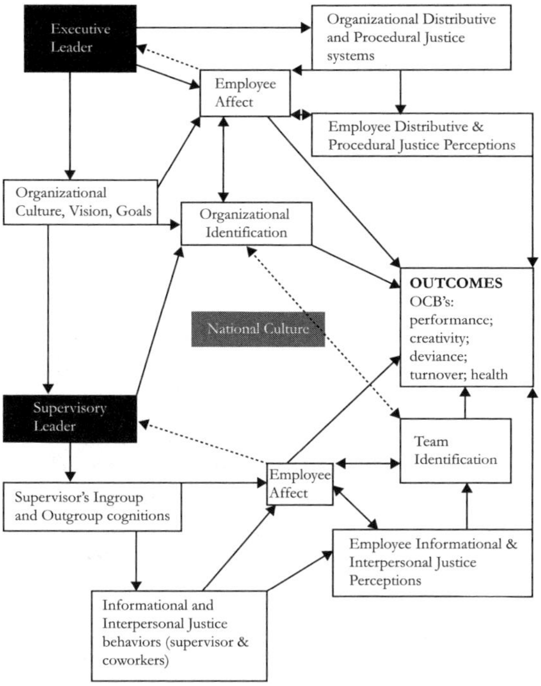

Fig. 12.1 Integrated model of multilevel justice, multilevel culture, constructs that link culture and justice, and organizational justice outcomes.

Social Identity Theory (SIT; Tajfel & Turner, 1979; Hogg & Terry, 2000) tells us that identity is responsive to contextual cues as well to chronic influences such as those from national culture (or those from personality; or those from genetics—see Weber, Johnson, & Arceneaux, 2011). That element of SIT fits with the Gelfand et al. (2007) situational explanation outlined previously for the differing results of the Sama and Papamarco's (2000) versus Fischer and Smith (2003) meta-analyses of cultural influences on allocation norms. The latter argument is also compatible with that of Zhao et al. (2012), who found that western-style organizational cultures and identities could overwhelm Chinese culture and identity in studies of Chinese participants' reactions to justice perceptions. Culture-level-based variations in active identity may, therefore, moderate scores for perceived justice, for justice behaviors in organizations, and of tests of justice relationships to other organizational outcomes.

Leadership

Masterson et al. (2000) and Scandura (1999) position leadership as a key moderator of employees' justice perceptions and outcomes. Does (national) culture shape leadership approaches, including the likelihood that transformational leadership approaches will be employed? House et al. (2004) indicate that national cultural influences tend to guide the development of organizational cultures for leadership. Shao and Webber (2006) similarly concluded in the affirmative, at least relative to Chinese culture. They argue, for instance, that high uncertainty avoidance in Chinese culture makes Chinese leaders reluctant to provide intellectually stimulating experiences/feedback to subordinates; intellectual stimulation is a major component of transformational leadership. A number of other authors (e.g., Shin & Zhou, 2007; Walumbwa, Wang, Lawler, & Shin, 2004), however, provide data indicating not only that Chinese leaders do use transformational leadership, but also that such a leadership style has similar positive effects (on, e.g., employee creativity, collective efficacy, organizational innovation) in China as in the west.

In line with the model shown in Figure 12.1, the results of Shao et al.'s (2013) meta-analysis add organizational levels to the picture by indicating that cultural values differentially moderate the effects of justice perceptions on supervisory versus organizational outcomes. Organizational-Systems Theory (OST—Jacobs & Jaques, 1987; Katz & Kahn, 1978; Robbins and Duncan, 1988), as well as organizational-strategy and transformational-leadership theories (Bass, 1996; House & Shamir, 1993; Kozlowski, Chao, & Jensen, 2010; Senge, 1990; Zaccaro and Banks, 2001), also include similar perspectives. Those theories indicate that executive leaders in an organization tend to develop the organization's mission, strategy, vision, values, and policies. Bateman, O'Neill and Kenworthy-U'Ren (2002), in fact, provide direct evidence that top organizational leaders' organizational vision is underpinned by taxonomic hierarchy of values that has "ultimate values" (i.e., the big and deep ideals being sought) at the top, subsuming lower-level goals for process, output, and effectiveness.

If, then, executive (top-level) leaders' decisions shape their organizations' procedural and distributive justice systems, their own justice actions may become symbolic of organizational justice values and principles (Jacobs & Jacques, 1987; Katz & Kahn, 1978). For instance, Jones (2009) found that executive leaders most strongly influenced organizational culture, distributive and procedural justice systems, and employees' levels of organizational identity. In Jones (2009), procedural justice predicted employees' counterproductive behaviors (or organizational deviance) directed toward the organization as a whole. According to a multilevel study of four Chinese IT companies by James and Yao (2014), this is how both Chinese and western executive leaders operate, and how their justice behaviors are viewed by employees.

Jones (2009) also found that supervisory leaders most strongly influenced interactional justice, team justice climate, and team identity. Supervisory leaders, although not generally responsible for developing their organizations' mission, policies, and values, tend to have more direct and day-to-day interaction with workers than do executive leaders (Bass 1996; James & Lahti, 2011; Katz & Kahn, 1978; Zaccaro & Banks, 2001). Their justice behaviors should, therefore, mainly be of the interpersonal variety and mainly influence individual-level (leader-member) identity, as well as team-level identity (Jones, 2009; see also Alban-Metcalfe & Alimo-Metcalfe, 2007; and Simons & Roberson, 2003—see also, though, Zacharatos et al.'s 2007 meta-analysis of studies of leadership levels in the automotive industry). For instance, interpersonal and informational (together, interactional) justice may be primary influences on employees' counterproductive behaviors toward their immediate supervisors in (Jones, 2009; c.f., Shao et al, 2013). James and Yao (2014) observed largely the same pattern of differential justice and outcome effects associated with executive versus supervisory leaders in their study of Chinese organizations. Along the same lines, Chi and Lo (2003) found that Taiwanese employees' perceptions of the fairness of treatment of co-workers who were punished was influenced by the perceivers' Leader-Member Exchange (LMX) relationships with her/his supervisor, as well as by the perceivers' relationship with the punished co-worker.

Affect, Health, and Multilevel Culture and Justice

Justice perceptions have also been shown to influence employees' affective states and outcomes. Barsky and Kaplan (2007), for instance, did a meta-analysis that yielded evidence that relatively high-state negative affect is associated with higher scores for perceived workplace injustice (see also Clay-Warner, 2006; De Cremer, 2007; and Weiss et al., 1999). Barsky and Kaplan (2007) found that both state and trait (and positive and negative) affect were significantly correlated with distributive and procedural justice perceptions, whereas trait affectivity was also related to interactional justice (no meta-analytic correlation could be computed between interactional justice and state positive affect because of lack of studies).

National-culture-based conflict in procedural preferences often produces negative emotional reactions, especially anger and stress (Mor Barak, Findler, & Wind, 2003; Vinokur, Schul, & Caplan, 1987). Clay-Warner (2006) reviews evidence to also support the view that organization-wide shared beliefs about justice, as well as about the legitimacy of authority figures to decide justice procedures, influence individual affect in ways that shape individual, supervisory, and organizational outcomes.

Legitimacy of leaders relates to trust in them, and trust has a strong affective component. Brass and Labianca (1999) discuss how social network relationships characterized by negative affect, negative interactions, and negative behaviors degrade trust in organization and leaders, weaken sense of social obligation, and undermine social norms for positive behaviors. Transformational leadership perceptions, on the other hand, are also a type of emotionally charged (but positive) evaluation of leaders (Bass, 1996). As was noted earlier in the Leadership section, there is evidence that transformational leadership is equally used and equally effective in (collectivistic) Chinese national organizations. Such leadership evaluations are represented in Figure 12.1 by the dashed (feedback) lines that indicate reverberation from employee affect back to (executive or supervisory) perceptions of leaders.

Justice climates and interteam (unit) justice patterns in organizations have similar emotional components and potential implications. Tyler (1999), for instance, argues that individual and group-level identities are each related to a distinct cluster of emotions that differs between them. Brass and Labianca (1999) conclude that member of teams that see themselves as out-groups in an organization experience relatively high feelings of work stress.

Organizational Justice Outcomes

Multiple potential outcomes of organizational justice are shown in Figure 12.1 (right center box). Shao et al.'s (2013) meta-analysis demonstrated that different various elements, and various justice types and motives, can yield distinct patterns of outcomes across levels of entities in an organization. For instance, leadership at different levels and justice-climate (culture) at different levels are potentially associated with both positive and negative outcomes for employees, supervisors, teams, and organizations by way of associated cultural, identity, and organizational justice levers. Dirks and Ferrin's (2002) meta-analytic review yielded, for instance, evidence that trust in executive leadership is likely to be more strongly related to organizational-level reciprocation, such as organizational commitment. On the other hand, trust in nonexecutive leadership was more strongly related to dyadic (supervisory) leader-follower reciprocity. Scandura (1999) also argued that employees who have positive LMX relationships with their supervisor are influenced mainly by perceived interactional justice, whereas employees who are part of their leaders' out-groups are mainly impacted by their perceptions of the distributive justice in their organizations. The logic behind Scandura's (1999) conclusion is essentially that leader-in-group relationships operate on principles of identity-based trust, whereas leader-out-group relationships operate on calculus-based trust. According to Scandura (1999), with greater degrees of identity-based trust come greater organizational commitment, higher levels of organizational citizenship behaviors, and improved learning.

Figure 12.1, therefore, lists a greater range of potential outcomes from organizational justice than are typically investigated by justice scholars. Across future research, careful consideration should be given to adequately representing the potential full range of outcomes of importance.

For example some studies of organizational justice and work health were summarized earlier. Ecosocial Theory and Stress-as-Offense-to-Self theory tie together organizational levels, identity, organizational justice, work stress, and employee health (Krieger, 2001; Meier, Semmer, & Hupfeld, 2009; Semmer, McGrath & Beehr, 2005; Semmer et al, 2007). The argument is that unfair treatment in the workplace can occur as a part of a general pattern of disrespect of a group or an individual that generally de-legitimizes a particular identity (Semmer et al., 2007), yielding "stress as disrespect" (SAD), and consequent negative impacts on health.

Robbins, Ford, and Tetrick (2012) similarly conclude from a meta-analysis that individual-level perceptions of unfairness are associated with stress and strain (negative health) outcomes. Robbins et al. (2012) also found that those effects were stronger for US samples than for samples workers from other countries. The cultural or other dynamics that were behind those differences in sample effects could not, however, be determined from the data available. Thus, health effects of the organizational justice process are also included in the outcome box of Figure 12.1. Future studies of culture and justice impacts in the workplace should explore further whether, when, and why culture moderates organizational justice to health effects, and such work should also incorporate different levels of culture and justice constructs. Out of multiple studies like that, meta-analyses such as Shao et al.'s (2013) could add stress and health to outcomes of culture x justice processes in the workplace.

Model Summary

The preceding review included multiple levels of both culture and justice, and future research should systematically attend to distinctions among the levels of each construct for relations to the other construct, as well as for the relationship of both to outcomes of interest. Putting all of these pieces together, executive leaders justice actions seem generally more important than supervisory leadership to the types of justice (distributive and procedural) that characterize organizational culture and individuals' organizational identity. When organizational identity is dominant or acutely salient, then, organizational culture will be the dominant cultural influence on justice perceptions and behaviors. In that case, perceived distributive and procedural justice are likely to be the mediate effects of organizational culture on individual behavior tendencies such as turnover intentions and OCB inclinations.

When team-level identity is dominant or acutely salient, though, interactional justice with supervisory and co-workers seems most important, and relational justice motives move to the fore. Team climate (culture) for justice will then be crucial in determining especially team-level outcomes such as collective performance. Supervisory (as opposed to organizational) outcomes such as supervisor-directed OCB's also seem more influenced by this level of organizational justice. However, individual outcome (such as individual performance) effects are clearly necessary to produce team-level effects. In addition, the team and interteam levels of justice seem to exert major impacts on individual stress and health outcomes.

When individual identity is dominant or salient, equity distributions and justice procedures that help reduce uncertainty and aid individual-level inputs into decisions seem to be critical. Individual perceptual, affective, performance outcomes, organizational deviance, and individual health are the outcomes that seem most likely to be associated with the individual level of justice perceptions and emotional reactions. National culture may still moderate these, through internalization of specific cultural elements such as values or behavior norms, as well as through general effects of national culture on personality inclinations (Triandis & Suh, 2002).

Thus, in Figure 12.1, the lower half links together team identity, supervisors, and teammates interpersonal and informational justice behaviors, and employees' interpersonal and informational justice perceptions. Interpersonal and informational justice perceptions are then shown in Figure 12.1 as significantly related to employee and organizational outcomes (far right, midpage box). Note also, however, the three dashed lines in Figure 12.1, which indicate feedback cycles. Organizational identity (as, largely, a mechanism for executive leadership and organizational-level processes and procedures), for instance, is shown in Figure 12.1 as influencing team identity, but team identity (a mechanism of supervisory leadership and team processes) is also shown as feeding back to influence organizational-level identity.

Practical Considerations and Practice Concerns

Some practical advice about managing organizational justice across cultures can be found in the literature. In particular, Shao et al (2013) lay out culture-values-to-justice profiles for approximately two dozen nations and use them to develop prescriptions for promoting perceptions of justice and positive outcomes from justice among workers from different backgrounds. Much caution should be used in considering such advice, however.

First of all, the evidence about effects of multiple levels of cultural constructs on justice perceptions and outcomes that was outlined earlier indicates that the national culture of a set of workers might neither, given a strong organizational and/or team culture with the proper characteristics, predict their justice reactions nor influence the impact of the latter on outcomes of interest. Related to the preceding is evidence that cultural values and norms, identity, and justice perceptions and behaviors are all situationally malleable (James et al., 2008; Sama & Papamarcos, 2002; Tajfel & Turner, 1979; Wegner, 1982).

Then there is the question of the validity of cultural- (and justice-) construct measures, given the multiple levels of entity that occur in organizations, generally, as well as specifically, to justice. Tyler, Lind, & Huo (2000), for instance, discuss how the Hofstede (1980; 2001) measures were designed for use in cross-national, not individual-level, assessment of cultural values and how Tyler et al. (2000) found Hofstede's uncertainty avoidance items, in particular, to have weak validity when applied at the individual level (cf., Shao et al., 2013). Similarly, Whitman et al. (2012) reported in their meta-analysis that instruments specifically developed and validated to assess *unit-level justice* yielded significantly greater predictive power for *unit-level outcomes* than did measures developed and validated at other levels.

In addition, the nations whose cultural profiles are given by Shao et al. (2013) are all, to some extent, culturally and ethnically diverse, such that even a management technique that works for members of the "mainstream" culture may not work for *all* people from that nationality. Shao et al. (2013) *do* acknowledge this. An obvious case in point is the United States of America, in which the growing minority population has received much attention. Triandis (1995b; Triandis et al., 1985), for instance, presents evidence that, although the "Anglo" majority of the US population is relatively high in individualism, Hispanics, Asian Americans, Native Hawaiians, and African Americans are all notably higher in collectivism. High levels of cultural diversity have also always existed in some countries such as India and Russia, and has grown rapidly recently within national populations in Europe, the UK, Canada, Australia, and elsewhere (see Mor Barak, 2013).

Although the "diversity" of some other nations such as China might be smaller, somewhat less publicized, and somewhat less visible, it exists nonetheless—in the form of, for instance, Uyghur, Tibetan, and ethnic Russian groups that are officially citizens of China. There is even considerable diversity evident within the dominant Han Chinese majority. The prevalence of cultural diversity within all nations should also give us pause about applying generic principles for managing organizational justice based on national citizenship.

Perhaps the strongest recommendation that the current state of the evidence justifies is that leaders should be aware that members of different national cultures often endorse different primary rules on, for instance, distributive and interpersonal fairness. Organizations should, therefore, select or train leaders for knowledge of culture and justice interactions. From that, leaders should have or develop (with or without systematic organizational aid) the ability to effectively present and detail the rationale for whatever justice procedures might be extant in their organizations to subordinates from different cultural backgrounds.

Barsky and Kaplan (2007) offered a different type of advice on managing organizational justice when they concluded (based on their meta-analysis of affect and justice sensitivity) that organizations would do well to intentionally place individuals high in trait-negative affect in some leadership positions. Barsky and Kaplan (2007) argue that such leaders would be highly sensitive to how justice-related behaviors will affect workers, clients, and the public. They would, therefore, act in ways that would promote positive justice perceptions by all of those groups, according to Barsky and Kaplan (2007). Of course, that tentative idea about leader selection for justice sensitivity is just that—very tentative and requiring further research to document the full pattern of constructs that Barsky and Kaplan (2007) postulate, as well as to examine whether it is cross-culturally valid.

Conclusions

The growth in works that examine culture and organizational justice has been impressive. Yet, the preceding review indicates that there are still too few studies, overall, to provide adequate exploration of the complexities of potential relationships between the two. Research in this area needs to be increased both in overall volume and in systematic exploration of components of each construct, as well as potential multilevel effects within and between the constructs. Theory building about how, when, and why culture and justice will be linked with each other and mutually associated with outcomes of importance will help promote the needed new research (c.f., Greenberg, 2001). Some of that is provided in the current work, but more is clearly needed.

In the articles cited in this chapter, the majority of comparative studies contrast East Asian (also known as Confucian Asian) and "Anglo-Cluster" of nations according to the taxonomy from the GLOBE studies of leadership (see Gupta et al., 2002 and House et al., 2004 for discussions of GLOBE methods, results, and interpretations). This is important especially given the size of East Asian populations, the growing economic power of East Asian nations and organizations in the globalized economy, and the traditional dominance of Anglo-culture-based organizational-science theory and research. Nonetheless, for full understanding of culture and justice effects in, on, and by organizations, we need systematic studies of all major cultural clusters; all major cultural constructs; and all major justice types, motives, and potential outcomes. Currently, there are gaps in the culture- and organizational-justice literature that need to be filled.

The GLOBE studies provide a model of systematic exploration across cultures that justice researchers should consider mimicking. As was noted (in the Culture x Justice x Levels section), the GLOBE instrument also includes multiple levels (types) of collectivism, and justice researchers should similarly consider including multiple levels of cultural constructs in their future studies. The argument presented in the current work, however, indicates that an extension beyond the view of culture in the GLOBE studies is also needed in the area of organizational justice. In particular, justice scholars need to carefully consider which possible situational moderators of cultural impacts on justice to study to advance understanding of when and how cultural factors shape organizational justice. In addition, in order to try to ensure that observed "emic" cultural or justice elements really are culturally unique, it is important to assess the full range of predictors and outcomes. Evidence of the cross-cultural fit of the posited measurement model, along with inferential tests of proposed nomological networks of cultural, justice, and outcome constructs will yield the knowledge needed by both science and practice.

Finally, meta-analyses such as Shao et al.'s (2013) make it clear that culture comes together with organizational justice in different ways for different important outcomes. The works on organizational justice and health outcomes that were reviewed in the current chapter but not addressed by Shao et al. (2013) add to the breadth of important outcomes that need to be considered in studies of cultural and justice effects at work. Researchers should strategically choose the outcomes to examine in a given study based on the cultural, justice, and mediating foci. Across studies, systematic exploration is needed of how major cultural factors influence and combine with major organizational-justice types and motives to impact all major individual, team, and organizational outcomes (and, perhaps also, societal-level outcomes—see James et al. 2008).

I made an effort in this chapter to interest justice scholars in expanding the scope of studies of culture and organizational justice. At the risk of pushing their patience too far, let me add a last set of ideas and literature that seem relevant but that contemporary organizational-behavior-justice scholars tend to ignore: works on culture and justice from the behavioral economics literature. In particular, Henrich et al. (2004) review data indicating that some cultures include an extreme exchange norm specifying high levels of future distributions if one accepts even a seemingly fair (equitable, equal) allocation from another. In such cultures, individuals may be motivated to avoid even "fair" distributions because of the future obligations that they carry. This is certainly a somewhat different type of justice motive than any of the four main types that management scholars and psychologists of organizational justice have identified. We might do well to incorporate and test this and other behavioral-economics-derived views of justice into our theories and research.

A tentative integration of the nomological networks for culture and organizational justice was presented here that focused on the constructs of identity, leadership, and affect. It points toward a number of aspects of the pattern of relationships among constructs and multiple levels that could be profitably investigated. Theories of culture and organizational justice also probably need to incorporate other constructs, however, to be fully informative of research and practice. Nonetheless, the current work should be a useful tentative step toward a more fully developed organizational science of distinctive and shared influences on, associations between, and outcomes from, culture and organizational justice.

References

Alban-Metcalfe, J., & Alimo-Metcalfe, B. (2007). Development of a private sector version of the (Engaging) Transformational Leadership Questionnaire. *Leadership & Organization Development Journal, 28*, 104–121.

Ashkanasy, N. M., Trevor-Roberts, N. M, & Earnshaw, L. (2002). The Anglo Cluster: Legacy of the British Empire. *Journal of World Business, 37*, 28–39.

Azzi, A. E. (1992). Procedural justice and the allocation of power in intergroup relations: Studies in the United States and South Africa. *Personality and Social Psychology Bulletin, 18*, 736–747.

Barsky, A., & Kaplan, S. A. (2007). If you feel bad, it's unfair: A quantitative synthesis of affect and organizational justice perceptions. *Journal of Applied Psychology, 92*, 286–295.

Bass, B. M. (1996). *A new paradigm of leadership: An inquiry into transformational leadership.* Alexandria, VA: U.S. Army Research Institute for the Behavioral and Social Sciences.

Bateman, T. S., O'Neill, H., & Kenworthy-U'Ren, A. (2002). A hierarchical taxonomy of top managers' goals. *Journal of Applied Psychology, 87*, 1134–1148.

Brass, D. J., & Labianca, G. (1999). Social capital, social liabilities, and social resource management. In R. T. A. J. Leenders & S. M. Gabbay (Eds.), *Corporate social capital liability* (pp. 323–338). Boston, MA: Kluwer Academic Publishers.

Brockner, J., Ackerman, G., Greenberg, J., Gelfand, M. J., Francesco, A. M., Chen, Z. X.,... Shapiro, D. (2001). Culture and procedural justice: The influence of power distance on reactions to voice. *Journal of Experimental Social Psychology, 37*, 300–315.

Beugre, C. D., & Acar, W. (2008). Offshoring and cross-border interorganizational relationships: A justice model. *Decision Sciences, 39*, 445–468.

Chen, C. C., Meindl, J. R., & Hui, H. (1998). Deciding on equity or parity: A test of situational, cultural, and individual factors. *Journal of Organizational Behavior, 19*, 115–129.

Chi, S.-C., & Lo, H.-H. (2003). Taiwanese employees' justice perceptions of co-workers' punitive events. *Journal of Social Psychology, 143*, 21–42.

Chick, G. (1997). Cultural complexity: The concept and its measurement. *Cross-Cultural Research, 31*, 275–307.

Child, J., & Markoczy, L. (1993). Host country managerial behavior and learning in Chinese and Hungarian joint ventures. *Journal of Management Studies, 30*, 611–631.

Chow, I. H. (1995). An opinion survey of performance appraisal practices in Hong Kong and the People's Republic of China. *Asia Pacific Journal of Human Resources, 32*, 67–79.

Chun, G., & Giacobbe-Miller, J. K. (2012). Understanding survivors' reactions to downsizing in China. *Journal of Managerial Psychology, 27*, 27–47.

Clay-Warner, J. (2006). Procedural justice and legitimacy: Predicting negative emotional reactions in to workplace injustice. In S. R. Thye & E. J. Lawler (Eds.), *Social psychology in the workplace: Advances in group processes* (Vol. 23, 207–227). Amsterdam, Netherlands: Elsevier/JAI.

Clayton, S., & Opotow, S. (2003). Justice and identity: Changing perspectives on what is fair. *Personality and Social Psychology Review, 7*, 298–310.

Colquitt, J. A. (2001). On the dimensionality of organizational justice: A construct validation of a measure. *Journal of Applied Psychology, 86*, 386–400.

Colquitt, J. A., Conlon, D. E., Wesson, M. J., Porter, C. O. L., & Ng, K. Y. (2001). Justice at the millennium: A meta-analytic review of 25 years if organizational justice research. *Journal of Applied Psychology, 86*, 425–445.

Coopey, J. (1995). The learning organization, power, politics and ideology, *Management Learning, 26*, 193–214.

Cropanzano, R., Li, A., & James, K. (2007). Intraunit justice and interunit justice and the people who experience them. In F. Dansereau & F. J. Yammarino (Eds.), *Research in multilevel issues* (Vol. 6, pp. 415–438). Englewood Cliffs, NJ: Erlbaum.

Cropanzano, R., Rupp, D. E., Mohler, C. J., & Schminke, M. (2001). Three roads to organizational justice. In J. Ferris (Ed), *Research in personnel and human resources management* (Vol. 20, pp. 1–113). Greenwich, CT: JAI Press.

Dbaibo, D., Harb, C., & van Meurs, N. (2010). Values and justice as predictors of perceived stress in Lebanese organisational settings. *Applied Psychology: An International Review, 59,* 701–720.
De Cremer, D. (2007). *Advances in the psychology of justice and affect.* Greenwich, CO: Information Age.
Dessler, G., & C. H. Tan (Eds., 2006). *Human resource management: An Asian perspective* (2nd Ed.). New York: Pearson Prentice Hall.
Deutsch, M. (1985). *Distributive justice.* New Haven, CT: Yale University Press.
Dirks, K. T., & Ferrin, D. L. (2002). Trust in leadership: Meta-analytic findings and implications for research and practice. *Journal of Applied Psychology, 87,* 611–628.
Ellemers, N., De Gilder, D., & Haslam, S. A. (2004). Motivating individuals and groups at work: A social identity perspective on leadership and group performance. *Academy of Management Review, 29,* 459–478.
Elovainio, M., Kivimaeki, M., Steen, N., & Vahtera, J. (2004). Job decision latitude, organizational justice and health: Multilevel covariance structure analysis. *Social Science & Medicine, 58,* 1659–1669.
Elovainio, M., Kivimaeki, M., & Vahtera, J. (2002). Organizational justice: Evidence of a new psychosocial predictor of health. *American Journal of Public Health, 92,* 105–108.
Erkutlu, H. (2011). The moderating role of organizational culture in the relationship between organizational justice and organizational citizenship behaviors. *Leadership & Organization Development Journal, 32,* 532–554.
Farh, J.-L., Earley, P. C., and Lin, S.-C. (1997). Impetus for action: A cultural analysis of justice and organizational citizenship behavior in Chinese society. *Administrative Science Quarterly, 42,* 421–444.
Fassina, N. E., Jones, D. A., & Uggerslev, K. L. (2008). Relationship clean-up time: Using meta-analysis and path analysis to clarify relationships among job satisfaction, perceived fairness, and citizenship behaviors? *Journal of Management, 34,* 161–188.
Finkelstein, R., Minibas-Poussard, J., & Bastounis, M. (2009). The moderating role of seeking social support on coping styles and perceptions of organizational justice: A study with French and Turkish students. *Social Behavior and Personality, 37,* 845–862.
Fischer R., & Smith P. B. (2003). Reward allocation and culture: A meta-analysis. *Journal of Cross-Cultural Psychology, 34,* 251–68.
Fisher, C. D., & Yuan, A. X. Y. (1998). What motivates employees? A comparison of US and Chinese responses. *International Journal of Human Resource Management, 9,* 516–528.
Fodchuk, K., & Sherman, H. D. (2008). Procedural justice and French and American performance evaluations. *Cross-cultural management: An international review, 15,* 285–299.
Folger, R. (1998). Fairness as a moral virtue. In M. Schminke (Ed.), *Managerial ethics: Moral management of people and processes* (pp. 13–34). Mahwah, NJ: Erlbaum.
Folger, R. (2001). Fairness as deonance. In S. W. Gilliland, D. D. Steiner, & D. P. Skarlicki (Eds.), *Research in social issues in management,* (Vol. 1, pp.3–33). New York, NY: Information Age.
Folger, R., Cropanzano, R., & Goldman, B. (2005). What is the relationship between justice and morality? In J. Greenberg & J. Colquitt (Eds.), *Handbook of organizational justice* (pp. 215–245). Mahwah, NJ: Lawrence Erlbaum Associates.
Gelfand, M. J., Erez, M., & Aycan, Z. (2007). Cross-cultural organizational behavior, *Annual Review of Psychology, 58,* 479–514.
Greenberg, J. (2001). Studying organizational justice cross-culturally: Fundamental challenges. *International Journal of Conflict Management, 12,* 365–375.
Gupta, V. Hanges, P. J., & Dorfman, P. (2002). Cultural clusters: Methodology and findings. *Journal of World Business, 37,* 11–15.
Hammer, T. H., Bayazit, M., & Wazeter, D. L. (2009). Union leadership and member attitudes: A multi-level analysis. *Journal of Applied Psychology, 94,* 392–410.
Haslam, S. A., Powell, C., & Turner, J. C. (2000). Social identity, self-categorization, and work motivation: Rethinking the contribution of the group to positive and sustainable organisational outcomes. *Applied Psychology: An International Review, 49,* 319–339.
He, W., Chen, C. C., & Zhang, L. (2004). Rewards-allocation preferences of Chinese employees in the new millennium: The effects of ownership reform, collectivism, and goal priority. *Organizational Science, 15,* 221–231.
Henrich, J., Boyd, R., Bowles, S., Camerer, C. F., Fehr, E., Gintis, H., & McElreath, R. (2004). Overview and synthesis. In J. Henrich, R. Boyd, S. Bowles, C. F. Camerer, E. Fehr & H. Gintis (Eds.), *Foundations of human sociality: Economic experiments and ethnographic evidence from fifteen small-scale societies* (pp. 8–54). Oxford, UK: Oxford University Press.
Hogg, M. A., & Terry, D. J. (2000). Social identity and self-categorization processes in organizational contexts. *Academy of Management Review, 25,* 121–140.
Hofstede, G. 1980. *Culture's consequences: International differences in work-related values.* Beverley Hills, CA: Sage.
Hofstede, G. (2001). *Culture's consequences: Comparing values, behaviors, institutions and organizations across nations* (2nd ed.). Thousand Oaks, CA: Sage.
Hofstede, G., & McCrae, R. R. (2004). Personality and culture revisited: Linking traits and dimensions of culture. *Cross-Cultural Research, 38,* 52–88.
House, R. J., Hanges, P. J., Javidan, M., Dorfman, P. W., & Gupta, V. (Eds.). (2004). *Culture, leadership and organizations: The GLOBE study of 62 societies.* Thousand Oaks, CA: Sage.
House, R. J., & Shamir, B. (1993). Toward an integration of charismatic, transformational, and visionary theories. In M. M. Chemers and R. Ayman (Eds.), *Leadership theory and research: Perspectives and directions.* Orlando, FL: Academic Press.
Ilies, R., Nahrgang, J. D., & Morgeson, F. P. (2007). Leader-member exchange and citizenship behaviors: A meta-analysis. *Journal of Applied Psychology, 92,* 269.
Jacobs, T. O., & Jaques, E. (1987). Leadership in complex systems. In J. Zeidner (Ed.), *Human productivity enhancement* (pp. 7–65). New York: Praeger.
James, K. (1993). The social context of organizational justice: Cultural, intergroup and structural effects on justice behaviors and perceptions. In R. Cropanzano (Ed.), *Justice*

in the workplace: Approaching fairness in human resource management (pp. 21–50). Hillsdale, NJ: Erlbaum.

James, K. (2006). Antecedents, processes, and outcomes of collective (group-level) politics in organizations. In E. Vigoda-Gadot & A. Drory (Eds.), *The handbook of organizational politics* (pp. 53–74). Cheltenham, UK: Elgar.

James, K., Burlacu, G., & Drown, D. (2011). Organizational justice and social capital. In S. Gilliland, D. Steiner, & D. Skarlicki (Eds.), *Research in social issues in management, Volume 7.* Greenwich, CT: Information Age.

James, K., Hiza, M., Hall, D., & Doppelt, R. (2008). Organizational environmental justice and community sustainability with a Navajo (Diné) case example. In S. Gilliland, D. Steiner, & D. Skarlicki (Eds.), *Research in social issues in management, Volume 6: Justice, morality and social responsibility* (pp. 263–290). Greenwich, CT: Information Age.

James, K., & Lahti, K. (2011). Organizational vision and system influences on employee inspiration and organizational performance. *Creativity and Innovation Management Journal, 20,* 1–14.

James, K., & Yao, X. (2014). *Multi-level inspirational leadership, organizational vision supports, and employee vision inspiration and creativity in China.* Unpublished manuscript, Portland State University.

Jones, D. A. (2009). Getting even with one's supervisor and one's organization: Relationships among types of injustice, desires for revenge and counterproductive work behaviors. *Journal of Organizational Behavior, 30,* 525–542.

Katz, D., & Kahn, R. J. (1978). *The social psychology of organizations* (2nd ed.). New York: Wiley.

Kepes, S., Delery, J., & Gupta, N. (2009). Contingencies in the effects of pay range on organizational effectiveness. *Personnel Psychology, 62,* 497–531.

Kim, K. I., Park, H.-J., & Suzuki, N. (1990). Reward allocations in the United States, Japan, and Korea: A comparison of individualistic and collectivistic cultures. *Academy of Management Journal, 33,* 188–198.

Kim, T-Y., & Leung, K. (2007). Forming and reacting to overall fairness: A cross-cultural comparison. *Organizational Behavior and Human Decision Processes, 104,* 83–95.

Kluckhohn, F. R., & Strodbeck, F. L. (1961). *Variations in value orientations.* New York: Harper & Row.

Kramer, R. M. (1991). Intergroup relations and organizational dilemmas: The role of categorization processes. In L. L. Cummings & B. M. Staw (Eds.), *Research in Organizational Behavior* (Vol. 13, pp. 191–228). Greenwich, CT: JAI.

Kozlowski, S. W. J., Chao, G. T., & Jensen, J. M. (2010). Building an infrastructure for organizational learning: A multilevel approach. In S. W. J. Kozlowski& E. Salas (Eds.), *Learning, training, and development in organizations* (pp. 363–403). New York: Routledge/Taylor & Francis.

Krieger, N. (2001). Theories for social epidemiology in the 21st century: An ecosocial perspective. *International Journal of Epidemiology, 30,* 668–677.

Kristof-Brown, A. L., Zimmerman, R. D., & Johnson, E. C. (2005). Consequences of individuals' fit at work: A meta-analysis of person-job, person-organization, person-group, and person-supervisor fit. *Personnel Psychology, 58,* 281–342.

Lam, S. S., Schaubroeck, J., & Aryee, S. (2002). Relationship between organizational justice and employee work outcomes: A cross-national study. *Journal of Organizational Behavior, 23,* 1–18.

Li, A., & Cropanzano, R. (2009). Do East Asians respond more/less strongly to organizational justice than North Americans? A meta-analysis. *Journal of Management Studies, 46,* 787–805.

Lind, E. A., & Tyler, T. R. (1988). *The social psychology of procedural justice.* New York, NY: Plenum.

Lind, E. A., & van den Bos, K. (2002). When fairness works: Toward a general theory of uncertainty management. In B. M. Staw & R. M. Kramer (Eds.), *Research in organizational behavior: An annual series of analytical essays and critical reviews* (pp. 181–223). Greenwich, CT: Elsevier Science/JAI Press.

Lindsley, D. H., Brass, D. J., & Thomas, J. B. (1995). Efficacy-performing spirals: A multilevel perspective. *Academy of Management Review, 20,* 645–678.

Lord, R. G, Brown, D. J, & Freiberg, S. J. (1999). Understanding the dynamics of leadership: The role of follower self-concepts in the leader/follower relationship. *Organizational Behavior & Human Decision Processes, 78,* 167–203.

Leung, K., Smith, P. B., Wang, Z., & Sun, H. (1996). Job satisfaction in joint venture hotels in China: An organizational justice analysis. *Journal of International Business Studies, 27,* 947–962.

Luo, Y. (2005). How important are shared perceptions of procedural justice in cooperative alliances? *Academy of Management Journal, 48,* 695–709.

Martin, J., & Siehl, C. 1983. Organizational culture and counter culture: An uneasy symbiosis. *Organizational Dynamics, 12,* 52–64.

Masterson, S. S., Lewis, K., Goldman, B. M., Taylor, M. S. (2000). Integrating justice and social exchange: The differing effects of fair procedures and treatment on work relationships. *Academy of Management Journal, 43,* 738–748.

McCauley, C. R., & Segal, M. E. (1987). Social psychology of terrorist groups. In C. Hendrick (Ed.) *Group processes and intergroup relations* (pp. 231–256). Newbury Park, CA: Sage.

Meier, L. L., Semmer, N. K., & Hupfeld, J. (2009). The impact of unfair treatment on depressive mood: The moderating role of self-esteem level and self-esteem instability. *Personality and Social Psychology Bulletin, 35,* 643–655.

Miles, J., & Greenberg, J. (1993). *Cross-national differences in preferences for distributive justice norms: The challenge of establishing fair resource allocations in the European community.* In J. B. Shaw, P. S. Kirbride, & K. M. Rowland (Eds.), *Research in personnel and human resources management* (No 3, pp. 133–156). Greenwich, CT: JAI Press.

Moliner, C., Martínez-Tur, V., Peiró, J. M., Ramos J., & Cropanzano, R. (2005). Relationships between organizational justice and burnout at the work-unit level. *International Journal of Stress Management, 12,* 99–116.

Mor-Barak, M. E. (2013). *Managing diversity: Toward a globally inclusive workplace* (3rd ed.). Thousand Oaks, CA: Sage.

Mor Barak, M. E, Findler, L., & Wind, L. H. (2003). Cross-cultural aspects of diversity and well-being in the workplace: An international perspective. *Journal of Social Work Research & Evaluation, 4,* 145–169.

More, K. V., & Tzafrir, S. S. (2009). The role of trust in core team employees: A three-nation study. *Cross Cultural Management, 16,* 410–433.

Opotow, S. (1995). Drawing the line: Social categorization, moral exclusion, and the scope of justice. In B. Bunker and J. Z. Rubin (Eds.), *Conflict, cooperation, and justice: Essays inspired by the work of Morton Deutsch* (pp. 347–369). San Francisco, CA: Jossey-Bass.

Opotow, S. (1996). Is justice finite? The case of environmental inclusion. In L. Montada & M. J. Lerner (Eds.), *Current societal concerns about justice* (pp. 213–230). New York, NY: Plenum.

Provan, K. G., Lamb, G., & Doyle, M. (2004). Building legitimacy and the early growth of health networks for the uninsured. *Health Care Management Review, 29*, 117–128.

Rego, A., & Cunha, M. P. (2010). Organisational justice and citizenship behaviors: A study in the Portuguese cultural context. *Applied Psychology: An International Review, 59*, 404–430.

Robbins, S. R., & Duncan, R. B. (1988). The role of the CEO and top management in the creation and implementation of strategic vision. In D. C. Hambrick (Ed.), *The executive effect: Concepts and methods for studying top managers* (pp. 205–236). Greenwich, CT: JAI Press.

Robbins, J. M., Ford, M. T., Tetrick, L. E. (2012). Perceived unfairness and employee health: A meta-analytic integration. *Journal of Applied Psychology, 97*, 235–272.

Rupp, D. E., Bashshur, M., & Liao, H. (2007). Justice climate past, present, and future: Models of structure and emergence. In F. Dansereau, & F. J. Yammarino (Eds.), *Research In multilevel issues* (pp. 357–396). New York, NY: Elsevier.

Rupp, D. E., Ganapathi, J., Aguilera, R. V., Williams, C. A. (2006). Employee reactions to corporate social responsibility: An organizational justice framework. *Journal of Organizational Behavior, 27*, 537–543.

Russo, K. W. (2000). Value orientations method: The conceptual framework. In K. W. Russo (Ed.), *Finding the middle ground: Insights and applications of the Value Orientations Method* (pp. 3–19). Yarmouth, ME,: Intercultural Press.

Sama L. M., & Papamarcos S. D. (2000). Hofstede's I-C dimension as predictive of allocative behaviors: A meta-analysis. *International Journal of Value-Based Management, 13*, 173–88.

Sarlicki, D. P. (2001). Cross-cultural perspectives of overall fairness. *International Journal of Conflict Management, 12*, 292–294.

Scandura, T. A. (1999). Rethinking leader-member exchange: An organizational justice perspective. *Leadership Quarterly, 10*, 25–40.

Schein, E. H. (2004). *Organizational culture and leadership.* San Francisco, CA: Jossey-Bass.

Schwartz, S. H. (1992). Universals in the content and structure of culture: Theoretical advances and empirical tests in 20 countries. *Advances in experimental psychology, 25*, 1–65.

Schwartz, S., & Boehnke, K. (2004). Evaluating the structure of human values with confirmatory factor analysis. *Journal of Research in Personality, 38*, 230–255.

Schwartz, S. H. Melech, G., Lehmann, A., Burgess, S., Harris, M., & Owens, V. (2001). Extending the cross-cultural validity of the theory of basic human values with a different method of measurement. *Journal of Cross-Cultural Psychology, 32*, 519–542.

Semmer, N. K., Jacobshagen, B, Meier, L. M., & Elfering, A. (2007). Occupational stress research: The "Stress-as-Offense-to-Self" perspective. In J. Houdmont & S. McIntyre (Eds.), *Occupational health psychology: European perspectives on research, education, and practice* (pp. 43–60). San Pedro, Portugal: Ismai.

Semmer, N. K., McGrath, J. E., & Beehr, T. A. (2005). Conceptual issues in research on stress and health. In C. L. Cooper (Ed.), *Handbook of stress and health* (2nd ed., pp. 1–43). New York, NY: CRC Press.

Senge, P. M. (1990). The fifth discipline. New York: Doubleday.

Shao, R., Rupp, D. E., Skarlicki, D. P., & Jones, K. S. (2013). Employee justice across cultures: A meta-analytic review. *Journal of Management, 39*, 263–301.

Shao, L., & Webber, S. (2006). A cross-cultural test of the 'five-factor model of personality and transformational leadership.' *Journal of Business Research, 59*, 936–944.

Sharoni, G., Tziner, A., Fein, E. C., Shultz, T., Shaul, K., & Zilberman, L. (2012). Organizational citizenship behavior and turnover intentions: Do organizational culture and justice moderate their relationship? *Journal of Applied Social Psychology, 42*(Suppl 1), E267–E294.

Shin, S., & Zhou, J. (2007). When is educational specialization heterogeneity related to creativity in research and development teams? Transformational leadership as a moderator. *Journal of Applied Psychology, 92*, 1709–1721.

Simons, T., & Roberson, Q. (2003). Why managers should care about fairness: The effects of aggregate justice perceptions on organizational outcomes. *Journal of Applied Psychology, 88*, 432–443.

Simonton, D. K., & Ting, S. S. (2010). Creativity in eastern and western civilizations: The lessons of historiometry. *Management and Organizational Review, 6*, 329–350.

St-Pierre, I., & Holmes, D. (2010). The relationship between organizational justice and workplace aggression. *Journal of Advanced Nursing, 66*, 1169–1182.

Tajfel, H., & Turner, J. C. (1979). An integrative theory of inter-group conflict. In W. G. Austin and S. Worchel (Eds.), *The social psychology of inter-group relations* (pp. 33–47). Monterey, CA: Brooks/Cole.

Tata, J., Fu, P. P., & Wu, R. (2003). An examination of procedural justice principles in China and the US. *Asia Pacific Journal of Management, 20*, 205–216.

Triandis, H. C. (1989). The self and social behavior in differing cultural contexts. *Psychological Review, 96*, 506–520.

Triandis, H. C. (1995a). *Culture and social behavior.* New York, NY: McGraw-Hill.

Triandis H. C. (1995b). *Individualism and collectivism.* Boulder, CO: Westview.

Triandis, H. C., Leung, K., Villareal, M. J., & Clack, F. L. (1985). Allocentric versus idiocentric tendencies: Convergent and discriminant validation. *Journal of Research in Personality, 19*, 395–415.

Triandis, H. C., & Suh, E. M. (2002). Cultural influences on personality. *Annual Review of Psychology, 53*, 133–160.

Tyler, T. R. (1991). Using procedures to justify outcomes: Testing the viability of a procedural justice strategy for managing conflict and allocating resources in work organizations. *Basic and Applied Social Psychology, 12*, 259–279.

Tyler, T. R. (1999). Why people co-operate with organizations: An identity-based perspective. In B. M. Staw & R. Sutton (Eds.), *Research in organizational behavior* (Vol. 21, pp. 201–246). Greenwich, CT: JAI.

Tyler, T. R., Lind, E. A., & Huo, Y. J. (2000). Cultural values and authority relations: The psychology of conflict resolution across cultures. *Psychology, Public Policy, and Law, 6*, 1138–1163.

van den Bos, K., & Lind, E. A. (2002). Uncertainty management by means of fairness judgments. In M. P. Zanna (Ed.), *Advances in experimental social psychology* (Vol. 34, pp. 1–60). San Diego, CA: Academic Press.

van Olffen, W., & de Cremer, D. (2007). Who cares about organizational justice? How personality moderates the effects of perceived fairness on organizational attachment. *European Journal of Work and Organizational Psychology, 16*, 386–406.

Vinokur, A., Schul, Y., & Caplan, R. D. (1987). Determinants of perceived social support: Interpersonal transactions, personal outlook, and transient affective states. *Journal of Personality and Social Psychology, 53*, 1137–1145.

Walumbwa, F. O., Wang, P., Lawler, J. J., & Shin, K. (2004). The role of collective efficacy in the relations between transformational leadership and work outcomes. *Journal of Occupational and Organizational Psychology, 77*, 515–530.

Weber, C., Johnson, M., & Arceneaux, K. (2011). Genetics, personality and group identity. *Social Science Quarterly, 92*, 1314–1337.

Wegner, D. M. (1982). Justice and the awareness of social entities. In J. Greenberg and R. Cohen, Eds.), *Equity and justice in social behavior* (pp. 77–117). New York, NY: Academic Press.

Weiss, H. M., Suckow, K., & Cropanzano, R. (1999). Effects of justice conditions on discrete emotions. *Journal of Applied Psychology, 84*, 786–794.

Whitman, D. S., Caleo, S., Carpenter, N. C., Horner, M. T., & Bernerth, J. B. (2012). Fairness at the collective level: A meta-analytic examination of the consequences and boundary conditions of organizational justice climate. *Journal of Applied Psychology, 97*, 776–791.

Zaccaro, S. J., & Banks, D. J. 2001. Leadership, vision, and organizational effectiveness. In S. J. Zaccaro & R. J. Klimoski (Eds.), *The nature of organizational leadership* (pp. 181–218). San Francisco, CA: Jossey-Bass.

Zacharatos, A., Herschcovis, M. S., Turner, N., & Barling, J. (2007). Human resource management in the North American automotive industry: A meta-analytic review. *Personnel Review, 36*, 231–254.

Zhao, H., Wu, J., Sun, J.-M., & Chen, C. W. (2012) Organizational citizenship behavior in Chinese society: A reexamination. *The International Journal of Human Resource Management*, 4145–4165.

CHAPTER

13 Justice Perception Formation in Social Settings

Suzanne S. Masterson *and* Nathan Tong

Abstract

Much of the justice literature implicitly treats the justice formation process as based primarily on an individual's experience of an event; however, this view ignores an important dimension that is highly relevant to justice perception formation: the social setting. There is clear evidence that justice perceptions generally do not develop in a vacuum, but instead rely on social information and the broader social context. Whether the social information stems from other individuals such as peers or supervisors, or from a larger setting such as one's work team or organization, studies have shown that people's individual justice perceptions are formed and influenced by one's social setting. In this chapter, we focus on the multiple mechanisms through which the social context plays a role in the formation of justice perceptions, from social comparison to social information and sensemaking.

Key Words: justice, fairness, social context, social comparison, social information, sensemaking

Justice Perception Formation in Social Settings

Much of the justice literature implicitly treats the justice formation process as based primarily on an individual's experience of an event (e.g., Cropanzano, Byrne, Bobocel, & Rupp, 2001): something happens (e.g., a hiring decision is made, a performance appraisal review occurs, etc.), and the individual employee experiences that event and forms justice perceptions based on three dimensions: was the outcome fair (distributive justice), was the procedure used to allocate the outcome fair (procedural fairness), and was the treatment during the event fair (interactional justice)? This perspective is pervasive throughout much of the justice literature, and research taking this view has provided a lot of good information about what factors employees consider relating to each of those dimensions (e.g., Colquitt, 2001) as well as the consequences associated with each of the dimensions (e.g., Colquitt, Conlon, Wesson, Porter, & Ng, 2001).

However, this view tends to overlook an important dimension that is highly relevant to justice perception formation: the social setting. From the earliest justice research on equity theory (Adams, 1965) to recently published meta-analytic reviews of justice climate (Whitman, Caleo, Carpenter, Horner, & Bernerth, 2012), researchers have recognized that justice perceptions do not develop in a vacuum, but instead rely on social information. This may occur through a social comparison process (e.g., Feinberg, 1974), meaning that individuals utilize a comparison point in order to put their own outcomes or treatment in perspective, and form justice perceptions accordingly. It may also occur through others intentionally providing information in order to shape the individuals' fairness perceptions, such as through offering explanations (Shaw, Wild, & Colquitt, 2003) which might manage others' impressions and perceptions of fairness (Greenberg, 1990).

Social information processing (Salancik & Pfeffer, 1978) also occurs, such as when organizational newcomers use information provided by coworkers in evaluating their organization's expected fairness (Hollensbe, Khazanchi, & Masterson, 2008), or when coworkers hear others talk about past experiences with a supervisor and use that information in assessing the supervisor's perceived fairness (Jones & Skarlicki, 2005). There is also evidence that social information processing occurs within teams and groups, such that individuals share information in the process of sensemaking (e.g., Weick, 1995), leading to shared perceptions of justice (e.g., Naumann & Bennett, 2000; Roberson, 2006).

Overall, there is strong evidence that, at times, justice perceptions are socially constructed, and that social information and the broader social context can play an important role in the formation of justice perceptions. In this chapter, we focus on the multiple mechanisms through which the social context plays a role, from social comparison to social information and sensemaking, looking at both targets' and actors' use of social information.

Social Comparison Processes

As Feinberg (1974) argued, justice can be separated into two categories: "the various contexts, criteria, and principles of justice...which essentially involve comparison between various persons and those which do not" (p. 298). This first category, comparative justice contexts, criteria, and principles, is of interest here, because it necessarily involves having some kind of social information about the outcomes and/or treatment of a comparison other in order for a fairness perception to be formed. As Kulik and Ambrose (1992) summarized, the comparison referent may be the self, an other internal to the organization, an other external to the organization, or even a system. Moreover, the comparison point can be temporally based such that it represents that referent in the past, present, or anticipated future, although the self is the one most likely to be grounded in a time other than the present (Kulik & Ambrose, 1992).

Feinberg (1974) further noted that there are three conditions under which comparative justice is most commonly appropriate: "(i) when comparative prizes are to be awarded, (ii) when burdens and benefits are to be distributed, and (iii) when general rules are to be made, administered, or enforced" (p. 299). These conditions relate to both distributive and procedural justice dimensions.

Distributive Justice

According to the first two conditions identified by Feinberg, distributive justice, or the perceived fairness of outcomes received, falls neatly into the comparative justice category. Equity theory (Adams, 1965) is a clear example of such a distributive justice application. Equity theory explicitly incorporates a social comparison process, proposing that individuals form fairness perceptions on the basis of a comparison of their own ratio of outcomes to inputs to that of a comparison other. Moreover, the selection of different comparison others can change one's perception of fairness from under-equity (when one's ratio is smaller than that of the comparison other) to over-equity (when one's ratio is larger than that of the comparison other). Relative deprivation (Martin, 1981) is another distributive justice-related framework that demonstrates that individuals' justice evaluations depend on the comparison of their own outcomes to those of others to whom the individuals regularly compare themselves. As Feinberg (1974) noted, different rules of comparison can be applied, so that one might consider the rules of equality (e.g., everyone gets the same outcome), equity (e.g., each gets outcomes in proportion to their inputs), or even need (e.g., each gets outcomes in proportion to their need), as outlined by Deutsch (1975). In the end, regardless of the decision rule applied, individuals should be motivated to seek comparison information in order to evaluate the fairness of the outcomes they receive.

Procedural Justice

According to the third condition outlined by Feinberg (1974), procedural justice, or the perceived fairness of the processes used to distribute outcomes, also falls into the comparative justice category, as it relates to the administration or enforcement of rules. Procedural justice is associated with a number of rules, including consistency, bias suppression, accuracy, correctability, representativeness, and ethicality (Leventhal, 1980) and voice (Lind & Tyler, 1988). Several of these rules have implications for social comparison processes, such as consistency, which holds that procedures should be consistent across persons and time, and representativeness, which holds that procedures should reflect the concerns and values of the individuals covered by the process. As Bies (2001) noted, "any deviation from equality of opportunity or the equality of administration of the rules forms the basis for claims of procedural injustice" (p. 109). Thus, individuals should be motivated to seek social comparison information in order to evaluate the fairness of the administration of the procedural justice rules.

Several early studies examined individuals' use of comparison information relating to both outcomes and procedures in assessing the overall fairness. For example, Cropanzano and Folger (1989) conducted a laboratory experiment in which subjects completed two tasks, only one of which would be used to determine whether the subject earned an extra research credit. In order to manipulate comparison of procedural information, subjects in the subject-decision condition were able to choose which task would count toward earning the extra credit, while subjects in the experimenter-decision condition were told which task would count toward earning the extra credit. In both conditions, the subjects were told that they failed to achieve a high enough score to earn the extra credit upon completing the two tasks. Moreover, subjects had comparison information about how they had performed in the task that did not count toward earning the extra credit (i.e., comparison to self). In the high referent condition, subjects learned that they would have performed high enough to earn the extra credit had the other task been chosen, while in the low referent condition, subjects learned that they would not have earned the extra credit regardless of which task had been chosen. The results revealed that only those subjects in the high referent, experimenter-decision condition felt unfairly treated as compared to the other three cells (high referent, subject-decision; low referent, experimenter-decision; low referent, subject-decision), demonstrating the importance of social comparison information to self (in terms of outcomes or performance) and others (in terms of procedures used).

Grienberger, Rutte, and van Knippenberg (1997), building on an earlier study by Ambrose, Harland, and Kulik (1991), took this a step forward by manipulating comparison information to others in terms of both outcomes and procedures. Rather than having subjects perform two tasks and compare possible outcomes based on their own performance as in Cropanzano and Folger (1989), Grienberger et al. incorporated a comparison other who subjects were told was able to choose or was assigned their task (high or low other-control) and who either earned or did not earn the bonus (high or low referent). Subjects either were able to choose or were assigned to their task (high or low self-control), and were always informed that they did not earn the bonus. The results replicated the findings of Cropanzano and Folger (1989), in that subjects who were assigned to a task and learned that the comparison other made the bonus reported higher levels of perceived unfairness than those who had chosen their task. Moreover, the results revealed that subjects who were assigned to a task but whose comparison other had been able to choose a task reported higher levels of perceived unfairness than the other cells. Again, these results demonstrate the importance of outcome and procedural comparison information, either to self or to others, in influencing perceptions of fairness.

Another way that social comparison plays a role in procedural justice is through the cues it provides regarding one's social status within a group. For example, under the group value model (Lind & Tyler, 1988), procedures are viewed as carrying information about one's intragroup status; to the extent that procedures are perceived as being unjust, the individual's status within the group is not recognized, and the individual's reactions should be strongly negative. Thus, individuals seek information regarding their social standing in comparison to other group members through their assessment of the fairness of procedures. This model was later reframed as the relational model (Tyler & Lind, 1992), and it was proposed that individuals care about procedural justice because of the information provided about their long-term relationships with the people employing the procedures. Thus, the procedural justice judgments provide essential information about one's relationship with the authority carrying out the procedures and the institution generating the procedures (Lind, 1994), which can then influence reactions to the procedures themselves (Van Prooijen, van den Bos, & Wilke, 2005). Again, the group value and relational models of procedural justice highlight the importance of the social context and the social comparison information gleaned from assessments of procedural fairness.

Interactional Justice

Feinberg's (1974) category of comparative justice does not appear to directly incorporate the subdimensions of interactional justice (Bies & Moag, 1986), which are interpersonal justice, or the perceived fairness of one's treatment in terms of dignity and respect, and informational justice, or the perceived fairness of the information given in terms of honest and full information (Greenberg, 1993). Bies (2001) argued that interactional justice is a form of noncomparative justice in that individuals have the right to be treated with dignity and respect as human beings, and treating everyone rudely or with abusive behavior would not make people feel better simply on the basis of their being treated equally. While this may be true, it is also likely that, just as with the group value and relational models above, individuals would use comparative information regarding their relative treatment in terms of dignity and respect and being provided with open and honest information as offering cues about their standing with the person carrying out the treatment and the larger group. Moreover, as Lamertz (2002) noted, "ambiguity exists about norms of interpersonal treatment, which may differ between organizational cultures" (p. 20). Thus, while comparative information is not at the heart of interactional justice perceptions (as it is with distributive and procedural), it likely is still sought for the additional information regarding social standing that it provides to the recipient, or the norms for expected fair treatment within a given organization.

Looking Across Justice Dimensions: The Fair Process Effect

One of the interesting questions, then, is how do individuals assess fairness, and particularly distributive fairness, in the absence of comparison information? As van den Bos, Lind, Vermunt, and Wilke (1997) noted, there are many occasions in life, and particularly in the workplace, where we know our own outcomes but do not know the outcomes of others. Thus, they proposed, on the basis of fairness heuristic theory, and found support for the fair process effect: when individuals do not have information about the outcomes of other people, they will look to information about the fairness of the process by which the outcomes were allocated, and judge their outcomes as more fair when the process itself was fair than when it was unfair (van den Bos et al., 1997). In the experiments, voice was manipulated as the procedural fairness condition, and the fair process effect was found: as compared to those who had outcome information about others, those without outcome information rated the outcomes as more fair and reported higher satisfaction when given voice (van den Bos et al., 1997). Overall, the findings associated with fairness heuristic theory, and the fair process effect in particular, point to how individuals "work around" situations in which they are unable to obtain the social information needed for comparisons. Still, the research also demonstrates that people use social comparison information when available, rather than relying on heuristics such as other fairness information.

Managers' Use of Social Information as a Means of Influencing Justice Perceptions

While employees engage in social comparison processes during justice perception formation, managers can use a different element of the social setting—social information—as a way to potentially influence and shape those justice perceptions.

Explanations

Explanations—also known as social accounts (Bies & Moag, 1986; Bies, 1987) and ideological accounts (Bies, 1987)—are known to increase perceptions of procedural justice as well as to temper the negative effects of perceptions of distributive injustice (Frey & Cobb, 2010). As the name suggests, explanations are the justifications offered by decision makers to explain, rationalize, or validate their decisions as well as their responsibilities in making those decisions (Bies & Shapiro, 1987). Scott and Lyman (1968), who are credited with starting scholarly interest in explanations (Shaw et al., 2003), made a distinction between two discrete types of explanations: excuses and justifications. Excuses are those explanations made by a manager in which he or she acknowledges that the decision or outcome is "unfavorable or inappropriate but denies full responsibility by citing some external cause or mitigating circumstance" (Shaw et al., 2003: 445), such as a strict company policy. Justifications, on the other hand, are explanations for which the manager takes full responsibility for the decision he or she made but refutes the impropriety of the decision based on some ultimate objective. For example, a company owner might withhold a customary annual raise normally given to the team but justify the decision by saying that the added financial burden would bankrupt the company. Explanations are often viewed by employees in terms of the explanation's provision, or the degree to which an explanation is provided for a given outcome or decision, and adequacy, or the degree to which a given explanation is thorough, unequivocal, and understandable (Shaw et al., 2003). Studies have demonstrated that managerial explanations that are evaluated as adequate by employees following an outcome that is viewed as unfavorable have enhanced those employees' perceptions of fair treatment (Bobocel & Farrell, 1996; Elkins, Bozeman, & Phillips, 2003).

Fairness theory (Folger & Cropanzano, 1998, 2001), which was previously known as and is derived from Folger's (1986, 1987) referent cognitions theory, posits that employees use explanations when cognitively processing or ultimately reacting to a managerial decision or outcome. In doing so, employees form counterfactuals, which are mental representations that simulate alternative courses of events that could have happened or alternative actions that a manager should have taken. Employees form counterfactuals based on multiple sources of reference, including past experiences, speculation, organizational norms, and social comparisons (Folger, 1987; Colquitt, 2004). Scholars have argued that people tend to turn to immediately available social comparison information first when judging the fairness of their treatment or allocation outcome, but if that information is not readily available, they utilize previous experiences (Folger & Kass, 2000). In both of these situations, it is clear that people reference some sort of social context when forming justice perceptions. Folger and Cropanzano (1998, 2001) suggest that counterfactuals can be divided into three types: (1) *could* counterfactuals, which compare the decision maker's actions to an alternative course of action or what the decision maker could have done, (2) *should* counterfactuals, which compare the decision that the decision maker made to some ethical standard, and (3) *would* counterfactuals, during which an employee compares his or her "current state of well-being with mental simulations of other, perhaps more positive, states" (Shaw et al., 2003: 446).

Shaw and his associates (2003) conducted a meta-analysis of the literature investigating explanations to examine its effects on justice perceptions and several associated outcomes (i.e., cooperation, retaliation, and withdrawal behaviors). Their findings demonstrated that both explanation provision and explanation adequacy, whether in the form of excuse or justification, had beneficial effects on perceptions of distributive and procedural justice. Furthermore, their results indicated that explanation provision was significantly related to increased cooperation and decreased retaliation but had no effect on withdrawal behaviors, whereas explanation adequacy was significantly related to all three outcomes (i.e., increased cooperation and decreased retaliation and withdrawal behaviors; Shaw et al., 2003). In contrast, however, the findings were equivocal as to whether explanations were beneficial: (1) when they were excuses rather than justifications, (2) when outcome favorability was low rather than high, and (3) in contexts where instrumental, relational, and moral virtue impacts were high rather than low (Shaw et al., 2003). Although these authors' findings most clearly demonstrated the effects of explanations on perceptions of distributive and procedural justice, they also found that the nature of explanations is directly related to the two subdimensions of interactional justice (interpersonal and informational justice). These findings suggest that while employees might have other contextual information to judge whether they have been treated fairly (e.g., the outcomes of their peers), the provision and adequacy of explanations offered to them by the decision maker significantly impacted their justice perceptions, as well as the consequences of those perceptions (i.e., their subsequent behaviors). Thus, the use of explanations by both managers and employees supports the view that justice perceptions are socially constructed.

Impression Management

Greenberg (1990; Greenberg, Bies, & Eskew, 1991) argued that individuals are often concerned about managing others' impressions of their image, particularly in terms of being seen as fair. Moreover, in organizations, managers must not only act fairly, but they have to ensure that others believe them to be fair; that is, they must manage others' impressions of their fairness. Certainly, there are times when managers believe that they are engaging in fair behaviors, but others (e.g., subordinates or superiors) might not perceive the behavior to be fair—as Greenberg et al. (1991) noted, "The major problem lies in the fact that fairness judgments rest in the eye of the beholder" (p. 112). Thus, it is important for managers to shift their perspective to understand what those others will perceive as fair.

Greenberg (1990) suggested multiple tactics that could be used to manage perceptions of fairness; for example, managers who need to address a situation that others might potentially view as unfair may use accounts (by offering excuses and justifications) and apologies (by showing remorse and taking responsibility), while managers who are trying to proactively create impressions of fairness might use entitlings (through attempting to take responsibility for positive events and outcomes) and enhancements (through attempting to make ambiguous situations appear to be positive, or positive situations to be even more positive; Greenberg, 1990). All of these actions involve providing information in an attempt to influence or control others' fairness perceptions. Thus, the impression management view of organizational justice supports a social constructionist view of justice perspectives, in that an individual's perceptions are influenced by the social information provided by the manager.

Greenberg et al. (1991) took this idea a step further, proposing additional actions that can be used to influence subordinates' perceptions of fairness, including actions that fall squarely into the procedural and interpersonal justice dimensions (e.g., providing voice, demonstrating neutrality, applying criteria consistently, and treating subordinates with dignity and respect), although the focus is often on how to communicate (i.e., provide information) that one is engaging in these behaviors. Overall, the clear message of the impression management perspective is that individuals can influence the formation of justice perceptions in others through providing social information.

One caution of justice-related impression management has to do with "hollow justice" (Greenberg, 1990: 139), or the attempt to appear fair without actually behaving in a fair manner. Greenberg (1990) noted that such attempts are not necessarily intentionally harmful, but instead may represent an inaccurate belief in one's own identity as a fair person. At the same time, there is also the possibility that social information can be used in an attempt to manipulate fairness perceptions such that they do not reflect the reality of the behaviors enacted by the manager.

Employees' Use of Social Information in the Formation of Justice Perceptions

Beyond the intentional provision of social information by managers as a means of influencing justice perceptions, employees seek out and use social information on their own, using information available in the broader social context beyond that intentionally provided by managers and organizations. We first examine social information's role in event-based justice perceptions, or the fairness associated with particular organizational events such as hiring decisions or performance appraisals, and then turn to the more recently developing area of entity-based justice perceptions, or the fairness associated with particular exchange partners such as supervisors or organizations (e.g., Cropanzano et al., 2001).

Event-based Justice Perceptions and Social Information

There is a fair amount of research, particularly research that has been performed in the laboratory, which demonstrates the role of social information, such as knowing whether others perceive a situation or event to be fair or unfair, in the formation of justice perceptions. In an early study, Folger and his colleagues examined whether voice would have the same relationship with fairness perceptions and other reactions under the conditions of information or no information about how peers viewed the fairness of the outcome. In this set of laboratory studies, Folger, Rosenfield, Grove, and Cockran (1979) manipulated whether the subject had voice or no voice regarding the outcome to be received upon completing a task, while also manipulating whether the subject received or did not receive information regarding the peer's opinion on the perceived fairness regarding the ultimate outcome. Folger et al.'s (1979) findings suggest that, when subjects were not sure they had been treated inequitably, either because they had no information about the peer's perceptions of fairness, or because the information they received indicated that the peer found the outcome to be fair, voice resulted in more positive outcomes in terms of perceived fairness of the process and outcome, and satisfaction. However, when subjects received confirmation that they had been treated inequitably via the peer's opinion, voice did not result in more positive outcomes and, in study 2, resulted in more negative outcomes with regard to perceived fairness of the process and outcome, and satisfaction. Overall, it appears that having direct information about a peer's fairness perceptions changes the way an individual reacts to procedural elements such as voice.

Greenberg (1979) examined the influence of having a group discussion on individuals' allocation decisions. In this laboratory study, there were three allocation decisions (T1 = individual decision; T2 = group decision; and T3 = individual decision) and, in each, an allocation had to be made between two data entry assistants who worked for an equivalent period of time but performed at different levels. Greenberg (1979) proposed that individuals who expected to have a future interaction with the allocation recipients would tend to use an equality-based allocation rule (i.e., give equal amounts to each of the data entry assistants) due to the desire to minimize embarrassment and present themselves positively. Conversely, he proposed that as these individuals came together as a group at T2, the group would tend to use an equity-based allocation rule (i.e., give more to the data entry assistant who performed at the higher level than the other), given the ability to diffuse responsibility across the group members. Finally, Greenberg (1979) expected that, when they again had to make decisions as individuals at T3, the exposure to the group discussion would carry over to the final allocation decision.

Greenberg's (1979) results supported the hypothesis that individuals would make equality-based allocations at T1 but would make equity-based allocations when part of a group at T2; however, at T3, individuals reverted to equality-based allocations, contrary to expectations. Still, individuals reported higher levels of confidence in the fairness of their allocations at both T2 and T3, indicating that there appeared to be some carryover effect from the group discussion. Overall, Greenberg's (1979) findings demonstrate that individuals' perceptions of fairness, in terms of which allocation rules to apply and confidence in the fairness of those allocation decisions, were influenced by group discussion, a clear indication that individual perceptions are changed through a social interaction process.

Lind, Kray, and Thompson (1998) examined the relative influence on justice perceptions and other related outcomes of personal justice-related experiences with a supervisor versus peer reports of justice-related experiences with the same supervisor. While they recognized that information about others' unfair treatment can provide important cues about the supervisor's tendencies to engage in unfair behaviors, Lind and his colleagues noted that both the self-interest and group value theories of justice suggest that this type of information will not be weighted as heavily as one's own experiences with the supervisor. As they stated, "it may be difficult for reports of others' unfair treatment to be incorporated in a truly effective way into personal assessments of fairness" (p. 3). Lind et al. proposed that: (1) personal experiences would hold much more influence over subsequent justice perceptions than would reported experiences by peers, such that when mild injustice is distributed across all members of a group as opposed to concentrated with one member of the group, the group will see the supervisor as more unfair and react more negatively; and (2) as a result of group discussions, groups would rate injustice more strongly than would individuals either before or after the group discussion. Their results supported both hypothesized effects: the subject who was treated unfairly in the concentrated condition rated supervisors as much less fair, polite, and unbiased than did the other two subjects, although their perceptions were influenced downward after hearing about their peer's unfair treatment. Moreover, group ratings of unfairness were always more extreme than were the averaged individual ratings of fairness, both before and after the group discussion (Lind et al., 1998). As Lind and his colleagues summarized, "People do consider and respond to the injustices of others, but that response pales relative to reactions to their own personal injustices. Our findings here suggest that widespread acceptance of the injustice reports of a few fellow workers may be difficult to achieve, absent some personal experiences with the injustice" (p. 17).

As a follow-up to the earlier Lind et al. (1998) study, van den Bos and Lind (2001) examined the effects of knowing the fairness of another individual's procedural treatment as well as the fairness of one's own procedural treatment on overall procedural justice judgments. In study 1, accuracy was manipulated so that the procedure was either accurate (all answers were graded) or inaccurate (only one out of twenty answers were graded), while in study 2, voice was manipulated so that the experimenter either gave the opportunity for voice or not. Subjects learned about the other's fair or unfair treatment through receiving direct information about the process during the experiment, as opposed to hearing it from the other him/herself; thus, information about the other's treatment was direct and unambiguous (van den Bos & Lind, 2001). Unsurprisingly, procedural justice perceptions were highest when both the self and other received the fair manipulation. Interestingly, procedural justice perceptions were equally low when either the self or the other received an unfair manipulation; that is, subjects rated the process as unfair regardless of whether they experienced the unfair manipulation or whether they witnessed the other experience the unfair manipulation (van den Bos & Lind, 2001). van den Bos and Lind (2001) proposed that an important factor in this study's findings is the nature of the information about the other's procedure: "[W]e are prompted to advance the hypothesis that certainty about whether a given procedure is fair or unfair is more important than whether the procedure is applied to oneself or another" (p. 1331).

De Cremer, van Dijke, and Mayer (2010) further proposed that individuals' perceptions of their own and others' fair treatment would be important in predicting cooperation behaviors, particularly under the condition of working with a prototypical leader who exemplifies the values of the overall group. In a series of four studies, their hypothesis was supported: cooperative behaviors were the highest when respondents reported that both they and their colleagues were treated fairly by a leader high on prototypicality, demonstrating again that employees do pay attention to the broader context of fairness and that this determines their resulting behaviors, in conjunction with their perceptions of their own fair treatment. De Cremer and Van Hiel (2010) continued this research, examining the relationship between own and others' fair treatment with regard to negative reactions. Their results suggest "that people do seem to care about the justice experiences of others" (p. 290), providing further evidence that social context does indeed matter and helps shape justice perceptions.

Colquitt (2004) examined the influence of consistency of treatment between self and others, specifically incorporating teams with varying levels of task interdependence. In a series of studies examining the interaction of the fairness of procedural administration and the level of team task interdependence, Colquitt (2004) found that people's own perceptions of procedural justice and level of performance was moderated by the perceived justice allocated to others on the same team, such that role performance increased when procedural justice was consistent between the individual and team members. Moreover, the effect was stronger when the team members had a high level of task interdependence as compared to a low level. Overall, these results demonstrate that individuals take both their own fair treatment as well as the fair treatment of others within their social group into account when acting within organizations.

Jones and Skarlicki (2005) conducted a study that further examined the role of social information processing, focusing specifically on the extent to which fairness perceptions might be influenced by hearing one's peers talk about their previous fairness-related experiences with an authority. In this laboratory study, information was obtained indirectly, through overhearing a confederate describe her treatment by the experimenter in a previous study as either fair or unfair. The subjects had no prior experience with the experimenter other than what occurred in the study. The results demonstrated that the social information had a significant incremental impact on subjects' ratings of interactional fairness above their own experience in the study (Jones & Skarlicki, 2005). Thus, it appears that individuals who have little experience with an authority are influenced by both their own experience as well as information from their peers about the authority's fairness, even when that information is obtained indirectly.

Tangirala and Alge (2006) argued that employees working together remotely will have lower exposure to the social cues and information that occur when peers work side by side at the same location, and thus experience higher informational uncertainty. Based on the tenets of uncertainty management theory (Lind & van den Bos, 2002), they proposed that teams working together via computer-mediated communication media would report lower fairness perceptions than working together face-to-face, and that the relationship would be mediated by the availability of social information. In a laboratory study in which face-to-face and computer mediated groups were exposed to the same fair and unfair situational elements, both hypotheses were supported: the students who worked remotely reported lower perceptions of fairness, and the relationship was mediated by students' self-reported familiarity with their peers. Tangiarala and Alge's (2006) findings point to the importance of the social cues that many employees are exposed to on a regular basis in influencing fairness judgments.

Entity-based Justice Perceptions

Traditionally, justice researchers have focused on employees' reactions to a particular event (Cropanzano et al., 2001), such as a hiring decision (e.g., Gilliland, 1994), performance appraisal (e.g., Taylor, Tracy, Renard, Harrison, & Carroll, 1995), or pay raise (e.g., Folger & Konovsky, 1989), among others. This event perspective generally focuses on the employee as experiencing the event first-hand and reacting to the event based on that personal experience, or what Rupp (2011) has recently termed "looking in." Some researchers have attempted to study the different protagonists or sources of justice-related events, such as supervisors and organizations, through a multi-foci approach (e.g., Masterson, Bartol, & Moye, 2000; Rupp & Cropanzano, 2002).

However, there is also evidence that individuals have entity-related justice perceptions, or evaluations of the fairness of exchange partners such as organizations, supervisors, and coworkers, among others (e.g., Cropanzano et al., 2001). Cropanzano et al. suggested that it is likely that entity-related justice perceptions are the result of an aggregation of a number of event-based justice perceptions where the entity was the agent responsible for the justice-related behaviors. That is, an employee would experience multiple events in which the supervisor enacted procedures and allocated outcomes (e.g., made work assignments, carried out performance reviews, allocated bonus money, etc.), and would have evaluated the fairness of each of the events as they occurred. Moreover, over time, those justice judgments would accumulate such that the employee would develop a perception of the supervisor's fairness, based in part on the social comparison processes previously discussed.

Hollensbe, Khazanchi, and Masterson (2008) raised the question as to how newcomers to an organization would assess the fairness of both the organization and the supervisor. That is, without having a number of justice-related events to aggregate, would new employees be able generate fairness perceptions of these two important entities? To answer this question, they conducted a qualitative study, interviewing 33 organizational newcomers within the first few weeks of entry, and again after three to five months of working at their organizations. Their results are interesting, and point to the importance of social information processing (Salancik & Pfeffer, 1978). When asked whether they expected the organization to be fair and on what they were basing this expectation, 45% of respondents indicated that they were using information based on their coworkers' experiences and perceptions of fairness when they first entered the organization (T1), and 54% reported using that information after three to five months on the job (T2) (Hollensbe et al., 2008). This was the single most used factor respondents cited in assessing organizational fairness, reflecting the importance of social information in the formation of justice perceptions of organizations. Respondents also reported using social information from coworkers and others in assessing the fairness of the supervisor at both times, although the percentages were lower (T1 = 9%, T2 = 21%) than for perceptions of organizational fairness. It is interesting to note that use of direct social information increased slightly as new employees gained experience in their new context, perhaps indicating that social information does not become less important as one gains experience, but perhaps gains a different kind of importance in grounding one's experiences in the broader social context.

New employees also reported using other types of indirect social context information as well in assessing the fairness of the organization, including the level of organizational support to employees (T1 = 24%, T2 = 21%), the amount of turnover (T1 = 12%, T2 = 0%), and the organization's commitment to organizational diversity (T1 = 15%, T2 = 12%) (Hollensbe et al., 2008). Each of these provides additional information about the overall organizational social context—how well cared for employees appear to be, how likely employees are to stay with the organization, and the make-up of the overall workforce—and may serve as proxies for direct information from coworkers about their treatment and organizational fairness perceptions. Interestingly, new employees did not appear to use such indirect social information in assessing supervisor fairness, instead using more direct personal experiences (such as supervisor support of the employee, supervisor flexibility, and other supervisor traits). Overall, the findings of Hollensbe and her colleagues highlight both the direct and indirect use of social information in the formation of entity-related justice perceptions in new settings.

Social Information as Provided via Social Networks

An interesting development has been the examination of social networks as a source of social information for processes such as justice perception formation (Shapiro, Brass, & Labianca, 2008). Lamertz (2002) proposed that employees' perceptions of procedural and interactional justice would be related to the procedural and interactional justice perceptions of their close peers, given that they look to their peers for information about organizational norms relating to fairness standards. Moreover, Lamertz proposed that the more relationships employees have with managers in the organization, the more positive their procedural and interactional justice perceptions would be, as they are motivated to maintain a positive evaluation of their treatment, given their elevated status in the group based on their inclusion in the in-group of managers (e.g., group value model; Lind & Tyler, 1988). As Lamertz (2002) summarized, "social cues from, as well as social comparison and social identification with, peers and managers to whom an employee has social relationships will influence his or her justice perceptions" (p. 21). In this study, Lamertz (2002) used social networking tools to identify a "social influence generating peer" with whom each focal employee had an embedded relationship as well as to indicate the number of managers with whom each focal employee interacted. The results demonstrated that both the peer's interactional justice perceptions as well as the number of relationships with managers had significant and positive influences on employees' interactional justice perceptions, but not on their procedural justice perceptions. Lamertz's (2002) results demonstrate the impact that social information and cues received through relationships with peers and managers have on individuals' justice perceptions, again reflecting the social nature of justice perception formation.

Umphress, Labianca, Brass, Kass, and Scholten (2003) also took a social networking approach to the study of justice perceptions, predicting that employees' organizational justice perceptions are influenced by the people with whom they interact in the workplace. In developing their hypotheses, Umphress and her associates emphasized that examining the social ties between employees goes beyond simple social comparisons to explore how coworkers can actually influence the development and transmission of justice perceptions. Based on social information processing (Salancik & Pfeffer, 1978), they proposed that interactional justice perceptions should be the most susceptible to influence from social ties, because these perceptions are the most ambiguous in terms of interpretation. As Umphress et al. (2003) noted, "when assessing interactional justice, an employee may have difficulty identifying whether a supervisor's remark was condescending, sarcastic, playful, or reflected stress from factors unrelated to the employee. Thus, when evaluating the interactional justice of the incident, an employee may be particularly sensitive to coworkers' opinions of his or her treatment, or coworkers' opinions of how they are treated" (p. 741). As Folger and Kass (2000) postulated, the opinions of others can be used as proxies for one's own "actual" perceptions.

In their study, conducted on employees in the finance area of a division of a Fortune 500 financial services company, Umphress and her associates demonstrated that positive expressive ties (e.g., friendship or liking relationships) were positively related to greater similarity in perceptions of interactional justice, while there were no such relationships found for procedural or distributive justice perceptions. In addition, Umphress et al. (2003) found that employees who had higher prestige, or a higher number of social ties as reported by other participants, had more similar perceptions of interactional justice with other employees. Thus, the results support the social information processing tenet that employees seek information from others when interpreting ambiguous environmental cues.

Chia, Foo, and Fang (2006) noted that, while research demonstrates the importance of social information, we do not know very much about the choice of sources to get information from and give information to. Using a social networking approach, Chia et al. (2006) found that employees of a Chinese electricity plant sought out, voluntarily gave, and accepted information from both expressive (close, intimate) and instrumental (weak, arm's length) ties relating to procedural justice. In contrast, for interactional justice related information, employees sought out, voluntarily gave, and accepted information primarily from expressive ties only. Chia et al.'s (2006) research provides insight into how social information relating to justice may travel within organizations. In later research, Fang and Shaw (2010) extended this research to demonstrate the importance of employee self-monitoring in conjunction with other network variables in determining justice-related information flow.

Although not specifically focused on an intact organizational social network, Kulik, Pepper, Shapiro, and Cregan (2012) conducted a study examining postings on an internet website regarding organizational fairness and unfairness. Interestingly, they found that "outsiders have a greater effect on how discussion board participants feel about organizations than insiders do. The power of the outsider lies in his or her description of the organization as fair or unfair. Discussion board participants responded to the cognitive content of the outsider's message, not the outsider's emotional tone" (Kulik et al., 2012: 581). This is another indication of how different kinds of status may play into reactions to social information.

Organizational Culture and Climate as Social Contexts for Justice

The social context of the organization can also be a source of information for the employee in interpreting cues and forming justice perceptions. Conversely, employees can create a social context through the sharing of their justice perceptions (i.e., climate for justice).

Organizational Culture

Mitrano (1997) conducted an interesting study as a participant-observer at a pediatric AIDS clinic in order to understand the influences of distributive, procedural, and interactional justice perceptions of professionals in this setting. During his time at the clinic, he identified the outcomes, procedures, and interactions that the professionals labeled as fair or unfair, and sought to understand how these perceptions were "created, shaped, managed, and negotiated" (Mitrano, 1997: 186). Mitrano found that organizational cultural norms were the primary influence on professionals' expectations with relation to outcome fairness (59.5%); prior work experiences were the primary influence on expectations with relation to procedural fairness (57.9%); and professional subcultural norms were the primary influence on their expectations with relation to interactional fairness (72.2%). Thus, when professionals experienced outcome injustice, it was primarily because they had not received the outcomes (e.g., payment, time, space, resources) that they felt entitled to based on the norms that had been codified into the organization's culture, or a social comparison between what the culture dictated and what they actually got. In contrast, when they experienced procedural injustice, it was primarily because the processes (e.g., hiring, training, evaluation) did not match with their past work or shared experiences—again, indicating a social comparison process between the current and past procedures. Finally, when they experienced interactional injustice, which generally involved communication issues (e.g., quantity, frequency, quality, form), the professionals were comparing their expectations based on their professional norms with what they were actually experiencing. The interactional injustices were particularly troublesome in this healthcare context, in which individuals representing a multitude of professional subcultures were present. In the case of both the organizational culture norms and the professional subculture norms, social construction played a major part, as the justice expectations were shaped by the individuals participating in them.

Climate for Justice

Within organizations, employees may come to have a set of shared perceptions regarding the organizational practices and policies that is developed through members of the group interacting with one another, or an organizational climate (Schneider & Reichers, 1983). Climate perceptions generally are directed at a particular set of policies and practices, such as a climate for service (Schneider, White, & Paul, 1998). In one of the earliest studies on a climate for procedural justice, Naumann and Bennett (2000) outlined several ways in which climates are believed to form, all of which demonstrate the potential influence that social interactions can have on employees' perceptions. One of the ways in which climates are believed to form is through the development of shared meanings through interactions with others within a group; in this way, different groups within an organization may develop different sets of shared perceptions regarding a particular set of policies or practices (i.e., the symbolic interaction explanation; Schneider & Reichers, 1983). A second way can be seen through the attraction-selection-attrition model (ASA; Schneider, 1987), which posits that work groups tend to become more similar over time, as individuals who "fit" with the other group members select in and remain, while those who don't fit select out and leave. As the members become more similar on multiple dimensions, their interests and perceptions may also become more alike (Naumann & Bennett, 2000). Finally, because individuals within a work group share a supervisor, that manager may have a strong influence on group perceptions by applying the same practices and policies and giving the same information to everyone in the group (Naumann & Bennett, 2000).

In their study, Naumann and Bennett (2000) found evidence for climates for procedural justice perceptions within bank branches; that is, there was evidence that employees within individual bank branches were in agreement in terms of their procedural justice perceptions. Moreover, their results demonstrated support for both the symbolic interaction explanation for a shared procedural justice climate as well as for the influence of the shared supervisor, but not for the ASA explanation of climate. Subsequent research by Colquitt, Noe, and Jackson (2002) did find that age diversity within groups led to a weaker procedural justice climate, thus implying that demographic similarity may lead to shared perceptions as would be predicted by the ASA model.

Roberson (2006) applied a sensemaking perspective in order to examine the development of team-level fairness perceptions, building on the work of Weick (1995) and Salancik and Pfeffer (1978). As Weick (1995) stated: "Sensemaking is what it says it is, namely, making something sensible" (p. 16). Thus, when individuals encounter a situation that is ambiguous or unexpected, they attempt to make sense of that situation, often through using social cues and information, both from the environment as well as from other people, in order to understand that situation and develop associated perceptions relating to it. Roberson (2006) noted that communication is the primary means for engaging in sensemaking, and as this communication occurs, it influences individuals' views of reality such that they can become shared. Roberson specifically set out to examine team sensemaking, "or the social interchanges through which members interpret their collective experiences and construe attributes of those experiences as fair or unfair" (p. 179).

In her laboratory study, two teams of three individuals each engaged in a team brainstorming task, and both teams received the same procedurally just or unjust manipulation, while one team received a favorable outcome and the other received an unfavorable outcome. Teams were then given an opportunity for individual team discussion (teams returned to separate rooms while they waited for the next stage of the experiment). Those team discussions were videotaped and coded for sensemaking behaviors: discussion of the simulation, discussion of the procedure, discussion of the outcome, and discussion of the team itself. Roberson's results indicated that teams which experienced fair procedural treatment and unfavorable outcomes were more likely to engage in sensemaking, and engaged in longer discussions, than did teams in the other conditions. This might be explained by the potential surprise of receiving an unfavorable outcome following a fair procedure. Roberson also found that teams that engaged in sensemaking discussions relating to the simulation and to the team itself had stronger procedural and distributive justice climates, as did those that engaged in longer discussions. Overall, Roberson's (2006) findings demonstrate the social construction of justice perceptions; through engaging in discussions in which they attempted to make sense of the simulation (i.e., what happened in the experiment) and the team (i.e., the team's identity and its comparison to the other team), teams developed shared perceptions of procedural and distributive justice.

Since 2000, a number of studies have examined justice climates, expanding to address climates for distributive, procedural, and interactional justice, as well as consequences of those shared perceptions of fairness. A recent meta-analysis by Whitman, Caleo, Carpenter, Horner, and Bernerth (2012) identified 66 studies focusing on the concepts of unit justice/fairness, team justice/fairness, and justice/fairness climate, demonstrating the importance of understanding how social influence processes can shape these shared perceptions.

Justice as a Contagious Process

In 2000, Degoey developed the concept of justice as a social contagion, highlighting that "people's perspectives on justice can, in part, be based on social interaction and exposure to others' thoughts and feelings" (p. 55). The image of contagion illustrates that justice perceptions can spread much like a virus, which is different than a goal-driven model in which individuals purposefully try to influence others' justice perceptions. Degoey (2000) suggested that simply talking about justice can create a shift in individuals' perceptions from their original position—an effect demonstrated in earlier research by Lind et al. (1998).

Degoey (2000) further distinguished between cognitive contagion of justice and emotional contagion of justice. Cognitive contagion of justice refers to processes by which gaining information about an event influences individuals to develop similar justice judgments. Specifically, under a cognitive contagion model, organizational employees share information with one another in order to make sense of an event, and the result is similar perceptions of justice regarding that event (Degoey, 2000). Degoey offered several studies which support the cognitive contagion model, including Greenberg (1979) and Lind et al. (1998). Subsequent studies also support Degoey's cognitive contagion model, through demonstrating that individuals share similar justice perceptions with important others in their social networks (e.g., Lamertz, 2002; Umphress et al., 2003). Overall, the cognitive contagion model demonstrates a social information processing effect such that individuals' attitudes are influenced through direct information provided by coworkers or peers (Salancik & Pfeffer, 1978).

Emotional contagion of justice refers to processes by which an individual's emotional reactions to a justice-related event are influenced by those of other people (Degoey, 2000). Degoey (2000) proposed two potential emotional contagion processes: (1) when an individual receives information about a potential negative consequence and seeks social support as a way of coping with that event, the sharing of information during the social interaction might lead to shared perceptions about the fairness of the situation; and (2) when an individual is treated in an unexpected way, he/she might turn to others to help interpret and define the experience, which again might lead to shared perceptions about the fairness of the situation.

Degoey (2000) proposed multiple factors that might promote the contagion of fairness, including exposure to others who have had a similar fairness-related experience (e.g., Lind et al., 1998), discussion with others with whom one has friendship ties (e.g., Umphress et al., 2003), ambiguous situations (e.g., Umphress et al., 2003), new situations (e.g., Hollensbe et al., 2008), and social identification (e.g., Mitrano, 1997), among others. Degoey (2000) also proposed that the fairness reputation of an entity may serve as a social mechanism through which justice perceptions can be influenced, which was directly supported by Jones and Skarlicki (2005) and indirectly supported by Hollensbe et al. (2008).

Beyond an individual's justice perceptions about a single situation being influenced through communication with others, the contagion model also proposes that shared perceptions relating to justice can be maintained across situations and collectives (Degoey, 2000). Moreover, Degoey suggested that these shared perceptions relating to justice may lead to different forms of collective action, including collective protests, group-based impression management efforts, and group-based antisocial behaviors. As Degoey (2000) argued, "As group or network members arrive at a shared perspective on justice, such a perspective can create a sense of solidarity and cohesion that makes collective action more likely" (p. 81). Roberson (2006) is an example of one study that demonstrates support for Degoey's proposals regarding the development of a shared perspective on justice through the actions of discussion and storytelling. As noted earlier, Roberson found that teams that engaged in different types of sensemaking discussions had stronger justice climates for both procedural and distributive justice.

As reflected in the above summary, subsequent research has provided some support for Degoey's propositions relating to justice contagion, particularly in terms of the factors which may make social contagion more likely, as well as in the demonstration of the importance of discourse in the transmission of justice perceptions between individuals and the development of shared justice perceptions in collectives.

Future Directions for Research on Justice Perception Formation in Social Settings

Our review of the literature suggests that we are starting to better understand the role that social information and the broader social context plays on the formation of justice perceptions, yet there is still much more to learn. There are several areas that we believe are particularly interesting in terms of the next set of research questions.

Changing Work Contexts

Past research has demonstrated that ambiguous situations clearly create a context in which social information becomes very important (e.g., uncertainty management theory; Lind & van den Bos, 2002). Currently, rapid advancements in communication technology are changing work contexts in ways that may open new avenues of research on social influences on justice perceptions. For example, there may be opportunities to build on Tangirala and Alge's (2006) formulation of social information uncertainty, to identify what other social information sources are used by employees who are not co-located with their peers. This is particularly important, given that the proliferation of the internet over the past thirty years has opened new avenues for organizations in the ways that they are able to conduct business. Workers no longer need to remain stationary in a single location as they have in the past. In fact, estimates show that roughly 30% of the worldwide workforce includes workers who are mobile (Morganson, Major, Oborn, Verive, & Heelan, 2009). With these new non-traditional work arrangements come a host of novel questions regarding the formation of justice perceptions. The accretion of technological advances such as smart phones and laptops with built-in webcams, along with the ever-increasing availability of internet connections, has resulted in an increased number of dispersed and virtual teams. Because these team members are not co-located and typically convene only to perform work tasks with little opportunity for extra-task activities (e.g., "water cooler" conversations, break and lunch interactions, etc.), there are numerous outside sources of social information that might be used in formulating justice perceptions—sources that organizations may not be able to influence, but should certainly try to understand.

An interesting category of worker that has previously been unexamined is those whose job duties take them off-site from the company operations and require that they regularly work alone or with an extremely limited number of peers or other members from the organization. Examples of such occupations include sales representatives, truck drivers, and district managers; all are occupations in which there is often not a "home" location within the organization's physical location, and the employee often interacts as much or more with organizational outsiders versus insiders. Such employees may not have a readily available internal comparison other with which to evaluate whether the outcomes, procedures, and interactions they receive from their supervisors and organizations are fair. One conjecture could be that they form and base their perceptions of justice on their previous employment; another is that perhaps they compare their work circumstances to their peers outside of the workplace, such as spouses, family, or friends and neighbors. Kulik and Ambrose (1992) proposed that individuals comparing extrinsic job facets are typically more likely to make comparisons using information garnered from others, as opposed to using one's own previous experience. Furthermore, they suggested that people tend to use physically proximate referent others when selecting a comparison referent rather than looking to others who might hold the same job or perform the same duties but are not physically adjacent. Certainly, as Kulik and Ambrose (1992) posited, there are a host of other personal factors, such as age, race, position, and tenure, and situational factors, such as compensation and resource allocation procedures, that workers may take into account when deciding whom they should use as a comparison other.

It is currently unknown as to whether these changes in job context, such as increased availability of technology and decreased physical interaction with other organizational employees, make a difference to employees' perceptions of justice. By examining the formation of justice perceptions of those employees who engage in changing and non-traditional work arrangements, and specifically of those workers who do not work in typical organizational settings, researchers may begin to shed new light on the formation of justice perceptions in all workers.

Increasing Availability of Information

Another byproduct of changes in information technology may be related to the increased availability of information resulting in the choice of particular comparison referents. As Kulik and Ambrose (1992) noted, the selection of a comparison referent is related both to the availability of information as well as the relevance of the referent to the individual. Both situational and personal characteristics are believed to influence the availability of information, and an important situation characteristic examined in the past has been physical proximity, with individuals believed to choose comparison referents who are physically proximate (Kulik & Ambrose, 1992). However, advancements in information technology make more information available than ever before, making it possible to find, for example, salary surveys and organizational procedures with a quick internet search. Moreover, the increasing use of social media such as Facebook has increased the number of virtual (non-proximal) "friends" and acquaintances from which individuals receive informational updates on a regular basis. Other information sources are likely to be used as well; the recent research by Kulik et al. (2012) points to internet discussion boards, where postings by both organizational insiders and outsiders are available to all as a new and relatively unknown source of social information. All of these advances point to the importance of re-examining the characteristics leading to the availability of information, and how availability of information interacts with the relevance of the referent in an individual's choice of a comparison referent in the fairness assessment process.

Generational Differences

An interesting area of research may be to explore the potential generational differences in utilizing social information during the justice evaluation process. There are currently a number of different generations co-existing in organizational settings (Society for Human Resource Management, 2005), and each brings with it different expectations related to organizational practices and outcomes. It may be that each generation also has different sources of social information as well as different usage patterns of that social information. Kulik and Ambrose (1992) offered propositions relating to age and tenure, but it may be that generation plays an important role in the choice of comparison others or in the incorporation of social information along with one's own experiences into perceptions of fairness. As Joshi, Dencker, Franz, and Martocchio (2010) noted, "unlike other forms of demographic differences, such as gender or ethnicity, the effect of generational differences on organizational outcomes has received relatively little attention among researchers" (p. 408). It may also be that other organizational members' perceptions of an individual based on his or her generation may influence the types of social information that are presented to that individual. Looking at generational identification, both from the recipient and actor perspectives, may provide additional understanding of the role of social information in justice perceptions as well as some practical advice for organizations dealing with multiple generations in the workplace. In particular, generational identification may play a role in the perceived relevance or salience of particular comparison referents, an important factor in the selection of a referent (Kulik & Ambrose, 1992).

Entity-based Justice Perceptions

To date, justice research has focused more on event-based versus entity-based justice perceptions; however, the management literature clearly demonstrates the importance of perceptions of and relationships with different work-related entities, including organizations (e.g., perceived organizational support; Eisenberger, Huntington, Hutchison, & Sowa, 1986), supervisors (leader-member exchange; Graen & Scandura, 1987), and team members (team-member exchange; Seers, 1989). Thus, it is reasonable to posit that employees' perceptions of the fairness of these entities are likely important in terms of the exchange relationships that are developed and maintained, as well as the behaviors that are reciprocated to these entities (e.g., Masterson, Lewis, Goldman, & Taylor, 2000). A closer examination of entity-based justice perceptions would provide an interesting opportunity to understand whether different kinds of social information processing effects might be at play; do individuals look to different sources of information when assessing events vs. entities? What about with different types of entities? Hollensbe et al. (2008) found strong reported use of social information from coworkers, especially with regard to assessing the fairness of the organization (as opposed to the supervisor). Perhaps personal interactions with specific individuals (such as a supervisor) are weighted more heavily into perceptions of justice of that person, while assessments of "global" entities such as teams or organizations rely more heavily on information from others. Moreover, as Jones and Skarlicki (2012) recently proposed, research needs to look more closely at the role of social information processing (Salancik & Pfeffer, 1978) and sensemaking (Weick, 1995) in terms of understanding entity-based justice perceptions.

Research Design Issues

Beyond potential topics for future research, it is also important to consider the implications of the social context for the design of future research. We note that much of the research examining the role of social information in justice perception formation has occurred in the laboratory. This research has done much to increase our understanding of the role that social information can play, but it is also important to incorporate the social context into field research, as has been done with the research examining social networks (e.g., Chia et al., 2006; Lamertz, 2002; Umphress et al., 2003) and climate for justice (e.g., Naumann & Bennett, 2000). For example, from experimental research, we have learned that direct information about peers' outcomes and procedures (e.g., Folger et al., 1979) influence individuals' fairness perceptions, and that personal experience is more influential than peers' experiences in those fairness perceptions (Lind et al., 1998). At the same time, experimental research has found that, under conditions of clear and unambiguous information, subjects rated procedures as equally unfair regardless of whether they experienced the procedure or merely witnessed another party experience the unfair procedure (van den Bos & Lind, 2003). Now, we need to translate these various scenarios into organizational settings, where employees are embedded in relationships in which fairness-related information and events occur frequently. We must conduct organizational-based, longitudinal research that can develop and test hypotheses based on what we have learned in the lab, in order to more fully understand how these situations unfold in the workplace and to develop practical advice for organizations for the fair treatment of employees.

We also extend a call for more qualitative research, such as that conducted by Mitrano (1997) and Hollensbe et al. (2008), in order to identify new areas for future quantitative research. Participant-observer research, such as Mitrano (1997) conducted, allows a full immersion in the organizational environment, and may reveal new sources of social information and aspects of the social context that have not yet been identified. Alternatively, interview studies across multiple individuals, such as Hollensbe et al. (2008) conducted, allow participants to identify those factors and sources most important to them, and the examination of the results can lead to new grounded theory and propositions to be tested in subsequent research. As an example, the Hollensbe et al. study revealed that individuals reported using information far beyond the decision rules commonly associated with distributive, procedural, and interactional justice in determining the fairness of their supervisor and organization. Without this study, research on entity-based justice perceptions might have proceeded by simply applying those well-established justice rules, missing out on the richness of the social information used in assessing entity-based fairness. A particularly ripe area for future research might be to qualitatively study a major change event occurring within or between organizations (e.g., a downsizing, an acquisition or merger, an adoption of a new technology or start-up of a new service line, etc.), and the progression of fairness-related perceptions throughout the event. Such situations are often characterized by surprising and unexpected events and ambiguity—conditions ripe for social information processing (Salancik & Pfeffer, 1978) and sensemaking (Weick, 1995).

Conclusion

Employees' judgments regarding their individual outcomes of each of the dimensions of justice (distributive, procedural, and interactional; Bies & Moag, 1986; Feinberg, 1974) derive from information they gather from numerous sources, both directly and indirectly. These sources could be peers, such as in Salancik and Pfeffer's (1978) social information processing model (e.g., Hollensbe et al., 2008); from supervisors in the form of explanations (e.g., Shaw et al., 2003); or from organizational norms (i.e., the justice climate; Naumann & Bennett, 2000).

Justice research demonstrates that, while employees often "look in" to determine whether an authority's actions should be deemed fair or unfair, they also "look around" to gather social information from proximal others (e.g., peers, fellow group or team members, supervisors) to decide whether the outcomes they receive and the processes used to reach those outcomes should be considered just (Rupp, 2011). Whether employees form their justice judgments based on information that stems from an event (Cropanzano et al., 2001) or an entity (Hollensbe et al., 2008), the social setting plays an important role in that formation process.

References

Adams, J.S. (1965). Inequity in social exchange. In L. Berkowitz (Ed.), *Advances in experimental social psychology* (Vol. 2, pp. 267–299). New York: Academic Press.

Ambrose, M.L., Harland, L.K., & Kulik, C.T. (1991). Influence of social comparisons on perceptions of organizational fairness. *Journal of Applied Psychology, 76*, 239–246. doi:10.1037//0021-9010.76.2.239

Bies, R.J. (1987). The predicament of injustice: The management of moral outrage. In L.L. Cummings & B.M. Staw (Eds.), *Research in Organizational Behavior* (Vol. 9, 289–319). Greenwich, CT: JAI Press.

Bies, R.J. (2001). Interactional (in)justice: The sacred and the profane. In J. Greenberg & R. Cropanzano (Eds.), *Advances in organizational justice* (pp. 89–118). Stanford: Stanford University Press.

Bies, R.G., & Moag, J.F. (1986). Interactional justice: Communication criteria of fairness. In R.J. Lewicki, B.H. Sheppard, & M.H. Bazerman (Eds.), *Research on negotiations in organizations* (Vol. 1, pp. 43–55), Greenwich, CT: JAI Press.

Bies, R.J. & Shapiro, D.L. (1987). Interactional fairness judgments: The influence of causal accounts. *Social Justice Research, 1*, 199–218. doi:10.1007/BF01048016

Bobocel, D.R. & Farrell, A.C. (1996). Sex-based promotion decision and interactional fairness: Investigating the influences of managerial accounts. *Journal of Applied Psychology, 81*, 22–35. doi:10.1037/0021-9010.81.1.22

Chia, H.-B., Foo, M.-D., & Fang, R. (2006). Workplaces as communities: The role of social networks in who seeks, gives, and accepts information on justice issues. *Journal of Community Psychology, 34*, 363–377. doi:10.1002/jcop.20104

Colquitt, J.A. (2001). On the dimensionality of organizational justice: A construct validation of a measure. *Journal of Applied Psychology, 86*, 386–400. doi:10.1037/0021-9010.86.3.386

Colquitt, J.A. (2004). Does the justice of the one interact with the justice of the many? Reactions to procedural justice in teams. *Journal of Applied Psychology, 89*, 633–646. doi:10.1037/0021-9010.89.4.633

Colquitt, J.A., Conlon, D.E., Wesson, M.J., Porter, C.O.L.H., & Ng, K.Y. (2001). Justice at the millennium: A meta-analytic review of 25 years of organizational justice research. *Journal of Applied Psychology, 86*, 425–445. doi:10.1037/0021-9010.86.3.425

Colquitt, J.A., Noe, R.A., & Jackson, C.L. (2002). Justice in teams: Antecedents and consequences of procedural justice climate. *Personnel Psychology, 58*, 83–109.

Cropanzano, R., Byrne, Z.S., Bobocel, D.R., & Rupp, D.E. (2001). Moral virtues, fairness heuristics, social entities, and other denizens of organizational justice. *Journal of Vocational Behavior, 58*, 164–209. doi:10.1006/jvbe.2001.1791

Cropanzano, R., & Folger, R. (1989). Referent cognitions and task decision autonomy: Beyond equity theory. *Journal of Applied Psychology, 74*, 293–299. doi:10.1037/0021-9010.74.2.293

Degoey, P. (2000). Contagious justice: Exploring the social construction of justice in organizations. In B.M. Staw & R.I. Sutton (Eds.), *Research in organizational behavior* (Vol. 22, pp. 51–102). Greenwich, CT: JAI Press. doi:10.1016/S0191-3085(00)22003-0

De Cremer, D., & Van Hiel, A. (2010). "Becoming angry when another is treated fairly": On understanding when own and other's fair treatment influences negative reactions. *British Journal of Management, 21*, 280–298. doi:10.1111/j.1467-8551.2009.00653.x

De Cremer, D., van Dijke, M., & Mayer, D.M. (2010). Cooperating when "you" and "I" are treated fairly: The moderating role of leader prototypicality. *Journal of Applied Psychology, 95*, 1121–1133. doi:10.1037/a0020419

Deutsch, M. (1975). Equity, equality and need: What determines which value will be used as the basis for distributive justice? *Journal of Social Issues, 31*, 137–149.

Eisenberger, R., Huntington, R., Hutchison, S., & Sowa, D. (1986). Perceived organizational support. *Journal of Applied Psychology, 71*, 500–507. doi:10.1037/0021-9010.71.3.500

Elkins, T.J., Bozeman, D.P., & Phillips, J.S. (2003). Promotion decisions in an affirmative action environment: Can social accounts change fairness perceptions? *Journal of Applied Social Psychology, 33*, 1111–1139. doi:10.1111/j.1559-1816.2003.tb01941.x

Fang, R., & Shaw, J.D. (2010). Self-monitoring, status, and justice-related information flow. *Journal of Occupational and Organizational Psychology, 82*, 405–430. doi:10.1348/096317908X311705

Feinberg, J. (1974). Noncomparative justice. *This Philosophical Review, 83*, 297–338.

Folger, R. (1986). A referent cognitions theory of relative deprivation. In J.M. Olson, C.P. Herman, & M.P. Zanna (Eds.), *Relative deprivation and social comparison: The Ontario symposium* (Vol. 4, 33–55). Hillsdale, NJ: Erlbaum.

Folger, R. (1987). Reformulating the preconditions of resentment: A referent cognitions model. In J.C. Masters & W.P. Smith (Eds.), *Social comparison, justice, and relative deprivation: Theoretical, empirical, and policy perspectives* (183–215). Hillsdale, NJ: Erlbaum.

Folger, R., & Cropanzano, R. (1998). *Organizational justice and human resource management.* Thousand Oaks, CA: Sage.

Folger, R., & Cropanzano, R. (2001). Fairness theory: Justice as accountability. In J. Greenberg & R. Cropanzano (Eds.), *Advances in organizational justice* (1–55). Palo Alto, CA: Stanford Press.

Folger, R., & Kass, E.E. (2000). Social Comparison and Fairness: A Counterfactual Simulations Perspective. In J. Suls & L. Wheeler (Eds.), *Handbook of Social Comparison: Theory and Research* (423–441). New York: Plenum Publishers.

Folger, R., & Konovsky, M.A. (1989). Effects of procedural and distributive justice on reactions to pay raise decisions. *Academy of Management Journal, 32*, 115–130.

Folger, R., Rosenfield, D., Grove, J., & Cockran, L. (1979). Effects of "voice" and peer opinions on responses to inequity. *Journal of Personality and Social Psychology, 37*, 2253–2261. doi:10.1037/0022-3514.37.12.2253

Frey, F.M., & Cobb, A.T. (2010). What matters in social accounts? The roles of account specificity, source expertise, and outcome loss on acceptance. *Journal of Applied Social Psychology, 40*, 1203–1234. doi:10.1111/j.1559-1816.2010.00616.x

Gilliland, S.W. (1994). Effects of procedural and distributive justice on reactions to a selection system. *Journal of Applied Psychology, 79*, 691–701. doi:10.1037/0021-9010.79.5.691

Graen, G., & Scandura, T. (1987). Toward a psychology of dyadic organizing. In L.L. Cummings & B.M. Staw (Eds.), *Research in organizational behavior* (Vol. 9, pp. 175–208). Greenwich, CT: JAI Press.

Greenberg, J. (1979). Group vs. individual equity judgments: Is there a polarization effect? *Journal of Experimental Social Psychology, 15*, 504–512. doi:10.1016/0022-1031(79)90012-X

Greenberg, J. (1990). Looking fair vs. being fair: Managing impressions of organizational justice. In B.M. Staw & L.L. Cummings (Eds.), *Research in organizational behavior* (Vol. 12, pp. 111–157). Greenwich, CT: JAI Press.

Greenberg, J. (1993). The social side of fairness: Interpersonal and informational classes of organizational justice. In R. Cropanzano (Ed.), *Justice in the workplace: Approaching fairness in human resource management* (pp. 79–103). Hillsdale, NJ: Erlbaum.

Greenberg, J., Bies, R.J., & Eskew, D.E. (1991). Establishing fairness in the eye of the beholder: Managing impressions of organizational justice. In R. Giacalone & P. Rosenfeld (Eds.), *Applied impression management: How image making affects managerial decisions* (pp. 111–132). Newbury Park, CA: Sage.

Grienberger, I.V., Rutte, C.G., & van Knippenberg, A.F.M. (1997). Influence of social comparisons of outcomes and procedures on fairness judgments. *Journal of Applied Psychology, 82*, 913–919. doi:10.1037/0021-9010.89.4.633

Hollensbe, E.C., Khazanchi, S., & Masterson, S.S. (2008). How do I assess if my supervisor and organization are fair? Identifying the rules underlying entity-based justice perceptions. *Academy of Management Journal, 51*, 1099–1116. doi:10.5465/AMJ.2008.35732600

Jones, D.A., & Skarlicki, D.P. (2005). The effects of overhearing peers discuss an authority's fairness reputation on reactions to subsequent treatment. *Journal of Applied Psychology, 90*, 363–372. doi:10.1037/0021-9010.90.2.363

Jones, D.A., & Skarlicki, D.P. (2012). How perceptions of fairness can change: A dynamic model of organizational justice. *Organizational Psychology Review*, 1–23. doi:10.1177/2041386612461665.

Joshi, A., Dencker, J. C., Franz, G., & Martocchio, J. J. (2010). Unpacking generational identities in organizations. *Academy of Management Review, 35*, 392–414. doi:10.5465/AMR.2010.51141800

Kulik, C.T., & Ambrose, M.L. (1992). Personal and situational determinants of referent choice. *Academy of Management Review, 17*, 212–237. doi:10.5465/AMR.1992.4279534

Kulik, C.T., Pepper, M.B., Shapiro, D.L., & Cregan, C. (2012). The electronic water cooler: Insiders and outsiders talk about organizational justice on the internet. *Communication Research, 39*, 565–591. doi:10.1177/0093650211429286

Lamertz, K. (2002). The social construction of fairness: Social influence and sense making in organizations. *Journal of Organizational Behavior, 23*, 19–37. doi:10.1002/job.128

Leventhal G.S. (1980). What should be done with equity theory? New approaches to the study of fairness in social relationships. In K. Gergen, M. Greenberg, & R. Willis (Eds.), *Social exchange: Advances in theory and research* (pp. 27–55). New York: Plenum Press.

Lind, E.A. (1994). Procedural justice and culture: Evidence for ubiquitous process concerns. *Zeitschrift für Rechtssoziologie, 15*, 24–36.

Lind, E.A., Kray, L., & Thompson, L. (1998). The social construction of injustice: Fairness judgments in response to own and others' unfair treatment by authorities. *Organizational Behavior and Human Decision Processes, 75*, 1–22. doi:10.1006/obhd.1998.2785

Lind, E.A., & Tyler, T.R. (1988). The social psychology of procedural justice. New York: Plenum Press.

Lind, E.A., & van den Bos, K. (2002). When fairness works: Toward a general theory of uncertainty management. In B.M. Staw & R.M. Kramer (Eds.), *Research in organizational behavior* (Vol. 24, pp. 181–223). Greenwich, CT: JAI Press.

Martin, J. (1981). Relative deprivation: A theory of distributive injustice for an era of shrinking resources. In L.L. Cummings & B.M. Staw (Eds.), *Research in organizational behavior* (Vol. 3, pp. 53–107). Greenwich, CT: JAI Press.

Masterson, S.S. Bartol, K.M., & Moye, N. (2000, April). *Interactional and procedural justice: Type vs. source of fairness.* Presented at the 15th Annual Conference of the Society for Industrial & Organizational Psychology. New Orleans, LA.

Masterson, S.S., Lewis, K., Goldman, B.M., & Taylor, M.S. (2000). Integrating justice and social exchange: The differing effects of fair procedures and treatment of work relationship. *Academy of Management Journal, 43*, 738–749. doi:10.2307/1556364

Mitrano, J.R. (1997). That's not fair!: The social construction of organizational (in)justice among professionals. *Sociological Inquiry, 67*, 182–206. doi:10.1111/j.1475-682X.1997.tb00439.x

Morganson, V.J, Major, D.A., Oborn, K.L, Verive, J.M., & Heelan, M.P. (2009). Comparing telework locations and traditional work arrangements. *Journal of Managerial Psychology, 25*, 578–595. doi:10.1108/02683941011056941

Naumann, S.E., & Bennett, N. (2000). A case for procedural justice climate: Development and test of a multilevel model. *Academy of Management Journal, 43*, 881–889.

Roberson, Q.M. (2006). Justice in teams: The activation and role of sensemaking in the emergence of justice climates. *Organizational Behavior and Human Decision Processes, 100*, 177–192. doi:10.1016/j.obhdp.2006.02.006

Rupp, D.E. (2011). An employee-centered model of organizational justice and social responsibility. *Organizational Psychology Review, 1*, 72–94. doi:10.1177/2041386610376255

Rupp, D.E., & Cropanzano, R., (2002). The mediating effects of social exchange relationships in predicting workplace outcomes from multifoci organizational justice. *Organizational Behavior and Human Decision Processes, 89*, 925–946. doi:10.1016/S0749-5978(02)00036-5

Salancik, G.R., & Pfeffer, J. (1978). A social information processing approach to job attitudes and task design. *Administrative Science Quarterly, 23*, 224–253.

Schneider, B. (1987). The people make the place. *Personnel Psychology, 40*, 437–453. doi:10.1111/j.1744-6570.1987.tb00609.x

Schneider, B., & Reichers, A. (1983). On the etiology of climates. *Personnel Psychology, 36*, 19–40.

Schneider, B., White, S.S., Paul, M.C., (1998). Linking service climate and customer perceptions of service quality: Tests of a causal model. *Journal of Applied Psychology, 83*, 150–163. doi:10.1037/0021-9010.2.150

Scott, M.B., & Lyman, S.M. (1968). Accounts. *American Sociological Review, 33*, 46–62.

Seers, A. (1989). Team-member exchange quality: A new construct for role-making research. *Organizational Behavior and Human Decision Processes, 43*, 118–136. doi:10.1016/0749-5978(89)90060-5

Shapiro, D.L., Brass, D., & Labianca, J. (2008). Examining justice from a social network perspective. In S.W. Gilliland, D. Skarlicki, & D. Steiner (Eds.), *Justice, morality, and social responsibility (Research on Social Issues in Management Series, pp. 201–226)*. Charlotte, NC: Information Age Publishing.

Shaw, J.C., Wild, E., & Colquitt, J.A. (2003). To Justify or Excuse?: A Meta-Analytic Review of the Effects of Explanations. *Journal of Applied Psychology, 88*, 444–458. doi:10.1037/002-9010.88.3.444

Society for Human Resource Management. (2005). *SHRM generational differences survey report: A study by the Society for Human Resource Management* (SHRM surveys series). Alexandria, VA: Society for Human Resource Management.

Tangirala, S., & Alge, B.J. (2006). Reactions to unfairness in computer-mediated groups: A test of uncertainty management theory. *Organizational Behavior and Human Decision Processes, 100*, 1–20. DOI:10.1016/j.obhdp.2005.11.002

Taylor, M.S., Tracy, K.B., Renard, M.K., Harrison, J.K., & Carroll, S.J. (1995). Due process in performance appraisal: A quasi-experiment in procedural justice. *Administrative Science Quarterly, 40*, 495–523.

Tyler, T.R., & Lind, E.A. (1992). A relational model of authority in groups. In M. Zanna (Ed.), *Advances in experimental social psychology*, (Vol. 25, pp. 115–192). New York: Academic Press.

Umphress, E.E., Labianca, G., Brass, D.J., Kass, E., & Scholten, L. (2003). The role of instrumental and expressive social ties in employees' perceptions of organizational justice. *Organization Science, 14*, 738–753.

Van den Bos, K., & Lind, E.A. (2001). The psychology of own versus others' treatment: Self-oriented and other-oriented effects on perceptions of procedural justice. *Personality and Social Psychology Bulletin, 27*, 1324–1333. doi:10.1177/01461672012710008

Van den Bos, K., Lind, E.A., Vermunt, R., & Wilke, H.A.M. (1997). How do I judge my outcome when I do not know the outcome of others? The psychology of the fair process effect. *Journal of Personality and Social Psychology, 72*, 1034–1046. doi:10.1037/0022-3514.72.5.1034

Van Prooijen, J.-W., van den Bos, K., & Wilke, H.A.M. (2005). Procedural justice and intragroup status: Knowing where we stand in a group enhances reactions to procedures. *Journal of Experimental Social Psychology, 41*, 664–676. doi:10.1016/j.jesp.2004.12.003

Weick, K.E. (1995). *Sensemaking in organizations.* Thousand Oaks, CA: Sage.

Whitman, D.S., Caleo, S., Carpenter, N.C., Horner, M.T., & Bernerth, J.B. (2012). Fairness at the collective level: A meta-analytic examination of the consequences and boundary conditions of organizational justice climate. *Journal of Applied Psychology, 97*(4), 776–791. doi:10.1037/a0028021

CHAPTER

14

The "When" of Justice Events and Why It Matters

David Patient, Irina Cojuharenco, *and* Marion Fortin

Abstract

This chapter reviews research and theory pertaining to the effect of temporal characteristics of events on perceptions of and reactions to organizational justice. In order to set the context for empirical findings, we first review dynamic aspects of classical and more recent justice theories. We then review findings on several temporal aspects of justice events, including dynamic features (timing, duration of event, and frequency) and temporal perspective (distance, orientation, and scale). Maintaining our focus on specific events, we conclude the chapter by proposing theoretical and empirical avenues for including time in future investigation of organizational justice.

Key Words: organizational justice, fairness, time, temporal, dynamic

Introduction

Employees are highly attuned to the fairness they receive from their organization. In appraising fairness, employees not only evaluate specific events but also form judgments relating to the fairness of the organization and of individuals, such as their supervisor. In either case, because employee perceptions of and reactions to fairness take place within ongoing work relationships, they are generally not instantaneous or isolated. Rather, employee fairness judgments regarding events and persons are both temporally bounded and also affected by past and anticipated experiences. Employee reactions to unfairness are also likely to vary over time in their targets, their expression in different behaviors, and their levels of intensity (Cojuharenco, Fortin & German, 2014).

Roe (2008) points out that, in spite of time being a highly salient facet of work life, most descriptions and explanations of human behavior in applied psychology are "essentially timeless" (p. 37). George and Jones (2000) emphasize that including time into the what, how, and when of our theories is necessary to improve our understanding of organizational behavior phenomena and the predictive value of our models. They call for our theories to consider and adopt additional aspects of time, including duration, rates of change, frequency, and how time is bracketed and aggregated. In the organizational justice area, too, researchers have focused almost exclusively on how fairness perceptions form or exist at a single point in time (Jones & Skarlicki, 2013) and much is still not known about justice over time (Hausknecht, Sturman, & Roberson, 2011).

The chapter is organized as follows. In order to set the context for empirical findings, we first review dynamic aspects of some classical and more recent justice theories. Next, we introduce our focus on justice events (for a more general review, see Fortin, Cojuharenco, Patient & German, in press). We then review findings on several temporal aspects of justice events, including temporal characteristics (when, for how long, how frequently) and temporal perspective (distance, orientation, and scale). Finally, we propose theoretical and empirical avenues for including time in future investigation.

In order to assess the state of the field, we started off by looking at articles relating to organizational justice published between 1990 and 2010 in six top journals: *Academy of Management Journal, Administrative Science Quarterly, Organizational Behavior and Human Decision Processes, Journal of Applied Psychology, Journal of Management*, and *Organization Science*. From our initial search, we identified 201 justice-related articles containing 295 studies. Fifty-two out of the 295 studies (43 of the 201 articles) directly considered some element of time, using the following criteria: (a) time or temporal effects were explicitly mentioned in hypotheses, (b) longitudinal (survey or archival) data was used for lagged effect or within person differences, or (c) temporal features of justice events (speed, timing, temporal perspective) were either manipulated or measured. Of these, only 15 studies focused specifically on events. Accordingly, we sought and included in our discussion important past work on temporal effects from other outlets (e.g., for anticipatory justice, Shapiro & Kirkman, 1999), more recent articles with explicit temporal focus (e.g., for justice trajectory, Hausknecht et al, 2011), and unpublished but potentially important work (e.g., for effect of phase-shifting on importance of overall justice to anticipatory justice, Soenen, Melkonian & Ambrose, 2012), along with theoretical work (e.g., the dynamic model of organizational justice, Jones and Skarlicki, 2013). Thus, though this is not a systematic or comprehensive review of the entire body of justice articles, we present many of the most interesting and important findings relating to time.

Our first preliminary conclusion is that most justice research remains steadfastly cross-sectional, in spite of frequent calls in the literature for justice phenomena to be investigated over time and the fact that doing so has "important practical, methodological, and conceptual ramifications" (Ambrose & Cropanzano, 2003, p. 266). Our second conclusion is that most of the articles that include time in their theory or design only do so in a very limited fashion. In the majority of those studies, the passage and measurement of time was simply used to either demonstrate causality or a certain sequence among variables. Few longitudinal studies have gone beyond using two or three data points, with the spacing between usually not theoretically justified. Only a handful were *fully temporal* (Roe, 2008), in terms of including time conceptually and methodologically, as an explicit part of the model tested. Thus, there is an apparent gap between an increasing recognition among organizational justice scholars of the need to incorporate time into our models and a low rate of actually doing so.

Our third conclusion, however, is that recent theoretical advances and empirical findings relating to time and justice give grounds for optimism and specific directions for moving forward. A small but important body of interesting findings has accumulated regarding different temporal aspects. In addition, several organizational justice models that have recently been proposed have strong and explicit temporal aspects, including Jones and Skarlicki (2013), Rupp (2011), and Rupp and Paddock (2010). Finally, although methodological challenges may previously have stymied attention to temporal aspects of justice, recent articles (e.g., Holtz & Harold, 2009; Hausknecht, et. al, 2011; Cojuharenco, Patient, & Bashshur, 2011) have demonstrated conceptually appropriate ways of examining time-related justice phenomena. We review all of these next.

Overview of Justice Theorizing in Relation to Time

In this section we review some temporal aspects of both recent and more established organizational justice theories. We also discuss advances in the literature between process and content theories, between event and entity justice, and between facet and overall perceptions, that are relevant to a review of justice over time.

Process Theories of Organizational Justice

A review of four decades of organizational justice research by Colquitt, Greenberg, and Zapata-Phelan (2005) suggests that, as the emphasis has shifted from justice judgment *content* to justice judgment *process*, more explicit attention is paid to time. The authors delineate organizational justice research into four distinctive waves. The first three waves focused, respectively, on identifying the variables influencing distributive, procedural, and interactional justice judgments. Frameworks such as equity theory (Adams, 1965), the group-value model (Tyler & Lind, 1992), and interactional justice (Bies & Moag, 1986) are largely taxonomic in nature (Cropanzano, Byrne, Bobocel, & Rupp, 2001) and focus primarily on identifying the components of each justice type. Only in the fourth, "integrative wave" of justice research did researchers begin to pay more explicit attention to process, in terms of how the variables influencing justice judgments interact and in what sequence.

Several of the earlier integrative theories pay explicit attention to the timing of justice events. Fairness heuristic theory (Lind, 1995; 2001) and the uncertainty management model (Van den Bos, 2001) propose that in forming justice judgments the timing and order of information matters. For example, procedural justice information will be scrutinized more closely by employees when they do not have direct prior information regarding the trustworthiness of the authority. Fairness heuristic theory proposes a primacy effect (Lind, 1995) whereby an employee's early fairness-related experiences with an entity will establish a standard that guides how subsequent experiences are evaluated (Van den Bos, Vermunt, & Wilke, 1997). Once a fairness heuristic has been established, employees will only (re)enter a judgment phase when the future actions of an authority are made less certain because of radical change in the organization, such as a merger or major restructuring (Soenen et al., 2012). Justice integration theory (Gilliland & Paddock, 2005) suggests another way that individuals use past fairness information: they use past schema to recognize, categorize, and decide how to respond to new justice-related events. These process theories show both that the fairness information people pay attention to can depend on when it is received, and that earlier justice experiences can influence later justice perceptions.

Entity and Event Judgments, Overall Justice and Justice Facets

Before introducing recent process models of organizational justice-judgment formation, it is important to review two further areas in which our understanding of justice judgments has become more nuanced: the distinction between entity and event justice and the distinction between facet and overall justice. First, research has distinguished two broad approaches to organizational justice research: the event paradigm versus the social entity paradigm (Cropanzano et al., 2001). The event paradigm investigates how people react to one or more specific events in the workplace, often using carefully controlled stimuli in laboratory experiments. The social entity paradigm investigates how people appraise a person or the organization, on the whole and across situations, often using correlational survey methodologies. Cropanzano and colleagues (2001) suggested that individual-event justice judgments are combined and aggregated into social entity judgments. Several justice researchers have recently begun to address the question posed by Cropanzano and colleagues (2001): "how do we get from unfair events to unfair people, groups, or organizations?" (p. 190). An abiding interest in recent dynamic models is elaborating how this process takes place over time.

A related issue that is also relevant to temporal justice dynamics lies in the distinction between facet justice and overall justice. Until recently, organizational justice was almost always considered in terms of specific facets, namely distributive, procedural, interpersonal, and informational. Only recently have scholars begun to investigate overall justice, defined as global evaluations of fairness based on an amalgam of past justice-related experiences (Ambrose & Schminke, 2009). Overall justice has been found to predict important work outcomes, over and above the specific justice facets, providing evidence that holistic perceptions regarding the overall fairness of a situation and/or entity can play an important role. Holtz and Harold (2009) suggest that overall justice can be viewed as an attitudinal construct that changes over time. Cojuharenco and Patient (2013) showed that once formed, overall positive versus negative justice judgments may in turn influence which facets of organizational justice become salient to employee fairness reasoning.

Two Dynamic Models of Organizational Justice

Two recent models are of particular interest: the dynamic model of organizational justice by Jones and Skarlicki (2013) and the multilevel temporal model of justice climate by Rupp and Paddock (2010). Jones and Skarlicki (2013) propose a sequence of processes through which fairness perceptions change and evolve over time. Central to their dynamic model of organizational justice is the distinction between facet judgments regarding specific events and more global perceptions regarding a particular source of justice. The initial entity judgment, and subsequent entity judgments, are usually a summary and interpretation of past event judgments. Thus, the authors propose that justice judgments evolve over time, as judgments regarding events potentially influence entity judgments, which in turn influence the subsequent interpretation of events. The influence that events have on entity judgments can be either in terms of increasing their strength (if consistent with prior judgments) or, if inconsistent with prior judgments, decreasing their strength or prompting a more effortful reassessment that supplants earlier entity judgments.

Rupp and Paddock's (2010) multilevel temporal model proposes that the building blocks of organizational justice are individual experiences of discrete events relating to the workplace outcomes, procedures, and interactions received. People then use emotional reactions to these events in forming fairness judgments regarding specific exchange partners. Over time, these entity judgments aggregate event information and emotional reactions. A critical component of the model is the time required not only for emotional reactions to different events to lead to entity judgments but also the time for individual entity-justice judgments to combine through social processes into aggregated entity-justice judgments and finally into shared cognitions regarding justice climate.

Focusing on Justice Events

Although both events and entities are important to justice judgments, there are several reasons why we focus in this chapter on temporal aspects of justice-related events. In all of the preceding models, discrete events are the basic building blocks of justice judgments. Managers and other social entities are evaluated in part on the basis of past events for which they are seen as the source. Although few studies have "drilled down to the level of a true fairness related event" (Rupp & Paddock, 2010, p. 249) versus, for example, focusing on a practice consisting of many events (e.g., a promotion), experience-sampling methodologies have shown that, indeed, justice perceptions occur at the level of specific events (Rupp & Paddock, 2010). In contrast to entities, which are judged across time, events occur at specific times. This makes them more amenable to being examined in terms of specific temporal characteristics. This is consistent with the suggestion by Roe (2008) that behaviors should be examined in terms of phenomena, that is, observable events with a specific beginning and end, though these can be implicit. Therefore, it becomes interesting to examine what temporal aspects of events have been considered in the justice literature and to propose promising areas and methodologies for considering additional temporal aspects, and to relate the temporal characteristics of events to their role in dynamic justice-judgment formation processes.

Temporal Dynamics of Justice Events

The specific question we address is as follows: What temporal characteristics of events influence justice judgments, regarding both the event and also social entities that are seen as the source of the event? We organize our review of relevant articles by two classes of temporal characteristics: (1) the dynamic features of the event, and (2) the temporal perspective taken on the event. For each, we first review studies in terms of interesting findings, and then we discuss what conclusions can be drawn and note potential avenues for future research.

The first, dynamic features of the event, includes when a justice event happens (timing), how many times it happens over a given interval (frequency), for how long (duration), and with what patterns (trajectory). These are considered in turn.

Timing of Justice Events

Timing refers to the onset (e.g., early, delayed) of a phenomenon. In jurisprudence, the importance of timing of procedures and remedies has long been acknowledged in the maxim "Justice delayed is justice denied." Likewise, work events undergo scrutiny in terms of fairness not only because of expectations in terms of what happened but also in terms of when it happened. Timeliness has been recognized as an explicit criterion of organizational justice, through statements used to measure informational justice, such as "Has (he/she) communicated details in a timely manner?" (Colquitt, 2001). A number of studies have investigated the timing of different types of fairness-related events, including the provision of feedback, dispute intervention, and denial of voice.

Sapienza and Korsgaard (1996) examined the effect of timeliness of feedback in a scenario experiment and a survey focused on entrepreneur-investor relations. In the first study, 44 business students were asked to take the perspective of an investor deciding whether to invest in an entrepreneurial venture. Whether the venture provided timely feedback to the investor was manipulated and found to positively influence the entrepreneur's willingness to invest. In a follow-up survey study, partners from 118 venture capital firms similarly reported that the timeliness of feedback (regarding performance and strategic decisions) from actual entrepreneurial ventures over the prior 12 month period positively influenced perceptions of fairness, trust in the ventures, and support for their strategic decisions. Only in Study 1, however, did timely feedback from entrepreneurs affect whether an investor invested or intended to invest in a venture. In both Study 1 and Study 2, procedural justice mediated the effect of feedback timeliness on investor trust in and acceptance of strategic decisions of the entrepreneurial venture.

In some situations, the timing of procedures can also violate expectations and be considered unfair if it comes too *early*. Such was the case in a study by Conlon and Fasolo (1990) that investigated the timing of third-party intervention in a dispute. In a simulated negotiation involving 197 undergraduate business students, the authors manipulated speed of third-party intervention (early versus late), role (negotiator versus a constituent who was affected but did not negotiate), and outcome (favorable versus unfavorable). Results showed that when a third party intervened early (following the second versus eighth round of nine possible rounds of negotiation), distributive justice, procedural justice, and satisfaction with the third party were all lower. Interestingly, the negative effect of early third-party intervention was far stronger for affected parties directly involved in the negotiation; that is, for negotiators versus constituents. This is consistent with the authors' reasoning that when a third-party intervenes too early it can be seen as reducing the control and voice of negotiating parties.

The effects of timing may also depend on whether events follow (or precede) unfair versus fair treatment. Theorizing on emotions and justice suggests that people start to think about justice when they experience negative affect (Mullen, 2007—see also Chapter 20, Justice and Affect: A Dimensional Approach in this volume). Because negative outcomes are, therefore, more likely than positive outcomes to undergo scrutiny in terms of fairness (Jones and Skarlicki, 2013; Greenberg, 2001), events directly following them are also more likely to become relevant to employee justice perceptions. The role of fairness versus unfairness of prior treatment has been investigated in several studies.

Van den Bos and colleagues (2005) demonstrated in two studies that how fair a neutral message from an authority is perceived to be can depend on the history of prior fair and unfair events experienced. In the first study, 99 students participated in a scenario exercise. The fairness experienced under a previous authority figure (fair versus unfair versus absent) and the person communicating the new, neutral message (same authority figure as before versus new authority figure) were manipulated. In a second study, 120 participants in an experiment completed two tasks and were supposedly sent a neutral message by the supervisor of the second task. In both studies, an *assimilation effect* was found whereby when participants had the same fair (unfair) authority figure as before they were more (less) likely to be satisfied and happy with the neutral message received and to accept the supervisor decision (only asked in Study 2). In addition, Study 1 also showed a *contrast effect*: when participants had a different authority figure from before, a neutral message was more likely to be regarded as fair following a history of unfair events with a prior authority figure.

Another type of contrast effect can occur when an event is regarded as more unfair (fair) because it is more negative (positive) than what was expected. Colquitt and Chertkoff (2002) investigated the effects of providing explanations on procedural and distributive justice in an experiment involving 168 undergraduate students. A 2 × 2 design (explanation versus no explanation × favorable versus unfavorable outcome) was used. In the favorable outcome condition, participants were able to select an additional member for their group, whereas in the unfavorable outcome condition their decision was overruled. Results showed that the positive effects of providing an explanation were stronger when the outcome was unfavorable versus favorable. The positive effects of providing an explanation were further strengthened when participants had high (unmet) expectations regarding the outcome.

Finally, the timing of events may be determined in relation to the start of the employment relationship or of a phase-shifting stage of the relationship. As discussed earlier, fairness heuristic theory (Lind, 2001; Van den Bos, 2001) proposes that events early in a relationship matter more to perceptions of fairness than subsequent events. Thus, a primacy effect occurs. For example, in a lab experiment with student work groups, Lind, Kray, and Thompson (2001) gave explanations to group members in each of three task rounds or they refused to provide explanations in the first, second, or third round. When the denial of explanations happened in earlier rather than later rounds, it exerted a stronger effect on fairness perceptions, on relational perceptions regarding the supervisor, and on acceptance of supervisor's authority. In addition, group identification was manipulated, and the researchers found that the effect of earlier rather than later unfairness on fairness perceptions (i.e., a primacy effect) was stronger for individuals in the high versus low group-identification condition. The fact that this was the case for fairness but not for other judgments regarding the supervisor (relational perceptions, authority acceptance) supports theory suggesting primacy effects on fairness judgments operate above and are separate from other primacy effects.

Frequency of Justice Events

The frequency of events refers to how many times an event occurs in a focal bracket of time, such as during a change process or since the beginning of a relationship Although event frequency is likely to be relevant to employee perceptions of organizational justice, in our sample, none of the articles directly examined the effect on fairness perceptions of repeated events. However, we discuss here some ways that theoretical papers and findings from other domains suggest event frequency might become important to organizational justice.

Some research suggests that repeated injustices may decrease the responsiveness of individuals to fair events. Davidson and Friedman (1998) conducted several studies to investigate the effect of explanations on the fairness perceptions of managers from a disadvantaged group observing unjust behaviors toward a victim from the same group. Using a scenario experiment and a 2 × 2 design in which victim race and provision of explanations were manipulated, the authors found that black managers responded less strongly to explanations about negative actions toward a hypothetical black victim than white managers did. In a subsequent study, they tested whether this "persistent injustice effect" among black managers resulted from personal experiences with injustice and from their empathy and in-group identification with the victim. The results showed that the black managers became less responsive to social accounts when they reported higher-levels of past personal experiences with injustice and higher levels of identification with their (and the victim's) race.

In a similar vein, Charness and Levine (2002) found that explanations for various pay cut scenarios did not improve perceptions of pay cut fairness in the 1990s as much as they did when respondents had been surveyed a decade earlier. The authors hypothesized that recent changes in the employment contract with less commitment between the employer and the employee, and more frequent experiences of pay cuts and job loss, may have lowered the tendency of individuals to regard pay cuts as unfair. Contrary to their hypothesis, pay cuts were not perceived as less unfair over time. Repeated exposure to this type of unfair event seems to have instead diminished respondent sensitivity to explanations.

Similarly, research has found that aspects of procedural justice can lose their positive effect, and even have a negative effect, when they repeatedly lead to a negative outcome. Folger (1977) suggested that this was the case when opportunities for voice were provided but had no impact, leading to a "frustration effect" whereby the positive effects of voice on fairness perceptions were reduced. More recently, Kulik and Clark (1993) showed that job applicant dissatisfaction with drug-testing procedures was highest when the outcome was believed to be incorrect in spite of the fact that the procedure used was generally accurate, though not completely accurate. The authors made the same argument as Folger (1977): that certainty regarding the unfair outcome tainted the usually positive procedural justice element, such as voice or accuracy. The difference was that in Kulik and Clark (1993) the unfairness of the outcome could be established immediately, whereas in Folger's (1977) original work on the frustration effect repeated negative outcomes were necessary to undermine an apparently fair procedure.

In fact, the frequency of events is likely to affect perceptions of justice differentially for fair and unfair events. Jones and Skarlicki (2005) suggest that whereas a single instance of an unfair event is likely to affect perceptions of entity justice, more than a single instance of a fair event will be necessary to have a similar impact. This prediction, which remains to be tested, is consistent with a more general postulate that "bad is stronger than good" (Baumeister, Bratslavsky, Finkenauer, & Vohs, 2001) and is also in line with the trust literature, whereby a single negative event can break trust but it takes a long time to restore trust (Gillespie & Dietz, 2009).

Speaking to the role of event frequency in making events justice relevant is the possibility of the so-called "threshold effects" (Robbins, Summers, & Miller, 2000). For example, one instance of rudeness from one's supervisor may be perceived as a one-off event that is unlikely to repeat in the future. Yet, repeated instances of rude treatment will at some point reach a threshold and trigger perceptions of unfair treatment, as well as the corresponding reactions. Robbins et al. (2000) suggest that "threshold effects" may help explain why relationships between justice perceptions and reactions may be stronger when they are measured at a time delay rather than simultaneously. In a field study they find that the relationship between fair treatment and fair information from one's supervisor and turnover intentions is stronger over a 10-month lag than when measured cross-sectionally. They propose additionally that the thresholds themselves may differ for events concerning interpersonal treatment versus those that have to do with outcome allocations. The authors reasoned that unfair distributions in an organization may be seen as something systemic and unlikely to change, whereby one single instance of unfair distributions may evoke negative expectations regarding future distributions. In contrast, up to a certain threshold instances of unfair interpersonal treatment may not be seen as stable and generalizable. In line with this reasoning, Robbins and colleagues find that the effects of distributive justice on turnover were more immediate. Similarly, a qualitative study of a strike at a biomed manufacturing plant showed that it was the repeated nature of layoffs for a particular category of workers that led workers to perceiving the practice as unfair and reacting against it (Devinatz, 2003).

Finally, Fortin and Fellenz (2008), make the provocative suggestion that repeated experience of injustice may not lead to more negative reactions. They argue that instead—especially if the victims of injustice are powerless—people can, over time, begin to regard unfair experiences as the "new normal." This "habituation effect" can be reinforced, firstly, if individuals are prevented over longer periods of time from voicing their concerns or reacting to experienced injustice, and secondly if the authority employs so-called "shaping mechanisms," whereby they succeed in redefining issues, norms and perceived wants, for example through rhetoric and socialization. Such effects have been documented by sociologists researching the exercise of power (Gaventa, 1980). Thus, over time, people may redefine fairness and accept treatment previously seen as unfair. This type of effect is, of course, difficult to discover even in longitudinal quantitative studies, as it implies so-called beta-change, whereby the subject under investigation is redefined during the course of the study.

Duration and Trajectory of Justice Events

The duration of an event refers to the length of time between onset and offset of a phenomenon. The trajectory of a justice event refers to the change over time in a justice phenomenon, in terms of slope, stability, start and end points, and inflection points. Justice events studied have varied considerably in their duration, from minute-long manipulations in experimental laboratory settings (e.g., Colquitt & Chertkoff, 2002) to organizational changes lasting several years (e.g., Mesch & Dalton, 1992). However, as in many other areas of applied psychology (Roe, 2008), the short-lived versus the long-lasting nature of specific events, have not been examined in terms of potential effects on overall assessments and the resulting attitudes and behaviors (Roe, 2008). However, research from other domains suggests some promising directions for future study.

Kahneman and colleagues (Kahneman, 2000; Kahneman, Wakker, & Sarin, 1997) identified the phenomenon of *duration neglect*, whereby the overall assessment of an event is largely independent of its duration That is, rather than duration, the intensity of peak and end moments, as well as increasing versus decreasing trends in intensity, can explain differences in overall assessments of events (e.g., Ariely & Carmon, 2000). To our knowledge, these predictions have only been directly examined in one justice article. Hausknecht and colleagues (2011) conducted research not at the level of a single event, but for perceptions of fairness over the course of one year at work. They show that trends in perceptions of justice over time explained additional variance in distal work outcomes such as job satisfaction, organizational commitment, and turnover intentions, after controlling for end-state levels of justice and (as noted in a footnote) for average levels of justice.

Measurement challenges in relation to the variability of event justice judgments are also illustrated by Paterson, Green and Cary (2002), who conducted two studies to develop measures of the perceived fairness of organizational change programs. In study 1, items for procedural, distributive and interpersonal justice were administered twice (measurement lag of 3 months) to participants who had undergone a collective bargaining process. Interestingly, in each of the three dimensions of justice several items showed no reliability and were therefore deleted. The biggest problem was found with the equity-based measure of distributive justice, where four out of five items had to be deleted, with the remaining item also showing low reliability. This may be because the equity norm was simply not suitable in this particular context, or it may have been because justice norm preferences of participants changed over the course of the three months. However, in this study, different justice dimensions are confounded with different sources, with procedural justice being linked to the organization, interpersonal justice being linked to the manager, and only distributive justice clearly being linked to the event (the negotiation). It is possible that the differences in reliability between distributive versus other justice items could be due to the event versus entity nature of the judgments.

SUMMARY AND FUTURE DIRECTIONS: TIMING, FREQUENCY AND DURATION OF JUSTICE EVENTS

Research shows that the timing can be an important aspect of fairness phenomena. Given that timeliness is a criterion of informational justice, it is hardly surprising that explanations can be less effective when they are regarded as too late (Sapienza & Korsgaard, 1996). Conlon and Fasolo (1990) show that procedures that occur too early can also be seen as less fair, which is the case when parties involved perceive certain procedures to be limiting their autonomy and control of the situation. Research should investigate what factors affect perceptions of the ideal timing for various types of organizational procedures, explanations, and remedies, from situation- to individual-specific variables. One situation-specific factor may have to do with the context in which procedures take place. For example, Cugueró-Escofet, Fortin and Canela (2013) find that remedies such as procedure changes, sincere apologies, and compensation reinforce each other when delivered simultaneously, yet we do not know whether the overall impact will change if one administers, for example, an apology a long time before or a long time after a procedure change. In other words, it is not just clock time that matters ("an apology *one month* later is too late"), but also ordering of events and actions ("the apology needs to come *before* we start to speak about the future"). Additionally, beliefs about the appropriate timing of events may differ by event type. For example, it would be interesting to test whether a conflict involving personal insults, sexist comments, or racial slurs may be seen as requiring faster intervention than a conflict that remains strictly task-focused.

As for individual-specific determinants of the perceptions of timeliness, because timeliness is a social construction (Bluedorn & Jaussi, 2008), individuals and cultures may differ in their interpretations of certain events as timely versus (unfairly) late. For example, individual or cultural differences in time urgency (Jansen & Kristof-Brown, 2005) and in preferences for pace or speed of action may produce such effects (Bluedorn & Jaussi, 2008). Taking time urgency as a case in point, individuals who are high in their sense of time urgency may perceive an organizational action, such as the provision of explanations for a pay cut, as slow if explanations take a day to arrive, whereas individuals who have a low sense of time urgency may consider the same explanations to be timely. As a result, the provision of explanations will be considered to be unfair by the former and fair by the latter.

The literature we reviewed suggests a number of ways in which current theoretical frameworks addressing time may be developed and expanded. For example, there seems to be a controversy regarding the impact of event novelty or how early an event is experienced on perceptions of organizational justice. On the one hand, there is evidence supporting a basic tenet of fairness heuristic theory regarding the primacy effect whereby early justice experiences are more influential. On the other hand, the evidence consistent with "threshold effects" (Robbins et al., 2000), suggests that events experienced early may not have the critical mass necessary for individuals to perceive them as fairness-relevant and react to them accordingly. Moreover, certain reactions may be observed only in relation to events experienced repeatedly (Jones & Skarlicki, 2013).

Further, the *substitutability* hypothesis in Fairness Heuristic Theory (Lind, 2001) suggests that events experienced early in the relationship, be they distributive or procedural in nature, will impact perceptions regarding other justice facets by means of assimilation. Yet, both assimilation and contrast effects seem to be possible (Van den Bos et al., 2005). For a review of evidence for both contrast and assimilation effects in the justice literature, see Fortin (2008).

Our review suggests that relatively understudied temporal features of fairness-related events are their duration and trajectory. For duration, we are not aware of any study that would use the duration of an organizational event as a potential determinant of its evaluation in terms of fairness and the corresponding reactions. As for event trajectories, the study by Hausknecht and colleagues (2011) suggests that the summary assessment of a relationship history may be better gauged by taking into account whether individuals experienced a decline or an increase in fairness perceptions over time rather than just by the most recent report of fairness perceptions. Applying this insight to fairness-related events, we can speculate that the effect of trajectories in fairness perceptions may be stronger with greater passage of time because trends may be especially salient in memory-based conceptions of the event (Kahneman, 2000). As a result, event-specific justice perceptions may change over time without objective changes in the event itself, solely based on the increasing importance of event trajectory to overall assessment.

Temporal Perspective on Justice Events

Not only can fairness related events be placed differently in time, vary in their relation to other events, and last varying durations, they can also be viewed from different perspectives. The temporal perspective from which an event is viewed includes: whether orientation is past or future (anticipatory justice and temporal orientation), how far away in time (temporal distance), and what period of time is bracketed (temporal scale). Research on anticipatory justice is considered first and separately. Temporal orientation and distance have tended to be examined in the same studies and so these are discussed together, especially as a common mechanism (psychological distance) has been proposed to explain findings relating to both. Work on temporal scale is considered last.

Anticipatory Justice: Expectations Regarding Fairness-Related Events

Perceptions of and reactions to injustice might not only be responses to a situation, but can also be the result of expectation (Shapiro & Kirkman, 2001). *Anticipatory justice*, defined as employee expectations regarding fairness-related events they may experience in the future, has been the subject of several studies. These have examined how expectations relate to experienced justice, the distinctive antecedents and consequences of anticipatory justice, and how it applies to overall and facet justice (distributive, procedural, interpersonal, and informational)

Shapiro and Kirkman (1999) first introduced the construct of anticipatory justice. From two large organizations that had just implemented self-managed work teams, 492 employees participated in the survey. Distributive injustice anticipated in relation to the introduction of the self-managed teams was found to predict higher employee resistance to change, higher quit intentions, and lower organizational commitment. However, in the case of resistance to change and organizational commitment (but not in the case of self-reported citizenship behaviors or quit intentions) this relationship was only present when procedural justice was low versus high. When procedural justice (which in this case also included items measuring interactional aspects) was high, anticipatory distributive justice did not predict the measured workplace outcomes.

In a selection context involving 1,832 individuals applying for employment as firefighters, Bell, Wiechmann, and Ryan (2006) investigated the effect on several outcomes of anticipatory justice, which they termed *justice expectations.* Prior expectations of distributive, procedural, informational, and (marginally) interpersonal justice all predicted applicant pretest motivation. Likewise, expectations regarding the four justice facets predicted job recommendation intentions and job acceptance intentions, except for procedural justice expectations which only predicted recommendation intentions. In addition, job applicant distributive, procedural, and informational justice expectations regarding the testing process predicted subsequent perceptions of the testing process as fair, with the strongest relationships (and sometimes the only ones) within rather than across facets. Only interpersonal justice expectations did not predict later interpersonal justice perceptions. The study also showed that, in the case of interpersonal justice expectations, these expectations moderated the relationship between interpersonal justice and two outcomes: negative affect and psychological withdrawal.

In a hospital context, Rodell and Colquitt (2009) had 113 employees (final sample) complete surveys three weeks before a smoking ban went into effect and also three months after the ban was implemented. In the preban survey, employees evaluated global fairness, and three dimensions of anticipatory justice: procedural, interpersonal, and informational. In the postban survey, employees rated three dimensions of experienced justice: procedural, interpersonal, and informational. All justice measures were related to the ban and targeted at immediate supervisors, since first-line supervisors were in charge of implementation. Results showed that global supervisory fairness predicted all three types of anticipatory justice, measured at the same time. All three dimensions of anticipatory justice related to their respective dimensions of experienced justice, measured four months later.

However, of the three dimensions of experienced justice, only interpersonal justice predicted support for the ban.

Rodell and Colquitt (2009) tested two moderators of the relationship between anticipated and experienced justice: uncertainty and the favorability of change. The relationship between anticipatory justice and experienced injustice was found to be stronger (a) when perceived uncertainty was higher, but only for interpersonal and informational justice, and (b) when perceived favorability was low, but only for interpersonal justice. Additionally, the same two moderators were tested for the relationship between global supervisory fairness and experienced justice. The relationship between global supervisory justice and experienced justice was found to be stronger when perceived uncertainty was higher, but only for interpersonal and informational justice. Perceived favorability did not moderate the relationship between global supervisory justice and experienced injustice.

There is also research suggesting that anticipations themselves are, in turn, influenced by previous experiences. To investigate the role of anticipatory procedural justice Patient, Sguera, and Saldanha (2013) conducted an experiment with a heterogeneous sample of U.S. workers (n=183) and a field study with employees working in a public sector organization during a large scale organizational change (n=315). The study's hypotheses were tested using moderated mediation analysis. Both studies showed that anticipatory procedural justice fully mediated the relationship between experienced procedural justice and organizational citizenship behavior intentions, with all variables measured at the same time. In the field study, support was found for two moderators of the mediation. First, the relationship between experienced procedural justice and anticipatory procedural justice was stronger when affective commitment to the organization was high versus low. Second, the positive relationship between anticipatory procedural justice and OCB intentions was only significant when professional identification was low.

In the context of an international merger involving a complete overhaul of the previous business model, Soenen and colleagues (2012) surveyed 115 Spanish and French employees. Levels of overall justice directly after the announcement of the merger (T1), predicted anticipatory procedural, distributive, and interactional justice six months later (T2). However, the relationship between T1 overall justice and T2 expectations regarding anticipatory procedural, distributive, and interactional justice was only significant for employees who did not regard the changes as different than expected and who did not regard them as fundamentally altering their relationship with the organization (i.e., phase-shifting). It appears that when employees perceive major organizational changes they enter a judgment phase whereby the fairness anticipated is more likely to diverge from fairness experienced in the past.

SUMMARY AND FUTURE DIRECTIONS: ANTICIPATORY JUSTICE

The preceding studies consistently show that anticipatory justice is distinct from experienced justice. Employees respond not only to experienced justice but also to future anticipated justice (Shapiro & Kirkman, 1999). Using longitudinal designs, several studies have shown that anticipatory justice predicts experienced justice. As Shapiro and Kirkman (2001) put it, "if employees expect to see injustice, they probably will, in the absence of unequivocal, objective evidence to indicate otherwise" (p. 152). This is consistent with the persistent injustice effect reviewed above (Davidson & Friedman, 1998), whereby people who have repeatedly experienced injustice appear unresponsive to events (explanations) that would typically be interpreted as fair.

The research suggests several conditions under which individuals' justice expectations have more or less of an impact. It appears that anticipated events play an especially important role during times of uncertainty. This can explain why research has tended to focus on situations of organizational change, whether major (e.g., a merger and major restructuring, as in Soenen et al., 2012) or minor (such as a smoking ban, as in Rodell & Colquitt, 2009). Soenen and colleagues (2012) showed that when employees perceive changes as major (i.e., phase-shifting events) rather than minor, employees are more likely to re-evaluate their perceptions of fairness of authorities rather than simply rely on existing judgments (Soenen et al., 2012). Rodell and Colquitt (2009) also show that when uncertainty is high, for example if previous entity fairness evaluations are called into doubt, employees engage in more predictive activity. They found that when uncertainty was high versus low employee global evaluations regarding an entity have less influence on subsequent experienced justice (for interpersonal justice), and employee anticipatory justice (for interpersonal and informational justice) has greater influence on subsequent experienced justice. This is consistent with Jones and Skarlicki's (2013) model of dynamic justice reasoning, which suggests that effortful processing of events in the workplace occurs in three instances: when an event brings an unfavorable outcome, when an event is particularly important, and when perceptions regarding the entity are uncertain.

The extent and valence of change also appear to play an important role. Rodell and Colquitt (2009) show that in the case of interpersonal justice the relationship between anticipatory and subsequently experienced justice was stronger when employees rated the favorability of change as low. The extent of change can also influence the differential importance of justice expectations. In a situation in which department supervisors were in charge of implementing a smoking ban, Rodell and Colquitt (2009) found that anticipatory interpersonal justice had greater effect on outcomes than other justice dimensions. In contrast, Melkonian, Soenen, and Ambrose (2012) found anticipatory procedural justice to be the dominant predictor of cooperation in a merger situation where decisions were being made at a high level in the organization. Which anticipatory dimension matters most appears to depend on the type of change and on who is perceived as administering the change.

Employees' justice expectations can be an important "leverage point" for enhancing employee fairness perceptions because of both their importance early in the change process and their subsequent effect on experienced fairness related events (Bell et al., 2006). However, our theoretical understanding of the types of fairness-related events that employees anticipate remains at an early stage. Relating justice expectations to existing theories of experienced justice can explain additional variance in employee attitudes and behaviors. Furthermore, anticipations may be a useful construct for researchers to link perceptions relating to earlier and later events because over time experiences and anticipations inform one another, in turn.

Temporal Orientation and Temporal Distance

Temporal orientation refers to whether a person focuses on a past versus future event. *Temporal distance* refers to whether the event is recent/near (e.g., in a few days) or more distant (e.g., in a year). Although orientation and distance are separate aspects of temporal perspective, several of the articles we review have looked at both in the same studies and sometimes at their interaction. In addition, Cojuharenco and colleagues (2011) propose that the findings for both temporal orientation and temporal distance can be explained by a common mechanism. Thus, we discuss both together in the following section.

The ability to re-visit the past and engage in prospective thought about the future is uniquely human. Employee attention can sometimes be directed to specific timeframes, such as when they are asked to evaluate the past (or anticipate the next) two weeks versus two months. In other situations a temporal perspective can be unspecified but implicit. For example, if an employee evaluates his or her organization or supervisor, the entire relationship with the target social entity will typically be examined (Hollensbe, Khazanchi, & Masterson, 2008). Several studies have directly investigated the effect of temporal orientation and temporal distance on the type of unfair events that employees focus on.

Using a longitudinal study of 83 university faculty members, Ambrose and Cropanzano (2003) examined the effect on organizational attitudes of the distributive and procedural fairness relating to a promotion and tenure decision, viewed at different points in time. Distributive (in)justice was measured in advance of the decision (future orientation), and distributive and procedural justice were measured at two points following the decision (past orientation, recent and distant). The authors proposed that procedures would be most important when employees had fewer details regarding the decision, but that outcomes will matter more when employees had the time to experience and evaluate decision outcomes. Consistent with this reasoning, procedural aspects of the promotion decision were important in advance of the decision in terms of predicting employee job satisfaction and organizational commitment. Directly following the decision, both procedural and distributive justice were influential, whereas long after the decision (approximately 20 months), only justice judgments regarding outcomes predicted employee attitudes. It is important to note that the effects discussed for the second and third time periods (directly after and long after the decision) refer only to effects of procedural and distributive justice *over and above* its influence in the prior time period, which was controlled for. As the authors point out, for this reason the results do not show that distributive justice at T3 is more important than procedural justice, only that distributive justice becomes more important and procedural justice less important with the passage of time since a decision. Since participants at time 1 (future orientation) were only asked to evaluate procedural justice and not distributive justice, the effect of past versus future orientation on salience of justice facets could not be shown.

Cojuharenco and colleagues (2011) examined the effect of employee temporal perspective on the type of unfair events—distributively, procedurally, or interactionally unfair—that employees reported being concerned with. Whereas the first and third of three studies focused on temporal orientation, study two looked at both temporal orientation and temporal distance. In Study 1, a diverse sample of 551 employees completed a survey in which individual differences in temporal focus were related to concerns about workplace injustice. Temporal orientation was measured as an individual difference variable using the Temporal Focus Scale (Shipp, Edwards & Shurer Lambert, 2009), and unfair events brought to mind were coded for the dominant concern being outcomes versus interpersonal treatment. Higher levels of future temporal focus were found to be associated with a focus on events emphasizing distributive injustice, whereas higher levels of present temporal focus were associated with a focus on events emphasizing interactional injustice.

In a second study, both temporal orientation and temporal distance were considered. Survey participants were randomly assigned to one of four conditions and asked to recall/anticipate an unfair event at work: (a) between 2 and 12 months (distant past), (b) over the past two weeks (recent past), (c) between 2 and 12 months (distant future), or (d) over next two weeks (near future). Event descriptions were then coded in terms of whether they primarily involved distributive or interactional injustice. Events involving distributive injustice were found to be more salient to participants asked to consider future versus past timeframes. In contrast, events involving interactional injustice were more salient when participants were asked to focus on past versus future timeframes. When temporal distance was low (i.e., participants focused on a near versus distant past or future time frame) interactional injustice was more likely to be reported but the salience of distributive justice was not affected.

In a third study, Cojuharenco and colleagues (2011) tested a mechanism for the differential salience of distributive versus interactional justice from different temporal perspectives: the concreteness versus abstractness with which workplace events were represented. Construal level theory (CLT) (Trope & Liberman, 2003) suggests that experiences are represented in more abstract versus concrete terms when they are more versus less *psychologically distant*, that is, in some way not part of one's direct and immediate perception and feelings (Trope, Liberman & Wakslak, 2007). Experiences become more psychologically distant when they are set in the distant versus near future, when they occur farther away geographically, and when they are hypothetical or less likely to occur (Liberman & Trope, 2008). Using CLT, Cojuharenco, Patient, and colleagues (2011) proposed that (a) future versus past events and (b) distant versus close events would primarily involve abstract, definitional aspects of work rather than concrete, contextual aspects. Abstract definitions of work were expected to focus on issues of compensation and other outcome allocations (i.e., distributive justice), whereas concrete, contextualized descriptions of work were expected additionally to focus on quality of interpersonal treatment (i.e., interactional justice). Study 3 used a 2 × 2 (abstract versus concrete reasoning induced x focus on unfair event in next/past two weeks) design to show that more abstract cognitions about employment were, in fact, the reason distributive injustice was more salient and interactional injustice less salient in future-oriented thinking.

Memory and cognition research suggests that self-relevance is a powerful principle for predicting the availability of information in memory (e.g., Ross & Sicoly, 1979; Schacter, 2001). In a study focused on third-party justice, Cojuharenco, van Prooijen, and Patient (2013) examined whether the effect of past unfair treatment experienced by others on overall justice judgments differed depending on temporal distance. With greater passage of time, individuals were expected to forget more of the details regarding what others experienced than what they experienced themselves, especially to the extent that the other people were more versus less socially distant. This was tested in two studies. In Study 1, there were 87 students who participated in a longitudinal lab experiment involving a scenario exercise. At T1, participants read about unfairness that happened to either a friend or a stranger and responded to it immediately and at T2 (two weeks later). Results showed that at T1, observer justice perceptions were not affected by what they observed happening to a third-party, whether friend or strangers. However, at T2, observer perceptions regarding the overall fairness of the situation were negatively affected by the unjust treatment of a close other, but not of a socially distant other. This result was partially replicated in a second study in which working adults were asked to recall how fairly they and co-workers had been treated at work in the last two weeks versus in the last month, and respondents reported their level of collective self-definition as a measure of social distance from colleagues.

Lilly, Virick, and Hadani (2010) conducted a study with 369 participants who recalled an important work event that they had experienced, such as promotion or salary increase, at four points in time six months apart. They found no fluctuations in the perceptions of interpersonal justice of the event. For procedural justice perceptions, individuals who had initially perceived low procedural justice increased their procedural justice perceptions over time. Lilly and colleagues suggested that the effects for procedural justice arose because memories are reconstructed to fit recent positive work experiences. However, they also posed a question that remains to be answered: "... if an individual reconstructs their memory, why would the individual only do this for procedural justice perceptions and not for interpersonal justice perceptions?" (p. 52). Future research is necessary to find out whether the higher retrospective fluctuation of procedural justice judgments (versus interpersonal justice judgments) lies in the nature of both constructs or might have been due to the fact that interpersonal justice was measured with reference to a person who enacted the event, whereas procedural justice was tied to the specific event.

SUMMARY AND FUTURE DIRECTIONS: TEMPORAL ORIENTATION AND TEMPORAL DISTANCE

It appears that different events (e.g., Cojuharenco et al., 2011), and different aspects of events (e.g., Ambrose & Cropanzano, 2003), can be salient depending on whether they are remembered or anticipated, and distant or close. Additionally, the fairness of a given workplace event may be recalled differently over time depending on social proximity to the victims of injustice and fairness perceptions held in the present (Cojuharenco et al., 2013; Lilly et al., 2010). The preceding effects of temporal orientation and past temporal distance are important given that organizational justice measures typically refer to past events (e.g., Colquitt, 2001; Konovsky, Folger, & Cropanzano, 1987; Moorman, 1991), and thus rely on participants' memory-based judgments.

In fact, future research may examine what temporal frames are naturally used in fairness reasoning. It may be that expectations regarding outcomes and procedures trigger thinking about the distant future, whereas concerns about interpersonal treatment refer to horizons only weeks away from the present. Also, in forming perceptions of distributive justice, individuals may be recalling events farther away in the past than in forming perceptions of interpersonal justice. Temporal perspective can also result from a predisposition, as some individuals tend to, for example, focus on the future more than on the present or the past, and on long term more than on short term (Hofstede, 2001; McGrath & Tschan, 2004; Zimbardo & Boyd, 1999). It would be interesting to examine to what extent cultural differences in emphasizing or de-emphaszing certain facets of organizational justice (e.g., Kim & Leung, 2007) might result from differences across cultures in habitual temporal perspective.

Temporal Scale: Over How Large a Slice of Time?

Temporal scale refers to the length of an episode in which fairness is evaluated. For example, the fairness of a phenomenon or entity can be evaluated during a relatively long period (e.g., in the past month) or short period (e.g., yesterday). George and Jones (2000) point out that the length of episodes examined can change the meaning of, variability of, and reactions to important constructs. As with temporal perspective, temporal scale can be set explicitly or implicitly. The length of the episode considered, which can be an event or an aggregation of events relating to a specific entity, will affect both the meaning attributed to it and its relationship to other phenomena (George & Jones, 2000).

Few studies directly compare the effect on fairness salience, judgments, and reactions of wider versus more narrow temporal frames. However, several recent studies using within-person designs, such as interval-contingent experience sampling, indirectly suggest important effects of temporal scale on the type and variability of justice perceptions. Within-person studies can provide insight into what experiences cause justice perceptions to fluctuate over short time intervals, and suggest ways in which employees focus on different types of justice-relevant events as a function of the temporal scale.

Inspired by affective events theory (Weiss & Cropanzano, 1996), Judge, Scott, and Ilies (2006) examined the perceived quality of daily interpersonal treatment at work as a predictor of daily hostility and workplace deviance. There were 64 employees who completed daily surveys over three weeks. Of the variance in employee workplace deviance, 53% was found to be within-individual. The authors focused on the interpersonal dimension of justice because of "practical constraints of an ESM design" (p. 135), but also suggested that interpersonal justice was likely to vary more on a daily basis than other justice facets. Results showed that fairness perceptions regarding daily interpersonal treatment related negatively to the state hostility and workplace deviance reported by employees, even when trait hostility was taken into account. It is important to note, however, that employees reported daily perceptions of interpersonal justice (e.g., Has he/she treated you in a polite manner?") rather than justice regarding specific events.

Similarly, Ferris, Spence, Brown, & Heller (2010) tested the impact of daily interpersonal treatment on daily deviance behaviors. One hundred employees completed daily diary questionnaires over a two-week period, regarding justice, affect, organizational-based self esteem (OBSE), job satisfaction, and workplace deviance. Like Judge and colleagues (2006), they found that a substantial part of the variance of workplace deviance was within person. Daily experiences of interpersonal justice predicted employee deviance, and this relationship was partially mediated by employee OBSE. The authors justified their focus on interpersonal justice in part because it was more likely than procedural or distributive justice to vary on a daily basis.

Loi, Yang, and Diefendorff (2009) investigated with a sample of 231 employees the effects of daily job satisfaction of the four facets of organizational justice. Consistent with the preceding reasoning, interpersonal and informational justice were expected to vary over time within person and, therefore, were measured on a daily basis. However, procedural and distributive justice were construed as structural forms of justice that are relatively stable over time (within person) and, therefore, were measured at a single point in time without temporal anchors and used as a between-person moderator of the effects of interpersonal and informational justice. For example, a typical item would ask: "Regarding your supervisor's behavior today, to what extent did your supervisor treat you in a polite manner?" As predicted, interpersonal and informational justice during the day related to daily job satisfaction, and this relationship was stronger when perceptions of the fairness of procedures and outcomes (measured only once) were low.

SUMMARY AND FUTURE DIRECTIONS: TEMPORAL SCALE

Just as temporal distance and orientation can affect the salience of specific events, temporal scale also invites a focus on specific event types. Methodological choices of justice researchers suggest that different justice dimensions may be most appropriately examined using different ways of bracketing time. For example, diary studies have asked respondents to report on interactional justice at work (Judge et al., 2006; Loi et al., 2009; Ferris et al., 2010) because interpersonal treatment and communication is most likely to vary on a daily basis (Bies, 2001; Ferris et al., 2010). Events that relate to organizational procedures or outcome allocations may occur less frequently, and are typically included in research relating to larger brackets of time, such as months or years (Loi et al., 2010). Naturally, the appropriate time scale for each dimension will depend on context and also on the source of justice (and how often one interacts with the source), and may also change depending on whether the relationship with the source or the organization is new or established.

Whether a construct, such as justice perceptions, is defined as stable will in many cases depend on the time scale (Roe, 2008). In the case of fairness, Holtz and Harold (2009) suggested that different findings regarding variability/stability of perceptions may result from more frequent measurement (measured at intervals of four weeks, rather than daily). It is important to note, however, that in diary studies, in addition to reducing the temporal scale that employees focus on, researchers may also be reducing employee attention to events that are longer in duration, in terms of not starting and ending during the temporal period examined. Thus the bracketing of something as "an event" may actually define both—the length of the event and the scale considered for the event. As a result, the effect of justice events that take place over or beyond several measurement periods can be underestimated if the methodology leads employees not to report on them. Similarly, studies using daily reporting can only include reactions for which there are likely to be opportunities on a daily basis (such as gossiping or helping, as opposed to sharing sensitive information with a competitive firm or finding a new employer). Unfortunately we could not locate any studies that compared different temporal scales and their respective explanatory power.

An interesting contextual factor to consider would be the perceived fairness or unfairness of an event. Because events perceived as unfair versus fair are likely to be examined in terms of concrete and contextual details (Cojuharenco & Patient, 2013; Mullen, 2007), which may include specific events leading up to the focal event, unfair events may, in general, be examined using greater temporal scales. In addition, individuals may differ in the temporal scale they typically take (Shipp et al., 2009), in terms of the amount of past or future they bring into present evaluations. Roe (2008) also points out that individuals can differ in the extent to which their attitudes and evaluations are stable over time versus frequently changing. This could reflect dispositional differences in sensitivity to justice events or in the strength of existing entity perceptions that, in turn, can anchor and dampen swings in justice evaluations, as suggested by Jones and Skarlicki (2013). In either case, some employees are likely to have justice perceptions that change less frequently and substantially than other employees'.

Discussion

In this chapter, we reviewed research on how two classes of temporal characteristics affect how people think about and perceive the fairness of events. The first class of temporal characteristics concerned the temporal dynamics inherent in the event itself, including its timing, frequency, duration, and trajectory. The second class focused on the perceiver's temporal perspective on the event, in terms of orientation (future versus past), distance (close versus far away), and scale (narrow versus broad slice of time).

Our review suggests that relatively few studies deal directly with time and justice, and that there appears to be little connection between these studies. This lack of integration may have to do with the fact that classical justice theory paid little attention to temporal aspects. Recent theoretical developments (Jones & Skarlicki, 2013; Rupp & Paddock, 2010), however, provide a theoretical foundation for conducting more sophisticated and explicitly temporal studies and also for integrating studies focused on different temporal aspects of justice phenomena.

We believe, however, that the temporal aspects considered may also inform and refine some of the classical theories regarding justice events. For example, the *would* counterfactual in fairness theory (did an event cause harm, relative to an easily imagined alternative?) is likely to be affected by the timing, frequency, duration, and trajectory of the negative outcome(s). Likewise, whether a perpetrator *could* reasonably be expected to have acted differently will depend on whether this is an event that has occurred frequently and whether it is recalled or anticipated. In the case of future versus past events, Trope and Liberman (2003) suggest that feasibility considerations are likely to receive less attention. This suggests weaker internal attributions for wrongdoing. Even the ethical taint accompanying an event (*should* the perpetrator have acted differently?) can be less or greater depending on whether preceding events were better, worse, or the same.

Fairness theory can also be helpful in establishing the link between an event (where a transgression occurred) and the justice judgment regarding an entity (whom do we blame, and how does this affect our overall justice judgment regarding this person or organization). Indeed, the importance of events to justice perceptions lies additionally in their effects on perceptions regarding social entities, such as supervisors, departments, or organizations. It is perhaps this relationship between event judgments and entity judgments that most urgently calls for further research and for which temporal aspects of events may be particularly relevant. Thus, we echo calls from Cropanzano and colleagues (2001) and Holtz and Harold (2009) for more work on models combining event justice and entity justice, including tests of the integrative model whereby event perceptions are aggregated over time to form entity perceptions, which in turn can inform event judgments (Choi, 2008).

The relationship between entity and event justice is unlikely to be straight forward, and qualitative research by Hollensbe and colleagues (2008) illustrates some of the challenges. Hollensbe and colleagues find that interview respondents based their justice judgments not only on classical justice antecedents (such as equity or voice), but also considered attributes such as supervisor flexibility or workforce diversity. Although these additional attributes are, in fact, based on specific past events, in this case the respondents were newcomers and used these attributes as cues without having experienced or even heard about the specific events. In addition, the distinction between judgments regarding events and entities can blur when larger time scales are used and when we use the word "event" to refer to processes, such as a performance appraisal, that can extend over time. This makes it all the more important that research continue to investigate the inter-relationships over time in fairness judgments regarding events and entities. Although recent theories (Cropanzano et al., 2001; Rupp & Paddock, 2010; Jones & Skarlicki, 2013) have proposed linkages, insufficient empirical work has focused on both event and entity justice judgments at the same time.

We expect that some temporal characteristics reviewed, such as event timing, may influence whether specific events prompt justice reasoning and impact ongoing entity justice perceptions. Other temporal characteristics, such as event duration, may matter for both ongoing perceptions of entity judgments and affect whether and how individuals recall the fairness of past interactions. It is important to acknowledge that events can impact entity justice perceptions not only immediately but also retrospectively. Even to the extent that past events contribute to judgments regarding entity fairness, it is likely that some of the events contributing to entity fairness perceptions (such as a supervisor flexibly interpreting a regulation, or the organization hiring an employee of different gender or race) may at the time they were experienced not have been seen as events substantially relating to fairness. Thus, an event not originally "registered" as justice relevant may later contribute to fairness reasoning regarding an entity, as employees look back at and re-interpret their experiences, and prospectively as employees anticipate future experience with an entity.

Temporal perspective can be set either explicitly or implicitly. Managers and researchers set an explicit temporal perspective when they ask people to evaluate treatment received in the past versus in the future, to fix their attention on a specific point that is close or distant in time, or to recall or anticipate treatment during a specified period, such as "over the past/coming six months." Temporal perspective can also be present implicitly, as is often the case when entity fairness is evaluated. Situational influences can also trigger the adoption of certain temporal perspectives. Depending on the specific context, an employee evaluating a promotion system in terms of procedural fairness might direct their attention to the period since its inception, or to the period leading up to a specific promotion decision. Researchers and managers asking employees to evaluate fairness need to carefully consider whether they wish to set an explicit time horizon, and what temporal perspective they would like to learn about. To facilitate knowledge in this area, we first may need to learn what temporal perspectives people "typically" (and naturally) use to evaluate specific types of justice aspects, when not prompted by a researcher. Individual differences may also be important here (Cottle, 1968; Shipp et al., 2009).

A major challenge for research is that "objective" temporal characteristics and subjective temporal experience and dynamics are not the same thing, yet both need to be considered. For example, imagine an employee receiving an unfair performance evaluation and appealing. It is important not only to know, for example, the number of days that an employee waited for their performance appraisal appeal but also to know how the employee situates the event vis-à-vis other events. Do they regard the appraisal process as part of a larger ongoing conflict with their manager or do they see it as a stand-alone event? By carefully examining these experiences in terms of what happens in different slices of time, in the past and in the future, in clock time and in subjectively experienced time, in isolation and in relation to other events, we can develop deeper understanding of how fairness is subjectively experienced. Of course, no single study can address all these questions. However, studies should aim at including some of the different "objective" temporal facets reviewed in this chapter (trajectories, duration, timing, frequency), as well as some of the subjective temporal aspects (temporal scale, distance, and orientation). These are likely to be interlinked. Imagine, for example, that a specific injustice event is repeated several times. This could also mean that after a certain number of occurrences, future events will not be considered on their own merit, but rather in the context of all the previous occurrences (i.e., temporal scale is changed), and that at a certain "tipping point" expectations regarding future similar treatment will be triggered (temporal orientation is changed).

The possibility that events may matter to fairness reasoning not only when they occur but also from the vantage point of a later temporal perspective highlights an important practical issue for the management of justice perceptions—there may be no safe way to "cut corners" when it comes to selectively upholding fairness standards. At least not, if as we suggest, the relevance of an event to fairness judgments can change over time as it combines and is juxtaposed with other events and as it is viewed differently and from different perspectives. Many events can have unanticipated consequences in terms of fairness, if not sooner than perhaps later. Accordingly, the specific effects of temporal characteristics of events on justice perceptions and reactions are an area ripe for further theoretical development and empirical research.

Conclusion

In this chapter, research on time and justice was reviewed, and promising avenues for future research were identified. In spite of the fact that most research in organizational justice has been cross-sectional and largely atemporal, we started this chapter and end it on an optimistic note. New dynamic theories of organizational justice are not only stressing the need for further empirical investigation but also providing frameworks for organizing and integrating findings. Slowly but surely, calls for greater attention to be paid to time in justice research are being heeded. In integrating the diverse findings, we hope this chapter will stimulate further work on justice and time.

References

Adams, J. S. (1965). Inequity in social exchange. In L. Berkowitz (Ed.), *Advances in experimental social psychology* (Vol. 2, pp. 267–299). New York, NY: Academic Press.

Ambrose, M. L., & Cropanzano, R. (2003). A longitudinal analysis of organizational fairness: An examination of reactions to tenure and promotion decisions. *Journal of Applied Psychology, 88*, 266–275.

Ambrose & Schminke, (2009). The role of overall justice judgments in organizational justice research: A test of mediation. *Journal of Applied Psychology, 94*, 491–500.

Ariely, D., & Carmon, Z. (2000). Gestalt characteristics of experienced profiles. *Journal of Behavioral Decision Making, 13*, 191–201.

Baumeister, R. F., Bratslavsky, E., Finkenauer, C., & Vohs, K. D. (2001). Bad is stronger than good. *Review of General Psychology, 5*, 323–370.

Bell, B. S., Wiechmann, D., & Ryan, A. M. (2006). Consequences of organizational justice expectations in a selection system. *Journal of Applied Psychology, 91*, 455–466.

Bies, R. J. (2001). International (in)justice: The sacred and the profane. In J. Greenberg & R. Cropanzano (Eds.), *Advances in organization justice* (pp. 89–118). Palo Alto, CA: Stanford University Press.

Bies, R. J., & Moag, J. S. (1986). Interactional justice: Communication criteria of fairness. In R. Lewicki, B. H. Sheppard & M. H. Bazerman (Eds.), *Research on negotiation in organizations* (Vol. 1, pp. 43–55). Greenwich, CT: JAI Press.

Bluedorn, A. C., & Jaussi, K. S. (2008). Leaders, followers, and time. *Leadership Quarterly, 19*, 654–668.

Charnesss, G., & Levine, D. (2002). Changes in the employment contract: Evidence from a quasi-experiment. *Journal of Economic Behavior and Organization, 47*, 391–405.

Choi, J. (2008). Event justice perceptions and employees' reactions: perceptions of social entity justice as a moderator. *Journal of Applied Psychology, 93*, 513–528.

Cojuharenco, I., Fortin, M., & German, H. (2014). Organizational justice and time: A review of the literature on justice reactions over time and directions for future research. In A. Shipp & Y. Fried (Eds.), *Time and work*, Current Issues in Work and Organizational Psychology Series.

Cojuharenco, I., & Patient, D. L. (2013). Workplace fairness versus unfairness: Examining the differential salience of facets of organizational justice. *Journal of Organizational and Occupational Psychology, 86*, 371–393.

Cojuharenco, I., Patient, D. L., & Bashshur, M. (2011). Seeing the forest or the trees of organizational justice: Effects of temporal perspective on employee concerns about unfair treatment at work. *Organizational Behavior and Human Decision Processes, 116*, 17–31.

Cojuhareco, I., Van Prooijen, J. W., & Patient, D. (2013). As fa(i)r as I remember it: How social and temporal distance affect judgments of organizational justice. Working paper.

Colquitt, J. (2001). On the dimensionality of organizational justice: A construct validation of a measure. *Journal of Applied Psychology, 86*, 386–400.

Colquitt, J. A., & Chertkoff, J. M. (2002). Explaining injustice: The interactive effect of explanation and outcome on fairness perceptions and task motivation. *Journal of Management, 28*, 591–610.

Colquitt, J. A., Greenberg, J., & Zapata-Phelan, C. P. (2005). What is organizational justice? A historical overview. In J. Greenberg & J. A. Colquitt (Eds.), *Handbook of organizational justice* (pp. 59–84). Mahwah, N.J: Erlbaum.

Conlon, D. E., & Fasolo, P. M. (1990). The influence of third-party intervention and outcome on negotiator and constituent fairness judgments, *Academy of Management Journal, 33*, 833–846.

Cottle, T. J. (1968). The location of experience: A manifest time orientation. *Acta Psychologica, 28*, 129–149.

Cropanzano, R., Byrne, Z. S., Bobocel, D. R., & Rupp, D. E. (2001). Moral virtues, fairness heuristics, social entities, and other denizens of organizational justice. *Journal of Vocational Behavior, 58*, 164–209.

Cugueró-Escofet, N., Fortin, M., Canela, M. A. (2013). Righting the wrong for third parties—How monetary compensation, procedure changes and apologies can restore justice for observers of injustice. *Journal of Business Ethics, 122*, 253–268.

Davidson, M., & Friedman, R. (1998). When excuses don't work: The persistent injustice effect among black managers. *Administrative Science Quarterly, 43*, 154–183.

Devinatz, V. G., (2003). "Imagine that—a wildcat at biomed!" Organizational justice and the anatomy of a wildcat strike at a non-union medical electronics factory. *Employee Responsibilities and Rights Journal, 15*, 55–70.

Ferris. D. L., Spence, J. R., Brown, D. J., & Heller, D. (2010). Interpersonal injustice and workplace deviance: The role of esteem threat. *Journal of Management*, 38, *38*, 1788–1811.

Folger, R. (1977). Distributive and procedural justice: Combined impact of "voice" and improvement on experienced inequity. *Journal of Personality and Social Psychology, 35*, 108–119.

Fortin, M. (2008). Perspectives on organizational justice: Concept clarification, social context integration, time and links with morality. *International Journal of Management Reviews, 10*, 93–126.

Fortin, M., Cojuharenco, I., Patient, D., & German, H. (in press). It is time for justice: How time changes what we know about justice judgments and justice effects. *Journal of Organizational Behavior.*

Fortin, M., & Fellenz, M. (2008). The hypocrisies of fairness—towards a more reflexive ethical base in organizational justice research and practice. *Journal of Business Ethics, 78*, 415–433.

Gaventa, J. (1980). *Power and powerlessness: Quiescence and rebellion in an appalachian valley.* Urbana and Chicago, IL: University of Illinois Press.

George, J., & Jones, G. (2000). The role of time in theory and theory building. *Journal of Management, 26*, 657–684.

Gillespie, N., & Dietz, G. (2009). Trust repair after organization-level failure. *Academy of Management Review, 34*, 127–145.

Gilliland, S. W., & Paddock, L. (2005). Images of justice: Development of justice integration theory. In S. W. Gilliland, D. D. Steiner, & D. P Skarlicki (Eds.), *What motivates fairness in organizations?* (pp. 49–78). Greenwich, CT: Information Age.

Greenberg, J. (2001). Setting the justice agenda: Seven unanswered questions about "what, why, and how." *Journal of Vocational Behavior, 58*, 210–219.

Hausknecht, J. P., Sturman, M. C., & Roberson, Q. M. (2011). Justice as a dynamic construct: Effects of individual trajectories on distal work outcomes. *Journal of Applied Psychology, 96*, 872–880.

Hofstede, G. (2001). *Culture's consequences: Comparing values, behaviors, institutions, and organizations across nations.* Thousand Oaks, CA: Sage.

Hollensbe, E. C., Khazanchi, S., & Masterson, S. S. (2008). How do I assess if my supervisor and organization are fair? Identifying the rules underlying entity-based justice perceptions. *Academy of Management Journal, 51*, 1099–1116.

Holtz, B. C., & Harold, C. M. (2009). Fair today, fair tomorrow? A longitudinal investigation of overall justice perceptions. *Journal of Applied Psychology, 94*, 1185–1199.

Jansen, K. J., & Kristof-Brown, A. L. (2005). Marching to the beat of a different drummer: Examining the impact of pacing congruence. *Organizational Behavior and Human Decision Process, 97*, 93–105.

Jones, D., & Skarlicki, D. P. (2005). The effects of overhearing peers discuss an authority's fairness reputation on reactions to subsequent treatment. *Journal of Applied Psychology, 90*, 363–372.

Jones, D., & Skarlicki, D. P. (2013). How perceptions of fairness can change: A dynamic model of organizational justice. *Organizational Psychology Review, 3*, 138–160.

Judge, T. A., Scott, B. A., & Ilies, R. (2006). Hostility, job attitudes, and workplace deviance: Test of a multilevel model. *Journal of Applied Psychology, 91*, 126–138.

Kahneman, D. (2000). Evaluation by moments: Past and future. In D. Kahneman, & A. Tversky (Eds.), *Choices, values and frames* (pp. 693–708). Cambridge, UK: Cambridge University Press.

Kahneman, D., Wakker, P. P., & Sarin, R. (1997). Back to Bentham? Explorations of experienced utility. *Quarterly Journal of Economics, 112*, 375–405.

Kim, T. Y., & Leung, K. (2007). Forming and reacting to overall fairness: A cross-cultural comparison. *Organizational Behavior and Human Decision Processes, 104*, 83–95.

Konovsky, M. A., Folger, R., & Cropanzano, R. (1987). Relative effects of procedural and distributive justice on employee attitudes. *Representative Research in Social Psychology, 17*, 15–24.

Kulik, C., & Clark, S. (1993). Frustration effects in procedural justice research: The case of drug testing legislation. *Social Justice Research, 6*, 287–299.

Liberman, N., & Trope, Y. (2008). The psychology of transcending the here-and-now. *Science, 322*, 1201–1205.

Lilly, J. D., Virick, M., & Hadani, M. (2010). The dynamic nature of justice: Influential effects of time and work outcomes on long-term perceptions of justice. *Social Justice Research, 23*, 37–59.

Lind, E. A. (1995). Justice and authority relations in organizations. In R. S. Cropanzano, & K. M. Kacmar (Eds.), *Organizational politics, justice, and support: Managing the social climate of the workplace* (pp. 83–96). Westport, CT: Quorum Books.

Lind, E. A. (2001). Fairness heuristic theory: Justice judgments as pivotal cognitions in organizational relations. In J. Greenberg & R. Cropanzano (Eds.), *Advances in organizational justice* (pp. 56–88). Stanford, CA: Stanford University Press.

Lind, E. A., Kray, L., & Thompson, L. (2001). Primacy effects in justice judgments: Testing predications from fairness heuristic theory. *Organizational Behavior and Human Decision Processes, 85*, 189–210.

Loi, R., Yang, J., & Diefendorff, J. M. (2009). Four-factor justice and daily job satisfaction: A multilevel investigation. *Journal of Applied Psychology, 94*, 770–781.

McGrath, J. E., & Tschan, F. (2004). *Temporal Matters in Social Psychology: Examining the role of time in the lives of groups and individuals.* Washington DC: APA Publications.

Melkonian, T., Soenen, G., & Ambrose, M. L. (2012). *The role of anticipatory justice perceptions on employees' cooperation in a merger context.* Paper presented at the *Workshop on Research Advances in Organizational Behavior and Human Resources Management*, Dauphine Université, Paris.

Mesch, D. J., & Dalton, D. R. (1992). Unexpected consequences of improving workplace justice: A six-year time series assessment. *Academy of Management Journal, 35*, 1099–1114.

Moorman, R. H. (1991). Relationship between organizational justice and organizational citizenship behaviors: Do fairness perceptions influence employee citizenship? *Journal of Applied Psychology, 76*, 845–855.

Mullen, E. (2007). The reciprocal relationship between affect and perceptions of fairness. In K. Tornblom & R. Vermunt (Eds.), *Distributive and procedural justice: Research and social implications* (pp. 15–38). Farnham, UK: Ashgate.

Paterson, J. M., Green, A., & Cary, J. (2002). The measurement of organizational justice in organizational change programmes: A reliability, validity and context-sensitivity assessment. *Journal of Occupational and Organizational Psychology, 75*, 393–408.

Patient, D., Sguera, F., and Saldanha, M. F. (2013). Past fairness, future fairness: Procedural justice expectations during times of change. Working paper.

Robbins, T. L., Summers, T. P., & Miller, J. L. (2000). Intra- and inter-justice relationships: Assessing the direction. *Human Relations, 53*, 1329–1355.

Rodell, J. B., & Colquitt, J. A. (2009). Looking ahead in times of uncertainty: The role of anticipatory justice in organizational change context. *Journal of Applied Psychology, 94*, 989–1002.

Roe, R. A. (2008). Time in applied psychology: The study of "what happens" rather than "what is". *European Psychologist, 13*, 37–52.

Ross, M., & Sicoly, F. (1979). Egocentric biases in availability and attribution. *Journal of Personality and Social Psychology, 37*, 322–336.

Rupp, D. E. (2011). An employee-centered model of organizational justice and social responsibility. *Organizational Psychology Review, 1*, 72–94.

Rupp, D. E., & Paddock, E. L. (2010). From justice events to justice climate: A multilevel temporal model of information aggregation and judgment. In E. A. Mannix, M. A. Neale, & E. Mullen (Eds.), *Fairness and groups: Research on managing groups and teams* (Vol. 13, pp. 245–273). Bingley, UK: Emerald.

Sapienza, H. J., & Korsgaard, M. A. (1996). Procedural justice in entrepreneur-investor relations. *Academy of Management Journal, 39*, 544–574.

Schacter, D. (2001). *The seven sins of memory: How the mind forgets and remembers*. Boston, MA: Houghton Mifflin.

Shapiro, D. L., & Kirkman, B. L. (1999). Employees' reaction to the change to work teams: The influence of "anticipatory" injustice. *Journal of Organizational Change Management, 12*, 51–66.

Shapiro, D. L., & Kirkman, B. L. (2001). Anticipatory injustice: The consequences of expecting injustice in the workplace. In J. Greenberg & R. Cropanzano (Eds.), *Advances in organizational justice* (pp. 152–178). Lexington, MA: New Lexington.

Shipp, A. J., Edwards, J. R., & Schurer Lambert, L. (2009). Conceptualization and measurement of temporal focus: The subjective experience of the past, present, and future. *Organizational Behavior and Human Decision Processes, 110*, 1–22.

Soenen, G., Melkonian, T., & Ambrose, M. L. (2012). The dynamics of justice judgments during organizational change: The antecedents and consequences of phase-shifting perceptions. Presented at *International Round Table on Innovations in Research on Organizational Justice*, Nice, France.

Trope, Y., & Liberman, N. (2003). Temporal construal. *Psychological Review, 110*, 403–421.

Trope, Y., Liberman, N., & Wakslak, C. (2007). Construal levels and psychological distance: Effects on representation, prediction, evaluation, and behavior. *Journal of Consumer Psychology, 17*, 83–95.

Tyler, T. R., & Lind, E. A. (1992). A relational model of authority in groups. *Advances in Experimental Social Psychology, 25*, 115–191.

Van den Bos, K. (2001). Uncertainty management: The influence of uncertainty salience on reactions to perceived procedural fairness. *Journal of Personality and Social Psychology, 80*, 931–941.

Van den Bos, K., Burrows, J. W., Umphress, E., Folger, R., Lavelle, J. J., Eaglestone, J., & Gee, J. (2005). Prior experiences as temporal frames of reference in social justice: The influence of previous fairness experiences on reactions to new and old supervisors. *Social Justice Research, 18*, 99–120.

Van den Bos, K., Vermunt, R., & Wilke, H. (1997). Procedural and distributive justice: What is fair depends more on what comes first than on what comes next. *Journal of Personality and Social Psychology, 72*, 95–104.

Weiss, H. M., & Cropanzano, R. (1996). Affective events theory: A theoretical discussion of the structure, causes and consequences of affective experiences at work. *Research in Organizational Behavior, 18*, 1–74.

Zimbardo, P., & Boyd, J. (1999). Putting time in perspective: A valid, reliable individual differences metric. *Journal of Personality and Social Psychology, 77*, 1271–1288.

PART 3

Psychological Processes and Motivation

CHAPTER

15 Justice and Deonance: "You Ought to Be Fair"

Robert Folger *and* David R. Glerum

Abstract

This chapter relates justice to *deonance*, or the psychology of behaviors required or forbidden by social codes of conduct (prescriptive and proscriptive duties), versus those that are permitted (rights). Initial sections review the origins of deonance as a perspective on organizational justice and then discuss subsequent developments—some of which connect directly to that original formulation and some of which are related concepts. The subsequent analysis looks forward rather than backward in the sense of tracing historical roots. On the one hand it revisits the conceptual foundation and extends it by noting some additional implications. On the other hand it goes beyond mere extensions of the original by suggesting some new directions. In particular, these indicate how a deonance perspective encompasses more than the justice phenomena that had been its source.

Key Words: deonance, organizational justice, duty, rights, morality, ethics, self-interest, reactance, bounded autonomy

> "[B]ehavior becomes a norm in the sense that the individuals think the behavior *ought* to be performed or that one has a *right* to perform the behavior."
>
> —Opp, 2004, p. 13

This is a two-layer chapter. The first layer is the foundation. It reviews the origins of deonance as a perspective on organizational justice, and then it discusses subsequent developments—some of which connect directly to that original formulation and some of which are related concepts. The second layer adds to the first in a different way. On the one hand it revisits the conceptual foundation and extends it by noting some additional implications On the other hand it goes beyond mere extensions of the original by suggesting some new directions. In particular, these indicate how a deonance perspective encompasses more than the justice phenomena that had been its source.

Beginnings, Extensions, and Parallel Developments: Looking Back on Deonance-Out-of-Justice

A Personal Note

The origins of deonance are best described autobiographically—in this subsection only—by the first author. I invented the word *deonance* (Folger, 2001) by drawing on the Greek root *deon*, translated variously as duty, obligation, and the like. There were several reasons why I decided to coin a new term. First, it's always easier to stipulate the meaning you want to go with a new construct when the name for it is not already taken by another construct. Second, I wanted to stress how it might be conceptualized as a psychological state along the lines of reactance (Brehm, 1966) and dissonance (Festinger, 1957). Third, I wanted to draw attention to the novelty and distinctiveness of a perspective on justice that might serve as an alternative to those existing at the time. In particular, that meant stressing how people might sometimes behave if they felt they had an obligation to be fair and to hold other people accountable to standards of justice (to respond toward other people as if they also had a duty to be fair).

In my view, fairness as an interpersonal obligation needed some attention because the very meaning of fairness was jeopardized by the assumptions of the existing approaches to justice. The theory of inequity (Adams, 1965) had included a duty-like hypothesis that people could feel guilty about receiving more than their due (being in a position called *advantageous inequity*) and that they might feel an obligation to re-align the situation in accord with distributive justice. Unfortunately, however, equity theory (Walster, Bersheid, & Walster, 1973) instead stipulated that seeking distributive justice was actually derived from concerns about one's own outcomes or was even merely a version of self-interest in disguise (during the same era, one early advocate of an extreme socio-biological doctrine had commented that you could "scratch an 'altruist' and see a 'hypocrite' bleed"; Ghiselin, 1974, p. 247.).

A self-interested outlook on fairness was perpetuated by the Thibaut and Walker (1975) approach to procedural justice, which described a disputant's "process control" as a supplement to the "decision control" of someone arbitrating a dispute. Disputants' participation in the decision-making process was said to give them a sense of control because they would see it as a chance to influence the outcome in directions favoring their own interests. I was uncomfortable at the time with the control terminology, so I substituted the term *voice* in my procedural justice research (Folger, 1977) because I thought its connotations were more neutral with respect to any implied assumptions about the psychological mechanisms involved.

Tyler and Lind (1992) also sought to move beyond an interpretation of procedural justice in terms of self-interested efforts to influence the outcome of a dispute. They reasoned that the fairness of a procedure might reassure people of their inclusion within a group important to one's self-identity (reinforcing self-image, feelings of self-worth and self-esteem, etc.). To me, this still posited a reliance on the assumption that people would react negatively to an unfair procedure because it produced a form of deprivation from a self-interested standpoint—a decline in the self's social standing as it were, even if not a deprivation of tangible resources per se.

Two things always struck me as ironic about that approach. First, Tyler and Lind (1992) said their model was an alternative to the Thibaut and Walker (1975) perspective, which they called an *instrumental model*. It seemed to me that evaluating procedures according to the effects on self-esteem was still evaluating them on instrumental grounds (judging a procedure's fairness based on how instrumental it was in sustaining one's self-esteem). Second, it seemed odd to assume that what a procedure implied about an affected party's worthiness, vis-à-vis symbolic inclusion in the group, would drive perceptions about the procedure's fairness, rather than perceptions about *the person in charge* of the procedure (e.g., as corrupt, callous, and so on).

For those reasons, I was always impressed by the research findings obtained by Kahneman, Knetsch, and Thaler (1986). They studied the reactions of people to someone else's decision when they were not directly affected by it. These research participants acted in opposition to their own self-interest in order to punish the other person's unfair decision-making. Carmelo Turillo was a doctoral student in a seminar of mine when we covered the Kahneman et al. (1986) research. He saw some methodological improvements worth trying, which we implemented in a string of studies that replicated the original results in an overwhelming way (Turillo, Folger, Lavelle, Umphress, & Gee, 2002). Part of the objective was to add one design feature after another to eliminate every possible form of self-interest we could imagine. When I thought we'd done that successfully, a co-author—Jim Lavelle—asked me what was going on if it was *not* self-interest. Thinking about that question led me to posit the psychological state of deonance as an experience based on considering fairness to be important in and of itself. To put it another way, I presumed that people think of fair treatment (whether in the form of distributive, procedural, or interactional justice) as something we owe one another, so my label for the underlying mechanism was a neologism whose Greek influence reflected that assumption.

I now regret some things I wrote about deonance at the outset, and correcting for them is one thing I hope this chapter will accomplish. For example, our title for those original findings referred to "virtue" as its own "reward" (Turillo et al., 2002). That might be a problem if someone assumed we had adopted a virtue ethic position, or if referring to a reward were taken to imply a self-interested outcome in the sense of virtue as the means to obtaining a reward. I also want to address another term that has cropped up from time to time—"deontic justice" (e.g., Cropanzano, Goldman, & Folger, 2003; Folger & Skarlicki, 2008)—lest it be misconstrued. As mentioned eariler, deonance is, in fact, a perspective that need not be restricted to topics addressed under the rubric of organizational justice; the concept of deonance is independent from the concept of justice.

I also want to make sure than no one associates deonance with the ethical philosophy known as deontology (e.g., referring to deonance as a deontological perspective). First, the features of the numerous variations on that philosophy have nothing to do with deonance, and vice versa. Second, deonance is independent of deontology in a very important way. One of the connotations sometimes associated with deontology is that it refers to a duty-based ethic, and it is in that respect differentiated from utilitarianism as an ethic focused on consequences (e.g., the greatest good for the greatest number) rather than duty. Deonance does have a bearing on duty, but it's quite possible for people to perceive a duty (directed toward themselves or others) in terms of bringing about certain types of consequences. Moreover, deonance is descriptive and empirically oriented, whereas ethical philosophies, such as deontology and consequentialism, are normative. For example, deonance applied to organizational justice issues is about people's *perceived* obligations regarding distributive, procedural, interpersonal, or informational justice. In fact, some of the research on each of those types of justice has dealt with the perceived *norms* that people have (e.g., about the role of voice in procedures; what kind of appeal process should be established; whether the proper distributive norm in a given context is equity, equality, or need). The essence of a norm is that it says what *ought* to be the case, and deonance is about perceived "oughts."

Deonance and Its Conceptual Cousins

Theorizing about deonance has been pursued in a number of articles or chapters (Cropanzano, Goldman, & Folger, 2003, 2005; Folger, 2001, 2011; Folger & Butz, 2004; Folger & Cropanzano, 2010; Folger, Cropanzano, & Goldman, 2005; Folger & Salvador, 2008; Folger & Skarlicki, 2005, 2008; Greenbaum, Folger, & Ford, 2011; Salvador & Folger, 2009; Turillo et al., 2002). Prior to the introduction of deonance, organizational justice research typically involved a strong emphasis focused on self-interest as a motive and neglected to consider moral or ought-based mechanisms for justice (Cropanzano et al., 2005; Folger, 2001; Folger & Salvador, 2008). In addition, several authors have drawn upon deontic concepts through explication of their own theoretical frameworks. Cropanzano, Byrne, Bobocel, and Rupp (2001) included the "need for meaning," or a "deontic model of justice" (Crawshaw, Cropanzano, Bell, & Nadisic, 2013) as a component of a multiple-needs model of organizational justice. The deontic component highlights the force of values, virtues, or norms as guiding ought forces in organizational justice. An additional application of deonance can be found in O'Reilly and Aquino's (2011) theoretical model of third-party reactions to injustice in which awareness of mistreatment is followed by an intuition of moral violation, which is, in turn, followed by moral anger and justice cognitions. In this model, centrality of moral identity (Aquino & Reed, 2002) also plays a role in moderating the relationships between awareness and intuition as well as between intuition and moral anger.

Prior justice theories have been organized by harkening to a series of metaphors, namely, homo economicus (e.g., self-interest), homo socialis (e.g., relational), and homo moralis (e.g., deonance), which specify overarching human motives to behavior, the last of which is concerned with right and wrong conceptions (Hegtvedt & Scheuerman, 2010; Skitka, Aramovich, Lytle, & Sargis, 2009). Similarly, Skitka and Wisneski (2012) mention a series of additional metaphors for justice approaches positing people as intuitive economists, politicians, scientists, prosecutors, and theologians in terms of ethical decision-making and interpreting justice concerns. Thierry Nadisic (2006) recently arranged these diverse moral and self-interest-driven motives into a hierarchical typology separated by those based on automatic versus rational processes. Nadisic notes that deonance is a second-order, metamotive that is primarily morally driven and based on automatic processes.

Linda Skitka and colleagues have given moral considerations a central role in the value protection model (Mullen & Skitka, 2006; Skitka, 2002; Skitka & Mullen, 2002) and the accessible identity model (Skitka, 2003; Skitka & Bravo, 2005). The former grounds moral decision-making in a sense of self through an emphasis on individual positions as moral convictions or mandates (see also Skitka & Houston, 2001). The latter emphasizes how the activation of relevant values and goals is governed by an aspect of one's self-concept. In the newest instantiation of the importance of moral conviction, Skitka and colleagues have advanced an integrated theory of moral conviction, which holds that moral convictions are strong and differ from other attitudes through a distinction between preferences, normative conventions, and morality (Skitka, 2010, 2014; Skitka, Bauman, & Mullen, 2008). This integrated theory of moral conviction has been applied to studies of leadership and compliance to authority (Skitka, Bauman, & Lytle, 2008, 2009), voice in procedural justice (Bauman & Skitka, 2009), religiosity and trust (Wisneski, Lytle, & Skitka, 2009), and moral courage (Skitka, 2012). Prior to introducing these models, Skitka and Tetlock (1992) forwarded a norm-driven theory of distributive justice in which determining whether there is a fair distribution of resources is contingent upon attributions of why claimants need help, whether they deserve to be helped, and whether they should have a priority to be helped (see also Skitka, McMurray, & Burroughs, 1991; Skitka & Tetlock, 1993a, 1993b). This work suggests that normative "ought forces" are important in distributive justice considerations beyond the establishment of equilibrium or acting in self-interest. Furthermore, the more recent work on moral mandates and moral conviction highlights the importance of norms in guiding ethical decision-making.

Beyond moral conviction, moral identity, and the multiple-needs model, a variety of other theoretical frameworks have incorporated deonance or deontic elements (in the way this chapter describes them). These include Skarlicki and Kulik's (2005) model of third-party reactions to employee mistreatment; Colquitt, Scott, Judge, and Shaw's (2006) exploration of individual differences in deontic anger expression and response; Beugré's (2009, 2010) models of neuro-organizational justice and deontic-justice model of organizational corruption; Rupp's (2011) employee-centered model of organizational justice; Barsky, Kaplan, and Beal's (2011) process model of affective context and fairness perceptions; and Jones and Skarlicki's (2013) dynamic model of organizational justice. These theories draw on deonance to potentially assist in explaining a multitude of aspects of organizational justice.

Deonance, Protected Values, Sacred Values, and Taboo Trade-offs

Perhaps the closest conceptual cousin to deonance can be found in Jonathan Baron and colleagues' protected values and Philip Tetlock and colleagues' sacred values (Baron & Ritov, 2009; Baron & Spranca, 1997; Tetlock, 1999; Tetlock, Peterson, & Lerner, 1996). Protected values are those that are based on rules for action, which people resist violating or trading off with other values (Baron & Spranca, 1997; Ritov & Baron, 1999). Relatedly, sacred values add an element of transcendental significance and isolation from secular values while also prohibiting trade-offs (Tetlock, 2003). Both sacred and protected values are closely related to deonance, and by nature they are predicated on a resistance to violating values, no matter the costs. This suggests that violating the value opens one to scorn, contempt, and reprehension by those who hold the value, even in the face of consequentialist reasoning. The resistance of sacred and protected values to consequentialist reasoning can be demonstrated by the employee who will not steal from the company (as a value) no matter the consequences (providing for his malnourished family). Although protected values are resistant to consequentialist reasoning, Tanner, Medin, and Iliev (2008) have demonstrated that the willingness to make a risky decision depends on the interplay between framing effects as a gain or loss, whether one adopts the protected value, if it is an act or omission, and if one tends to be oriented toward consequentialist thinking. Even if one adopts a protected value, if the situation is framed in a way that suggests a loss and if the individual making the decision holds a consequentialist orientation, they tend to gravitate toward the risky decision (Tanner et al., 2008). This qualified Tanner and Medin's (2004) finding that those who hold protected values tend to be resistant in general to riskiness or certainty in ethical decision-making to include consequentialist orientation. Regardless, protected values were relatively highly correlated with a deontological orientation, suggesting that they are closely related (Tanner et al., 2008).

The normative forces underlying the prohibition or reluctance of violating sacred and protected values suggests a similarity with deonance, as both are grounded in the notion that normative ought forces serve to guide behavior. One example of a protected value in organizational contexts is the notion of exploitative child labor (Ritov & Baron, 1999). The underpayment, subjugation, and mistreatment of children in organizations would be considered by many to be a value that resists trade-off with other values (e.g., maximized production, increased profits, minimized selection costs). Baron and Spranca (1997) note that these values have certain properties, namely that the quantity of consequences is irrelevant (e.g., child labor should not be implemented regardless of whether profits would be increased by $1.00 or $300,000,000.00 as a result of the action), although data suggesting that the quantity might be relevant have been provided by Bartels and Medin (2007); that they are agent relative (e.g., one would only feel directly responsible for preventing child labor from being implemented in one's organization as a participating decision maker or stakeholder); they are seen as moral obligations (e.g., people are morally obligated not to exploitatively conscript children to work); people tend to think they are impervious to trade-offs (e.g., people deny that child labor would be permissible under conditions such as the only way to provide food, shelter, and clothing for the laborer's family); and people tend to become angry at the idea of a violated protected value.

Ritov and Baron (1999) expanded the idea of protected values to demonstrate through a series of experiments that protected values will tend to show an omission bias in trade-offs, which suggests that people are more concerned with harms associated with violating a protected value through action, rather than through omission (see also Ritov & Baron, 1990, 1992; Spranca, Minsk, & Baron, 1991). For example, with regard to child labor laws, people would be more concerned with the action of buying a product from or stock in an organization that has been known to engage in child labor practices as opposed to the omission of such an action. Ritov and Baron (1999) noted that measuring omission bias is usually accomplished through having the participant establish the threshold between levels of harm for commission of an act while holding the level of harm for an omission constant (e.g., an organization conscripts 4,000 children worldwide to work in sweatshops; how much money would you have to earn before you would allow investing in that organization?). Baron (2000) revised the prior trade-off measurement approach by recommending that trade-offs be elicited through prompting participants to resolve their inconsistencies by determining which of the two options is worse and in turn specifying which quantity of either amount would have to be increased or decreased in order to make the two equivalent. However, people still tend to believe that these situations of resolving inconsistencies between values do not occur in real life, despite findings that their invocation is dependent on the magnitude of the violation (Baron & Leshner, 2000). In addition to an omission bias, Baron and Ritov (2004) have also provided evidence for the existence for the opposite, an action bias, to occur. They note that with regard to this bias, it is likely to stem from a reaction to inaction and passivity. Similarly, Tanner and Medin (2004) did not find evidence for omission bias but did find a bias toward actions and also noted that those with strong protected values were immune to framing effects. Beliefs of human nature (Bain, Kashima, & Haslam, 2006) as well as the endorsement of moral rules and thinking style (Bartels, 2008) have also been shown to affect perceptions of protected values and willingness to commit trade-offs.

In a similar fashion, The Sacred-Value-Protection Model (SVPM) suggests that moral outrage wrought with anger, disgust, and contempt follows observing the violation of a sacred value. These violations can come in the form of actual or "entertained" commissions of taboo trade-offs, forbidden base rates, and heretical counterfactuals (Tetlock, Kristel, Elson, Green, and Learner, 2000). Taboo trade-offs occur in a similar fashion to the trade-offs between protected values and can result in eliciting negative emotions (Hanselmann & Tanner, 2008; e.g., attaching a monetary value of benefit to the neglect of organizational justice concerns). Hanselmann and Tanner (2008) note that the type of trade-off also makes a difference, and tragic trade-offs that involve choosing between two sacred values are perceived as extremely difficult and stressful, whereas routine trade-offs involving no violation of sacred values are fairly easy to commit. Entertaining or drawing on forbidden base rates also posit a violation of sacred values, because these are empirical generalizations that are morally offensive as they suggest religious, political, racial, ethnic, or gender insensitivity (e.g., lower cognitive ability test scores for people of different backgrounds). Lastly, heretical counterfactuals are those that cross normative boundaries through heretical what-if speculation by violating religious or political norms, especially with regard to founders of movements (e.g., the suggestion that Steve Jobs has been described as ruthless, narcissistic, and abrasive by some may be considered a heretical counterfactual). Furthermore, even just thinking about or entertaining the idea of a taboo trade-off, heretical counterfactual, or forbidden base rate can cause one to engage in acts of moral cleansing and atonement to make up for a sense of impurity

(Tetlock, 1999; Tetlock et al., 2000). Relatedly, in some taboo trade-off situations, people refuse to make a choice altogether (Lichtenstein, Gregory, & Irwin, 2007).

Because normative ought forces underlie our propensity to uphold and resist trade-offs and uphold our own values and mandates, it is perhaps tempting to conclude that sacred and protected values, tragic and taboo trade-offs, moral mandates, and deonance are all referencing explicitly similar phenomena. However, deonance diverges from these traditions of moral psychology in its conceptualization of ought forces. Whereas sacred and protected values, tragic and taboo trade-offs, and moral mandates are rigidly resistant to violations and grounded in inviolable principles, deonance, on the other hand, suggests that ought forces can be multidirectional and multidimensional in nature. Sacred values, protected values, and moral mandates are only violated or traded off with much hesitation. This trade-off point results in a threshold that treats the acceptability of an action or its omission as a dichotomous, "all-or-nothing" phenomenon. This absolute focus on the avoidance of value or mandate violation can perhaps be considered as proscriptive (rather than prescriptive) in nature, focusing on the avoidance of the commission of a harmful or wrong action (Janoff-Bulman & Carnes, 2013; Janoff-Bulman, Sheikh, & Hepp, 2009). These moral frameworks rarely provide direction that is prescriptive in nature or focused on the action itself or on what we should do (cf. Baron & Ritov, 2004; Tanner & Medin, 2004). For example, child labor as a sacred value, protected value, or moral mandate would posit that child labor should be avoided at all costs, and only with much reluctance would this constraint be lifted. This is also implicit in the agent-relativity characteristic of protected values; as Baron and Spranca (1997) note, assuming the responsibility for enforcing a protected value at all times and across all situations would be next to impossible.

Deonance would treat ought forces underlying the moral permissiveness or rightness of child labor as dimensional and not absolutely inviolable. The rightness of an action with respect to deonance could be clarified with the introduction of "switching variables." These can be thought of as contextual or situational characteristic variables that act as boundary conditions and alter one's perception of the rightness of an action. Their presence or absence in any given context or situation could alter perceptions of the rightness of an action. For example, with regard to child labor, exploitative procedural measures taken to employ children could typically be regarded as switching variables that would make such a practice impermissible. These might include making children work long hours, keeping them away from school, exposing them to excessively burdensome labor or work, abusing or unduly coercing them into working, and severely underpaying them, which would result in poverty. On the other hand, child labor or work involving voluntary employment, not interfering with school, commensurate with the child's abilities, in assistance with a family business, or to teach the "value of money" as a part of learning (e.g., a lemonade stand or a paperboy/girl position) could be considered as not only permissible aspects of a developmental experience, but as a valuable developmental milestone for children. Sacred values, protected values, or moral mandates perhaps apply multiple constraints on situations (à la switching variables) to craft principles that others would rarely deem permissible and that are resistant to trade-offs. Deonance recognizes these switching variables and the dimensional nature of ought forces as opposed to conceptualizing rightness and wrongness as a dichotomous condition or value that transcends situational or contextual variations. In addition to the rightness considerations levied in deonance, sacred and protected values, tragic and taboo trade-offs, and moral mandates, moral emotions play a large role in their emergence with moral reasoning and behavior often accompanied with emotions of deontic anger, outrage, disgust, guilt, and impurity, among others. In the following section, the role of emotions in deonance and justice will be explicated.

The Role of Moral Emotions

Moral emotions are inextricably linked to the experience of injustice, whether as a recipient, a transgressor, or a third-party observer. Moral emotions are laden with considerations of others' interests or welfare and thus provide a motivational impetus for engaging in right and wrong behaviors (Haidt, 2003b, Tangney, Stuewig, & Mashek, 2007). Bies and Tripp (2001) note that "the experience of injustice is 'hot and passionate,' reflecting the intense and personal pain of a violated psyche and sense of self" (p. 202). Furthermore, adhering to or violating moral standards can result in either positive or negative affective states, respectively (Cropanzano & Rupp, 2002; Tangney et al., 2007). Dimensions of emotion may be present during all components of ethical decision-making (Rest, 1986, 1994), with arousal and feeling states permeating sensitivity to ethical issues and prescriptive reasoning (Gaudine & Thorne, 2001). Others, like Jonathan Haidt, have taken a social-intuitionist approach and suggest that moral intuitions and emotions preclude or cause moral judgments (Haidt, 2001, 2003a). Haidt (2003b) outlined two separate components of moral emotions: elicitors (i.e., triggering events or conditions) and action tendencies (i.e., a form of behavioral response coupled with or following the experience of the moral emotion). These emotional components are important in understanding the link between injustice experiences, the experience of moral emotions, and the behavioral reactions people exhibited along with these experiences.

Why do we experience such strong emotions in conjunction with our experiences with justice or injustice? Fiske (2002) argues that the experience of emotion serves to inspire action with the ultimate adaptive goals of relationship maintenance and upkeep function. Furthermore, he argues that it was adapted for emergencies—emotions help us buy time through an evolutionarily resourceful situational assessment and subsequent behavior (Fiske, 2004). Anger may have served an evolutionary purpose to cause those who were threatened to leap to the defense of their own resources and loved ones (Fiske, 2002; Folger & Skarlicki, 2008). Furthermore, Salvador and Folger (2009) outlined the neurobiological basis supporting the critical role of emotion in ethical decision-making in their review of emerging themes in neuroethics. In particular, the role of anger has been linked to certain brain regions by localizing the function of anger to the RAGE system; humans can experience anger and uncontrollable retaliatory urges (Folger & Skarlicki, 2005; Panksepp, 1998). The evolutionary and adaptive bases along with advancements in neuroethics support the notion that we have evolutionarily adaptive emotional responses to injustice.

With regard to deonance, the primary moral emotion experienced as the result of directly experiencing injustice or in a breach of a moral contract (Greenbaum et al., 2011) as a recipient or third-party observer is the deontic response (see also deontic state, righteous anger, or moral antipathy). The deontic response is characterized by outrage, fury, hostility, resentment, and anger (Folger, 1998, 2001; Folger & Butz, 2004; Folger, Cropanzano, & Goldman, 2005; Folger & Skarlicki, 2005). As a result of the deontic response, organizational retaliatory behaviors (ORB) or deontic retaliation can occur as the behavioral manifestation, or as the action tendency following the elicitor (Haidt, 2003b). Folger and Skarlicki (2005) suggest that the deontic response is rooted in an adaptive function of imposing a check on rampant powers that some might try to take—to hold transgressors morally accountable for violating moral standards. Relatedly, Rozin, Lowery, Imada, and Haidt (1999) note that the experience of anger is linked to violations of individual rights in their Contempt Anger and Disgust (CAD) triad hypothesis. The deontic response occurs as an automatic response to injustice, can be irrational in nature, sees retribution as an end in itself, factors in mechanisms for reconciliation, and treats emotion as the driver of behavior (Folger et al., 2005; Folger & Skarlicki, 2008). Although the deontic response is automatic, it can also result in rumination in which the injustice stagnates and hangs around to the point of obsession, although its intensity can vary and taper off over time (Folger & Skarlicki, 2008). Furthermore, the deontic response should be seen as a social, interpsychic, and intrapsychic process in which emotional states between people are interdependent (Folger et al., 2005). Folger and Cropanzano (2010) drew upon Boehm's (1999) ambivalence-compromise model to highlight the impact of the social hierarchy in the context of deonance, which posits that we attempt to strike a compromise between social dominance and submission. As such, combinations of the nature of our duties, as well as the moral impetus of restraint of self versus the constraints imposed by others, guide the emergence of moral emotions such as guilt, shame, resentment, and indignation (Folger & Cropanzano, 2010).

Guilt and shame could also play a role in understanding deonance and the moral emotions surrounding the transgressors behind the commission of injustice (Eisenberg, 2000; Folger et al., 2005). Weiss, Suckow, and Cropanzano (1999) suggest that this might be true in conditions in which one is benefiting from a positive outcome of a favorably biased procedure. The experience of guilt in these situations might lead the individual who benefited from the injustice to seek atonement or reparation (Gausel & Brown, 2012; Tangney et al., 2007). A related emotion of disgust could emerge, and this is related to violations of purity, which may occur in situations in which the unjust act involves violation of human rights (e.g., disgust toward sweatshop worker conditions; Rozin et al., 1999). Overall, moral emotions (especially deontic anger) play a major role in the experience of injustice in organizations, serving as the evolutionarily and neurobiologically grounded impetus for retaliatory responses. Establishing anger as an experienced moral emotion preceding retaliatory behaviors has been important to advancing empirical work on deonance.

Empirical Work on Deonance

Along with theoretical work on deonance theory over the past decade, empirical evidence is beginning to emerge providing support for deonance and moral considerations as an alternative to self-interest motives as well as support for its cross-cultural significance (e.g., Shao, Rupp, Skarlicki, & Jones, 2013). The work of Turillo et al. (2002), in which people sacrificed self-interest in order to punish others' moral violations, suggests that people are not consistently driven toward maximizing personal gain. This study was an early indicator of the opposing nature of ought forces: although motivated to distribute resources to individuals based on effort and merit (efficiency), ought forces may drive a compromise when other citizens are in danger of lapsing into poverty as a result of the decision. Similarly, Johansson and Svedsäter (2009) found that fairness motives were weaker in a reward allocation task when payoff level was determined by a coin flip, suggesting that external factors or internal norms were in play. Retaliatory behaviors against self-interest coupled with a deontic response can also occur for employee perceptions of supervisor rudeness when employees reduce their performance to "punish" the supervisor (Porath & Erez, 2007; Porath, MacInnis, & Folkes, 2011), through forms of retaliation (Mitchell & Ambrose, 2012), and in third-party reactions to abusive supervision (Mitchell, Vogel, & Folger, in press). Typically, deonance has been inferred through interpretation of the effects of experimental manipulations, although recent work by Beugré (2012) involved the development and validation of a scale for measuring deontic justice, which has shown initial evidence for construct validity. Future research regarding the scale's psychometric properties and criterion-related validity would further improve and broaden the methods for deonance research.

Additional support for deonance can be found in studies on the nature of the deontic response and moral cognition. Upon witnessing (as a third-party) or personally being affected by a moral norm-violating behavior, a deontic response may follow that manifests as deontic anger or fury. For example, Barclay, Skarlicki, and Pugh (2005) found that negative emotions varied as a function of justice violation and outcome favorability for layoff victims, with different observed interactions for the experience of shame and guilt and of anger and hostility, both as sets of emotions reflecting accountability for moral standards (Folger, Cropanzano, & Goldman, 2005). Spencer and Rupp (2009) also provide support for deonance (and fairness theory) as they found increased emotional labor for workers when observing unfairness toward employees by customers (which was mediated by deontic anger and counterfactual thinking). Skarlicki and Rupp (2010) explored the effect of rational and experiential processing frames on retribution tendencies. When adopting a rational frame, individuals reported lower retribution tendencies. On the other hand, those high in moral identity tended to be less affected by the framing procedure. This suggests that when norms guiding perceptions of morally consistent behaviors are strong enough, the automatic processes engaged in engendering a deontic response and subsequent consistent reaction are strong to the point of overriding a rational frame.

In a study examining the retaliation of layoff victims, the perceptions of employer integrity and perceived sincerity helped clarify the informational justice-retaliation relationship (Skarlicki, Barclay, & Pugh, 2008). These results suggest that employee attempts to set the record straight with their employer through retaliation were diminished when the employer was perceived as having integrity and sincerity, under conditions of informational justice (i.e., removing conditions that may lead to perceptions of unfairness may reduce deontic anger and retaliation). Additional attitudinal and perceptual information like this has been shown to inform moral decision-making and is consistent with a deontic perspective in that the perpetrator then becomes a target of interest for the observer. Bell and Main (2011) acknowledged that people are deontically motivated to seek out information regarding the perpetrator regardless of decision relevance, valence of the information, and other factors, as well as by ruling out distrust as a motivator. Even the mere intention of causing injustice can generate negative reactions in observers without an explicit victim (Umphress, Simmons, Folger, Ren, & Bobocel, 2013). Furthermore, the process of fairness judgments can be automatic and, once primed, have the potential to influence one's own fairness toward a third party (Zdaniuk & Bobocel, 2013). This is consistent with a deonance perspective, because fairness perceptions of a leader primed fairness behaviors with a third party, perhaps demonstrating compliance with an observed fairness norm.

Ideology, values, norms, self-regulation, moral development, and moral identity have contributed to the understanding of deonance and its manifestations in the experience of the deontic response and the expression of reactionary behaviors. Goldman et al. (2008a) demonstrated that perceived justice was related negatively to "ideological-based perceptions," or perceptions of the involvement of moral principles and human decency, in claimants of EEOC-sponsored mediation cases. Goldman, Slaughter, Schmit, Wiley, and Brooks (2008b) linked perceptions of discrimination strongly and negatively to deontic need fulfillment in their application of the multiple-needs model to explaining the relationship between perceived discrimination with experienced job attitudes and turnover intentions. Furthermore, Triana, Wagstaff, and Kim (2012) found that those who value diversity tend to react more strongly to perceived discrimination reflecting moral accountability and norm compliance as components of deonance and justice (Folger, 2001). Rupp and Bell (2010) extended the deontic model of justice to suggest that sometimes (depending on the person and situation), the deontic response might actually trigger inaction. They found evidence for this in individuals who engaged in moral self-regulation (as coded from verbal protocols). Skarlicki, van Jaarsveld, and Walker (2008) found support for inaction as an alternative to retaliation following deontic response in a study seeking to determine for whom customer-instigated interpersonal injustice inspires customer-directed sabotage. This study examined moral identity as a potential moderating factor and found that the relationship depends on whether employees internalize or symbolize their behavior (Aquino & Reed, 2002). Similarly, employees higher in moral identity may engage in nonretributive or constructive forms of action (Greenbaum, Mawritz, Mayer, & Priesemuth, 2013).

Overall, deonance has benefited from a decade of theoretical refinement, empirical examination, and incorporation as an explanatory mechanism for organizational justice theories. There is still much empirical and theoretical work to be done, but the advances so far have been informative and promising. In the next section, deonance will be further illustrated and characterized by moving beyond the domain of organizational justice.

Looking Ahead to Deonance-Beyond-Justice

In this part of the chapter we expand the deonance framework beyond the justice context of the first deonance studies (Turillo et al., 2002), which focused on third parties (a) who had not suffered injustice and merely knew of someone else's unfair treatment, and (b) who had an opportunity to make a personal sacrifice in response to finding out about that injustice. Those studies were also limited in scope in another way: They only addressed punitive responses to another person's apparent injustice. An expansion to that scope can be traced to the roots of deonance (Folger, 2001) as related to Brehm's (1966) theory of reactance, and as amplified in a more recent treatment of deonance (Folger, Ganegoda, Rice, Taylor, & Wo, 2013).

Our discussion will highlight that a theory about the psychology of perceived duties (deonance) goes beyond considerations about justice to also address the relationship between *rights* and duties. One link, therefore, is a characterization of rights in relation to the notion of *free behaviors* as the cornerstone of reactance theory (Brehm, 1966). Striking out in that direction will mean moving away from the more narrow confines of the initial deonance studies and into the realm where rights have implications about duties and vice versa. Moreover, by relating rights with free behaviors, we will show how establishing a connection between rights and duties implies that reactance is, in a sense, encompassed by deonance. We also draw upon Folger et al. (2013) in relating the central idea of deonance—an association with the *ought* translation of the Greek *deon*—to Heider's (1958) discussion about the *properties of ought*.

The Force of Oughts

> "Freedom of behavior is a pervasive and important aspect of human life.... [M]ost of the time people will feel that they are relatively free to engage in a variety of different behaviors and that they can select among these as they please."
>
> —*Brehm*, 1966, p. 1.

> "We often have the feeling that someone ought to get a reward or a punishment, that we or other people should do something, that someone does not deserve his bad or good luck, or that he has a right to act in a certain way. These oughts or

obligations play a major role... in the evaluation and determination of behavior and its consequences."
—*Heider*, 1958, p. 218

"[R]estrictions of freedom are a pervasive aspect of daily life."
—*Brehm*, 1966, p. v.

Generalities about human nature sometimes seem contradictory, such as "Birds of a feather flock together" versus "Opposites attract." The above quotes from Brehm indicate his awareness of this type of apparent contradiction between pervasive freedom and pervasive restrictions on freedom. He briefly touched on an apparent resolution of that contradiction, and in a subsequent section we will discuss how Folger et al. (2013) took up where Brehm left off.

Opposing forces—such as threats to freedom and resistance to those threats—need not seem unusual, of course, from the perspective that Lewin (1943) called a *force-field analysis*. Lewin suggested that opposing forces sometimes resolve themselves into a relatively stable condition, or at least a quasi-stationary equilibrium, especially when these opposing forces can be considered to be pervasive aspects of human life (cf. Brehm, 1966). Forms of unacceptable conduct run up against what Heider (1958) called the *ought force* of moral norms, however, and its strength in general acts to curb the extent to which unfettered self-interest might otherwise make the equilibrium of civil order difficult to sustain. That is the rationale behind developments of deonance outlined below.

The Context of Deonance: Freedom and Its Limits

Folger et al. (2013) discussed reactance and deonance in terms of perceived freedoms about how to behave. The reactance orientation of defending your perceived freedoms contrasts with the deonance orientation about normative limits to freedom. Under other circumstances, a person can feel these two tugging against each other—for example, when people want to do something but realize that morally they shouldn't. Norms for conduct circumscribe free behaviors: The more internalized the norm, the more such limitations make it seem as if the behaviors were not free to begin with (e.g., there is no desire to engage in them), so reactance is virtually absent (Brehm, 1966). Folger et al. (2013) noted that a diminished or nullified reactance motivation corresponds to what Folger (1998) called *bounded autonomy*. Quite simply, bounded autonomy means freedom is never infinite because various socio-moral norms represent limits to the freedoms people might otherwise defend in a reactance-like fashion. Indeed, if certain kinds of normative restrictions on freedom are fully internalized, they can act in a self-regulating fashion.

Bounded autonomy, along with the tension of deonance and reactance pitted against one another as opposing forces, can also be understood in terms of pairings such as rights versus duties. Perceptions of free behaviors are equivalent to beliefs about having the right to behave in certain ways. Each perceived duty, on the other hand, represents an aspect of bounded autonomy, which is equivalent to the absence of the right to behave in a certain way. The resolution of the conflict between the two depends on their relative strengths in the sense of a Lewinian force field. To make explicit what perhaps was only implicit in the Folger et al. (2013) discussion, we stress that each side of the field involves an ought force in Heider's terms. One side represents the perception that you ought to be free to behave in a particular way, that it is a right you ought to have. In the passage quoted earlier, for example, recall the statement about "a right to act in a certain way" within the list of "oughts or obligations" (Heider, 1958, p. 218). The opposing perception is that you ought to act in accord with a duty that imposes a negation of those freedoms, denying you the right to behave in a particular way. An implication of a Lewinian force-field analysis is that the equilibrium between these two forces can change depending on the firmness of beliefs about rights or about duties.

This notion of opposing ought forces indicates how reactance fits within the scope of deonance as a broader concept. The psychological state of deonance is based on perceptions about what ought to be. The psychological state of reactance is based on what people perceive they ought to be free to do as their right. In that sense, therefore, reactance is a special case of deonance. The reactance-based inclination to defend what you ought to be freely allowed to do can cause negative responses toward people who try to limit those freedoms (Brehm, 1966). Analogously, participants in the studies by Turillo et al. (2012) showed negative responses toward people who tried to exceed what ought to have been the limits of freedom.

Earlier, we spoke of contradictory generalities in the context of quotes from Brehm (1966) that, on the one hand, referred to freedom of behavior as a pervasive aspect of life, yet, on the other hand, noted that restrictions on freedom are also pervasive. Brehm was in essence pointing to something like the equivalent of the bounded autonomy idea. Although he did not pursue that idea, he briefly alluded to ways that the fettered and unfettered aspects of life could avoid being constantly at war with one another. He used the terms *justification* and *legitimacy* in that context. To illustrate (without defining his terms), he used separate examples referring to two different types of restrictions on the same thing that someone had come to regard as included within the domain of free behaviors. Each example, however, illustrated a different way in which that freedom could be restricted without arousing reactance (or at least keeping it at a subthreshold level). One example indicated how emergency circumstances could provide a justification for restricting the freedom; the other involved freedom restriction based on legitimate authority. Folger et al. substituted the terms *instrumental* and *inherent* in place of justification and legitimacy, respectively, as we describe in the next two subsections.

Instrumental Deontic Framing

Sometimes a restriction to freedom (bounded autonomy) produces little or no reactance because of the perceived instrumental relations between the restriction and a favorable state of affairs. Put another way, the conditions with the restriction seem—all things considered—preferable to the conditions that would exist without it. A restriction implemented to deal with an emergency (e.g., in case of fire, don't use the elevators) illustrates this type of situation: The restriction is perceived as something that *ought* to be in place because otherwise, without the restriction in place, conditions presumably would be worse (e.g., people might get burned if trapped in elevators). Imagine, for example, believing that you should be free to take the elevator up to your office or not, depending on whether you feel like taking the stairs on any given day. One day you see for the first time a sign telling you not to take the elevator if you hear a fire alarm. You have no idea that people can be trapped in elevators during fires, so it seems as if there is no good reason for this new policy. You are annoyed and are ready to start a petition drive calling for the policy's elimination. When you learn of the potential danger that led to the policy's implementation, however, your annoyance subsides and you lose all interest in trying to get signatures on any petition.

An instrumental (re-)framing establishes bounded autonomy by associating the restriction of freedom with several perceived features. One is a deontic perspective, namely that the situation is perceived as including normative features regarded as duties, responsibilities, codes of conduct, and the like (e.g., a job description for an employee will have such features, as will the policies in employee handbooks and company codes of ethics). Another is that some such features can be seen as contours on freedom that govern behaviors prescriptively (e.g., check in with a supervisor upon arrival at work) and some as governing proscriptively (e.g., no smoking). We emphasize framing and perceptions because sometimes the same normative element might come across in either of two ways (e.g., "be on time" or "don't be late"). Either way, the behavior-governing element involves the perception of an instrumental relation regarding what it takes to bring about some desirable state of affairs (e.g., standardized procedures that help to produce quality products consistently) or to avoid some undesirable state of affairs (e.g., safety regulations).

Note that deontic framing, in the broad sense of the conditions needed to bring about some state of affairs, might have nothing to do with ethical considerations. If you want outdoor paint not to wash off during the first good storm, you'd better not mix it with a lot of thinner (you owe it to yourself not to be too cheap!). Deonance applied in the context of organizational justice or similar arenas of interpersonal relations, however, is instead a theory about behavioral options limited for reasons perceived as related to considerations that seem moral in nature. These reasons are deontic because they relate to *ought*, to *must*, and to a variety of similar terms that linguists and logicians designate as "deontic" within a specific classification system; that is, they in some sense are deontic by definition or because of the stipulation that such a category exists. They are instrumentally deontic if they refer to what ought to *be*, what must *be*, and the like (desirable versus undesirable states of affairs as conditions in the world).

Deonance theory does not try to stipulate the nature of ethical criteria applicable to instrumental relations. Like beauty, morality is in the eye of the beholder. Put another way, deonance is a theory of behavioral ethics, which is a descriptive approach regarding whatever people happen to perceive as being ethical. It is not a normative discipline (e.g., ethical philosophy) about the proper criteria to apply. "Instrumentally deontic moral reasons" are descriptive of when people make a particular judgment about behaviors (their own or the behavior of others) based on the presumed instrumental contributions those behaviors can make or have made to a state of affairs perceived as *morally* desirable, by whatever kinds of criteria seem moral. Quite commonly, for example, such a state of affairs will be one judged as better, rather than worse, with regard to the general welfare in some sense (e.g., a society in which theft is discouraged). Also, the moral criteria applied instrumentally in support of restrictions on behavior might vary in the extent to which they seem onerous ("I wish I didn't have to show up today, but I know I should—I owe it to the rest of my team because they are counting on my contribution to the work that needs doing") versus tapping into internalized values of a completely positive nature ("I'm going to work hard because the company will make a donation to the charities chosen by members of the team that finishes first").

Inherent Deontic Framing

"It just seems like the right thing to do" is the essence of perceptions consistent with contours on freedom perceived as inherently deontic by virtue of their nature—in this case, expressed prescriptively. Speaking proscriptively, an employee might say something like "Yes, Marketing Plan X would bring in more customers than Plan Y, but let's not go with Plan X—it just seems deceptive." In extreme cases of behavioral norms perceived with regard to inherent qualities, people might be unable to say why something seems right or wrong. Haidt (2001) referred to such cases as examples of a phenomenon he called moral dumbfounding—when pressed hard to defend a proscriptive norm even after all arguments about why it might be harmful were stripped away, some research participants still called it wrong despite being unable to give any reason; "they would stutter, laugh, and express surprise at their inability to find supporting reasons, yet they would not change their initial judgments of condemnation" (Haidt, 2001, p. 817). Such reactions can also be described as based on the *perceptions* of a "behavior's inherent status as a basis for conduct" (Folger et al., 2013, p. 909). Just as an instrumental status as a basis for conduct refers to what a behavior *does*, an inherent basis refers to what type of perceived behavior it *is*. The moral status of an act is at times more symbolic than anything else, such as things that might be done to dead bodies when no one would find out (i.e., the essence of a "harmless" act that nonetheless seems offensive). Once again this situation boils down to *perceived* morality, but in this case the perceptions stop after evaluating the nature of the act itself, without considering (or in deciding that there is no need to consider) what state of the world might be instrumentally related to the act.

Note that *inherent* in this sense doesn't mean an innate, eternal quality. Often the perceived inherent properties will depend on the customs, mores, rules, and the like associated with a given form of activity and its behavioral elements. Sometimes a normative aspect of social life is treated as if it were inherent in an even stronger sense, of course, such as the way the US Declaration of Independence says that certain "truths" are "self-evident" (although the act of perception is even here acknowledged implicitly, because the full phrase says it is the writers who "hold" those ideas as being self-evident). Likewise, employees might perceive that they have certain kinds of things they would include in an Employee Bill of Rights. On inherent grounds this might be, for example, simply because of a perception that the company should not be allowed to require a certain kind of activity (employees should be allowed to forego participating in that kind of activity—such as the requirement of helping to elect a political candidate favored by the company's top executives) or that the company has no right to forbid a certain kind of activity, as "the principle of the thing" rather than for any particular reason having to do with the nature of the activity (e.g., employees should be allowed to do what they want on their own time, when not at work, such as supporting the candidate of their own choice).

The point is that although certain kinds of things—such as freedom of religion—might be defended because of what might happen if they were not permitted, for example, they might also come to be perceived as rights simply because it is (perhaps for no particular reason) perceived as wrong to forbid them. We do not insist that certain kinds of activities (e.g., freedoms) *are* right by their nature or *are* wrong by their very nature (e.g., slavery); that would constitute a normative philosophy. Our aim is an empirical, descriptive science. What we are suggesting or hypothesizing or proposing is that people *perceive* certain things—activities or states of the world—as inherently right or wrong; that is, as a matter of principle, in and of themselves, by their very nature.

When thinking about what might fit into the inherent category, therefore, it is essential to recognize that it can be completely a function of mere perception. Some or all of its content under a given set of circumstances might be based on certain values internalized in such a way that a person will defend them without being able to explain why. Certain kinds of things can seem right or wrong for purely symbolic reasons or as a function of what seems as if should be a way of expressing an attitude toward something, such as its inherent importance on religious grounds (e.g., to honor God or your parents; not to eat fish on Fridays). For that reason, people might believe they have certain inherent rights in the workplace, such as stopping for prayer at certain times during the day.

Although we stress that considering something to be inherent is subjective and in the eye of the beholder, the same is true, for that matter, with the instrumental category. Depending on numerous situational contingencies, for example, the same thing might be perceived as inherent by one person and instrumental by another. Moreover, someone might perceive something as having both qualities (e.g., right or wrong on both instrumental and inherent grounds) or might perceive one kind of attribute on some occasions and another on other occasions.

Folger et al. (2013) illustrated this point by referring to a famous quote by Milton Friedman, in which he claimed that a business's only (moral) responsibility is "to increase its profits so long as it stays within the rules of the game, which is to say, engages in open and free competition without deception and fraud" (Friedman, 1962, p. 133). On the one hand, such statements can be seen as referring to moral duties that are instrumental in nature:

> [H]ow a company conducts its business is supposed to be based on contingencies regarding profits and losses as a function of different business practices. As the moral duty of a manager, making money for stockholders provides a specific criterion by which to judge what should and should not be done: Behave in ways that make money and don't behave in ways that don't make money; choose among courses of action based on how much the company stands to gain or lose. The behavioral contingencies of responsibility stem from projected risk–reward relationships. The bottom line influences the boundaries of autonomy.
>
> —Folger et al., 2013, p. 909

On the other hand, the same statement by Friedman also indicated that companies ought to be conducting themselves in ways that could be perceived as inherent to the very nature of commerce itself, at least within certain systems of government:

> By invoking the moral dictate of staying "within the rules of the game," he [Friedman] was referring to business conducted within an economic system of market capitalism. Doing business in a communist regime *inherently* involves a different set of rules, as a function of the nature of the difference between capitalism and communism. Similarly, different cultures have different moral norms as regards Friedman's dictate about conducting business "without deception and fraud." The proscriptions against certain kinds of business practices seen as deceptive in one culture might be *perceived* in another culture as simply a part of the very nature of doing business (e.g. deliberately posting prices that are not "real" because of norms about haggling).
>
> —*Folger* et al., 2013, p. 909

Justice, Morality, and all That (Future) Jazz

> "How people manage to recognize matters of fairness and justice seems to be just as much in need of explanation as how they recognize matters of morality."
>
> —*Waldmann, Nagel, & Wiegmann*, 2012, p. 286

Discussing the relationship(s) between justice and morality could fill an entire chapter—and that's already happened several times! We won't review the conclusions reached elsewhere (e.g., Skitka et al., 2009; Hegtvedt & Scheuerman, 2010), but we will focus instead on the account directed most exclusively toward deonance (Folger et al., 2005). Moreover, we don't want to attempt a definitive statement, because our view coincides with the view expressed in the quote from Waldmann et al. (2012). Because fairness/justice and ethics/morality can each be conceptualized in many different ways, the relations among them quickly multiply as a function of the possible permutations and combinations. Next, we tackle the issue in two ways. First we review the Folger et al. (2005) discussion, noting some differences from the perspective we've adopted here. Second, we describe some future research directions as a way of illustrating that "you say toe-may-toe, I say toe-mah-toe"—in other words, suggesting that much the same kinds of studies would be pursued regardless of the labels used to describe them.

The Justice/Morality Relationship—A Decade Later

It has been about a decade since Folger et al. (2005) wrote on "What Is the Relationship Between Justice and Morality?" as their assignment for an edited collection of essays on organizational justice (Greenberg & Colquitt, 2005). Their answer to that question covered a lot of ground, but some snippets from the abstract point to differences in the approach we've taken:

> This chapter discusses the relationship between injustice and moral *accountability*.... [W]e argue that the sense of fairness is grounded in basic ethical assumptions of *normative treatment*.... [or] acceptable *conduct*. We term this the deontic *response*.
>
> —*Folger et al.*, 2005, p. 216, emphases added

The key is a focus on a specific type of response and on mistreatment as its instigator. As we noted at the outset, the deonance perspective on organizational justice originated primarily to account for third-party responses. Reactions such as moral outrage about injustice otherwise made little sense when the responding person had no stake in what had occurred; in other words, when the absence of "normative treatment" (less than "acceptable conduct") resulted in nothing directly harmful to the third party. Although that describes *what* people do when they learn about others who have been mistreated, it says little about *why*. To the extent that deonance makes some headway on the latter issue, work on justice and morality tend to merge.

The force-field perspective can generate some of that progress because it focuses on both sides of any norm regarding behavior and, hence, on the boundaries between acceptable conduct and actions that count as injustice. Socio-moral norms are two-sided. On the one hand, they address what is allowed and, hence, the fairness of perceived rights of discretion. On the other hand, they address what is required or not allowed, which highlights areas where discretion is limited (bounded autonomy) and would be unfair to exercise. As we have shown, various literatures all deal with these same deontic concepts—the forbidden, the mandated, and the areas of nonforbidden, nonmandated freedoms. Norms of social conduct shape the regulatory contours of human life, and people whose actions exceed those boundaries behave unfairly to the extent that they are not playing by the same deontic rules as others.

Justice and Deonance: Research in the Decades Ahead

To illustrate prospects for future deonance research, we use the example of how collective moral intensity might mediate the relationship between (un)ethical climates and sexual harassment. Presumably the existence of a climate that fosters unethical behavior in general would increase tendencies in the direction of specific unethical behaviors such as sexual harassment. Beyond that blanket assertion, however, questions about possible moderators and mediating processes need attention. Arnaud and Schminke (2012) found evidence for collective moral emotion and collective ethical efficacy as moderators of the relationship between ethical climate and ethical behavior. Jones's (1991) model of moral intensity is a source of ideas about possible mediators, namely the components of intensity, and we suggest that these might operate at the collective level.

Two of those components—social consensus and magnitude of consequences characteristics—have emerged as major contributors to the process of ethical decision-making and behavior (Lefkowitz, 2003). These mirror the deonance elements of inherent and instrumental concerns, respectively (see Table 15.1). Social consensus refers to the perceived agreement that an act is right or wrong, acceptable or unacceptable (inherent), whereas magnitude of consequences is concerned with the degree of benefit or harm (instrumental). A deonance-based, multilevel conceptualization of collective moral intensity as an organization-level construct would thus involve aggregate perceptions of the severity of consequences from sexual harassment and of social endorsement about its wrongness as an action. This conceptualization of collective moral intensity as an organization-level general construct fits well with integrative models of climate, such as Ostroff, Kinicki, and Tamkins' (2003) multilevel model of organizational culture and climate.

The enactment of policies, practices, and procedures regarding sexual harassment will tend to influence perceptions about harassment in terms of intensity attributes such as social consensus about its inherent wrongness (internalized proscriptions against it) and its magnitude of harm (instrumental grounds for proscriptions). Reductions to levels of sexual harassment, therefore, will tend to occur as a function of those intensity perceptions. Deonance theory also highlights that the domain of ethicality of actions can be over- and underincluded so as to contain omissions or excesses of applicability to agents, patients, and categories of actions (especially in terms of inherent qualities) or conditions (especially as considered from an instrumental perspective). In short, a deonance analysis encourages studies of how (un)ethical climate might affect

Table 15.1 Inherent and Instrumental Approaches as Dual Deonance Considerations for Morality

Inherent	Instrumental
Means	Ends
Deontology	Consequentialism
"Rightness/Wrongness"	Outcomes
Social Consensus	Magnitude
Legitimacy	Justification

(un)ethical behavior to the extent that such climates influence the intensity of perceptions about (a) the inherent ethical rightness or wrongness of the behavior itself, and (b) the magnitude of good or bad consequences that might result from the behavior. Moreover, the likelihood of engaging in a specific act under specific circumstances will depend on the perceived over- or underinclusiveness of the relevant moral norm as a potentially entrenched generalization[1] (e.g., whether a specific comment to a specific person is perceived as falling into a category of actions prohibited because they constitute sexual harassment).

Deonance also points to a force-field analysis of moral intensity perceptions regarding consensus about a norm's inherent applicability and the instrumental effect of a behavior on the magnitude of consequences. An organization's efforts to inculcate an ethical climate, therefore, needs to take into account the potential force of reactance based on its members' perceptions of their rights. A relevant context could involve an organization's members who think their constitutional rights to certain freedoms extend to their behavior within the organization, such as when employees think that standards of political correctness can encroach on the right to free speech. That belief could come into play, for example, when employees would normally (outside the organization) not refrain from using double entendres just because someone might take offense. Any reactance-based tendency to resist restrictions on free speech would represent a force potentially in opposition to the inherent and instrumental force of the organization's proscriptions against sexual innuendoes. The equilibrium (Figure 15.1) or balance of forces (Figure 15.2) would, in general, be based on factors that influence the relative strengths involved.

To illustrate at the individual level, imagine Employee A as someone who thinks that, although in principle people should not have to change their patterns of speech just because of some organizational rule, the harmfulness of sexual innuendoes for a work-team's effectiveness outweighs the importance of exercising that right. In a given situation for Employee B, on the other hand, the force-field's resolution is more a function of the perceived over- or underinclusiveness of the rule's applicability to a particular remark. Suppose this employee is a male familiar with "You ignorant slut" as a remark intended for comedic effect on TV in Saturday Night Live shows. He will not refrain from using it in workplace conversations if he thinks the organization's rules against sexually offensive conduct don't apply to that remark (e.g., would be overinclusive when the remark obviously can't be taken seriously), whereas he will refrain if he thinks this expression falls into a category that might be perfectly fine in TV skits but needs to be inhibited at work (i.e., using it would be underinclusive vis-à-vis the applicability of the organization's proscriptions about sexual harassment).

Conclusion

Norms of proscription, prescription, fairness, and rights all illustrate mental representations in deontic terms. A sense of the way things ought to be—regarding someone's conduct or existing conditions—will provide the lens through which the world is perceived under certain kinds of circumstances. Based on the regulatory contours that mark where the right to behavioral freedom stops

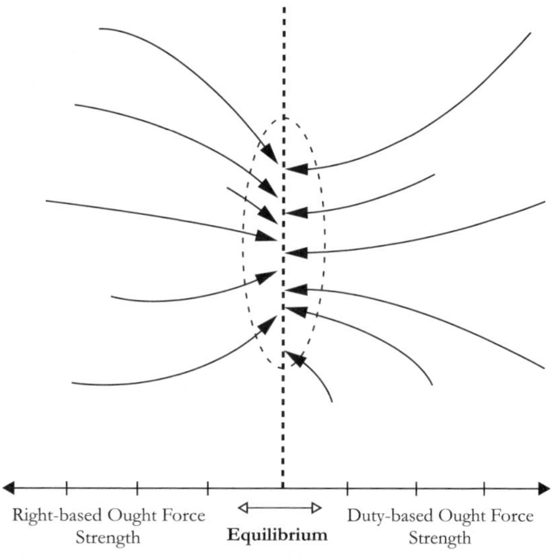

Fig. 15.1 Force-Field Analysis (cf. Lewin, 1943). Arrows represent ought forces of varying strength. The strength and number of ought forces determine the nature of the state of equilibrium.

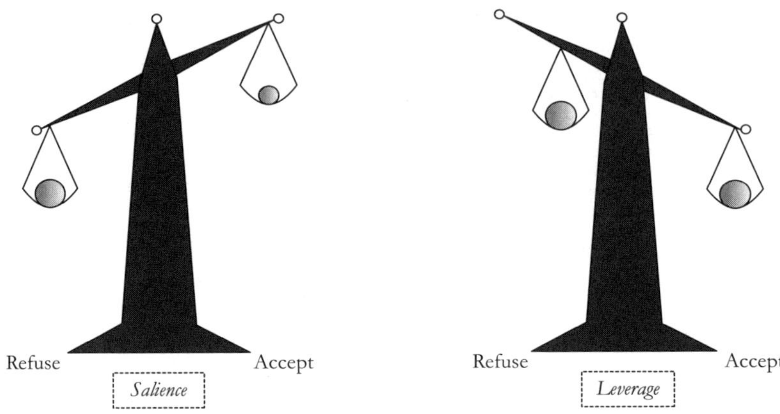

Fig. 15.2 Application of Leverage-Salience Theory of Survey Participation to Deonance. The scale metaphor illustrates opposing forces that are a function of attributes guiding decisions to accept or refuse a decision. Balls correspond to attributes of the decision. The size of the ball corresponds to the salience of the attribute. The distance between the fulcrum of the scale and the location of the attribute on the scale corresponds to the leverage of the attribute. Adapted from "Leverage-Saliency Theory of Survey Participation" by R. M. Groves, E. Singer, and A. Corning, 2000, *Public Opinion Quarterly*, *64*, p. 300.

and restrictions on it start, the members of a civil society are able to maintain a reasonable degree of equilibrium and order in their dealings with one another. The psychology of deonance captures those features of the social order. All of us take them for granted in our daily lives, but the comprehensive study of them has only just begun. This chapter represents steps in that direction.

Note

1. The terms *overinclusive, underinclusive*, and *entrenched generalization* are drawn from Schauer (1991).

References

Adams, J. S. (1965). Inequity in social exchange. In L. Berkowitz (Ed.), *Advances in experimental social psychology* (Vol. 2, pp. 267–299). doi:10.1016/s0065-2601(08)60108-2

Aquino, K., & Reed, A. (2002). The self-importance of moral identity. *Journal of Personality and Social Psychology*, *83*, 1423–1440. doi:10.1037//0022-3514.83.6.1423

Arnaud, A., & Schminke, M. (2012). The ethical climate and context of organizations: A comprehensive model. *Organization Science*, *23*, 1767–1780. doi:10.1287/orsc.1110.0698

Bain, P. G., Kashima, Y., & Haslam, N. (2006). Conceptual beliefs about human values and their implications: Human nature beliefs predict value importance, value trade-offs, and responses to value-laden rhetoric. *Journal of Personality and Social Psychology*, *91*, 351–367. doi:10.1037/0022-3514.91.2.351

Barclay, L. J., Skarlicki, D. P., & Pugh, S. D. (2005). Exploring the role of emotions in injustice perceptions and retaliation. *Journal of Applied Psychology*, *90*, 629–643. doi:10.1037/0021-9010.90.4.629

Baron, J. (2000). Measuring value tradeoffs: Problems and some solutions. In E. U. Weber, J. Baron, & G. Loomes (Eds.), *Conflict and tradeoffs in decision making: Essays in honor of Jane Beattie*. New York, NY: Cambridge University Press.

Baron, J., & Leshner, S. (2000). How serious are expressions of protected values? *Journal of Experimental Psychology: Applied*, *6*, 183–194. doi:10.1037//1076-898X.6.3.183

Baron, J., & Ritov, I. (2004). Omission bias, individual differences, and normality. *Organizational Behavior and Human Decision Processes*, *94*, 74–85. doi:10.1016/j.obhdp.2004.03.003

Baron, J., & Ritov, I. (2009). Protected values and omission bias as deontological judgments. In D. Bartels, C. W. Bauman, L. J. Skitka, & D. Medin (Eds.), *Moral judgment and decision making. Psychology of learning and motivation* (pp. 133–167). San Diego, CA: Academic Press. doi:10.1016/S0079-7421(08)00404-0

Baron, J., & Spranca, M. (1997). Protected values. *Organizational Behavior and Human Decision Processes*, *70*, 1–16. doi:10.1006/obhd.1997.2690

Barsky, A., Kaplan, S. A., & Beal, D. J. (2011). Just feelings? The role of affect in the formation of organizational fairness judgments. *Journal of Management*, *37*, 248–279. doi:10.1177/0149206310376325

Bartels, D. M. (2008). Principled moral sentiment and the flexibility of moral judgment and decision making. *Cognition*, *108*, 381–417. doi:10.1016/j.cognition.2008.03.001

Bartels, D. M., & Medin, D. L. (2007). Are morally motivated decision makers insensitive to the consequences of their choices? *Psychological Science*, *18*, 24–28. doi:10.1111/j.1467-9280.2007.01843.x

Bauman, C. W., & Skitka, L. J. (2009). In the mind of the perceiver: Psychological implications of moral conviction. In D. M. Bartels, C. W. Bauman, L. J. Skitka, & D. L. Medin (Eds.), *Moral judgment and decision making. The psychology of learning and motivation* (pp. 341–364). San Diego, CA: Academic Press. doi:10.1016/s0079-7421(08)00411-8

Bell, C. M., & Main, K. J. (2011). Deonance and distrust: Motivated third party information seeking following disclosure of an agent's unethical behavior. *Journal of Business Ethics*, *102*, 77–96. doi:10.1007/s10551-011-0801-5

Beugré, C. D. (2009). Exploring the neural basis of fairness: A model of neuro-organizational justice.

Organizational Behavior and Human Decision Processes, 110, 129–139. doi:10.1016/j.obhdp.2009.06.005

Beugré, C. D. (2010). Resistance to socialization into organizational corruption: A model of deontic justice. *Journal of Business Psychology, 25*, 533–541. doi:10.1007/s10869-010-9176-3

Beugré, C. D. (2012). Development and validation of a deontic justice scale. *Journal of Applied Social Psychology, 42*, 2163–2190. doi:10.1111/j.1559-1816.2012.00935.x

Bies, R. J., & Tripp, T. M. (2001). A passion for justice: The rationality and morality of revenge. In R. Cropanzano (Ed.), *Justice in the workplace: From theory to practice* (Vol. 2, pp. 197–208). Mahwah, NJ: Erlbaum.

Boehm, C. (1999). *Hierarchy in the forest*. Cambridge, MA: Harvard University Press.

Brehm, J. W. (1966). *A theory of psychological reactance*. New York, NY: Academic Press.

Colquitt, J. A., Scott, B. A., Judge, T. A., & Shaw, J. C. (2006). Justice and personality: Using integrative theories to derive moderators of justice effects. *Organizational Behavior and Human Decision Processes, 100*, 110–127. doi:10.1016/j.obhdp.2005.09.001

Crawshaw, J. R., Cropanzano, R., Bell, C. M., & Nadisic, T. (2013). Organizational justice: New insights from behavioural ethics. *Human Relations, 66*, 885–904. doi:10.1177/0018726713485609

Cropanzano, R., Byrne, Z. S., Bobocel, D. R., & Rupp, D. E. (2001). Moral virtues, fairness heuristics, social entities, and other denizens of organizational justice. *Journal of Vocational Behavior, 58*, 164–209. doi:10.1006/jvbe.2001.1791

Cropanzano, R., Goldman, B., & Folger, R. (2003). Deontic justice: The role of moral principles in workplace fairness. *Journal of Organizational Behavior, 24*, 1019–1024. doi:10.1002/job.228

Cropanzano, R., Goldman, B., & Folger, R. (2005). Self-interest: Defining and understanding a human motive. *Journal of Organizational Behavior, 26*, 985–991. doi:10.1002/job.353

Cropanzano, R., & Rupp, D. E. (2002). Some reflections on the morality of organizational justice. In S. Gilliland, D. Steiner, & D. Skarlicki (Eds.), *Emerging perspectives on managing organizational justice* (pp. 225–278). Greenwich, CT: Information Age.

Eisenberg, N. (2000). Emotion, regulation, and moral development. *Annual Review of Psychology, 51*, 665–697. doi:10.1146/annurev.psych.51.1.665

Festinger, L. (1957). *A theory of cognitive dissonance*. Stanford, CA: Stanford University Press.

Fiske, A. P. (2002). Socio-moral emotions motivate action to sustain relationships. *Self and Identity, 1*, 169–175. doi:10.1080/152988602317319357

Fiske, A. P. (2004). *Emotions are proximate motives to sustain social relationships*. Unpublished manuscript.

Folger, R. (1977). Distributive and procedural justice: Combined impact of "voice" and improvement of experienced inequity. *Journal of Personality and Social Psychology, 35*, 108–119. doi:10.1037//0022-3514.35.2.108

Folger, R. (1998). Fairness as moral virtue. In M. Schminke (Ed.), *Managerial ethics: Moral management of people and processes* (pp. 13–34). Mahwah, NJ: Erlbaum.

Folger, R. (2001). Fairness as deonance. In S. W. Gilliland, D. D. Steiner, & D. P. Skarlicki (Eds.), *Research in social issues in management: Theoretical and cultural perspectives on organizational justice* (pp. 3–31). Charlotte, NC: Information Age.

Folger, R. (2011). Deonanace: Behavioral ethics and moral obligation. In D. DeCremer & A. E. Tenbrunsel (Eds.), *Behavioral business ethics: shaping an emerging field* (pp. 123–142). New York, NY: Routledge.

Folger, R., & Butz, R. (2004). Relational models, "deonance," and moral antipathy toward the powerfully unjust. In N. Haslam (Ed.), *Relational models theory: A contemporary overview* (pp. 217–242). Mahwah, NJ: Erlbaum.

Folger, R., & Cropanzano, R. (2010). Social hierarchies and the evolution of moral emotions. In M. Schminke (Ed.), *Managerial ethics: Managing the psychology of morality* (pp. 207–234). New York, NY: Routledge.

Folger, R., Cropanzano, R., & Goldman, B. (2005). What is the relationship between justice and morality? In J. Greenberg & J. A. Colquitt (Eds.), *Handbook of organizational justice* (pp. 215–246). Mahwah, NJ: Erlbaum.

Folger, R., Ganegoda, D. B., Rice, D. B., Taylor, R., & Wo, D. X. (2013). Bounded autonomy and behavioral ethics: Deonance and reactance as competing motives. *Human Relations, 66*, 905–924. doi:10.1177/0018726713482013

Folger, R., & Salvador, R. (2008). Is management theory too "self-ish"? *Journal of Management, 34*, 1127–1151. doi:10.1177/0149206308324321

Folger, R., & Skarlicki, D. P. (2005). Beyond counterproductive work behavior: Moral emotions and deontic retaliation versus reconciliation. In S. Fox & P. E. Spector (Eds.), *Counterproductive work behavior: Investigations of actors and targets* (pp. 83–105). doi:10.1037/10893-004

Folger, R., & Skarlicki, D. P. (2008). The evolutionary bases of deontic justice. In S. W. Gilliland, D. D. Steiner, & D. P. Skarlicki (Eds.), *Research in social issues in management: Justice, morality, and social responsibility* (Vol. 6, pp. 29–62). Charlotte, NC: Information Age.

Friedman, M. (1962). *Capitalism and freedom*. Chicago, IL: University of Chicago Press.

Gaudine, A., & Thorne, L. (2001). Emotion and ethical decision-making in organizations. *Journal of Business Ethics, 31*, 175–187. doi:10.1023/A:1010711413444

Gausel, N., & Brown, R. (2012). Shame and guilt—do they really differ in their focus of evaluation? Wanting to change the self and behavior in response to ingroup immorality. *The Journal of Social Psychology, 152*, 547–567. doi:10.1080/00224545.2012.657265

Ghiselin, M. (1974). *The economy of nature and the evolution of sex*. Berkeley, CA: University of California Press.

Goldman, B. M., Cropanzano, R., Stein, J. H., Shapiro, D. L., Thatcher, S., & Ko, J. (2008a). The role of ideology in mediated disputes at work: A justice perspective. *International Journal of Conflict Management, 19*, 210–233. doi:10.1108/10444060810875787

Goldman, B. M., Slaughter, J. E., Schmit, M. J., Wiley, J. W., & Brooks, S. M. (2008b). Perceptions of discrimination: A multiple needs model perspective. *Journal of Management, 34*, 952–977. doi:10.1177/0149206308318613

Greenbaum, R. L., Folger, R., & Ford, R. C. (2011). Moral contracts. In S. W. Gilliland, D. D. Steiner, & D. P. Skarlicki (Eds.), *Research in social issues in management: Emerging perspectives on organizational justice and ethics* (pp. 199–221). Charlotte, NC: Information Age.

Greenbaum, R. L., Mawritz, M. B., Mayer, D. M., & Priesemuth, M. (2013). To act out, to withdraw, or to constructively resist? Employee reactions to supervisor abuse of customers and the moderating role of employee moral identity. *Human Relations*, *66*, 925–950. doi:10.1177/0018726713482992

Greenberg, J., & Colquitt, J. A. (Eds.). (2005). *Handbook of organizational justice*. Mahwah, NJ: Erlbaum.

Haidt, J. (2001). The emotional dog and its rational tail: A social intuitionist approach to moral judgment. *Psychological Review*, *108*, 814–834. doi:10.1037//0033-295X.108.4.814

Haidt, J. (2003a). The emotional dog does learn new tricks: A reply to Pizarro and Bloom (2003). *Psychological Review*, *110*, 197–198. doi:10.1037/0033-295X.110.1.197

Haidt, J. (2003b). The moral emotions. In R. J. Davidson, K. R. Scherer, & H. H. Goldsmith (Eds.), *Handbook of affective sciences* (pp. 852–870). Oxford, UK: Oxford University Press.

Hanselmann, M., & Tanner, C. (2008). Taboos and conflicts in decision making: Sacred values, decision difficulty, and emotions. *Judgment and Decision Making*, *3*, 51–63. doi:10.5167/uzh-5948

Hegtvedt, K. A., & Scheuerman, H. L. (2010). The justice/morality link. In S. Hitlin & S. Vaisey (Eds.), *Handbook of the sociology of morality* (pp. 331–360). doi:10.1007/978-1-4419-6896-8_18

Heider, F. (1958). *The psychology of interpersonal relations*. doi:10.1037/10628-000

Janoff-Bulman, R., & Carnes, N. C. (2013). Surveying the moral landscape: Moral motives and group-based moralities. *Personality and Social Psychology Review*, *17*, 219–236. doi:10.1177/1088868313480274

Janoff-Bulman, R., Sheikh, S., & Hepp, S. (2009). Proscriptive versus prescriptive morality: Two faces of moral regulation. *Journal of Personality and Social Psychology*, *96*, 521–537. doi:10.1037/a0013779

Johansson, L, & Svedsäter, H. (2009). Piece of cake? Allocating rewards to third parties when fairness is costly. *Organizational Behavior and Human Decision Processes*, *109*, 107–119. doi:10.1016/j.obhdp.2009.02.001

Jones, T. M. (1991). Ethical decision-making by individuals in organizations: An issue-contingent model. *Academy of Management Review*,*16*, 366–395.

Jones, D. A., & Skarlicki, D. P. (2013). How perceptions of fairness can change: A dynamic model of organizational justice. *Organizational Psychology Review*, *3*, 138–160. doi:10.1177/2041386612461665

Kahneman, D., Knetsch, J. L., & Thaler, R. H. (1986). Fairness and the assumptions of economics. *The Journal of Business: Part 2: the behavioral foundations of economic theory* [Special Issue], *59*(4). S285–S300. doi:10.1086/296367

Lefkowitz, J. (2003). *Applied Psychology Series: Ethics and values in industrial-organizational psychology*. Mahwah, NJ: Erlbaum.

Lewin, K. (1943). Defining the "field at a given time." *Psychological Review*, *50*, 292–310. doi:10.1037/h0062738

Lichtenstein, S., Gregory, R., & Irwin, J. (2007). What's bad is easy: Taboo values, affect, and cognition. *Judgment and Decision Making*, *2*, 169–188.

Mitchell, M. S., & Ambrose, M. L. (2012). Employees' behavioral reactions to supervisor aggression: An examination of individual and situational factors. *Journal of Applied Psychology*, *97*, 1148–1170. doi:10.1037/a0029452

Mitchell, M. S., Vogel, R. M., & Folger, R. (in press). Third-party reactions to abusive supervision of coworkers. *Journal of Applied Psychology*.

Mullen, E., & Skitka, L. J. (2006). Exploring the psychological underpinnings of the moral mandate effect: Motivated reasoning, group differentiation, or anger? *Journal of Personality and Social Psychology*, *90*, 629–643. doi:10.1037/0022-3514.90.4.629

Nadisic, T. (2006). *The motives of organizational justice*. Unpublished manuscript, HEC School of Management, Paris, France.

Opp, K. D. (2004). "What is is always becoming what ought to be." - How political action generates a participation norm. *European Sociological Review*, *20*, 13–29. doi:10.1093/esr/20.1.13

Ostroff, C., Kinicki, A. J., & Tamkins, M. M. (2003). Organizational culture and climate. In W. C. Borman, D. R. Ilgen, & R. J. Klimoski (Eds.), *Handbook of psychology: Industrial and organizational psychology* (Vol. 12, pp. 565–593). doi:10.1002/0471264385.wei1222

O'Reilly, J., & Aquino, K. (2011). A model of third parties' morally motivated responses to mistreatment in organizations. *Academy of Management Review*, *36*, 526–543. doi:10.5465/amr.2011.61031810

Panksepp, J. (1998). *Affective neuroscience: The foundations of human and animal emotions*. New York, NY: Oxford University Press.

Porath, C. L., & Erez, A. (2007). Does rudeness really matter? The effects of rudeness on task performance and helpfulness. *Academy of Management Journal*, *50*, 1181–1197. doi:10.2307/20159919

Porath, C. L., MacInnis, D., & Folkes, V. S. (2011). It's unfair: Why customers who merely observe an uncivil employee abandon the company. *Journal of Service Research*, *14*, 302–317. doi:10.1177/1094670511404393

Rest, J. (1986). *Moral development: Advances in research and theory*. New York, NY: Praeger.

Rest, J. (1994). Background: Theory and research. In J. R. Rest & D. Narvaez (Eds.), *Moral development in the professions: Psychology and applied ethics* (pp. 1–25). Hillsdale, NJ: Erlbaum.

Ritov, I., & Baron, J. (1990). Reluctance to vaccinate: Omission bias and ambiguity. *Journal of Behavioral Decision Making*, *3*, 263–277. doi:10.1002/bdm.3960030404

Ritov, I., & Baron, J. (1992). Status-quo and omission bias. *Journal of Risk and Uncertainty*, *5*, 49–61. doi:10.1007/BF00208786

Ritov, I., & Baron, J. (1999). Protected values and omission bias. *Organizational Behavior and Human Decision Processes*, *79*, 79–94. doi:10.1006/obhd.1999.2839

Rozin, P., Lowery, L., Imada, S., & Haidt, J. (1999). The CAD triad hypothesis: A mapping between three moral emotions (contempt, anger, disgust) and three moral codes (community, autonomy, divinity). *Journal of Personality and Social Psychology*, *76*, 574–586. doi:10.1037/0022-3514.76.4.574

Rupp, D. E. (2011). An employee-centered model of organizational justice and social responsibility. *Organizational Psychology Review*, *1*, 72–94. doi:10.1177/2041386610376255

Rupp, D. E., & Bell, C. M. (2010). Extending the deontic model of justice: Moral self-regulation in third-party responses to injustice. *Business Ethics Quarterly*. *20*, 89–106. doi:10.5840/beq20102017

Salvador, R., & Folger, R. (2009). Business ethics and the brain. *Business Ethics Quarterly, 19,* 1–31. doi:10.5840/beq20091911

Schauer, F. 1991. *Playing by the rules: A philosophical examination of rule-based decision-making in law and in life.* New York, NY: Oxford University Press.

Shao, R., Rupp, D. E., Skarlicki, D. P., & Jones, K. S. (2013). Employee justice across cultures: A meta-analytic review. *Journal of Management, 39,* 263–301. doi:10.1177/0149206311422447

Skarlicki, D. P., Barclay, L. J., & Pugh, S. D. (2008). When explanations for layoffs are not enough: Employer's integrity as a moderator of the relationship between informational justice and retaliation. *Journal of Occupational and Organizational Psychology, 81,* 123–146. doi:10.1348/096317907X206848

Skarlicki, D. P., & Kulik, C. T. (2005). Third-party reactions to employee (mis)treatment: A justice perspective. *Research in Organizational Behavior, 26,* 183–229. doi:10.1016/S0191-3085(04)26005-1

Skarlicki, D. P., & Rupp, D. E. (2010). Dual processing and organizational justice: The role of rational versus experiential processing in third-party reactions to workplace mistreatment. *Journal of Applied Psychology, 95,* 944–952. doi:10.1037/a0020468

Skarlicki, D. P., van Jaarsveld, D. D., & Walker, D. D. (2008). Getting even for customer mistreatment: The role of moral identity in the relationship between customer interpersonal injustice and employee sabotage. *Journal of Applied Psychology, 93,* 1335–1347. doi:10.1037/a0012704.

Skitka, L. J. (2002). Do the means always justify the ends, or do the ends sometimes justify the means? A value protection model of justice reasoning. *Personality and Social Psychology Bulletin, 28,* 588–597. doi:10.1177/0146167202288003

Skitka, L. J. (2003). Of different minds: An accessible identity model of justice reasoning. *Personality and Social Psychology Review, 7,* 286–297. doi:10.1207/S15327957PSPR0704_02

Skitka, L. J. (2010). The psychology of moral conviction. *Social and Personality Psychology Compass, 4,* 267–281. doi:10.1111/j.1751-9004.2010.00254.x

Skitka, L. J. (2012). Moral convictions and moral courage: Common denominators of good and evil. In M. Mikulincer & P. Shaver (Eds.), *Social psychology of morality: Exploring the causes of good and evil* (pp. 349–365). doi:10.1037/13091-019

Skitka, L. J. (2014). The psychological foundations of moral conviction. In H. Sarkissian & J. Wright (Eds.), *Advances in experimental moral psychology* (pp. 148–166). New York, NY: Bloomsbury Academic Press.

Skitka, L. J., Aramovich, N. P., Lytle, B. L., & Sargis, E. G. (2009). Knitting together an elephant: An integrative approach to understanding the psychology of justice reasoning. In D. R. Bobcel, A. C. Kay, M. P. Zanna, & J. M. Olson (Eds.), *The psychology of justice and legitimacy: The Ontario Symposium* (Vol. 11). Philadelphia, PA: Psychology Press.

Skitka, L. J., Bauman, C. W., & Lytle, B. L. (2008). Morality as a foundation of leadership and a constraint on deference to authority. In D. Forsyth & C. Hoyt (Eds.), *Social psychology and leadership* (pp. 300–315). Westport, CN: Praeger.

Skitka, L. J., Bauman, C. W., & Lytle, B. L. (2009). Limits on legitimacy: Moral and religious convictions as constraints on deference to authority. *Journal of Personality and Social Psychology, 97,* 567–578. doi:10.1037/a0015998

Skitka, L. J., Bauman, C. W., & Mullen, E. (2008). Morality and justice: An expanded theoretical perspective and review. In K. A. Hedgvedt & J. Clay-Warner (Eds.), *Advances in group processes* (Vol. 25, pp. 1–27). doi:10.1016/s0882-6145(08)25001-0

Skitka, L. J., & Bravo, J. (2005). An accessible identity approach to understanding fairness in organizational settings. In S. W. Gilliland, D. D. Steiner, & D. P. Skarlicki, & K. Van Den Bos (Eds.), *Research in social issues in management: What motivates fairness in organizations?* (Vol. 4, pp. 105–128). Charlotte, NC: Information Age.

Skitka, L. J., & Houston, D. A. (2001). When due process is of no consequence: Moral mandates and presumed defendant guilt or innocence. *Social Justice Research, 14,* 305–326. doi:10.1023/A:1014372008257

Skitka, L. J., McMurray, P. J., & Burroughs, T. E. (1991). Willingness to provide post-war aid to Iraq and Kuwait: An application of the contingency model of distributive justice. *Contemporary Social Psychology, 15,* 179–188.

Skitka, L. J., & Mullen, E. (2002). Understanding judgments of fairness in a real-world political context: A test of the value protection model of justice reasoning. *Personality and Social Psychology Bulletin, 28,* 1419–1429. doi:10.1177/014616702236873

Skitka, L. J., & Tetlock, P. E. (1992). Allocating scarce resources: A contingency model of distributive justice. *Journal of Experimental Social Psychology, 28,* 491–522. doi:10.1016/0022-1031(92)90043-J

Skitka, L. J., & Tetlock, P. E. (1993a). Of ants and grasshoppers: The political psychology of allocating public assistance. In B. Mellers, & J. Baron (Eds.), *Psychological perspectives in justice* (pp. 205–233). doi:10.1017/cbo9780511552069.011

Skitka, L. J., & Tetlock, P. E. (1993b). Providing public assistance: Cognitive and motivational processes underlying liberal and conservative policy preferences. *Journal of Personality and Social Psychology, 65,* 1205–1223. doi:10.1037/0022-3514.65.6.1205

Skitka, L. J., Wisneski, D. C. (2012). Justice theory and research: A social functionalist perspective. In I. B. Weiner, H. A. Tennen, & J. M. Suls (Eds.), *Handbook of psychology: Personality and social psychology* (2nd ed., pp. 407–428). doi:10.1002/9781118133880.hop205019

Spencer, S., & Rupp, D. E. (2009). Angry, guilty, and conflicted: Injustice toward coworkers heightens emotional labor through cognitive and emotional mechanisms. *Journal of Applied Psychology, 94,* 429–444. doi:10.1037/a0013804

Spranca, M., Minsk, E., & Baron, J. (1991). Omission and commission in judgment and choice. *Journal of Experimental Social Psychology, 27,* 76–105. doi:10.1016/0022-1031(91)90011-T

Tangney, J. P., Stuewig, J., & Mashek, D. J. (2007). Moral emotions and moral behavior. *Annual Review of Psychology, 58,* 345–372. doi:10.1146/annurev.psych.56.091103.070145

Tanner, C., & Medin, D. L. (2004). Protected values: No omission bias and no framing effects. *Psychonomic Bulletin & Review, 11,* 185–191. doi:10.3758/BF03206481

Tanner, C., Medin, D. L., & Iliev, R. (2008). Influence of deontological versus consequentialist orientations on act choices and framing effects: When principles are more important than consequences. *European Journal of Social Psychology, 38*, 757–769. doi:10.1002/ejsp.493

Tetlock, P. E. (1999). Coping with trade-offs: Psychological constraints and political implications. In S. Lupia, M. McCubbins, & S. Popkins (Eds.), *Political reasoning and choice*. doi:10.1017/cbo9780511805813.011

Tetlock, P. E. (2003). Thinking the unthinkable: Sacred values and taboo cognitions. *Trends in Cognitive Sciences. 7*, 320–324. doi:10.1016/S1364-6613(03)00135-9

Tetlock, P. E., Kristel, O. V., Elson, S. B., Green, M. C., & Lerner, J. S. (2000). The psychology of the unthinkable: Taboo trade-offs, forbidden base rates, and heretical counterfactuals. *Journal of Personality and Social Psychology, 78*, 853–870. doi:10.1037/0022-3514.78.5.853

Tetlock, P. E., Peterson, R., & Lerner, J. (1996). Revising the value pluralism model: Incorporating social content and context postulates. In C. Seligman, J. Olson, & M. Zanna (Eds.), *Ontario symposium on social and personality psychology: Values*. Hillsdale, NJ: Erlbaum.

Thibaut, J. W., & Walker, L. (1975). *Procedural justice: A psychological analysis*. Hillsdale, NJ: Erlbaum.

Triana, M. D. C., Wagstaff, M. F., & Kim, K. (2012). That's not fair! How personal value for diversity influences reactions to the perceived discriminatory treatment of minorities. *Journal of Business Ethics, 111*, 211–218. doi:10.1007/s10551-012-1202-0

Turillo, C. J., Folger, R., Lavelle, J. J., Umphress, E. E., & Gee, J. O. (2002). Is virtue its own reward? Self-sacrificial decisions for the sake of fairness. *Organizational Behavior and Human Decision Processes, 89*, 839–865. doi:10.1016/S0749-5978(02)00032-8

Tyler, T. R., & Lind, E. A. (1992). A relational model of authority in groups. In M. P. Zanna (Ed.), *Advances in experimental social psychology* (Vol. 25, pp. 115–191). doi:10.1016/s0065-2601(08)60283-x

Umphress, E. E., Simmons, A. L., Folger, R., Ren, R., & Bobocel, R. (2013). Observer reactions to interpersonal injustice: The roles of perpetrator intent and victim perception. *Journal of Organizational Behavior, 34*, 327–349. doi:10.1002/job.1801

Waldmann, M. R., Nagel, J., & Wiegmann, A. (2012). Moral judgment. In K. J. Holyoak & R. G. Morrison (Eds.), *The Oxford handbook of thinking and reasoning* (pp. 364–389). doi:10.1093/oxfordhb/9780199734689.013.0019

Walster, E., Berscheid, E., & Walster, G. W. (1973). New directions in equity research. *Journal of Personality and Social Psychology, 25*, 151–176. doi:10.1037/h0033967

Weiss, H. M., Suckow, K., & Cropanzano, R. (1999). Effects of justice conditions on discrete emotions. *Journal of Applied Psychology, 84*, 786–794. doi:10.1037/0021-9010.84.5.786

Wisneski, D. C., Lytle, B. L., & Skitka, L. J. (2009). Gut reactions: Moral conviction, religiosity, and trust in authority. *Psychological Science, 20*, 1059–1063. doi:10.1111/j.1467-9280.2009.02406.x

Zdaniuk, A., & Bobocel, D. R. (2013). The automatic activation of (un)fairness behavior in organizations. *Human Resource Management Review, 23*, 254–265. doi:10.1016/j.hrmr.2012.12.006

CHAPTER

16 Relational Models of Procedural Justice

Steven L. Blader *and* Tom R. Tyler

Abstract

The relational models of procedural justice refer to three theoretical models: The *group value* model (Lind & Tyler, 1988), the *relational model of authority* (Tyler & Lind, 1992), and the *group engagement model* (Tyler & Blader, 2000). The three models share a focus on the fundamental psychological concerns that procedural justice addresses, highlighting the perspective that people care about and react to procedural justice because of the relational message conveyed by fair process. Procedural justice conveys a positive message to justice recipients about their relationship with the entity enacting justice, whereas procedural injustice conveys a negative message about that relationship. We review the development of the relational models of procedural justice, explain their contribution to several critical issues at the heart of procedural justice research, highlight recent developments in the relational model perspective, and identify important avenues for future research.

Key Words: procedural justice, relational models, group value model, relational model of authority, group engagement model

It has recently been noted that organizational justice research has focused primarily on four recurring issues: (1) why justice matters; (2) how justice judgments are formed; (3) the consequences of justice; and (4) the factors antecedent to justice judgments (Crawshaw, Cropanzano, Bell & Nadisic, 2013). We suggest one additional issue that has received the attention of justice researchers (5) a focus on for whom and under what conditions justice matters most. These five issues represent a broad range of questions that have occupied justice researchers for many years. Indeed, thousands of studies have been conducted on these issues over the past 40 years, and our understanding of justice dynamics has been greatly enhanced as a result.

Within the voluminous justice literature, the three *relational models of procedural justice* (Lind & Tyler, 1988; Tyler & Blader, 2000, 2003; Tyler & Lind, 1992) represent an important stream of work. The significance of the relational models can be attributed to their ability to address each of these five major issues mentioned above. Although the primary objective of the relational models has always been to address the question of why procedural justice matters, research on (or inspired by) the relational models has had a dramatic impact on our understanding of procedural justice judgments and reactions. As a result, the relational models have had a widespread influence on the key issues considered by justice researchers. By focusing on the underlying psychological concerns that drive people's focus on procedural justice, the relational models have helped paint a more complete picture of the implications of recognizing that the procedural justice people encounter conveys important information about their relationships to the individuals and entities with whom they interact.

In this chapter, we review the key premises and research that constitute the relational models of procedural justice. We do so with an eye toward explaining how relational models have contributed to the five major issues listed earlier. Moreover, we devote our attention not only to reviewing the foundational work on the relational models, but also to highlighting a number of important studies and innovations on the models conducted over the past 10 years. In discussing some of this most recent work, we highlight issues and questions that we believe require further investigation. We see the discussion of recent work as particularly important since this work is potentially quite fruitful for advancing both the relational perspective on procedural justice and organizational justice research more broadly.

What Are the Relational Models? An Historical Overview

The "relational models" actually refer to a family of three models that were developed and tested over a period of approximately 15 years, with each one building on and extending the insights of those preceding it. The three models are the group-value model of procedural justice (Lind & Tyler, 1988); the relational model of authority (Tyler & Lind, 1992); and the group engagement model (Tyler & Blader, 2000; 2003). The common denominator of these models—and of all subsequent research inspired by them—is that people use the procedural justice they encounter in an interaction (or across interactions) as a cue for evaluating the nature of their relationship with the party enacting the procedure. Fair procedures communicate a positive message about the nature of that relationship, while unfair procedures communicate the opposite message. These relationships can involve bilateral relationships, people's relationships with group authorities, and their relationships with organizations, communities, institutions or society. The importance of such relational messages, in turn, broadly explains the reactions that people have to the procedural justice they encounter. Although the models involve a far more specific and complex set of arguments, this premise is what underlies the relational perspective on procedural justice.

The Group-Value Model

The first effort at articulating the relational perspective was by Lind and Tyler (1988), in their book, *The Social Psychology of Procedural Justice*. This book represented an important milestone in the progression of procedural justice research. First, it integrated the research on procedural justice that had been conducted subsequent to Thibaut and Walker's (1975) seminal book on the topic. In the process, it clearly laid out the procedural justice argument and the relevance of that argument not only (or even especially) for organizations, but also for other hierarchical contexts such as the law and the political arena. Second, it introduced the group-value model, presented initially as an effort to explain a range of procedural justice phenomena that the self-interest model of procedural justice was unable to explain. In particular, the group-value model was the first articulation of the argument that procedural justice communicates information to group members about their relationship to the group. Fair procedures communicate a positive relationship, whereas unfair procedures communicate a negative relationship.

To understand the contribution of this idea, it is necessary to consider the context of early theories about procedural justice: that is, the work of Thibaut and Walker (1975). That pioneering research argued that people care about procedural justice because they care about receiving desirable/fair outcomes. In disputes, the parties are seeking a fair outcome, something that requires the authority to have information from both sides. Voice (i.e., process control) allows people to present evidence to the decision maker and, hence, promotes the likelihood that that authority will make fair decisions. Fair procedures, therefore, are valued because they allow voice and, through that voice, give the parties indirect control over their outcomes. This instrumental control model develops from social-exchange theories (Thibaut & Kelley, 1959). In contrast, the group-value model's emphasis on relationship with the group is a product of theories of social identification (Hogg & Abrams, 1988; Tajfel & Turner, 1986). Social identity theory, as compared to social exchange theory, represents a dramatically different conception of what people want from groups. In particular, social identity theory argues that people want their group membership to serve as a positive source of self-esteem and identity, whereas social exchange theory argues that people want their group membership to be a source of achieving desired long-term outcomes. Lind and Tyler (1988) extended the social identity argument about what people seek from their groups to the domain of procedural justice. They did so by emphasizing that procedural justice provides people with information about their relationship to the group, insofar as people make inferences about that relationship based on the congruence between the group's procedures and their values.

That relationship is viewed positively when group procedures are congruent with the individual's values (including values that the individual may have internalized from the group). Therefore, the procedural justice that people encounter is interpreted as a cue regarding their relationship to their group. This, in turn, shapes their identity and influences their feelings of well-being and self-esteem.

The group-value model's premise that procedures are valued because of the message they convey about relationship to the group and not because of self-interest had widespread implications for thinking about the antecedents of procedural justice judgments. That is, because the group-value model emphasized that procedural justice was valued for noninstrumental reasons, it brought greater attention to noninstrumental factors that influence procedural justice judgments. This insight is reflected in various studies that have shown effects of noninstrumental factors on procedural justice. For instance, studies have shown effects for voice even in cases in which it is made clear that voice will not have an impact on the decisions that are made (Lind, Kanfer, & Earley, 1990; Tyler, 1987). The seminal article by Lind, Kanfer, and Earley (1990) provides an excellent example of this point. That study included a condition in which participants were given voice *after* a decision had been made (in particular, a goal-setting decision). If voice had been valued only because it made preferred outcomes more likely—reflecting the self-interest model's perspective on voice—then reactions in this postdecision voice condition should have been indistinguishable from those in the no-voice condition. However, the results indicated that reactions (e.g., justice judgments) in the postdecision voice condition were significantly more positive than in the no-voice condition. This study put forth one of the earliest and most definitive findings about the role of noninstrumental factors in procedural justice judgments.

Further evidence of the role of noninstrumental concerns in procedural justice is demonstrated by findings that people care more about procedural justice when it comes from a member of their own group rather than from an out-group member, even though the impact on outcomes does not vary between such cases. For instance, Smith, Tyler, Huo, Ortiz, and Lind (1998) found that the effect of treatment quality (a key element of procedural justice) on outcomes such as felt respect and self-esteem varied as a function of whether the group authority was an in-group or out-group member. Their experimental studies manipulated fairness of treatment, outcome favorability, and the group affiliation of the authority. The last variable was manipulated by varying whether the experimenter was ostensibly from participants' own university or a different university. When they were identified as being from the other university (i.e., out-group), fairness of treatment did not matter as much as when they were from one's own university (in-group). This insight is consistent with the relational models since interactions with in-group authorities convey information about one's relationship to the group that is not relevant or involved in dealings with out-group authorities. In other words, noninstrumental concerns critically shape reactions to the procedural justice encountered.

More generally, Lind and Tyler (1988, pg. 237) specifically highlighted that a primary contribution of the group-value model is that it explains why procedural factors such as impolite or undignified treatment carry such significance to individuals. Although such treatment may have relatively little bearing on outcomes received, they are significant when it comes to evaluating one's relationship with the group. In contrast, the control model of procedural justice focuses exclusively on how decisions are made, the element of procedural justice most related to people's outcomes.

The Relational Model of Authority

The relational model of authority (Tyler & Lind, 1992) built on the early insights of the group-value model, although it did so with a somewhat different primary goal. In particular, the relational model of authority focused on understanding the factors that shape reactions to authorities. Yet that focus returned the model to an emphasis on theorizing about procedural justice, which, in a manner of speaking, serves as testament to the importance of procedural justice for understanding groups. Indeed, a key insight of the relational model of authority was the point that procedural justice shapes reactions to authorities, an argument that has subsequently been supported with regard to legal, political, managerial, familial, and educational authorities (Tyler, Boeckmann, & Smith, 1997).

According to the relational model of authority, procedural justice plays a critical role in judgments of the legitimacy of a leader, and these legitimacy judgments, in turn, shape whether group members voluntarily defer to a leader's directives. In addition to the emphasis on the importance of procedural justice for understanding reactions to authorities, the relational model of authority also brought more specificity to the initial point made by the group-value model about the importance of noninstrumental factors as antecedents of justice judgments. In particular, the relational model of authority specifically highlighted that the relational concerns of neutrality, trustworthiness, and status recognition will impact procedural justice judgments, an argument also has received extensive empirical support (Tyler, 1989, 1994; Tyler, Degoey & Smith, 1996). One of the most important demonstrations of this effect is presented in the seminal work by Tyler, Degoey, & Smith (1996). These researchers found that relational factors such as evaluations of an authority's neutrality, trustworthiness, and status recognition—procedural elements that have little to do with outcomes received—had greater impact on downstream reactions than did instrumental and control factors (i.e., those directly tied to outcomes received). Most impressive was that this field research explored this effect in a wide variety of settings, including family, work, university, and political contexts.

The argument that people care how authorities treat them is linked to the role of authorities as representatives of their group. In this role, authorities communicate socially relevant information about people's standing/status in the group. This is reflected in studies such as Smith et al. (1998), discussed earlier, in which the authority's status as an in-group versus out-group member had a critical impact on whether participants reacted to fairness of treatment. It is also reflected in work that shows that treatment from group authorities matters more to those who are highly identified with a group (Smith et al., 1998). These insights are, in turn, linked to two fundamental human concerns. First, is a person included in the group and entitled to the identity of a group member? In organized groups, this standing is reflected in such privileges as the right to vote and the right to the protection of the group's rules (e.g., the group's laws). Second, within the group, what status does the person have (Smith & Tyler, 1997)? Is he or she respected, valued and esteemed by others or merely a marginal member of the group? This latter issue shapes feelings of self-esteem and well-being.

The Group-Engagement Model

The third framework to develop out of the relational model perspective was the group engagement model (Blader & Tyler, 2009; Tyler & Blader, 2000, 2003; *see also* Tyler, 1999). This model was heavily influenced by the group-value model and the relational model of authority that preceded it. By the time the group-engagement model was developed, work inspired by these earlier models had already paved the way for understanding procedural justice judgments as shaped by noninstrumental factors and, moreover, for acknowledging that people valued procedural justice for noninstrumental reasons. Indeed, research findings in support of this perspective had amassed to the point that little remained of the argument that procedural justice was valued *solely* for instrumental reasons. Instead, evidence seemed to support the notion that both instrumental and relational processes were in operation with regard to procedural justice, and that work was needed to sort out their relationship (Lind & Tyler, 1988). Such efforts would include, for example, work indicating that the relative importance of instrumental versus relational factors was likely dependent on a variety of person-based and situation-based factors (DeCremer & Tyler, 2005; Tyler & DeCremer, 2005; Tyler & Degoey, 1995).

These insights—and, in particular, the insights regarding the role of relational concerns—enabled the group-engagement model to adopt a far broader and more comprehensive perspective on procedural justice's relational function. Indeed, the aims of the group-engagement model were far broader in scope than these earlier models, as it set out to understand the key drivers of attitudes, values, and cooperative behaviors in groups. In other words, the group-engagement model "broadens the focus of justice studies and its predecessor models of justice by positing a general model of the relationship between people and groups" (Tyler & Blader, 2003, pg. 352). Yet despite the broader aims of the group-engagement model, procedural justice once again takes center stage, serving as testament to the power of the procedural justice effect.

More specifically, the group-engagement model builds on the prior insight that procedural justice communicates valuable information about one's standing in the group from which they are encountering justice or injustice. It does so by focusing on the mechanism by which procedural justice impacts group-relevant attitudes and behaviors—in particular, by arguing that procedural justice impacts these important outcomes due to its influence on people's identities. That is, the group engagement model argues that the relational message conveyed by fair or unfair procedures will, over time, have an impact on whether people identify with their group. It will shape how they think and feel about themselves, a profound impact which, in turn, explains their orientation toward their organization as expressed in their attitudes and behaviors. This is, perhaps, the key contribution of the group-engagement model to the relational model perspective of the psychology of procedural justice.

By explicitly pinpointing identity as the mechanism by which procedural justice shapes engagement in groups, the group-engagement model advances the relational model perspective. The model specifically explains how the message about standing that is communicated by procedural justice is transformed into cooperative group attitudes and behaviors. Moreover, the group-engagement model highlights the link between procedural justice and identity—a link that connects procedural justice research to social psychological research on social identity and its emphasis on people's need to develop a positive sense of themselves through the groups to which they belong (Tajfel & Turner, 1986). Even more fundamentally, it links procedural justice to one of people's most fundamental needs, the need to belong (DeCremer & Blader, 2006).

Blader & Tyler (2009) provides an illustrative example of the key premises and powerful predictions of the model. In that article, we present two field studies that propose—among a number of other predictions—that the effect of procedural justice on extra-role behavior is mediated by social identity. Between the two studies, there were nearly one thousand participants for whom we had supervisor ratings of extra-role behavior. The results of the studies are striking. Like other justice researchers, we found that employees' procedural justice judgments were key predictors of engagement in extra-role behavior (Cohen-Charash & Spector, 2001; Colquitt, Conlon, Wesson, Porter, & Ng, 2001; LePine, Erez, & Johnson, 2002; Moorman, 1991; Organ & Ryan, 1995). The more novel insight, however, was our finding that the impact of procedural justice on extra-role behavior was fully mediated by social identity. There was no significant remaining effect of procedural justice on extra-role behavior once the mediating effects of social identity were accounted for.

These findings provide powerful evidence in support of the relational models because they indicate that the arguments of the relational models fully account for the well-documented relationship between procedural justice and extra-role behavior. In addition, the group-engagement model incorporates instrumental concerns into its theorizing, but posits and finds that instrumental judgments shape extra-role behavior because they, too, shape social identity. Both procedural justice and instrumental judgments shape extra-role behavior because they send a powerful message about the group and one's standing in the group, messages that shape the nature of the relationship between group members and the group. Two notable characteristics about these samples of participants are worth mentioning. The first study was conducted in a financial services firm, and the respondents in our sample were quite well-compensated individuals working in an industry and a job where money is, ostensibly, their primary concern. The second study's sample, in contrast, was a large and highly representative sample of the US working population. These studies demonstrate the usefulness of the relational perspective to procedural justice both a) among individuals for whom we might be least likely to expect such effects and b) across a broad range of individuals (importantly, we did not find any evidence of moderation by any key job-related characteristics).

This does not mean that social identity is the only mechanism by which procedural justice and instrumental concerns lead to extra-role behavior. Other mechanisms may be at play, mechanisms unexplored by the group-engagement model because of its distinct focus on relational factors and, moreover, the grounding of the group-engagement model in prior relational models of justice. Our results provide support the group-engagement model, but they do less to explain how the social identity mechanism operates in relation to other mechanisms. We regard research exploring the integration of the relational perspective (and, in particular, the social identity mechanism) with other perspectives as a critical avenue for future research.

In closely related work, Olkonnen & Lipponen (2006) similarly hypothesized and found a significant indirect effect of procedural justice on extra-role behavior that was mediated by social identity. However, this study took a more-detailed approach and focused on the source of procedural justice and the target of social identification, arguing that there would be consistency between these. On the one hand, the authors argued and found that procedural justice attributed to the organization would primarily impact organizational identification and, subsequently, extra-role behavior targeted at the organization. On the other hand, procedural justice attributed to a supervisor would primarily impact work-unit identification and, subsequently, extra-role behavior targeted at the work unit. Their findings corroborate the arguments of the group-engagement model while also highlighting the importance of focusing on the source of justice and the target of social identification.

Summary

The trajectory of the relational models is informative for understanding the growth and impact of procedural justice research more generally. What started out as an observation that procedural justice is shaped by noninstrumental factors and is valued (at least in part) for noninstrumental reasons evolved, over time, into a broad psychological model of how people relate to their groups and to the groups' authorities. The finding that procedural justice can have such a profound impact—and that such an impact is at least partially (if not mostly) due to the relational message conveyed by procedural justice—helps explain why procedural justice research has become one of the most active research areas in the social sciences. Moreover, the support that the relational models has received over the years (e.g., DeCremer & Tyler, 2005, 2007; Stahl, Vermunt & Ellemers, 2008; van Laar, Derks, Ellemers & Bleeker, 2010; Van Prooijen, Van den Bos & Wilke, 2004; as well as many of the studies discussed later) helps explain why this perspective—along with several others—has remained the focus of so much research activity.

The Impact of the Relational Models

We began this chapter by highlighting the key issues that have grabbed the attention of justice researchers for the past 40 years. As noted, relational models, at their core, are focused on addressing the first of those issues—namely, the issue of why procedural justice matters. The relational models explain that procedural justice matters because it communicates a message about how the party dispensing justice regards the other party; as a result, it sends a message that shapes the nature of the relationship that develops between these interacting parties. In group contexts, this leads group members to tie their sense of self to the group. In the context of authority relations, this leads followers to view authorities as more legitimate and to voluntarily follow their directives. In either case, the relational message conveyed by procedural justice taps into core psychological concerns that people have in groups and in all kinds of hierarchical settings. That is, they seek to feel respected and included by the other party, to feel a positive social bond that, in turn, satisfies their fundamental need for belongingness (Baumeister & Leary, 1995) and contributes more generally to a positive sense of self and of their place in the world. The relational models answer the question of why procedural justice matters by indicating that procedural justice addresses some of people's most fundamental psychological concerns.

This hallmark of all the relational models—that they connect with core psychological drives that people have in social settings—is important because it helps explain why such models have had such a broad impact on justice theorizing. Indeed, the influence of the relational models extends beyond work on why procedural justice matters and has brought attention to the other key issues outlined rlier.

The Factors Antecedent to Procedural Justice Judgments

To start, let's consider the factors that people consider when evaluating procedural justice. The relational models make clear that they will focus on noninstrumental factors. Indeed, this was one of the key insights to develop from the group-value model (Lind & Tyler, 1988), which was further specified in the relational model of authority (Tyler & Lind, 1992; Tyler, Degoey & Smith, 1996). Early efforts to examine what people care about when thinking about issues of justice strongly support the argument that people focus heavily on noninstrumental issues (Tyler, 1989).

The four-component model of procedural justice (Blader & Tyler, 2003a, 2003b) is a framework that was inspired by the relational models to directly address the question of what factors people consider when evaluating procedural justice; this framework focuses on organizing the variety of noninstrumental factors that relate to procedural justice. As such, the four-component model entered into the debate about the appropriate conceptualization of procedural justice. For several years, researchers debated (and continue to debate, though less so) whether concepts such as interactional justice and informational justice represent distinct forms of justice—at the same level at which procedural justice is distinct from distributive justice—or whether they are best conceptualized as elements of procedural justice.

We refer readers interested in the specifics of this debate elsewhere (e.g., Blader & Fortin, 2013;

Blader & Tyler, 2003a, 2003b; Tyler & Blader, 2000). The key point to emphasize here is that, consistent with its roots in the relational perspective, the four-component model addresses this question by starting with an approach strongly grounded in the justice literature. That is, the four-component model emphasizes that our understanding of how to best conceptualize procedural justice should be guided by our understanding of why procedural justice matters. If it matters because of the relational message conveyed via procedures, then all elements that convey this relational message should be conceptualized as elements of procedural justice. This, of course, does not exclude the possibility of making more-fine-grained distinctions, but it does suggest, at its broadest level, that we should decide which factors comprise procedural justice based on whether they share a common psychological function. This is precisely the argument that the four-component model makes. Although the model's specific arguments are important, somewhat more critical for current purposes is recognition that grounding in the relational models shaped the development of the four-component model. It did so by stipulating that the question of how to best conceptualize procedural justice should be answered with a focus on the relational concerns that procedural justice addresses.

Other efforts to conceptualize procedural justice or to identify the factors antecedent to procedural justice that take a different approach—such as descriptive or empirical efforts that are not guided by an overriding theoretical perspective—have their benefits, but are not as likely to contribute to the advancement of justice theorizing itself. This is because they do not coalesce around a central message about the psychology that underlies procedural justice. For instance, factor-analytic efforts to identify different aspects of justice (Colquitt, 2001) do not provide a framework for theoretically linking different aspects of justice to one another or to the reasons that people care about justice.

Another approach to relational issues is to ask what it is that most fundamentally defines the link between people and groups. Huo (2002) approaches this issue by examining what types of deprivations are most upsetting. She contrasts three types of deprivation: withholding monetary resources; abandoning procedural protections; and denying people respectful treatment. Her results suggest that people view disrespectful treatment as the most fundamental deprivation and the withholding of material resources as the least important. This experimental support for the relational argument suggests that identity-relevant concerns are the most central to people's relationship with groups.

The Consequences of Justice

Relational models also speak to the other issues that have been the focus of justice research. With regard to the consequences of procedural justice, research on relational models emphasizes that justice will impact primarily those consequences that reflect the nature of the relationship between the parties. In the case of authority relations, those consequences will include the perceived legitimacy of the authority, support for the authority, and deference to the authority's directives (Tyler, 2006a, 2006b).

In group contexts, those consequences will include discretionary efforts expended on behalf of the group (Tyler & Blader, 2000; 2001). Discretionary efforts—such as extra-role behaviors—represent the behavioral manifestation of a group member's orientation and relationship with the group. Since these behaviors are optional, they provide leeway for expression of the group member's relationship with the group. This contrasts with behaviors that are mandated (i.e., in-role performance) and that, as a result, provide less of a window into the member's sentiments toward the group. So, with regard to this issue, the relational model's emphasis on how procedural justice shapes the justice recipient's relationship toward the group guides the search for consequences of procedural justice. Consistent with this finding, justice research typically finds far stronger effects of procedural justice on discretionary as compared to mandatory behaviors (Colquitt et al., 2001).

For Whom and When Will Justice Matter Most?

Relational models also provide clear guidance about the issue of for whom and when—that is, under what circumstances—procedural justice will matter most. Indeed, the logic of the relational models has been extended in a number of different studies to examine moderators of procedural justice effects. Once again, this issue is informed by a focus on how the relational significance of fair procedure explains the effect of procedural justice. In particular, the relational models have inspired work showing that procedural justice will matter less when the relationship with the justice agent (i.e., a specific authority, the organization overall, etc.) matters less—that is, when it is less identity relevant. This basic insight has been shown in a number of different ways. For instance, earlier, we discussed the findings of Smith et al., 1998, who showed that procedural justice matters less when the justice agent is an out-group rather than an in-group member. This is because in-group authorities (unlike out-group authorities) have the ability to represent the entire group to a group member—the relational message they convey through the procedural fairness they implement is informative about a group member's standing in the entire group. This explanation also helps explain a somewhat recent finding that procedural fairness has a stronger impact on cooperation among leaders who are regarded as relatively more prototypical since such leaders are seen as embodying the group's values and norms (DeCremer, van Dijke, & Mayer, 2010). Like interactions with in-group authorities, encounters with more prototypical authorities (as compared to less prototypical authorities) are seen as communicating relatively more diagnostic information to group members about their standing in the group.

The same logic also explains the finding that procedural justice matters more to those who are strongly identified with a group (Smith et al., 1998). Identification with a group leads group members to care more about their relations with the group and their standing in the group since these factors will more strongly impact their sense of self. However, procedural justice will matter less for those who are weakly identified with the group since their relationship to the group has less bearing on their self-esteem. One recent and intriguing demonstration of this is presented in Smith, Olson, Agronick, & Tyler (2009), who found that these effects can emerge even prior to entry to a new organization and can shape socialization to the group. That study found that among a group of college freshmen, their level of identification with the university prior to actually arriving on campus moderated the influence of procedural justice on academic engagement three months later. This is particularly remarkable since it shows that identification even prior to actual membership (i.e., identification with a future group) can moderate the impact of the relational message behind procedural justice.

An interesting twist on these ideas was presented in Mayer, Kuenzi, Greenbaum, Bardes, & Salvador (2009), who found that there is no effect of voice on procedural justice judgments when outcomes violate central aspects of an individual's personal or social identity. This pattern of moderation is consistent with the relational models, insofar as outcomes that violate one's identity should prompt individuals to psychologically distance themselves from the authority and from the group responsible for those outcomes. Indeed, not distancing oneself from an entity that is dispensing identity-threatening outcomes could potentially lead to identity conflict. This psychological distancing, in turn, will make relational information from that group (in the form of procedural justice) or authority less relevant—just like low-identification, out-group justice agents, as well as other, as yet unexplored, factors that may intervene in the orientation that individuals have towards their groups.

How Justice Judgments Are Formed

Finally, relatively less work inspired by the relational models has been done on the issue of the procedural justice judgment process itself. An exception—one with a variety of implications and suggestions for future work—is the finding that those with a stronger need to belong engage in more careful and systematic processing of procedural fairness information (DeCremer & Blader, 2006). This work hypothesized that those with a strong need to belong are more interested in evaluating acceptance by their groups, and, thus, they will be more vigilant in processing information about inclusion such as procedural justice. This prediction was tested using a common paradigm in social psychology for assessing processing motivation (Correll, Spencer & Zanna, 2004; Petty & Cacioppo, 1984; Petty & Wegener, 1998). In particular, the authors varied the quality and the credibility of the reasons provided to participants for a fictitious manager providing voice. Some participants were provided a compelling set of reasons (e.g., the manager believes in democratic values; the manager wants everyone to feel heard and valued by the company), whereas others were given a poor set of reasons (e.g., the manager heard about giving voice and thought it was a fun idea; the manager thought that giving voice would feel good at the moment). The dependent variable in this study was perceived procedural fairness. It was expected and found that participants with a stronger need to belong—those who the relational models would predict are more concerned about the message conveyed by procedural fairness—were more reactive to variations in the reasons for giving voice than their lower-need-to-belong counterparts. This finding provides tentative evidence that the relational models can be used not only to think about the factors that shape justice judgments but also about the cognitive processing associated with justice reasoning.

Mayer et al. (2009), discussed earlier, provided another interesting examination of relational influences on the justice judgment process. The authors pursued an important extension of their work by exploring the process by which identity-threatening outcomes diminish the impact of procedural justice. In particular, they found that when encountering an identity-threatening outcome, participants encountering fair procedures (i.e., voice) were less likely to believe that the procedures were authentically implemented (e.g., they were skeptical that authorities actually considered the opinions expressed before making their decision). This finding indicates that motivated reasoning processes can intervene in the procedural justice judgment process and, moreover, that those motivated reasoning processes may act in the service of the relational concerns that are prompted by identity-threatening outcomes. Indeed, this process is consistent with the mechanism that underlies the findings by Blader (2007), who found that identification with a group had a strong positive impact on procedural justice judgments when definitive procedural information was absent. Blader (2007) attributed these findings to motivations spurred by identification, motivations that lead individuals to want to regard the group with which they are identified as fair. Doing so helps ensure that the group will continue to serve as a source of positive social identity for the individual; it also reflects the motivation to feel a sense of presumptive trust (Kramer, 2001) with the group.

Summary

In sum, what we have emphasized in this section is that, although the relational models are primarily theoretical models about why people care about justice, their insights have significance for the full range of issues that have captured the attention of justice researchers. We feel that this is made possible by the relational models' emphasis on linking justice to a core set of psychological concerns that people have in social contexts; we believe that the models would not have had as far-reaching implications if they had not focused on psychological concerns as their foundation. The relational models are by no means alone in this regard—the uncertainty theories of justice, the deontic models, and others also attempt to understand justice with a guiding psychological principle about why justice matters. However a great deal of the current work on procedural justice lacks this grounding. We see this as a threat to the progression of justice research. Moreover, we see this as a possible obstacle to organizational justice research having a broader influence on other areas of organizational research.

With this concern in mind, we now consider some recent—and particularly promising— innovations in procedural justice research that build on the relational perspective. Important work is being done on procedural justice, and the topics covered next are by no means exhaustive; rather, they represent a selective consideration of some important new directions.

Advances in the Relational Model Perspective

Although relational models are primarily models about justice, their influence spans multiple literatures, such as the organizational identity literature (e.g., Bartel, Wrzsniewski, & Wiesenfeld, 2012; Brickson, 2013); the relational identification literature (e.g., Sluss & Ashforth, 2007); the status and respect literatures (e.g., Huo, Binning & Molina, 2010; Ellemers, Sleebos, Stam, & de Gilder, 2013); and, more generally, the social identity literature. These models have such a wide influence because they link justice to broader social concerns, such as authority relations (Tyler & Lind, 1992) and group processes (Tyler & Blader, 2000). Although several of these literatures represent valuable extensions of the relational models, we focus here on just a few recent developments and extensions that are grounded in the justice literature.

The Role of the Self

We regard one of the most important developments in the relational models to be work that focuses on linking justice to self-construal (DeCremer & Tyler, 2005). This work suggests that people care about treatment most strongly when they use relational treatment to construct their identities. An implicit and critical foundation of the relational models is that justice concerns relate to the social self, which is that part of the self-concept that is based on relationships with others. This premise is inherent in the point that people value the relational message conveyed by fair procedure because it shapes their social self. Thus, the link between justice and the social self is critical to the relational models.

The link between justice and self-construal is corroborated by findings that the effects of procedural justice are accentuated when aspects of the social self-concept are more accessible (Johnson, Selenta, & Lord, 2006). More specifically, this work finds that the effect of organization-level fairness is accentuated when the collective self-concept is more active, whereas the effect of supervisor-level fairness is accentuated when the relational self-concept is more active. This echoes the findings discussed earlier regarding the moderating effect of organizational identification on justice effects, but it does so by focusing on the self-concept (which is general and not group specific), rather than on the cognitive merging that group members may have with a specific group.

Johnson and Lord (2010) conducted a particularly compelling demonstration of the link between justice and the social self. Their studies explored the extent to which encountering (un) fairness activates individual versus interdependent self-identities, and whether any such activation mediated the effect of justice on trust and cooperation. Note that the social self is reflected in one's interdependent self-construal (by one's tendency to define the self in terms of relationships and group memberships), which is distinct from (and orthogonal to) individual self-construal. The authors' research explored this issue at both the explicit (i.e., conscious) and the implicit (i.e., subconscious) levels, providing a more comprehensive and arguably more direct "window" into the impact of justice on self-construal (and, thus, a superior test of the link between justice and the social self). The results of this work provide compelling confirmation for the relational model perspective. Participants in their highly involved experimental study demonstrated a positive relationship between justice and both implicit and explicit measures of interdependent self-construal. Moreover, they also found a negative relationship between justice and both implicit and explicit measures of independent self-construal.

This latter finding is particularly intriguing since, although the relational models would predict activation of the interdependent self, they would not necessarily predict that the individual self is actually subordinated by justice processes. Indeed, Johnson and Lord (2010) point out that their work is among the first to demonstrate this pattern, which suggests an important mechanism by which unfairness leads people to focus on self-interest (since it activates individual identity). Moreover, their findings further indicate that interdependent self-construal mediates the effects of justice on trust and cooperation, as would be predicted by the relational models in general and the group engagement model (Tyler & Blader, 2000) in particular. Especially fascinating is that these mediation effects were considerably stronger for the implicit self-construal measures, serving as testament to the automaticity of these processes. This is particularly intriguing because justice researchers rarely (indeed, to our knowledge, never) examine implicit measures, and the Johnson and Lord (2010) findings suggest that this may be an important gap in justice research.

Another important study examining the role of self-construal is by Holmvall and Bobocel (2008), who found that interdependent and independent self-construal had opposite effects on reactions to unfavorable outcomes that result from fair procedures. As the relational models would predict, interdependent self-construal led to relatively more positive reactions to negative outcomes that were achieved through fair process. However, like Johnson and Lord (2010), Holmvall and Bobocel (2008) found an interesting effect for independent self-construal, such that reactions to unfavorable outcomes achieved through fair process were especially negative. Due to their self-focus, these individuals were relatively more focused on the fact that fair process made it more likely that the individuals themselves were responsible for the negative outcome. Differential effects in reactions to justice as a function of self-construal are likewise found in Bobocel (2013). That study found that overall entity fairness judgments interacted with interdependent self-construal to shape forgiveness (a prosocial relational reaction to unfairness) in the face of an unfair discrete event, but that overall entity fairness judgments interacted with independent self-construal to shape revenge (an antisocial reaction to unfairness). Collectively, these studies extend the insights of the relational model with regard to interdependent self-construal and, in the process, provide intriguing insights into the role of individual self-construal in justice dynamics. This is certainly an area worthy of additional research.

Overall, this line of research that links justice to self-construal does a great deal to corroborate the major premises of the relational models. Moreover, it extends justice theorizing in new directions by highlighting the key yet underexplored role of the individual's self-concept in justice dynamics.

However, despite its importance, the role of the relational self with regard to justice (cf. Johnson, Selenta, & Lord, 2006) remains relatively less explored. Although the relational models emphasize that justice is a cue used to evaluate the quality and nature of all social relationships, the preponderance of work has focused on the relationship between group members and their groups. The focus on groups means that most procedural justice research has essentially been focused only on dynamics related to the collective self. Yet the relational model perspective is equally relevant to interpersonal interactions: Justice can be a signal of respect and a positive relational bond among interacting individuals even when occurring outside a group context. Indeed, needs for belongingness and positive social bonds exist at the interpersonal level (Baumeister & Leary, 1995; Hornsey & Jetten, 2004) just as much as they do at the group level. This point served as the basis for DeCremer & Blader's (2006) investigation of the moderating effect of need to belong on procedural justice reactions. This work argued that the need to belong, which does not rely on a group context, accentuates the effects of justice even in interpersonal contexts and that it does so because of the dynamics articulated by the relational models. This insight has paved the way for work applying the relational model perspective to interpersonal exchanges. Indeed, it highlights the potential opportunities for the relational models to contribute to justice research topics that, though already well developed, have thus far not done much to integrate the insights of the relational models. Research on justice and negotiations represent one prime example of this; although a great deal of work has been conducted on this topic, relatively little of it has adopted the insights of the relational models (see Tyler & Blader (2004) for a discussion of the relational models of justice and negotiations).

Do Higher-Ranked Parties Care About Being Treated Fairly?

Arguably one of the most significant gaps in the justice literature has been the near-exclusive focus on those of relatively lower hierarchical rank, with very little attention paid to those of higher hierarchical rank. That is, the focus of most justice research has been on the justice that lower-ranked parties encounter in their interactions with higher-ranked parties, with scant attention paid to the justice that higher-ranked parties encounter in their interactions with lower-ranked parties. This limited focus implies that justice is relevant only to lower-ranked parties and that higher-ranked parties are not concerned about the justice they encounter in their interactions.

There are, however, a few exceptions that are largely consistent with the insights of the relational models. As noted, the primary question to address in examining justice dynamics among relatively higher-ranked parties in an encounter is to determine whether justice is even of concern to them. It is possible that it may not be: Since they are not subject to the same vulnerabilities as lower-ranked parties, they may not be concerned about justice (van den Bos & Lind, 2002). This might be expected, to the extent that the primary function of justice is to alleviate concerns about exploitation and resources. Some prior work is consistent with this prediction. For instance, Begley, Lee, and Hui (2006) predicted that procedural justice was less predictive of outcomes for employees higher up in the organization's hierarchy, a hypothesis that they supported with a field study in China.

The relational perspective suggests a different conclusion since it focuses on social relations and social acceptance and since these are universal concerns that operate across all levels of hierarchical rank (Baumeister & Leary, 1995). This perspective is confirmed by research exploring justice concerns among higher-ranked parties (Chen, Brockner, & Greenberg, 2003), which found that they do, indeed, care about the justice they encounter in their interactions with lower-ranked counterparts. More specifically, the three experiments presented by Chen et al. (2003) (two using MBA students engaging in a negotiation simulation, and the other using employees at an organization engaging in a work simulation) found that individuals who have higher status (based on role or membership in a higher-status group) show positive reactions to procedural justice, much as their lower-status counterparts do. Interestingly, however, these positive reactions emerge more strongly when outcomes are also positive. This contrasts with the reactions traditionally found for lower-status parties (Brockner & Wiesenfeld, 1996), for whom positive reactions to procedural justice are attenuated when outcomes are positive.

Somewhat more recent work (Blader & Chen, 2011) confirmed that relatively higher-ranked parties care about justice, and that this concern is rooted in the relational message conveyed by justice. However, differences between higher-ranked and lower-ranked parties in the pattern of the procedural justice by outcome favorability interaction reflect differences in the relational concern that is most prominent for each of these parties. For lower-ranked parties interacting with higher-ranked parties, the primary relational concern is about inclusion in the group. For higher-ranked parties interacting with lower-ranked parties, the primary relational concern is less about inclusion in the group and more about recognition of the higher-ranked parties' standing and status (Blader & Chen, 2011; Chen et al., 2003). That is, the relational concern among higher-ranked parties is whether the lower-ranked interaction partner acknowledges the relative hierarchical difference and, thus, recognizes their high-ranking position as deserved and legitimate. Yet these, too, are relational messages conveyed by justice—signals about the nature of the relationship between the parties; thus, research confirms that higher-ranked parties do care about the justice they encounter in their interactions with lower-ranked parties. This validates the argument that justice research should be more comprehensive in investigating justice dynamics at all levels of hierarchy.

Although the foregoing discussion considers how higher-ranked parties react to justice, a related but distinct question concerns the justice that they encounter in the first place. Interestingly, prior work has shown that those higher up in an organization's hierarchy tend to experience greater fairness in the first place (Schminke, Cropanzano, & Paddock, 2002) and are less sensitive to how elements of the organizational structure effect their justice perceptions. This raises a number of important issues, such as the distinction between the justice experienced in interpersonal encounters (which are the focus of Blader & Chen (2011) and Chen et al. (2003)) and the justice that relates to formal organizational processes and characteristics (such as elements of the organization's structure). This distinction highlights that different results may emerge for different types of dependent variables and, in particular, that for higher-ranked individuals, it may be important to focus on dependent variables that describe the relationship with the other party (such as one's desire for future interaction with the other person). Moreover, it highlights that when it comes to higher-ranked parties, the relational models may be relevant primarily for understanding the justice of interpersonal encounters and not other types of encounters.

Do Higher-Ranked Parties Care About Enacting Fairness?

Although the research just discussed considers whether higher-ranked parties care about being the recipients of fairness, a somewhat different question is whether they are concerned with enacting fairness. This is particularly important because it is those at higher hierarchical ranks who most typically determine the justice that others encounter when it comes to formal organizational processes. That is, these are the justice agents (e.g., supervisors, managers, and leaders) who serve as the starting point of the justice process when it comes to key decisions such as performance appraisals, layoffs, resource allocations, and so forth. Knowing that these individuals care about the justice they experience as justice recipients is a start to better understanding the psychology of their justice concerns, but it does not tell us how these concerns shape their enactment of justice or injustice. Remarkably little prior work has considered this issue. Indeed, the lack of attention to justice agents was observed 10 years ago (Colquitt & Greenberg, 2003; Scott, Colquitt & Paddock, 2009), yet relatively little has changed since then (Blader & Chen, 2012).

However, recent research has begun to study justice agents to better understand the factors that determine whether they enact fairness or unfairness. The relational models have likewise played a strong role in some of this work. For instance, Blader and Chen (2012) recently investigated the influence of both power and status on the enactment of justice toward others. In particular, they found that while power has a negative effect on the enactment of fairness, status has a positive effect. That is, those with a psychological sense of high power will act less fairly than those with a sense of low power; and those with a psychological sense of high status will act more fairly than those with a sense of low status.

Relational concerns are theorized to drive both effects, and, in particular, the effects are theorized as linked to the divergent effects of power and status on relational concerns. It is well documented in the power literature that power makes people more self-focused at a cost to their focus on others (Fiske, 2010; Galinsky, Magee, Inesi, & Gruenfeld, 2006; Lee & Tiedens, 2001). They attend to others less (Fiske, 1993; Galinsky et al., 2006; Galinsky, Magee, Gruenfeld, Whitson, & Liljenquist, 2008; Gruenfeld, Inesi, Magee, & Galinsky, 2008), are less inherently concerned about others and, instead, are more concerned about their own goals and needs

(Gruenfeld et al., 2008; Overbeck & Park, 2006). Put simply, power diminishes social and relational concerns. Relatively less work has focused on the psychology of status, but Blader and Chen (2012) theorized that since holding a high-status position depends on status conferral from others (i.e., people can't have status unless others bestow it upon them), maintaining positive relations with others will be a critical goal among high-status parties. As such, high status (and the associated concern over maintaining one's desirable high-status position) will prompt a focus on others and, in particular, on the quality of relations with others (Blader & Chen, 2012; Flynn, Reagans, Amanatullah, & Ames, 2006). Status, in other words, accentuates social and relational concerns. In sum, Blader and Chen (2012) theorized that power will *diminish* the focus on relational concerns, and status will *accentuate* the focus on relational concerns.

Most importantly for current purposes, this work suggests that the enactment of justice will track the focus on relational concerns—justice will be more likely among justice agents who are relatively more concerned about relationships with others since justice is a means by which justice agents can build positive relationships. In this way, the fundamental premise of the relational models was used in this prior work to predict the opposite effects of power and status—two fundamental elements of the psychology of holding higher rank—on justice.

Another noteworthy study that used a relational perspective to understand justice agents is that by Cornelis, van Heil, DeCremer, and Mayer (2013). In both field and laboratory contexts, this work found that those in leadership positions are influenced by their judgments of a follower's belongingness needs. In particular, they are more likely to adhere to procedural fairness when they have the sense that a follower has a high (versus low) need to belong. This is based on the premise that they recognize the follower's relational needs (which flow from the follower's need to belong), recognize that procedural justice provides a means to meet those needs, and act accordingly. That is, these findings show that leaders have an implicit sense that procedural justice communicates a relational message and satisfies relational needs. Expecting this of leaders is no small order. It suggests that they are intuitive justice researchers. Indeed, the work by Cornelis et al. (2013) proposes an important moderating trait: They find that it is primarily leaders high in empathy (either dispositional or through situation induction) who demonstrate in their justice enactment this pattern of being influenced by followers' need to belong.

Given the propensity for leadership to be associated with a sense of high power and for a sense of power to be associated with an egocentric focus (and, thus, diminished empathic focus), Cornelis et al. (2013) does not put forth a promising forecast for the enactment of procedural justice in actual organizations. Indeed, this is an issue with several of the relatively few studies that have focused on justice enactment: Common to most of them is the perspective that follower characteristics determine agents' justice enactment (e.g., follower charisma shapes justice enactment (Scott, Colquitt, Zapata-Phelan, 2007)), which doesn't seem to reflect the insight that having high hierarchical rank diminishes focus on others in the first place. That said, integration of Cornelis et al.'s (2013) insights with Blader and Chen's (2012) findings might suggest some fruitful approaches for a relational perspective to fostering greater procedural justice in organizations. This is because status may operate in much the same way as empathy—it focuses individuals on others (albeit for different reasons). As such, perhaps orienting leaders to be more concerned about how others see them (i.e., orienting them toward a greater concern with status conferral) may not only prompt main effects of status, as shown in Blader and Chen (2012), but also may prompt interactive effects with perceived follower belongingness needs. Indeed, just as both status and empathy draw individuals outward and make relational concerns more prominent, other variables that also make the social context more salient may be a means to greater fairness enactment.

In general, prior research seems to suggest that when the relationship matters more, justice will be important to both justice recipients and justice agents: Recipients will demonstrate stronger reactions to justice, whereas agents will be more likely to enact justice. This relational perspective to when justice agents are likely to enact fairness has great potential for spurring additional work on the antecedents of leader fairness. This work would go far beyond Blader and Chen's (2012) focus on power and status to possibly include a host of factors that may make justice agents more or less concerned about their relationships with those on the receiving end of their justice enactment.

In sum, one of the most underexplored yet important areas for future research is the question of what prompts leaders to enact fairness or unfairness. Although justice research may know a great deal about why, when, and who cares about being treated fairly, these insights are of limited value in creating real change in organizations and in fostering more procedurally just institutions if we don't understand the factors that shape specific justice agents' justice-oriented behaviors. Moreover, we argue that the relational model perspective can be a fruitful approach to addressing this issue. The relational needs and concerns of justice agents may hold the key to helping understand their justice enactment, much in the same way that they shape justice recipients' reactions to justice. In many ways, this insight seems quite natural. Relationships are two-party situations, and relational concerns obviously operate on both sides of those relationships. Therefore, it makes sense that the relational models' perspective that justice conveys relational information affects both parties to the relationship. It affects how recipients react to relational information in the form of justice experienced, and it shapes the relational messages that justice agents intend to send toward others in the form of justice enacted.

More on the Intersection of Power and Justice

Power dynamics are not only relevant to justice agents, of course, but also to justice recipients. Investigating the role of power among justice recipients, a new line of study also suggests that procedural justice can remove some of the threats inherent to having less power by changing subordinates' subjective perception of power in two important ways (Mentovich, 2012). First, procedural justice *empowers* subordinates; when treated fairly by an authority figure, subordinates experience themselves as having more autonomy and more power compared with when they are treated unfairly. Second, procedural justice *equalizes* power relations; the use of procedural justice causes the hierarchical power relations between subordinates and authorities to be seen more similarly to relations between equals.

These effects have been demonstrated in how citizens view their power in law enforcement settings and with regard to legal authorities (Mentovich, 2012). In describing their encounter with a police officer, citizens reported feeling more autonomous, more powerful, and more equal to a police officer who treated them fairly as opposed to unfairly. These findings have important implications for our understanding of the role of procedural justice in fostering legitimacy and cooperation, not only among citizens but also for employees.

A sense of subjective empowerment may be particularly conducive to cooperation that is based on a sense of volition, choice, and the belief that one's actions will make an impact. Although disempowered subordinates are more likely to obey, those who are empowered are more likely to cooperate. In addition, since empowerment is a positive psychological experience in itself, subjectively empowered employees may continue to cooperate with their manager and their organization simply because they view this experience as altogether positive. Conversely, although some degree of power inequality may be necessary in organizations, it is easier for those who are on the lower rungs of the power ladder to accept arrangements that minimize power disparities. It is, therefore, possible that employees—particularly those in societal or organizational cultures characterized by relatively lower levels of power distance—are more likely to legitimize systems and authorities that maintain a relatively minimal degree of power differentials over them. Overall, this suggests some intriguing new paths by which the relational perspective explains the relationship between procedural justice and cooperation.

Identity Security and Identity Enhancement

The relational models argue that a key concern in relationships with authorities and groups is how those relationships are anticipated to shape people's identities, with people's actions reflecting a desire to promote their self-esteem and feelings of positive identity. This argument is consistent with a general recognition in social psychology that people want to have positive self-esteem and a favorable identity (Leary & Baumeister, 2000). Recent research has clarified this by emphasizing that people have two types of identity concerns: identity security and identity enhancement (Tyler & Mentovich, 2013). Procedural justice is important, first, because it communicates to people in groups that merging their identities with a group does not pose a threat to their sense of well-being—that is, that their identities will be secure. Second, justice suggests to people that if they merge their sense of self with the group, then there will be opportunities for their identities to be validated and enhanced and their well-being increased.

The distinction between security and enhancement flows from the psychological literature on avoidance and approach motivation (Elliott & Covington, 2001). This distinction is central to Lewin's (1935) work. However, it is most closely associated with the work of Maslow (1943, 1955), who distinguished between the need to reduce negative states of tension and the need to seek positive stimulation. More recently, this motivational distinction has emerged from a theoretical analysis of people's strategies when interacting with others. That analysis distinguishes the motivation for self-protection from the motivation for self-enhancement (Alicke & Sedikides, 2009). Alicke and Sedikides examine how people shape their interpretation of events to promote feelings of security and enhancement. They propose that people minimize their shortcomings and exaggerate their virtues to achieve these objectives by pursuing "purposive strategies... to explain or remember their decisions, actions, and characteristics in a way that maintains or advances their desired self-views" (p. 2).

The first concern is *identity security*. Although using a group to determine one's identity can facilitate positive feelings of self-worth and self-esteem, it also contains risks. People can receive favorable identity-relevant information, but they can also have their identities damaged when they receive negative feedback from others. For example, people who identify more strongly with an organization are more strongly impacted when they see that the group operates in unfair ways (Brockner, Tyler, & Cooper-Schneider, 1992). Opening one's self to others creates vulnerabilities and the possibility of receiving negative feedback that damages one's identity, perhaps best illustrated by the impact that corporate scandals can have on employees' sense of self. People are sensitive to the potential pitfalls of identifying with others who might provide them with negative status information, and, thus, they maintain distance. They are motivated to avoid negative experiences.

The idea of identity security is illustrated by the literature on stereotype threat (Steele, 1997), which argues that when people are potentially subject to the application of negative stereotypes, they are unwilling to engage in tasks for which their performance might result in damage to their identities and feelings of self-worth. The members of minority groups seek identity safety (Purdie-Vaughns & Walton, 2011) and are sensitive to cues of potential identity threats (Purdie-Vaughns, Steele, Davies, Ditlmann, & Crosby, 2008; Schmader, Major, & Gramzow, 2001). Schmader, Major, and Gramzow suggested that "psychological disengagement is a defensive detachment of self-esteem from a particular domain" (2001, p. 93). One already documented approach to addressing identity threat concerns is to provide people with information that bolsters their identity, thereby motivating engagement in achievement tasks (Cohen, Garcia, Purdie-Vaughns, Apfel & Brzustoski, 2009; Cook, Purdie-Vaughns, Garcia, & Cohen, 2011).

Another approach is to demonstrate to people that authorities or organizations act through fair procedures (Brooke & Tyler, 2011). Such procedures, which are neutral and do not reflect personal opinions or biases, provide evidence of identity security because actions are fact and rule based. Fair procedures also mandate fair and respectful treatment. To the degree that people feel that an authority or organization acts via fair procedures, they are more likely to judge that their identity can be safely and securely merged with that of the group. Justice, in other words, alleviates people's concerns that group membership will result in negative consequences for the self.

A second identity concern is that interaction with others leads to opportunities for *identity enhancement*. People have a fundamental need to have their positive sense of self affirmed, and interaction with others provides a way to affirm and enhance one's identity and self-esteem (Baumeister & Leary, 1995; Baumeister, Schmeichel, & Vohs, 2007; Crocker & Nuer, 2004). Studies show that such enhancement opportunities lead to favorable attitudes and behaviors. For example, Kawakami, Steele, Cifa, Phills, and Dovidio (2008) show that when people associate mathematics with approach motivations, their attitudes toward and performance in mathematics improve.

Theories of justice have long argued that an important role of justice is to provide people with reassurance that the world is ordered and structured, with people's fates flowing reasonably from their actions (Kay, Whitson, Gaucher, & Galinsky, 2009; Lerner, 1980). This motivates people to believe that investing themselves in activities with others is a reasonable strategy for pursuing high status and supporting a favorable sense of self (Laurin, Fitzsimons, & Kay, 2011). This is the case because fair procedures communicate to people both that their efforts will be evaluated in neutral, factual ways that are linked to objective and unbiased evaluations and that others will consider their needs and concerns in decision-making (Brooke & Tyler, 2011). Hence, the use of fair procedures communicates that engagement with an authority or organization offers opportunities for identity enhancement.

Using both experimental and nonexperimental approaches, Tyler and Mentovich (2013) demonstrated that identity security and identity enhancement are empirically distinct and have distinct consequences for attitudes and behaviors. Further identity security and identity enhancement mediate the impact of procedural justice on attitudes and behaviors, suggesting that they encompass people's key relational concerns. This very recent work on identity security sheds greater light on the psychological dynamics that undergird the relational models. They take the insight that procedural justice shapes social identity and dig much deeper into the underlying reasons that people are drawn toward this relational function of procedural justice. As a result, they offer an even deeper understanding of why and when employees will care about procedural justice the most.

Conclusion

The relational models of justice have done much to advance the progress of justice theorizing. We attribute their influence to the fact that their origins lie in answering the question: Why do people care about justice? Their focus on this fundamental psychological question may have, at least at first, made it seem as if they would have little impact on understanding organizational life. Indeed, it is likely that some organizational researchers regarded exploration of the psychology that underlies employees' concern with fairness as somewhat esoteric. Perhaps all that matters was evidence that employees react so strongly to justice? The story of the relational models shows this was not the case. By addressing the reasons that employees care about justice, the relational models have impacted all the key issues considered in organizational justice research. One primary goal of this chapter was to review the relational models and their impact on organizational justice research. More importantly, we sought to highlight some of the recent and innovative work that has been inspired by the relational perspective. To be sure, there are many questions left unanswered and there is much more work to be done, especially with regard to how the relational perspective relates to other predominant justice theories. We look forward to seeing the insights that emerge from the next wave of justice research, and we particularly hope that future work takes a more integrative approach than has been the case in the justice literature to date.

References

Alicke, M., & Sedikides, C. (2009). Self-enhancement and self-security: What they are and what they do. *European Review of Social Psychology, 20*, 1–48.

Bartel, C. A., Wrzesniewski, A., & Wiesenfeld, B. M. (2012). Knowing where you stand: Physical isolation, perceived respect, and organizational identification among virtual employees. *Organization Science, 23*, 743–757.

Baumeister, R., & Leary, M. (1995). The need to belong: Desire for interpersonal attachments as a fundamental human motivation. *Psychological Bulletin, 117*, 497–529.

Baumeister, R. F., Schmeichel, B. J., & Vohs, K. D. (2007). Self-regulation and the executive function. In A. Kruglanski and E. T. Higgins (Eds.), *Social Psychology: Handbook of basic principles* (2nd ed.). New York, NY: Guilford.

Begley, T. M., Lee, C., & Hui, C. (2006). Organizational level as a moderator of the relationship between justice perceptions and work-related reactions. *Journal of Organizational Behavior, 27*, 705–721.

Blader, S. L. (2007). What determines people's fairness judgments? Identification and outcomes influence procedural justice evaluations under uncertainty. *Journal of Experimental Social Psychology, 43*, 986–994.

Blader, S. L., & Chen, Y. R. (2011). What influences how higher status people respond to lower status others? Effects of procedural fairness, outcome favorability, and concerns about status. *Organization Science*, 22, 1040–1060.

Blader, S. L., & Chen, Y. R. (2012). Differentiating the effects of status and power: A justice perspective. *Journal of Personality and Social Psychology, 102*, 994–1014.

Blader, S. L., & Fortin, M. (2013). Revisiting the four component model of procedural justice. Unpublished manuscript.

Blader, S., & Tyler, T. R. (2003a). What constitutes fairness in work settings? A four-component model of procedural justice. *Human Resource Management Review, 12*, 107–126.

Blader, S., & Tyler, T. R. (2003b). A four component model of procedural justice: Defining the meaning of a "fair" process. *Personality and Social Psychology Bulletin, 29*, 747–758.

Blader, S. L., & Tyler, T. R. (2009). Testing and extending the group engagement model: Linkages between social identity, procedural justice, economic outcomes and extra-role behavior. *Journal of Applied Psychology, 94*, 445–464.

Bobocel, D. R. (2013). Coping with unfair events constructively or destructively: The effects of overall justice and self-other orientation. *Journal of Applied Psychology, 98*(5), 720–731.

Brickson, S. L. (2013). Athletes, best friends, and social activists: An integrative model accounting for the role of identity in organizational identification. *Organization Science, 24*, 226–245.

Brockner, J., Tyler, T. R., & Cooper-Schneider, R. (1992). The higher they are, the harder they fall: The effects of prior commitment and procedural injustice on subsequent commitment to social institutions. *Administrative Science Quarterly, 37*, 241–261.

Brockner, J., & Wiesenfeld, B. M. (1996). An integrative framework for explaining reactions to decisions: interactive effects of outcomes and procedures. *Psychological Bulletin, 120*, 189–208.

Brooke, J., & Tyler, T. R. (2011). Diversity and corporate performance: A review of the psychological literature. *North Carolina Law Review, 89*, 715–789.

Chen, Y., Brockner, J., & Greenberg, J. (2003). When is it "a pleasure to do business with you?" The effects of relative status, outcome favorability, and procedural fairness. *Organizational Behavior and Human Decision Processes, 92*, 1–21.

Cohen-Charash, Y., & Spector, P. E. (2001). The role of justice in organizations: A meta-analysis. *Organizational Behavior and Human Decision Processes, 86*, 278–321.

Cohen, G. L., Garcia, J., Purdie-Vaughns, V., Apfel, N., & Brzustosk, P. (2009). Recursive processes in self-affirmation. *Science, 324*, 400–403.

Colquitt, J. A. (2001). On the dimensionality of organizational justice: A construct validation of a measure. *Journal of Applied Psychology, 86*, 386–400.

Colquitt, J. A., Conlon, D. E., Wesson, M. J., Porter, C. O., & Ng, K. Y. (2001). Justice at the millennium: a meta-analytic review of 25 years of organizational justice research. *Journal of Applied Psychology, 86*, 425–445.

Colquitt, J. A., & Greenberg, J. (2003). Organizational justice: A fair assessment of the state of the literature. In J. Greenberg (Ed.), *Organizational behavior: The state of the science* (2nd ed.) (pp. 165–210). Mahwah, NJ: Erlbaum.

Cook, J. E., Purdie-Vaughns, V., Garcia, J., & Cohen, G. L. (2011). Chronic threat and contingent belonging: Protective benefits of values affirmation on identity development. *Journal of Personality and Social Psychology, 47*, 274–277.

Cornelis, I., van Heil, A., DeCremer, D., & Mayer, D. M. (2013). When leaders choose to be fair: Follower belongingness needs and leader empathy influences leaders' adherence to procedural fairness rules. *Journal of Experimental Social Psychology, 49*, 605–613.

Correll, J., Spencer, S. J., & Zanna, M. P. (2004). An affirmed self and an open mind: Self-affirmation and sensitivity to argument strength. *Journal of Experimental Social Psychology, 40*, 350–356.

Crawshaw, J. R., Cropanzano, R., Bell, C. M., & Nadisic, T. (2013). Organizational justice: New insights from behavioural ethics. *Human Relations, 66*, 1–20.

Crocker, J., & Nuer, N. (2004). The insatiable quest for self-worth. *Psychological Inquiry, 14*, 31–34.

De Cremer, D., & Blader, S. L. (2006). Why do people care about procedural fairness? The importance of belongingness in responding and attending to procedures. *European Journal of Social Psychology, 36*, 211–228.

De Cremer, D., & Tyler, T. R. (2005). Managing group behavior: The interplay between procedural justice, sense of self, and cooperation. *Advances in Experimental Social Psychology, 37*, 151–218.

De Cremer, D., & Tyler, T. R. (2007). The effects of trust in authority and procedural fairness on cooperation. *Journal of Applied Psychology, 92*, 639–649.

De Cremer, D., van Dijke, M., & Mayer, D. M. (2010). Cooperating when "you" and "I" are treated fairly: The moderating role of leader prototypicality. *Journal of Applied Psychology, 95*, 1121–1133.

Ellemers, N., Sleebos, E., Stam, D., & de Gilder, D. (2013). Feeling included and valued: How perceived respect affects positive team identity and willingness to invest in the team. *British Journal of Management, 24*, 21–37.

Elliot, A. J., & Covington, M. V. (2001). Approach and avoidance motivation. *Educational Psychology Review, 13*, 73–92.

Fiske, S. T. (1993). Controlling other people: The impact of power on stereotyping. *American Psychologist, 48*, 621–628.

Fiske, S. T. (2010). Interpersonal stratification: Status, power, and subordination. *Handbook of Social Psychology, 5*, 941–982.

Flynn, F. J., Reagans, R. E., Amanatullah, E. T., & Ames, D. R. (2006). Helping one's way to the top: Self-monitors achieve status by helping others and knowing who helps whom. *Journal of Personality and Social Psychology, 91*, 1123–1137.

Galinsky, A. D., Magee, J. C., Gruenfeld, D. H., Whitson, J. A., & Liljenquist, K. A. (2008). Power reduces the press of the situation: implications for creativity, conformity, and dissonance. *Journal of Personality and Social Psychology, 95*, 1450–1466.

Galinsky, A. D., Magee, J. C., Inesi, M. E., & Gruenfeld, D. H. (2006). Power and perspectives not taken. *Psychological Science, 17*, 1068–1074.

Gruenfeld, D. H., Inesi, M. E., Magee, J. C., & Galinsky, A. D. (2008). Power and the objectification of social targets. *Journal of Personality and Social Psychology, 95*, 111–127.

Hogg, M., & Abrams, D. (1988). *Social identifications.* London: Routledge.

Holmvall, C. M., & Bobocel, D. R. (2008). What fair procedures say about me: Self-construals and reactions to procedural fairness. *Organizational Behavior and Human Decision Processes, 105*, 147–168.

Hornsey, M. J., & Jetten, J. (2004). The individual within the group: Balancing the need to belong with the need to be different. *Personality and Social Psychology Review, 8*, 248–264.

Huo, Y. J. (2002). Justice and the regulation of social relations: When and why do group members deny claims to social goods? *British Journal of Social Psychology, 41*, 535–562.

Huo, Y. J., Binning, K. R., & Molina, L. E. (2010). Testing an integrative model of respect: Implications for social engagement and well-being. *Personality and Social Psychology Bulletin, 36*, 200–212.

Johnson, R. E., & Lord, R. G. (2010). Implicit effects of justice on self-identity. *Journal of Applied Psychology, 95*, 681–695.

Johnson, R. E., Selenta, C., & Lord, R. G. (2006). When organizational justice and the self-concept meet: Consequences for the organization and its members. *Organizational Behavior and Human Decision Processes, 99*, 175–201.

Kawakami, K., Steele, J. R., Cifa, C., Phills, C. E., & Dovidio, J. F. (2008). Approaching math increases math=me, math=pleasant. *Journal of Experimental Social Psychology, 44*, 818–825.

Kay, A. C., Whitson, J. A., Gaucher, D., & Galinsky, A. D. (2009). Compensatory control: Achieving order through the mind, our institutions, and the heavens. *Current Directions in Psychological Science, 18*, 264–268.

Kramer, R. M. (2001). Identity and trust in organizations: One anatomy of a productive but problematic relationship. In M. Hogg & D. Terry (Eds.), *Social identity processes in organizational contexts* (pp. 167–180). Philadelphia, PA: Psychology Press.

Laurin, K., Fitzsimons, G. M., & Kay, A. C. (2011). Social disadvantage and the self-regulatory function of justice beliefs. *Journal of Personality and Social Psychology, 100*, 149–171.

Leary, M. R., & Baumeister, R. F. (2000). The nature and function of self-esteem: Sociometer theory. In M. Zanna (Ed.), *Advances in experimental social psychology* (Vol. 32, pp. 1–62). San Diego, CA: Academic Press.

Lee, F., & Tiedens, L. Z. (2001). Who's being served? "Self-serving" attributions in social hierarchies. *Organizational Behavior and Human Decision Processes, 84*, 254–287.

LePine, J. A., Erez, A., & Johnson, D. E. (2002). The nature and dimensionality of organizational citizenship behavior: a critical review and meta-analysis. *Journal of Applied Psychology, 87*, 52.

Lerner, M. J. (1980). *The belief in a just world: A fundamental delusion*. New York, NY: Plenum.

Lewin, K. (1935). *A dynamic theory of personality*. New York, NY: McGraw-Hill.

Lind, E. A., Kanfer, R., & Earley, P. C. (1990). Voice, control, and procedural justice: Instrumental and noninstrumental concerns in fairness judgments. *Journal of Personality and Social Psychology, 59*, 952.

Lind, E. A., & Tyler, T. R. (1988). *The social psychology of procedural justice*. New York, NY: Plenum.

Maslow, A. H. (1943). A theory of human motivation. *Psychological Review, 50*, 370–396.

Maslow, A. H. (1955). Deficiency motivation and growth motivation. In M. Jones (Ed.), *Nebraska Symposium on Motivation*. University of Nebraska Press.

Mayer, D. M., Kuenzi, M., Greenbaum, R., Bardes, M., & Salvador, R. B. (2009). How low does ethical leadership flow? Test of a trickle-down model. *Organizational Behavior and Human Decision Processes, 108*, 1–13.

Mentovich, A. (2012). *The power of fair procedures: The effect of procedural justice on perceptions of power and hierarchy*. Unpublished doctoral thesis, New York University.

Moorman, R. H. (1991). Relationship between organizational justice and organizational citizenship behaviors: do fairness perceptions influence employee citizenship? *Journal of Applied Psychology, 76*, 845–855.

Olkkonen, M. E., & Lipponen, J. (2006). Relationships between organizational justice, identification with organization and work unit, and group-related outcomes. *Organizational Behavior and Human Decision Processes, 100*, 202–215.

Organ, D. W., & Ryan, K. (1995). A meta-analytic review of attitudinal and dispositional predictors of organizational citizenship behavior. *Personnel Psychology, 48*, 775–802.

Overbeck, J. R., & Park, B. (2006). Powerful perceivers, powerless objects: Flexibility of powerholders' social attention. *Organizational Behavior and Human Decision Processes, 99*, 227–243.

Petty, R. E., & Cacioppo, J. T. (1984). Source factors and the elaboration likelihood model of persuasion. *Advances in Consumer Research, 11*, 668–672.

Petty, R. E., & Wegener, D. T. (1998). Matching versus mismatching attitude functions: Implications for scrutiny of persuasive messages. *Personality and Social Psychology Bulletin, 24*, 227–240.

Purdie-Vaughns, V., Steele, C., Davies, P. G., Ditlmann, R., & Crosby, J. R. (2008). Social identity contingencies: How diversity cues signal threat or safety for African Americans in mainstream institutions. *Journal of Personality and Social Psychology, 94*, 615–630.

Purdie-Vaughns, V., & Walton, G. M. (2011). Is multiculturalism bad for African Americans? Redefining inclusion through the lens of identity safety. In Troop, L. R. & Mallett, R. K. (Eds.), *Moving beyond prejudice reduction* (pp. 159–177). Washington, D.C.: American Psychological Association.

Schmader, T., Major, B., & Gramzow, R. H. (2001). Coping with ethnic stereotypes in the Academic domain: Perceived injustice and psychological disengagement. *Journal of Social Issues, 57*, 93–111.

Schminke, M., Cropanzano, R., & Rupp, D. E. (2002). Organization structure and fairness perceptions: The moderating effects of organizational level. *Organizational Behavior and Human Decision Processes, 89*, 881–905.

Scott, B. A., Colquitt, J. A., & Paddock, E. L. (2009). An actor-focused model of justice rule adherence and violation: the role of managerial motives and discretion. *Journal of Applied Psychology, 94*, 756–769.

Scott, B. A., Colquitt, J. A., & Zapata-Phelan, C. P. (2007). Justice as a dependent variable: Subordinate charisma as a predictor of interpersonal and informational justice perceptions. *Journal of Applied Psychology, 92*, 1597–1609.

Sluss, D. M., & Ashforth, B. E. (2007). Relational identity and identification: Defining ourselves through work relationships. *Academy of Management Review, 32*, 9–32.

Smith, H. J., Olson, G., Agronick, G., & Tyler, T. (2009). Everyday interactions with university authorities: Authority treatment quality, outcome favorability and first-year students' university adjustment. *Group Processes & Intergroup Relations, 12*, 209–226.

Smith, H. J., & Tyler, T. R. (1997). Choosing the right pond: The influence of the status of one's group and one's status in that group on self-esteem and group-oriented behaviors. *Journal of Experimental Social Psychology, 33*, 146–170.

Smith, H. J., Tyler, T. R., Huo, Y. J., Ortiz, D. J., & Lind, E. A. (1998). The self-relevant implications of the group-value model: Group membership, self-worth, and procedural justice. *Journal of Experimental Social Psychology, 34*, 470–493.

Stahl, T., Vermunt, R., & Ellemers, N. (2008). For love or money?: How activation of relational versus instrumental concerns affects reactions to decision-making procedures. *Journal of Experimental Social Psychology, 44*, 80–94.

Steele, C. (1997). A threat in the air: How stereotypes shape intellectual identities and performance. *American Psychologist, 52*, 613–629.

Tajfel, H., & Turner, J. C. (1986). The social identity theory of intergroup behaviour. In S. Worchel & W. G. Austin (Eds.), *Psychology of intergroup relations* (pp. 7–24). Chicago, IL: Nelson-Hall.

Thibaut, J. W., & Kelly, H. (1959). *The social psychology of groups*. New York, NY: Wiley.

Thibaut, J. W., & Walker, L. (1975). *Procedural justice: A psychological analysis*. Hillsdale, NJ: Erlbaum.

Tyler, T. R. (1987). Conditions leading to value-expressive effects in judgments of procedural justice: A test of four models. *Journal of Personality and Social Psychology, 52*, 333-.

Tyler, T. R. (1989). The psychology of procedural justice: A test of the group-value model. *Journal of Personality and Social Psychology, 57*, 830–838.

Tyler, T. R. (1994). Psychological models of the justice motive: Antecedents of distributive and procedural justice. *Journal of Personality and Social Psychology, 67*, 850–863.

Tyler, T. R. (1999). Why do people help organizations?: Social identity and pro-organizational behavior. In B. Staw & R. Sutton (Eds.), *Research on organizational behavior* (Vol. 21, pp. 201–246). Greenwich, CT: JAI.

Tyler, T. R. (2006a). *Why people obey the law.* Princeton, NJ: Princeton University Press.

Tyler, T. R. (2006b). Legitimacy and legitimation. *Annual Review of Psychology 57,* 375–400.

Tyler, T. R., & Blader, S. L. (2000). *Cooperation in groups: Procedural justice, social identity, and behavioral engagement.* Philadelphia, PA.: Psychology Press.

Tyler, T. R., & Blader, S. L. (2001). Identity and cooperative behavior in groups. *Group Processes & Intergroup Relations, 4,* 207–226.

Tyler, T. R., & Blader, S. L. (2003). Procedural justice, social identity and cooperative behavior. *Personality and Social Psychology Review, 7,* 349–361.

Tyler, T., & Blader, S. L. (2004). Justice and negotiation. In M. Gelfand & J. Brett (Eds.), *The handbook of negotiation and culture* (pp. 295–312). Stanford, CA: Stanford University Press.

Tyler, T. R., Boeckmann, R., Smith, H. J., & Huo, Y. J. (1997). *Social justice in a diverse society.* Denver, CO: Westview.

Tyler, T. R., & De Cremer, D. (2005). Process-based leadership: Fair procedures and reactions to organizational change. *The Leadership Quarterly, 16,* 529–545.

Tyler, T. R., & Degoey, P. (1995). Collective restraint in social dilemmas: Procedural justice and social identification effects on support for authorities. *Journal of Personality and Social Psychology, 69,* 482–497.

Tyler, T. R., Degoey, P., & Smith, H. (1996). Understanding why the justice of group procedures matters: A test of the psychological dynamics of the group-value model. *Journal of Personality and Social Psychology, 70*(5), 913.

Tyler, T. R., & Lind, E. A. (1992). A relational model of authority in groups. *Advances in Experimental Social Psychology, 25,* 115–191.

Tyler, T. R., & Mentovich, A. (2013). Two functions of procedural fairness: Protecting identity security and promoting identity enhancement. Unpublished manuscript.

Van den Bos, K., & Lind, E. A. (2002). Uncertainty management by means of fairness judgments. *Advances in Experimental Social Psychology, 34,* 1–60.

Van Laar, C., Derks, B., Ellemers, N., & Bleeker, D. (2010). Valuing social identity. *Journal of Social Issues, 66,* 602–617.

Van Prooijen, J. W., van den Bos, K., & Wilke, H. A. M. (2004). The role of standing in the psychology of procedural justice. *European Review of Social Psychology, 15,* 33–58.

CHAPTER

17 Fairness Heuristic Theory, the Uncertainty Management Model, and Fairness at Work

Devon Proudfoot *and* E. Allan Lind

Abstract

This chapter provides an overview of Fairness Heuristic Theory and the Uncertainty Management Model as they endeavor to answer the questions of when and why employees are likely to attend to fairness in the workplace. Emphasis is given to the implications of these theoretical perspectives for workplace manager–report (and leader–follower) interactions and for organizational policies. We conclude the chapter with a discussion of how these theories relate to perspectives emerging from System Justification Theory on how people construct fairness judgments and when they may be more or less likely to attend to fairness in the workplace.

Key Words: Fairness Heuristic Theory, Uncertainty Management Model, System Justification Theory, organizational policies, manager-report interactions, leader-follower interactions, attention to fairness

Decades of research on organizational justice have demonstrated that fairness in the workplace is immensely important to people. Employees respond very positively to work situations they deem to be fair and react very negatively to work situations they deem unfair (e.g., Adams, 1965; Brockner & Wiesenfeld, 1996; Weiss, Suckow, Cropanzano, 1999). Consequently, workplace fairness, or lack thereof, predicts a multitude of employee attitudes and behaviors (see generally Greenberg & Colquitt, 2005; Lind & Tyler, 1988; Tyler & Lind, 1992).

Perceiving one's organization to be fair and just has been demonstrated to have a variety of desirable consequences, including higher job satisfaction (Ambrose & Schminke, 2009; Folger & Cropanzano, 1998; Greenberg, 1982; McFarlin & Sweeney, 1992), greater organizational commitment (Ambrose & Schminke, 2009; Korsgaard, Schweiger, & Sapienza, 1995; Moorman, 1991) and increased acceptance of workplace policies (Greenberg, 1994, 2000; Greenberg & Scott, 1996). Employees who judge their workplace to be fair engage in more organizational citizenship behaviors (OCBs) (Karriker & Williams, 2009; Konovsky & Folger 1991; Podsakoff & McKenzie, 1993), exhibit higher job performance (Colquitt, Noe, & Jackson, 2002; Lind, Kanfer, & Early, 1990) and are less likely to quit (Ambrose & Schminke, 2009; Simons & Roberson, 2003).

Conversely, perceptions of organizational unfairness or injustice have been linked to several undesirable outcomes, including decreased cooperation and less obedience toward authority figures (Huo, Smith, Tyler, & Lind, 1996; Lind, Kulik, Ambrose, & de Vera Park, 1993), increased absenteeism and turnover (Alexander & Ruderman, 1987; De Boer, Bakker, Syroit, Schaufeli, 2002) and lack of organizational citizenship behaviors (Moorman, Nieghood, & Organ, 1993; Niehoff & Moorman, 1993). Moreover, employees who believe their treatment in the workplace to be unfair are more likely to participate in counterproductive work behaviors (Cohen-Charash & Spector, 2001; Fox, Spector, & Miles, 2001), steal from their workplace (Greenberg, 1990; 1993), engage in workplace violence (Dietz, Robinson, Folger, Baron, & Schulz, 2003; Folger & Baron, 1996), and sue their organization (Lind, Greenberg, Scott, & Welchans, 2000).

The powerful effect of fairness on workplace attitudes and behavior has led to the development of a substantial literature on the psychology of justice in organizations. Much of the classic research on organizational justice focused on exploring the consequences of perceptions of fairness and unfairness (see, e.g., Lind & Tyler, 1988; Tyler & Lind, 1992) and on distinctions between distributive, procedural, and interactive justice experiences (Ambrose & Arnaud, 2005; Bies, 2005; Cropanzano & Ambrose, 2001; Folger, 1977; Thibaut & Walker, 1975, 1978). More recently, some scholars have directed their attention toward answering the question of *when* fairness is likely to matter more to people and when it is likely to matter less. As we have sought to understand *when* fairness matters, we have also found ourselves giving substantial consideration to the question of *why* judgments of how fair or unfair one's treatment or outcomes are have such a robust effect on so many aspects of organizational life.

The goal of this chapter is to provide an overview of two related theoretical works—Fairness Heuristic Theory (Lind, 2001; Van den Bos, Lind, & Wilke, 2001) and the Uncertainty Management Model (Lind & Van den Bos, 2002; Van den Bos, 2001a; Van den Bos & Lind, 2002) as they endeavor to answer these questions. We focus on the implications of these theoretical perspectives for leader–follower interactions in the workplace and for organizational policies. We then discuss these theories in relation to perspectives emerging from System Justification Theory (Jost & Banaji, 1994), which also provide insight into when people may be more or less likely to attend to organizational justice.

Fairness Heuristic Theory

Fairness Heuristic Theory (Lind, 2001; Van den Bos, Lind, & Wilke, 2001) seeks to provide a coherent account of *when* and *why* people form and use fairness judgments. In doing so, the theory also describes *how* people's beliefs about the fairness of a given context are psychologically constructed.

The Fairness Heuristic

A central tenet of Fairness Heuristic Theory is its conceptualization of fairness in terms of cognitions, focusing specifically on how subjective *beliefs* about organizational fairness drive key workplace attitudes and behaviors. According to this theory, employees adopt early, relatively quickly formulated judgments about the fairness of a given work context and incorporate these judgments into an overall evaluation of the fairness of their work situation, which they then use as a heuristic or cognitive shortcut to guide their behavior and interpretation of subsequent fairness-relevant information in that context. This *fairness heuristic* is also used to regulate their emotional involvement at work. One important implication of this is that rather than constantly scanning their environment for new fairness-related information, people heavily draw from their early workplace experiences to construct a general impression of how fair their organization is. Thus, newly hired employees, or those recently transferred to a new team or department, are likely to use information available during early interactions with coworkers and authority figures to form a stable global fairness judgment about their new work environment.

In suggesting *when* people are most likely to form their beliefs about whether a context is fair or not, Fairness Heuristic Theory proposes a multiphase process through which people construct, then use, and then re-construct their fairness judgments. Early workplace experiences (or, as we will note later, experiences following an exceptional event that triggers re-evaluation of the fairness heuristic) constitute the "judgment phase" of fairness cognition process. Once an initial fairness assessment has been formulated, people tend to use this judgment, more or less uncritically, as a heuristic to guide their subsequent workplace reactions and evaluations. Fairness Heuristic Theory calls this second period of time the "use phase." In this phase, the global fairness judgment, if positive, facilitates trust, engagement, and acceptance of authority in everyday work life. Feelings of fairness enable the person to cooperate and identify with their team or organization, whereas feelings of unfairness block this type of psychological engagement and instead prompt a strict quid-pro-quo approach to responding to requests. According to the initial statement of the theory, the use phase persists until there is a striking change or inconsistency that makes it clear that "all bets are off." Certain environmental changes (phase shifting events) may trigger a reassessment of the cognitive shortcut that the fairness heuristic supplies and may provoke the person to recalibrate by seeking out new fairness information and constructing a new fairness heuristic to rely on in later decisions about how much to cooperate or engage.

Thus Fairness Heuristic Theory introduced two novel theoretical ideas. First, rather than delineating the unique effects of different types of justice on organizational outcomes, as is common in justice research (see e.g., Bies, 2005), Fairness Heuristic Theory posits that, from the psychological perspective of employees, different types of justice experiences are cognitively integrated to form an overall global judgment of organizational fairness, which then influences employees' workplace-relevant attitudes and behaviors (also see Ambrose & Schminke, 2009). Fairness Heuristic Theory labels this global judgment a *fairness heuristic*. Second, in contrast to the assumption in many justice analyses that people are constantly vigilant to fairness information, Fairness Heuristic Theory posits that people's attention to fairness is, in reality, episodic. Specifically, the theory advances the idea that employees use initial cues about the fairness of their workplace to form a judgment about whether their organization is fair. Once constructed, this fairness judgment acts as cognitive heuristic—a relatively change-resistant lens through which subsequent organizational experiences are interpreted.

Why Do People Use Fairness Heuristics?

Fairness Heuristic Theory takes the view that people think about fairness in terms of their relationships with other people. The theory draws on the group-value model of justice and the relational model of authority (Lind & Tyler, 1988; Tyler & Lind, 1992) in its view of how and why people care about fairness. The relational or group-based nature of fairness has been demonstrated empirically in numerous studies. Fair treatment has been shown to have a greater impact on overall fairness perceptions when people are dealing with members of their in-group compare to when they are dealing with members of an out-group (Huo et al. 1996). For example, the fairness of in-group authorities has been shown to matter more to people than the fairness of out-group authorities (Platow et al. 2012; Smith, Tyler, Huo, Ortiz, & Lind, 1998). These studies and others all demonstrate that fairness is closely connected to judgments about one's relationship to the organizational authorities, teams, and groups at whose hands fair or unfair treatment is received (also see Tyler and Lind, 1992).

Consistent with this research, Fairness Heuristic Theory argues that people seek to form judgments about the fairness of their environment early on because fairness is a readily constructed indicator that suggests they are safe from exclusion and exploitation by others in their group. That is, attending to fairness information helps people resolve what Lind (1994) terms the "fundamental social dilemma," a dilemma posed by the tension between the potential advantages and disadvantages associated with engaging as a group member. Although group membership may come with psychological and material benefits, including an increased sense of structure and identity and the possibility of partaking in group rewards that are greater than would be had as an individual, it also comes with the risk of potential losses in terms of individual rewards, identity, personal freedom, and control over one's future. The fairness heuristic, then, acts as a "pivotal cognition" in resolving this dilemma, allowing people to assess whether they are safe or unsafe as they move from a self-interested orientation to an orientation that favors the interests of their group or organization.

Building on the idea that fairness is relational in nature, original formulations of Fairness Heuristic Theory conceptualized fairness acts as a proxy for interpersonal trust (Lind, 2001; Van den Bos, Wilke, & Lind, 1998). In support of this notion, Van den Bos and colleagues (1998) have shown that, in a laboratory experiment, people who lack information about whether they can trust an authority figure rely more on procedural fairness information when assessing their outcomes and satisfaction with their experience. Similarly, in a field survey, Jones & Martens (2009) found that employees use fairness information as a heuristic to infer trust when the trustworthiness of organizational authority is uncertain.

What Are the Consequences of Fairness Heuristic Processes?

A major feature of Fairness Heuristic Theory is its proposition that the cognitive construction of fairness judgments is episodic in nature. That is, the theory conceives of the fairness judgment process as fundamentally changing over time. People in a new situation (e.g., those who are just joining a team, those who suddenly find themselves with a new boss, or even students who find themselves in an unfamiliar psychology experimental procedure) will be motivated to find any available fairness-relevant information in the environment in order to develop a fairness judgment that can guide their behavior. Once they have generated a fairness judgment, however, people will then begin to assimilate later experiences to this initial fairness judgment. A key idea here is that, in order for one's fairness judgment to be useful as a decision heuristic, helping a person answer the question of whether to engage and cooperate with his or her team or organization, the judgment has to be generated quickly and it needs to be reasonably stable (and, therefore, not open to radical revision at each small variation in treatment, process, or outcome). This set of propositions leads to some novel predictions about how time and context affect the fairness judgment process.

PRIMACY EFFECT

Fairness Heuristic Theory predicts a primacy effect in the fairness judgment process, whereby early fairness information receives greater weight than does later fairness information. Stated slightly differently, the same fair or unfair action (or outcome) will have greater impact if it is encountered early on in a new context than if it is encountered later on.

Lind, Kray, and Thompson (2001) empirically demonstrate just such a primacy effect. In a simulated work context, they found that early experiences of a fair or unfair procedure (in this experiment, being given or denied voice) had a greater impact on people's ultimate fairness judgments than did later experiences of the same procedures. Specifically, people who were treated fairly versus unfairly by a new supervisor on the first round of a three-round work assignment showed greater differences in ratings of their supervisor's fairness than did people who received the same fair or unfair treatment on the third round of the assignment. Consistent with what one would expect from the group-value and relational-authority foundations of Fairness Heuristic Theory, this effect was found to be stronger for people who identified more strongly with their work group.

More recent work has applied Fairness Heuristic Theory's primacy effect hypothesis to study individuals' dispositional characteristics and their judgments about future events. People's chronic propensity to trust others has been shown to act as a preexisting fairness heuristic through which their workplace experiences are interpreted (Bianchi & Brockner, 2012; Colquitt, Scott, Judge, & Shaw, 2006). In addition, existing global fairness judgments can influence the extent to which people anticipate being treated fairly by a future organizational policy that has not yet been implemented (Rodell & Colquitt, 2009). In this research, these anticipatory justice judgments also predict the fairness workers report experiencing in relation to the policy three months after it was enacted.

SUBSTITUTABILITY EFFECT

A phenomenon closely related to the primacy effect involves the substitutability of different kinds of justice information in informing overall fairness judgments. That is, the global judgment used as a fairness heuristic can be derived from distributive, procedural, or interactional justice information and, according to the theory, subsequent fairness experiences and information are assimilated to this early global judgment. Van den Bos, Vermunt, & Wilke (1997) used this aspect of Fairness Heuristic Theory, the notion of primacy effects, and the idea that fairness heuristics are resistant to change, to predict that early fairness information of one type would affect the interpretation of later fairness information of a different type. Thus, early fair or unfair outcomes should affect the evaluation of subsequent procedures or later interpersonal treatment. The basic idea here is that a person encountering multiple "waves" of fairness information will rely on his or her existing generalized fairness judgment from the first wave of experiences rather than a full evaluation of the fairness of later waves of information.

The substitutability of fairness information is particularly important when people find themselves in situations in which information is missing or ambiguous. In these contexts, people are especially likely to use aspects of the situation about which they *do* have fairness information to guide their interpretation of the fairness of aspects of the situation for which they lack information or when available information is difficult to interpret (cf. Van den Bos, Lind, Vermunt, & Wilke, 1997; Van den Bos, Wilke, & Lind, 1998). Consistent with this, empirical evidence demonstrates that when the fairness of one's outcome is difficult to decipher (as is the case when one does not know the outcome of others relative to one's own outcome), procedural fairness has a greater impact on overall fairness judgments (Van den Bos, Lind, Vermunt, & Wilke, 1997). Similarly, when information about the fairness of a process or procedure is ambiguous, as in the case of procedures that implicitly (rather than explicitly) deny people the opportunity to voice their opinions, people are more likely to rely on outcome information when assessing the fairness of the process (Van den Bos, 1999).

Interestingly, the primacy and substitutability effects predicted by Fairness Heuristic Theory and found in the studies described earlier provide a novel explanation for the especially strong influence of procedural justice on overall fairness perceptions and related attitudes. Based on the finding that procedural fairness has a stronger impact on overall fairness judgments and satisfaction than outcome fairness, a substantial body of scholarship put forth the view that procedural justice may matter more to people than distributive justice (e.g., Alexander & Ruderman, 1987; Tyler & Caine, 1981; see generally Lind & Tyler, 1988). However, Fairness Heuristic Theory points to the possibility that procedures might influence global fairness perceptions more than outcomes do, not necessarily because processes are more important to people than outcomes, but because process information tends to come *before* outcome information (primacy effect), and later outcome information might be assimilated to the general fairness judgment already formed on the basis of the early process information (substitutability effect).

When Are Fairness Heuristics More or Less Likely to Be Re-evaluated?

According to Fairness Heuristic Theory, preexisting fairness heuristics normally color expectations about the fairness of one's organization and thus determine how subsequent events are interpreted. However, the theory also predicts that "phase shifting events" can trigger a re-evaluation of a given fairness heuristic. Such events generally constitute a violation of expectations. They may include extreme norm transgressions, such as in the case of violation of moral mandates (Skitka, 2002), extremely negative treatment, or evidence that the relationship between the individual and organization is changing. For instance, Jones and Skarlicki (2005) demonstrate that workers who are given initial social cues indicating that an authority was fair but then received unfair treatment by that authority (thus violating their expectations) react more negatively to this treatment than workers who had no previous information about the reputation of the authority (also see Folger, Rosenfield, Grove, & Corkran, 1979). Furthermore, Lind and his colleagues (Lind, Greenberg, Scott, & Welchans, 2000) present evidence that workers who had recently been fired or laid off were very sensitive to how fairly they were treated by their organization, specifically at their time of termination (a time when the relationship between the organization and the individual is obviously changing), and perceptions of how fair their termination was significantly predicted workers' intentions to file wrongful termination claims.

Fairness Heuristic Theory suggests that reevaluation of fairness heuristics will occur during shifts in organizational structure or fundamental changes in organizational relationships, such as during mergers and acquisitions. When we consider the Uncertainty Management Model later in this chapter, we will see that feelings of personal uncertainty and insecurity may act as the mechanism by which many of these situations trigger reevaluation of the general fairness assessment underlying the fairness heuristic.

Conversely, drawing on what is known about general heuristic processing, we can also speculate about contexts in which fairness heuristics are less likely to be re-evaluated. The original statements of Fairness Heuristic Theory (Lind, 2001; Van den Bos et al. 2001) did not include consideration of many of these factors, but theoretical advances in social cognition allow us to make some predictions based on what we now know about cognitive processes. Specifically, people who lack cognitive resources have been shown to rely more on heuristic processing of other types. In the domain of social judgments, for instance, people who are cognitively busy or depleted (for example, when they are distracted by other tasks or tired) are more likely to use heuristic shortcuts when making judgments about other people (e.g., Gilbert & Hixon, 1991; Gilbert, Pelham, & Krull, 1988; Bodenhausen, 1990). Van den Bos, Peters, Bobocel, and Ybema (2006) also demonstrate that being cognitively busy may make people less likely to react negatively to inequity. Specifically, in their studies, they present evidence that although people are generally less satisfied when given better outcomes than others' compared to when they are given outcomes that are equitable, this difference in satisfaction goes away when people's available cognitive resources are strongly limited. The authors suggest that, under cognitive load, people are less likely to correct for their initial preferences to incorporate fairness concerns.

We would expect, then, to use the terminology of Fairness Heuristic Theory, that when people are operating under high cognitive load, or when they are cognitively "stretched thin," or depleted by either their workload or the nature of their job, they will be less likely to transition from the heuristic-based use phase back into the more detail-oriented judgment phase in terms of how they assess the fairness of their environment. In this circumstance, it is possible, as Lind (2001) notes, that unfair experiences may be stored in memory and not evaluated until the cognitive load is reduced. At that time, insecurity, uncertainty, or sudden recognition of a large discrepancy between a previous fairness judgment and one's current experience might trigger a rapid transition into the judgment phase, with attendant re-evaluation of both overall fairness and willingness to cooperate and identify with the team or organization.

Practical Implications

There are a number of interesting implications of Fairness Heuristic Theory, as well as the research it has stimulated on primacy and substitutability effects. First, the theory predicts that organizational leaders would do well to focus on impressing those they lead with fairness-relevant behaviors early in their tenure in leadership positions. At least one empirical study has provided support for this prediction: Janson, Levy, Sitkin, and Lind (2008) found evidence of a fairness heuristic in leadership evaluations. In their study, which used data from a leadership survey conducted in several different countries and in a variety of different industries, positive early fairness judgments seemed to overwhelm later information about other positive or negative leadership behaviors. Fairness Heuristic Theory also suggests that special attention should be devoted to fairness at times when situational changes in the organization might prompt people to move from the "use phase" of fairness judgments into a new judgment phase. Mergers and acquisitions, or changes aimed at restructuring units, tasks, or reporting relationships are all the sort of phase-shifting events that seem likely to push people back into devoting cognitive resources to assessing (or re-assessing) the fairness judgments that underlie the fairness heuristic.

Note that there might be times when an organization may benefit from shifting its employees away from the use phase and into the judgment phase. If previous unfair treatment (real or perceived) had generated the perception of an unfair leader or organization, it might be advisable to "induce" feelings of a change in situation so that a new, more positive, heuristic can be generated. Sometimes, we suspect, organizations make a show of restructuring because those in charge intuit that this might allow for a "fresh start" with new fairness judgments based on new (and better) treatment experiences. Of course, if such a deliberate induction of a new judgment phase for fairness beliefs is not followed by experiences that are, in fact, perceived to be fair, then this exercise is likely to be unsuccessful.

That said, the line of reasoning just described does point out that changes intended to induce new fairness perceptions need to be both obvious and proximal to the people whose fairness judgments need to be changed. It seems unlikely that shuffling C-suite personnel would stimulate rank-and-file employees to shift into judgment phase processing of fairness information, but a change of membership in the employee's immediate team might well have that effect.

On the other hand, Fairness Heuristic Theory also suggests that there are times when organizational leaders can rely on the cooperation generated by employees' positive fairness heuristics without being concerned deeply with how their every action is judged with respect to fairness. When team members are deeply in the use phase posited by the theory, for example, they might be relatively insensitive to unfair treatment; this is similar to the experimental participants who first received and then were denied voice in the Lind et al. (2001) primacy study. It would never be wise to push this "buffer" against later unfair treatment too far, of course, even if the theory is correct and minor injustices are disregarded in the use phase, there is always the danger that memories of these injustices will be processed the next time events push the person in question into a new judgment phase.

Furthermore, Fairness Heuristic Theory's contention that global fairness judgments matter most in determining people's attitudes and behaviors related to cooperation and group identification has important workplace implications. Although specific types of fairness (distributive, procedural) may indeed show stronger or weaker relationships on some specific organizational attitudes or behaviors, Fairness Heuristic Theory notes that it is the rapidly formed global fairness judgment that will have the strongest impact on those attitudes and behavior that are specifically related to one's tendency to engage with and contribute to their group. Ambrose and Schminke (2009) provide striking evidence for this pattern of effects. Their data imply that a top priority for managers should be fairness in any form; Fairness Heuristic Theory suggests that this is true especially early in employees' organizational relationships.

In general, the practical implications of Fairness Heuristic Theory point to the wisdom of being attentive to events that might prompt organizational members to shift into the judgment phase of processing information about fairness. When members are likely to be in this phase, organizational leaders would be well-advised to quickly make fairness-relevant information and experiences salient. The substitutability effect tells us that it does not really matter much what sort of fairness information is put forward, only that this information be presented early on and be unambiguous. The implication of the Lind et al. (2001), Van den Bos, Vermunt, & Wilke (1997), and Van den Bos et al. (1998) studies is that the judgment phase is quite limited in duration. Thus, if positive fairness judgments are quickly engendered, they will facilitate cooperation and generally positive team-orientated behavior. Once the use phase is in full force, organizational leaders might then focus their efforts on avoiding any substantial injustice, since such experiences may push employees into a new judgment phase. Instead, at this point, leaders should focusing on making good use of the cooperation and engagement prompted by employees' positive fairness heuristic to secure good results for all.

Uncertainty Management Model

Extending many of the propositions put forth by Fairness Heuristic Theory, the Uncertainty Management Model (Lind & Van den Bos, 2002; Van den Bos, 2001a; Van den Bos & Lind, 2002) mainly focuses on further exploring *when* and *why* fairness matters to people. The Uncertainty Management Model also provides new insight into the process by which fairness judgments are formed. One of the model's principal contributions to the organizational justice literature is its conceptualization of the link between fairness concerns and uncertainty management; it argues that fairness beliefs serve a specific psychological function: they help people manage feelings of uncertainty. Consequently, the model predicts that people are more likely to attend to fairness during times of high uncertainty, that psychological uncertainty plays a crucial role in the construction of fairness beliefs, and that positive fairness beliefs help people deal with uncertainty.

Psychological Uncertainty

The Uncertainty Management Model begins with the notion, both inside and outside of organizations.[1] From fluctuations in the economy to the increasingly diverse ways in which organizations and the labor force are structured, today's workers must deal with high levels of unpredictability. An abundance of social psychological research shows that people are generally averse to feelings of uncertainty and are motivated to reduce subjective feelings that the world is an uncertain place (e.g., Fiske & Taylor, 1991; Hogg, 2007; McGregor, Zanna, Holmes, & Spencer, 2001). People may cope with uncertainty by seeking out information (Ashford & Cummings, 1985) or as Hogg and colleagues argue, they may look to the structure that groups and organizations afford (Hogg 2000; Hogg & Mullin, 1999). Yet, although uncertainty is common, the Uncertainty Management Model emphasizes that it is also variable. Levels of uncertainty fluctuate in organizational life and these fluctuations, the theory suggests, are central to understanding the relationship between uncertainty and fairness concerns.

Uncertainty and Fairness Concerns

Building on Fairness Heuristic Theory's proposition regarding the role played by fairness beliefs in solving the fundamental social dilemma, the Uncertainty Management Model argues that people are motivated to seek information related to fairness in order to reduce feelings of uncertainty elicited by the situations they find themselves in. As noted earlier in our discussion of Fairness Heuristic Theory, the belief that one will be treated fairly by others is a way to cope with the many sources of uncertainty that come with entering into a new relationship with an organization. But the Uncertainty Management Model recognizes that uncertainty can come from a variety of sources or events. When a person is in a state of personal uncertainty or insecurity, the model suggests, he or she will seek to gather new information and revisit the fairness judgment process, in order to assess whether he or she can expect fair treatment in the future. In the terms used in Fairness Heuristic Theory, feelings of personal uncertainty or insecurity push people out of the use phase of fairness judgments and into the judgment phase wherein new beliefs are constructed. Hence, in times of high personal uncertainty, the impact of fairness should be particularly pronounced. Thus, uncertainty is seen as a moderating variable in the impact of fairness-relevant experiences. When uncertainty is high, people are more sensitive to fairness; when it is low, they are less sensitive.

Some of the empirical evidence reviewed earlier in support of Fairness Heuristic Theory also provides support for predictions about informational uncertainty in the Uncertainty Management Model. For instance, Van den Bos, Lind, Vermunt, & Wilke's (1997) finding that procedural fairness matters more when others' outcomes are unknown provides evidence for the idea that uncertainty about how one is being treated in relation to others may prompt an increased vigilance toward fairness concerns. Similarly, Lind et al. (2000)'s demonstration that the impact of fairness is greater during employee terminations than during their work tenure suggests that fairness may increase in subjective importance during times of informational uncertainty.

Furthermore, research on individual differences in how people deal with, or attend to, uncertainty is consistent with the main proposition put forth by the model. For instance, Colquitt and his colleagues (2006) provide evidence that chronic differences in risk aversion moderate justice effects in the way that the Uncertainty Management Model would predict. That is, people who were highly risk averse, or chronically sensitive to uncertain situations and outcomes, are found to react more strongly to unfairness than people low on risk aversion. This moderating effect of risk aversion on justice concerns is found to impact employees' tendency to engage in counterproductive workplace behaviors as well as their task performance. Similarly, Thau, Aquino, and Wittek (2007) show that individual differences in self-uncertainty (or the degree to which people tend to feel insecure about themselves in relation to others) moderate the interactive effect of situational uncertainty and fairness experiences on workplace behavior. Specifically, this research found that the relationship between unfairness and employee antisocial behavior was stronger for employees high in chronic self-uncertainty.

Recent research conducted both in the field and in the laboratory provides further support for the main hypothesis put forward by the Uncertainty Management Model—that feelings of uncertainty moderate the psychological impact of experiences of fairness and unfairness. In a field sample of subordinates working in different industries, the relationship between unfairness (operationalized as abusive supervision in this study) and employee deviance was stronger when situational uncertainty was high rather than low (in this study, lack of authoritarian management style was used as an indicator of uncertainty; Thau, Bennett, Mitchell, & Marrs, 2009). In another field study, uncertainty (operationalized in this case as lack of work-time control and negative changes at work) moderated the effect of fairness on employee absenteeism (Elovainio et al. 2005). Furthermore, in a survey of technology firm teams, Li, Bingham, and Umphress (2007) found that the positive relationship between perceived procedural fairness and collaborative problem-solving was moderated by environmental uncertainty. Specifically, for team members who perceived a high level of uncertainty, procedural fairness was positively related to collaborative problem-solving, but no relationship existed between these variables when uncertainty was perceived to be low.

There is a great deal of evidence for the basic assertion of the Uncertainty Management Model that the salience of uncertainty enhances the impact of fairness information. In a series of experimental studies, Van den Bos (2001a) found that people who were asked to write about a time when they had experienced uncertainty reacted more strongly to a subsequent unfair procedure than people who were not made to think about experiences of uncertainty. Similarly, people who were asked to think about an uncertain aspect of their life (their own mortality) reacted more strongly to receiving an unfair outcome when compared to people who were not asked to contemplate their own death (Van den Bos, 2001b). In addition, Van den Bos and Miedema (2000) showed that people who thought about their own mortality showed enhanced positive reactions to fair processes compared to people who had not thought of their mortality, suggesting that uncertainty may enhance the extremity of fairness judgments in both positive and negative directions. Van den Bos, Poortvliet, Maas, Miedema, and Ham (2005) demonstrated that mortality salience prompts greater personal uncertainty and that this uncertainty is the source of the fairness effects observed in these studies.

In addition, people appear to use fairness judgments to guide behavior in uncertain situations, as the Uncertainty Management Model predicts. For instance, a field study investigating people's attitudes toward environmental issues found that community members who felt a high level of informational uncertainty regarding an environmental policy relied more on perceived procedural fairness of the initiative when determining their level of support for it (See, 2009).

Fairness Concerns and the Human Alarm System

Empirical work relating justice concerns to the human alarm system (see Van den Bos et al. 2008; Van den Bos & Lind, 2009) demonstrates how general feelings of uncertainty can affect fairness judgments. That is, the way that personal uncertainty affects fairness judgments is through the activation of a very fundamental set of processes that humans use to respond to potential threats. Thus, Van den Bos and colleagues (2008) demonstrated that cultural symbols that cue feelings of alarm and uncertainty can produce increased vigilance toward fairness information. Specifically, they show that people presented with alarm-signaling stimuli such as flashing lights and exclamation points showed more extreme reactions to fair and unfair processes and outcomes. This research suggests that uncertainty does not need to be produced by, or even to be especially relevant to, a particular context, in order to significantly affect how people attend to fairness in that context. In addition, this work points to a very fundamental, perhaps even physiological, basis for the relationship between uncertainty management and fairness concerns. Indeed, in Van den Bos et al.'s (2008) article, the authors note that there is some research using fMRI imaging that suggests a connection between the presentation of cultural symbols of alarm and the activation of brain areas known to be involved in moral judgments.

The importance of the human alarm system research and the conceptual analyses linking it to the Uncertainty Management Model lies in the demonstration of how basic and how fundamental to human psychology this pattern of fairness responses might be. When events that provoke alarm and uncertainty occur, the response of greater sensitivity to fairness—or in Fairness Heuristic Theory terms, the shift to judgment phase processing—might well be more or less automatic. And as we will point out in the next section, there are some important implications of this for organizations.

Practical Implications

Following the basic premise put forth by the Uncertainty Management Model, organizational leaders should focus most on fairness in situations in which their employees are likely to experience feelings of uncertainty, as these situations are likely to increase the psychological impact of fair and unfair experiences. For example, performance evaluations and promotions are contexts that may provoke an unusually high level of employee uncertainty. Devoting more time and resources to voice in these contexts would, according to the model, yield optimal results.

Furthermore, a strong practical implication of research on the human alarm system is that general personal uncertainty, or uncertainty produced by factors outside the workplace, can affect vigilance toward fairness at work. In many of the studies on uncertainty management and fairness, the stimuli that provoked greater uncertainty and then greater attention to fairness information had little or nothing to do with the situation within which fairness sensitivity was examined. This is evident in the studies just reviewed, which used cultural symbols such as exclamation points or flashing lights to prompt uncertainty. In addition, in most empirical work that tests the Uncertainty Management Model, feelings of uncertainty are experimentally induced using an episodic recall task that is completely unrelated to the contexts or scenarios later used in these studies to assess fairness sensitivity (e.g., Van den Bos 2001a, 2001b). The participants in these experiments responded with greater fairness sensitivity when they had merely been asked to recall what it felt like to be uncertain in an ostensibly unconnected prior study.

The Uncertainty Management Model's propositions related to when fairness matters most also have interesting practical implications for the workplace (also see Lind & Van den Bos, 2002). We mentioned earlier that Fairness Heuristic Theory suggests that, during times of leadership change or organizational transformation, people are likely to be pushed into the judgment phase and thus it may be more important to be fair during such times. The Uncertainty Management Model adds an additional set of times and situations in which it is most advisable to be fair. Specifically, when an employee's personal life is in flux, encountering fair processes, procedures, and outcomes at work is likely to have greater psychological impact than in other circumstances. Thus, when designing workplace benefits, rules and procedures for serious illness or for maternity/paternity leave, it would be wise to minimize unnecessary bureaucracy and instead focus on communicating compassion and respect for claimants.

If one accepts the notion that being attentive to fairness is not without cost—for example, an organization must invest time and effort in order to provide voice or give explanations to employees—then the earlier discussion suggests *when* a manager is likely to derive the most substantive benefits from devoting resources to being fair. Allocating resources to fairness when an employee's life, job, or personality does not suggest any personal uncertainty may yield less robust results (see for example, Desai, Sondak, & Diekmann, 2011). A savvy manager would be well-advised, then, to stay attuned to signs of uncertainty in his or her reports in order to determine when to devote the most time and effort to fairness.

That said, a completely instrumental view of when it "pays" to be fair is unlikely to be successful for several reasons. First, it is difficult to read with precision when people are uncertain and when they are not, and a mistake in making that judgment could lead a manager to neglect fairness when it is quite important. Second, it is worth noting that, even in experiments showing an uncertainty-moderated effect of fairness treatment, the effect of fairness was not always zero in the uncertainty-absent conditions. That is, even without inducing feelings of uncertainty, fair treatment or lack thereof still generally mattered to people. Finally, there is always the danger that unfair treatment, especially if repeated, will itself produce feelings of uncertainty, instigating a psychological need for fair treatment. It is better on all counts, we believe, to always maintain a reasonable level of fairness but to focus special efforts on being fair in those situations and for those people that most need it.

In general, the Uncertainty Management Model, viewed in the context of the larger organizational justice literature on the many positive effects of fair treatment, suggests that any material costs associated with being fair would be well recompensed by the beneficial outcomes produced by the positive feelings that fairness induces in the organization's employees. However, this effect should be magnified when employees are dealing with feelings of uncertainty produced by their work life or personal life.

Fairness Heuristics, Uncertainty Management, and System Justification Theory

Recently, some scholars (Van den Bos, 2009a; Tost & Lind, 2010; Lind, 2011) have started working toward bringing the predictions suggested by Uncertainty Management Model and Fairness Heuristic Theory together with those put forth by System Justification Theory (Jost & Banaji, 1994), a seemingly contrasting account of what drives people's concern with fairness and how justice judgments are constructed. Drawing on the ideas they discuss, and on some recent empirical work, we aim, in this next section, to further the discussion of how fairness heuristic and uncertainty management theories might be reconciled with system justification perspectives; in doing so, we highlight some potential directions for future research.

System Justification Theory (Jost & Banaji, 1994) argues that people possess a motivated tendency to perceive the systems they function within to be just and legitimate. That is, individuals *want* to believe that their institutional and organizational systems operate in a fair and reasonable manner. Instances of unfairness, then, tend to be psychologically threatening because they run counter to this belief. In order to manage the psychological threat or anxiety caused by encountering unfairness and maintain a positive view of their system, people oftentimes are motivated to justify or defend injustices that they encounter in their environment (cf. Jost & Hunyady, 2003; Kay & Zanna, 2009). Hence, while Fairness Heuristic Theory and the Uncertainty Management Model focus on explaining when and why people have negative reactions to instances of unfairness, System Justification Theory seeks to explain why people sometimes may not perceive instances of unfairness in such a negative light.

To reconcile these two perspectives, Tost and Lind (2010) argue that system justification processes may predominate in what Fairness Heuristic Theory calls the "use" phase of justice judgments. They propose two distinct psychological modes of justice evaluation—a system justification mode (predominating in the use phase) and a system critique mode (predominating during the judgment and re-evaluation phase). Furthermore, they make predictions regarding specific kinds of phase-shifting events that facilitate a move out of the system justification mode into the system critique mode (for more detail on their theoretical model, see Tost & Lind, 2010; Lind, 2011).

We build on Tost & Lind's (2010) model to suggest factors that might inhibit, rather than facilitate, people's transition out of the use phase of the fairness heuristic. That is, drawing on recent research emerging from System Justification Theory, we outline several factors that may increase people's tendency to interpret new experiences of unfairness through the lens of their positive global beliefs about the fairness of their system, rather than re-evaluating this global belief. In doing so, we emphasize the role that psychological rationalization processes may play in prolonging the use phase of the fairness heuristic.

A central proposition put forth by System Justification Theory is that people have a tendency to rationalize away or downplay instances of unfairness and injustice, especially under conditions in which their system justification motive is heightened. In other words, people often engage in cognitive restructuring of reality in order to maintain their belief that their system is just and fair. Thus, as long as people are able to psychologically rationalize and justify instances of unfairness in their system and instead make them seem reasonable and deserved, they will likely remain in the use phase of the fairness heuristic. However, when people encounter injustice that is so extreme or unexpected that they are unable to rationalize it (i.e., a phase shifting event), the system-justification mode of justice judgments may be replaced with the system critique mode.

In addition to the absence of phase-shifting events, recent empirical work suggests specific organizational contexts in which system-justifying processes are likely to persist over system-critique processes. People have been shown to be more likely to justify their systems when these systems face external threats (Kay, Jost, & Young, 2005), when people feel especially dependent on their systems (Kay et al. 2009), when their systems seem inescapable (Laurin, Shepherd, & Kay, 2010) or are perceived as stable and unchanging (Laurin, Gaucher & Kay, 2013) and when people's sense of personal control is low (Kay, Gaucher, Napier, Callan, & Laurin, 2008). Under these conditions, the psychological threat posed by acknowledging system unfairness is purported to be especially high, and thus people are increasingly motivated to engage in rationalization of unfairness that they encounter (cf. Kay & Friesen, 2011). Next, we provide two illustrative examples of the effects of two contextual factors that enhance people's tendency to rationalize away instances of unfairness: system dependence and system inescapability.

In one experimental study looking at the effect of system dependence on people's motivation to perceive their system as fair, participants were either led to believe that they were quite dependent on their university for influencing their life outcomes (high university dependence condition) or they were made to believe instead that the government influenced their life outcomes (low university dependence condition; Kay et al., 2009). Participants were then asked to rate the fairness of their university's funding policies. Results indicated that when people were made to feel dependent on their university, they rated the university's funding policies to be significantly fairer than when they were made to feel dependent on the alternative system (the government). The same effect was found for people who were asked to rate the fairness of their government's funding policy—people's who were made to feel dependent on their government rated its funding policy as significantly fairer than people who were, instead, made to feel dependent on their university. These findings suggest a motivated tendency to perceive one's elements of one's system as fair when one feels dependent on that particular system.

In another experiment, participants were made to believe that their socio-political system (the nation of Canada) was either easy or difficult to leave (Laurin et al. 2010). Participants were then asked to rate the extent to which gender inequality in Canada was caused by systemic unfairness or by biological differences between men and women. Results revealed that, compared to participants who were made to think that emigrating out of Canada was easy (low inescapability condition), participants who were made to think that emigrating out of Canada was difficult (high inescapability condition) increasingly attributed gender inequality in Canada to biological differences between men and women instead of systemic unfairness. These findings demonstrate that perceptions of system inescapability may enhance people's motivation to defend their system and avoid seeing it as unjust. This study also provides an example of the kind of specific rationalizations people may use to order to maintain their belief in system fairness when faced with evidence to the contrary.

In addition to research suggesting some specific conditions or contexts in which the system justification mode is likely to be enhanced and predominate, other empirical work emerging from System Justification Theory directly investigates one potential moderator of people's tendency to rationalize unfairness rather than react negatively to it. Laurin, Kay, and Fitzsimons (2012) experimentally demonstrate that when an unfavorable policy is framed as absolute or unchangeable, people tend to downplay or rationalize away that policy's negative qualities, consistent with a system justification perspective. However, when the same policy is construed as changeable, people react against it, a finding that is consistent with the Uncertainty Management Model's prediction that, in situations with low certainty, people are increasingly likely to react negatively to instances of unfairness. For instance, in one experiment, Laurin and colleagues (2012) presented three groups of participants with information about a new policy that restricted their ability to use their cell phones while driving. They then varied, between groups, how changeable the policy was. When this policy was framed as changeable, participants indicated that they were more bothered by the policy than did participants who were given no information about how changeable the policy was. However, when the policy was framed as absolute (nonchangeable), participants indicated that they were *less* bothered by the policy than participants given no changeability information, suggesting a rationalization effect. Although this study does not specifically focus on attention to fairness information per se, it highlights another moderator (i.e., changeability) of people's tendency to engage in the psychological processes suggested by Fairness Heuristic or Uncertainty Management theory versus those suggested by System Justification Theory. When a particular policy change is certain (i.e., absolute), people tend to rationalize away its negative qualities; however, when there is uncertainty regarding whether a policy change will endure, people react against it. Future research could directly explore the application of these findings to people's vigilance to fairness.

Thus, as these examples suggest, people may be more likely to rationalize away instances of unfairness and remain in the use phase of the fairness heuristic when they find themselves in organizations that they feel dependent on or are unable to escape. In addition, the implementation of unfair organizational policies that are perceived as unchangeable may be more likely to induce people's rationalization processes rather than encourage them to re-assess their fairness heuristic. Though not covered in depth in this section, there is also strong evidence to suggest that system threat, system stability, and low personal control are three other factors that enhance people's system justification motive and thus may prolong the use phase of the fairness heuristic (cf. Kay & Friesen, 2011; Laurin et al., 2013).

Conversely, when people find themselves in work contexts that induce feeling of personal uncertainty or when they encounter unfair experiences that they are unable to rationalize away, they may be more likely to switch to the judgment phase suggested by Fairness Heuristic Theory. What is clearly needed in the future is research that addresses more directly the phenomenon of phase-shifting in justice judgment processes (which, to date, is supported empirically mainly by the Jones & Martens, 2009, research and by inference from the primacy and substitutability studies). We need to look especially at how factors like changeability, uncertainty, and strength of identification play against each other to affect system justification versus system critique reactions.

Conclusion

According to Fairness Heuristic Theory, the Uncertainty Management Model, *and* System Justification Theory, sometimes people at work think about fairness differently than they do at other times. The theories and research that we have reviewed in this chapter point to a number of situations that are likely to provoke special reactions to justice and justice-related information. The task remains to us researchers and theorists to resolve the details of when and which episodic reactions prevail, but we have certainly begun to explore when, how, and why justice will matter more or less in organizational contexts.

Note

1. The Uncertainty Management Model addresses both "information uncertainty" and "personal uncertainty." We will be focusing more on the latter, but we will note some aspects of the former when we discuss how the "substitutability" effects that support Fairness Heuristic Theory predictions are ways of dealing with informational uncertainty.

References

Adams, J. S. (1965). Inequity in social exchange. In L. Berkowitz (Ed.), *Advances in experimental psychology* (Vol. 2, pp. 267–299). San Diego, CA: Academic Press.

Alexander, S., & Ruderman, M. (1987). The role of procedural and distributive justice in organizational behavior. *Social Justice Research, 1*(2), 177–198.

Ambrose, M. L., & Arnaud, A. (2005). Are procedural justice and distributive justice conceptually distinct?. In J. Greenberg & J. Colquitt (Eds.), *The handbook of organizational justice* (pp. 59–84). Mahwah, NJ: Erlbaum

Ambrose, M. L., & Schminke, M. (2009). The role of overall justice judgments in organizational justice research: a test of mediation. *Journal of Applied Psychology, 94*(2), 491.

Ashford, S. J., & Cummings, L. L. (1985). Proactive feedback seeking: The instrumental use of the information environment. *Journal of Occupational Psychology, 58*(1), 67–79.

Bodenhausen, G. V. (1990). Stereotypes as judgmental heuristics: Evidence of circadian variations in discrimination. *Psychological Science, 1*(5), 319–322.

Bianchi, E. C., & Brockner, J. (2012). In the eyes of the beholder? The role of dispositional trust in judgments of procedural and interactional fairness. *Organizational Behavior and Human Decision Processes, 118*(1), 46–59.

Brockner, J., & Wiesenfeld, B. M. (1996). An integrative framework for explaining reactions to decisions: interactive effects of outcomes and procedures. *Psychological Bulletin, 120*(2), 189.

Bies, R. J. (2005). Are procedural justice and interactional justice conceptually distinct?.?. In J. Greenberg & J. Colquitt (Eds.), *The handbook of organizational justice*. Mahwah, NJ: Erlbaum

Cohen-Charash, Y., & Spector, P. E. (2001). The role of justice in organizations: A meta-analysis. *Organizational behavior and human decision processes, 86*(2), 278–321.

Colquitt, J. A., Noe, R. A., & Jackson, C. L. (2002). Justice in teams: Antecedents and consequences of procedural justice climate. *Personnel Psychology, 55*(1), 83–109.

Colquitt, J. A., Scott, B. A., Judge, T. A., & Shaw, J. C. (2006). Justice and personality: Using integrative theories to derive moderators of justice effects. *Organizational Behavior and Human Decision Processes, 100*(1), 110–127.

Cropanzano, R., & Ambrose, M. L. (2001). Procedural and distributive justice are more similar than you think: A monistic perspective and a research agenda. *Advances in organizational justice, 119*, 151.

De Boer, E. M., Bakker, A. B., Syroit, J. E., & Schaufeli, W. B. (2002). Unfairness at work as a predictor of absenteeism. *Journal of Organizational Behavior, 23*(2), 181–197.

Desai, S. D., Sondak, H., & Diekmann, K. A. (2011). When fairness neither satisfies nor motivates: The role of risk aversion and uncertainty reduction in attenuating and reversing the fair process effect. *Organizational Behavior and Human Decision Processes, 116*(1), 32–45.

Dietz, J., Robinson, S. L., Folger, R., Baron, R. A., & Schulz, M. (2003). The impact of community violence and an organization's procedural justice climate on workplace aggression. *Academy of Management Journal, 46*, 317–326

Elovainio, M., van den Bos, K., Linna, A., Kivimäki, M., Ala-Mursula, L., Pentti, J., & Vahtera, J. (2005). Combined effects of uncertainty and organizational justice on employee health: testing the uncertainty management model of fairness judgments among Finnish public sector employees. *Social science & medicine, 61*(12), 2501–2512.

Fiske, S. T., & Taylor, S. E. (1991). *Social cognition* (2nd ed.). New York, NY: McGraw-Hill.

Folger, R. (1977). Distributive and procedural justice: Combined impact of voice and improvement on experienced inequity. *Journal of Personality and Social Psychology, 35*(2), 108.

Folger, R., & Baron, R. A. (1996).Violence and hostility at work: a model of reactions to perceived injustice. In *Violence on the job: Identifying risks and developing solutions*. In G. Van den Bos, E. Bulatao (pp. 51–85). Washington, DC: American Psychological Association.

Folger, R. G., & Cropanzano, R. (1998). *Organizational justice and human resource management* (Vol. 7). Thousand Oaks, CA: Sage.

Folger, R., Rosenfield, D., Grove, J., & Corkran, L. (1979). Effects of" voice" and peer opinions on responses to inequity. *Journal of Personality and Social Psychology, 37*(12), 2253.

Fox, S., Spector, P. E., & Miles, D. (2001). Counterproductive work behavior (CWB) in response to job stressors and organizational justice: Some mediator and moderator tests for autonomy and emotions. *Journal of vocational behavior, 59*(3), 291–309.

Gilbert, D. T., & Hixon, J. G. (1991). The trouble of thinking: Activation and application of stereotypic beliefs. *Journal of Personality and Social Psychology, 60*(4), 509.

Gilbert, D. T., Pelham, B. W., & Krull, D. S. (1988). On cognitive busyness: When person perceivers meet persons perceived. *Journal of Personality and Social Psychology, 54*(5), 733.

Greenberg, J. (1982). Approaching equity and avoiding inequity in groups and organizations. *Equity and justice in social behavior*, 389–435.

Greenberg, J. (1990). Employee theft as a response to underemployment inequity: The hidden costs of pay cuts. *Journal of Applied Psychology, 75*, 561–568.

Greenberg, J. (1993). Stealing in the name of justice: Informational and interpersonal moderators of theft reactions to underpayment inequity. *Organizational Behavior and Human Decision Processes, 54*, 81–103.

Greenberg, J. (1994). Using socially fair treatment to promote acceptance of a work site smoking ban. *Journal of Applied Psychology, 79*, 288–297.

Greenberg, J. (2000). Promote procedural justice to enhance acceptance of work outcomes. In E. A. Locke (Ed.), *Handbook of principles of organizational behavior* (pp. 181–195). Oxford, England: Blackwell.

Greenberg, J. E., & Colquitt, J. A. (2005). *Handbook of organizational justice*. Mahwah, NJ: Erlbaum.

Greenberg, J., & Scott, K. S. (1996). Why do workers bite the hands that feed them? Employee theft as a social exchange process. In B. M. Staw & L. L. Cummings (Eds.), *Research in organizational behavior: Vol. 18. An annual series of analytical essays and critical reviews*. (pp. 111–156): Greenwich, CT: JAI.

Hogg, M. A. (2000). Subjective uncertainty reduction through self-categorization: A motivational theory of social identity processes. *European Review of Social Psychology, 11*(1), 223–255.

Hogg, M. A. (2007). Uncertainty–identity theory. *Advances in Experimental Social Psychology, 39*, 69–126.

Hogg, M. A., & Mullin, B. A. (1999). Joining groups to reduce uncertainty: Subjective uncertainty reduction and group identification. In D. Abrams & M. A. Hogg (Eds.), *Social identity and social cognition*, (pp. 249–279). Malden, UK: Blackwell Publishing.

Huo, Y. J., Smith, H. J., Tyler, T. R., & Lind, E. A. (1996). Superordinate identification, subgroup identification, and justice concerns: is separatism the problem; is assimilation the answer?. *Psychological Science, 7*, 40–45.

Janson, A., Levy, L., Sitkin, S. B., & Lind, E. A. (2008). Fairness and other leadership heuristics: A four-nation study. *European Journal of Work and Organizational Psychology, 17*(2), 251–272.

Jones, D. A., & Martens, M. L. (2009). The mediating role of overall fairness and the moderating role of trust certainty in justice–criteria relationships: The formation and use of fairness heuristics in the workplace. *Journal of Organizational Behavior, 30*(8), 1025–1051.

Jones, D. A., & Skarlicki, D. P. (2005). The effects of overhearing peers discuss an authority's fairness reputation on reactions to subsequent treatment. *Journal of Applied Psychology, 90*(2), 363.

Jost, J. T., & Banaji, M. R. (1994). The role of stereotyping in system-justification and the production of false consciousness. *British Journal of Social Psychology, 33*(1), 1–27.

Jost, J., & Hunyady, O. (2003). The psychology of system justification and the palliative function of ideology. *European Review of Social Psychology, 13*(1), 111–153.

Kay, A. C., & Friesen, J. (2011). On social stability and social change understanding when system justification does and does not occur. *Current Directions in Psychological Science, 20*(6), 360–364.

Kay, A. C., Gaucher, D., Napier, J. L., Callan, M. J., & Laurin, K. (2008). God and the government: Testing a compensatory control mechanism for the support of external systems. *Journal of Personality and Social Psychology, 95*(1), 18.

Kay, A. C., Jost, J. T., & Young, S. (2005). Victim derogation and victim enhancement as alternate routes to system justification. *Psychological Science, 16*(3), 240–246.

Kay, A. C., Gaucher, D., Peach, J. M., Laurin, K., Friesen, J., Zanna, M. P., & Spencer, S. J. (2009). Inequality, discrimination, and the power of the status quo: Direct evidence for a motivation to see the way things are as the way they should be. *Journal of Personality and Social Psychology, 97*(3), 421.

Kay, A. C., & Zanna, M. P. (2009). A contextual analysis of the system justification motive and its societal consequences. *Social and Psychological Bases of Ideology and System Justification*, 158–181.

Karriker, J. H., & Williams, M. L. (2009). Organizational justice and organizational citizenship behavior: A mediated multifoci model. *Journal of Management, 35*(1), 112–135.

Konovsky, M. A., & Folger, R. (1991). The effects of procedures, social accounts, and benefits level on victims' layoff reactions. *Journal of Applied Social Psychology, 21*(8), 630–650.

Korsgaard, M. A., Schweiger, D. M., & Sapienza, H. J. (1995). Building commitment, attachment, and trust in strategic decision-making teams: The role of procedural justice. *Academy of Management Journal, 38*, 60–84.

Laurin, K., Gaucher, D., & Kay, A. (2013). Stability and the justification of social inequality. *European Journal of Social Psychology, 43*(4), 246–254.

Laurin, K., Kay, A. C., & Fitzsimons, G. J. (2012). Reactance versus rationalization divergent responses to policies that constrain freedom. *Psychological Science, 23*(2), 205–209.

Laurin, K., Shepherd, S., & Kay, A. C. (2010). Restricted emigration, system inescapability, and defense of the status quo system-justifying cnsequences of restricted exit opportunities. *Psychological Science, 21*(8), 1075–1082.

Li, H., Bingham, J. B., & Umphress, E. E. (2007). Fairness from the top: perceived procedural justice and collaborative problem solving in new product development. *Organization Science, 18*(2), 200–216.

Lind, E. A. (1994). Procedural justice and culture: Evidence for ubiquitous process concerns. *Zeitschrift für Rechtssoziologie*, 15, 24–36.

Lind, E. A. (2001). Fairness heuristic theory: Justice judgments as pivotal cognitions in organizational relations. In J. Greenberg & R. Cropanzano (Eds.), *Advances in organizational justice* (pp. 56–88). Stanford, CA: Stanford University Press.

Lind, E. A. (2011). Culture and fairness: Some possible dynamics of cultural variation in the psychology of fairness. In N. Asai, K. Ohbuchi (Eds.), *Inequality, discrimination and conflict in Japan: Ways to social justice and cooperation* (pp. 1–23). Melbourne: Trans Pacific Press.

Lind, E. A., Greenberg, J., Scott, K. S., & Welchans, T. D. (2000). The winding road from employee to complainant: Situational and psychological determinants of wrongful-termination claims. *Administrative Science Quarterly, 45*(3), 557–590.

Lind, E. A., Kanfer, R., & Earley, P. C. (1990). Voice, control and procedural justice; Instrumental and non-instrumental concerns in fairness judgments. *Journal of Personality and Social Psychology, 59*, 952–959.

Lind, E. A., Kray, L., & Thompson, L. (2001). Primacy effects in justice judgments: Testing predictions from Fairness Heuristic Theory. *Organizational Behavior and Human Decision Processes, 85*, 189–210.

Lind, E. A., Kulik, C. T., Ambrose, M., & de Vera Park, M. V. (1993). Individual and corporate dispute resolution: Using procedural fairness as a decision heuristic. *Administrative Science Quarterly, 38*, 224–251.

Lind, E. A., Greenberg, J., Scott, K. S., & Welchans, T. D. (2000). The winding road from employee to complainant: Situational and psychological determinants of wrongful termination claims. *Administrative Science Quarterly, 45*, 557–590.

Lind, E. A., & Tyler, T. R. (1988). *The social psychology of procedural justice.* New York, NY: Plenum.

Lind, E. A., & Van den Bos, K. (2002). When fairness works: Toward a general theory of uncertainty management. In B. M. Staw & R. M. Kramer (Eds.), *Research in organizational behavior* (Vol. 24, pp. 181–222). Boston, MA: JAI.

McFarlin, D. B., & Sweeney, P. D. (1992). Research notes. Distributive and procedural justice as predictors of satisfaction with personal and organizational outcomes. *Academy of Management journal, 35*(3), 626–637.

McGregor, I., Zanna, M. P., Holmes, J. G., & Spencer, S. J. (2001). Compensatory conviction in the face of personal uncertainty: going to extremes and being oneself. *Journal of personality and social psychology, 80*(3), 472.

Moorman, R. H. (1991). Relationship between organizational justice and organizational citizenship behaviors: do fairness perceptions influence employee citizenship? *Journal of applied psychology, 76*(6), 845.

Moorman, R. H., Niehoff, B. P., & Organ, D. W. (1993). Treating employees fairly and organizational citizenship behavior: Sorting the effects of job satisfaction, organizational commitment, and procedural justice. *Employee Responsibilities and Rights Journal, 6*(3), 209–225.

Niehoff, B. P., & Moorman, R. H. (1993). Justice as a mediator of the relationship between methods of monitoring and organizational citizenship behavior. *Academy of Management journal*, 527–556.

Platow, M. J., Eggins, R. A., Chattopadhyay, R., Brewer, G., Hardwick, L., Milsom, L., . . . Welsh, J. (2012). Two experimental tests of relational models of procedural justice: Non-instrumental voice and authority group membership. *British Journal of Social Psychology, 52*, 361–376.

Podsakoff, P. M., & MacKenzie, S. B. (1993). Citizenship behavior and fairness in organizations: Issues and directions for future research. *Employee Responsibilities and Rights Journal, 6*(3), 257–269.

Rodell, J. B., & Colquitt, J. A. (2009). Looking ahead in times of uncertainty: The role of anticipatory justice in an organizational change context. *Journal of Applied Psychology, 94*(4), 989.

See, K. E. (2009). Reactions to decisions with uncertain consequences: Reliance on perceived fairness versus predicted outcomes depends on knowledge. *Journal of Personality and Social Psychology, 96*, 104–118.

Simons, T., & Roberson, Q. (2003). Why managers should care about fairness: the effects of aggregate justice perceptions on organizational outcomes. *Journal of Applied Psychology, 88*(3), 432.

Skitka, L. J. (2002). Understanding judgments of fairness in a real-world political context: A test of the value protection model of justice reasoning. *Personality and Social Psychology Bulletin, 28*, 1419–1429.

Smith, H. J., Tyler, T. R., Huo, Y. J., Ortiz, D. J., & Lind, E. A. (1998). The self-relevant implications of the group-value model: Group membership, self-worth, and treatment quality. *Journal of Experimental Social Psychology, 34*, 470–493.

Thau, S., Aquino, K., & Wittek, R. (2007). An extension of uncertainty management theory to the self: the relationship between justice, social comparison orientation, and antisocial work behaviors. *Journal of Applied Psychology, 92*(1), 250.

Thau, S., Bennett, R. J., Mitchell, M. S., & Marrs, M. B. (2009). How management style moderates the relationship between abusive supervision and workplace deviance: An uncertainty management theory perspective. *Organizational Behavior and Human Decision Processes, 108*(1), 79–92.

Thibaut, J. W., & Walker, L. (1975). *Procedural justice: A psychological analysis.* Hillsdale, NJ: Erlbaum.

Thibaut, J., & Walker, L. (1978). Theory of procedure, *Annals of the California Law Review, 66*, 541.

Tost, L. P., & Lind, E. A. (2010). Sounding the alarm: Moving from system justification to system condemnation in the justice judgment process. *Research on Managing Groups and Teams, 13*, 3–27.

Tyler, T. R., & Caine, A. (1981). The influence of outcomes and procedures on satisfaction with formal leaders. *Journal of Personality and Social Psychology, 41*(4), 642.

Tyler, T. R., & Lind, E. A. (1992). A relational model of authority in groups. In M. Zanna (Ed.), *Advances in Experimental Social Psychology, 25*, 115–191. New York, NY: Academic Press.

Van den Bos, K. (1999). What are we talking about when we talk about no-voice procedures? On the psychology of the fair outcome effect. *Journal of Experimental Social Psychology, 35*, 560–577.

Van den Bos, K. (2001a). Uncertainty management: The influence of uncertainty salience on reactions to perceived procedural fairness. *Journal of Personality and Social Psychology, 80*, 931–941.

Van den Bos, K. (2001b). Reactions to perceived fairness: The impact of mortality salience and self-esteem on ratings of negative affect. *Social Justice Research, 14*(1), 1–23.

Van den Bos, K. (2009). The social psychology of uncertainty management and system justification. In J. T. Jost & A. C. Kay (Eds.), *Social and Psychological Bases of Ideology and System Justification* (pp. 185–20). New York: NY: Oxford University Press.

Van den Bos, K., Ham, J., Lind, E. A., Simonis, M., van Essen, W. J., & Rijpkema, M. (2008). Justice and the human alarm system: The impact of exclamation points and flashing lights on the justice judgment process. *Journal of Experimental Social Psychology, 44*(2), 201–219.

Van den Bos, K., & Lind, E. A. (2002). Uncertainty management by means of fairness judgments. In M. P. Zanna (Ed.), *Advances in experimental social psychology* (Vol. 34, pp. 1–60). San Diego, CA: Academic Press.

Van den Bos, K., & Lind, E. A. (2009). The social psychology of fairness and the regulation of personal uncertainty. In R. M. Arkin, K. C. Oleson, & P. J. Carroll (Eds.), *Handbook of the uncertain self* (pp. 122–141). New York, NY: Psychology Press.

Van den Bos, K., Lind, E. A., Vermunt, R., & Wilke, H. A. (1997). How do I judge my outcome when I do not know the outcome of others? The psychology of the fair process effect. *Journal of Personality and Social Psychology, 72*(5), 1034.

Van den Bos, K., Lind, E. A., & Wilke, H. A. (2001). The psychology of procedural and distributive justice viewed from the perspective of fairness heuristic theory. *Justice in the Workplace: From Theory to Practice, 2*, 49–66.

Van den Bos, K., & Miedema, J. (2000). Toward understanding why fairness matters: The influence of mortality salience on reactions to procedural fairness. *Journal of Personality and Social Psychology, 79*(3), 355.

Van den Bos, K., Peters, S. L., Bobocel, D. R., & Ybema, J. F. (2006). On preferences and doing the right thing: Satisfaction with advantageous inequity when cognitive processing is limited. *Journal of Experimental Social Psychology, 42*(3), 273–289.

Van den Bos, K., Poortvliet, P. M., Maas, M., Miedema, J., & van den Ham, E. J. (2005). An enquiry concerning the principles of cultural norms and values: The impact of uncertainty and mortality salience on reactions to violations and bolstering of cultural worldviews. *Journal of Experimental Social Psychology, 41*(2), 91–113.

Van den Bos, K., Vermunt, R., & Wilke, H. (1997). Procedural and distributive justice: What is fair depends more on what comes first than on what comes next. *Journal of Personality and Social Psychology, 72*, 95–104.

Van den Bos, K., Wilke, H. A., & Lind, E. A. (1998). When do we need procedural fairness? The role of trust in authority. *Journal of Personality and Social Psychology, 75*(6), 1449.

Van den Bos, K., Wilke, H. A., Lind, E. A., & Vermunt, R. (1998). Evaluating outcomes by means of the fair process effect: Evidence for different processes in fairness and satisfaction judgments. *Journal of Personality and Social Psychology, 74*(6), 1493.

Weiss, H. M., Suckow, K., & Cropanzano, R. (1999). Effects of justice conditions on discrete emotions. *Journal of Applied Psychology, 84*(5), 786.

CHAPTER

18

The Role of Concern for Others in Reactions to Justice: Integrating the Theory of Other Orientation with Organizational Justice

M. Audrey Korsgaard, Bruce M. Meglino, *and* Matthew L. Call

Abstract

Prevelant theory on justice allows that individual may be motivated by both self-interested and relatively selfless, deontic motivations. However, current theory fails to directly address the role of other oriented motivations. We describe how the theory of other orientation can foster a greater understanding of the process whereby individuals make and react to decisions involving justice. We propose that persons who are higher in other orientation will be less motivated by self-interested concerns (e.g., protect their long-term self-interests; preserve their self-worth) as well as deontic concerns, leading to circumstances where individuals are both unselfish and unjust. We report the findings of seven studies that support our expectations about the dispositional and situational effects of other orientation on persons' behavior and reactions to justice. We finish by recommending future research avenues that explore further the role of other orientation in fairness actions and reactions.

Key Words: justice, work values, altruism, other orientation, fairness, self-interest

Justice in the workplace is beneficial to an organization in numerous ways in that perceptions of justice are positively related to a variety of individual and unit-level outcomes (Cohen-Charash & Spector, 2001; Colquitt, Conlon, Wesson, Porter, & Yee Ng, 2001). Theoretical advances over the last 20 years have produced important insight into why fairness is important (see Cropanzano, Rupp, Mohler, & Schminke, 2001 for a review). Specifically, justice affords recipients protection of their material self-interests and protects and affirms the self-esteem of persons who receive fair treatment. As a result, individuals are willing to remain in, and invest in, exchange relationships in which they believe they will materially benefit and/or feel psychologically validated. Thus, it is in the best interests of decision makers and leaders to act justly if they want committed exchange partners. Further, justice is a fundamental social value that individuals are committed to uphold. Depending on the strength of this value, recipients, bystanders, and decision makers act in ways to uphold or restore justice because it is an inherent good, regardless of the personal cost or benefits. In short, research and theory suggest three main mechanisms underlying justice: material self-interest, self-esteem, or deontological (moral) values.

The other orientation of the individual is an important motivational force that has been neglected in organizational justice research. The phenomenon of justice is inherently social, occurring in the context of an exchange relationship involving the decision maker, the recipient, and possibly bystanders. The previously noted mechanisms suggest that individuals enact and react to justice based on their own concerns (material or psychological) and their own emphasis on the value of justice. However, these actions affect the other party or parties in the social context. Thus, individuals' choices and actions may be driven by their concern for the other party as much as by their concerns for the self or for justice in the abstract. This additional motive can be an important qualifier to the effects of justice, as protecting or promoting the concerns for others may conflict with self-interests or the abstract principle of justice.

The purpose of this chapter is to explore how other orientation as a motive shapes actions and reactions to justice. We employ theory and research on other orientation (Meglino & Korsgaard, 2004; 2006) to demonstrate ways in which the motivation to help others and avoid harming others alters the meaning and role of organizational justice from the perspective of the decision maker and the recipient.

Mechanisms Underlying Organizational Justice

Theories of organizational justice pose three broad mechanisms through which justice perceptions lead to important attitudes and behaviors (Cropanzano et al., 2001): an instrumental approach (Thibaut & Walker, 1978), which emphasizes self-interest vis-à-vis gains and losses; an interpersonal approach (sometimes referred to as noninstrumental, group value or group engagement; Lind & Tyler, 1988), which is rooted in the value, or self-esteem, one receives from personal relationships and group membership; and, finally, the moral approach (often referred to as the deontic approach, Folger & Cropanzano, 2001), which focuses on one's ethical or moral commitment to justice.

The enactment of, and reactions to, justice occur within exchange relationships and social systems wherein other parties have vested interests. Thus, the actions and reactions of focal persons directly affect specific others within these relationships and systems. Yet, curiously absent from all three perspectives is the possibility that the focal actor may consider the welfare of other parties. That is, none of these perspectives directly addresses the potential role of other oriented motivations, an oversight that creates a void in the explanation of justice effects. For example, the instrumental mechanism pertains to the desire to protect or promote one's own interests. When motivated by this mechanism, individuals will accept less than optimal personal outcomes to the extent that the procedures and interactions signal that their long-term self-interests are protected (Lind, Kray, & Thompson, 2001). From this perspective, the interests or needs of the other parties in the exchange relationship are irrelevant. That is, theory and research on interpersonal motivations suggests that individuals' identity or esteem concerns may trump their material self-interest. In contrast to material self-interest, this approach focuses on the role of psychological, ego-based concerns such as self-worth, uncertainty reduction and belongingness needs (Blader & Tyler, 2009) Again, the interests and needs of the other party are deemed not pertinent to explaining or predicting such justice reactions.

The moral perspective on justice provides an alternative to self-interested motivations underlying justice effects in that individuals motivated by moral consideration will sacrifice their self-interests to uphold principles of justice. Broadly speaking, this explanation is prosocial in that the morally motivated actor seeks to preserve social order from which the collective may benefit. However, the deontically motivated individual is focused on an abstract principle (Cropanzano, Goldman, & Folger, 2003), which can lead him or her to be relatively indifferent to the other parties involved in the immediate situation. Thus, the morally motivated individual may inflict harm on those who violate just principles and take steps to restore justice that do not particularly benefit the victim of injustice (Turillo, Folger, Lavelle, Umphress, & Gee, 2002). In sum, all three perspectives share a common thread: the impact that the focal person has on other parties is incidental to the focal person's goals—whether those goals are to protect material self-interests, preserve self-esteem or uphold principles of justice. As such, prevailing perspectives on organizational justice do not account for other-oriented motivation in an individual's enactment of and reaction to justice.

In this chapter we present a greater role for individuals' concern for others. Our perspective is stimulated by theory and research suggesting that individuals are driven by dual motives, to serve the self and to address the needs of others. For example, Pruitt and Rubin (1986) advance a theory of dual concern that identifies two motivations in interdependent relationships: self-concern and other-concern. The intensity of each varies as a function of the person and context. Moreover, theory and evidence suggest that concern for others may be a powerful motivating force that is often neglected in justice research (Moon, Kamdar, Mayer, & Takeuchi, 2008). Concern for others may be especially relevant to justice in light of the fact that justice is often embedded in social exchange relationships that involve a commitment to others and to interpersonal relationships (Blau, 1964).

Although justice perceptions affect work-related attitudes and behaviors that can be positive (e.g., organizational citizenship or commitment) or negative (e.g., stealing, suing the organization; Lind, Greenberg, Scott, & Welchans, 2000), these actions and reactions are not always consistent in magnitude. Contextual factors and individual differences influence the strength of the justice—outcome relationship (Liao & Rupp, 2005), and some of these factors have implications for other-oriented concerns. For example, agreeableness, a broad trait that includes altruistic or other-oriented concerns, is one factor that qualifies a person's reactions to justice. Individuals high in agreeableness are less likely to be angry in response to a distributively unjust allocation (Stouten, Kuppens, & Decoster, 2013). Similarly, the impact of distributive and interactional justice on counterproductive work behavior is mitigated by agreeableness (Chang & Smithikrai, 2010; Flaherty & Moss, 2007; Skarlicki, Folger & Tesluk, 1999). These findings suggest that a fourth mechanism, concern for others, should be considered when seeking a comprehensive explanation for justice motivations. In the remainder of this chapter, we will expand on this notion of including concern for others in justice research by first, reviewing the theory of other orientation focusing on its mechanisms, motivations, and various representations and operationalizations; second, examining evidence of the role of other orientation in enacting and reacting to justice; and third, discussing the implications of other orientation for managing justice in organizations and influencing future research.

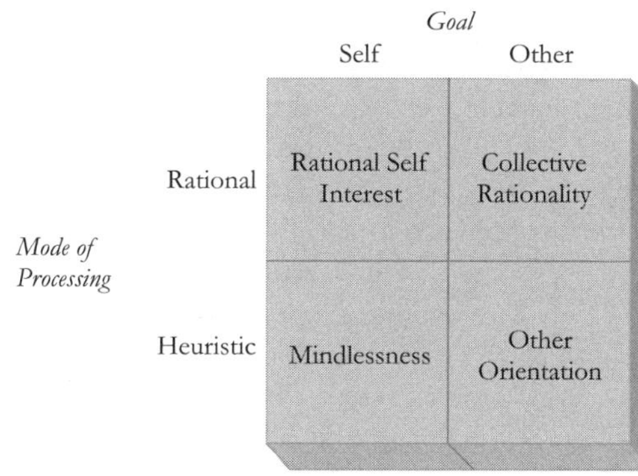

Fig. 18.1 Interrelationship between rational and heuristic processing and self-versus-other goals.

Theory of Other Orientation

As noted earlier, in addition to concern for the self, individuals' motives for justice can also encompass concern for others. To address the implications of these two motives, we employed the theory of other orientation (Meglino & Korsgaard, 2004, 2006), which addresses self- versus other-oriented goals and the judgment processes underlying the pursuit of these goals. The theory, illustrated in Figure 18.1, proposes that under certain conditions, individuals will be motivated by instrumental concerns and will employ rational cognitive processing wherein they systematically consider the consequences of their actions. Under other circumstances, persons will be motivated by noninstrumental concerns and will engage in heuristic processing wherein they respond based on factors such as social norms and group identity without carefully considering the implications of their actions. Although these modes of processing are depicted as separate categories in Figure 18.1, the distinction between rational and heuristic processing is more appropriately conceived of as a continuum.

The theory also maintains that rational and heuristic modes of processing can be directed at self- or other-oriented goals. Consistent with the mechanisms underlying goal setting, self- versus other-oriented goals act to focus one's attention on the self or on another person or persons to the exclusion of acts and outcomes that are inconsistent with the goal. The interaction resulting from the different modes of processing and goals yields the 2 × 2 matrix of motivations shown in Figure 18.1.

The theory of other orientation specifically addresses the distinction between rational modes of processing that serve self-oriented goals, and heuristic modes of processing directed at other-oriented goals (the cells along the main diagonal of the matrix in Figure 18.1). We discuss these two motivations first.

The upper left cell (Rational Self-Interest) is the motivational condition in which individuals focus on personal gain and pursue self-interested goals in a way that maximizes their expected personal outcomes. This motivational condition forms the basis for classical economics and value-expectancy models of attitudes and motivation. When persons act according to rational self-interest, they pursue self-oriented goals in a deliberative manner with little or no regard for the interests of others.

The lower right cell (*Other Orientation*) represents the condition wherein individuals are focused on other-oriented goals but engage in a low level of rational processing, that is, they focus on benefiting others without considering personal consequences.

Persons who act consistently with the assumptions underlying this cell are more likely to rely on heuristic or normative processing, which eliminates the need to carefully consider the consequences of one's actions. As such, factors that focus attention and concerns on others are likely to contribute to sensitivity to norms and are likely to induce this form of reasoning. Depending on the norms involved, behavior in this cell may not always benefit the target of one's actions. For example, one theory (Fehr & Fischbacher, 2003) holds that altruists are "strong reciprocators," who not only abide by norms but also enforce or maintain these norms by punishing defectors, even when such actions are costly to themselves.

The lower left cell (Mindlessness) describes the motivational condition in which individuals pursue self-oriented goals without carefully considering the consequences to the self and without the intent to maximize their self-interests. This category includes spontaneous behavior such as impulsive retaliation, which is clearly self-gratifying, as well as certain prosocial actions (e.g., spontaneous helping) that are undertaken to maintain one's pleasant mood (Cropanzano, Goldman, & Folger, 2005). This cell also encompasses situations in which the individual is focused on self-oriented goals but is unable to engage in rational processing due to factors such as distraction, fatigue, time pressure, or fear.

The upper right cell (Collective Rationality) depicts the condition in which individuals pursue other-oriented goals and engage in rational judgment. Individuals acting within the parameters of this cell are likely to be simultaneously focused on the outcomes of others and their own interests while engaging in rational processing. Persons acting on the basis of collective rationality can rationally pursue other-oriented goals with little concern for the self (e.g., risking one's life while engaging in deliberative actions aimed at rescuing another person).

As noted earlier, the theory of other orientation is primarily concerned with the distinction between rational self-interest and other orientation. These motives have dominated research because, although one's mode of processing and the target of his or her behavior are distinct constructs, they are correlated in that self-interested goals are positively associated with high levels of rational information processing. This is evident from research in behavioral decision theory and theories of attitude formation, which indicate that persons employ more rational processing when their personal outcomes are greater (Eagly & Chaiken, 1993; McAllister, Mitchell, & Beach, 1979). Moreover, the nature of rational processing indicates that the reverse must also be true, that is, stimulating rational processing (encouraging a deliberative consideration of relevant beliefs and valences) must necessarily involve a consideration of self-relevant outcomes.

Considering the positive relationship between rational information processing and self-oriented goals, maintaining an enduring focus on other-oriented goals is more sustainable when individuals employ less instrumental heuristic processing. Indeed, unless stimulated to act differently, the "default" tendency for most individuals is to avoid effortful rational processing. This occurs because individuals are *cognitive misers* (Fiske & Taylor, 1984) in that they generally prefer less effortful heuristic processing over more cognitively taxing rational processing. This tendency has received increased attention in the bias and decision making literatures, which indicate that individuals prefer to employ automatic (System 1) thinking over effortful (System 2) thinking (Stanovich & West, 2000). This preference was evident in a study by De Dreu and his colleagues (De Dreu, Koole, & Steinel, 2000) showing that participants had to be specifically compelled to adopt the more effortful rational mode of processing required for joint (self and other) optimization under collective rationality. Thus, mindlessness and collective rationality represented in the off-diagonal cells in Figure 18.1 (upper right and lower left cells) are more appropriately conceived of as transitory motivational states.

Dispositional and Situational Approaches to Other Orientation

Other orientation as a motive can originate from dispositional and situational factors. As a trait, other orientation is defined as the dispositional tendency to be concerned with and helpful to other persons (Meglino & Korsgaard, 2004). This trait is manifest in numerous measures of other-oriented constructs that include agreeableness, empathy, social responsibility, prosocial values, and concern for the welfare of others (Rushton, Chrisjohn, & Fekken, 1981; Schroeder, Penner, Dovido, & Piliavin, 1995). Indeed, Penner and his associates discovered that measures of other-oriented values were so highly related that they could be captured in a single measure of prosocial tendency (Penner, Fritzsche, Craiger, & Freifeld, 1995). Moreover, cross-cultural research shows that individuals from collectivist cultures display a greater orientation toward others as indicated by cultural differences in the value of individualism–collectivism (Hofstede, 1984; Triandis, 1995). Therefore, various indicators such as values (e.g., concern for others, Ravlin & Meglino, 1987a; 1987b), traits (e.g., dispositional empathy, Archer, 1991; social interest, Crandall, 1975), and cross-cultural differences in individualism–collectivism are likely to represent similar manifestations of other orientation. In our research, we have operationalized dispositional concern for others using both Davis's (1983) trait-based measure of empathic concern and a value-based measure, the Concern for Others subscale of the Comparative Emphasis Scale (Ravlin & Meglino, 1987a; 1987b). Both of these measures are reproduced in the Appendix.

Various situational factors may also prompt individuals to act in accordance with other oriented motives. The context motivates prosocial behavior when other-oriented concerns are made salient or when individuals are prone to think heuristically or intuitively, thus prompting a reliance on prevailing prosocial norms. The salience of other-oriented concerns have been induced by having the individual take the perspective of a target other (Batson & Shaw, 1991) or by priming the individual to think about situations in which prosocial concerns or behaviors are present (Korsgaard, Meglino, Lester, & Jeong, 2010). Inducing individuals to process information heuristically—as opposed to deliberatively—has been experimentally manipulated through priming wherein research participants work on a preliminary task requiring either intuitive, heuristic thinking or rational deliberation (Korsgaard, Meglino, Thomas, and Au, 2001; Zhong, 2011). These manipulations lead individuals to be more or less prosocial in their actions and intentions (Zhong, 2011; Skarlicki & Rupp, 2010). In our research, we have employed perspective-taking and heuristic-versus-deliberative processing manipulations, which are listed in the Appendix.

In summary, other orientation as either a dispositionally or situationally induced motive, is associated with greater concern for others (and lower concern for the self), and with the tendency to engage in a comparatively low level of rational processing. Thus, other-oriented individuals are more likely to accept and act on social information such as norms, even when the requisite actions are inconsistent with their self interests. These characteristics contain important implications for attitudes and behavior. Specifically, (a) when faced with a self-versus-other trade-off, persons higher in other orientation will give greater weight to others' outcomes than will people lower in other orientation, (b) compared to those who are lower in other orientation, people higher in other orientation will be more sensitive to normative pressure even when the associated actions are personally costly to them, and (c) the tendency to engage in rational, deliberative processing will mute these effects.

Implications of Other Orientation for Justice

Our core thesis is that other orientation will affect how individuals act and react to organizational justice. We specifically propose that persons who are higher in other orientation will act in ways that are less consistent with self-interest motives or deontological values. For example, among individuals who are high in other orientation, the motivation to benefit others and, by extension, to avoid harming others, can potentially overwhelm the mechanisms seen to affect organizational justice. These mechanisms include self-interest and the deontological motive to uphold fairness (see e.g., Batson, Klein, Highberger, & Shaw, 1995).

Impact of Other Orientation on Being Fair

Although the benefits of organizational justice are well documented (Cohen-Charash & Spector, 2001; Colquitt et al., 2001), accounts of organizational injustice are quite commonplace, suggesting that leaders and managers are often unwilling or unable to be fair. One reason that this occurs is because leaders and managers often seek to maximize their own outcomes at the expense of their employees. The principle of meritocracy espoused in corporate settings allows for the uneven distribution of resources. In such cases, one follows the norm of equity as opposed to equality (Deutsch, 1975), but the degree to which equitable allocations are unequal is subject to interpretation. Aside from pure greed, self-serving bias is apt to exacerbate inequality in allocations. Research suggests that persons in charge of resource allocations tend to see themselves as more deserving. For example, in making allocation between themselves and others with less power, individuals in the position of leadership tend to believe they are entitled to a larger allocation (De Cremer & Van Dijk, 2005). Decision makers are thus apt to make decisions that result in excessive gaps between the resources allocated to themselves versus others. Our proposition suggests that this tendency would be less prevalent for individuals higher in other orientation. Because of the strong motivation to benefit others and avoid harming them, individuals higher in other orientation should tend toward more equal distribution of rewards, even when the other individual is less deserving.

We tested this prediction in Study 1, a scenario-based study in which participants assumed the role of a team member in a class project for a course. They were asked to allocate 100 points among themselves, two other "good" team members, and a low performing team member. To induce other orientation, we used Batson's manipulation of empathy (Batson & Shaw, 1991; see Appendix) by asking participants to remain objective (low empathy) or put themselves "in the shoes" of the low performing member (high empathy). As shown in Figure 18.2, participants were more forgiving (i.e., they awarded more points) of the low performing member in the high empathy condition than in the low empathy condition. More importantly, the difference in the amount participants gave themselves versus the low performing other was significantly less in the high empathy condition than in the low empathy condition. These findings suggest that other orientation promotes avoidance of harm over the harsher enforcement of distributive justice.

DISTRIBUTIVE JUSTICE AND EMPATHY

One potential interpretation of this finding is that other orientation may lead to compromising on the principle of distributed justice. However, research suggests that other orientations leads to a heightened sensitivity to prevailing norms, including fair exchanges (Korsgaard et al., 2010). Thus, individuals higher in other orientation should abide by the justice norms unless abiding by the norm directly conflicts with the principle of benevolence. For example Batson and his colleagues (Batson et al., 1995) found that, in comparison to individuals low in empathy, empathetic individuals were more likely to move a target patient to a higher position on the waiting list for an organ donation in violation of the allocation procedure. In this case, upholding the norm of fairness would harm the patient who was the focus of the actor's concerns. Only by violating the principle of fairness could this patient be helped. Ironically, although one person was generously helped, another was unintentionally disadvantaged. This study suggests that other orientation can lead to compromises in distributive justice when the decision involves harming a particular, focal individual. This effect was demonstrated in Study 2, a scenario-based study (Rymph, 1999) in which participants read about an employee who deserved a raise (potential benefit) or deserved a pay cut (potential harm). As in Study 1, empathy was manipulated through instructions to take the employee's perspective or to remain objective (Batson & Shaw, 1991; Appendix). The findings revealed a significant interaction between empathy and potential harm versus benefit. As illustrated in Figure 18.3, in the potential benefit condition, there was no difference between high versus low empathy, but in the potential harm condition, the average pay reduction was significantly smaller for the high-empathy versus the low- empathy participants. These findings suggest that, rather than leading to wholesale violations of distributive

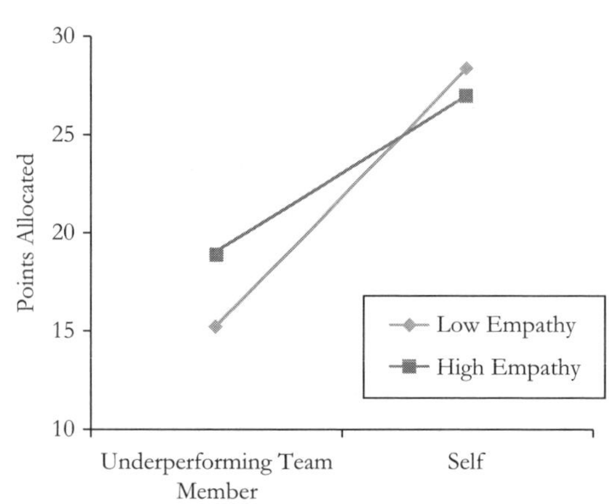

Fig. 18.2 Relationship of empathy to allocations to the self versus underperforming team member (Study 1).

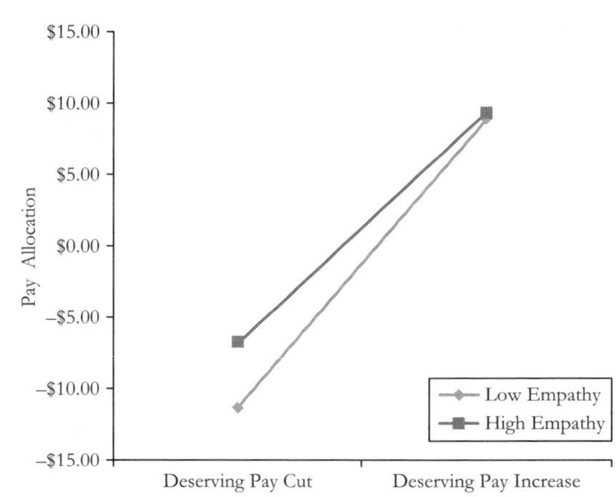

Fig. 18.3 Relationship among empathy, deservingness, and pay allocations (Study 2).

justice, other orientation is most relevant to decisions involving potential harm, leading individuals to temper justice with mercy.

THE CHURCHILL EFFECT

Managerial injustice is not restricted to violation of distributive justice; interactional, information, and procedural justice are also lacking in many common allocation decisions. Deficits in these forms of justice have been attributed to a phenomenon known as the Churchill Effect (Folger & Skarlicki, 1998). Leaders and managers are responsible for making sound business decisions that can be harmful to their employees. For example, managers are required to make decisions about who is denied a pay raise or promotion and who is terminated or laid off. These decisions can lead to feelings of discomfort such as guilt and anxiety, causing the manager to psychologically distance him or herself from the employee (Folger & Skarlicki, 1998). Psychological distancing—minimizing interactions with the victim, blaming the victim, being cold or impolite toward the victim, etc.—can make the manager appear to be interactionally or procedurally unjust (Folger & Skarlicki, 2001). The theory of other orientation suggests that this effect is less likely to occur when individuals are higher in other orientation. The trade-off underlying the Churchill effect is between fairness toward another versus personal comfort. In cases in which self-interest is pitted again others' interest, other orientation is likely to "move the needle" closer to protecting the interests of the other. As such, other orientation should lead to greater interactional fairness when decision makers have to make a harmful decision.

We tested this proposition in Study 3, a scenario-based study with 105 undergraduate students enrolled in a public university in the southeast United States. In the scenario, participants assumed the role of a hiring manager preparing to interview a candidate. After reading a profile of the job requirements and the resume and background of a particular candidate, participants were asked how long they would spend interviewing the candidate. Half the participants considered a candidate who was highly qualified and the other half considered a candidate who was clearly unqualified. Other orientation was captured by a trait measure of empathy (Davis, 1983; see Appendix). The Churchill effect would suggest a significant effect for candidate qualifications such that decision makers would avoid spending time with a candidate that they would not hire. The results show that the effect of candidate qualifications on the amount of time spent was qualified by empathy. As illustrated in Figure 18.4a, participants lower in empathy intended to spend slightly less time with unqualified candidates. In contrast, participants higher in empathy intended to spend significantly more time with the unqualified candidate than with the qualified candidate. In other words, when the candidate was unqualified, participants higher in empathy intended to spend substantially more time with the candidate than did participants lower in empathy.

In Study 4, we replicated this study with a group of 78 working adults attending part time MBA programs at two public universities in the United States. In this case, we manipulated empathy by having participating engage in perspective taking (Batson & Shaw, 1991). We found a marginally significant interaction between the favorableness of the candidate and empathy. Consistent with the Churchill effect, individuals overall were likely to spend significantly less time with an unqualified as opposed to qualified candidate. However, this effect was significant only for participants low in empathy; individual high in empathy were apt to spend nearly equal amounts of time with both qualified and unqualified candidates.

Taken together, these studies suggest that other orientation may be an important differentiator of how decision makers handle making or delivering unfavorable allocation decisions. Such decisions involve real or imaged personal costs, such as guilt and potential retaliation, which may motivate

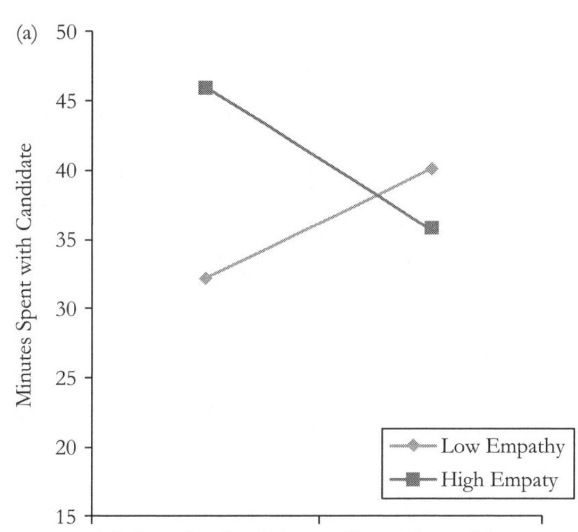

Fig. 18.4a Relationship among empathy, candidate merit, and time with candidate: Undergraduates (Study 3).

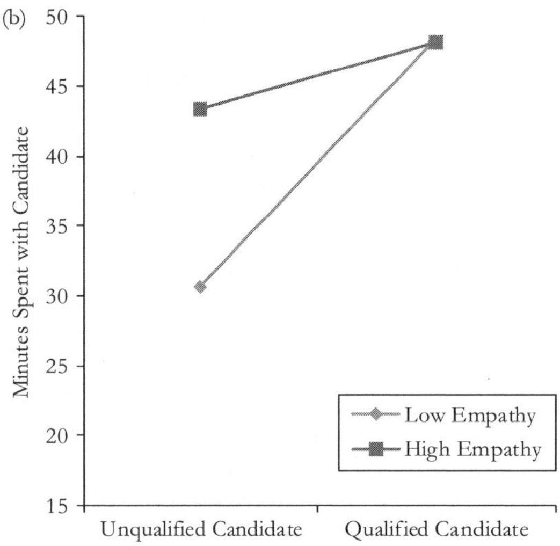

Fig. 18.4b Relationship among empathy, candidate merit, and time spent with candidate: Working adults (Study 4).

avoidance and psychological distance. Because distancing behavior can result in less fair treatment (i.e., less voice, fewer demonstrations of concern), it can further exacerbate the harm to the recipient. Thus, making decisions that harm others and delivering such news poses a trade-off between self-interest and the needs of the other party. Our findings, illustrated in Figure 18.4b, suggest that other orientation tips the scales in favor of the needs of the other party, resulting in less distancing behavior. In contrast, when the decision maker has greater ego involvement in the situation—for example, when he or she is personally responsible for harming another (Folger & Skarlicki, 1998)—distancing behavior is more likely to win out over fair treatment.

Impact of Other Orientation on Reactions to Unfairness

The preceding discussion considered how other orientation influences the way decision makers address fairness in making allocation decisions and enacting those decisions. Other orientation is also likely to play a role in how individuals react as recipients of potentially unfair allocations or treatment.

One implication that flows from the theory of other orientation is that, among persons who are higher in other orientation, actions in response to injustice are likely to be less contingent on the potential harm or benefit to the self. One reason that individuals respond to injustice is to restore a balanced exchange or somehow preserve their self-interest going forward. Given that individuals higher in other orientation are less prone to rational deliberation regarding choices and decisions (Korsgaard, Meglino, & Lester, 1996), their responses to injustice should be less calculating. For example, one response to injustice is to exit the relationship (Hirschman, 1970), but research also suggests that the relationship between justice and exit is contingent on satisfaction (Iverson & Currivan, 2003). This contingency reflects a rational and deliberative process wherein individuals tend to weigh their current job satisfaction in deciding to leave the firm (Mobley, Griffeth, Hand, & Meglino, 1979). This relationship is apt to be stronger among persons who are lower in other orientation and thus more likely to engage in rational deliberations. In contrast, for persons higher in other orientation who are apt to respond based on heuristic processing and adherence to prevailing norms, the response to injustice should be less dependent of whether their reaction will produce beneficial effects to the self.

This proposition was tested in two scenario studies (Studies 5 & 6) in which participants read about a situation in which they were denied a promised and deserved promotion (Korsgaard et al., 2001). Half the subjects read that they were very satisfied with their job, whereas the other half were told that they were very dissatisfied with their job. We expected that dissatisfaction would be a significant determinant of exit intentions. In Study 5, we directly assessed the role of deliberativeness in responses to injustice among 126 working professionals enrolled in an MBA program. We used a priming task based on Chen, Shechter, and Chaiken (1996) in which participants either answered a series of questions involving deliberative and objective thought (e.g., conducting a background check on a prospective employee) or questions involving less-deliberative thought (e.g., sitting next to a talkative bore on a long airplane flight; see Appendix). Participants were then asked their intention to exit the organization depicted in the scenario (Rusbult et al., 1988). As expected there was a significant interaction between satisfaction and deliberativeness such that job dissatisfaction had a strong impact on exit intentions for participants in the high-deliberative condition (Figure 18.5a).

Study 6 involved 253 business students for a southeastern US university and a university in New Zealand. In this study, instead of manipulating deliberativeness, we measured other orientation using the Concern for Others subscale of the Comparative Emphasis values scale (Ravlin &

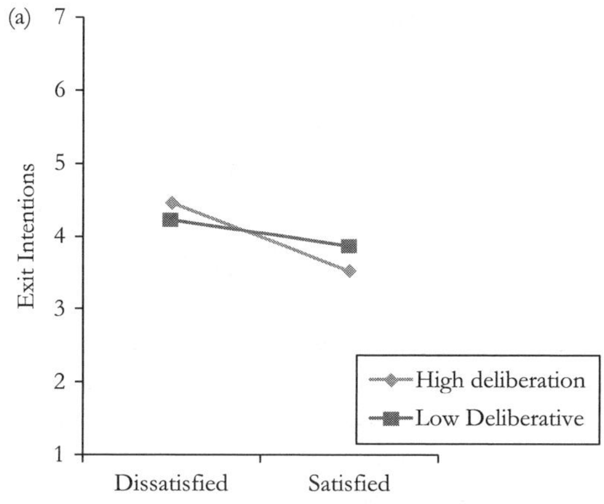

Fig. 18.5a Relationship among deliberations, job satisfaction, and exit intentions (Study 5).

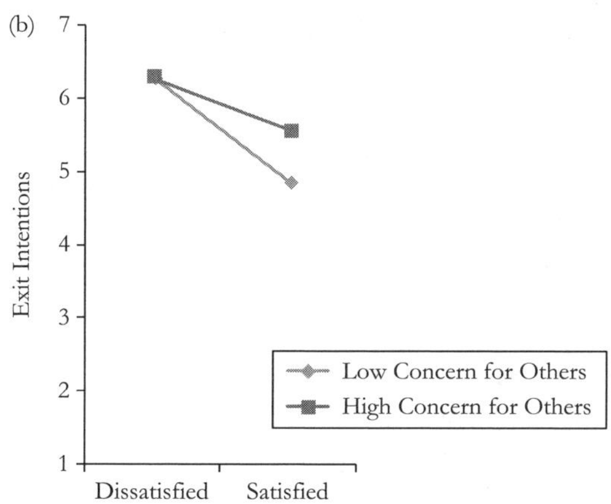

Fig. 18.5b Relationship among concern for others, job satisfaction, and exit intentions (Study 6).

Meglino, 1987a; 1987b; see Appendix). We obtained a similar finding in Study 6 as in Study 5: the impact of job satisfaction was significantly moderated by other orientation such that the effect on intention to remain was stronger for individuals lower on other orientation (Figure 18.5b). In both studies, more-deliberative, less-other-oriented individuals were more likely to respond to an injustice in a calculating way by exiting the organization when they were dissatisfied (Study 5) and by remaining with the organization when they were satisfied (Study 6).

A second important implication that flows from the theory of other orientation is that other orientation should influence how individuals interpret potentially unjust decisions. The theory of other orientation suggests that the attitudes and beliefs of individuals higher in other orientation are less likely to be filtered through egoistic or self-enhancement concerns (Korsgaard & Meglino 2008). Thus, individuals higher in other orientation should be less prone to self-inflation in assessments of their performance and should have perceptions of their performance that are more in line with their those of their superiors (Korsgaard, Meglino & Lester, 2004). In contrast, because unfavorable evaluations can pose a threat to self-esteem, such evaluations are apt to be rejected when viewed through the lens of the self. In seeking to maintain a positive self-image, persons lower in other orientation are likely to reject negative evaluations and hold a negative attitude toward the evaluator (Korsgaard, Meglino, & Lester, 1996). In short, persons lower in other orientation are more likely to take negative evaluations as a personal affront. Such reactions are likely to adversely affect perceptions of interactional justice (Bies, Tripp, & Kramer, 1997).

In Study 7 we tested in this prediction using student reactions to on-campus recruitment interviews. Following the recruiting interview, we administered a survey to 193 students asking their perceptions of the interview and their intentions. To assess the favorableness of the interview, students indicated the likelihood that they would be hired. Students also indicated the extent to which they were treated in an interactionally fair manner. We measured other orientation using the Concern for Others subscale of the Comparative Emphasis values scale (Ravlin & Meglino, 1987a; 1987b; see Appendix). The findings, illustrated in Figure 18.6a, show that other orientation significantly moderated the impact of the favorability of the interview on perceived interactional

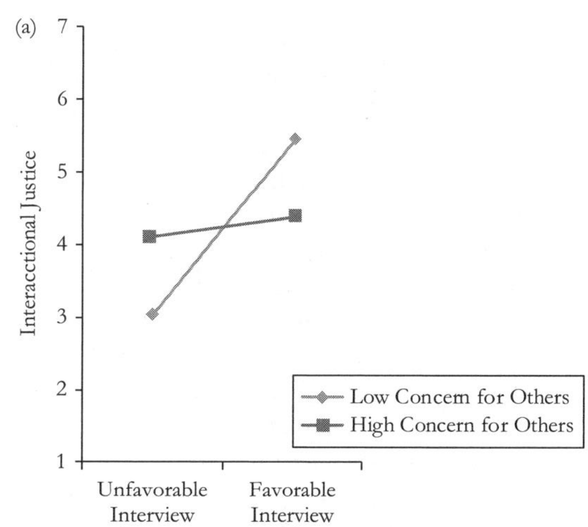

Fig. 18.6a Relationship among concern for others, interview favorableness, perceived interactional justice (Study 7).

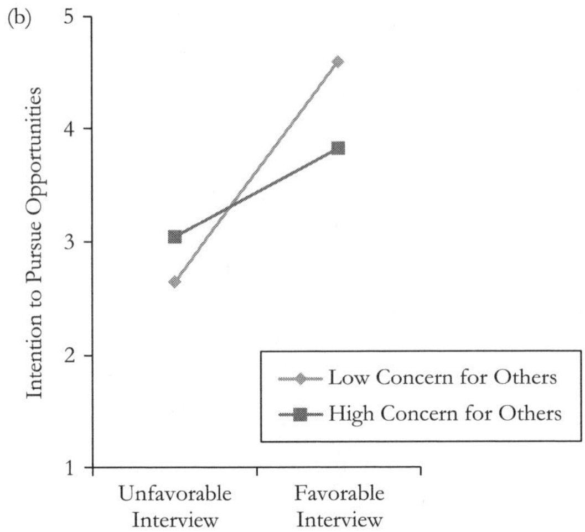

Fig. 18.6b Relationship among concern for others, interview favorableness, and intention to pursue opportunities (Study 7).

justice. Individuals higher in concern for others generally perceived the interview as more interactionally just and their perceptions were less contingent on the favorableness of the interview.

When individuals are treated disrespectfully, they are apt to consider vengeful responses (Bies et al., 1997). Indeed, one broad category of responses to injustice is some form of punishment or retribution (Lind, 1997). In response to unfairness, a deontological view of fairness can lead individual to punish others even when it comes at a personal cost (Turillo et al., 2002). However because the intent in such cases is to harm the perpetrator, other orientation should lead individuals to refrain from such responses to injustice. In the context of the recruitment interview study, one way to "punish" the recruiter was to refuse an offer or other potential opportunity with the organization. We found that other orientation moderated the relationship between expected outcome and willingness to work for the organization in another capacity. Simple slopes show a stronger, significant relationship for persons lower in concern for others. Further, this relationship was mediated by interactional justice (Figure 18.6b). These findings suggest that other orientation reduces the likelihood that individuals are personally offended by unfavorable evaluations and whether such evaluations are apt to lead to retribution responses to perceived injustice.

Summary and Conclusions

In this investigation we outlined how the theory of other orientation can be integrated with organizational justice research to understand how individuals make and react to decisions involving justice. Specifically, the theory of other orientation describes how an individual's motivational orientation influences his or her reactions and behavior. It maintains that persons who are motivated by rational self-interest are less concerned with the interests of others and tend to pursue self-oriented goals in a deliberative manner. In contrast, those who are motivated by other orientation are more concerned with benefiting others, and are more likely to employ normative or heuristic processing that minimizes the need to carefully consider the consequences of their actions.

The theory of other orientation contributes to research on organizational justice because justice mechanisms that rely on self-interested processes are likely to be more descriptive of individuals who are motivated by rational self-interest. Therefore, instrumental justice motives such as the desire to maintain equity, to control personal outcomes, and/or to protect one's long-term self-interests should be more operative when persons are motivated by rational self interest.

Our findings for this investigation support the proposed intersection between justice related processes and the theory of other orientation. Specifically, when persons were responsible for making decisions involving distributive justice, those who were higher in other orientation awarded greater outcomes (grade points) to an underperforming group member (Study 1) and gave less of a pay cut to persons who deserved such a cut (Study 2). These findings are consistent with those obtained by Batson and his colleagues (1995) indicating that persons will compromise distributive justice principles in order to avoid harming a specific individual.

In the case of procedural justice, persons who were higher in other orientation preferred to spend more time with an unqualified interview applicant (Study 3). Moreover, in contrast with persons low in other orientation who indicated they would be more dismissive of an unqualified job applicant, those who were higher in other orientation reported they would spend nearly equal time with an unqualified versus a qualified applicant (Study 4). Taken together, these studies indicate that other-oriented persons are more willing to minimize social distance and tolerate the personal discomfort associated with delivering bad news to another person. Since administering procedural and interactional fairness requires one to sacrifice some personal comfort, such findings suggest that other oriented leaders will be more adept at administering procedural and interactive justice.

Studies 5, 6, and 7 examined how other orientation affects individuals' reactions to a potentially unjust decision. Low-other-oriented participants in Study 5 showed a greater likelihood of leaving a dissatisfying job in response to an injustice and, in Study 6, a greater likelihood of remaining with a satisfying job in response to the same injustice. Similar egoistic reactions were evident among low-other- oriented participants in Study 7 who were more likely to evaluate the interactional fairness of an employment interview based on whether the interview was favorable to them in terms of their likelihood of being hired. Moreover, persons who were lower in other orientation were more likely to refuse other potential employment opportunities with the interviewing organization if they judged the interview to be unfavorable to them. As predicted from the theory of other orientation, these studies indicate that individuals who were lower in other orientation were more calculating and more likely to react in egoistic, self-enhancing ways.

The findings of the previous studies also support the robustness of other orientation as a dispositional and situational phenomenon. As a disposition, other orientation was assessed using two different measures: the concern for others subscale of the Comparative Emphasis Scale (Ravlin & Meglino, 1987a; 1987b) and Davis's (1983) measure of empathic concern. Likewise, similar results were obtained using two different situational manipulations: Batson's method of priming empathy (Batson & Shaw, 1991) and, in producing low levels of other orientation, Chen, et al.'s (1996) method of priming deliberativeness.

Taken as a whole, the similar results obtained for various operationalizations of other orientation suggest that other orientation can be triggered in numerous ways in actual organizations. With respect to dispositions, organizations or subunits within an organization may, through the attraction–selection–attrition cycle (Schneider, 1987), be composed of employees who share a common level of other orientation. At the situational level, organizations may promulgate values stressing concern for employees and others, which can act to prime constituents to be more other oriented. Research suggests that units composed of individuals high in agreeableness (a trait that encompasses other orientation) tend to have climates for procedural and interactional justice (Mayer, Nishii, Schneider, & Goldstein, 2007). To the extent that organizations foster other orientation, they are likely to encourage a climate that promotes greater fairness.

Future Research

The previous studies suggest a number of fruitful avenues for research aimed at integrating organizational justice with the motivational processes defined in the theory of other orientation. Although research objectivity must certainly be maintained in any systematic investigation, we believe that the findings of such research are likely to yield contingency as opposed to universal conclusions for other orientation. That is, rather than indicating that organizations should uniformly focus their efforts at becoming either more rationally self-interested or more other orientated, the findings of such investigations are likely to suggest that efforts aimed at stimulating greater or lesser orientation toward others will depend on the specific evaluations and behaviors that the organization or work unit wishes to encourage. In this regard, we believe that future findings will have much in common with the traditional "structure follows strategy" approach that underlies much of strategic management (Chandler, 1962). Thus, given the multifaceted nature of manager and employee relations, we believe that managers will ultimately select the appropriate orientation toward others based on their desired approach to organizational justice and the organizational functions they wish to encourage.

Our expectation that future research will yield contingent findings can be seen most dramatically in the findings of Studies 1–5, which are relevant to persons in leadership positions. One obvious contingency in this research is evident in the immediate versus long-term costs and benefits for a leader being highly other oriented. In Study 1, these persons were more likely to sacrifice their own outcomes to support a lower performing team member. Although costly in the short run, research suggests that such forms of self-sacrificial behavior can advance the long-term interests of the leader. Specifically, such behavior signals that the leader will help others at a later time, leading to higher follower performance via the norm or reciprocity. Additionally, this behavior should produce a greater sense of collective identity and common mission that can lead to higher leader effectiveness, greater levels of commitment and motivation, and greater willingness on the part of team members to make personal sacrifices in the future (van Knippenberg & van Knippenberg, 2005).

It is important to note that the leader's largesse in Study 1 came at the expense of the leader himself/herself. This was not necessarily the case in Study 2 where the leader awarded less of a pay cut to an employee who deserved such a cut. Leaders and employees instinctively understand that pay raises and cuts among employees amount to a zero-sum game wherein a pay cut for one employee may amount to a pay raise to another. Therefore, in contrast to Study 1, the leader's distributive injustice in Study 2 could easily come at the financial expense of other employees, who could grow to resent the leader in the long run.

Such self-sacrificial behavior was also evident in Studies 3 and 4. In these studies, the scarce resource at issue was the leader's time and attention, which, when lavished on others, generally casts the leader in a positive light (Grant, 2013). Albeit less consequential than grade points and pay raises, time and attention devoted to unqualified or underperforming employees could also be seen as a violation of distributive justice by other employees. Thus, depending on the dynamics of the work environment, the likelihood that other oriented leaders would engage in greater helpfulness, while enhancing procedural and interactive justice in the short run, could come at the expense of broader resentment in the work unit. Clearly, determining the desirable implicit balance between various forms of justice on the one hand and compassionate behavior on the other is an area that can benefit from substantial systematic research.

The contingent aspects of future research can also be seen in the findings of Studies 5, 6, and 7, which cast the individual as the recipient of a real or imagined injustice. The findings of Studies 5 and 6, which specifically deal with turnover intentions, indicate that persons who are low in other orientation are more calculating in their decision to exit an organization when they are the recipient of an injustice, preferring to leave when the job is less satisfying (Study 5) and choosing to stay when the job is more satisfying (Study 6). From a traditional perspective, which views turnover as costly to an organization and something to be avoided or otherwise discouraged (Mobley, 1982), one might conclude that it is more beneficial for the organization to utilize practices that enhance other orientation among employees. Reducing turnover in such cases would be less onerous that attempting to address the numerous sources of job satisfaction that influence one's intentions to quit.

One might reach a different conclusion when considering the functional aspects of turnover. Functional turnover occurs when the organization has a negative evaluation of an employee and is unconcerned about whether the employee leaves (Dalton, Krackhardt, & Porter, 1981). As was evident in Study 7, an employee who is low in other orientation may interpret a negative performance evaluation as a violation of interactional justice, prompting the employee to exit the organization if the job is less satisfying (Studies 5 & 6). Although we would not suggest that organizations violate procedural or interactional justice for low-performing employees, low-other-oriented employees may interpret the organization's actions in such a light, prompting them to consider leaving. Under these conditions, it may be functional for an organization to encourage low levels of other orientation and to avoid extraordinary efforts to increase job satisfaction. Such actions may be functional in that they encourage low performers to leave the organization.

Finally, consistent with the theory of other orientation, the findings of all studies reported here show that other-oriented persons are less likely to engage in rational self-interested calculation when considering their actions. Thus, they are more likely to sacrifice their resources for others, are less jealous of their time, and are more likely to tolerate negative aspects of their job without leaving. These qualities are extremely important in reaching a successful reconciliation of previous grievances with another person or entity such as an organization. Since forgiveness requires that one suspend his or her negative evaluation of another and relinquish the egoistic desire for retaliation (Aquino, Tripp, & Bies, 2006), other-oriented persons may be more willing to forgive past transgressions. In many respects, this may be a positive quality if it reestablishes a relationship that is supportive for both parties. On the other hand, it can also constitute a form of "pathological altruism" (see Oakley, 2013) that appears beneficial in the short run but ultimately casts the forgiving party as one who enables the continuing transgressions of the other. As with the other contingency aspects outlined earlier, the characteristics of the particular circumstance overwhelm our desire to offer universal prescriptions about the desired motivational orientation of others.

References

Aquino, K., Tripp, T. M., & Bies, R. J. (2006). Getting even or moving on? Power, procedural justice, and types of offense as predictors of revenge, forgiveness, reconciliation, and avoidance in organizations. *Journal of Applied Psychology, 91*, 653–668.

Archer, R. L. (1991). Dispositional empathy and a pluralism of prosocial motives. *Psychological Inquiry, 2*, 123–124.

Batson, C. D., & Shaw, L. L. (1991). Evidence for altruism: Toward a pluralism of social motives. *Psychological Inquiry, 2*, 107–122.

Batson, C. D., Klein, T. R., Highberger, L., & Shaw, L. L. (1995). Immorality from empathy-induced altruism: When compassion and justice conflict. *Journal of Personality and Social Psychology, 68*, 1042–1054.

Bies, R. J., Tripp, T. M., & Kramer, R. M. (1997). At the breaking point: Cognitive and social dynamics of revenge in organizations. In R. A. Giacalone & G. Greenberg, *Antisocial behavior in organizations.* 18–36. Thousand Oaks, CA: Sage.

Blader, S. L., & Tyler, T. R. (2009). Testing and extending the group engagement model: Linkages between scial identity, procedural justice, economic outcomes, and extrarole behavior. *Journal Of Applied Psychology, 94*(2), 445–464.

Blau, P. M. (1964). *Exchange and power in social life.* New York, NY: Wiley.

Chandler, A. (1962). *Strategy and structure.* Cambridge, MA: M.I.T. Press.

Chang, K., & Smithikrai, C. (2010). Counterproductive behaviour at work: an investigation into reduction strategies. *The International Journal of Human Resource Management, 21*, 1272–1288.

Chen, S., Shechter, D., & Chaiken, S. (1996). Getting at the truth or getting along: Accuracy-versus impression-motivated heuristic and systematic processing. *Journal of Personality and Social Psychology, 71*, 262–275.

Cohen-Charash, Y., & Spector, P. E. (2001). The role of justice in organizations: A meta-analysis. *Organizational Behavior and Human Decision Processes, 86*, 278–321.

Colquitt, J. A., Conlon, D. E., Wesson, M. J., Porter, C. O. L. H., & Ng, K. Y. (2001). Justice at the millennium: a meta-analytic review of 25 years of organizational justice research. *Journal of Applied Psychology, 86*, 425.

Crandall, J. E. (1975). A scale for social interest. *Journal of Individual Psychology, 31*, 187–195.

Cropanzano, R., Goldman, B., & Folger, R. (2003). Deontic justice: the role of moral principles in workplace fairness. *Journal of Organizational Behavior, 24*, 1019–1024.

Cropanzano, R., Goldman, B., & Folger, R. (2005). Self-interest: defining and understanding a human motive. *Journal of Organizational Behavior, 26*, 985–991.

Cropanzano, R., Rupp, D. E., Mohler, C. J., & Schminke, M. (2001). Three roads to organizational justice. *Research in Personnel and Human Resources Management, 20*, 1–113.

Dalton, D. R., Krackhardt, D. M., & Porter, L. W. (1981). Functional turnover: An empirical assessment. *Journal of Applied Psychology, 66*, 716–721.

Davis, M. H. (1983). Measuring individual differences in empathy: Evidence for a multidimensional approach. *Journal of Personality and Social Psychology, 44*, 113–126.

De Cremer, D., & Van Dijk, E. (2005). When and why leaders put themselves first: Leader behaviour in resource allocations as a function of feeling entitled. *European Journal of Social Psychology, 35*, 553–563.

De Dreu, C. K. W., Koole, S. L., & Steinel, W. (2000). Unfixing the fixed pie: A motivated information-processing approach to integrative negotiation. *Journal of Personality and Social Psychology, 79*, 975–987.

Deutsch, M. (1975). Equity, equality, and need: What determines which value will be used as the basis of distributive justice? *Journal of Social Issues, 31*, 137–149.

Eagly, A. H., & Chaiken, S. (1993). *The psychology of attitudes.* San Diego, CS: Harcourt Brace Jovanovich.

Fehr, E., & Fischbacher, U. (2003). The nature of human altruism. *Nature, 425*, 785–791.

Fiske, S. T., & Taylor, S. (1984). Social cognition. (2nd ed.). New York, NY: McGraw-Hill.

Flaherty, S., & Moss, S. A. (2007). The impact of personality and team context on the relationship between workplace injustice and counterproductive work behavior. *Journal of Applied Social Psychology, 37*, 2549–2575.

Folger, R., & Cropanzano, R. (2001). Fairness theory: Justice as accountability. *Advances in Organizational Justice, 1*, 1–55.

Folger, R., & Skarlicki, D. (1998). When tough times make tough bosses: Managerial distancing as a function of layoff blame. *Academy of Management Journal, 41*, 79–87.

Folger, R., & Skarlicki, D. P. (2001). Fairness as a dependent variable: Why tough times can lead to bad management. *Justice in the workplace: From theory to practice* (2nd ed., 97–118). Psychology Press.

Grant, A. M. (2013). *Give and take: A revolutionary approach to success.* New York, NY: Penguin Group.

Hirschman, A. O. (1970). *Exit, voice, and loyalty: Responses to decline in firms, organizations, and states.* Cambridge, MA: Harvard University Press.

Hofstede, G. (1984). Cultural dimensions in management and planning. *Asia Pacific Journal of Management, 1*, 81–99.

Iverson, R. D., & Currivan, D. B. (2003). Union participation, job satisfaction, and employee turnover: An event-history analysis of the exit-voice hypothesis. *Industrial Relations: A Journal of Economy and Society, 42*, 101–105.

Korsgaard, M. A., & Meglino, B. M. (2008). Beyond the individualistic self: A framework for prosocial motives and judgments. In H. A. Wayment & J. J. Bauer (Eds.), *Transcending self-interest: Psychological explorations of the quiet ego* (pp. 183–196). Washington, DC: American Psychological Association.

Korsgaard, M. A., Meglino, B. M., & Lester, S. W. (1996). The Effect of Other-Oriented Values on Decision Making: A Test of Propositions of a Theory of Concern for Others in Organizations. *Organizational Behavior and Human Decision Processes, 68*(3), 234–245.

Korsgaard, M. A., Meglino, B. M., & Lester, S. W. (2004). The effect of other orientation on self–supervisor rating agreement. *Journal of Organizational Behavior, 25*, 873–891.

Korsgaard, M A., Meglino, B. M, Lester, S. W., & Jeong, S. S. (2010). Paying you back or paying me forward: Understanding rewarded and unrewarded organizational citizenship behavior. *Journal of Applied Psychology, 95*, 277–290.

Korsgaard, M. A., Meglino, B. M., Thomas, D., & Au, K. (2001, April). *How deliberative are employee responses to violations of expectations.* Paper presented at the annual meeting of the Society for Industrial and Organizational Psychology, San Diego, CA.

Liao, H., & Rupp, D. E. (2005). The impact of justice climate and justice orientation on work outcomes: a cross-level multifoci framework. *Journal of Applied Psychology, 90*, 242–256.

Lind, E. A. (1997). Litigation and claiming in organizations. In *Antisocial behavior in organizations* (pp. 150–171). Thousand Oaks: Sage Publications.

Lind, E., Kray, L., & Thompson, L. (2001). Primary Effects in Justice Judgments: Testing Predictions from Fairness Heuristic Theory. *Organizational Behavior & Human Decision Processes, 85*(2), 189–210.

Lind, E. A., & Tyler, T. R. (1988). *The social psychology of procedural justice*. New York: Plenum.

Lind, E., Greenberg, J., Scott, K., & Welchans, T. (2000). The winding road from employee to complainant: Situational and psychological determinants of wrongful-termination claims. *Administrative Science Quarterly, 45*, 557–590.

Mayer, D., Nishii, L., Schneider, B., & Goldstein, H. (2007). The precursors and products of justice climates: Group leader antecedents and employee attitudinal consequences. *Personnel Psychology, 60*, 929–963.

McAllister, D. W., Mitchell, T. R., & Beach, L. R. (1979). The contingency model for the selection of decision strategies: An empirical test of the effects of significance, accountability, and reversibility. *Organizational Behavior and Human Performance, 24*, 228–244.

Meglino, B. M., & Korsgaard, A. (2004). Considering rational self-interest as a disposition: organizational implications of other orientation. *Journal of Applied Psychology, 89*, 946–959.

Meglino, B. M., & Korsgaard, M. A. (2006). Considering situational and dispositional approaches to rational self-interest: an extension and response to de Dreu (2006). *Journal of Applied Psychology, 91*, 1253–1259.

Mobley, W. H. (1982). Some unanswered questions in turnover and withdrawal research. *Academy of Management Review, 7*, 111–116.

Mobley, W. H., Griffeth, R. W., Hand, H. H., & Meglino, B. M. (1979). Review and conceptual analysis of the employee turnover process. *Psychological Bulletin, 86*, 493–522.

Moon, H., Kamdar, D., Mayer, D. M., & Takeuchi, R. (2008). Me or we? The role of personality and justice as other-centered antecedents to innovative citizenship behaviors within organizations. *Journal of Applied Psychology, 93*, 84–94.

Oakley, B. A. (2013). Concepts and implications of altruism bias and pathological altruism, *Proceedings of the National Academy of Sciences*, 1–8.

Penner, L. A., Fritzsche, B. A., Craiger, J. P., & Freifeld, T. R. (1995). Measuring the prosocial personality. In J. N. Butcher & C. D. Spielberger (Eds.), *Advances in Personality Assessment* (Vol. 10, pp. 147–163). Hillsdale, NJ: Erlbaum.

Pruitt, D. G., & Rubin, J. Z. (1986). *Social conflict: Escalation, stalemate, and settlement*. New York, NY: Random House.

Ravlin, E. C., & Meglino, B. M. (1987a). Effect of values on perception and decision making: A study of alternative work values measures. *Journal of Applied Psychology, 72*, 666.

Ravlin, E. C., & Meglino, B. M. (1987b). Issues in work values measurement. In *Research in corporate social performance and policy* (Vol. 9, pp. 153–183). Greenwich, CT: JAI.

Rusbult, C. E., Farrell, D., Rogers, G., & Mainous, A. G. (1988). Impact of exchange variables on exit, voice, loyalty, and neglect: An integrative model of responses to declining job satisfaction. *Academy of Management Journal, 31*(3), 599–627.

Rushton, P. J., Chrisjohn, R. D., & Cynthia Fekken, G. (1981). The altruistic personality and the self-report altruism scale. *Personality and Individual Differences, 2*, 293–302.

Rymph, R. D. (1999). *Why kind people can seem so unfair: Empathy's impact on resource allocations and interpersonal justice.* (Doctoral Dissertation). Available from the ProQuest Dissertation and Thesis database. (UMI no. 9952749)

Schneider, B. (1987). The people make the place. *Personnel Psychology, 40*, 437–453.

Schroeder, D. A., Penner, L. A., Dovido, J. F., & Piliavin, J. A. (1995). *The psychology of helping and altruism*. New York, NY: McGraw-Hill.

Skarlicki, D. P., Folger, R., & Tesluk, P. (1999). Personality as a moderator in the relationship between fairness and retaliation. *Academy of Management Journal, 42*, 100–108.

Skarlicki, D. P., & Rupp, D. E. (2010). Dual processing and organizational justice: The role of rational versus experiential processing in third-party reactions to workplace mistreatment. *Journal of Applied Psychology, 95*, 944–952.

Stanovich, K. E., & West, R. F. (2000). Individual differences in reasoning: Implications for the rationality debate? *Behavioral and Brain Sciences, 23*, 645–665.

Stouten, J., Kuppens, P., & Decoster, S. (2013). Being angry for different reasons: The role of personality in distributive justice. *Journal of Applied Social Psychology, 43*, 795–805.

Thibaut, J., & Walker, L. (1978). A theory of procedure. *California Law Review, 66*, 541.

Triandis, H. C. (1995). *Individualism & collectivism* (Vol. 5). Boulder, CO: Westview.

Turillo, C. J., Folger, R., Lavelle, J. J., Umphress, E. E., & Gee, J. O. (2002). Is virtue its own reward? Self-sacrificial decisions for the sake of fairness. *Organizational Behavior and Human Decision Processes, 89*, 839–865.

Van Knippenberg, B., & Van Knippenberg, D. (2005). Leader self-sacrifice and leadership effectiveness: The moderating role of leader prototypicality. *Journal of Applied Psychology, 90*, 25–37.

Zhong, C. (2011). The Ethical Dangers of Deliberative Decision Making. *Administrative Science Quarterly, 56*(1), 1–25.

Appendix

Operationalizations of Other Orientation

A. Manipulation of Perspective Taking (Batson & Shaw, 1991; Studies1, 2, and 4)

High Empathy

While you are reading this, try to imagine how this person feels about what is described. Try to imagine how it has affected this person's life and how this person feels as a result.

Low Empathy

While you are reading this, try to take an objective perspective about what is described. Try not to get caught up in how this person feels; just remain objective and detached.

B. Empathic Concern (Davis, 1983; Study 3)

C. Manipulation of Deliberative versus Heuristic Thinking (Based on Chen, et al., 1996; Studies 5 and 6)

Deliberative Priming

1. Imagine you work for a magazine that evaluates consumer products. You have been assigned to write an article evaluating various "pocket-size" computer devices that have Internet and personal computing capabilities. The companies that manufacture these devices all claim that they are helpful, easy to use, and that people are satisfied after the purchase. You want to investigate and report on these claims for your article. What would you do?

2. Suppose a manager is seeking to hire someone for a position in your company. Several people have recommended that a certain person might be good for this position. The manager has interviewed this applicant and would like to hire the individual. At the same time, however, the manager has an uneasy feeling that some of the facts on the resume (for example, education, work experience) are not accurate. Imagine that it is your job to verify the applicant's background and make the final approval for hiring the applicant. What would you do?

3. Your monthly credit card statement indicates that you were charged for a number of goods or services that you do not recall purchasing. Unfortunately, a company without a clear description of the particular item or service lists the charges on your statement. Therefore, it is difficult for you to determine what these purchases involved. You believe that you did not make these purchases, but you may be wrong. You would like to determine what these purchases are, verify that you in fact made these purchases, and correct any mistakes that might exist. What would you do?

Heuristic Priming

1. You are on a 3-hour airplane flight by yourself and have no work to do and nothing to read. The person seated next to you starts up a conversation on a topic that you find extremely boring. The airplane is full, so you cannot change seats. You do not want to be rude, but you would very much like to stop this boring conversation. What do you do?

2. You are at a large dinner party hosted by a co-worker with whom you have a friendly but not close relationship. When you arrive, you find out that no other co-workers will be attending the party. Most of the guests are from the co-worker's neighborhood. They seem to know each other quite well, but you do not know any of the guests. You do not expect dinner to be served for at least an hour. What do you do?

3. You are having lunch with a business contact. This person is talking in great detail about a new home he is building. He has been involved in every step of the process and describes the new house with pride. You have just finished building a house yourself. You think he may be

1	2	3	4
Does not describe me well			Describes me very well

1. I often have concerned feelings for people less fortunate than myself.
2. I sometimes do not feel very sorry for other people when they are having problems.
3. When seeing someone taken advantage of, I feel kind of protective toward him or her.
4. I am not disturbed by other peoples' problems a great deal.
5. When seeing someone treated unfairly, I sometimes don't feel much pity for him or her.
6. I am often quite touched by things that I see happen.
7. I would describe myself as a pretty softhearted person.

using the wrong materials in certain aspects of the construction. If he has made this error and continues, it may cost tens of thousands of dollars in repairs. What do you do?

D. Concern for Others Subscale of the Comparative Emphasis Scale (Ravlin & Meglino, 1987a; 1987b; Studies 6 and 7)

Read each pair of statements carefully and place a check next to the statement that you feel you *should* emphasize more in your behavior at work.

1.	☐ Taking care of all loose ends on a job or project ☐ Being impartial in dealing with others	13.	☐ **Trying to be helpful to a friend at work** ☐ Being sure that work assignments are fair to everyone
2.	☐ Taking actions which represent your true feelings ☐ **Trying to avoid hurting other people**	14.	☐ Refusing to take credit for ideas of others ☐ Maintaining the highest standard for your performance
3.	☐ **Encouraging someone who is having a difficult day** ☐ Considering different points of view before taking action	15.	☐ Being determined to be the best at your work ☐ **Trying not to hurt a friend's feelings**
4.	☐ Speaking your mind even when your views may not be popular ☐ Working to meet job requirements even when your personal schedule must be rearranged	16.	☐ Trying to bring about a fair solution to a dispute ☐ Admitting responsibility for errors made
5.	☐ Making decisions which are fair to all concerned ☐ Expressing your true opinions when asked	17.	☐ Finishing each job you start even when others do not ☐ Making sure that rewards are given in the fairest possible way
6.	☐ Continuing to work on a problem until it is resolved ☐ **Trying to help a fellow worker through a difficult time**	18.	☐ Refusing to tell a lie to make yourself look good ☐ **Helping those who are worried about things at work**
7.	☐ **Trying to help reduce a friend's burden** ☐ Admitting an error and accepting the consequences	19.	☐ Trying as hard as you can to learn as much as possible about your job ☐ Taking a stand for what you believe in
8.	☐ Being impartial in judging disagreements ☐ **Helping others on difficult jobs**	20.	☐ **Sharing information and ideas which others need to do their job** ☐ Always setting high performance goals for yourself
9.	☐ Taking on additional tasks to get ahead ☐ Admitting to making a mistake rather than covering it up	21.	☐ Refusing to do something you think is wrong ☐ Providing fair treatment for all employees
10.	☐ **Offering help to others when they are having a tough time** ☐ Doing whatever work is required to advance in your career	22.	☐ Allowing each employee to have an equal chance to get rewards ☐ Taking on more responsibility to get ahead in an organization
11.	☐ Always being truthful in dealing with others ☐ Giving everyone an equal opportunity at work	23.	☐ **Correcting others' errors without embarrassing them** ☐ Holding true to your convictions
12.	☐ Judging people fairly based on their abilities rather than only on their personalities ☐ Seeking out all opportunities to learn new skills	24.	☐ Providing fair treatment for each employee ☐ **Lending a helping hand to someone having difficulty**

Note: Items in the Concern for Others Subscale are in bold.

CHAPTER

19 Humans Making Sense of Alarming Conditions: Psychological Insight into the Fair Process Effect

Kees van den Bos

Abstract

This chapter examines the psychology of the fair process effect, which is defined as the positive effect that people's perceptions of experienced treatment fairness have on their subsequent reactions. The chapter argues that when people are confronted with potentially problematic events or personal uncertainty-provoking experiences, this signals to them that something alarming may be going on that warrants their attention. As a result, the individuals involved are likely to engage in psychological processes of trying to make sense of what is going on and what they should expect will be happening. Because perceived procedural fairness has important informational value for people, it follows that people are susceptible to issues of treatment fairness in many alarming or sense-making triggering situations. The current chapter describes this alarm-system perspective on the psychology of the fair process effect and discusses implications of this perspective for our understanding of organizational behavior and human resource management.

Key Words: fair process effect, treatment fairness, human reactions, sense making, alarm system, informational value, organizational behavior, human resource management

In this chapter, I focus on the psychology of the fair process effect, the positive effect that people's perceptions of procedural fairness (also referred to in this chapter as experienced treatment fairness[1]) have on their subsequent reactions (Folger, Rosenfield, Grove, & Corkran, 1979; Van den Bos, 2005; Walker, LaTour, Lind, & Thibaut, 1974). A central outcome of the research that I will review in the chapter is that an important reason that this effect is so robust and so prevalent in many different situations is because the experience of fair treatment serves important functions in processes of sense-making. That is, when people are confronted with events such as economic problems, reorganization processes, potential lay-offs (Brockner, 2010), but also more general personal uncertainty-provoking experiences (Van den Bos, 2001a), this signals to them that something potentially alarming may be going on that warrants their attention (Van den Bos et al., 2008). As a result, the individuals involved are likely to engage in sense-making and social appraisal processes in order to make sense of what is going on and what they should expect will be happening (Van den Bos & Lind, 2013; Weick, 1995).

Because perceived procedural fairness has important informational value for people (Hulst, Van den Bos, & Akkermans, 2013; Lind, 2001; Van den Bos, 2001b), it follows that people are susceptible to issues of treatment fairness in many alarming or sense-making triggering situations (Van den Bos & Lind, 2009), especially when they are interacting with supervisors, management, or other social authorities (Lind, 1995; Tyler & Lind,

I thank Maureen Ambrose, Russell Cropanzano, and Liesbeth Hulst for their comments and suggestions on an earlier draft of this chapter.

1992; see also Weick, 1995). Therefore, information that conveys fair treatment by authorities or other important people will yield various types of positive reactions among the individuals involved, such as increased organizational commitment, job performance, conflict resolution, decision acceptance, and job satisfaction (Van den Bos, 2005). In contrast, information that indicates unfair treatment instigates all sorts of negative responses, such as increased retaliation, theft, work stress, overt or covert disobedience, and decreased mental and physical health (Folger & Cropanzano, 1998).

Thus, a central premise of the current chapter is that perceived procedural or treatment fairness fulfills important psychological functions for people trying to make sense of their worlds, especially when they are trying to manage potentially alarming situations in those worlds. Figure 19.1 illustrates this alarm-system perspective on the psychology of the fair process effect. In what follows in this chapter, I will define the fair process effect and will give a brief overview of instances in which the effect has been found. I then will go on and discuss basic psychological insights into the fair process effect. The chapter will end by drawing some conclusions of these insights for our understanding of organizational behavior and human resource management.

The Fair Process Effect: Instances of the Effect and Conceptualizing the Effect

In the organizational justice literature, there continues to be some misunderstanding and ambiguity about how the term *the fair process effect* should be understood (Van den Bos, 2005). It is important, therefore, to delineate how I think the term should be defined and what I mean with the term when discussing instances of the effect, basic psychological mechanisms underlying the effect, and implications of the effect for our understanding of organizational behavior and more general social behavior. This discussion will necessarily rely and build on what I said earlier about these issues in my earlier review of the fair process effect (see Van den Bos, 2005).

A review of the fair process effect should start with the 1974 experiment by Walker et al. This

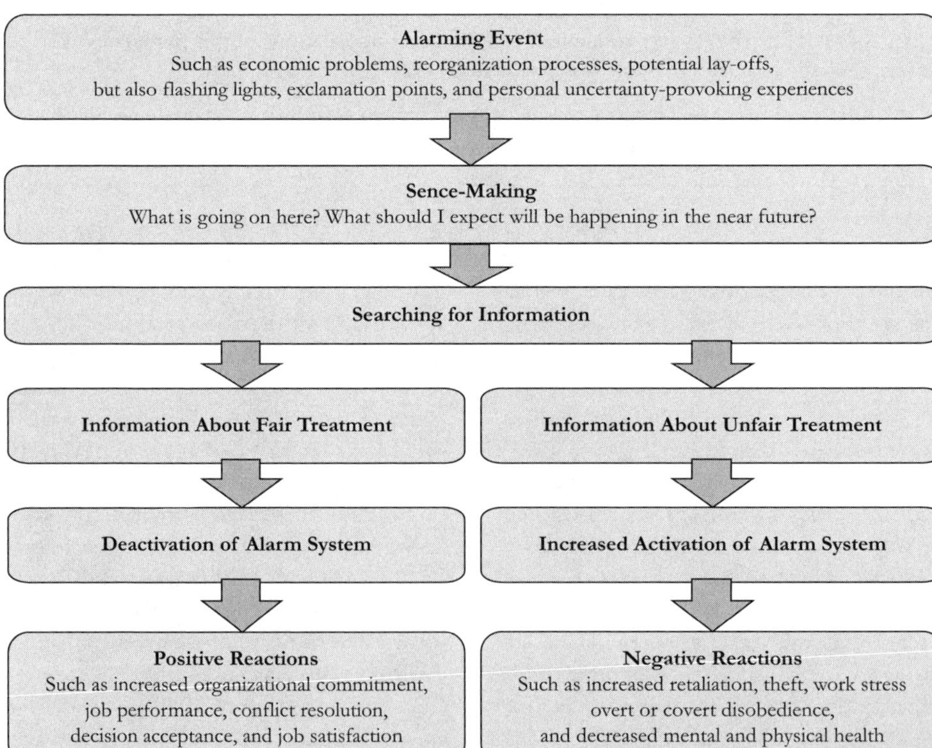

Fig. 19.1 An alarm-system perspective on the psychology of the fair process effect.

Note. The model assumes that people try to make sense of alarming events and that information about fair treatment encountered in processes of sense-making will calm people down and hence yield positive reactions, whereas information about unfair treatment will lead to increased activation of the alarm-system and hence instigate negative reactions among humans.

experiment was the first procedural justice study that revealed a fair process effect. The experiment investigated the effects of adversary and inquisitorial procedures on the reactions of disputants toward either a favorable or an unfavorable verdict in a simulated court trial. Adversary and inquisitorial procedures differ on multiple dimensions, but the key distinction that Thibaut and Walker were interested in is that adversary procedures allow people involved in court trials greater levels of control over the process used in the court trial than inquisitorial procedures do. Findings of the Walker et al. study indicated that defendants judged the way in which they had been treated to be more fair when they had experienced the adversary procedure than when they had been subjected to the inquisitorial procedure. These effects are interpreted to reflect that, compared to inquisitorial procedures, adversary procedures allow people greater levels of process control (Thibaut & Walker, 1975, 1978) and more opportunities to voice their opinions (Folger et al., 1979). More important for the current purposes is that the findings also revealed a fair process effect such that participants judged their verdict to be more fair and were more satisfied with the verdict in case of the fair (adversary) procedure as opposed to the unfair (inquisitorial) procedure.

Building on the Walker et al. (1974) findings, Folger and colleagues (1979) were the first to come up with the term *the fair process effect.* Extending on Hirschman's (1970) conception of voice, Folger et al. suggested that getting the opportunity to present evidence supporting one's own case in a court trial has a strong positive effect on the defendant's reactions toward the verdict. Folger et al. (1979) tested their line of reasoning by manipulating whether participants in an experimental set-up either received or did not receive an opportunity to voice their opinions about how the experimenter should divide lottery tickets between participants themselves and the other participants. As predicted, findings revealed a fair process effect such that voice procedures resulted in higher ratings of overall satisfaction than no-voice procedures.

Following the pioneering studies by Walker et al. (1974) and Folger et al. (1979) as well as the groundbreaking review of the psychological literature on procedural justice by Lind and Tyler (1988), many positive reactions have been reported of employees who felt they had been treated in a fair way by their management or their organization. These positive reactions include higher commitment to organizations and institutions (Folger & Konovsky, 1989; Korsgaard, Schweiger, & Sapienza, 1995; McFarlin & Sweeney, 1992; Moorman, 1991), more extra-role citizenship behavior (Konovsky & Folger, 1991; Podsakoff & MacKenzie, 1993), greater likelihood of conflict prevention and resolution (Bobocel, Agar, Meyer, & Irving, 1998), better job performance (Lind, Kanfer, & Earley, 1990), more widespread acceptance of company policy (Greenberg, 1994; Lind, 1990) and supervisor directives (Huo, Smith, Tyler, & Lind, 1996), higher levels of job satisfaction (Folger & Cropanzano, 1998), and more positive emotional feelings (Weiss, Suckow, & Cropanzano, 1999). In contrast, when employees perceive that they have been treated in an unfair way, they are more likely to leave their jobs (Alexander & Ruderman, 1987), are less likely to cooperate (Lind, 2001), show lower levels of morale and higher levels of work stress and overt and covert disobedience (Huo et al., 1996), are more likely to initiate lawsuits (Lind, Greenberg, Scott, & Welchans, 2000), and may even start behaving in antisocial ways (Greenberg, 1993, 1997; Greenberg & Lind, 2000).

In other social contexts than organizations, the fair process effect as defined here yields reliable and important effects on human reactions as well. For example, the belief that one has been treated fairly by judges, the police, or other social authorities enhances acceptance of legal decisions (Lind, Kulik, Ambrose, & De Vera Park, 1993), obedience to laws (Tyler, 1990), more positive evaluations of public policies (Lind, 1990; Tyler, Rasinski, & McGraw, 1985), and more trust in government (Van den Bos, Van der Velden, & Lind, 2014) whereas the belief that one has been treated unfairly has been shown to prompt protest behavior (Vermunt, Wit, Van den Bos, & Lind, 1996) and recidivism among spousal abuse defendants (Paternoster, Brame, Bachman, & Sherman, 1997). Indeed, what makes the fair process effect so important is that the effect has been shown on a wide variety of human responses (for overviews, see, e.g., Lind & Tyler, 1988; Van den Bos, 2005).

I want to emphasize explicitly that the definition of the fair process effect that is used in this chapter is that the effect refers to the positive effect that people's perceptions of treatment fairness have on their subsequent reactions. Thus, *treatment fairness* is a term I use here to signify the fairness of how people are treated. This term refers not only (or primarily) to the perceived fairness of formal procedures but also (or especially) to the fairness people experience in interactions with other persons. I am proposing, therefore, that the perceived fairness of interpersonal treatment is what is driving large parts of what has become known in the literature as the fair process effect.

Following my take on the fair treatment effect, it is important to specify what I think researchers often mean when they refer to the concept of *procedure*. The terms *procedure* and *procedural justice* are derived from the law literature and especially from the 1975 work by social psychologist John Thibaut and law professor Lawrence Walker. These authors and their colleagues were inspired by the psychological differences they saw between different legal procedures, and in their pioneering procedural justice experiments they took these differences as starting point for their investigation of participants' reactions toward procedures that varied the amount of process control that participants experienced in simulated court trials. Thus, Thibaut and Walker (1975) combined their mutual interests in social psychology and law and as a result they placed their studies under the heading of "procedural justice" research. However, this should not be taken too literally, since these authors clearly saw their experiments as a first step toward understanding the psychology involved in fairness and justice issues (Thibaut & Walker, 1978) and were intrigued by the implication of their findings that how people are treated in courts of law can have strong impact on their reactions to judges' verdicts (Walker et al., 1974).

Following the pioneering research by Thibaut and Walker (1975, 1978), scientists have deepened our understanding of the psychological processes hinted upon in this earlier work (e.g., Folger et al., 1979; Folger, 1986; Greenberg, 2000; Greenberg & Folger, 1983; Lind & Tyler, 1988; Tyler & Lind, 1992; Van den Bos & Lind, 2002) and rightfully noted that the psychological processes involved in the Thibaut and Walker simulations could be adequately expanded to incorporate how people react to fairness and justice in other contexts than legal settings. Most notably, the role of procedural justice in the workplace was recognized to be very important (Colquitt, Conlon, Wesson, Porter, & Ng, 2001; Greenberg, 2000; Greenberg & Folger, 1983; Moorman, 1991). Even more important for the current purposes, during the 1975-1985 advancement of research and theory on procedural justice it became clear that what by then had become known as procedural justice effects were really effects of how fairly people felt they had been treated in the particular context under investigation (for an overview, see, e.g., Lind & Tyler, 1988).

In correspondence with this latter observation, the fair process effect research that is reviewed in this chapter is about the effect of the fairness of the way in which people feel they have been treated in the workplace or elsewhere. Thus, "procedural fairness" and "procedural justice" as they are being used here, and as I think that John Thibaut really intended it to be, refer to the way people are treated. So, in essence, fair or unfair treatment in interpersonal and social interactions is the issue here. This is also the reason why in this chapter I equate the fair process effect with an effect of fair treatment. Indeed, it may be more accurate to refer to the "fair process effect" as the *fair treatment effect*.

It is important to note that this conception of procedural justice overlaps to some extent with a notion that was developed later in the organizational justice literature, the concept of "interactional justice" (see, e.g., Bies & Moag, 1986; Bies & Shapiro, 1987). One could argue that a danger of using the procedural justice label is that it may be a bit of a misnomer and that people may wrongfully misinterpret the concept to refer to formal, lawlike procedures. The interactional justice label has the advantage of clearly referring to the justice and fairness aspects of social interactions that are so important in understanding the majority of the fairness effects reported in the psychological literature.

The main disadvantage of "international justice," however, is that when, in addition to the two earlier developed notions of distributive and procedural justice, researchers start using this concept they have to redefine the concept of procedural justice. That is, because of the obvious overlap of interactional justice with informal procedural justice (Tyler & Bies, 1990), introducing the concept of interactional justice forces researchers to start redefining procedural justice in terms of *formal* decision-making procedures. In the modern organizational justice literature, there is a strong tendency to do this. However, this formal aspect was never meant to be important in the work by the founders of procedural justice. On the contrary, they were really referring to the more informal way in which people were treated in decision-making processes. It is this latter conception, the fairness of informal treatment, that I think the literature should focus on (for a similar argument, see Tyler & Bies, 1990), and I will refer to this by means of the notions that were originally developed for these effects: procedural justice (Thibaut & Walker, 1975) and the fair process effect (Folger et al., 1979).

Thus, the term *fair process* in organizational justice should be used to refer primarily to the informal way in which people are treated in decision-making processes, and not (or not only) to formal procedures. Formal aspects of procedures may have a role in the fair process effect, but the fairness of the informal ways in which people are treated by other persons is what is really driving the large part of the effect. Therefore, treating the concepts of "procedural justice" and "the fair process effect" in formal ways, as opposed to informal ways, would be a major error.

I should emphasize that I am not stating that perceived procedural justice or treatment fairness should be equated with perceptions of distributive justice. Research has shown clearly that procedural justice or treatment fairness have quite different effects than distributive justice has (Lind & Tyler, 1988). Furthermore, it is often or typically the combined effect of procedural and distributive justice that yield precise and important insight into organizational behavior (Brockner, 2010; Brockner & Wiesenfeld, 1996).

I also would like to note that thus far there is not a good scale that always will reliably measure the fair process effect or will assess people's procedural or treatment fairness perceptions in valid ways. This noted, recent evidence suggests that the Moorman (1991) scale might be a very good scale to measure experienced procedural justice in organizations (Miller, Konopaske, & Byrne, 2012), especially when items are tailored to fit the organization where the study is conducted and also fit the employees' experiences accurately (Lind & Tyler, 1988). It would be important for the progress in organizational justice if future studies would come up with a reliable scale of the fair process effect as defined here.

Interesting in this respect is that Miller et al. (2012) recently examined the criterion-related validity of two commonly used measures of organizational justice Colquitt, 2001; Moorman, 1991). To this end, the authors conducted a dominance analysis on the three-dimension measure of organizational justice by Moorman (1991) versus the four-dimension measure of Colquitt (2001) in the prediction of Colquitt's own outcomes. Results suggested that Moorman's measures may dominate Colquitt's measures on some dependent variables. These findings need further replication in different samples and different work settings, but when replicated suggest that renewed consideration should be given to Moorman's scales, as it appears that this three-factor measure of organizational justice may outperform the four-factor measure in at least some instances. More generally, Miller et al. note that Moorman's parsimonious representation of justice may be more useful than Colquitt's version for explaining the nuances of perceptual differences regarding fairness and justice in the workplace. Clearly, attention is warranted to sort out the implications of this very interesting research, because it may help to come up with a robust scale that reliably measures procedural and other justice perceptions in many different work settings.

It is also important to note here that a precondition before fair process effects can occur is that the experience of a particular procedure leads to the perception of a certain level of procedural fairness. It is this procedural fairness perception that influences the person's subsequent reactions and in this way creates a fair process effect. Thus, for example, when individuals get an opportunity to voice their opinions about the way in which tasks will be distributed among employees in their department, the individuals involved may perceive the way in which they have been treated as fair. This perception of procedural fairness may then lead the department members to be more satisfied with the final decision of exactly how task assignments are distributed among them. The label "the voice effect" should be reserved, therefore, for the enhancement of procedural fairness when a procedure allows people a chance to express themselves, and "the fair process effect" is the enhancement of people's evaluations, attitudes, behaviors, and other reactions following this procedural fairness perception. Thus, in contrast with what sometimes is done in the literature, a voice effect should not be equated with a fair process effect (Van den Bos, 2005). Rather the experience of voice, or encountering an accurate, a consistent, or any other particular procedure (Leventhal, 1980; Van den Bos, Vermunt, & Wilke, 1996, 1997) can affect people's fairness perceptions, and these perceptions are a prerequisite before fair process effects can be found. Making a clear distinction between voice and fair process effects is also important because different psychological processes may be driving voice versus fair process effects (Van den Bos, 2001a; Van den Bos, Maas, Waldring, & Semin, 2003; Van den Bos & Miedema, 2000).

I think it is important to highlight the importance of the role of *perceptions* in the fair process effect. Fairness and justice as psychologists study these concepts are really in the eye of the beholder (e.g., Adams, 1965; Lind, Kanfer, et al., 1990; Mikula & Wenzel, 2000; Tyler, Boeckmann, Smith, & Huo, 1997; Van den Bos & Lind, 2002). Although it might be possible to derive rational-normative principles of procedural justice, and although it might be possible to come up with an objective fair process effect (see, e.g., Hare, 1981; Rawls, 1992/1971; see also Jasso, 1994, 1999), I argue that the fair process effect in essence is a *psychological* effect, constructed in the head of the recipient of the procedure. Thus, the psychology of the fair process effect examines how fairness and justice judgments are constructed by people. This implies that objective conditions that researchers, organizational behaviorists, and employers think are fair or unfair do not have to be viewed that way by employees and other recipients of the procedure under consideration.

I also would like to emphasize the importance of the concept of *fairness* in our understanding of "the fair process effect" and the larger literature on "organizational justice." That is, compared to the related notions of justice and morality, fairness better connotes the subjective, ready judgment that is and has long been the true topic of psychological study (Van den Bos & Lind, 2002). Related to this, participants and respondents in research studies typically find it easier and more relevant to provide judgments of fairness than judgments of justice or morality. This is the reason that most psychologists in our field usually ask people to rate fairness rather than to rate justice or morality (cf. Tyler & Lind, 1992). This is also a main cause of why morality researchers often use "good" or "bad" judgments or "thumbs up" or "thumbs down" judgments as their dependent variables (e.g., Greene, Sommerville, Nystrom, Darley, & Cohen, 2001). These variables may be conceptually related to judgments of what is moral and immoral but obviously are very different from what Kant (1959/1785) and other rationalist moral philosophers (Beauchamp, 2001) are focusing on. Returning to the fair process effect, these considerations constitute the reason that the central topic of consideration of this chapter is called "the fair process effect" and not "the just process effect" or "the moral process effect." The former simply reflects better both common research practices and the core belief under study. An implication of this observation is that although organizational psychologists usually call this area "organizational justice," we are in effect referring to fairness perceptions as the major antecedent of the effects we are interested in (Lind & Van den Bos, 2002; Van den Bos & Lind, 2009).

Related to this is the concern about whether what usually is called the fair process effect should be really conceived of as a *fair* process effect or that it would it be more accurate to start talking about an *unfair* process effect instead (cf. Greenberg & Folger, 1983). Whereas the former perspective is in line with how the effect generally is known, the latter view corresponds with observations that unfair events affect lay people's cognitions and reactions stronger than fair events (Brockner & Wiesenfeld, 1996; Folger, 1984; Van den Bos & Spruijt, 2002; Van den Bos & Van Prooijen, 2001; Van den Bos et al., 1997). This finding is probably caused by the important role that people's expectations have in the psychology of fairness judgments (e.g., Van den Bos et al., 1996) and the fact that unfair events may strongly violate these expectations (Van den Bos & Van Prooijen, 2001). The psychological mechanism behind this finding may well be an instance of the more general negativity effect that indicates that negative things typically have a bigger impact on psychological processes than positive things (see, e.g., Fiske & Taylor, 1991; Peeters & Czapinski, 1990). Thus, *un*fairness, in fact, may play a more prominent role and it may be better to focus on the psychology of *un*fairness as opposed to fairness (Folger & Cropanzano, 1998). In the current chapter, I will use the traditional term "the fair process effect," with the understanding that, unless explicitly stated otherwise, this may involve the effects of both fair and unfair procedures on people's reactions.

Psychological Insight into the Fair Process Effect: Alarming Conditions and Sense-Making Processes

Many studies have reported fair process effects in many different contexts using different research methods. The effect has been observed most often within the organizational context (Lind & Van den Bos, 2002), but it has frequently been found elsewhere as well (e.g., Paternoster, Brame, Bachman, & Sherman, 1997; Vermunt et al., 1996). Furthermore, an exciting aspect of research on the effects of procedural fairness perceptions is that effects of these perceptions have been found on very different human reactions (Lind & Tyler, 1988). This is important because it suggests that fair process studies may have substantial implications for a multitude of domains of human and organizational behavior (Greenberg, 2000). Because fair procedures enhance so many important cognitions, feelings, attitudes, and behaviors, insight into what is responsible for the fair process effect is crucial for understanding how people think, feel, and behave in their social and organizational environments (Cropanzano & Folger, 1989, 1991; Cropanzano & Greenberg, 1997; Greenberg, 2000; Folger & Konovsky, 1989; Greenberg, 1990, 1993; Lind & Tyler, 1988; Tyler & Lind, 1992). To this end, this chapter will examine the psychology of the fair process effect.

Different psychological explanations of the fair process effect exist in the organizational justice literature. These include instrumental explanations of the effect (see, e.g., Shapiro & Brett, 2005; Thibaut & Walker, 1975, 1978; Walker, Lind, & Thibaut, 1979), which emphasize the amount of control procedures give people over the outcomes they hope to get. Other explanations focus on processes of social influence (e.g., Greenberg & Folger, 1983) and note that the fair process effect can be explained in terms of people being susceptible to influence via social comparison of others' opinions about whether certain outcome distributions are fair or unfair (Folger et al., 1979).

Yet another important account of the fair process effect points at the role of referent cognitions in explaining and understanding the effect (Cropanzano & Folger, 1989; Folger, 1986, 1987, 1993; Folger & Baron, 1996; Folger & Skarlicki, 1998). Referent cognitions theory tends to focus on *unfair* procedures and argues that experiences of procedural unfairness are psychologically so meaningful to people because when a procedural rule is broken people use a frame of reference for evaluating what happened that consists of a mental comparison to what might have happened instead. In contrast, relational models focus on experiences of *fair* procedures. Relational models argue that fair treatment by authorities signals that important persons in your society or organization value and respect you and, therefore, treat you with dignity and respect (Lind & Tyler, 1988; Tyler & Lind, 1992).

Instrumental, social influence, referent cognitions, and relational models have been reviewed and discussed earlier (see, e.g., Folger & Cropanzano, 1998; Tyler & Lind, 1992; Van den Bos, 2005). Here I concentrate on a more recent psychological explanation of the effect that perhaps has the potential to integrate many aspects of the earlier proposed explanations. That is, the alarm-system perspective on the fair process effect argues that people show positive reactions to fair treatment because being treated fairly gives them a way to cope with alarming circumstances. The alarm-system account explains people's negative responses to unfair treatment by pointing out that being treated unfairly constitutes an alarming experience in itself (Van den Bos et al., 2008; Van den Bos & Lind, 2009).

The alarm-system explanation focuses on how people make sense of alarming experiences, such as economic problems, reorganization processes, and potential lay-offs, but also flashing lights, exclamation points, and personal uncertainty-provoking experiences (Van den Bos et al., 2008; Van den Bos & Lind, 2009). The alarm-system perspective on the fair process effect is inspired by an earlier body of research that shows that people react more vigilantly to issues of treatment fairness when they are coping with personal uncertainty (Van den Bos & Lind, 2002, 2009). One of the first studies on uncertainty and the fair process effect was a series of experiments published in 2001. In these experiments, half the participants were asked to think about, and write a description of, the emotional experiences they feel when they encounter uncertainty in their personal lives (Van den Bos, 2001a). The other half of the participants thought about and wrote about the emotional experiences involved in their watching television, an issue that does not salientize personal uncertainty among the population of university students with whom we conducted our studies. In a later, ostensibly unrelated study, the same participants were exposed to standard procedural fairness manipulations: In some of the experiments, this involved participants, after completing a task in which they worked with another person, either being or not being allowed to voice their views about how much they should be paid relative to the other participant. In another experiment, participants were informed that, in a selection process in which they took part, either all (accurate procedure) or only some (inaccurate procedure) of their test items would be taken into account. These voice and accuracy manipulations are common procedural fairness manipulations, reliably leading those who do not receive voice or who experience inaccurate procedures to feel they have been unfairly treated and those who receive voice or are accurately treated to feel they have been fairly treated.

The principal dependent variable in the Van den Bos (2001a) experiments was the participants' ratings of positive or negative affect toward the way they were treated. The results support the uncertainty salience hypothesis proposed in the article: When personal uncertainty had been made salient, the fair procedures resulted in more positive and less negative affect whereas the unfair procedures yielded more negative and less positive affect than was the case when uncertainty had not been made salient. In other words, when personal uncertainty was salient, the fair process effect (Van den Bos, 2005) on participants' affective treatment ratings was magnified.

Other fairness studies have found similar effects not just for the salience of personal uncertainty, but also for real experienced personal uncertainty (Maas & Van den Bos, 2011) and for stable individual differences in uncertainty orientation in organizational contexts or other important real-world situations (see, e.g., Elovainio et al. 2005; Kausto, Elo, Lipponen, & Elovainio, 2005; Patterson, Cowley, & Prasongsukarn, 2006; See, 2009; Thau, Aquino, & Wittek, 2007). Devon Proudfoot and Allan Lind (2015) talk more about these and other uncertainty findings in Chapter 17, in this volume. Here I would like to note that the implication of what I have discussed thus far seems to be that there is something about personal uncertainty that makes people react more strongly and more vigorously toward fair and unfair events.

An important way to understand these research results is provided by the idea that personal uncertainty often leads people to react more strongly toward fair and unfair events because being uncertain or being reminded about things one is uncertain about often instigates strong affective-experiential processes (Maas & Van den Bos, 2009). Thus, the idea is that experiencing feelings of uncertainty would lead people to start processing information they subsequently receive in experiential-intuitive ways (Epstein & Pacini, 1999).

Cognitive-experiential self-theory distinguishes between two conceptual systems that people use to process information, namely the experiential-intuitive and the rational-cognitive systems (Epstein & Pacini, 1999). The experiential way of processing information is intuitive, preconsciously encoding information into concrete images or metaphors, and making associative connections. In experiential modes, events are experienced passively, and people can be seized by their emotions. The rationalistic way of processing information, on the other hand, is analytic, encoding information in abstract ways, based on making logical cause-and-effect connections, and requiring intentional, effortful processing. In rationalistic modes of information processing, people experience events actively and consciously while thinking things over and making justifications for what happened in these events, and in these modes people are in control of their thoughts.

Cognitive-experiential self-theory also assumes that the operation of experiential mindsets is intimately associated with affect-related experiences (see, e.g., Epstein & Pacini, 1999). If experiential mindsets do indeed make people's fairness reactions more susceptible to affect-related processes, then the intensity with which people react affectively to daily life events (Larsen, Diener, & Cropanzano, 1987) should interact with people's mindsets. Earlier fairness studies had shown that individual differences in affect intensity can moderate people's fairness reactions (Van den Bos et al., 2003). Integrating this line of work with cognitive-experiential self-theory, Maas and Van den Bos (2009) predicted that under conditions of uncertainty, individual differences in affect intensity (Larsen, Diener, & Emmons, 1986) would moderate people's fairness reactions, especially when they have been primed with experiential (as opposed to rationalistic) modes of information processing.

To test these predictions, Maas and Van den Bos (2009) brought people in either experiential or rationalistic mindsets. To this end, we developed a manipulation that varied the mindsets (experiential or rationalistic) people are in, such that people react more based on their gut feelings when in experiential mindsets and more deliberately when in rationalistic mindsets. After thus having been brought in either experiential or rationalistic mindsets, participants responded to procedures that allowed them opportunities to voice their opinions or that denied them such opportunities (Maas & Van den Bos, 2009, Study 2). As predicted, the findings reported showed that people who had been primed with experiential mindsets and who score high on the affect intensity scale (Larsen et al., 1986) reacted more strongly to fair and unfair events (compared to those who had been brought in rationalistic mindsets and/or who scored low on affect intensity). These findings suggest that focusing on the combination of affective and experiential processes is important for the social psychology of uncertainty effects reported in the literature. Affective and experiential reactions may be more likely in alarming conditions in which people are trying to assess frantically what to do and how to behave. It is to a discussion of this alarm-system based work that I now turn.

The alarm-system perspective on the justice judgment process argues that the affective-experiential effects that are found under conditions of uncertainty (Maas & Van den Bos, 2009) occur because experiencing feelings of personal uncertainty constitutes an alarming experience (Van den Bos et al., 2008). Specifically, in this line of research we examined a possible connection between, on the one hand, the augmentation of fairness effects in the presence of personal uncertainty (e.g., Van den Bos, 2001a; Van den Bos, Poortvliet, Maas, Miedema, & Van den Ham, 2005) and other self-threatening conditions (Miedema, Van den Bos, & Vermunt, 2006) and, on the other hand, related phenomena in social cognition and social neuroscience showing the possible existence of a "human alarm system" (Eisenberger, Lieberman, & Williams, 2003).

In the literatures on close relationships and on social neuroscience, it has been suggested that personal uncertainty and self-threats lead to the activation of the "human alarm system," a psychological system that people use to detect and handle alarming situations and that prompts people to process more alertly what is going on in the situations in which they find themselves. For example, Murray, Holmes, and Collins (2005) suggested that personal uncertainty and felt insecurity in close relationships activate the human alarm system with the result that people process more alertly what is happening in their relationships.

Along similar lines, Eisenberger et al. (2003) have argued that being ostracized or experiencing other self-threatening events activates parts of the human brain that Eisenberger et al. have labeled the "human alarm system." The alarm system is responsible for detecting cues that might be harmful to survival and, after activation, for recruiting attention and coping responses to minimize threat. Eisenberger et al. (2003) have argued that experiencing social exclusion or other self-threatening events may be an experience of social pain. Like physical pain, the experience of social pain may trigger the human alarm system, "alerting us when we have sustained injury to our social connections" (Eisenberger et al., 2003, p. 292). From an evolutionary perspective, the working of such an alarm system would be adaptive: An activated alarm system prompts the human organism to act and respond more quickly or otherwise more alertly to what is going on in the organism's environment; this in turn makes the survival of the organism more likely.

One way to triangulate the relationships linking personal uncertainty, the human alarm system, and the fairness literature is to conceptualize an overlap between the alarm system and the fairness judgment process. An intriguing hypothesis that can be derived from such a postulated overlap is that factors that people associate with alarming conditions would be expected to enhance the sensitivity of the alarm system and thus, given the postulated overlap, potentiate sensitivity to the fairness-related events people subsequently experience. This hypothesis was not unlike Eisenberger and Lieberman (2004) who postulated that the brain bases of social pain are similar to those of physical pain and predicted that "factors that enhance the sensitivity to one type of pain should enhance the sensitivity of this alarm system and thus potentiate sensitivity to the other type of pain as well" (p. 297). In our 2008 article, my co-authors and I postulated that presenting alarm-related symbols to people would activate the human alarm system and hence potentiate sensitivity to other types of processes associated with it as well, including enhanced sensitivity to the fairness judgment process. This would be expected to make people react more sensitively to subsequently experienced fair or unfair events (Van den Bos et al., 2008).

More specifically, the literature reviewed thus far suggests two conclusions in line with this analysis: (1) personal uncertainty and other self-threatening conditions activate the human alarm system (Eisenberger et al., 2003; Murray et al., 2005); (2) personal uncertainty and self-threatening conditions lead to more extreme fair process effects (Miedema et al., 2006; Van den Bos 2001a; Van den Bos et al., 2005). Thus, we now know that the same conditions that are thought to activate the human alarm system, might also lead to more extreme fairness effects. Given this observation, we proposed that activating the human alarm system directly, by presenting alarm-related stimuli to people, would lead to more extreme reactions toward fair and unfair events.

Thus, an intriguing hypothesis that follows from the alarm-system perspective is that the presentation of cues that are closely, even subtly, related to alarming conditions might lead people to form more extreme judgments about subsequently presented fair and unfair events. Findings of various experiments (scenario studies, an experiential experiment, and fMRI testing) in fact provided evidence for this line of reasoning (Van den Bos et al., 2008; Van den Bos & Rijpkema, 2008). Specifically, we found that viewing large exclamation points prior to responding to accurate or inaccurate procedures and voice or no-voice procedures indeed made people react more extremely to the procedures. Similar effects were also found on participants' reactions to good versus bad outcomes, suggesting that an alarm-system perspective on fairness reactions applies not only to the fair process effect but to fair outcome effects as well (Van den Bos, 1999). The overlap between reactions to procedural and distributive justice has been discussed elsewhere as well (see, e.g., Ambrose & Arnaud, 2005; Ambrose & Schminke, 2009; Cropanzano & Ambrose, 2001; but see also Brockner, 2010; Brockner & Wiesenfeld, 1996).

Another experimental study replicated and extended these findings. Participants in this study were people from various parts of the Netherlands, with different educational backgrounds and from different age groups, who were interviewed in a shopping area of a medium-sized city located in the middle of the Netherlands. Specifically, people who were walking in the shopping area of the city center of Amersfoort were asked whether they would like to participate in a study on how people process information and which would take a maximum of 10 minutes of their time. Two meters behind the experimenter, an orange flashing light of 17 × 14 × 14 centimeters of the sort used on emergency vehicles had been placed on a small pedestal of 1 meter high. Both the flashing light and pedestal were ostensibly unrelated to our study and the flashing light was connected by means of an electric cable of 1.5 meters long to a large store (Vroom & Dreesmann; a Dutch equivalent of Macy's). As our alarm-related manipulation, the flashing light had been switched on for half the participants and the flashing light was off for the other half of the participants.

In this setting, participants responded to scenarios in which they were asked to image that fair or unfair events happened at their workplace. In accord with the alarm-system view of the justice judgment process, the findings revealed that when the flashing light had been switched on, people showed more extreme justice judgments in response to variations in good and bad outcomes than when the flashing light had been switched off. A finding not reported in the article but that is interesting to note here was that participants also showed more extreme reactions in response to accurate versus inaccurate procedures when the flashing light was on as opposed to off.[2] Thus, we found similar effects of our alarm manipulation on both reactions to variations in distributive fairness and procedural fairness, again suggesting that the alarm-system perspective is not limited to the fair process effect only but applies to fair outcome effects as well. More generally, perhaps this is an indication that as our field evolves our thinking about the fair process effect, the fair treatment effect, and other fairness judgment processes needs to evolve as well. Perhaps this suggests that "fair process" was a specific example of a more general phenomenon.

The studies reported in the Van den Bos et al. (2008) paper were in part inspired by the conjecture that the uncertainty management findings reported in the fairness literature (see, e.g., Van den Bos, 2001a; Van den Bos & Lind, 2002; Van den Bos et al., 2005) might be explained by the notion that experiences of personal uncertainty often constitute alarming events to people and that it is this alarm-related component of uncertainty manipulations that is driving some or perhaps all of the uncertainty effects reported in the social psychological literature.

Especially interesting in this respect are some findings from functional magnetic resonance imaging (fMRI) testing (Van den Bos & Rijpkema, 2008). This study showed that watching an exclamation point leads to a brain activation pattern that shares areas (medial frontal gyrus, Brodmann area 9) with the brain regions that have been found to be active in personal moral judgment tasks. These brain areas are known to be sensitive to tapping the combined effects of cognitive and emotional responses (Greene et al., 2001). This might indicate that a combination of cognition and emotion best explains how people will form and respond to fairness and justice perceptions (Van den Bos et al., 2008) and make personal moral decisions (cf. Greene et al., 2001). In other words, the social psychology of personal uncertainty and fairness judgments may well involve hot-cognitive, not cold-cognitive, processes (Van den Bos, 2007).

Figure 19.1 illustrates the current thinking on the alarm-system perspective on the fair process effect. Related to other ideas of sense-making in organizations (e.g., Weick, 1995), the model assumes that issues of treatment fairness serve important functions in processes of sense-making. Especially when people encounter alarming events such as economic problems, reorganization processes, potential lay-offs, personal uncertainty-provoking experiences, and other stimuli, this signals to them that something potentially alarming may be going on that warrants their attention (Van den Bos et al., 2008). As a result, the individuals involved are likely to engage in sense-making and social appraisal processes in order to make sense of what is going on and what they should expect will be happening. Therefore, the model assumes that people will start to look for information about what is going on and how they should behave and what will be happening in their near future. Information about fair and unfair treatment may have special importance in these kinds of situations. In particular, information that conveys fair treatment will calm people down (Vermunt & Steensma, 2003) and hence deactivate the alarm system. This is assumed to be associated with strong positive reactions among the individuals encountering the fair treatment. In contrast, information about unfair treatment will further activate the alarm system (Van den Bos et al., 2005), resulting in strong negative responses among the individuals involved.

Conclusions: Toward an Alternate View on Organizational Behavior

This chapter studied the fair process effect, defined explicitly as an effect of perceptions of treatment fairness on human reactions. The research reviewed in this chapter shows that experienced fair treatment has various positive effects on people's reactions, whereas perceived unfair treatment yields all kinds of negative reactions. A central hypothesis put forward in this chapter is that the fair process effect is found in so many circumstances on so many different dependent variables among so many different research participants and respondents because many people in many different situations are trying to make sense of what is going on in their immediate environments. This insight fits a growing recognition that sense-making in organizations and in other social situations makes up an important component of what people do in the modern world (Van den Bos & Lind, 2013; Weick, 1995). The perception of treatment fairness is assumed to fulfill important functions in these processes of sense-making (Hulst et al., 2013).

Future research is needed to examine all the implications of the alarm-system model of the fair process effect and to fill in empirically all the components of the view of the sense-making individual discussed here. For example, issues that should be studied include the basic psychological mechanisms underlying the fair process effect. This includes the cognitive fluency with which information pertaining to fair and unfair treatment is processed in different circumstances (e.g., Winkielman, Schwarz, Fazendeiro, & Reber, 2003). This also includes identifying the conditions and applied contexts under which the alarm system holds particularly well, as well as the circumstances in which the model might be less relevant. Fair process effect may also be contingent on other information people receive, such as information about their outcomes (Brockner, 2010; Brockner & Wiesenfeld, 1996), and may depend on the organizational structure in which the fair treatment is experienced (Schminke, Ambrose, & Cropanzano, 2000). Besides organizational contexts, a particularly relevant situation in which the fair process effect should be studied more intensively is the courtroom (Lind, Ambrose, et al., 1990) and other judicial settings (Lind et al., 1993; Tyler, 1990; Van den Bos et al., 2014). Appropriate attention should also be paid to cross-cultural differences on how people respond to fair and unfair procedures (e.g., Leung, 2005; Van den Bos, Brockner, et al., 2010; Van den Bos, Brockner, Van den Oudenalder, Kamble, & Nasabi, 2013).

Thus, many issues need to be studied in future research. This noted, I think that some of the implications that already follow from an alarm-system perspective on the fair process effect and a sense-making view on organizational behavior stand in contrast with the view that humans are primarily interested in material gain and try to achieve this gain by rational means. A basic assumption underlying the model presented here is that people are individuals who are frequently busy appraising what is going on in their social surroundings and how to behave in these surroundings. I argue, therefore, that the *Rational-Economic Man* view that one finds so often in the fields of business, economics, law, and elsewhere in society (cf. Kahneman, Knetsch, & Thaler, 1986) should be replaced or at least complemented by a view of humans as *Social-Appraising Individuals* (Van den Bos & Lind, 2013).

Of course, I am not denying that some people engage in selfish, exploitative, or even fraudulent behavior. This noted, although people's primitive core may sometimes (e.g., when their cognitive capacities have been severely limited) push them in an egoistic direction, it may well be the case that frequently people try to free cognitive resources to do the right thing (Van den Bos, Peters, Bobocel, & Ybema, 2006). Thus, I work from the assumption that fairness is frequently a very real concern to people (Miller, 1999; Miller & Ratner, 1998) and that people use their fairness perceptions to try to make sense of what is going on and how to behave in appropriate manners (Lind & Van den Bos, 2013; Van den Bos & Lind, 2013). It is my hope that, with the current chapter, I have contributed a bit to what I see as a modern, sense-making perspective on organizational behavior and human resource management.

Notes

1. In fact, later in this chapter I will argue that *fair treatment* better captures what we know about the phenomenon than *fair process*. This fits with my line of reasoning that it is important to conceptualize the "fair process effect" more broadly than sometimes is done in the literature, an issue to which I will return later.
2. These fair process reactions were measured after the dependent variables that were reported in Experiment 4 of the Van den Bos et al. (2008) paper.

References

Adams, J. S. (1965). Inequity in social exchange. In L. Berkowitz (Ed.), *Advances in experimental social psychology* (Vol. 2, pp. 267–299). New York, NY: Academic Press.

Alexander, S., & Ruderman, M. (1987). The role of procedural and distributive justice in organizational behavior. *Social Justice Research, 1*, 117–198.

Ambrose, M. L., & Arnaud, A. (2005). Are procedural and distributive justice conceptually distinct? In J. Greenberg & J. A. Colquitt (Eds.), *Handbook of organizational justice: Fundamental questions about fairness in the workplace* (pp. 59–84). Mahwah, NJ: Erlbaum.

Ambrose, M. L., & Schminke, M. (2009). The role of overall justice judgments in organizational justice research: A test of mediation. *Journal of Applied Psychology, 94*, 491–500.

Beauchamp, T. L. (2001). *Philosophical ethics: An introduction to moral philosophy* (3rd ed.). Boston, MA: McGraw-Hill.

Bies, R. J., & Moag, J. S. (1986). Interactional justice: Communication criteria of fairness. In R. Lewicki, B. H. Sheppard, & M. H. Bazerman (Eds.), *Research on negotiation in organizations* (pp. 43–55). Greenwich, CT: JAI.

Bies, R. J., & Shapiro, D. L. (1987). Interactional fairness judgments: The influence of causal accounts. *Social Justice Research, 1*, 199–218.

Bobocel, D. R., Agar, S. E., Meyer, J. P., & Irving, P. G. (1998). Managerial accounts and fairness perceptions in conflict resolution: Differentiating the effects of minimizing responsibility and providing justification. *Basic and Applied Social Psychology, 20*, 133–143.

Brockner, J. (2010). *A contemporary look at organizational justice: Multiplying insult times injury*. New York, NY: Routledge.

Brockner, J., & Wiesenfeld, B. M. (1996). An integrative framework for explaining reactions to decisions: Interactive effects of outcomes and procedures. *Psychological Bulletin, 120*, 189–208.

Colquitt, J. A. (2001). On the dimensionality of organizational justice: A construct validation of a measure. *Journal of Applied Psychology, 86*, 386–400.

Colquitt, J. A., Conlon, D. E., Wesson, M. J., Porter, C. O. L. H., & Ng, K. Y. (2001). Justice at the millennium: A meta-analytic review of 25 years of organizational justice research. *Journal of Applied Psychology, 86*, 425–445.

Cropanzano, R., & Ambrose, M. L. (2001). Procedural and distributive justice are more similar than you think: A monistic perspective and a research agenda. In J. Greenberg & R. Cropanzano (Eds.), *Advances in organizational behavior* (pp. 119–151). Stanford, CA: Stanford University Press.

Cropanzano, R., & Folger, R. (1989). Referent cognitions and task decision autonomy: Beyond equity theory. *Journal of Applied Psychology, 74*, 293–299.

Cropanzano, R., & Folger, R. (1991). Procedural justice and worker motivation. In R. M. Steers & L. W. Porter (Eds.), *Motivation and work behavior* (Vol. 5, pp. 131–143). New York, NY: McGraw-Hill.

Cropanzano, R., & Greenberg, J. (1997). Progress in organizational justice: Tunneling through the maze. In C. L. Cooper & I. T. Robertson (Eds.), *International review of industrial and organizational psychology* (pp. 317–372). New York, NY: Wiley.

Eisenberger, N. I., & Lieberman, M. D. (2004). Why rejection hurts: A common neural alarm system for physical and social pain. *Trends in Cognitive Sciences, 8*, 294–300.

Eisenberger, N. I., Lieberman, M. D., & Williams, K. D. (2003). Does rejection hurt? An fMRI study of social exclusion. *Science, 302*, 290–292.

Elovainio, M., Van den Bos, K., Linna, A., Kivimäki, M., Ala-Mursula, L., Pentti, J., & Vahtera, J. (2005). Combined effects of uncertainty and organizational justice on employee health: Testing the uncertainty management model of fairness judgments among Finnish public sector employees. *Social Science & Medicine, 61*, 2501–2512.

Epstein, S., & Pacini, R. (1999). Some basic issues regarding dual-process theories from the perspective of cognitive-experiential self-theory. In S. Chaiken & Y. Trope (Eds.), *Dual-process theories in social psychology* (pp. 462–482). New York, NY: Guilford.

Fiske, S. T., & Taylor, S. E. (1991). *Social cognition* (2nd ed.). New York, NY: McGraw-Hill.

Folger, R. (1984). (Ed.). *The sense of injustice: Social psychological perspectives*. New York, NY: Plenum.

Folger, R. (1986). Rethinking equity theory: A referent cognitions model. In H. M. Bierhoff, R. L. Cohen, & J. Greenberg (Eds.), *Justice in social relations* (pp. 145–162). New York, NY: Plenum.

Folger, R. (1987). Reformulating the preconditions of resentment: A referent cognitions model. In J. C. Masters, & W. P. Smith (Eds.), *Social comparison, social justice, and relative deprivation: Theoretical, empirical, and policy perspectives* (pp. 183–215). Hillsdale, NJ: Erlbaum.

Folger, R. (1993). Reactions to mistreatment at work. In K. Murnigham (Ed.), *Social psychology in organizations: Advances in theory and research* (pp. 161–183). Stanford, CA: Stanford University Press.

Folger, R., & Baron, R. A. (1996). Violence and hostility at work: A model of reactions to perceived injustice. In G. R. VandenBos & E. Q. Bulatao (Eds.), *Violence on the job: Identifying risks and developing solutions* (pp. 51–85). Washington, DC: American Psychological Association.

Folger, R., & Cropanzano, R. (1998). *Organizational justice and human resource management*. Thousand Oaks, CA: Sage.

Folger, R., & Konovsky, M. (1989). Effects of procedural and distributive justice on reactions to pay raise decisions. *Academy of Management Journal, 32*, 115–130.

Folger, R., Rosenfield, D., Grove, J., & Corkran, L. (1979). Effects of "voice" and peer opinions on responses to inequity. *Journal of Personality and Social Psychology, 37*, 2253–2261.

Folger, R., & Skarlicki, D. P. (1998). A popcorn metaphor for employee aggression. In R. Griffin, A. O'Leary-Kelly, & J. Collins (Eds.), *Dysfunctional behavior in organizations: Volume 1. Violent behavior in organizations* (pp. 43–82). Greenwich, CT: JAI.

Greenberg, J. (1990). Organizational justice: Yesterday, today, and tomorrow. *Journal of Management, 16*, 399–432.

Greenberg, J. (1993). Stealing in the name of justice: Informational and interpersonal moderators of theft reactions to underpayment inequity. *Organizational Behavior and Human Decision Processes, 54*, 81–103.

Greenberg, J. (1994). Using socially fair treatment to promote acceptance of a work site smoking ban. *Journal of Applied Psychology, 79*, 288–297.

Greenberg, J. (1997). A social influence model of employee theft: Beyond the fraud triangle. In R. J. Lewicki, R. J. Bies, & B. H. Sheppard (Eds.), *Research on negotiation in organizations* (Vol. 6, pp. 29–52). Greenwich, CT: JAI.

Greenberg, J. (2000). Promote procedural justice to enhance acceptance of work outcomes. In E. A. Locke (Ed.), *A handbook of principles of organizational behavior* (pp. 181–195). Oxford, UK: Blackwell.

Greenberg, J., & Folger, R. (1983). Procedural justice, participation, and the fair process effect in groups and organizations. In P. B. Paulus (Ed.), *Basic group processes* (pp. 235–256). New York, NY: Springer-Verlag.

Greenberg, J., & Lind, E. A. (2000). The pursuit of organizational justice: From conceptualization to implication to application. In C. L. Cooper & E. A. Locke (Eds.), *I/O psychology: What we know about theory and practice* (pp. 72–105). Oxford, UK: Blackwell.

Greene, J. D., Sommerville, B., Nystrom, L. E., Darley, J. M., & Cohen, J. D. (2001). An fMRI investigation of emotional engagement in moral judgment. *Science, 293*, 2105–2108.

Hare, R. M. (1981). *Moral thinking: Its levels, method, and point*. Oxford, UK: Clarendon Press.

Hirschman, A. O. (1970). *Exit, voice and loyalty: Responses to declines in firms, organizations, and states*. Cambridge, MA: Harvard University Press.

Hulst, L., Van den Bos, K., & Akkermans, A. (2013, January). *Citizens processing information when interacting with legal decision-making authorities: The role of the behavioral inhibition system in the fair process effect*. Poster paper presented at the Social Psychology and Law Preconference of the Fourteenth Meeting of the Society for Personality and Social Psychology, New Orleans, LA.

Huo, Y. J., Smith, H. J., Tyler, T. R., & Lind, E. A. (1996). Superordinate identification, subgroup identification, and justice concerns: Is separatism the problem; is assimilation the answer? *Psychological Science, 7*, 40–45.

Jasso, G. (1994). Assessing individual and group differences in the sense of justice: Framework and application to gender differences in the justice of earnings. *Social Science Research, 23*, 368–406.

Jasso, G. (1999). How much injustice is there in the world? Two new justice indexes. *American Sociological Review, 64*, 133–168.

Kahneman, D., Knetsch, J. L., & Thaler, R. H. (1986). Fairness and the assumptions of economics. *Journal of Business, 59*, 285–300.

Kant, I. (1959). *Foundation of the metaphysics of morals*. Indianapolis, IN: Bobbs-Merrill. (Original work published in 1785).

Kausto, J., Elo, A. L., Lipponen, J., & Elovainio, M. (2005). Moderating effects of job insecurity in the relationships between procedural justice and employee well-being: Gender differences. *European Journal of Work and Organizational Psychology, 14*, 431–452.

Konovsky, M., & Folger, R. (1991, August). *The effects of procedural and distributive justice on organizational citizenship behavior*. Paper presented at the annual meeting of the Academy of Management, Miami Beach, FL.

Korsgaard, M. A., Schweiger, D. M., & Sapienza, H. J. (1995). Building commitment, attachment, and trust in strategic decision-making teams: The role of procedural justice. *Academy of Management Journal, 38*, 60–84.

Larsen, R. J., Diener, E., & Cropanzano, R. S. (1987). Cognitive operations associated with individual differences in affect intensity. *Journal of Personality and Social Psychology, 53*, 767–774.

Larsen, R. J., Diener, E., & Emmons, R. A. (1986). Affect intensity and reactions to daily life events. *Journal of Personality and Social Psychology, 51*, 803–814.

Leventhal, G. S. (1980). What should be done with equity theory? New approaches to the study of fairness in social relationships. In K. J. Gergen, M. S. Greenberg, & R. H. Willis (Eds.), *Social exchange: Advances in theory and research* (pp. 27–54). New York, NY: Plenum.

Leung, K. (2005). How generalizable are justice effects across cultures? In J. Greenberg & J. A. Colquitt (Eds.), *Handbook of organizational justice: Fundamental questions about fairness in the workplace* (pp. 555–586). Mahwah, NJ: Erlbaum.

Lind, E. A. (1990). *Arbitrating high-stakes cases: An evaluation of court-annexed arbitration in a United States district court*. Santa Monica, CA: Rand Corporation.

Lind, E. A. (1995). *Social conflict and social justice: Lessons from the social psychology of justice judgments*. Inaugural oration, Leiden University, Leiden, The Netherlands.

Lind, E. A. (2001). Fairness heuristic theory: Justice judgments as pivotal cognitions in organizational relations. In J. Greenberg & R. Cropanzano (Eds.), *Advances in organizational behavior* (pp. 56–88). Stanford, CA: Stanford University Press.

Lind, E. A., Ambrose, M., De Vera Park, M., & Kulik, C. T. (1990). Perspective and procedural justice: Attorney and litigant evaluations of court procedures. *Social Justice Research, 4*, 325–336.

Lind, E. A., Greenberg, J., Scott, K. S., & Welchans, T. D. (2000). The winding road from employee to complainant: Situational and psychological determinants of wrongful termination claims. *Administrative Science Quarterly, 45*, 557–590.

Lind, E. A., Kanfer, R., & Earley, P. C. (1990). Voice, control, and procedural justice: Instrumental and noninstrumental concerns in fairness judgments. *Journal of Personality and Social Psychology, 59*, 952–959.

Lind, E. A., Kulik, C. T., Ambrose, M., & De Vera Park, M. V. (1993). Individual and corporate dispute resolution: Using procedural fairness as a decision heuristic. *Administrative Science Quarterly, 38*, 224–251.

Lind, E. A., & Tyler, T. R. (1988). *The social psychology of procedural justice*. New York, NY: Plenum.

Lind, E. A., & Van den Bos, K. (2002). When fairness works: Toward a general theory of uncertainty management. In B. M. Staw & R. M. Kramer (Eds.), *Research in organizational behavior* (Vol. 24, pp. 181–223). Greenwich, CT: JAI.

Lind, E. A., & Van den Bos, K. (2013). Freeing organizational behavior from inhibitory constraints. *Research in Organizational Behavior, 33*, 79–95.

Maas, M., & Van den Bos, K. (2009). An affective-experiential perspective on reactions to fair and unfair events: Individual differences in affect intensity moderated by experiential mindsets. *Journal of Experimental Social Psychology, 45*, 667–675.

Maas, M., & Van den Bos, K. (2011). Real personal uncertainty induced by means of task-related feedback: Effects on reactions to voice and no-voice procedures. *Social Justice Research, 24*, 107–125.

McFarlin, D. B., & Sweeney, P. D. (1992). Distributive and procedural justice as predictors of satisfaction with personal and organizational outcomes. *Academy of Management Journal, 35*, 626–637.

Miedema, J., Van den Bos, K., & Vermunt, R. (2006). The influence of self-threats on fairness judgments and affective measures. *Social Justice Research, 19*, 228–253.

Mikula, G., & Wenzel, M. (2000). Justice and social conflict. *International Journal of Psychology, 35*, 126–135.

Miller, B. K., Konopaske, R., & Byrne, Z. S. (2012). Dominance analysis of two measures of organizational justice. *Journal of Managerial Psychology, 27*, 264–282.

Miller, D. T. (1999). The norm of self-interest. *American Psychologist, 54*, 1053–1060.

Miller, D. T., & Ratner, R. K. (1998). The disparity between the actual and assumed power of self-interest. *Journal of Personality and Social Psychology, 74*, 53–62.

Moorman, R. H. (1991). Relationship between organizational justice and organizational citizenship behaviors: Do fairness perceptions influence employee citizenship. *Journal of Applied Psychology, 76*, 845–855.

Murray, S. L., Holmes, J. G., & Collins, N. L. (2005). *The relational signature of felt security*. Paper presented at the 2005 Conference of the Society of Experimental Social Psychology, San Diego, USA.

Paternoster, R., Brame, R., Bachman, R., & Sherman, L. W. (1997). Do fair procedures matter? The effect of procedural justice on spouse assault. *Law and Society Review, 31*, 163–204.

Patterson, P. G., Cowley, E., & Prasongsukarn, K. (2006). Service failure recovery: The moderating impact of individual-level cultural value orientation on perceptions of justice. *International Journal of Research in Marketing, 23*, 263–277.

Peeters, G., & Czapinski, J. (1990). Positive-negative asymmetry in evaluations: The distinction between affective and information negativity effects. In W. Stroebe & M. Hewstone (Eds.), *European review of social psychology* (Vol. 1, pp. 33–60). Chichester, UK: Wiley.

Podsakoff, P. M., & MacKenzie, S. B. (1993). Citizenship behavior and fairness in organizations: Issues and directions for future research. *Employee Responsibilities and Rights Journal, 6*, 235–247.

Proudfoot, D., & Lind, E. A. (2015). Fairness heuristic theory, the uncertainty management model, and fairness at work. In M. L. Ambrose & R. S. Cropanzano (Eds.), *Oxford handbook of justice in work organizations* (pp. 371–385). Oxford, UK: Oxford University Press.

Rawls, J. (1992). *A theory of justice*. Oxford: Oxford University Press. (Original work published in 1971)

Schminke, M., Ambrose, M. L., & Cropanzano, R. S. (2000). The effect of organizational structure on perceptions of procedural fairness. *Journal of Applied Psychology, 85*, 294–304.

See, K. E. (2009). Reactions to decisions with uncertain consequences: Reliance on perceived fairness versus predicted outcomes depends on knowledge. *Journal of Personality and Social Psychology, 96*, 104–117.

Shapiro, D. L., & Brett, J. M. (2005). What is the role of control in organizational justice? In J. Greenberg & J. A. Colquitt (Eds.), *Handbook of organizational justice: Fundamental questions about fairness in the workplace* (pp. 155–178). Mahwah, NJ: Erlbaum.

Thau, S., Aquino, K., & Wittek, R. (2007). An extension of uncertainty management theory to the self: The relationship between justice, social comparison orientation, and antisocial work behaviors. *Journal of Applied Psychology, 92*, 286–295.

Thibaut, J., & Walker, L. (1975). *Procedural justice: A psychological analysis*. Hillsdale, NJ: Erlbaum.

Thibaut, J., & Walker, L. (1978). A theory of procedure. *California Law Review, 66*, 541–566.

Tyler, T. R. (1990). *Why do people obey the law? Procedural justice, legitimacy, and compliance*. New Haven, CT: Yale University Press.

Tyler, T. R., & Bies, R. J. (1990). Beyond formal procedures: The interpersonal context of procedural justice. In J. S. Caroll (Ed.), *Applied social psychology and organizational settings* (pp. 77–98). Hillsdale, NJ: Erlbaum.

Tyler, T. R., Boeckmann, R. J., Smith, H. J., & Huo, Y. J. (1997). *Social justice in a diverse society*. Boulder, CO: Westview.

Tyler, T. R., & Lind, E. A. (1992). A relational model of authority in groups. In M. P. Zanna (Ed.), *Advances in experimental social psychology* (Vol. 25, pp. 115–191). San Diego, CA: Academic Press.

Tyler, T. R., Rasinski, K. A., & McGraw, K. M. (1985). The influence of perceived injustice on the endorsement of political leaders. *Journal of Applied Social Psychology, 15*, 700–725.

Van den Bos, K. (1999). What are we talking about when we talk about no-voice procedures? On the psychology of the fair outcome effect. *Journal of Experimental Social Psychology, 35*, 560–577.

Van den Bos, K. (2001a). Uncertainty management: The influence of uncertainty salience on reactions to perceived procedural fairness. *Journal of Personality and Social Psychology, 80*, 931–941.

Van den Bos, K. (2001b). Fairness heuristic theory: Assessing the information to which people are reacting has a pivotal role in understanding organizational justice. In S. W. Gilliland, D. D. Steiner, & D. P. Skarlicki (Eds.),

Theoretical and cultural perspectives on organizational justice (pp. 63–84). Greenwich, CT: Information Age Publishing.
Van den Bos, K. (2005). What is responsible for the fair process effect? In J. Greenberg & J. A. Colquitt (Eds.), *Handbook of organizational justice: Fundamental questions about fairness in the workplace* (pp. 273–300). Mahwah, NJ: Erlbaum.
Van den Bos, K. (2007). Hot cognition and social justice judgments: The combined influence of cognitive and affective factors on the justice judgment process. In D. de Cremer (Ed.), *Advances in the psychology of justice and affect* (pp. 59–82). Greenwich, CT: Information Age.
Van den Bos, K., Brockner, J., Stein, J. H., Steiner, D. D., Van Yperen, N. W., & Dekker, D. M. (2010). The psychology of voice and performance capabilities in masculine and feminine cultures and contexts. *Journal of Personality and Social Psychology, 99*, 638–648.
Van den Bos, K., Brockner, J., Van den Oudenalder, M., Kamble, S. V., & Nasabi, A. (2013). Delineating a method to study cross-cultural differences with experimental control: The voice effect and countercultural contexts regarding power distance. *Journal of Experimental Social Psychology, 49*, 624–634.
Van den Bos, K., Ham, J., Lind, E. A., Simonis, M., Van Essen, W. J., & Rijpkema, M. (2008). Justice and the human alarm system: The impact of exclamation points and flashing lights on the justice judgment process. *Journal of Experimental Social Psychology, 44*, 201–219.
Van den Bos, K., & Lind, E. A. (2002). Uncertainty management by means of fairness judgments. In M. P. Zanna (Ed.), *Advances in experimental social psychology* (Vol. 34, pp. 1–60). San Diego, CA: Academic Press.
Van den Bos, K., & Lind, E. A. (2009). The social psychology of fairness and the regulation of personal uncertainty. In R. M. Arkin, K. C. Oleson, & P. J. Carroll (Eds.), *Handbook of the uncertain self* (pp. 122–141). New York, NY: Psychology Press.
Van den Bos, K., & Lind, E. A. (2013). On sense-making reactions and public inhibition of benign social motives: An appraisal model of prosocial behavior. In J. M. Olson & M. P. Zanna (Eds.), *Advances in experimental social psychology* (Vol. 48, pp. 1–58). San Diego, CA: Academic Press.
Van den Bos, K., Maas, M., Waldring, I. E., & Semin, G. R. (2003). Toward understanding the psychology of reactions to perceived fairness: The role of affect intensity. *Social Justice Research, 16*, 151–168.
Van den Bos, K., & Miedema, J. (2000). Toward understanding why fairness matters: The influence of mortality salience on reactions to procedural fairness. *Journal of Personality and Social Psychology, 79*, 355–366.
Van den Bos, K., Peters, S. L., Bobocel, D. R., & Ybema, J. F. (2006). On preferences and doing the right thing: Satisfaction with advantageous inequity when cognitive processing is limited. *Journal of Experimental Social Psychology, 42*, 273–289.
Van den Bos, K., Poortvliet, P. M., Maas, M., Miedema, J., & Van den Ham, E.-J. (2005). An enquiry concerning the principles of cultural norms and values: The impact of uncertainty and mortality salience on reactions to violations and bolstering of cultural worldviews. *Journal of Experimental Social Psychology, 41*, 91–113.
Van den Bos, K., & Rijpkema, M. (2008). *Studying effects of exclamation point primes using functional neuroimaging.* Unpublished manuscript.
Van den Bos, K., & Spruijt, N. (2002). Appropriateness of decisions as a moderator of the psychology of voice. *European Journal of Social Psychology, 32*, 57–72.
Van den Bos, K., Van der Velden, L., & Lind, E. A. (2014). On the role of perceived procedural justice in citizens' reactions to government decisions and the handling of conflicts. *Utrecht Law Review, 10*(4), 1–26.
Van den Bos, K., & Van Prooijen, J.-W. (2001). Referent cognitions theory: The role of closeness of reference points in the psychology of voice. *Journal of Personality and Social Psychology, 81*, 616–626.
Van den Bos, K., Vermunt, R., & Wilke, H. A. M. (1996). The consistency rule and the voice effect: The influence of expectations on procedural fairness judgements and performance. *European Journal of Social Psychology, 26*, 411–428.
Van den Bos, K., Vermunt, R., & Wilke, H. A. M. (1997). Procedural and distributive justice: What is fair depends more on what comes first than on what comes next. *Journal of Personality and Social Psychology, 72*, 95–104.
Vermunt, R., & Steensma, H. (2003). Physiological relaxation: Stress reduction through fair treatment. *Social Justice Research, 16*, 135–150.
Vermunt, R., Wit, A. P., Van den Bos, K., & Lind, E. A. (1996). The effects of unfair procedure on affect and protest. *Social Justice Research, 9*, 109–119.
Walker, L., LaTour, S., Lind, E. A., & Thibaut, J. (1974). Reactions of participants and observers to modes of adjudication. *Journal of Applied Social Psychology, 4*, 295–310.
Walker, L., Lind, E. A., & Thibaut, J. (1979). The relation between procedural and distributive justice. *Virginia Law Review, 65*, 1401–1420.
Weick, K. E. (1995). *Sensemaking in organizations.* Thousand Oaks, CA: Sage.
Weiss, H. M., Suckow, K., & Cropanzano, R. (1999). Effects of justice conditions on discrete emotions. *Journal of Applied Psychology, 84*, 786–794.
Winkielman, P., Schwarz, N., Fazendeiro, T., & Reber, R. (2003). The hedonic marking of processing fluency: Implications for evaluative judgment. In J. Musch & K. C. Klauer (Eds.), *The psychology of evaluation: Affective processes in cognition and emotion* (pp. 189–217). Mahwah, NJ: Erlbaum.

CHAPTER

20 Justice and Affect: A Dimensional Approach

Marion Fortin, Steven L. Blader, Batia M. Wiesenfeld, *and* Sara L. Wheeler-Smith

Abstract

Scholarship on justice and affect has expanded dramatically in recent years, spanning investigations of the relationships between justice and discrete emotions as well as justice and affective dimensions (e.g., valence).The present chapter summarizes and builds on the latter developments by exploring how several leading theories of justice can organize and lend insight to research that takes a dimensional approach to affect. In particular, we explore the valence dimension of affect in relation to the self-interest model of justice, the uncertainty dimension of affect in relation to the uncertainty management model of justice, the morality dimension of affect in relation to the deontic model of justice, and the social dimension of affect in relation to the relational models of justice. We also discuss the value of the dimensional approach for organizing prior findings, highlighting novel insights, and identifying new pathways for justice research.

Key Words: justice, affect, emotions, instrumental model, uncertainty management, deontic model, relational models, discrete emotions, emotion dimensions

Imagine your organization is merging with another organization. Your colleague Tina is deeply angry about how the resulting changes will likely affect her. She also feels that the way the decision to merge has been made and communicated is unfair. In contrast, Tina's manager, Adam, feels quite positively about the changes and is happy about the rumors that if the merger goes through he'll be promoted. In a meeting, you and your colleagues witness a heated discussion between Tina and Adam. Adam, who usually has a very calm demeanor, becomes agitated when being reproached by Tina. Tina is offended and argues that Adam is not involving her as much as other team members. You feel empathy with Tina, who has been a loyal colleague for many years. Another of your colleagues later remarks contemptuously that Tina is probably just envious of Adam.

The preceding example, which is representative though fictitious, illustrates some of the close linkages between justice and affect. The emotions Tina and Adam feel for one another—and that observers, including you, feel toward each of them—will critically impact justice judgments, actions, and reactions. Moreover, the moods that you or any other party feels will likely impact the justice-related dynamics in this situation. This fundamental insight about the interdependence of justice and affect was acknowledged in some of the earliest social psychological research on justice (e.g., Adams, 1965). Initially, the focus was on affective reactions to injustice, with a great deal of accumulated evidence demonstrating that people who feel unfairly treated experience negative emotions. For example, a seminal study by Mikula, Scherer, and Athenstaedt (1998) found that anger, fear, sadness, disgust, shame and guilt were all reactions to perceived injustice. Recent neuroimaging studies represent the new wave of work exploring this connection, demonstrating activation of the brain regions associated with the experience of emotion in people making moral judgments (for a review, see Barsky, Kaplan & Beal, 2011; e.g., Greene & Haidt, 2002).

Recent justice research greatly extends these insights and highlights the complex, reciprocal interrelationships between mood, emotion, and dispositional affect on the one hand and fairness perceptions and reactions on the other (for recent reviews on justice and affect, see Cohen-Charash & Byrne, 2008; Cropanzano, Stein, & Nadisic, 2011; De Cremer, 2007).[1] It is now well recognized that justice not only prompts affective reactions, but that affect can also operate as a mediator and a moderator of reactions to justice. That is, current research makes clear that the interplay of justice and affect is quite complex. In this chapter, we review prototypical examples of the work on justice and affect, with an eye toward bringing greater clarity to their complex relationship.

Two critical attributes define our approach to clarifying the literature on justice and affect. First, we anchor our review around the predominant theories concerning why people care about justice. That is, we organize our thinking (and the prior research) on justice and affect according to the fundamental reasons that people care about justice. Consideration of these different justice motives has been largely absent in the literature linking justice and affect. We argue that this is unfortunate, because each of the predominant theories about why people care about justice is associated with an extensive—and different—set of affect-based processes (Cropanzano et al., 2011). That is, the various theories make distinct predictions about the emotions and moods that will matter in terms of shaping justice judgments, predicting justice reactions, and understanding mediating processes. Our approach is consistent with the recent theorizing of Cropanzano et al. (2011), who suggest that the emotions that follow from a given injustice experience will greatly depend on the justice motives (i.e., control, social identity, morality) that are at play for a given individual as they encounter that experience. For example, moral motives are expected to elicit anger and disgust, whereas social identity motives are expected to elicit feelings of loneliness. By anchoring our review in terms of key theories of why people care about justice, we hope to understand those theories through a new lens—the affect-based lens—and as a result we hope to shed greater light on the psychology of justice. Moreover we hope to bring greater understanding and organization to prior research findings on justice and affect, moving away from a somewhat dispersed set of interesting findings to a more coherent framework that has the psychology of justice at its core.

The second key and distinctive characteristic of our review is that we take a dimensional approach to affect. In particular, we use each of the prevailing theories about why people care about justice as our starting point, and then we identify an affective dimension that is suggested by each theory. Affective dimensions focus on a defining affective element and organize discrete affective responses according to where they fall along that element. For instance, consider valence—an archetypical dimension of affect defined by negativity and positivity. Discrete emotions can be organized according to valence (e.g., anger, sadness, serenity, happiness, joy; arrayed respectively from negative to positive on the valence dimension), and in this way they can be placed on a continuum with regard to their implied negativity and positivity. Moreover, action tendencies that follow from negativity and positivity can be understood and predicted based on where the relevant emotion being experienced falls on the valence dimension. We explain the dimensional approach in more detail below, but suffice it to say at this point that our review of the literature emphasizes this approach because we see great value in it.

Before we proceed, some clarity about terms and definitions is in order. Our analysis is focused on the intersection of justice and affect. Yet affect (defined as consciously accessible feelings; Cropanzano et al., 2011; Frederickson, 2001) is present in an array of phenomena including the distinct constructs of emotions and moods. Emotions and moods differ with regard to whether they have a defined target: emotions are felt toward a specific person and/or linked to an eliciting event (e.g., one's manager or recent performance appraisal), whereas moods are more diffuse feelings not related to a specific target or cause (Frijda, 1986). When appropriate, we distinguish emotions and moods in our discussion later, and in some places, when appropriate, we refer to them collectively as affect. For the most part, however, we distinguish them as is consistent with how they have been treated in research on justice and affect.

In sum, our goal in this chapter is to draw attention to a dimensional approach to affect, and to organize our review of research on justice and affect around a set of dimensions that relate to the reasons people care about justice. Our approach, therefore, complements (rather than repeats) previous reviews that have, for example, focused on conceptual and theoretical models that explain the links between justice and emotions (Cropanzano, Stein, &

Nadisic, 2011), the possible causal mechanisms relating justice and emotion (Cohen-Charash & Byrne, 2008), and affect as a mediator between justice and outcomes (Colquitt et al. 2013). Those reviews provide a comprehensive analysis of these issues and we recommend them to the interested reader.

Justice and Affect: Setting the Stage

We begin our analysis by noting that we take a very broad approach to the concept of justice. Our analysis is inclusive of all types of justice discussed in the literature (distributive, procedural, interactional). It also covers both sides of the (in) justice equation—overadvantage and underadvantage. Research has generally focused on the injustice experienced when someone receives less or is treated less well than others, but this approach misses a critical side of the story. For instance, emotional reactions to underadvantage or unfavorably biased procedures (e.g., anger) will differ from emotions in response to overadvantage or favorably biased procedures (e.g., guilt) (Weiss, Suckow et al. 1999). We, therefore, take a more comprehensive approach by drawing attention to unfairness involving both negative and positive deviations from justice standards, and the emotions associated with these instances.

Moreover, our analysis examines the perspectives of all parties to justice events. Research on how emotions and justice can be linked has primarily focused on the affect that is experienced by the recipient of fair or unfair treatment. Specifically, most studies have addressed the emotional reactions that follow from the fairness personally encountered by an individual and—to a lesser extent—how a person's moods and emotions may shape how they judge the treatment and the outcomes that they personally receive. Although victims of injustice and recipients of justice are, of course, worthy of attention, the emotions and moods experienced by other parties are also deserving of attention. Of particular importance are the perspectives of the "agents" of justice and of third parties.

Justice agents are those who make decisions or provide the treatment that is the subject of other people's justice judgments. Justice agents are often organizational authorities, but other sources of (un)just treatment exist, such as peers and customers. The agent's actions lie at the root of the justice process; they are the origins of justice or injustice and understanding their psychology is essential to remedying injustice when it occurs. The agents' emotions toward the recipient, as well as their incidental emotions and mood states, are all intertwined with their justice enactment. In this way, an affect-based analysis of justice agents can help provide insight to a critically underdeveloped issue in justice research, namely when and why justice agents enact fairness or unfairness.

Third parties in the justice process are those who witness or learn about injustices that happen to others. There is extensive research evidence to suggest that people react to injustice even if they are not personally victims of it (for a review, see Skarlicki & Kulik, 2005). Third-party perspectives are particularly important because people tend to witness many more injustices than they personally experience. The injustice experienced by one person can thus reverberate throughout an organization. Third-parties' emotions toward recipients and agents, as well as their incidental emotions and moods, may all impact justice judgments and reactions.

A more complete understanding of the intersection of affect and justice in organizations requires a thorough understanding of each of these three perspectives (recipient, agent, and third party), as well as an understanding of the interactions between these different parties. As our introductory example illustrates, one person's emotional displays may influence the emotions and reactions of colleagues, which, in turn, feed back into further justice-relevant experiences for the initial person. More directly, the emotional display of any one party may influence other parties' reactions to justice events. That is, people make inferences about justice based on the emotional displays they see in others (e.g., DeCremer, Wubben & Brebels, 2008). As such, in applying our dimensional lens, we focus on all parties to the justice encounter (target, observer, agent) in our consideration of the interplay of justice dynamics and affect.

As previous reviews have pointed out, research on justice and affect includes studies that show how justice judgments influence mood or emotion, and how emotion or moods influence justice judgments. The majority of this work focuses on justice as a predictor of moods and emotions. Several theories from both the emotions and the justice literature suggest that the experience of (in-)justice leads to emotional reactions (for a thorough summary of these theoretical models, see Cropanzano, Stein, & Nadisic, 2011). For example, both fairness theory and deontic justice models suggest that the perception of injustice leads to anger (Folger & Cropanzano, 2001, Folger, Cropanzano & Goldman, 2005), whereas affective events theory (Weiss & Cropanzano, 1996) suggests more generally that event appraisals lead to emotions that subsequently predict workplace attitudes and behaviors. Emotions that are found to be reactions to justice and injustice experiences include anger, envy, guilt, and pride, but multiple discrete emotions are often combined into larger categories (Cohen-Charash & Byrne 2008), making it unclear whether emotions or moods are measured.

The influence of emotions and mood on justice judgments is a more recent research area and draws generally on broader theory that explains the influence of affect on cognitive processes. For example, the affect-as-information model (Schwarz & Clore, 1983) suggests that mood influences current judgments both directly and through effects on information search. Drawing on this broader literature, several models were proposed specifically to explain the effects of emotions and moods on justice judgments (e.g., Scher & Heise, 1993; Mullen, 2007; Barsky, Kaplan & Beal, 2011). There is a smaller but growing body of empirical research supporting the notion that mood affects justice judgments (e.g., Sinclair & Mark, 1991, Van den Bos, 2003) and also that emotions affect justice judgments (e.g., Van den Bos, 2003). However, as Cohen-Charash and Byrne (2008) point out, there are relatively few studies that examine the effect of discrete emotions on justice judgments. In our effort to complement prior reviews, we focus greater attention on those areas that have received less attention in the past, not only with respect to our dimensional approach to affect but also our attention to fairness and overadvantage; agents and third parties; and the effect of affect on justice judgments.

A Dimensional Approach to Affect

The study of affect can be characterized as taking either a discrete or dimensional approach, both of which are represented in prior justice research. However, there is some debate about their relative merits (see for example Lindquist, Siegel, Quigley & Barrett, 2013, p. 255). On the one hand, a focus on discrete emotions brings with it richness and nuance regarding each distinct emotion. On the other hand, a dimensional approach focuses on commonalities between multiple discrete emotions, shedding light on how they relate to one another and to particular outcomes. Emotions that are similar with respect to some underlying dimension are thought to have similar effects on judgments and choices (e.g., Lerner & Keltner, 2000). The dimensional approach pays less attention to differences between distinct emotions in the belief that a focus on central defining elements that discrete emotions share with one another can tell us a great deal about the specific emotions as well as the overall dimension itself. As an illustrative example, consider the relationship between emotional valence (an affective dimension) and happiness. Positively valenced emotions capture a wide range of discrete emotions, whereas happiness refers to something more specific but with greater depth in meaning. Indeed, happiness (like other discrete emotions) can be classified not only in terms of its valence, but also in terms of other widely accepted dimensions of emotions such as arousal and approach/avoidance (Lang, Bradley, & Cuthbert, 1997; Russell & Barrett, 1999; Schneirla, 1959; Watson, Wiese, Vaidya, & Tellegen, 1999). It may also be characterized by a host of other experiential, physiological, and behavioral responses (Ekman, 1999; Panksepp, 2007). That said, focusing on the valence aspect of happiness gives prominence to this particular element of the discrete emotion and indicates what happiness might have in common with other emotions such as joy, excitement, and contentment, among others.

As is readily evident, this is a fundamental difference in perspective, and, as with all fundamental differences, there are camps on each side advocating for the value of one approach over the other. The proponents of the discrete emotions approach argue that research in organizational contexts will benefit from considering discrete emotions because each emotion has unique relational themes and may explain specific outcomes (Lazarus & Cohen-Charash, 2001). On the other hand, scholars advocating the dimensional approach have pointed out that the distinctions between discrete emotions may often be overstated, and that a dimensional approach not only offers greater parsimony but also explains greater variance than the discrete emotions approach (Barrett, 2006; Mauss & Robinson, 2009; Watson, 2000). This perspective has, in turn, prompted research attention to identify additional dimensions of emotion, beyond those most commonly recognized (i.e., valence and arousal). For example, emotions such as anger and anxiety both have negative valence and high arousal, and, thus, initial research recognizing only the valence and arousal dimensions might lead scholars to expect them to be highly correlated.

However, they lie on opposite ends of a continuum with respect to the level of certainty or uncertainty associated with the emotion. Specifically, anger is resolute and certain whereas anxiety is marked by uncertainty (a more complete description of the certainty/uncertainty dimension and how it relates to discrete emotions follows below). Ignoring the uncertainty dimension of these emotions may lead scholars to overlook important differences in how anger and anxiety shape justice perceptions and reactions.

How has prior work at the intersection of justice and emotions navigated the discrete/dimensional affect divide? Prior reviews of the literature relating emotion to justice (e.g., Cohen-Charash & Byrne, 2008; Cropanzano et al., 2011; DeCremer 2007) have focused on discrete emotions (such as anger in response to unfair treatment, happiness in response to fair treatment, or empathy as an antecedent of justice) or have touched on common dimensions such as valence. However, other potentially relevant affective dimensions have been relatively neglected. As a result, the justice literature has not yet fully leveraged advances in the literature on affect that can offer new insights regarding how justice perceptions form and how people react to them. We address this gap in the remainder of this chapter, where we review prior work on justice and affect but do so by adopting a dimensional affect lens in relation to justice. In adopting this dimensional lens, we hope to develop novel insights and spur new thinking about the intersection of justice and affect.

Importantly, as we discussed earlier, we focus on novel affective dimensions that follow from the major theories about why people care about justice. This approach highlights the affective processes (both subjective affective experiences and consequent action tendencies) linked to each of the major justice theories. Notably, the affective aspect of the major theories about why people care about justice has received relatively little attention (Cropanzano et al, 2011), and, more generally, research on justice and affect has developed largely detached from the very theories that are the building blocks of justice theorizing.

We start with one of the earliest approaches to justice: the instrumental models. These models emphasize that justice is valued because it serves people's self-interest (Thibaut & Walker, 1975). We draw upon valence as the affective dimension that is most related to this perspective. We next consider the uncertainty-management theory of justice (van den Bos & Lind, 2002), which we explore in relation to the certainty dimension of affect. Following this we consider the deontic model of justice, which has clear relevance to the moral dimension of affect (Brown & Trevino, 2006; Folger, 2001). Finally, we turn our attention to the relational models of justice (Lind & Tyler, 1988, Tyler & Blader, 2003) that can be illuminated with reference to the social dimension of affect.

Note that although valence is one of the most well-established and researched dimensions, the other dimensions on which we focus (the certainty, moral, and social dimensions) have received less attention in the literature. Later, we describe and develop these dimensions more. It is also worth noting that although dimensions can refer to a characteristic on which every affective response can be arrayed, some of the dimensions we highlight are not relevant to all discrete emotions or moods, but merely to a subclass. Nevertheless, in all cases, the dimensions capture a characteristic on which discrete emotions or moods within that subclass can be arrayed, generating testable predictions about how placement on that continuum relates to critical justice dynamics. Finally, we do not consider a dimension that has received a great deal of attention in the literature, namely activation. Although this dimension may also have relevance for justice, our focus on dimensions that relate to the major justice theories led us to exclude it. That is, we do not regard the affective dimension of activation as clearly reflective of nor implicated by any of the major justice theories, and thus we do not consider it here.

Instrumental Justice Models: The Valence Dimension

The affective circumplex (Russell, 1980) is one of the most widely adopted dimensional models of affect. It describes affect with respect to two underlying dimensions corresponding to two neurophysiological systems: valence and arousal. Arousal, or alertness, has received relatively little attention, but the valence dimension has been the subject of much research in the justice literature. Valence emphasizes the degree to which experienced affect is marked by pleasurable or displeasureable feelings (Barrett & Russell, 1999).

We suggest that valence is related to instrumental self-interest-based models of the justice motive (e.g., Deutsch, 1975; Walster, Walster & Berscheid, 1978). These models assume that instrumentality, or the desire to maximize the favorability of outcomes over the long term, is the motivator driving the desire for both procedural and distributive justice. Emotional valence is a metric of value or perceived favorability, and people are assumed to desire and derive value from maximizing their experience of positively valenced emotion and minimizing their experience of negatively valenced emotion.

Many studies that investigate emotional reactions to justice have focused on the valence of the emotions felt by justice recipients, differentiating between positive versus negative affect[2] (for example, van den Bos & Miedema 2000; Vermunt, Wit, van den Bos and Lind, 1996). Indeed, the body of literature that has accumulated regarding affect as an outcome of justice has become important enough for both positive and negative state affect to be included in the most recent meta-analysis of organizational justice (Colquitt et al. 2013). Overall, moderate relationships are found among all four types of justice and both positive affect (between $r=.29$ and $r=.39$) and negative affect (between $r=-.23$ and $r=-.32$). Colquitt and colleagues conclude, "Justice seems to make people feel good to the same degree that injustice makes them feel bad." (p. 216).

Colquitt and colleagues (2013) also find that affect mediates some of the relationships between justice and outcomes. Specifically, procedural and distributive justice had indirect effects on task performance and on organizational citizenship behaviors (OCBs), and distributive, procedural and interpersonal justice had indirect effects on counterproductive work behaviors (CWBs).

Overall, the evidence indicates that injustice triggers negative affect, which in turn can lead to behaviors that are harmful for the organization. Likewise, justice may also apparently trigger positive affect that leads to helpful behaviors. Barclay and Kiefer (2014) potentially shed more light on the mediating role of affect by differentiating between approach-related behaviors (performance and helping) and avoidance-related behaviors (withdrawal). In two field studies, they find that positive emotions mediated the relationship between overall justice and approach-related behaviors, while negative emotions mediated the relationship between justice and avoidance-related behaviors (with inconclusive results for negative emotions and approach behaviors). Overall, these findings underscore the potential usefulness of the valence distinction for understanding justice dynamics and predicting behaviors.

More recently, valence has also been included in theorizing to explain the effect of emotions and moods on justice judgments (Mullen, 2007; Barsky et al., 2011). This work suggests that valence may shape: (a) whether someone makes a justice judgment, (b) how they make the justice judgment, and (c) how likely they are to be treated unfairly and thus experience injustice.

Mullen (2007) argues that the valence of decision recipients' emotion related to a justice encounter determines whether they initiate justice reasoning in the first place. Specifically, people may only spontaneously think about justice when they experience negative emotions in response to the primary assessment of an event (such as frustration when they are recipients of injustice or guilt when they observe injustice in others). When they experience positive emotions, however, they are reassured that everything is fine in their environment and are not motivated to engage in justice reasoning. Thus the valence dimension has a primary role in the justice judgment process. Moreover, put in terms of our link to core justice motives, this suggests that justice reasoning follows primarily when self-interest is threatened, not when it is served.

Although Mullen's theorizing focuses on victims of unfairness, it also has interesting implications for third party justice concerns. If positive affect dampens justice reasoning, then when the majority of people are "happy," such as because they are advantaged by a decision or justice event, they may show little concern for the injustice experienced by a minority in their midst. In other words, third parties may be less likely to be concerned about the underdog when times are good (for them). Moreover, their inaction may not be a motivated outcome driven by self-interest (i.e., fear of rocking the boat and potentially threatening the source of their happiness) but rather the result of a cognitive blind spot whereby they fail to think about justice in these cases.

Valence of affect may not only determine whether people initiate justice reasoning, but also whether they judge justice events as more or less fair. Typically, there is some ambiguity when people experience justice-relevant events, and incidental moods can sway the interpretation of events (van den Bos, 2003). Furthermore, the valence of mood can influence fairness judgments by influencing which justice norms people choose and implement. Sinclair and Mark (1991) explain that those in a negative mood engage in more systematic justice processing, which is necessary when applying cognitively demanding justice rules such as equity. In their study, participants in a positive mood showed less preference for equity and made less precise equity allocations. Of course, if justice reasoning is less likely among people in a positive mood (Mullen, 2007) then positive mood may only affect norm choice (and justice reasoning in general) when an alternate trigger (such as uncertainty) makes justice salient. Some existing research may be biased because widely adopted justice scales and other instruments may direct attention toward justice issues that would not be salient otherwise.

Valence may also bias recollections of the past and expectations of the future. For example, moods bring congruent memories to mind (Ellis & Moore, 2005). Thus, when people evaluate the justice of their organization or supervisor while they are in a good mood, they are more likely to think of positive past experiences than when they are in a bad mood. Mood may also influence anticipatory injustice because negative mood is linked to pessimistic expectations (Forgas, 2003).

Barsky et al. (2011) suggest a third way that valence of affect can shape justice; they argue that the valence of moods can change how fairly a person is actually treated, thus changing the underlying experience of injustice in addition to the justice judgment. Specifically, they argue that targets in a good mood engender a more positive mood in justice agents through a contagion process, which, in turn, elicits agents' helpfulness and prosocial behavior (George & Brief, 1992). In other words, those in a good mood are more likely to be treated fairly because they put justice agents in a good mood. These contagion processes are generally nonconscious and are likely to be stronger when they come from a source seen as a referent. Unfortunately, we are not aware of research that empirically tests this logic, but it is worthy of study if only because it suggests that affect may shape the actions of agents as well as the judgments of the recipients of justice. Moreover, little research has been focused on how the valence of the agent's emotions influences their justice reasoning and actions.

The preceding discussion illustrates the potential usefulness of the valence dimension, because it explains how a full range of emotions can shape and be shaped by justice. Moreover, it links those effects to a working model of why people care about justice. In this way, the preceding discussion demonstrates the potential insights a dimensional emotions approach to justice may yield. However, no single dimension—not even valence—can capture affect's inherent richness. It is, therefore, understandable that previous reviews of justice and emotion have criticized over-reliance on the valence dimension (e.g., Cropanzano et al., 2011). Moreover, similarly valenced emotions (or moods) can have opposing effects. For example, Cropanzano and colleagues (2011) review evidence suggesting that some negative emotions, such as anxiety, seem to promote more careful fairness processing, but that others, such as anger, may elicit more heuristic processing. Although these findings lead some to advocate for the importance of a discrete emotions approach (Cohen-Charash & Byrne, 2008; Cropanzano et al., 2011), we suggest that a worthwhile complementary path is to explore other affective dimensions in addition to valence that help explain these differences among similarly valenced emotions (e.g., in the example provided, perhaps differences between anxiety and anger are explained by their differences in certainty, reflecting a different core justice motive).

Uncertainty Management Theory: The Certainty Dimension

Uncertainty reduction and security are, according to uncertainty management theory (UMT), central reasons that people care about justice (van den Bos & Lind, 2002). Uncertainty is an uncomfortable experience, and UMT holds that justice makes the environment more predictable and, therefore, can reduce uncertainty and the discomfort resulting from it. Interestingly, this is even the case if the fairness experience is unrelated to the source of the uncertainty. Therefore, people become more concerned with justice when they feel any form of uncertainty, such as mortality salience (Van den Bos & Lind, 2002). Recent models have built on this research, suggesting that people who experience emotions high in uncertainty would also think and care more about fairness than those who experience more certain emotions (Mullen, 2007; Barsky et al., 2011). We argue that the degree to which an emotion reflects uncertainty or certainty is a relevant dimension in relation to the uncertainty reduction motive of justice.

Although this dimension has received little attention from affect scholars to date, there is good evidence that the judgments that people make about the certainty of the situation (ranging from highly certain to highly uncertain) influence which discrete emotion is experienced, and that the same is true for a number of other appraisal dimensions (Smith & Ellsworth 1985; 1987). Smith and

Ellsworth (1985) identified certainty as one of eight possible appraisal dimensions in the literature (the other seven were: pleasantness, attention, control, perceived obstacle, legitimacy, responsibility, and anticipated effort). They asked 16 students to recall and describe past emotional experiences regarding each of 15 specific emotions (e.g., happiness, sadness, fear, anger), and then to rate the experience they described with respect to uncertainty and the other appraisal dimensions. They found that whereas fear and surprise were associated with appraisals of particularly high uncertainty, pride, happiness, and anger were associated with appraisals of high certainty. Importantly, certainty was the main dimension that distinguished fear, hope, and surprise from the other emotions in their study.

The certainty dimension may help to explain differential effects of specific discrete emotions that valence alone cannot explain. In a study of emotions and economic decision making, Lerner, Small, and Loewenstein (2004) induced sadness (a low certainty emotion), disgust (a high certainty emotion) or neutral emotions (through video clips) in 199 student participants. Then, an endowment effect paradigm was adapted, with students in each emotion condition divided into "sell" or "choice" conditions. In the "sell" condition they received a highlighter set and were asked to indicate the price at which they would sell it. In the "choice" condition, they were shown the set and asked what cash amount they would pay for it. The endowment effect is in evidence when people who possess the item perceive its value as higher than those who do not yet possess it (i.e., higher "sell" than "choice" prices). They found that disgust reduced both the choice and sell prices, and eliminated the endowment effect. Sadness reversed the endowment effect, with participants setting higher choice than sell prices. This study shows how emotions of the same valence (but different levels of certainty) may have different effects. Future research is needed to understand the impact of the certainty dimension on resource valuations and moreover how that might impact justice dynamics that relate to resources.

Lerner also shows that fear versus anger are related to different risk perceptions (Lerner, Gonzalez, Small & Fischhoff, 2003; Lerner & Keltner, 2001). In a study with 97 students, Lerner and Keltner (2001) measured dispositional anger and fear of participants and then showed that fear, which is related to appraisals of high uncertainty, was linked to pessimistic assessments and risk-averse choices, whereas anger, related to appraisals of low uncertainty, was linked to optimistic risk assessment and risk-seeking choices. In a second paper, Lerner and Keltner (2001) go on to show that the differential effects for fear and anger emerge not only for naturally occurring but also for experimentally induced fear and anger, and that appraisals of certainty and control can explain these effects. The same effects were also replicated on a nationally representative US sample regarding risk estimates for terrorism and explaining public-policy preferences (Lerner, Gonzalez, Small & Fischhoff, 2003).

Together, Lerner's studies suggest that angry people tend to engage in risky behavior, whereas fearful people do not. In the justice literature, emotions as an outcome of justice have typically been assessed as negative/positive bundles. By separately measuring certain versus uncertain emotions, justice researchers may be able to predict different downstream behavioral reactions (e.g., sabotage versus withdrawal). Moreover, the salience of the uncertainty reduction motive may influence the emotions people experience in response to justice; for example, fear may be more dominant than anger when uncertainty dynamics are more salient.

Differentiating between uncertain versus certain emotions may not only improve our understanding of reactions to justice but may also shed new light on the justice judgment process as well. We first discuss UMT's general predictions regarding the justice judgment process before discussing two recent models that explicitly treat the uncertainty of emotion as a determinant of justice judgments.

Uncertainty management theory not only explains why people care about justice (to reduce uncertainty), but also how justice judgments are made. In response to uncertainty, people monitor their environment for fairness-relevant data, which is often incomplete and ambiguous. The information that is available can be used as a heuristic substitute when assessing justice. Therefore, according to UMT, uncertainty is a crucial moderator of how justice judgments are formed. Although initial theorizing on uncertainty management concentrated on how people gather different pieces of information (regarding procedures, outcomes, etc.) and how they cognitively process the information, Van den Bos (2003) extended the model to include feelings as input for justice judgments under uncertainty. In three studies, he explored when affect is used to evaluate justice. In one experiment, participants were asked to imagine they were either happy or angry. Participants learned that their reward was better, worse, or the same as that of an equally performing other, or received no information about the other's outcome. Thus, the study had a balanced factorial design of 2 (affective state) by 4 (outcome better, worse, equal, unknown). Van den Bos found that the affect manipulation only influenced participants' justice judgments when they did not know about the others' outcomes. In a second experiment with 120 students, the same effects were replicated regarding procedural justice (voice). As hypothesized, there was no influence of affect on procedural justice judgments in the explicit voice and the explicit nonvoice conditions. However, in the no-information condition, those in the positive affect group felt they were treated more fairly than those in the negative affect condition. A third experiment with 243 students included a no affect control condition to assess whether the effect of affect was driven by positive or negative affect or both. This third study showed that both negative and positive affective states impact justice judgments under conditions of uncertainty, although the negative affect condition differed more strongly from the control condition than the positive affect condition.

In conclusion, the Van den Bos (2003) studies provide evidence that UMT can be extended to include affect as a source of information that people draw on to make judgments under conditions of uncertainty. At the same time, these studies suggest that both the valence *and* the uncertainty of affect may need to be considered in order to more fully understand how people make justice judgments. That is, whereas these studies rely on situationally manipulated uncertainty, it is also quite likely that the degree of uncertainty inherent in the emotion itself may produce some of the same effects, and, thus, where an emotion falls with regard to certainty may determine how other aspects of the emotion (e.g., valence or any of the other dimensions we consider) shape the justice judgment process.

Related to this point, two recent models similarly consider valence and uncertainty as two crucial inputs into justice judgments, but directly focus on the degree of uncertainty of emotions felt, rather than uncertainty more generally. First, Mullen's (2007) affective model of justice reasoning (AMJR) argues that although the valence of emotion felt as a response to the initial appraisal of an event decides *whether* justice reasoning is triggered, it is the degree of *certainty* or uncertainty that will decide how justice reasoning and processing occurs. Specifically, when the primary appraisal of an event elicits negative emotions, then people start to reason about fairness. If the emotion is associated with high uncertainty (e.g., sadness or disappointment), then people will engage in more substantive and careful processing of information in order to understand the event. If the emotion is associated with high certainty (e.g., anger), then people will engage in motivated processing, looking for evidence that the event was unfair. This does not mean that they will conclude that the event was unfair, but (as shown by Van den Bos, 2003) when the information is ambiguous and they are in a negative emotional state they are more likely to perceive unfairness. Combined with UMT, this logic suggests that uncertainty makes people care about justice and think about it more carefully.

Barsky and colleagues (2011) add that the certainty of emotions felt will also influence the aggregation of justice perceptions over time. In other words, the certainty of current emotions may determine how large a window of time is retrieved and aggregated when making more global fairness judgments. In support of this argument, Van den Bos, Wilke, Lind, & Vermunt (1998) found that if individuals feel fear (high uncertainty emotion) they are less likely to show substitutability effects in their justice judgments (an aspect of heuristic processing) and, instead, collect and use as much information as possible. In other words, fear was found to lead to more thorough aggregation and less heuristic processing. Similarly, we expect that those experiencing more uncertain emotions will consider larger timespans of experiences when making overall judgments. Uncertainty may not only make people think further back into the past but also look more carefully for cues to predict the future, thus extending people's temporal scale (see Chapter 14 by Patient et al., this volume). To conclude, it seems that the degree of uncertainty that is inherent in an emotion can impact when people (a) gather more information, (b) gather information relating to longer time spans, and (c) process this information more carefully.

The uncertainty dimension of emotions may also stimulate new research on the third party and agent perspectives of justice. For example, if uncertain emotions increase careful and systematic justice processing, then uncertain emotions in managers and other decision makers may lead to more considerate and less biased decisions. This presents an intriguing paradox, since the uncertain emotions that we propose will enhance the enactment of fairness are not emotions typically associated with leadership or power. Indeed, these very emotions may run counter to leadership, because it is those individuals who most demonstrate certainty who are perceived as dominant and thus likely to assume leadership positions. Perhaps one reason that we do not see greater fairness enacted in hierarchical contexts such as organizations is because emotional certainty increases the likelihood that an individual will be selected for a leadership role at the same time that it reduces the likelihood they will behave fairly (by reducing their tendency to engage in systematic justice processing).

The extent to which justice recipients display certain or uncertain emotions may also influence third parties and agents through emotional contagion processes. Specifically, recipients displaying more (less) certain emotions may make other parties feel more (less) certain. Because certainty of affect influences how systematic justice processing will be, this emotional contagion indirectly influences the justice processing of these parties. For example, observing a fearful colleague may evoke feelings of fear in an observing team member, leading the observer to be more systematic in their justice processing. These indirect justice contagion effects may also contribute to the similarity of justice judgments within groups. The emotional contagion processes that can lead to group justice dynamics may not only be due to the valence of the emotion, but also (or instead) to the certainty of the emotion.

Deontic Justice Models: The Morality Dimension

Deontic models of justice suggest that justice motives and reactions to injustice originate not in rational self-interest, concern about uncertainty, or concern about status and exclusion, but rather in the motivation to uphold previously established moral and social standards (Folger, 2001). Deontic models are, therefore, founded upon research in moral psychology, which has recently begun to recognize the importance of emotion. Indeed, both the deontic perspective and moral psychology research on the moral emotions have come to highlight the primacy of the emotional response over the rational and cognitive one (Folger, Cropanzano, & Goldman, 2005; Haidt, 2001; Mullen, 2007; Mullen & Skitka, 2006). This primacy has served as the basis for linking moral motives to specific emotional reactions to injustice (Cropanzano et al., 2011).

Moral emotions refers to a class or subset of emotions that are viewed as a critical component of human's moral apparatus (Tangney, Steuwig, & Mashek, 2007) and are thought to provide the motivational energy driving people to do good and avoid doing bad (Kroll & Egan, 2004). Much of the research on moral emotions focuses on discrete emotions such as guilt and shame (Tangney et al., 2007). However, Haidt (2003) explicitly argues that morality be construed as a dimension of emotion. In particular, Haidt (2003) argues that any emotion can be evaluated on a continuum with respect to how prototypically *moral* the emotion is. The two key attributes serving as the basis for classifying the morality of an emotion are: (a) the elicitors of the emotion; and (b) the nature of the emotion's action tendencies.[3] More prototypically moral emotions (e.g., elevation, compassion, disgust, and guilt) are those that are elicited by the interests of society or people other than the self, and they tend to motivate prosocial behavior (Haidt, 2003).

Efforts to assess how prototypically moral an emotion is are complicated by the fact that moral emotions can be said to be more prototypical based on whether they reflect both disinterested elicitors and prosocial action tendencies (rather than one or the other), as well as how consistently they reflect each of those elicitors and action tendencies. For example, fear is a less prototypical moral emotion because although it may sometimes be elicited by a threat to others, it is most commonly elicited by a threat to the self and thus is not consistently elicited by moral concerns. Disgust takes at least two (and possibly three) forms, with "pure disgust" differentiated from moral disgust with respect to its neural substrates as well as its elicitors and action tendencies (Moll et al., 2005). Haidt (2003) suggests that emotions that reflect only one of the two characteristics (e.g., disinterested elicitors but self-interested action tendencies, or prosocial action tendencies but self-focused elicitors) are more marginal or less prototypical moral emotions. This discussion raises the observation that, although the dimensional approach may hold great value, it can also present complications when it comes to organizing emotions along the dimension.

The dimensional approach to moral emotion is not prominent in the justice literature but the moral relevance of emotions has certainly been an issue of concern for justice scholars (Cropanzano et al., 2011). Most prominently, a number of scholars have explored moral outrage in association with perceived injustice (e.g., Bies, 1987). However, justice research examining moral outrage does not always distinguish it from related emotions, such as anger, that may be invoked by self-interest (rather than social concerns) and may motivate actions that are not prosocial. Inattention to this distinction may be attributed to a focus solely on discrete emotions and not also on the moral dimension of emotions. For example, recipients of injustice may feel angry simply because they perceive that their outcomes are unfair or unfavorable, and thus selfish concerns rather than concern about the violations of moral codes that govern society may elicit their emotion. Furthermore, the anger they feel may motivate them to reduce their effort or diminish their engagement on the job for instrumental or identity-based reasons (e.g., to conserve personal resources), rather than in response to prosocial motives.

Like the valence and certainty dimensions described earlier, the moral dimension of emotion has implications for both reactions to injustice as well as the nature of justice reasoning. According to the CAD triad hypothesis, contempt, anger and disgust (CAD) are three moral emotions triggered across cultures by different violations of moral codes (Rozin, Lowery, Imada, & Haidt, 1999). Although injustice has long been known to elicit anger as indicated earlier, recent evidence suggests that it also elicits disgust and contempt. For example, Skarlicki, Hoegg, Aquino, & Nadisic (2013) recently showed in three experiments that interactional injustice not only triggers an anger response but also elicits moral disgust both for those experiencing the injustice and for third parties. Moreover, they found that experiencing or observing injustice alters both taste and smell consistent with, and indeed mediated by, a disgust response. Recent evidence also suggests that distributive injustice experienced in the context of an ultimatum bargaining game triggers contempt even when controlling for other (not prototypically moral) emotions such as happiness (Tabibnia, Satpute, & Lieberman, 2008).

Moral emotion may also be integral to deontic justice reasoning in that such emotions are recruited to arouse moral motives and thus "moralize" issues, events, and objects. Rozin, Markwith, & Stoess (1997) argue that moral emotions are used to convert preferences into values. By extension, moral emotions such as disgust may imbue events with apparent moral relevance, triggering deontic justice reasoning about those events. For example, Moretti and di Pelligrino (2010) manipulated whether subjects experienced more or less prototypically moral negative emotions (i.e., disgust vs. sadness) or neutral emotion. Then, all subjects were given an unfair offer from a partner in an ultimatum bargaining game, which they could accept or reject. Rejecting the offer conflicts with their rational self-interest because neither partner is paid when offers are rejected. Subjects who experienced disgust were more likely to reject offers than those experiencing sadness or neutral emotion, suggesting that the experience of disgust imbued the injustice event with moral implications.

A dimensional approach to the moral emotions may offer new insight into research regarding the deonance model by emphasizing the underlying motives that drive responses to injustice (i.e., the desire to maintain moral codes and prosocial action orientation). These motives suggest very different subsequent reactions to the experience of injustice than we might otherwise expect. We may be able to distinguish deontic from instrumental or relational reactions to injustice not only with respect to the primacy of the emotional response or the nature of the emotions triggered, but also with respect to the extent to which the behavioral reactions triggered are prosocial versus self-interested. The same action may have different motivations: for example, recipients of injustice may take resources from those that behave unfairly toward them in order to enrich themselves (instrumental concern) or to punish and discourage perpetrators (deontic concerns). Alternatively, different responses may be triggered by moral versus nonmoral emotion (such as effects on taste and smell demonstrated by Skarlicki and colleagues' (2013) research described earlier). To the extent that moral emotions are triggered by justice violations, recipients and observers may be motivated to engage in proactive and constructive efforts to change the system and insure justice rather than more destructive efforts to merely retaliate. Moral emotions in response to injustice may elicit productive engagement rather than the withdrawal and disengagement suggested by equity theory. This discussion demonstrates how taking a moral dimension approach may offer novel insight into the possible consequences of injustice.

Moral emotions may influence our expectations of agents as well as recipients and third parties. Agents' moral emotions, such as guilt and remorse, play a crucial role in restorative justice (e.g., Fehr &

Gelfand, 2012), serving as the basis for repairing injustice. Research on restorative justice (Fehr & Gelfand, 2012; Okimoto, Wenzel & Feather, 2009) is explicitly focused on the interdependent roles of agents, recipients, and third parties in producing justice. Although the deontic model has primarily focused on the immediate experience of and reactions to injustice, restorative justice takes a long-term focus, emphasizing how injustices may be addressed and relationships repaired. Moral emotions, such as agents' feeling of guilt and recipients' empathy for agents of injustice, serve as a bridge linking deontic justice perspectives to restorative justice, and thus broadening the temporal scope of scholarship from before and during justice events to long afterward, when reparation is made.

Moreover, although deontic perspectives assume that justice violations trigger emotional reactions, a dimensional approach to the moral emotions raises the possibility that justice (in addition to injustice) may elicit socially beneficial emotions. Specifically, research on the moral emotions highlights a host of other-praising moral emotions elicited by moral behavior, such as awe, elevation, and gratitude (Haidt, 2003). Thus, the moral dimension highlights a wider and more diverse spectrum of discrete emotions that may be implicated in justice events, providing scholars with a vocabulary and theoretical basis for exploring the emotional responses to justice as a complement to emotional responses to injustice. Research might consider which parties are more likely to experience other-praising emotions such as gratitude in response to justice. For example, those who experience fairness when they did not expect it and third parties who are highly identified with the group might feel moral emotions such as gratitude in response to justice, perhaps motivating them to strengthen their engagement and effort.

Likewise, work on moral emotions suggests that people's tendencies toward norm enforcement or norm obedience may interact with their justice experiences to shape the emotions they experience. For example, those oriented toward norm enforcement may experience other-condemning emotions such as disgust and anger in response to injustice, whereas those oriented toward norm obedience may experience guilt. Orientation toward norm enforcement or norm obedience may vary by role—for example, agents may be particularly aware of their failure to obey norms and thus may experience guilt. Guilt has been relatively neglected in the deontic justice literature to date, although it has important implications for whether prior deontic violations will reduce or increase the likelihood of future violations (because guilt has been shown to elicit prosocial subsequent behaviors when opportunities for reparation are present; Amodio, Devine, & Harmon-Jones, 2007).

Relational Models of Justice: The Social Dimensions

The relational models of justice (Lind & Tyler, 1988; Tyler & Blader, 2000, 2003; Tyler & Lind, 1992) represent the fourth prevailing justice theory that we will cover. The relational models primarily emphasize the relational function served by justice. According to these models, justice judgments serve as a signal of the nature of the relationship between interacting parties and thus reactions to justice are explained by this function served by justice. In other words, these theories argue that people care about justice because they care about their relationships with others, with their groups, and with group authorities. The relational models have strong connections to affect and affective dimensions, since social relationships are affect-laden. Social relationships both shape affect and are shaped by affect, and since justice is a proxy for the nature of those relationships we likewise expect that the relational signals cued by justice shape the affect experienced in reaction to a justice encounter, and that affect associated with social relationships will shape the evaluation of justice in the first place.

The relational models of justice are, therefore, relevant to any affective dimension that relates to social dynamics. Indeed, the relational models provide the theoretical grounding for linkages between justice and affect that reflects the social relationship between parties. This refers to affect that reveals and influences the connection between the individual experiencing the affect and their social world. Next in our discussion, we focus on three affective dimensions that describe a person's relationship to their social context: social orientation, inward (versus outward) focus and congruence.

SOCIAL ORIENTATION

The social orientation dimension emerges from studies that reveal that self-construal differs substantially across cultures, although it can also vary within cultures (Chen, Brockner, & Chen, 2002; Markus & Kitayama, 1991, 2001). This work demonstrates that, on average, East Asians construe the self as being inherently embedded in and interdependent with others, and, thus, social harmony is a primary goal. In contrast, those in the West construe the self as being independent from others and focused on individual agency. Based on these insights, Kitayama and colleagues proposed that there are systematic cultural differences in emotional experience and expression between East and West, differences that they describe as based on the "social orientation" of the emotion (Kitayama, Karasawa & Mesquita, 2004; Kitayama, Markus & Kurokawa, 2000; Kitayama, Mesquita & Karasawa, 2006; Markus & Kitayama, 1991, 2001).

At one end of the social orientation continuum are the socially engaging emotions, which reflect and reinforce an interdependent self-construal and social harmony and hence are more likely to be experienced by those with an interdependent self construal. Kitayama and colleagues suggest that when those with an interdependent self-construal achieve goals that support or enhance valued relationships, they will experience positively valenced socially engaging emotions such as respect (an emotion that includes a concern for others and an aspect of mutuality, Frei & Shaver, 2002). However, when such individuals fail to achieve such goals, they will experience negatively valenced socially engaging emotions such as guilt. Guilt is a prototypical socially engaging emotion in that it reflects feelings that one has violated a norm and, hence, harmed others (Ortony, Clore, & Collins, 1988; Tangney & Dearing, 2002) and motivates restoration of the harmed relationship (Baumeister, Stillewell, & Heatherton, 1994; Leith & Baumeister, 1998; Tangney, Stuewig, & Mashek, 2007). Hence, guilt motivates individuals to act in the service of social harmony.

In contrast, the socially disengaging emotions reflect and bolster an independent self-construal, and the associated value placed on individual agency and the pursuit of individualized goals. Hence, those with an independent self-construal are more likely to experience these emotions. As an illustration, when someone with an independent self-construal achieves a personal goal or acts in a way that is consistent with their individual values, they will experience feelings of pride in their own accomplishments. If they fail, they will experience negative socially disengaging emotions like anger and frustration.

Importantly, the same event may prompt very different appraisals and affective reactions depending on prevailing culture, and hence self-construal. For example, individuals with an independent self-construal are likely to experience pride after being singled out for praise by a manager. This event is consistent with the goals of individualized achievement and agency that are critical for those with an independent self-construal, and the event itself is likely to be appraised as being a deserved fulfillment of a central goal. In contrast, an employee with an interdependent self-construal is likely to appraise the same event as revealing that he/she has sought to differentiate him/herself from the group, thus potentially threatening group harmony. Such appraisals may lead an employee to experience shame and embarrassment.

To date, the social orientation dimension of emotions has received little attention outside of cultural psychology. However, related work reveals that justice recipients' emotional reactions to justice are similarly influenced by their self-construal. In particular, those with a more interdependent self-construal are particularly tolerant of unfavorable outcomes reached via a fair process (Holmvall & Bobocel, 2008; Brockner, De Cremer, van den Bos & Chen, 2005). These findings are consistent with the relational models of justice which suggest that people care about fairness because it provides important information about their standing in the group—which is particularly important to those with an interdependent self-construal (e.g., Tyler & Lind, 1992; Tyler & Blader, 2000).

Extending this work to justice agents and incorporating the social orientation dimension leads to several novel predictions about the emotional responses of justice agents to their own enactment of fairness and unfairness. For instance, justice agents with an interdependent self-construal may be particularly likely to experience positively valenced, socially engaging emotions (e.g., feelings of closeness and mutual respect) when enacting high outcome and process fairness. In contrast, justice agents with an independent self-construal may experience socially disengaging emotions such as pride when they make fair decisions, which can, in turn, undermine some of the benefits to group members' engagement that follow from the enactment of fairness.

The social orientation dimension also provides new insight into emotional responses to different types of fairness and unfairness. For instance, self-construal alters justice judgments such that those with a more strongly independent self-construal perceive justice through a more egocentric lens than those with a more interdependent self-construal (Gelfand et al, 2002). For those with an independent self-construal (who thus interpret justice more egocentrically) underadvantage is likely to be perceived as particularly unfair and undeserved and hence prompt anger (a negative, socially disengaging emotion). However, these same individuals may be particularly likely to view treatment that unfairly overadvantages them as deserved and facilitating differentiation from others, hence prompting pride and other positive, socially disengaging emotions.

In contrast, individuals with an interdependent self-construal may be particularly likely to experience negative socially engaging emotions like embarrassment and guilt following overadvantage, and, instead, experience positive socially engaging emotions when receiving treatment that is equivalent to others' (whether fair or unfair) as this does not disrupt social harmony. Indeed, for those with an interdependent self construal, past research reveals that who is enacting unfairness also shapes justice reactions, such that they react especially negatively to unfair treatment by a close other (Chen, Chen, & Portnoy, 2009, Study 2). Extending this logic to justice agents, we might expect those with interdependent self-construals to feel particularly guilty (a negatively valenced socially engaging emotion) when they treat a close other unfairly.

In sum, although relatively less justice research has directly examined the social-orientation dimension, we see great potential value in thinking about this dimension. At a minimum, it has the potential of bringing an affective lens toward research that integrates justice and self-construal. Beyond that, however, it raises the potential for predicting and explaining a new range of phenomena particularly related to justice agents and recipients.

INWARD- VERSUS OUTWARD-FOCUSED EMOTIONS

Inward-focused emotions reflect internal attributions of responsibility (e.g., guilt and shame), whereas outward-focused emotions occur when the other party is held responsible (e.g., anger and hostility) Tangney & Dearing, 2002). This affective dimension was shown to be pivotal for specific justice dynamics by Barclay, Skarlicki, and Pugh (2005), who argue that when outcomes are negative, people use procedural and interactional justice to make attributions of responsibility for the outcome. Drawing on Spreecher's work (1986), they suggest that when procedural and interactional justice is high then the person is likely to attribute responsibility for the negative outcome to themselves. This leads to negative inward-focused emotions such as guilt, but low outward-focused emotion such as anger, which, in turn, has a complex set of implications for both the self as well as for social relations.

Barclay et al. (2005) tested these predictions on a sample of 173 people who had been laid off during cost cutting or restructuring programs. Participants' emotions regarding their layoff experienced were measured, including two negative inward-focused emotions: shame and guilt, and two negative outward-focused emotions: anger and hostility. The perceived outcome favorability of the layoff was also measured. The predictions were confirmed, insofar as people were found to react with more shame and guilt when procedural or interpersonal justice were high and outcomes were unfavorable, but they reacted with more anger and hostility when procedural or interpersonal justice were low and outcomes were unfavorable. Interestingly, inward- and outward-focused emotions were highly correlated, suggesting that people can experience both at the same time.

Overall, these results demonstrate the usefulness of the inward- versus outward-focused dimension in explaining different patterns for emotions that have the same valence (negative). Further stressing the importance of the distinction between outward-versus inward-focused emotions, Barclay and her colleagues found that it was only outward-focused emotions that mediated the interaction of outcome favorability and interactional justice with organizational retaliatory behaviors. This highlights the linkage between these emotions and the relational models, since it indicates that it is primarily those emotions and moods that speak to social relations (e.g., emotions that orient individuals away from others, such as anger and hostility) that lead to outcomes that reflect social relations. Although the Barclay et al. (2005) study focuses on negative outward emotions and thus on organizational retaliatory behaviors, it is likely the case that positive outward emotions (e.g., pride, respect) and affect more generally would produce positive group-oriented outcomes. Indeed, this is precisely the findings in much of the research on the relational models, which often show that pride and respect follow from justice judgments and moreover that they may mediate the effect of justice on downstream outcomes such as engagement. Notably, inward social emotions—either positive or negative—will not likely shape outcomes that reflect nor enrich social relations, and in this way the inward versus outward dimension is extremely relevant to understanding when and why the relational models may be more or less relevant to understanding a particular justice encounter and its subsequent consequences.

Much additional research is needed on the inward versus outward dimension. As is the case with all the dimensions discussed in this chapter, such work should focus on how inward- versus outward-focused affect impacts justice judgments; how it may follow from justice judgments; when justice matters; and in what ways justice matters (i.e., justice reactions). Of course, it is critical to understand the full range of factors (including those related to the justice encounter) that may lead to the experience of inward versus outward affect in the first place.

CONGRUENCE

Perhaps the most recent affective dimension that has been theorized and tested for its relationship to justice dynamics is congruence (Blader, Wiesenfeld, Fortin, & Wheeler-Smith, 2013; Blader, Wiesenfeld, Rothman, & Wheeler-Smith, 2010). This dimension applies to a specific class of emotions, namely evaluative social emotions, defined as feelings that represent an appraisal of a social target. Such emotions include empathy, love, pride in other, vicarious joy, schadenfreude, envy, and resentment. Because they describe how one feels about social targets, social emotions capture the social relationship between individuals (Blader et al., 2010). They are, therefore, an omnipresent and powerful factor in social contexts and when thinking about the relational models of justice.

The congruence dimension organizes evaluative social emotions according to the orientation toward the target of the emotion (as opposed, for instance, to the valence or level of arousal of the emotion). The dimension itself runs from congruent to incongruent. The congruence end of the dimension refers to an orientation that indicates being aligned with (i.e., "in step with") the target. When a perceiver experiences a congruent social emotion (such as empathy, pride in other, vicarious joy, love, and admiration), the psychological distance between themselves and the target is reduced and they come to think and feel in ways similar to their impressions of how the target thinks and feels. For instance, they come to think about and react to situations from the target's perspective, rather than their own perspective. The incongruence end of the dimension refers to an orientation marked by being oppositionally oriented to the target (i.e., repulsed by). When a perceiver experiences an incongruent social emotion (such as schadenfreude, resentment, envy, hate, and contempt), not only is the psychological distance between them increased, but that distance is driven by an effort to distinguish oneself from the target. Incongruence is, therefore, not merely disengagement; it reflects repulsion from the target. Since congruence varies as a function of the target in question, congruence—unlike the social orientation discussed earlier—may vary not only across individuals but also within individuals.

Both congruence and incongruence prompt engagement with the target—a defining feature of evaluative social emotions—but congruence pulls parties together, whereas incongruence pushes them apart. This is critical for drawing linkages with the relational models of justice, since those models argue that justice concerns take on particular emphasis when parties are engaged with one another. Social emotions, therefore, make justice reasoning and concerns more prominent—as per the relational models—but congruence shapes the nature of a social emotion's influence on justice.

The congruence dimension has been particularly valuable for conceptualizing third party reactions to under- and overadvantage (the latter being a relatively neglected form of injustice). For example, in one study (Blader et al., 2013; Study 2) participants in the role of third parties were led to feel congruent, incongruent, or neutral toward a target recipient of injustice. The injustice was either objective under- or overadvantage. Participants primed to feel congruence reacted quite favorably to the target being overadvantaged, and indeed regarded the treatment as fair. In contrast, participants in the incongruent conditions reacted quite negatively to the target being overadvantaged and perceived it as extremely unfair in comparison to their neutral emotion counterparts.

Participants who observed a target being underadvantaged displayed the opposite pattern. Specifically, congruence led participants to view underadvantage as quite negative and unfair, but justice judgments and reactions were relatively favorable in the incongruent conditions. Notably, in all cases, the effects of congruence on downstream reactions to the situation were mediated by justice judgments, suggesting that congruence shapes whether third parties perceive unfair situations as fair.

Blader and colleagues (2013) validate the congruence dimension by demonstrating that manipulations of various discrete emotions—instead of congruence itself—can prompt the same effects. Moreover, they consistently find that congruence manipulations prompt variations in a variety of discrete social emotions felt toward the target. These findings demonstrate that dimensions themselves (rather than the discrete emotions they characterize) can be manipulated in empirical research and thus provide insight into the influence of a wide array of affective states at once. That is, they corroborate our emphasis on dimensions and show that research can directly examine given dimensions without relying on discrete emotions themselves.

The social relations—and thus felt social emotions—between third parties and justice agents may likewise reflect congruence. Consider a third party feeling a social emotion characterized by congruence toward a justice agent—for example, a top executive who feels empathy toward a supervisor who must lay off his/her subordinates. The alignment that the executive feels toward the supervisor may have positive consequences, such as greater appreciation for the balancing act often involved in behaving fairly. That alignment may also have negative consequences, such as if the executive experiences some of the same biased ethical reasoning, justification processes, and ultimately favoritism that may influence the supervisor herself. Furthermore, incongruence (and its oppositional orientation) with agents may lead to the tendency to deride an agent's decisions as unfair, even when they are fair. Note that this is more than healthy skepticism; rather, it is a uniform bias to regard any actions agents undertake as unfair (in opposition to agents themselves who are likely to see their actions as fair).

Although necessarily more engaged, the effects of congruence (and of social emotions in general) cannot be said to be consistently positive or negative. Congruence may prevent third parties from objectively evaluating a situation (as when it leads them to perceive overadvantage as fair), but we also highlighted cases in which congruence may prompt greater insight and perspective (as when it leads them to better understand agents' trade-offs and perspectives).

Since congruence is a dimension of social emotions, and since social emotions can be present in all social contexts, every justice encounter is open to influence by the social emotions felt toward the respective parties. In other words, not only third parties but also justice agents and decision recipients may be impacted by congruence. For example, justice agents who experience congruent social emotions may operate less as dispassionate authorities and instead embrace the perspectives, concerns, and reactions of the decision recipient, perhaps enacting unfairness as a consequence. Indeed, Blader and Rothman (2014) found that decision makers who felt empathy (a congruent social emotion) toward a decision recipient showed favoritism for the target of their emotions even though doing so comes at a cost to others (in the form of reduced resource pools) and may come at a cost to themselves (in the form of being perceived as unfair by the affected third parties, and the loss of trust and legitimacy associated with those perceptions). These effects are due to the effect of congruence on justice judgments: empathy led these decision makers to see what is objectively preferential treatment as fair. Ironically, their unfairness was in the service of the justice motive.

A congruence-focused analysis of recipients would suggest an affect-based and nonrational mechanism to explain recipients' orientation to justice agents. This complements the decidedly rational and information-based approach offered in existing research (e.g., Tyler, Degoey & Smith, 1996; Tyler & Lind, 1992). As such, a congruence analysis may add to an accumulating body of evidence that justice judgments can be impacted by factors that are not inherently rational (e.g., Bianchi & Brockner, 2012; Blader, 2007) and perhaps have little to do with the actual justice encountered.

When justice recipients feel social emotions marked by congruence toward the justice agent, they will be more likely to analyze the fairness of the encounter—and react to the encounter—from the justice agent's perspective. This may prompt more comprehensive reasoning about fairness in the situation, and may lead them to see fairness where they may not otherwise. In this way, congruence can have both positive and negative consequences for justice recipients. On one hand, congruence may lead to more balanced justice evaluations, moving people away from their tendency to egocentrically evaluate fairness and to instead factor in a wider range of considerations that the justice agent faces. On the other hand, congruence may prompt recipients to evaluate justice with an overly benevolent lens, which can, in turn, provide leeway for justice agents to, in fact, treat their recipients less justly. (The extent to which agents do so is likely determined by many factors, not the least important of which might be the congruence they feel toward the recipient.) In contrast, recipients feeling incongruent social emotions have an oppositional orientation toward the justice agent that will predispose them to distrust the agent (e.g., to take a stance of presumptive mistrust) and to maintain psychological distance from those agents. By maintaining a view of those agents as unfair, they are able to maintain this distance and more generally to sustain a negative dynamic with those parties.

Overall, a congruence-dimension analysis of justice has the potential to shed a great deal of light on justice dynamics. That is, the congruence of the social emotions that are active in a given justice encounter can tell us a great deal about how justice will be evaluated from the perspective of all parties to the encounter (recipients, agents, and third parties). Importantly, the congruence approach can also shed light on divergence in opinions about whether fairness is occurring. Disagreements among parties about whether a given encounter is fair or unfair are common and present a vexing paradox for justice researchers. One explanation for this lack of consensus may be rooted in social emotions. Since social emotions are relationship-specific, two people in the same role (and with the same information) may well arrive at very different justice judgments due to their respective social emotions felt toward the justice agent and recipient. The value of a dimension-based approach is also apparent in this analysis. Although the range of social emotions that justice agents may feel toward decision recipients is vast, focusing on a dimension along which they vary enables us to use one basic premise to generate a number of predictions about how a range of social emotions impact justice parties' fairness perceptions, decisions, and actions. Although there may be attributes of discrete social emotions that moderate the overall pattern implied by the congruence of the social emotion, the dimensional approach provides a starting point by capturing the baseline effect.

Conclusion

Prior research linking justice and affect has been largely focused on discrete emotions and the affective experience of justice recipients. In this chapter, we suggest that opportunities to advance the literature may emerge from taking a complementary approach, leveraging new research in the literature on affective dimensions and expanding our scope to consider multiple parties (recipients, agents, and third-party observers) as both the targets and the experiencers of affect. Although the dimensional approach that we outline cannot replace the rich and nuanced exploration of discrete emotions and moods, we suggest that it may help scholars generate new insight in multiple ways. Moreover, scholarship in the area of affect has not extensively focused on justice (whether perceptions, judgments, behaviors or reactions) as either antecedents or consequences of emotion. Instead, justice scholars have conducted most of the work linking justice and affect. And yet, according to affective events theory (Weiss & Cropanzano, 1996), justice events have all the hallmarks of affect-provoking and affect-laden instances. Justice is inherently social, with multiple parties involved, all of whom experience, express, and perceive an incredible range of emotions and moods. Thus, justice may be an area ripe for exploration by affect researchers.

It is also worth considering that key elements of procedural justice have the effect of putting parties into closer contact with one another, of providing greater opportunity for affect to arise, of spreading via contagion processes or otherwise conveyed, and, thus, of impacting important outcomes. For example, providing opportunities for voice, giving advance notice, demonstrating consideration and dignified and respectful treatment, and providing a customized account are all ways in which justice agents and recipients are brought into intimate contact and by which justice events become more personalized. These conditions are fertile for affect to arise and to critically shape evaluations of and reactions to those events.

The approach that we take in the present chapter may also generate new opportunities to advance the justice literature. We have mapped recent research on dimensions of affect onto some of the most prominent models of justice. For example, the uncertainty dimension of emotion corresponds with the uncertainty management model in that both focus on the discomfort of uncertainty; the moral dimension of emotion corresponds with deontic models of justice in that both highlight the prominence of moral and ethical values; and the social dimension of emotion corresponds with the relational model in that both draw attention to the role and importance of social relationships and inclusion. Linkages between these affective dimensions and corresponding justice models can help create new insights. For example, third parties and justice agents may feel congruent emotions toward justice recipients, altering what they perceive as fair and thus explaining their concern with recipients' experiences. Similarly, injustice, may elicit a wide range of uncertain emotions, including anxiety and ambivalence. These emotional consequences of justice may be just as likely among third parties and agents as recipients. Survivors of layoffs may be extremely anxious merely from observing the injustice that victims experience, and agents may feel ambivalence from perpetrating injustice. Moreover, these emotions may, in turn, generate consequences that are not yet anticipated in current justice theory. For example, ambivalence has been shown to make people more deliberative (Rothman, 2011) and to have important consequences for decision-making.

Although our analysis provides one form of integration (mapping affective dimensions to justice theories and thus deriving new insights for each), additional forms of integration lie outside our scope and, therefore, offer opportunities for future advancement. For example, although we have identified and differentiated the moral, certainty, and social dimensions, these different dimensions can also be mapped onto one another or onto the original dimensions of the affective circumplex (i.e., valence and arousal). Intriguing insights may emerge when thinking about insights that can emerge at the intersection of multiple affective dimensions. Likewise, scholars have treated the various justice motives as distinct but possibly co-occurring (e.g., people may be pulled in different directions by simultaneous self-interest, uncertain management, and moral motives in relation to justice). Defining how different affective dimensions relate to one another may lend insight into how different justice theories relate to one another, potentially bringing greater clarity to both literatures.

One important issue that justice scholars are struggling to identify conceptually is collective justice perceptions and reactions—that is, how justice perceptions are meaningfully shared across a group of individuals in a way that shapes group-level behaviors, outcomes, norms, and so forth. Affect may be an important mechanism through which individual-level justice cognitions and atomized justice events shape collectives. Our analysis of multiple parties involved in justice events (recipient, agent, third party) and research on emotion cycles in the affect literature may be usefully leveraged to understand these dynamic processes (Hareli & Raphaeli, 2008). In particular, because emotions spread through nonconscious contagion processes such as mimicry, as well as through conscious and even rational pathways, emotion may shape the justice judgments and reactions of even fairly large groups in a consistent way. For example, it is possible that it is only when individual justice events elicit emotional reactions among third-party observers that individual-level injustice elicits collective-level processes. The emotion that arises from such justice events may spread and reverberate, thus shaping collective outcomes such as social movements. For example, the Occupy movement was based on widespread feelings of outrage among third parties over social inequality, and it channeled that outrage into social pressure to redefine inequality not as a functional effect of capitalist economies and competition but as a referendum on the fairness of our society, which influenced political rhetoric and perhaps shaped outcomes like Federal elections. Absent emotions such as outrage among third parties, the collectivization that defined the Occupy movement may not have taken hold nor might consensus have developed around the justice issues at hand.

In closing, we wish to emphasize that justice is a mature field of scholarship and, therefore, novel theoretical insights are likely to emerge less from incremental advances and more from entirely new approaches. In this chapter, we emphasize work that broadens the scope of research on justice and affect, beyond discrete emotions and the emotional reactions to injustice of recipients. We highlight emergent affective dimensions (e.g., certainty, morality, congruence), the effect of emotion on justice judgments, and the emotional experiences and expressions of third parties and agents, as well as recipients. Future research informed by these approaches is likely to contribute both to justice scholarship and to our understanding of affect.

Notes

1. In this chapter, we adopt a broad focus, and thus consider research that relates justice to all types of affect; namely moods, emotions, and dispositional affect. Later, we define and differentiate these types of affect.
2. Often utilizing the PANAS scale to measure affect, these studies do not reliably distinguish between moods and emotions
3. The moral dimension is thus more likely to characterize emotions than moods or affect in general because emotions have more specific elicitors and action tendencies.

References

Adams, J. S. (1965). Inequity in social exchange. *Advances in Experimental Social Psychology, 2*, 267–299.

Amodio, D. M., Devine, P. G., & Harmon-Jones, E. (2007). A dynamic model of guilt implications for motivation and self-regulation in the context of prejudice. *Psychological Science, 18*(6), 524–530.

Barclay, L. J., & Kiefer, T. (2014). Approach or avoid? Exploring overall justice and the differential effects of positive and negative emotions. Journal of Management. *40*(7), 1857–1898.

Barclay, L. J., Skarlicki, D. P., & Pugh, S. D. (2005). Exploring the role of emotions in injustice perceptions and retaliation. *Journal of Applied Psychology, 90*, 629–643.

Barrett, L. F. (2006). Are emotions natural kinds? *Perspectives on Psychological Science, 1*, 28–58.

Barrett, L. F., & Russell, J. A. (1999). The structure of current affect controversies and emerging consensus. *Current Directions in Psychological Science, 8*(1), 10–14.

Barsky, A., Kaplan, S. A., & Beal, D. J. (2011). Just feelings? The role of affect in the formation of organizational fairness judgments. *Journal of Management, 3*, 248–279.

Baumeister, R. F., Stillwell, A. M., & Heatherton, T. F. (1994). Guilt: an interpersonal approach. *Psychological Bulletin, 115*, 243–267.

Bianchi, E. C., & Brockner, J. (2012). In the eyes of the beholder? The role of dispositional trust in judgments of procedural and interactional fairness. *Organizational Behavior and Human Decision Processes, 118*, 46–59.

Bies, R. J. (1987). The predicament of injustice: The management of moral outrage. *Research in Organizational Behavior, 9*, 289–313.

Blader, S. L. (2007). What determines people's fairness judgments? Identification and outcomes influence procedural justice evaluations under uncertainty. *Journal of Experimental Social Psychology, 43*, 986–994.

Blader, S. L., & Rothman, N. B. (2014). Paving the road to preferential treatment with good intentions: Empathy, accountability and fairness. *Journal of Experimental Social Psychology, 50*, 65–81.

Blader, S. L., Wiesenfeld, B. M., Fortin, M., &Wheeler-Smith, S. L. (2013). Fairness lies in the heart of the beholder: How the social emotions of third parties influence reactions to injustice. *Organizational Behavior and Human Decision Processes, 121*, 62–80.

Blader, S. L., Wiesenfeld, B., Rothman, R., & Wheeler-Smith, S. (2010). Social emotions and justice: How the emotional fabric of groups determines justice enactment and reactions. In E. A. Mannix, M. A. Neale (Series Eds.) & E. Mullen (Vol. Ed.), *Research on managing groups and teams: Fairness & groups* (pp. 29–62). Bingley, UK: Emerald.

Brockner, J., De Cremer, D., van den Bos, K., & Chen, Y. R. (2005). The influence of interdependent self-construal on procedural fairness effects. *Organizational Behavior and Human Decision Processes, 96*, 155–167.

Brown, M. E., & Treviño, L. K. (2006). Ethical leadership: A review and future directions. *The Leadership Quarterly, 17*, 595–616.

Chen, Y. R., Brockner, J., & Chen, X. P. (2002). Individual–collective primacy and ingroup favoritism: Enhancement and protection effects. *Journal of Experimental Social Psychology, 38*, 482–491.

Chen, Y. R., Chen, X. P., & Portnoy, R. (2009). To whom do positive norm and negative norm of reciprocity apply? Effects of inequitable offer, relationship, and relational-self orientation. *Journal of Experimental Social Psychology, 45*, 24–34.

Cohen-Charash, Y., & Byrne, Z. S. (2008). Affect and justice—current knowledge and future directions. In N. M. Ashkanasy, & C. L. Cooper (Eds.), *Research Companion to Emotion in Organizations* (pp. 360–391). Edward Elgar, Northampton, MA.

Colquitt, J. A., Scott, B. A., Rodell, J. B., Long, D. M., Zapata, C. P., Conlon, D. E., & Wesson, M. J. (2013). Justice at the millennium, a decade later: A meta-analytic test of social exchange and affect-based perspectives. *Journal of Applied Psychology, 98*, 199–236.

Cropanzano, R., Stein, J. H., & Nadisic, T. (2011). *Social justice and the experience of human emotion.* New York, NY: Routledge.

De Cremer, D. (2007). *Advances in the psychology of justice and affect.* Information Age.

De Cremer, D., Wubben, M. J., & Brebels, L. (2008). When unfair treatment leads to anger: The effects of other people's emotions and ambiguous unfair procedures1. *Journal of Applied Social Psychology, 38*, 2518–2549.

Deutsch, M. (1975). Equity, equality, and need: What determines which value will be used as the basis of distributive justice?. *Journal of Social Issues, 31*, 137–149.

Ekman, P. (1999). Basic emotions. *Handbook of cognition and emotion, 4*, 5–60.

Ellis, H. C., & Moore, B. A. (2005) Mood and memory. In T. Dalgleish and M. J. Power (Eds.), *Handbook of Cognition and Emotion.* Chichester, UK: Wiley.

Fehr, R., & Gelfand, M. J. (2012). The forgiving organization: A multilevel model of forgiveness at work. *Academy of Management Review, 37*, 664–688.

Folger, R. (2001). Fairness as deonance. *Theoretical and Cultural Perspectives on Organizational Justice*, 3–33.

Folger, R., & Cropanzano, R. (2001). Fairness theory: Justice as accountability. *Advances in Organizational Justice*, 1–55.

Folger, R., Cropanzano, R., & Goldman, B. (2005). What is the relationship between justice and morality? In J. Greenberg & J. Colquitt (Eds.), *The handbook of organizational justice* (pp. 215–245). Mahwah, NJ: Lawrence Erlbaum Associates.

Forgas, J. P. (2003). Affective influences on attitudes and judgments. In R. J. Davidson, K. R. Scherer and H. Goldsmith, (Eds.), *Handbook of affective sciences* (pp. 596–618). Oxford University Press.

Fredrickson, B. L. (2001). The role of positive emotions in positive psychology: The broaden-and-build theory of positive emotions. *American Psychologist, 56*, 218–226.

Frei, J. R., & Shaver, P. R. (2002). Respect in close relationships: Prototype definition, self report assessment, and initial correlates. *Personal Relationships, 9*, 121–139.

Frijda, N. H. (1986). *The emotions.* Cambridge University Press.

Gelfand, M. J., Higgins, M., Nishii, L. H., Raver, J. L., Dominguez, A., Murakami, F., . . . & Toyama, M. (2002). Culture and egocentric perceptions of fairness in conflict and negotiation. *Journal of Applied Psychology, 87*, 833.

George, J. M., & Brief, A. P. (1992). Feeling good-doing good: a conceptual analysis of the mood at work-organizational spontaneity relationship. *Psychological Bulletin, 112*, 310.

Greene, J., & Haidt, J. (2002). How (and where) does moral judgment work? *Trends in Cognitive Sciences, 6*(12), 517–523.

Haidt, J. (2001). The emotional dog and its rational tail: a social intuitionist approach to moral judgment. *Psychological Review, 108*, 814.

Haidt, J. (2003). The moral emotions. *Handbook of affective sciences* (pp. 852–870).

Hareli, S., & Rafaeli, A. (2008). Emotion cycles: On the social influence of emotion in organizations. *Research in organizational behavior, 28*, 35–59.

Holmvall, C. M., & Bobocel, D. R. (2008). What fair procedures say about me: Self-construals and reactions to procedural fairness. *Organizational Behavior and Human Decision Processes, 105*, 147–168.

Kitayama, S., Karasawa, M., & Mesquita, B. (2004). Collective and personal processes in regulating emotions: Emotion and self in Japan and the United States. *The regulation of emotion*, 251–273.

Kitayama, S., Markus, H. R., & Kurokawa, M. (2000). Culture, emotion, and well-being: Good feelings in Japan and the United States. *Cognition & Emotion, 14*, 93–124.

Kitayama, S., Mesquita, B., & Karasawa, M. (2006). Cultural affordances and emotional experience: socially engaging and disengaging emotions in Japan and the United States. *Journal of Personality and Social Psychology, 91*(5), 890–903.

Kroll, J., & Egan, E. (2004). Psychiatry, moral worry, and the moral emotions. *Journal of Psychiatric Practice, 10*, 352–360.

Lang, P. J., Bradley, M. M., & Cuthbert, B. N. (1997). Motivated attention: Affect, activation, and action. In P. J. Lang, R. F. Simons, & M. T. Balaban (Eds.), Attention and orienting: Sensory and motivational processes (pp. 97–135). Hillsdale, NJ: Erlbaum.

Lazarus, R. S., & Cohen-Charash, Y. (2001). Discrete emotions in organizational life. *Emotions at work: Theory, research and applications for management*, 45–81.

Leith, K. P., & Baumeister, R. F. (1998). Empathy, shame, guilt, and narratives of interpersonal conflicts: Guilt prone people are better at perspective taking. *Journal of Personality, 66*, 1–37.

Lerner, J. S., Gonzalez, R. M., Small, D. A., & Fischhoff, B. (2003). Effects of fear and anger on perceived risks of terrorism A national field experiment. *Psychological Science, 14*, 144–150.

Lerner, J. S., & Keltner, D. (2000). Beyond valence: Toward a model of emotion-specific influences on judgement and choice. *Cognition & Emotion, 14*, 473–493.

Lerner, J. S., & Keltner, D. (2001). Fear, anger, and risk. *Journal of Personality and Social Psychology, 81*, 146.

Lerner, J. S., Small, D. A., & Loewenstein, G. (2004). Heart strings and purse strings: Carryover effects of emotions on economic decisions. *Psychological Science, 15*, 337–341.

Lind, E. A., & Tyler, T. R. (1988). *The social psychology of procedural justice*. New York, NY: Plenum.

Lindquist, K. A., Siegel, E. H., Quigley, K., & Barrett, L. F. (2013). The hundred-year emotion war: are emotions natural kinds or psychological constructions? Comment on Lench, Flores, and Bench (2011). *Psychological Bulletin, 139*, 255–263.

Markus, H. R., & Kitayama, S. (1991). Culture and the self: Implications for cognition, emotion, and motivation. *Psychological Review, 98*, 224.

Markus, H. R., & Kitayama, S. (2001). The cultural construction of self and emotion: Implications for social behavior. *Emotions in social psychology: Essential reading*, 119–137.

Mauss, I. B., & Robinson, M. D. (2009). Measures of emotion: A review. *Cognition and Emotion, 23*, 209–237.

Mikula, G., Scherer, K. R., & Athenstaedt, U. (1998). The role of injustice in the elicitation of differential emotional reactions. *Personality and Social Psychology Bulletin, 24*, 769–783.

Moll, J., de Oliveira-Souza, R., Moll, F., Ignácio, F., Bramati, I., Caparelli-Dáquer, E., & Eslinger, P. (2005). The moral affiliations of disgust: A functional MRI study. *Cognitive & Behavioral Neurology, 18, 68–78.*

Moretti, L., & di Pellegrino, G. (2010). Disgust selectively modulates reciprocal fairness in economic interactions. *Emotion, 10*(2), 169–180.

Mullen, E. (2007). The reciprocal relationship between affect and perceptions of fairness. In K. Tornblom & R. Vermunt (Eds.), *Distributive and Procedural Justice: Research and Social Applications* (pp. 15–37). Burlington, VT: Ashgate.

Mullen, E., & Skitka, L. J. (2006). Exploring the psychological underpinnings of the moral mandate effect: Motivated reasoning, group differentiation, or anger? *Journal of Personality and Social Psychology, 90*, 629.

Okimoto, T. G., Wenzel, M., & Feather, N. T. (2009). Beyond retribution: Conceptualizing restorative justice and exploring its determinants. *Social Justice Research, 22*, 156–180.

Ortony, A., Clore, G., & Collins, A. (1988). *The cognitive structure of emotions*. New York: Cambridge University Press.

Panksepp, J. (2007). Neurologizing the psychology of affects: How appraisal-based constructivism and basic emotion theory can coexist. *Perspectives on Psychological Science, 2*, 281–296.

Rothman, N. B. (2011). Steering sheep: How expressed emotional ambivalence elicits dominance in interdependent decision making contexts. *Organizational Behavior and Human Decision Processes, 116*, 66–82.

Rozin, P., Lowery, L., Imada, S., & Haidt, J. (1999). The CAD triad hypothesis: a mapping between three moral emotions (contempt, anger, disgust) and three moral codes (community, autonomy, divinity). *Journal of Personality and Social Psychology, 76*, 574.

Rozin, P., Markwith, M., & Stoess, C. (1997). Moralization and becoming a vegetarian: The transformation of preferences into values and the recruitment of disgust. *Psychological Science, 8*, 67–73.

Russell, J. A. (1980). A circumplex model of affect. *Journal of Personality and Social Psychology, 39*, 1161–1178.

Russell, J. A., & Barrett, L. F. (1999). Core affect, prototypical emotional episodes, and other things called emotion: Dissecting the elephant. *Journal of Personality and Social Psychology, 76*, 805.

Scher, S. J., & Heise, D. R. (1993). Affect and the perception of injustice. *Advances in Group Processes, 10*, 223–252.

Schneirla, T. C. (1959). An evolutionary and developmental theory of biphasic processes underlying approach and withdrawal. *Nebraska Symposium on Motivation: Vol. 7* (pp. 1–43). Lincoln, NE: University of Nebraska Press

Schwarz, N., & Clore, G. L. (1983). Mood, misattribution, and judgments of well-being: Informative and directive functions of affective states. *Journal of Personality and Social Psychology, 45*, 513.

Sinclair, R. C., & Mark, M. M. (1991). Mood and the endorsement of egalitarian macrojustice versus equity-based microjustice principles. *Personality and Social Psychology Bulletin, 17*, 369–375.

Skarlicki, D. P., Hoegg, J., Aquino, K., & Nadisic, T. (2013). Does injustice affect your sense of taste and smell? The mediating role of moral disgust. *Journal of Experimental Social Psychology.*

Skarlicki, D., & Kulik, C. (2005) Third party reactions to employee mistreatment: A justice perspective. In B. Staw and R. Kramer (Eds.), *Research in Organizational Behavior,* 183–230. Greenwich CT: JAI.

Smith, C. A., & Ellsworth, P. C. (1985). Patterns of cognitive appraisal in emotion. *Journal of Personality and Social Psychology, 48,* 813.

Smith, C. A., & Ellsworth, P. C. (1987). Patterns of appraisal and emotion related to taking an exam. *Journal of Personality and Social Psychology, 52,* 475.

Sprecher, S. (1986). The relation between inequity and emotions in close relationships. *Social Psychology Quarterly, 49,* 309–321.

Tabibnia, G., Satpute, A. B., & Lieberman, M. D. (2008). The sunny side of fairness preference for fairness activates reward circuitry (and disregarding unfairness activates self-control circuitry). *Psychological Science, 19,* 339–347.

Tangney, J. P., & Dearing, R. (2002). *Shame and guilt.* New York, NY: Guilford.

Tangney, J. P., Stuewig, J., & Mashek, D. J. (2007). Moral emotions and moral behavior. *Annual Review of Psychology, 58,* 345.

Thibaut, J. W., & Walker, L. (1975). *Procedural justice: A psychological analysis.* Hillsdale: L. Erlbaum.

Tyler, T. R., & Blader, S. L. (2000). *Cooperation in groups: Procedural justice, social identity, and behavioral engagement.* Philadelphia, PA.: Psychology Press.

Tyler, T. R., and Blader, S. L. (2003). Procedural justice, social identity and cooperative behavior. *Personality and Social Psychology Review, 7,* 349–361.

Tyler, T. R., Degoey, P., & Smith, H. (1996). Understanding why the justice of group procedures matters: A test of the psychological dynamics of the group-value model. *Journal of Personality and Social Psychology, 70,* 913.

Tyler, T. R., & Lind, E. A. (1992). A relational model of authority in groups. *Advances in Experimental Social Psychology* (Vol. 25, pp. 115–191).

Van den Bos, K. (2003). On the subjective quality of social justice: the role of affect as information in the psychology of justice judgments. *Journal of Personality and Social Psychology, 85*(3), 482.

Van den Bos, K., and Lind, E. A. (2002). Uncertainty management by means of fairness judgments. *Advances in Experimental Social Psychology, 34,* 1–60.

Van den Bos, K., & Miedema, J. (2000). Toward understanding why fairness matters: The influence of mortality salience on reactions to procedural fairness. *Journal of Personality and Social Psychology, 79,* 355.

Van den Bos, K., Wilke, H. A., Lind, E. A., & Vermunt, R. (1998). Evaluating outcomes by means of the fair process effect: Evidence for different processes in fairness and satisfaction judgments. *Journal of Personality and Social Psychology, 74,* 1493.

Vermunt, R., Wit, A., van den Bos, K., & Lind, E. A. (1996). The effects of unfair procedure on negative affect and protest. *Social Justice Research, 9,* 109–119.

Walster, E., Walster, G. W., & Berscheid, E. (1978). *Equity: Theory and research.* Boston, MA: Allyn & Bacon.

Watson, D. (2000). *Mood and temperament.* New York, NY: Guilford.

Watson, D., Wiese, D., Vaidya, J., & Tellegen, A. (1999). The two general activation systems of affect: Structural findings, evolutionary considerations, and psychobiological evidence. *Journal of Personality and Social Psychology, 76,* 820.

Weiss, H. M., & Cropanzano, R. (1996). Affective events theory: A theoretical discussion of the structure, causes and consequences of affective experiences at work. In: B. M. Staw & L. L. Cummings (Eds.), *Research in Organizational Behavior, 19,* 1–74. Greenwich, CT: JAI Press.

Weiss, H. M., Suckow, K., & Cropanzano, R. (1999). Effects of justice conditions on discrete emotions. *Journal of Applied Psychology, 84,* 786.

PART 4

Justice and Conflict

CHAPTER

21 The Role of Conflict in Managing Injustice

Debra L. Shapiro *and* Elad N. Sherf

Abstract

In this chapter we define *conflict, injustice,* and what is meant by "managing" each of these perceptions. We illuminate the ease with which perceived conflict can become perceived injustice and vice-versa. We posit that perceived conflict becomes perceived injustice when goal blockage is seen as norm violating and that perceived injustice becomes perceived conflict when seemingly unfair goal blockages are not removed. Therefore, perceived conflict and perceived injustice can reciprocally influence each other. We conclude that better integration of the justice and conflict literatures is needed to strengthen understanding of how to manage injustice so that it does not escalate into conflict and how, if conflict occurs, to resolve conflict in ways that will be deemed mutually satisfying and fair. With these conflict management-insights in mind, we also propose ways to design future studies of organizational (in)justice.

Key Words: goal blockage, norm violation, perceived conflict, perceived injustice, conflict-management strategies, injustice-management strategies, third-party strategies, integrative communications

This chapter regards the role of conflict in managing injustice. For this to be understood requires us to clarify what it means to perceive "conflict" and "injustice," and to "manage" each of these perceptions. Clarifying these terms' meanings will help to explain what the role of conflict is in managing perceived injustice.

This chapter proceeds by discussing these issues, each in turn. Therefore, in the first section we review literature pertaining to the meaning of *conflict* and the various forms that conflict can take. In the second section we review the meaning of injustice and its various potential forms. In the third section we note the negative consequences of unmanaged, or festering, conflict and injustice and describe conflict-managing and injustice-managing strategies aimed at reducing or eliminating these negative consequences. Lastly, in the fourth section, we note how an understanding of conflict-related insights can help manage perceived injustice and, therefore, also, help guide future research on organizational justice.

Defining *Conflict*

Conflict has been defined objectively as well as perceptually. Objectively, conflict has been described as present when: (a) parties hold divergent goals; (b) one or more party attempts to block another party's goal achievement; and (c) parties compete for scarce resources (Pondy, 1967; M. S. Schmidt & Kochan, 1972). *Perceived* conflict has been described this same way but with the following additional requirements: one or more of the parties need to be aware that their viewpoint or goal is divergent or in opposition with the view or goal of another party and to feel nontrivially concerned about this. Consistent with this, DeDreu and Gelfand (2008, p. 8) say that conflict exists when "... [an] individual or group perceives differences and opposition between itself and another individual or group about interests and resources, beliefs, values, or practices that matter to them." Similarly, other scholars emphasize the need for at least one party to be aware of differences and to perceive these as conflict-creating, or goal-blocking, in nature (cf., Fink, 1968; Mannes, 2008; Thomas, 1998; Wall & Callister, 1995).

For two reasons, in this chapter we focus on dynamics relating to *perceived* conflict. First, in the absence of perceived conflict, there is no felt-need to manage conflict on the part of anyone (e.g., those for whom conflict exists or those who witness this). Second, a perceptual focus has dominated the way conflict has been empirically assessed. Evidence of this includes the perceptual assessments of conflict management-styles (Cosier & Ruble, 1981; Euwema, van de Vliert, & Bakker, 2003; Rahim & Magner, 1995; Rahim, 1983; van de Vliert & Euwema, 1994; van de Vliert & Kabanoff, 1990) and the perceptual assessment of team-conflicts— namely, the measures comprising what Jehn (1995, 1997) introduced as "task conflict," "relationship conflict," and "process conflict" (i.e., team members' perceptions of how frequently they experience each of these) (see also Pearson, Ensley, & Amason, 2002). Table 21.1 shows how these three types of team conflicts have been defined and examples of each.

When comparing the descriptions of task versus process conflict, it becomes clear that they differ from each other in terms of what the disagreement regards. If the disagreement regards the decision itself, it is task conflict; but if the disagreement instead regards what process ought to be used to make a decision and/or to achieve a task-assignment, then it is process conflict (Jehn, 1997; Jehn, Northcraft, & Neale, 1999). In contrast to each of these conflict types, relational conflict pertains to disagreements among group members that have interpersonal rather than task-related sources. Sources may be differences in personality, norms, or values that cause team members to feel negative emotions (e.g., tensions, discomfort, annoyance) toward each other and/or to engage in personal attacks that express interpersonal dislike (Jehn, 1997; Rispens, Greer, Jehn, & Thatcher, 2011). Thus, it is possible for relational conflict to be provoked by qualities of organizational members that do not necessarily relate to a task decision or the process used to guide it (e.g., personality and personal values or behavioral mannerisms, cf., De Dreu & Van Vianen, 2001). In Table 21.1 we have chosen "relational conflict" over other terms that have been used interchangeably in the literature to describe this type of conflict (e.g., emotional or affective conflict as seen in work by Amason, 1996; Von Glinow, Shapiro, & Brett, 2004). Our term-choice is due to our desire to clarify that this type of conflict involves *relational* strain. In their meta-analysis, de Wit, Greer, and Jehn (2011) found that

Table 21.1 Types of Conflicts (Goal-blockages)

Type of Conflict	Definition[a]	Example of this Conflict
Task	"Task conflicts entail disagreements among group members about the content and outcomes of the task being performed"	• Employees cannot agree who to hire as a new employee • Employees cannot agree on a future course of action for the team (i.e., whether to focus on increasing market share or on obtaining more value from current customers)
Process	"Process conflicts are disagreements among group members about the logistics of task accomplishment, such as the delegation of tasks and responsibilities"	• Employees cannot agree on what the selection criteria ought to be to guide their selection of a new hire in their department • Employees cannot agree on who is in charge of various group or team-tasks
Relational	"Relationship conflicts involve disagreements among group members about interpersonal issues, such as personality differences or differences in norms and values"	• An employee calls another "stupid" and/or shows other demeaning behaviors toward that person, due to obvious feelings of interpersonal dislike and animosity

Note: [a]Definitions are based on a meta-analysis by de Wit et al. (2011: 360), which is the most updated comprehensive treatment of the team conflict literature.

70% of the 116 studies examining team-conflicts assessed the types of conflicts shown in Table 21.1, and did this by using variants of the perceptual-oriented measures introduced by Jehn (1995) to empirically capture these.

In addition to the types of team-conflicts shown in Table 21.1, various types of perceived conflict, or goal blockage, can occur within individuals, between individuals, between groups or teams, within one organization's divisional or departmental units (which is why intra-organizational and intergroup studies involving organizational members are interchangeable), between organizations, and between nations. The terms *intra-individual, interpersonal, intergroup, intra-organizational, inter-organizational,* and *international* describe each of these types of conflicts, respectively. Examples of each of these conflict-types are shown in Table 21.2. Regardless of who is experiencing conflict (e.g., one or more individuals, groups, organizations, nations), perceived conflict at any of these levels of analysis exists when one or more participants become aware of divergent or opposing goals held by them versus other parties, and this divergence or opposition is concerning to them (cf., De Dreu & Gelfand, 2008; Fink, 1968; Mannes, 2008; Thomas, 1998; Wall & Callister, 1995). The existence of perceived conflict at potentially all these levels of analysis is why strategies that have been identified as effective for managing conflict between two or more people (which is the predominant focus of strategies reviewed in the third section of this chapter) apply to dyadic-, intragroup, and intergroup conflicts, although the practical feasibility of conflict-management is always greater when the number of participants are fewer rather than greater in number (cf., Hanges, Lyon, & Dorfman, 2005; Lovelace, Shapiro, & Weingart, 2001).

Defining *Injustice*

Rawls (1971) is among the earliest scholars to theorize about what leads people to perceive injustice. Key to Rawls's thesis is the notion that perceived injustice (or more accurately, what he called "social justice" given his societal focus) involves insufficient fulfillment, or "violation," of agreed upon societal norms. More specifically, Rawls said,: "... [a] conception of social justice... is to be regarded as providing... a standard whereby the distributive aspects of the basic structure of society are to be assessed" (p. 9).

The perceived violation of norms is identified as a "trigger" of perceived injustice in fairness theory, too, proposed by Folger and Cropanzano (2001) and by Cropanzano, Goldman, and Folger (2003). More specifically, these scholars name two specific types of norm violations—deviation from moral standards and deviation from psychological contracts (or relation-based expectations)—as likely triggers of perceived injustice. Understanding what the norms are among people (dyads, teams, organizational members, etc.) can thus aid prediction regarding when anyone will likely perceive injustice since norm *violation* instantiates this.[1]

Although many potential norms exist, such as equality, need, and equity norms (Tornblom & Jonsson, 1985), one of the most universal norms held in work contexts is the need for employees' rewards to be reflective of the level of their contribution, hence merit-based (Kabanoff, 1991; Miller & Komorita, 1995). The concept of merit is seen, too, in descriptions of what it means to ensure that employees perceive "equity"—that is, similar levels of reward-allocations to employees whose contributions are similar (Adams, 1965). Guided by Rawls's (1971) theorizing, if equity is perceived as insufficient, then this violation of an equity-norm ought to provoke perceived injustice. Consistent with this, Adams (1965) theorized that violations of perceived equity—termed *inequity*— create perceptions of unfairness. The term *distributive injustice* has been used interchangeably with inequity, and has been defined as the perceived unfairness of work-related allocations (Folger & Martin, 1986; Homans, 1961; Leventhal, 1976; Walster, Berscheid, & Walster, 1973). When the perception of unfairness regards not the allocated outcome itself but, rather, the procedure used to determine work outcomes (e.g., performance appraisal procedures), this has been called "procedural injustice" (Brockner & Wiesenfeld, 1996; Folger & Greenberg, 1985; Leventhal, 1980; van den Bos, Lind, Vermunt, & Wilke, 1997).

When the perception of unfairness regards insufficient interpersonal sensitivity in the enactment of procedures (e.g., providing critical performance feedback to employees in a manner that is publicly humiliating), this has been called "interactional injustice" (cf., Bies & Shapiro, 1987, 1988), which later was parsed by Greenberg (1990a) into two subcategories (interpersonal and informational). When the perception of organizational justice is a gestalt that results from an accumulation of various types of injustice-related events in

Table 21.2 Types of Conflict at Varying Levels of Analysis

Type of Goal Blockage/Conflict	Realm of occurrence	Examples	Relevant Cites
"Intra-individual"	An individual is confronted with competing (i.e., mutually exclusive) aims or roles	• When a dedicated employee yet devoted family member cannot decide whether to work overtime at the expense of his/her time with family or, instead, to refuse to work overtime at the expense of meeting his/her organization's needs • When an employee faces two urgent and equally important projects that require time and attention	(King & King, 1990) (A. M. Schmidt & DeShon, 2007)
"Interpersonal"	Two (or more) individuals goals, behaviors or perceptions are in disagreement	• When a buyer and seller cannot agree on transaction-related terms • When two group members cannot agree on the steps needed to reach the group goals	(Jehn, 1995)
"Intergroup"	Two (or more) groups have opposing goals, ideas or actions	• When two groups compete for the same organizational resource, such as budgets or additional human capital • When one group of employees (i.e., medical stuff) actively prevent the implementation of another group's (i.e., administrative team) vision	(Sherif, 1966) (Fiol, Pratt, & O'Connor, 2009)
"Intra-organizational"	The goals, behaviors or perceptions of two (or more) groups within an organization are in disagreement	• [Vertical] When two departments in the organization work to maximize their local performance measures at the expense of another unit (i.e., marketing department makes sales that the manufacturing department can't deliver) • [Horizontal] When management and employees (unionized or not) disagree about compensation levels for employees	(Kramer, 1991)
"Inter-organizational"	Two (or more) organizations compete for the same resources or attempt to advance different goals with a shared market or field	• When two organizations compete for the same client • When two organizations make competing arguments about a required public policy	(Katz & Khan, 1978)
"International"	Between nations	• Trade agreements disputes between nations • Aggressive military action	

a place of work, this has been called "overall (in) justice" (Ambrose & Schminke, 2009); however, this global assessment has been predicted and found to be significantly influenced by the "facets" of (in)justice named earlier, namely by the extent to which employees have perceived distributive, procedural, and interpersonal (in)justice. Box 21.1 and Box 21.2 show the items used to assess the facets of (in)justice and overall (in)justice, respectively.

Numerous investigations regarding antecedents to each of these types of perceived (in)justice have occurred, and their findings have been reviewed elsewhere (Cohen-Charash & Spector, 2001; Colquitt, Conlon, Wesson, Porter, & Ng, 2001; Cropanzano,

Box 21.1 Colquitt (2001) Measure of Justice-Facets

Procedural Justice

The following items refer to the procedures used to arrive at your (outcome). To what extent:

1. Have you been able to express your views and feelings during those procedures?
2. Have you had influence over the (outcome) arrived at by those procedures?
3. Have those procedures been applied consistently?
4. Have those procedures been free of bias?
5. Have those procedures been based on accurate information?
6. Have you been able to appeal the (outcome) arrived at by those procedures?
7. Have those procedures upheld ethical and moral standards?

Distributive Justice

The following items refer to your (outcome). To what extent:

1. Does your (outcome) reflect the effort you have put into your work?
2. Is your (outcome) appropriate for the work you have completed?
3. Does your (outcome) reflect what you have contributed to the organization?
4. Is your (outcome) justified, given your performance?

Interpersonal Justice

The following items refer to (the authority figure who enacted the procedure). To what extent:

1. Has (he/she) treated you in a polite manner?
2. Has (he/she) treated you with dignity?
3. Has (he/she) treated you with respect?
4. Has (he/she) refrained from improper remarks or comments?

Informational Justice

The following items refer to (the authority figure who enacted the procedure). To what extent:

1. Has (he/she) been candid in (his/her) communications with you?
2. Has (he/she) explained the procedures thoroughly?
3. Were (his/her) explanations regarding the procedures reasonable?
4. Has (he/she) communicated details in a timely manner?
5. Has (he/she) seemed to tailor (his/her) communications to individuals' specific needs?

Rupp, Mohler, & Schminke, 2001; Shao, Rupp, Skarlicki, & Jones, 2013). In general, outcome-allocations are deemed unfair or "distributively unjust" when the equity norm is perceived as violated. This means distributive injustice is perceived when people view their outcome-allocations as "disadvantaged" relative to the outcomes being allocated to similar others, or others with similar "inputs" (e.g., level of work effort and quality). Despite the social comparative nature of the conceptualization of inequity (cf., Adams, 1965), empirical assessments of distributive injustice refer only to the extent to which outcome-allocations are deemed insufficient or unfair relative to one's own work contributions. This becomes clear when examining the items used to assess distributive (in) justice, as shown in Box 21.1.

Procedures are generally deemed more fair when their qualities include as many as possible of those identified by Leventhal (1980). These

Box 21.2 Ambrose and Schminke's (2009) Overall Justice Measure

1. Overall, I am treated fairly by my organization.
2. In general, I can count on this organization to be fair.
3. In general, the treatment I receive around here is fair.
4. Usually the way things work in this organization are not fair (reverse scored).
5. For the most part this organization treats its employees fairly.
6. Most of the people who work here would say they are often treated unfairly (reverse scored).

qualities include a neutral or impartial procedural administrator, a procedure that is applied with consistency, and guided by informational accuracy and moral and ethical standards, as well as by input from procedural participants, including participants' chance to appeal the authority's decision. The items seen in Box 21.1 that are used to empirically assess procedural justice reflect these qualities. Lower levels of procedural justice are typically perceived when one or more of these qualities are weak.

With regard to interpersonal justice, as can be seen in Box 21.1, empirical assessments of this suggest that interpersonal treatment is generally deemed unfair when this violates universally sacred actions that enable people to feel a sense of dignity and respect (for an elaboration of this view, see Bies & Moag, 1986; Bies, 1987, 2001). Although Box 21.1 distinguishes interpersonal justice from informational justice, these two facets of justice are often nondistinct from each other in empirical studies, and thus often collapsed together (cf., Goldman, Cropanzano, Stein, Shapiro, et al., 2008). This is not surprising since, as Box 21.1 shows, empirical assessments of informational justice pertain to qualities of a procedural enactor's communication with participants, during which there is ample opportunity for participants to perceive how respectfully they are being treated.

Thus far in this chapter, we have defined perceived conflict and perceived injustice; and as such, we have treated these concepts as though they are distinct from each other. But might perceived conflict evoke perceived unfairness and might perceived unfairness evoke conflict? The answer is "yes" and "yes," respectively, depending on the circumstances. More specifically, perceived injustice is likely to trigger perceived conflict (or blocked goals) if the events seen as unfair prevent their perceivers (or those with whom they identify, Friedman & Davidson, 1999; Skarlicki & Kulik, 2005) from achieving goals they value. For example, if people perceive their outcome-allocations as unfair, hence they perceive distributive injustice, this becomes a conflict if they express a desire for more outcomes and receivers of this request block or refuse this. As another example, if people perceive the procedures used to determine their outcome-allocations as unfair, hence they perceive procedural injustice, this becomes a conflict if they express a desire for procedural improvements and receivers of this request block or refuse this. As another instance, if people perceive the interpersonal treatment they are receiving as unfair, hence they perceive interpersonal injustice, this becomes a conflict if they express a desire for more sensitivity and receivers of this request block or refuse this. This means that *how perceived injustice gets responded to* ultimately determine whether perceived conflict results.

With regard to when perceived conflict is likely to trigger perceived injustice, our thinking is guided by Rawls (1971) and fairness theory (Cropanzano et al., 2003; Folger & Cropanzano, 2001), which identify a key determinant of perceived injustice to be one's perception that agreed upon norms have been violated. Therefore, when people perceive conflict, hence when they are aware of divergent goals between themselves and others that risk blocking them from obtaining a desirable scarce resource, this conflict ought to be seen as unfair *only if these differences violate their expectations of norm-appropriate behavior.* To make this point vivid, let us use a sports analogy: Members of different sports teams certainly recognize that their goals are divergent and that they are competing for a scarce resource (i.e., to be the upcoming game's sole winner). But because it is normative for members of opposing sports-teams to block each other (literally in the physical sense in the case of sports games), injustice is unlikely to be perceived by participants of sports competitions. That said, if there are rules that normatively guide sportsmanlike behavior, and those rules are violated during the course of play, then the team that is disadvantaged by the rule-infraction will perceive procedural injustice. And if the injustice goes uncorrected (hence unmanaged), then perceived injustice will lead, also, to perceived conflict if achieving the goal of victory matters much to the team who believes they have been blocked from achieving this. As a result, perceived conflict and perceived injustice have the potential to reciprocally influence each other; and whether they do depends on how expressed concerns about injustice or goal blockages get managed. We thus turn attention to this next.

Managing Conflict and/or Injustice

Managing Conflict

Numerous strategies identified as illustrative of "conflict management" exist. We place quotation marks around this term here because, as will be seen later in the descriptions of the various strategies, some are better suited than others to actually enable each side's underlying interests to be satisfied, thus better able to resolve conflict in a mutually satisfying, lasting way. To parsimoniously represent these, several taxonomies have been created. One of the most influential taxonomies in the conflict management literature is the dual-concern model (Pruitt, 1983; Pruitt & Carnevale, 1993; Rahim, 1983), which is depicted in Figure 21.1. The reason this model has been so influential is because the two concerns it names—concern for one's own and the opposing side's welfare—applies across contexts and disputes and levels of analysis. Other taxonomies associated with managing conflict pertain to third-party dispute resolution procedures (for a review of these, see Goldman, Cropanzano, Stein, & Benson, 2008). Since Thibaut and Walker's (1975, 1978) conceptualization of "process control" and "decision control" have illuminated differences across third-party interventions, we rely on the latter concepts to guide the four intervention strategies we describe. Process and outcome control refer to disputants' (versus the third party's) level of participation and decision authority in the hearing and settlement of their cases, respectively. We describe conflict-managing strategies and third-party dispute-resolution strategies next, each in turn.

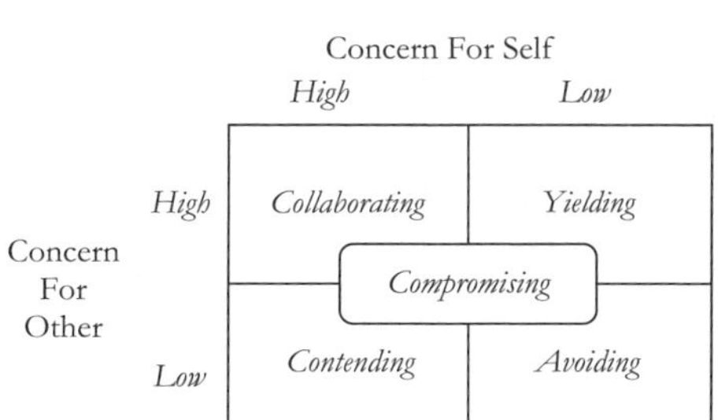

Fig. 21.1 The Dual Concerns Model.

DUAL-CONCERN MODEL AND ITS FIVE CONFLICT-MANAGING STRATEGIES

The pivotal role that the dual-concern model has played in generating understanding and empirical investigations by conflict-management scholars has been noted by Olekalns, Putnam, and Weingart (2008) in their extensive review of the conflict-management literature. The dual-concern model clarifies why, in any given conflict-managing situation, the behaviors exhibited by each side vary in their degree of cooperation. As Figure 21.1 depicts, the reason for each side's level of (non) cooperation is due to how much concern each side has for its own welfare and the opposing side's welfare.

How do these two concerns at high versus low levels translate into conflict-management strategies? If one who perceives a blocked goal has little concern about resolving this in a manner that protects his/her own welfare and is highly concerned about resolving the goal-blockage in a manner that protects the other's welfare, this means one is highly concerned about pleasing the other side. The strategy orientation reflecting this is "yielding," also called "obliging." As a result, any possible discussion about blocked goals ought to be relatively brief since the yielder will readily concede.

The antithesis of a yielder is a disputing party who is highly concerned about the welfare of only him or herself. Under these circumstances, the likely behavior one will exhibit is "contending" (Pruitt & Carnevale, 1993), also referred alternately as taking an approach that is "distributive" (Putnam, 1990), "dominating" (De Dreu & Van Vianen, 2001), and "rights or power oriented" (Brett, Shapiro, & Lytle, 1998). The risk of managing conflict with dominating, or distributive, behaviors is that aggressive communications, such as demands and threats, typically escalate tensions into a "conflict spiral," which often ends with high costs to all sides or with a lopsided win for one side (cf., Brett et al., 1998). Such outcomes typically also strain relationships among the participants, potentially beyond "relationship repair"—that is, beyond any chance of restoring it to an initially positive state (Dirks, Lewicki, & Akbar, 2009).

If blocked goals cause one to feel little concern about both his or her own and the opposing side's welfare, then this means the blocked goal matters little. As such, this state, which the dual-concern model identifies as likely to coincide with "avoiding conflict resolution," poorly matches the definition of conflict provided earlier in this chapter.

If someone who perceives blocked goals is highly concerned about resolving this in a manner that protects both his or her own and the opposing side's welfare, this means she or he is oriented toward resolving conflict via "problem solving." Other construct-names used to describe this orientation include: "integrating" (Putnam, 1990), "interest-oriented" (Brett et al., 1998), "collaborating" (De Dreu & Van Vianen, 2001), and "constructive controversy" (Johnson, Johnson, & Tjosvold, 2006).

Communications illustrating the integrating-versus distributive-oriented conflict-management strategies are, not surprisingly, more cooperative versus noncooperative, respectfully. And, thus, also not surprisingly, the probability of resolving conflict in a mutually satisfying way is greater when the communications expressed by disputing parties are more integrative rather than distributive. Consistent with this, Rotondo, Carlson, and Kincaid (2003) and Tidd and Friedman (2002) found lower levels of stress among employees who managed role conflicts via approaches that were more direct and problem-solving in nature rather than more passive in nature. The more passive approaches to manage role conflict included employees' attempts to view the situation positively by changing their initial perceptions of role conflict or to avoid the role conflict altogether. Moreover, extensive reviews of the effects of various conflict-handling strategies document that, relative to the other conflict-managing strategies, the integrating approach generally produces more satisfying outcomes in dyads (De Dreu, Weingart, & Kwon, 2000) and teams (DeChurch, Mesmer-Magnus, & Doty, 2013). Exceptions to this are when the conflict is relational, rather than task-based (De Dreu & Van Vianen, 2001; Weingart & Jehn, 2009), the reasons for which probably relate to the difficulty under relational strain to communicate noncontentiously (as discussed later in this chapter).

Until now our review of conflict-managing strategies has made no mention of the compromising strategy. As can be seen in Figure 21.1, compromise is centrally located and, thus, represents a moderate level of concern for one's own and the opposing side's well-being. With the compromise approach, although it is somewhat cooperative, typically solutions are less creative than those that can be discovered when disputing parties seek to more fully satisfy their own and the other side's underlying interests (for an elaboration of this point, see Shapiro & Kulik, 2004). This is why "win-win" is reserved for the integrative approach, not the compromise approach. Win-win is vividly illustrated by Mary Parker Follet's (1940) classic story of two sisters who wanted an orange (there was only one available) and discovered, after cutting the orange in half and seeing one squeeze her half for juice and the other sister use the peel to bake a cake, that each could have had 100% of the orange (better-than-compromise, or win-win) if they had explored their underlying needs and better integrated them.

To this point our chapter has reviewed literature finding that the integrative approach is generally more effective than others for managing conflict. However, the constructive controversy, or mutual cooperation, required to use the integrative approach is not always feasible. This is because it is challenging to restrain oneself from expressing contentious remarks (e.g., demands for concessions, threats if requests get refused), especially when one believes him/herself to be a victim of injustice. This is why, when a conflict's intensity is marked by high levels of anger, distrust, or hostility, third parties typically get involved to aid conflict resolution. We turn our attention to third-party interventions next.

THIRD-PARTY STRATEGIES FOR MANAGING CONFLICT

Disputing parties sometime call upon others for assistance, either informal or formal third parties, whose role is to help them reach agreement. Third-party process-interventionists, such as mediators, typically set ground-rules for disputants' discussions that include encouraging integratively oriented communications (e.g., interest-oriented remarks). Conflict management scholars use the term *third party* to refer to individuals who help others who are disputing to reach an agreement, also referred to as a settlement. These third parties are "formal" when they are external to the organization, such as mediators or arbitrators. In contrast, third parties are "emergent" when they are internal to the organization, such as direct supervisors or even co-workers or team members who spontaneously attempt to facilitate peace-making among disputing employees (Conlon & Meyer, 2004).

Theorizing by Thibaut and Walker (1975, 1978) has enabled third-party procedures to be differentiated with regard to how much control they give to disputing parties versus to the third-parties in terms of: (a) determining the data or information that gets presented during the presentation of the dispute (called "process control" and later, more simply called "voice," cf., Folger, 1977); and (b) determining the dispute's settlement (called "decision, or outcome, control"). Examples of third-party dispute-resolving procedures that deny disputing parties decision control are those, such as arbitration and inquisition, that occur in courtroom settings and, thus, that involve a court-appointed judge who renders his/her decision after hearing the case. Although arbitration and inquisition are both autocratic forms of third-party intervention, they differ from each other in terms of how much process control, or voice, they give to the disputing parties. More specifically, during an inquisition, disputants are permitted only to answer questions that an inquisitor opts to ask them, whereas during arbitration, disputants are asked to tell the arbitrator their perspective (either directly or via a representative they choose). The extent of control that disputants have over the information and/or evidence that the third party hears about their grievance is, thus, greater in arbitration relative to inquisition. Consequently, from the disputants' perspective, inquisition is characterized by low levels of both process and outcome control, whereas arbitration is characterized by high process control but low decision control.

In contrast to inquisition and arbitration, mediation gives disputants both process and outcome control. This is because a mediator asks each side to explain their view of the dispute (thereby giving voice to each disputant) and then facilitates discussion between them that includes proposals of various possible settlements that the disputing parties ultimately decide on (thereby giving the disputants decision control). The greater decision-control that disputing parties have in mediation relative to arbitration led Shapiro and Brett (1993) to predict that mediation would be evaluated by disputants as more satisfying and fair; their findings supported this prediction. Moreover, as they also predicted, Shapiro and Brett found that disputants' perceptions of fairness and level of satisfaction with the outcome of their dispute tended to be higher when they also perceived themselves to have more process control. This led them to conclude that organizations aiming to enhance procedural justice ought to design dispute resolution systems that give, both, process and outcome control to those who express grievances about conflict they perceive.

The tendency for disputants to perceive greater fairness when they have more process control, or voice, has been termed the *voice effect* (Folger, 1977) due to the consistency with which this positive relationship has been found. The effect of disputants' having versus lacking decision control on their degree of perceived fairness is less clear. Guided by their review of the justice literature, Shapiro and Brett (2005) suggest this lack of clarity is due to the paucity of studies that varied decision control as well as process control (an impossibility for studies using courtrooms as settings) and to reasons relating to differential operationalizations of mediation across studies.

Regarding the latter point, authors have differentially defined and differentially operationalized mediation. Indeed, in the taxonomy of third-party interventions proposed by Thibaut and Walker (1975, 1978), mediation is described as third-parties (rather than disputants) retaining process control. Such a description runs counter to qualitative observations of professional mediators (cf. Shapiro & Kolb, 1994) and to quantitatively assessed reports by disputants of their level of process control in mediation (cf. Shapiro & Brett, 1993) The variance in mediator styles (cf., Brett, Drieghe, & Shapiro, 1986; Shapiro, Drieghe, & Brett, 1985) probably contributes to the difficulty of operationalizing mediation uniformly. Consistent with this, Goldman, Cropanzano, Stein, and Benson (2008, p. 302) say, "... [T]here is not a unanimously accepted or commanding definition of mediation or mediator behavior...," a view that is expressed also by Lewicki, Weiss, and Lewin (1992).

Our discussion to this point has been focused on the perspective of the disputing parties; this is in keeping with our chapter's focus on perceived conflict as the impetus for managing perceived conflict and injustice. Nevertheless, we note here that, from the perspective of the third party, especially when this is a manager, the more autocratic forms of dispute-intervention are often preferred over mediation. This is because it takes less time to use procedures in which the third party mandates a decision (hence to use procedures that deny decision control to the disputants), and time-efficiency is sometimes a necessity (cf., Elangovan, 1995; Goldman, Cropanzano, Stein, & Benson, 2008). Therefore, disputing parties who feel a need for a third-party interventionist may not necessarily be able to find one who is willing to engage them in a procedure that enables them the level of process and/or decision control they may prefer. This can potentially add complexity to the conflict that disputing parties are already perceiving.

Regardless of whether mediation is the preferred third-party dispute-resolving intervention over others, much has been learned about conflict managing by watching what professional mediators do (for elaborate qualitative descriptions, see Shapiro et al., 1985; Shapiro & Kolb, 1994). One of the actions taken by mediators is to set ground rules for discussion at the start of the session, the overarching purpose of which is to encourage disputing parties be open-minded to learning the other side's perspective and to refrain from contentious communications, even if they are occasionally targets of aggression. Such restraint is called "accomodation" by Rusbult, Verette, Whitney, Slovik, and Lipkus (1991). Rusbult et al.'s descriptions of this include choosing to not answer a threat with a threat, hence not reciprocating the domination of communications. Such a choice is counter to the "norm of reciprocity" (cf., Gouldner, 1960), that is, people's instinct to reciprocate how they are treated. Not surprisingly, therefore, self-control is needed to accommodate.

The setting of ground rules for encouraging constructive discussion is akin to what Jehn (1995, 1997) has called setting "conflict process norms" in teams. As noted earlier, self-control is needed to act on conflict-process norms, especially since these get acted on when people are perceiving conflict and, therefore, likely also feeling angry (Jehn, 1997). People with higher versus lower levels of dispositional self-control, or a greater ability to deliberately and consciously respond to situations in ways that are *not* their first inclination, (Baumeister, Bratslavsky, Muraven, & Tice, 1998) have generally been found to respond less aggressively to various types of provocations (Tangney, Baumeister, & Boone, 2004), to abusive supervisors (Lian et al., 2012), and to demeaning remarks or relationship-ending threats from their romantic partners (Finkel & Campbell, 2001). Mediators help ensure that disputing parties exercise self-control (in the form of restrained contentiousness even if feeling personally attacked during the session), by starting the session by articulating the conflict-process-norms that will govern discussion.

These process-norms, along with mediators' tendency to call caucuses, or to physically separate the disputants when they violate these norms with contentious remarks (cf., Brett et al., 1986; Shapiro et al., 1985; Shapiro & Kolb, 1994) help to defuse negative emotions. Since cooperative actions tend to be greater when people's moods and emotions are more positive (cf., Cropanzano, Becker, & Feldman, 2012), mediators' emotion-defusing actions also help to ensure that more constructive dialogue and concession making will subsequently occur on the part of the disputing parties.

SUMMARY

In summary, guided by the dual-concern model (Pruitt, 1983; Pruitt & Carnevale, 1993), we have described five conflict-managing strategies (integrating, dominating, yielding, compromising, and avoiding), but we have identified integrating as the most likely of these to resolve conflict in mutually satisfying ways. Additionally, guided by Thibaut and Walker's (1975, 1978) illumination of third-party intervention distinctions along the lines of disputants' degree of process and outcome control, we have described three third-party intervention procedures (mediation, arbitration, and inquisition), and noted the tendency for employees to prefer procedures that give them, minimally, voice (process control), called the "voice effect" (Folger, 1977). Due to the dynamic nature of communication during dispute resolution, including the possibility that initial cooperation may end and turn contentious when a particular issue gets raised, these strategies are often combined (cf., Barry & Shapiro, 2000; Brett et al., 1998; Shapiro & Rosen, 1994). Even mediation and arbitration have been combined in ways that create a hybrid procedure of the two (cf. Shapiro & Brett, 1993). Indeed, for this reason, Putnam (1990) has suggested that the labels "integrative" versus "distributive" communication falsely suggest a dichotomy that in practice does not exist. For this reason, conflict management scholars typically predict and assess the proportionality (e.g., the percentage of comments reflecting interest-oriented versus contentious remarks, cf., Brett et al., 1998) as well as patterns of communications that occur between disputing parties (see Olekalns et al., 2008, for a review).

Managing Perceived Injustice

Several strategies exist for managing perceived injustice, namely actions that enhance the perceived fairness of distributive-justice, procedural-justice, and interpersonal justice. We review these next, each in turn.

STRATEGIES FOR ENHANCING THE PERCEIVED FAIRNESS OF OUTCOMES

One of the strategies that enhance the extent to which employees perceive fairness is to provide them with outcomes they will view as equitable, hence fair. Consistent with this, more fairness has been reported by managers who described themselves as having more rather than less satisfying job assignments and rewards given to them by their superiors (Sheppard & Lewicki, 1987); by citizens in traffic appeals court who received reduced or eliminated traffic-fines from the court-appointed judge (Conlon, 1993); by students who, in a simulated interview, received a more- rather than less-praiseworthy performance review (Stoffey & Reilly, 1997); and by students who, in a laboratory experiment, received from the experimenter fewer lottery tickets than they saw other laboratory participants receive (Peters & van den Bos, 2008; van den Bos et al., 1997; van den Bos, Wilke, Lind, & Vermunt, 1998).

STRATEGIES FOR ENHANCING THE PERCEIVED FAIRNESS OF PROCEDURES GUIDING OUTCOME-ALLOCATIONS

A second strategy for enhancing perceived justice is to make salient to recipients of decisions, such as job assignments and rewards, or organizational changes, such as layoffs, that the qualities of the procedure guiding the decision are fair. With regard to what these procedural qualities need to be, these are shown in the substance of the items used to empirically assess procedural justice and informational justice, shown in Box 21.1 (Colquitt, 2001). Therefore, the procedural qualities that need to be made salient pertain to the fact that decisions were guided or influenced by input from employees, and by norms, standards, criteria, or other reasons that are likely to be deemed adequate. Typically, making procedural qualities salient requires explaining their presence to decision recipients; this is why giving explanations for decisions generally enhances perceived justice. Evidence supporting this abounds and has been reviewed elsewhere (Colquitt et al., 2001; Greenberg, 1990a). Examples include greater levels of perceived justice being reported by: (a) employees, even those who had received critical performance reviews, when they had more rather than less input into the performance-appraisal process (Landy, Barnes, & Murphy, 1978; Landy, Barnes-Farrell, & Cleveland, 1980), and similarly, by managers and employees of a governmental agency who had more input into their performance-appraisals (Taylor, Tracy, Renard, Harrison, & Carroll, 1995); (b) disputants, even when they lacked decision control, when they felt they had a proper amount of influence over the process (i.e., an opportunity to voice their point of view to a tribunal, sufficient time to provide evidence and present their case) (Thibaut & Walker, 1975); (c) students, even those who had been denied extra-credit points for participating in a study, when they had been given the chance to choose the study task rather than assigned this by the experimenter (Cropanzano & Folger, 1989); and (d) employees making budget requests, even when these request were denied (Bies & Shapiro, 1987).

In summary, providing people (e.g., employees, disputants, students) with increased control of the process of the decision-making, including allowing them to voice their concerns and opinions about the desired outcome, has consistently been shown to improve perceptions of fairness. Indeed, this is why the "voice-effect," termed by Folger (1977), is among the most documented findings in the organizational justice literature. Importantly, however, the latter finding has been identified in more recent work to be possibly Western biased since Western cultures tend to be more egalitarian and less hierarchical than non-Western cultures (Brockner et al., 2001; Shapiro & Brett, 2005; Von Glinow et al., 2004). Therefore, future research on voice effects needs to consider the cultural norms of the context in which the study is occurring.

STRATEGIES FOR ENHANCING THE PERCEIVED FAIRNESS OF INTERPERSONAL TREATMENT

A third strategy for enhancing perceived justice is to treat recipients of decisions as well as procedures in ways that accord them respect and dignity. Bies and Moag (1986) identified what the communication qualities need to be to convey this. Building on this, Shapiro and colleagues (Barry & Shapiro, 2000; Shapiro, 1991, 1993) theoretically and empirically identified behaviors associated with providing "adequate explanations" and providing grievants "consideration." Findings documenting the tendency for more fairness to be perceived when people are treated respectfully are difficult to find since interpersonal sensitivity tends to be operationalized in the form of explanation giving whose fairness-enhancing effects were reviewed earlier. However, findings that show the fairness-enhancing effect of informational justice, even under the dire circumstances of explaining the reason for paycuts (Greenberg, 1990b) and the reason for smoking bans (Greenberg, 1994), to be significantly stronger when the information provider shows rather than lacks interpersonal sensitivity (i.e., did versus did not express remorse, respectively) and documents the importance of treating others respectfully when communicating decisions and/or explanations for them. More recently, Kernan and Hanges (2002) similarly found that, in a study of employees at a major multinational pharmaceutical corporation that was undergoing a significant reorganization, the quality of the communication employees received from management about the reorganization process (in terms of quantity, timeliness, adequacy, and accuracy), was positively associated with employees' degree of perceived fairness.

In summary, in this section, we have described strategies for managing perceived conflict and injustice, respectively. In so doing, we see similarities as well as differences between the management of these two perceptions. The similarities pertain to the reliance that managing perceived conflict and injustice each have on communications. The shared emphasis on communications when managing perceived conflict and injustice is not surprising. This is because perceived conflict often involves competing claims of what the right thing is to do (Brett et al., 1998; Felstiner, Abel, & Sarat, 1981) and because communications are essential in enabling people to gain understanding of each side's perspective (Olekalns et al., 2008). Moreover, until people express their privately held grievances, including perceived injustice, it is not possible for others to know of their existence (Ren & Gray, 2009). This is why Ren and Gray identify alerting others to grievances they feel, or what they call "challenge," as an essential first-step in repairing relationships. Linking challenge to relationship repair, as Ren and Gray (2009) do, illuminates the fact that positive consequences are possible when perceived conflict or injustice is *managed,* or resolved.

The differences in strategies for managing perceived conflict and managing perceived injustice pertain to whether the communication is top-down versus more broadly construed and whether emphasis is placed on what gets said (substantive communication qualities) rather than how it is said (dynamic communication qualities). The tendency for injustice-management strategies to be, nearly exclusively, a top-down communication was noted first by Shapiro and Brett (2005) and more recently, too (cf., Bies & Tripp, 2012; Conlon & Ross, 2012). The top-down communication descriptions of managing perceived injustice is undoubtedly due to the tendency for organizational justice phenomena to be studied in contexts involving the communication of decisions that authorities control. Such decisions include job assignments and rewards (Sheppard & Lewicki, 1987), smoking bans (Greenberg, 1994), pay-cuts (Greenberg, 1990b), layoffs (Brockner, DeWitt, Grover, & Reed, 1990), resource-request rejections (Bies & Shapiro, 1987), performance appraisals (Folger & Greenberg, 1985), and traffic appeals (Conlon, 1993). In these contexts, it makes sense that the person who is communicating reasons, explanations, and possibly also apologies and/or other impression-managing remarks (Greenberg, 1990a) is an authority figure (e.g., a boss or policeman or court judge) relative to their communication receiver. However, perceptions of injustice occur among peers, too, such as in situations involving perceived offensive remarks by co-workers (Kim, Shapiro, Aquino, Lim, & Bennett, 2008) or other sources of relational strain (Ren & Gray, 2009). Moreover, employees' increased tendency to work in self-managing work teams means that decisions that have traditionally been only the purview of organizational authorities, including goal prioritizing, task-assignments, and performance appraisals, are being made by team members, hence by peers (cf., Kirkman & Shapiro, 2001). Therefore, there is practical as well as theoretical need for future studies of organizational justice to examine the effectiveness of strategies for managing perceived injustice in contexts involving peer communications, not only top-down communications.

The second distinction we see in descriptions of managing perceived conflict versus perceived injustice pertains to a greater emphasis in the justice literature than in the conflict-management literature on what gets said (substantive communication qualities) in the organizational justice literature rather than on how it is said (dynamic communication qualities). In contrast, the conflict-management literature has placed more equal emphasis on both of these things, reflected in part by the greater use of audio- or videotaping and then content analysis in studies assessing the effectiveness of conflict-management strategies (cf., Olekalns et al., 2008; Weingart, 1997). The importance of assessing nonverbal qualities (e.g., volume and tonality of one's voice, facial, and hand-expressions) in addition to substantive qualities of communications is that the bulk of message interpretation, especially with regard to assessing the communicator's sincerity or honesty, is guided by nonverbal cues (Lewicki & Hanke, 2012; Zuckerman, DePaulo, & Rosenthal, 1981). Even greater understanding of when justice-managing communications will have their intended effect thus seems likely if qualitative, as well as quantitative, methods are used in future studies to assess justice-managing communications.

How Do Conflict-Related Insights Aid "Injustice-Management"?

The conflict-related insights that emerge in this chapter that seem likely to aid "injustice-management" are several. We review them next and note their implications for future research needs, each in turn.

First, it is helpful to understand that perceived conflicts of various kinds (e.g., task, process, and relational conflicts) are more likely to trigger perceptions of injustice when these conflicts violate agreed-upon norms for desired employee behavior. Such understanding illuminates the powerful role that norm setting plays in determining how damaging (if at all) the effect of conflicts will be. By applying this to injustice management, employees may be less likely to perceive conflicts as evidence of someone behaving unjustly if norms in organizations are set that lead employees to desire and expect employees to challenge task-related ideas and to challenge existing procedures, in a constructive manner, with the goal of quality improvement. Additionally, this possibility suggests that strategies for managing injustice need to be less reactive or "impression-managing" in nature (cf., Greenberg, 1990a) and more preventative, hence proactive, in nature (cf., Marks, Mathieu, & Zaccaro, 2001). Recent theorizing by Fehr and Gelfand (2012) regarding the benefits of a forgiveness climate to organizations and employees is one example of proactively minimizing the likelihood of conflict and, when it does occur, minimizing the likelihood that conflict will be managed ineffectively and thereby escalate into perceived injustice and related negative consequences. The effects of forgiveness climate or other types of prosocial cultures on organizational justice-dynamics is in need of empirical research.

A second way conflict-related insights aid injustice-management pertains to the emphasis placed in the conflict literature on the need for communications to be phrased in interest-oriented, or integrative (win-win), ways if they are to incentivize a cooperative response. Applying this to injustice management, employees may be more likely to revise initially held perceptions of injustice associated with goal blockages (such as an inability to obtain a valued resource or to change a procedure they think is improper) if the reasons for these blockages illuminate new routes to the goal that they seek. Training decision makers in organizations (at all levels) to explain decisions via "interest-oriented remarks," and, therefore, to be genuinely open to new ways to meet the spirit of the decision, as well as the other side's needs, will likely enhance perceived justice. To test this speculation requires future justice studies assessing the extent to which interest-oriented remarks accompany communications intended to raise perceptions of justice. Such assessment can be done via qualitative communication-observing methods (Olekalns et al., 2008) and/or quantitative methods (cf., Lovelace et al., 2001).

Finally, a third conflict-related insight that may aid injustice management regards the fact that strategies for resolving conflict can occur among peers, with the help of a third-party, and/or with the intervention of organizational authorities. As a result, it may be time to revise the notion of "injustice managers" so that the communicators of justice-enhancing messages are *not* only organizational authorities. As we noted earlier, there is need for future justice studies to examine justice managing among peers, including team members. Although scholars have theorized that relationship repair among peers involves restoring perceptions of fairness (Ren & Gray, 2009) as well as trust (Tomlinson & Mayer, 2009), this has not been empirically tested with relation to injustice. Similarly, recommendations for how to resolve relational conflict in teams abounds (De Dreu & Weingart, 2003; Jehn & Bendersky, 2003; Weingart & Jehn, 2009), but these prescriptions have generally not been empirically tested, with few exceptions (e.g., De Dreu & Van Vianen, 2001;

Jehn, 1995, 1997; Jehn, Greer, Levine, & Szulanski, 2008; Tekleab, Quigley, & Tesluk, 2009; Tjosvold, Law, & Sun, 2006). However, perceptions of justice are excluded from these studies.

Conclusion

In this chapter we have defined perceptions of conflict and injustice and what it means to "manage" these, and we have described strategies identified in conflict and organizational justice literatures for managing perceived conflict and injustice, respectively. In so doing, we discovered the prominent role of communication in managing, both, perceived conflict and perceived injustice; additionally, we discovered that the conflict management literature has theoretically and empirically examined these communications more broadly (beyond top-down communications) and more qualitatively (in terms of nonverbal as well as verbal cues). Given the ease with which unmanaged conflict becomes perceived injustice, conflict-related insights can aid injustice management, as discussed earlier. Incorporating these insights, also, into the design of future justice-studies promises to better integrate the conflict management and organizational justice literatures. Such integration promises to strengthen understanding about how to manage injustice so that it does not escalate into conflict and, if conflict nevertheless occurs, how to resolve it in ways most likely to be deemed mutually satisfying and fair.

Note

1. It is possible for agreed-upon norms of society to be discrepant with the values or norms held by some of its citizens. This is why "within-group variance" on cultural values and their associated norms is said to exist within national cultures (cf., Hofstede, 1980), especially those whose population is more heterogeneous (cf., Brett, Tinsley, Shapiro, & Okumura, 2007). If a society's or organization's norms (e.g., institutionalized slave labor or normalized corruption) are discrepant with the values and related norms held by some of its citizens, then these citizens will likely perceive norm violation. This is why *perceived norm violation*, hence perceived injustice, may occur for some, but not others, within cultures.

References

Adams, J. S. (1965). Inequity in social exchange. *Advances in Experimental Social Psychology, 62*, 267–299.

Amason, A. C. (1996). Distinguishing the effects of functional and dysfunctional conflict on strategic decision making: Resolving a paradox for top management teams. *Academy of Management Journal, 39*(1), 123–148.

Ambrose, M. L., & Schminke, M. (2009). The role of overall justice judgments in organizational justice research: A test of mediation. *Journal of Applied Psychology, 94*(2), 491–500. doi:10.1037/a0013203

Barry, B., & Shapiro, D. L. (2000). When will grievants desire voice?: A test of situational, motivational, and attributional explanations. *International Journal of Conflict Management, 11*(2), 106–134.

Baumeister, R. F., Bratslavsky, E., Muraven, M., & Tice, D. M. (1998). Ego depletion: Is the active self a limited resource? *Journal of Personality and Social Psychology, 74*(5), 1252–1265.

Bies, R. J. (1987). The predicament of injustice: The management of moral outrage. In L. L. Cummings & B. M. Staw (Eds.), *Research in organizational behavior* (pp. 289–319). Greenwich, CT: JAI.

Bies, R. J. (2001). Interactional (in)justice: The sacred and the profane. In J. Greenberg & R. Cropanzano (Eds.), *Advances in organizational justice* (pp. 89–118). Palo Alto, CA: Stanford University Press.

Bies, R. J., & Moag, J. S. (1986). Interactional justice: Communication criteria for fairness. In B. H. Sheppard (Ed.), *Research on negotiation in organizations* (pp. 43–55). Greenwich, CT: JAI.

Bies, R. J., & Shapiro, D. L. (1987). Interactional fairness judgments: The influence of causal accounts. *Social Justice Research, 1*(2), 199–218.

Bies, R. J., & Shapiro, D. L. (1988). Voice and justification: Their influence on procedural fairness judgments. *Academy of Management Journal, 31*(3), 676–685. doi:10.2307/256465

Bies, R. J., & Tripp, T. (2012). Negotiating the peace in face of modern distrust: Dealing with anger and revenge in the 21st century workplace. In B. M. Goldman & D. L. Shapiro (Eds.), *The psychology of negotiations in the 21st century workplace: New challenges and new solutions* (pp. 181–210). New York, NY: Routledge.

Brett, J. M., Drieghe, R., & Shapiro, D. L. (1986). Mediator style and mediation effectiveness. *Negotiation Journal, 2*(3), 277–285.

Brett, J. M., Shapiro, D. L., & Lytle, A. L. (1998). Breaking the bonds of reciprccity in negotiations. *Academy of Management Journal, 41*(4), 410–424.

Brett, J. M., Tinsley, C. H., Shapiro, D. L., & Okumura, T. (2007). Intervening in employee disputes: How and when will managers from China, Japan and the USA act differently? *Management and Organization Review, 3*(2), 183–204. doi:10.1111/j.1740-8784.2007.00070.x

Brockner, J., Ackerman, G., Greenberg, J., Gelfand, M. J., Francesco, A. M., Chen, Z. X., . . . Shapiro, D. L. (2001). Culture and procedural justice: The influence of power distance on reactions to voice. *Journal of Experimental Social Psychology, 37*(4), 300–315. doi:10.1006/jesp.2000.1451

Brockner, J., DeWitt, R. L., Grover, S., & Reed, T. (1990). When it is especially important to explain why: Factors affecting the relationship between managers' explanations of a layoff and survivors' reactions to the layoff. *Journal of Experimental Social Psychology, 26*(5), 389–407.

Brockner, J., & Wiesenfeld, B. M. (1996). An integrative framework for explaining reactions to decisions: Interactive effects of outcomes and procedures. *Psychological Bulletin, 120*(2), 189–208.

Cohen-Charash, Y., & Spector, P. E. (2001). The role of justice in organizations: A meta-analysis. *Organizational*

Behavior and Human Decision Processes, 86(2), 278–321. doi:10.1006/obhd.2001.2958

Colquitt, J. A. (2001). On the dimensionality of organizational justice: A construct validation of a measure. *Journal of Applied Psychology, 86*(3), 386–400. doi:10.1037//0021-9010.86.3.386

Colquitt, J. A., Conlon, D. E., Wesson, M. J., Porter, C. O. L. H., & Ng, K. Y. (2001). Justice at the millenium: A meta-analytic review of 25 years of organizational justice research. *Journal of Applied Psychology, 86*(3), 425–445. doi:10.1037//0021-9010.86.3.425

Conlon, D. E. (1993). Some tests of the self-interest and group-value models of procedural justice: Evidence from an organizational appeal procedure. *Academy of Management Journal, 36*(5), 1109–1124.

Conlon, D. E., & Meyer, C. J. (2004). Contractual and emergent third-party intervention. In M. J. Gelfand & J. M. Brett (Eds.), *The handbook of negotiation and culture* (pp. 258–279). Stanford, CA: Stanford Business Books.

Conlon, D. E., & Ross, W. H. (2012). The effect of perceived/felt injustice on cooperativeness: Implications for negotiators as "justice-enhancing communicators" in an era of social networking. In Barry M. Goldman & D. L. Shapiro (Eds.), *The psychology of negotiations in the 21st century workplace: New challenges and new solutions* (pp. 17–44). New York, NY: Routledge.

Cosier, R. A., & Ruble, T. L. (1981). Conflict-handling behavior: An experimental approach. *Academy of Management Journal*, *24*(4), 816–831.

Cropanzano, R., Becker, W. J., & Feldman, J. (2012). The effect of moods and discrete emotions on negotiator behavior. In Barry M. Goldman & D. L. Shapiro (Eds.), *The psychology of negotiations in the 21st century workplace: New challenges and new solutions*. New York, NY: Routledge.

Cropanzano, R., & Folger, R. (1989). Referent cognitions and task decision autonomy: Beyond equity theory. *Journal of Applied Psychology, 74*(2), 293–299. doi:10.1037//0021-9010.74.2.293

Cropanzano, R., Goldman, B., & Folger, R. (2003). Deontic justice: The role of moral principles in workplace fairness. *Journal of Organizational Behavior, 24*(8), 1019–1024. doi:10.1002/job.228

Cropanzano, R., Rupp, D. E., Mohler, C. J., & Schminke, M. (2001). Three roads to organizational justice. *Research in Personnel and Human resources Management, 20*, 1–113.

De Dreu, C. K. W., & Gelfand, M. J. (2008). Conflict in the workplace: Sources, functions, and dynamics across multiple levels of analysis. In C. K. W. De Dreu & M. J. Gelfand (Eds.), *The psychology of conflict and conflict management in organizations* (pp. 3–54). New York, NY: Erlbaum.

De Dreu, C. K. W., & Van Vianen, A. E. M. (2001). Managing relationship conflict and the effectiveness of organizational teams. *Journal of Organizational Behavior, 22*(3), 309–328.

De Dreu, C. K. W., & Weingart, L. R. (2003). Task versus relationship conflict, team performance, and team member satisfaction: A meta-analysis. *Journal of Applied Psychology, 88*(4), 741–749. doi:10.1037/0021-9010.88.4.741

De Dreu, C. K. W., Weingart, L. R., & Kwon, S. (2000). Influence of social motives on integrative negotiation: A meta-analytic review and test of two theories. *Journal of Personality and Social Psychology, 78*(5), 889–905.

De Wit, F. R. C., Greer, L. L., & Jehn, K. A. (2011). The paradox of intragroup conflict: A meta-analysis. *Journal of Applied Psychology, 97*(2), 360–390. doi:10.1037/a0024844

DeChurch, L. A., Mesmer-Magnus, J. R., & Doty, D. (2013). Moving beyond relationship and task conflict: Toward a process-state perspective. *Journal of Applied Psychology.* doi:10.1037/a0032896

Dirks, K. T., Lewicki, R. J., & Akbar, Z. (2009). Repairing relationships within and between organizations: Building a conceptual foundation. *Academy of Management Review, 34*(1), 68–84.

Elangovan, A. R. (1995). Managerial third-party dispute intervention: A prescriptive model of strategy selection. *Academy of Management Review, 20*(4), 800–830. doi:10.5465/AMR.1995.9512280022

Euwema, M. C., van de Vliert, E., & Bakker, A. B. (2003). Substantive and relational effectiveness of organizational conflict behavior. *International Journal of Conflict Management, 13*(2), 119–139.

Fehr, R., & Gelfand, M. J. (2012). The forgiving organization: A multilevel model of forgiveness at work. *Academy of Management Journal, 37*(4), 664–688.

Felstiner, W. L. F., Abel, R. L., & Sarat, A. (1981). The emergence and transformation of disputes: naming, blaming, claiming. . . *Law & Society Review, 15*(3), 631–654.

Fink, C. F. (1968). Some conceptual difficulties in the thoery of social conflict. *Journal of Conflict Resolution, 12*, 412–460.

Finkel, E. J., & Campbell, W. K. (2001). Self-control and accommodation in close relationships: An interdependence analysis. *Journal of Personality and Social Psychology, 81*(2), 263–77.

Fiol, C. M., Pratt, M. G., & O'Connor, E. J. (2009). Managing intractable identity conflicts. *Academy of Management Review, 34*(1), 32–55.

Folger, R. (1977). Distributive and procedural justice: Combined impact of voice and improvement on experienced inequity. *Journal of Personality and Social Psychology, 35*(2), 108–119. doi:10.1037//0022-3514.35.2.108

Folger, R., & Cropanzano, R. (2001). Fairness theory: Justice as accountability. In R. Cropanzano & J. Greenberg (Eds.), *Advances in organizational justice* (pp. 1–55). Stanford, CA: Stanford University Press.

Folger, R., & Greenberg, J. (1985). Procedural justice: An interpretive analysis of personnel systems. In K. Rowland & G. Ferris (Eds.), *Research in personnel and human resources management* (pp. 141–183). Greenwich, CT: JAI.

Folger, R., & Martin, C. (1986). Relative deprivation and referent cognitions: Distrbutive and procedural justice effects. *Journal of Experimental Social Psychology, 22*, 531–546.

Follett, M. P. (1940). Constructive conflict. In C. Metcalf & L. Urwick (Eds.), *Dynamic administration: The collected papers of Mary Parker Follett.* New York, NY: Harper.

Friedman, R., & Davidson, M. N. (1999). The Black-White gap in perceptions of discrimination: Its causes and consequences. *Research on negotiation in organizations, 7*, 203–230.

Goldman, B. M., Cropanzano, R., Stein, J., & Benson, L. I. (2008). The role of third-parties/mediation in resolving conflict in organizations. In M. J. Gelfand & C. K. W. De Dreu (Eds.), *The psychology of conflict and conflict management in organizations* (pp. 291–320). Mahwah, NJ: Erlbaum.

Goldman, B. M., Cropanzano, R., Stein, J. H., Shapiro, D. L., Thatcher, S., & Ko, J. (2008). The role of ideology in mediated disputes at work: A justice perspective. *International Journal of Conflict Management, 19*(3), 210–233. doi:10.1108/10444060810875787

Gouldner, A. W. (1960). The norm of reciprocity: A preliminary statement. *American Sociological Review, 25*(2), 161–178.

Greenberg, J. (1990a). Organizational justice: Yesterday, today and tomorrow. *Journal of Management, 16*(2), 399–432.

Greenberg, J. (1990b). Employee theft as a reaction to underpayment inequity: The hidden cost of pay cuts. *Journal of Applied Psychology, 75*(5), 561–568. doi:10.1037//0021-9010.75.6.667

Greenberg, J. (1994). Using socially fair treatment to promote acceptance of a work site smoking ban. *Journal of Applied Psychology, 79*(2), 288–297.

Hanges, P. J., Lyon, J. S., & Dorfman, P. W. (2005). Managing a multinational team: Lessons from Project Globe. In D. L. Shapiro, M. A. Von Glinow, & J. L. C. Cheng (Eds.), *Advances in International Management* (Vol. 18, pp. 337–360). San Diego, CA: Elsevier.

Hofstede, G. (1980). *Culture's consequences*. Newbury Park, CA: Sage.

Homans, G. C. (1961). *Social behavior: Its elementary forms*. London: Routledge & Kegan Paul.

Jehn, K. A. (1995). A multimethod exanimation of the benefits and detriments of intragroup conflict. *Administrative Science Quarterly, 40*(2), 256–282.

Jehn, K. A. (1997). A qualitative analysis of conflict types and dimensions in organizational groups. *Administrative Science Quarterly, 42*(3), 530. doi:10.2307/2393737

Jehn, K. A., & Bendersky, C. (2003). Intragroup conflict in organizations: A contingency perspective on the conflict-outcome relationship. *Research in Organizational Behavior, 25*, 187–242. doi:10.1016/S0191-3085(03)25005-X

Jehn, K. A., Greer, L., Levine, S., & Szulanski, G. (2008). The effects of conflict types, dimensions, and emergent states on group outcomes. *Group Decision and Negotiation, 17*(6), 465–495. doi:10.1007/s10726-008-9107-0

Jehn, K. A., Northcraft, G. B., & Neale, M. A. (1999). Why differences make a difference: A field study of diversity, conflict, and performance in workgroups. *Administrative Science Quarterly, 44*(4), 741–763.

Johnson, D. W., Johnson, R. T., & Tjosvold, D. (2006). Constructive controversy: The value of intellectual opposition. In M. Deutsch, P. T. Coleman, & E. C. Marcus (Eds.), *The Handbook of conflict resolution* (2nd ed., pp. 69–91). San Francisco, CA: Wiley.

Kabanoff, B. (1991). Equity, equality, power, and conflict. *Academy of Management Review, 16*(2), 416–442.

Katz, D., & Khan, R. L. (1978). *The social psychology of organizations* (2nd ed.). New York, NY: Wiley.

Kernan, M. C., & Hanges, P. J. (2002). Survivor reactions to reorganization: Antecedents and consequences of procedural, interpersonal, and informational justice. *Journal of Applied Psychology, 87*(5), 916–928. doi:10.1037//0021-9010.87.5.916

Kim, T.-Y., Shapiro, D. L., Aquino, K., Lim, V. K. G., & Bennett, R. J. (2008). Workplace offense and victims' reactions: The effects of victim-offender (dis)similarity, offense-type, and cultural differences. *Journal of Organizational Behavior, 29*(3), 415–433. doi:10.1002/job

King, L. A., & King, D. W. (1990). Role conflict and role ambiguity: A critical assessment of construct validity. *Psychological Bulletin, 107*(1), 48–64. doi:10.1037//0033-2909.107.1.48

Kirkman, B. L., & Shapiro, D. L. (2001). The impact of cultural values on job satisfaction and organizational commitment in self-managing work teams: the mediating role of employee resistance. *Academy of Management Journal, 44*(3), 557–569.

Kramer, R. M. (1991). Intergroup relations and organizational dilemmas: The role of categorization process. In B. M. Staw & L. L. Cummings (Eds.), *Research in organizational behavior* (pp. 191–228). Greenwich, CT: JAI.

Landy, F. J., Barnes, J. L., & Murphy, K. R. (1978). Correlates of perceived fairness and accuracy of performance evaluation. *Journal of Applied Psychology, 63*(6), 751–754. doi:10.1037//0021-9010.63.6.751

Landy, F. J., Barnes-Farrell, J. L., & Cleveland, J. N. (1980). Perceived fairness and accuracy of performance evaluation: A follow-up. *Journal of Applied Psychology, 65*(3), 355–356. doi:10.1037//0021-9010.65.3.355

Leventhal, G. S. (1976). The distribution of rewards and resources in groups and organizations. In L. Berkowitz & W. Walster (Eds.), *Advances in experimental social psychology* (pp. 91–131). New York, NY: Academic Press.

Leventhal, G. S. (1980). What should be done with equity theory? New approaches to the study of fairness in social relationships. In K. Gergen, M. Greenberg, & R. Willis (Eds.), *Social exchange: Advances in theory and research*. New York, NY: Plenum.

Lewicki, R. J., & Hanke, R. (2012). Once fooled, shame on you! Twice fooled, shame on me! What deception does to deceivers and victims: Implications for negotiators when ethicality is unclear. In Barry M. Goldman & D. L. Shapiro (Eds.), *The psychology of negotiations in the 21st century workplace: New challenges and new solutions* (pp. 211–243). New York, NY: Routledge.

Lewicki, R. J., Weiss, S. E., & Lewin, D. (1992). Models of conflict, negotiation and third party intervention: A review and synthesis. *Journal of Organizational Behavior, 13*(3), 209–252. doi:10.1002/job.4030130303

Lian, H., Brown, D. J., Ferris, D. L., Liang, L. H., Keeping, L. M., & Morrison, R. (2012). Abusive supervision and retaliation: A self-control framework. *Academy of Management Journal, 57*(1), 116–139. doi:10.5465/amj.2011.0977

Lovelace, K., Shapiro, D. L., & Weingart, L. R. (2001). Maximizing cross-functional new product teams' innovativeness and constraint adherence: A conflict communications perspective. *Academy of Management Journal, 44*(4), 779–793. doi:10.2307/3069415

Mannes, A. E. (2008). An integrative solution to the conflict over conflict. *Academy of Management Proceedings, 2008*(1), 1–5.

Marks, M. A., Mathieu, J. E., & Zaccaro, S. J. (2001). A temporally based framework and taxonomy of team processes. *Academy of Management Review, 26*(3), 356. doi:10.2307/259182

Miller, C. E., & Komorita, S. S. (1995). Reward allocation in task-performing groups. *Journal of Personality and Social Psychology, 69*(1), 80–90. doi:10.1037//0022-3514.69.1.80

Olekalns, M., Putnam, L. L., & Weingart, L. R. (2008). Conflict management and Communication processes. In C. K. W. De Dreu & M. J. Gelfand (Eds.), *The psychology of conflict and conflict management in organizations* (pp. 81–114). New York, NY: Erlbaum.

Pearson, A. W., Ensley, M. D., & Amason, A. C. (2002). An assessment and refinement of Jehn's intragroup conflict scale. *International Journal of Conflict Management, 13*(2), 110–126.

Peters, S. L., & van den Bos, K. (2008). When fairness is especially important: Reactions to being inequitably paid in communal relationships. *Social Justice Research, 21*(1), 86–105. doi:10.1007/s11211-007-0056-6

Pondy, L. R. (1967). Organizational conflict: Concepts and models. *Administrative Science Quarterly, 12*, 269–320.

Pruitt, D. G. (1983). Strategic choice in negotiation. *American Behavioral Scientist, 27*(2), 167–194.

Pruitt, D. G., & Carnevale, P. J. (1993). *Negotiation in social conflict.* Buckingham, UK: Open University Press.

Putnam, L. L. (1990). Reframing integrative and distributive bargaining: A process perspective. In B. H. Sheppard, M. H. Bazerman, & R. J. Lewicki (Eds.), *Research on negotiation in organizations.* Greenwich, CT: JAI.

Rahim, M. A. (1983). A measure of styles of handling interpersonal conflict. *Academy of Management Journal, 26*(2), 368–377.

Rahim, M. A., & Magner, N. R. (1995). Confirmatory factor analysis of the styles of handling interpersonal conflict: First-order factor model and its invariance across groups. *Journal of Applied Psychology, 80*(1), 122–132.

Rawls, J. (1971). *A theory of justice.* Cambridge, MA: Harvard University Press.

Ren, H., & Gray, B. (2009). Repairing relationship conflict: how violation types and culture influence the effectiveness of restoration rituals. *Academy of Management Review, 34*(1), 105–126.

Rispens, S., Greer, L., Jehn, K. A., & Thatcher, S. M. B. (2011). Not so bad after all: How relational closeness buffers the association between relationship conflict and helpful and deviant group behaviors. *Negotiation and Conflict Management Research, 4*(4), 277–296. doi:10.1111/j.1750-4716.2011.00083.x

Rotondo, D. M., Carlson, D. S., & Kincaid, J. F. (2003). Coping with multiple dimensions of work-family conflict. *Personnel Review, 32*(3), 275–296. doi:10.1108/00483480310467606

Rusbult, C. E., Verette, J., Whitney, G. A., Slovik, L. F., & Lipkus, I. (1991). Accommodation processes in close relationships: Theory and preliminary empirical evidence. *Journal of Personality and Social Psychology, 6*(1), 53–78.

Schmidt, A. M., & DeShon, R. P. (2007). What to do? The effects of discrepancies, incentives, and time on dynamic goal prioritization. *Journal of Applied Psychology, 92*(4), 928–941. doi:10.1037/0021-9010.92.4.928

Schmidt, M. S., & Kochan, T. A. (1972). Conflict: Toward conceptual clarity. *Administrative Science Quarterly, 17*, 359–370.

Shao, R., Rupp, D. E., Skarlicki, D. P., & Jones, K. S. (2013). Employee justice across Cultures: A meta-analytic review. *Journal of Management, 39*(1), 263–301. doi:10.1177/0149206311422447

Shapiro, D. L. (1991). The effects of explanations on negative reactions to deceit. *Administrative Science Quarterly, 36*(4), 614. doi:10.2307/2393276

Shapiro, D. L. (1993). Reconciling theoretical differences among procedural justice researchers by re-evaluating what it means to have one's views "considered": Implications for third-party managers. In R. Cropanzano (Ed.), *Justice in the workplace: Approaching fairness in human resource management* (pp. 51–78). Mahwah, NJ: Erlbaum.

Shapiro, D. L., & Brett, J. M. (1993). Comparing three processes underlying judgments of procedural justice: A field study of mediation and arbitration. *Journal of Personality and Social Psychology, 65*(6), 1167–1177. doi:10.1037//0022-3514.65.6.1167

Shapiro, D. L., & Brett, J. M. (2005). What is the role of control in organizational justice? In J. Greenberg & J. Colquitt (Eds.), *Handbook of organizational justice* (pp. 155–177). Mahwah, NJ: Erlbaum.

Shapiro, D. L., Drieghe, R., & Brett, J. M. (1985). Mediator behavior and the outcome of mediation. *Journal of Social Issues, 41*(2), 101–114.

Shapiro, D. L., & Kolb, D. M. (1994). Reducing the "litigious mentality" by increasing employees' desire to communicate grievances. In S. Sitkin & R. J. Bies (Eds.), *The legalistic organization* (pp. 304–326). Newbury Park, CA: Sage.

Shapiro, D. L., & Kulik, C. T. (2004). Resolving disputes between faceless disputants: New challenges for conflict management theory. In Michele J. Gelfand & J. M. Brett (Eds.), *The handbook of negotiation and culture* (pp. 177–192). Standford, CA: Stanford Business Books.

Shapiro, D. L., & Rosen, B. (1994). An investigation of managerial interventions in employee disputes. *Employee Responsibilities and Rights Journal, 7*(1), 37–51.

Sheppard, B. H., & Lewicki, R. J. (1987). Toward general principles of managerial fairness. *Social Justice Research, 1*(2), 161–176.

Sherif, M. (1966). *Group conflict and cooperation: Their social psychology.* London: Routledge & Kegan Paul.

Skarlicki, D. P., & Kulik, C. T. (2005). Third-party reactions to employee (mis)treatment: A justice perspective. In Barry M. Staw & R. M. Kramer (Eds.), *Research in organizational behavior* (pp. 183–230). Greenwich, CT: JAI.

Stoffey, R. W., & Reilly, R. R. (1997). Training appraisees to participate in appraisal: Effects on appraisers and appraisees. *Journal of Business and Psychology, 12*(2), 219–240.

Tangney, J. P., Baumeister, R. F., & Boone, A. L. (2004). High self-control predicts good adjustment, less pathology, better grades, and interpersonal success. *Journal of Personality, 72*(2), 271–324.

Taylor, M. S., Tracy, K. B., Renard, M. K., Harrison, J. K., & Carroll, S. J. (1995). Due process in performance appraisal: A quasi-experiment in procedural justice. *Administrative Science Quarterly, 40*(3), 495. doi:10.2307/2393795

Tekleab, A. G., Quigley, N. R., & Tesluk, P. E. (2009). A longitudinal study of team conflict, conflict management, cohesion, and team effectiveness. *Group & Organization Management, 34*(2), 170–205. doi:10.1177/1059601108331218

Thibaut, J., & Walker, L. (1975). *Procedural justice: A psychological analysis.* Hillsdale, NJ: Erlbaum.

Thibaut, J., & Walker, L. (1978). A theory of procedure. *California Law Review, 66*(3), 541–566. doi:10.2307/3480099

Thomas, K. W. (1998). Conflict and conflict management: Reflections and update. *Journal of Organizational Behavior, 13*(3), 265–274.

Tidd, S. T., & Friedman, R. A. (2002). Conflict style and coping with role conflict: An extension of the uncertainty model of work stress. *International Journal of Conflict Management, 13*(3), 236–257.

Tjosvold, D., Law, K. S., & Sun, H. (2006). Effectiveness of Chinese teams: The role of conflict types and conflict management approaches. *Management and Organization Review*, *2*(2), 231–252. doi:10.1111/j.1740-8784.2006.00040.x

Tomlinson, E. C., & Mayer, R. C. (2009). The role of causal attribution dimensions in trust repair. *Academy of Management Review*, *34*(1), 85–104. doi:10.5465/AMR.2009.35713291

Tornblom, K. Y., & Jonsson, D. R. (1985). Subrules of the equality and contribution principles: Their perceived fairness in distribution and retribution. *Social Psychology Quarterly*, *48*(3), 249–261.

Van de Vliert, E., & Euwema, M. C. (1994). Agreeableness and activeness as components of conflict behaviors. *Journal of Personality and Social Psychology*, *66*(4), 674–687.

Van de Vliert, E., & Kabanoff, B. (1990). Toward theory-based measures of conflict management. *Academy of Management Journal*, *33*(1), 199–209.

Van den Bos, K., Lind, E. A., Vermunt, R., & Wilke, H. A. M. (1997). How do I judge my outcome when I do not know the outcome of others? The psychology of the fair process effect. *Journal of Personality and Social Psychology*, *72*(5), 1034–1046.

Van den Bos, K., Wilke, H. A. M., Lind, E. A., & Vermunt, R. (1998). Evaluating outcomes by means of the fair process effect: evidence for different processes in fairness and satisfaction judgments. *Journal of Personality and Social Psychology*, *74*(6), 1493–1503.

Von Glinow, M. A., Shapiro, D. L., & Brett, J. M. (2004). Can we talk, and should we? Managing emotional conflict in multicultural teams. *Academy of Management Review*, *29*(4), 578–592.

Wall, J. A. J., & Callister, R. R. (1995). Conflict and its management. *Journal of Management*, *21*(3), 515–558.

Walster, E., Berscheid, E., & Walster, G. W. (1973). New directions in equity research. *Journal of Personality and Social Psychology*, *25*(2), 151–176. doi:10.1037/h0033967

Weingart, L. R. (1997). How did they do that? The ways and means of studying group process. *Research in Organizational Behavior*, *19*, 189–239.

Weingart, L. R., & Jehn, K. A. (2009). Manage intra-team conflict through collaboration. In E. A. Locke (Ed.), *Handbook of principles of organizational behavior: Indispensable knowledge for evidence-based management* (2nd ed., pp. 327–346).

Zuckerman, M., DePaulo, B. M., & Rosenthal, R. (1981). Verbal and nonverbal communication of deception. *Advances in experimental social psychology*, *14*(1), 1–59.

CHAPTER

22 "Doing Justice": The Role of Motives for Revenge in the Workplace

Thomas M. Tripp *and* Robert J. Bies

Abstract

This chapter reviews research on workplace aggression that is motivated by perceptions of injustice, covering mostly the last five years. In particular, the motive to "do justice" to an injustice by engaging in revenge is examined. As several emerging domains make clear—including new contexts in which revenge is being studied, such as customer-service encounters, and other disciplines, such as neuroscience—the motives for much workplace aggression are justice-driven, though not always as justice-driven nor as rational as avengers claim. Indeed, strong emotions often precede and prime perceptions of injustice that motivate revenge; it is not always the case that a sense of injustice precedes the moral outrage that drives the desire for revenge. This argument, and recent findings from which it emerges, are discussed within a model of the antecedents, consequences, and moderators of the desire for workplace revenge.

Key Words: revenge, justice, conflict, aggression, anger, forgiveness, coping

Introduction

> "Revenge is the act of passion; vengeance is an act of justice. Injuries are revenged; crimes are avenged."
> —*Samuel Johnson*, Dictionary of the English Language (1755)

It has been almost two decades since we published our first paper on revenge in the workplace (Bies & Tripp, 1996). Since the publication of that paper, there has been an explosion of research on revenge and related topics, such as retaliation (Allred, 1999; Skarlicki & Folger, 1997), deviant workplace behaviors (Robinson & Bennett, 1995), workplace aggression (Neuman & Baron, 1997; O'Leary-Kelly, Griffin, & Glew, 1996), incivility (Anderssen & Pearson, 1999), bullying (Zapf, Einarson, Hoel & Vartia, 2003), violence in the workplace (Folger & Skarlicki, 1998), workplace forgiveness (Bradfield & Aquino, 1999), and consumer retaliation against firms (Grégoire & Fisher, 2008). Several reviews of research on revenge have occurred over the past decade (e.g., Bies & Tripp, 2004; Fox & Spector, 2005; McCullough, 2008; McCullough, Kurzban, & Tabak, 2013; Miller, 2001; Tripp & Bies, 2009; Tripp, Bies, & Aquino, 2007), as well as meta-analyses of related constructs (e.g., Fehr, Gelfand, & Nag, 2010, on forgiveness; Hershcovis et al., 2007, on aggression).

This chapter has three sections. First, we distinguish revenge from related constructs (e.g., aggression, bullying). Second, rather than reviewing the same literature in the earlier reviews just noted, we instead provide an overview of recent research findings on revenge. In this section, we highlight domains of research on revenge research, including new organizational processes in which revenge is being studied (e.g., customer service encounters), and revenge research guided by new frameworks of analysis (e.g., neuroscience). In this review, we identify antecedents, consequences, and moderators of the revenge response. In doing so, we highlight the importance of understanding the motives for revenge, with a particular focus on the justice motivation for revenge. Finally, we take stock of where we are in the current state of research on revenge.

Revenge and Related Constructs: Making Conceptual Distinctions

In this section, we discuss revenge as a construct relative to related constructs, and how a justice lens shapes theories of revenge. Although revenge may not always *do* justice, it is important for scholars to understand and analyze revenge in justice terms; for, in phenomenological terms, that is what a person *perceives* and *feels* when engaging in an act of revenge. The study of revenge has occurred in a field of many related constructs (Bies & Tripp, 2005; Tepper, 2007). Some scholars have called for the field to reconcile overlapping constructs (Hershcovis, 2011). Taking up this call, Benson (2013) found evidence that suggests that many of these constructs are the same.

We agree with these scholars that the field would benefit from using fewer constructs. Workplace aggression seems the most neutral of the possible constructs, and perhaps the one that scholars will feel the least territorial about. That said, however, our interest here is not merely nor wholly the study of workplace aggression, *whatever the cause* (e.g., frustration, sadism, inattentiveness). We are interested in what employees *do* after perceiving an injustice. Employees may do many things, including aggression, avoidance, forgiveness and reconciliation (Tripp, Bies & Aquino, 2007). When they aggress, in response to an injustice, such aggression has a common name, that is, *revenge*. Thus, we study not just any form of workplace aggression, but revenge-motivated workplace aggression. However, for the sake of brevity and clarity, we use the label *revenge* throughout this chapter.

In a previous review, we analyzed the relationship of revenge to related constructs (Bies & Tripp, 2005). In that analysis, we argued that revenge is uniquely different from other workplace aggression constructs. Briefly, our analysis argued that:

- Revenge is not always, if even usually, the same thing as incivility, which can be motivated by competitiveness, sadistic impulses, or inattentiveness, none of which are revenge motives (Andersson & Pearson, 1999; Lim, Cortina, & Magley, 2008).
- Revenge is not the same thing as bullying (Randall, 2001; Einerasen, Hoel & Notelaers, 2009), which is about individuals who instigate aggression for sadistic pleasure, not about those who feel provoked to respond to aggression with more aggression.
- Revenge is not the same thing as abusive supervision (Tepper, 2000, 2007), because, though abusive supervisors may engage in revenge, so do many other employees who are not supervisors or not "abusive."
- Revenge is not the same thing as deviance, either in terms of normative deviance or statistical deviance (Robinson & Bennett, 1995). Nor is revenge necessarily a "counter-productive work behavior" because sometimes it may actually resolve conflicts, create trust, and improve workplace conditions (Axelrod, 1984; Bies & Tripp, 1998; Tripp & Bies, 1997).

In sum, what makes "revenge" unique is that, unlike these other constructs, revenge includes a specific motive: to get even. Revenge is concerned with reactions to perceived workplace *injustices*. Thus, we define revenge as an action in response to some perceived harm or wrongdoing by another party that is intended to inflict damage, injury, discomfort, or punishment on the party judged responsible (Aquino, Tripp, & Bies, 2001).

The preceding approach and definition means that when we examine revenge-motivated aggression, we focus on the aggressor's motives for the act of revenge. Motives are essential. For example, one reason one employee may be uncivil to another is that the employee is getting even for a past transgression. In such cases, *incivility* is perhaps better understood as an act of revenge. Sometimes the same may go for acts of organizational deviance and abuse. We are not claiming that all uncivil and deviant acts are motivated by the urge to get even; indeed, many such acts may occur due to negligence (e.g., social clumsiness). (As the Hanlon's razor prescribes, "never attribute to malice that which can be explained by stupidity.") Moreover, in our work, we focus on the justice-related motives for revenge because we are justice scholars. That is, our theoretical question, which has guided us over the past 20 years, is not "why do employees aggress?" but, rather, "once employees are treated unfairly, what do they do next?" Answers to the second question contribute to what had been a neglected area in organizational justice theory: the field spent decades parsing out various fairness perceptions and causes of such perceptions (e.g., breaking interactional justice off from procedural justice; splitting interactional justice into interpersonal and informational justices), but after Stacy Adams' seminal work on equity theory (Adams, 1963, 1965), the field spent little effort determining how employees react to unfairness once they perceive it. In the next section, we turn our attention to what people do in response to a perceived injustice—and why.

Engaging in Revenge: Antecedents, Consequences, and Moderators

In Tripp et al. (2007), we laid out a model of revenge that incorporates what we knew up to that time, regarding antecedents, consequences, and moderators of revenge. We summarize that model here to provide a framework for considering new findings. The model follows a sequence: (a) Revenge is "triggered" by an event; (b) the victim blames the offender responsible for the trigger, (c) the victim becomes motivated to seek revenge; and (d) the victim copes with the motivation/desire to seek revenge by choosing to actually get revenge, avoid the offender, forgive the offender and/or reconcile with offender. Moreover, various factors moderate the choice of which coping response the avenger chooses, including power differences, procedural justice climate, and personality traits. Since we published this model in 2007, other research has explored better how motives shape revenge—both the victim's perceptions of the offender's motives, and the victim's motives—including how emotion accelerates these processes. We also note that much of this research comes from nonorganizational domains such as marketing and neuroscience.

Triggers of Revenge

Our research (e.g., Bies & Tripp, 1996), and that of others (e.g., Allred, 1999; Jones, 2010; Skarlicki & Folger, 1997), makes it quite clear that revenge is a provoked, or "triggered," behavior.

Triggers include (a) goal obstruction (e.g., inadequate resource support); (b) violation of rules, norms, and promises (e.g., shirking job responsibilities, taking undue credit for a team's performance); and (c) status and power derogation (e.g., public ridicule, destructive criticism). In general, the perception of injustice is a major driver of revenge. Thus, not surprisingly, in Hershcovis et al.'s (2007) meta-analysis of aggression, injustice shows up as a predictor of aggression, including revenge. Similarly, Jones (2009) finds that injustice predicts the desire for revenge, which, in turn, strongly predicts counterproductive workplace behaviors. DiMatteo, Bird, and Colquitt (2011) show that perceptions of unfair employment discharges lead to increased retaliation and litigation (see also Goldman, 2003). The perception of un-remedied injustice may also inhibit forgiveness. According to Worthington's injustice gap theory (Worthington, 2006), until a victim sees that justice is served to the offender, forgiveness is much harder. In short, forgiveness is conditional on justice.

Other studies show that injustice predicts other aggressive actions. For instance, in the deviance literature, Holtz and Harold (2013) find that perceived injustice predicts organizational deviance. Semmer, Tschan, Meier, Facchin, and Jacobshagen (2010) show that when employees are asked to perform illegitimate tasks, which employees perceive as unfair, employees engage in more counterproductive work behaviors. Jensen, Opland, and Ryan (2010) find that psychological contract breaches predict counterproductive workplace behaviors. Although Jensen et al. did not measure perceptions of injustice, other scholars note that psychological contract breaches are often perceived as unfair (e.g., Dimatteo et al., 2011; Kickul, Neuman, Parker, & Finkl, 2001) and that injustice predicts counterproductive workplace behaviors (Kickul et al., 2001). Similarly, Coyle-Shapiro (2002) finds that psychological contract breaches predict perceptions of injustice, which, in turn, negatively correlate with organizational citizenship behaviors. Note that, if injustice predicts these other actions, then these actions could be better understood as being motivated by revenge. Supporting this interpretation, in a multisource survey of supervisor–employee pairs, Hung, Chi, and Lu (2009) find that the relationship between social loafing and counterproductive workplace behaviors is fully mediated by the revenge motive. Also, Mitchell and Ambrose (2007) find that the belief in negative reciprocity moderates the effect between abusive supervision and employee deviance. Clearly, such effects can be understood as acts of revenge (Mitchell & Ambrose, 2012).

The Assignment of Blame

How much a victim blames an offender for the offense affects how motivated the victim is to seek revenge (Barclay, Skarlicki, & Pugh, 2005; Bechwati & Morrin, 2007, Grégoire, Laufer, & Tripp, 2010; Weiner, 2000). To a victim, blame justifies seeking revenge; that is, it provides the justification that is perhaps necessary for committing such a taboo act (Jacoby, 1983).

Recent research sheds light on how the victim's perceptions and inferences of the offender's motive for the offense affects how much the victim blames the offender. For example, in the management literature, Crossley (2009) conducted a scenario experiment, where he varied the motives that victims perceive the offender to have. He finds that the more the victim infers that the offender was motivated to harm that particular victim (i.e., "malice" motive)—as opposed to being willing to harm any person who would advance the offender's agenda (i.e., "greed" motive)—the angrier the victim becomes, and the more revenge and avoidance, and less reconciliation, the victim seeks.

The marketing literature also has investigated how victims perceive offenders' motives. The marketing scholars are especially concerned with the context of "service failures," when a firm fails to provide quality service or product, and of "double-deviations" when not only did a service failure occur but also the firm "doubled" the harm by not recovering from the failure with some kind of accommodation or repair. In such situations, some customers seek revenge. Forms of customer revenge include: (a) private negative word of mouth to others, (b) voicing their concerns to the firm, and (c) seeking third-party help by contacting a consumer agency, legal experts, mass media, or the Internet (Gelbrich, 2010; Johnson, Matear, & Thomson, 2011; Singh, 1988). Note that not all such complaining is merely an instrumental means to secure a better service or product; recent research shows that customers may also engage in *vindictive* complaining by verbally attacking firm employees in order to upset them, and by complaining to third parties to cause inconvenience to firms (Bonifield & Cole 2007). Indeed, a recent form of vindictive complaining involves online review sites, such as rippedoffreport.com, consumeraffairs.com, and yelp.com (Gregoire, Tripp, & Legoux, 2009), where upset customers can spread negative word of mouth much farther than before.

Examining why consumers engage in such revenge, Joireman, Gregoire, Devezer, and Tripp (2013) confirm that consumers do spontaneously consider firms' motives for service failures before responding. Moreover, in a field study of airline passengers who complained about poor service, Joireman et al. show that customers' inferences of firms' motives mediate the effect of failure severity, blame attribution, perceived fairness on the desire for revenge. In a follow-up scenario experiment, Joireman et al. manipulate perceived motives for a service failure as positive or negative (i.e., greedy), and show that perceived firm motives affect the desire for revenge and the desire for reconciliation. Specifically, when customers perceive a positive motive for the double deviation, they are more likely to desire reconciliation than to desire revenge. In contrast, when customers perceive a negative motive, they are more likely to desire revenge than to desire reconciliation. Grégoire et al. (2010) investigate inferences of the specific negative motives of firm greed, using two critical incident studies (one of online complainers and one of students). Similarly, they find that perceived greed fully mediates the effects of blame attribution and perceived fairness (all three types) on the desire for revenge and on actual direct revenge behaviors (i.e., vindictive complaining, marketplace aggression) and indirect revenge behaviors (i.e., online complaining for negative publicity, negative word of mouth).

Recent advances in neuroscience also speak to the importance of victims' inferences of the offender's motives in how victims respond to offenses. Much research in the last decade uses brain-imaging equipment (e.g., fMRI and PET-scan machines) to explore the locations in the human brain where various processes lie, including anger, perceived injustice, and revenge. For instance, Sanfey, Rilling, Aronson, Nystrom, and Cohen (2003) had subjects play the "ultimatum game," while lying in a functional Magnetic Resonance Imaging (fMRI) machine. In the ultimatum game, two people are given a fixed sum of money to divide. One person, the proposer, gets to propose a split of the money, and the other person, the decider, decides to accept or reject the split. If the decider rejects the proposed split, neither person gets any money. Typically, offers that allocate 80% or more for the proposer (and thus 20% or less for the decider) are usually rejected. That is, the deciders get even when proposers make such "greedy" offers. In Sanfey et al.'s experiment, each subject saw 30 offers believed to be from either another subject or from a computer. Some offers were even (i.e., $5 each), and some were uneven (e.g., $9 to the proposer, $1 to the decider). When subjects received even offers from persons, or any kind of offer from the computer, the dorsolateral prefrontal cortex (DLPFC)—where thought, but not feeling, occurs—was involved. When subjects saw uneven offers from people, however, then not only the DLPFC was involved, but also the anterior insula region of the brain, which is associated with negative emotion.

The significance of the Sanfey et al. finding here is that people get angry only when they believe a person has acted stingy, but not when a computer has acted stingy. One essential difference between the computer and the person is that only persons can form greedy intent. As such, there is really no reason to become angry with a computer as there is with a person, whose intent may be to "cheat" another. Also, note that, because these ultimatum games were one-shot games, acts of revenge could have no instrumental value, only deontic value. Thus, this research suggests that victim-cum-avengers consider the offender's intent, which can make the victims genuinely angry. Other neuroscience research shows that information about intentions affects moral judgments of others. For instance, studies, such as those conducted by Rebecca Saxe and colleagues (e.g., Young, Scholz, & Saxe, 2011), show that a specific brain area (the right temporo-parietal junction) is involved when people make moral judgments about other people's intentions. Young et al. (2011) conclude there is neurological evidence that one must have a theory of the (offender's) mind, what her or his intentions are, to form moral judgments.

In forgiveness, inferences of the offenders' intent also play a role. Indeed, in the Fehr et al. (2010) meta-analysis of forgiveness studies, offenders' intent had corrected $r = -.49$ with forgiveness. That is, the greater the victim's belief of the offender's intent to harm is, then the less forgiving the victim is. And the less forgiving the victim is, then the more likely the victim will seek revenge, because revenge and forgiveness are conceptually antithetical and empirically negatively correlated [though far from perfectly negatively correlated, e.g., $r = -.32$ in Aquino et al. (2006); similarly, in Joireman et al. (2013), $r = -.33$ and $-.25$, between desire for revenge and desire for reconciliation across two studies].

Motives for Revenge

So far we have discussed the role the victims' perceptions of the *offender's* motives plays in the victims' reactions to injustice. But what of the *victim's* motives? What do victims hope to accomplish in seeking revenge? For instance, how much of customers' vengeful behavior is motivated by the wish to the see the firm suffer versus bullying the firm to provide better service?

When we asked this question of workers who had sought revenge (Tripp & Bies 1997), answers they gave us included: restoring justice, deterrence, improving self-esteem (by "standing up" for oneself), restoring status and identity (see also Aquino & Douglas, 2003), and helping others. Zdaniuk and Bobocel (2012) show that often revenge restores victims' self-esteem when the self-esteem was diminished by the offense. Jones (2010) argues that such motives may also reflect a need to reassert control (see also, Cropanzano, Byrne, Bobocel, & Rupp, 2001). These motives are also found in non-workplace contexts, and deterrence in particular may be why humans evolved revenge mechanisms (McCullough et al., 2013). Another motive, implicit in the deterrence motive, is to "teach a lesson" to the offender (Miller, 2001). Arguably, revenge may not create deterrence unless the offender learns the lesson that offenses are punished with revenge acts (Axelrod, 1984).

A limitation of much of this research is that it relies too much on self-report data. One of the conclusions from neuroscience research is that motives are often formed subconsciously, informed by implicit attitudes of which respondents may be unaware, and thus asking respondents what motivated certain actions results in, at best, incomplete answers, and at worst, incorrect answers (Becker, Cropanzano, & Sanfey, 2011). For example, an emotion such as envy can be automatic and not deliberative (Joseph, Powell, Johnson & Kedia, 2008). As Becker et al. (2011) argue, "we have little insight into where implicit attitudes come from, often confusing a nonconscious bias with a self-justifying rationalization" (p. 940). Avengers, who should be as egocentrically biased as anyone, may have and report self-justifying rationalizations instead of their actual motives. This could be one reason that, in Jones's (2010) interviews with people who had committed workplace revenge, he finds their accounts filled with justifications based on "doing justice" to an injustice. How many of those who reported that their revenge was intended to deter future aggression, may have acted first and then invented the rationalization later? Might some avengers invent rationalizations *post*-revenge to make themselves feel better about committing such a taboo act (Haidt, 2001)?

If so, injustice may not be the cause of aggression as often as aggressors might have us believe. However, injustice must be the cause at least some of the time, because too many studies have shown a correlation between perceived injustice and workplace aggression (Hershcovis et al., 2007) and forgiveness (Worthington, 2006). In such studies, not all rely on self-reports for why the aggressor aggressed.

Neuroscience research, which does not rely on self-reports, reveals some of the motives for revenge. Sanfey et al.'s (2003) experiment shows that revenge is not merely an attempt to secure economic gain. Rather, avengers feel injustice and anger that is quite real, which is evident from the fact that the part of the brain associated with negative emotion is activated. This study strongly suggests that avengers have a deontic motive in addition to whatever other motives they may have. Such a motive could explain "altruistic punishment," in which someone punishes another who violates social norms, even though the punisher cannot benefit economically (indeed, may pay economic costs to administer the punishment). Other neuroscience research supports this conclusion. For instance, recent studies (Singer et al., 2006; de Quervain et al., 2004) show that witnessing punishment of others who have acted unfairly activates the "reward circuits" of the brain (i.e., left ventral striatum/nucleus accumbens). Note that were revenge solely motivated by instrumental reasons, then there should be no pleasure in witnessing unfair people, with whom one will not have future interactions, get punished.

Exactly what kind of deontic motive may avengers have? One reason victims report avenging is to teach the offender a lesson (Tripp & Bies, 1997). If such self-reports are accurate, perhaps avengers will enjoy revenge more if, postrevenge, the offender learns a lesson. Gollwitzer and Denzler (2009) tested whether avengers really do feel better when they see that offenders learn their lessons. Gollwitzer and Denzler (2009, and Gollwitzer, Meder, & Schmitt, 2011) argue that if teaching a lesson is *not* important, then just seeing the offender suffer (as much as the victim suffered from the original offense) should be satisfactory enough. However, in several experiments they show that when the avenger can see that the offender *understands* that the suffering is in retribution for the offense, the avenger experiences more satisfaction than when the avenger sees that the offender believes the suffering is due to chance. The authors conclude, "Revenge does not seem to be merely about paying back, it is also about delivering a message" (Gollwitzer et al., 2011, p. 372).

Other evidence suggests that although victims may seek certain goals and payoffs, they do not always achieve them. Tripp and Bies (1997) report that one reason avengers judge their own actions as "bad" is because they lead to consequences the avengers did not predict, such as escalating a conflict rather than resolving it. In short, revenge may not lead to the satisfying emotions avengers hope. As the affective forecasting literature has demonstrated (Wilson & Gilbert, 2005), people often misforecast how they will feel when certain choices turn out as hoped. For instance, certain choices may not make people as happy as they predict it will (Loewenstein & Schadke, 1999). Regarding the choice to seek revenge, evidence suggests that angry avengers expect revenge will produce catharsis, but, in fact, it does not (Geen & Quanty, 1977). For example, Wiltermuth and Tiedens (2011) show that angry people think they would enjoy evaluating others and that evaluating others' low quality ideas would make them feel better. Yet, other research shows that these angry people are wrong: they do not feel better after revenge, they feel worse. In a series of experiments, Carlsmith, Wilson, and Gilbert (2008) show that avengers often do not receive the cathartic closure they seek and expect but, instead, end up ruminating even more, extending their anger. In Carlsmith et al.'s experiments, some subjects were given the chance to punish free riders. Subjects predicted that they would feel better if they could punish free riders, yet subjects who could punish free riders (experimental condition) felt *worse* (i.e., more negative affect, and more rumination) than subjects who could not punish free riders (control condition). However, Konecni (2013) notes that revenge may make people feel better when it successfully removes the "irritant" trigger that otherwise may keep upsetting the victim, for example, when deterrence is successful.

Recent research also explores the motives behind workplace forgiveness (e.g., Aquino, Grover, Goldman, & Folger, 2003; Bright, Fry, & Cooperrider, 2006). Cox, Bennett, Tripp, and Aquino (2012) use factor analysis to analyze data from a series of critical-incident-based field surveys and find five motives for forgiveness:

- *Moral*, when the victim believes forgiveness is the most ethical choice.
- *Relationship*, when the victim believes that not forgiving would jeopardize a highly-valued relationship.
- *Apology*, when the victim forgives because the offender apologized.
- *Religious*, when the victim follows religious norms that proscribe forgiveness.
- *Lack of alternatives*, when the victim believes that any act other than forgiveness would bring about even worse consequences (e.g., severe counter-retaliation).

Moreover, Cox et al. find that how effective forgiveness is at reducing negative emotions depends on the motive for forgiveness: moral motives to forgive lead to health benefits (e.g., reduced stress), but religious and lack-of-alternatives motives lead to reduced health.

Emotions as Accelerators for Revenge

Although we have discussed the emotions of revenge elsewhere as hot, intense, and enduring (e.g., Bies & Tripp, 2002), we did not include emotions in our 2007 model beyond the recognition that anger accompanies revenge (Tripp et al., 2007). Rather, our model reflected the more conscious, rational approach to revenge as cost-benefit calculation to restore justice, similar (in this respect) to McCullough et al.'s cognitive system model of revenge and forgiveness that led the 2013 *Behavioral and Brain Science* special issue on revenge. But as most of the published peer commentaries in the same issue attest (e.g., Aureli & Schaffner, 2013; Holbrook, Fessler, & Gervais, 2013; Konecni, 2013; Leiser & Joskowicz-Jabloner, 2013; O'Conner & Adams, 2013; Potegal, 2013; Sell, 2013; Uhlmann, 2013; Yu, 2013), any complete model of revenge must better account for emotions, because revenge is not just a calculated decision to restore justice; quite often, it is emotionally driven (O'Conner & Adams, 2013), and can be visceral in nature (Bies & Tripp, in press). Strong emotions such as anger amplify the desire for revenge (Darley & Pittman, 2003; O'Conner & Adams, 2013). For this and other reasons, justice scholars are now advocating an integration of affect into justice theories (e.g., Cropanzano, Stein, & Nadisic, 2010; DeCremer, 2007; Hillebrandt & Barclay, 2013). Thus, in this section, we explore recent research that reveals some of the ways emotion shapes revenge.

Beugré (2009) proposes a "neuro-organizational justice" model that incorporates emotional and neural aspects of employee's reactions to injustice. He argues the aim of this model is "specifying how the individual thinks from the moment the first stimuli are encountered through the transmission of electrochemical signals in the brain, to the engagement of actual behavior" (p. 130). Summarizing much neuroscience research (especially, Lieberman, Gaunt, Gilbert, and Trope, 2002), Beugré details how cognitions and emotions are not separate, but influence each other reciprocally through neural circuits. In short, an emotional, usually subconscious, automatic, perceptual pattern-matching system ("X-system" in Lieberman et al.'s terms, or "System 1" in Kahneman's, 2011, terminology) determines our reactions and preferences. Sometimes the other system—the cognitive, reflective, deliberative, conscious mind (the "C" system in Lieberman et al.'s terms, or "System 2" in Kahneman's, 2011, terminology)—gets involved. It gets involved after receiving outside information that contradicts one's initial judgments by double-checking the X-system's perceptions and preferences, and when System 1 cannot handle a novel stimulus that does not match known patterns and prototypes. Regarding these systems' roles in fairness judgments, Beugré notes, "the C-system is capable of rule-based analysis and performs a regulatory role over the X-system. Thus the X-system is dependent on the C-system for its supply of prototypes" (p. 131). Rules include standards such as equity or voice; prototypes include scripts or templates about fair outcomes and fair treatments (Ambrose & Kulik, 2001). When others' behavior violates such scripts and prototypes, emotion may arise before cognitive judgment does (because the X-system is much faster than the C-system). More simply, as van den Bos (2007) put it: "in some situations people seem to construct justice judgments in a thorough way, weighing all the relevant information carefully in an impartial manner... whereas in other circumstances... people's gut reactions seem to lead to snap judgments" (p. 62). Thus, justice judgments are not always reflective and deliberative, nor are they always the driver of emotions such as moral outrage; often justice judgments are quick and automatic, and as much as justice judgments influence affect, affect also influences judgment (for a review of research on the reciprocal influence of justice and affect, see Cohen-Charash & Byrne, 2008).

Revenge, because it depends on justice judgments, requires that we consider the preceding neuroscience and affect research. Also, because revenge runs both hot and cold (i.e., has both cognitions and emotions, which both mediate perceptions and reactions; e.g., Gregoire et al., 2010), revenge theory would benefit from a better understanding of how emotions arise from the subconscious and influence decisions to seek revenge.

Some research already addresses this issue. For instance, anger from unfair offers in ultimatum games causes negotiators to reject profitable offers (Pillutla & Murnighan, 1996). However, concerns about injustice do not simply serve to foul up negotiations and undermine decision-making.

Lerner and Tiedens (2006) show that anger can improve decision-making when anger spotlights issues as urgent and important, and thus motivates action. Thus, anger is not merely a bias that makes decision-making less logical, but it also can serve as an "alarm" to motivate System 2 to analyze a novel threat. Peters, Vastfjall, Garling, and Slovic (2006) propose that affect has four helpful roles in improving decision-making: (1) affect as a "spotlight" to mark important issues; (2) affect as a motivator of information processing and decision-making; (3) affect as information about how the choice should be made; and, (4) affect as a "common currency" that allows comparison of qualitatively different alternatives. What the preceding research supports is that specific emotions often precede justice judgments.

What about moods? Byrne, Rupp, and Eurich (2003) find that positive moods increase favorable justice perceptions. Can such moods extend beyond judgments to actions, namely, influencing revenge? The Wiltermuth and Tiedens' (2011) experiment, described earlier, suggests so. What's interesting about the anger in the Wiltermuth and Tiedens' (2011) experiment is that the anger their evaluators felt was incidental to the task of evaluating, the subjects were not angry at the people they were evaluating, and the evaluatees did not offend or provoke the evaluators. Yet, the angry evaluators believed that rating these evaluatees harshly would lead to catharsis nonetheless. Our point here is that even *incidental* anger primed vengeful responses.

If incidental anger, and more generally negative moods, can make revenge more likely, then recent research on visceral reactions to environmental stimuli becomes important. These visceral factors have direct hedonic consequences and a disproportionate effect on behavior, "crowding out" virtually all goals other than that of mitigating the visceral factor (Loewenstein, 1996). That is, sometimes people can experience negative emotions not due to any act of another person, but simply due to their environment. When this happens, does revenge follow? Research on heat and aggression suggests the answer is yes.

Criminologists have known for some time that more violent crimes are committed when temperatures rise (though up to a point where it becomes so hot that people remain indoors instead of going out to commit crimes; Rotton & Cohn, 2004). Hsiang, Burke, and Miguel (2013) reviewed studies of heat, conflict, and war, across a wide variety of disciplines, including: archaeology, criminology, economics, geography, history, political science, and psychology. They find that for each standard deviation change in climate toward warmer temperatures, the frequency of interpersonal violence rises 4% and the frequency of intergroup conflict rises 14%.

In an earlier review of heat and aggression, Anderson (2001) proposes a mechanism that can explain how heat causes aggression. Mainly, Anderson says:

> heat makes people "cranky," which then distorts the social interaction process toward revenge. That is, such distortion increases anger... which in turn primes aggressive thoughts, attitudes, preparatory behaviors (e.g., fist clenching), and behavioral scripts (such as "retaliation" scripts). A minor provocation can quickly escalate, especially if both participants are affectively and cognitively primed for hostility by their heightened level of discomfort. A mild insult is more likely to provoke a severe insult in response when people are hot than when they are more comfortable. This may lead to further increases in the aggressiveness of responses and counter-responses. An accidental bump in a hot and crowded bar can lead to the trading of insults, punches, and (eventually) bullets (p. 36).

As an example of heat-induced retaliation, Larrick, Timmerman, Caron, and Abrevaya (2011) analyzed nearly 60,000 Major League Baseball games to see if high temperatures increase the prevalence of batters being hit by a pitch. They found that probability of a pitcher hitting a batter, when the pitcher's teammates are hit by the opposing team's pitcher earlier in the game, increases abruptly at higher temperatures.

Responses to the Desire for Revenge

When feeling unfairly treated, revenge is but one of several possible responses that people can take. Other responses could be avoidance, forgiveness, or reconciliation. Several scholars (e.g., Bies & Tripp, 1996; Bradfield & Aquino, 1999; McCullough, 2008; Tripp & Bies, 2009; Tripp et al. 2007) have identified many possible responses to perceived injustice. Next, we summarize recent research on possible responses to perceived injustice.

Recently, the marketing literature has begun to study how consumers get even with firms for bad service (Ariely, 2007; Bechwati & Morrin, 2003, 2007; Bonnifield & Cole, 2007), especially in the form of online public complaining (Gregoire et al., 2009; Ward & Ostrom, 2006). Other responses include negative word of mouth, vindictive complaining to the firm (e.g., giving customer service representatives "a hard time"), and reducing patronage. In this literature, they find that perceptions of injustice predict revenge (e.g., Gregoire et al., 2009, 2010; Joireman et al., 2013).

Common experience suggests that, just because victims may desire revenge does not mean that they always, in fact, seek revenge. The research generally supports this common wisdom. In no study that we know of that has measured both the desire for revenge and revenge actions, is the correlation perfect. For instance, in a recent study (Joireman et al., 2013) where both the desire for revenge and the act of revenge were measured in the consumer context of service failure and failed service recovery attempts, zero-order correlations were only about r =.6, on average. This quite imperfect correlation begs the question: what else do victims do with the desire for revenge?

Justice researchers have turned to studying other responses to the desire for revenge, especially forgiveness. Since Bradfield and Aquino's (1999) seminal research on workplace forgiveness, dozens of studies in the field on workplace forgiveness have appeared (many of which we have discussed earlier), and on related topics of trust repair and effective apologies (see Fehr et al., 2010, for a review), not counting the scores of studies in psychology on interpersonal forgiveness (see McCullough, 2008, for a review). New avenues in workplace forgiveness research include taking a macro perspective on how organizational practices and institutions shape the choice and acts of forgiveness and reconciliation. For example, Fehr and Gelfand (2012) propose a multilevel model of forgiveness that takes into account organizational culture and how that may create a forgiveness climate. Bies, Tripp, and Barclay (2012) also explore how organizational institutions, such as formal grievance systems, may create barriers to forgiveness and reconciliation among employees. Another related avenue is the recent increase in research on restorative justice (e.g., Goodstein & Aquino, 2010; Kidder, 2007, Pfarrer, DeCelles, Smith, & Taylor, 2008, Wenzel & Okimoto, 2010, Okimoto, Wenzel & Feather, 2009; Wenzel, Okimoto, Feather, & Platow, 2008), including a forthcoming special issue of *Business Ethics Quarterly* on reintegrating individuals and organizations following a transgression.

Finally, McCullough continues to work on understanding forgiveness. He recently developed an evolutionary model of revenge and forgiveness that stipulates that revenge and forgiveness evolved to deter aggressors and incentivize others to cooperate (McCullough et al., 2013). Moreover, according to the model, the choice to choose revenge or forgiveness depends largely on cost-benefit ratio calculations, including how much the victim values the welfare of the target.

Moderators of the Desire for Revenge

Which response victims choose in order to cope with their desire for revenge depends on several factors. In our 2007 review (Tripp et al., 2007), we identified three such groups of moderating factors: power, procedural justice climate, and individual differences. Since then, research has confirmed and expanded the list of moderators.

POWER

Several recent studies show how power affects the choice to seek revenge. Porath and Pearson (2012) study incivility spirals and find that greater incivility is accompanied by greater anger, fear, and sadness. However, although anger leads to direct incivility, fear leads to *indirect* incivility. That is, fearful employees avoid forms of incivility where they might be identified, or "get caught." In a related review, Klaussner (2014) examines how conflict between supervisors and subordinates spiral to the point of no return. He proposes that when subordinates perceive their supervisors as unjust, and supervisors see the subordinates as inadequate, these views reinforce each other, creating a conflict spiral or feedback loop, to the point where the subordinate judges the supervisor to be "abusive." Furthermore, power asymmetries among supervisor and subordinates inhibit reconciliation attempts: subordinates who feel inferior react more passively than actively. Similarly, Jones (2010) finds that people avoid revenge against powerful supervisors. One reason would-be avengers avoid direct confrontation with powerful others may be that the would-be avengers see fewer opportunities (Tripp & Bies, 1997). Supporting this explanation, Jones (2004) finds that the perceived opportunity for revenge predicts counter-productive workplace behaviors beyond other variables (e.g., demographics, perceived norms about revenge).

Another reason would-be avengers avoid direct confrontation with powerful others is fear of counter-retaliation (Tripp & Bies, 1997; Tripp et al., 2007). Mitchell and Ambrose (2012) in their study of employees' behavioral reactions to supervisor aggression, where they measured employees' fear of counter-retaliation, find that employees who fear counter-retaliation are less likely to retaliate. The effect of power on direct versus indirect revenge is similar in the consumer context. Gregoire et al. (2010) find that power moderates the choice to engage in direct acts of consumer revenge (i.e., vindictive complaining; marketplace aggression), but has no effect on indirect consumer revenge (i.e., negative word of mouth; online complaining for negative publicity).

PROCEDURAL JUSTICE CLIMATE

Aquino, Tripp, & Bies (2006) also find that the procedural justice climate of the organization influences the choice of coping response. When victims perceive an organization to have fair grievance procedures, victims more likely pursue justice through official, organizational channels; however, when victims perceive that organizations have unfair grievance procedures, then victims will consider pursuing justice on their own, much as vigilantes "take the law into their own hands." Recently, Bobocel (2013) confirms this effect. She finds that perceptions of overall organizational justice facilitates forgiveness and suppresses revenge.

INDIVIDUAL DIFFERENCES

Regarding the role of individual differences, studies reveal many variables that help predict who is more likely to act on the desire for revenge, which include: trait anger, attitude toward revenge, gender, attribution style, justice sensitivity, belief in the norm of negative reciprocity, and, especially, negative affectivity (for reviews, see Douglas and Martinko, 2001; Hershcovis et al., 2007). Recent research adds to this growing list of variables. Holtz and Harold (2013) find that those employees with strong interpersonal justice values and a justice orientation tend not to engage in workplace deviance, no matter how strong their perceptions that an injustice has occurred. Yet, Graso, Tripp, Bies, and Goodspeed, (2010) find that those people who collect injustices—that is, perceive injustices more easily, are more bothered by injustices, and recall injustices more quickly than others—are more likely to seek revenge. Zdaniuk and Bobacel (2012) find that victims who are high in vertical individualism (i.e., motivated by self-enhancement values, such as achievement and power, and accept hierarchy and inequality) are more likely to seek revenge than those who are low in vertical individualism. Pronk, Karremans, Overbeek, Vermuist, and Wigboldus (2010) find that executive, cognitive control increases forgiveness, at least for severe offenses, and does so by reducing rumination, which inhibits revenge.

Taking Stock of Research on Revenge: Concluding Thoughts

The modern study of revenge in the workplace began with the foundational theory of organizational justice—Adams' equity theory (1965). Adams' research clearly demonstrates that when people feel underpaid, they contribute less in response to that injustice. In other words, they engage in revenge. Adams work helped incite decades of research on injustice in the workplace. Interestingly, the vast majority of that work built on only the first part of equity theory—that is, how workers perceive injustice. As to what employees actually do *after* they perceive an injustice, that question remained relatively unexplored for 30 years, until we started studying it in the mid 1990s—save for those who, while studying various forms of workplace aggression or productivity, would sometimes stumble into revenge. Fortunately, in writing this chapter, we were amazed where research on revenge has gone over the past two decades, and especially the last 5 years. There is promising research being conducted in new organizational domains and processes, reflecting the 21st-century workplace (Goldman & Shapiro, 2012). This research is important because the role of technology and new work arrangements both instigate and shape acts of revenge (Bies & Tripp, 2012). For instance, the customer-service experience and service-recovery failures have become rich contexts for the study of revenge, including the role of social media as a channel for engaging in revenge (e.g., Gregoire et al., 2009).

The promise of revenge research is also found in the new conceptual frameworks that are now guiding research. The neuroscience perspective (e.g., Beugré, 2009; Becker et al., 2011) is one such framework. To get inside the brain to understand the emotions that motivate revenge is clearly exciting, and very useful for moving beyond fallible self-reports. New perspectives on the role of emotions (Cropanzano et al., 2010), and its experience and intensity (Barclay & Whiteside, 2011), also hold tremendous promise for future research on revenge. As Kahneman (2011) makes clear, we cannot understand choices—such as the choice to choose revenge, forgiveness, reconciliation or avoidance—unless we understand how affect, and related subconscious processing, prime these choices.

This great promise for the future of research on revenge will be better realized if scholars can see revenge for what it is. By this we mean two things. First, it would help if those who study related constructs—such as counterproductive workplace behaviors, deviance, incivility, abuse, and so forth—could more uniformly pay attention to the motives for these behaviors, which often include revenge, especially when scholars are exploring the connection between injustice and such behaviors. Second, it may help to view revenge less judgmentally and with more empathy for those who commit it. That is, when revenge is viewed as counter-productive workplace behaviors or as a deviant act, it is seen as dysfunctional. Yet, the reality of revenge is that it is multifaceted—it has good, bad, and ugly faces. Revenge can be destructive and antisocial, but not always. There is evidence that revenge can also be constructive and pro-social. If revenge can stop the perpetrator, or protect the victim or the organization from future harms or wrongdoing, then it serves a very valuable social function. Not only has this been our view the last 20 years (e.g., Bies & Tripp, 1998, 2004), but also McCullough (2013), who is perhaps best known for studying forgiveness, promotes this view that revenge, alongside forgiveness, is functional and serves a purpose.

Perhaps, it is the word *revenge* that is the problem. It is a taboo word (Jacoby, 1983). Perhaps, if we used the phrase *getting even* it would feel more "justice"-like in tone and meaning. And that is exactly what subjects did in the groundbreaking research of Adams (1963)—they were "getting even," and maybe they even thought "doing justice."

Since Adams (1965), however, a clear lesson is that even if functional, revenge and getting even are not as rational as they perhaps once seemed to justice scholars like us. Perhaps we should drop the notion that in the realm of getting even, emotion is solely a product of judgment, that moral outrage always *follows* careful, cognitive deliberation of the facts. Quite often, and to the contrary, revenge may be outrage that burns beneath the surface, looks for an outlet, surfaces in the form of getting even, and then uses—post hoc—the rhetoric of injustice and doing justice to justify the outlet. Evidence increasingly suggests that this may be the way we are hardwired. If we are to make useful theoretical headway, we must better understand how these circuits work.

References

Adams, J. S. (1963). Towards an understanding of inequity. *The Journal of Abnormal and Social Psychology, 67,* 422–436.

Adams, J. S. (1965). Inequity in social exchange. In L. Berkowitz (Ed.), *Advances in experimental social psychology* (Vol. 2, pp. 267–299). New York, NY: Academic Press.

Allred, K. G. (1999). Anger driven retaliation: Toward an understanding of impassioned conflict in organizations. In R. J. Bies, R. J. Lewicki, & B. H. Sheppard (Eds.) *Research on negotiations in organizations* (Vol. 7, pp. 27–58). Greenwich, CT: JAI Press.

Ambrose, M. L., & Kulik, C. T. (2001). How do I know that's fair? A categorization approach to fairness judgments. *Research in Social Issues in Management, 1,* 35–62.

Anderson, C. A. (2001). Heat and violence. *Current Directions in Psychological Science, 10,* 33–38.

Andersson, L. M., & Pearson, C. M. (1999). Tit for tat? The spiraling effect of incivility in the workplace. *Academy of Management Review, 24,* 452–471.

Aquino, K., & Douglas, S. (2003). Identity threat and antisocial behavior in organizations: The moderating effects of individual differences, aggressive modeling, and hierarchical status. *Organizational Behavior and Human Decision Processes, 90,* 195–208.

Aquino, K., Grover, S. L., Goldman, B., & Folger, R. (2003). When push doesn't come to shove Interpersonal forgiveness in workplace relationships. *Journal of Management Inquiry, 12,* 209–216.

Aquino, K., Tripp, T. M., & Bies, R. J. (2001). How employees respond to personal offense: The effects of blame attribution, victim status, and offender stat us on revenge and reconciliation in the workplace. *Journal of Applied Psychology, 86,* 52–59.

Aquino, K., Tripp, T. M., & Bies, R. J. (2006). Getting even or moving on? Power, procedural justice, and types of offense as predictors of revenge, forgiveness, reconciliation, and avoidance in organizations. *Journal of Applied Psychology, 91,* 653–658.

Ariely, D. (2007). HBR case study: The customers' revenge. *Harvard Business Review, 85,* 31–42.

Aureli, F., & Schaffner, C. M. (2013). Why so complex? Emotional mediation of revenge, forgiveness, and reconciliation. *Brain and Behavioral Science, 36,*15–16.

Axelrod, R. (1984). *The evolution of cooperation.* New York, NY: Basic Books.

Barclay, L. J., Skarlicki, D. P., & Pugh, S. D. (2005). Exploring the role of emotions in injustice perceptions and retaliation. *Journal of Applied Psychology, 90,* 629–643.

Barclay, L. J., & Whiteside, D. B. (2011). Moving beyond justice perceptions: The role of experience and intensity. In S. W. Gilliland, D. D. Steiner, & D. P. Skarlicki (Eds.), *Research in social issues in management,* Volume 7: Emerging perspectives on organizational justice and ethics (pp. 49–74). Greenwich, CT: Information Age.

Bechwati, N. N., & Morrin, M. (2003). Outraged consumers: getting even at the expense of getting a good deal. *Journal of Consumer Psychology, 13,* 440–53.

Bechwati, N. N., & Morrin, M. (2007). Understanding voter vengeance. *Journal of Consumer Psychology, 17,* 277–291.

Becker, W. J., Cropanzano, R., & Sanfey, A. G. (2011). Organizational neuroscience: Taking organizational theory inside the neural black box. *Journal of Management, 37*, 933–961.

Benson. W. L. (2013). Workplace psychological aggression: Resolving the battle of competing constructs. Dissertation. Washington State University.

Beugré, C. D. (2009). Exploring the neural basis of fairness: A model of neuro-organizational justice. *Organizational Behavior and Human Decision Processes, 110*, 129–139.

Bies, R. J. (2001). Interactional (in)justice: The sacred and the profane. In J. Greenberg & R. Cropanzano (Eds.), *Advances in organizational behavior* (pp. 89–118) Palo Alto, CA: Stanford University Press.

Bies, R. J., & Tripp, T. M. (1996). Beyond distrust: "Getting even" and the need for revenge. In R. M. Kramer & T. Tyler (Eds.), *Trust and organizations* (pp. 246–260). Thousand Oaks, CA: Sage.

Bies, R. J., & Tripp, T. M. (1998). The many faces of revenge: The good, the bad, and the ugly. In R. W. Griffin, A. O'Leary-Kelly, & J. Collins (Eds.), *Dysfunctional behavior in organizations, Vol. 1: Violent behaviors in organizations.* Vol. 23: 49–68. Greenwich, CT: JAI.

Bies, R. J., & Tripp, T. M. (2002). Hot flashes, open wounds: Injustice and the tyranny of its emotions. In S. Gilliland, D. Steiner, and D. Skarlicki (Eds.) *Emerging perspectives on managing organizational justice* (pp. 203–223). Greenwich, CT: IAP.

Bies. R. J., & Tripp, T. M. (2004). Badmouthing the company: Bitter employee or concerned citizen? In R. Kidwell & C. Martin (Eds.), *Managing organizational deviance.* Sage.

Bies, R. J., & Tripp, T. M. (2005). The study of revenge in the workplace: Conceptual, ideological, and empirical issues. In S. Fox & P. E. Spector (Eds.), *Counterproductive work behavior: Investigations of actors and targets* (pp. 65–81). Washington, DC: American Psychological Association.

Bies, R. J., & Tripp, T. M. (2012). Negotiating the peace in the face of modern distrust: Dealing with anger and revenge in the 21st century workplace. In B. M. Goldman and D. L. Shapiro (Eds.), *The psychology of negotiations in the 21st century workplace.* New York, NY: Rutledge.

Bies, R. J., & Tripp, T. M. (in press). In the heat of the moment: The influence of visceral factors on retaliation. In B. Turner and C. Hilleman's, *On Retaliation*. Berghahn Publishing, Germany.

Bies, R. J., Tripp, T. M., Barclay, L. J. (2012). Barriers on the road to forgiveness: a macro perspective. In L. J. Barclay and R. J. Bies, *Barriers and Gateways to Forgiveness in the Workplace: New Directions in Theory and Research.* Presented at the annual meeting of the Academy of Management, Boston, MA, August, 2012.

Bobocel, D. R. (2013). Coping with unfair events constructively or destructively: The effects of overall justice and self–other orientation. *Journal of Applied Psychology*, May 13, 2013 (online).

Bonifield, C., & Cole, C. (2007). Affective responses to service failure: Anger, regret, and retaliatory and conciliatory responses. *Marketing Letters, 18*, 85–99.

Bradfield, M., & Aquino, K. (1999). The effects of blame attributions and offender likableness on forgiveness and revenge in the workplace. *Journal of Management, 25*, 607–631.

Bright, D. S., Fry, R. E., & Cooperrider, D. L. (2006). Forgiveness from the perspectives of three response modes: Begrudgement, pragmatism and transcendence. *Journal of Management Spirituality and Religion, 2/3*, 78–103.

Byrne, Z. S., Rupp, D. E., & Eurich, T. (2003). Effects of discrete emotions on distributive, procedural, and interactional justice. In *Poster presented at the 18th Annual Conference of the Society for Industrial/Organizational Psychology, Orlando, FL.*

Carlsmith, K. M., Wilson, T. D., & Gilbert, T. D. (2008). The paradoxical consequences of revenge. *Journal of Personality and Social Psychology, 95*, 1316.

Cohen-Charash, Y., & Byrne, Z. S. (2008). Affect and justice: Current knowledge and future directions. In N. M. Ashkanasy & C. L. Cooper (Eds.), *Research companion to emotion in organizations* (pp. 360–391). Cheltenham, UK: Edward Elgar.

Cox, S. S., Bennett, R. J., Tripp, T. M., & Aquino, K. (2012). An empirical test of forgiveness motives' effects on employees' health and well-being. *Journal of Occupational Health Psychology, 17*, 330.

Coyle-Shapiro, J. A. M. (2002). A psychological contract perspective on organizational citizenship behavior. *Journal of Organizational Behavior, 23*, 927–946.

Cropanzano, R., Byrne, Z. S., Bobocel, D. R., & Rupp, D. E. (2001). Moral virtues, fairness heuristics, social entities, and other denizens of organizational justice. *Journal of Vocational Behavior, 58*, 164–209.

Cropanzano, R., Stein, J. H., & Nadisic, T. (2010). *Social justice and the experience of emotions.* New York, NY: Routledge.

Crossley, C. D. (2009). Emotional and behavioral reactions to social undermining: a closer look at perceived offender motives. *Organizational Behavior and Human Decision Processes, 108*, 14–24.

Darley, J. M., & Pittman, T. S. (2003). The psychology of compensatory and retributive justice. *Personality and Social Psychology Review, 7*, 324–336.

De Cremer, D. (2007). *Advances in the psychology of justice and affect.* Greenwich, CT: Information Age.

de Quervain, D. J. F., Fischbacher, U. Treyer, V., Schellhammer, M., Schnyder, U., Buck, A., & Fehr, E. (2004). The neural basis of altruistic punishment. *Science, 305*, 1254–1258.

DiMatteo, L., Bird, R., & Colquitt, J. (2011). Justice, employment, and the psychological contract. The selected w of Larry A DiMatteo. Available at: http://works.bepress.com/larry_dimatteo/6

Douglas, S. C., & Martinko, M. J. (2001). Exploring the role of individual differences in the prediction of workplace aggression. *Journal of Applied Psychology, 86*, 547–559.

Einarsen, S., Hoel, H., & Notelaers, G. (2009). Measuring exposure to bullying and harassment at work: Validity, factor structure and psychometric properties of the Negative Acts Questionnaire-Revised. *Work & Stress, 23*, 24–44.

Fehr, R., & Gelfand, M. J. (2012). The forgiving organization: A multilevel model of forgiveness at work. *Academy of Management Review, 37*, 664–688.

Fehr, R., Gelfand, M. J., & Nag, M. (2010). The road to forgiveness: a meta-analytic synthesis of its situational and dispositional correlates. *Psychological Bulletin, 136*, 894.

Folger, R., & Skarlicki, D. P. (1998). A popcorn metaphor for workplace violence: In R. W. Griffin, A. O'Leary-Kelly, & J. Collins (Eds.), *Dysfunctional behavior in organizations*

(Vol. 1: 43–82): Violent behaviors in organizations. Greenwich, CT: JAI Press.

Fox, S., & Spector, P. (2005). *Counterproductive work behavior: Investigations of actors and targets.* Washington, DC: American Psychological Association.

Geen, R. G., & Quanty, M. B. (1977). The catharsis of aggression: An evaluation of a hypothesis. *Advances in experimental social psychology, 10,* 1–37.

Gelbrich, K. (2010). Anger, frustration, and helplessness after service failure: coping strategies and effective informational support. *Journal of the Academy of Marketing Science, 38,* 567–585.

Goldman, B. M. (2003). The application of referent cognitions theory to legal-claiming by terminated workers: The role of organizational justice and anger. *Journal of Management, 29,* 705–728.

Goldman, B. M., & Shapiro, D. L. (Eds.). (2012). *The psychology of negotiations in the 21st century workplace: New challenges and new solutions.* New York, NY: Routledge.

Gollwitzer, M., & Denzler, M. (2009). What makes revenge so sweet: Seeing the offender suffer or delivering a message? *Journal of Experimental Social Psychology, 45,* 840–844.

Gollwitzer, M., Meder, M., & Schmitt, M. (2011). What gives victims satisfaction when they seek revenge? *European Journal of Social Psychology, 41,* 364–374.

Goodstein, J., & Aquino, K. (2010). And restorative justice for all: Redemption, forgiveness, and reintegration in organizations. *Journal of Organizational Behavior, 31,* 624–628.

Graso, M., Tripp, T., Bies, R., & Goodspeed, J. "Collectors of injustice": A new trait to predict revenge in the workplace. In A. Turner & S. Robinson's, *Revenge in (and toward!) organizations.* Presented at the annual meeting of the Academy of Management, Montreal, Canada, August 2010.

Gregoire, Y., & Fisher, R. (2008). Customer betrayal and retaliation: When your best customers become your enemies. *Journal of the Academy of Marketing Science, 36,* 247–261.

Grégoire, Y., Laufer, D., & Tripp T. M. (2010). A comprehensive model of customer direct and indirect revenge: understanding the effects of perceived greed and customer power. *Journal of the Academy of Marketing Sciences, 28,* 738–758.

Gregoire, Y., Tripp T. M., & Legoux, R. (2009). Customer revenge and avoidance over time: Insights about a longitudinal "love becomes hate" effect. *Journal of Marketing, 73,* 18–32.

Haidt, J. (2001). The emotional dog and its rational tail: a social intuitionist approach to moral judgment. *Psychological Review, 108,* 814.

Hershcovis, M. S. (2011). Incivility, social undermining, bullying...oh my!: A call to reconcile constructs within workplace aggression research. *Journal of Organizational Behavior, 32,* 499–519.

Hershcovis, M. S., Turner, N., Barling, J., Aronold, K. A., Dupre, K. E., Inness, M. . . . Sivanathan, N. (2007). Predicting workplace aggression: A meta-analysis. *Journal of Applied Psychology, 92,* 228–238.

Hillebrandt, A., & Barclay, L. J. (2013). Integrating Organizational Justice and Affect: New Insights, Challenges, and Opportunities. *Social Justice Research, 26,* 1–19.

Holbrook, C., Fessler, D. M., & Gervais, M. M. (2013). Revenge without redundancy: Functional outcomes do not require discrete adaptations for vengeance or forgiveness. *Behavioral and Brain Sciences, 36,* 22–23.

Holtz, B. C., & Harold, C. M. (2013). Interpersonal justice and deviance the moderating effects of interpersonal justice values and justice orientation. *Journal of Management, 39,* 339–365.

Hsiang, S. M., Burke, M., & Miguel, E. (2013). Quantifying the influence of climate on human conflict. *Science.* Published Online August 1 2013: http://www.sciencemag.org/content/early/2013/07/31/science.1235367

Hung, T. K., Chi, N. W., & Lu, W. L. (2009). Exploring the relationships between perceived coworker loafing and counterproductive work behaviors: The mediating role of a revenge motive. *Journal of Business and Psychology, 24,* 257–270.

Jacoby, S. (1983). *Wild justice: The evolution of revenge.* New York, NY: Harper & Row.

Jensen, J. M., Opland, R. A., & Ryan, A. M. (2010). Psychological contracts and counterproductive work behaviors: Employee responses to transactional and relational breach. *Journal of Business and Psychology, 25,* 555–568.

Johnson, A. R., Matear, M., & Thomson, M. (2011). A coal in the heart: Self-relevance as a post-exit predictor of consumer anti-brand actions. *Journal of Consumer Research, 38,* 108–125.

Joireman, J., Gregoire, Y., Devezer, B., & Tripp, T. M. (2013). When do customers offer firms a "second chance" following a double deviation? The impact of inferred firm motives on customer revenge and reconciliation. *Journal of Retailing, 89,* 315–337.

Jones, D. A. (2004). Counterproductive work behavior toward supervisors and organizations: Injustice, revenge, & context. In *Academy of management proceedings* (Vol. 2004, No. 1, pp. A1–A6). Academy of Management.

Jones, D. A. (2009). Getting even with one's supervisor and one's organization: relationships among types of injustice, desires for revenge, and counterproductive work behaviors. *Journal of Organizational Behavior, 30,* 525–542.

Jones, D. A. (2010). Getting even for interpersonal mistreatment in the workplace: Triggers of revenge motives and behavior. In J. Greenberg's (Ed.), *Insidious workplace behavior,* (pp. 101–148). New York, NY: Routledge.

Joseph, J. E., Powell, C. A., Johnson, N. F., & Kedia, G. (2008). The functional neuroanatomy of envy. *Envy: Theory and Research,* 290–314.

Kahneman, D. (2011). *Thinking, fast and slow.* New York, NY: Macmillan.

Kickul, J. R., Neuman, G., Parker, C., & Finkl, J. (2001). Settling the score: The role of organizational justice in the relationship between psychological contract breach and anticitizenship behavior. *Employee Responsibilities and Rights Journal, 13,* 77–93.

Kidder, D. L. (2007). Restorative justice: Not "rights," but the right way to heal relationships at work. *International Journal of Conflict Management, 18,* 4–22.

Klaussner, S. (2014). Engulfed in the abyss: The emergence of abusive supervision as an escalating process of supervisor–subordinate. *Human Relations, 67,* 311–322.

Konecni, V. J. (2013). Revenge: Behavioral and emotional consequences. *Brain and Behavioral Science, 36,* 25–26.

Larrick, R. P., Timmerman, T. A., Carton, A. M., and Abrevaya, J. (2011). Temper, temperature, and temptation: Heat-related retaliation in baseball. *Psychological Science, 22,* 423–428.

Leiser, D., & Joskowicz-Jabloner, L. (2013). On the differential mediating role of emotions in revenge and reconciliation. *Behavioral and Brain Sciences, 36*, 27–28.

Lerner, J. S., & Tiedens, L. Z. (2006). Portrait of the angry decision maker: how appraisal tendencies shape anger's influence on cognition. *Journal of Behavioral Decision Making, 19*, 115–117.

Lieberman, M. D., Gaunt, R., Gilbert, D. T., & Trope, Y. (2002). Reflexion and reflection: A social cognitive neuroscience approach to attributional inference. *Advances in experimental social psychology, 34*, 199–249.

Lim, S., Cortina, L. M., & Magley, V. J. (2008). Personal and workgroup incivility: Impact on work and health outcomes. *Journal of Applied Psychology, 93*, 95–107.

Loewenstein, G. (1996). Out of control: Visceral influences on behavior. *Organizational Management Inquiry, 12*, 209–216.

McCullough, M. L. (2008). *Beyond revenge: The evolution of the forgiveness instinct*. San Francisco, CA: Jossey-Bass.

McCullough, M. L., Kurzban, R., & Tabak, B. A. (2013). Cognitive systems of revenge and forgiveness. *Behavioral and Brain Sciences, 36*, 1–15.

Miller, D. T. (2001). Disrespect and the experience of injustice. *Annual Review of Psychology, 52*, 527–553.

Mitchell, M. S., & Ambrose, M. L. (2007). Abusive supervision and workplace deviance and the moderating effects of negative reciprocity beliefs. *Journal of Applied Psychology, 92*, 1159–1168.

Mitchell, M. S., & Ambrose, M. L. (2012). Employees' behavioral reactions to supervisor aggression: An examination of individual and situational factors. *Journal of Applied Psychology, 97*, 1148–1170.

Neuman, J. H., & Baron, R. A. (1997). Aggression in the workplace. In R. A. Giacalone & J. Greenberg (Eds.), *Antisocial behavior in organizations* (pp. 37–67). Thousand Oaks, CA: Sage.

O'Connor, K., & Adams, G. S. (2013). Affective antecedents of revenge. *Behavioral and Brain Sciences, 36*, 29–30.

O'Leary-Kelly, A. M., Griffin, R. W., & Glew, D. J. (1996). Organization-motivated aggression: A research framework. *Academy of Management Review, 21*, 225–253.

Okimoto, T. G., Wenzel, M., & Feather, N. T. (2009). Beyond retribution: Conceptualizing restorative justice and exploring its determinants. *Social Justice Research, 22*, 156–180.

Peters, E., Vastfjall, D., Garling, T., & Slovic, P. (2006). Affect and decision making: A hot topic. *Journal of Behavioral Decision Making, 19*, 79–85.

Pfarrer, M. D., DeCelles, K. A., Smith, K. G., & Taylor, S. M. (2008). After the fall: Reintegrating the corrupt organization. *Academy of Management Review, 33*, 730–749.

Pillutla, M. M., & Murnighan, J. K. (1996). Unfairness, anger, and spite: Emotional rejections of ultimatum offers. *Organizational Behavior and Human Decision Processes, 68*, 208–224.

Porath, C. L., & Pearson, C. M. (2012). Emotional and behavioral responses to workplace incivility and the impact of hierarchical status. *Journal of Applied Social Psychology, 42*, E326–E357.

Potegal, M. (2013). Revenge: An adaptive system for maximizing fitness, or a proximate calculation arising from personality and social-psychological processes? *Behavioral and Brain Sciences, 36*, 33–34.

Pronk, T. M., Karremans, J. C., Overbeek, G., Vermulst, A. A., & Wigboldus, D. H. (2010). What it takes to forgive: When and why executive functioning facilitates forgiveness. *Journal of Personality and Social Psychology, 98*, 119.

Randall, P. (2001). *Bullying in adulthood: Assessing the bullies and their victims*. New York, NY: Brunner-Routledge.

Robinson, S. L., & Bennett, R. J. (1995). A typology of deviant workplace behaviors: A multidimensional scaling study. *Academy of Management Journal, 38*, 555–572.

Rotton, J., & Cohn, E. G. (2004). Outdoor temperature, climate control, and criminal assault: The spatial and temporal ecology of violence. *Environment and Behavior, 36*, 276–306.

Sanfey, A. G., Rilling, J. K., Aronson, J. A., Nystrom, L. E., & Cohen, J. D. 2003. The neural basis of economic decision-making in the ultimatum game. *Science, 300*, 1755–1758.

Sell, A. N. (2013). Revenge can be more fully understood by making distinctions between anger and hatred. *Behavioral and Brain Sciences, 36*, 36–37.

Semmer, N. K., Tschan, F., Meier, L. L., Facchin, S., & Jacobshagen, N. (2010). Illegitimate tasks and counterproductive work behavior. *Applied Psychology, 59*, 70–96.

Singer, T., Seymor, B., O'Doherty, J. P., Sephan, K. E., Dolan, R. J., & Frith, C. D. (2006). Empathic neural responses are modulated by the perceived fairness of others. *Nature. 439*, 466–469.

Singh, J. (1988). Consumer Complaint Intentions and Behavior: Definitional and Taxonomical Issues. *Journal of Marketing, 52*, 93–107.

Skarlicki, D. P., & Folger, R. (1997). Retaliation in the workplace: The roles of distributive, procedural, and interactional justice. *Journal of Applied Psychology, 82*, 434–443.

Tepper, B. J. (2000). Consequences of abusive supervision. *Academy of Management Journal, 43*, 178–190.

Tepper, B. J. (2007). Abusive supervision in work organizations: Review, synthesis, and research agenda. *Journal of Management, 33*, 261–289.

Tripp, T. M., & Bies, R. J. (1997). What's good about revenge? The avenger's perspective. In R. J. Lewicki, R. J. Bies, and B. H. Sheppard (Eds.), *Research on negotiation in organizations* (Vol. 6, pp. 145–160). Greenwich, CT: JAI.

Tripp, T. M., & Bies, R. J. (2009). *Getting even: The truth about workplace revenge—and how to stop it*. San Francisco, CA: Jossey-Bass.

Tripp, T. M., Bies, R. J., & Aquino, K. (2007). A vigilante model of justice: revenge, reconciliation, forgiveness, and avoidance. *Social Justice Research, 20*, 10–34.

Uhlmann, E. L. (2013). The logic of moral outrage. *Behavioral and Brain Sciences, 36*, 38–38.

van den Bos, K. (2007). Hot cognition and social justice judgments. In. D. DeCremer (Ed.), *Advances in the psychology of justice and affect* (pp. 59–82). Greenwich, CT: Information Age.

Ward, J. C., & Ostrom, A. L. (2006). Complaining to the masses: The role of protest framing in customer-created complaint web sites. *Journal of Consumer Research, 33*, 220–230.

Weiner, B. (2000). Attributional thoughts about consumer behavior. *Journal of Consumer Research, 27*, 382–387.

Wenzel, M., & Okimoto, T. G. (2010). How acts of forgiveness restore a sense of justice: Addressing status/power and value concerns raised by transgressions. *European Journal of Social Psychology, 40*, 401–417.

Wenzel, M., Okimoto, T. G., Feather, N. T., & Platow, M. J. (2008). Retributive and restorative justice. *Law and Human Behavior, 32*, 375–389.

Wilson, T. D., & Gilbert, D. T. (2005). Affective forecasting knowing what to want. *Current Directions in Psychological Science, 14*, 131–134.

Wiltermuth, S. S., & Tiedens, L. Z. (2011). Incidental anger and the desire to evaluate. *Organizational Behavior and Human Decision Processes, 116*, 55–65.

Worthington, E. L. (2006). *Forgiveness and reconciliation: Theory and application*. New York, NY: Routledge.

Young, L., Scholz, J., & Saxe, R. (2011). Neural evidence for "intuitive prosecution": The use of mental state information for negative moral verdicts. *Social Neuroscience, 6*, 302–315.

Yu, R. (2013). Revenge, seen though it is not your fault. *Brain and Behavioral Science, 36*,40–41.

Zapf, D., Einarsen, S., Hoel, H., & Vartia, M. (2003). Empirical findings on bullying in the workplace. In S. Einarsen, H. Hoel, D. Zapf, & C. Cooper (Eds.), *Bullying and emotional abuse in the workplace* (pp. 103–125). New York, NY: Taylor & Francis.

Zdaniuk, A., & Bobocel, D. R. (2012). Vertical individualism and injustice: The self-restorative function of revenge. *European Journal of Social Psychology, 42*, 640–651.

CHAPTER

23 Compensatory Justice

Elizabeth Mullen *and* Tyler G. Okimoto

Abstract

Compensatory justice refers to the provision of resources to a victim of injustice with the goal of minimizing or reversing the impact of harm done by the injustice. We propose a conceptual framework for understanding people's reactions to compensatory justice. In particular, we review theory and research relevant to understanding how compensatory justice affects individuals' instrumental, relational, and moral concerns following a transgression. Moreover, we explain how characteristics of (a) the transgression (e.g., offense severity, type of violation), (b) the compensatory response (e.g., source of compensation, type of compensation), and (c) victims and third parties (e.g., emotions, power) are likely to influence reactions to and desires for compensatory justice. Given the relative lack of empirical attention devoted to compensatory justice in the literature, we conclude with a call for future research investigating how, when, and why victims and third parties will perceive the provision of compensation to be an appropriate response to injustice in organizational contexts.

Key Words: compensatory justice, injustice, victims, compensation, transgression

Even in the most exemplary organizations, injustice exists. The most commonly reported experiences of injustice in everyday life involve some form of disrespectful treatment or violation of interpersonal codes of conduct (Baron & Neuman, 1996; Lupfer, Weeks, Doan, & Houston, 2000; Messick, Bloom, Boldizar, & Samuelson, 1985; Mikula, 1986; Mikula, Scherer & Athenstaedt, 1998; Miller, 2001). In organizational settings, instances of injustices reported by workers include humiliation and wrongful accusation by superiors (Bies & Tripp, 1996), violation of codes of conduct (Aram & Salipante, 1981), and betrayal by co-workers (Bies, 1993). Moreover, these experiences of injustice are consequential: perceived injustice in the workplace can lead to anger (Weiss, Suckow & Cropanzano, 1999), withdrawal (e.g., increased noncompliance with authorities; Conlon, Meyer, & Nowakowski, 2005), theft (Greenberg, 1993), sabotage (Giacalone & Greenberg, 1997) and violence (Folger & Skarlicki, 1998) on the part of victims (see Skarlicki & Folger, 1997 for a review).

It is not only victims who have adverse reactions to injustice; witnessing another's unfair treatment can evoke comparable feelings of injustice as when individuals experience the injustice themselves (Van den Bos & Lind, 2001, but see Lind, Kray, & Thompson, 1998). Moreover, when witnessing an injustice, observers may express compassion toward victims and a desire to help them and to see that justice is restored (Folger & Cropanzano, 2001; Kray & Lind, 2002; Lerner, 1980; Meindl & Lerner, 1983), even when it is costly to do so (Lotz, Okimoto, Schlosser, & Fetchenhauer, 2011). For example, survivors of workplace layoffs often react sympathetically to the unfair treatment of co-workers and seek ways to restore justice to victims of unfairness (Brockner, 1990). If such restoration is not possible, lingering perceptions of injustice may cause their work effort to decrease (Brockner, Grover, Reed, & DeWitt, 1992), and their work performance and organizational commitment to diminish (Brockner, 1990; Brockner et al., 1986; Brockner, Grover, Reed, DeWiit, & O'Malley, 1987). Thus, when a transgression occurs, organizational authorities must know how to appropriately repair the wrong and the harm done to the victims in an effort to restore a sense of justice in the workplace.

How then should organizational authorities and representatives go about restoring justice following a transgression? Restoration could entail punishing perpetrators for their wrongs (i.e., retributive justice) or compensating victims for the harm they have suffered (i.e., compensatory justice), among other responses. *Retributive justice* refers to negative sanctions intentionally applied to a perpetrator who has violated a rule, norm, or law (Vidmar & Miller, 1980). In contrast, *compensatory justice* involves the provision of resources to a victim with the goal of minimizing or reversing the impact of the harm done by the injustice (Darley & Pittman, 2003; Okimoto & Tyler, 2007; Van Prooijen, 2010). Although both are common responses to transgressions (Van Prooijen, 2010), prior research has generally focused more on punishment (e.g., the psychological motives for punishment; see Carlsmith & Darley, 2008 for a review) than on compensation. Indeed, compensation has been a relatively ignored variable in the justice literature, despite evidence that people may actually prefer compensation over punishment as a response to injustice (e.g., Lotz et al, 2011). To address this shortcoming and provide groundwork for future research in this understudied domain, we review relevant theory and research on the psychology underlying compensatory justice, and discuss principles and practices of compensatory justice for organizational settings. In particular, we review research in psychology, organizational behavior and service recovery to outline how compensatory justice might help to alleviate victims' and observers' instrumental, relational or moral concerns following an injustice. We then review factors that influence when victims and third parties will likely find compensation effective and appropriate following a transgression. Finally, we conclude with a call for future research, both theoretical and applied, on the use, effectiveness, and function of compensation as a response to injustice in the workplace.

Psychological Function of Compensatory Justice

Within the organizational justice literature, discussion of the psychological function of compensatory justice is scant, particularly when compared to the traditional focus on retributive justice (e.g., sanctions, penalties, revenge) or the rapidly growing interest in reconciliation (e.g., Goodstein & Aquino, 2010; Kidder, 2007; Okimoto, Wenzel, & Platow, 2010) and forgiveness (e.g., Fehr, Gelfand, & Nag, 2010). The lack of research on compensatory justice may be at least partly due to the assumption that monetary compensation is only suitable as a response to instrumental violations. Although such compensation may be preferred when a justice violation elicits primarily instrumental concerns (e.g., Reb, Goldman, Kray, & Cropanzano, 2006), compensation may also function more symbolically as a way to address relational and moral concerns. Thus, we review how compensation can serve all three concerns.

In the following section, we outline the consequences of compensation as a response to injustice (see right half of Figure 23.1); we discuss the instrumental importance of compensation while also acknowledging the symbolic psychological functions of compensation for addressing an individual's salient justice motives and concerns. We adopt the theoretical distinction between instrumental, relational, and moral motives for why people care about justice (see Cropanzano, Byrne, Bobocel, & Rupp, 2001; Cropanzano, Rupp, Mohler, & Schminke, 2001; Skitka, 2003; Skitka, Bauman, & Mullen, 2008), and use these multiple "need-based" models to analyze the applicability of monetary or material compensation as a response to injustice. This approach is particularly useful as a framework for the current discussion given that it focuses on the psychological concerns that follow from injustice (i.e., *why* are people upset by injustice?), rather than the specific injustice event triggers (see arguments by Cropanzano, Byrne, Bobocel, & Rupp, 2001).

Instrumental Concerns

Injustice elicits demands for some response partly because individuals are fundamentally motivated to seek and maintain control, particularly over desired outcomes (e.g., Skinner, 1996; Bandura, 1995); echoing norms in the literature, we refer to this as the instrumental aspect of justice motivation. Instrumental concerns are often

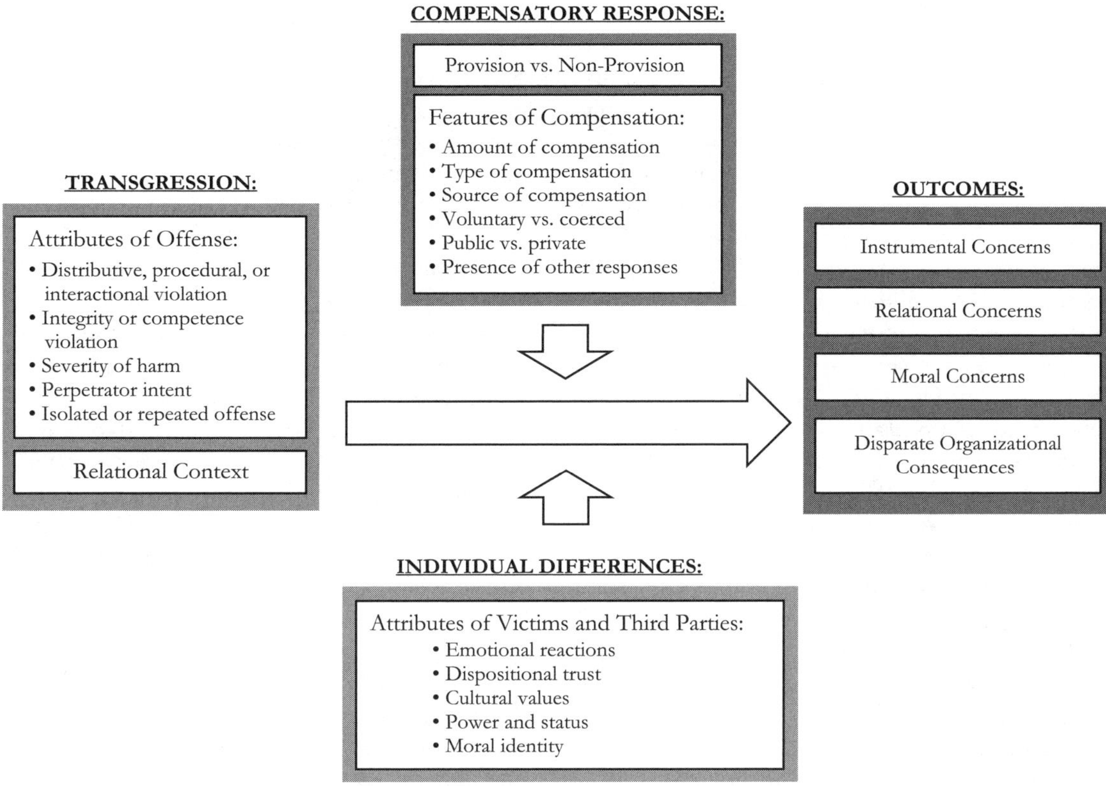

Fig. 23.1 Conceptual model of compensatory justice.

elicited following violations of distributive justice, when individuals judge their material outcomes to be inequitable relative to others (Adams, 1965; Walster & Walster, 1975) or relative to some expected value for exchange (Blau, 1964; Thibaut & Kelley, 1959). Procedural injustice (e.g., violation of the rules used to allocate outcomes) also elicits instrumental concerns; Thibaut and Walker (1975; also Walster, Berscheid, & Walster, 1976) argued that people's preoccupation with procedural fairness (esp. "voice") can be explained by self-interest because fair procedures facilitate predictability (and thus control) over future or long-term outcomes. Some research has even suggested that interpersonal treatment can also function as an instrumental, albeit socioemotional, outcome (Greenberg, 1993), and may be used as a means to interpret the fairness of material outcomes in the absence of clear information regarding distributive fairness (Brockner & Wiesenfeld, 1996). Thus, violations of interactional justice (i.e., unfair interpersonal treatment) may also elicit instrumental concerns.

Monetary compensation can be an appropriate response to justice violations (esp. distributive and procedural) as it speaks directly to the instrumental concerns of the victims. Distributive injustice, in particular, motivates people to seek a fair rebalancing of inputs and rewards (see Greenberg & Cohen, 1982); inequity prompts reduction of inputs and/or attempts to gain greater material outcomes (e.g., Pritchard, 1969; Pritchard, Dunnette, & Jorgenson, 1972). For example, victims of organizational injustice may steal from their organization to alleviate feelings of inequity (Greenberg, 1990; see also Hollinger & Clark, 1983). In consumer service- failure contexts (i.e., contexts where organizations have failed to provide adequate service to consumers), a recent meta-analysis shows that the provision of compensation as a service recovery strategy shows a moderately strong positive correlation with perceptions of distributive justice, suggesting the effectiveness of such compensatory repair strategies (Gelbrich & Roschk, 2011).

Compensation may also follow as a response to procedural violations, addressing victims' instrumental concerns following the injustice. For example, a field study of recently terminated employees revealed that (when accounting for their intercorrelation) procedural injustice was positively associated with preferences for monetary compensation whereas interactional injustice was associated with preferences for punishing the party responsible for their termination (Reb et al., 2006). Judgments of procedural injustice co-occurred with desires for monetary compensation; but the absence of a parallel effect for interactional injustice (which is argued to carry relatively greater relational meaning and less instrumental meaning) suggests that the desire for compensation in this context was driven by heightened instrumental concern. Further evidence of the instrumental nature of compensation comes from theoretical work by Darley and Pittman (2003) who argue that victims' demands for compensation follow from losses that can be attributed to a perpetrator who is responsible for those losses. Notably, the provision of nonmonetary resources following an injustice may also satisfy instrumental needs. For example, the allocation of office space (Greenberg, 1988) or other discretionary resources (Nadisic, 2008) might be used to compensate employees for the losses resulting from past injustices, thereby addressing their instrumental concerns.

Third parties may also desire that victims of distributive injustice be compensated. In an empirical extension of the classic altruistic punishment paradigm typically used to illustrate the third-party retributive justice motive (Fehr & Gächter, 2002), Lotz and colleagues (2011) showed evidence of a third-party compensatory justice motive via an altruistic compensation paradigm (see also Lelieveld, Van Dijk, & Van Beest, 2012). Student participants in an experimental game observed an unfair allocation in a dictator game between two other participants, and were then given the opportunity to sacrifice their own outcomes to punish the offender (i.e., reduce the offender's payment) and/or compensate the victim (i.e., increase the victim's payment). Supporting the argument that third parties are motivated to compensate victims of distributive injustice, 32% of participants chose to compensate the victim, while only 6.7% chose to punish, and 42.6% chose to do both (Lotz et al., 2011). Interestingly, this preference for compensation was reduced when the victim was unaware of the offense and subsequent compensation, suggesting that third parties may provide compensation strategically, and may be aware of the social capital that compensating others can provide (see Adams & Mullen, 2013). Although it seems that third parties may (under some conditions) choose to compensate for the losses incurred by victims of distributive justice violations, future research should investigate whether they would do the same in response to procedural violations.

Importantly, injustice (distributive, procedural, *and* interactional) may affect victims' symbolic resources (e.g., power), and thus may elicit additional instrumental motives beyond any current or future material losses. For example, victims of injustice often report feeling diminished and disempowered following a transgression (Bies & Tripp, 1996; Heider, 1958; Miller, 2001). The offender's actions rob the victim of symbolic resources by degrading and diminishing the victim (Murphy & Hampton, 1988), and provoking feelings of inferiority (Foster & Rusbult, 1999), powerlessness (Baumeister, Stillwell, & Heatherton, 1994), dishonor (Bies & Moag, 1986; Scheff, 1994), disrespect (Lind & Tyler, 1988; Tyler & Smith, 1998), and diminished self-worth (Koper, Van Knippenberg, Bouhuijs, Vermunt, & Wilke, 1993; Scobie & Scobie, 1998). Thus, injustice may elicit an instrumental desire to seek reparations for these symbolic resources, even though such resources may not carry any material value.

Recent research and theory support the claim that power and control are valuable resources that must be compensated to restore a sense of justice. Okimoto and Wenzel (2008) argued that when victimization undermines feelings of power and control, victims are motivated to restore those psychological resources through some compensatory action that empowers victims and rebalances the relative status between victims and offenders. Such recompense of power and control may be a requisite response to achieve justice. For example, injustice responses that empower victims increase their willingness to reconcile with offenders (Shnabel & Nadler, 2008). Moreover, Wenzel, Okimoto, Feather, and Platow (2010) demonstrated that victims demand compensation of these symbolic resources. When victims of injustice felt demeaned and disempowered following a hypothetical case of workplace theft, they were more likely to seek responses that imbued victim empowerment and imposed suffering on the offender. In other words, feelings of diminished power and control (the same symbolic resources that are critical to securing future outcomes; Walster et al., 1976) may themselves be considered a deserved resource that must be compensated after a transgression (Okimoto & Wenzel, 2008).

However, it is not yet clear whether the provision of material outcomes can actually compensate for symbolic losses, or if symbolic losses simply elicit a compensatory motive. Moreover, if material compensation can make up for symbolic losses in power and control, what are the boundary conditions that specify the scope of such an effect? To the extent that offender-provided compensation (i.e., restitution) is construed as a form of punishment for the offender (Van Prooijen, 2010), material compensation may serve to restore these symbolic losses (as punishment disempowers the offender, rebalancing relative levels of power/control; Okimoto & Wenzel, 2008). However, research has not yet shown whether material compensation actually functions in this way.

Notably, if the goals of compensation are indeed instrumental, the source of that compensation should not matter to compensation recipients. That is, if instrumental concern (e.g., resources, power) underlies desires for compensation, it should not matter whether that compensation comes at the expense of the offender, the organization as a whole, or even uninvolved third parties. However, it is still unclear whether offenders, observers, or organizational decision makers see such third-party compensation as appropriate; future research may identify potential discrepancies between the perceived legitimacy of compensation when provided by different organizational stakeholders, or when viewed from the perspective of different stakeholders.

Relational Concerns

Beyond instrumental concerns, injustice in the workplace also elicits concerns over fundamental needs for belongingness, attachment (Baumeister & Leary, 1995), and social esteem (Maslow, 1943; Steele, 1988), which we refer to as the relational aspect of justice motivation. Research has shown that although these relational concerns can follow as a consequence of unfavorable outcomes or distributive violations (Blader & Tyler, 2009), they are particularly salient following procedural and interactional violations (Lind, 2001; Tyler & Lind, 1992). As explicated in relational models of justice (Lind & Tyler, 1988; Tyler & Blader, 2003; Tyler & Lind, 1992), employees use fairness information to infer the quality of their relationships and status within the organization. These relational judgments are central to the self-concept (Luhtanen & Crocker, 1992; Tajfel & Turner, 1986; Turner, Hogg, Oakes, Reicher, & Wetherell, 1987) and become particularly salient when threatened, necessitating some response that reaffirms ones sense of belonging (Hazan & Shaver, 1994). For example, victims of a procedural injustice have been shown to be more vigilant for social cues that provide information regarding the status of their membership in the group (De Cremer & Blader, 2006).

Can monetary compensation make up for the relational concerns elicited by injustice? Some theoretical work has suggested that substituting money for noninstrumental transgressions should elicit moral outrage and exacerbate the initial injustice (Fiske & Tetlock, 1997; Tetlock, Peterson, & Lerner, 1996). In particular, Tetlock, Kristel, Elson, Green, and Lerner (2000) argue that such exchange of profane material goods for sacred values such as honor, love, and justice are considered to be "taboo." Nevertheless, they also suggest that monetary exchanges can be symbolically framed in ways that make the trade-off between money and justice less taboo (Aaker, Fournier, & Brasel, 2004; McGraw & Tetlock, 2005), or at least license people to use injustice as a legitimate justification for accepting unearned material goods.

Thus, despite the potential "taboo" that such exchanges may elicit, monetary compensation can act symbolically as relational concern, addressing the relational needs of employees after a justice violation. Drawing from more general work suggesting that money can have symbolic meaning (Furnham & Argyle, 1998; Opsahl & Dunnette, 1966), and research suggesting that favorable outcomes can positively affect the same relational motives implicated by procedural and interactional justice (Blader & Tyler, 2009; Tyler & Blader, 2003), Okimoto (2008) proposed that material compensation paid from third-party administrators to victimized group members can protect the organization from suffering the negative consequences of the injustice (e.g., disengagement, dissatisfaction, intent to turnover). Specifically, material compensation awarded to victimized organizational members was shown to improve the feelings of diminished membership status that were elicited by injustice, an effect that mediated subsequent increases in their organizational identification and more positive attitudes toward the organization as a whole. Notably, the benefit of compensation appeared to be symbolic and not the consequence of the outcomes themselves—identification and attitudes increased after compensation irrespective of whether the victim saw that material resource as valuable, only when compensation was attributed to benevolent intent (i.e., an act motivated by genuine concern for the victim), and only when provided by an ingroup authority (Okimoto, 2008).

Third parties also believe compensation can repair relational concerns following an injustice (Nadisic, Skarlicki, Cropanzano, & Fortin, 2013). In particular, Nadisic and colleagues (2013) found that managers sometimes engage in "Robin Hood" behaviors; they break organizational rules or protocols to allocate discretionary resources to victimized employees in an effort to compensate them for injustice they experience in the workplace, particularly when such injustice was perpetrated by higher authorities. For example, 18% of managers in one sample reported providing additional time off, nominal gifts, or a larger bonus to employees who had been victimized by the organization or higher authorities, and they provided such resources largely without the knowledge of those higher authorities (Nadisic et al., 2013). Moreover, of the managers who had engaged in Robin Hood behaviors, 30% indicated they did so for relational reasons (e.g., to foster a satisfying relationship with the employee). Thus, such compensatory responses are argued to address instrumental as well as relational concerns, by conveying a symbolic expression of solidarity and concern that bolsters relational ties between employee and manager, albeit at the expense of the organization.

Additional evidence of the symbolic meaning of compensation comes from the service recovery literature, which also recognizes the importance of relational repair, particularly following procedural or interactional service failures (Johnston, 1995; Krishnan & Valle, 1979; McColl-Kennedy & Sparks, 2003; Valle & Wallendorf, 1977; Zeithaml, Parasuraman, & Berry, 1990). After a service failure, material compensation has a generally positive effect on customer attitudes and future purchase intentions (Goodwin & Ross, 1992; Mattila & Patterson, 2004; Webster & Sundaram, 1998; Wong, 2004). For example, small token compensation following a service failure results in greater customer satisfaction and judgments of fairness when offered in addition to an apology (Goodwin & Ross, 1992). Although shown in the consumer rather than employee context, these findings exhibit the potential relational value of compensation.

However, critical to the effectiveness of compensation to communicate relational information is the symbolic framing of the compensatory act (McGraw & Tetlock, 2005). In order for compensation to be acceptable as a proxy for relational concern, it must first be perceived as benevolent—as indicative of and attributed to the organization's concern for the victim. Thus, pairing compensation (from either a third party or from the offender) with an expression of concern is more likely to promote benevolent attributions for that compensation and contribute to its effectiveness in addressing relational concerns. For example, explicitly framing compensation as a gesture of concern or pairing the compensation with an apology leads victims to view that compensation as symbolic of concern, resulting in more favorable reactions compared to compensation alone or concern/apology alone (with third-party compensators, Okimoto, 2008; and with offender compensators, Schmitt, Gollwitzer, Förster, & Montada, 2004). Similarly, individuals who trust the organization, either because of a personal history with that organization or because of contextual cues influencing its trustworthiness, are more likely to interpret compensation from that organization as symbolic of relational concern and react positively to it (Lotz & Okimoto, 2013; Okimoto, 2008). This work is also consistent with research in service repair (Goodwin & Ross, 1992; Hocutt, Chakraborty, & Mowen, 1997; Sparks & McColl-Kennedy, 2001) and trust repair (Bottom, Gibson, Daniels, & Murnighan, 2002; Dirks, Kim, Ferrin, & Cooper, 2011; Gillespie & Dietz, 2009) which shows that the pairing of compensation and apology is particularly effective in repairing organizational relationships. Notably, the pairing of compensation with expressions of relational concern (such as acknowledging or apologizing for the harm the victim experienced) can also amplify the favorability of reactions to instrumental violations. In particular, even following accidental distributive inequities that arguably do not elicit relational concern (Darley & Pittman, 2003), the co-occurrence of compensation and expressions of concern (e.g., apologies) can result in significantly more favorable reactions toward the compensating organization (Okimoto & Tyler, 2007).

Importantly, although research is quite clear regarding the symbolic function and value of compensation for victims of an injustice, research investigating the scope of its effect within non-consumer organizational contexts is quite limited. Another major limitation of the literature is the almost exclusive focus on one particular compensatory script: an organizational representative offering compensation to the victim of an injustice perpetrated by another organizational member.

However, compensation may be offered by the offending actor him/herself (i.e., restitution) rather than the organization as a whole (i.e., third-party compensation). Moreover, such compensation from either party may be provided voluntarily or involuntarily. The lack of clarity about how these and other important dimensions influence the perceived effectiveness of compensation is a substantial gap in the literature.

On a related note, the interplay between different levels of relational concern may also be critically important in determining the effectiveness of compensation. If relational concerns of belonging and self-regard are indeed grounded in an individual's level of social identification with the organization (Tyler & Blader, 2003), an injustice event is likely to trigger relational concern at one specific level of identity (Hogg & Terry, 2000). For example, an employee may interpret his low salary to suggest that the organization does not value his contribution; if his direct supervisor compensates for this unfair wage by offering him some form of discretionary compensation (e.g., the best office, the easy work assignments), would it address the organizational-level identity concerns elicited by the injustice? In this case, the relational concern is at the organizational level, but the compensatory response is at the supervisory level. Further research is needed to determine whether (and when) cross-level compensation is effective, or if compensation must be provided by the source of the injustice. The limited evidence suggests that compensation from company representatives may prevent employee disengagement from the organization after a violation at the peer-level (Okimoto, 2008); however, it remains unclear whether an organizational compensatory response actually addresses the relational threat between an individual transgressor and the victim (i.e., relational identity), or if such organizational-level compensation only serves to protect an employee's relationship with the wider group (i.e., social identity).

It is also unclear how third-party observers would interpret the provision and acceptance of compensation between two organizational members. Given the ambiguity surrounding the circumstances that precede the act of compensating, combined with normative beliefs about the use of money (Tetlock et al., 2000), observers may see compensation as inappropriate and/or driven by purely instrumental motives. However, when observers are certain that an injustice has occurred, they should be more likely to support managers who provide compensation to victimized employees (O'Connor & Mullen, 2012). In addition, it is unclear whether compensatory responses outside of the consumer context are seen as legitimate expenditures by organizational decision makers, leaders, and shareholders.

In summary, there is some evidence that providing compensation to victims of injustice can repair their relational concerns, and that managers and organizational members at times offer compensation as an attempt at relational repair following an injustice. However, there is a notable lack of empirical work, and field work in particular, on the use and meaning of compensation as a form of relational repair. Future research should seek to understand when, how, and why compensation will repair individuals' relational needs following an injustice.

Moral Concerns

People can also be concerned with fairness because they have a basic respect for human dignity and worth (Folger, 1998) and feel a sense of moral obligation to follow certain principles (Cropanzano, Goldman, & Folger, 2003). Thus, a third concern that is elicited by workplace transgressions is tied to an individual's principled moral standards and fundamental notions of right and wrong (Skitka, 2003; Skitka, Bauman, & Mullen, 2008; Tetlock, 1985). This moral motive is evidenced by a tradition of research showing that third-party observers are willing to incur a cost to see justice done, even when the original injustice has no instrumental implications for those observers and those observers have no relationship with the involved parties (e.g., Fehr, & Gächter, 2002; Kahneman, Knetsch & Thaler, 1986; Turillo, Folger, Lavelle, Umphress, & Gee, 2002). Instead, people seek to satisfy an intrinsic motive for "just deserts" (Darley, Carlsmith, & Robinson, 2000), also commonly referred to as the deontological motive (Cropanzano, Goldman, & Folger, 2003; Folger, 1998, 2001). Indeed, people react more strongly to observed injustice when they have strong moral convictions about the violation (Mullen & Skitka, 2006; Skitka, 2002; Skitka & Mullen, 2002), or if morality plays a central role in their self-definition (Aquino, Freeman, Reed, Lim, & Felps, 2009; Aquino & Reed, 2002; Skarlicki & Folger, 1997). Such moral concerns cut across justice types, prompting reactions to distributive, procedural, and interactional violations (Skitka, 2002), although they are more commonly associated with distributive (Skitka, 2002; Skitka et al., 2008) and interactional injustice (Ambrose, Seabright & Schminke 2002; Folger & Cropanzano, 1998; Skarlicki & Folger, 1997).

Significantly, the moral concerns elicited following a workplace violation require some response that helps to re-establish the moral order. Perhaps the most prominent reaction to moral violations is a retributive impulse that seeks offender suffering through punishment or revenge (Bies & Tripp, 1996; Bies, Tripp, & Kramer, 1997; Folger, Cropanzano, & Folger, 2005; Goldman, 2003; Turillo et al., 2002). In the face of injustice, people seek retributive responses that they subjectively perceive to be morally proportional to the violation (Carlsmith & Darley, 2008); and although punishment may arguably speak to instrumental (i.e., utility; see Nagin, 1998) and relational (see Okimoto & Wenzel, 2011) concerns, it is typically motivated by a desire to restore the moral order (Bies & Tripp, 1996; Cropanzano et al., 2003; Folger et al., 2005). Punishment achieves a restoration of the moral order by reasserting the validity of important social values and norms (Durkheim, 1964; Miller & Vidmar, 1981; Tyler & Boeckmann, 1997) through the symbolic communication of those values (Okimoto & Wenzel, 2011; Vidmar, 2002).

Can monetary compensation address the moral concerns elicited by injustice, helping to re-establish the moral order? Some research suggests that compensation may be effective in addressing moral concerns, but, specifically, compensation that is imposed upon the offender as a form of retaliation or punishment (i.e., as a just deserts reaction to the offense), a justice approach we refer to as *compensatory retaliation* (i.e., using compensatory interventions with the goal of punishing or retaliating against the offender). For example, replicating field research (Greenberg, 1990), participants who were treated poorly or inequitably in a laboratory study were more likely to steal from the experimenter when given the opportunity (Greenberg, 1997), presumably to remedy the inequity they experienced. Recent cross-sectional research also showed that the absence of perceived organizational support implied by experienced injustice predicts victims' self-reported retaliatory deviance behaviors such as workplace theft, falsely reporting working hours/expenses, or "slacking-off" (Lim & Okimoto, 2013). It is important to note that such compensatory retaliation is argued to be driven by moral concerns (Greenberg, 2002); workers who believed that their organization violated distributive justice principles attempted to compensate for the injustice by stealing, an effect that was particularly strong among those with high (rather than low) levels of moral reasoning. This moderation pattern implicates the relevance of moral judgment in the motivation to impose compensatory retaliation, as salient moral concern heightened rather than inhibited the compensatory response.

Third-party observers may also find imposed compensation provided from the offender to be a satisfactory response, but a response that may be targeted toward alleviating their own moral concerns after an injustice rather than the victim's concerns. Compensation from the offender is more satisfying to observers when framed as a punishment (Van Prooijen, 2010); thus, compensation may address symbolic moral concerns, particularly when such compensation functions as a punitive response. Therefore, compensation from the offender may be effective in addressing the moral motives of third parties, even (or possibly even particularly) when that compensation is provoked through force or coercion. This contrasts with the relational function of compensation which is likely to only follow from the voluntary (as compared to involuntary) provision of compensation (Desmet, DeCremer, & Van Dijk, 2010).

Although forced compensation may satisfy third parties' moral concerns, victims may not necessarily view forced compensation as sufficient to restore justice. For example, Desmet and colleagues (2010) found that although victims are sensitive to the size of financial compensation they receive from offenders (with larger compensation amounts restoring trust to a greater degree), size of compensation only mattered when it was provided voluntarily. Victims responded with similarly low levels of trust to offenders who were ordered by a third party to pay them larger versus smaller amounts of compensation. These findings again suggest that victims are not solely motivated by instrumental concerns (or they would always preference the larger compensation amount over the smaller one); rather, they highlight the importance of victims' relational and moral concerns following injustice.

Interestingly, moral concerns may also motivate third parties to provide compensation indirectly, not necessarily from the source of the injustice (i.e., *third-party compensation*). Nadisic and colleagues (2013) work on the "Robin Hood Effect" (reviewed earlier) supports the notion that managers' moral motivations drive them to compensate victims of organizational injustice. In particular, 45% of the managers who engaged in Robin Hood behaviors (e.g., providing a discretionary bonus to a victimized employee) in their sample, indicated they did so because they believed it was the "right" thing to do. Moreover, this tendency to compensate victimized employees is particularly strong among managers with a high moral identity (Reynolds & Ceranic, 2007). These cases of third-party compensation suggest that observers are driven to compensate by their moral imperative to see justice done. Consistent with this notion, observers who felt the most empathy for victimized employees were the strongest supporters of managers who violated the rules to compensate those employees (O'Connor & Mullen, 2012). Thus, compensation may be seen as a route to restoring the moral order *even without a punitive meaning*. However, it is unclear whether the victims of injustice would view such third-party compensation as effectively restoring justice.

It is also unclear whether the symbolic communication implied by retaliatory compensation actually helps to reaffirm important justice principles, or whether such compensation only satisfies internal moral imperatives to seek just deserts. Research in the legal domain suggests that although often justified by instrumental motives of deterrence and behavior control (Carlsmith, 2008), punishments are actually driven by internal drives for moral proportionality (Carlsmith & Darley, 2008). That is, people want to see offenders suffer in proportion to the wrong they caused (i.e., just deserts) but profess deterrence and behavior control motives to justify that suffering. Applied to compensation, the compensatory impulse may be justified by instrumental motives to help the victim, but may actually be driven by an internal moral motive to take positive action toward balancing the scales of justice. The fact that both theft and third-party compensation are often "invisible" to the perpetrators of injustice suggests that the latter may be true. However, future research is necessary to specify precisely how compensation addresses people's moral concerns, while also considering the perspective of all involved parties.

Summary of the Instrumental, Relational, and Moral Consequences of Compensation

In summary, providing compensation to victims of injustice can help to alleviate people's instrumental, relational, and moral concerns following a transgression. The extent to which compensation is effective at restoring justice likely depends on the extent to which its effect matches the salient concern aroused by the transgression. This general idea applies the "multiple needs" models of justice (Cropanzano et al., 2001) to understand reactions to compensatory justice, although this broader argument has been evoked in other injustice theories and research (e.g., Okimoto & Wenzel, 2008; Reb et al., 2006).

This perspective makes it critical to understand precisely when different instrumental, relational, and/or moral concerns may be evoked. Skitka and colleagues developed a contingency model of justice reasoning (e.g., Skitka, 2003; Skitka et al., 2008; Skitka & Wisneski, 2012) that proposes that how people judge what is fair or unfair is contingent on which aspect of identity is currently most accessible in people's working self-concept, that is, their material (i.e., instrumental), social (i.e., relational), or moral identity. Drawing on research on the self, Skitka and colleagues argue that these various identities cannot all be equally accessible at any given time. Moreover, (a) the relative accessibility of a given identity in the working self-concept is influenced by the perceiver's past experience, present expectations, current motives and goals, in combination with cues from the social context; and (b) a shift in identity focus similarly shifts the accessibility of associated expectations, motives, values, knowledge, and goals (see Baumeister, 1999; Brewer, 1991; Carver & Scheier, 1998; Markus & Kunda, 1986; McGuire, McGuire, & Cheever, 1986; Turner, 1999, for relevant reviews and research). Given this, a shift in identity focus triggered by a particular injustice or context is likely to also affect the symbolic meaning people ascribe to an injustice, the affective reactions they have to it, and their salient justice-repair motives (Okimoto & Wenzel, 2013). For example, compensation paired with expressions of relational concern (e.g., an apology) may be most effective following transgressions that threaten people's social identity or arouse relational concerns. Such expressions of relational concern may be unnecessary, however, if people's instrumental (rather than relational) needs were threatened by the transgression. Future research is needed to test whether and under what circumstances various types of compensation will satisfy individuals' instrumental, relational, and moral concerns.

Organizational Consequences of Compensation

In addition to influencing individuals' instrumental, relational, and moral concerns, the provision of compensation should also influence a number of variables that are particularly important in organizational contexts. We reviewed how compensation may serve to increase customer loyalty (Goodwin & Ross, 1992), restore trust (Desmet et al., 2010; Gillespie & Dietz, 2009), increase organizational identification (Okimoto, 2008), and facilitate reconciliation (Shnabel & Nadler, 2008) following transgressions. Although this research is a good starting point for investigating how compensatory justice influences organizational outcomes, more research is needed. For example, future research should explore how compensation influences organizational performance.

Moreover, given that victims sometimes feel it is fair to enact revenge to restore justice in the workplace (Jones, 2009), and may be particularly likely to do so when they perceive that formal methods in the organization are incapable of restoring justice (Aquino, Tripp & Bies, 2006), it is particularly important to understand the factors that allow the provision of compensation to restore victims' sense of justice and reduce their desires for revenge. Thus, future research is required to more fully understand how the provision of various types of compensation (e.g., voluntary versus coerced; public versus private) provided by various parties (e.g., perpetrator, third party) can help to restore justice from the perspective of various organizational stakeholders.

Consequences of Compensating Victims for the Injustice Responder

Managers and organizational authorities are often in positions of power that require them to respond to injustice. Thus, it is important to understand how observers and victims of the injustice view the injustice responder. When viewed from the perspective of the three need-based models for why people care about (in)justice, providing compensation to a victim could lead the compensator to be evaluated more favorably because compensating victims could help to: (a) assure victims and observers that their instrumental needs will be met (i.e., they will get what is due to them in the long run), (b) assuage their relational concerns, and/or (c) restore the moral order. If compensation effectively alleviates any of these concerns, people should view the compensator more positively.

Indeed, recent research suggests that leaders who provide compensation to victims are evaluated more positively by observers and fellow group members relative to those who do not compensate victims (Adams & Mullen, 2013). For example, people were more likely to vote for candidates for leadership positions who responded to various transgressions (the Darfur crisis, campus bike theft, and domestic violence) by compensating victims (or simultaneously compensating victims and punishing perpetrators) rather than solely punishing the perpetrator or not responding. This was because participants' perceived compensators to be warmer and more likable than punishers, and this increased warmth led to an increased willingness to elect compensators to leadership positions (Adams & Mullen, 2013). Other recent research parallels these findings, showing that both male and female managers who provided compensation to a victim of a workplace transgression were viewed by third-party observers as more benevolent than managers who took no action to restore justice, and through these benevolent perceptions, compensation had an indirect effect on subsequent leadership evaluations (Beaton, 2013).

Thus, it appears that by providing compensation to victims when dealing with workplace transgressions (instead of solely focusing on punishing), managers can help to mitigate the potential for negative perceptions that sometimes accompany meting out punishment (Ball, Trevino, & Sims, 1993). For example, although some research suggests that observers hold punishers in higher esteem for enforcing group norms (Barclay, 2006; Beaton, 2013), other research reveals that employees sometimes report becoming less trusting, less respecting, and more fearful of managers who punish other employees (Atwater, Waldman, Carey, & Carter, 2001; Niehoff, Paul, & Bunch, 1998; Schnake, 1986), and subordinate employees sometimes exhibit lower performance after observing their leader punish other employees (Podsakoff, Bommer, Podsakoff, & Mackenzie, 2006). Thus, providing compensation to victims (in addition to or in lieu of punishing) may afford managers greater status and help them retain perceived legitimacy in the eyes of their employees. However, additional research is needed to determine potential moderators of these effects.

Having reviewed the consequences of providing compensation for individuals' instrumental, relational, and moral concerns, as well as various other consequences that are relevant for organizational life (status, trust), in the remaining sections we turn to more fully articulating the remaining links in the model in Figure 23.1. In particular, we review (a) how characteristics of the transgression (e.g., severity of harm) influence desires for compensation, (b) how characteristics of the compensatory response influence its effectiveness, and (c) how individual characteristics of victims and third parties influence individuals' desires for compensation as well as their reactions to the provision of compensation. We argue that various characteristics of the transgression threaten different needs to varying degrees, and, therefore, the type of compensation that is necessary to restore justice.

Characteristics of the Transgression

The relational context in which a transgression occurs as well as characteristics of the transgression (e.g., the severity of the offense) should influence people's desires for compensatory justice. For example, research suggests that people will be more satisfied with compensation when: (a) the crime is less severe, and (b) the perpetrator did not intend to cause harm (Darley & Pittman, 2003).

Relational Context

Workplace injustice often entails an event that occurs in the context of an ongoing relationship, whereas many other types of injustice are more likely to occur as a one-shot encounter; thus, aspects of that relationship (e.g., the level of trust prior to the injustice) are likely to influence victims' evaluations of the injustice. For example, employees with more commitment to the organization may respond more favorably to compensation for organizational wrongs, whereas those who are less committed to the organization may instead choose to exit the organization following the injustice (Andiappan & Trevino, 2010). Similarly, victims of workplace injustice may be more open to compensation and other efforts to restore justice in general relative to victims of other types of injustice, because victims of workplace justice may prefer to keep their jobs rather than exit the relationship (Andiappan & Trevino, 2010). Relative to criminal contexts, compensation in organizational contexts might also be preferred by the organization over unilaterally punitive approaches that might jeopardize important relationships with the offender and/or incur turnover costs, particularly in response to minor, nonfiring offenses. Transgressions committed by fellow in-group members are also more likely to elicit relational threats compared to transgressions committed by out-group members (Smith, Tyler, Huo, Ortiz, & Lind, 1998), thus enhancing the importance of symbolically framing any compensation as a benevolent act of concern (Okimoto, 2008, Study 5). Finally, whether the injustice represents an initial or repeated occurrence will likely influence people's desires for compensation. Individuals may demand more compensation for organizational failings when those failings are repeated, because individuals feel the problem should have already been addressed (Grewal, Roggeveen, & Tsiros, 2008). Thus, a promising avenue for future research is to investigate how the relational context influences people's responses to compensatory justice.

Perpetrator Blame

Attributions of responsibility and intent influence observers' reactions to transgressions and what they feel is necessary to restore justice (Folger & Cropanzano, 2001; Gromet & Darley, 2009). Fairness theory predicts that when individuals witness or experience injustice, they engage in counterfactual thinking to understand what happened and why (Folger & Cropanzano, 2001). In particular, they evaluate whether the perpetrator *could* have behaved differently (e.g., were there situational constraints?), and if so, if he *should* have behaved differently (e.g., what behavior is normatively or ethically appropriate in the situation?). In addition, they also evaluate how the situation would have been different had the perpetrator behaved differently (e.g., what the fair outcome would have felt like). Thus, individuals' counterfactuals contribute to the attributions of responsibility they make for the perpetrator's behavior as well as their affective reactions. If the perpetrator could and should have behaved differently, victims and observers are likely to blame the perpetrator for his actions and experience anger. In contrast, if the perpetrator could not have behaved differently, victims and observers might be more likely to make situational attributions for the behavior and experience sadness or disappointment about the injustice (see also Weiner, 1995).

Thus, attributions of responsibility predict what victims and observers feel is necessary following an injustice. When perpetrators are deemed responsible for their transgressions, individuals may feel that compensation alone is not enough to restore justice and that punishment is also warranted. In contrast, when perpetrators are not blamed for their transgressions, individuals may be more satisfied with material compensation following the injustice (Darley & Pittman, 2003). Interestingly, some research suggests that people's perceptions of the perpetrator's intent to harm also influence how much compensation they think victims should receive, with higher intent associated with higher compensation (Miller & McCann, 1979). Thus, attributions of responsibility and intent should be strong predictors not only of how much punishment is warranted following a transgression but also whether compensation is deemed an appropriate response.

Severity of the Offense

When defining the severity of an offense, researchers refer to the severity of harm to the victim or the perceived wrongfulness of the offense (see Gromet & Darley, 2009 for a review). For our purposes, both versions of offense severity likely influence the acceptability of compensation following an offense. People may be more willing to overlook small injustices or be satisfied with token compensation following such injustices, but will think more is required to restore justice following more serious offenses (Andiappan & Trevino, 2010). Consistent with this notion, work in service recovery suggests that the larger the inconvenience caused by a failed service delivery (e.g., a delay in delivery), the larger the need for compensation to retain loyalty to the organization (Kim, Kim, & Kim, 2009). Moreover, people are willing to forgo punishment in favor of restorative options that are more focused on helping the victim when the offense is low in severity (Gromet & Darley, 2006). Therefore, in the case of serious wrongs, people may only be satisfied with compensation if it is also paired with punishment for the offender.

Characteristics of the Compensatory Response

There are a variety of attributes of the compensatory response that will influence victims' and third parties' reactions to it (see Figure 23.1). For example, people should be more satisfied when compensation helps to restore equity relative to token (or no) compensation. Moreover, as described earlier, whether compensation is voluntarily provided or coerced influences people's reactions to it (e.g., voluntary compensation is better at satisfying relational concerns than forced compensation). Finally, the presence of additional injustice responses (such as punishment or an apology) may also influence reactions to compensation.

Amount of Compensation

Whether compensation is perceived as appropriate is likely to vary as a function of the degree to which it sufficiently repairs the harm that was caused. For example, numerous studies in the service recovery literature suggest that the provision of material compensation (e.g., a gift, a discount) increases people's perceptions of fairness following a service failure, and that increased perceived fairness increases people's satisfaction with the organization and their willingness to continue patronizing or purchasing products from the organization (e.g., Chebat & Slusarczyk, 2005; Karatepe, 2006; Lin, Wang, & Chang, 2011; Maxham & Netemeyer, 2002; 2003; Smith, Bolton, & Wagner, 1999). In addition, research on service recovery has also demonstrated that overcompensation (being given more than the equitable amount) for prior harm results in more positive attitudes (i.e., satisfaction) than exactly equitable compensation or undercompensation (Boshoff, 1997; Davidow, 2003; Gilly & Hansen, 1985; Webster & Sundaram, 1998). Similarly, overcompensation for an injustice in an economic exchange fosters more trust in the transgressor than equitable compensation, when that compensation was provided voluntarily but not when provided involuntarily (Desmet et al., 2011).

Thus, equitable or overcompensation for instrumental harms is likely to be more effective at restoring justice in the eyes of victims than token compensation amounts. When compensation is designed to repair relational harms, however, the material value of the compensation may be less important. Preliminary research evidence suggests that compensation can repair relational concerns irrespective of its actual material value to its recipient (Okimoto, 2008, Study 4). Finally, although the amount of compensation for instrumental harms influences victims' perceptions of justice, it is less clear whether compensation amount would have similar effects on observers' perceptions of justice. For example, research on revenge demonstrates that observers evaluate equitable acts of revenge as fairer than acts of revenge that extract more harm from the perpetrator than the perpetrator originally caused to the victim (Tripp, Bies, & Aquino, 2002); thus, observers may not evaluate overcompensation as positively as victims do. Future research should, therefore, further investigate how the amount of compensation (as well as whether it was provided voluntarily or involuntarily) influences observers' perceptions of fairness.

Compensation Paired with Other Repair Strategies

Reactions to and demands for compensation also vary as a function of the presence of other justice restoration strategies (e.g., punishment, apology). As reviewed previously, compensation is more effective when paired with expressions of remorse or an apology (Schmitt et al., 2004) because such a pairing of responses more effectively alleviates individuals' instrumental *and* relational concerns (e.g., Goodwin & Ross, 1992; Okimoto & Tyler, 2007; Okimoto, 2008). Similarly, when adequate compensation is offered for a service failure, customers are even more satisfied when such compensation is accompanied by high procedural fairness (e.g., when they are told compensation for such service failures is standard company policy; Sparks & McColl-Kennedy, 2001). Thus, the pairing of compensation with some additional justice restoration strategies can increase perceptions of justice and satisfaction.

However, the pairing of compensation with other strategies may also diminish the *amount* of compensation observers deem warranted following a transgression. Some theorists have argued that punishment is the default response to transgressions and effectively restores justice following transgressions (see Gromet & Darley, 2009 for a review). Thus, if observers learn that the perpetrator has been punished, their sense of justice may increase (e.g., Goldberg, Lerner, & Tetlock, 1999), and their willingness to engage in additional injustice responses (e.g., victim compensation) may decrease. Consistent with this idea, when punishment recommendations or allocations precede compensation recommendations or allocations, people generally endorse giving less compensation (i.e., monetary aid) to victims than when punishment follows compensation (Adams & Mullen, 2015); this is true even in cases in which punishment does not entail any transfer of resources from the perpetrator to the victim (e.g., jail time). In contrast, learning that victims have been compensated does not influence people's punishment recommendations (Adams & Mullen, 2015), suggesting that compensation may not effectively alleviate individuals' moral outrage in response to intentional harms. Thus, the order in which people are asked to consider compensating victims and punishing perpetrators may determine the amount of assistance victims receive. Future research should explore whether the presence of other justice restoration strategies (e.g., apology) similarly reduce compensation amounts.

Characteristics of Victims and Third Parties

Theory would dictate a variety of characteristics of victims and third parties that should influence demands for compensation following an injustice as well as moderate reactions to the provision of compensation. However, there is very little empirical work testing such effects; therefore, we focus on only those variables with known empirical support (see Figure 23.1). Future research will doubtless uncover others.

Empathy

Empathy is a prosocial, moral emotion, as it involves the emotional matching and perspective taking of another (Batson, 1987, 1991; Batson & Coke, 1981; DeWaal, 2008; Eisenberg, 2000; Eisenberg & Miller, 1987). Thus, individuals who are higher in empathy may be more likely to sympathize with a victim's negative emotional state and, therefore, be more likely to want to alleviate the victim's suffering, relative to those who are lower in empathy (Batson, 1987). Consistent with this view, observers of injustice who are higher in empathic concern (trait empathy) are more likely to compensate victims than those lower in empathic concern, and will even pay a financial cost to do so (Lelieveld et al., 2012). Empathy for victims of injustice can even lead individuals to behave dishonestly to compensate those victims (Gino & Pierce, 2009). Similarly, observers who experienced heightened empathy for a victim of a workplace injustice were more likely to support managers who bent the rules to compensate the victim relative to observers who felt less empathy for the victim (O'Connor & Mullen, 2012). Thus, individual differences in trait-level empathic concern as well as state-level differences in empathy for victims predicts third parties' willingness to compensate victims and their reactions to the provision of compensation.

Cultural Value Orientation

Cultural value orientation (e.g., individualism versus collectivism, interdependence versus independence) has been shown to influence consumers' perceptions of what type of compensation is necessary following a service failure (Patterson, Cowley, & Prasongsukarn, 2006) and their satisfaction with various service recovery efforts (Mattila & Patterson, 2004). Thus, culture is also likely to influence the type of compensation deemed necessary to restore justice following other types of transgressions. Patterson and colleagues argue that given the emphasis individuals from more collectivist societies place on social harmony, collectivists dislike having to voice a complaint. Thus, customers with more collectivistic value orientations are more satisfied when the organization recognizes a service failure and initiates the service recovery attempt than when they have to point out the failure themselves. Similarly, within an organization, employees with more collectivistic value orientations may desire their managers to take the initiative to correct injustices, and may be less satisfied with injustice responses when they have to personally initiate the grievance process.

Power

Finally, the power of victims and third parties influences how likely victims are to be compensated. Power, or an individual's relative capacity to modify others' states by providing or withholding resources (Keltner, Gruenfeld & Anderson, 2003), has been shown to increase third parties' willingness to compensate victims of injustice (Mullen, Adams, Chow, & Zak, 2013). In particular, high power perceivers are more likely to compensate victims of injustice than are low power perceivers, whereas low power perceivers are more likely to punish offenders. This is consistent with work suggesting that power can lead individuals to show more concern for others and behave in more socially responsible ways, at least among those high in a communal orientation (Chen, Lee-Chai, & Bargh, 2001). Similarly, the power of recipients in ultimatum games has been shown to influence allocations to those recipients; completely powerless recipients actually receive more generous allocations than those who have modest amounts of power, because the recipients' powerlessness transforms the situation into one where norms of social responsibility are evoked (Handgraaf, Van Dijk, Vermunt, & Wilke, 2008). Thus, third parties who view victims as powerless to recover from the harm they experienced may be more willing to provide compensation to those victims, although this is a question that should be addressed in future research.

In addition, the power of victims should also influence their willingness to accept compensation rather than retaliate (e.g., Aquino, Tripp & Bies, 2006). Power influences people's beliefs about their abilities to effectively act on their environment and the extent to which they follow norms and procedures (Keltner et al., 2003). Thus, low power individuals may be more willing to accept token compensation than high power individuals because they may not feel they have other ways to correct the injustice (i.e., low power individuals may not feel they can effectively retaliate and thus may take what they are given). Consistent with this notion, work by Aquino et al., (2006) suggests that high status individuals (a concept related, but not identical, to power) were more likely to retaliate against injustice than their low status counterparts, but only when perceptions of procedural justice climate were low (i.e., when they likely did not believe the organization would effectively correct the injustice).

In summary, there are a variety of contextual and individual difference factors that will influence desires for compensation following a transgression. Our review was certainly not exhaustive, but was constrained by the limited amount of research on compensatory justice. Future research is needed to further explore how contextual and individual difference variables shape people's desires for and reactions to compensation.

Directions for Future Research

Although we reviewed literature in psychology, organizational behavior and service recovery, there are many gaps in our understanding of the psychological function and perceived effectiveness of compensatory justice and thus many avenues for future research. Despite the simplicity of the model depicted in Figure 23.1, if one considers the number of perspectives (e.g., victim, observer), varieties of compensation, and features of transgressions that occur in organizational contexts, the scope of future research necessary to more fully understand the effects (both symbolic and concrete) of compensatory justice phenomena is quite large. Throughout this chapter, we have highlighted the need for additional research supporting each of the sections in the model in Figure 23.1.

In addition to the areas we already mentioned, promising directions for future research include further exploration of how reactions to compensation vary as a function of who provides the compensation (e.g., perpetrator or third-party), and whether third parties and victims similarly perceive specific acts of compensation. In particular, there is considerable need to explore whether third parties can accurately understand the needs of victims following a transgression (i.e., whether instrumental, relational, or moral concerns were threatened by the transgression) so as to be able to effectively tailor the compensatory response to meet those concerns. If third parties offer compensation that they perceive is adequate in light of their own understanding of victims' needs and this compensation is viewed as inadequate by victims, such compensation may serve to further fuel perceived injustice on the part of victims. Similarly, future research should explore whether there is a psychological difference between *accepting* compensation for an injustice and *requesting* compensation for an injustice, and whether the latter is typically only driven by the pursuit of material self-interest or just appears that way to observers.

Future research should also address whether organizations should offer compensation for some types of violations but not others. For example, work on apologies and trust repair suggests that apologies are more effective for competence than integrity-based violations (Kim, Ferrin, Cooper & Dirks, 2004). It would be interesting to explore whether similar parallels exist with compensation. Perhaps providing compensation is more effective for competence than integrity-based violations, because monetary compensation for a competence-based violation may effectively alleviate concerns about injustice, whereas people may continue to worry about recurrence with integrity-based violations. Future research should also address whether the timing of the provision of compensation influences its effectiveness (e.g., can compensation atone for historical wrongs?). Scholars should also seek to understand when compensation will not only increase perceptions of justice but also effectively lead to reconciliation and forgiveness (see Bradfield & Aquino, 1998) and repair trust (e.g., Dirks, et al., 2011). Finally, in our review, we largely omitted questions about perpetrators' motivations to correct their wrongs by offering compensation. Thus, future research should also explore how characteristics of the perpetrator (e.g., moral identity, guilt proneness), the victim (e.g., status), and the transgression may motivate perpetrators to voluntarily offer compensation to those they have victimized.

Conclusion

Our review attempted to organize the scant literature on compensatory justice using a multiple needs-based model to understand how compensatory justice can fulfill individuals' instrumental, relational, and moral concerns following a transgression, as well as mitigate other negative reactions to injustice. In addition, our review highlighted characteristics of (a) the transgression, (b) the compensatory response, and (c) victims and third parties that influence when people will view compensation as an appropriate response to injustice. In doing so, we have identified gaps in our existing knowledge as well as promising directions for new research. It is clear that the dominant focus on retributive justice in the psychological and organizational literatures have left many interesting questions about compensatory justice unanswered. Fortunately, the scope of inquiry about how people respond to transgressions has recently begun to expand to include alternative approaches to justice such as reconciliation (e.g., Goodstein & Aquino, 2010; Kidder, 2007; Okimoto, Wenzel, & Platow, 2010) and forgiveness (Fehr, Gelfand, & Nag, 2010). We hope that our review will inspire increased empirical inquiry into compensatory justice as well.

References

Aaker, J., Fournier, S., & Brasel, S. A. (2004). When good brands do bad. *Journal of Consumer Research, 31,* 1–16. doi:10.1086/383419

Adams, G. S., & Mullen, E. (2013). Increased voting for candidates who compensate victims rather than punish offenders. *Social Justice Research, 26,* 168–192. doi:10.1007/s11211-013-0179-x

Adams, G. S., & Mullen, E. (2015). Punishing the perpetrator decreases compensation for victims. *Social Psychological and Personality Science.* doi:10.1177/1948550614542346

Adams, J. S. (1965). Inequity in social exchange. In L. Berkowitz (Ed.), *Advances in experimental social psychology* (Vol. 2, pp. 267–299): Academic Press.

Ambrose, M. L., Seabright, M. A., & Schminke, M. (2002). Sabotage in the workplace: The role of organizational injustice. *Organizational Behavior and Human Decision Processes, 89,* 947–965. doi:10.1016/S0749-5978(02)00037-7

Andiappan, M., & Trevino, L. K. (2010). Beyond righting the wrong: Supervisor-subordinate reconciliation after an injustice. *Human Relations, 64,* 359–386.

Aquino, K., Freeman, D., Reed, A.II, Lim, V. K., & Felps, W. (2009). Testing a social-cognitive model of moral behavior: The interactive influence of situations and moral identity centrality. *Journal of Personality and Social Psychology, 97,* 123–141.

Aquino, K., & Reed, A.II, (2002). The self-importance of moral identity. *Journal of Personality and Social Psychology, 83,* 1423–1440.

Aquino, K. Tripp, T. M., & Bies, R. (2006). Getting even or moving on? Power, procedural justice, and types of offense as predictors of revenge, forgiveness, reconciliation, and avoidance in organizations. *Journal of Applied Psychology, 91,* 653–668.

Aram, J. D., & Salipante, P. F. (1981). An evaluation of organizational due process in the resolution of employee/employer conflict. *Academy of Management Review, 6,* 197–204.

Atwater, L. E., Waldman, D. A., Carey, J. A., & Cartier, P. (2001). Recipient and observer reactions to discipline: Are managers experiencing wishful thinking? *Journal of Organizational Behavior, 22,* 249–270.

Ball, G. A., Trevino, L. K, & Sims, H. P. (1993). Justice and organizational punishment: Attitudinal outcomes of disciplinary events. *Social Justice Research, 6*, 39–67.

Bandura, A. (1995). *Self-efficacy in changing societies.* Cambridge: Cambridge University Press.

Barclay, P. (2006). Reputational benefits for altruistic punishment. *Evolution and Human Behavior, 27*, 325–344.

Baron, R. A., & Neuman, J. H. (1996). Workplace violence and workplace aggression: Evidence on their relative frequency and potential causes. *Aggressive Behavior, 22*, 161–173.

Batson, C. D. (1987). Prosocial motivation: Is it ever altruistic? In L. Berkowitz (Ed.), *Advances in experimental social psychology* (Vol. 20, pp. 65–122). New York, NY: Academic Press.

Batson, C. D. (1991). *The altruism question.* Hillsdale, NJ: Erlbaum.

Batson, C. D., & Coke, J. S. (1981). Empathy: A source of altruistic motivation for helping? In J. P. Rushton & R. M. Sorrentino (Eds.), *Altruism and helping behavior: Social, personality, and developmental perspectives* (pp. 167–211). Hillsdale, NJ: Erlbaum.

Baumeister, R. (1999). The nature and structure of the self: An overview. In R. Baumeister (Ed.), *The self in social psychology* (pp. 1–20). Philadelphia, PA: Psychology Press.

Baumeister, R. F., & Leary, M. R. (1995). The need to belong: Desire for interpersonal attachments as a fundamental human motivation. *Psychological Bulletin, 117*, 497–529. doi:10.1037/0033-2909.117.3.497

Baumeister, R. F., Stillwell, A. M., & Heatherton, T. F. (1994). Guilt: An interpersonal approach. *Psychological Bulletin, 115*, 243–267.

Beaton, J. (2013). *Do managers' justice restoration styles influence third party's leadership evaluations of them, and if so, why?* (Unpublished masters thesis). The University of Queensland, Brisbane, Australia.

Bies, R. J. (1993). Privacy and procedural justice in organizations. *Social Justice Research, 6*, 69–86.

Bies, R. J., & Moag, J. S. (1986). Interactional justice: Communication criteria of fairness. *Research on negotiation in organizations, 1*, 43–55.

Bies, R. J., & Tripp, T. M. (1996). Beyond distrust:" Getting even" and the need for revenge. In R. M. Kramer & T. R. Tyler (Eds.), *Trust in organizations: Frontiers of theory and research* (pp. 246–260). Thousand Oaks, CA: Sage.

Bies, R. J., Tripp, T. M., & Kramer, R. M. (1997). At the breaking point: Cognitive and social dynamics of revenge in organizations. In R. A. Giacalone & J. Greenberg (Eds.), *Antisocial behavior in organizations* (pp. 18–36). Thousand Oaks, CA: Sage.

Blader, S. L., & Tyler, T. R. (2009). Testing and extending the group engagement model: Linkages between social identity, procedural justice, economic outcomes, and extrarole behavior. *Journal of Applied Psychology, 94*, 445–464.

Blau, P. M. (1964). *Exchange and power in social life.* New York, NY: Wiley.

Boshoff, C. (1997). An experimental study of service recovery options. *International Journal of Service Industry Management, 8*, 110–130.

Bottom, W. P., Gibson, K., Daniels, S. E., & Murnighan, J. K. (2002). When talk is not cheap: Substantive penance and expressions of intent in rebuilding cooperation. *Organization Science, 13*, 497–513.

Bradfield, M., & Aquino, K. (1998). The effects of blame attributions and offender likeableness on revenge and forgiveness in the workplace. *Journal of Management, 25*, 607–631.

Brewer, M. B. (1991). The social self: On being the same and different at the same time. *Personality and Social Psychology Bulletin, 17*, 475–482.

Brockner, J. (1990). Scope of justice in the workplace: How survivors react to co-worker layoffs. *Journal of Social Issues, 46*, 95–106.

Brockner, J., Greenberg, J., Brockner, A., Bortz, J., Davy, J., & Carter, C. (1986). Layoffs, equity theory, and work performance: Further evidence of the impact of survivor guilt. *Academy of Management Journal, 29*, 373–384.

Brockner, J., Grover, S., Reed, T. F., & DeWitt, R. L. (1992). Layoffs, Job Insecurity, and Survivors' Work Effort: Evidence of an Inverted-U Relationship. *Academy of Management Journal, 35*, 413–425.

Brockner, J., Grover, S., Reed, T. F., Dewitt, R. L., & O'Malley, M. (1987). Survivors' reactions to layoffs: We get by with a little help for our friends. *Administrative Science Quarterly, 32*, 526–541.

Brockner, J., & Wiesenfeld, B. M. (1996). An integrative framework for explaining reactions to decisions: Interactive effects of outcomes and procedures. *Psychological Bulletin*, 120, 189–208.

Carlsmith, K. M. (2008). On justifying punishment: The discrepancy between words and actions. *Social Justice Research, 21*, 119–137.

Carlsmith, K. M., & Darley, J. M. (2008). Psychological aspects of retributive justice. *Advances in Experimental Social Psychology, 40*, 193–236.

Carver, C. S., & Scheier, M. F. (1998). *On the self-regulation of behavior.* New York, NY: Cambridge University Press.

Chebat, J., & Slusarczyk, W. (2005). How emotions mediate the effects of perceived justice on loyalty in service recovery situations: an empirical study. *Journal of Business Research, 58*, 664–673.

Chen, S. Lee-Chai, A. Y., & Bargh, J. (2001). Relationship orientation as a moderator of the effects of social power. *Journal of Personality and Social Psychology, 80*, 173–187.

Conlon, D. E., Meyer, C. J., & Nowakowski, J. M. (2005). How does organizational justice affect performance, withdrawal, and counterproductive behavior? In J. Greenberg & J. A. Colquitt (Eds.), *Handbook of Organizational Justice* (pp. 301–327). Mahwah, NJ: Erlbaum.

Cropanzano, R., Byrne, Z. S., Bobocel, D. R., & Rupp, D. E. (2001). Self-enhancement biases, laboratory experiments, george wilhelm friedrich hegel, and the increasingly crowded world of organizational justice. *Journal of Vocational Behavior, 58*, 260–272. doi:10.1006/jvbe.2001.1798

Cropanzano, R., Goldman, B., & Folger, R. (2003). Deontic justice: The role of moral principles in workplace fairness. *Journal of Organizational Behavior, 24*, 1019–1024.

Cropanzano, R., Rupp, D. E., Mohler, C. J., & Schminke, M. (2001). Three roads to organizational justice. In J. Ferris (Ed.), *Research in personnel and human resource management* (Vol. 20, pp. 1–113). New York, NY: JAI.

Darley, J. M., Carlsmith, K. M., & Robinson, P. H. (2000). Incapacitation and just deserts as motives for punishment. *Law and Human Behavior, 24*, 659–683.

Darley, J. M., & Pittman, T. S. (2003). The psychology of compensatory and retributive justice. *Personality and Social Psychology Review, 7*, 324–336.

Davidow, M. (2003). Organizational responses to customer complaints: What works and what doesn't. *Journal of Service Research, 5*, 225–250.

De Cremer, D., & Blader, S. L. (2006). Why do people care about procedural fairness? The importance of belongingness in responding and attending to procedures. *European Journal of Social Psychology, 36*, 211–228.

Desmet, P. T., De Cremer, D., & van Dijk, E. (2010). On the psychology of financial compensations to restore fairness transgressions: When intentions determine value. *Journal of Business Ethics, 95*, 105–115.

Desmet, P. T. M., De Cremer, D., & van Dijk, E. (2011). Trust recovery following voluntary or forced financial compensations in the trust game: The role of trait forgiveness. *Personality and Individual Differences, 51*, 267–273.

De Waal, F. B. M. (2008). Putting the altruism back into altruism: The evolution of empathy. *Annual Review of Psychology, 59*, 279–300.

Dirks, K. T., Kim, P. H., Ferrin, D. L., & Cooper, C. D. (2011). Understanding the effects of substantive responses on trust following a transgression. *Organizational Behavior and Human Decision Processes, 114*, 87–103.

Durkheim, E. (1964). *The division of labor in society*. New York, NY: Free Press. (Originally published in 1893.)

Eisenberg, N. (2000). Emotion, regulation, and moral development. *Annual Review of Psychology, 51*, 665–697.

Eisenberg, N., & Miller, P. A. (1987). The relation of empathy to prosocial and related behaviors. *Psychological Bulletin, 101*, 91–119.

Fehr, E., & Gächter, S. (2002). Altruistic punishment in humans. *Nature, 415*, 137–140.

Fehr, R., Gelfand, M. J., & Nag, M. (2010). The road to forgiveness: A meta-analytic synthesis of its situational and dispositional correlates. *Psychological Bulletin, 136*, 894–914.

Fiske, A. P., & Tetlock, P. E. (1997). Taboo trade-offs: Reactions to transactions that transgress the spheres of justice. *Political Psychology, 18*, 255–297.

Folger, R. (1998). Fairness as a moral virtue. In M. Schminke (Ed.), *Managerial ethics: Moral management of people and processes* (pp. 13–34). Mahwah, NJ: Erlbaum.

Folger, R. 2001). Fairness as deonance. In S. W. Gilliand, D. D. Steiner, & D. P. Skarlicki (Eds.), Research in social issues in management (Vol. 1, pp. 3–33). New York, NY: Information Age.

Folger, R., & Cropanzano, R. (1998). *Organizational justice and human resource management. Foundations for organizational science.* Thousand Oaks, CA: Sage.

Folger, R., & Cropanzano, R. (2001). Fairness theory: Justice as accountability. In J. Greenberg & R. Cropanzano (Eds.), *Advances in organizational justice* (pp. 1–55). Stanford, CA: Stanford University Press.

Folger, R., Cropanzano, R., & Goldman, B. (2005). What is the relationship between justice and morality? *Handbook of organizational justice* (pp. 215–245). Mahwah, NJ: Erlbaum.

Folger, R., & Skarlicki, D. P. (1998). A popcorn metaphor for workplace violence. In R. W. Griffin, A. O'Leary-Kelly, & J. Collins (Eds.), *Dysfunctional behavior in organizations, Vol. 1: Violent behaviors in organizations* (pp. 43–81). Greenwich, CT: JAI.

Foster, C. A., & Rusbult, C. E. (1999). Injustice and powerseeking. *Personality and Social Psychology Bulletin, 25*, 834–849.

Furnham, A., & Argyle, M. (1998). *The psychology of money.* Florence, KY: Taylor & Frances/Routledge.

Gelbrich, K., & Roschk, H. (2011). A meta-analysis of organizational complaint handling and customer responses. *Journal of Service Research, 14*, 24–43.

Giacalone RA, Greenberg J. (1997). *Anti-social behavior in organizations.* Thousand Oaks, CA: Sage.

Gillespie, N., & Dietz, G. (2009). Trust repair after an organization-level failure. *Academy of Management Review, 34*, 127–145.

Gilly, M. C., & Hansen, R. W. (1985). Consumer complaint handling as a strategic marketing tool. *Journal of Consumer Marketing, 2*, 5–16.

Gino, F., & Pierce, L. (2009). Dishonesty in the name of equity. *Psychological Science, 20*, 1153–1160.

Goldberg, J. H., Lerner, J. S., & Tetlock, P. E. (1999). Rage and reason: the psychology of the intuitive prosecutor. *European Journal of Social Psychology, 29*, 781–795.

Goldman, B. M. (2003). The application of referent cognitions theory to legal-claiming by terminated workers: The role of organizational justice and anger. *Journal of Management, 29*, 705–728.

Goodstein, J., & Aquino, K. (2010). And restorative justice for all: Redemption, forgiveness, and reintegration in organizations. *Journal of Organizational Behavior, 31*, 624–628.

Goodwin, C., & Ross, I. (1992). Consumer responses to service failures: Influence of procedural and interactional fairness perceptions. *Journal of Business Research, 25*, 149–163.

Greenberg, J. (1988). Equity and workplace status: A field experiment. *Journal of Applied Psychology, 73*, 606–613.

Greenberg, J. (1990). Employee theft as a reaction to underpayment inequity: The hidden cost of pay cuts. *Journal of Applied Psychology, 75*, 561–568.

Greenberg, J. (1993). The social side of fairness: Interpersonal and informational classes of organizational justice. In R. Cropanzano (Ed.), *Justice in the workplace: Approaching fairness in human resource management.* (pp. 79–103). Hillsdale, NJ: Erlbaum.

Greenberg, J. (1997). The steal motive: Managing the social determinants of employee theft. In R. A. G. J. Greenberg (Ed.), *Antisocial behavior in organizations* (pp. 85–108). Thousand Oaks, CA: Sage.

Greenberg, J. (2002). Who stole the money, and when? Individual and situational determinants of employee theft. *Organizational Behavior and Human Decision Processes, 89*, 985–1003.

Greenberg, J., & Cohen, R. L. (1982). Why justice? Normative and instrumental interpretations. In J. Greenberg & R. L. Cohen (Eds.), *Equity and justice in social behavior* (pp. 437–466). San Diego, CA: Academic Press.

Grewal, D., Roggeveen, A. L., & Tsiros, M. (2008). The effect of compensation on repurchase intentions in service recovery. *Journal of Retailing, 84*, 424–434.

Gromet, D., & Darley, J. M. (2006). Restoration and retribution: How including retributive components affects the acceptability of restorative justice procedures. *Social Justice Research, 19*, 395–432.

Gromet, D. M., & Darley, J. M. (2009). Retributive and restorative justice: Importance of crime severity and shared identity in people's justice responses. *Australian Journal of Psychology, 61*, 50–57.

Handgraaf, M. J. J., Van Dijk, E., Vermunt, R. C., & Wilke, H. A. M. (2008). Less power or powerless? Egocentric empathy gaps and the irony of having little versus no power in social decision making. *Journal of Personality and Social Psychology, 95*, 1136–1149.

Hazan, C., & Shaver, P. R. (1994). Attachment as an organizational framework for research on close relationships. *Psychological Inquiry, 5*, 1–22.

Heider, F. (1958). *The psychology of interpersonal relations.* Hoboken, NJ: Wiley.

Hocutt, M. A., Chakraborty, G., & Mowen, J. C. (1997). The impact of perceived justice on customer satisfaction and intention to complain in a service recovery. *Advances in Consumer Research, 24*, 457–463.

Hogg, M. A., & Terry, D. I. (2000). Social identity and self-categorization processes in organizational contexts. *Academy of Management Review, 25*, 121–140.

Hollinger, R. C., & Clark, J. P. (1983). *Theft by employees.* Lexington, MA: Lexington Books.

Johnston, R. (1995). The determinants of service quality: Satisfiers and dissatisfiers. *International Journal of Service Industry Management, 6*, 53–71.

Jones, D. A. (2009). Getting even with one's supervisor and one's organization: relationships among types of injustice, desires for revenge, and counterproductive work behaviors. *Journal of Organizational Behavior, 30*, 525–542.

Kahneman, D., Knetsch, J. L., & Thaler, R. (1986). Fairness as a constraint on profit seeking: Entitlements in the market. *The American Economic Review, 76*, 728–741.

Karatepe, O. M. (2006). Customer complaints and organizational responses: The effects of complainants' perceptions of justice on satisfaction and loyalty. *International Journal of Hospitality Management, 25*, 69–90.

Keltner, D., Gruenfeld, D. H., Anderson, C. (2003). Power, approach and inhibition. *Psychological Review, 110*, 265–284.

Kidder, D. L. (2007). Restorative justice: Not "rights", but the right way to heal relationships at work. *International Journal of Conflict Management, 18*, 4–22.

Kim, P. H., Ferrin, D. L., Cooper, C. D., & Dirks, K. T. (2004). Removing the shadow of suspicion: The effects of apology vs. denial for repairing ability- vs. integrity-based trust violations. *Journal of Applied Psychology, 89*, 104–118.

Kim T., Kim W., & Kim, H. (2009). The effects of perceived justice on recovery satisfaction, trust, word-of-mouth, and revisit intention in upscale hotels. *Tourism Management, 30*, 51–62.

Koper, G., Van Knippenberg, D., Bouhuijs, F., Vermunt, R., & Wilke, H. (1993). Procedural fairness and self-esteem. *European Journal of Social Psychology, 23*, 313–325.

Kray, L. J., & Lind, E. A. (2002). The injustices of others: Social reports and the integration of others' experiences in organizational justice judgments. *Organizational Behavior and Human Decision Processes, 89*, 906–924.

Krishnan, S., & Valle, V. A. (1979). Dissatisfaction attributions and consumer complaint behavior. *Advances in Consumer Research, 6*, 445–449.

Lelieveld, M. C., Van Dijk, E., & Van Beest, I. (2012). Punishing and compensating others at your own expense: The role of empathic concern on reactions to distributive injustice. *European Journal of Social Psychology, 42*, 135–140.

Lerner, M. J. (1980). *The belief in a just world: A fundamental delusion.* New York, NY: Springer.

Lim, L. Y. H., & Okimoto, T. G. (2013). *Deviant workplace behaviors and the psychological concerns elicited by organizational injustice.* Manuscript submitted for publication.

Lin, H.-H., Wang, Y.-S., & Chang, L.-K. (2011). Consumer responses to online retailer's service recovery after a service failure: A perspective of justice theory. *Managing Service Quality, 21*, 511–534.

Lind, E. A. (2001). Fairness heuristic theory: Justice judgments as pivotal cognitions in organizational relations. In J. Greenberg & R. Cropanzano (Eds.), *Advances in organizational justice* (pp. 56–88): Stanford University Press.

Lind, E. A., Kray, L., & Thompson, L. (1998). The social construction of injustice: Fairness judgments in response to own and others' unfair treatment by authorities. *Organizational Behavior and Human Decision Processes, 75*, 1–22.

Lind, E. A., & Tyler, T. R. (1988). *The social psychology of procedural justice.* New York, NY: Plenum.

Lotz, S., & Okimoto, T. G. (2013). *The symbolic value of customer compensation: Outcomes as socio-emotional reparation for service failures.* Manuscript submitted for publication.

Lotz, S., Okimoto, T. G., Schlösser, T., & Fetchenhauer, D. (2011). Punitive versus compensatory reactions to injustice: Emotional antecedents to third-party interventions. *Journal of Experimental Social Psychology, 47*, 477–480.

Luhtanen, R., & Crocker, J. (1992). A collective self-esteem scale: Self-evaluation of one's social identity. *Personality and Social Psychology Bulletin, 18*,302–318.

Lupfer, M. B., Weeks, K. P., Doan, K. A., & Houston, D. A. (2000). Folk conceptions of fairness and unfairness. *European Journal of Social Psychology, 30*, 405–428.

Markus, H., & Kunda, Z. (1986). Stability and malleability of the self-concept. *Journal of Personality and Social Psychology, 51*, 858–866.

Maslow, A. H. (1943). A theory of human motivation. *Psychological Review, 50*, 370–396.

Mattila, A. S., & Patterson, P. G. (2004). The impact of culture on consumers' perceptions of service recovery efforts. *Journal of Retailing, 80*, 196–206.

Maxham, J. G. III, & Netemeyer, R. G. (2002). Modeling customer perceptions of complaint handling over time: The effects of perceived justice on satisfaction and intent. *Journal of Retailing, 78*, 239–252.

Maxham, J. G. III, & Netemeyer, R. G. (2003). Firms reap what they sow: The effects of shared values and perceived organizational justice on customers' evaluations of complaint handling. *Journal of Marketing, 67*, 46–62.

McColl-Kennedy, J. R., & Sparks, B. A. (2003). Application of fairness theory to service failures and service recovery. *Journal of Service Research, 5*, 251–266.

McGraw, A. P., & Tetlock, P. (2005). Taboo trade-offs, relational framing, and the acceptability of exchanges. *Journal of Consumer Psychology, 15*, 2–15.

McGuire, W. J., McGuire, C. V., & Cheever, J. (1986). The self in society: Effects of social contexts on the sense of self. *British Journal of Social Psychology, 25*, 259–270.

Meindl, J., & Lerner, M. J. (1983). The heroic motive in interpersonal relations. *Journal of Experimental Social Psychology, 19*, 1–20.

Messick, D. M., Bloom, S., Boldizar, J. P., & Samuelson, C. D. (1985). Why we are fairer than others. *Journal of Experimental Social Psychoogy, 21*, 480–500.

Mikula, G. (1986). The experience of injustice: Toward a better understanding of its phenomenology. In H. W. Bierhoff,

R. L. Cohen, & J. Greenberg (Eds.), *Justice in social relations* (pp. 103–123). New York, NY: Plenum.

Mikula, G., Scherer, K. R., & Athenstaedt, U. (1998). The role of injustice in the elicitation of differential emotional reactions. *Personality and Social Psychology Bulletin, 24*, 769–783.

Miller, D. T. (2001). Disrespect and the experience of injustice. *Annual Review of Psychology, 52*, 527–553.

Miller, D. T., & Vidmar, N. (1981). The social psychology of punishment reactions. In M. Lerner & J. S. Lerner (Eds.), *The justice motive in social behavior* (pp. 145–172). New York, NY: Plenum.

Miller, D. T, & McCann, C. D. (1979). Children's reactions to the perpetrators and victims of injustices. *Child Development, 50*, 861–868.

Mullen, E., & Skitka, L. J. (2006). Exploring the psychological underpinnings of the moral mandate effect: Motivated reasoning, group differentiation, or anger? *Journal of Personality and Social Psychology*, 90, 629–643.

Mullen, E., Adams, G. S., Chow, R., & Zak, S. (2013). *Power influences preferences for compensatory and retributive justice.* Unpublished manuscript.

Murphy, J. G., & Hampton, J. (1988). *Forgiveness and mercy.* New York, NY: Cambridge University Press.

Nadisic, T. (2008). The Robin Hood Effect: Antecedents and consequences of managers using invisible remedies to correct workplace injustice. In S. W. Gilliland, D. D. Steiner, & D. P. Skarlicki (Eds.), *Justice, morality and social responsibility.* Charlotte, NC: Information Age.

Nadisic, T., Skarlicki, D., Cropanzano, R., & Fortin, M. (under review). *Responding to workplace injustice: Managers as modern-day Robin Hoods.* Manuscript submitted for publication.

Nagin, D. (1998). Criminal deterrence research at the outset of the twenty - first century. In M. Tonry (Ed.), *Crime and justice: A review of research* (Vol. 23, pp. 1–42). Chicago, IL: University of Chicago Press.

Niehoff, B. P., Paul, R. J., & Bunch, J. F. S. (1998). The social effects of punishment events: the influence of violator past performance record and severity of the punishment on observers' justice perceptions and attitudes. *Journal of Organizational Behavior, 19*, 589–602.

O'Connor, K., & Mullen, E. (2012, August). *Two wrongs make a right: When rule violations can restore justice.* Paper presented at the annual meeting of the Academy of Management, Boston, MA.

Okimoto, T. G. (2008). Outcomes as affirmation of membership value: Material compensation as an administrative response to procedural injustice. *Journal of Experimental Social Psychology, 44*, 1270–1282.

Okimoto, T. G., & Tyler, T. R. (2007). Is compensation enough? Relational concerns in responding to unintended inequity. *Group processes & intergroup relations, 10*, 399–420.

Okimoto, T. G., & Wenzel, M. (2008). The symbolic meaning of transgressions: Towards a unifying framework of justice restoration. *Advances in group processes, 25*, 291–326.

Okimoto, T. G., & Wenzel, M. (2011). Third-party punishment and symbolic intragroup status. *Journal of Experimental Social Psychology, 47*, 709–718.

Okimoto, T. G., & Wenzel, M. (2014). Bridging diverging perspectives and restoration goals in the aftermath of workplace transgressions. *Business Ethics Quarterly, 24*, 443–473.http://dx.doi.org/10.5840/beq201471515

Okimoto, T. G., Wenzel, M., & Platow, M. J. (2010). Restorative justice: Seeking a shared identity in dynamic intragroup contexts. *Research on managing groups and teams, 13*, 205–242.

Opsahl, R. L., & Dunnette, M. D. (1966). Role of financial compensation in industrial motivation. *Psychological Bulletin, 66*, 94–118.

Patterson, P. G., Cowley, E., & Prasongsukarn, K. (2006). Service failure recovery: The moderating impact of individual-level cultural value orientation on perceptions of justice. *International Journal of Research in Marketing, 23*, 263–277.

Podsakoff, P. M., Bommer, W. H., Podsakoff, N. P., & MacKenzie, S. B. (2006). Relationships between leader reward and punishment behavior and subordinate attitudes, perceptions, and behaviors: A meta-analytic review of existing and new research. *Organizational Behavior and Human Decision Processes, 99*, 113–142.

Pritchard, R. D. (1969). Equity theory: A review and critique. *Organizational Behavior and Human Performance, 4*, 176–211.

Pritchard, R. D., Dunnette, M. D., & Jorgenson, D. O. (1972). Effects of perceptions of equity and inequity on worker performance and satisfaction. *Journal of Applied Psychology, 56*, 75–94.

Reb, J., Goldman, B. M., Kray, L. J., & Cropanzano, R. (2006). Different wrongs, different remedies? Reactions to organizational remedies after procedural and interactional injustice. *Personnel Psychology, 59*, 31–64.

Reynolds, S. J., & Ceranic, T. L. (2007). The effects of moral judgment and moral identity on moral behavior: An empirical examination of the moral individual. *Journal of Applied Psychology, 92*, 1610–1624.

Scheff, T. J. (1994). *Bloody revenge: Emotions, nationalism, and war.* Boulder, CO: Westview Press.

Schmitt, M., Gollwitzer, M., Förster, N., & Montada, L. (2004). Effects of objective and subjective account components on forgiving. *The Journal of Social Psychology, 144*, 465–486.

Schnake, M. E. (1986). Vicarious punishment in a work setting. *Journal of Applied Psychology, 71*, 343–345.

Scobie, E., & Scobie, G. (1998). Damaging events: The perceived need for forgiveness. *Journal for the Theory of Social Behaviour, 28*, 373–402.

Shnabel, N., & Nadler, A. (2008). A needs-based model of reconciliation: Satisfying the differential emotional needs of victim and perpetrator as a key to promoting reconciliation. *Journal of Personality and Social Psychology, 94*, 116–132.

Skarlicki, D., & Folger, R. (1997). Retaliation in the workplace: The roles of distributive, procedural, and interactional justice. *Journal of Applied Psychology, 82*, 434–443.

Skinner, E. A. (1996). A guide to constructs of control. *Journal of Personality and Social Psychology, 71*, 549–570.

Skitka, L. J. (2002). Do the means always justify the ends, or do the ends sometimes justify the means? A value protection model of justice reasoning. *Personality and Social Psychology Bulletin, 28*, 588–597.

Skitka, L. J. (2003). Of different minds: An accessible identity model of justice reasoning. *Personality and Social Psychology Review, 7*, 286–297.

Skitka, L. J., Bauman, C. W., & Mullen, E. (2008). Morality and justice: An expanded theoretical perspective and empirical review. *Advances in group processes, 25*, 1–27.

Skitka, L. J., & Mullen, E. (2002). Understanding judgments of fairness in a real-world political context: A test of the value protection model of justice reasoning. *Personality and Social Psychology Bulletin, 28*, 1419–1429.

Skitka, L. J., & Wisneski, D. (2012). Justice theory and research: A social functionalist perspective. In J. Suls & H. Tennen (Eds.), *The handbook of psychology* (2nd ed., pp. 407–428). Hoboken, NJ: Wiley.

Smith, A. K., Bolton, R. N., & Wagner, J. (1999). A model of customer satisfaction with service encounters involving failure and recovery. *Journal of Marketing Research, 36*, 356–372.

Smith, H. J., Tyler, T. R., Huo, Y. J., Ortiz, D. J., & Lind, E. A. (1998). The self-relevant implications of the group-value model: Group membership, self-worth, and procedural justice. *Journal of Experimental Social Psychology, 34*, 470–493.

Sparks, B. A., & McColl-Kennedy, J. R. (2001). Justice strategy options for increased customer satisfaction in a services recovery setting. *Journal of Business Research, 54*, 209–218.

Steele, C. M. (1988). The psychological of self-affirmation: Sustaining the integrity of the self. In L. Berkowitz (Ed.), *Advances in experimental social psychology* (Vol. 24, pp. 261–302). New York: Academic Press.

Tajfel, H., & Turner, J. C. (1986). The social identity theory of intergroup behaviour. In S. Worchel & W. G. Austin (Eds.), *Psychology of intergroup relations* (2nd ed., pp. 7–24). Chicago, IL: Nelson-Hall.

Tetlock, P. E. (1985). Accountability: The neglected social context of judgment and choice. In B. Staw & L. Cummings (Eds.), *Research in organizational behavior* (Vol. 7, pp. 297–332). Greenwich, CT: JAI.

Tetlock, P. E., Kristel, O. V., Elson, S. B., Green, M. C., & Lerner, J. S. (2000). The psychology of the unthinkable: Taboo trade-offs, forbidden base rates, and heretical counterfactuals. *Journal of Personality and Social Psychology, 78*, 853–870.

Tetlock, P. E., Peterson, R. S., & Lerner, J. S. (1996). Revising the value pluralism model: Incorporating social content and context postulates. In C. Seligman, J. M. Olson & M. P. Zanna (Eds.), *The psychology of values: The Ontario symposium* (Vol. 8, pp. 25–51).

Thibaut, J. W., & Kelley, H. H. (1959). *The social psychology of groups*. Oxford, UK: Wiley.

Thibaut, J. W., & Walker, L. (1975). *Procedural justice: A psychological analysis*. Hillsdale, NJ: Erlbaum.

Tripp, T. M., Bies, R., & Aquino, K. (2002). Poetic justice or petty jealousy? The aesthetics of revenge. *Organizational Behavior and Human Decision Processes, 89*, 966–984.

Turillo, C. J., Folger, R., Lavelle, J. J., Umphress, E. E., & Gee, J. O. (2002). Is virtue its own reward? Self-sacrificial decisions for the sake of fairness. *Organizational Behavior and Human Decision Processes, 89*, 839–865.

Turner, J. C. (1999). Some current issues in research on social identity and self-categorization theories. In N. Ellemers, R. Spears, & B. Doosje (Eds.), *Social identity* (pp. 6–34). Malden, MA: Blackwell.

Turner, J. C., Hogg, M. A., Oakes, P. J., Reicher, S. D., & Wetherell, M. S. (1987). *Rediscovering the social group: A self-categorization theory*. Cambridge, MA: Basil Blackwell.

Tyler, T. R., & Blader, S. L. (2003). The group engagement model: Procedural justice, social identity, and cooperative behavior. *Personality and Social Psychology Review, 7*, 349–361.

Tyler, T. R., & Boeckmann, R. J. (1997). Three strikes and you are out, but why? The psychology of public support for punishing rule breakers. *Law and Society Review, 31*, 237–265.

Tyler, T. R., & Lind, E. A. (1992). A relational model of authority in groups. *Advances in Experimental Social Psychology, 25*, 115–191.

Tyler, T. R., & Smith, H. J. (1998). Social justice and social movements. In D. T. Gilbert, S. T. Fiske & G. Lindzey (Eds.), *The handbook of social psychology* (4th ed., pp. 595–629). New York, NY: McGraw-Hill.

Valle, V., & Wallendorf, M. (1977). Consumers' attributions of the cause of their product satisfaction and dissatisfaction. In R. L. Day (Ed.), *Consumer satisfaction, dissatisfaction, and complaining behavior* (pp. 26–30). Bloomington, IN: Indiana University.

Van den Bos, K., & Lind, E. A. (2001). The psychology of own versus others' treatment: Self-oriented and other-oriented effects on perceptions of procedural justice. *Journal of Personality and Social Psychology, 27*, 1324–1333.

Van Prooijen, J. W. (2010). Retributive versus compensatory justice: Observers' preference for punishing in response to criminal offenses. *European Journal of Social Psychology, 40*, 72–85.

Vidmar, N. (2002). Retributive justice: Its social context. In M. Ross & D. T. Miller (Eds.), *The justice motive in everyday life* (pp. 291–313). Cambridge, UK: Cambridge University Press.

Vidmar, N., & Miller, D. T. (1980). Social psychological processes underlying attitudes towards legal punishment. *Law & Society Review, 14*, 565–602.

Walster, E., Berscheid, E., & Walster, G. W. (1976). New directions in equity research. *Advances in Experimental Social Psychology, 9*, 1–42.

Walster, E., & Walster, G. W. (1975). Equity and social justice. *Journal of Social Issues, 31*, 21–43.

Webster, C., & Sundaram, D. S. (1998). Service consumption criticality in failure recovery. *Journal of Business Research, 41*, 153–159. doi:10.1016/S0148-2963(97)00004-0

Weiner, B. (1995). *Judgments of Responsibility: A Foundation for a Theory of Conduct*. New York, NY: Guilford.

Weiss, H. M., Suckow, K., & Cropanzano, R. (1999). Effects of justice conditions on discrete emotions. *Journal of Applied Psychology, 84*, 786–794.

Wenzel, M., Okimoto, T. G., Feather, N. T., & Platow, M. J. (2010). Justice through consensus: Shared identity and the preference for a restorative notion of justice. *European Journal of Social Psychology, 40*, 909–930.

Wong, A. (2004). The role of emotional satisfaction in service encounters. *Managing Service Quality, 14*, 365–376.

Zeithaml, V., Parasuraman, A., & Berry, L. (1990). *Delivering quality service: Balancing customer perceptions and expectations*. New York, NY: Free Press.

CHAPTER

24 Recovering from Organizational Injustice: New Directions in Theory and Research[1]

Laurie J. Barclay *and* Maria Francisca Saldanha

Abstract

In this chapter, we address the question of what it means to recover from organizational injustice. We begin by briefly overviewing the existing literature on remedying justice violations, including individual and organizational responses to perceived injustice. Next, we offer a definition of *recovery* that focuses on moving beyond the initial violation to include the aftermath of injustice and the dynamic process through which individuals may interact, negotiate, and work with others to resolve and move past the situation. We also explore what recovery means from the perspective of employees and managers and how recovery may be facilitated within organizations, including interventions that may be particularly helpful in this process. Finally, we conclude by discussing theoretical, methodological, and practical implications that arise from this approach.

Key Words: organizational justice, fairness, injustice, recovery, remedy, repair, violation, intervention, process, justice episode

"I feel exhausted because I'm tired of being angry, and this anger just has no outlet since I cannot do anything about the situation. I feel tired because every time I recall the situation the emotions engulf me over and over again. There should be peace, and I feel that dwelling on the situation does not give me peace. I feel a desire for contentment and settlement, without the hatred, the anger, and the wanting for revenge."

"I get terribly upset when random thoughts of this incident just pop into my head. I pray that they would go away but they wouldn't. These thoughts are a nightmare and reliving them is just awful. Feelings of disgust with myself for having lived through those few months surface quite often."[2]

The toll of experiencing injustice in the workplace can be profound and pervasive. As evidenced by the preceding quotes, in the aftermath of a workplace injustice, people can experience damaging emotional, psychological, and even physical consequences. Moreover, these negative consequences are not limited to employees but can also have significant implications for organizations—employees who feel unfairly treated, for example, may be less productive, less committed to the organization, or may even wish to harm the organization in order to "get even" for the injustice (see Colquitt, Conlon, Wesson, Porter, & Ng, 2001; Colquitt et al., 2013 for meta-analytic reviews). To date, contemporary research has heavily focused on why people care about fairness, what employees appraise when forming justice perceptions, and how experiencing (in)justice impacts employees' attitudes and behaviors (cf. Cropanzano, Byrne, Bobocel, & Rupp, 2001). Although numerous calls have been made for shifting our focus to how people can *recover* from experiences of workplace injustice (e.g., Barclay & Skarlicki, 2008; Barclay, Skarlicki, & Latham, 2009; Shapiro, 2001), research examining how to address the aftermath of an injustice has focused on how to "fix" injustice rather than how individuals can *recover* from these experiences.

In this chapter, we aim to make several contributions. First, whereas previous research has focused on *responding to* or *remedying* organizational injustice, we argue that justice scholars should also consider how to help individuals *recover* from organizational injustice.[3] Specifically, we argue that recovery goes beyond "fixing what is broken" and includes helping the individual manage the aftermath of an injustice and perhaps even gain positive benefits from these experiences. We focus on violations that occur between employees/managers where the manager is the perceived responsible party given that this is likely the most frequent situation within the workplace. Second, we explore recovery from the perspective of the employee and manager. Previous research has focused on the perspective of managers/organizations when exploring how to remedy injustice (e.g., Reb, Goldman, Kray, & Cropanzano, 2006) and the perspective of the aggrieved employee when exploring how individuals can cope with injustice (e.g., Barclay & Skarlicki, 2008, 2009). However, we argue that these approaches are narrowly focused and limited; research on recovery needs to consider a more comprehensive approach that delves deeper into the experiences of employees and managers, addresses the relational concerns that can arise in the aftermath of a violation, and considers the process that unfolds as a result of experiencing a violation. Third, despite calls in the literature to develop interventions within the context of organizational justice (e.g., Greenberg, 2001; Shapiro, 2001), few studies have explored interventions and those that have typically focus on how to promote justice as opposed to how to recover from injustice (e.g., Greenberg, 2006; Skarlicki & Latham, 1996). We argue for the importance of interventions and suggest two potential interventions that may facilitate recovery within the context of organizational justice. Finally, we conclude the chapter by exploring the theoretical, methodological, and practical implications as well as future research directions that emerge when this shift in paradigm is adopted.

Remedying and Responding to Injustice

Research exploring how people respond to injustice has primarily adopted an event-based approach that focuses on reactions to specific violations. Given the emphasis on discrete violations, it is perhaps not surprising that this approach has been associated with attempts to respond to and/or remedy injustice with specific actions—for example, by "fixing what is broken" or by engaging in a particular behavioral response (e.g., retaliation), depending on the perspective being explored. We argue that responding to or attempting to remedy an injustice may help individuals and organizations manage the discrete event, however, this may not be sufficient to help individuals "recover" from injustice. Specifically, we propose that recovery requires a more comprehensive approach that not only addresses the event but also its aftermath. In this section, we briefly overview research exploring remedies and responses to injustice (from the perspective of the manager/organization and employee, respectively). Next, we explore differences in what it means to "remedy" versus "recover" from injustice.

Managerial-Centered Perspective

Traditionally, research exploring how to remedy injustice has emphasized the "managerial-centered" perspective, in which justice issues have been viewed through the interests of managers and the organization (cf. Bies & Tripp, 2002; Scott & Hart, 1979). From this perspective, attempts to remedy injustice are initiated by the manager or organization, with the aggrieved employee often treated as a passive recipient (Barclay & Skarlicki, 2008). The goal of the remedy is to rectify the injustice and address the harm that was created by the violation (Reb et al., 2006). If successful, remedies have been found to increase justice perceptions (O'Malley & Greenberg, 1983) and decrease negative employee reactions (e.g., legal claiming, retaliation) as well as prevent the escalation of conflict (Reb et al., 2006). Managerial-centered approaches to remedying injustice have primarily focused on two main categories: (a) mitigating the injustice or (b) addressing the harm that was incurred (i.e., "fixing what is broken").

Scholars attempting to answer the question of how to mitigate injustice have typically focused on the importance of managing different facets of fairness as well as the role of explanations. With respect to the former, perhaps one of the most robust findings within the justice literature is the notion that negative reactions to unfavorable outcomes can be mitigated by fair procedures or fair interpersonal treatment (e.g., Brockner, 2010; Brockner & Wiesenfeld, 1996). In other words, one way to prevent or manage negative reactions to unfavorable outcomes is to ensure that the procedures used to derive those outcomes and/or the interpersonal treatment that accompanies these outcomes is perceived to be fair. Interestingly, procedural and interactional justice can substitute for each other, such that high levels of either of these dimensions can offset negative reactions to outcomes (cf. Skarlicki & Folger, 1997).

Given the early focus on outcomes, it is perhaps not surprising that a vast literature on explanations emerged since these can help employees understand why negative outcomes occurred and may reduce the sense of injustice associated with the violation (Shaw, Wild, & Colquitt, 2003). Termed informational justice, this form of justice is related to the explanations that outline the procedures used to derive an outcome and/or why a particular outcome was received (Colquitt, 2001; Greenberg, 1993a). Explanations can serve a variety of purposes including legitimatizing actions, managing attributions and impressions, diverting blame, as well as helping to reframe events and/or consequences (Colquitt & Chertkoff, 2002). Within this literature, the adequacy of explanations has been found to be critical—adequate explanations have been found to be more beneficial than cursory explanations because adequate explanations are better able to address why the event occurred and whether the decision maker could have acted differently (Shapiro, Buttner, & Barry, 1994). Meta-analytic evidence, however, suggests that not all explanations are created equal—although justifications can help individuals understand why an unfavorable event might have been appropriate, excuses have been found to be more beneficial since they suggest that no other actions were feasible (Shaw et al., 2003).

The managerial-centered perspective has also explored how managers/organizations can remedy or atone for justice violations. Whereas explanations focus on managing individuals' reactions to the event, remedies focus on rectifying the injustice by addressing the harm through socio-emotional (e.g., apologies), instrumental (e.g., compensation), and/or punitive (e.g., punishment) means (see Barclay & Skarlicki, 2008 for a review). In general, research on remedies has focused on "fixing what is broken"—that is, the type of remedy offered should "match" the type of injustice that was perceived and/or the need that was violated.[4] Using the multiple needs model of justice, for example, Reb et al. (2006) found that people who had experienced procedural injustice preferred instrumental remedies (e.g., monetary compensation) since this addressed their need for control, whereas people who had experienced an interactional injustice preferred punitive remedies (e.g., disciplinary action against the perpetrator) since this addressed their need for meaning. Similarly, Fehr and Gelfand (2010) found that apologies should be consistent with the recipient's self-views (i.e., their self-construals)—that is, people who perceive their relationships with other people to be more independent, relational, or collective, are more likely to forgive their offender following offers of compensation, expressions of empathy, and the acknowledgement of violated norms, respectively. Taken together, this line of research suggests that a successful remedy is one that matches the violation and the individual's needs, which in turn "restores justice perceptions and eliminates the desire to engage in revenge for a perceived injustice" (Reb et al., 2006, p. 34).

Employee Perspective

Employees have been found to use several different "coping strategies" for dealing with a workplace offense (e.g., Aquino, Tripp, & Bies, 2001, 2006). Specifically, research has focused on employees' responses to injustice, such as revenge, reconciliation, forgiveness, and avoidance. Revenge is defined as an effort to inflict harm on the party deemed responsible, whereas avoidance reflects the distancing of oneself from the perpetrator (Aquino et al., 2001). In contrast, reconciliation involves the offering of acts of goodwill toward the offender in an effort to restore the relationship, whereas forgiveness reflects the internal act of relinquishing anger, resentment, and the desire to seek revenge (Aquino et al., 2001, 2006; McCullough et al., 1998; McCullough, Worthington, & Rachal, 1997).

Although individuals can have a variety of reactions to injustice, research has emphasized "dark side" behaviors, such as revenge, retaliation, and counterproductive work behaviors (CWBs). We suggest that the managerial-centered perspective has also pervaded this literature; studies have focused on questions that are important from a managerial perspective, such as why people engage in these behaviors and how dark side behaviors can be prevented. Skarlicki and Folger (1997), for example, found that employees were more likely to retaliate against their organization when low distributive justice (i.e., unfair outcomes) was combined with low procedural or low interactional justice. Barclay, Skarlicki, and Pugh (2005) found that outward-focused emotions (e.g., anger) are a key mechanism that link fairness perceptions and retaliation, whereas Aquino et al. (2001) found that people who blamed their offender were more likely to seek revenge against their offender, particularly when the offender's status was lower than their own. Using an agent-system model, Jones (2009) found that CWBs are often driven by a desire for revenge and people tend to direct these behaviors toward the source of the perceived mistreatment; people were more likely to engage in CWBs directed toward their supervisors when interpersonal and informational justice were violated, whereas they directed CWBs toward the organization when procedural justice was violated. Despite the managerial focus, some research has explored why people may seek revenge. Tripp and Bies (1997), for example argued that revenge may serve functional purposes—it can "balance the scales," re-establish moral norms, and discourage further exploitation. Aquino et al. (2006) also found that contextual factors predict revenge responses—individuals with lower status seek revenge when the organization's procedural justice climate is low since they cannot count on the organization to re-establish justice. From an employee-centered perspective, however, it is also important to understand how this act can help aggrieved individuals manage the emotional and cognitive toll of experiencing an injustice and how engaging in revenge can impact these individuals (e.g., by creating a sense of guilt) and their relationships as well as their recovery process over the long term.

Although research initially focused on the "dark side," there has been a growing interest in forgiveness within the workplace. Fehr, Gelfand, and Nag (2010) recently conducted a meta-analysis that summarized the situational and dispositional characteristics that predict *when* people are likely to forgive. This research demonstrated the importance of peoples' cognitions (i.e., sensemaking, attitudes, and thoughts), affect (i.e., moods and emotions), and constraints (i.e., correlates that extend beyond the offense at hand, including the degree to which the individual is embedded in the relationship and his or her own socio-moral standards) in predicting the decision to forgive. There have also been numerous studies indicating the importance of justice in the decision to forgive. Worthington (2003) argued that interpersonal offenses can create an *injustice gap*—a discrepancy between current and desired outcomes—with larger gaps being associated with a lower likelihood of forgiveness. This line of research suggests that forgiveness is more likely to the degree that offenders can close the gap (e.g., by apologizing, offering restitution, etc.). In a field study, Bobocel (2014) showed that employees' perceptions of overall justice facilitated forgiveness among employees with a strong other-orientation. Wenzel and Okimoto (2010) demonstrated that expressing one's forgiveness to the offender can increase a sense of justice in victims by restoring their power and perceived value consensus with the offender. Moreover, this sense of justice can reduce hostile emotions, revenge motivation, and increase their desire to reconcile.

Although these studies shed light on when and why individuals may forgive as well as the benefits of forgiving, most of the studies in this area have focused on forgiveness as a *decision*. From an employee-centered perspective, however, forgiveness is more effectively viewed as a *process* that occurs over time and requires the processing of negative emotions, thoughts, and the development of empathy for the perpetrator (cf. Baskin & Enright, 2004). This suggests that more research is needed focusing on the individual and understanding the process that they go through in order to forgive and how this process impacts their long-term recovery.

One approach that focuses on individuals' recovery is restorative justice—an approach that focuses on providing *justice for all* (i.e., the victim, perpetrator, and broader community)—by not only providing restitution but also reintegrating offenders into the community and reaffirming values that may have been violated by the offense (Braithwaite, 1999, 2002; Roche, 2003; Wenzel, Okimoto, Feather, & Platow, 2008). Wenzel and Okimoto (2014) found that restorative processes can create feelings of justice, which can enhance individuals' ability to forgive their offender. This approach can be particularly effective when a transgression has raised concerns about shared values since this approach can reaffirm value consensus (Wenzel et al., 2008) and when the victim and offender have a shared identity (Okimoto, Wenzel, & Feather, 2009; Wenzel et al., 2008). However, it is critical that all parties *voluntarily* participate in the process and that the restorative justice process is not used to shame or lecture offenders into taking accountability in order for restorative justice attempts to be effective (Roche, 2003).

Although this approach has been effective within the criminal justice literature (e.g., Roche, 2003), it has received less attention within organizational contexts. An important exception is Kidder (2007), who argued that restorative justice processes can empower employees, relieve the need for managerial interventions, and provide training/

coaching opportunities. With respect to the latter point, Kidder (2007) proposes that restorative justice practices encourage individuals to deal with interpersonal conflicts early, which can not only prevent larger conflicts from developing but may also strengthen relationships by building trust and developing individuals' skills for dealing with conflict. Although Kidder (2007) suggests that restorative justice may not be appropriate for all offenses within the organization, the boundary conditions for restorative justice are unclear. We echo Goodstein and Aquino's (2010) recent call for more research that explores how this approach can be used effectively with justice violations and within organizational contexts.

Defining Recovery from Injustice

Although managers and employees can deal with justice violations in a variety of different ways, we argue that research has primarily focused on the managerial-centered perspective, event-based violations, and short-term "fixes" that can address the specific violation that occurred. For example, an individual who retaliates may "balance the scales" and/or demonstrate to the perpetrator that the egregious behavior will not be tolerated in the future, but this "coping strategy" does not necessarily address the emotional and cognitive needs of the individual or the longer-term ramifications of the injustice (e.g., broken trust, threatened identity, etc). Similarly, the primary objective of organizational remedies is to "restore justice perceptions" and prevent retaliation and/or the escalation of conflict (Reb et al., 2006). Although research from the service recovery (complaint handling) and marketing literatures suggests that justice perceptions can be restored (and even enhanced) after a violation has occurred (e.g., Hess & Olver, this volume; Liao, 2007; Tax et al., 1998), these studies have focused on customer reactions to injustice, which are likely to be quite different than relationships between employees/managers. This raises the question of whether remedies can truly address the issues that may emerge when violations occur within manager/employee relationships and whether these remedies can effectively manage the aftermath of an injustice.

Recently, Barclay and Skarlicki (2008) suggested that justice researchers should shift perspectives and focus on understanding the perspective of the aggrieved employee. That is, it is important to not only explore managerial or organizational efforts to repair fairness violations but also explore how violations are experienced by individuals (e.g., how they emotionally, cognitively, and behaviorally experience the violation), as well as how repairs can address the needs of these individuals. The authors argued that remedying injustice is particularly important from the perspective of the aggrieved individual given the severe negative consequences that they may experience (e.g., detriments to ones' physical and psychological health). Moreover, the authors introduced the term *remedial justice*, which refers to "efforts to recover from, remedy, correct, and/or repair violations of fairness" (Barclay & Skarlicki, 2008, pp. 156–157), and called for justice scholars to further explore the experiences and recovery of aggrieved individuals.

We argue that although this perspective and definition was helpful for advancing research in this area, this approach may not go far enough toward understanding recovery. For example, the term *remedial justice* suggests a longer-term approach that deals with the experience over time; however, the wording of the definition also tends to suggest the importance of focusing on the precipitating violation and reducing the harm associated with this violation but not necessarily addressing the aftermath of the violation. In other words, it assumes that by addressing the harm incurred by the violation, the implications of experiencing the injustice will also be addressed, including how this violation may impact individuals over time (e.g., when approaching similar situations in the future) and how it may influence their relationships with their managers, the organization, and others (e.g., co-workers who observed the violation; family and friends who provided social support during and in the aftermath of the violation).

We propose that *recovering* from injustice requires that the violation *and* its aftermath be effectively addressed. Whereas remedying injustice reflects the desire to correct the harm to the individual thereby making the person "whole" again, recovery should go beyond this to include managing the aftermath of the violation, such as issues and questions that arise as a result of the violation. For example, an individual who felt demeaned by his/her manager in front of a group of co-workers may accept an apology for the violation, but the violation has also raised additional issues about the individual (e.g., Did I deserve this treatment? Do other people share this view of me?), their manager (e.g., Can this person be trusted in the future?), the relationship between the individual and their manager (e.g., Does this person value me? Are there issues that we need to work on?), as well as others (e.g., I feel embarrassed, how can I face my coworkers?). Thus, although an apology may "fix" the violation, it may not address these other issues. Moreover, this example suggests the need to adopt a dyadic approach to exploring recovering since many situations are likely to be "negotiated" by employees and managers through multiple interactions over the course of time (Whiteside & Barclay, 2015).

We define *recovery* as the process through which individuals manage the implications arising from the initial violation as well as the aftermath of an injustice. This involves movement toward a sense of resolution surrounding the injustice. We should note that recovery does not stop when the harm is corrected (i.e., the person is "made whole"). Instead, we suggest that by virtue of experiencing injustice, individuals and their relationships are likely to be changed in some way. Thus, recovery goes beyond "restoring" the individual to the previolation state and includes understanding how the experience of injustice has changed the individual and how they are coping with these changes. Moreover, recovery is not limited to the person who perceived the injustice; rather recovery involves the process through which each party involved in the violation manages their experience as well as negotiates and manages their relationships with others in the aftermath of a justice violation. This definition implies the importance of exploring (a) the nature and magnitude of the violation, (b) the aftermath of violations, (c) how to capture and organize these experiences, (d) the dynamic nature of recovery, and (e) the influence of dyads and others in the recovery process. We address each of these considerations next.

Nature and Magnitude of the Violation

Our definition of recovery includes the initial violation as well as the aftermath of that violation. With respect to the initial violation, previous research has demonstrated that not all justice violations are created equal—that is, different unfair events or episodes may elicit different recovery needs. Bies (2001), for example, argued that violations of interactional justice can be particularly harmful since these violations threaten individuals' sacred sense of self. Moreover, in contrast to distributive injustice, which may be offset by high procedural or interactional justice (Skarlicki & Folger, 1997), violations of interactional justice are unlikely to be mitigated by distributive justice (cf. Barclay et al., 2005). Instead of focusing on what facet of justice was violated, it may be more insightful to focus on the psychological needs involved in the violation (e.g., control, belonging, positive regard, meaningfulness; cf. Cropanzano et al., 2001); these needs may be differentially influential and/or may need to be attended to different ways. For example, an individual whose sense of belonging is threatened by the violation is likely to have different recovery needs (e.g., recovery may need to involve re-establishing status within the group, reinforcing social relationships) as compared to an individual whose sense of meaning or morality has been threatened (e.g., recovery may need to involve re-establishing moral norms).

We argue that it is also important to consider the magnitude of the violation—including the depth and breadth of the violation. Previous research has demonstrated that the larger the *injustice gap*—a discrepancy between current and desired outcomes—the more difficult it is to forgive (Worthington, 2003). We suggest that the magnitude of this gap will also make recovery more difficult. Additionally, violations that have deep (e.g., fundamentally change the nature of work relationships, threaten individuals' identity) and/or pervasive implications (e.g., impacting work relationships and also personal relationships) are more likely to require recovery than violations that have a small set of implications that are limited to an isolated unfair event. Further, the severity of the violation may not only influence individual's reactions to the event (e.g., Aquino et al., 2001), but it may also influence recovery attempts—similar to the way that some violations are unforgiveable (Zechmeister & Romero, 2002), it is possible that individuals may not be able to fully recover from some violations, particularly severe violations.

Within the context of recovery, it is also important to explore contextual and individual factors related to the violation. In their review, Barclay and Skarlicki (2008) argued that contextual considerations, such as the history of the relationship and whether the individual has experienced similar violations in the past (from the same or other perpetrtators) may influence individuals' recovery. Additionally, there are a variety of individual differences that can influence recovery. Research has demonstrated, for example, that some individuals may be more attuned to observing and experiencing violations (e.g., Liao & Rupp, 2005) and may be more likely to engage in justice-motivated reactions (e.g., Dalbert, 2002). Further, individuals may be differentially motivated to recover from the injustice—whereas some individuals may wish to move on as quickly as possible, others may not be ready to move on and/or may even wish to prolong their anger in order to make changes in their environment (Tice & Baumeister, 1993).

Going Beyond the Violation: Addressing the Aftermath

Although it is important to explore the violation, we propose that recovery is fundamentally different from the approaches to justice violations discussed above since it also includes the aftermath of the violation (e.g., issues that were raised by and the changes that occurred as a result of the violation). In other words, recovery involves not only dealing with the precipitating violation but also how the parties cope with and manage the ensuing aftermath. From this perspective, responding to an injustice (e.g., engaging in behavioral strategies, such as revenge or reconciliation) represents an individuals' attempt to address a violation but does not necessarily reflect how that individual is *recovering* from the violation and its aftermath. For example, they may engage in revenge as a way to show the perpetrator that the injustice will not be tolerated or they may reconcile because they are forced to work with the person and it is easier to reconcile than hold a grudge (Bies & Tripp, 1996). However, neither of these responses reflects the toll of the violation on the individual, how the individual can recover from this violation, how this influences their relationships with the perpetrators and others who are impacted by the violation (e.g., co-workers, family), and how this may change how the individual experiences and deals with similar issues in the long term.

Similarly, remedying injustice reflects the organization's attempt to correct the harm incurred by the violation. In other words, it is focused on fixing what is broken, with the ultimate aim of preventing retaliation and the escalation of conflict (Reb et al., 2006). However, remedies are unlikely to address the issues that have been raised by the violation and how this has changed the parties' emotions, cognitions, and ways of interacting. Recovery, in contrast, involves not only the violation but also the aftermath of an injustice; it includes dealing with the issues inherent in the violation and also how the affected parties manage the changes that have occurred as a result of the violation. This suggests that recovery happens over the course of time and may be influenced by subsequent interactions between parties.

Exploring Recovery Episodes

An initial violation may create issues that *broaden* and/or *evolve* over the course of time as the parties work through the violation, interact, and manage new concerns that arise as a result of the precipitating violation. In order to capture this phenomenon, we argue that it is important to expand our perspective from an event-based to an episode-based approach. Specifically, drawing on the notion of emotion episodes (e.g., Frijda, 1993; Weiss & Cropanzano, 1996), Whiteside and Barclay (2015) recently introduced the notion of a *justice episode,* defined as a series of interactions that are initiated by a precipitating event, unfold over the course of time, and may include related subevents that are all related to the initial event. Within the context of recovery, this conceptualization may be particularly beneficial because it can organize the experience of recovery. A justice episode, for instance, may include the initial precipitating event, attempts to respond to and/or remedy the injustice, as well as the interactions that occur between parties as they negotiate and manage the aftermath of the violation. Additionally, as discussed later (in the section on dyadic considerations and the influence of others), other parties may be involved in the episode—for example, third parties may intervene, individuals may seek out the support of others and even attempt to build coalitions to deal with the offender. These subevents may influence how the process of recovery unfolds. For example, the recovery process may be different for an employee who received a sincere apology from his/her manager than for an employee who must approach his/her manager and request an apology. Similarly, a manager who reacts to the employee's concerns by expressing surprise or sadness is likely to influence the recovery process differently than a manager who reacts with anger (and may even be creating a subsequent violation as a result; Hillebrandt & Barclay, 2013). Thus, the episode may also incorporate other events (e.g., additional violations occur that are perceived to be a continuation of the initial event). By exploring the overall episode and how it unfolds over time, this approach can shed light on how parties are coping with the violation as well as how their interactions and additional events influence both parties' recovery from the violation.

Recovery as a Dynamic Phenomenon

Despite the fact that most research examines justice at one point in time, justice is not a static phenomenon—justice perceptions change (e.g.,

Ambrose & Cropanzano, 2003; Holtz & Harold, 2009; Jones & Skarlicki, 2013; Lilly, Virick, & Hadani, 2010) and fluctuations in justice perceptions can predict variations in daily satisfaction (Loi, Yang, & Dienfendorff, 2009) as well as distal outcomes such as commitment and turnover (Hausknecht, Sturman, & Roberson, 2011). Similar to justice perceptions, we suggest that recovery is also a dynamic phenomenon that may change over time. Specifically, as individuals work through the issues raised by the violation, their perceptions and emotions can change. Some research has demonstrated these changes.

Using an expressive writing intervention in which individuals wrote about their unfair experience for 20 minutes per day over four days, for example, Barclay and Skarlicki (2009) found that individuals who expressed their thoughts and emotions about a justice violation were less angry, better able to make sense of the violation, and more likely to experience a sense of resolution. For these individuals, venting emotions and embedding the violation into their broader experiences allowed them to better understand the event and put it behind them. Similarly, Dhensa (2011) found that talking about an injustice with others facilitated individuals' ability to take meaning and recover from the experience. Throughout this process of sense and meaning making, individuals may experience changes in their perceptions of justice, the perceived severity of the event, and even their expectations. For example, an individual may initially be angry about not receiving a desired outcome, but upon reflection may discover that this anger emerged from a sense of disappointment from not feeling valued by his/her manager. Moreover, as individuals engage in sensemaking, they may retrospectively change their perceptions as new information is incorporated and old information is reinterpreted (Weick, 1995). This suggests that it is not only important to explore how individuals' perceptions, emotions, and coping strategies change over time but also how individuals may reconceptualize what it means to recover from this incident and what is needed to facilitate this recovery.

Dyadic Considerations and the Influence of Others

Our definition also suggests that recovery is not limited to the individual who perceived the violation. As noted earlier, individuals who experience an injustice are likely to undergo a process in which they attempt to make sense of the violation, deal with their emotions and cognitions, and ultimately cope with or develop a sense of resolution about the experience. However, the manager (i.e., perpetrator) may also be influenced by the violation. Given that fairness is a deeply held virtue in society (e.g., Cropanzano et al., 2001; Folger, 2001) and that individuals typically want to perceive themselves as fair and protect this self-conception/identity (e.g., Diekmann, Samuels, Ross, & Bazerman, 1997; Gonzales, Manning, & Haugen, 1992; Messick, Bloom, Boldizar, & Samuelson, 1985), engaging in behaviors that are perceived to be unfair by others can be self-threatening and may motivate the manager to deal with this discrepancy (Whiteside & Barclay, 2015). Moreover, managers may also be influenced by having to engage in attempts to remedy the injustice. For example, consider a manager who recognizes that a violation occurred and believes that the employee would like an apology. A manager who apologizes because he/she believes that they did something wrong may feel better by approaching the victim. However, the manager may also feel threatened by the realization that s/he behaved unfairly. Moreover, the manager may need to address how this realization impacts his/her identity and how he/she wishes to prevent unfairness in the future. Conversely, a manager who believes that no unfairness occurred may experience some psychological benefits by refusing to apologize, but must then also deal with the fallout of refusing to apologize with the aggrieved employee. Okimoto, Wenzel, and Hedrick (2012), for example, found that offenders who refused to apologize experienced increased feelings of power/control and integrity, which resulted in higher self-esteem. This suggests that it is critically important to understand how the violation, remedy, and aftermath may influence managers. Moreover, it suggests that the manager's perspective and actions can have implications for how these two parties interact and how the process of recovery unfolds.

The process of recovery may also be influenced by others outside the dyad. When individuals experience injustice, they can seek social support and guidance from other sources (e.g., family, friends, counselors, union officers, legal advisors, etc.). Although voicing one's concerns to others can provide social support and guidance, it can also influence individuals' interpretations and reactions to the event. Eaton, Struthers, and Santelli (2006), for example, found that acknowledgement of the transgression by third parties can increase forgiveness by validating the individual and acknowledging that the person has been hurt by the transgression. On the other hand, third parties (e.g., family and friends) can also validate the aggrieved individual's perspective (rather than the individuals themselves), which can influence the attributions that are made for the transgression. Goldman and colleagues, for instance, found that receiving social guidance from others encouraged aggrieved individuals to engage in legal claiming (Goldman, 2001; Groth, Goldman, Gilliland, & Bies, 2002). Moreover, by sharing their experiences, individuals are often made aware of others' judgments and expectations. Since third parties tend to be less forgiving than the victim (Green, Burnette, & Davis, 2008), people who share their experiences may also feel that they need to fulfill the third party's expectations for how they should react to the situation. Third parties may also intervene in situations, which can influence the dynamic between the aggrieved individual and the perpetrator. Taken together, it is important to understand how the broader context influences this process.

Summary

Our definition of recovery suggests that a broader, dynamic, and process-oriented perspective is needed to understand this phenomenon. Moreover, recovery is not limited to the aggrieved individuals, but may also involve others including the perceived perpetrator as well as other stakeholders. In the next section, we explore how to facilitate recovery from injustice.

Recovering from Injustice: Considering Employees, Managers, and Relationships

The toll of experiencing injustice can have long lasting, pervasive, and even devastating effects. Aggrieved individuals, for example, can ruminate about injustice for years after the violation (Matthews, 1988). Although an extensive volume of studies have demonstrated the negative impact of unfairness on employee outcomes (see Colquitt et al., 2001; 2013 for meta-analytic reviews), the implications of unfairness extend beyond organizational bounds to impact personally relevant outcomes, including physical and psychological health. Experiencing unfairness, for example, has not only been associated with short-term negative consequences (e.g., increased anger, anxiety; Harlos & Pinder, 2000) but also long-term implications, such as insomnia (Greenberg, 2006), depression (Tepper, 2001), exhaustion (Elovainio, Kivimaki, & Helkama, 2001; Elovainio, Kivimaki, & Vahtera, 2002), psychiatric disorders (Kivimaki Elovainio, Vahtera, & Ferrie; 2003; Kivimaki, Elovainio, Vahtera, Virtanen, & Stansfeld, 2003), and coronary heart disease (Kivimaki et al., 2005). Moreover, perceived unfairness is a significant predictor of aggressive acts, including psychological aggression and violence (Barclay & Aquino, 2010; Folger & Baron, 1996).

From a managerial and organizational perspective, recovering from injustice is important to mitigate and manage negative employee reactions (e.g., increased theft, retaliation; Greenberg, 1993b; Skarlicki & Folger, 1997), which can negatively influence organizational effectiveness, not only by detracting from performance (Colquitt, 2001), but also by creating team dysfunction (Tyler & Blader, 2003) and poorer customer service (Masterson, 2001). This has potentially long-term and pervasive effects for the organization as well. Rupp and Paddock (2010), for example, argued that individuals' experiences of injustice are often aggregated (i.e., combined) over the course of time and shared with others, which over time can negatively contribute to justice climates within the organization and may also impact the ability of organizations to attract and retain valued employees. In this section, we explore recovery from the perspective of the aggrieved employee and the manager. We also examine the relational aspects of recovery, including how to rebuild damaged relationships and create a foundation for recovery.

Recovery from the Perspective of the Aggrieved Employee

Despite the pervasive physical, psychological, and emotional consequences that can be associated with experiencing injustice (see Barclay & Skarlicki, 2008 for a review), research has demonstrated that these consequences can be mitigated and prevented by helping individuals understand the negative event, develop a sense of resolution, and find positive meaning and/or learn from the experience (Barclay & Skarlicki, 2009; Pennebaker, 1997). Embedded in this perspective is the notion that individuals must "cope" with the injustice. Although some research has conceptualized justice as a stressor (Vermunt & Steensma, 2001), surprisingly little research has explored what it means to cope with injustice and how this can be facilitated.

Within the stress literature, coping has been defined as responses to adversity and the resulting distress (Carver & Connor-Smith, 2010). Individuals may engage in a variety of coping strategies. Problem-focused coping, for example, refers to the tendency for individuals to focus on addressing the stressor itself (e.g., by removing, mitigating, or escaping from the situation), whereas emotion-focused coping focuses on reducing the aversive state provoked by the stressor (Carver & Connor-Smith, 2010). Approach coping focuses on dealing with the stressor itself or with the emotions generated in the process, drawing the individual toward the stressor; whereas avoidance coping involves evading the situation or associated emotions, drawing the individual away from the situation (Roth & Cohen 1986; Skinner, Edge, Altman, & Sherwood, 2003). Coping responses are not limited to behaviors, but can also involve attention, emotions, and goals (Skinner, 1999). Skinner and colleagues (2003), for example, proposed twelve categories of coping responses, which include problem solving, support seeking, avoidance, distraction, positive cognitive restructuring, rumination, helplessness, social withdrawal, emotional regulation, information seeking, negotiation, and opposition.

Within the coping paradigm, an individual's access to resources is critical to facilitate coping. Specifically, employees who have resources available have more confidence that they can successfully overcome obstacles and achieve desired goals (Bandura, 1986), which in turn may influence the way individuals perceive potentially stressing situations (Lazarus & Folkman, 1984), as well as their attainment and maintenance of other resources (Hobfoll, 2001). Resources relevant in this context can be either job-related (such as job control and social support) or person-related (such as self-esteem and optimism; Grebner, Elfering, & Semmer, 2010; Meier, Semmer, Elfering, & Jacobshagen, 2008). Fredrickson (1998, 2001) has also demonstrated that experiencing positive emotions can build individuals' resources and buffer negative experiences.

Within the justice literature, "coping" has often been depicted as engaging in a single behavioral response to a fairness event (e.g., Aquino et al., 2001, 2006). We suggest that justice scholars would be well served to adopt a more comprehensive approach to coping that includes individuals' attempts to work through the issues, deal with the adversity, and even learn and/or grow from the experience. We argue that coping is important because it provides the foundation for the individual to re-engage with their environment—for example, individuals who have had the time to process and deal with their own issues may be in a better position to interact with their manager and others in the situation. Although coping with the injustice is a necessary condition for recovery, as we discuss further below, an individual's own coping process is likely not sufficient for "recovery" since individuals must also deal with the relational concerns that arise in the aftermath of a violation.

Recovery from the Perspective of the Manager

Throughout our discussion, we have emphasized the importance of understanding how individuals recover from an injustice. In contrast to previous research that has focused on how the aggrieved individual responds to the violation, we argue that recovery also needs to consider the person who was responsible (or perceived to be responsible) for the violation. Within organizations, this is often an individual's manager. Whereas previous research exploring the manager's perspective has focused on how managers can deliver or enact justice (e.g., Patient & Skarlicki, 2010), we propose that it is also important to understand how managers cope with justice violations and the aftermaths themselves. Within organizational settings, despite their best intentions, managers may have to treat employees in ways that can violate their own standards of fairness. For example, managers who deliver bad news must cope not only with the employees' emotions but also their own emotions (Folger & Skarlicki, 2001). In other words, managers may become focused on their own experiences, which can leave them with fewer resources to address their employees' concerns. Moreover, they must reconcile discrepancies between how they must act and how they believe that they should act. This may take a significant toll on managers and influence their ability to respond to their employees. Thus, it is important to not only understand why managers may treat employees unfairly but also how engaging in these behaviors (and remedy attempts) can impact the manager and influence the recovery process.

Additionally, although it is often assumed that a violation of justice primarily impacts the aggrieved employee, it is possible that some situations may create a sense of violation for the manager as well. Managers, for example, may have to enact organizational procedures or be a part of a larger situation that they deem to be unfair (e.g., enacting layoffs). Moreover, in some cases, they may not agree with the employee that a violation has occurred—that is, a predicament of injustice may arise, such that the manager believes that he or she is being fair, however, the employee does not perceive this to be the case (cf. Bies, 1987; Cooper & Scandura, 2012). These predicaments can threaten the manager's identity and create a motivation to defend him- or herself and/or influence the employee to adopt their perspective (Whiteside & Barclay, 2015). Thus, it is important to explore the manager's experience of the violation and his or her recovery needs.

Managers must not only deal with their own issues and reactions to the violation and its aftermath, they often must facilitate employees in their recovery. This suggests that managers need to prepare themselves so that they can provide remedies and social support to the aggrieved employee to facilitate the recovery process. However, as research on fairness as a dependent variable indicates, managers often find interacting with an aggrieved employee to be difficult, and they avoid engaging in these situations (e.g., Folger & Skarlicki, 2001). Moreover, managers may feel constrained by organizational policies around events and even fear litigation from employees if they provide apologies (i.e., accept responsibility). This suggests that some managers may feel tensions between how they would like to help their employees and what their organization will allow them to do, which may create stress for managers.

Taken together, we propose that when recovery is viewed from the perspective of the manager, it is important to consider not only how they are experiencing the violation and its aftermath but also how they prepare themselves for dealing with their employees and facilitating the recovery of others. This includes taking into consideration the role of other contextual factors that may influence how they can and should respond.

The Influence of Other Stakeholders and Contextual Factors in the Recovery Process

Although the focus of the present chapter is on the perspectives of managers and employees, it is important to note that others outside this dyad may influence the process of recovery. In addition to the influence of friends and family that we noted earlier, we also acknowledge the importance of considering third party observers (e.g., co-workers and/or others who witness the violation) and other stakeholders in the recovery process. Specifically, these other stakeholders can often experience their own reactions to the perceived violation (e.g., Spencer & Rupp, 2009) and may be motivated to respond, for example, by correcting the injustice and/or punishing the perpetrator (e.g., Turillo, Folger, Lavelle, Umphress, & Gee, 2002). It is unclear, however, how these responses impact the parties involved. Thus, it is important to explore how interactions with others can influence the recovery process.

The recovery process may also be influenced by other processes within and outside the organization. Employees, for example, who choose to grieve or litigate a perceived violation can find that these formalized processes can create a win-lose mentality in which individuals may feel compelled to strengthen their position (i.e., that they have been unfairly treated) to "win" the case. Moreover, these formalized processes can prolong the situation (e.g., when individuals must meet over an extended period of time for a lawsuit), which may make it difficult for individuals to focus on recovery. Taken together, although we argue for a focus on dyadic interactions, it is also important to consider the context in which these dyads are embedded and how contextual factors and other stakeholders can influence the recovery process.

Rebuilding Relationships in the Aftermath of Injustice: The Role of Trust Repair

Throughout our argument, we have emphasized not only remedying injustice, but also managing the aftermath of the violation and the relational concerns that may be raised. Inherent in this discussion is the notion of trust. Trust is defined as a person's willingness to be vulnerable to another based on positive expectations of his/her behavior and intentions, whereas trustworthiness relates to the attributes or characteristics of the trustee that inspire trust (Mayer, Davis, & Schoorman, 1995; Rousseau, Sitkin, Burt, & Camerer, 1998). Trust, trustworthiness, and justice have strong theoretical and empirical relationships. For example, trust is a central feature of key justice theories, including relational models (e.g., Lind & Tyler, 1988) and fairness heuristic theory (e.g., Lind, 2001a, 2001b), to name a few examples. Trust has also been argued to be an antecedent and consequence of justice and may also co-evolve with justice perceptions (e.g., Brockner & Siegel, 1996). There are also likely to be reciprocal relationships between these constructs. Using a longitudinal field study, Colquitt and Rodell (2011), for example, found that informational justice predicted trust (after controlling for prior trust and trustworthiness) whereas procedural and interpersonal justice predicted benevolence and integrity (components of trustworthiness), and integrity, in turn, significantly predicted subsequent justice perceptions. Empirically, justice and trust have been shown to have moderate to strong positive correlations (see Cohen-Charash & Spector, 2001; Colquitt et al., 2001, 2013 for meta-analytic reviews). Despite this strong association, the inter-relationships between these constructs have not been fully elaborated (Lewicki, Wiethoff, & Tomlinson, 2005).

Given the strong inter-relationships between these constructs, we argue that the literature on repairing trust can be helpful for repairing and rebuilding relationships within the context of a justice violation. Within the trust repair literature, Kim, Dirks, and Cooper (2009) argued that, in the wake of a violation, it is important to not only address the negative expectations that have arisen due to the violation but also re-build the relationship. In order to be effective, the process of rebuilding trust must go beyond re-establishing behaviors that reinforce trust and involve how both parties resolve discrepancies in their beliefs through repeated interactions. Specifically, these authors argue that typically there is a tension between the trustee who wants to be considered trustworthy, the trustor who tends to believe that trust in the trustee is not deserved, and the interplay that emerges as trustees and trustors attempt to resolve these discrepant beliefs. We argue that a similar dynamic is likely to emerge within the context of a justice violation—with individuals attempting to resolve the "predicament of injustice" through repeated interactions (cf. Bies, 1987). That is, within the context of a justice violation, it is important to not only address the violation, but also the relational concerns that may emerge and the dynamic interplay that may emerge between the parties as they attempt to "negotiate" and rebuild their relationship. In order for justice scholars not to "re-invent the wheel," we suggest that the literature on trust repair may be particularly helpful for exploring how to do this given the strong inter-relationships between these constructs.

It is also important for research to distinguish how recovery may be different within the context of justice as compared to trust. Within the trust literature, for example, efforts to repair trust often focus on repairing trustworthiness (e.g., Gillespie & Dietz, 2009; Tomlinson & Mayer, 2009). However, it is possible that injustice can be restored through different mechanisms. Moreover, Lewicki and Bunker (1996) argued that trust may be repaired primarily through cognitive or emotional means, depending on the type of trust that was violated. Given the inherently emotional nature of injustice, however, it is likely that emotional repair will be central to injustice recovery attempts. Thus, it is important to explore whether there are different antecedents, consequences, and mediators/moderators for recovery from trust violations versus injustice.

Additionally, it is critical that justice and trust scholars explore the interplay between these constructs in the (re-)building of a relationship. Some scholars, for example, have argued that fairness and trust can substitute for each other. Van den Bos, Wilke, and Lind (1998), for instance, argued that justice is likely to be particularly important when individuals lack information about an authority's trustworthiness. Moreover, it is possible that recovering from injustice may help facilitate trust repair efforts. Dirks and De Cremer (2010, p. 214), for example, noted that once trust is broken, it can be "notoriously difficult to repair" and may not ever be restored to the previolation state. However, given that justice can often facilitate trust, it is possible that focusing on recovering from injustice and re-establishing justice can set the foundation for trust repair and/or that combined efforts to recover from injustice and trust may be mutually reinforcing.

Trust may also create a context for justice concerns. Lewicki et al. (2005), for example, argued that justice may be viewed very differently depending on whether the relationship in which the violation occurs is characterized by calculus-based or identification-based trust. For example, within a calculus-based relationship, individuals are focused on transactional exchanges and view trust in a primarily cognitive manner. Accordingly, distributive and procedural justice can be particularly important because these dimensions allow individuals to judge the exchange partner's reliability and dependability. Within this context, violations typically result in short-term reactions that are focused on correcting the "balance" in the relationship. In contrast, identification-based trust relates to compatibility of the parties' interests, needs, and values. Within this relational context, fairness is socially constructed with the other parties, and the norms that are specific to the relationship dictate what is perceived as "fair." In other words, justice is "calibrated" by the relationship between the two parties. Violations in this context typically occur when a highly unanticipated or inappropriate act occurs, often focus on interactional justice, and involve a threat to the employee's identity. Embedded in this argument is the notion that standards of fairness can vary and evolve depending on the type of trust relationship that has been established. Moreover, repairing and rebuilding relationships may need to involve different types of fairness and trust efforts at different times, and it is possible that some violations may not be repairable, whereas in other cases it will be possible to "repair" the violation but it may be difficult to re-establish the relationship. Thus, significant insights are likely to be gained by integrating these two literatures and exploring the interplay between the constructs; however, it is also important to ensure that distinctions between the constructs are maintained.

Building a Foundation for Recovery

Although rebuilding relationships in the aftermath of injustice is important in order to address relational issues sparked by the violation, we propose that the seeds of an effective recovery are likely planted long before the violation actually occurs. A growing body of literature has demonstrated that how individuals interpret justice events can be strongly influenced by their prior perceptions and relationship with the perpetrator. Drawing upon fairness heuristic theory, for example, Choi (2008) found that entity perceptions moderated the relationship between the perceived fairness of an event and their reactions to the event. Specifically, individuals who believed that their manager was a generally fair person had less negative reactions to events than individuals who perceived their manager to be unfair. Similarly, Skarlicki, Barclay, and Pugh (2008) found that prior trust in one's manager significantly influenced individuals' reactions to a layoff, with individuals who had low prior trust reacting particularly poorly to manager's attempts to be "fair" during the layoff since these attempts were perceived to be insincere.

These studies are important for at least two reasons. First, entity perceptions of fairness can be relatively stable (Cropanzano et al., 2001). Managers who are perceived to be unfair may have difficultly changing this perception and building trust. Alternatively, when employees perceive their manager to be fair, this may buffer negative events, thereby decreasing the toll on the individuals involved as well as reducing potential damage to the relationship as a result of a violation. In other words, one way to lessen the sense of violation, and by extension increase recovery from injustice, is to ensure that employees feel fairly treated and that employees and managers have developed trusting relationships prior to a violation occurring. Second, we argue that by developing open and trusting relationships prior to the violation, employees and managers are likely to be better able to work together in the aftermath of a violation. Specifically, in order to work through the recovery process, it is often important to understand the other person's perspective. When a strong relationship has already been established, this may help individuals understand the other person's perspective and can make them more willing to interact, provide and accept apologies, as well as reconcile/forgive in the wake of a violation (e.g., Galinsky, Ku, & Wang, 2005; Ho, 2012; Hodgins & Liebeskind, 2003).

Summary

In this section, we proposed that it is important to explore what recovery means from the perspective of the aggrieved employee and the manager. Specifically, we argued that it is not only critical to examine how both parties experience the violation, but also how both parties prepare themselves to interact with the other person and manage, as well as rebuild, the relationship in the aftermath of the violation. In the next section, we build on this foundation by suggesting interventions that may help facilitate this process.

Promoting Recovery: The Role of Interventions

Despite numerous calls in the literature for interventions that can help promote fairness in the workplace and manage experiences of injustice (e.g., Greenberg, 2001; Shapiro, 2001), there has been a dearth of empirical research in this area. Although some research has demonstrated that training managers in justice principles can promote fairness (e.g., Greenberg, 2006; Skarlicki & Latham, 1996, 1997) and numerous suggestions have been offered for the types of interventions that may help employees manage their experiences (cf. Barclay & Skarlicki, 2008), few studies have explored how to recover from injustice (for exceptions see Barclay & Skarlicki, 2009; Dhensa, 2011, discussed earlier).

When considering interventions, it may be useful to draw upon occupational health frameworks, which suggest that there are three main types of intervention strategies: primary, secondary, and tertiary (e.g., Quick, Murphy, Hurrell, & Orman, 1992). Primary interventions focus on preventing the issue from emerging (in this case, ensuring that people feel fairly treated to begin with and preventing violations, where possible).

Secondary interventions assume that individuals have been exposed to the issue (i.e., violation) and are aimed at minimizing the negative effects of the violation or managing/modifying individuals' reactions. Tertiary interventions focus on seeking to ameliorate harm that has been caused by exposure to the issue (i.e., violation). As noted earlier, an extensive literature has focused on how to prevent unfairness and remedy/mitigate the damages associated with violation. Thus, we focus on this last category, tertiary interventions, with a specific focus on two types of interventions that may be particularly helpful for facilitating *recovery*—positive psychology and forgiveness interventions.

Positive Psychology Interventions

Positive psychology interventions are aimed at overcoming challenges by fostering the strength and inner resources of individuals with the objective of increasing well-being and producing lasting positive changes (Rashid, 2009; Schueller, 2010). Rather than remedying a problem, positive psychology interventions are aimed at building the resources and strength of individuals (Sin & Lyubomirsky, 2009). Thus, these interventions acknowledge that experiences can be perceived and experienced as negative and unpleasant, but encourage individuals to use their strength to restore and foster resources (e.g., courage, social and emotional intelligence; Rashid, 2009). As such, positive interventions frequently include an initial reflection on the individual's negative experiences, including the pain and distress associated with the experience, but move toward shifting attention and memory from negative to positive experiences (Calhoun & Tedeschi, 1998; Rashid, 2009).

Some positive psychology interventions also focus on promoting growth after a negative experience. Posttraumatic growth-based interventions, for example, challenge individuals to use negative and/or challenging life events to foster positive psychological change (Tedeschi & Calhoun, 2004). These interventions assume that the negative experience will remain distressing to the individual. Thus, growth results not from the event itself but from its aftermath and how it can help transform the individual's usual functioning and established schemas. One example of a posttraumatic growth intervention that could be applied within the context of organizational injustice is OTHERS (Fazio, 2009; Fazio & Fazio, 2006; Fazio, Rashid, & Hayward, 2008). OTHERS interventions seek to promote growth after a traumatic event by fostering positive emotions and a set of inner strengths composed by optimism, true meaning, humor, emotional intelligence, resilience, spirituality, self-confidence, and relationships with others (Fazio, 2009). In general, posttraumatic growth interventions involve a sense of increased personal strength and wisdom and the strengthening of social ties through the increased awareness of the importance of close relationships (Calhoun & Tedeschi, 1998).

Although positive psychological interventions are often used to help individuals foster positive changes and recovery in the wake of a violation (i.e., tertiary interventions), they may also be used on an ongoing basis to help build resources that can buffer individuals against unfairness (i.e., primary interventions) as well as help individuals cope with future violations (i.e., secondary interventions). Specifically, positive psychology interventions can be used not only at the time of the negative experience but also as a regular strategy in individuals' daily lives (Sin & Lyubomirsky, 2009). Common exercises that may be beneficial include savoring (i.e., daily reflection on pleasurable experiences with a focus on intensifying the positive emotions associated with experiences), three good things in life (i.e., daily identification of three positive events and their causes), identifying signature strengths (i.e., identification of one's five greater strengths, and using them more often each day), and using signature strengths in a new way (i.e., identification of one's five greater strengths, and finding a new way to use one of the identified strengths each day) (e.g., Seligman, Rashid, & Parks, 2006; Seligman, Steen, Park, & Peterson, 2005). Each of these strategies can help individuals build emotional and psychological resources that can help buffer them against stresses and violations.

Within the context of recovery from injustice, we argue that positive psychology interventions may be helpful not only for the aggrieved individual but also for their manager. With respect to the aggrieved individual, experiencing unfairness can trigger intense negative emotions and a deep sense of sacred-self violation (Bies, 2001; Bies & Tripp, 2002). Positive psychology interventions foster positive emotions, which have been shown to facilitate recovery from negative emotions and their negative consequences (cf. Fredrickson & Levenson, 1998; Tugade & Fredrickson, 2004). Moreover, positive emotions broaden not only the momentary thought-action repertoire but also long-term physical, intellectual, and social resources, which can be used as reserves to facilitate coping at other times (Fredrickson, 1998, 2001; Fredrickson & Branigan, 2005). Importantly, positive emotions facilitate coping with difficult and stressful situations (Fredrickson & Joiner, 2002), which can include situations of unfairness at work.

With respect to managers, these interventions may help them in dealing with their own issues related to the injustice as well as how they can help the aggrieved individual. Specifically, similar to employees, positive psychology interventions can help managers build their physical, emotional, intellectual, and social resources (Fredrickson, 1998, 2001). This may be helpful for managers as they attempt to manage their own emotions, thoughts, and reactions to the situation and its aftermath and may be especially helpful when managers are experiencing their own negative reactions to the situation and/or feel that they are not entirely to blame for the situation. Moreover, this intervention may help managers interact in a positive manner with aggrieved employees. Research has shown that managers often distance themselves from aggrieved employees and/or negative situations (e.g., when they must deliver bad news)—for example, managers may avoid the situation because they do not feel as though they have the resources available to deal with the situation, the employee, and/or their own emotional reactions (Brockner, 2010; Skitka, Mullen, Griffin, Hutchinson, & Chamberlin, 2002). Positive psychology interventions that promote positive emotions may help managers in expanding the resources they have available in a given moment and act as a buffer against the negative situation (Fredrickson, 1998, 2001). When managers are better able to cope with the situation themselves, their ability to facilitate other's coping is also likely increased. Additionally, the use of positive psychology interventions may encourage managers to reflect and learn from negative experience, which may not only help them prevent future situations from occurring, but may also enhance their abilities to effectively manage negative experiences in the future. Thus, exploring positive psychology interventions with aggrieved individuals and managers is likely to not only shed light on the recovery process but it can also reply to calls for more research on how to enhance fair behavior from managers (i.e., justice as a dependent variable; Folger & Skarlicki, 2001).

Forgiveness Interventions

Although individuals may respond to violations with forgiveness, and forgiveness may help facilitate the process of recovery, many individuals find it difficult to forgive and may not consider forgiveness as an option (McCullough et al., 1997; 1998). However, the benefits of forgiveness for aggrieved individuals have been established on a multitude of outcomes—forgiveness has been associated with fewer negative emotions (Freedman & Enright, 1996), increased positive emotions (Al-Mabuk, Enright, & Cardis, 1995; Coyle & Enright, 1997; Freedman & Enright, 1996), fewer retaliatory behaviors, (McCullough, 2000; McCullough et al., 1997; Rusbult, Verette, Whitney, Slovik, & Lipkus, 1991; Subkoviak et al., 1995), as well as increased physical and psychological health (e.g., Coyle & Enright, 1997; Witvliet, Ludwig, & Laan, 2001).

A number of interventions have been developed that focus on facilitating forgiveness. Although the justice literature has tended to focus on forgiveness as a decision as opposed to a process, meta-analytic research suggests that a process-based perspective is more effective in promoting forgiveness and emotional well-being (Baskin & Enright, 2004). Whereas decision-based interventions have a cognitive emphasis and are focused on the aggrieved individuals' decision to forgive a perpetrator (Baskin & Enright, 2004; Neblett, 1974), process-based interventions view forgiveness as a process that starts with the initial feelings of resentment and anger, leading to a decision to forgive, followed by a struggle to feel empathy and compassion toward the offender. This approach sees the decision to forgive as only one part of the process (Baskin & Enright, 2004; North, 1987).

Research on forgiveness interventions has demonstrated that although time is important for facilitating forgiveness, the simple passage of time is not as effective at eliciting forgiveness as an intervention (Wade, Worthington, & Meyer, 2005). There have been a number of different forgiveness interventions that have been advocated (see Wade et al., 2005 for a meta-analytic review and Wade & Worthington, 2005 for a content analysis of forgiveness interventions). Enright and colleagues, for example, developed a multistage model of forgiveness that has focused on steps that individuals must go through before forgiving (e.g., Enright & The Human Development Study Group, 1991). The model initially focused on 17 steps (cf. Hebl & Enright, 1993) but was later expanded to 20 steps (Enright & Fitzgibbons, 2000)—the steps include activities such as releasing anger, identifying and accepting the hurt, developing empathy, and so forth. Worthington and colleagues have developed a five-stage model of forgiveness (REACH) that focuses on ***R***ecalling the hurt, building ***E***mpathy for the offender, giving an ***A***ltruistic gift of forgiveness, ***C***ommitting to forgiveness, and ***H***olding on or maintaining the forgiveness (e.g., Worthington, 2003). Baskin and Enright (2004) suggested that most process-based interventions involve four phases: uncovering, decision, work, and outcome. In the first phase, individuals focus on the violation, including the emotions that have been sparked (as well as releasing their anger), exploring how the violation has impacted them and/or altered their beliefs (e.g., belief in a just world), and explore their psychological defenses that may be preventing the violation from being processed. In the decision phase, individuals may examine their resolution strategies and begin to consider forgiveness as an option. In the work phase, individuals start working toward forgiveness by engaging in activities such as reframing the event, developing empathy toward the transgressor, and accepting the event. Finally, in the last phase (outcome), individuals recognize what forgiving means to them and begin to attach meaning to the event and move past it.

The vast majority of these interventions have been developed in clinical settings, are facilitated by clinicians, and may focus on individuals and/or groups (Wade & Worthington, 2005). Within organizational settings, they may also be facilitated by employee assistance programs. Research has demonstrated that these process-based interventions tend to be most effective when (a) forgiveness is introduced explicitly with clients giving their consent to participate in a forgiveness intervention prior to the start of the intervention, (b) individuals are guided through the entire process, and (c) individuals are committed to the *process* of forgiveness as well as the forgiveness achieved during the intervention (Wade et al., 2005).

Within the context of recovery from injustice, adopting a process-based approach may facilitate recovery by aiding both employees and managers. From the perspective of the aggrieved individual, not only can forgiveness have the beneficial effects noted earlier, but it can also create empathy and compassion toward the perpetrator as well as ready the individual to receive reparation attempts and also increase the potential that the reparation will be effective (Decety & Jackson, 2004). Studies have shown, for example, that apologies are often more effective after aggrieved individuals have had a chance to work through their own thoughts and feelings (e.g., Frantz & Bennigson, 2005), and perpetrators are more willing to apologize to the extent that the other party is willing to forgive (Leunissen, De Cremer, & Folmer, 2012). From the perspective of the manager, viewing forgiveness as a process can also be helpful because it may facilitate an understanding that aggrieved employees may need time to heal and help manage expectations about how soon forgiveness is likely to occur after the violation. Moreover, managers may also need to engage in forgiveness—often times, managers can feel that they are unfairly bearing the brunt of an employee's negative reactions and may experience resentment toward the employee (Whiteside & Barclay, 2015). Thus, managers may also need time to heal and forgive. Taken together, we propose that further investigating forgiveness is important to understanding recovery for both employees and managers.

Interventions: What, When, Where, and Why?

We have provided two examples of potential interventions. However, many other possibilities exist and much more empirical research is needed in this area. Moreover, it is important to explore a number of questions, including what interventions should be used, why interventions may be effective, when interventions should be adopted, and where interventions are most effective. We briefly explore these questions below.

WHAT INTERVENTIONS SHOULD BE DEVELOPED?

We have offered two types of interventions that may be particularly helpful for facilitating recovery from injustice. However, these interventions are likely only the tip of the iceberg and many more possibilities exist. Interventions in the aggression literature, for example, suggest that training and educating individuals on how they can identify, prepare themselves, and cope with negative experiences can be effective in order to prevent and manage negative experiences (cf. Schat & Kelloway, 2006). Moreover, training managers not only on how to implement justice principles (e.g., Greenberg, 2006; Skarlicki & Latham, 1996) but also developing their communication and conflict management skills may help them facilitate employees' recovery. Interventions that have been developed in the conflict management and clinical psychology literatures may be particularly helpful given the conceptual overlap of injustice with conflict and traumatic experiences, respectively.

WHY ARE INTERVENTIONS EFFECTIVE?

In addition to exploring what interventions can be used, it is also important to explore why the interventions are effective. In other words, researchers should also focus on identifying the underlying mechanisms. This is important not only for understanding why a particular intervention is effective but also because it has the potential to help advance our theoretical understanding of recovery, as well as to develop more interventions that specifically target these mechanisms.

WHEN SHOULD INTERVENTIONS BE USED?

More work is also need on *when* these interventions are likely to be most effective. Pennebaker and Chung (2007), for example, argued that some interventions (e.g., expressive writing) may be most appropriate several weeks or months after the precipitating violation, whereas implementing these interventions in the immediate aftermath of a violation may prevent the use of defense mechanisms that can be quite healthy in the wake of an upheaval. More research is also needed on when different interventions should be used. It is possible that the interventions are differentially effective depending on the violation (e.g., nature and magnitude of the violation, whether the violation is ongoing and/or a series of violations), the individuals involved (e.g., their willingness and/or preparedness to participate in an intervention, the psychological needs that need to be addressed), and the relationship between the employee and manager (e.g., the nature of the trust between the parties). Clearly, a great deal of research is needed in order to explore the boundary conditions of interventions.

In addition to exploring when interventions can be used, it may also be important to explore opportunities for intervention. Research in the aggression literature suggests that when injustice occurs, it often creates a spiral in which the conflict escalates and may become violent (cf. Andersson & Pearson, 1999). However, there are many points of prevention that present organizations with opportunities to intervene and prevent aggression from occurring (cf. Hershcovis & Barling, 2006). It may be helpful to explore whether similar spirals exist for recovery efforts and/or whether opportunities for intervention can be identified. Taken together, it is important to explore not only what and how interventions should be used but also when and toward what purpose.

WHERE SHOULD INTERVENTIONS BE USED AND WHO SHOULD IMPLEMENT THEM?

When it comes to implementing interventions, it is important to consider who will be using the intervention and why. If used improperly, interventions have the potential to backfire and cause more harm than good. Barclay and Skarlicki (2009), for example, argued that expressive writing should not be used as a first line of defense for organizations after a violation occurs. Rather, this intervention should be used for people who are having trouble overcoming an injustice and need help working through their own issues. Moreover, they suggested that this intervention should only be used by employees on their own time. The authors argued that if individuals believe that their managers or organization may have access to their writing, they may be less willing to engage in the type of writing that has been found to be most effective. It may also introduce ethical issues for the organization and manager. In these cases, it may be important to educate employees about the availability of such resources but allow them to engage in these interventions alone.

In many organizations, there are dispute resolution processes and other formal mechanisms that are available to employees and managers. In some cases, these can help de-escalate conflict and may be particularly useful if aggression or violence is likely to result from the violation. However, in other cases, formal procedures can reinforce injustice, and the bureaucracy involved may make recovery more difficult by prolonging the process. Thus, it is important to further explore who should implement the different types of interventions and where these interventions should take place.

Summary

Taken together, although individuals can be motivated to recover from injustice, they may need help in doing so. The few studies that have explored interventions within the justice literature have had promising results, not only for promoting justice but also facilitating recovery. However, a great deal of research is needed in order to develop empirically supported interventions. We encourage justice researchers to not only work toward understanding recovery from a theoretical perspective, but also aim to develop direct applications and interventions that can reduce the research–practice gap by benefitting individuals experiencing this phenomenon in the workplace.

Moving Forward: Theoretical, Methodological, and Practical Implications

We began this chapter by suggesting that current focus on remedying and responding to injustice does not capture what it means to *recover* from injustice. Moreover, we argued that recovery is a dynamic process that represents not only how an individual copes with and moves past a violation, but also involves the interplay between individuals (e.g., managers/employees) as the recovery process is negotiated. This shift in paradigm has a number of theoretical, methodological, and practical implications that create opportunities for future research. In this section, we overview a sampling of these implications and argue that addressing these questions can foster our understanding of recovery within the context of organizational justice.

Theoretical Implications

Our focus on recovery has a number of potential theoretical implications for the justice literature. First, this perspective suggests a focus on overall justice. Although the justice literature has devoted a great deal of attention toward delineating the various dimensions of justice (cf. Colquitt, 2001; Colquitt et al., 2001, 2013), a number of scholars have argued that individuals are more likely to focus on their overall sense of justice rather than distinguishing between these dimensions (e.g., Shapiro, 2001). Moreover, there have been repeated calls in the literature to focus on overall justice since this construct can provide a more phenomenologically accurate and parsimonious depiction of employees' actual experience of justice (e.g., Ambrose & Arnaud, 2005; Ambrose & Schminke, 2009; Lind, 2001a; Lind 2001b; Shapiro, 2001; Tornblom & Vermunt, 1999). Although it is likely appropriate to explore justice dimensions when examining attempts to remedy injustice, overall (in)justice may be more appropriate for recovery. Whereas remedies focus on whether the dimension that was violated is corrected, recovery has potentially broader outcomes. Bandwidth fidelity theory suggests that it is important to match the breadth or generality of the predictor to the outcome being predicted (Cronbach, 1970; Cronbach & Gleser, 1965). We argue that overall justice may be better able to match the generality of the outcomes that are likely to be important for recovery (e.g., sense of resolution, etc.). Taken together, this suggests that justice researchers need to be cognizant of the implications of focusing on the justice dimensions versus overall justice and ensure that they adopt the conceptualization that will allow them to address the research question at hand.

Second, although our discussions have focused on recovery from *injustice*, there is considerable ambiguity in the literature about the distinctions between justice and injustice. Numerous scholars have suggested that justice and injustice are distinct constructs (e.g., Bies, 2001; Gilliland, 2008). Moreover, Colquitt, Long, Rodell, and Halvorsen-Ganepola (2010) demonstrated empirically that measures that focus on "injustice" (e.g., that focus on being treated disrespectfully rather than respectfully, etc.) account for variance above and beyond those that focus on "justice." However, these constructs are often used interchangeably; many scholars focus on justice when they aim to study injustice and vice versa (cf. Bies & Tripp, 2002) and researchers often use scales that focus on justice criteria when exploring individuals' experience of injustice (cf. Colquitt, 2001). Barclay and colleagues (Barclay & Whiteside, 2011; Hillebrandt & Barclay, 2013; Whiteside & Barclay, 2015) recently argued that the experience of injustice and justice are likely to be different—whereas justice is likely to be a more cognitively based phenomenon, injustice is likely to be laden with emotion and is unlikely to be captured solely by individuals' perceptions. Rather, injustice is likely better understood by exploring how individuals *experience* injustice (Barclay & Whiteside, 2011; Hillebrandt & Barclay, 2013; Shapiro, 2001). This also suggests that measures of injustice need to go beyond perceptual criteria to include the experience of injustice. Moreover, this distinction also suggests that restoring justice is likely to be a different phenomenon than recovery from injustice. Clearly, more research is needed to differentiate these constructs (as well as develop measures that can assess both justice and injustice). Thus, within the context of recovery, it is important to explore the experience of injustice, what injustice means for individuals, as well as how the interrelationships between justice and injustice and the interplay between these constructs may facilitate recovery.

Third, despite numerous calls in the literature to further integrate (in)justice and affect, there are still significant gaps in our understanding of the inter-relationships between these constructs (e.g., Cropanzano, Stein, & Nadisic, 2011; De Cremer, 2007). Within the context of recovery, this is important since emotions are likely to influence the experience of injustice, as well as be an integral part of the recovery process—through the venting of negative emotion and the fostering of positive emotions in order to build resources that can be used to facilitate recovery (Barclay & Skarlicki, 2009; Fredrickson, 1998, 2001). This suggests that a deeper appreciation of the linkages between these constructs will not only facilitate our understanding of (in)justice and affect, but also our understanding of the recovery process.

Finally, throughout the chapter, we have focused on recovery from *organizational* injustice. However, individuals can experience injustice in other domains (e.g., personal relationships) as well as experience negative situations that are not necessarily justice-related. This raises the question of whether recovery from organizational injustice is a unique or a specific case of a broader phenomenon (e.g., recovery from negative experiences). We argue that recovery from organizational injustice is likely to share numerous characteristics with other violations—for example, these experiences are likely to act as a stressor for the individual and invoke the need to respond in some way (Vermunt & Steensma, 2001). However, we also argue that there are likely to be differences between organizational injustice and other negative experiences. These differences may be related to factors that are uniquely related to the experience of injustice (versus other negative phenomenon), contextual factors related to the workplace (e.g., organizational culture, constraints on the ability to express certain emotions or behaviors within organizational settings; cf. Barclay & Kiefer, 2014), and differences related to the nature of work relationships (e.g., norms, roles, power/status, etc.), to name a few. We propose that more theoretical and conceptual work is needed in order to further clarify the commonalities and differences between recovery within the context of organizational injustice and other phenomenon.

Methodological Implications

Due to the focus in the literature on responses and remedies to violations of justice, it is perhaps not surprising that researchers have tended to use between-subject designs that tap into justice issues at one point in time (i.e., cross-sectionally; Greenberg, 2001). However, in order to fully explore the process of recovery, significant changes in the way we investigate these topics are needed. First, although justice is a relatively mature field, the question of recovery has received relatively little attention in this context, and many constructs need further development (e.g., *recovery from injustice* and *justice episodes*). Moreover, this approach to recovery represents a significant departure from previous work and a change in paradigm (i.e., away from cross-sectional studies to a more dynamic process-oriented approach). Thus, theoretical development and empirical studies that reflect this new paradigm are needed—although we can leverage previous research in other fields (e.g., coping, conflict management), it is important to explore the unique ways that recovery may occur within the context of workplace injustice and the mechanisms that underlie this process. Given the nature of these questions, we suggest that the field may benefit from qualitative investigations since this can provide rich and detailed data that can deeply delve into the phenomenon and increase our understanding (cf. Edmondson, & McManus, 2007).

Second, our discussions have highlighted the importance of exploring within-person variations and processes. As individuals work through the issues raised by the violation, they may experience a number of different processes, including engaging in sensemaking, processing their emotions and cognitions, retrospectively re-interpreting events, and evoking coping mechanisms (e.g., Barclay & Skarlicki, 2009). This suggests that it is important to explore the dynamic psychological and experiential processes that influence and shape individuals' changing experiences of justice and recovery. Moreover, it is critical to delve into these processes and identify the mechanisms that underlie them. In order to capitalize on this opportunity, researchers may be well-served to focus on within-person approaches. An example of this approach is the *person-centric perspective* advocated by Rupp and colleagues (e.g., Guo, Rupp, Weiss, & Trougakos, 2011; Weiss & Rupp, 2011). This approach argues that contemporary paradigms reduce individuals to abstractions (e.g., skills, attitudes, properties) and, in doing so, lose the essence of the individuals themselves. In contrast, the person-centric perspective advocates a focus on individuals as a whole—emphasizing their experiences and the meaning of work through their eyes and perspectives. This approach is characterized by (a) a subjective stance (i.e., individuals' subjective experiences are fundamental to understanding the individual), (b) lived through experience (i.e., "what it is like" to experience things like injustice and how this is related to time and the individual's search for meaning) and (c) an active self (i.e., the self is a source of perspective and is central to understanding experiences). By focusing on individuals' subjective experiences, this perspective allows researchers to delve into within-person processes as well as how these processes unfold over the course of time and relate to individuals' search for meaning. For example, within the context of recovery, a person-centric approach will allow researchers to better understand how the individual experiences the injustice, what recovery means to the individual, and how living through the experience can take on and create meaning for the individual.

Third, this focus on recovery suggests the importance of exploring justice events and episodes from the perspective of both the aggrieved employee and the manager. As noted earlier, both parties are likely to have issues that need to be worked through—thus, it is important to understand how both parties are interpreting, managing, and responding to the experience. Moreover, in order to truly tap into the unfolding of these experiences over time, it is also critical to explore the dyadic interactions that emerge and influence the recovery. In other words, our methodologies may need to explore multiple perspectives and how these perspectives interact over the course of time in order to capture and understand these experiences.

Fourth, there have been numerous calls within the justice literature for more longitudinal research (e.g., Ambrose & Cropanzano, 2003; Holtz & Harold, 2009). Within this context, longitudinal designs may be particularly helpful to (a) explore how justice episodes emerge, (b) understand how recovery is influenced by prior and ongoing interactions and processes, and (c) identify possible points of intervention that may help the recovery process.

Taken together, these methodological approaches can help capture these experiences and provide a deeper understanding of the processes that underlie this phenomenon. An important consideration to note is that our earlier discussion assumes that field research will be required in order to fully understand these experiences. In addition to the significant amount of time, effort, and resources that is required for field work, this approach also brings unique ethical considerations. For example, investigating ongoing justice and recovery episodes may influence how individuals respond and cope. Moreover, following individuals through an ongoing process (and repeatedly asking questions about that experience) may highlight the unfairness and prevent some coping mechanisms (e.g., inhibition) from operating and/or influence how they react to the other party. Further, Barclay and Skarlicki (2008) argued that the employees' willingness to participate in employee-centered interventions as well as the effectiveness of interventions may be compromised if employees believe that managers may have access to this information, which suggests the importance of ensuring that the intervention is suited to the context and issues at hand. Given the importance of these phenomena, it is critical that a greater understanding is developed so that we can facilitate recovery and prevent negative consequences in the workplace. However, this also requires that researchers exercise an extreme amount of care and caution as well as a strict adherence to ethical codes when investigating these issues.

Practical Implications

Throughout our discussion, we have highlighted the importance of examining recovery from multiple perspectives, not just the perspective of the aggrieved individual. Similarly, we suggest that it is important to explore how organizations can support and facilitate recovery for different individuals involved in the recovery experience. Thus, it is important to further investigate *how* organizations can effectively support recovery—whether it is providing resources and tools that can be used to facilitate recovery (e.g., counseling, interventions) and/or educating and training individuals on how to implement justice and manage conflict (e.g., Greenberg, 2006; Skarlicki & Latham, 1996, 1997). It is also important to explore how the organizational context may influence recovery. Fehr and Gelfand (2012), for example, suggested that organizations can create forgiveness climates that may facilitate prosocial responses to conflict (e.g., justice violations). Specifically, this research suggests that embedding core cultural values that support forgiveness (e.g., restorative justice, compassion, temperance) in the organization can allow a climate of forgiveness to emerge. This climate may guide the sensemaking of organizational members and provide direction on appropriate responses to conflict. Thus, it is important to investigate how contextual factors may also facilitate the recovery of organizational members.

Finally, the profound and pervasive toll of injustice can have long-lasting consequences not only for individuals' physical and psychological health but it can also impact their ability to secure new employment (Spera, Buhrfeind, & Pennebaker, 1994) and detract from their relationship with a new organization (Pugh, Skarlicki, & Passell, 2003). We propose that organizations have a responsibility to facilitate recovery even when individuals are no longer part of the organization. That is, organizations should aim to "do no harm" and, where possible, mitigate the harm that may have been inadvertently caused to their employees.

Conclusion

Despite extensive research exploring how employees appraise and react to (in)justice, relatively little is known about how individuals can *recover* from injustice. Although some research has explored how organizations can remedy injustice and how employees can cope with these experiences, few studies have explored how individuals can recover beyond the initial violation. In this chapter, we argued that justice researchers should adopt a new definition of recovery that focuses on the dynamic and process-oriented nature of this phenomenon. Shifting our paradigms and questioning our assumptions about what it means to recover from injustice has the potential to not only address critical questions within the literature but it also opens a number of new research directions. Given these benefits, we hope that justice researchers will answer the call to further explore recovery from injustice. Doing so will not only benefit employees and organizations but it will likely expand our theoretical understanding of (in) justice and ensure that our field remains relevant and influential (cf. Shapiro, 2001).

Notes

1. The research was supported by a grant from the *Social Sciences and Humanities Research Council of Canada* awarded to the first author and a Ontario Trillium Scholarship awarded to the second author.
2. Quotes from employees who had experienced unfairness in the workplace and were participating in an expressive writing intervention (cf. Barclay, 2006).
3. We focus on *organizational* (in)justice. Hereafter, we simply use the term (in)justice to refer to organizational (in)justices.
4. Although we focus on remedying violations between managers and employees, this approach to "correcting" justice violations has also pervaded the service recovery (complaint handling) and marketing literatures. Research on "service recoveries" (i.e., attempts to correct a service failure; Tax, Brown, & Chandrashekaran, 1998) has demonstrated that treating customers fairly and addressing their fairness-related concerns throughout the service recovery process has been associated with higher customer satisfaction and individuals may be even more satisfied with an organization after a successful service recovery (Liao, 2007).

References

Al-Mabuk, R. H., Enright, R. D., & Cardis, P. A. (1995). Forgiveness education with parentally love-deprived late adolescents. *Journal of Moral Education, 24*, 427–444.

Ambrose, M. L., & Arnaud, A. (2005). Distributive and procedural justice: Construct distinctiveness, construct interdependence, and overall justice. In J. Greenberg & J. Colquitt (Eds.), *Handbook of organizational justice* (pp. 59–84). Mahwah, NJ: Erlbaum.

Ambrose, M. L., & Cropanzano, R. (2003). A longitudinal analysis of organizational fairness: An examination of reactions to tenure and promotion decisions. *Journal of Applied Psychology, 88*, 226–275.

Ambrose, M. L., & Schminke, M. (2009). The role of overall justice judgments in organizational justice research: A test of mediation. *Journal of Applied Psychology, 94*, 491–500.

Andersson, L. M., & Pearson, C. M. (1999). Tit for tat? The spiraling effect of incivility in the workplace. *Academy of Management Review, 24*, 452–471.

Aquino, K., Tripp, T. M., & Bies, R. J. (2001). How employees respond to personal offense: The effects of blame attribution, victim status, and offender status on revenge and reconciliation in the workplace. *Journal of Applied Psychology, 86*, 52–59.

Aquino, K., Tripp, T. M., & Bies, R. J. (2006). Getting even or moving on? Power, procedural justice, and types of offense as predictors of revenge, forgiveness, reconciliation, and avoidance in organizations. *Journal of Applied Psychology, 91*, 653–668.

Bandura, A. (1986). *Social foundations of thought and action: A social cognitive theory.* Upper Saddle River, NJ: Prentice Hall.

Barclay, L. J. (2006). *Healing the wounds of injustice: The effectiveness of writing interventions on the physiological, psychological, and behavioral consequences of workplace mistreatment* (Unpublished doctoral dissertation). Vancouver, Canada: University of British Columbia.

Barclay, L. J., & Aquino, K. (2010). Workplace aggression and violence. In S. Zedeck (Ed.), *APA handbook of industrial and organizational psychology, Volume 3: Maintaining, expanding, and contracting the organization* (pp. 615–640). Washington, DC: American Psychological Association.

Barclay, L. J., & Kiefer, T. (2014) Approach or avoid? Exploring overall justice and the differential effects of positive and negative emotions. *Journal of Management, 40*, 1857–1898.

Barclay, L. J., & Skarlicki, D. P. (2008). Shifting perspectives: Helping victims recover from organizational justice violations. In S. W. Gilliland, D. D. Steiner, & D. P. Skarlicki (Eds.), *Research in social issues in management: Justice, morality, and social responsibility* (Vol. 6, pp. 155–199). Greenwich, CT: Information Age.

Barclay, L. J., & Skarlicki, D. P. (2009). Healing the wounds of organizational injustice: Examining the benefits of expressive writing. *Journal of Applied Psychology, 94*, 511–523.

Barclay, L. J., Skarlicki, D. P., & Latham, G. (2009). Greenberg doth protest too much: Application always has been, and victims and morality always will be critical for advancing organizational justice research. *Industrial and Organizational Psychology: Perspectives on Science and Practice, 2*, 201–204.

Barclay, L. J., Skarlicki, D. P., & Pugh, S. D. (2005). Exploring the role of emotions in injustice perceptions and retaliation. *Journal of Applied Psychology, 90*, 629–643.

Barclay, L. J., & Whiteside, D. B. (2011). Moving beyond justice perceptions: The role of experience and intensity. In S. W. Gilliland, D. D. Steiner, & D. P. Skarlicki (Eds.), *Research in social issues in management: Emerging perspectives on organizational justice and ethics* (Vol. 7, pp. 49–74). Greenwich, CT: Information Age.

Baskin, T. W., & Enright, R. D. (2004). Intervention studies on forgiveness: A meta-analysis. *Journal of Counseling and Development, 82*, 79–90.

Bies, R. J. (1987). The predicament of injustice: The management of moral outrage. *Research in Organizational Behavior, 9*, 289–319.

Bies, R. J. (2001). Interactional (in)justice: The sacred and the profane. In J. Greenberg & R. Cropanzano (Eds.), *Advances in organizational justice* (pp. 89–118). Stanford, CA: Stanford University Press.

Bies, R. J., & Tripp, T. M. (1996). Beyond distrust: "Getting even" and the need for revenge. In R. M. Kramer & T. R. Tyler (Eds.), *Trust in organizations: Frontiers of theory and research* (pp. 246–260). Thousand Oaks: Sage.

Bies, R. J., & Tripp, T. M. (2002). "Hot flashes and open wounds": Injustice and the tyranny of its emotions. In S. W. Gilliland, D. D. Steiner, & D. P. Skarlicki (Eds.), *Emerging perspectives on managing organizational justice* (pp. 203–221). Greenwich, CT: Information Age.

Bobocel, D. R. (2014). Coping with unfair events constructively or destructively: The roles of overall justice and self-other construal. *Journal of Applied Psychology, 98*, 720–731.

Braithwaite, J. (1999). Restorative justice: Assessing optimistic and pessimistic accounts. In M. Tonry (Ed.), *Crime and justice: A review of research* (Vol. 25, pp. 1–127). Chicago, IL: University of Chicago Press.

Braithwaite, J. (2002). *Restorative justice and responsive regulation*. New York, NY: Oxford University Press.

Brockner, J. (2010). *A contemporary look at organizational justice: Multiplying insult times injury*. New York, NY: Routledge.

Brockner, J., & Siegel, P. A. (1996). Understanding the interaction between procedural and distributive justice: The role of trust. In R. Kramer & T. Tyler (Eds.), *Trust in organizations: Frontiers of theory and research* (pp. 390–413). Thousand Oaks, CA: Sage.

Brockner, J., & Wiesenfeld, B. M. (1996). An integrative framework for explaining reactions to decisions: Interactive effects of outcomes and procedures. *Psychological Bulletin, 120*, 189–208.

Calhoun, L. G., & Tedeschi, R. G. (1998). Beyond recovery from trauma: Implications for clinical practice and research. *Journal of Social Issues, 54*, 357–371.

Carver, C. S., & Connor-Smith, J. (2010). Personality and coping. *Annual Review of Psychology, 61*, 679–704.

Choi, J. (2008). Event justice perception and employees' reactions: Perceptions of social entity justice as a moderator. *Journal of Applied Psychology, 93*, 513–528.

Cohen-Charash, Y., & Spector, P. E. (2001). The role of justice in organizations: A meta-analysis. *Organizational Behavior and Human Decision Processes, 86*, 278–321.

Colquitt, J. A. (2001). On the dimensionality of organizational justice: A construct validation of a measure. *Journal of Applied Psychology, 86*, 386–400.

Colquitt, J. A., & Chertkoff, J. M. (2002). Explaining injustice: The interactive effect of explanation and outcome on fairness perceptions and task motivation. *Journal of Management, 28*, 591–610.

Colquitt, J. A., Conlon, D. E., Wesson, M. J., Porter, C. O. L. H., & Ng, K. Y. (2001). Justice at the millennium: A meta-analytic review of 25 years of organizational justice research. *Journal of Applied Psychology, 86*, 425–445.

Colquitt, J. A., Long, D. M., Rodell, J. B., & Halvorsen-Ganepola, M. D. K. (2010, August). Measuring organizational (in)justice. In J. Greenberg (Chair), *Issues in the measurement of organizational justice*. Symposium at the Annual Meeting of the Academy of Management, Montreal, Quebec.

Colquitt, J. A., & Rodell, J. B. (2011). Justice, trust, and trustworthiness: A longitudinal analysis integrating three theoretical perspectives. *Academy of Management Journal, 54*, 1183–1206.

Colquitt, J. A., Scott, B. A., Rodell, J. B., Long, D. M., Zapata, C. P., Conlon, D. E., & Wesson, M. J. (2013). Justice at the millennium, a decade later: A meta-analytic test of social exchange and affect-based perspectives. *Journal of Applied Psychology, 98*, 199–236.

Cooper, C. D., & Scandura, T. A. (2012). Was I unfair? Antecedents and consequences of managerial perspective taking in a predicament of injustice. In C. A. Schriesheim & L. L. Neider (Eds.), *Research in management: Perspectives on justice and trust in organizations* (pp. 107–138). Charlotte, NC: Information Age.

Coyle, C. T., & Enright, R. D. (1997). Forgiveness intervention with post-abortion men. *Journal of Consulting and Clinical Psychology, 65*, 1042–1045.

Cronbach, L. J. (1970). *Essentials of psychological testing*. New York, NY: Harper & Row.

Cronbach, L. J., & Gleser, G. C. (1965). *Psychological tests and personnel decisions* (2nd ed.). Urbana, IL: University of Illinois Press.

Cropanzano, R., Byrne, Z. S., Bobocel, D. R., & Rupp, D. E. (2001). Moral virtues, fairness heuristics, social entities, and other denizens of organizational justice. *Journal of Vocational Behavior*, 58, 164–209.

Cropanzano, R., Stein, J. H., & Nadisic, T. (2011). *Social justice and the experience of emotions*. New York, NY: Routledge.

Dalbert, C. (2002). Beliefs in a just world as a buffer against anger. *Social Justice Research, 15*, 123–145.

Decety, J., & Jackson, P. L. (2004). The functional architecture of human empathy. *Behavioral and Cognitive Neuroscience Reviews, 3*, 71–100.

De Cremer, D. (2007). Justice and affect: When two friends meet. In D. De Cremer (Ed.), *Advances in the psychology of justice and affect* (pp. 1–11). Greenwich, CT: Information Age.

Dhensa, R. K. (2011). *It's good to talk: Examining the effectiveness of talking as a victim-centered recovery from organizational injustice*. Best Paper Proceedings of the Seventy-First Annual Meeting of the Academy of Management, 2011 (CD).

Diekmann, K. A., Samuels, S. M., Ross, L., & Bazerman, M. H. (1997). Self-interest and fairness in problems of resource allocation: Allocators versus recipients. *Journal of Personality and Social Psychology, 72*, 1061–1074.

Dirks, K. T., & De Cremer, D. (2010). The repair of trust: Insights from organizational behavior and social psychology. In D. De Cremer, R. van Dick, & J. K. Murnighan

(Eds.), *Social psychology and organizations* (pp. 211–230). New York, NY: Routledge.

Eaton, J., Struthers, C. W., & Santelli, A. G. (2006). The mediating role of perceptual validation in the repentance-forgiveness process. *Personality and Social Psychology Bulletin, 32*, 1389–1401.

Edmondson, A. C., & McManus, S. E. (2007). Methodological fit in management field research. *Academy of Management Journal, 32*, 1155–1179.

Elovainio, M., Kivimaki, M., & Helkama, K. (2001). Organizational justice evaluations, job control, and occupational strain. *Journal of Applied Psychology, 86*, 418–424.

Elovainio, M., Kivimaki, M., & Vahtera, J. (2002). Organizational justice: Evidence of a new psychosocial predictor of health. *American Journal of Public Health, 92*, 105–108.

Enright, R. D., & Fitzgibbons, R. P. (2000). *Helping clients forgive: An empirical guide for resolving anger and restoring hope*. Washington: American Psychological Association.

Enright, R. D., & The Human Development Study Group (1991). The moral development of forgiveness. In W. Kurtines & J. Gerwirtz (Eds.), *Handbook of moral behavior and development* (Vol. 1, pp. 123–152). Hillsdale, NJ: Erlbaum.

Fazio, R. J. (2009). Growth consulting: Practical methods of facilitating growth through loss and adversity. *Journal of Clinical Psychology: In Session, 65*, 532–543.

Fazio, R. J., & Fazio L. M. (2006). Growth through loss: Promoting healing and growth in the face of trauma, crisis and loss. *Journal of Loss and Trauma, 10*, 221–252.

Fazio, R. J., Rashid, T., & Hayward, H. S. (2008). Growth through loss and adversity: A choice worth making. In S. J. Lopez (Ed.), *Positive psychology: Exploring the best in people* (Vol. 3, 1–27). Westport, CT: Praeger Publishers/Greenwood.

Fehr, R., & Gelfand, M. J. (2010). When apologies work: How matching apology components to victims' self-construals facilitates forgiveness. *Organizational Behavior and Human Decision Processes, 113*, 37–50.

Fehr, R., & Gelfand, M. J. (2012). The forgiving organization: A multilevel model of forgiveness at work. *Academy of Management Review, 37*, 664–688.

Fehr, R., Gelfand, M. J., & Nag, M. (2010). The road to forgiveness: A meta-analytic synthesis of its situational and dispositional correlates. *Psychological Bulletin, 136*, 894–914.

Folger, R. (2001). Fairness as deonance. In S. W. Gilliland, D. D. Steiner, & D. P. Skarlicki (Eds.), *Research in social issues in management: Theoretical and cultural perspectives on organizational justice* (Vol. 1, pp. 3–33). Greenwich, CT: Information Age.

Folger, R., & Baron, R. A. (1996). Violence and hostility at work: A model of reactions to perceived injustice. In G. R. Van den Bos & E. Q. Bulatao (Eds.), *Violence on the job: Identifying risks and developing solutions* (pp. 51–85). Washington, DC: American Psychological Association.

Folger, R., & Skarlicki, D. P. (2001). Fairness as a dependent variable: Why tough times can lead to bad management. In R. Cropanzano (Ed.), *Justice in the workplace: Volume II - From theory to practice* (pp. 97–118). Mahwah, NJ: Erlbaum.

Frantz, C. M., & Bennigson, C. (2005). Better late than early: The influence of timing on apology effectiveness. *Journal of Experimental Social Psychology, 41*, 201–207.

Fredrickson, B. L. (1998). What good are positive emotions? *Review of General Psychology, 2*, 300–319.

Fredrickson, B. L. (2001). The role of positive emotions in positive psychology: The broaden-and-build-theory of positive emotions. *American Psychologist, 56*, 218–226.

Fredrickson, B. L., & Branigan, C. (2005). Positive emotions broaden the scope of attention and thought-action repertoires. *Cognition and Emotion, 19*, 313–332.

Fredrickson, B. L., & Joiner, T. (2002). Positive emotions trigger upward spirals toward emotional well-being. *Psychological Science, 13*, 172–175.

Fredrickson, B. L., & Levenson, R. W. (1998). Positive emotions speed recovery from the cardiovascular sequelae of negative emotions. *Cognition and Emotion, 12*, 191–220.

Freedman, S. R., & Enright, R. D. (1996). Forgiveness as an intervention goal with incest survivors. *Journal of Consulting and Clinical Psychology, 64*, 983–992.

Frijda, N. H. (1993). Moods, emotion episodes, and emotions. In M. Lewis & J. M. Haviland (Eds.), *Handbook of emotions* (pp. 381–403). New York, NY: Guilford.

Galinsky, A. D., Ku, G., & Wang, C. S. (2005). Perspective-taking and self-other overlap: Fostering social bonds and facilitating social coordination. *Group Processes Intergroup Relations, 8*, 108–124.

Gillespie, N., & Dietz, G. (2009). Trust repair after an organization-level failure. *Academy of Management Review, 34*, 127–145.

Gilliland, S. (2008). The tails of justice: A critical examination of the dimensionality of organizational justice constructs. *Human Resource Management Review, 18*, 271–281.

Goldman, B. M. (2001). Toward an understanding of employment discrimination claiming: An integration of organizational justice and social information processing theories. *Personnel Psychology, 54*, 361–386.

Gonzales, M. H., Manning, D. J., & Haugen, J. A. (1992). Explaining our sins: Factors influencing offender accounts and anticipated victim responses. *Journal of Personality and Social Psychology, 62*, 958–971.

Goodstein, J., & Aquino, K. (2010). And restorative justice for all: Redemption, forgiveness, and reintegration in organizations. *Journal of Organizational Behavior, 31*, 624–628.

Grebner, S., Elfering, A., & Semmer, N. K. (2010). The success resource model of job stress. In P. L. Perrewé & D. C. Ganster (Eds.), *New developments in theoretical and conceptual approaches to job stress: Research in occupational stress and well being* (Vol. 8, pp. 61–108). Bingley, UK: Emerald.

Green, J. D., Burnett, J. L., & Davis, J. L. (2008). Third-party forgiveness: (Not) forgiving your close other's betrayer. *Personality and Social Psychology Bulletin, 34*, 407–418.

Greenberg, J. (1993a). The social side of fairness: Interpersonal and informational classes of organizational justice. In R. Cropanzano (Ed.), *Justice in the workplace: Approaching fairness in human resource management* (pp. 79–103). Hillsdale, NJ: Erlbaum.

Greenberg, J. (1993b). Stealing in the name of justice: Informational and interpersonal moderators of theft reactions to underpayment inequity. *Organizational and Human Decision Processes, 54*, 81–103.

Greenberg, J. (2001). The seven loose can(n)ons of organizational justice. In J. Greenberg & R. Cropanzano (Eds.), *Advances in organizational justice* (pp. 245–271). Stanford, CA: Stanford University Press.

Greenberg, J. (2006). Losing sleep over organizational injustice: Attenuating insomniac reactions to underpayment inequity with supervisory training in interactional justice. *Journal of Applied Psychology, 91*, 58–69.

Groth, M., Goldman, B., Gilliland, S., & Bies, R. (2002). Commitment to legal claiming: Influences of attributions, social guidance, and organizational tenure. *Journal of Applied Psychology, 87*, 781–788.

Guo, J., Rupp, D. E., Weiss, H. W., & Trougakos, J. P. (2011). Justice in organizations: A person-centric perspective. In S. W. Gilliland, D. D. Steiner, & D. P. Skarlicki (Eds.), *Research in social issues in management: Emerging perspectives on organizational justice and ethics* (Vol. 7, pp. 3–32). Greenwich, CT: Information Age.

Harlos, K. P., & Pinder, C. C. (2000). Emotions and injustice in the workplace. In S. Fineman (Ed.), *Emotion in organizations* (2nd ed., pp. 255–276). London, UK: Sage.

Hausknecht, J. P., Sturman, M. C., & Roberson, Q. M. (2011). Justice as a dynamic construct: Effects of individual trajectories on distal work outcomes. *Journal of Applied Psychology, 96*, 872–880.

Hebl, J. H., & Enright, R. D. (1993). Forgiveness as a psychotherapeutic goal with elderly females. *Psychotherapy, 30*, 658–667.

Hershcovis, M. S., & Barling, J. (2006). Preventing workplace violence. In E. K. Kelloway, J. Barling, & J. Hurrell (Eds.), *Handbook of workplace violence* (pp. 607–632). Thousand Oaks, CA: Sage.

Hillebrandt, A., & Barclay, L. J. (2013). Integrating organizational justice and affect: New insights, challenges, and opportunities. *Social Justice Research, 26*, 513–531.

Ho, B. (2012). Apologies as signals: With evidence from a trust game. *Management Science, 58*, 141–158.

Hobfoll, S. E. (2001). The influence of culture, community, and the nested-self in the stress process: Advancing conservation of resources theory. *Applied Psychology: An International Review, 50*, 337–421.

Hodgins, H. S., & Liebeskind, E. (2003). Apology versus defense: Antecedents and consequences. *Journal of Experimental Social Psychology, 39*, 297–316.

Holtz, B. C., & Harold, C. M. (2009). Fair today, fair tomorrow? A longitudinal investigation of overall fairness perceptions. *Journal of Applied Psychology, 94*, 1185–1199.

Jones, D. A. (2009). Getting even with one's supervisor and one's organization: Relationships among types of injustice, desires for revenge, and counterproductive work behaviors. *Journal of Organizational Behavior, 30*, 525–542.

Jones, D. A., & Skarlicki, D. P. (2013). How perceptions of fairness can change: A dynamic model of organizational justice. *Organizational Psychology Review, 3*, 138–160.

Kidder, D. L. (2007). Restorative justice: Not "rights", but the right way to heal relationships at work. *International Journal of Conflict Management, 18*, 4–22.

Kim, P. H., Dirks, K. T., & Cooper, C. D. (2009). The repair of trust: A dynamic bilateral perspective and multilevel conceptualization. *Academy of Management Review, 34*, 401–422.

Kivimaki, M., Elovainio, M., Vahtera, J., & Ferrie, J. E. (2003). Organisational justice and health of employees: Prospective cohort study. *Occupational Environmental Medicine, 60*, 27–34.

Kivimaki, M., Elovainio, M., Vahtera, J., Virtanen, M., & Stansfeld, S. A. (2003). Association between organizational inequity and incidence of psychiatric disorders in female employees. *Psychological Medicine, 33*, 319–326.

Kivimaki, M., Ferrie, J. E., Brunner, E., Head, J., Shipley, M. J., Vahtera, J., & Marmot, M. G. (2005). Justice at work and reduced risk of coronary heart disease among employees: The Whitehall II study. *Archives of Internal Medicine, 165*, 2245–2251.

Lazarus, R. S., & Folkman, S. (1984). *Stress, appraisal, and coping*. New York, NY: Springer.

Leunissen, J. M., De Cremer, D., & Folmer, C. P. R. (2012). An instrumental perspective on apologizing in bargaining: The importance of forgiveness to apologize. *Journal of Economic Psychology, 33*, 215–222.

Lewicki, R. J., & Bunker, B. B. (1996). Developing and maintaining trust in work relationships. In R. M. Kramer & T. R. Tyler (Eds.), *Trust in organizations: Frontiers of theory and research* (pp. 114–139). Thousand Oaks, CA: Sage.

Lewicki, R. J., Wiethoff, C., & Tomlinson, E. C. (2005). What is the role of trust in organizational justice? In J. Greenberg & J. A. Colquitt (Eds.), *Handbook of organizational justice* (pp. 247–270). Mahwah, NJ: Erlbaum.

Liao, H. (2007). Do it right this time: The role of employee service recovery performance in customer-perceived justice and customer loyalty after service failure. *Journal of Applied Psychology, 92*, 475–489.

Liao, H., & Rupp, D. E. (2005). The impact of justice climate and justice orientation on work outcomes: A cross-level multifoci framework. *Journal of Applied Psychology, 90*, 242–256.

Lilly, J. D., Virick, M., & Hadani, M. (2010). The dynamic nature of justice: Influential effects of time and work outcomes on long-term perceptions of justice. *Social Justice Research, 23*, 37–59.

Lind, E. A. (2001a). Fairness heuristic theory: Justice judgments as pivotal cognitions in organizational relations. In J. Greenberg & R. Cropanzano (Eds.), *Advances in organizational justice* (pp. 56–88). San Francisco, CA: New Lexington Press.

Lind, E. A. (2001b). Thinking critically about justice judgments. *Journal of Vocational Behavior, 58*, 220–226.

Lind, E. A., & Tyler, T. R. (1988). *The social psychology of procedural justice*. New York, NY: Plenum.

Loi, R., Yang, J., & Diefendorff, J. M. (2009). Four-factor justice and daily job satisfaction: A multilevel investigation. *Journal of Applied Psychology, 94*, 770–781.

Masterson, S. S. (2001). A trickle-down model of organizational justice: Relating employees' and customers' perceptions of and reactions to fairness. *Journal of Applied Psychology, 86*, 594–604.

Matthews, C. (1988). *Hardball: How politics is played—told by one who knows the game*. New York, NY: Summit Books.

Mayer, R. C., Davis, J. H., & Schoorman, F. D. (1995). An integrative model of organizational trust. *Academy of Management Review, 20*, 709–734.

McCullough, M. E. (2000). Forgiveness as human strength: Theory, measurement, and links to well-being. *Journal of Social and Clinical Psychology, 19*, 43–55.

McCullough, M. E., Rachal, C. K., Sandage, S. J., Worthington, E. L., Jr., Brown, S. W., & Hight, T. I. (1998). Interpersonal forgiving in close relationships II: Theoretical elaboration and measurement. *Journal of Personality and Social Psychology, 75*, 1586–1603.

McCullough, M. E., Worthington, E. L., Jr., & Rachal, C. K. (1997). Interpersonal forgiving in close relationships. *Journal of Personality and Social Psychology, 73*, 321–336.

Meier, L. L., Semmer, N. K., Elfering, A., & Jacobshagen, N. (2008). The double meaning of control: Three-way interactions between internal resources, job control, and stressors at work. *Journal of Occupational Health Psychology, 13*, 244–258.

Messick, D. M., Bloom, S., Boldizar, J. P., & Samuelson, C. D. (1985). Why we are fairer than others. *Journal of Experimental Social Psychology, 21*, 480–500.

Neblett, W. R. (1974). Forgiveness and ideals. *Mind, 83*, 269–275.

North, J. (1987). Wrongdoing and forgiveness. *Philosophy, 62*, 499–508.

Okimoto, T. G., Wenzel, M., & Feather, N. T. (2009). Beyond retribution: Conceptualizing restorative justice and exploring its determinants. *Social Justice Research, 22*, 156–180.

Okimoto, T. G., Wenzel, M., & Hedrick, K. (2012). Refusing to apologize can have psychological benefits (and we issue no mea culpa for this research finding). *European Journal of Social Psychology, 43*, 22–31.

O'Malley, M. N., & Greenberg, J. (1983). Sex differences in restoring justice: The down payment effect. *Journal of Research in Personality, 17*, 174–185.

Patient, D. L., & Skarlicki, D. P. (2010). Increasing interpersonal and informational justice when communicating negative news: The role of the manager's empathic concern and moral development. *Journal of Management, 36*, 555–578.

Pennebaker, J. W. (1997). *Opening up: The healing power of expressing emotions*. New York, NY: Guilford.

Pennebaker, J. W., & Chung, C. K. (2007). Expressive writing, emotional upheavals, and health. In H. Friedman & R. Silver (Eds.), *Handbook of health psychology* (pp. 263–284). New York, NY: Oxford University Press.

Pugh, S. D., Skarlicki, D. P., & Passell, B. S. (2003). After the fall: Layoff victims' trust and cynicism in re-employment. *Journal of Occupational and Organizational Psychology, 76*, 201–212.

Quick, J. C., Murphy, L. R., Hurrell, J. J., & Orman, D. (1992). The value of work, the risk of distress, and the power of prevention. In J. C. Quick, L. R. Murphy, & J. J. Hurrell (Eds.), *Stress and well-being at work: Assessment and interventions for occupational mental health* (pp. 3–13). Washington, DC: American Psychological Association.

Rashid, T. (2009). Positive interventions in clinical practice. *Journal of Clinical Psychology: In Session, 65*, 461–466.

Reb, J., Goldman, B. M., Kray, L. J., & Cropanzano, R. (2006). Different wrongs, different remedies? Reactions to organizational remedies after procedural and interactional injustice. *Personnel Psychology, 59*, 31–64.

Roche, D. (2003). *Accountability in restorative justice*. Oxford: Oxford University Press.

Roth, S., & Cohen, L. (1986). Approach, avoidance, and coping with stress. *American Psychologist, 41*, 813–819.

Rousseau, D. M., Sitkin, S. B., Burt, R. S., & Camerer, C. (1998). Not so different after all: A cross-discipline view of trust. *Academy of Management Review, 23*, 393–404.

Rupp, D. E., & Paddock, E. L. (2010). From justice events to justice climate: A multi-level temporal model of information aggregation and judgment. *Research on Management Groups and Teams, 13*, 245–273.

Rusbult, C. E., Verette, J., Whitney, G. A., Slovik, L. F., & Lipkus, I. (1991). Accommodation processes in close relationships: Theory and preliminary empirical evidence. *Journal of Personality and Social Psychology, 60*, 53–78.

Schat, A. C. H., & Kelloway, E. K. (2006). Training as a workplace aggression intervention strategy. In E. K. Kelloway, J. Barling, & J. Hurrell (Eds.), *Handbook of workplace violence* (pp. 579–605). Thousand Oaks, CA: Sage.

Schueller, S. M. (2010). Preferences for positive psychology exercises. *Journal of Positive Psychology, 5*, 192–203.

Scott, W. G., & Hart, D. K. (1979). *Organizational America: Can individual freedom survive within the security it promises?* Boston MA: Houghton Mifflin.

Seligman, M. E., Rashid, T., & Parks, A. C. (2006). Positive psychotherapy. *American Psychologist, 61*, 774–788.

Seligman, M. E. P., Steen, T. A., Park, N., & Peterson, C. (2005). Positive psychology progress: Empirical validation of interventions. *American Psychologist, 60*, 410–421.

Shapiro, D. L. (2001). The death of justice theory is likely if theorists neglect the "wheels" already invented and the voices of the injustice victims. *Journal of Vocational Behavior, 58*, 235–242.

Shapiro, D. L., Buttner, E. H., & Barry, B. (1994). Explanations: What factors enhance their perceived adequacy? *Organizational Behavior and Human Decision Processes, 58*, 346–368.

Shaw, J. C., Wild, E., & Colquitt, J. A. (2003). To justify or excuse? A meta-analytic review of the effects of explanations. *Journal of Applied Psychology, 88*, 444–458.

Sin, N. L., & Lyubomirsky, S. (2009). Enhancing well-being and alleviating depressive symptoms with positive psychology interventions: A practice-friendly meta-analysis. *Journal of Clinical Psychology: In Session, 65*, 467–487.

Skarlicki, D. P., Barclay, L. J., & Pugh, S. D. (2008). When explanations for layoffs are not enough: Employer's integrity as a moderator of the relationship between informational justice and retaliation. *Journal of Occupational and Organizational Psychology, 81*, 123–146.

Skarlicki, D. P., & Folger, R. (1997). Retaliation in the workplace: The roles of distributive, procedural, and interactional justice. *Journal of Applied Psychology, 82*, 434–443.

Skarlicki, D. P., & Latham, G. P. (1996). Increasing citizenship behavior within a labor union: A test of organizational justice theory. *Journal of Applied Psychology, 81*, 161–169.

Skarlicki, D. P., & Latham, G. P. (1997). Leadership training in organizational justice to increase citizenship behavior within a labor union: A replication. *Personnel Psychology, 50*, 617–633.

Skinner, E. A. (1999). Action regulation, coping, and development. In J. B. Brandtstädter & R. M. Lerner (Eds.), *Action and self-development* (pp. 465–503). Thousand Oaks, CA: Sage.

Skinner, E., Edge, K., Altman, J., & Sherwood, H. (2003). Searching for the structure of coping: A review and critique of category systems for classifying ways of coping. *Psychological Bulletin, 129*, 216–269.

Skitka, L. J., Mullen, E., Griffin, T., Hutchinson, S., & Chamberlin, B. (2002). Dispositions, scripts, or motivated correction? Understanding ideological differences in explanations for social problems. *Journal of Personality and Social Psychology, 83*, 470–487.

Spencer, S., & Rupp, D. E. (2009). Angry, guilty, and conflicted: Injustice toward coworkers heightens emotional labor through cognitive and emotional mechanisms. *Journal of Applied Psychology, 94*, 429–444.

Spera, S. P., Buhrfeind, E. D., & Pennebaker, J. W. (1994). Expressive writing and coping with job loss. *Academy of Management Journal, 37*, 722–733.

Subkoviak, M. J., Enright, R. D., Wu, C. R., Gassin, E. A., Freedman, S., Olson, L. M., & Sarinopoulos, I. (1995). Measuring interpersonal forgiveness in late adolescence and middle adulthood. *Journal of Adolescence, 18*, 641–655.

Tax, S. S., Brown, S. W., & Chandrashekaran, M. (1998). Customer evaluations of service complaint experiences: Implications for relationship marketing. *Journal of Marketing, 62*, 60–76.

Tedeschi, R. G., & Calhoun, L. G. (2004). Posttraumatic growth: Conceptual foundations and empirical evidence. *Psychological Inquiry, 15*, 1–18.

Tepper, B. J. (2001). Health consequences of organizational injustice: Tests of main and interactive effects. *Organizational Behavior and Human Decision Processes, 86*, 197–215.

Tice, D. M., & Baumeister, R. F. (1993). Controlling anger: Self-induced emotion change. In D. M. Wegner & J. W. Pennebaker (Eds.), *Handbook of mental control* (pp. 393–409). Englewood Cliffs, NJ: Prentice-Hall.

Tomlinson, E. C., & Mayer, R. C. (2009). The role of causal attribution dimensions in trust repair. *Academy of Management Review, 34*, 85–104.

Tornblom, K. Y., & Vermunt, R. (1999). An integrative perspective on social justice: Distributive and procedural fairness evaluations of positive and negative outcome allocations. *Social Justice Research, 12*, 39–64.

Tripp, T. M., & Bies, R. J. (1997). What's good about revenge? The avenger's perspective. In. R. J. Lewicki, R. J. Bies, & B. H. Sheppard (Eds.), *Research on negotiation in organizations* (Vol. 6, pp. 145–160). New York, NY: JAI.

Tugade, M. M., & Fredrickson, B. L. (2004). Resilient individuals use positive emotions to bounce back from negative emotional experiences. *Journal of Personality and Social Psychology, 86*, 320–333.

Turillo, C. J., Folger, R., Lavelle, J. J., Umphress, E., & Gee, J. (2002). Is virtue its own reward? Self-sacrificial decisions for the sake of fairness. *Organizational Behavior and Human Decision Processes, 89*, 839–865.

Tyler, T., & Blader, S. (2003). The group engagement model: Procedural justice, social identity, and cooperative behavior. *Personality and Social Psychology Review, 7*, 349–361.

Van den Bos, K., Wilke, H. A. M., & Lind, E. A. (1998). When do we need procedural fairness? The role of trust in authority. *Journal of Personality and Social Psychology, 75*, 1449–1458.

Vermunt, R., & Steensma, H. (2001). Stress and justice in organizations: An exploration into justice processes with the aim to find mechanisms to reduce stress. In R. Cropanzano (Ed.), *Justice in the workplace: From theory to practice* (Vol. 2, pp. 27–48). Mahwah, NJ: Erlbaum.

Wade, N. G., & Worthington, E. L. Jr. (2005). In search of a common core: A content analysis of interventions to promote forgiveness. *Psychotherapy, Research, Practice, Training, 42*, 160–177.

Wade, N. G., Worthington, E. L. Jr., & Meyer, J. E. (2005). But do they work? A meta-analysis of group interventions to promote forgiveness. In E. L. Worthington (Ed.), *Handbook of forgiveness* (pp. 423–439). New York, NY: Routledge.

Weick, K. E. (1995). *Sensemaking in organizations.* Thousand Oaks, CA: Sage.

Weiss, H. M., & Cropanzano, R. (1996). Affective events theory: A theoretical discussion of the structure, cases, and consequences of affective experiences at work. In B. M. Staw & L. L. Cummings (Eds.), *Research in organizational behavior* (Vol. 18, pp. 1–74). Greenwich, CT: JAI.

Weiss, H. M., & Rupp, D. E. (2011). Experiencing work: An essay on a person-centric work psychology. *Industrial and Organizational Psychology, 4*, 83–97.

Wenzel, M., & Okimoto, T. G. (2010). How acts of forgiveness restore a sense of justice: Addressing status/power and value concerns raised by transgressions. *European Journal of Social Psychology, 40*, 401–417.

Wenzel, M., & Okimoto, T. G. (2014). On the relationship between justice and forgiveness: Are all forms of justice made equal? *British Journal of Social Psychology, 53*, 463–483.

Wenzel, M., Okimoto, T. G., Feather, N. T., & Platow, M. J. (2008). Retributive and restorative justice. *Law and Human Behavior, 32*, 375–389.

Whiteside, D. B., & Barclay, L. J. (2015). The justice tug-of-war: A dyadic approach to conflicting perceptions of fairness. In S. W. Gilliland, D. D. Steiner, & D. P. Skarlicki (Eds.), *Research in social issues in management: Volume 8* (pp. 3–36). Greenwich, CT: Information Age.

Witvliet, C. V. O., Ludwig, T. E., & Laan, K. L. V. (2001). Granting forgiveness or harboring grudges: Implications for emotion, physiology, and health. *Psychological Science, 12*, 117–123.

Worthington, E. L., Jr. (2003). *Forgiving and reconciling.* Downers Grove, IL: Intervarsity Press.

Zechmeister, J. S., & Romero, C. (2002). Victim and offender accounts of interpersonal conflict: Autobiographical narratives of forgiveness and unforgiveness. *Journal of Personality and Social Psychology, 82*, 675–686.

CHAPTER

25 Restorative Justice

Jerry Goodstein *and* Kenneth D. Butterfield

Abstract

Restorative justice represents an emerging perspective within the field of organizational justice. In this chapter, we first provide an overview of the restorative justice perspective, discussing its historical roots as well as more contemporary considerations. Next, we review conceptual and empirical work in organizational science that is relevant to the restorative justice perspective. We then identify directions for future research, emphasizing the potential for restorative justice to contribute to theoretical and empirical work on the topic of how managers and organizations respond to interpersonal wrongdoing. We believe that restorative justice holds significant promise both for scholars and practicing managers by bridging and integrating traditionally divergent views of organizational justice.

Key Words: restorative justice, organizational justice, interpersonal wrongdoing, making amends, forgiveness, reintegration, retributive justice

Compared with other areas of focus in the organizational justice literature, it is only within the past 10–15 years that organizational scholars have taken note of the topic of restorative justice. The initial reference to restorative justice in the management literature was made by Bradfield and Aquino (1999), who noted that distributive justice is concerned with perceived fairness in relation to outcome distributions, procedural justice with perceived fairness of rules and procedures as they relate to decision-making processes, and interactional justice with perceived fairness of treatment by higher status individuals. In contrast, restorative justice is fundamentally concerned with the response of parties following an act of harm by one person against another. Kidder (2007), Goodstein and Aquino (2010), and Goodstein and Butterfield (2010) further recognized the importance of restorative justice as a process that through practices such as forgiveness, making amends, and reintegration, addresses in an integrated manner the justice concerns of multiple parties affected by wrongdoing, i.e., the offender, the victim(s), and third-parties affected by the offender's actions.

Despite the relevance and promise of restorative justice as a focus for organizational scholars, the development of this topic within the field of organizational justice has been limited to date. The purpose of this chapter is threefold: (1) to provide a broad overview of the restorative justice perspective, emphasizing its historical and more contemporary roots; (2) to highlight current conceptual and empirical work in the organizational sciences of relevance to the restorative justice perspective; and (3) to identify ways researchers can build on and extend the existing work to further advance the restorative justice perspective within the field of organizational justice.

An Overview of the Restorative Justice Perspective

At the heart of restorative justice is a process undertaken in the aftermath of an offense to repair harm and relationships damaged by this harm.

Wenzel, Okimoto, and Cameron (2012, p. 28) note that this process is fundamentally based on, "a dialogue between stakeholders—victims, offenders, and possibly other community members—ideally designed to reach a shared understanding of the transgressions, the rules or values violated, and the actions that repair the harm done." From a restorative justice perspective, wrongdoing is conceptualized as "first and foremost a violation of people and their relationships, rather than merely a violation of the law" (Roche, 2003, p. 26). As such, although sanctions and punishment are not precluded by this approach, emphasis is placed on being forward looking, solving problems, actively involving all participants, and repairing relationships (Kidder, 2007; Marshall, 2003).

Restorative justice is a practice with historical roots in ancient Greek, Roman, and Arab civilization, a variety of indigenous cultures (e.g., Native American, Australian Aborigine), and various religious traditions, including Confucianism, Taoism, Buddhism, Hinduism, and early Christianity. The rise of retributive justice that began in medieval Europe over time became the dominant model for responding to transgressions. From this perspective, "justice can be conceptualized as retributive in nature—as an assertion against the offender that requires the unilateral assignment of punishment, which is necessary and sufficient for justice to be achieved" (Okimoto, Wenzel, & Feather, 2009: 157). Underlying the retributive justice perspective is a desire for just deserts for the offender, reflected in suffering, humiliation, and degradation, and a kind of moral compensation for the victim that is achieved primarily by punishing the offender in a way that is proportional to the harm done to the victim and broader society (Okimoto et al., 2009; Trevino & Weaver, 2010). In the early 1970s critics began to raise concerns regarding the use of retributive justice approaches, arguing that they focus on the past, are detached from the direct participants, suffer from an over-reliance on due process, and ignore the victim (Zehr, 1990). This criticism gave rise to a revival of restorative justice practices throughout much of Western society in the 1970s, most notably in Canada, Australia, New Zealand, the United States, South Africa, and the United Kingdom (Braithwaite, 2002).

Restorative justice has three core objectives for those involved in the process: reintegrating *offenders* back into the community, restoring *victims*, and facilitating *community* healing (Braithwaite, 1999). The key practice in offender reintegration is making amends, which involves the offender accepting responsibility and accountability for the wrongdoing, expressing remorse, seeking forgiveness from the victim and other affected parties, and offering a sincere apology and/or other restitution to these parties (e.g., Braithwaite, 1999, 2003; Marshall, 2003; Roche, 2006).

For victims, restoring justice involves having one's material, emotional, and moral needs attended to, obtaining material compensation, symbolic amends (e.g., an apology) or other reparations from the offender, receiving community support, healing, and finding closure. Meeting victims' needs opens up the possibility for victims to extend forgiveness to the offender. Forgiveness is a core practice of restorative justice in which negative emotions toward and judgments about the offender are diminished by trying to view the offender with compassion (Aquino, Grover, Goldman, & Folger, 2003; Enright, Gassin, & Wu, 1992; McCullough, Worthington, & Rachal, 1997; North, 1987). Forgiveness helps victims relieve themselves of the burden of resentment, anger, vengefulness, and other negative feelings toward the offender, by restoring damaged or broken relations between victim and offender, and by settling a wrong from the past "while releasing the future from its impact" (Walker, 2006, p. 154).

Facilitating community healing involves supporting the victim (e.g., helping them become healed, compensated, or otherwise repaired), supporting the offender (e.g., by offering forgiveness and restoring the offender's sense of integrity), building trust, encouraging dialogue, promoting collective learning, and restoring a sense of morality (e.g., Braithwaite, 1999, 2003; Kidder, 2007; Tyler, 2006; Walker, 2006). However, the key principle in community healing is to provide offenders with an opportunity to earn redemption and reintegrate back into the community through mechanisms such as restorative justice conferences (Goodstein & Aquino, 2010). Braithwaite offers the following description of these conferences:

> a facilitator invites to a conference the offender and the people who the offender and his family say care about them most. That structures reintegration into the conference. Also invited are the victim plus family and friends of the victims. Their concerns structure shaming into the conference. Shaming happens naturally through the process of the

victim and their supporters simply describing the consequences of the crime for them personally and for their loved ones" (2000: 20).

Process considerations are central to restorative justice conferences and are critical in fostering the practices highlighted earlier. Three primary features of the restorative justice process are of particular importance: dialogue, relationship building, and communication of moral values (Presser & Van Voorhis, 2002). Dialogue that is respectful, impartial, and voluntary is critical to the quality and effectiveness of restorative justice practices. Mending relationships that have been harmed through wrongdoing is a critical component of victim healing and strengthening the social bonds critical to offender reintegration. The communication of moral values represents a third feature of restorative justice conferences vital to their effectiveness. The expression of moral values the offender violated by victims and community members guides the offender in understanding what actions were not acceptable, how those actions harmed others, and what steps may be necessary to take to repair the harm (Bush & Folger, 1994; Kuo, Longmire, & Cuvelier, 2010).

Evaluating the outcomes associated with restorative justice processes has been a central focus for restorative justice researchers in a variety of academic disciplines including criminal justice (e.g., Braithwaite, 1999, 2000; 2003; Daly & Immarigeon, 1998; Zehr, 1990), social welfare (e.g., Roche, 2006), and education (e.g., Karp & Conrad, 2005). A number of studies demonstrate high rates of satisfaction with the process and outcomes for both victims and offenders (Strang, 2002; Umbreit & Bradshaw, 1999; Umbreit, Vos, Coates, & Brown, 2003). Participation in restorative justice conferences also lowers significantly the likelihood of offender recidivism in comparison with participation in traditional court procedures (Bradshaw & Roseborough, 2005; McGarrell, 2001). A recent study by Kuo et al. (2010) focused on the process features of restorative justice conferences. Kuo et al. (2010) found that in comparison with traditional court proceedings, participants involved in restorative justice conferences experienced significantly greater levels of dialogue, relationship building, and moral communication.

Scholars have also explored restorative justice outcomes through experimental research. A number of these studies found that individuals who have been victims or who imagined themselves as being victims in the studies reacted positively toward restorative justice as a response to transgressions. Victims of transgressions also preferred the use of restorative procedures (e.g., direct meetings with the offender) to more punitive measures (e.g., formal punishment) when they shared an identity with the offender and/or a desire to establish consensus about the violated values (e.g., Wenzel, Okimoto, Feather, & Platow, 2008, 2010; Wenzel et al., 2012). Experimental studies also highlight the effect of restorative justice processes on the emotional responses of individuals. People have lessened negative emotional experiences and calmer physiological reactions to imagined transgressions against them with restorative, as compared to retributive, responses (Gromet, 2012; Witvliet et al., 2008).

The Dynamics of Restorative Justice in Organizations

Although restorative justice, as noted earlier, has a long tradition in multiple disciplines, it has only recently begun to receive explicit attention in the organizational justice literature. As noted earlier, Bradfield and Aquino (1999) first explored restorative justice in the context of studying the enactment of revenge and forgiveness in organizations. They argued that whether victims would engage in revenge or forgiveness behaviors was a function of five key considerations, the severity of the transgression, attributions of blame, offender likableness, and revenge or forgiveness cognitions. Their empirical tests generally supported their model. They found for example that revenge/forgiveness cognitions are positively associated with revenge/forgiveness behaviors and that more severe offenses are associated with greater attributions of blame, which, in turn, are positively associated with revenge cognitions. Building on this initial work, Kidder (2007) directed attention to restorative justice as an important process for resolving workplace disputes and healing damaged or broken relationships in the workplace. Kidder argued that restorative justice has the potential to be an effective response to workplace transgressions improving interpersonal relations, rebuilding trust, and fostering perceptions of organizational justice.

In an effort to synthesize insights from the restorative justice, social science, and ethics literatures, Goodstein and Butterfield (2010) developed a conceptual framework focused on responses to ethical transgressions in the workplace that represented a significant extension of prior work by integrating into their framework multiple parties (offender, victim, and third parties) and multiple restorative practices (making amends, forgiveness, and reintegration). In addition, their framework, (a) elaborated the interrelationships among the core practices of restorative justice (restoring victims through forgiveness, restoring offenders through providing opportunities for making amends, and facilitating community healing through offender reintegration), (b) identified several moderators of the relationships among these core practices (e.g., whether the offender intended to commit the unethical act, psychological safety of the workplace culture), and (c) related the effects of these combined practices to critical outcomes of the restorative justice process, some of which have been confirmed in empirical research (e.g., recidivism, offender/victim satisfaction, perceived justice in the workplace, and interpersonal trust).

Each of these core practices associated with restorative justice—making amends, forgiveness, and reintegration—has separate research streams that have developed over time and in direct and indirect ways have influenced organizational justice scholarship. Next, we discuss these streams and in particular draw attention to variables identified by Goodstein and Butterfield (2010) as important moderators of the interrelationships among making amends, forgiveness, and reintegration. We review as well relevant research that has tested the effects of restorative justice practices on offender recidivism, offender and victim satisfaction, perceived justice in the workplace, and interpersonal trust.

Making Amends

The concessions literature (e.g., Gonzales, Manning & Haugen, 1992; Mikula, 1994; Schonbach, 1990; Tata, 2000) points to important cognitive and affective factors that might influence the likelihood that individuals who have harmed others through wrongdoing will take steps to make amends for these harms. Perceptions of accountability, attributions of responsibility and causality, and the severity of the offense represent important cognitive moderating variables influencing whether individuals will concede wrongdoing and take additional steps such as expressing regret and making amends (Gonzales et al., 1992; Mikula, 1994; Schonbach, 1990; Tata, 2000; Tavuchis, 1991; Walker, 2006; Weiner, Graham, & Zmuidinas, 1991). Gonzales et al. (1992) found, for example, that when there is a greater degree of "blameworthiness," as reflected in higher levels of responsibility and accountability, there is a great likelihood of offenders making concessions to those who they had harmed. Walker (2006) notes that the restorative justice processes can "create the conditions to leverage responsibility, that is, move people from a minimal or peripheral sense of connection and responsibility for a wrong to a richer and more demanding perception of what is wrong and how they might be related to it" (Walker, 2006, p. 215).

Affective responses on the part of the employee such as experienced guilt and shame (Radzik, 2009; Tangney & Dearing, 2002; Taylor, 1985) and empathy (Mikula, 1994; Radzik, 2009) are also potentially important moderators of the motivation of the offender to make amends (Hareli & Eisikovits, 2006; Hareli, Shomat, & Biger, 2005; Tangney & Dearing, 2002). With regard to feelings of guilt, these feelings can indicate that the individual experiencing them is aware of the harm they have caused, takes responsibility for the action, and intends to avoid further harmful actions (Hareli & Eiskovitz, 2006). Expressions of shame can also represent an attempt by the offender to restore the relationship by lowering his status in an effort to equalize status between the offender and victim (Hareli & Eiskovitz, 2006). Empirical research suggests that feelings of guilt and shame can motivate offenders to make amends with victims through apology and direct compensation (Hareli & Eiskovitz, 2006; Hareli, Shomrat, & Biger, 2005; Tangey & Dearing, 2002).

Forgiveness

Researchers from a variety of disciplines have contributed as well to a richer understanding of forgiveness. These researchers define forgiveness as a process involving affective, cognitive, and behavioral responses in which negative emotions toward and judgments about the offender are diminished by trying to view the offender with compassion, understanding, and perhaps even love (Aquino et al., 2003; Enright et al.,1992; McCullough et al., 1997; North, 1987). In making a choice to forgive, the victim makes a conscious effort to give up resentment and retaliation, even if the opportunity to punish the offender presents itself and opens up the potential for victims to make some effort to reconcile with the offender by extending acts of goodwill in an attempt to repair a damaged relationship (Aquino, Tripp, & Bies, 2006; McCullough et al., 1997).

Empirical research has identified a number of factors likely to moderate the relationship between offender efforts to make amends and victim forgiveness. One critical consideration is whether the victim is satisfied that offenders have meaningfully acknowledged harms and losses, for example, by expressing remorse through apologies and offering some form of penance or compensation to victims (Bottom, Gibson, Daniels, & Murnighan, 2002; Radzik, 2009; Strang, 2002). Strang (2002) evaluated restorative justice conference outcomes and found that victim forgiveness is more likely when offenders apologize directly to victims in these conferences. Bottom et al. (2002) found in their experimental studies that, although apologies can be effective as a response to breaches of cooperation, offering more substantive amends is even more effective in restoring cooperation. Perceptions of the severity of the harm and attributions of intentionality can also influence whether victims accept efforts to make amends and forgive offenders. More serious offenses against victims tend to lead to less forgiving responses by victims (Gonzales et al., 1992; Gromet & Darley, 2009). Forgiveness is also less likely when the offense is perceived by the victim as, "intentional, callous, and significant (Walker, 2006, p. 203). Victim forgiveness may be influenced as well by social and broader cultural factors. Wenzel et al. (2008) and Okimoto et al. (2009) note that as the strength of shared social identity and values between the offender and victim increases, there is a great likelihood of victims forgiving offenders for transgressions that violate these values. Third parties can influence victim forgiveness as well. Eaton, Struthers, and Santelli (2006) found that, when third parties were more forgiving of offender transgressions, this influenced victims as well to be more forgiving. Ren and Gray (2009) draw attention to how broad societal influences beyond organizations, such as national culture, influence the extension of forgiveness by a victim to an offender. For example in more collectivistic (as compared with individualistic) cultures, there may be a greater emphasis on interdependence rather than autonomy. Within these cultures, there is a greater emphasis, therefore, on "maintaining relatedness, and promoting others' needs or those of the group as a whole." (Ren & Gray, 2009, p. 113)

Offender Reintegration

With respect to offender reintegration, a body of empirical work is developing that specifically examines factors that influence how third-parties respond to offenders who have harmed a victim. This work draws attention to the potential for transgressions to violate important group norms and values and the role played by shared identity. To the extent that a transgression is perceived as a violation of shared norms and values, individuals are more likely to favor a restorative response that is aimed at reintegrating the offender and supporting the victim, whereas perceptions of the offense as one of power and status is likely to be associated with individuals favoring a more retributive response directed to punishing the offender (Wenzel et al., 2012). Complementary studies also show that when a shared identity exists between the victim/observers and the offender, the victim and observers are more likely to endorse a restorative response to the transgression (e.g., Wenzel et al., 2008; Wenzel et al., 2012).

With regard to more conceptually oriented work, Goodstein, Aquino, and Skarlicki (2011) developed a model of offender reintegration based on a synthesis and integration of a variety of literatures. They defined offender reintegration as "other employees' psychological willingness to maintain working relationships with the offender (Goodstein et al., 2011, p. 76)" and posited three primary sources of influence on the likelihood of offender reintegration: employees' perceptions of moral (e.g., employee's moral identity), social (e.g., shared identity with offender), and instrumental (e.g., perceived ability of the offender to advance employee success) considerations.

Restorative Justice Practices and Key Justice/Interpersonal Outcomes

Goodstein and Butterfield (2010) suggest in their conceptual model that the combined practices associated with restorative justice will influence important outcomes of interest to justice scholars: participant satisfaction with processes and outcomes, participant perceptions of justice, offender recidivism, and interpersonal trust. Studies undertaken in traditional criminal contexts are the primary source of insight regarding the effects of these core practices of restorative justice on these outcomes. Research comparing traditional court processes with restorative justice processes for similar acts of wrongdoing confirms that there is greater satisfaction associated with both the process and outcomes of the process for offenders and victims (Braithwaite, 2002; Strang, 2002). Restorative justice processes provide a context within which victims can communicate directly to offenders the nature of how they were harmed and offenders, in turn, can make amends. Third parties (e.g., family members, invited participants) have an opportunity as well to support the victim and offender and contribute to the reintegration of the offender (Braithwaite, 2002, Strang, 2002. Empirical research suggests as well that offenders who have participated in restorative justice conferences have significantly lower rates of recidivism as compared with traditional court processes (Menkel-Meadow, 2007; Presser & Vorhees, 2002). Offenders are better able to repair harm and strengthen relationships through interaction and dialogue with victims and third parties, strengthening social bonds and reinforcing more positive prosocial behaviors that reduce the likelihood of re-offending (Presser & Vorhees, 2002).

Goodstein and Butterfield (2010) also argued that restorative justice processes would have a positive effect on perceptions of justice and interpersonal trust. Restorative justice conferences provide opportunities for participants to exercise voice (procedural justice), foster an environment of interpersonal respect (interactional justice), and allow for participants to determine what is appropriate in terms of consequences for the offender (distributive justice). The core practices of restorative justice can also enhance the repair of interpersonal trust weakened by wrongdoing in organizations. Dirks, Lewicki, & Zaheer (2009, p. 71) note, "in order to repair trust, the wronged party must perceive that the transgression does not reflect the violator's true nature, or must perceive that the violator has experienced redemption following the transgression". Actions taken by an offender to make amends (e.g., expressing remorse, offering an apology, returning stolen materials) can play an important role in victim and third-party perceptions of reduced harm. Similarly, it can be important to the repair of interpersonal trust for offenders to feel as if victims and third parties have forgiven them and reintegrated them through extending emotional support. These actions can lessen the offender's perceived guilt and loss of self-respect and further the repair of interpersonal trust.

Although more research is being conducted on the dynamics of restorative justice, there are still significant gaps in the understanding of which of the core practices (i.e., making amends, forgiveness, reintegration) or how these practices either individually or in combination influence the outcomes discussed earlier. This represents an important area for additional theoretical and empirical development.

Organizational Perspectives on Restorative Justice

Although to date the restorative justice literature highlighted earlier has focused primarily on the dynamics of repairing harm and restoring relationships at the individual and group level, there are some strands of relevant work at the organizational level that draw on the core ideas of restorative justice and relate them to important organizational and interorganizational outcomes. Reb, Goldman, Kray, and Cropanzano (2006) developed and tested a needs-based model of organizational remedies (i.e., organizational efforts to make amends) for perceived procedural and interactional injustices. They posited three sets of general needs for individuals: instrumental, meaning, and belonging. In focusing on instrumental and meaning needs, they argued that violations of procedural justice are most likely to undermine instrumental needs, whereas violations of interactional justice will be most likely to undermine meaning needs. They further hypothesized and confirmed empirically that individuals prefer instrumental remedies for violations of procedural justice (e.g., compensation), whereas meaning-based remedies (e.g., punishment) are preferred for violations of interactional justice. They suggested as well (but did not formally test) a third form of remedy, one that is socio-emotional in nature, such as a public apology, when belonging needs are violated.

Gillespie and Dietz (2009) offer a model of repairing organization-level trust following an incident (e.g., accounting fraud, significant environmental accidents, significant downsizing) directed primarily internally with respect to employees. The process of restoring employee perceptions of trustworthiness begins with a set of immediate responses involving acknowledgment of the incident, expressions of remorse and regret, and the initiation of a diagnosis of causes of the incident. Immediate action is taken to address known causes of the incident while the diagnosis proceeds to uncover more systematic causes. The diagnosis stage is followed by reforming interventions such as apologies and organizational changes. The process concludes with an evaluative stage designed to assess the effectiveness of the repair process.

Fehr and Gelfand (2012) focus specifically on forgiveness as an attribute of the workplace, highlighting the importance of restorative justice values and practices in fostering organizational forgiveness climates. They suggest, furthermore, that more forgiving workplace climates will encourage restorative changes, that is, the extension of forgiveness by victims and the expression of remorse and apologies by offenders, and in addition strengthen employee relationships in the aftermath of interpersonal harm.

Pfarrer, DeCelles, Smith, and Taylor (2008) focused their attention on transgressions that harm stakeholders, in particular external organizations and institutions, and the process of reintegration and restoring legitimacy with these stakeholders for corporations that have engaged in corrupt or unethical behavior. They highlight the significant role played by stakeholders (e.g. customers, industry partners) in assessing reparative actions taken by organizations and whether offending organizations should be reintegrated back into the organizational/stakeholder community. Pfarrer et al. (2008) posit a series of stages consisting of discovering the nature of the transgression (discovery), explaining why the transgression occurred (explanation), determining what punishment is appropriate (penance), implementing changes to limit future transgressions (rehabilitation), and regaining lost legitimacy with stakeholders (reintegration). Reintegration with stakeholders in this process is more likely when organizations take actions consistent with the restorative justice perspective such as acknowledging and taking responsibility for harms to stakeholders, expressing regret and offering amends to stakeholders, accepting punishment, and making organizational changes that demonstrate a commitment to prevent future transgressions with stakeholders.

Before turning to a discussion of how organizational justice scholars might build on this existing work, it is important to note limiting factors influencing the effectiveness of restorative justice processes. Menkel-Meadow (2007) summarizes a number of these considerations. First, in practice, restorative justice processes are applied to crimes of intermediate levels of seriousness, suggesting that there are boundaries on when restorative justice may be most effective. With transgressions of low seriousness, employing restorative justice processes may represent too great a commitment of effort, whereas with very serious transgressions, especially those of an interpersonal nature, victim participation may be precluded. Second, some have questioned whether restorative justice processes by virtue of their relative informality and flexibility in comparison with traditional court procedures, for example, might threaten important procedural and retributive justice concerns such as due process and equity and proportionality in punishment. Third, to the extent that restorative justice requires "well intentioned, non-manipulated participants," any sense that victims have been coerced into forgiving an offender or offenders coerced into apologizing and making amends will compromise the process (Menkel-Meadow, 2007, p. 172). A related consideration is the extent to which participants have the capacity for empathy (Presser & Vorhees, 2002). Fourth, restorative justice can be viewed as resource intensive, requiring skilled facilitators and significant commitments of time and resources.

Taking Restorative Justice and Organization Justice in New Directions

Despite the fact that restorative justice scholarship has continued to develop in traditional literatures such as criminal justice, restorative justice remains largely at the margins of organizational justice scholarship. Few books and articles in the organizational and management literature directly examine restorative justice or appeal to it as a primary conceptual framework. Research that has addressed restorative justice has tended to do so in a fragmented, rather than integrated manner, focusing on specific topics such as forgiveness or apology (e.g., Fehr & Gelfand, 2012) independently, rather than in an integrated manner that includes concerns and issues relevant to victims, offenders, and third parties. As a result, important gaps remain in developing the restorative justice literature in the organizational context and within organizational justice scholarship.

In this section, we consider some potential ways to build on the current restorative justice literature that are more integrative in nature and of relevance to organizational justice research. Rather than offer a "laundry list" of potential topics, we focus on an area of inquiry that that we believe holds significant promise for bridging the gap between the restorative justice and organizational justice literatures and opening up new possibilities for theoretical and empirical development: how managers and organizations respond to interpersonal wrongdoing. As we discuss below, restorative justice represents an integrative perspective on responding to interpersonal wrongdoing, both in terms of *integrating multiple stakeholders* and *integrating approaches.*

Managers and the Integration of Multiple Stakeholders

We first explore the topic of responding to interpersonal wrongdoing from the manager's perspective, a point of view that has received limited attention in the restorative justice literature. From a managerial perspective, a restorative justice approach involves managers integrating multiple stakeholders (offender, victim, affected third parties) into the process of responding to wrongdoing and fostering restorative practices such as making amends, extending forgiveness, and supporting the reintegration of offenders. Restorative justice scholars have argued that traditional retributive approaches to wrongdoing, that is, those that rely on punishment, focus largely on the offender and often neglect important concerns from the perspective of other organizational members, particularly the victim (e.g., Kidder, 2007). Directing attention to victims and other organizational stakeholders prompts a series of important but largely overlooked questions regarding who matters in organizational justice, such as: "What does it mean for victims of wrongdoing and affected third parties to give and receive justice when they have been directly or indirectly harmed?" "How can managers assist in compensating, healing, and otherwise repairing victims, affected third parties, and the offender, as well as relationships among these parties?" "How can an organization reintegrate offenders back into the organizational community?" Restorative justice practices are inherently inclusive, explicitly focusing attention on the needs of victims and other organizational stakeholders such as group members, others who may play a significant role in fostering the reintegration of offenders back into the organization (e.g., managers), and the larger organizational community. By explicitly considering the needs of all affected parties, restorative justice helps shift thinking about who matters in organizational justice by emphasizing the needs and interests of a variety of participants and stakeholders beyond the offender.

A more inclusive view of who matters in the aftermath of organizational wrongdoing has the potential to generate important topics for future research. For example, researchers are increasingly discovering that one's choice of the appropriate response to wrongdoing can depend on one's perspective (e.g., victim, offender, manager, co-worker). This has important implications for managers who are often in the position of responding to incidents of wrongdoing within a work unit. In the organizational punishment literature, research has shown that managers tend to focus on issues of procedural justice, whereas offenders tend to emphasize distributive concerns (e.g., Ball, Treviño, & Sims, 1994; Butterfield, Treviño, & Ball, 1996). However, from a restorative justice perspective, the effectiveness of a manager's response will depend on the ability of the manager to encourage restorative practices (e.g., making amends) that are responsive to the needs of the offender, victim, and third parties. For example, recent research on reconciliation (e.g., Shnabel & Nadler, 2008; Shnabel, Nadler, Ullrich, Dovidio, & Carmi, 2009) shows that, in the wake of wrongdoing, victims and offenders often have different unresolved needs. Victims' restorative needs can be material, such as financial compensation, as well as emotional, such as a need for a sincere apology and restoring their power and status (e.g., Reb et al., 2006; Shnabel & Nadler, 2008; Shnabel et al., 2009; Walker, 2006). Offenders' restorative needs might include regaining a sense of dignity, self-respect, and personal integrity or restoring their image and identity as moral actors (Goodstein & Butterfield, 2010; Shnabel & Nadler, 2008; Shnabel et al., 2009). Other stakeholders might also have restorative needs, such as desiring an apology from the offender or finding ways to support the victim (e.g., Goodstein & Butterfield, 2010).

To the extent that managers are able to respond to wrongdoing in an integrated way that takes account of multiple parties and encourages the key practices of making amends, forgiveness, and offender reintegration, we suggest that the promotion of restorative justice will have important implications for a number of important individual and interpersonal outcomes, in particular justice-oriented outcomes. We noted earlier research undertaken in other contexts (e.g. criminal proceedings) that shows high levels of satisfaction with process and outcome considerations when restorative justice processes are employed. Within organizational settings, we might expect the manager's efforts to encourage parties to repair harm associated with wrongdoing will generally be viewed by affected parties in a favorable light, for example, as representing acts of benevolence, kindness, caring, or compassion. Having received benevolent treatment, participants may respond in kind by finding ways to reciprocate by extending caring and compassionate treatment to others. Reciprocation is a common theme in restorative justice research; participants often attempt to keep their "social accounts in relative balance... rooted in a desire to pay back what we owe, both the good and the evil" (Sharpe, 2007, p. 24). For example, when a manager treats an offender in a benevolent manner (e.g., by facilitating his or her reintegration back into the organizational community), the offender may be motivated to reciprocate by responding in a meaningful way to the victim, such as apologizing and asking what else can be done to make amends. The victim (and perhaps other affected third parties) may, in turn, express appreciation and forgiveness that helps the offender relieve feelings of guilt and restore a sense of integrity and self-respect. We speculate that such positive exchanges may further reinforce traditional justice-oriented outcomes (i.e. perceived distributive, retributive, procedural, and interactional fairness) and foster restorative justice-oriented outcomes such as a reduced sense of harm and improved interpersonal relationships (e.g., Bottom et al., 2002; Dirks et al., 2009).

Organizations and the Integration of Retributive and Restorative Approaches to Wrongdoing

Restorative justice not only extends our thinking about who matters it also reorients our thinking about what matters in organizational justice. Applying restorative justice in many organizations (particularly corporate contexts) is likely to involve at least some element of retributive justice, specifically in the form of formal punishment. This is particularly likely in environments (e.g., corporations) where managers may believe that a punitive response is necessary in the aftermath of wrongdoing (e.g., to avoid legal problems), where punishment is deeply entrenched in the organizational culture, where organizational members (e.g., victims, co-workers) expect wrongdoers to be punished for their actions (e.g., Treviño, 1992), and in cases involving "serious" harm (e.g., interpersonal violence or sexual harassment; Griffin & Lopez, 2005; Robinson & Bennett, 1995). Applying restorative justice is, therefore, likely to involve integrating restorative justice (in the form of formal punishment) with restorative responses. As such, restorative justice complements the traditional retributive approach that has dominated the organizational and management literature as a method of responding to employee wrongdoing (e.g., Brett, Atwater, & Waldman, 2005; Butterfield et al., 1996; Carlsmith, Darley, & Robinson 2002; Treviño, 1992). This raises an important set of questions: "What would an integration of retributive and restorative justice in response to wrongdoing look like?" and "What are the organizational implications of organizational systems that are more restorative in nature?" We offer some initial thoughts on these questions beginning with a discussion of similarities and differences between restorative justice and retributive approaches as manifested in organizational settings. We adopt the more familiar organizational term *punishment* in what follows to characterize the retributive approach in organizations.

The restorative justice approach and traditional punishment approach to wrongdoing have important similarities. Both approaches emphasize considerations such as fairness, deterrence, and organizational learning (e.g., Atwater, Waldman, Carey, & Cartier, 2001; Ball et al., 1994; Butterfield et al., 1996; Cole, 2004, 2008; Podsakoff, Bommer, Podsakoff, & MacKenzie, 2006; Treviño, 1992). These approaches also have significant areas of overlap. Although not a point of emphasis, punishment often plays an important role in restorative justice. As noted by Kidder, "the focus on repairing harm should not be misinterpreted as avoiding punishment for the offender" (2007, p. 12). Restorative justice meetings generally result in offender punishments such as paying restitution. Conversely, restorative results can be achieved through punishment. Punishment is sometimes viewed as "paying one's debt to society," which can facilitate the process of offender reintegration (e.g., Goodstein & Butterfield, 2010; Treviño & Weaver, 2010).

Differences between the restorative justice and traditional punishment approaches can be characterized along several key dimensions, including *inclusiveness, interaction among participants, transparency, time orientation, empowerment, flexibility, and mutual accountability* (e.g., Braithwaite, 2003; Goodstein & Butterfield, 2010; Strang & Braithwaite, 2000; Van Ness & Strong, 2002). We consider these dimensions at the system level, reflecting organizations as actors who can adopt systems of wrongdoing that are relatively retributive or restorative in nature.

INCLUSIVENESS

The traditional punishment approach is relatively individualistic and offender-centered in nature, placing an emphasis on due process intended to protect individuals' rights and provide retributive justice (e.g., Braithwaite, 2003; Van Ness, 1993). The restorative justice approach is less formalized, more community-centered, and emphasizes inclusiveness in the sense that affected parties, including the offender, victim, and third parties, are encouraged to participate in the process and to accept mutual responsibility in restoring relationships harmed through wrongdoing.

INTERACTION AMONG PARTICIPANTS

In systems characterized by a punishment approach, interaction is often limited and the process is relatively adversarial, impersonal, and detached from direct participants (e.g., Van Ness, 1993). Third parties (e.g., managers) are responsible for following established rules and procedures, determining who is right and wrong, and meting out punishment to offenders as appropriate. Restorative justice approaches to wrongdoing emphasize collaborative and interactive approaches in determining how misconduct will be handled. Restorative justice meetings bring offenders, victims, and interested stakeholders together to engage in open dialogue, share feelings, and solve problems in a personal and cooperative manner.

TRANSPARENCY

Another distinguishing feature of punishment approaches in organizations is a focus on privacy and confidentiality. Those who apply due process generally go to great lengths to keep sensitive information confidential and ensure the privacy of all parties (e.g. Braithwaite, 2003). Restorative justice approaches emphasize open and candid dialogue among offenders, victims, and third parties. This enables affected parties to take direct action to address harm and repair relationships.

TIME ORIENTATION

Although punishment can reflect retributive (focused primarily on the past) or consequentialist (focused on the future) views (Treviño & Weaver, 2010), research suggests that managers' punishment decisions are more likely to be driven by retribution (Carlsmith et al., 2002). Punishment approaches, therefore, tend to be reactionary in nature, focusing largely "on the past, determining who was right and who was wrong, assessing blame, and then deciding on punishment" (Kidder, 2007, p. 8). Restorative justice approaches are generally more "forward looking," taking a proactive problem-solving perspective that emphasize developing long-term strategies for restoring all affected parties in the aftermath of wrongdoing (Goodstein & Butterfield, 2010; Kidder, 2007).

EMPOWERMENT

Restorative justice scholars (e.g., Johnstone & Van Ness, 2007; Sawin & Zehr, 2007) have argued that punishment approaches to wrongdoing often fail to engage and empower those stakeholders (e.g., victims, offenders, third parties) who are most directly affected by wrongdoing. Within the restorative justice approach, empowerment plays a key role; managers give those who were most responsible for and affected by the wrongdoing the power and freedom to identify problems and resolve issues among themselves (Johnstone & Van Ness, 2007; Sawin & Zehr, 2007).

FLEXIBILITY

Traditional punishment approaches in organizations generally promote consistency; to maintain procedural and distributive fairness, punishment should be applied consistently across people, time, and location (e.g., Treviño, 1992). Flexibility is typically greater in restorative justice responses to wrongdoing; each situation is considered unique, and participants are encouraged to tailor the process and outcomes to the particular circumstances, including participants' distinct needs, perceived harms, and objectives (e.g., Sharpe, 2007; Van Ness & Strong, 2002).

MUTUAL ACCOUNTABILITY

In punishment approaches, accountability is focused on offenders and their responsibility to the organization to "pay for" the act of wrongdoing. Restorative justice approaches similarly emphasize the importance of offenders taking responsibility for their actions and accepting punishment. However, they typically are also held accountable for acknowledging the harm that they have done, offering an apology or other amends, expressing regret, and making changes that demonstrate to victims and third parties a commitment to prevent future misconduct (Van Ness & Strong, 2002). In turn, victims and third parties are asked to join the offender in assuming mutual responsibility and accountability for restoring all affected parties, including the offender. This allows all participants to focus on understanding the harm that been done and to decide together how to address the harm and repair damaged relationships.

IMPLICATIONS

Building on these dimensions, one can conceptualize punitive (i.e., grounded primarily in a punishment approach) and restorative (i.e., grounded primarily in a restorative justice approach) responses as a continuum that has implications for how managers might respond to wrongdoing. At the ends of the continuum, the manager's response is solely punitive or solely restorative in nature. In between, the manager's response integrates the two approaches. In practical terms, this means determining an appropriate punishment (e.g., a formal suspension) that reflects distributive (e.g., ensuring that the penalties fit the offense), retributive, procedural (e.g., due process), and interactional fairness (e.g., Treviño & Weaver, 2010) as well as repairing damaged relationships and healing those (offender, victim, and third parties) who have experienced harm. Relationship repair may be enabled within systems characterized by greater degrees of empowerment, flexibility, and accountability, for example, and in which managers might take explicit steps to bring willing parties together for a meeting to open a dialogue about the harm caused to the victim (e.g., public embarrassment) and co-workers (e.g., stress from witnessing the incident), to discuss ideas for appropriate amends, strategies for reintegration and healing, and to identify underlying causes of problems and generate plans for preventing future problems.

There are potentially important organizational implications of the use of these approaches to responding to wrongdoing. We specifically direct attention to emerging phenomena in the positive organizational scholarship (POS) literature that are of particular relevance for the restorative justice perspective and have received less significant attention by organizational justice scholars: caring and compassion. POS research places "a special emphasis on uncovering and interpreting what is affirmative in organizations" (Cameron & Caza, 2004, p. 731-732), including previously neglected emotional phenomena such as virtuousness, compassion, and caring (e.g., Dutton, Frost, Worline, Lilius, & Kanov, 2002; Dutton, Worline, Frost, & Lilius, 2006; Cameron, Dutton, and Quinn, 2003).

The concept of the organization as a caring entity is generally viewed through the lens of feminine ethics, particularly in the "ethics of care" tradition (e.g., Burton & Dunn, 1996; Gilligan, 1982; Lawrence & Maitlis, 2012; Liedtka, 1996; Noddings, 1984;). The ethics of care places an emphasis on the self and its fundamental connection with particular others (Gilligan, 1982; Noddings, 1984). Although not inconsistent with an ethic of justice, the ethics of care emphasizes caring, nurturing, connectedness, interdependence, dialogue-based processes, and building close relationships. The ethics of care views traditional ethics topics such as autonomy and responsibility through the lens of caring, stressing the importance of attending to the contextual details of the situation in order to be responsive to one's own needs and the needs of particular others (e.g., Derry, 1999; Lawrence & Maitlis, 2012; Liedtka, 1996). According to Liedtka:

> in order for an organization to "care" in the sense that feminist ethicists have used the term, such caring would need to be: (a) focused entirely on persons, not "quality," "profits," or any of the other kinds of ideas that much of today's "care-talk" seems to revolve around, (b) undertaken as an end in and of itself, and not merely a means toward achieving quality, profits, etc., (c) essentially personal, in that it ultimately involves particular individuals engrossed, at a subjective level, in caring for other particular individuals, (d) growth-enhancing for the cared-for, in that it moves them towards the use and development of their full capacities, within the context of their self defined needs and aspirations. (1996, p. 185).

We propose that varying organizational approaches to wrongdoing (as reflected in Table 25.1) will have different implications for motivating caring and compassionate actions by affected parties. As discussed earlier, punishment approaches grounded in retributive justice can be characterized as more individualistic, impersonal, adversarial, secretive, focused on the past, and limited in interaction in comparison with restorative justice approaches. This can create a context that limits that attention to harm experienced by affected parties and may be less likely to evoke caring and compassionate responses on the part of offenders, victims, and other affected stakeholders.

The restorative justice approach is characterized by a process that by virtue of being more inclusive, participative, transparent, and placing greater emphasis on addressing harm and rebuilding relationships, in comparison with punishment oriented approaches, is more likely to create a context that encourages compassionate and caring responses on the part of offenders, victims, and other affected third-party stakeholders (e.g., co-workers, managers). With regard to offenders, "making good" on the harm one has inflicted involves repairing damaged relationships by personally responding to the needs of the victim and other stakeholders, genuinely expressing remorse, offering a sincere apology, and engaging in other actions that demonstrate a high level of connectedness with the victim and other affected parties. From an ethics of care perspective, this means engaging with the victim and other affected parties at a highly personal level, attending to the contextual details of the situation (e.g., offering

Table 25.1 Key Dimensions of Organizational Responses to Workplace Wrongdoing

Dimensions	Punishment Approach	Restorative Justice Approach
Inclusiveness	Low inclusiveness. Offender centered, individualistic, emphasis on individuals' rights.	High inclusiveness. Community centered, emphasis on collectively engaging all willing offenders, victims, and third parties.
Interaction among participants	Low interaction. Impersonal, adversarial, detached from direct participants.	High interaction. Personal, emphasis on dialogue & discussion among willing participants.
Transparency	Low transparency. Emphasis on secrecy and privacy.	High transparency. Emphasis on openness and candor.
Time orientation	Emphasis on past (reactive).	Emphasis on future (proactive problem solving).
Empowerment	Low empowerment. Power and control remain largely with managers.	High empowerment. Those most responsible for and affected by the wrongdoing are given power and freedom to identify and resolve issues among themselves.
Flexibility	Low flexibility. Emphasis on consistency across people, time, and location.	High flexibility. Emphasis on tailoring the process and outcomes for different participant needs, harms, and goals.
Degree of mutual accountability	Low mutual accountability. Offender centered—offender forced to take responsibility. Accountability is primarily to the organization.	High mutual accountability. Although offender is expected to take responsibility for the offense, offender, victim, and third parties are jointly accountable to each other for determining appropriate response to wrongdoing.

compensation that is appropriate for the given situation), viewing amends and expressing remorse as ends-in-themselves (not as a means to other ends, such as saving one's job), and viewing the process as a growth-enhancing experience. In the case of victims, it is the victim who cares for the offender—establishing dialogue, extending understanding, kindness, and other acts of goodwill to the offender, attending to the contextual details of the situation (e.g., building relationships as appropriate), offering forgiveness as an end-in-itself, and viewing the forgiveness process as a growth-enhancing experience. Other stakeholders beyond the offender-victim dyad also play a key role in the caregiving process. Restorative justice conferences are ultimately personal in nature, with a variety of particular individuals intimately involved in attempting to build relationships and restore other particular individuals in the aftermath of wrongdoing. Restorative justice conferences are also highly sensitive to the context and the particulars of a given offense. Reintegration is viewed as an important end-in-itself and is growth-enhancing for those who participate, encouraging ongoing learning among offenders, victims, and other interested parties (e.g., Goodstein & Butterfield, 2010).

Over time, the modeling of restorative behaviors by managers, offenders, victims, and third-party stakeholders may deepen values and principles that reflect the extent to which the organization cares about its employees and reinforce a culture of caring and compassion (Lawrence & Maitlis, 2012), as well as foster the development of organizational virtues important to restorative justice processes in organizations. We specifically highlight the virtues of courage, humanity, temperance, and transcendence (Peterson & Park, 2006) and relevant character strengths because of their importance to restorative justice practices such as making amends and offering forgiveness.

Restorative justice meetings foster courage by testing participants' will to pursue goals and resilience while confronting internal and external challenges and sources of resistance (Lawrence & Maitlis, 2012; Peterson & Park, 2006). For offenders, making amends with victims requires personal honesty and authenticity and a considerable degree of courage to overcome guilt and shame in admitting wrongdoing. For victims and third parties, restorative responses to wrongdoing and the extension of caring and compassion can promote the virtues of temperance and humanity. Acting with temperance involves overcoming anger and strengthening character through extending forgiveness to offenders, while acting with humanity is demonstrated by showing kindness and providing social and emotional support to offenders.

Restorative responses also have important implications for personal meaning and transcendence, and in particular, gratitude. McCullough, Kilpatrick, Emmons, and Larson (2001, p. 252) write, "Whereas empathy and sympathy operate when people have the opportunity to respond to the plight of another person, and guilt and shame operate when people have not met moral standards or obligations, gratitude operates typically when people are the recipients of prosocial behavior." Offender gratitude is expanded by having the opportunity to be forgiven and to make amends. Victims may experience gratitude by offender's acknowledging harm and taking steps to make amends. Victims may even be grateful for being given the opportunity to forgive the offender and let go of anger and resentment. Third parties may be grateful for also being included in the process of repairing relationships and having their concerns acknowledged and responded to by the offender.

Before we conclude this chapter, we offer a few thoughts related to potential obstacles in advancing a restorative justice perspective within organizations, particularly with respect to formalizing restorative justice in organizations. First, it is important to note that we conceptualize restorative responses as complementing, rather than replacing, punishment-based responses. Punishment plays an important role in establishing perceptions of fairness (distributive, procedural, interactive, and retributive) in the wake of interpersonal offenses. However, research suggests that when people are given an opportunity to use restorative responses to wrongdoing together with retributive responses, they prefer both, rather than the forced choice of one or the other (Gromet & Darley, 2009).

There is also reason to believe that restorative responses, in tandem with punitive responses, have the potential to address root causes of interpersonal offenses. When managers surface and address the underlying causes of the offenders' behavior, this can represent an act of compassion that helps offenders understand why they committed acts of wrongdoing. Rather than compound the problem, restorative responses allow for "deep" interventions that may prevent or break emerging cycles of interpersonal harm and offender recidivism. Contrast that to, strictly punitive systems, where, at times, what is punished is the interpersonal offense, without understanding what may have provoked the harming behavior (Bies & Tripp, 2005).

Nevertheless, organizations and managers interested in adopting a restorative justice approach and implementing restorative practices to address wrongdoing may confront a number of potential barriers. Their efforts might be met with a degree of skepticism and resistance, particularly from those who are unfamiliar with this approach. Managerial resistance may be rooted in a belief that restorative responses do not represent a realistic option in their organization or department. One critical barrier is time. Responding solely with punishment is more expedient and involves limited coordination and interaction, whereas restorative practices are likely to be more time intensive and can require more coordination by the manager and interaction among the offender, victim, and relevant third parties.

Managers may also have basic fairness concerns. Restorative processes are generally contextual; that is, the process that is followed and the agreed-upon outcomes (e.g., manager's action plans, the amount and type of restitution offered by the offender) are situated in the circumstances of the particular case. Some managers, particularly those who are accustomed to traditional punishment processes, may disapprove of a system in which the dynamics of the restorative process and outcomes might differ for different participants. Such managers may express a preference for punishment, as opposed to restorative responses to harming behavior, particularly for high severity offenses (e.g., Carlsmith et al., 2002; Gromet & Darley, 2009). However, to the extent that justice, compassion, and sensitivity to context is a primary objective in the aftermath of a transgression, bringing together both punishment and restorative justice approaches to address interpersonal offenses can be of value to managers, offenders, victims, and other critical parties.

Conclusion

Significant progress has been made on specifying the myriad violations of distributive, procedural, and interactional justice in organizations and examining the antecedents and consequences of these injustices. Understanding how justice is restored in the aftermath of injustice, particularly with respect to wrongdoing and interpersonal harm in organizations, represents a central challenge for organizational justice scholars and practitioners. The domain of restorative justice and the growing body of conceptual and empirical work produced by researchers holds great promise in furthering this understanding and contributing to the development of organizational justice theory and research.

References

Aquino, K., Grover, S. L., Goldman, B., & Folger, R. (2003). When push doesn't come to shove: Interpersonal forgiveness in workplace relationships. *Journal of Management Inquiry, 12*, 209–216.

Aquino, K., Tripp, T. M., & Bies, R. J. (2006). Getting even or moving on: Power, procedural justice, and types of offense as predictors of revenge, forgiveness, reconciliation, and avoidance in organizations. *Journal of Applied Psychology, 91*, 653–668.

Atwater, L. E., Waldman, D. A., Carey, J. A., & Cartier, P. (2001). Recipient and observer reactions to discipline: Are managers experiencing wishful thinking? *Journal of Organizational Behavior, 22*, 249–270.

Ball, G. A., Treviño, L. K., & Sims, H. P. Jr. (1994). Just and unjust punishment: Influences on subordinate performance. *Academy of Management Journal, 37*(2), 299–323.

Bies, R. J., & Tripp, T. M. (2005). The study of revenge in the workplace: Conceptual, ideological, and empirical issues. *Counterproductive Work Behavior: Investigations of Actors and Targets*, 65–81. Washington D.C.: American Psychological Association.

Bottom, W. P., Gibson, K. S, Daniels, S., & Murnighan, J. K. (2002). When talk is not cheap: Substantive penance and expression of intent in rebuilding cooperation. *Organization Science, 13*, 497–513.

Bradfield, M., & Aquino, K. (1999). The effects of blame attributions and offender likableness on forgiveness and revenge in the workplace. *Journal of Management, 25*(5), 607–631.

Bradshaw, W., & Roseborough, D. (2005). Restorative justice dialogue: The impact of mediation and conferencing on juvenile recidivism. *Federal Probation, 69*, 15.

Braithwaite, J. (1999). Restorative justice: Assessing optimistic and pessimistic accounts, *Crime and Justice, 25*, 1–127.

Braithwaite, J. (2000). Decomposing a holistic vision of restorative justice. *Contemporary Justice Review, 3*, 433–440.

Braithwaite, J. (2002). *Restorative justice and responsive regulation*. Boston, MA: Oxford University Press.

Braithwaite, J. (2003). Restorative justice and social justice. In McLaughlin, E., Fergusson, R., Hughes, G. and Westmarland, L. (Eds.) *Restorative justice: Critical issues* (pp. 157–163). London, UK: Sage.

Brett, J. F., Atwater, L. E., & Waldman, D. A. (2005). Effective delivery of workplace discipline. *Group and Organization Management, 30*, 487–511.

Burton, B. K., & Dunn, C. P. (1996). Feminist ethics as moral grounding for stakeholder theory. *Business Ethics Quarterly, 6*(2), 133–147.

Bush, R. A. B., & Folger, J. P. (1994). *The promise of mediation: Responding to conflict through empowerment and recognition* (pp. 1996–133). San Francisco, CA: Jossey-Bass.

Butterfield, K. D., Treviño, L. K., & Ball, G. A. (1996). Punishment from the manager's perspective: A grounded investigation and inductive model. *Academy of Management Journal, 39*(6), 1479–1512.

Cameron, K. S., & Caza, A. (2004). Introduction: Contributions to the discipline of positive organizational scholarship. *American Behavioral Scientist, 47*(6), 731–739.

Cameron, K. S., Dutton, J. E., & Quinn, R. E. (2003). *Positive organizational scholarship: Foundations of a new discipline*. San Francisco, CA: Berrett-Koehler Publishers.

Carlsmith, K. M., Darley, J. M., & Robinson, P. H. (2002). Why do we punish? Deterrence and just desserts as motives for punishment. *Journal of Personality and Social Psychology, 83*(2), 284–299.

Cole, N. D. (2004). Gender differences in perceived disciplinary fairness. *Gender, Work, and Organization, 11*, 254–279.

Cole, N. D. (2008). Consistency in employee discipline: an empirical exploration. *Personnel Review, 37*(1), 109–117.

Daly, K., & Immarigeon, R. (1998). The past, present, and future of restorative justice: Some critical reflections, *Contemporary Justice Review, 1*, 21–45.

Derry, R. (1999). Feminist theory and business ethics. In R. E. Frederick (Ed.), *A Companion to Business Ethics* (pp. 81–87). Oxford, UK: Blackwell Publishers.

Dirks, K. T., Lewicki, R. J., & Zaheer, A. (2009). Repairing relationships within and between organizations: Building a conceptual foundation. *Academy of Management Review, 34*(1), 68–84.

Dutton, J. E., Frost, P. J., Worline, M. C., Lilius, J. M., & Kanov, J. M. (2002), January. Leading in times of trauma. *Harvard Business Review, 80*, 54–62.

Dutton, J. E., Worline, M. C., Frost, P. J., & Lilius, J. (2006). Explaining compassion organizing. *Administrative Science Quarterly, 51*(1), 59–96.

Eaton, J., Struthers, C. W., & Santelli, A. G. (2006). The mediating role of perceptual validation in the repentance-forgiveness process. *Personality and Social Psychology Bulletin, 32*, 1389–1401.

Enright, R. D., Gassin, E. A., & Wu, C. (1992). Forgiveness: A developmental view. *Journal of Moral Education*, 2, 99–114.

Fehr, R., & Gelfand, M. (2012). The forgiving organization: A multilevel model of forgiveness at work. *Academy of Management Review, 37*(4), 664–688.

Gillespie, N., & Dietz, G. (2009). Trust repair after an organization-level failure. *Academy of Management Review, 34*(1), 127–145.

Gilligan, C. (1982). *In a different voice*. Cambridge, MA.: Harvard University Press.

Gonzales, M. H., Manning, D. J., & Haugen, J. A. (1992). Explaining our sins: Factors influencing offender accounts and anticipated victim responses. *Journal of Personality and Social Psychology, 62*(6), 958–971.

Goodstein, J. D., & Aquino, K. (2010). And restorative justice for all: Redemption, forgiveness, and reintegration in organizations. *Journal of Organizational Behavior, 31*, 624–628.

Goodstein, J. D., Aquino, K., & Skarlicki, D. (2011). Opening a new conversation in organizational justice: A conceptual model of offender reintegration in organizations.

In S. W. Gilliland, D. D. Steiner, & D. P. Skarlicki (Eds.), *Emerging perspectives on organizational justice and ethics* (pp. 75–104). Charlotte, NC: Information Age.

Goodstein, J. D., & Butterfield, K. D. (2010). Extending the horizon of business ethics: Restorative justice and the aftermath of unethical behavior. *Business Ethics Quarterly, 20*(3), 453–480.

Griffin, R. W., & Lopez, Y. P. (2005). "Bad behavior" in organizations: A review and typology for future research. *Journal of Management, 31*, 988–1005.

Gromet, D. M. (2012). Restoring the victim: Emotional reactions, justice beliefs, and support for reparation and punishment. *Critical Criminology, 20*(1), 1–15.

Gromet, D. M., & Darley, J. M. (2009). Retributive and restorative justice: Importance of crime severity and shared identity in people's justice responses. *Australian Journal of Psychology, 61*(1), 50–57.

Hareli, S., & Eisikovits, Z. (2006). The role of communicating social emotions accompanying apologizing in forgiveness. *Motivation and Emotion, 30*, 189–197.

Hareli, S., Shomrat, N., & Biger, N. (2005). The role of emotions in employees' explanations for failure in the workplace. *Journal of Managerial Psychology, 20*, 663–680.

Johnstone, G., & Van Ness, D. W. (2007). The meaning of restorative justice. In G. Johnstone and D. Van Ness (Eds.) *Handbook of restorative justice* (pp. 5–23). Cullompton, UK: Willan Publishing.

Karp, D., & Conrad, S. (2005). Restorative justice and college student misconduct, *Public Organization Review: A Global Journal, 5*, 315–333.

Kidder, D. L. (2007). Restorative justice: Not "rights," but the right way to heal relationships at work, *International Journal of Conflict Management, 18*(1), 4–22.

Kuo, S. Y., Longmire, D., & Cuvelier, S. J. (2010). An empirical assessment of the process of restorative justice. *Journal of Criminal Justice, 38*(3), 318–328.

Lawrence, T. B., & Maitlis, S. (2012). Care and possibility: Enacting an ethic of care through narrative practice. *Academy of Management Review, 37*(4), 641–663.

Liedtka, J. M. (1996). Feminist morality and competitive reality: A role for an ethic of care? *Business Ethics Quarterly, 6*(2), 179–200.

Marshall, T. F. (2003). Restorative justice: An overview. In Johnstone, G. (Ed.) *A restorative justice reader: Texts, sources, and context* (pp. 28–45). Devon, UK: Willan Publishing.

McCullough, M. E., Kilpatrick, S. D., Emmons, R. A., & Larson, D. B. (2001). Is gratitude a moral affect? *Psychological Bulletin, 127*, 249–266.

McCullough, M. F., Worthington, E. L., & Rachal, K. C. (1997). Interpersonal forgiving in close relationships. *Journal of Personality and Social Psychology, 73*, 321–336.

McGarrell, E. F. (2001). *Restorative justice conferences as an early response to young offenders*. Washington, DC: US Department of Justice, Office of Justice Programs, Office of Juvenile Justice and Delinquency Prevention.

Menkel-Meadow, C. J. (2007). Restorative justice: What is it and does it work? *Annual Review of Law and Social Science, 3*(10), 1–10.

Mikula, G. (1994). Perspective-related differences in interpretations of injustice by victims and victimizers: A test with close relationships. In M. J. Lerner & G. Mikula (Eds.), *Entitlement and the affectional bond* (pp. 175–204). New York, NY: Plenum.

Noddings, N. (1984). *Caring: A feminine approach to ethics and moral education*. Berkeley, CA: University of California Press.

North, J. (1987). Wrongdoing and forgiveness. *Philosophy, 62*, 499–508.

Okimoto, T. G., Wenzel, M., & Feather, N. T. (2009). Beyond retribution: Conceptualizing restorative justice and exploring its determinants. *Social Justice Research, 22*, 156–180.

Peterson, C., & Park, N. (2006). Character strengths in organizations. *Journal of Organizational Behavior, 27*, 1149–1154.

Pfarrer, M. D., DeCelles, K. A., Smith, K. G., & Taylor, M. S. (2008). After the fall: Reintegrating the corrupt organization. *Academy of Management Review, 33*, 730–749.

Podsakoff, P. M., Bommer, W. H., Podsakoff, N. P., & MacKenzie, S. B. (2006). Relationships between leader reward and punishment behavior and subordinate attitudes, perceptions, and behaviors: A meta-analytic review of existing and new research. *Organizational Behavior and Human Decision Processes, 99*(2), 113–142.

Presser, L., & Van Voorhis, P. (2002). Values and evaluation: Assessing processes and outcomes of restorative justice programs. *Crime and Delinquency, 48*, 162–188.

Radzik, L. (2009). *Making Amends: Atonement in Morality, Law, and Politics*. New York, NY: Oxford University Press.

Reb, J., Goldman, B. M., Kray, L. J., & Cropanzano, R. (2006). Different wrongs, different remedies? Reactions to organizational remedies after procedural and interactional injustice. *Personnel Psychology, 59*(1), 31–64.

Ren, H., & Gray, B. (2009). Repairing relationship conflict: How violation types and culture influence the effectiveness of restoration rituals. *Academy of Management Review, 34*(1), 105–126.

Robinson, S. L., & Bennett, R. J. (1995). A typology of deviant workplace behaviors: A multidimensional scaling study. *Academy of Management Journal, 38*(2), 555–572.

Roche, D. (2003). *Accountability in restorative justice*. Oxford, UK: Oxford University Press.

Roche, D. (2006). Dimensions of restorative justice, *Journal of Social Issues, 62*(2), 217–238.

Sawin, J. L., & Zehr, H. (2007). The ideas of engagement and empowerment. In G. Johnstone and D. Van Ness (Eds.) *Handbook of restorative justice* (pp. 41–58). Cullompton, UK: Willan Publishing.

Schonbach, P. (1990). *Account episodes: The management and escalation of conflict*. Cambridge, UK: Cambridge University Press.

Sharpe, S. (2007). The Idea of Reparation. In G. Johnstone and D. Van Ness (Eds.) *Handbook of restorative justice* (pp. 24–40). Cullompton, UK: Willan Publishing.

Shnabel, N., & Nadler, A. (2008). A needs-based model of reconciliation: Satisfying the differential emotional needs of victim and perpetrator as a key to promoting reconciliation. *Journal of Personality and Social Psychology, 94*(1), 116.

Shnabel, N., Nadler, A., Ullrich, J., Dovidio, J. F., & Carmi, D. (2009). Promoting reconciliation through the satisfaction of the emotional needs of victimized and perpetrating group members: The needs-based model of reconciliation. *Personality and Social Psychology Bulletin, 35*(8), 1021–1030.

Strang, H. (2002). *Repair or revenge: Victims and restorative justice*. Oxford, UK: Oxford University Press.

Strang, H., & Braithwaite, J. (2000). Restorative Justice. Aldershot, UK: Ashgate.

Tangney, J. P., & Dearing, R. L. (2002). *Shame and guilt.* New York, NY: Guilford.

Tata, J. (2000). She said, he said: The influence of remedial accounts on third-party judgments of coworker sexual harassment. *Journal of Management, 26*(6), 1133–1156.

Tavuchis, N. (1991). *Mea culpa: A sociology of apology and reconciliation.* Stanford, CA: Stanford University Press.

Taylor, G. (1985). *Pride, shame, and guilt: Emotions of self-assessment.* New York, NY: Oxford University Press.

Treviño, L. K. (1992). The social effects of punishment in organizations: A justice perspective. *Academy of Management Review, 17*(4), 647–676.

Treviño, L. K., & Weaver, G. R. (2010). Advances in research on punishment in organizations: Descriptive and normative perspectives. In M. Schminke (Ed.) *Managerial ethics: Managing the psychology of morality.* New York, NY: Routledge.

Tyler, T. R. (2006). Restorative justice and procedural justice: Dealing with rule breaking. *Journal of Social Issues, 62*(2), 307–326.

Umbreit, M. S., & Bradshaw, W. (1999). Factors that contribute to victim satisfaction and mediated offender dialogue in Winnipeg: An emerging area of social work practice. *Journal of Law and Social Work, 9*(1), 67–84.

Umbreit, M. S., Vos, B., Coates, R. B., & Brown, K. A. (2003). *Facing violence: The path of restorative justice and dialogue* (pp. 45–52). Monsey, NY: Criminal Justice Press.

Van Ness, D. W. (1993). New wine and old wineskins: Four challenges of restorative justice. *Criminal Law Forum, 4*(2), 251–276.

Van Ness, D. W., & Strong, K. H. (2002). *Restoring justice.* Cincinnati, OH: Anderson Publishing.

Walker, M. U. (2006). *Moral repair: Reconstructing moral relations after wrongdoing.* New York, NY: Cambridge University Press.

Weiner, B., Graham, S., Peter, O., & Zmuidinas, M. (1991). Public confession and forgiveness. *Journal of Personality, 59*, 281–312.

Wenzel, M., Okimoto, T. G., & Cameron, K. (2012). Do retributive and restorative justice processes address different symbolic concerns? *Critical Criminology, 20*(1), 25–44.

Wenzel, M., Okimoto, T. G., Feather, N. T., & Platow, M. J. (2008). Retributive and restorative justice. *Law and Human Behavior, 32*, 375–389.

Wenzel, M., Okimoto, T. G., Feather, N. T., & Platow, M. J. (2010). Justice through consensus: Shared identity and the preference for a restorative notion of justice. *European Journal of Social Psychology, 40*(6), 909–930.

Witvliet, C. V. O., Worthington, E. L., Jr., Root, L. M., Sato, A. F., Ludwig, T. E., & Exline, J. J. (2008). Retributive justice, restorative justice, and forgiveness: An experimental psychophysiology analysis. *Journal of Experimental Social Psychology, 44*(1), 10–25.

Zehr, H. (1990). *Changing lenses: A new focus for criminal justice.* Scottsdale, PA.: Herald Press.

PART 5

Applications of Justice

CHAPTER

26 Justice and Organizational Structure: A Review

Marshall Schminke, Michael A. Johnson, *and* Darryl Rice

Abstract

The literature on organizational justice has come a long way in the past three decades, but a significant gap still exists. Relatively little attention has been paid to the context in which justice experiences emerge and the role of the organization itself. In this chapter we seek to narrow this gap by reviewing justice research that considers the critical role organizational structure plays in how justice judgments are formed, and the impact they have on the organization and its employees. We examine 30 years of empirical research linking justice and structure, and catalog these efforts across a variety of structural dimensions. We identify patterns in this research and offer suggestions for future research aimed at putting the "organization" back in organizational justice.

Key Words: organizational justice, organizational structure, structural dimensions

To understand organizational justice, one must understand the organizational context in which it exists. This chapter explores the role organizational structure plays in shaping justice experiences at work. We focus on structure because it represents one of the most ubiquitous aspects of organizations (Clegg & Hardy, 1996).

Our goal in this chapter is to review empirical research over the last three decades that has linked organizational justice and structure. We seek to enlighten justice researchers as to the breadth and depth of evidence linking justice and structure in meaningful ways. We also hope it will draw scholars to the possibility that structural considerations represent new paths to understanding the issues they wrestle with in their own justice research.

Our review is organized into three sections. The first establishes the boundaries of our efforts in this chapter. The second presents the core of the review, which summarizes existing work across distinct structural dimensions, in chronological order within each dimension. To help guide the reader, an overview of this summary appears in table form as well. The third section provides a commentary on the state of knowledge in the area, and outlines directions for future work.

Boundaries of the Review

This chapter reviews *empirical* work linking organizational justice and structure. Sound conceptual and theoretical treatments of the potential impact of organizational context on justice have existed for some time (e.g., Leventhal, 1980; Lind & Tyler, 1988; Tyler, 1996; Cropanzano & Greenberg, 1997). Building on this work, others have focused on structure in particular and theorized about its relationship with justice perceptions (Ambrose, 2002; Ambrose & Schminke, 2001; Greenberg, 1993; Keeley, 1988; Lansberg, 1988; Nowakowski & Conlon, 2005; Rupp & Paddock, 2010; Sheppard, Lewicki, & Minton, 1992). Most of the empirical studies examined in this chapter provide quality conceptual foundations as well. Therefore, we focus our attention on empirical work, and we refer the reader to these other sources for greater conceptual insights.

Second, we examine research that focuses on formal organizational structure. Organizational structure refers to an organization's internal pattern of relationships, authority, and communication (Thompson, 1967). Its focus is an organization's formal reporting relationships, groupings, and systems (Daft, 2007). This description of structure highlights its multidimensional nature. First, it specifies reporting relationships, the number of levels in the organizational hierarchy, and the span of control of supervisors and managers. Second, it identifies how individuals are grouped together into departments and how those departments are grouped together in comprising the organization. Finally, it specifies how systems are designed to ensure effective communication, coordination, and integration between departments (Daft, 2007).

The formal nature of structure is important. With its focus on the formal aspects of the organizational context, structure is distinct from the informal organizational context that includes factors such as organizational culture, climate, norms, politics, and values. Each of these represents an important component of the overall organizational context, but none falls within the conceptual space of structure. Therefore, they are not included in the review.

In addition to its formal nature, we conceptualize structure as a work-unit level construct. Although scholars sometimes refer to *organizational* structure, it is a rare organization that exhibits similar structural characteristics across all departments and work units. For example, most organizations would embrace flexibility, creativity, and responsiveness in advertising or research departments, but few would welcome those characteristics in their accounting and audit groups. Across the organization, departments perform distinct functions. They employ different production technologies and face different operating environments. As we will see later in our discussion of structural contingency theory, these departmental differences demand different structural adaptations.

Third, in conducting our search, we gathered published empirical works that linked any aspect of organizational justice or fairness to constructs that fall under our definition of structure. We were able to identify research linking justice to a host of structural elements, including bureaucracy, organic-mechanistic structure, formalization, centralization, formal power and authority, size and complexity, task interdependence, communication systems, structure as a form of leadership, and hierarchical level in the organization. Although other facets of structure appear in the organizational studies literature (e.g., integration, differentiation, horizontal complexity), not all have been linked to justice research. Therefore, the entire spectrum of possible structural dimensions is not represented in our review.

Finally, in establishing the boundaries of our review, we also need to specify what structure is not. First, as noted earlier, structure does not include the informal aspects of organizational context like culture, climate, norms, politics, and values. Second, we did not include conceptualizations of structure that are illustrated primarily in organization charts, such as product structures, divisional structures, matrix structures, hybrid structures, and so on. The most important influence of structure on individuals in organizations is not captured in organization charts but rather, in the finer-grained dimensions of structure enumerated earlier. Organization charts may depict structure, but they are not structure.

We also did not classify human resource management (HRM) practices and policies as structure. Our review, therefore, does not include justice research related to the fairness of various compensation systems, performance evaluation systems, monitoring systems, and so on. Such HRM systems may be formalized, and the role of fairness in HRM practices is important, but in our view these represent a distinct area of study from structure. Further, our review includes only a subset of justice research related to teams. Although structure occurs at the work unit level and, therefore, often manifests itself through team processes, the mere presence of a team context (versus an individual context) does not dictate any particular structural features. Therefore, we have not included research that simply explores the relationship between justice and working in a team setting (of no particular structural form), team diversity, and so on. Finally, strategy is not structure. Recent research has begun to integrate fairness principles into work on strategic issues like managing acquisitions, diversification, multinationals, and strategic alliances (e.g., Argawal, Croson, & Mahoney, 2010). This is important work, but we leave these issues for another review.

All these research areas represent promising avenues for enhancing our understanding of justice in organizational settings. However, although they may occupy space in the global domain of organizational context, they are not structure and, therefore, fall outside our purview.

In addition to these notes about structure, three clarifications about justice are in order. First, the terms *justice* and *fairness* are often used interchangeably in the literature, and we do the same here. Second, we follow a conventional history of justice research, focusing primarily on the issues of distributive, procedural, and interactional (sometimes informational and interpersonal) justice. Finally, our review involves only issues of organizational justice. Clearly, issues of justice and fairness permeate many other areas of scholarship (e.g., law, family, community), but we limit our focus here to those involving organizations and the people in them.

Before moving on to the review, a final note is in order regarding how we have categorized and reported relationships between justice and structure. Some studies are complicated to codify. For example, consider a study in which justice is hypothesized to mediate the relationship between structure and job satisfaction. Because our interest is in relationships between structure and justice, in this case our attention rests on the direct effect of structure on justice. In our narrative description of a study, we certainly convey the author's interest in the mediating role of justice. But in the summary table of what we have learned about the functional relationship between justice and structure, we report structure as an independent variable (IV) and justice as a dependent variable (DV). Therefore, the reader should be aware that in studies involving constructs beyond structure and justice, their roles in the study may be represented somewhat differently in the narrative than in the summary table. In this way, the two components of the review (narrative and table) work in a complementary fashion.

The Review

We present our review of justice and structure in a top-down fashion. We begin by exploring two relatively global conceptualizations of structure: Weber's (1946) bureaucracy and Burns and Stalker's (1961) mechanistic and organic structural forms. We continue with work that has explored specific structural subdimensions often associated with Burns and Stalker's mechanistic and organic structures: formalization, centralization, formal power and authority, size and complexity. We conclude by examining structural factors not as commonly associated with the Burns and Stalker framework (task interdependence and communication systems) as well as two constructs that relate to structure in important ways (the initiating structure aspect of leader behavior, and the level of the organization hierarchy at which one resides).

As the review progresses, we refer the reader to the Table 26.1 as an aid in organizing the disparate literature encompassing justice and structure. Table 26.1 provides the essential information necessary for categorizing what we learn about the relationship between justice and structure from each study: (a) the structural dimensions involved (e.g., formalization, centralization); (b) the justice dimensions involved (e.g., distributive, procedural, interactional); (c) the role played by each (e.g., IV, DV, mediator, moderator), (d) the sample employed, and (e) a summary of results.

Bureaucracy

> "You will never understand bureaucracies until you understand that for bureaucrats, procedure is everything and outcomes are nothing."
>
> —*Thomas Sowell*, 2003

For many, the idea of organizational structure conjures a clear image of modern bureaucracy: senseless rules and regulations dominating every aspect of organizational life, and alienated employees with no ability to think, innovate, or use discretion in their work. However, this has not always been the case. Bureaucracy has not always been a derogatory word. In its earliest form, bureaucracy represented a sound structural response to the needs of the large scale industrial enterprises emerging from the industrial revolution (Victor & Stephens, 1994). Scholars like Weber (1946) identified bureaucracy as the most rational and efficient means of organizing, and of meeting the challenges of an industrialized society dominated by large firms. For Weber, bureaucracy reflected organizational departments with fixed and identifiable duties, a clear chain of command, stable, written rules and regulations for governing behavior, and hiring for specific competencies to perform particular jobs. These design features contrasted sharply with the structures of smaller, more traditional, often family-based organizations such as guild, craft, or farming entities prevalent prior to the industrial revolution.

In terms of empirical research, organizational scholars interested in issues of structure have more typically embraced later conceptualizations of structure such as that of Burns and Stalker (1961, see the next subsection). However, some research does speak to the relationship between organizational justice and structure in the form of bureaucracy.

Table 26.1 Justice and Structure

Author(s)	Date	Structural dimension(s) and (role)[a]	Justice dimension(s) and (role)[a]	Sample	Results
Ambrose & Schminke	2003	Mech (mod) Org (mod)	PJ (IV) IJ (IV)	506 employees, 98 departments, 64 organizations	Mech + mod PJ → POS Org + mod IJ → supervisory trust
Ambrose et al.	In press	Org (mod)	Super IJ (IV) IJ Climate (DV, med)	489 individuals (406 employees and 83 supervisors), 83 work units, 72 organizations	Org + mod Super IJ → IJ Climate, and overall moderated mediation model supported
Andrews et al.	2008	Cent-HA (mod)	DJ (IV) PJ (IV) IJ (IV)	489 purchasing managers	Cent-HA + mod PJ → Job satisfaction Cent-HA + mod IJ → Job satisfaction Cent-HA did not mod DJ → job satisfaction
Andrews & Kacmar	2001	Form (IV) Cent-HA (IV)	PJ (DV) DJ (corr)	408 employees of a water treatment firm, multiple levels and departments	Form + related to PJ Cent-HA – related to PJ Form + corr w/ DJ Cent-HA + corr w/ DJ
Ang et al.	2003	TI (mod)	DJ (DV) PJ (DV)	466 ethnic Chinese workers in Singapore (253 local, 213 foreign)	TI + mod Employment status → DJ TI + mod Employment status → PJ
Aryee et al.	2004	Form (IV) Cent-Part (IV) Cent-HA (IV)	PJ (DV)	211 employees in 66 work groups, Indian marble mfg. firm	Form + related to PJ Cent-Part + related to PJ Cent-HA not related to PJ
Begley et al.	2006	Level (mod)	PJ (IV) DJ (IV)	605 employee-supervisor dyads, Chinese steel conglomerate	PJ → most outcomes stronger @ low levels DJ → most outcomes stronger @ high levels
Bollen et al.	2012	Level (IV) Level (mod)	PJ (IV)	100 participants in 50 Dutch mediation cases	Level – related to PJ Level – mod PJ → mediation effectiveness
Colquitt	2004	TI (mod)	Own PJ (IV) Others' PJ (IV)	1: 314 undergraduates 2: 300 undergraduates	TI + mod Justice consistency (own/others) → performance
Greenberg	1988	Level (IV)	Equity theory inputs	198 salaried employees, life insurance company	"Unearned" level of office related to performance change (+ and –)
Holtz & Harold	2012	IS (IV)	DJ (DV) PJ (DV) IntJ (DV) InfJ (control)	1: 158 employees, 122 supervisors, variety of firms 2: 105 employee-coworker dyads via StudyResponse	1: IS + related to DJ, PJ, IntJ 2: IS + related to DJ, PJ, IntJ, InfJ (InfJ not hypothesized)

Homburg & Furst	2005	Mech (IV) Org (IV)	Cust DJ (DV) Cust PJ (DV) Cust IJ (DV)	110 complaint managers & 550 complaining customers	Mech + related to customer DJ, PJ, & IJ Org + related to customer DJ, PJ, & IJ (Mech effect stronger)
Hulland, et al.	2012	Com-Int (mod)	DJ (IV) PJ (IV) IJ (IV)	203 sales and marketing managers, 38 firms, consumer packaged goods industry	Com-Int + mod DJ → relat. effectiveness Com-Int + mod PJ → RE Com-Int did not mod IJ → RE
Karambayya et al.	1992	Auth (corr)	DJ (corr) PJ (corr)	351 MBA & executive program students	Auth not corr w/ DJ or PJ (or fairness of invited 3rd party mediator)
Kim	2007	Org (IV)	Combined PJ & IJ (DV)	1,191 employees of 31 Korean firms	Org + related to combined PJ & IJ measure of justice
Kurland & Egan	1999	Form-Job Form-Com (corr only)	DJ (corr) PJ (corr)	206 public-sector employees 210 private-sector employees	Form-Job + corr w/ DJ & PJ Form-Com + corr w/ DJ (n.s. w/ PJ)
Lambert et al.	2006	Cent-Part (corr) Cent-HA (corr)	DJ (corr) PJ (corr)	272 correctional facility employees	Cent-Part + corr w/ DJ & PJ Cent-HA – corr w/ DJ & PJ
Lansberg	1984	Level (mod)	Fairness of 6 distribution rules	70 HR dept. employees, research and development firm	Level related to distribution rule preferences (Mid & upper managers prefer equity, clerical view equality and equity equally)
Long et al.	2011	Bureaucracy, Market, Clan (all IV)	Monitoring of PJ, DJ, IJ (all DV)	1: 138 Qualtrics respondents 2: 624 Qualtrics respondents	DJ, PJ, IJ monitoring + related to market, bureaucratic, clan control structures, respectively
Liden et al.	2004	TI (corr)	DJ (corr) PJ (corr)	168 employees (35 electronics firm, 133 machinery producing firm), 23 supervisors (5 electronics, 18 machinery)	TI not corr w/ DJ or PJ
Martin	1980	Cent (corr)	DJ (corr)	250 employees, education and services firm	Cent – corr w/ DJ
Mossholder et al.	1998	Pow-Leg (IV) Pow-Rew (IV)	PJ (DV)	1: 122 employees, public utility & computer services firms 2: 123 employees of a U.S. metropolitan hospital	1: Pow-Leg not related to PJ Pow-Rew not related to PJ 2: Pow-Leg not related to PJ Pow-Rew – related to PJ

(continued)

Table 26.1 Continued

Pearce et al.	1998	Bureaucracy (IV)	PJ (DV)	1604 managerial & professional employees of 5 electronics mfg. firms (four U.S., one Lithuanian)	Bureaucracy + related to PJ
Riolli & Savicki	2006	Pow-Leg (corr) Pow-Rew (corr)	PJ (corr)	103 employees, engineering firm	Pow-Leg – corr w/ PJ Pow-Rew – corr w/ PJ
Rosier et al.	2010	Org (IV, mod)	PJ (DV)	115 mid-level marketing managers in UK-based business-to-business service-based organizations	Org + related to PJ Org^2 – related to PJ (in top 30% Org structures, Org – related to PJ)
Schminke et al.	2000	Form (IV) Cent-Part (IV) Cent-HA (IV) Size (IV)	PJ (DV) IJ (DV)	209 employees of 11 organizations	Form, $Form^2$ not related to PJ Cent-Part + related to PJ Cent-HA – related to PJ (strongest effect) Size – related to IJ
Schminke et al.	2002	Form (IV) Cent-Part (IV) Cent-HA (IV) VC (IV) Size (IV) Level (mod)	DJ (DV) PJ (DV) IJ (DV)	212 employees in 45 departments of 35 organizations	Form + related to DJ, PJ, IJ Cent-Part + related to DJ, PJ Cent-HA – related to DJ, PJ, IJ VC not related to DJ, PJ, or IJ Size not related to DJ, PJ, or IJ Level + related to DJ, PJ Level mod 9 of 15 relationships between 5 structure and 3 justice types
Spell & Arnold	2007a	Mech (mod) Org (mod)	PJ (IV) IJ (IV)	677 employees in 72 work groups	Mech did not mod PJ → depression Mech + mod PJ → anxiety
Spell & Arnold	2007b	Mech (mod) Org (mod)	PJ climate (IV) IJ climate (IV)	483 employees in 56 work groups	Mech did not mod PJ Climate → mental health Org did not mod IJ Climate → mental health
Tripp	1993	Auth (IV)	Fairness goal (mod)	110 MBA students in negotiation exercise	Fairness goals – mod Auth → resources taken
Yen & Teng	2012	Cent-HA (IV)	PJ (DV)	318 employees of Taiwanese international tourist hotels	Cent-HA (IV) – related to PJ

[a]Role of variable indicates the relationship of structure and justice variables to each other in each study. The actual role in the overall model tested in the study may differ, for example, due to the presence of additional "upstream" or "downstream" variables in the model.

Abbreviations:

Roles/relationships: IV = independent variable, DV = dependent variable, mod = moderating variable, corr = correlational relationship only

Justice: DJ = distributive justice, PJ = procedural justice, IJ = interactional justice, IntJ = interpersonal justice, InfJ = informational justice, Cust = customer justice, Super IJ = Supervisor's interactional justice

Structure: Auth = formal authority, Cent = centralization, Com = communication, Com-Int = Interfunctional communication, Form = formalization, Form-Job = job formalization; Form-Com = Communication formalization, HA = hierarchy of authority, IS = Initiating structure, Level = organizational level, Mech = mechanistic structure, Org = organic structure, Part = participation, Pow = formal power, Pow-Leg = Legitimate power, Pow-Rew = Reward power, TI = Task interdependence, VC = Vertical complexity

Driven by an interest in how the impact of social structures and processes might be linked to employee psychology, Pearce, Bigley, and Branyiczki (1998) examined the impact of bureaucratic structure on the procedural justice perceptions of employees. The authors argued that multiple theories of social institutions have the potential to improve our understanding of how employees respond to fairness, observing that many of the characteristics of procedurally fair organizations (e.g., voice, bias suppression) parallel foundations of Weber's (1946) bureaucracy. They compared the responses of workers employed in organizations utilizing what they term "modern" bureaucratic structure (merit-based, rule-governed, with limited supervisory discretion on treatment of specific individuals) with those employed by an organization with a "neotraditional" structure (based on political or tribal histories, with wide discretion for managers in treatment of particular individuals). Modern bureaucratic structures were represented by US firms, and neotraditional structures were represented by a Lithuanian firm. Results of a study involving more than 1600 employees indicated that those in bureaucratic structures reported higher levels of procedural fairness.

More recently, Long, Bendersky, and Morrill (2011) were interested in what factors might determine the type of fairness to which employees might attend most closely, that is, which fairness issues are most professionally relevant for them. They explored how organizational control structures influence the type of fairness monitoring in which employees engage. The authors predicted that specific types of control structures (bureaucratic, market, and clan) would be related to specific types of fairness monitoring (procedural, distributive, and interactional). Bureaucratic controls convey to employees that successful performance involves executing task procedures successfully. Thus, employees will most closely monitor procedural fairness. Market controls convey to employees the importance of individual production outputs. Therefore, employees will most closely monitor distributive fairness. Clan controls emphasize the importance of developing collegial relationships and common values with organizational others. Thus, employees will monitor most closely interactional fairness. Results of two studies utilizing Qualtrics participants (N = 138, 624) supported these predictions.

The relationship between bureaucratic structures and justice has not been widely explored in the organizational literature. However, these two studies point to interesting results. They suggest bureaucratic structures, properly understood to mean those designed to engage in universalistic and merit-based treatment of employees, lead not only to greater levels of procedural fairness, but a greater focus on procedural fairness monitoring as well.

The Burns and Stalker (1961) Structural Contingency Framework

Structural contingency theory is based on the premise that no single organizational structure represents "the one best way to organize." Rather, the best structure for an organization depends on a series of contingencies it faces, such as degree of uncertainty involved in its production process, the degree of uncertainty in its markets, its strategies, its size, and so on. Some structures are better for stable, predictable settings, whereas others are better for volatile, unpredictable situations. The aim of structural contingency theory is to identify which organizational structures represent the best fit with the various organizational contingencies (Donaldson, 1996). Burns and Stalker's (1961) distinction between mechanistic and organic structures represents the most widely adopted framework for categorizing organizational structures at a general level and identifying the contingencies for which each represents the best fit.

Mechanistic forms of structure display certain structural characteristics, including high levels of task specialization, formalized rules and procedures, strict lines of authority, hierarchical systems of control, highly centralized power, vertical communication, and an internal (local) rather than general (cosmopolitan) focus on knowledge and skills. Accordingly, they are tight, rigid, and efficient, and best in stable conditions. Organic forms, by contrast, are characterized by tasks that involve a broader range of skills, sharing of knowledge and responsibility, decentralized decision-making, horizontal communication (of the advise-and-consult rather than command-and-control type), and a stronger sense of professionalism. As such, they are more adaptive and flexible, innovative, and best in changing conditions (Burns & Stalker, 1961; Donaldson, 1996).

The Burns and Stalker (1961) framework has been called "the most widely received contribution in the structural contingency theory literature" (Donaldson, 1996, p. 59). It is, therefore, not surprising that its influence has spread to scholars interested in organizational justice. This has happened in two ways. Some scholars have embraced the mechanistic-organic distinction in its general form. General measures of structure that capture overall rigidity and tightness versus overall flexibility and looseness have made this possible. Other scholars have embraced the Burns and Stalker framework in a more fine-grained way. Rather than employing an overall measure of the organic or mechanistic nature of structure, they have delved into its component parts, exploring specific components of structure (e.g., formalization, centralization, complexity) and how they relate to justice concerns. We review these studies next.

The Organic-Mechanistic Perspective

Although empirical research exploring the relationship between justice and structure examined specific dimensions of the Burns and Stalker (1961) framework (e.g., formalization, centralization, complexity) as early as 1980, Ambrose and Schminke (2003) were the first to assess the relationship between structure and justice from an overall organic-mechanistic perspective. Their work proposed that structure moderates the relationship between justice judgments and two types of social-exchange relationships experienced by an employee: organizational (represented by perceived organizational support [POS]) and supervisory (represented by supervisory trust). Ambrose and Schminke (2003) theorized that because formal rules and procedures define the environment of mechanistic organizations, these procedural rules will come to be seen as the standard by which fairness judgments are made, and individuals' justice concerns will focus primarily on procedural justice. In contrast, organic structures rely more on interpersonal interactions and relationships. Thus, in organic settings, individuals will focus more on interactional justice. Results of a study of 506 employees from 98 departments across 64 organizations supported both moderating hypotheses.

Homburg and Fürst (2005) extended the literature by exploring the impact of mechanistic and organic structure on the fairness judgments of customers. In particular, they examined the impact of mechanistic and organic approaches to complaint handling on customer justice judgments. They argued that the specific behavioral guidelines provided by a mechanistic approach would enhance customer perceptions of procedural justice, and the supportiveness of the internal environment with respect to complaint handling offered by an organic approach would enhance customer perceptions of distributive justice. In a study involving 110 complaint managers and 550 complaining customers, they found both mechanistic and organic approaches for handling customer complaints influenced customer perceptions of the distributive, procedural, and interactional fairness. Results further showed the mechanistic influence to be stronger overall than the organic influence. However, interaction effects revealed a complementary relationship between mechanistic and organic approaches, with a stronger organic mode softening the positive impact of a mechanistic approach.

In a study of employee mental health, Spell and Arnold (2007a) built on Ambrose and Schminke's (2003) assertion that a mechanistic structure will reinforce employee perceptions of procedural justice, and hypothesized that organizational structure would, therefore, moderate the relationship between justice judgments and the mental health of employees. In particular, Spell and Arnold (2007a) predicted mechanistic structure would strengthen the influence of procedural justice in lessening employee depression and anxiety. Results of a study of 677 employees in 72 different work units showed partial support for this hypothesis. Mechanistic structure strengthened the relationship between procedural justice and anxiety, but not between procedural justice and depression.

In a closely related study, Spell and Arnold (2007b) broadened their model of mental health in two ways. First, they raised the level of analysis of justice to the climate level. Second, they extended their view of the potential moderating effects of structure. In addition to their previous hypothesis that mechanistic structure would enhance the relationship between procedural justice (in this study, procedural justice climate) and mental health outcomes, they also hypothesized that organic structure would strengthen the relationship between interactional justice climate and mental health outcomes. A study of 483 employees across 56 work groups did not reveal support for their interaction hypotheses. Structure did not enhance the relationship between fair climates and the mental health of employees. The authors speculate this may mean structure does not represent as powerful a force in shaping the impact of collective constructs like climate, as it does on individual factors like individual justice judgments.

Other studies have considered whether justice or structure might represent components of larger mediating relationships. For example, building on Schminke, Ambrose, and Cropanzano's (2000) results that demonstrated a link between structure and fairness perceptions, Kim (2007) hypothesized that procedural and interactional justice would mediate the relationship between structure and organizational relationship type and quality. In the process of testing this mediation effect, Kim explored the direct effect of organic structure on justice on a sample of 1,191 employees of 31 Korean firms representing a variety of industries. Combining measures of procedural and interactional justice into a single justice construct, Kim found organic structure was significantly and positively related to justice perceptions.

Another study of the direct impact of organic structure on justice perceptions considered whether the relationship between structure and justice was necessarily linear. In contrast with earlier work positing a positive relationship between mechanistic structure and procedural justice, Rosier, Morgan, and Cadogan (2010) suggested a generally positive relationship between organic structure and procedural justice perceptions of midlevel marketing managers due to the additional midlevel manager empowerment offered by an organic structure. However, they also hypothesized that the benefits of an organic structure may decrease, even turning negative at very high levels, due to the lack of role and goal clarity that may be present in extremely organic settings. Results from 115 UK-based marketing managers supported their theorizing. Overall, more organic structures were related to higher levels of procedural justice. However, for firms with very organic structures (i.e., the top 30%), the relationship between structure and procedural justice perceptions became negative.

A final study exploring the impact of organic structure on organizational justice did so in exploring the trickle-down effects of justice. Ambrose, Schminke, & Mayer (2013) posited that an organic structure would moderate (strengthen) the relationship between a supervisor's perceptions of his or her own interactional fairness experiences and the interactional justice climate reported by his or her subordinates. They reasoned that the weak situation represented by organic structures would enhance the impact of one's personal fairness experiences. Further, they argued the increased ambiguity and more frequent face-to-face interaction of organic settings would make supervisor behaviors more salient and influential. Results of a study involving 489 individuals (406 employees and 83 supervisors) from 83 work units spanning 72 organizations supported this prediction.

Ambrose et al. (2013) further hypothesized an overall moderated mediation model in which both justice and structure play important roles. They predicted supervisor interactional justice would be related to group outcomes (group organizational citizenship behavior [OCB], group interpersonal deviance, and group organizational deviance) via conditional indirect effects, such that its relationship with outcomes would be moderated by workgroup structure and mediated by justice climate. Results of normal theory tests and bootstrapping procedures to create confidence intervals around the parameter estimates supported the moderated mediation hypotheses. That is, the moderating effect of organic structure on the relationship between supervisor interactional justice and interactional justice climate exerted a significant indirect (mediated) effect on outcomes at more organic levels of work-group structure.

In all, these studies demonstrate the potential power of mechanistic-organic structures to influence justice experiences in organizational settings. In most studies, hypothesized relationships between structure and justice emerged as predicted. They suggest that whether as a direct driver of justice judgments, or as a moderator of the relationship between justice and other constructs, mechanistic-organic structures play a significant role in the emergence and impact of justice perceptions. However, results also indicated some possible contradictions, both conceptually and empirically. For example, although the literature has regularly linked rules-oriented mechanistic structures with procedural fairness, Rosier et al. (2010) turned this view on its head by predicting—and finding—a positive relationship between organic structure and procedural fairness.

As noted earlier, mechanistic and organic are global descriptions of structures that display a related set of structural characteristics like formalization, centralization, complexity, and so on. Although broadly related in terms of comprising tight and efficient (mechanistic) or loose and flexible (organic) structures, these structural components describe distinct structural characteristics that do not always move together and operate on individual and organizational processes in distinct ways. Thus, in an attempt to understand more fully the relationship between structure and justice, researchers have unpacked the mechanistic-organic construct further, exploring the relationship between justice and individual structural components. In the next subsections, we review this work.

Formalization

Structural formalization is the extent to which organizations seek to ensure uniformity in job behavior and system operations through formal, written rules, procedures, instructions, and communications (Pugh, Hickson, Hinings, & Turner, 1968). Perhaps the earliest empirical evidence of a relationship between justice and formalization appears in Kurland and Egan's (1999) research comparing the differences between public- and private-sector employees. The authors distinguished between two types of formalization. Job formalization refers to the structure of the work process itself, and communication formalization refers to the structure of communication between supervisors and subordinates. Although they did not expressly hypothesize about the relationship between justice and formalization, correlational results reported in their work are suggestive. Correlational data from 206 public-sector employees (two organizations) and 210 private-sector employees (five organizations) show job formalization was positively related to both distributive and procedural justice. Communication formalization was positively related to distributive justice as well.

Schminke et al. (2000) were the first to hypothesize a specific relationship between formalization and justice perceptions. They noted the positive impact of consistency that formalized procedures and rewards impart, thus suggesting a positive relationship between formalization and procedural justice (Leventhal, 1980). However, they also noted the threat that too much formalization represents, potentially leading to what Sitkin and Bies (1993) have termed the legalistic organization. They therefore hypothesized that these opposing forces of consistency and legalism may result in a nonlinear "inverted U" relationship between formalization and justice judgments. That is, although some formalization may enhance justice, too much of a good thing may harm justice perceptions. Results, based on 209 participants across 11 organizations, did not support either a linear or inverted-U relationship between formalization and procedural justice. The authors speculated this may be due to a conceptual confusion between the amount of formalization (which they measured) and the appropriateness of the formalization (which they did not).

However, subsequent research provides stronger support for a relationship between formalization and procedural justice. Schminke, Cropanzano, and Rupp (2002) examined the justice perceptions of 212 employees in 45 departments representing 35 organizations. Building on the parallel between consistency as a foundation for both procedural justice (Leventhal, 1980) and formalized structures, Schminke et al. hypothesized a positive relationship between formalized structures and justice judgments. They found formalization to be positively related to distributive, procedural, and interactional justice.

Similarly, in a study of 418 employees representing various levels and departments of a water management firm, Andrews and Kacmar (2001) argued that the rules and policies dictated by formalized systems will be viewed as more procedurally fair than systems in which such practices are absent. They predicted and found that structural formalization was positively related to perceptions of procedural fairness. Although the Andrews and Kacmar model did not formally predict a relationship between formalization and distributive justice, correlational evidence indicated a positive relationship between the two.

Aryee, Chen, and Budhwar (2004) also hypothesized a positive relationship between formalization and procedural justice because formalized systems constrain individual discretion in behavior in favor of rules-oriented behavior, which should be employed impartially and thus perceived as more fair. Their results, based on a sample of 211 employees representing 66 work groups of an Indian marble manufacturing firm, supported this prediction.

In all, evidence suggests structural formalization is positively related to organizational justice, in particular procedural justice. Notwithstanding the results of Schminke et al. (2000), research linking formalization and justice has demonstrated a strong positive impact of formalized systems on the procedural fairness that employees experience at work.

Centralization

Perhaps the most-studied structural factor related to justice is centralization, which refers to the concentration of power or authority in an organization. The literature often identifies two subcomponents of centralization: participation in decision-making and hierarchy of authority. Participation in decision-making refers to how concentrated decision-making power with respect to establishing policy is, and how involved employees are in those issues. Hierarchy of authority refers to how concentrated decision-making power with respect to performing tasks is, such as the structural autonomy one has in one's job (Hage & Aiken, 1967). Low participation and high hierarchy of authority each reflect more centralized structures.

As with formalization, the first evidence of a relationship between centralization and justice was not hypothesized explicitly. Rather, it emerged in Martin's (1980) study of turnover at an education and services firm located in the central United States. Correlational data from the 250 employees participating in the study showed a significant and negative relationship between structural centralization and distributive justice perceptions. It would be 20 years before this relationship was revisited in a formal way.

The first formally hypothesized relationship between centralization and justice appeared in Schminke et al. (2000). This research examined the two subcomponents of centralization—participation in decision making and hierarchy of authority—and their relationship with procedural justice. The authors predicted that lower levels of centralization (i.e., higher participation and lower hierarchy of authority) would be related to higher levels of procedural fairness through the structure of organizational procedures. Process control (voice) and decision control (choice) have long been identified as attributes of procedural fairness (Thibaut & Walker, 1975), and they align closely with the two dimensions of centralization. Results supported both predictions. In a subsequent paper, Schminke et al. (2002) expanded this analysis to include distributive and interactional justice as well. Results indicated hierarchy of authority was negatively related to all three justice types. Participation was positively related to distributive and procedural justice, but unrelated to interactional justice.

Andrews and Kacmar (2001) also predicted centralization would be negatively related to procedural justice, due to the positive impact a decentralized structure would have on employee opportunity for input and thus, perceptions of voice. They operationalized centralization as hierarchy of authority and results supported their prediction. In addition, although they did not formally model a relationship between centralization and distributive justice, correlational evidence indicated a negative relationship between the two.

Similarly, following arguments offered by Schminke et al. (2000), Aryee et al. (2004) predicted higher levels of participation and lower levels of hierarchy of authority (both indicative of lower centralization) would be related to higher levels of procedural fairness. Results indicated that as predicted, participation was positively related to procedural justice. However, hierarchy of authority was not.

With the exception of Martin (1980), the studies examined thus far in this section also explored structural formalization (see earlier). However, more recent studies have examined the relationship between centralization and justice absent any focus on formalization. A study of correctional officer job stress (Lambert, Hogan, & Allen, 2006) did not explicitly model a relationship between centralization and justice perceptions. However, because both centralization and justice were examined as predictors of job stress, correlational evidence is available. These data, from 272 employees of a Midwestern correctional facility, show higher centralization—as indicated by both lower levels of participation and higher levels of hierarchy of authority—was related to lower levels of procedural and distributive justice.

Beyond studies of the impact of centralization on justice perceptions, scholars have also examined centralization as a moderator. Andrews, Baker, and Hunt (2008), for example, argued that centralization should moderate the relationship between justice and outcomes. Building on arguments based in referent cognitions theory (Folger, 1986) regarding the amount of control an individual has over his or her actions and outcomes, they predicted that centralization in the form of hierarchy of authority would strengthen the relationship between all three justice types they explored (distributive, procedural, and interactional) and job satisfaction. A study of 489 purchasing managers found that centralization moderated the relationship for procedural and interactional justice, but not for distributive justice.

Research exploring the link between centralization and justice continues. Yen and Teng (2012) explored the role of procedural justice as a mediator of the relationship between centralization and employee outcomes (OCB and deviance). Following arguments presented by Schminke et al. (2002) and Ambrose and Schminke (2003), Yen and Teng hypothesized that increased centralization would exert a negative effect on perceptions of procedural justice, which in turn would impact both deviant and citizenship behaviors on the part of employees. In a study of 318 employees of Taiwanese international tourist hotels, Yen and Teng utilized a measure of centralization that reflected hierarchy of authority, and found it to be negatively related to procedural justice.

Taken together, these studies indicate justice and structural centralization are related in meaningful ways. Both components of centralization have been shown to negatively impact procedural fairness, although hierarchy of authority has been explored more deeply than participation. Evidence also links centralization to other aspects of justice, and recent evidence suggests the relationships may go beyond direct effects to include moderating effects as well.

Formal Power and Authority

Closely related to centralization are studies of formal power and authority. The distinction lies in the fact that formal power and authority exist and exert influence throughout the organization, irrespective of how concentrated that power is (i.e., centralization). Because we are interested in formal structure and its relationship to justice, we now turn to studies exploring potential links between formal power or formal authority and justice. By limiting our attention to formal power and authority, we bypass nonstructural (individual) sources of power and authority like charisma and expertise as part of our review. These may be impactful with respect to justice, but fall outside our focus on formal organizational structures.

Perhaps the earliest available evidence regarding the relationship between formal authority and justice emerges in Karambayya, Brett, and Lytle's (1992) exploration of third party participation in resolving disputes. Although the power distinction between third party participants who had formal authority over the disputing parties (supervisors) versus those who did not (peers) was not part of the formal hypothesis development of the paper, correlational evidence provides some insights. In all, 351 participants from MBA and executive programs participated in a simulated organizational dispute experience. Correlational results indicate that whether a third-party participant (who is asked to intervene in the dispute) had formal authority over the disputants was not related to subsequent disputant ratings of procedural fairness, distributive fairness, or the fairness of the third party.

Research has explored the potential moderating effect of justice on the use of formal authority. In a study of 110 MBA students, Tripp (1993) explored this relationship by examining the moderating effect of fairness goals on the tendency for negotiators high on formal authority (those with unilateral rather than bilateral decision control) to take more of the negotiated resources. In one experimental condition of the negotiation exercise, high-authority negotiators were provided a goal of appearing fair in their decisions. In the other, high-authority negotiators were provided a goal of maximizing their personal returns. As hypothesized, fairness goals moderated the tendency for high-authority negotiators to take more resources.

In addition to the moderating effects of justice, research has also examined fairness as a mediator of the impact of formal power on outcomes. Mossholder, Bennett, Kemery, and Wesolowski (1998) suggested procedural justice would mediate the relationship between supervisors' use of various bases of power and subordinates' job satisfaction and organizational commitment. In this study, the authors examined five bases of power based on French and Raven's (1959) framework: referent power, expert power, coercive power, reward power, and legitimate power. Three of these (referent, expert, and coercive) are often seen primarily as personal rather than positional (formal) in nature and, therefore, lie outside our focus. Referent power is the ability to convey to others feelings of personal acceptance or approval. Expert power reflects the ability to deliver knowledge and expertise. Coercive power is the ability to deliver undesired outcomes or to remove desired outcomes. Although coercive power may be positional, it is most often characterized as including threats, confrontation, and punishment outside of normal role expectations (Hinkin & Schriesheim, 1990; 1994) and, therefore, also lies outside our interests.

The other two bases of power, reward and legitimate, more clearly reflect formal positional power and are, therefore, within our scope of interest. However, Mossholder et al. (1998) found little evidence that procedural justice mediated the relationship between these formal bases of power and employee attitudes. In Study 1, which involved 122 employees of two organizations (a public utility and a computer-services firm), neither reward nor legitimate power was significantly related to procedural justice. In Study 2, which involved 123 employees of a metropolitan hospital in the United States, only reward power was significantly related to procedural justice. Legitimate power was not.

In all, this paper suggests informal, individual sources of power appear to be more strongly related to fairness than formal, structural sources of power. However, correlational data from a later study calls that result into question. Riolli and Savicki (2006) explored the impact of fairness and leadership [operationalized according to the French and Raven (1959) bases of power] on employee outcomes during periods of organizational change. They did not hypothesize a relationship between fairness and power bases. However, correlational data from their study of 103 employees of a nationwide engineering firm showed reward and legitimate power were both significantly and negatively correlated with ratings of procedural justice.

These studies demonstrate varied patterns of relationships between justice and formal power and authority. Direct effects, mediation effects, and moderating effects have all emerged in the literature and in these studies. However, in spite of the conceptual overlap between formalized power or authority and structural centralization, these studies suggest there is something fundamentally different at work in the relationship between formal power and justice than we saw in the relationship between centralization and justice. Whereas centralization has demonstrated fairly consistent relationships with fairness, the evidence regarding the relationship between formalized power or formal authority and justice is far less clear.

Size and Structural Complexity

Some scholars treat size as a structural component in its own right (Meyer, 1972), whereas others view it as a proxy for organizational complexity (Fredrickson, 1984; Wally & Baum, 1994). Although justice scholars have often treated size and complexity as distinct variables, the structure literature considers them closely related, and, thus, for the purposes of this review, we will present them together.

Schminke et al. (2000) hypothesized large organizations (measured by number of employees) would be associated with lower levels of interactional justice for two reasons: the increasing dependence on impersonal rules and regulations often required in large-scale enterprises, and the greater propensity for political behavior in large organizations. Results supported that hypothesis. In a subsequent study, Schminke et al. (2002) explored both the impact of size and vertical complexity (the number of levels in an organization's hierarchy) on distributive, procedural, and interactional justice. Both sets of arguments followed those of Schminke et al. (2000), although results demonstrated no relationship between size or vertical complexity and any of the three justice types. Taken together, these studies suggest the relationship between size, vertical complexity, and justice remains unclear.

Beyond these aspects of structure, commonly ascribed to Burns and Stalker's (1961) conceptualization of mechanistic and organic structures, lie other structural dimensions. Although they have not garnered the attention that the Burns and Stalker dimensions have, they nonetheless offer important insights about the relationship between justice and structure. In the following sections, we explore task interdependence, communication systems, structure resulting from leadership, and hierarchical level.

Task Interdependence

Task interdependence reflects the extent to which work unit members must interact with one another in order to accomplish the unit task successfully. Three studies offer insights into the relationship between justice and this aspect of structure.

In a study examining how foreign workers respond to their jobs relative to local workers, Ang, Van Dyne, and Begley (2003) hypothesized foreign workers would report lower levels of distributive and procedural fairness. Further, they predicted higher levels of task interdependence would moderate those relationships, such that the relationships would be stronger under high task interdependence, because the greater interaction required of task interdependent employees would emphasize differences that exist between them. Their study involving ethnic Chinese workers in Singapore (253 local employees and 213 foreign workers from the People's Republic of China) showed support for this hypothesis. Task interdependence strengthened the relationship between employment status (foreign versus local) and both distributive and procedural justice. Although not a hypothesized relationship, task interdependence did not exert a direct effect on either procedural or distributive justice.

A second study reinforces this finding that task interdependence does not appear to influence justice judgments directly. Liden, Wayne, Jaworski, and Bennett (2004) conducted a field examination of social loafing. No relationships were hypothesized between task interdependence and distributive and procedural fairness, but all three were predicted to influence social loafing and therefore, correlational evidence of their relationship was presented. Results from a sample of 168 employees (35 from an electronics firm, 133 from a machinery producing firm) and 23 supervisors (5 electronics, 18 machinery) revealed no significant correlation between task interdependence and either distributive justice or procedural justice.

Finally, Colquitt (2004) explored how the interaction of one's own justice experiences interacts with one's perception of the justice experienced by other team members to influence team performance. He hypothesized that consistency between own and others' justice experiences would enhance team performance. He further reasoned that task interdependence would moderate this effect, so as to strengthen the effect under conditions of high interdependence, by increasing the likelihood of social comparisons between teammates. Study 1, involving 314 undergraduate participants, supported this prediction. (In addition, task interdependence was not significantly correlated with participant ratings of own and others' justice.) Study 2, involving 300 undergraduate participants, demonstrated similar results. Task interdependence interacted significantly with the degree of consistency between participant ratings of own and others' fair treatment in predicting team conflict, cooperation, and decision accuracy. Task interdependence was again not significantly correlated with participant ratings of either own or others' fair treatment.

In all, these studies point to task interdependence as playing a potential moderating role in how the effects of fair treatment play out in organizational settings. However, they are consistent in demonstrating task interdependence appears to play no direct role in determining justice judgments.

Communication Systems

The justice literature has a strong interest in communication, such as its focus on the role of voice. Therefore, structural mechanisms for establishing and maintaining communication within and between departments may play an important role in shaping fairness perceptions and their impact on employee and organization outcomes. One study has explicitly addressed this issue. Hulland, Nenkov, and Barclay (2012) reasoned that the existence of effective communication channels between functional departments like marketing and sales would improve integration, harmony, understanding, and commitment between the departments. Thus, they hypothesized that effective communication channels would moderate—in this case enhance—the positive impact of justice on the quality of interdepartmental relationships. Further, they suggested higher levels of distributive, procedural, and interactional justice should enhance the quality of relationship between sales and marketing departments. They surveyed 203 sales and marketing managers from 38 firms in the consumer packaged goods industry and found that interfunctional communication moderated the relationship between distributive justice and relationship effectiveness, and procedural justice and relationship effectiveness. It did not moderate the effect of interactional justice on relationship effectiveness. Overall however, these results point to the potential power of communication structures to enhance the positive impacts of justice in organizational settings.

Structure via Leadership

Leadership is not generally considered a structural factor. However, one aspect of leadership has a significant conceptual link to structure. The initiating structure dimension of what is known as the Ohio State leadership behaviors (Judge, Piccolo, & Ilies, 2004) involves leader action aimed at defining and organizing roles, specifying goals, and establishing well-defined patterns and channels of communication (Fleishman, 1973). Scholars have suggested links between initiating structure and justice. For example, Judge et al. (2004) suggested (but did not investigate) that justice judgments may mediate the effect of initiating structure on outcomes.

Recent research has explored this thinking. Holtz and Harold (2012) hypothesized employee perceptions of justice would mediate the relationship between initiating structure and counterproductive work behaviors. In doing so, they predicted that the consistent, standardized work environments resulting from structure would be positively related to distributive, procedural, and informational (but not interpersonal) justice and explored these predictions in two studies. Study 1 involved 158 employees and 122 supervisors from a variety of organizations. Results supported all their predictions, irrespective of whether employee or supervisor ratings of leader initiating structure were considered. Study 2 involved 105 employee–co-worker dyads, recruited through the Study Response Project. Again, results supported all their predictions that initiating structure was positively related to distributive, procedural, and informational justice. In addition, Study 2 revealed a nonhypothesized positive relationship between initiating structure and interpersonal justice.

Hierarchical Level

Before concluding our review, we turn to one final aspect of structure and its relationship with justice. It involves the question of whether where one lies in the organization's structural hierarchy influences justice perceptions.

Considerable research has explored this question, beginning with Lansberg (1984). This study hypothesized a contingency (moderating) relationship between an employee's level in the organizational hierarchy and his or her views of what constitutes fair distribution rules. Participants, 70 employees of a human resource department within a research and development laboratory (12 upper managers, 24 middle managers, and 34 clerical employees), were asked to choose from among six possible allocation choices as the fairest for distributing a lump-sum bonus pool among employees: (1) Winner take all: Allocate the entire amount to the top performer in the organization, (2) Equity-all: Allocate proportionally to each employee's contribution to the organization overall, (3) Equity-unit: Allocate proportionally to each employee's contribution to his or her work unit, (4) Current: Allocate proportionally to each employee's current salary, (5) Need: Allocate so those who earn least get proportionally more than those who earn more, or (6) Equality: Allocate an equal dollar amount to each employee. Results indicated an employee's position within the organizational hierarchy was related to his or her judgments of the fairness of the various distribution rules. For example, upper and middle managers showed a strong preference for equity principles, whereas clerical workers did not differentiate between the fairness of equity and equality principles.

The level one occupies in an organization may be related to fairness in other ways as well. For example, Greenberg (1988) demonstrated that the occupied level need not be real or permanent to deliver effects related to justice. Greenberg's study followed 198 salaried employees of a life insurance underwriting department who were temporarily displaced from their offices during remodeling. During a two-week remodeling period, employees were randomly assigned to higher-status, equal-status, or lower-status offices than they normally occupied. In accordance with equity theory principles (Adams, 1965), employees assigned to higher status offices than they had "earned" significantly raised their level of performance, whereas those assigned to lower status offices than they had earned exhibited significant declines in performance. Thus, in relation to equity theory, structural factors like the position one occupies in an organization (even if temporary and unearned) may be among the critical factors employees consider when making judgments about the equity of their position.

Organizational level has been conceptualized as a predictor of justice as well as a moderator of the relationship between structural facets of organizations and the fairness perceptions related to them. Schminke et al. (2002) hypothesized that because of their positions, individuals at higher organizational levels would experience higher levels of distributive, procedural, and interactional fairness. Results supported the prediction for distributive and procedural justice, but not for interactional justice. Schminke et al. also predicted higher organizational level would moderate (weaken) the relationships between five structural components [formalization, centralization (participation and hierarchy of authority), size, and vertical complexity] and the three types of justice. Level moderated 9 of 15 possible relationships (five structural dimensions by three justice types) in the anticipated direction.

Others have conceptualized organizational level as a moderator as well, although in a different form. Begley, Lee, and Hui (2006) posited that organizational level would moderate the relationship between justice perceptions and employee attitudes and behavior. Specifically, they predicted that because procedural justice is of greater concern to lower-level employees, it would be a better predictor of outcomes for lower-level employees (and distributive justice would be a better predictor of outcomes for higher-level employees) including job satisfaction, organizational trust, organizational commitment, intent to quit, altruism, conscientiousness, and civic virtue. Results from a study of 605 employee-supervisor pairs from a Chinese steel conglomerate mostly supported their predictions.

Bollen, Ittner, and Euwema (2012) also framed level as both an IV and a moderator in the same study. In a study of mediation processes in Holland between individuals in different hierarchical positions, they predicted that lower-level employees would experience lower levels of procedural justice due to the lower levels of control and higher levels of uncertainty they face. Results from 50 dyads engaged in mediation supported their prediction. They also predicted that level would moderate the positive relationship between perceptions of procedural justice and assessments of mediation effectiveness, such that the relationship would be stronger for lower-level employees. Results also supported this prediction.

Together, these studies provide evidence that it is not just the type of structure that matters, but where an employee finds him or herself within that structure also matters. Research suggests organizational level exerts both direct and moderating effects on justice processes in organizational settings. That is, it plays an important role not only in how much justice an employee experiences but also in how those judgments are made.

Discussion and Conclusions

When it comes to matters of organizational justice, these studies demonstrate that context matters. However, as James (1993, p. 44) notes, some justice scholars appear to be of the opinion that contextual factors "generally have such complex patterns of influence and interrelationship that it is, in fact, best to simply ignore them." Poppycock! The notion that an action or an outcome in an organizational setting can be judged as fair or not, without considering the context in which it happens, is misguided. Context matters, and when it comes to organizations, structure is perhaps the most important of all contextual factors.

In this review we have explored structure and its relationship with justice from multiple perspectives. We have seen structure presented as a global construct conveying a general sense of looseness and adaptability (organic) or rigidity and efficiency (mechanistic). We have seen structure presented at a more fine-grained level, so as to explore the impact of specific aspects of structure including formalization, centralization, power and authority, size and complexity, task interdependence, and communication systems. We have examined how some organizational constructs that may not appear to have structural consequences actually do (e.g., leadership initiating structure). We have also considered how one's position within the organizational structure, in addition to the structure itself, may shape justice judgments in the organization.

Lessons Learned

Beyond the specifics of the individual studies reviewed, what does this exercise teach us? Many things. For example, it is clear that "justice and structure" does not constitute a defined field of study. Although a great deal of work has addressed questions related to both justice and structure, it has done so in a piecemeal fashion. As a body of research, this work has demonstrated no identifiable focus, patterns, or direction. In all, it is less a field of study than an accumulation of studies.

Nevertheless, a lack of organizing focus does not mean we cannot draw important insights from this work. Structure and justice may not represent a formal field of study, but over the past 30 years, many leading scholars have asked—and answered—interesting and important questions about the relationship between justice and structure. Even fragmented, disconnected, disjointed research can contribute to our understanding of a phenomenon. That has happened here, and at least four themes emerge from this work.

First, our review suggests that incorporating organizational structure into organizational justice research greatly enhances our understanding of fairness, its antecedents, and its consequences in organizational settings. Whether we view this important contextual factor from a broad theoretical perspective (e.g., Ambrose & Schminke, 2003; Burns & Stalker, 1961) or a more focused perspective (e.g., Aryee et al., 2004; Schminke et al., 2000, 2002), structure is tightly interwoven with the emergence and impact of justice judgments. Further, in addition to displaying direct effects on justice judgments, research shows organizational structure may play important moderating and mediating roles with respect to justice perceptions and justice-relevant antecedents and outcomes (Ang et al., 2003; Begley et al., 2006; Bollen et al., 2012; Schminke et al., 2002).

Second, the research reviewed in this review point to issues of power and authority as central to understanding justice in context. Studies that involve centralization—which span both participation and hierarchy of authority—combined with studies of formal power and authority, represent nearly half of all studies that have explored the link between justice and structure (see table). Because the relationship between justice and many aspects of structure has yet to be explored, we cannot say centralization and power necessarily represent the most significant structural component involved in issues of organizational fairness. However, most of the papers reviewed tested theory-driven models of structure, in which issues related to power bubbled to the surface for conceptual reasons, prior to the emergence of empirical evidence. This pattern of reasonable theoretical explanations, combined with a stable set of empirical outcomes, points to centralization and power as a sound starting point for future conceptualizations of organizational justice.

Third, there does not appear to be a linear, evolutionary pattern to scholars' exploration of structure and justice. In many literatures, when a new family of constructs is introduced to the conversation, research progresses in a somewhat predictable pattern. IVs are converted to DVs. Main effects give way to mediating and moderating effects. Over time, the literature moves from antecedents to consequences (or vice versa), direct to indirect effects, and boundary conditions of the emergent phenomena. Our presentation of justice and structure research shows no such patterns. Earlier, we noted that structure and justice does not represent a field of study as we commonly envision it, because it is not driven by a focused, coherent set of research questions. However, the situation is even more freeform than that. Not only have researchers failed to converge on a fixed set of themes, but the emergent patterns of their work has not started to mirror a typical pattern of empirical progression, either accidentally or by intent. We have plenty of studies from which to draw insights. But viewed as a whole, the positioning of structure and justice variables within those studies appears haphazard.

Finally, our review reveals that organizational authorities have substantial control regarding many of these structural relationships. Consider the work of Holtz and Harold (2012), who demonstrated that leaders can effectively influence justice perceptions by initiating structure in the workplace. Work like this illustrates that structure may be viewed as an organizational asset or resource that managers may use to promote justice and alleviate the negative repercussions of injustice in the workplace. As a characteristic of the formal side of organizational context, structure offers managers the opportunity to modify the organizational context in a manner not always as possible with the informal characteristics like climate, culture, and politics. Thus, structural characteristics represent a manageable facet of organizational context for managers concerned with justice. Furthermore, even in instances in which informal facets of organizational climate may underlie justice concerns, they may be difficult to change without addressing formal considerations as well. For example, if a culture of corruption exists in an organization, it is unlikely that this culture will change without modifying formal contextual factors first (e.g., clarifying rules, procedures, and expectations).

Future Research

Our review also points to several promising areas for additional research. First, we have described empirical work that shows the justice and structure relationship as fragmented and piecemeal. Structure and justice are both, by nature, multidimensional. Yet few studies employ a comprehensive approach to either; most explore only one or two aspects of structure and the relationship with one or two facets of justice. Only by crafting more comprehensive models will we be able to isolate the most meaningful relationships between specific aspects of structure and those of justice.

Second, although research has explored the relationship between a number of specific structural dimensions and justice, we still know little about how other structural elements (e.g., integration, differentiation, horizontal complexity) may impact this relationship. These elements comprise important aspects of the organizational context. As justice researchers, we should not ignore them simply because they have not received attention in our literature to date.

Third, the structure of teams and work units is changing (Cramton & Webber, 2005). For example, more organizations are taking advantage of benefits found in geographically dispersed work groups, which rely on strong, healthy communication and integration systems (Mohrman 1999). Understanding the role justice plays in these structures can provide insightful recommendations for practice. For example, justice should be an important mediator in the relationship between these communication systems and work outcomes. Interactional justice should mediate the relationship between communication systems and relationship quality (Leader-member exchange theory [LMX] and team cohesion). The communication systems will not be effective if they are not used to transmit information appropriately (informational justice), or are used to treat employees disrespectfully (interpersonal justice).

The role of leadership suggests another interesting path for future research. For example, Holtz and Harold (2012) argue that if a supervisor does not define and enforce clear rules and performance standards (i.e., exhibits weak structure), employees may feel it is okay to slack on the job. However, they also suggest that, if a supervisor provides too much structure, employees may feel they lack autonomy and control, which may lead to counterproductive behavior (e.g., Fox & Spector, 1999). Therefore, future researchers may aim their endeavors at identifying the ideal level of structure.

Similarly, we do not know much about whether and how employees differentiate between individual and structural sources of (in)justice. Although some evaluations of organizational mistreatment may be easily connected to the specific individuals involved, other beliefs that such conduct is prevalent and ongoing in the organization are more likely to be linked to organizational structural features (Dutton, Dukerich, & Harquail 1994). Thus, recent research suggesting employees may hold the organization responsible for injustices that occur in the workplace (Shoss, Eisenberger, Restubog, & Zagenczyk, 2013) provides another possibility for interesting research.

Of course, these are not the only potentially productive paths to making significant additional inroads into our understanding of justice, structure, and the relationship between them. For example, structure and fairness may be fluid, and this fluidity may alter our perspectives on the most important research questions. For instance, as conditions change, structure also changes. Therefore, studies of the relationship between fairness and structure may give way to studies of fairness and changes in structure. Likewise, the role of justice expectations, mainly in the form of anticipatory justice and injustice (e.g., Rodell & Colquitt, 2009; Shapiro & Kirkman, 2001), rather than justice judgments, may move to the forefront in our research. These examples point to the potential richness of research in this area, as research in the two underlying domains—justice and structure—continues to evolve.

Conclusion

Shafritz and Ott declared that "Most problems in an organization result from structural flaws and can be solved by changing the structure" (1996, p. 204). It is unclear whether such a strong statement applies literally to issues of organizational fairness, but we admire their boldness nonetheless. This review points to an important and recurring set of relationships between the various aspects of justice, and the multiple components of structure. Our hope is that justice scholars will embrace the opportunity to put the "organization" back in organizational justice, by paying heed to the critical role of organizational context, in the form of organizational structure.

References

Adams, J. S. (1965). Inequity in social exchange. In L. Berkowitz (Ed.), *Advances in experimental social psychology* (Vol. 2, pp. 267–299). New York, NY: Academic Press.

Agarwal, R., Croson, R., & Mahoney, J. T. (2010). The role of incentives and communication in strategic alliances: An experimental investigation. *Strategic Management Journal, 31*, 413–437.

Ambrose, M. L. (2002). Contemporary justice research: A new look at familiar questions. *Organizational Behavior and Human Decision Processes, 89*(1), 803–812.

Ambrose, M. L., & Schminke, M. (2001). Are flexible organizations the death knell for the future of procedural justice? In R. Cropanzano (Ed.), *Justice in the workplace II: From theory to practice* (pp. 229–244). Hillsdale, NJ: Erlbaum.

Ambrose, M. L., & Schminke, M. (2003). Organization structure as a moderator of the relationship between procedural justice, interactional justice, perceived organizational support, and supervisory trust. *Journal of Applied Psychology, 88*(2), 295–305.

Ambrose, M. L., Schminke, M., & Mayer, D. M. (2013). Trickle-down effects of supervisor perceptions of interactional justice: A moderated mediation approach. *Journal of Applied Psychology, 98*, 678-689.

Andrews, M. C., Baker, T. L., & Hunt, T. G. (2008). The interactive effects of centralization on the relationship between justice and satisfaction. *Journal of Leadership & Organizational Studies, 15*(2), 135–144.

Andrews, M. C., & Kacmar, K. M. (2001). Discriminating among organizational politics, justice, and support. *Journal of Organizational Behavior, 22*(4), 347–366.

Ang, S., Van Dyne, L., & Begley, T. M. (2003). The employment relationships of foreign workers versus local employees: A field study of organizational justice, job satisfaction, performance, and OCB. *Journal of Organizational Behavior, 24*(5), 561–583.

Aryee, S., Chen, Z. X., & Budhwar, P. S. (2004). Exchange fairness and employee performance: An examination of the relationship between organizational politics and procedural justice. *Organizational Behavior and Human Decision Processes, 94*(1), 1–14.

Begley, T. M., Lee, C., & Hui, C. (2006). Organizational level as a moderator of the relationship between justice perceptions and work-related reactions. *Journal of Organizational Behavior, 27*(6), 705–721.

Bollen, K., Ittner, H., & C. Euwema, M. (2012). Mediating hierarchical labor conflicts: Procedural justice makes a difference-for subordinates. *Group Decision & Negotiation, 21*(5), 621–636.

Burns, T., & Stalker, G. M. (1961). *The management of innovation*. London, UK: Tavistock.

Clegg, S. R., & Hardy, C. (1996). Organizations, organization, and organizing. In S. R. Clegg, C. Hardy, & W. R. Nord (Eds.), *Handbook of organization studies* (pp. 1–28). Thousand Oaks, CA: Sage.

Colquitt, J. A. (2004). Does the justice of the one interact with the justice of the many? Reactions to procedural justice in teams. *Journal of Applied Psychology, 89*(4), 633–646.

Cramton, C. D., & Webber, S. S. (2005). Relationships among geographic dispersion, team processes, and effectiveness in software development work teams. *Journal of Business Research, 58*(6), 758–765.

Cropanzano, R., & Greenberg, J. (1997). Progress in organizational justice: Tunneling through the maze. In L. T. Robertson & C. L. Cooper (Eds.), *International review of industrial and organizational psychology* (pp. 317–372). New York, NY: Wiley.

Daft, R. L. (2007). Fundamentals of organization structure. In R. L. Daft, *Organization Theory and Design* (pp. 88–133). Mason, OH: Thomson.

Donaldson, L. (1996). The normal science of structural contingency theory. In S. R. Clegg, C. Hardy, & W. R. Nord (Eds.), *Handbook of organization studies* (pp. 57–76). Thousand Oaks, CA: Sage.

Dutton, J. E., Dukerich, J. M., & Harquail, C. V. (1994). Organizational images and member identification. *Administrative Science Quarterly, 39*(2), 239–263.

Fleishman, E. A. (1973). Twenty years of consideration and structure. In E. A. Fleishman & J. G. Hunt (Eds.), *Current developments in the study of leadership* (pp. 1–40). Carbondale, IL: Southern Illinois University Press.

Folger, R. (1986). Rethinking equity theory: A referent cognitions model. In H. W. Biefhoff, R. L., Cohen, & J. Greenberg (Eds.), *Justice in social relations* (pp. 145–162). New York, NY: Plenum.

Fox, S., & Spector, P. E. (1999). A model of work frustration–aggression. *Journal of Organizational Behavior, 20*(6), 915–931.

Fredrickson, J. W. (1984). The comprehensiveness of strategic decision processes: Extension, observations, future directions. *Academy of Management Journal, 27*(3), 445–466.

French, J., & Raven, B. H. (1959). The bases of social power. In D. Cartwtight (Ed.), *Studies in social power* (pp.150–167). Ann Arbor, MI: University of Michigan, Institute for Social Research.

Greenberg, J. (1988). Equity and workplace status: A field experiment. *Journal of Applied Psychology, 73*(4), 606–613.

Greenberg, J. (1993). The social side of fairness: Interpersonal and informational classes of organizational justice. In R. Cropanzano (Ed.), *Justice in the workplace: Approaching fairness in human resource management* (pp. 79–103). Hillsdale, NJ: Erlbaum.

Hage, J., & Aiken, M. (1967). Relationship of centralization to other structural properties. *Administrative Science Quarterly, 12*(1), 72–92.

Hinkin, T. R., & Schriesheim, C. A. (1990). Relationships between subordinate perceptions of supervisor influence tactics and attributed bases of supervisory power. *Human Relations, 43*, 221–237.

Hinkin, T. R., & Schriesheim, C. A. (1994). An examination of subordinate-perceived relationships between leader reward and punishment behavior and leader bases of power. *Human Relations, 47*(7), 779–800.

Holtz, B. C., & Harold, C. M. (2012). Effects of leadership consideration and structure on employee perceptions of justice and counterproductive work behavior. *Journal of Organizational Behavior, 34*(4), 492–519.

Homburg, C., & Fürst, A. (2005). How organizational complaint handling drives customer loyalty: An analysis of the mechanistic and the organic approach. *Journal of Marketing, 69*(3), 95–114.

Hulland, J., Nenkov, G. Y., & Barclay, D. W. (2012). Perceived marketing–sales relationship effectiveness: A matter of justice. *Journal of the Academy of Marketing Science, 40*(3), 450–467.

James, K. (1993). The social context of organizational justice: Cultural, intergroup, and structural effects on justice behaviors and perceptions. In Cropanzano, R. E. (ed.), *Justice in the workplace: Approaching fairness in human resource management.* (pp. 21–50). Hillsdale, NJ: Erlbaum.

Judge, T. A., Piccolo, R. F., & Ilies, R. (2004). The forgotten ones? The validity of consideration and initiating structure in leadership research. *Journal of Applied Psychology, 89*(1), 36–51.

Karambayya, R., Brett, J. M., & Lytle, A. (1992). Effects of formal authority and experience on third-party roles, outcomes, and perceptions of fairness. *Academy of Management Journal, 35*(2), 426–438.

Keeley, M. (1988). *A social contract theory of organizations.* Notre Dame, IN: University of Notre Dame Press.

Kim, H. S. (2007). A multilevel study of antecedents and a mediator of employee—organization relationships. *Journal of Public Relations Research, 19*(2), 167–197.

Kurland, N. B., & Egan, T. D. (1999). Public v. private perceptions of formalization, outcomes, and justice. *Journal of Public Administration Research and Theory, 9*(3), 437–458.

Lambert, E., Hogan, N., & Allen, R. (2006). Correlates of correctional officer job stress: The impact of organizational structure. *American Journal of Criminal Justice*, 30(2), 227–246.

Lansberg, I. (1984). Hierarchy as a mediator of fairness: A contingency approach to distributive justice in organizations. *Journal of Applied Social Psychology, 14*(2), 124–135.

Lansberg, I. (1988). Social categorization, entitlement, and justice in organizations: Contextual determinants and cognitive underpinnings. *Human Relations, 41*(12), 871–899.

Leventhal, G. S. (1980). What should be done with equity theory? New approaches to the study of fairness in social relationships. In K. Gergen, M. Greenberg, & R. Willis (Eds.), *Social exchange: Advances in theory and research* (pp. 27–55). New York, NY: Plenum.

Liden, R. C., Wayne, S. J., Jaworski, R. A., & Bennett, N. (2004). Social loafing: A field investigation. *Journal of Management, 30*(2), 285–304.

Lind, E. A., & Tyler, T. R. (1988). *The social psychology of procedural justice.* New York, NY: Plenum.

Long, C. P., Bendersky, C., & Morrill, C. (2011). Fairness monitoring: Linking managerial controls and fairness judgements in organizations. *Academy of Management Journal, 54*(5), 1045–1068.

Martin, T. N. (1980). Modelling the turnover process. *Journal of Management Studies, 17*(3), 261–274.

Meyer, M. W. (1972). Size and the structure of organizations: A causal model. *American Sociological Review, 37*(4), 434 – 441.

Mohrman, S. A. (1999). The contexts of geographically dispersed teams and networks. *Trends in organizational behavior, 6*, 63–80.

Mossholder, K. W., Bennett, N., Kemery, E. R., & Wesolowski, M. A. (1998). Relationships between bases of power and work reactions: The mediational role of procedural justice. *Journal of Management, 24*(4), 533–552.

Nowakowski, J. M., & Conlon, D. E. (2005). Organizational justice: Looking back, looking forward. *International Journal of Conflict Management, 16*(1), 4–29.

Pearce, J. L., Bigley, G. A., & Branyiczki, I. (1998). Procedural justice as modernism: Placing industrial/organisational psychology in context. *Applied Psychology, 47*(3), 371–396.

Pugh, D. S., Hickson, D. J., Hinings, C. R., & Turner, C. (1968). Dimensions of organization structure. *Administrative Science Quarterly, 13*(1) 65–105.

Riolli, L., & Savicki, V. (2006). Impact of fairness, leadership, and coping on strain, burnout, and turnover in organizational change. *International Journal of Stress Management, 13*(3), 351–377.

Rodell, J. B., & Colquitt, J. A. (2009). Looking ahead in times of uncertainty: The role of anticipatory justice in an organizational change context. *Journal of Applied Psychology, 94*(4), 989–1002.

Rosier, E. R., Morgan, R. E., & Cadogan, J. W. (2010). Marketing strategy and the efficacy of procedural justice: The mid-level marketing manager in industrial service firms. *Industrial Marketing Management, 39*(3), 450–459.

Rupp, D. E., & Paddock, E. L. (2010). From justice events to justice climate: A multilevel temporal model of information aggregation and judgment. In B. Mannix, M. Neal, & E. Mullen (Eds.), *Research on managing groups and teams: Fairness and groups* (Vol. 13, pp. 239–267). Bingley, UK: JAI Emerald.

Schminke, M., Ambrose, M. L., & Cropanzano, R. S. (2000). The effect of organizational structure on perceptions of procedural fairness. *Journal of Applied Psychology, 85*(2), 294–304.

Schminke, M., Cropanzano, R., & Rupp, D. E. (2002). Organization structure and fairness perceptions: The moderating effects of organizational level. *Organizational Behavior and Human Decision Processes, 89*(1), 881–905.

Shafritz, J. M., & Ott, J. S. (1996). *Classics of organization theory*. Belmont, CA: Wadsworth.

Shapiro, D. L., & Kirkman, B. L. (2001). Anticipatory injustice: The consequences of expecting injustice in the workplace. In J. S. Greenberg, & R. Cropanzano (eds.), *Advances in organizational justice* (pp. 152–178). Stanford, CA: Stanford University.

Sheppard, B. H., Lewicki, R. J., & Minton, J. W. (1992). *Organizational justice: The search for fairness in the workplace*. New York, NY: Lexington Books.

Shoss, M. K., Eisenberger, R., Restubog, S. L. D., & Zagenczyk, T. J. (2013). Blaming the organization for abusive supervision: The roles of perceived organizational support and supervisor's organizational embodiment. *Journal of Applied Psychology, 98*(1), 158–168.

Sitkin, S. B., & Bies, R. J. (1993). The legalistic organization: Definitions, dimensions, and dilemmas. *Organization Science, 4*(3), 354–351.

Sowell, T. (2003). Random thoughts. http://admin.townhall.com/columnists/thomassowell/2003/11/27/random_thoughts

Spell, C. S., & Arnold, T. J. (2007a). An appraisal perspective of justice, structure, and job control as antecedents of psychological distress. *Journal of Organizational Behavior, 28*(6), 729–751.

Spell, C. S., & Arnold, T. J. (2007b). A multi-level analysis of organizational justice climate, structure, and employee mental health. *Journal of Management, 33*(5), 724–751.

Thibaut, J., & Walker, L. (1975). *Procedural justice: A psychological analysis*. Hillsdale, NJ: Erlbaum.

Thompson, J. D. (1967). *Organizations in action: Social science bases of administrative theory*. New York, NY: McGraw-Hill.

Tripp, T. M. (1993). Power and fairness in negotiations. *Social Justice Research, 6*(1), 19–38.

Tyler, T. R. (1996). The relationship of outcome and procedural fairness: How does knowing the outcome influence judgments about the procedure? *Social Justice Research, 9*(4), 311–325.

Victor, B., & Stephens, C. (1994). The dark side of the new organizational forms: An editorial essay. *Organization Science, 5*(4), 479–482.

Wally, S., & Baum, J. R. (1994). Personal and structural determinants of the pace of strategic decision making. *Academy of Management Journal, 37*(4), 932–956.

Weber, M. (1946). Bureaucracy. In H. H. Gerth, C. W. Mills & M. Weber (Eds. and Trans.), *Max Weber: Essays in sociology* (pp.196–244). New York, NY: Oxford University Press.

Yen, C. H., & Teng, H. Y. (2012). The effect of centralization on organizational citizenship behavior and deviant workplace behavior in the hospitality industry. *Tourism Management, 36*, 401–410.

CHAPTER

27 The Fork in the Road: Diversity Management and Organizational Justice

Carol T. Kulik *and* Yiqiong Li

Abstract

The diversity management literature frequently makes reference to justice constructs, but diversity researchers rarely draw explicitly upon organizational justice frameworks. In this chapter, we use Cropanzano, Rupp, Mohler and Schminke's (2001a) three "roads" to organizational justice to examine how instrumental, relational, and deontic concerns are enacted in the diversity management literature. We describe the "fork in the road" that reflects the two dominant ways organizations approach diversity management: identity blind vs identity conscious. We review research on diversity climate and affirmative action to demonstrate how diversity management research does not (climate) and does (affirmative action) link organizational management practices with employee perceptions of justice. Finally, we suggest some ways that diversity management research can more effectively engage with organizational justice theory to predict, and understand, the consequences of organizations' diversity management choices.

Key Words: diversity management, organizational justice, diversity climate, affirmative action, identity blind management, identity conscious management

The Fork in the Road: Diversity Management and Organizational Justice

Imagine this: It's a beautiful sunny day and you're about to embark on a road trip. Before you swing onto the highway you stop at the 7-11 convenience store. The store has two maps and you buy them both. One map is very detailed, showing both the major arteries and secondary roads. The other is a colorful tourist map that highlights the scenic viewpoints, monuments, wineries, and amusement parks without reporting the actual distance between them or identifying efficient routes to reach them. If only you could overlay the two maps to get the most value from your big day out!

The organizational justice and diversity management literatures are a lot like those two maps. The academic literature on organizational justice has mushroomed since the 1980s, and the body of research is sprawling and detailed. Organizational justice research increasingly uses sophisticated data collection and analysis techniques that illustrate the complexity of justice phenomena, operating across levels (e.g., Liao & Rupp, 2005) and over time (e.g., Holtz & Harold, 2009). In contrast, while the term "diversity management" first appeared in the literature in the 1980s, academic research on diversity management got off to a slow start (Kulik & Roberson, 2008). Today, while scholars who attempt to review the organizational justice literature often comment on its "diversity in theoretical approach" (Colquitt, Conlon, Wesson, Porter & Ng, 2001: 425), scholars in the diversity management literature are more likely to beg for "additional theory development and testing" (Olsen & Martins, 2012: 1169). Rather than re-inventing the wheel and generating new diversity management theory, we suggest that the literature would benefit from a stronger consideration of organizational justice theory as a basis for predicting, and understanding, the consequences of diversity management. This chapter is designed as a first step in that direction.

The developing diversity management literature frequently makes reference to justice constructs. For example, researchers who study diversity "climates" regularly include justice and fairness items in their climate measures (e.g., Mor Barak, Cherin & Berkman, 1998). Diversity researchers emphasize the importance of treating members of underrepresented demographic groups with respect and dignity (Ely & Thomas, 2001), reflecting classic themes from the organizational justice literature (Lind & Tyler, 1988; Tyler & Lind, 1992). And yet, surprisingly, the diversity management and organizational justice literatures have developed largely independent of one another (Roberson & Stevens, 2006). Diversity researchers routinely discuss fairness (e.g., McKay, Avery & Morris, 2008), but rarely draw directly upon organizational justice frameworks or typologies (see Cropanzano, Slaughter & Bachiochi, 2005 and Roberson & Stevens, 2006 for exceptions to the rule).

In this chapter, we deliberately adopt an organizational justice framework to interpret organizations' diversity management choices. We present Cropanzano, Rupp, Mohler and Schminke's (2001a) "three roads" to organizational justice and describe the "fork in the road" characterizing the two dominant ways organizations approach diversity management. We review the emerging literature on diversity climate to illustrate how we are measuring employee reactions to diversity management, and highlight how our understanding is being constrained by those measures. We use affirmative action plans as one specific illustration of diversity management—and demonstrate how different employees can converge on fairness impressions even though they travel different "roads." Finally, we gaze out to the horizon and make some suggestions about how diversity management research can more effectively engage with organizational justice theory to better understand the consequences of organizations' diversity management choices.

Three Roads to Organizational Justice

Cropanzano et al. (2001a) conducted an extensive review of the organizational justice literature and identified three major perspectives ("roads") on organizational justice. The first road emphasizes *instrumental* models of justice positing that people care about justice because they are motivated to maximize self-interest in the long run (Thibaut & Walker, 1975). We value fair procedures because we expect, on average, that fair procedures will deliver fair outcomes (or, better still, favorable outcomes). We think procedures are more fair when they deliver outcomes that favor us (e.g., Ambrose, Harland & Kulik, 1991) and we are more willing to accept unfavorable outcomes if we are confident they are delivered by a fair system which will deliver better outcomes over time (Thibaut & Walker, 1975).

The second road focuses on *interpersonal relationships* (Cropanzano et al., 2001a). People have relationships with organizations and with organizational representatives. Instead of self-interest being the driving concern, researchers argue that people care about justice as a signal about the extent to which they are valued and respected by the organization (Lind & Tyler, 1988; Tyler, 1989). Fair procedures send positive signals; unfair procedures send negative signals and suggest that people are not fully included or accepted by the organization. On this road, procedures have an impact far beyond the tangible economic outcomes that they deliver. Procedural fairness influences emotional and affective responses to the organization and its agents (Tyler, Degoey & Smith, 1996) and impacts the long-term sustainability of the organizational relationship (Restubog, Hornsey, Bordia & Esposo, 2008).

As Folger (1998) first argued, and Cropanzano, Byrne, Bobocel and Rupp (2001b) reiterated, the first and second roads to organizational justice are both driven by self-interest, but with different emphases on instrumental and relational outcomes. A job is an instrumental resource that people value, but getting or losing that job also conveys relational meaning. Identity concerns figure prominently in organizational relationships, but organizational relationships also impact instrumental outcomes. The distinction between these first two roads may be clearer in theory than it is in practice (and perhaps clearer in academics' and managers' minds than it is in the minds of non-managerial employees).

The final road described by Cropanzano et al. (2001a) involves *moral principles.* Cropanzano et al. (2001a) point out that the instrumental road defines fairness in terms of gains and losses. The interpersonal road defines fairness in terms of relationships. But a third approach defines fairness in relation to universal moral standards. We care about justice because we have a basic respect for human dignity and worth (Folger, 1998, 2001). When people experience critical events, they want explanations that are both causal and moral (Cropanzano et al., 2001b). This third road is most visible in the ethics literature—it has received limited attention in the mainstream justice literature and even less attention in the diversity literature that is the focus of this chapter.

These three roads are based on different assumptions about human motivation and offer unique perspectives on organizational justice (Cropanzano et al., 2001a), and so they might lead to different destinations. Echoing Cropanzano et al. (2001a: 2), "it would work against our purpose to combine them." Instead, we drive between and across the justice "roads" to better understand the justice implications of organizations' diversity management choices.

Diversity Management's Fork in the Road

Fueled by the 1960s Civil Rights movement, American managers developed practices designed to increase employment opportunities available to racial minorities (Dobbin & Kalev, 2013). Then, in the late 1980s, when managers faced a labor force characterized by more women, a greater variety of cultural and racial backgrounds, and multiple generations, organizations began to view diversity through a "business case" lens (Robinson & Dechant, 1997) and became motivated to gain a "competitive advantage" by taking full advantage of a diverse talent pool (Thomas & Ely, 1996). Today, diversity management is a global concept. Many European and English-speaking countries have mimicked North American practices, but other geographic locations are developing context-specific diversity definitions and culturally-appropriate diversity management practices (Özbilgin, Jonsen, Tatli, Vassilopoulou & Surgevil, 2013).

As workforce diversity has increased, we have observed a simultaneous increase in the diversity of diversity management strategies adopted by modern organizations. Organizations implement different practices depending on their beliefs about diversity and their expectations about diversity's role in the organization (Dass & Parker, 1999; Ely & Thomas, 2001; Kulik & Roberson, 2008). Different authors use different terms to describe organizations' approaches to diversity management (identity blind vs identity conscious human resource management structures—Konrad & Linnehan, 1995; discrimination-and-fairness vs learning-and-effectiveness perspectives—Ely & Thomas, 2001; colorblind vs multicultural models—Plaut, Garnett, Buffardi & Sanchez-Burks, 2011), but these typologies converge onto a single important choice: a question of whether the organization's human resource management activities will ignore (identity blind) or consider (identity conscious) an employee's social identity (e.g., their gender, race, age, or other demographics).

In a *blind* approach to diversity management, organizations do not explicitly or formally include social group identity in their human resource decisions (Konrad & Linnehan, 1995). Identity blind approaches assume that prejudice has kept members of certain groups out of organizations, but that with equal access and fair treatment under the law, previous inequities can be corrected (Dass & Parker, 1999; Ely & Thomas, 2001). Therefore, the organization focuses attention on providing equal opportunities in hiring and promotion, suppressing prejudicial attitudes and eliminating discrimination in its practices. These human resource management practices are designed to reduce discrimination and bias, and create a level playing field for employees.

In a *conscious* approach to diversity management, organizations explicitly incorporate social group identity in its human resource decisions (Konrad & Linnhan, 1995). Organizations adopting an identity conscious approach take steps to remove discriminatory language from their job descriptions and eliminate bias from their decision procedures, but they supplement these with other identity conscious practices. Identity conscious practices could include designing recruitment materials to attract members of underrepresented identity groups (Avery, 2003), engaging in preferential hiring to increase the representation of some identity groups (Heilman & Blader, 2001), tailoring mentoring and development programs to the needs of specific identity groups (Ely, Ibarra & Kolb, 2011), and redesigning jobs so that they can be performed by identity groups that would otherwise be excluded from the workplace (Konrad, Moore, Ng, Doherty & Breward, 2012). These practices are intended to attract women, racial minorities, people with disabilities, and members of other identity groups historically underrepresented in organizations—and to give them a stronger say in organizational processes and decisions (Yang & Konrad, 2011). But how do these two approaches impact the *justice* of diversity management?

Identity Blind Diversity Management

Most organizations choose the identity blind option; this is the dominant approach to diversity management (Thomas & Ely, 1996). Employees are encouraged to view people of different colors, genders, or national origins as the same, and to make sure that differences among them "do not count" (Thomas & Ely, 1996: 81). Identity blind structures ensure that the human resource decision making process is the same for each individual (Konrad & Linnehan, 1995). They apply the same procedures consistently across time and across people (Leventhal, 1976). By adopting standard procedures, organizations increase confidence that employees are receiving fair outcomes. The identity blind organization signals that it places a higher value on people's achievements and merit than on their social identities. These principles of meritocracy and equality are highly valued by employees (Konrad & Linnehan, 1995; Thomas, Mack & Montagliani, 2004).

The identity blind approach to diversity management primarily reflects concerns of Cropanzano et al.'s (2001a) first road to justice—it is based on an instrumental model of organizational justice that emphasizes modifying procedures to ensure a fair distribution of outcomes. Managers who adopt identity blind practices "value due process and equal treatment" (Thomas & Ely, 1996: 81). But does an identity blind approach to diversity management in fact produce fair outcomes? On the one hand, yes. Organizations adopting identity blind practices are motivated to remove the most visible barriers that block the progress of women and racial minorities. But on the other hand, maybe not. Identity blind approaches emphasize merit, and ostensibly "merit-based" systems may reassure managers that non-discrimination is already "built in" to the process. For example, Castilla and Benard (2010) demonstrated that managers whose organizations explicitly emphasized meritocracy values showed *greater* bias—were more likely to favor a male employee for promotion over an equally qualified female employee—than managers whose organizations did not emphasize meritocracy. Identity blind practices might fail to achieve their intended purposes, if they encourage managers to relax their vigilance and allow personal biases greater sway in decision-making.

Further, identity blind approaches to diversity management may suppress employees' ability to recognize discrimination when it occurs. Employees are motivated to view their organizations as fair and non-discriminatory, so employees who work in an identity blind organization are more likely to dismiss evidence of inequity as isolated incidents and see it as the responsibility of individual employees to overcome them. For example, Bailyn (2003) describes the experience of female scientists at the Massachusetts Institute of Technology (MIT) who were doing significant work and nonetheless had fallen behind their male colleagues in compensation, lab space, and other critical resources. Academia's emphasis on merit, and MIT's own emphasis on equal opportunity, were so ingrained that "each person assumed that what happed to her was entirely due to her own behaviour and thus must be deserved" (Bailyn, 2003: 149). In an identity blind organization, employees may lose their ability to identify a group-based disadvantage. But in the absence of a perceived group-based disadvantage they are unmotivated to pursue organizational change and inequities are perpetuated within the system (Spoor & Schmidt, 2011). MIT acted to correct gender inequities after internal champions amassed enough data to make male-female group comparisons, but it was the public release of a report documenting those comparisons that galvanized deeper inquiries into the processes generating gender inequities (Bailyn, 2003).

Further, while organizations are traveling the first road to justice and emphasizing instrumental models, their employees may be traveling the second road and reflecting on their interpersonal relationships within the organization. In identity blind organizations, members of minority groups may not experience psychological safety (Purdie-Vaughns, Steele, Davies, Ditlmann & Crosby, 2008). An identity blind organization usually emphasizes assimilation to a dominant majority group standard (e.g., White and male) (Ely & Thomas, 2001; Härtel, 2004) so that members of minority groups may feel undermined, devalued and disrespected (Ely & Thomas, 2001). Because their identity group is not acknowledged or supported, employees may suspect that identity blind practices are disingenuous; the organization may be claiming a concern for fairness without actually practicing fairness (Plaut et al., 2011). For example, Purdie-Vaughns et al. (2008) demonstrated that African Americans were skeptical of identity blind philosophies expressed in a company brochure unless the brochure also included photographs of racial minority employees.

Identity Conscious Diversity Management

So, what happens when organizations choose the other option and adopt an identity conscious approach to diversity management? Organizations that take an identity conscious approach to diversity management are more proactive; they go beyond legal compliance (Dass & Parker, 1999). Organizations adopting an identity conscious approach believe that different kinds of employees bring different important and competitively relevant knowledge and perspectives about how the work should be done (Thomas & Ely, 1996). Employees are encouraged to bring their whole selves to the workplace and identify more fully with the work that they do. The identity conscious perspective explicitly recognizes employee differences as potentially valuable resources that will generate learning and adaptive change. It thus encourages employees to utilize their entire set of insights, skills, and experiences gained from their identity group membership.

The identity conscious approach to diversity management is an example of Cropanzano et al.'s (2001a) second road to justice—it emphasizes the relationship between employer and employee and actively sends signals to the employee about the value the employer places on that relationship. Importantly, these signals operate on two different levels (Tyler, Degoey & Smith, 1996). Identity conscious practices tell an employee that they are valued and respected. Moreover, they tell the employee that people *like them* are valued and respected. As a result, employees can express themselves as members of their identity group and take pride in their identity group membership. In work teams that recognize identity concerns of their members, members demonstrate higher creativity and lower absenteeism (Thatcher & Greer, 2008). Therefore, identity conscious practices might have a positive impact on both employee well-being and the organization's bottom line.

Does an identity conscious approach deliver more organizational justice than an identity blind approach? It might. Identity conscious practices usually offer faster and substantial change (Kalev, Dobbin & Kelly, 2006; Konrad & Linnehan, 1995). For example, Konrad and Linnehan (1995) found that identity conscious practices (including affirmative action plans, targeting women and racial minorities for management development training, and resource groups for women and racial minorities) were more successful than identity blind ones in getting women and racial minorities into management positions. Organizations establishing affirmative action plans, diversity committees, and diversity staff positions experienced increases in managerial diversity (Kalev et al., 2006). Homosexual employees working in organizations that had adopted sexual orientation policies and practices (e.g., a policy that forbids discrimination based on sexual orientation; gay and lesbian employee resource groups; health insurance, bereavement leave, and sick care leave that extend to domestic partners) reported less experience of discrimination based on their sexual orientation (Button, 2001; Ragins & Cornwell, 2001). Organizations adopting identity conscious practices are more likely to monitor the outcomes of their decision making procedures, ensuring that women and racial minorities are not disadvantaged (Konrad & Linnehan, 1995). Decision makers who are primed with an identity conscious philosophy exhibit less racial bias (Richeson & Nussbaum, 2004), more inclusive attitudes on social policies (Wolsko, Park & Judd, 2006) and greater openness to others (Verkuyten, 2005; Vorauer, Gagnon & Sasaki, 2009).

Women and racial minorities are particularly sensitive to signals sent by identity conscious practices; identity issues are more salient for minority groups (Buttner, Lowe & Billings-Harris, 2010; Phinney, 1992). As a result, minority members with a strong sense of their social identity may be particularly likely to bring diversity problems to management's attention in an identity conscious organization (Leslie & Gelfand, 2008), creating a positive force for change. However, organizations that adopt identity conscious practices may inadvertently "turn up the volume" on racial identity for majority group members. For example, Mollica (2003) demonstrated that Whites who learned that a layoff had disproportionately affected White employees saw the layoff as especially unfair when it occurred alongside identity conscious management practices (e.g., creating a diversity action team, emphasizing diversity in recruiting, training and employee development, and holding managers accountable for diversity management). Majority group members may view these practices as a threat to their own instrumental outcomes (first road; Cropanzano et al., 2001a) or as disrespectful of their own social identity (second road; Cropanzano et al., 2001a). But minority group members may also reject identity conscious practices for relational reasons (second road; Cropanzano et al., 2001a): They fear being stigmatized (Konrad &

Linnehan, 1995) or valued only because they are "different" (Purdie-Vaughns et al., 2008). These relational concerns may have implications for the instrumental outcomes they can expect from the organizational relationship (first road; Cropanzano et al., 2001a).

Further, identity conscious practices may "look" fair without "being" fair (Greenberg, 1990). Identity conscious practices may be "window dressing" (Edelman, Krieger, Eliason, Albiston & Mellema, 2011) that mask unfair outcomes. Racial minorities are skeptical of diversity conscious practices unless they are accompanied by strong objective evidence that these practices benefit their identity group. For example, racial minorities only felt that an identity conscious organization acted fairly when it laid off White employees in disproportionate numbers relative to nonWhites (Mollica, 2003).

The skepticism minority employees have about identity conscious organizations may be warranted. In a persuasive series of experiments, Kaiser et al. (2012) demonstrated that directing research participants' attention to an organization's identity conscious practices (e.g., emphasizing diversity in the company's mission statement or delivering mandatory diversity training to managers) caused them to overlook objective evidence of racial and gender discrimination and to view employees' discrimination claims as less valid. Observers may erroneously use the presence of identity conscious structures at a company as indicators of the efficacy of diversity efforts, even though these structures might not actually achieve equity.

Identity Blind vs Identity Conscious Diversity Management

Our review of the diversity management literature highlights three useful observations:

First, the attentive reader will note that our review to this point makes very little use of Cropanzano et al.'s (2001a) "third road" to organizational justice—the road that emphasizes a moral approach to justice. That's because there is surprisingly little discussion of moral imperatives in the diversity management literature. The personal values of business owners, chief executives, and senior management are frequently described as important motivators of diversity management (e.g., Gentile, 1996) and research suggests that a leader with a high appreciation for social justice is likely to be more influential in getting his or her organization to adopt diversity management practices (Ng & Sears, 2012). However, the organization is more likely to justify its activities in terms of the "business case" (Cox & Blake, 1991; Robinson & Dechant, 1997) and a "business case" justification is likely to be positively received by stakeholders (Kidder, Lankau, Chrobot-Mason, Mollica & Friedman, 2004). Recently, scholars have criticized organizations and diversity management scholars for neglecting the moral dimension of diversity management (e.g., Demuijnck, 2009; O'Leary & Weathington, 2006) but in the literature moral issues are more likely to be discussed in relation to single specific practices (e.g., affirmative action; Burns & Schapper, 2008) rather than in relation to an organization's overall diversity management strategy.

Second, the available literature demonstrates that the jury is still out about whether an identity blind or identity conscious approach to diversity management is more or less fair—whether fairness is measured as employee reactions (e.g., engagement; Plaut, Thomas & Goren, 2009) or as objective outcomes (e.g., minority representation in senior management; Kalev et al., 2006). People use a variety of cognitive shortcuts to ensure that they have a fairness judgment available when they need to make decisions within an organizational context, and either identity blind or identity conscious practices can trigger heuristic assessments of organizational fairness (Lind, Kulik, Ambrose & Park, 1993; Lind, 2001). Heuristic fairness judgments are especially likely when one has limited information, and so we might expect to see more of these "kneejerk" reactions when decision makers are presented with organizational scenarios (as in Castilla & Benard, 2010 and Kaiser et al., 2012). Employees, in contrast, are a more skeptical lot, and likely to interpret diversity practices in conjunction with other available evidence (e.g., the representation of racial minorities in the organization's management ranks; McKay & Avery, 2005; Purdie-Vaughns et al., 2008).

Third, management philosophy guides an organization's adoption of identity blind or identity conscious approaches to diversity management. But managerial preferences for the instrumental or relational road to justice may or may not be shared by non-managerial employees. Management may adopt an identity blind approach in order to demonstrate instrumental fairness, but employees may interpret identity blind practices as devaluing their relational needs. Alternatively, management may adopt an identity conscious approach that explicitly demonstrates the value they place on relational issues, but employees may object to the impact of those identity conscious practices on their instrumental outcomes. Differences in manager-employee perspectives pose a challenge for researchers who want to study diversity management fairness (we'll return to this issue later when we discuss diversity climate). It is very important that researchers distinguish between the *content* of an organization's diversity management practices and employee *reactions* to those practices (Kuenzi & Schminke, 2009). That might sound obvious, but as our review will demonstrate, diversity management researchers frequently conflate practices and content by asking employees to simultaneously report their organization's diversity management activities and their own reactions to those activities.

Organizations usually bundle individual practices into a larger diversity management strategy (Kulik & Roberson, 2008), and so it would be very useful to understand how an organization's diversity management strategy is interpreted by employees as demonstrating (or not demonstrating) fairness. Unfortunately, the link between an organization's overall portfolio of diversity management practices and employee fairness reactions has received limited attention. The closest the diversity management literatures comes to assessing employee reactions to diversity management as an overall strategy is in its focus on diversity climate—and that's where we turn in the next section.

Employee Reactions to Organizational Choices

Diversity climate reflects employees' "perceptions of the organizational context related to women and minorities" (Mor Barak, Cherin & Berkman, 1998: 83) and is represented by "aggregate member perceptions about the organization's diversity-related formal structure characteristics and informal values" (Gonzalez & DeNisi, 2009: 24). In other words, diversity climate is an outcome of the organization's diversity management practices and could be useful in helping us to understand how these practices impact organizational fairness. However, researchers studying diversity climate usually conceptualize it simultaneously as employee perceptions of, *and* reactions to, the organization's approach to diversity management—making it impossible to separate the actual diversity practices in operation from the reactions to those practices (see Kuenzi & Schminke, 2009 for a similar concern about the broader organizational work climate literature).

A sizable body of research has examined diversity climate and demonstrated that it has important effects on organizational commitment (Buttner, Lowe, Billings-Harris, 2012; Gonzalez & DeNisi, 2009; Hicks-Clarke & Ilies, 2000), turnover intentions (Buttner et al., 2012; Gonzalez & DeNisi, 2009; McKay et al., 2007), individual performance (McKay, Avery & Morris, 2009), and organizational performance (Gonzalez & DeNisi, 2009). Unfortunately, researchers are more likely to use diversity climate as a predictor or a moderator variable rather than an outcome variable, and so "little is known about how diversity strategies, espoused or enacted, contribute to building a... climate that is effective at attracting and retaining minority employees" (Buttner et al., 2012: 248). Researchers are more likely to use employee and supervisor demographics as predictors of diversity climate (e.g., Avery, McKay, Wilson & Tonidandel, 2007; Kossek & Zonia, 1993; Mor-Barak, Cherin & Berkman, 1998) than the organization's diversity management practices. Further, when researchers do include a measure of diversity management practices as an antecedent of diversity climate, they tend not to be specific about the nature of those practices (e.g., "we have processes and programs in place to incorporate the perspectives of all backgrounds and experiences in decisions at this hotel"; Herdman & McMillan-Capehart, 2010).

Most measures of diversity climate do not differentiate whether the respondent is being asked about their perceptions of either identity blind or identity conscious management practices. One of the earliest, and still the most popular, measures of diversity climate (Mor Barak et al., 1998) distinguished between an Organizational Fairness factor that focused on identity blind practices (e.g., "Managers here have a track record of hiring and promoting employees objectively, regardless of their race, sex, religion, or age") and an Organizational Inclusion factor that included identity conscious practices (e.g., "Management here encourages the formation of employee network support groups" and "There is a mentoring program in use here that identifies and prepares all minority and female employees for promotion"). However, later research used either only the Organizational Inclusion scale (Buttner et al., 2010) or integrated items from both factors into a single summary measure (e.g., Buttner et al., 2012; Gonzalez & DeNisi, 2009). One very promising step in this area of research is Nishii's (2012) "climate for inclusion" measure that explicitly distinguishes between management practices that ignore demographic differences (e.g., "Employees in this unit receive equal pay for equal work") and those that embrace differences (e.g., "This unit is characterized by a non-threatening environment in which people can reveal their true selves"). As a result, this measure might be more likely to capture both the instrumental and relational responses that employees have to their organization's diversity management practices.

We might learn more about diversity management and organizational fairness by taking a closer look at an individual diversity management practice, where researchers can systematically vary the content of the practice and measure reactions to the practice. This research strategy has been heavily utilized in the study of affirmative action, and so we turn our attention to that part of the literature now.

Affirmative Action Programs—the Fork as a Continuum

"Affirmative action" describes a wide range of organizational activities designed to improve the employment opportunities for members of underrepresented groups, especially racial minorities and women (Kovach, Kravitz & Hughes, 2004). Affirmative action is usually focused at organizational entry, although organizations may adopt affirmative action policies with respect to other decisions (e.g., training opportunities or layoffs). We focus here on affirmative action at organizational entry for two reasons. First, when organizations launch diversity management programs, their attention is likely to be initially directed toward increasing their workforce diversity by changing their recruitment and selection practices (Kulik & Roberson, 2008). Second, entry-stage affirmative action practices are themselves very diverse, and so they provide a good opportunity to view diversity management from different justice perspectives (the three "roads").

Affirmative action practices can be arrayed along a continuum. This continuum is sometimes described as "strength" (Lowery, Unzueta, Knowles & Goff, 2006) or "prescriptiveness" (Harrison, Kravitz, Mayer, Leslie & Lev-Arey, 2006) but can also be characterized as "blind-conscious" (Cropanzano, Slaughter & Bachiocci, 2005). At the identity blind end of the affirmative action continuum, an organization might consider race or gender *before* the hiring decision, but not *during* the hiring decision. Identity blind examples of affirmative action include strategies like targeted recruitment or training that are designed to increase the representation of racial minorities and women in the applicant pool. However, hiring decisions are based on merit criteria and ignore identity group membership. Identity conscious examples include strategies like "tiebreaks" (in which demographics might be used to choose between two equally qualified candidates) or quotas (in which demographics are explicitly weighted and valued in the hiring decision).

The very large literature on affirmative action is surprisingly consistent in its overall conclusion: Both beneficiaries (racial minorities and women) and non-beneficiaries (White men) usually express a clear preference for identity blind practices and see identity blind affirmative action as more fair than identity conscious affirmative action (see Harrison et al., 2006 for a review). However, the literature also suggests that beneficiaries and non-beneficiaries evaluate affirmative action practices by traveling along different justice "roads" (Cropanzano et al., 2001a).

Non-beneficiaries (e.g., White men) view affirmative action primarily through an instrumental lens (first road; Cropanzano et al., 2001a)—their assessments of affirmative action are heavily influenced by self-interest and concerns about personal loss (Shteynberg, Leslie, Knight & Mayer, 2011). For example, research demonstrates that Whites react most negatively to affirmative action when their own job security is threatened (Levi & Fried, 2008; Mollica, 2003). But Whites' reactions reflect relational concerns as well. Whites' discomfort with affirmative action is most acute when their own social identity is salient (second road; Cropanzano et al., 2001a). For example, Lowery et al. (2006) found that Whites' support for affirmative action was mediated by how Whites expected the plan to affect their group outcomes. The more strongly respondents identified with the White racial group, the more they opposed an affirmative action plan that might harm their group outcomes.

In contrast, beneficiaries (e.g., racial minorities and women) view affirmative action primarily through a relational lens (second road; Cropanzano et al., 2001a)—their assessments of affirmative action are motivated by how preferential treatment will be viewed by other members of the organization and affect their organizational relationships. For example, Cropanzano, Slaughter and Bachiochi (2005) demonstrated that Black students viewed identity conscious affirmative action plans as less fair and more stigmatizing than identity blind plans. Similarly, beneficiaries of gender-based affirmative action believed that other people had lower expectations of their competence (Heilman & Alcott, 2001). But stigmatization has instrumental implications as well (first road; Cropanzano et al., 2001a). Non-beneficiaries do view beneficiaries of preferential selection (one of the most potent forms of identity conscious affirmative action) as less competent (Heilman & Blader, 2001), and thus beneficiaries might be less likely to be given developmental opportunities or fast tracked for promotions.

So, potential beneficiaries and non-beneficiaries of affirmative action reach the same conclusion (preferring identity blind hiring strategies that consider social identity only before selection decisions are made) but for different reasons. The affirmative action literature demonstrates that the first and second roads to justice do not run along strictly parallel lines; they sometimes converge and intertwine (Folger, 1998; Cropanzano et al., 2001b). At a minimum, this suggests that organizations adopting diversity management practices should be aware that both instrumental and relational concerns will surface in employee reactions—and that both types of concerns may surface for both beneficiaries and non-beneficiaries. But, in addition, the research on affirmative action suggests that organizations may be able to mitigate negative reactions by providing information to employees that addresses their concerns (Kovach et al., 2004)—leading us to a consideration of the role that social accounts play in diversity management.

Getting Organizations and Employees onto the Same Road

Our review suggests that employees may not perceive organizational diversity management programs positively—even when they are likely to experience instrumental benefits from those programs. Here's where concepts originating in the organizational justice literature may be very helpful to the diversity management literature. We know that explanations, or social accounts, are very effective in helping people to view organizational practices as fair—even when they receive unfavorable outcomes from those practices. Employees have little direct knowledge of the procedures by which organizational decisions are made, and so organizational explanations may be a key factor in understanding whether those decisions are fair or unfair (Bies & Moag, 1986; Tyler & Bies, 1990). The justice literature distinguishes among three types of accounts: (1) excuses, in which an organizational actor acknowledges a negative event but takes no responsibility for it; (2) apologies, in which the actor accepts responsibility and expresses regret for the outcomes; and (3) justifications, in which the actor admits personal responsibility but denies the severity of the outcome. Justification further takes two forms (Bies, 1987): an ideological account in which the actor attempts to reframe the event or its consequences by appealing to superordinate values or a referential account, in which the actor attempts to reduce the severity of the event by providing a more favorable standard. The only type of account that has received any substantive attention in the diversity management literature is the ideological account, in which an organization justifies a diversity management practice by pointing out that the practice will allow the organization to achieve some desirable superordinate goal.

Some research suggests that, at least in the abstract, people prefer certain types of ideological accounts as justifications for diversity management activities. For example, Whites were more favorable to an organization's diversity management program when it was accompanied by a "competitive advantage" justification (the organization was reacting to a diverse customer base) than a "reactive" justification (the organization was responding to equal employment opportunity guidelines and affirmative action goals) (Kidder et al., 2004). Among six arguments for diversity management, employees most preferred an argument that diversity management would give the firm a competitive advantage (Kirby & Richard, 2000).

However, in the diversity management literature, explanations don't mitigate non-beneficiary reactions to unfavorable outcomes the way the organizational justice literature would predict. For example, neither the "competitive advantage" nor the "reactive" justification mitigated White participants' reactions to missing out on a promotion (Kidder et al., 2000). Knowing that an employee's time extension was an accommodation for a learning disability didn't stop coworkers from feeling unfairly treated when the employee won a prize for her high performance (Paetzold et al., 2008). Instead, in the diversity management literature, explanations are more likely to mitigate *beneficiary* reactions to *favorable* outcomes. For example, Richard, Fubara and Castillo (2000) demonstrated that racial minorities told that they had been hired through a diversity program anticipated better reactions from their coworkers when the program was justified either as offering a competitive advantage or as correcting past inequities. Similarly, women told that they had been hired through a diversity program anticipated more positive reactions from their coworkers when the program was justified as offering a competitive advantage (compared to no justification) (Richard & Kirby, 1998). Organizational justifications provide information to beneficiaries about how much relational stigma "baggage" will accompany their instrumental gains. Without an explicit explanation for the hire, selecting a solo woman into a male-dominant group is viewed as gender-based preferential selection, even if no affirmative action policy is explicitly stated (Heilman & Blader, 2001).

Further, employee interpretations of the explanations organizations offer for their diversity management practices are affected by the employee's prior experience. Williamson, Slay, Shapiro and Shivers-Blackwell (2008) investigated how White, Black, and Asian job applicants reacted to organizations that engaged in "aggressive recruiting" of underrepresented groups (women, racial minorities, people with disabilities, and veterans). They contrasted two types of explanations: a rational, business case justification explaining that this identity conscious practice would help the organization gain a competitive advantage, and an ideological justification suggesting that the firm had a moral obligation to ensure fair treatment (third road; Cropanzano et al., 2001a). The effects of these justifications differed by racial group and prior experience. Whites who had experienced high levels of discrimination in the past reacted more favorably to the business case justification, while Whites who had experienced low levels of discrimination in the past reacted more favorably to the ideological justification. For Blacks who had experienced low levels of discrimination in the past, neither justification made a big difference in organizational attraction. But Blacks who had experienced high levels of discrimination reacted more favorably to the ideological justification. Williamson et al.'s (2008) conclusion is that justifications do not provide a simple universal solution because no one type of justification was received positively by all types of applicants.

Eyes on the Horizon: An Emerging Research Agenda

Nearing the end of our road trip, we acknowledge that our review raises questions rather than delivering answers. Our review demonstrates that research in the diversity management literature is not really designed to understand the justice implications of identity blind and identity conscious management practices, and we offer several suggestions to move the field forward.

First, we would love to see more research that examines the justice implications of an organization's overall approach to diversity management (e.g., the identity blind vs identity conscious choice). We need to think about how multiple diversity-relevant indicators contribute to *entity-based* justice perceptions rather than studying isolated *event-based* justice perceptions of individual practices (Hollensbe, Khazanchi & Masterson, 2008). A systematic configuration of diversity management practices is likely to send a stronger signal to employees about the organization's diversity philosophy than any single practice (Bowen & Ostroff, 2004). Some authors have argued that an identity conscious strategy will produce better, more sustainable, long-range outcomes than an identity blind one (Ely & Thomas, 2001); others have argued for equifinality, suggesting that either diversity management approach will be effective as long as it is consistent with the organization's culture (Thomas & Gabarro, 1999). Employee perceptions of fairness are one important indicator of organizational effectiveness, and these perceptions are likely to have implications for the durability of the employment relationship (Restubog et al., 2008). We encourage researchers to directly compare employee justice perceptions of identity blind and identity conscious practice portfolios.

Implicitly, this recommendation to compare identity blind and identity conscious diversity management strategies is a plea for diversity management research that is simultaneously multilevel and multisource. The diversity management literature almost exclusively relies on *employee* reports of *management* practices. Employee perceptions of practices do matter, both in the organizational justice literature (Whitman, Caleo, Carpenter, Horner & Bernerth, 2012) and in the diversity management literature (e.g., Gonzalez & DeNisi, 2009). But we need to know how to influence those perceptions by introducing tangible changes within organizations, and only managers can report on the "global" formal policies and programs that are in place (Arthur & Boyles, 2007). If we focus only on "configural" reports about employee experiences with those policies and programs, we risk developing meso-theories about differences across organizational units at the expense of organization-level theories about differences across firms (Kulik, 2011) and we will fail to distinguish between cases where the diversity management policy is unfair or just poorly implemented (Brown, Bemmels, & Barclay, 2010).

Second, if researchers continue to study individual practices, at least we should expand the empirical database beyond organizational entry practices. Hiring practices, especially affirmative action, have been given extensive attention, but the fairness of identity conscious training programs (Ely et al., 2011) or job accommodations (Konrad et al., 2012) are less frequently studied. These practices are important to study because their ultimate success depends on employee support. This support can be displayed by positively reinforcing a coworker for using newly-learned diversity skills on the job (Roberson, Kulik & Pepper, 2009), publicly identifying as an "ally" to gay and lesbian coworkers (Griffith & Hebl, 2002), or swapping tasks with a coworker to accommodate the coworker's disability (Colella, Paetzold & Belliveau, 2004). We already know that fairness perceptions impact organizational citizenship (Colquitt et al., 2001), but establishing the fairness of organization-level diversity management practices (offering diversity training, incorporating sexual orientation into antidiscrimination policies, or hiring people with disabilities) might motivate employees to view these individual-level helping behaviors as part of their organization-level exchange relationship and engage in them more frequently (Rupp & Cropanzano, 2002).

Once we start positioning organizational justice as an endogenous variable (i.e., as a mediator or a dependent variable), it becomes more appropriate to incorporate *direct* measures of organizational justice that explicitly ask how fair the organization's diversity management procedures are (Colquitt & Shaw, 2005). However, the diversity management literature is more likely to import *indirect* measures from the general organizational justice literature (e.g., Triana & Garcia, 2009) or to use measures of diversity climate. Diversity climate measures are indirect measures of organizational justice because they ask research participants to report "a descriptive judgment of the characteristics of a decision event" (Colquitt & Shaw, 2005: 120)—they ask about the extent to which the organization enacts certain "justice rules" (Colquitt & Shaw, 2005: 134). Unfortunately, as we explained earlier in this review, the items included in diversity climate measures do not clearly distinguish between fairness arising from identity blind and identity conscious "rules". There are probably multiple diversity climates (e.g., identity blind climates and identity conscious climates), in the same way that there are multiple justice climates (e.g., distributive, procedural, and interactional justice; Whitman et al., 2012) but we are not distinguishing them. This blurring of the identity blind/conscious distinction even extends to experimental methodologies. As one example, Leslie and Gelfand (2008) manipulated climate by describing one organization as a "boy's club" and describing the other as valuing male and female leaders equally—but it's unclear whether the positive diversity climate condition was describing an identity blind or identity conscious organization. We need to be as explicit about the diversity practices that contribute to diversity climate as we are about the safety practices that contribute to safety climate (Zohar & Luria, 2005).

And, when we do include measures of organizational fairness, we need to specify "fair to whom?" Usually we expect research participants to adopt personal frames of reference, but recently researchers have been asking participants whether organizations have been fair to members of underrepresented groups (Kaiser et al., 2012; Triana, Wagstaff & Kim, 2012). Asking a participant whether "I am treated with dignity and respect" (beneficiary perspective; Liao & Rupp, 2005); "Has your organization's treatment of minority employees been free of bias?" (non-beneficiary perspective; Triana et al., 2012); or "The way the victim was laid off was fair" (observer perspective; Skarlicki, Ellard & Kellen, 1998) prime different perspectives and can trigger different answers. The way we ask questions matters (Schwartz, 1999): Asking about the self may rouse instrumental concerns, asking about other groups may rouse relational concerns, and asking about fairness in the abstract may rouse deontic concerns. It is important that researchers be explicit about the perspective they want respondents to adopt, and present theory-driven rationales for the wording of their survey questions.

Finally, we need more research on the third road that considers the moral approach to organizational justice. Employees' personal values have received surprisingly little attention in the diversity management literature. But a recent study by Triana et al. (2012) examined the relationship between employee ratings of the extent to which their organizations engaged in several diversity management practices (e.g., "actively recruits members of traditionally underrepresented groups" and "strives to retain employees who are members of traditionally underrepresented groups") and employee ratings of procedural justice for minorities. Overall, there was a positive relationship—more engagement in those practices was associated with higher ratings of procedural justice. However, the relationship was significantly stronger for employees who personally valued diversity. Interpreting these findings through a deontic lens (third road; Cropanzano et al., 2001a; Folger, 2001) suggests that non-beneficiaries of diversity conscious management practices may respond positively if those practices are consistent with their personal values.

Conclusion

The diversity management and organizational justice literatures have many natural affinities and areas of overlap, but our review suggests that diversity management researchers are not actively incorporating justice constructs into their theory-building or theory-testing. We hope that our review inspires diversity management researchers to more systematically test the justice implications of different approaches to diversity management (e.g., identity blind vs. identity conscious). The diversity management literature has demonstrated that employee perceptions of fairness (measured as diversity climate) impact individual and organizational outcomes. What we need now is more attention to the management practices that first create and then sustain employee perceptions of fairness.

References

Ambrose, M. L., Harland, L. K., & Kulik, C. T. (1991). Influence of social comparisons on perceptions of organizational fairness. *Journal of Applied Psychology, 76*(2), 239–246. doi:10.1037/0021-9010.76.2.239

Arthur, J. B., & Boyles, T. (2007). Validating the human resource system structure: A levels-based strategic HRM approach. *Human Resource Management Review, 17*(1), 77–92. doi:http://dx.doi.org/10.1016/j.hrmr.2007.02.001

Avery, D. R. (2003). Reactions to diversity in recruitment advertising: Are differences black and white? *The Journal of Applied Psychology, 88*(4), 672–679. doi:10.1037/0021-9010.88.4.672

Avery, D. R., McKay, P. F., Wilson, D. C., & Tonidandel, S. (2007). Unequal attendance: The relationships between race, organizational diversity cues and absenteeism. *Personnel Psychology, 60*(4), 875–902. doi:10.1111/j.1744-6570.2007.00094.x

Bailyn, L. (2003). Academic careers and gender equity: Lessons learned from MIT 1. *Gender, Work & Organization, 10*(2), 137–153. doi:10.1111/1468-0432.00008

Bies, R. J. (1987). The predicament of injustice: The management of moral outrage. *Research in Organizational Behavior, 9*, 289–319.

Bies, R. J., & Moag, J. S. (1986). Interactional justice: Communication criteria of fairness. In R. J. Lewicki, B. H. Sheppard & M. H. Bazerman (Eds.), *Research on negotiations in organizations* (pp. 43–55). Greenwich, CT: JAI Press.

Bowen, D. E., & Ostroff, C. (2004). Understanding hrm–firm performance linkages: The role of the "strength" of the HRM system. *Academy of Management Review, 29*(2), 203–221. doi:10.5465/amr.2004.12736076

Brown, G., Bemmels, B., & Barclay, L. J. (2010). The importance of policy in perceptions of organizational justice. *Human Relations, 63*(10), 1587–1609. doi:10.1177/0018726710362273

Burns, P., & Schapper, J. (2008). The ethical case for affirmative action. *Journal of Business Ethics, 83*(3), 369–379. doi:10.1007/s10551-007-9625-8

Buttner, E. H., Lowe, K., & Billings-Harris, L. (2012). An empirical test of diversity climate dimensionality and relative effects on employee of color outcomes. *Journal of Business Ethics, 110*(3), 247–258. doi:10.1007/s10551-011-1179-0

Buttner, E. H., Lowe, K. B., & Billings-Harris, L. (2010). Diversity climate impact on employee of color outcomes: Does justice matter? *Career Development International, 15*(3), 239–258. doi:10.1108/13620431011053721

Button, S. B. (2001). Organizational efforts to affirm sexual diversity: A cross-level examination. *Journal of Applied Psychology, 86*(1), 17–28. doi:10.1037/0021-9010.86.1.17

Castilla, E. J., & Benard, S. (2010). The paradox of meritocracy in organizations. *Administrative Science Quarterly, 55*(4), 543–676. doi:10.2189/asqu.2010.55.4.543

Colella, A., Paetzold, R., & Belliveau, M. A. (2004). Factors affecting coworkers' procedural justice inferences of the workplace accommodations of employees with disabilities. *Personnel Psychology, 57*(1), 1–23. doi:10.1111/j.1744-6570.2004.tb02482.x

Colquitt, J. A., Conlon, D. E., Wesson, M. J., Porter, C. O. L. H., & Ng, K. Y. (2001). Justice at the millennium: A meta-analytic review of 25 years of organizational justice research. *Journal of Applied Psychology, 86*(3), 425–445. doi:10.1037/0021-9010.86.3.425

Colquitt, J. A., & Shaw, J. (2005). How should organizational justice be measured? In J. Greenberg & J. A. Colquitt (Eds.), *Handbook of organizational justice.* (pp. 113–152). Mahwah, NJ: Erlbaum.

Cox, T. H., & Blake, S. (1991). Managing cultural diversity: Implications for organizational competitiveness. *The Academy of Management Executive, 5*(3), 45–56. doi:10.2307/4165021

Cropanzano, R., Byrne, Z. S., Bobocel, D. R., & Rupp, D. E. (2001b). Moral virtues, fairness heuristics, social entities, and other denizens of organizational justice. *Journal of Vocational Behavior, 58*(2), 164–209. doi:http://dx.doi.org/10.1006/jvbe.2001.1791

Cropanzano, R., Rupp, D. E., Mohler, C. J., & Schminke, M. (2001a). Three roads to organizational justice. *Research in Personnel and Human Resources Management, 20*, 1–113.

Cropanzano, R., Slaughter, J. E., & Bachiochi, P. D. (2005). Organizational justice and black applicants' reactions to affirmative action. *Journal of Applied Psychology, 90*(6), 1168–1184. doi:10.1037/0021-9010.90.6.1168

Dass, P., & Parker, B. (1999). Strategies for managing human resource diversity: From resistance to learning. *The Academy of Management Executive, 13*(2), 68–80. doi:10.5465/ame.1999.1899550

Demuijnck, G. (2009). Non-discrimination in human resources management as a moral obligation. *Journal of Business Ethics, 88* (1), 83–101. doi:10.1007/s10551-009-0100-6

Dobbin, F., & Kalev, A. (2013). The origins and effects of corporate diversity programs. In Q. M. Roberson (Ed.), *Oxford handbook of diversity and work* (pp. 253–281). New York: Oxford University Press.

Edelman, L. B., Krieger, L. H., Eliason, S. R., Albiston, C. R., & Mellema, V. (2011). When organizations rule: Judicial deference to institutionalized employment structures. *American Journal of Sociology, 117*(3), 888–954. doi:10.1086/661984

Ely, R. J., Ibarra, H., & Kolb, D. M. (2011). Taking gender into account: Theory and design for women's leadership development programs. *Academy of Management Learning & Education, 10*(3), 474–493. doi:10.5465/amle.2010.0046

Ely, R. J., & Thomas, D. A. (2001). Cultural diversity at work: The effects of diversity perspectives on work group processes and outcomes. *Administrative Science Quarterly, 46*(2), 229–273. doi:10.2307/2667087

Folger, R. (1998). Fairness as a moral virtue. In M. Schminke (Ed.), *Managerial ethics: Moral management of people and processes* (pp. 13–34). Mahwah, NJ: Erlbaum.

Folger, R. (2001). Fairness as deonance. In S. Gilliland, D. D. Steiner & D. P. Skarlicki (Eds.), *Theoretical and cultural perspectives on organizational justice* (pp. 3–31). Greenwich, CT: Information Age.

Gentile, M. C. (1996). Managerial effectiveness and diversity: Organizational choices. In M. C. Gentile (Ed.), *Managerial excellence through diversity* (pp. 225–256). Chicago: Irwin.

Gonzalez, J. A., & DeNisi, A. S. (2009). Cross-level effects of demography and diversity climate on organizational attachment and firm effectiveness. *Journal of Organizational Behavior, 30*(1), 21–40. doi:10.1002/job.498

Greenberg, J. (1990). Organizational justice: Yesterday, today, and tomorrow. *Journal of Management, 16*(2), 399–432. doi:10.1177/014920639001600208

Griffith, K. H., & Hebl, M. R. (2002). The disclosure dilemma for gay men and lesbians: 'Coming out' at work. *Journal of Applied Psychology, 87*(6), 1191–1199. doi:10.1037/0021-9010.87.6.1191

Harrison, D. A., Kravitz, D. A., Mayer, D. M., Leslie, L. M., & Lev-Arey, D. (2006). Understanding attitudes toward affirmative action programs in employment: Summary and meta-analysis of 35 years of research. *Journal of Applied Psychology, 91*(5), 1013–1036. doi:10.1037/0021-9010.91.5.1013

Härtel, C. E. J. (2004). Towards a multicultural world: Identifying work systems, practices and employee attitudes that embrace diversity. *Australian Journal of Management, 29*(2), 189–200. doi:10.1177/031289620402900203

Heilman, M. E., & Alcott, V. B. (2001). What I think you think of me: Women's reaction to being viewed as beneficiaries of preferential selection. *Journal of Applied Psychology, 86*(4), 574–582. doi:10.1037/0021-9010.86.4.574

Heilman, M. E., & Blader, S. L. (2001). Assuming preferential selection when the admissions policy is unknown: The effects of gender rarity. *Journal of Applied Psychology, 86*(2), 188–193. doi:10.1037/0021-9010.86.2.188

Herdman, A., & McMillan-Capehart, A. (2010). Establishing a diversity program is not enough: Exploring the determinants of diversity climate. *Journal of Business and Psychology, 25*(1), 39–53. doi:10.1007/s10869-009-9133-1

Hicks-Clarke, D., & Iles, P. (2000). Climate for diversity and its effects on career and organisational attitudes and perceptions. *Personnel Review, 29*(3), 324–345. doi:10.1108/00483480010324689

Hollensbe, E. C., Khazanchi, S., & Masterson, S. S. (2008). How do I assess if my supervisor and organization are fair? Identifying the rules underlying entity-based justice perceptions. *Academy of Management Journal, 51*(6), 1099–1116. doi:10.5465/AMJ.2008.35732600

Holtz, B. C., & Harold, C. M. (2009). Fair today, fair tomorrow? A longitudinal investigation of overall justice perceptions. *Journal of Applied Psychology, 94*(5), 1185–1199. doi:10.1037/a0015900

Kaiser, C. R., Major, B., Jurcevic, I., Dover, T. L., Brady, L. M., & Shapiro, J. R. (2012). Presumed fair: Ironic effects of organizational diversity structures. *Journal of Personality and Social Psychology, 104*(3), 504–519. doi:10.1037/a0030838

Kalev, A., Dobbin, F., & Kelly, E. (2006). Best practices or best guesses? Assessing the efficacy of corporate affirmative action and diversity policies. *American Sociological Review, 71*(4), 589–617. doi:10.1177/000312240607100404

Kidder, D. L., Lankau, M. J., Chrobot-Mason, D., Mollica, K. A., & Friedman, R. A. (2004). Backlash toward diversity initiatives: Examing the impact of diversity program justification, personal and group outcomes. *International Journal of Conflict Management, 15*(1), 77–102. doi:10.1007/s10672-006-9024-9

Kirby, S. L., & Richard, O. C. (2000). Impact of marketing workplace diversity on employee job involvement and organizational commitment. *Journal of Social Psychology, 140*(3), 367–377. doi:10.1080/00224540009600477

Konrad, A. M., & Linnehan, F. (1995). Formalized HRM structures: Coordinating equal employment opportunity or concealing organizational practices? *The Academy of Management Journal, 38*(3), 787–820. doi:10.2307/256746

Konrad, A. M., Moore, M. E., Doherty, A. J., Eddy, S. W. N., & Breward, K. (2012). Vocational status and perceived well-being of workers with disabilities. *Equality, Diversity and Inclusion: An International Journal, 31*(2), 100–123. doi:10.1108/02610151211202772

Kossek, E. E., & Zonia, S. C. (1993). Assessing diversity climate: A field study of reactions to employer efforts to promote diversity. *Journal of Organizational Behavior, 14*(1), 61–81. doi:10.1002/job.4030140107

Kovach, K. A., Kravitz, D. A., & Hughes, A. A. (2004). Affirmative action: How can we be so lost when we don't even know where we are going? *Labor Law Journal, 55*(1), 53–61.

Kuenzi, M., & Schminke, M. (2009). Assembling fragments into a lens: A review, critique, and proposed research agenda for the organizational work climate literature. *Journal of Management, 35*(3), 634–717. doi:10.1177/0149206308330559

Kulik, C. T. (2011). Climbing the higher mountain: The challenges of multilevel, multisource, and longitudinal research designs. *Management and Organization Review, 7*(3), 447–460. doi:10.1111/j.1740-8784.2011.00226.x

Kulik, C. T., & Roberson, L. (2008). Diversity initiative effectiveness: What organizations can (and cannot) expect from diversity recruitment, diversity training, and formal mentoring programs. In A. P. Brief (Ed.), *Diversity at work* (pp. 265–317). Cambridge: Cambridge University Press.

Leslie, L. M., & Gelfand, M. J. (2008). The who and when of internal gender discrimination claims: An interactional model. *Organizational Behavior and Human Decision Processes, 107*(2), 123–140. doi:http://dx.doi.org/10.1016/j.obhdp.2008.02.004

Leventhal, G. S. (1976). The distribution of rewards and resources in groups and organizations. In L. Berkowitz & W. Walster (Eds.), *Advances in experimental social psychology* (Vol. 9, pp. 91–131). New York: Academic Press.

Levi, A. S., & Fried, Y. (2008). Differences between African Americans and Whites in reactions to affirmative action programs in hiring, promotion, training, and layoffs. *Journal of Applied Psychology, 93*(5), 1118–1120. doi:10.1037/0021-9010.93.5.1118

Liao, H., & Rupp, D. E. (2005). The impact of justice climate and justice orientation on work outcomes: A cross-level multifoci framework. *Journal of Applied Psychology, 90*(2), 242–256. doi:10.1037/0021-9010.90.2.242

Lind, E. A. (2001). Thinking critically about justice judgments. *Journal of Vocational Behavior, 58*(2), 220–226. doi:http://dx.doi.org/10.1006/jvbe.2001.1793

Lind, E. A., Kulik, C. T., Ambrose, M., & De Vera Park, M. V. (1993). Individual and corporate dispute resolution: Using procedural fairness as a decision heuristic. *Administrative Science Quarterly, 38*(2), 224–251. doi:10.2307/2393412

Lind, E. A., & Tyler, T. R. (1988). *The social psychology of procedural justice.* New York: Plenum Press.

Lowery, B. S., Unzueta, M. M., Knowles, E. D., & Goff, P. A. (2006). Concern for the in-group and opposition to affirmative action. *Journal of Personality and Social Psychology, 90*(6), 961–974. doi:10.1037/0022-3514.90.6.961

McKay, P. F., & Avery, D. R. (2005). Warning! Diversity recruitment could backfire. *Journal of Management Inquiry, 14*(4), 330–336. doi:10.1177/1056492605280239

McKay, P. F., Avery, D. R., & Morris, M. A. (2008). Mean racial-ethnic differences in employee sales performance: The moderating role of diversity climate. *Personnel Psychology, 61*(2), 349–374. doi:10.1111/j.1744-6570.2008.00116.x

McKay, P. F., Avery, D. R., & Morris, M. A. (2009). A tale of two climates: Diversity climate from subordinates' and managers' perspectives and their role in store unit sales performance. *Personnel Psychology, 62*(4), 767–791. doi:10.1111/j.1744-6570.2009.01157.x

McKay, P. F., Avery, D. R., Tonidandel, S., Morris, M. A., Hernandez, M., & Hebl, M. R. (2007). Racial differences in employee retention: Are diversity climate perceptions the key? *Personnel Psychology, 60*(1), 35–62. doi:10.1111/j.1744-6570.2007.00064.x

Mollica, K. A. (2003). The influence of diversity context on white men's and racial minorities' reactions to disproportionate group harm. *The Journal of Social Psychology, 143*(4), 415–431. doi:10.1080/00224540309598454

Mor Barak, M. E., Cherin, D. A., & Berkman, S. (1998). Organizational and personal dimensions in diversity climate: Ethnic and gender differences in employee perceptions. *The Journal of Applied Behavioral Science, 34*(1), 82–104. doi:10.1177/0021886398341006

Ng, E., & Sears, G. (2012). CEO leadership styles and the implementation of organizational diversity practices: Moderating effects of social values and age. *Journal of Business Ethics, 105*(1), 41–52. doi:10.1007/s10551-011-0933-7

Nishii, L. (2012). The benefits of climate for inclusion for gender diverse groups. *Academy of Management Journal.* doi:10.5465/amj.2009.0823

O'Leary, B., & Weathington, B. (2006). Beyond the business case for diversity in organizations. *Employee Responsibilities and Rights Journal, 18*(4), 283–292. doi:10.1007/s10672-006-9024-9

Olsen, J. E., & Martins, L. L. (2012). Understanding organizational diversity management programs: A theoretical framework and directions for future research. *Journal of Organizational Behavior, 33*(8), 1168–1187. doi:10.1002/job.1792

Özbilgin, M., Jonsen, K., Tatli, A., Vassilopoulou, J., & Surgevil, O. (2013). In Q. M. Roberson (Ed.), *Oxford handbook of diversity and work* (pp. 419–441). New York: Oxford University Press.

Paetzold, R. L., Garcia, M. F., Colella, A., Ren, L. R., Triana, M. d. C., & Ziebro, M. (2008). Perceptions of people with disabilities: When is accommodation fair? *Basic & Applied Social Psychology, 30*(1), 27–35. doi:10.1080/01973530701665280

Phinney, J. S. (1992). The multigroup ethnic identity measure: A new scale for use with diverse groups. *Journal of Adolescent Research, 7*(2), 156–176. doi:10.1177/074355489272003

Plaut, V. C., Garnett, F. G., Buffardi, L. E., & Sanchez-Burks, J. (2011). "What about me?" perceptions of exclusion and whites' reactions to multiculturalism. *Journal of Personality and Social Psychology, 101*(2), 337–353. doi:10.1037/a0022832

Plaut, V. C., Thomas, K. M., & Goren, M. J. (2009). Is multiculturalism or color blindness better for minorities? *Psychological Science, 20*(4), 444–446. doi:10.1111/j.1467-9280.2009.02318.x

Purdie-Vaughns, V., Steele, C. M., Davies, P. G., Ditlmann, R., & Crosby, J. R. (2008). Social identity contingencies: How diversity cues signal threat or safety for African Americans in mainstream institutions. *Journal of Personality and Social Psychology, 94*(4), 615–630. doi:10.1037/0022-3514.94.4.615

Ragins, B. R., & Cornwell, J. M. (2001). Pink triangles: Antecedents and consequences of perceived workplace discrimination against gay and lesbian employees. *Journal of Applied Psychology, 86*(6), 1244–1261. doi:10.1037/0021-9010.86.6.1244

Restubog, S. L. D., Hornsey, M. J., Bordia, P., & Esposo, S. R. (2008). Effects of psychological contract breach on organizational citizenship behaviour: Insights from the group value model. *Journal of Management Studies, 45*(8), 1377–1400. doi:10.1111/j.1467-6486.2008.00792.x

Richard, O. C., Fubara, E. I., & Castillo, M. N. (2000). The impact of explanations and demographic group membership: Reactions to diversity initiatives. *Journal of Applied Social Psychology, 30*(5), 1039–1055. doi:10.1111/j.1559-1816.2000.tb02509.x

Richard, O. C., & Kirby, S. L. (1998). Women recruits' perceptions of workforce diversity program selection decisions: A procedural justice examination.

Journal of Applied Social Psychology, 28(2), 183–188. doi:10.1111/j.1559-1816.1998.tb01700.x

Richeson, J. A., & Nussbaum, R. J. (2004). The impact of multiculturalism versus color-blindness on racial bias. *Journal of Experimental Social Psychology, 40*(3), 417–423. doi:http://dx.doi.org/10.1016/j.jesp.2003.09.002

Roberson, L., Kulik, C. T., & Pepper, M. B. (2009). Individual and environmental factors influencing the use of transfer strategies after diversity training. *Group & Organization Management, 34*(1), 67–89. doi:10.1177/1059601108329732

Roberson, Q. M., & Stevens, C. K. (2006). Making sense of diversity in the workplace: Organizational justice and language abstraction in employees' accounts of diversity-related incidents. *Journal of Applied Psychology, 91*(2), 379–391. doi:10.1037/0021-9010.91.2.379

Robinson, G., & Dechant, K. (1997). Building a business case for diversity. *The Academy of Management Executive, 11*(3), 21–31. doi:10.5465/ame.1997.9709231661

Rupp, D. E., & Cropanzano, R. (2002). The mediating effects of social exchange relationships in predicting workplace outcomes from multifoci organizational justice. *Organizational Behavior and Human Decision Processes, 89*(1), 925–946. doi:http://dx.doi.org/10.1016/S0749-5978(02)00036-5

Schwartz, S. H. (1999). A theory of cultural values and some implications for work. *Applied Psychology, 48*(1), 23–47. doi:10.1111/j.1464-0597.1999.tb00047.x

Shteynberg, G., Leslie, L. M., Knight, A. P., & Mayer, D. M. (2011). But affirmative action hurts us! Race-related beliefs shape perceptions of white disadvantage and policy unfairness. *Organizational Behavior and Human Decision Processes, 115*(1), 1–12. doi:http://dx.doi.org/10.1016/j.obhdp.2010.11.011

Skarlicki, D. P., Ellard, J. H., & Kellen, B. R. C. (1998). Third-party perceptions of a layoff: Procedural, derogation, and retributive aspects of justice. *Journal of Applied Psychology, 83*(1), 119–127. doi:10.1037/0021-9010.83.1.119

Spoor, J. R., & Schmitt, M. T. (2011). "Things are getting better" isn't always better: Considering women's progress affects perceptions of and reactions to contemporary gender inequality. *Basic and Applied Social Psychology, 33*(1), 24–36. doi:10.1080/01973533.2010.539948

Thatcher, S. M. B., & Greer, L. L. (2008). Does it really matter if you recognize who i am? The implications of identity comprehension for individuals in work teams. *Journal of Management, 34*(1), 5–24. doi:10.1177/0149206307308909

Thibaut, J. W., & Walker, L. (1975). *Procedural justice: A psychological analysis.* Hillsdale, N.J.: Lawrence Erlbaum Associates.

Thomas, D. A., & Ely, R. J. (1996). Making differences matter: A new paradigm for managing diversity. *Harvard Business Review, 74*(5), 79–90.

Thomas, D. A., & Gabarro, J. J. (1999). *Breaking through: The making of minority executives in corporate America.* Boston: Harvard Business School Press.

Thomas, K. M., Mack, D. A., & Montagliani, A. (2004). Arguments against diversity: Are they valid? In F. Crosby & P. Stockdale (Eds.), *The psychology and management of diversity in organizations* (pp. 31–52). Malden, MA: Blackwell.

Triana, M. C., Wagstaff, M., & Kim, K. (2012). That's not fair! How personal value for diversity influences reactions to the perceived discriminatory treatment of minorities. *Journal of Business Ethics, 111*(2), 211–218. doi:10.1007/s10551-012-1202-0

Triana, M. C., & García, M. F. (2009). Valuing diversity: A group-value approach to understanding the importance of organizational efforts to support diversity. *Journal of Organizational Behavior, 30*(7), 941–962. doi:10.1002/job.598

Tyler, T., Degoey, P., & Smith, H. (1996). Understanding why the justice of group procedures matters: A test of the psychological dynamics of the group-value model. *Journal of Personality and Social Psychology, 70*(5), 913–930. doi:10.1037/0022-3514.70.5.913

Tyler, T. R. (1989). The psychology of procedural justice: A test of the group-value model. *Journal of Personality and Social Psychology, 57*(5), 830–838. doi:10.1037/0022-3514.57.5.830

Tyler, T. R., & Bies, R. J. (1990). Beyond formal procedures: The interpersonal context of procedural justice. In J. Carroll (Ed.), *Applied social psychology and organizational settings* (pp. 77–98). Hillsdale, NJ: Erlbaum.

Tyler, T. R., & Lind, E. A. (1992). A relational model of authority in groups. In P. Z. Mark (Ed.), *Advances in experimental social psychology* (Vol.25, pp. 115–191): Academic Press.

Verkuyten, M. (2005). Ethnic group identification and group evaluation among minority and majority groups: Testing the multiculturalism hypothesis. *Journal of Personality and Social Psychology, 88*(1), 121–138. doi:10.1037/0022-3514.88.1.121

Vorauer, J. D., Gagnon, A., & Sasaki, S. J. (2009). Salient intergroup ideology and intergroup interaction. *Psychological Science, 20*(7), 838–845. doi:10.1111/j.1467-9280.2009.02369.x

Whitman, D. S., Caleo, S., Carpenter, N. C., Horner, M. T., & Bernerth, J. B. (2012). Fairness at the collective level: A meta-analytic examination of the consequences and boundary conditions of organizational justice climate. *Journal of Applied Psychology, 97*(4), 776–791. doi:10.1037/a0028021

Williamson, I. O., Slay, H. S., Shapiro, D. L., & Shivers-Blackwell, S. L. (2008). The effect of explanations on prospective applicants reactions to firm diversity practices. *Human Resource Management, 47*(2), 311–330. doi:10.1002/hrm.20214

Wolsko, C., Park, B., & Judd, C. (2006). Considering the tower of babel: Correlates of assimilation and multiculturalism among ethnic minority and majority groups in the united states. *Social Justice Research, 19*(3), 277–306. doi:10.1007/s11211-006-0014-8

Yang, Y., & Konrad, A. M. (2011). Understanding diversity management practices: Implications of institutional theory and resource-based theory. *Group & Organization Management, 36*(1), 6–38. doi:10.1177/1059601110390997

Zohar, D., & Luria, G. (2005). A multilevel model of safety climate: Cross-level relationships between organization and group-level climates. *Journal of Applied Psychology, 90*(4), 616–628. doi:10.1037/0021-9010.90.4.616

CHAPTER

28 The Roles of Workplace Justice in the Midst of Organizational Change

M. Susan Taylor

Abstract

Based on a literature review of 19 scholarly journals and research annals, the chapter examines 17 focal articles published between 1987–2012. It categorizes them according to the role that workplace justice plays in two types of change, transitional and transformational, and whether that role is serving as a dependent, independent mediator, or moderator variable. Review of the focal articles revealed: (a) strong support for workplace justice as a primary determinant of employees' reactions to transitional change; (b) differences in the outcome variables change commitment and organizational commitment when operating at different levels of analysis; (c) consistent results across three studies that employees' negative reactions to change occur much earlier than expected, even before the change actually begins; and (d) growing support for the *impact of change* construct in shaping individuals,' commitment to and behavioral support of change. Practical implications and future research directions are discussed.

Key Words: workplace justice, organizational change, transitional change, transformational change, procedural justice, levels of analysis, anticipatory justice

A number of years ago, after providing only a week's notice, the business school where I worked as an assistant professor purchased and configured the first round of personal computers ever, for all of its faculty and staff. It also began to digitalize its budget and travel reimbursement records, going back more than a decade. The school's then associate dean, let's call her Jennifer, was assigned to manage the overall task, and a long-time, administrative employee who had handled the processing of the school's travel reimbursements for more than a decade, let's call her Sonia, was assigned to develop, pilot, and maintain a new computerized process for travel reimbursements.

Associate Dean Jennifer, no stranger to the general nature of organizational change, sensed there might be some resistance on the part of Sonia, a strong-willed, hard- working but rather inflexible woman, and Jennifer quickly initiated what some might call "a change intervention." She shared with Sonia the logic behind the school's adoption of personal computers, a big picture of the proposed process for digitally recording and storing travel reports, and the time, effort, and cost saving benefits that would accrue to the school as a whole and to the faculty and staff, once employees' gained proficiency in using their new computers and developing new processes. Much to Jennifer's consternation, Sonia responded that the changes were wasteful and unfair, as her new computer was expensive, difficult to operate, and very time consuming, making it twice as hard for her to achieve even mediocre results on her work assignments. And by the way, no other staff member had received such an assignment. "Further," Sonia stated, "the existing method of recording travel reimbursement information and storing it in file folders is easy to use, fairly secure (e.g., "we have not lost any travel records in quite some time," requires much less time, and only about half as much effort." Sonia then reiterated that the school and Jennifer were treating her unfairly by requiring her to both learn the new computer technology *and* to develop a new, process for storing travel information.

Disappointed, although not really surprised by Sonia's negativity, Jennifer asserted that the new computers were definitely here to stay and again, would ultimately yield many time saving benefits for Sonia and other staff and faculty. She pointed out that Sonia' extensive knowledge of the travel reimbursement records clearly made her the best person to develop a new computerized process for travel records and reimbursements. Jennifer asked Sonia to keep working on the assignment, offered to help her with any problems, and encouraged her to ask if she needed any assistance. She decided to give Sonia a week to 10 days to adjust to the new computer, and the inevitability of developing the new computerized process. Each time Jennifer walked by Sonia's office, however, she could hear the woman complaining bitterly to co-workers about both the unnecessary expense of the new computers and the needless loss of her valuable work time.

At the end of a week, Jennifer was growing increasingly frustrated but still wanted to treat Sonia fairly, rather than manipulate or coerce her. After all, the woman was a conscientious employee who certainly hadn't requested this change, received little advance notice, and was well known for her inflexibility. After mulling things over a bit longer, she finally responded by walking up to Sonia's desk and asked for her "input on an important issue." "Sonia," Jennifer asked, "in the past, when you have experienced change in the work place, what exactly did it take for you to adjust to the change, reduce your frustration, learn the new process and once again become a happy and productive employee?" "About six weeks," Sonia responded almost instantly, seemingly without thinking. "Ah," thought Jennifer, "this may be a case where finding the balance between change and status quo is quite important," and made a note to extend the length of Sonia's adjustment period.

Sure enough, some five weeks later, almost to the day, Sonia was at her desk, humming to herself while working comfortably and competently on her computer, and putting the final touches on the computerized travel record process.

Introduction

Organizational change, defined as a planned or unplanned response to pressures and forces of many types (competitive, economic, political, regulatory, social, technological, etc. (Jick & Peiperl, 2010) is an increasingly frequent phenomenon. Even relatively small changes such as that faced by Jennifer and Sonia, often create feelings of anxiety, stress, unfairness, and dissatisfaction for employees and their managers. In some cases, managers receive advance notice and sufficient resources (Shin, Taylor, & Seo, 2012) that enable them to buffer their employees and themselves from many of the strains, stresses, and negative emotions stimulated by organizational change and to empower their unit to work together in making their part of the focal change successful. Unfortunately, however, often, this is not the case. Instead, much work time and effort is lost, and many negative attitudes emerge, as parties muddle through, and ultimately come to some kind of terms with the change. This, in fact, is exactly what happened in the organizational change experienced by Jennifer and Sonia, although their own change was relatively small, their frustrations fairly minor, and their success greater than is the general case. It seems quite possible that the ultimately positive outcomes of that change resulted, in part, from Jennifer's determination to treat Sonia fairly by being respectful and courteous to Sonia throughout the change process even though their views of the situation differed considerably. Jennifer also provided information about why the school-wide adoption of personal computers was undertaken and why Sonia was singled out to develop a new computerized process for the school's travel reimbursements. Jennifer also allowed Sonia to voice her concerns and express her feelings relatively openly, and ultimately gave her the time she typically needed to adapt to a new workplace change.

Building on the opening vignette, this chapter examines the role of organizational fairness or justice, terms that are used interchangeably in this paper, within the midst of organizational change. Although the linkages between organizational change and workplace justice have not been extensively researched, based on the literature review conducted for this chapter, the growing number of empirical articles in the literature to date appears sufficient to examine the role of workplace justice in the midst of organizational change, and draw some preliminary conclusions about whether significant interrelationships exist, have yielded valuable outcomes to date and have the potential to offer more.

If so, there is much reason to suspect that such findings could certainly benefit the growing number of organizations currently involved in organizational change efforts. For example, a 2011 IBM global study (Jorgesen, Owen, & Neus, 2011) reported that the percentage of CEOs expecting substantial change in their organizations rose from 65% to 83% between 2006–2008. Yet despite the increasing frequency with which organizational change occurs, its success rate, as assessed by a variety of outcomes (market share, productivity, revenues, speed, etc.) selected by the change organization, is quite disappointing, and indicates that such changes fail more often than not, that is, more than 50% of the time (Balogun & Johnson, 2004;Jorgesen, Owen, & Neus, 2011; McKinsey, 2008).

Although there are undoubtedly many determinants of change success, scholarly and applied research indicates that the human element, in the form of disgruntled and alienated employees are a major cause of change failure (Fugate, Kinicki, Prussia, 2008; Keifer, 2005; Schweiger & DeNisi, 1991). The generally negative experiences of employees during organizational change, strongly suggest that workplace justice plays an important role in the change process and its outcomes. Further, it seems very possible that understanding more about the interrelationships between workplace justice and organizational change will add value for both bodies of literature.

This chapter, entitled The Roles of Workplace Justice in the Midst of Organizational Change, reviews the literature on justice and organizational change, and categorizes articles, first according to the type of change pursued, and then by the role that workplace justice plays in the article. In addition to examining the findings emerging from the articles identified by the literature search, the chapter includes a final integrative section that is built around the following research questions:

1. What types of justice are most frequently associated with organizational change in prior studies and what, if any, effects do different types of justice have on various change processes, as well as employees' attitudinal and behavioral outcomes?

2. Which theories or conceptual frameworks have been applied by prior research to develop and explain hypothesized effects of workplace justice, and to what extent have they been supported empirically?

3. What if any, impact do empirically supported relationships between perceived justice and organizational change have on the overall effectiveness of change, and thus, the success level, of organizational change?

4. What are the major theoretical and practical contributions resulting from these articles?

5. What are the high priority future research needs that would enable researchers and managers to better understand and use the role that workplace justice plays in the processes of organizational change?

As a roadmap for the reader, I begin exploring the these issues with a brief discussion of how the literature search for empirical literature reviewed for this chapter was conducted, and then introduce a typology of different kinds of organizational change and their differences. I use this typology to sort the selected organizational change articles identified by my literature search into different types of change, and then further categorize them by identifying the different roles that workplace justice plays within these types, I then qualitatively review one exemplar article for each role in order to illustrate the nature of published research that currently exists and its findings, and also providing shorter reviews for the remaining articles within a given role. Based on the literature reviewed for each role of workplace justice, I summarize and, where possible, integrate their results. Finally, in a closing, integrative session, I draw conclusions about the different types of organizational fairness found within the identified articles on organizational change, their effects on change processes and outcomes, the major theoretical and practical contributions to the change literature, and high priorities for future research examining the impact of workplace justice on organizational change.

Literature Search

To search for relevant empirical and conceptual research at the intersect of workplace justice and organizational change, I used the key words *justice/fairness/change* and initially identified 69 potential articles from the 19 scholarly journals and research annals listed in footnote 1.[1] By reading the abstracts and papers, I narrowed the remaining articles down to 17, based on whether: (a) they were empirical in nature, (b) workplace justice was actually included as a variable in the article, and (c) could be linked to different roles that workplace justice played in the articles. The 17 articles were published in the period between 1987 and 2012, with the vast majority (13) falling between 2000 and 2012. The articles appeared in the following outlets: Administrative Science Quarterly (1), Journal of Applied Behavioral Science (4), Journal of Applied Psychology (4), Journal of Management (2), Journal of Organizational Behavior (2), Journal of Organizational Change Management (2) Leadership Quarterly (1), and Personnel Psychology (1). I move now to briefly discuss an established typology of organizational change that I used to classify the articles emerging from the literature review.

A Typology for Organizational Change

Differences in the terminology used for various types of change abound in the scholarly literature. As an example, in the second edition of his popular book, *Organizational Change, Theory and Practice*, Burke (2008), describes the "nature" of organizational change as either evolutionary or revolutionary. Evolutionary change, according to Burke (2008), is comprised of small improvements or incremental steps that resolve problems and/or change a part of a larger system. Conversely, revolutionary change occurs both because of internal disruptions that alter the alignment of activities and subsystems, and because changes in the system's external environment sometimes bring a jolt to the organization's system that is so significant that "nothing will ever be the same again" (Burke, 2008). Still other scholars use the term *transformational change* as a large-scale alteration of the overall nature of the organization, particularly its culture and design, as well as its attention to the people and members within the organization (Cummings & Worely; 1997; Tushman, Newman & Romanelli, 1986) Reger et al. (1994) provide further variety in naming types of change by referring to second-order discontinuous change that is very much transformational and radical in nature, and intended to alter the very core of the organization. Clearly, both transformational and second-order change shows strong similarities with evolutionary and revolutionary change.

Given many different terminologies to choose from despite strong underlying similarities in the two major types of change, in this chapter, I rely on one developed by Anderson and Ackerman (2010). Observing the types of changes that occur frequently in organizations, they identify two main types. First, similar in nature to the evolutionary change mentioned earlier, *transitional change* is used to assist an organization evolve slowly over time and solve old problems. The management of the transition is required in order to tear down the old state while putting in the new one, and all the while meeting an established timetable. Examples of this change include restructuring, divestitures, simple mergers or consolidations, installation and integration of new technology, and the creation of new products, services, technologies, and processes that take the place of old ones. Anderson and Ackerman (2010) argue that during the transition period, an organization is in some kind of middle ground, neither what it was at the beginning of change, nor what it aspires to become. Transition steps include temporary arrangements, pilots, or phased in operations among many others. They are key to the success of this type of change. Further, the management task for transitional change is complex and can require the launching of several new processes simultaneously, assessing uncertainty and risk, and meeting the needs of change recipients. Gradually, the transition steps are implemented and the organization reaches its desired new state.

A second type of organizational change identified by Anderson and Ackerman (2010) is called transformational. Often galvanized by a change in the beliefs of management and employees regarding what is possible and critical for the organization, transformational change is typically not initiated until other options have failed. In many ways, it is most similar to the revolutionary change mentioned previously in this section. Unlike transitional change, the end state of transformational change is not known until it begins to unfold; thus transformational change necessitates a leap of faith by the organization and its members. Typically, such change is accomplished through the radical re-conceptualization of the organization's mission, culture, strategy, leadership, and so forth. Further, careful planning and implementation may be less central to change success than the ability to quickly recognize and respond to opportunities and threats in the environment. Similarly, envisioning the look and feel of the organization in the future is instrumental for successful transformational change. Anderson and Ackerman (2010) point out that, in the first and second decades of the 2000s, transformational change emerged in many industries such as automobile and steel, banking and financial markets, computer, and so forth.[2] Having identified these two types of change, I begin with transitional change, by far the most frequent type emerging from the articles identified by the literature search, and, ultimately, further categorized articles, based on my initial reading, into four types of roles that workplace justice plays in organizational change.

The Roles of Workplace Justice in Change

Burke (2008) argues that transitional change tends to account for 95% of all existing changes, a percentage quite consistent with the percentage of transitional changes found in my reading of the articles selected from the literature search (94%). This section of the paper includes 16 articles examining different kinds of transitional changes, for example, mergers, reorganization/layoffs, divestiture, self-managing work teams, along with one article that examines a transformational change. In the sections that follow, I further categorize the different roles workplace justice plays within the change. I begin with the role of workplace justice as a dependent variable.

The Role of Workplace Justice as a Dependent Variable

Only one article illustrates the role of workplace justice as a dependent variable—Liu, Caldwell, Fedor, and Herold (2012)—and although virtually all articles in the literature search include more complexity than a simple relationship between antecedent and justice, I place the article in this category as the only one that providing such a direct antecedent, even though it also includes a significant three-way interaction. Please note that a third section entitled The Role of Workplace Justice as a Moderator appears later.

LIU ET AL. (2012)

Liu et al. (2012) built on the argument that the uncertainty and challenges that employees experience during organizational change causes them to become concerned about justice violations. Yet despite the importance of justice for successful change, neither justice nor change scholars have given much attention to this issue. The oversight is important, because research studies indicate that when organizational leaders show their care and commitment to employees by providing a sufficient amount of support for change, employees will reciprocate with favorable reactions including forming judgments that the change is being conducted justly. Yet, even when management intends to do everything "the right way" to support the change, other factors may negatively influence employees' reactions.

Therefore, in this paper, Liu et al. (2012, p. 442) ask the research question, "What will affect fairness judgments beyond specific actions to support change?" Using a multilevel research design, they examine two moderators of the change support–change fairness relationship suggested by the literature: (1) employee internal and external attributions about the reason that a change is being implemented; and (2) employee conscientiousness (individual level of analysis) such that high conscientiousness employees are predicted to have a bias to expect that management will take personal responsibility for change, whereas low conscientiousness employees will be less likely to personally hold management to a higher standard of change support. Thus, it seems likely that high and low conscientiousness employees also differ in their expectations about how fairly they are treated by management during change (Liu et al., 2012).

Liu et al.'s (2012) article focused on (1) change support, defined as the material and socioemotional support provided to employees by management to help them cope with organizational change (Caldwell, Herold & Fedor, 2004; e.g. providing necessary resources and training); and (2) change fairness, defined as employees' view of the procedural justice nature of the change process. The researchers proposed three hypotheses:

> *H1:* Change support, as perceived at the work-unit level, will be positively related to individual employees' perceptions of change fairness.
>
> *H2:* Change attributions at the work-unit level will moderate the positive relationship between change support and individual employees' perceptions of change fairness. The relationship will be stronger when change is attributed to internal causes such as management initiatives, and weaker when the change is attributed to external environmental factors.
>
> *H3:* Change support, change attributions, and employee conscientiousness will interact to affect perceptions of change fairness. The interaction effects of change support and change attributions will be weaker for more conscientious employees and stronger for less conscientious employees.

Methodology

Much of the methodology for this study is the same or similar to that of Fedor, Caldwell and Herold (2006): sample (693), multilevel design, and some 29 different change organizations. Analyses included aggregation, confirmatory factor analysis to assess the validity of measures used in the study, and hierarchical linear modeling (HLM) to test hypotheses.

FINDINGS

Results supported H1 regarding the positive relationship between change support at the work-unit level and employee's perception of change fairness. They did not support H2, that change attributions at the work-unit level would moderate the relationship between change support and individual employee perceptions of change fairness. Hypothesis 3 predicting a three-way interaction between change support, change attributions, and conscientiousness on change fairness was also supported and indicated that for highly conscientious employees, the level of change support was directly related to perceived change fairness. For less conscientious employees, change fairness was positively related to change support *only* when employees attributed responsibility for the change initiative to management.

Conceptual and Practical Implications

Findings revealed that management's strong support of change may compensate for weaknesses in other policy and structural aspects of the change initiative and directly affect employee's perceptions of change fairness. Further, both change attributions and level of employee conscientiousness moderated the change support–change fairness relationship, indicating that employees low in conscientiousness displayed a positive change support–change fairness relationship *only* when the change was attributed internally to the organization and its managers, whereas employees who were high in conscientiousness displayed a positive change support–change fairness relationship regardless of whether change attributions were internal or external. Practically, results suggest that management should note the importance of the attributions that employees make about the decision to implement change and to highlight internal factors where possible. In addition, managers leading change should consider devoting more time to the motivation of highly conscientious employees who likely possess both an achievement orientation and the dependability to contribute to change success. Next, I examine the role of workplace justice as an independent variable.

The Role of Workplace Justice as an Independent Variable

Four articles fall within this category, Bernerth, Walker, Walter, and Hirschfeld (2011), which examines a transitional change; and a subsection of three other articles that examine the role of procedural justice (PJ) as an effective leadership tool: Tyler and de Cremer (2005); Gopinath and Becker (2000), and Michel, Stegmaier, and Sonntag (2010). The last is the only article in the literature search examining a transformational change. I begin with Bernerth et al. (2010), which treats justice as an independent variable and then moves on to the subsection examining PJ as an effective leadership tool.

Bernerth et al. (2011) used social comparison and fairness theories to compare individuals' assessment of the level of just or fair treatment that they received personally with the level they believed that their co-workers received. Studying a US manufacturing plant that had carried out several cost-saving initiatives (e.g., the transfer of several employees to another location, cutbacks in fringe benefits, and employee layoffs), the researchers matched two surveys collecting information on personal and other-party differences for 214 employees out of 500. They predicted that the negative difference between the two would affect employees' affective change commitment, turnover intentions, and emotional exhaustion. Specifically, this negative difference was predicted to:

H1. Negatively relate to employees' commitment to change. ***Supported***

H2. Positively relate to their intentions to turnover. **Not Supported**

H3. Positively relate to their level of emotional exhaustion. ***Supported***

Finally,

H4. Emotional exhaustion was predicted to mediate the indirect relationship between differences in justice perceptions and change commitment (***Supported)***, as well as that between indirect differences in justice perceptions and turnover intentions (***Supported)***.

THEORETICAL IMPLICATIONS

Implications include findings suggesting that self-interest is not the primary determinant of assessing fairness during change, and findings that replicated previous research showing that individuals distinguish between their own fair treatment and the fair treatment and outcomes of others. Overall, findings indicate that employees react negatively to any differences between personal and other-party justice, whether more or less than those of other parties. *Practically*, results indicate that management should emphasize the importance of treating employees consistently fairly across the organization in order that they experience psychological health and positive work attitudes during change. Further, employees' own personal fair treatment and their perceptions of the treatment of their co-workers predicted important employee responses to change, that is, affective organizational commitment and emotional exhaustion (Bernerth et al. (2011). I now examine the subsection of Justice as an IV and begin with Tyler and de Cremer (2005).

Justice as an IV and a Leadership Tool

In addition to the four studies mentioned earlier, I include three additional studies that are a relevant special case to the role of workplace justice as an independent variable (IV). The three studies—Tyler and De Cremer (2005), Gopinath and Becker (2000), and Michel, Stegmaier, and Sonntag (2010)—focus on the role of leaders during change, and include justice dimensions as IVs, and employee reactions or outcomes of change. I begin with Tyler and De Cremer (2005), as an exemplar.

TYLER AND DE CREMER

Tyler and de Cremer (2005) sought to determine whether PJ serves as a valuable leadership tool that motivates employees' cooperation with the acquiring (merger and acquisition) organization. Building on the Group Engagement Model (Tyler & Blader, 2000, 2003) proposing that leaders are able to enhance employees' internal motivation by consistently demonstrating the fairness of procedures used to manage work groups, the researchers proposed that leaders attain followers' acceptance of their vision and motivate them by basing their leadership on fair decision-making procedures, in this case where the organization involved a recent merger, through the policies and practices used to implement the merger (Lind & Tyler, 1988; Tyler & Smith, 1998).

Tyler and de Cremer (2005) argued that if leaders enact their authority in a manner that employees believe is fair, then the individuals will, in turn, display high support for their employer's goals and cooperate by supporting it during change. The researchers viewed leaders' effectiveness in increasing employees' cooperation as primarily a function of procedural fairness (PJ) that stimulates employees to see the goals of the company as their own goals, rather than the economic or instrumental outcomes associated with distributive justice (Tyler, 2004), although both variables, PJ and a combination of economic and instrumental outcomes, were included in the empirical test of the proposed model.

In addition, the researchers proposed a chain of relationships such that employees' perceptions of their leaders' application of fair procedures would influence two variables capturing employees' evaluations of their leaders: (1) leader's *legitimacy*, that is, employees' beliefs that the actions of their leaders ought to be accepted; and (2) leaders' *competence*, that is, employees' beliefs that management understands how to keep the organization competitive and successful. Tyler and de Cremer (2005) proposed that these two leadership evaluations would subsequently mediate the relationship between PJ and two dependent variables reflecting their acceptance of the merger: (a) acceptance of the leaders' vision that merger is a good strategic decision; and (b) employees' motivation to work for the new company, such as their motivation, acceptance of the leader's vision, and so forth. Finally, based on social identity theory, Tyler and de Cremer (2005) also included a moderator in the chain of relationships, employees' social identification with the new company, and proposed that employees' perceptions of the fairness of procedures managers used to implement the merger would be stronger when employees highly identified with the new organization.

METHODOLOGY

To test their model, Tyler and de Cremer (2005) used a sample of 540 employees (40% response rate) working for the US division of a large multinational financial organization. Another company took over the division in a hostile merger that justifiably generated concern among employees about the loss of their jobs as many subsequently were terminated or had their salary and job status reduced. Thus employees' acceptance of the new organizational leader's vision and their support for the new organization were questionable. Multiple regression analysis was used to test hypotheses.

FINDINGS

Results indicated that PJ emerged as an important determinant of leader legitimacy and trust in leader competence, whereas the combined outcome variable capturing valued economic and instrumental outcomes (e.g., satisfactory salary/benefit changes, more and improved job opportunities, etc.) was not significantly linked to leader legitimacy, only to leader competence. Whereas PJ significantly related to the two acceptance-dependent variables-- acceptance of leaders' vision that the merger was a good strategic decision, and motivation to support the new organization--the combined economic and instrumental outcome variable significantly influenced only the acceptance of leader's vision that the merger was a good strategic decision. Results also supported the mediating hypothesis only for PJ, not for the combined economic and instrumental outcome variable. Thus, employees' views of their leaders' legitimacy and competence mediated the PJ→acceptance of vision relationship and the PJ→motivation to support the new organization relationship. Finally, findings on the moderator hypotheses were significant only for PJ, not for the combined economic and instrumental outcome variable. When employees' identification with the new organization was high, the effect of PJ on a combined index of both acceptance measures—whether employees viewed the merger as a good strategic decision and whether they were motivated to work for the new organization—was significant. Conversely, when identification was low, the effect of PJ on the combined index was not significant. Overall, PJ more consistently affected employees' evaluation of their leaders' legitimacy and competence, and the two acceptance outcomes—supporting leader's vision and being motivated to support the new organization during the change, than did the combined tangible economic and instrumental outcome variable.

IMPLICATIONS

There were three implications: (1) Faced with merger situations, leaders should be aware that providing tangible resources to employees is not the only method to motivate their acceptance of the leader's vision and their general support of the organization during the change. (2) Rather, leaders must be sensitive to the importance of implementing fair decision-making processes. (3) Those leaders who clearly demonstrate their interest and concerns in employees' well-being, and reflect this in their decision- making processes, are more likely to stimulate employees' acceptance of, and cooperation with, the change, rather than resisting change. Tyler and de Cremer (2005) argued that the chances of change success are much greater when: (a) employees' embrace change; and (b) when leaders understand how displaying fairness in their exercise of authority motivates employees to believe in the benefits of change and accept the newly merged organization.

Gopinath and Becker

Gopinath and Becker (2000) examined relationships between managerial communication, survivors perceptions of the procedural justice of layoffs, and their reactions within the context of a divestiture situation in which the medical products division of a large, well-established chemical company was sold to a recently created corporation. The researchers proposed:

H1. Higher levels of perceived procedural justice regarding divestiture are predictive of higher levels of trust in new ownership and higher levels of postdivestiture commitment to the organization. **Supported**

H2. Perceptions of PJ regarding divestitures account for variance in trust in new ownership and postdivestiture commitment to the organization over and above variance due to perceptions of PJ regarding layoffs. **Supported**

H3. Communications from management that help employees understand the events (including layoffs) relating to the sale enhance employees' perceptions of PJ regarding the divestiture and layoffs. **Supported**

H4. Controlling for perceptions of PJ, helpful company communications lead to higher levels of trust in new ownership and greater postdivestiture commitment to the organization. **Supported for Commitment, Not Supported for Trust13**

The study was conducted on the sale of the medical products division of a large, established chemical company to a recently created corporation for the stated reasons that the division no longer fit the parent company's strategy. Employees were led to believe that only the ownership of the division would change, whereas jobs and benefits would be protected. Closer to the sale, it became clear that layoffs would occur and that several employee benefits would also change. The sale process took eight months and on its completion, the division leaders enacted three rounds of layoffs affecting five percent of the employee numbers. Two rounds of data collection were beginning five weeks after the layoffs were completed and after division management informed the researchers that layoffs were completed and no more were under immediate consideration. Wave 1 included measures of the management communication and the procedural justice of both the sale and the layoffs (IVs). It was collected through surveys requesting an anonymous ID number that was sent to all 950 survivors. The wave led to the return of 314 usable surveys (33.1%). Wave 2 was sent two months later, and included the following DVs—trust in ownership, postdivestiture commitment to the organization, and social desirability as a control variable. Wave 2 yielded 318 usable responses, and ultimately, complete data on 144 employees (response rate approximately 15%).

THEORETICAL IMPLICATIONS

Findings support that:

1. Employees who perceived greater procedural justice vis–a-vis the divestiture at one point in time had higher levels of trust in the new ownership and a higher degree of postdivestiture commitment.
2. Perceptions of PJ divestiture are not the result of perceived layoff PJ but rather explained variance in trust and commitment unrelated to that yielded by the PJ of layoffs; thus results indicate that the context of layoffs must be better understood in order to predict employee reactions.
3. Communications from management that help employees understand the events of divestiture increased the individuals' PJ perceptions for both divestiture and layoffs, affecting trust and commitment both directly and indirectly. However these results are expected to replicate only when leaders enact and communicate authentic PJ, not when they seek to create the impression, rather than the substance, of PJ.

Michel et al.

Michel et al.'s (2010) research builds on Tyler and Blader's (2000) group engagement model proposing that: (a) employees engage and cooperate with an organization in order to receive feedback allowing them to develop and/or maintain a favorable organizational identity; and (b) that procedural justice (PJ) is an important source of feedback affecting individual employees' organizational identity, a variable that influences employees' cooperation with the change in the form of supportive attitudes, values, and behaviors (Blader & Tyler, 2005). The researchers conducted their study at a German university undergoing transformational change for the purpose of increasing its competitiveness in the domain of higher education. University management and faculty associations jointly restructured academic departments, implemented bachelors and masters programs, developed new partnerships with external and international schools, created attractive research positions with tenure options for young academics, and established a process for maintaining work-life balance. Based on the group engagement model, the researchers expected that employees who are treated procedurally fairly by management will begin to view themselves as appreciated members of the organization. Thus, they posited:

H1. PJ is positively related to organizational identification.

Further, if employees identify with their organization, they will tend to view the organizational change as necessary and beneficial and reflect this in their level of affective change commitment. Therefore,

H2. Organizational identification mediates the positive relationship between PJ and affective commitment to change.

Group engagement theory suggests that employees identifying with the organizational collective will tend to view their place in the world as consistent with the organization's values, ideology, and culture. Values–congruence fit is defined as the sharing of values, goals and norms between employees and their organization (Lauver and Kristof-Brown, 2001). Thus,

H3. Organizational identification mediates the positive relationship between PJ and values–congruence fit.

Employees who identify with their organization are also motivated to support change processes in order to maintain a positive self-concept emerging from their membership in the organization. Therefore,

H4. Organizational identification mediates the positive relationship between PJ and change supporting behavior.

Employees who engage cooperatively with the organization's change initiative are likely to hold favorable, change specific attitudes, possess common values with the organization, and support the change with their behavior across different phases of the change. Thus,

H5. Organizational identification at Time 1 mediates the positive relationship between PJ and affective change commitment at Time 2, after controlling for the Time 1 level of change commitment.

H6. Organizational identification at Time 1 mediates the positive relationship between PJ at Time 1 and values-congruence fit at Time 2, after controlling for the Time 1 level of values–congruence fit.

H7. Organizational identification at Time 1 mediates the positive relationship between PJ at Time 1 and Time 2 change supporting behavior, after controlling for the Time 1 level of change supporting behavior.

METHODOLOGY

Phase 1 took place one year after the announcement of the change initiative. Thirteen hundred surveys were distributed to academic staff members and graduate students yielding a final sample of 315 (23.83% response rate). Phase 2 occurred six months later with the initial changes still in progress. Matching members' two surveys yielded a sample of 110 people in the longitudinal analysis. There was no significant difference between those responding at both Time 1 and Time 2 and those responding only at Time 1. Analyses were conducted with structural equation modeling (Amos 7.0).

FINDINGS

All predicted model paths were significant. A post hoc analysis indicated that supportive change attitudes, values, and change-supportive behavior at the beginning of the change process influenced the three forms of cooperation some six months later as the change progressed. All hypotheses were supported except for H7, and model fit was better at Time 2 than Time 1.

IMPLICATIONS

Results provided strong support for the group engagement model, identifying PJ as an important, direct determinant of individuals' identification with the organization, that, in turn, mediated the effects of PJ on employees' change-related outcomes of affective change commitment, values-congruence fit, and change-supportive behavior, together comprising the meta variable of employee cooperation with change. PJ reassured employees that they were valued, respected, and honored by the organization during the change, and encouraged them to identify with the organization. Subsequently, the individuals tended to cooperate with the change to increase the likelihood that it would be successful. The authors also note the importance that decisions are made in a procedurally just way during change in order that employees are able to develop perceptions of high PJ, and initiate a chain of relationships that ultimately results in their cooperation with change.

The Role of Workplace Justice as a Mediator

Four transitional change articles illustrate the workplace justice role of mediator. To illustrate the nature of this role, I present Kernan and Hanges (2002), as an exemplar and provide shorter summaries of the three remaining articles within this role.

Kernan and Hanges

Kernan and Hanges (2002) studied employees working in the research and development facility of a division within a major multinational pharmaceutical corporation undergoing a significant reorganization. Building on the group value model (Lind & Tyler, 1988), the agent-system model (Bies & Moag, 1986); the value-expressive role of organizational justice, and Colquitt's justice findings, Kernan and Hanges (2002) conceptually developed and longitudinally tested a comprehensive model of survivor reactions to their organization by incorporating three sets of variables: antecedents, fairness, and consequences. Thus, three justice dimensions serve as mediators between the antecedents and outcomes of Kernan and Hanges' (2002) model. Based on a review of the literature, Kernan and Hanges (2002) identified four possible antecedents—employee input, organizational support, quality of information received from supervisors (communication), and the consistency between the reorganization objectives communicated at the beginning of the change process and managements' subsequent actions (implementation). They also included three dimensions of justice based on the work of Colquitt (2001) and predicted the effect of each antecedent on the relevant justice dimension. The researchers hypothesized that procedural justice (PJ) would be stimulated by employee input or voice because of the process decisions occurring during reorganizations:

H1. Employee input will be positively related to perceptions of procedural justice.

Although employee input was expected to be most strongly related to PJ, the group value model of Lind and Tyler (1988) suggests that it also may be linked to interpersonal justice, (INTERJ), defined as the quality of interpersonal treatment individuals receive as procedures are enacted (Colquitt, 2001).

H2. Employee input will be positively related to perceptions of INTERJ.

Kernan and Hanges (2002) built on the value-expressive component of justice to argue that support activities reflect respect and sensitivity for employees by their management and, thereby, enhance employees' INTERJ (Naumann, Bennett, Bies, & Manin,1998).

H3. Employee perceptions of support for victims will be positively related to their perceptions of INTERJ.

Because change situations are often marked by high levels of uncertainty and chaos (Tombaugh & White, 1990), the quality of information that employees receive from their managers during reorganization is important but often deteriorates during change, limiting their access to information (Cascio, 1993). Thus, ongoing communication about all phases of the reorganization that employees view as accurate, timely, and helpful is believed central to their sense making and uncertainty reduction (Schweiger & DeNisi, 1991), and critical for their views of fairness (Novelli, Kirkman, & Shapiro, 1995).

H4. The perceived quality of the communications received during the reorganization process will be positively related to INTERJ.

Both Greenberg (1993) and Colquitt (2001) have argued that informational justice (INFOJ) includes the justifications that management offers for its decisions that, in turn, affect employee perceptions of informational justice. Thus:

H5. The perceived quality of the communications received during the reorganization process will be positively related to INFOJ.

Finally, the researchers proposed that employees who perceived that the reorganization, as implemented, accomplished management's stated objectives, would experience higher levels of justice. Whitener, Brodt, Korsgaard, and Werner (1998) asserted that employees form attributions based on the consistency between management's words and actions, which then affect employees' perceptions of managers' trustworthiness (Whitener et al., 1998). The researchers expected that implementation perceptions would shape employees' feelings of being treated with respect and dignity and thus their perceptions of INTERJ.

H6. Implementation perceptions will be positively related to perceptions of INTERJ. That is, the more employees perceive consistency between management objectives and behavior, the greater their perceptions of INTERJ.

Further, the researchers argued that employees' judgments about the consistency of change objectives and implementation influence their assessment of the fairness of particular processes, interpersonal interactions, and information received.

H7. Implementation perceptions will be positively related to perceptions of INFOJ.

Remaining study hypotheses examined how employees' perceptions of informational, interpersonal, and procedural justice related to outcomes previously found in many prior justice studies: job satisfaction (Davey, Kinicki, & Scheck, 1991; Martin & Bennett, 1996) affective organizational commitment (Folger & Konovsky, 1989), trust in management (Bruning, Keup, & Cooper, 1996), and turnover intentions (Daly & Geyer, 1994). Relying on Colquitt's (2001) results and Bies and Moag's (1986) agent-system model, Kernan and Hanges (2002) proposed that individuals rely on their INTERJ and INFOJ perceptions to determine their reactions to individual authority figures or agents (i.e., supervisors) and on PJ perceptions when determining how to react to the larger organization. Past research has consistently categorized affective organizational commitment and turnover intentions as system-level outcomes Colquitt et al. (2001). Thus, Kernan and Hanges (2002) hypothesized:

H8. PJ perceptions will be positively related to affective organizational commitment.

H9. PJ perceptions will be negatively correlated with intentions to leave the organization.

Although job satisfaction is considered to result from both supervisory and organizational-level factors, Colquitt et al.'s (2001) meta-analyses found PJ to be a better predictor of satisfaction than INTERJ or INFOJ. Thus, they hypothesized:

H10. PJ will be positively correlated with job satisfaction.

Based on the agent-system model the researchers also proposed PJ, INTERJ, and INFOJ as significant predictors of trust in management (Tyler & Bies, 1990).

H11. PJ will be positively correlated with trust in management.

H12. INTERJ will be positively correlated with trust in management.

H13. INFOJ will be positively correlated with trust in management.

METHODOLOGY

The researchers studied employees working in the research and development facility of a division within a major multinational pharmaceutical corporation undergoing a significant reorganization. After the new organization had been in place for approximately 2 months (Time 1), researchers administered a survey assessing demographic indicators, and all justice, antecedents, and outcome variables to all 328 employees. The response rate was 69%. A second survey, conducted 10 months after the first (Time 2), collected data on demographics and outcome variables. The researchers matched 82 Time 2 and Time 1 surveys and used EQS to assess the fit between the proposed model and the data.

FINDINGS

All hypothesized paths in the model were significant and consistent with Hypotheses 1–7, proposed antecedents, significantly related to the predicted justice variables. Hypotheses 8–11 were also strongly supported, such that employees' perceptions of PJ were significantly related to the four outcome variables in the hypothesized direction. As predicted by H12 and H13, INTERJ and INFOJ added unique variance to the trust in management variable. Examination indicated that all antecedents were equally important in influencing perceptions of fair treatment for PJ. Implementation emerged as the strongest predictor of INTERJ. Results also showed that the PJ-management trust relationship was stronger than that for INFOJ. The reorganization effort remained stable over time, and two years later still predicted employee outcomes through PJ.

In summary, Kernan and Hanges (2002) developed a comprehensive (antecedents, justice dimensions, consequences) model of survivors' reactions to two reorganizations that included layoffs. The categorization of justice dimensions as mediators of the antecedent—employee reaction outcomes within the research is based on the nature of the model, rather than on empirical tests for mediation and the belief that the mediation category is the best fit of the four categories. The researchers identified four antecedents (1) perceived employee input or voice—PJ, INTERJ; (2) perceived organizational support for victims of reorganization—INTERJ; (3) perceived quality of information received from supervisors—INTERJ, INFOJ, and (4) the perceived consistency of change objectives and implementation—INTERJ that directly influenced three different types of work place justice, and, subsequently affected change related outcomes. Despite predictions, all antecedents were equally important in influencing PJ. The consistency of change objectives and implementation emerged as the strongest antecedent for INTERJ. In terms of justice effects on employees' reactions to change, Kernan and Hanges (2002) also proposed differential predictions for the three types of justice, on both system and agent outcomes.[3] PJ directly predicted system outcomes of affective organizational commitment and job satisfaction, and negatively predicted employees' intention to turnover, as well as positively predicting trust in management, as did INTERJ and INFOJ, with the effect of PJ on trust in management being stronger than that of INFOJ.

Daly and Geyer

Daly and Geyer (1994), a second study in this justice role, studied transitional changes in seven facilities in the Chicago area, and predicted that PJ would mediate the relationship between two interventions intended to reduce employee resistance to change (operationalized as turnover): (1) employee voice or input; and (2) education about the nature of the change and the justification for it, and the outcome variable of intention to leave. Findings supported the mediating effect of PJ on the education intervention—resistance to change relationship but not on the voice/input—resistance to change one. This result is somewhat surprising given Kernan and Hanges' (2002) finding that voice was a significant antecedent for PJ. The researchers suggested that the absence of a voice effect on PJ was due to the fact that respondents did not expect to have voice in relocation decisions.

Wu, Neubert, and Yi

Wu, Neubert, and Yi (2007) conducted their research in a large Chinese oil company undergoing major administrative changes including, abolishing lifetime employment, implementing a new performance management system; and initiating continuous improvement programs. Study objectives included: (a) Determining whether employees' INFOJ and INTERJ mediate the influence of transformational leadership (TFL), a style that stimulates followers to change their beliefs, values, capabilities, and motivates them to raise performance beyond their own self-interest to the benefit of the organization, Avolio (1999), on employees' cynicism (frustration, disillusionment, and negative feelings toward, and distrust of, a person, ideology, social convention or institution) about organizational change (CAOC) (Reichers, Wanous, & Austin, 1997); and (b) examining INFOJ and INTERJ perceptions as mechanisms mediating the effects of TFL on employee CAOC.

The researchers expected that immediate supervisors would influence employee justice perceptions through various dimensions of TFL, for example, supervisors' individualized consideration and inspirational motivation. Relying on both theoretical logic about TFL dimensions and their effects on followers' reaction (Bass. 1985), as well as meta-analytic results (Judge and Piccolo, 2004), Wu et al. (2007) expected TFL to negatively affect employees' CAOC *and* that workplace justice perceptions would then mediate the effects of TFL on employees' CAOC.

Wu et al. (2007) proposed and tested the following hypotheses:

H1. Supervisor TFL will be negatively related to follower CAOC ***Supported***

H2. INFOJ perceptions will mediate the relationship between supervisor TFL and employee CAOC. ***Supported***

H3. INTERJ perceptions will mediate the relationship between supervisor TFL and employee CAOC. ***Supported***

Finally, the researchers also expected that the bonding and closeness of unit members would enhance INFOJ and INTERJ perceptions and hypothesized:

H4. INFOJ will mediate the moderated relationship between TFL, group cohesion perceptions, and employee CAOC such that the higher the group cohesion perceptions, the stronger the influence of TFL on INFOJ and the stronger the influence of INFOJ on CAOC. ***Not Supported***

H5. INTERJ will mediate the moderated relationship between TFL, group cohesion perceptions, and employee CAOC such that the higher the group cohesion perceptions, the stronger the influence of TFL on interpersonal justice and the stronger the influence of interpersonal justice on CAOC. ***Supported***

METHODOLOGY

Wu et al. (2007) administered a survey a year after the changes started to provide employees time to form opinions about the change. Some 467 surveys were returned (72% response rate). Hierarchical regression was used to examine hypotheses.

CONCEPTUAL AND PRACTICAL CONTRIBUTIONS

Wu et al.'s (2007) research: (a) Identified the psychological processes through which transformational leadership influences the CAOC; (b) Confirmed the mediating effects of INFOJ and INTERJ on the TFL–CAOC relationship; (c) Supported the proposed mediating effect of INTERJ, but not INFOJ, on the moderated relationship among TFL, group cohesion perceptions, and employee CAOC. Higher group cohesion perceptions served to strengthen the influence of TFL on INTERJ and that of INTERJ on CAOC. Practically, the researchers encouraged top Chinese leaders to provide TFL training to reduce their employees' level of cynicism at work, and to increase resources that aid in building cohesive work groups, thus enhancing the strength of TFL effects on CAOC. Finally, top leaders of Chinese organizations should recognize that their own and supervisors' TFL skills are an effective mechanism for managing change.

Rodell and Colquitt

Rodell and Colquitt (2009) developed and tested a model of anticipatory justice in the context of one specific organizational change—a smoking ban. Drawing, on work introducing anticipatory justice, defined as expectations regarding whether individuals would experience justice in the context of a future event by Shapiro and Kirkman (1999, 2001), the researchers sought to extend what is currently known about the construct. Specifically they sought to address questions such as how perceptions of anticipatory justice develop, how and when anticipatory justice impacts experienced justice, and how it fits with the models and theories that drive the mainstream justice literature. The development of their model was based on pairing Shapiro and Kirkman's (2001) "seminal theorizing on anticipatory justice with fairness heuristic theory" (p. 989), which focuses on the forming and use of fairness perceptions (Lind, 2001). Drawing from initial studies that suggested the theoretical importance of the anticipatory justice construct, Rodell and Colquitt (2009) wished to address the important question of where justice perceptions came from, and whether they emerged from anticipations that were experienced either weeks or months before a target event.

The researchers noted that Fairness Heuristic Theory helps people determine whether to cooperate with those of higher authority (e.g. supervisor), by taking a cognitive shortcut and forming a global impression of fairness from readily available information and then relying on it to interpret their experiences and to guide their reactions. They proposed that global fairness is derived from a blend of important past justice experiences, and is generally linked to an entity such as a supervisor or an organization. Thus, Rodell and Colquitt (2009) propose that global fairness predicts anticipatory fairness, which, then, predicts experienced justice; however, global fairness also directly affects experienced justice yielding partial mediation, and. Thus, they hypothesized:

H1. Global perceptions of supervisory fairness are positively related to anticipatory justice perceptions. ***Supported***

H2. Anticipatory procedural, procedural interpersonal, and informational justice are positively related to experienced procedural interpersonal and informational justice respectively. ***Supported***

H3. Global perceptions of supervisory fairness are positively related to experienced justice perceptions. ***Partially Supported, Not Supported For Experienced Procedural Justice***

H4. The relationship between global supervisory fairness is partially mediated by anticipatory justice. ***Supported***

Rodell & Colquitt (2009) also propose that anticipatory justice is an event judgment because it involves a specific assessment of one action or a related group of actions.

Thus, organizational change characteristics that enhance employees' emphasis on the event, rather than the entity, will strengthen the linkage between anticipatory and experienced justice. The researchers chose to focus on two well-recognized change characteristics: (1) uncertainty—when employees do not possess the adequate information or understanding to predict the future; and (2) outcome favorability—when employees' outcome is beneficial. Rodell and Colquitt (2009) also note Shapiro and Kirkman's (2001) proposal that uncertainty heightens individuals' anticipatory activity—meaning their contemplation and rumination on a forthcoming event; they also note Wong and Weiner's (1981) finding that individuals who experience a negative outcome of an event are more likely to search for information. Thus, the researchers hypothesized:

H5. The perceived uncertainty created by the change moderates the relationship between anticipatory and experienced justice such that the relationship is more positive when perceived uncertainty is high. ***Partially Supported, Not Supported for PJ***

H6. The perceived outcome favorability of the change moderates the relationship between anticipatory justice and experienced justice such that the relationship is more positive when perceived favorability is low. ***Partially Supported, Not Supported for PJ, INFOJ***

Noting Lind's (2001) argument that changes like leadership, restructuring, mergers, and so forth cause individuals to reduce their focus on global impressions in favor of a new examination of justice relevant information, Rodell and Colquitt (2009) hypothesized

H7. The perceived uncertainty created by the change moderates the relationship between global supervisory fairness and experienced justice such that the relationship is less positive when perceived uncertainty is high. ***Partially Supported, Not Supported for PJ***

H8. The perceived outcome favorability of the change moderates the relationship between global supervisory fairness and experienced justice such that the relationship is less positive when perceived favorability is low. ***Not Supported***

Finally, based on prior work by Novelli et al.,(1995) examining the role of change on anticipatory justice, Rodell & Colquitt (2009) proposed that high levels of INTERJ and INFOJ can increase the effectiveness of change-management steps (e.g. such as promoting a shared vision of the change, spreading change effectively through the organization, modifying policies, processes, and structures to stabilize change), thereby providing high levels of support for it. Thus, the researchers hypothesized:

H9. Experienced justice is positively related to smoking ban support. ***Partially Supported, Not Supported for Experienced PJ, INFOJ***

THEORETICAL AND PRACTICAL IMPLICATIONS

Results indicate that global perceptions of supervisory fairness (fairness heuristic) were strongly related to anticipated justice with respect to PJ, INTERJ, and INFOJ. Further, the fairness heuristic also directly related to experienced justice. Individuals' experienced justice levels were affected by two preexisting beliefs: the anticipatory justice attached to the impending ban and the global sense of fairness attached to the respective supervisor. Anticipatory INTERJ and INFOJ effects were strengthened when employees perceived the ban as high in uncertainty and low in outcome favorability. The global fairness effect decreased when uncertainty perceptions were high in the case of INTERJ and INFOJ. Support for change (the smoking ban) was significantly related to experienced INTERJ but not to INFOJ or PJ, possibly, the researchers suggested, because information about INTERJ was more readily available than for INFOJ and PJ, that is, employees may have found it easier to assess politeness and respectfulness than to judge consistency, bias suppression, or truthfulness. Practically, the results of this study show the importance of managers' developing a strong reputation for fairness early in their tenure as professionals.

Overall the four preceding studies provide evidence of the mediation effects of three justice dimensions, INFOJ, INTERJ and PJ, in the relationship between different change antecedents, including voice, anticipatory justice, interventions such as transformational leadership, education about resistance to change, *and* employee reactions such as job-satisfaction organizational commitment, intention to turnover, emotional exhaustion, and support for change. As a result, I agree with Kernan and Hanges' (2002) statement that both the antecedents of justice dimensions and the justice dimensions themselves provide valuable inputs into the effective management of organizational change.

The Role of Workplace Justice as a Moderator

Eight studies fall into the moderating-workplace-justice role, with two, Greenberg (2006) and Shapiro and Kirkman (1999), falling into a subsection on equity-theory concerns. I review Korsgaard, Sapienza, and Schweiger (2002) as the exemplar study to begin this role category.

Korsgaard, et al.

Korsgaard, et al. (2002) conducted their research in two coal-powered electric generation plants owned by a single utility undergoing a transitional change to re-engineer core business processes and increase its competitiveness with new organizations rapidly entering its market. The authors reasoned that employees' would experience change as disconcerting and highly ambiguous and thus attempt to make sense out of the change process as soon as the organization began to plan for the change, rather than after it was in place. They also asserted that as employees are unlikely to experience new benefits during the change process, they will tend to grow apprehensive about potentially unfavorable outcomes that they will soon begin to experience and, thus, will begin to display a number of negative affective reactions, even before the change is implemented. These negative reactions will tend to undermine the employment relationship between the employees and their organizational employer, affecting: (a) employees' perceptions of the obligations they have to the organization; (b) their trust of management; and (c) their intention to remain a part of the organization in the future.

HYPOTHESES

Based on employees' vicarious learning from individuals in other organizations, and prior research (Rousseau & Tijoriwala, 1999), Kosgaard et al. (2002) posited that employees would view the planning stage of the organizational change as a signal that the organization was reducing its obligations to them and hypothesized:

H1. Employees' perceptions of their organization's obligations to them will decline following the planning of organizational change.

Assuming the validity of H1, employees were expected to perceive a weaker employment relationship with their employer, and thus, to begin reneging on their own obligations to the organization, their trust of management, and their intention to remain with the organization. However, employees' perceptions of PJ were predicted to moderate the relationship between the planning of the change and employees' negative reactions such that high levels of PJ would lead them to believe that the organization held positive views of their standing and worth, would protect their interests, and would provide them with fair outcomes in the long term. Korsgaard et al. (2002) posited:

H2. PJ will negatively moderate the negative relationship between the planning of organizational change and employees' perceived obligations to the organization such that when PJ is high, the relationship will remain the same, whereas when PJ is low, the quality of the employment relationship will decrease.

H3. PJ will moderate the negative relationship between the planning of organizational change and employees' trust of management such that when PJ is high, the relationship will remain the same, whereas when PJ is low, the relationship will decrease.

H4. PJ will positively moderate the relationship between the planning of organizational change and employees' intention to leave the organization, such that when PJ is high, the relationship will be negative, whereas when PJ is low, the relationship will be positive.

METHODOLOGY

A longitudinal design was used for the study. A sample of 115 employees participated in both baseline and the follow-up surveys, separated by 45 days. A multivariate test showed that the two plants did not differ in terms of study variables. Repeated measure regression was used to test hypotheses.

FINDINGS

HI, positing the relationship between planning for the change, employees' perceptions of a decline in the organizations' obligations to them over time, was not supported. The researchers' explanation of this lack of support was that employees believed that employer obligations *should* remain the same, even if they expected the opposite. H2, PJ's negative moderation of the relationship between the planning of change and employees' perceived obligations to the organization was supported, such that when PJ was high, the relationship remained the same, whereas when PJ was low, the relationship decreased. H3: This hypothesis posited PJ's negative effect on trust of management was not supported but instead, reversed. When PJ was low, trust remained the same, whereas when PJ was high, trust increased. Finally, H4 positing a positive moderating effect of PJ on the positive relationship between the organization's planning for change and employees intention to leave the organization was also supported.

THEORETICAL AND PRACTICAL IMPLICATIONS

Results indicated that even in the earliest stages of organizational change, management's development of a change plan might negatively impact employee perceptions, attitude, and intentions. However, the presence of high PJ signals employees that the organization values, respects, and honors their contributions, tends to reduce their tendency to rigidly resist the change and, instead, to support it through their attitudes and behaviors, a proposal indirectly supported by the work of Brockner, Wiesenfield and Martin (1995) in studying workforce reduction. Practically, findings suggest that managers may underestimate the impact of the planning process and its cumulative effects at subsequent change stages. Thus, executives should carefully consider how to orchestrate and enact change across its different stages, not just at the point of implementation. Finally, research results indicate that executives should better understand the elements that comprise PJ (e.g., voice, consideration, feedback and justification, etc.) and learn to apply them wisely in order to build change success, rather than to undermine it.

Brockner, Grover, Reed, De Witt, & O'Malley

Brockner, Grover, Reed, De Witt, & O'Malley (1987) studied survivor reactions in the midst of layoffs, and found that the perceived fair treatment of victims during layoffs moderated the relationship between survivors' identification with victims, higher employee performance (lab study), and higher levels of organizational commitment (field study), such that outcomes such as performance/organizational commitment were lowest when fair treatment of employees during layoffs were perceived as low and survivors closely identified with layoff victims.

Greenberg

Greenberg (1994), drawing on considerable research and theory on the social drivers of justice (Bies, 1987; Greenberg, 1990), examined the moderating effects of INFOJ and INTERJ on 312 nonsmoking and smoking clerical employees' acceptance of a nonsmoking ban. The ban was comprised of their affective organizational commitment, their behavioral intention to turnover, and their intention to go along with the ban and to stop smoking completely while at work. He hypothesized:

H1a. A smoking ban will be better accepted when employees receive high amounts of information about the ban than when they receive low amounts of information about the ban. **Supported**

H1b. A smoking ban will be better accepted when it is announced in a manner demonstrating a high amount of social sensitivity than when it is announced in a manner demonstrating a low amount of social sensitivity. **Supported**

H1c. The lowest amount of acceptance will occur when levels of both information and social sensitivity are low, and the highest degree of acceptance will occur when levels of both information and social sensitivity are high. **Supported**

Greenberg (1994) drew on Cropanzano and Folger's (1989) referent cognitions theory arguing that peoples' resentment is triggered by the receipt of negative outcomes when they believe that they would have received more favorable outcomes had decision makers implemented the procedures they should have implemented. Thus, he reasoned that explanations of outcomes aid acceptance of negative outcomes because they are likely to provide justifiable ground for the undesirable outcomes, and he noted research confirming the role of interpersonal justice variables in promoting the acceptance of negative outcomes (Bies, 1987). Greenberg (1994) further reasoned that INFOJ and INTERJ would each interact with outcome severity and thus have a greater impact in promoting acceptance of the ban by those who are most adversely affected by the smoking band than by those who are least adversely affected. He posited:

H2a. Nonsmokers will perceive the ban as acceptable regardless of the thoroughness of the information imparted and the interpersonal treatment received when it is explained. **Supported**

H2b. Heavy smokers will perceive the ban as more acceptable when informational justice is high (i.e., when high amounts of information were presented) than when it is low. **Supported**

H2c. Heavy smokers will perceive the ban as more acceptable when interpersonal justice is high (i.e., high amounts of social sensitivity about the effects of the smoking ban are shown) than when it is low. **Supported**

THEORETICAL IMPLICATIONS

Benefits of using fair social treatment to promote the acceptance of a smoking ban proved greater for the heaviest smokers who were most influenced by that treatment. Greenberg's 1994 article also provided early supportive conceptual evidence for separating informational and interpersonal justice into two separate dimensions. Results also provided further evidence supporting existing findings of a self-serving bias in the acceptance of outcomes, such that individuals are likely to accept outcomes that are more beneficial to them personally. Other findings of this study provided tentative evidence of why providing information about an outcome, or expressing concern about its potential impact is at least partially due to the tendency for fair social treatment to reduce negative reactions to the event—in this case, the smoking ban. However, Greenberg (1994) agreed that evidence is currently far from definitive and that additional explanations likely exist. Thus he asserted that there was a strong need for further research on this issue.

Kikul, Lester, & Finkl

Kikul, Lester, & Finkl (2002) also examined the moderation of workplace justice. Specifically, the researchers examined the moderating effect of workplace justice on the relationship between both intrinsic (freedom, autonomy, participation, development and support opportunities) and extrinsic aspects (flexible work schedules, competitive salaries, safe work environment, and rewards) of psychological contract breach, and four change-related outcomes—job satisfaction, intentions to leave the organization, in-role (task) performance, and organizational citizenship behavior during organizational change. They proposed that INTERJ would negatively moderate the intrinsic aspects of the contract and outcome relationships because of employees' greater concern about interpersonal justice. Conversely, they expected that PJ would negatively moderate the extrinsic aspects of the contract and the outcomes, because of the employer's greater ease in developing formal procedures for these outcomes. Both hypotheses were fully supported, providing strong support for the moderating effects of

PJ and INTERJ on different aspects of the psychological contract.

Fedor et al.

Fedor et al. (2006) examined the impact of organizational change on employees' commitment to both the change and to their organizational employer. The authors argued that the way management treats and involves its employees is particularly important in shaping their reactions to large-scale organizational change. The researchers used a multilevel design to examine work-unit members' *shared* perceptions (unit level of analysis) about the impact of fairness in the change process on members' (individual level) commitment to the change and to their organization. They hypothesized:

H1. Change fairness at the work-unit level will be positively related to perceptions of both change commitment and changes in organizational commitment. **Not Supported**

Arguing that employees' negative reactions to change might have resulted from poor change implementation or outcomes that benefit the organization, rather than its employees, Fedor et al. (2006) proposed:

H2. The positive relationships between change fairness and the favorable impact of change on an employee (termed *changed favorableness*) and the two commitment-related outcomes (change commitment and organizational commitment) will be moderated by the size of job and work-unit-level changes. More directly, the relationships between change fairness and change favorableness and the commitment outcomes (a) will be greater when both levels of change (work-unit level and job level) are high, and (b) will be greater when job-level change is high and unit-level change is low, rather than vice versa.

METHODOLOGY

The research examined 32 different organizational changes, including nine reorganizations or restructuring initiatives, eight implementations of new technology or reengineering, several mergers/consolidations of units, and several leadership and strategy changes. In order to reduce same source bias, the sample of 764 respondents were *assigned by their managers to one of two surveys*: (a) an organizational-change survey capturing data on specific change and change practices, or (b) a personal-change survey that examined individual reactions to change and the impact of change on the individual's own job.

MEASURES

Work-unit-level measures included work-unit change, change favorableness—the way employees of a work unit felt about the consequences of the change for unit members, and change fairness. To this writer they seem to be a composite of both interpersonal and informational justice—comprised of five items with a 5-point, Likert response scale.[4] *At the individual level,* measures included job-level change (Caldwell et al., 2004); measures included change commitment (Herscovitch & Meyer, 2002) and organizational commitment (Mowday et al., 1979 adapted for the change context).

FINDINGS

Results revealed no support for H1. Although the three-way interaction of change fairness, size of work-unit change, and size of job-level change on change commitment predicted by H2 was not supported, the two-way interaction of change fairness and job- level change *on change commitment* was significant. Further, *the moderation of change fairness on the work-unit change and organizational commitment was significant.*

Conceptual implications included: (a) Change fairness was important for organizational commitment when work-unit-change levels were increasing. The explanation given for the failure of predicted fairness effects was that prior studies have generally tested these effects in situations in which the outcomes of change are not available and thus, not assessed. Testing this argument with the favorability of change variable omitted from the equation, they found a significant three-way interaction with fairness and the two change levels. Overall, Fedor et al. (2006) make a strong case for the importance of more multilevel studies of organizational change and more dynamic measures of important change variables, that is, commitment that is collected at strategic points of the change.

One caveat however, is that, although preliminary analyses for the study found evidence that change favorability and change fairness are two separate factors, simple correlation ($r = .35$), much prior research in the justice area indicates that judgments of outcome favorability and outcome fairness *are* psychologically similar, often load as a single factor in a confirmatory factor analysis, and generally have been "viewed as reflecting the same psychology" (Tyler, 1994; Tyler & De Cremer, 2005;Tyler & Lind,1992). Thus, it seems important to test this issue further at the group level of analysis, rather than at the individual level.

Bernerth, Armenakis, Field, and Walker

Bernerth, Armenakis, Field, and Walker (2007) studied a spinoff of a subsidiary manufacturer of durable goods from its parent company. They proposed that when employees find the outcomes of change undesirable or the procedures that shape change, unfair, explanations given in a timely manner might mitigate these reactions. The researchers examined the moderating effect of interactional justice (INTERACTJ) on the relationships between distributive justice (DJ) and employees' level of change commitment, as well as between procedural justice (PJ) and employees' level of change commitment. They also examined the moderating effect of DJ on the relationship between PJ and employees' level of change commitment because research by Lind and Tyler (1988) has shown that PJ influences perceptions of fairness and acceptability of outcomes, similar to Wu et al.'s (2007) research, Further, Bernerth predicted a negative main effect for all three types of justice on employees' organizational change cynicism—"a pessimistic viewpoint about change efforts being successful because those responsible for making change are blamed for being unmotivated, incompetent or both" (Wanous, Reichers, & Austin, 2000, p.133). Finally, the researchers predicted that organizational cynicism—defined as "a belief on the part of individuals that their organization lacks integrity, and that principles such as fairness, honesty and sincerity are sacrificed in favor or organizational self-interest" (Atwater L.E., Waldman, Atwater D., & Cartier, 2000, p. 279)—would negatively moderate the positive relationship between each of the three types of justice and change commitment.

FINDINGS

Results partially supported the positive moderation of INTERACTJ on the relationship of both DJ and PJ with change commitment, showing that the relationship was strongest when employees perceived high levels of INTERACTJ. However, high levels of one justice dimension did not compensate for low levels of the other as expected by the authors. Further, the moderation of DJ on the PJ change commitment relationship was not significant. Additional analyses indicated that DJ mediated, rather than moderated, the positive relationship between PJ and change commitment. Only DJ and INTERACTJ, not PJ, proved negatively related to employees' cynicism about organizational change. Finally, the moderating effect of organizational cynicism on the relationship between justice and change commitment, a moderation that could also be conceptualized as justice dimensions moderating cynicism and change, was significant for the two justice dimensions, as well as INTERACTJ, that is not currently considered to be a justice dimension. The reader should note that there is potential for substantial overlap of INTERACTJ and justice dimensions as interactional justice contains several different dimensions including PJ, INTERJ, and INFOJ (Colquitt, 2001).

The relationship between justice dimension and change commitment was strongest when organizational cynicism was low, rather than high.

In combination, the three preceding studies provide evidence that justice dimensions such as PJ, INTERJ, and DJ, as well as INTERACTJ, frequently play a moderating role on the relationship between change phases or relationships (e.g. the planning phase; Korsgaard et al., 2002), the quality of the employment relationship (Kikul et al., 2002), or other types of justice (INTERACTJ; Bernerth et al., 2007) and a variety of change-related outcomes (e.g., job satisfaction, employee psychological contract obligations, change commitment, intention to leave, and task performance).

The Role of Workplace Justice as a Moderator: Deterring Change-Related Inequity Effects on Valued Outcomes

Two final studies of this chapter fall within a subsection of the moderator role for workplace justice in the context of organizational change, Greenberg (2006), Shapiro and Kirkman (1999). I present Greenberg (2006) as an exemplar showing how change may stimulate strong inequity effects that subsequently influence employees' health.

Greenberg

Greenberg (2006) studied nurses working in four different hospitals in order to examine the distributive injustice effects of a decrease in pay policy (pay reduction) that had been implemented in two of the four facilities, and the subsequent physiological effects of participants' insomnia that was expected to occur as a result. As a second part of the research, Greenberg (2006) also trained nursing supervisors in the process of promoting INTERACTJ, in order to assess the predicted effectiveness of interactional justice in reducing insomnia.

The research built on the small amount of existing research identifying *distributive injustice*, DJ, employees' belief that they have not reaped benefits proportional to their investment in an event (Adams, 1965). Greenberg (2006) noted prior evidence that the greatest amount of stress occurred when injustice was experienced from both interactional and distributive justice (Elovainia, Kivimaki & Vahtera, 2002). Drawing on the demand, control, and support model of stress (Theorell & Karasek, 1996), he suggested that managers may change their behavior to provide greater social support to employees and thereby promote the individuals' perceptions of high levels of INTERACTJ (Bies, 2001; Bies and Moag, 1986). Greenberg (2006) proposed two hypotheses:

H1. Employees who encounter underpayment inequity on their jobs will experience higher levels of insomnia than those who do not encounter underpayment inequity.

H2. Underpaid workers whose supervisors are trained in techniques for promoting INTERACTJ will experience lower insomniac reactions than underpaid workers whose supervisors are not so trained.

METHODOLOGY

All total, 467 nurses participated in the study. The research design was an interrupted time series with a nonequivalent no-treatment control group series. A 2 × 2 (between) × 4 (within) mixed design was used for the research. The two between-subjects variables were pay (no change or underpaid), and interactional justice training (trained or untrained). One hospital was assigned to each of four groups created by cross-cutting the two between-subjects variables. The researcher collected reports of insomnia at two times following training.

Overall, underpaid employees reported greater insomnia than those whose pay was unchanged. Although differences decreased in magnitude over time as participants became accustomed to the new pay system, significant differences were found at all time periods following the change in pay. Nurses whose supervisors were trained in INTERACTJ displayed a lower level of insomnia over time. Taken together, these results support the effectiveness of training in INTERACTJ that was predicted in H2.

CONCEPTUAL AND PRACTICAL IMPLICATIONS

Conceptually, findings support the idea that perceived injustice may be viewed as an affective event stimulating stress reactions and that distributive injustice can be a strong determinant of emotional reactions (Weiss & Cropanzano, 1996). Further, results regarding nurses' insomnia indicate that perceived injustice is a determinant of psychosocial health risk factors (Vermunt & Steensma, 2005). Results provide evidence of a link between management training and insomnia, an indicator of workplace stress. Practically, findings offer strong support for developing greater opportunities for managers to use INTERACTJ training as a mechanism for decreasing the effect of a newly experienced stressor.

Shapiro and Kirkman

Shapiro and Kirkman (1999) examined two transitional changes resulting from the implementation of self-managing work teams (SMWTs) situated in Fortune 500 companies. The researchers expected that *employees' anticipation of distributive injustice,* defined as the anticipated receipt of unfair outcomes such as undesirable job assignments and added responsibilities, rather than distributive justice (Shapiro & Kirkman, 1999) caused SMWT-related concerns and resistance behavior [reduced work commitment and organizational citizenship behavior (OCB), intention to leave). Shapiro and Kirkman (1999) noted that past research shows that employees who perceive distributive injustice tend to display negative attitudes and behaviors (e.g., stealing from employer; Greenburg, 1990), and decreasing productivity (Pritchard, Dunnette, & Jorgenson, 1972), that are consistent with equity theory. They predicted that such employee responses (i.e., resisting the change to SMWT, lowering organizational commitment, intention to leave their jobs, and the display of low levels of OCB) would occur in their study when employees anticipated that they *would be* receiving unfair outcomes such as moving to SMWTs.

Fortunately, however, PJ has previously been found to offset the negative effects of distributive injustice for cases in which management decisions concerned layoffs and pay cuts, if employees perceive that the decision process itself was fair (Brockner et al., 1990). Thus, Shapiro and Kirkman (1999) also proposed that PJ would moderate the relationship between anticipatory distributive justice and employees' change-related work behaviors and attitudes. Findings strongly supported both predictions such that the level of anticipatory distributive injustice was negatively related to all but one of the aforementioned change-related outcomes (OCBs). Further, PJ moderated the positive relationship between anticipatory distributive injustice on employees' resistance responses such that high anticipatory distributive justice reduced employee resistance to change and increased their affective organizational commitment. No effect was found for employees' intention to leave. Please note that only one type of anticipatory justice was included in this study, distributive (inequity) anticipatory justice and see the Rodell and Colquitt (2009) article in The Role of Workplace Justice as a Mediator section of this chapter for an update on the determinants of anticipatory justice.

Both studies in this justice-moderator-role subsection provide strong evidence that change-related inequity occurs and tends to be deterred or reduced by the positive moderating effect of PJ, in the case of the longitudinal, correlational field design of Shapiro and Kirkman (1999), or the positive main effect of INTERACTJ, in the case of the longitudinal experimental design of Greenberg (2006). Again, readers should recall that there is potential for substantial overlap of INTERACTJ and justice dimensions, because interactional justice contains several different dimensions including PJ, INTERJ, and INFOJ (Colquitt, 2001).

Summary

In summary, the eight studies in The Role of Workplace Justice as a Moderator section strongly support the importance of justice dimensions and types as moderators of relationships between aspects of change, (e.g. the plan for change Kosgaard (2002), organizational identification Brockner et al. (1987), acceptance of a nonsmoking ban, psychological contract breach Kikl (2002), change favorability Fedor et al. (2006), anticipatory distributive injustice, and environment context effects Shapiro and Kirkman (1999), and outcomes reflecting employees' reactions to change (e.g., employees'/faculty's trust of, commitment to, cooperation with, and behavioral support of, organizational leaders and the change they initiated, change and organizational commitment, individual performance, insomnia, intention to leave, job satisfaction, and in-role performance). These significant findings provide strong support for the effect of justice on valued change outcomes such as those described earlier, and it is worth noting that the moderator role includes most articles (8) on any of the other three roles.

Discussion: The Integration of Findings Across Justice Roles

This section of the paper integrates findings across the 17 articles selected from the literature search and draws conclusions about the role of workplace justice in the context of organizational change by responding to the research questions presented earlier in the chapter Introduction. I begin with justice dimensions.

Justice Dimensions, and Effects of Workplace Justice in Organizational Change

PJ was, by far, the most widely studied type of justice within the 17 articles of the literature review, appearing in some nine out of the total 17 articles. The *second* most frequent justice types were interactional (INTERACTJ) and distributive (DJ) (often described as distributive injustice) that were each included in three studies, and both INFOJ and INTERJ that also were included in three articles each. Finally, three studies examined general types of justice that were developed by researchers to fit the context of their research. For example Fedor et al. (2006) and a related study by Liu et al. (2012) each examined "change fairness," defined as the overall fairness with which employees were treated during change. In addition, Bernerth et al. (2011) used variables termed "personal justice" ("I have been treated fairly) and "third-party justice" (termed other's justice in this chapter to avoid confounding due to other meanings of "third-party justice") that assessed how individuals viewed the level of justice experienced by their co-workers. Both variables were then used to compute a difference score that was converted to a major independent variable that was used as a mediator in the relationship between change-related variables and the outcomes of the change.

I speculate that the stronger presence of PJ within the 17 organizational change articles likely resulted from a number of different causes including: (a) researchers' greater familiarity and comfort with procedural justice due to its early development by Thibaut and Walker in 1975; (b) the fact that the fairness of different processes (layoffs, staffing of position assignments during mergers and acquisitions, the allocation process for awards, etc.)

within organizational change often emerge as quite important in organizational changes. Further, justice research by scholars such as Tom Tyler, Allan Lind, and Steven Blader among others has led to the development and testing of a number of different models and theories that have frequently used PJ as the cornerstone (e.g., the self-interest model of Thibaut and Walker, 1975, the group value model of Lind and Tyler, 1988, the group engagement model of Tyler and Blader,(2000, 2003), and (c) the fact that several articles were published at a time when the term *procedural justice* also included the dignity and respect content that subsequently were incorporated into what is now termed interpersonal justice (INTERJ) and informational justice (INFOJ; Colquitt, 2001), and may have provided a lower-cost "one-stop solution" in terms of questionnaire length for researchers wishing to conduct some early exploration about the role of justice in organizational change. In general, it is clear that PJ holds considerable sway, as an independent variable, mediator, and moderator affecting many important chains of relationships within organizational change, whereas DJ (usually referred to as distributive injustice), INFOJ, and INTERJ comparatively attract much less interest in organizational change research to date.

Overall, it is disappointing to see very little attention across the articles culled from the literature search given to Colquitt's (2001) caveat about the importance of including all four justice dimensions in research that tests justice effects in order to more accurately determine the relative contribution made by each type of justice to important outcome variables, particularly now that more research on anticipatory justice is appearing on the horizon. For articles published later than 2004, which I view as a sufficient period of time for researchers to have begun using Colquitt's (2001) typology of justice dimensions, it is also disturbing to find that INTERACTJ is included within studies examining DJ, PJ, INTERJ, and INFOJ that seem certain to include a fair amount of overlap in content domain and, thus, may cause instability in findings, making it very difficult to draw strong conclusions about the effects of particular dimensions and types of justice. It seems likely that such instability occurred in the findings of Bernerth et al's (2007) research on a divestiture where interactions of justice effects were used to predict outcomes such as employees' cynicism about change and their affective change commitment. Finally, this chapter identified several studies incorporating researchers using general justice scales believed to better capture the research question being examined [e.g., Fedor et al.'s (2006) fairness of change process, and Bernerth et al.'s (2011) evaluation of the difference between employees' assessment of their personal (individual) and their co-workers' fair treatment of change]. It would be helpful to correlate these scales with measures of the justice dimensions identified by Colquitt (2001) in order to more accurately determine the justice types that are most strongly related to change process and outcome variables.

Theories and Conceptual Frameworks Supporting the Research

Several theories and conceptual frameworks appeared frequently across the 15 articles identified in the literature search, including the agent system model (Kernan & Hanges, 2002), equity theory (Greenberg, 2006; Shapiro & Kirkman, 1999), group value model (Kernan & Hanges, 2002; Kikul et al. 2002), and the group engagement model (Tyler & De Cremer, 2005; Michel et al., 2010). Models appearing in the 15 articles used in this chapter were generally used as a conceptual foundation supporting the research topic rather than the conduct of specific tests of the research questions themselves. Although a recent meta-analysis of justice effects (Colquitt et al., 2013) failed to find support for the validity of the agent-system model excepting the role of supervisor as entity, this model often tests many different outcomes and it appears difficult to avoid finding partial support for it in individual studies (e.g., Kernan & Hanges, 2002).

Justice Effects on the Outcomes of Change

Many of the 17 articles provided evidence of justice effects on important outcomes of change, for example, performance (Brockner et al, 1987); change commitment (Bernerth et al. 2011; Fedor et al., 2006); organizational commitment (Fedor et al., 2006; Kernan & Hanges, 2002); insomnia (Greenberg, 2006); intention to quit (Bernerth et al., 2011; Kernan & Hanges, 2002; Shapiro & Kirkman, 1999); and job satisfaction (Kernan & Hanges, 2002). Further, as noted in the section on justice roles, different justice dimensions (e.g., PJ, INTERJ, etc.) and types (e.g., change fairness, etc.) also mediated the relationships between antecedents (e.g., TFL, voice, education about change, etc.), and change outcomes (Daly and Geyer, 1994) or they moderated relationships between different phases or elements of change (e.g., planning for change and various outcome variables, employees' obligations to their organization, their trust in management; Korsgaard et al., 2002), or the relationship between psychological contract breach of intrinsic and extrinsic outcomes and employee attitudes and behaviors (Kikul et al., 2002). Only a very few articles (Fedor et al., 2006; Liu et al., 2012) studied changes sufficiently far along to determine whether the change was successful in meeting set goals (e.g., profitability, revenue, organizational performance, etc.), and even these articles did not attempt to examine the success of various changes.

Selected Theoretical and Practical Contributions Emerging from Articles

Several insightful theoretical and practical contributions emerged from the group of 17 articles examining the effects of workplace justice on organizational change:

1. Kernan and Hanges (2002) developed a comprehensive model of justice antecedents, three justice dimensions, and a variety of outcomes displayed by survivors who experienced a major reorganization. Their findings provide strong support for workplace justice as a primary determinant of how employees react to this type of transitional change, while also acknowledging the importance of other factors, such as the nature of job changes. To this, I also suggest studying a general "impact of change" construct initially operationalized by Herold and colleagues (Herorld, Fedor, Caldwell & Liu, 2008). The measure of this construct encompasses a number of favorable and unfavorable change outcomes that, when combined into a single measure, have been shown to account for considerable variance in employee change related outcomes.

2. Fedor et al. (2006) used a multilevel design to examine the impact of some 32 different organizational changes. They proposed that change fairness at the work-unit level would positively relate to individual employees' change commitment and organizational commitment. Noting that their findings showed that organizational change did not influence change commitment and organizational commitment in the same manner, they argued that individuals' reactions to change are best understood by focusing on more than one level of analysis. Further, Fedor et al. (2006, p. 23) also observed that the outcome of the change is very important in shaping employee's commitment to change because change favorableness may at least partially outweigh the effect of change fairness, stating:

> . . . One of the most important implications of this study is doing a good job on the process side . . . may simply not be enough. Although providing advanced notice, soliciting input from those affected, and developing a rationale for the change are all important (Brockner, 2002), they are apparently not sufficient to override the favorableness of the change or the change's impact on the individual's job situation. This may be why managers often feel like they are in a no-win situation when it comes to change

3. Research findings by Korsgaard et al. (2002) Shapiro and Kirkman (1999), and Rodell and Coquitt (2009) build strong, although different, cases for the fact that employees are likely to experience much angst during the process of organizational change and often respond with very negative attitudes and unfavorable behaviors toward it and/or the organization even before the change begins. Korsgaard et al. (2002) found these reactions occurred once top management's planning of change began, and could be reduced by employees' perceptions that managers' displayed high levels of PJ. Similarly, Shapiro and Kirkman (1999) hypothesized and supported the effects of *employees' anticipation of distributive injustice,* defined as the anticipated receipt of unfair outcomes, such as undesirable job assignments and added responsibilities, and so forth, stimulated attitudinal concerns and resistance behavior (reduced work commitment and organizational citizenship behavior-OCB, intention to leave) from the mere anticipation of implementing SMWT. Shapiro and Kirkman (1999) also found that PJ moderated the negative effects of anticipated distributive injustice on the above outcomes. Finally, Rodell and Colquitt (2009), relied on considerable justice theory to determine that global supervisory fairness predicts different dimensions of anticipatory justice, that both global supervisory fairness and anticipatory justice dimensions predict different dimensions of experienced justice, and that experienced justice as well as individual difference variables predict support for change. The results of their research have much relevance for the future success of transitional changes, given that popular applied

change models (e.g., Kotter, 2012) place little emphasis on workplace justice or how to prepare employees to deal effectively with change before it begins.

4. Research by Tyler and de Cremer (2005) on whether PJ can serve as a valuable leadership tool that motivates employees' cooperation with an acquiring organization regarding a merger yields the following applied implications. Leaders in a merger situation should recognize that providing tangible resources to employees is only one method that might be used to motivate employees' acceptance of the leader's vision and their general support during the change. Beyond these resources, leaders should note the importance of developing and implementing fair decision-making processes such that when they clearly demonstrate their interest and concern for employees' well-being, and reflect them in the organization's decision-making processes, they (the leaders) are more likely to stimulate employees' acceptance of and cooperation with the change rather than to resist it. Thus, the likelihood that the change will be successful is much higher when leaders understand how displaying fairness in their exercise of authority motivate employees to believe in the benefits of change and to accept and embrace the merged organization.

High Priority Future Research Needs

Overall, Fedor et al. (2006) make a strong case for the greater use of multilevel designs in future studies examining the role of workplace justice within organizational change and for developing dynamic measures to be used with important change variables such as commitment to change. As noted earlier, only two out of 17 articles, Fedor et al. (2006), and Liu et al, (2012) used a multiple-level design for their research. Nevertheless, one caveat seems warranted given the researchers' prior statements about the roles of change fairness and favorability. Although preliminary analyses in the researchers' study showed that change favorability and change fairness are distinct variables, much prior research on justice indicates that: (a) judgments of outcome favorability and outcome fairness are psychologically similar; (b) they often load as a single factor in a confirmatory factor analysis; and (c) they have been viewed as "reflecting the same psychology" (Tyler, 1994; Tyler & De Cremer, 2005; Tyler & Lind, 1992). Thus, it also seems quite important to further test the distinctiveness of change fairness and change favorability at different levels of analysis in order to fully understand the impact of each on change related outcomes. In addition, Colquitt and his colleagues (Colquitt et al., 2013) recently published a meta-analysis of the justice literature that has emerged in the last decade. Although the meta-analysis focuses on how workplace justice directly and indirectly affect employees' behavioral reactions by working through two mediators, social exchange quality and state affect, rather than through organizational change, the state affect discussion within the article raises some interesting research questions for the organizational change domain. Whereas prior change research (Seo et al., 2012) and Shin et al. (2012) have pursued both of the two mediating pathways proposed by Colquitt et al. (2013), few or no change studies to date have examined the role of justice as the primary driver of these two pathways. Rather they have relied on both the impact of organizational change variable and/or other factors such as leadership style as primary drivers.

Given the growing frequency of organizational change, and repeated findings that more often than not it fails to meet the goals or standards set for it, future research is badly needed to examine the role of justice in influencing the success of change as mediated by these social exchange and affect pathways. Last but not least, future research is badly needed to examine the impact of large scale transitional or transformational organizational change with its myriad of strains and stresses, uncertainties anxiety, and guilt that are often transferred to the organization's workforce through the health and wellness of the organization's employees. As Greenberg's (2006) research indicates, inequitable changes can stimulate negative health-related outcomes, yet very little change research has examined the nature of these health and wellness effects on employees or, equally important, the extent to which they can be offset by providing supervisors, managers, and/or high-level organizational leaders with training in select justice dimensions, that is, DJ, PJ, INTERJ, INFOJ, and/or types, for example, INTERACTJ.

In Conclusion

This chapter has examined and qualitatively analyzed existing, but limited, empirical research on the role of workplace justice and organizational change. Its findings suggest that justice currently plays four roles in the organizational change domain—(1) the role of workplace justice as a dependent variable; (2) the role of workplace justice as an independent variable; (3) the role of workplace justice as a mediator; and (4) the role of workplace justice as a moderator. I classify the 17 empirical articles from my literature review into these roles and discuss their findings and, to the extent possible, commonalities within a given role. I also identify the frequency with which different justice dimensions appear within the different roles, select conceptual and applied contributions of the papers, and, make suggestions for future research. I seek not only to explore the role of workplace justice in organizational change but also to explain it to others in ways that increase their understanding and encourage them to extend what is currently known about justice as a driver of successful change.

Notes

1. *Academy of Management Journal, Academy of Management Review, Administrative Science Quarterly, Industrial and Corporate Change, Journal of Applied Behavioral Science, Journal of Applied Psychology, Journal of Applied Behavioral Science, Journal of Change Management, Journal of International Business Studies, Journal of Management, Journal of Organizational Behavior, Journal of Organizational Change Management, Management Science, Organizational Behavior and Human Decision Processes, Organization Science, Research in Personnel/Human Resource Management, Research in Organizational Behavior, Research in Organizational Change and Development,* and the *Strategic Management Journal.*
2. Anderson & Ackerman (2010) also identified a third type of change termed *developmental* that is used to fine tune or improve skills, methods, or conditions that for a variety of reasons, fail to reach existing expectations or goals. By itself, developmental change is rarely of concern within organizations. Because none of the articles in the literature review I conducted fell into the developmental change classification, I mention only the two remaining categories, transitional and transformational, that are more frequently of concern within organizations, far-reaching, possibly damaging in their implications and effects, and requiring of considerable leadership and management.
3. As Colquitt et al.'s (2013) recent meta-analysis shows, there is little evidence of differential system and agent effects; I reviewed the dependent variables as simply outcomes.
4. The items are: "Sufficient advance notice was given to employees affected by the change," "My input was sought by those responsible for the change," "The organization kept everyone fully informed during the change," "An adequate explanation for why change was necessary was provided," and "The organization did a good job of communicating about the change."

List of Organizational Change and Role of Workplace Justice Articles

Bernerth, J. B., Armenakis, A. A., Field, H. S., & Walker, H. J. (2007). Justice, Cynicism, and Commitment: A study of important organizational change variables. *Journal of Applied Behavioral Science, 43,* 303–325.

Bernerth, J. B., Walker, H. J., Walter, F., & Hirschfeld, R. R. (2011). A study of workplace justice differences during times of change: It's not all about me. *Journal of Applied Behavioral Science. 47,* 336–359.

Brockner, J., Grover, S., Reed, T., DeWitt, R., & O'Malley, M. (1987). Survivor's reactions to layoffs: We get by with a little help for our friends. *Administrative Science Quarterly, 32,* 526–541.

Cascio, W. (1993). Downsizing: What do we know? What have we learned? *Academy of Management Executive, 7,* 95–104.

Daly, J. P., & Geyer, P. D. (1994). The role of fairness in implementing large-scale change: Employee evaluations of process and outcome in seven facility locations. *Journal of Organizational Behavior, 15,* 623–638.

Fedor, D. B., Caldwell, S., & Herold, D. M. (2006). The effects of organizational changes on employee commitment: A multilevel investigation. *Personnel Psychology, 59,* 1–29.

Fugate, M., Kinicki, A., & Prussia, G. E. (2008). Employee coping with organizational change: An examination of theoretical perspectives and models. *Personnel Psychology, 61,* 1–36.

Gopinath, C., & Becker, T. (2000). Communication, procedural justice and employee attitudes: Relationships under conditions of divestiture. *Journal of Management, 26,* 63–83.

Greenberg, J. (1994). Using socially fair treatment to promote acceptable work site smoking ban. *Journal of Applied Psychology, 79,* 288–297.

Greenberg, J. (2006). Losing sleep over organizational injustice: Attenuating insomniac reactions to underpayment inequity with supervisory training in interactional justice. *Journal of Applied Psychology, 91,* 58–69.

Kernan, M. C., & Hanges, P. J. (2002). Survivor reactions to reorganization: Antecedents and consequences of procedural, interpersonal, and informational justice. *Journal of Applied Psychology, 87,* 916–928.

Kikul, J., Lester, S., & Finkl, J. (2002). Promise breaking during radical organizational change: Do justice interventions make a difference. *Journal of Organizational Behavior, 23,* 469–488.

Korsgaard, M. A., Sapienza, H. J., & Schweiger, D. M. (2002). Beaten before begun: The role of procedural justice in planning change. *Journal of Management, 28,* 497–516.

Liu, Y., Caldwell, S. D., Fedor, D. B., & Herold, D. M. (2012). *Journal of Applied Behavioral Science, 48,* 441–462.

Michel, A., Stegmaier, R., & Sonntag, K. (2010). I scratch your back-you scratch mine. Do procedural justice and organizational identification matter for cooperation during organizational change. *Journal of Change Management, 10,* 41–59.

Reger, R. K., Gustafson, L. T., DeMarie, S. M., & Mullane, J. V. (1994). Reframing the organization: Why implementing total quality is easier said than done. *Academy of Management Review, 19,* 565–584.

Rodell, J. B., Colquitt, J. A. (2009), Looking ahead in times of uncertainty: The role of anticipatory justice in an organizational change context. *Journal of Applied Psychology, 94,* 989–1002.

Shapiro, D. L., & Kirkman, B. L. (1999). Employees' reaction to the change to work teams: The influence of "anticipatory" injustice. *Journal of Organizational Change Management, 12,* 51–66.

Tyler, T. R., & de Cremer, D. (2005). Process-based leadership: Fair procedures and reactions to organizational change. *The Leadership Quarterly, 16*, 529–545.

Wu, C., Neubert, M. J., & Yi, X. (2007). Transformational leadership, cohesion perceptions, and employee cynicism about organizational change: The mediating role of justice perceptions. *Journal of Applied Behavioral Science, 43*, 327–351.

References

Adams, J. S. (1965). Inequality in Social Exchange. In L. Berkowitz (Ed.), Advances in Experimental Psychology (pp. 267–299). Academic Press, New York, NY.

Anderson, D., & Ackerman, L. A. (2010). *Beyond change management: How to achieve breakthrough results through conscious change leadership* (2nd ed., pp. 1–279). San Francisco, CA: Pfeiffer.

Atwater, L. E., Waldman, D. A., Atwater, D., & Cartier, P. (2000). An upward, feedback field experiment. Supervisors' cynicism, reactions, and commitment to subordinators. *Personnel Psychology, 53*, 275–297.

Avolio, B. Full (1999) leadership development: Building the vital forces in organizations. Thousand Oaks, CA: Sage.

Balogun, J., & Johnson, G. (2004). Organizational restructuring and middle manager sensemaking. *Academy of Management Journal, 47*, 523–549.

Bass, B. M. (1985). Leadership: Good, better, best. *Organizational Dynamics, 13*, 26–40.

Bies, R., & Moag, J. (1986). Interactional justice: Communication criteria of fairness. In R. Lewicki, B. Sheppard, & M. Bazerman (Eds.), *Research on negotiation in organizations* (pp. 43–55). Greenwich, CT: JAI.

Bies, R. J. (1987). Beyond "voice": The influence of decision-maker justification and sincerity on procedural fairness judgments. *Representative Research in Social Psychology, 17*, 3–14.

Bies, R. J. (2001). Interactional (in)justice: The sacred and the profane. In J. Greenberg & R. Cropanzano (Eds.), *Advances in organizational justice* (pp. 85–108). Stanford, CA: Stanford University.

Blader, S. L., & Tyler, T. R. (2003). Advancing the assessment of procedural justice: What constitutes fairness in work settings? *Human Resource Management Review, 13*, 107–126.

Brockner, J. Dewitt, R. L., Grover, S., & Reed, T. (1990). When is it expecially important to explain why: factors affecting the relationship between managers' explanations of a layoff and survivors' reactions to the layoff. *Journal of Experimental Social Psychology, 26*, 389–407.

Brockner, J. (2002). Making sense of procedural fairness: How high procedural fairness can reduce or heighten the influence of outcome favorability. *Academy of Management Review, 27*, 58–76.

Brockner, J., Wiesenfield, B., & Martin, C. L. (1995). Decision frame, procedural justice and survivors to job layoffs. *Organizational Behavior and Human Decision Processes, 63*, 59–68.

Bruning, N. S., Keup, L., & Cooper, C. L. (1996). *Justice perceptions and outcomes in a restructured organization: A longitudinal study.* Paper presented at the annual meeting of the Society for Industrial and Organizational Psychology, San Diego, CA.

Burke, W. (2008). Organization change: Theory and practice. Thousand Oaks, CA: Sage.

Caldwell, S. D., Herold, D. M., & Fedor, D. B. (2004).Toward an understanding of the relationships between organizational change, individual differences, and changes in person-environment fit: A cross-level study. *Journal of Applied Psychology, 89*, 868–882.

Colquitt, J. A. (2001). On the dimensionality of organizational justice: A construct validation of a measure. *Joumal of Applied Psychology, 86*, 386–400.

Colquitt, J. A., Conlon, D. E., Wesson, M. J., Porter, C. O. L. H., & Ng, K. Y. (2001). Justice at the millennium: A meta-analytic review of 25 years of organizational justice research. *Journal of Applied Psychology, 86*, 425–445.

Colquitt, J. A., Scott, B. A., Rodell, J. B., Long, D. M., Zapata, C. P., Conlon, D. E., & Wesson, M. J. (2013). Justice at the millennium, a decade later: A meta-analytic test of social exchange and affect-based perspectives. *Journal of Applied Psychology, 98*,199–236.

Cropanzano, R., & Folger, R. (1989). Referent cognitions and task decision autonomy: Beyond equity theory. *Journal of Applied Psychology, 74*, 293–299.

Cummings, T. G., & Worley, C. G. (1997). Organizational Development and Change. Cincinnati, OH: Southwest College.

Davey, J. A., Kinicki, A. J., & Scheck, C. L. (1991). Developing and testing a model of survivor responses to layoffs. *Journal of Vocational Behavior, 38*, 302–317.

Elovainio, M., Kivimaki, M., & Vahtera, J. (2002). Organizational justice: Evidence of a new psychosocial predictor of health. *American Journal of Public Health, 92*, 105–108.

Greenberg, J. (1990). Employee theft as a reaction to underpayment inequity: The hidden cost of pay cuts. *Journal of Applied Psychology, 75*, 561–568.

Greenberg, J. (1993). The social side of fairness: Interpersonal and informational classes of organizational justice. *Justice in the workplace: Approaching fairness in*

Herold, D. M., Fedor, D. B., Caldwell, S., & Liu, Y. (2008). The effects of transformational and change leadership on employees' commitment to change: A multilevel study. *Journal of Applied Psychology, 93*, 346–357.

Herscovitch, L., & Meyer, J. P. (2002). Commitment to organizational change: Extension of a three-component model. *Journal of Applied Psychology, 87*, 474–487.

Jick, T., & Peiperl, M. (2010). Managing change: Cases and concepts. 3rd Edition, pp. xx–xxi. McGraw-Hill/Irwin, New York, NY.

Judge, T. A., & Piccolo, R. F. (2004). Transformational and transactional leadership. A meta-analytic test of their relative validity. *Journal of Applied Psychology, 89*, 755–768.

Jorgesen, H. H., Owen, L., & Neus, A. (2011). Making change work. In *IBM Global business services strategy & change.* (6th ed.), (1997). Cincinnati, OH: Southwestern College.

Keifer, T. (2005). Feeling bad: Antecedents and consequences of negative emotions in ongoing change. *Journal of Organizational Behavior, 26*, 875–897.

Kotter, J. P. (2012). Leading change. Boston, MA: Harvard Business Review Press.

Lauver, K. J., & Kristof-Brown, A. (2001) Distinguishing between employees' perceptions of person-job and person-organization fit. *Journal of Vocational Behavior, 59*, 454–470.

Lind, E. A. (2001). Fairness Hueristic Theory: Justice judgments as pivotal cognitions in organizational relations. In

B. M. Staw and R. M. Kramer (Eds.), *Research in organizational behavior* (Vol. 24, pp.181–223). Boston, MA: Elsevier.

Lind, E. A., & Tyler, T. (1988). *Procedural justice in organizations. The social psychology of procedural justice* (pp.173–202). New York, NY: Plenum.

Martin, C. L., & Bennett, N. (1996). The role of justice judgements in explaining the relationship between job satisfaction and organizational commitment. *Group and Organization Management, 21*, 84–104.

McKinsey Global Survey Results. (2008). *Creating organizational transformation.* The McKinsey Quarterly.

Mowday, R. T. (1979). The measurement of organizational commitment. *Journal of Vocational Behavior, 26*, 224–247.

Naumann, S. E., Bennett, N., Bies. R. J., & Manin, C. L. (1998). Laid off, but still loyal: The influence of perceived justice and organizational support. *The International Journal of Conflict Management, 9*, 356–368.

Novelli, K. Jr., Kirkman, B. L., & Shapiro, D. L. (1995). Effective implementation of organizational change: An organizational justice perspective. In C. I. Cooper& D. M. Rousseau (Eds.), *Trends in organizational behavior* (Vol. 2, pp. 15–36). New York, NY: Wiley.

Pritchard, R. D. A., Dunnette, M. D., & Jorgenson, D. O. (1972). Effects of perceptions of equity and inequity on worker performance and satisfaction. *Journal of Applied Psychology, 56*, 75–94.

Reicher, A. E., Wanous, J. P., & Austin, J. T. (1997). Understanding and managing cynicism about organizational change. *Academy of Management Executive, 11*, 48–59.

Rousseau, D., & Tijoriwala, S. A. (1999). What's a good reason to change? Motivated reasoning and promoting social accounts in promoting organizational change. *Journal of Applied Psychology, 84*, 514–528.

Schweiger, D. M., & DeNisi, A. S. (1991). Communication with employees following a merger: A longitudinal field experiment. *Academy of Management Journal, 24*, 110–135.

Seo, M. G., Taylor, M. S., Hill, N. S., Zhang. X., Tesluk, P. E., & Lorinkova, N. M. (2012). The role of affect and leadership during organizational change. *Personnel Psychology, 65*, 121–165.

Shin, J., Taylor, M. S., & Seo, M. G. (2012). Resources for change: The relationships of organizational inducements and psychological resilience to employees' attitudes and behaviors toward organizational change. *Academy of Management Journal, 65*, 121–165.

Shapiro, D. L., & Kirkman, B. L. (2001). Anticipatory injustice: The consequences of expecting injustice in the workplace. In J. Greenberg & R. Cropanzano (Eds.), *Advances in organizational justice* (pp. 152–178). Lexington, MA: New Lexington.

Thibaut, J. W., & Walker, L. (1975). *Procedural justice: A psychological analysis*. Hillsdale, N.J.: Lawrence Erlbaum Associates.

Theorell, T., & Karasek, R. A. (1996). Current issues relating to psycho- social job strain and cardiovascular disease. *Journal of Occupational Health Psychology, 1*, 9–26.

Tombaugh, J. R., & White, L. P. (1990). Downsizing: An empirical assessment of survivors' perceptions in a post-layoff environment. *Organizational Development Journal, 8*, 32–43.

Tushman, M. L., Newman, W. H., & Romanelli, E. (1986). Convergence and upheaval: Managing the unsteady pace of organizational evolution. *California Management Review, 29*, 29–44.

Tyler, T. R. (1994). Psychological models of the justice motive. *Journal of Personality and Social Psychology, 67*, 850–863.

Tyler, T. R. (2004). Process based leadership: How do leaders lead? In R. Kramer & D. Messick (Eds.), *New thinking about the psychology of leadership* (pp. 431–505). Mahwah, NJ: Erlbaum.

Tyler, T. R., & Bies. R. (1990). Beyond formal procedures: The interpersonal aspects of procedural justice. In J. S. Carroll (Ed.), *Applied social psychology and organizational settings* (pp. 77–98). Hillsdale, NJ: Erlbaum.

Tyler, T. R., & Blader, S. L. (2000). Cooperation in groups. Philadelphia, PA: Psychology.

Tyler, T. R, & Lind, E. A. (1992). A relational model of authority in groups. *Advances in Experimental Social Psychology, 25*, 115–191.

Tyler, T. R., & Smith (1998). Social justice and social movements. In D. Gilbert, S. Fiske, & G. Lindzey (Eds.), *Handbook of social psychology* (4th ed., Vol. 2, pp. 595–629). New York, NY: McGraw-Hill.

Tyler, T. R., & Blader, S. L. (2003). The group engagement model: Procedural justice, social identity, and cooperative behavior. *Personality and Social Psychology Review, 7*, 349–361.

Vermunt, R., & Steensma, H. (2005). How can justice be used to manage stress in organizations. In J. Greenberg & J. A Colquitt (Eds.), *Handbook of Organizational Justice* (pp. 383–410). Mahwah, NJ: Erlbaum.

Wanous, J. P., Reichers, A. E., & Austin, J. T. (2000). Cynicism about organizational change: Measurements, antecedents, and correlates. *Group and Organization Management, 25*, 132–153.

Weiss, H. M., & Cropanzano, R. (1996). Affective events theory: A theoretical discussion of the structure, causes, and consequences of affective experiences at work. In B. M. Staw & L. L. Cummings (Eds.), *Research in organizational behavior* (Vol. 18, pp. 1–74). Greenwich, CT: JAI.

Whitener, E. M., Brodt, S. E., Korsgaard, M. A., & Werner, J. M. (1998). Managers as initiators of trust: An exchange relationship framework for understanding managerial trustworthiness. *Academy of Management Review, 23*, 513–530.

Wong, R., & Weiner, R. (1981). When people ask "why" questions and the heuristics of attributional search. *Journal of Personality and Social Psychology, 40*, 650–663.

CHAPTER

29 The Role of Due Process in Performance Appraisal: A 20-Year Retrospective

Paul E. Levy, Caitlin M. Cavanaugh, Noelle B. Frantz, *and* Lauren A. Borden

Abstract

Folger, Konovsky, and Cropanzano (1992) introduced the due process metaphor for performance appraisal that shifted the focus from measurement to justice in performance appraisal with an emphasis on social and communication processes. In this chapter, we review the 20 years of published work based on the due process metaphor. First, we review work that has empirically examined the due process approach to performance appraisal and its influence on important organizational outcomes. We continue by discussing the systemic and interpersonal elements that may influence successful use of the due process approach. Finally, we address the applicability of the western notion of due process to a global context by examining the body of published research on due process elements in non-American cultures. We conclude with a discussion of the limitations of our current knowledge and understanding of due process, and provide directions for future work that could strengthen the due process metaphor's applicability to performance appraisal research and practice.

Key Words: due process, test metaphor, performance appraisal, organizational justice, fairness, social processes, communication, global context

In many ways the Due Process Clauses of the Fifth and Fourteenth Amendments are the foundation for our legal system. In sum, they state that individuals should not be deprived the right to life, liberty, or property without due process of law. We won't suggest that performance appraisal belongs on the same stage as the Fifth Amendment. However, it is important to organizational and individual effectiveness. In a critical chapter published in 1992, Rob Folger, Mary Konovsky, and Russell Cropanzano proposed a *due process metaphor* for performance appraisal. At the time this was a very different and novel approach. The authors discussed two more traditional approaches to performance appraisal and categorized them as part of a *test metaphor,* which was largely focused on measurement, rating formats, and rating errors or a *political metaphor* with its emphasis on power, judgment, and accountability.

Folger et al. (1992) relied on the work of Thibaut and Walker (1978) in proposing the due process metaphor. Thibaut and Walker (1975; 1978) described their theory of dispute resolution with an emphasis on both distributive and procedural justice. Their novel approach suggested that disputants were as concerned and motivated by the process—how conflict was resolved—as the resolution or what outcome was achieved. Folger et al. argued that performance measurement and the psychometric qualities of the measurement were central, but that the process was just as important or even more important to performance appraisal. In the conclusion of their paper they say, "... appraising people is a matter of judging them, not simply measuring them as if they were to be fitted for new clothes. The due process metaphor argues for procedures appropriate to the management of disagreement rather than for procedures suited only for testing employees" (p.171).

Folger et al. (1992) borrowed from the work of Morris D. Forkosch (1958), a legal scholar who identified the essential features of due process as: adequate notice, a fair hearing, and judgment based on evidence. *Adequate notice* suggests that employees should be provided information about the performance management process such as standards, policies, and procedures. Adequate notice should provide employees with the opportunity to question procedures or standards they do not understand or to even disagree with a policy. Without adequate notice, employees do not have enough information to have any voice in the process. The provision of adequate notice provides the foundation for a *fair hearing,* which gives employees the opportunity to challenge any element of the performance management process and to be heard with respect to his or her perspective. This may involve the opportunity to provide a self-assessment or at least input into one's overall evaluation. Finally, *judgment based on evidence* is the element of the due process metaphor that seems to call most ideally for reasonableness. Decisions must be based on fair and accurate evidence, which means that they must be free from bias and external pressures. In addition, the reasonableness extends beyond the actual decision and includes the process as well (Folger et al.)—this requires a willingness on the part of raters to discuss issues related to the employees' appraisals.

Many researchers (Cawley, Keeping, & Levy, 1998; Ferris, Judge, Rowland, & Fitzgibbons, 1994; Ilgen, Barnes-Farrell, & McKellin, 1993; Levy & Williams, 2004; Murphy & Cleveland, 1991) have argued that the test metaphor's focus on measurement and psychometrics was misplaced and that the social context in which performance takes place should be considered as essential in understanding the appraisal process and designing and implementing effective performance management systems. Certainly, the due process approach is one steeped in the social context tradition, with each of the three components (adequate notice, fair hearing, and judgment based on evidence) being social in nature and involving social interactions between raters and ratees.

It is clear from even a casual familiarity with the evolution of the performance appraisal literature that the due process metaphor has played an important role in identifying the importance of social constructs such as fairness, voice, reasonable evidence, adequate hearing, participation, and so forth. The purpose of this chapter is to provide a systematic review of the role played by the due process metaphor in the advancement of the performance appraisal literature since the publication of Folger et al. (1992). Our approach was to review the literature that cited the original paper and then to dig deeper into those relevant studies with a goal to provide a description and integration of the major issues and findings that can be traced back to the due process metaphor as described by Folger et al. As a result of our analysis, the chapter is divided into three main areas. First, we discuss those empirical studies that set out to specifically test the due process metaphor. Although there are few studies that formally tested the model, they do provide important and useful information. Second, our reading of the literature uncovered quite a few papers that were clearly built on the due process approach and that emphasized the role of the rater or the ratee; these studies cite the due process metaphor extensively as the foundation for their work with its emphasis on the interaction and communication between raters and ratees. Finally, and surprising to us, we found many studies that have extended the due process metaphor outside North America. This was not an a priori focus of ours, but as we extended our search of the literature we found that even though the due process approach is built on what most would consider North American principles, this approach has been applied in many other countries that differ considerably from the cultural characteristics that describe North America. This provides some very interesting implications and applications for going forward.

Formal Tests of the Due Process Approach

The due process approach has been used in Industrial/Organizational (I/O) Psychology to define areas of selection and recruitment procedures (Mahony, Klaas, McClendon, & Varma, 2005), human resource policies (Dyer & Reeves, 1995; Whitener, 1998), employee development (Minter & Thomas, 1999), areas of performance management such as performance appraisal (Gupta & Kumar, 2013; Kataoka, Cole, & Flint, 2006; Kavanagh, Benson, & Brown, 2007; Masterson & Taylor, 1996), employee voice and communication (Ipsas, Ilies, Johnson, Iliescu, & Borman, 2010; Korsgaard & Roberson, 1995; Spencer, 1986), and the manager's role in performance appraisal

(Folger & Bies, 1989; Heslin & VandeWalle, 2011; Whitener, Brodt, Korsgaard, & Werner, 1998).

Although many studies have researched the effects of the three due process components separately, two empirical studies in particular have been pivotal in the successful application of the full due process model to performance appraisal: Taylor, Tracy, Renard, Harrison, and Carroll (1995) and Taylor, Masterson, Renard, and Tracy (1998).

Taylor et al. (1995) examined the effects of a due process performance appraisal system on both employee and manager reactions. The authors built from the due process model presented by Folger et al. (1992) and argued that the reactions of managers and employees must be considered in the performance appraisal process because they are central to obtaining performance information for employee development, reward allocation, and legal documentation.

Using a sample of government employees, manager–employee dyads were either placed in the experimental group where the performance appraisal process was built on a due process model, or in the control group where they continued with their current performance appraisal system for a period of three months. The results of this longitudinal study showed that both employees and managers in the experimental group reported perceiving significantly higher levels of all the due process variables than did the control group with one exception: employees did not have significantly higher perceptions of feedback frequency, which is an element of adequate notice.

Interestingly, employees who experienced the due process based performance appraisal were rated significantly lower on performance than those who continued with their traditional performance appraisal system. Although these employees in the due process group received lower performance ratings overall, they perceived the process and their personal ratings to be fairer and more accurate than did those in the control group; they were more satisfied with the process and their performance rating, and they rated their managers more favorably. Managers' perceptions were also significantly different for the two groups. In the due process model group, managers reported increased conflict resolution, greater satisfaction with the performance appraisal process, greater job satisfaction, and were less likely to bias appraisal results for personal gain than those managers in the control group.

Taylor et al. (1995) successfully supported the Folger et al. (1992) due process model of performance management. The research provided an empirical example of the benefits of a due process model of justice in the performance appraisal process experienced by not only the employee, but also the manager and ultimately, the organization.

In the second study, Taylor et al.'s (1998) focus was on managers' reactions to a procedurally just performance management system. The authors predicted that a due process performance appraisal system would lead managers to be more satisfied with the performance appraisal system, have better professional relationships with their employees, and to be less likely to knowingly bias performance appraisal ratings. The authors also predicted that the relationship between a due process (or procedurally just) performance appraisal and the manager's reaction would be moderated by the perceived fairness of the manager's own past performance appraisals.

Using a sample of managers (nonfaculty) from a large public university, Taylor et al. (1998) divided participants into two groups: a control group that continued with the current performance appraisal procedures and an experimental group that was introduced to a new, due process performance management system during a three month period. Results supported their first hypothesis that a due process performance appraisal system would lead managers to be more satisfied with the performance appraisal system, have better professional relationships with their employees, and to be less likely to knowingly bias performance appraisals.

Results indicated that a manager's own experiences in performance appraisal influenced the outcomes of the due process system. In other words, the extent to which the manager perceived his or her performance appraisal results as fair affected the relationship between the due process performance appraisal system and resulting manager reactions, such that managers who have perceived unfairness in their own performance appraisals exhibited more favorable reactions (i.e., more favorable relationships with their employees and less tendency to distort appraisal results) to a due process performance appraisal model than did those who perceived their most recent performance appraisal to be fair. The authors suggested that managers who had experienced the negative consequences of unfairness would be less likely to see the costs of implementing a due process system as a barrier to doing so, because the costs of an unfair system outweigh the costs of more effortful performance management. Additionally, Taylor et al.

(1998) retested the moderating hypothesis on the data from Taylor et al. (1995) and found support for the same moderating effect on the relationship between a due process performance appraisal and the resulting manager reactions.

In sum, Taylor et al.'s findings (1995; 1998) suggest that managers will likely react favorably and positively to a due process performance management system even though such a system produces more work for the manager and limits the manager's ability to evaluate employees independent of employee participation. This is particularly true of managers who have received prior negative evaluations of themselves. Because these managers are sensitized to the affective consequences of such an evaluation, they are more likely to avoid giving knowingly biased performance appraisals and more likely to follow policies that lead to better professional relationships with their employees.

Although research supports the use of due process performance appraisal systems in organizations, it is not always feasible or realistic for organizations to implement a complete due process approach. As Cropanzano, Bowen, and Gilliland (2007) pointed out, implementation of the three components of due process (i.e., adequate notice, fair hearing, and judgment based on evidence) in performance appraisal systems is complicated. Organizations must train and prepare managers to execute systems using due process and trust that these processes are being followed on a continual basis. Cropanzano et al. (2007) also mentioned the role of the employee and employee sense-making processes in a due process approach. Because employees may expect due process, systems that do not include the relevant components can increase expectations and result in more discontent for employees (Cropanzano et al., 2007). Further, if due process procedures are not designed and implemented appropriately, they could create unnecessary problems, possibly causing more harm than good.

Understanding that implementation of all three components of due process may be cumbersome or impossible; it is valuable to understand the effects of partial due process models on organizational justice perceptions. Although the general assumption about due process effectiveness may tend toward an "all or nothing" approach, results from one study suggest that a due process approach does not have to include all three components to be successful in increasing perceived procedural justice. Kataoka et al. (2006) empirically studied varying combinations of the due process components in both promotion and termination scenarios. Results showed that the number of due process components included in the promotion and termination scenarios had a significant, positive effect on perceptions of procedural fairness. Specifically, using two or three of the due process components resulted in significantly higher perceptions of procedural fairness than using zero or one component in promotion scenarios, whereas adding one, two, or all three components in a termination scenario significantly increased perceptions of procedural fairness as each component was added (Kataoka et al., 2006). These findings suggest that even in situations in which organizations may not be able to implement a performance appraisal system that is built on all the elements of a due process approach, using varying combinations of the three components can increase employee perceptions of procedural fairness and enhance the quality of the appraisal process.

In sum, tests of due process performance appraisal systems (e.g., Kataoka et al., 2006; Taylor et al., 1995; 1998) demonstrate that developing performance appraisal systems based on components of due process improves the experience for both supervisors and subordinates. Additionally, Kataoka et al. (2006) expands our understanding of the influence of the full due process model by demonstrating the usefulness of components of the model, which may be especially helpful for practitioners seeking to improve justice under organizational constraints.

Bridging the Gap Between Systemic and Interpersonal Aspects of Due Process

As suggested earlier, incorporating facets of the due process model into performance appraisal systems is associated with a variety of positive outcomes (Cloutier & Vilhuber, 2008; Findley, Giles, & Mossholder, 2000; Jawahar, 2010; Kataoka et al., 2006; Kavanagh et al., 2007; Taylor et al., 1995; 1998). Specifically, due process elements of performance appraisal systems foster positive justice perceptions and high levels of performance (Cloutier & Vilhuber, 2008; Kavanagh et al., 2007; Jawahar, 2010). However, for these systems to exert their positive effects, they must also be implemented fairly and effectively. In other words, in order for due process components to be maximally effective, they not only have to be incorporated into the system itself but also into the social interactions and communications that occur between supervisors and their subordinates. With this in mind, the successful application of the due process model to performance appraisal places the rater in a position of critical importance.

Research has highlighted this point, identifying the system, rater, and interpersonal interactions as distinct, and yet as critical sources of fairness perceptions throughout the performance appraisal process. For example, Erdogan, Kraimer, and Liden (2001) conducted a study on a sample of employees from a Turkish organization, which examined the underlying dimensions of the procedural justice construct. Specifically, the study sought to identify the due process characteristics that correlate with the perceived fairness of system procedural justice (i.e., of performance appraisal procedures and policies adopted by the company) and rater procedural justice (i.e., of the evaluation procedures implemented by the rater, irrespective of those put in place by the company). Results supported their two-dimensional conceptualization, because system and rater dimensions were associated with different components of the due process model. In particular, it appears that knowledge and validity of appraisal criteria are important precursors to employee perceptions of system procedural justice, whereas performance feedback and fair hearing are more strongly associated with perceptions of rater procedural justice. Although these findings suggest that due process components differentially correspond with each of these facets, they also highlight the point that due process components are necessary antecedents to ratee perceptions of both system and rater procedural justice perceptions (Erdogan, 2002; Erdogan et al., 2001).

Findley, Giles, and Mossholder (2000) also highlighted the multifaceted nature of fairness perceptions by emphasizing the contrast between system facets, which refer to organizational policies and procedures, and process facets, which refer to the extent to which these policies and procedures are fairly implemented by raters. In this case, they compared the effects of system and process facets on employees' contextual performance and perceived appraisal accuracy. Survey results revealed that only appraisal process facets uniquely predicted variance in both perceived accuracy and contextual performance above and beyond that accounted for by system facets. On the other hand, system facets only appeared to offer unique predictive ability for employee accuracy perceptions. In other words, both system and process facets foster contextual performance and perceived appraisal accuracy; however, fair implementation of policies and procedures are more uniquely predictive of desired organizational outcomes.

Other research has also emphasized the interpersonal component of performance appraisal, identifying interactional justice as a separate determinant of justice perceptions and as a precursor to positive attitudes toward appraisals and higher levels of trust in one's manager (Brockner et al., 1994; Erdogan, 2002; Konovsky, 2000; Korsgaard, Roberson, & Rymph, 1998). These findings highlight the multidimensional conceptualization of justice perceptions in performance appraisals. Furthermore, they underscore the importance of not only incorporating due process elements into the system itself, but into the relational aspects of performance appraisal processes.

In sum, these constructs and conceptualizations of fairness are not interchangeable and, therefore, must each work in tandem. In other words, for the due process model to exert its full range of positive effects in the performance appraisal context, its characteristics need to be incorporated into not only the system but also into rater behaviors and social interactions (Erdogan et al., 2001).

Communication

Recent research has placed considerable emphasis on the importance of system transparency and the availability of information to employees. For example, Cloutier and Vilhuber (2008) conducted a study examining which factors influence employee justice perceptions in the context of salary determination. Based on a survey of Canadian employees, results indicated that system transparency was one of the most significant determinants of employee justice ratings. Similarly, Kavanaugh and colleagues (2007) examined precursors to perceived performance appraisal fairness in a sample of Australian public sector employees. The study revealed that employee knowledge of the performance appraisal process was positively associated with employee perceptions of fairness. Lastly, according to a survey conducted by Findley and colleagues (2000), systems that exhibit low levels of complexity and are easily understood by employees are more conducive to accurate performance appraisals and are also associated with higher levels of contextual performance among employees (Findley et al., 2000). Taken together, results from these studies suggest that transparency in communication of performance systems has an important effect on employee fairness perceptions and performance.

However, the questions of whether a system is transparent, information is available, or the system is simple enough that employees are capable of understanding it are functionally irrelevant unless employees or ratees understand or are aware of the system itself. With this in mind, it is no surprise that since the due process model was first introduced, research has demonstrated the importance of fostering an understanding of the performance appraisal system. Specifically, Williams and Levy (1992) identified the importance of perceived system knowledge in the performance appraisal process. The study examined the effects of perceived system knowledge on the discrepancy between rater and ratee performance evaluations in a sample of employees working in banking institutions. Results revealed that ratees who felt as though they understood appraisal system processes and the evaluation criteria used were more likely to agree with their supervisors' evaluations (Williams & Levy, 1992).

Other studies have also drawn attention to the positive effects of perceived system knowledge. For example, Erdogan et al. (2001) demonstrated that employees who reported feeling as though they have a thorough understanding of performance criteria were also more likely to rate the performance appraisal system as being fair. Similarly, Levy and Williams (1998) conducted a survey study examining the effects of perceived system knowledge on appraisal reactions and job attitudes. Results indicated that individuals with higher levels of perceived system knowledge were more likely to react positively to evaluations, and to report high levels of job satisfaction and organizational commitment.

Ultimately, these findings make it clear that both system transparency and perceived system knowledge are worth promoting in the workplace. However, employees' perceptions of the extent to which they know and understand the system are often a direct result of leaders' ability to effectively and accurately communicate necessary information to them. These perceptions of informational justice are a critical component of due process implementation (Gupta & Kumar, 2013), and require that the rater deliberately communicates with ratees, clarifying performance expectations, explaining and providing well-reasoned justification for decisions, and suggesting specific strategies for improving (Jawahar, 2010; Korsgaard et al., 1998; Martin & Bartol, 2003; Thurston & McNall, 2010).

Aside from providing employees with advance notice and increasing informational justice perceptions, this kind of communication has been shown to lead to a variety of positive outcomes. For instance, Gupta and Kumar (2013) conducted a survey study on a sample of employees from a multinational Indian corporation, which examined the relationship between engagement and justice perceptions. Results indicated that employees who perceive that they have been provided with necessary information throughout the performance appraisal process also tend to exhibit higher levels of work engagement. Similarly, perceptions of informational justice have also been shown to lead to organizational citizenship behaviors (Thurston & McNall, 2010), more positive attitudes toward appraisal, higher levels of trust in one's manager (Korsgaard et al., 1998), and performance improvements (Jawahar, 2010).

Research has also identified the critical role of feedback in rater-ratee communication processes. For example, a qualitative case study conducted by Narcisse and Harcourt (2008) sought to identify the various components that contribute to employee justice perceptions. Analyses of data collected from completed appraisal forms and employee interviews revealed that frequent feedback is a critical component of one's due process in performance appraisal, because it allows for the clarification of objectives and provides opportunities for seeking feedback. Other studies have also highlighted the importance of feedback, indicating that ratees who have been provided with continuous and consistent feedback tend to report higher levels of procedural justice perceptions (Erdogan et al., 2001), satisfaction with the performance review (Kataoka et al., 2006; Narcisse & Harcourt, 2008; Noeverman, 2010), and are also more likely to engage in organizational citizenship behaviors (Thurston & McNall, 2010). In addition, research has indicated that employees who perceive their evaluations as accurate and the feedback source as credible also tend to report experiencing higher levels of informational justice during their performance appraisal review, which increases employees' motivation to improve their performance (Roberson & Stewart, 2006). In sum, communication between participants is an important component beyond the system itself that helps to enhance the benefits of implementing a due process system.

The Importance of the Rater Role

The above review brings to light the criticality of the rater's ability to interact and communicate with his or her subordinates in an effective way. However, research has also indicated that raters often vary in their ability to do so for a variety of reasons. For example, research has suggested that raters' proclivity toward implementing due process procedures may be a function of individual differences in Implicit Person Theory (IPT), or the extent to which they believe ratees can change and improve over time (Heslin & VandeWalle, 2011). Specifically, Heslin and Vandewalle (2011) conducted a survey study to examine this possibility within a sample of working professionals enrolled in a university MBA course. Results indicated that ratees who received evaluations from incrementalist superiors, or those who believe ratees can change or improve over time, were more likely to perceive their performance appraisal as being procedurally just. In turn, these procedural justice perceptions were predictive of higher levels of employee- and supervisor-rated organizational citizenship behaviors (Heslin & Vandewalle, 2011).

Similarly, research has suggested that employees' perceptions of fairness regarding performance appraisal systems are a function of not only *what* raters communicate (i.e., clarification, justification, suggestion, feedback, etc.), but *how* information is communicated. For this reason, rater differences in their utilization of interpersonal communication styles and strategies can have important implications regarding fairness in performance appraisal. For example, Yamaguchi (2005a) conducted a study on a sample of Japanese white-collar employees in order to identify the antecedents to procedural justice perceptions. Specifically, he evaluated the effects of interpersonal communications that incorporated voice, explanations for decisions, and the expression of social sensitivity. Results indicated that all of these variables significantly predicted procedural justice perceptions. Specifically, raters who are more socially sensitive during their communications are more likely to promote their employees' perceptions that performance appraisal procedures are fair (Yamaguchi, 2005a).

Yamaguchi also conducted another study (2005b) comparing the effects of hard, soft, and rational interpersonal communication tactics on employee procedural justice perceptions. According to Yamaguchi (2005b), hard tactics emphasize legitimacy and positional power, and they put pressure on others by using a high-handed manner, demands, orders, warnings, or threats. Conversely, soft interpersonal tactics involve ingratiation, personal appeal, and inspirational appeal. These tactics aim at improving interaction quality before asking the subordinate to complete a task, and include being friendly and using praise or flattery during communications. Lastly, rational communication tactics capitalize on reasoning, conditional and unconditional promises, and normative appeals. Employees completed questionnaires assessing the degree to which they felt their supervisors engaged in each category of communication tactic, as well as their perceptions of procedural justice. As expected, results indicated that higher levels of procedural justice perceptions are associated with having a supervisor who uses kind, friendly, sympathetic, and rational interpersonal communication, rather than authoritative tactics that capitalize on giving orders and making demands or threats (Yamaguchi, 2005b).

Recent research has also posed the question of whether impression management tactics used by raters influence subordinate interactional justice perceptions. Specifically, Erdogan (2002) proposed a theoretical model in which supervisor-focused impression-management tactics, which involve attempts to improve one's likeability through politeness and friendliness, and through subordinate-focused tactics involving praise, doing personal favors for the subordinate, and inquiring about reasons for poor performance, are more likely to result in employee perceptions that communications were fair, considerate, kind, and respectful. However, if raters are more inclined toward job-focused tactics, which involve attempts to give the impression that they are doing a good job by taking responsibility for the rating recipient's positive outcomes or minimizing the extent to which they are responsible for negative outcomes, ratees should be more likely to view interactions surrounding the performance appraisal as unjust (Erdogan, 2002).

Throughout this process, it is also important for raters to not only maintain neutrality and give unbiased ratings, but for the rating recipients to perceive this as being the case (Kavanagh et al., 2007; Poon, 2004). This is highlighted in a study conducted by Kavanagh and colleagues (2007), which showed that perceived rater neutrality is positively related to perceptions of fairness in performance appraisal (Kavanagh et al., 2007). Similarly, Poon (2004) studied the influence of politics, defined as the absence of judgment based on evidence in the performance appraisal process, on fairness perceptions. As hypothesized, results indicated that when employees perceive that their performance ratings were influenced by personal bias and intention to punish subordinates, they are more likely to exhibit decreased satisfaction, and subsequently, increased turnover intentions.

Furthermore, a study conducted by Jawahar (2010) also emphasized the rater role in due process. Specifically, this study examined the effects of various performance feedback characteristics pertaining to due process model components, and it revealed that rater job knowledge, job relatedness of the criteria, the use of goal setting, and having the rater suggest ways to improve were the strongest predictors of ratee reactions (Jawahar, 2010). In fact, even when receiving negative evaluations, individuals who experienced these factors perceived their ratings as being more accurate and useful, and were more satisfied with the feedback they received (Jawahar, 2010). In addition to highlighting the positive effects of due process facets, this further emphasizes the centrality of the rater's behaviors and strategies for implementing these systems in a way that maximizes positive justice perceptions and reactions (Jawahar, 2010). This is also consistent with literature indicating that negative feedback can be more beneficial than positive feedback, as it aids in employee development and performance advancements by diagnosing behaviors in need of improvement (Medvedeff, Gregory, & Levy, 2008; Smither & Walker, 2004).

However, although some rater behaviors have been identified as beneficial, theoretical work has also suggested that certain behaviors might not have a universally positive effect. According to Holbrook (2002), ratee justice perceptions, affective reactions, satisfaction, acceptance of the decision, organizational commitment, and turnover intentions are functions of a complex interaction of variables. For example, providing an explanation may have varying effects depending on the type of explanation for an outcome and on the favorability of the feedback being given (Holbrook, 2002). Specifically, internal explanations highlighting personal characteristics or behaviors may help magnify positive reactions to favorable feedback, whereas external explanations focusing on forces outside of one's control may minimize negative reactions to unfavorable feedback (Holbrook, 2002). This stresses the importance of interpersonal communication skills and the rater's ability to determine when to use each strategy in a way that encourages positive reactions and perceptions of fairness (Holbrook, 2002).

Ultimately, these findings and theoretical work highlight the importance of effective communication skills among raters, and yet underscore the complexities and difficulties that inhibit effective communication. Not only must raters provide the right information throughout the performance appraisal process in a fair and respectful manner (Gupta & Kumar, 2013; Jawahar, 2010; Korsgaard et al., 1998; Martin & Bartol, 2003; Thurston & McNall, 2010) but they also must tailor their communication style to the situation (Holbrook, 2002), give effective feedback (Erdogan et al., 2001; Kataoka et al., 2006; Narcisse & Harcourt, 2008; Noeverman, 2010; Thurston & McNall, 2010), utilize sensitive and rational communication tactics (Yamaguchi, 2005a; Yamaguchi, 2005b), convey neutrality (Kavanagh et al., 2007; Poon, 2004), and employ supervisor- and subordinate-focused impression-management strategies (Erdogan, 2002). Implementing fair performance appraisal procedures within a context of due process is, without a doubt, a complex and difficult endeavor, but one with great benefits.

The Importance of the Ratee Role

Although the literature clearly tends to focus on the importance of the rater role, recent research has revealed that justice perceptions in performance appraisals are a product of the combination of both rater and ratee characteristics and behaviors. The quality of the superior-subordinate relationship (LMX) has been identified as an important precursor to both interactional and procedural justice perceptions (Elicker, Levy, & Hall, 2006; Erdogan, 2002), drawing further attention to the criticality of social interactions in performance appraisal outcomes.

Furthermore, several studies have shed light on the idea that fair rater behavior is often a function of the behavior of the subordinate. For example, two studies conducted by Korsgaard, Roberson, and Rymph (1998) examined the possibility that subordinate communication style may influence supervisor's fairness during decision-making. First, a laboratory study was conducted that indicated that raters engage in more interactionally just behavior when interacting with an assertive ratee than a more passive ratee. Next, a quasi-experimental field study demonstrated that training employees to be more assertive ultimately leads to more positive attitudes toward the appraisal and higher levels of trust in one's manager. On a related note, a study conducted by Yamaguchi (2005a) suggested that information-seeking behaviors on the part of the ratee could induce interactionally just behavior from the rater. Specifically, higher levels of information seeking were associated with increased opportunity for voice, the provision of more explanations, more rational interpersonal communication, and, ultimately, higher levels of procedural justice perceptions (Yamaguchi, 2005a).

Rater-Ratee Training

The findings from these studies bring up several important points. First, as discussed previously, it is important for the due process model to be in place within the performance appraisal system to establish a framework for effective and fair communication and social interactions. For example, as Yamaguchi (2005b) suggests, subordinate information seeking is more likely when the performance appraisal system incorporates mechanisms that facilitate inquiry and provide individuals with the information they desire. Second, the rating recipient is capable of changing his or her behavior in a way that elicits fair treatment and due process during performance evaluations. In this sense, system characteristics based on the due process model (e.g., information-seeking mechanisms) set the stage for beneficial ratee behavior. Lastly, although acting assertively or deliberately pursuing desired information can provoke fair treatment, such behavioral changes are only beneficial when raters are capable of reacting appropriately (Korsgaard et al., 1998; Yamaguchi, 2005a). In other words, the recipients' behavior can only lead to these positive outcomes if raters respond by providing more information or communicating more effectively.

These points further emphasize the dynamic interplay between the system, rater, and rating recipient in determining justice perceptions. Some researchers have questioned whether the due process model accounts for this complex interaction, pointing out that it seems to focus on the structural and systemic factors that lead to fair performance appraisals (Thurston & McNall, 2010). However, the due process model provides a framework for fair social interactions, because multiple studies have identified associations between due process components and system-, rater-, process-, informational-, and interpersonally based conceptualizations of procedural justice (Erdogan, 2002; Erdogan et al., 2001; Findley et al., 2000; Gupta & Kumar, 2013). The literature discussed earlier supports these ideas, but also suggests that the situations in which due process-based performance appraisal systems fail to translate into justice perceptions may involve these social interactions. For example, the necessary systemic due process components may be in place, but raters may inhibit due process effectiveness in a variety of ways by failing to communicate the needed information. Further, they may communicate in a disrespectful or confusing way, they may provide feedback that is lacking in details or specifics, or they may unknowingly give off the impression that they are politically motivated. Conversely, systemic and rater factors may be in place, but perhaps the rating recipient is not taking the initiative to seek information when necessary. In this sense, the due process model is a necessary framework for interactional justice in performance appraisal, but there are times when it may not be sufficient because of these interpersonal issues.

To address this, due process model components must be incorporated into the system, rater, and interpersonal aspects of the performance appraisal system. With this in mind, rater–ratee training would complement due process-based performance appraisal systems by promoting fair interactions, effective communication, and more positive justice perceptions. In fact, according to Narcisse and Harcourt (2008), rater–ratee training is a critical part of the judgment based on evidence component of due process, because it ensures that both parties understand the performance appraisal systems and procedures. Furthermore, as discussed previously, the rater role is of central importance for fair performance appraisals, but it is also extremely complicated. Therefore, training both the ratee and rater would facilitate this process by promoting a more thorough understanding of appeal mechanisms, performance criteria, and other aspects of performance appraisal procedures, while training employees to act assertively and seek desired information when necessary (Korsgaard et al., 1998; Yamaguchi, 2005b). Such practices would address recent calls for an expansion of the due process model to include rater and ratee training (Narcisse & Harcourt, 2008), and would also more thoroughly address the importance of social aspects of the performance appraisal context by training both parties in how to navigate these interactions (Palaiologos, Papazekos, & Panayotopoulou, 2011; Thurston & McNall, 2010).

By expanding our conceptualization of performance appraisal fairness and due process implementation, training both the raters and the ratees would ensure that systemic factors aimed at promoting justice succeed in doing so by targeting problematic areas of communication and interaction. In this sense, building mechanisms into the system that directly target the rater, ratee, and the interactions between them would allow the due process model to produce its full range of positive individual- and organizational-level outcomes.

Applications of Due Process in a Global Context

As noted at the outset, the due process model stems from the Western legal context (Folger et al., 1992), and is rooted in Anglo-American notions of justice and fairness, dating back to the Magna Carta and US Constitution hundreds of years ago. The value of the due process model has been established in North American studies as an influence of fairness perceptions in the performance appraisal process. As the due process approach has become a more popular model in performance management research in the United States, researchers have begun to look at a due process approach to performance management in various countries and cultures (Erdogan et al., 2001; Kanwetuu, 2012; Kavanagh et al., 2007; Konovsky, 2000; Martin & Bartol, 2003; Narcisse & Harcourt, 2008).

With the globalization of business practices and increase in cultural awareness over the past 20 years, performance appraisals are subjected to the additional challenge of crossing cultural boundaries. A logical question is whether a due process approach to performance appraisal is appropriate and effective in organizations employing non-Western cultures, or with constituents from more than one culture. Since the publication of Folger et al.'s chapter in 1992, a surprising amount of research has been conducted internationally, investigating elements of the due process model and their influence on fairness perceptions of performance appraisal. Although few studies have directly tested the due process model (see the first section of this chapter), and tests with non-Western populations are fewer still, the research including components of the model suggests, at least, that due process has flowed into performance appraisal globally. For example, results from a survey of performance appraisal practices in Ghana suggested that employees with greater participation in the appraisal process (consistent with adequate-notice and fair-hearing principles) were more satisfied with the process and outcomes. Additionally, employees viewed these procedures as fair, and were motivated by the interactions with supervisors (Kanwetuu, 2012).

Zheng, Zhang, and Li (2011) examined the extent to which a structured performance appraisal process, rooted in due process elements, was associated with organizational citizenship and affective commitment in a sample of Chinese employees from a variety of industries. Findings suggested that performance appraisals laden with these elements resulted in more citizenship behaviors and that a strong rating-reward linkage strengthened the performance appraisal–citizenship behavior relationship. That is, performance appraisal processes that involved subordinates in planning, involved direct supervisor observation of performance, and considered subordinate viewpoints during discussions of performance were related to more citizenship behaviors when there was a clear relationship between performance rating and reward outcomes.

By examining due process elements together, these studies provide initial support for the transportability of the model cross-culturally. More research has focused on specific elements of due process in performance appraisal by exploring causes and consequences of adequate notice, fair hearing, and judgment based on evidence separately.

Adequate Notice

Research on the adequate notice principle in other cultures has focused on knowledge of the system and participation in the formation of objectives and standards, as well as the regularity of feedback conversations. Kavanagh et al. (2007) found that participation in and knowledge of the appraisal process influenced fairness perceptions of public-sector employees in Australia. Similarly, Erdogan et al. (2001) related knowledge of criteria to *system justice* and provided evidence for the influence of level in the organization on perceptions of knowledge in a sample of bank employees in Turkey. A qualitative exploration of factors influencing fairness in a Saint Lucian sample suggested that appraisal frequency was critical to employee perceptions of fairness (Narcisse & Harcourt, 2008)—appraisals occurring long after a designated appraisal time period or on an unpredictable basis were viewed as less fair and violated employees' sense of due process.

Taken together, these studies demonstrate the importance of adequate notice as an influence of fairness perceptions in other cultures. Employees generally view the performance appraisal process as more fair when they are informed about the standards and process, and when feedback is provided in a timely and regularly occurring fashion.

Fair Hearing

In addition to their examination of adequate-notice influences on system procedural justice, Erdogan et al. (2001) also examined the influence of fair hearing on employee perceptions of rater procedural justice in a Turkish sample. They determined that when employees were permitted open and active participation in the performance appraisal session, they perceived a greater level of justice regarding the rater versus the system itself. Even when a due process performance appraisal system is implemented, a supervisor can influence perceptions of justice and fairness by providing the employee an actual opportunity to contribute to an open conversation about the employee's performance.

Hartmann and Slapničar (2012) investigated the role of performance appraisal elements, including voice, in procedural justice perceptions of managers in several Slovenian banks. Findings suggested that, of four variables examined, only voice had a consistently strong and positive effect on perceptions of justice. Employees who had the opportunity to participate and provide input about their performance viewed the process as more just. Additionally, this effect was strengthened for ratees (in this case, managers) with high task uncertainty. Hartmann and Slapničar concluded that perceptions of procedural justice may be more severely damaged by the absence of voice for these managers in particular.

In summary, both studies strengthen the argument that employees who are able to contribute to the performance appraisal conversation leave the performance appraisal with more favorable justice perceptions. Employee awareness of and input in the standard-setting and evaluation components of performance appraisal are not likely to be harmful in other cultures and can be helpful, despite the fact that these elements derive from westernized definitions of justice.

Judgment Based on Evidence

One major difference between individualistic and collectivist societies stems from the standards that are used to make employment decisions. Specifically, individualist cultures emphasize individual performance and merit as the basis for personnel decisions, whereas collectivist cultures may make decisions based on loyalty, longevity, and harmony within the organization (Ramamoorthy, Flood, MacCurtain, Gupta, & Kulkarni, 2012). In the Western understanding of judgment based on evidence, performance appraisal ratings should be made based on consistently applied standards that are free from prejudice, corruption, or outside influence (Folger et al., 1992). Although this is not inconsistent with a collectivist emphasis on loyalty and seniority, research has suggested that the formality of Western appraisal systems tends to be viewed unfavorably in collectivist cultures because of the strict adherence to standards that do not permit consideration of nonperformance information (Ramamoorthy & Carroll, 1998).

With regard to this concern, Ramamoorthy et al. (2012) explored justice perception differences between samples in Ireland and India to see if the individualist and collectivist cultures differed in their relative value of procedural versus distributive justice with regard to intention to remain with the orgainzation, affective commitment, and normative commitment. Contrary to expectations, procedural justice was important for both cultures as a predictor of affective commitment and intention to remain. The authors concluded that despite the assumption that due process has a weaker role in performance appraisal in more collectivist societies, the real difference may lie in how rewards are allocated (e.g., distributive justice), rather than how ratings are assigned.

In a Malaysian sample, Poon (2004) studied the influence of politics, framed as the absence of judgment based on evidence in the performance appraisal process. Consistent with expectations, the perception that performance ratings were influenced by personal bias and intention to punish subordinates resulted in decreased satisfaction and indirectly resulted in increased turnover intentions. However, when employees perceived that ratings were intentionally distorted to serve motivational purposes, satisfaction and turnover were unaffected. These findings are similar to other research on the influence of politics and nonperformance information in performance appraisal (see Ferris et al., 1994), and consistent with hypotheses about cultural differences in the acceptance of nonperformance information in ratings. That is, when organizational goals (e.g., motivating employees to perform better) are the reason for distortion, employees are unaffected by inaccurate performance appraisal ratings, but perceptions of individual treatment and bias have negative effects on employee outcomes.

Limitations to the Influence of Due Process

Findings from extant research on performance appraisal seem to suggest that despite its foundation in Western notions of justice, the due process metaphor has had an impact on research on performance appraisal across the globe. However, researchers and practitioners alike should carefully consider the extent to which the model *should* be applied in other contexts. Several factors may influence the viability of a due process performance appraisal system globally.

First, it is important to note that cultural differences in the relative value of procedural justice are likely to influence the extent to which the due process model is accepted and useful in structuring performance appraisal systems. Research by Konovksy and colleagues (Konovsky, Elliot, & Pugh, 1995; Konovsky & Pugh, 1994) and others (e.g., Gupta & Kumar, 2013; Pillai & Williams, 1999) has supported cultural differences in the value of procedural versus distributive justice. However, Ramamoorthy et al. (2012) found that procedural justice was equally important in both individualistic and collectivist cultures. Future research should aim to clarify whether various aspects of justice in performance appraisal are valued differently in general, or only in relation to specific outcomes (i.e., trust, overall fairness perceptions, satisfaction with performance appraisal) in an effort to build a more comprehensive understanding of justice in other cultures.

Second, cultural differences in the standards used to make performance decisions may make a due process model more difficult to implement in global organizations. As individualistic cultures value subordinate involvement and decisions made primarily on the basis of performance and merit, a system that exclusively plays to these tendencies may not be favorably viewed in a collectivist or high power-distance culture valuing seniority, harmony, and teamwork as the basis for decision-making. Although some elements of due process may still be useful, for example, providing adequate notice of standards and procedures, the fair-hearing and judgment- based-on-evidence components may need to be altered for suitability to different cultural norms.

Finally, although a wide sampling of culture and ethnicity is represented in the extant research on the due process model, additional research explicitly examining due process in other cultural samples and in multicultural scenarios is likely warranted. Findings do suggest that, despite cultural differences in power distance or collectivism, elements of due process seem to increase perceptions of fairness, but these findings may only generalize when both supervisor and subordinate are of the same ethnicity. For example, Konovsky (2000) noted that differences in individualism–collectivism and power distance may influence cultural preferences for control and influence in the performance appraisal process. These cultural differences may play out differently when both parties in a supervisor–subordinate dyad are of the same cultural background than when two very different cultures are represented. Future research should investigate consequences of using a due process performance appraisal system in a context in which employees from widely diverse backgrounds interact, for instance, an organization relying on expatriate managers to review the performance of employees from a different cultural background. Doing so could further our understanding of cultural elements that might affect perceptions of fairness when one culture's norms are not valued in the performance appraisal process.

Conclusion

Although it may be hard to separate the impact that scholarly work on organizational justice has had on performance appraisal at both the conceptual and applied levels from the impact of due process specifically, it is clear that elements of due process have been investigated in high-quality research and implemented in organizations quite broadly. Folger et al. (1992) have done us a great service by outlining and clarifying the due process metaphor as applied to performance appraisal. Further, distinguishing it from the other more traditional metaphors (test metaphor and political metaphor) opened the door for researchers to both ask important and intriguing questions while also testing notions built on the existing due process structure. In this chapter we have reviewed the extant literature on due process in performance appraisal and tried to integrate this research in a more comprehensive way than has been done to date. Throughout, we presented some conclusions and suggestions for how to move research forward. We would like to end with a few final thoughts.

First, there have not been very many direct tests of the due process metaphor, but to do so would likely require a field experiment and these are difficult to conduct. The good news is that, in addition to a couple of field experiments that have tested the due process metaphor in a rigorous way (Taylor et al., 1995; Taylor et al., 1998) and demonstrated important benefits of the approach, other studies have tested and examined important components either directly or indirectly. From all these studies and experiments we can conclude that subordinates experiencing a due process performance appraisal system as opposed to those who do not perceive a due process system perceive their ratings as fairer and more accurate, are more satisfied with the process and their rating, and rate their managers more favorably. Managers who experience a due process system report increased conflict resolution, greater satisfaction with the appraisal process, and greater job satisfaction than do those managers not experiencing due process. There appears to be ample evidence that incorporating elements of the due process system into performance appraisals has positive benefits on both raters and ratees. However, there does not appear to be any evidence that speaks to how these due process systems impact organizational outcome variables. This seems to be an important next step—we know that raters and ratees respond favorably to due process systems in a variety of ways, but we need to explore the impact of due process systems on organizational outcomes like effectiveness, efficiency, absenteeism, turnover, counterproductive behavior, and so on.

Second, the existing research suggests that due process is important for promoting organizational justice in performance appraisal systems, but it is not sufficient. Our review indicates that the structure of a due process approach lays the foundation for implementing fair and just performance appraisal systems, but that, invariably, in addition to these systemic factors, organizations need to emphasize the social interactions inherent in performance management. Relationships between rater and ratee are critical. It is important to recognize that both systemic and interpersonal factors are essential for establishing fairness and justice in performance appraisal. We identified communication between rater and ratee as absolutely key along with due process components to creating a just performance appraisal process. Specific elements of communication include amount of communication, communication style, prevalence, and quality of feedback shared, and transparency regarding feedback. The relationship between the rater and ratee along with personality and individual differences of each partner also play important roles in perceptions of justice of the appraisal process. Finally, we agree with one of the conclusions of Narcisse and Harcourt (2008) that training of both raters and ratees is instrumental in developing and implementing a due process performance appraisal system that is perceived by all as fair and just. We think future work in this area would benefit from designing performance appraisal training that is built around the components of due process along with the elements of communication that have been discussed. This type of training should improve justice perceptions and through these perceptions both individual and organizational outcomes.

Third, it is clear that the due process metaphor originates from a very Western cultural outlook with its emphasis on rights and responsibilities of employees across all levels of the organization. With respect to Hofstede's cultural dimensions, Western countries tend to be low on Power Distance and high on Individualism (among others), which is reflected quite clearly in an emphasis on fairness and justice for all employees and the associated rights and responsibilities. One of the more intriguing findings from our review and synthesis is that, despite the very Western foundation for due process, the due process metaphor for performance appraisal has been developed for, implemented in, and successfully applied in many non-Western countries and cultures (Erdogan et al., 2001; Kanwetuu, 2012; Kavanagh et al., 2007). Given the globalization of work in the 21st century, this has huge implications for how performance appraisal systems develop and adapt. The due process model highlights the importance of active participation and communication among raters and ratees, which is somewhat consistent to the Theory Y approach to management that has developed over the past 50 years. However, the spread of the due process approach across varied countries (e.g., China, Australia, Saint Lucia, Turkey) suggests more widespread implications for the model than we would have anticipated prior to writing this chapter. This, of course, makes continued research on the key components, processes, and effectiveness of the due process metaphor all the more important. Further, it is conceivable that justice or fairness perceptions in the United States might be very different than justice or fairness perceptions in China and due process models may need to be adapted or adjusted for these cultural differences. The bottom line, however, is that the due process metaphor is alive and well in non-Western countries as it is in the western world where it originated. Cross-cultural and multinational research that examines the components and outcomes of due process performance appraisal initiatives is much needed.

The due process model has advanced theory, research, and practice regarding justice in performance appraisal by delineating elements that can directly influence justice perceptions and other valued organizational outcomes. Our review and synthesis reveals that due process in performance appraisal has been studied empirically with a focus on justice perceptions and individual-level outcomes. Folger et al.'s (1992) due process model articulates ways in which justice can be enhanced in performance appraisal with very clear mechanisms. Our review of the published literature since the original introduction of the model suggests strong support for its impact in making performance appraisal systems fairer and better received by raters and ratees. In addition, recent work has demonstrated that the due process metaphor is important and relevant across cultures, which further substantiates its importance in the big picture of performance management.

References

Brockner, J., Konovsky, M., Cooper-Schneider, R., Folger, R., Martin, C., & Bies, R. J. (1994). Interactive effects of procedural justice and outcome negativity on victims of job loss. *The Academy of Management Journal, 37*(2), 397–409.

Cawley, B. D., Keeping, L. M., & Levy, P. E. (1998). Participation in the performance appraisal process and employee reactions: A meta-analytic review of field investigations. *Journal of Applied Psychology, 83*, 615–633.

Cloutier, J., & Vilhuber, L. (2008). Procedural justice criteria in salary determination. *Journal of Managerial Psychology, 23*(6), 713–740.

Cropanzano, R., Bowen, D. E., & Gilliland, S. W. (2007). The management of organizational justice. *Academy of Management Perspectives, 21*(4), 34–48.

Dyer, L., & Reeves, T. (1995). Human resource strategies and firm performance: what do we know and where do we need to go? *International Journal of human resource management, 6*(3), 656–670.

Elicker, J. D., Levy, P. E., & Hall, R. J. (2006). The role of leader-member exchange in the performance appraisal process. *Journal of Management, 32*(4), 531–551.

Erdogan, B. (2002). Antecedents and consequences of justice perceptions in performance appraisals. *Human Resource Management Review, 12*, 555–578.

Erdogan, B., Kraimer, M. L., & Liden, R. C. (2001). Procedural justice as a two-dimensional construct: An examination in the performance appraisal context. *Journal of Applied Behavioral Science, 37*(2), 205–222.

Ferris, G. R., Judge, T. A., Rowland, K. M., & Fitzgibbons, D. E. (1994). Subordinate influence and the performance evaluation process: Test of a model. *Organizational Behavior and Human Decision Processes, 58*, 101–101.

Findley, H. M., Giles, W. F., & Mossholder, K. W. (2000). Performance appraisal process and system facets: Relationships with contextual performance. *Journal of Applied Psychology, 85*(4), 634–640.

Folger, R., & Bies, R. J. (1989). Managerial responsibilities and procedural justice. *Employee Responsibilities and Rights Journal, 2*(2), 79–90.

Folger, R., Konovsky, M. A., & Cropanzano, R. (1992). A due process metaphor for performance appraisal. *Research in organizational behavior, 14*, 129–129.

Forkosch, M. D. (1958). American democracy and procedural due justice. *Brooklyn Law Review, 24*, 173–252.

Gupta, V., & Kumar, S. (2013). Impact of performance appraisal justice on employee engagement: a study of Indian professionals. *Employee Relations, 35*(1), 61–78.

Hartmann, F., & Slapničar, S. (2012). The perceived fairness of performance evaluation: The role of uncertainty. *Management Accounting Research, 23*, 17–33.

Heslin, P. A., & VandeWalle, D. (2011). Performance appraisal procedural justice: The role of a manager's implicit person theory. *Journal of Management, 37(6)*, 1694–1718.

Holbrook, R. L. (2002). Contact points and flash points: Conceptualizing the use of justice mechanisms in the performance appraisal interview. *Human Resource Management Review, 12*, 101–123.

Ilgen, D. R., Barnes-Farrell, J. L., & McKellin, D. B. (1993). Performance appraisal process research in the 1980s: What has it contributed to appraisals in use? *Organizational Behavior and Human Decision Processes, 54*, 321–368.

Ipsas, D., Ilies, A., Johnson, R. E., Iliescu, D., & Borman, W. C. (2010, April). Participation in the Development of Performance Appraisal Systems: A Quasi-experiment. Paper presented at the annual meeting of the Society of Industrial Organizational Psychology, Atlanta, GA.

Jawahar, I. (2010). The mediating role of appraisal feedback reactions on the relationship between rater feedback-related bhaviors and ratee performance. *Group & Organization Management, 35*(4), 494–526.

Kanwetuu, V. D. P. (2012). *Performance appraisal as employee motivation mechanism in financial institutions in Ghana: a study of employees of selected financial institutions in Kumasi* (Unpublished master's thesis). Kwame Nkrumah University of Science and Technology Department of Sociology and Social Work, Kumasi, Ghana.

Kataoka, H. C., Cole, N. D., & Flint, D. A. (2006). Due process model of procedural justice in performance appraisal: Promotion versus termination scenarios. *Psychological Reports, 99*, 819–832.

Kavanagh, P., Benson, J., & Brown, M. (2007). Understanding performance appraisal fairness. *Asia Pacific Journal of Human Resources, 45*(2), 132–150.

Konovsky, M. A. (2000). Understanding procedural justice and its impact on business organizations. *Journal of Management, 26*(3), 489–511.

Konovsky, M. A., Elliot, J., & Pugh, S. D. 1995. Citizenship behavior and its determinants in Mexico. Paper presented at the National Academy of Management Meetings, Vancouver, CA.

Konovsky, M. A., & Pugh, S. D. 1994. Citizenship behavior and social exchange. *Academy of Management Journal, 37*, 656–669.

Korsgaard, M. A., & Roberson, L. (1995). Procedural justice in performance evaluation: The role of instrumental and non-instrumental voice in performance appraisal decisions. *Journal of Management, 21*(4), 657–669.

Korsgaard, A. M., Roberson, L., & Rymph, R. D. (1998). What motivates fairness? The role of subordinate assertive behavior on managers' interactional fairness. *Journal of Applied Psychology, 83*(5), 731–744.

Levy, P. E., & Williams, J. R. (1998). The role of perceived system knowledge in predicting appraisal reactions, job satisfaction, and organizational commitment. *Journal of Organizational Behavior, 19*, 53–65.

Levy, P. E., & Williams, J. R. (2004). The social context of performance appraisal: A review and framework for the future. *Journal of Management, 30*(6), 881–905.
Mahony, D. M., Klaas, B. S., Mcclendon, J. A., & Varma, A. (2005). The effects of mandatory employment arbitration systems on applicants' attraction to organizations. *Human Resource Management, 44*(4), 449–470.
Martin, D. C., & Bartol, K. M. (2003). Factors influencing expatriate performance appraisal system success: an organizational perspective. *Journal of International Management, 9*(2), 115–132.
Masterson, S. S., & Taylor, M. S. (1996). Total quality management and performance appraisal: An integrative perspective. *Journal of Quality Management, 1*(1), 67–89.
Medvedeff, M. Gregory, J. B., & Levy, P. E. (2008). How attributes of the feedback message affect subsequent feedback seeking: The interactive effects of feedback sign and type. *Psychologica Belgica, 48*, 109–125.
Minter, R. L., & Thomas, E. G. (1999). Employee development through coaching, mentoring and counseling: A multidimensional approach. *Review of Business- Saint Johns University, 21*(1), 43–47.
Murphy, K. R., & Cleveland, J. N., (1991). *Performance appraisal: An organizational perspective.* Needham Heights, MA: Allyn & Bacon.
Narcisse, S., & Harcourt, M. (2008). Employee fairness perceptions of performance appraisal: a Saint Lucian case study. *International Journal of Human Resource Management, 19*(6), 1152–1169.
Noeverman, J. (2010). Not just because it is fair—The role of feedback quality and voice in performance evaluation. *ERIM Report Series Reference No. ERS-2010-048-ORG.*
Palaiologos, A., Papazekos, P., & Panayotopoulou, L. (2011). Organizational justice and employee satisfaction in performance appraisal. *Journal of European Industrial Training, 35*(8), 826–840.
Pillai, R., & Williams, E. S. (1999). Are the scales tipped in favor of procedural or distributive justice? An investigation of the U.S., India, and Germany. Paper presented at the National Academy of Management Meetings, Chicago, IL.
Poon, J. M. L. (2004). Effects of performance appraisal politics on job satisfaction and turnover intention. *Personnel Review, 33*(3), 322–334.
Ramamoorthy, N., & Carroll, S. J. (1998). Individualism/Collectivism orientations and reactions toward alternative human resource management practices. *Human Relations, 51*(5), 571–88.
Ramamoorthy, N., Flood, P., MacCurtain, S., Gupta, A., & Kulkarni, S. (2012). Role of organizational justice perceptions in India and Ireland: An empirical examination. *IIM Bangalore Research Paper*, 383.
Roberson, Q. M., & Stewart, M. M. (2006). Understanding the motivational effects of procedural and informational justice in feedback processes. *British Journal of Psychology, 97*, 281–298.
Smither, J. W., & Walker, A. G. (2004). Are the characteristics of narrative comments related to improvement in multirater feedback ratings over time? *Journal of Applied Psychology, 89*(3), 575–581.
Spencer, D. G. (1986). Employee voice and employee retention. *Academy of Management Journal, 29*(3), 488–502.
Taylor, S. M., Masterson, S. S., Renard, M. K., & Tracy, K. B. (1998).Managers' reactions to procedurally just performance management systems. *Academy of Management Journal, 41*(5), 568–579.
Taylor, S. M., Tracy, K. B., Renard, M. K., Harrison, J. K., & Carroll, S. J. (1995). Due process in performance appraisal: A quasi-experiment in procedural justice. *Administrative Science Quarterly, 40*(3), 495–523.
Thibaut, J. W., & Walker, L. (1975). *Procedural justice: A psychological analysis.* Hillsdale: Erlbaum.
Thibaut, J., & Walker, L. (1978). Theory of Procedure, A. *California Law Review*, 66, 541.
Thurston, P. W., & McNall, L. (2010). Justice perceptions of performance appraisal practices. *Journal of Managerial Psychology, 25*(3), 201–228.
Whitener, E. M. (1998). The impact of human resource activities on employee trust. *Human Resource Management Review, 7*(4), 389–404.
Whitener, E. M., Brodt, S. E., Korsgaard, M. A., & Werner, J. M. (1998). Managers as initiators of trust: An exchange relationship framework for understanding managerial trustworthy behavior. *Academy of Management Review, 23*(3), 513–530.
Williams, J. R., & Levy, P. E. (1992). The effects of perceived system knowledge on the agreement between self-ratings and supervisor ratings. *Personnel Psychology, 45*, 835–847.
Yamaguchi, I. (2005a). Effective interpersonal communication in Japanese companies under performance-based personnel practices. *Corporate Communications: An International Journal, 10*(2), 139–155.
Yamaguchi, I. (2005b). Interpersonal communication tactics and procedural justice for uncertainty management of Japanese workers. *Journal of Business Communication, 42*(2), 168–194.
Zheng, W., Zhang, M., & Li, H. (2011). Performance appraisal process and organizational citizenship behavior. *Journal of Managerial Psychology, 27*(7), 732–752.

CHAPTER

30 Applicant Fairness Reactions to the Selection Process

Donald M. Truxillo, Talya N. Bauer, *and* Julie M. McCarthy

Abstract

Although for much of its history of the personnel selection literature has taken the organization's perspective, the last 25 years has seen an increasing interest in how applicants themselves perceive the hiring process. The primary theoretical basis of the applicant reactions literature has been organizational justice theory, that is, the perceived fairness of selection systems. In this chapter, we review the dominant models of selection fairness and subsequent research on them, including the effects of selection fairness on attitudinal and behavioral outcomes. We discuss key research design issues in this literature, potential differences in how applicants react to selection in different cultures, and provide recommendations for organizations. We conclude with recommended research paths forward for this evolving area of study.

Key Words: applicant reactions, applicant perceptions, applicant fairness perceptions, organizational justice, test-taker predispositions

Applicant Fairness Reactions to the Selection Process

Throughout most of the history of industrial and organizational psychology, the focus of personnel selection has been on advancing organizational goals, particularly in terms of increased performance. Although concerns had long been raised about "face validity" through the years (that is, whether a test looks valid to the applicant), the concerns of applicants had been generally ignored. However, over the last 20 years, selection researchers have shown sustained interest in applicant perspectives, perhaps due to increased legal exposure to discrimination claims in the United States and concerns for the fair treatment of applicants in Europe.

This increase in "applicant reactions" research—that is, research focused on how applicants perceive the hiring situation, and how these perceptions affect applicants' attitudes about the company and their subsequent behavior—was facilitated by the development of key applicant reactions models in the early 1990s (Arvey & Sackett, 1993; Gilliland, 1993; Schuler, 1993). Perhaps the most comprehensive and theoretical of these reactions models was that developed by Gilliland, who framed applicant reactions in terms of how well selection procedures adhere to 10 procedural justice rules, and how these in turn affect applicant attitudes and behavior. This robust theoretical basis put organizational justice at front and center in the applicant reactions literature. Moreover, this fairness perceptions approach fits at intuitively with the study of applicant reactions (Singer, 1993).

In this chapter we review the applicant reactions research that is based in organizational justice theory and how well these justice variables relate to outcomes for the organization and for the employee. We begin by describing the three key models of selection fairness (Arvey & Sackett, 1993; Gilliland, 1993; Schuler, 1993), the various justice frameworks used to study selection fairness, and the effects (or lack of effects) of selection fairness on individual and organizational outcomes. We then discuss essential design issues in justice research on applicant reactions, and how these original models of applicant reactions may need to be updated as a result of the changes in personnel selection practices over the last 20 years. Next, we focus on international differences in applicant reactions, what employers can do to improve applicant fairness reactions, and suggestions for future research.

The Application of Organizational Justice in the Selection Context

It is well established that organizational justice matters in a wide variety of organizational settings (e.g., Ambrose & Cropanzano, 2003; Folger & Cropanzano, 2001). In the selection context, organizational justice research has focused on the extent to which applicants perceive a selection system or a specific selection procedure (e.g., test, work sample, interview) to be fair, and how this affects their subsequent behaviors and attitudes. It is important to note that organizational justice in selection (or selection fairness) is not synonymous with the broader applicant reactions literature, which includes topics such as test-taker predispositions, including test-taking anxiety (e.g., Lievens, De Corte, & Brysse, 2003; McCarthy, Hrabluik & Jelley, 2009; McCarthy et al., 2013; Proost, Derous, Schreurs, Hagtvet, & De Witte, 2008), test-taking motivation (e.g., Arvey, Strickland, Drauden, & Martin, 1990; Sanchez, Truxillo, & Bauer 2000), and perceptions of recruitment in general (e.g., Slaughter, Zickar, Highhouse, & Mohr, 2004). Rather, the selection fairness literature focuses on perceptions of applicants' fair treatment during the actual application and selection process, including the period after either being hired or rejected; and how applicants' perceptions affect their perceptions of the process itself, the organization, and themselves, and future behavioral intentions and behaviors such as job offer acceptance or steps toward litigation. This selection fairness approach has dominated the reactions literature.

As originally described by Gilliland (1993), the selection outcome (that is, whether an applicant is hired or promoted, which is usually framed as distributive justice or outcome fairness in this literature) is a primary determinant of applicant reactions. Indeed, subsequent applicant reactions research has shown that the applicant's outcome is a primary determinant of how they will react to the selection situation (e.g., Ryan & Ployhart, 2000). However, effective selection procedures are developed to pass and fail applicants, and thus many, if not most, applicants are destined to fail and not proceed to the final selection stage. Rather, the key contribution to this selection fairness approach is the identification and reinforcement of *fair processes* on applicant reactions. Put differently, there is little the employer can do to reduce the fact that some applicants will fail a test or not get a job, but there may be much they can do to mitigate negative reactions by providing applicants with a fair process. In this vein, Gilliland's model describes a series of organizational justice rules that map onto the theoretical approaches to justice that existed at that time (e.g., Leventhal, 1980; Thibaut & Walker, 1975; Tyler & Bies, 1990) as well as selection system characteristics (job-relatedness of procedures, treatment by test administrators), which, if respected by the employer, can help improve applicant reactions in terms of attitudes and behaviors. In other words, applicants may not like the fact that they didn't get the job (the outcome they wanted), but if they feel that they took a job-related (valid) test and were treated with respect, they will be less likely to speak badly about the organization or to sue. In short, the selection fairness approach treats organizational justice as the primary mediating/explanatory mechanism in understanding how applicants react to selection procedures.

Early Models of Selection Fairness

As noted, Gilliland (1993) proposed a justice model of applicants' reactions to selection systems. Gilliland's model includes 10 procedural justice "rules," which are discussed later and summarized in Table 30.1. The model posited that procedural justice could be summarized as containing three components including formal characteristics of the procedures (i.e., what organizations *do*), explanation of procedures and decision-making (i.e., what organizations *say* they do and why), and interpersonal treatment (i.e., how organizations interact with applicants).

Under the *formal characteristics* umbrella are four dimensions. *Job relatedness* is the extent to which a test is thought to measure aspects of the actual job situation, which is likened to Leventhal's (1980) *accuracy rule,* which requires that decisions be made based on "good" information. *Opportunity to perform* is defined consistent to concepts by Thibaut and Walker (1975) as giving recipients of the decision (in this case applicants)

Table 30.1 Gilliland's (1993) 10 Selection Procedural Justice Rules

Justice Rules	Definitions
Formal Characteristics	
Job relatedness	The extent to which a test is thought to measure aspects of the actual job situation.
Opportunity to perform	Giving applicants a chance to express themselves before a decision is made.
Reconsideration opportunity	The ability of applicants to challenge or modify the decision-making process.
Consistency	Ensuring consistency across all candidates for the selection procedures.
Explanations	
Feedback	Provision of both timely and useful information.
Selection information	Giving applicants a justification for a given decision.
Honesty	Truthfulness of information given to applicants during the selection process.
Interpersonal Treatment	
Interpersonal effectiveness of the administrator(s)	Respect and warmth given to applicants during the selection process.
Two-way communication	The opportunity that applicants have to offer input or to have their views considered during the selection process.
Propriety of questions	Being asked appropriate and non-prejudicial statements during the selection process.

a chance to express themselves *before* the decision is made. *Reconsideration opportunity* relates to the ability of applicants to challenge or modify the decision-making evaluation process. *Consistency* refers to ensuring consistency across all candidates for the selection procedures. Under the *explanations umbrella* are three factors. *Feedback* refers to the provision of both timely and useful information. *Selection information* involves giving applicants a justification for a given decision. *Honesty* refers to the truthfulness of information given to applicants during the selection process. Under the *interpersonal treatment umbrella* are also three justice rules. *Interpersonal effectiveness of the administrator(s)* refers to the amount of respect and warmth that applicants are treated with during the selection process. *Two-way communication* refers to the opportunity that applicants have to offer input or to have their views considered during the selection process. Finally, *propriety of questions* is defined as applicants being asked to respond to queries which are considered improper or having to endure prejudicial statements during the process. Potential moderators to the model were also proposed, such as the prior experience of applicants and the stage in the selection process that the applicant is in. For example, an applicant may not be aware that a delayed organizational response to an application is common and may take this personally (Rynes, Bretz, & Gerhart, 1991). Similarly, the further an applicant advances in an application system, the more invested an applicant may become in terms of time and emotions.

Although this model has been influential, it should be remembered that this was not the first attempt to create such a model of applicant reactions, and two other contemporaneous models of selection fairness contributed to this literature as well. First, Arvey and Sackett (1993) developed a model of applicant reactions with multiple facets similar to those of Gilliland. Their model explicitly considered selection fairness not only from the viewpoint of the applicant, but also from the viewpoint of the organization and its decision makers. As such, they included technical aspects of selection tests, such as their basis in job analysis, as well as organizational context, such as the selection ratio, as additional components of fairness. Although relatively few subsequent studies have considered fairness from this standpoint (see Kohn & Dipboye, 1998; Lemons & Jones, 2001; Madigan & Macan, 2005; Nicolaou & Judge, 2007; Viswesvaran & Ones, 2004, for exceptions), the consideration of fairness from multiple perspectives—including decision-makers in the organization—may be important for understanding why certain selection procedures are actually used by organizations.

Second, Schuler (1993) proposed a model that focuses on the extent to which applicants are treated with dignity and respect. Specifically, social validity theory highlights the importance of ensuring that the selection methods are unambiguous (*transparency*), the information provided is useful (*informativeness*), the feedback about performance is sufficient (*feedback*), and opportunities for applicants to participate are clear (*participation*). In short, social validity theory focuses very specifically on the applicant's experience and his or her interpretation of it. Although there have been very few direct tests of social validity theory, it serves as a robust model of considering selection from the applicant's point of view.

Clarification of Selection Fairness from the Applicant's Perspective

Research subsequent to the development of these original applicant reactions models has clarified the fairness construct from the applicant's perspective. In the development of their 39-item selection procedural justice scales (SPJS), Bauer et al. (2001) found that in addition to Gilliland's (1993) 10 original justice rules, the job-relatedness dimension split into two dimensions, job-relatedness/predictive validity (e.g., "Doing well on this test means a person can do the *[insert job title]* job well.") and job-relatedness/content validity (e.g., "The content of the test was clearly related to the *[insert job title]* job."), for a total of 11 facets of selection procedural justice (see Table 30.2 for the complete list of items). Further, these 11 facets factored into two higher-order factors, which Bauer et al. called "structure fairness," which focuses on the selection procedures themselves; and "social fairness," which focuses on how applicants are treated during the process. These two higher-order factors map onto the two justice dimensions described by Greenberg (1993), that is, the fairness of processes themselves and the fairness of how people are treated. This two-factor approach to applicant reactions is also consistent with the approach taken by Cropanzano and Wright (2003). In short, selection fairness from the applicants' perspective may be a two-factor construct—the fairness of the process itself and the fairness of applicant treatment—rather than three factors described in Gilliland's model.

Additional Frameworks for Explaining Applicant Fairness Reactions

Although organizational justice theory permeates and undergirds the entire applicant reactions research, two specific theoretical approaches deserve additional attention. These are counterfactuals from fairness theory (Folger & Cropanzano, 1998) and the applicant attribution-reaction theory (AART; e.g., Ployhart & Harold, 2004).

COUNTERFACTUALS FROM FAIRNESS THEORY

Fairness theory (Folger & Cropanzano, 1998, 2001) is highly relevant to applicant reactions, because it holds that individuals develop "counterfactuals" to explain negative events, such as negative experiences during the selection process. As LaHuis, MacLane, and Schlessman (2007) note, "The basic tenets of fairness theory suggest that when confronted with a decision-based event, individuals first gauge how the events affect them. If there is a negative impact, individuals will attempt to assign blame to the decision makers, but only if the decision makers can be held accountable." In other words, fairness theory argues that people try to make greater sense of the situations they encounter by attempting to answer three counterfactual arguments (could, would, and should). For example, if an applicant felt that they received a negative result because of a test, he or she might ask: *Could* the organization have given a more job-related test? Explanations that are designed to reduce the effects of could counterfactuals would be *excuses,* for example, that the organization had no other choice but to use the test. An applicant might also ask: *Would* I have gotten the job offer if a more job-related test was used? Finally, an applicant might ask: *Should* the organization have used a different test? Explanations that are designed to reduce such counterfactuals are *justifications,* that is, that the organization did, in fact, use a valid test. In a meta-analysis of organizational decisions

Table 30.2 Items for the Selection Procedural Justice Scales (SPJS; Bauer et al., 2001)

A. Structure Fairness Factor
Job-relatedness—Predictive
1. Doing well on this test means a person can do the [insert job title] job well.
2. A person who scored well on this test will be a good [insert job title].
Information Known
3. I understood in advance what the testing processes would be like.
4. I knew what to expect on the test.
5. I had ample information about what the format of the test would be.
Chance to Perform
6. I could really show my skills and abilities through this test.
7. This test allowed me to show what my job skills are.
8. This test gives applicants the opportunity to show what they can really do.
9. I was able to show what I can do on this test.
Reconsideration Opportunity
10. I was given ample opportunity to have my test results rechecked, if necessary.
11. There was a chance to discuss my test results with someone.
12. I feel satisfied with the process for reviewing my test results.
13. Applicants were able to have their test results reviewed if they wanted.
14. The opportunities for reviewing my test results were adequate.
Feedback
15. I had a clear understanding of when I would get my test results.
16. I knew what I would receive feedback about my test results.
17. I was satisfied with the amount of time it took to get feedback on my test results.
B. Social Fairness Factor
Consistency
18. The test was administered to all applicants in the same way.
19. There were no differences in the way the test was administered to different applicants.
20. Test administrators made no distinction in how they treated applicants.
Openness
21. I was treated honestly and openly during the testing process.
22. Test administrators were candid when answering questions during the tests.

(*continued*)

Table 30.2 (Continued)

23. Test administrators answered procedural questions in a straightforward and sincere manner.
24. Test administrators did not try to hide anything from me during the testing process.
Treatment
25. I was treated politely during the testing process.
26. The test administrators were considerate during the test.
27. The test administrators treated applicants with respect during today's testing process.
28. The testing staff put me at ease when I took the test.
29. I was satisfied with my treatment at the test site.
Two-way Communication
30. There was enough communication during the testing process.
31. I was able to ask questions about the test.
32. I am satisfied with the communication that occurred during the testing process.
33. I would have felt comfortable asking questions about the test if I had any.
34. I was comfortable with the idea of expressing my concerns at the test site.
Propriety of Questions
35. The content of the test did not appear to be prejudiced.
36. The test itself did not seem too personal or private.
37. The content of the test seemed appropriate.
C. Job-relatedness Content Factor
Job-relatedness—Content
38. It would be clear to anyone that this test is related to the [insert job title] job.
39. The content of the test was clearly related to the [insert job title] job.

(i.e., not only hiring decisions), Shaw, Wild, and Colquitt (2003) showed that excuses are more effective explanations than justifications.

With respect to empirical support in the applicant reactions context, Gilliland, Groth, Baker, Dew, Polly, and Langdon (2001) conducted three studies of explanations in the selection context and found greater effects on applicant reactions for could-reducing counterfactuals or excuses. However, in their meta-analysis, Truxillo, Bodner, Bertolino, Bauer, and Yonce (2009) did not find any difference in the effectiveness of excuse and justification explanations when given to applicants. More work is needed on the application of fairness theory to applicant reactions to better understand when and how much these different counterfactuals matter to applicants.

APPLICANT ATTRIBUTION-REACTION THEORY

Applicant attribution-reaction theory (AART; Ployhart & Harold, 2004) posits that "attributional processing occurs between the presence of an event...and the formation of perceptions (e.g., fairness, attitudes) and behavior (e.g., motivation, test performance)" (p. 89). Their model seeks to illuminate what causes and explains applicant perceptions and behaviors beyond simply describing them. They argue that, by themselves, the actual situations that applicants find themselves in are relatively neutral until attributions (Fiske & Taylor, 1991) about situations are made by applicants. In other words, individuals imagine or process situations they find themselves in to determine why people are treated in different ways as well as why they receive the outcomes they do. Over time, attributional patterns become automated (Forsterling, 2001), but when individuals encounter new situations, more attentional processes take place. Some studies that have used the attributional approach (e.g., Ployhart, Ehrhart, & Hayes, 2005; Ployhart & Ryan, 1997) to explain applicant perceptions suggest that attributions may affect applicant self-perceptions, at least under conditions when the selection procedures are considered fair. Although more research is needed into the effectiveness of AART in explaining applicant reactions, recent research has shown the value of AART, finding that fairness perceptions affect applicant attributions, which, in turn, affect applicant attitudes and behavioral intentions (Ababneh, Hackett, & Schat, 2014). The extent to which applicant reactions are influenced by the interactive effect of attributional style and distributive fairness has also been explored. Although no evidence for the moderating role of attributional style on applicant reactions was found, individuals with a positive attributional style exhibited higher levels of well-being after a rejection decision than did individuals with a negative attributional style (Schinkel, van Dierendonck, van Vianen, & Ryan, 2011). Although AART shows promise for applicant reactions research, it has not generated a great deal of work to date. We encourage additional research using this theoretical framework.

What Are the Effects of Selection Fairness?

Interest in applicant fairness perceptions comes primarily from their presumed effects on outcomes of interest. In Europe, the key outcomes have especially focused on the individual applicant, such as treating the applicant with respect (e.g., Anderson, Salgado, & Hülsheger, 2010; Schuler, 1993). In North America, the outcomes of interest have been more focused on the interests of the organization, such as organizational attractiveness, willingness to purchase company products, and litigation (Truxillo & Fraccaroli, 2011). In his model, Gilliland (1993) proposed that the outcomes of selection fairness fall into three categories: reactions during hiring (e.g., attraction to the employer, satisfaction with the process, legal battles), reactions after hiring (e.g., performance, job satisfaction), and self-perceptions (e.g., self-efficacy, future job-search decisions). Details regarding the relationship between fairness perceptions and attitudinal and behavioral outcomes can be found in Truxillo and Bauer's (2011) review as well as Hausknecht, Day, & Thomas's (2004) meta-analysis, and we direct the reader to these sources. As summarized by Truxillo, Steiner, & Gilliland (2004), the link between fairness perceptions and "soft outcomes," such as organizational attractiveness and recommendation intentions, has been more clearly established than has the relationship with "hard outcomes," such as actual applicant behavioral outcomes (e.g., litigation) and job performance.

"SOFT" OUTCOMES

A number of reviews of the applicant reactions literature (e.g., Gilliland & Steiner, 2012; Hausknecht et al., 2004; Ryan & Huth, 2008; Ryan & Ployhart, 2000; Sackett & Lievens, 2008; Truxillo & Bauer, 2011; Truxillo, Steiner, & Gilliland, 2004) have noted that the effects of fairness perceptions are more likely to affect attitudinal outcomes and those behavioral intentions that are proximal to the selection process (e.g., organizational attractiveness, job purchase intentions). For example, in their meta-analysis Hausknecht et al. found that organizational attractiveness and recommendation intentions are significantly related to applicant reactions at $r = -.44$ and .46 respectively. Intentions to accept a job and self-esteem are related at $r = .28$ and .26, respectively.

"HARD" OUTCOMES

In contrast, there has been scant support for the effects of selection fairness on the most important behavioral outcomes (e.g., actual litigation, job performance)—meaning that not only have there been no relationships found between selection fairness and later behavioral outcomes, such as continuation in actual the hiring process and later turnover on the job (e.g., Truxillo, Bauer, Campion, & Paronto, 2002) but also that there have been few studies that even include behavioral outcomes, as noted in Hausknecht et al.'s (2004) meta-analysis. Moreover, early hopes that applicant reactions including justice perceptions might lead to a comprehensive explanation for subgroup differences on tests (e.g., Chan, 1997; Chan, Schmitt, DeShon, Clause, & Delbridge, 1997) did not come to fruition.

A recent paper by McCarthy and colleagues (2013) illustrates the difficulty of linking applicant reactions to these more distal outcomes such as test validity and work performance. McCarthy et al. developed and tested a conceptual framework that examined whether and how candidate reactions might (or might not) influence job performance and under what conditions. Across four studies, which included 6,480 job candidates completing a variety of selection tests, McCarthy et al. examined five key candidate reactions (anxiety, motivation, belief in tests, self-efficacy, procedural justice). Findings revealed that the relation between applicant reactions and job performance is partially contingent on the extent to which reactions are situational (e.g., belief in tests, procedural fairness) or dispositional (e.g., test-taking anxiety, motivation, self-efficacy) in nature. They also found that when reactions are situational in nature (e.g., justice), they have an indirect effect on job performance (through their relation with test performance). However, when reactions are dispositional in nature (e.g., anxiety), then test scores mediate the relation between test reactions and job performance (e.g., they have a direct effect on job performance *and* indirect effect on job performance via test scores). Finally, candidate reactions had little effect on the relation between test performance and performance on the job. In other words, reactions did not appear to have any influence on the criterion-related validity of various selection tests. Thus, this study confirms previous conclusions (Truxillo et al., 2004) that selection fairness has less of a direct effect on "hard outcomes," such as test validity and job performance, than it does on "soft outcomes" and outcomes more proximal to the selection situation (e.g., organizational attractiveness.)

In short, the effects of selection fairness on "soft outcomes" (Truxillo et al., 2004), such as organizational-attractiveness ratings during the selection process, seem to be fairly consistent and robust. This is not surprising given that during the hiring process applicants have little else to base their attitudes and behaviors on than the perceived fairness of the selection process to which they have been exposed. In contrast, the effects on "hard outcomes" such as actual behavior after hire have been little examined. In other words, the optimistic expectations during the early years of the applicant reactions literature that the fairness perceptions of applicants while they were being screened would affect their actual job performance months or years later (as was suggested by Gilliland, 1993) were not realistic. However, we also note that the effects of selection fairness on the most important outcome for employers, applicant litigation behavior, has not been studied at all, although the effects of fairness on litigation intentions in simulated studies has been established (Bauer et al., 2001).

Applicant Reactions-Research Design Issues

LABORATORY VERSUS FIELD STUDIES

By necessity applicant reactions studies are often conducted in laboratory settings (e.g., Chan & Schmitt, 1997; Ployhart & Ryan, 1998; Ployhart, Ryan, & Bennett, 1999), especially since many applicant reactions issues (e.g., inconsistent treatment) cannot be studied in field settings. Whether the effects of fairness found in laboratory versus field settings are stronger is unclear from meta-analytic work: Although Hausknecht et al. (2004) found weak support for their hypothesis that selection fairness would be stronger in the laboratory versus field settings, Truxillo, Bodner, et al. (2009) found stronger effects for fairness explanations in field settings, suggesting that laboratory studies may underestimate the effects of selection justice in actual selection contexts.

MEASUREMENT

"Fairness" in this literature has either been measured at a global level, where overall justice is measured (Macan, Avedon, Paese, & Smith, 1994); at a dimensional level, in which separate procedural and distributive justice dimensions are measured (Arvey & Sackett, 1993; Bauer, Maertz, Dolen & Campion, 1998; Truxillo & Bauer, 1999); or at a more fine-grained level that focuses on the specific rules from Gilliland's model (Bauer et al., 2001). The global and dimensional approaches have the advantage of ease of measurement and may be practical in terms of many applied settings. However, the more fine-grained approach offers a richer theoretical understanding of fairness and a better diagnostic tool for employers. It was this that motivated Bauer et al. to develop the 39-item selection procedural justice scales (SPJS), described earlier (see Table 30.1). The SPJS can either be used in its entirety, or specific facets of the scales can be used when the researcher wishes to focus on perceptions of particular aspects of the selection process and when survey space is limited.

RESEARCH DESIGN ISSUES

In early selection fairness studies (e.g., Smither, Reilly, Milsap, Pearlman, & Stoffey, 1993), applicant reactions were often measured only after the selection process. However, this approach only indicates whether applicants felt fairly treated *after* the selection process, not whether their perceptions *changed* as a result of the selection procedure. For this reason, most selection fairness studies control for applicant perceptions prior to the selection process as a baseline (Bauer et al., 1998; Chan et al., 1997). These preselection perceptions may either be perceptions of fairness, or, for situations in which applicants have no basis for fairness perceptions, some other surrogate measure (e.g., attitudes toward tests; perceptions of the employer) are measured instead. Second, given that applicant outcomes are a primary determinant of applicant reactions (Ryan & Ployhart, 2000), some measure of outcome fairness or outcome favorability (e.g., pass/fail) should be used as a control variable in assessing applicants' fairness perceptions and their effects on subsequent outcomes such as organizational attractiveness. Relatedly, although fairness perceptions measured during the selection process, such as immediately after a test, may be useful for a better understanding of the selection process, studies of selection justice should include measures of applicant perceptions after applicants have received their results to better understand the perceptions that applicants have after the conclusion of the selection process.

Note that one key gap in the selection justice research noted by past reviews of this literature (e.g., Chan & Schmitt, 2004) and which is still not addressed in the present literature is research on how applicants' perceptions develop throughout the selection process at multiple time points. Research on fairness within the recruitment literature suggests the value in such longitudinal research. For example, Walker et al. (2012) examined the effects of justice during the recruitment process over time and found that the effects of justice signals on organizational attraction changes over time and that organizations should manage these justice signals throughout the entire recruitment process.

International Issues

With increased globalization comes the need to understand cross-cultural issues in applicant reactions. To date, the bulk of research in the area of applicant reactions has occurred in North America and Europe. In North America, this research has focused on how applicant reactions impact *organizations*, examining outcomes such as organizational attractiveness, intentions to recommend the organization to others, and propensity for litigation. In contrast, European research has emphasized how the selection process impacts *individual applicants*, examining outcomes such as applicant self-esteem, stress, and self-worth (e.g., Salgado, Anderson, & Hülsheger, 2010; Schinkel, van Vianen, & van Dierendonck, 2013). Emblematic of this European work is Schuler's (1993) social validity theory, which focuses on the extent to which applicants are treated with dignity and respect. In terms of research content, international research has tended to focus on which selection procedures applicants prefer, as well as on explaining which (if any) cross-cultural differences actually exist.

WHICH METHODS DO APPLICANTS PREFER?

There has been extensive work comparing reactions to different selection methods across countries. When applicant preferences for selection techniques are considered, a similar cross-cultural pattern emerges. Hausknecht et al. (2004) found that interviews are the most preferred selection tool, followed by work samples, résumés, and written tests (Hausknecht et al., 2004). These findings also apply to the perceived fairness of different selection procedures, with studies across several countries, including Belgium, France, Germany, Greece, the Netherlands, Portugal, Romania, Saudi Arabia, Singapore, South Africa, Spain, Turkey, and the United States, revealing that interviews and work sample tests (including assessment centers; Macan et al., 1994) are judged the highest in fairness; résumés, cognitive tests, references, biodata, and personality inventories are judged moderate in fairness; and honesty tests, personal contacts, and graphology are judged lowest in fairness (e.g., Anderson, Ahmed, & Costa, 2012; Anderson, et al., 2010; Anderson & Witvliet, 2008; Banki & Latham, 2010; Bertolino & Steiner, 2007; Bilgiç, & Acarlar, 2010; Ispas, Ilie, Iliescu, Johnson, & Harris, 2010; Kravitz, Stinson, & Chavez, 1996; Marcus, 2003; Nikolaou & Judge, 2007; Steiner & Gilliland, 1996; Stinglhamber, Vandenberghe, & Brancart, 1999; Visser & DeJong, 2001). In short, what is most remarkable in considering the effects of international differences on reactions to different selection methods is that there are so few differences across countries, as confirmed in a meta-analysis by Anderson and colleagues (2010). Specifically, across 38 studies, Anderson et al. found that the most favored selection methods are work samples and interviews, followed by resumes, cognitive and personality tests, and biodata. The least preferred tests are honesty tests, personal contacts, and graphology. In other words, as noted in many previous reviews (e.g., Truxillo et al., 2004; Truxillo & Bauer, 2011) applicants tend to prefer obviously job-related methods (work samples) and methods in which they believe that they have control (interviews).

EXPLAINING CROSS-CULTURAL DIFFERENCES

When examined at a more nuanced level, however, cross-cultural variability may emerge, particularly when cultural dimensions (e.g., collectivism, uncertainty avoidance; Hofstede, 1980) and environmental factors (e.g., current economy) are considered. For example, there is evidence that candidates demonstrate more positive reactions to panel interviews, structured interviews and/or group interviews in highly collectivistic countries (Salgado, Gorriti, & Moscoso, 2008). Further, a large-scale study of 959 organizations across 20 countries (Ryan, McFarland, Baron, & Page, 1999) found that cultures high in uncertainty avoidance used more test types, conducted more interviews, and were more likely to audit their processes. Individual-level cultural values have also been found to be important, with research suggesting that individuals high in independence (i.e., viewing oneself as autonomous), which corresponds to country-level "individualism," tend to perceive biodata and personality measures as more job-related than a situational judgment test (Ryan et al., 2009). In addition, Hiemstra, Derous, Serlie, and Borne (2012) found, in a study in the Netherlands, that ethnic minorities (e.g., Moroccan, Surinamese/Antillean) preferred video resumes over paper format compared to their majority counterparts, perhaps because the video resume takes a more personalized approach to selection.

A study by Hoang, Truxillo, Erdogan, and Bauer (2012) also found evidence for subtle cross-cultural differences, as applicants in the United States rated selection procedures involving human interaction (i.e., interviews, references, and personal contacts) higher than did applicants in Vietnam, whereas Vietnamese applicants rated work sample tests, personality tests, and written ability tests higher than did United States applicants. Hoang et al. note that this difference may be because Vietnamese applicants prefer more objective methods that do not allow for favoritism and the use of personal biases in hiring decisions. Further, applicants in the United States were more concerned about an employer's right to obtain information, and they used this in their judgments of procedural favorability.

It is notable, however, that few studies have examined cross-national applicant reactions using a specific cultural framework (for an exception see Phillips & Gully, 2002). Building on this cross-cultural applicant reactions work, we encourage more work to develop an updated theoretical model that uses cross-cultural research and emic and etic concepts as a guide. We see a recent meta-analysis by Shao, Rupp, Skarlicki, and Jones (2013) as providing a foundation for such a model, because it simultaneously considers general perceptions of employee justice alongside cultural dimensions. Specifically, Shao and colleagues position Hofstede's (1980) cultural dimensions as moderators of the relation between general perceptions of justice and key outcomes. Consistent with predictions, justice effects are stronger for cultures that are high in individualism, femininity, uncertainty avoidance, and that are low in power distance. Future research that considers this model in the context of applicant reactions is likely to prove invaluable to understanding the subtle differences in applicant fairness perceptions across countries and cultures.

How Can Employers Affect Selection Fairness?

Because perceptions of unfairness during the hiring process can have detrimental effects for both organizations and job applicants, strategies for the management of applicant perceptions are critical (Bauer, McCarthy, Anderson, Truxillo, & Salgado, 2012). Although some authors have pointed out that much more work is needed on how to improve applicant reactions in the field (Ryan & Huth, 2008), we offer four recommendations that employers can adopt to facilitate fairness perceptions: they can change existing selection methods, alter the way in which applicants are treated, provide explanations to applicants, and provide applicants with feedback.

CHANGE EXISTING SELECTION METHODS

First, organizations should take a careful look at their existing selection techniques with the goal of improving and/or replacing current procedures. Given that applicants have preferences for particular selection methods, and that these preferences are relatively consistent across cultures, employers could start by adopting methods that are viewed as fair by applicants. As noted, the most preferred techniques have been found to be job interviews and work samples, followed by résumés, cognitive tests, references, biodata, and personality inventories (e.g., Anderson et al., 2010; Hausknecht et al., 2004). In contrast, honesty tests, personal contacts, and graphology rank among the least preferred techniques (Anderson et al., 2010; Hausknecht et al., 2004). Fortunately, the selection methods that are viewed most favorably by applicants (e.g., job interviews, work samples) are also those that are generally the most valid (Anderson et al., 2010). Unfortunately, some of the least expensive methods that can be used on large numbers of applicants (e.g., cognitive, personality, and honesty tests) may be perceived as less fair. Therefore, simply using methods that are attractive to applicants may result in cases in which inexpensive and valid tests, such as biodata tests and personality inventories, are excluded. This is a concern, because these instruments have been found to explain variance in job performance when used in combination with other selection tools (see Goffin, Rothstein, & Johnson, 1996; McHenry, Hough, Toquam, Hanson, & Ashworth, 1990; Mount, Witt, & Barrick, 2000; Schmidt & Hunter, 1998). Thus, under many circumstances, organizations must administer a battery of selection tools, which includes not only valid and fair selection procedures but also includes tools that may be lower in fairness and yet make a significant incremental contribution to the prediction of job performance (Cropanzano & Wright, 2003). Ultimately, a combination of selection tools can maximize perceptions of fairness *and* validity (Gilliland & Steiner, 1999).

Organizations should also ensure that their selection techniques are based on job-relevant knowledge, skills, abilities, and other characteristics (KSAOs), because the selection methods that are perceived to be relevant for the job, or face valid, are also viewed as more fair (i.e., Bauer et al., 1998; Gilliland, 1994; Hausknecht et al., 2004). This includes avoiding and/or eliminating items that are abstract in nature, as selection tests have been found to be viewed as more fair when concrete items are used (Smither et al., 1993). There is also evidence that field-vetting test items—a process that involves comprehensive item-review sessions with applied subject matter experts—is positively related to candidate perceptions of fairness (Jelley & McCarthy, 2013). Finally, irrelevant questions, such as inappropriate personal information and discriminatory questions should be discarded, because they have a negative effect on applicant reactions, applicant perceptions (e.g., organizational attractiveness) and applicant intentions (e.g., recommendation to others; Saks & McCarthy, 2006). Muchinsky (2004) provides specific recommendations on how to achieve some of these objectives, and in doing so he describes how to teach subject matter experts to write, edit, and validate test items, as well as how to validate and score measures. On a final note, it is important to ensure that selection procedures give applicants the opportunity to perform, because this, too, is a key aspect of fairness from the applicant's standpoint (Schleicher, Venkataramani, Morgeson, & Campion, 2006). This can be accomplished in a number of ways, such as soliciting applicant questions during the selection process, ensuring that multiple selection instruments are used, and incorporating work sample tests (or similarly clearly job-related tests such as situational judgment tests) into the selection battery.

Finally, a note of caution is warranted for organizations considering a change to their selection procedures in order to improve applicant reactions. As noted by Ryan and Huth (2008), just because a selection procedure is considered "less fair" by applicants is not to say that it is necessarily considered to be "unfair." Moreover, it is possible for applicants to like some things about a selection procedure (e.g., its face validity) but not others (e.g., its lack of control for the applicant (Ryan & Huth, 2008). In short, applicant preferences are just one, complex factor to consider among many in choosing selection procedures (Bauer, Truxillo, Paronto, Weekley, & Campion, 2004; Ryan & Huth, 2008).

CHANGE APPLICANT TREATMENT

Organizations can also change the manner in which they treat job applicants. Social fairness, which reflects the interpersonal treatment of applicants, is particularly relevant in this regard and has been found to be one of two broad dimensions that explain applicant reactions (Bauer et al., 2001). Ensuring high levels of social fairness is paramount, because applicants rightfully expect to be treated with warmth and respect (Schreurs, Derous, Proost, Notelaers, & De Witte, 2008). Further, social fairness dimensions have been found to be related to important outcomes, such as intentions to recommend the organization to others and increased perceptions of organizational attractiveness (Bauer et al., 1998, 2001; Uggerslev, Fassina, & Kraichy, 2012).

There are many ways to increase social fairness. Most important, test administrators should be trained on interpersonal sensitivity, as the application process is a highly stressful event that can trigger strong emotions (Carless & Imber, 2007). In support of this recommendation, providing sensitive explanations to job applicants has been found to facilitate justice perceptions and promote positive organizational attitudes (Ployhart et al., 1999). Furthermore, test administrators should be trained on the importance of fair treatment. This involves ensuring that administrators understand the importance, as well as the logistics, of making the testing process consistent across all applicants (Madigan & Macan, 2005). This is critical, because inconsistent administration has been found to lead to perceptions of unfairness—even for cases in which the inconsistency worked in the applicant's favor (Ployhart & Ryan, 1998).

PROVIDE APPLICANTS WITH EXPLANATIONS

Fairness perceptions can also be improved by providing applicants with explanations that detail why they were selected or rejected for the job (Gilliland et al., 2001; Ployhart et al., 1999; Truxillo et al., 2002). Based in fairness theory (e.g., Folger & Cropanzano, 1998), this information may be presented in the form of a *justification*, which provides a logical rationale for why the decision was made (e.g., "We recognize that this is disappointing news. However, we used scientifically developed selection methods to make our decision."), or in the form of an *excuse*, which attributes the decision to an external cause or circumstance (e.g., "We recognize that this is disappointing news, but extenuating economic circumstances restricted the number of applicants we could accept this year." Truxillo, Bodner, et al., 2009). Practically, providing this type of information is simple and inexpensive, because it can easily be communicated to applicants in written or video formats (Truxillo, Bauer et al., 2009) and can affect perceptions of fairness, perceptions of the hiring organization, test performance, and test-taking motivation (Truxillo, Bauer, et al., 2009).

Empirical support for the effectiveness of explanations is consistent with meta-analytic evidence indicating that the provision of explanations has a significant effect on applicant perceptions of fairness, perceptions of the hiring organization, test performance, and test-taking motivation (Truxillo, Bodner, et al., 2009). The strength of this effect is the same for applicants with positive versus negative outcomes, as well as for the provision of excuses versus justifications (Truxillo et al., 2009b). Differences do occur, however, when the type of test is considered—explanations exhibit stronger effects on personality tests than on assessments of cognitive ability (Truxillo, Bodner, et al., 2009), which may be attributable to the fact that personality tests are generally viewed less favorably by job applicants. There is also evidence that providing pretest information to applicants (e.g., why the test was selected, how it will be scored) can have a significant influence on fairness perceptions (Holtz, Ployhart, & Dominguez, 2005; Horvath, Ryan, & Stierwalt, 2000; Truxillo et al., 2002).

Overall, there is consistent support for the use of explanations. Providing explanations is also much more feasible than modifying the selection system or training test administrators. The key, however, is to ensure that the information is a statement of facts and not a tool for manipulating the attitudes of job applicants (Truxillo, Bodner, et al., 2009).

PROVIDE APPLICANTS WITH FEEDBACK

Finally, fairness perceptions can be improved by providing applicants with feedback on their test performance. Given that outcome favorability (e.g., pass/fail, accept/reject) has been found to be a central determinant of applicant reactions (see Bauer et al., 1998; Ryan & Ployhart, 2000), consideration of how to notify applicants about their performance is crucial. Further, the provision of feedback is something that job applicants expect (Derous, Born, & De Witte, 2004; Schreurs et al., 2008) and is in line with professional testing standards (SIOP, 2003). At the very least, applicants should be told the results of the selection process (e.g., did they get the job or not).

Comprehensive and accurate feedback has been found to facilitate perceptions of justice (Anseel & Lievens, 2009; Schinkel, van Dierendonck, & Anderson, 2004; van Vianen, Taris, Scholten, & Schinkel 2004), as has feedback that is presented in a timely fashion (Waung & Brice, 2000, 2007). Timely feedback has also been found to result in higher levels of applicant attraction (Chapman, Uggerslev, Carroll, Piasentin, & Jones, 2005) and job-offer acceptance (Becker, Connolly, & Slaughter, 2010). In terms of feedback content and method, providing personal information about the individual who actually received the job has been found to enhance fairness perceptions (Gilliland et al., 2001), whereas providing test scores in feedback interviews is related to job attractiveness (van Vianen et al., 2004).

A note of caution is in order, however, as the provision of feedback to unsuccessful applicants has been found to have harmful effects on applicant well-being (Ployhart et al., 1999; Schinkel et al., 2011). Thus, future research that considers techniques for providing feedback that is detailed, timely and accurate, but at the same time is designed to protect the self-image of rejected applicants, would be particularly valuable. One possibility would be to highlight the strengths of the overall applicant pool.

Future Research Directions

Although the literature has advanced understanding of applicant fairness perceptions, a number of important questions and opportunities remain, which prompt several valuable avenues for future research. We have highlighted a number of these in this chapter, such as the need for applicant reactions models to incorporate cultural differences. Next, we offer additional areas for future research.

EXPLORE ADDITIONAL OUTCOME VARIABLES AND EXPLANATORY VARIABLES

As previously noted, the majority of studies on applicant reactions have focused on "soft" outcomes, such as organizational attractiveness. Although this research has proved useful, research on "hard" outcomes, such as applicant withdrawal or pursuit of litigation, is greatly needed (Truxillo et al., 2004). We recommend that researchers consider Anderson's (2011) detailed model of perceived job discrimination (PJD) as a theoretical foundation. This model extends earlier theoretical frameworks on applicant reactions (i.e., Gilliland, 1993; Haushnecht et al., 2004; Ryan & Ployhart, 2000) and is tailored to PJD. Specifically, Anderson proposed that PJD is an outcome of selection fairness which leads, in turn, to outcomes such as complaint initiation and actual litigation. More specifically, the model suggests that in addition to common personal (e.g., demographics, personality) and procedural characteristics (e.g., justice violations, selection decision), PJD is influenced by the legal context for selection (e.g., employment legislation, union support), as well as violations of the psychological contract. Patterson and Zibarras (2011) also offer valuable insight into research on perceived job discrimination, and highlight the value of attribution theory, self-serving bias theory, and the theory of relational demography when considering the effects of perceived job discrimination. Ultimately, an empirical test of the effects of fairness perceptions on applicant PJD and intentions to litigate could go far in advancing the field.

There is also reason to believe that selection fairness perceptions in certain cases can affect outcomes such as self-perceptions and even performance. In an online experiment, Gillespie and Ryan (2012) found that fairness in terms of gender-based preferential selection affected self-evaluations through its effects on posthire performance.

We conclude this discussion of outcomes by pointing out the importance of matching applicant perceptions of fairness to outcomes that are conceptually aligned. This idea is consistent with Ajzen and Fishbein's (1977) compatibility principle, which asserts that relations will be strongest when constructs are conceptually matched. For example, job applicant perceptions of interpersonal justice are likely to demonstrate the strongest relations with organizational citizenship behaviors and social identity (Colquitt, Conlon, Wesson, Porter, & Ng, 2001; Lind, 2001), as well as LMX and trust (Truxillo et al., 2004). On the other hand, applicant perceptions of procedural justice are likely to demonstrate the strongest relations with task-based and counterproductive performance (Cohen-Charash, & Spector, 2001; Colquitt et al., 2001; Zapata-Phelan, Colquitt, Scott, & Livingston, 2009), as well as withdrawal (Colquitt et al., 2001) and litigation behaviors.

EXAMINE INDIVIDUAL DIFFERENCES IN REACTIONS

In addition to effects of characteristics of the selection system itself that are under the organization's control (e.g., test types, explanations), some research also suggests that certain applicants may be predisposed to perceive the process more favorably than others (e.g., Honkaniemi, Feldt, Metsapelto, & Tolvanen, 2013; Truxillo, Bauer, Campion, & Paronto, 2006; Visvesvaran & Ones, 2004). The research thus far is promising. For example, Truxillo et al. (2006) found that neuroticism and agreeableness were the most consistent predictors of applicant reactions. Honkanemi et al. found that the personality types they classified as "bohemian" and "resilient" had the most positive applicant reactions. Taken together, these few results suggest that the effects of individual differences on applicant fairness reactions is deserving of further study to better understand the many antecedents of applicant reactions.

EXAMINE MODERATORS

Research has examined the possibility of moderators in the selection fairness–outcomes relationship, implying that selection fairness may in fact have stronger effects under certain conditions. Walsh, Tuller, Barnes-Farrell, and Mathews (2010) found that the effects of selection fairness are moderated by national culture. Using a multinational sample, they found that the relation between structure fairness and organizational attractiveness varied by culture, with the relationship being strongest in performance-oriented countries. Geenen, Proost, van Dijke, Witte, and Grumbkow (2012) found across two samples that the relationship between expectations of procedural justice and recommendation intentions were stronger among applicants with positive affect, whereas the relationship between distributive justice expectations and litigation intentions was stronger among applicants with negative affect. In addition to organizational perceptions, Schinkel and colleagues (2011) examined well-being—a potentially important outcome for the individual applicant. Specifically, they found that outcome fairness and attributional style interacted to affect applicant well-being, with an optimistic style leading to higher well-being for those who perceived low outcome fairness. A number of additional variables that may moderate the relationship between perceived fairness and outcome variables, for example, continuance commitment, job insecurity, and role overload, should be examined in future research, as well as other variables.

FOCUS ON FAIRNESS PERCEPTIONS FOR PROMOTIONAL PROCESSES

Ford, Truxillo, and Bauer (2009) pointed out that the effects of selection fairness could be particularly acute among current employees up for promotion, with negative fairness perceptions affecting outcomes such as performance, satisfaction, well-being, and even health. They further pointed out that these effects may also be important to the organization because rejected applicants for promotion stay with the organization and their performance may be affected as well. Indeed, Garcia-Ezquierdo, Moscoso, and Ramos-Villagrasa (2012) found that selection fairness actually did affect the job satisfaction of employees up for promotion.

However, the number of studies that has considered the promotional process (e.g., Ambrose & Cropanzano, 2003; McCarthy et al., 2009; Truxillo & Bauer, 1999) remains scant in this literature, and this area is ripe for further study. Reactions to promotions could be a crucial line of inquiry, as internal employees who are turned down for promotions are likely to become disgruntled, but may, nevertheless, end up staying with the organization (Ford et al., 2009). This can have direct effects on outcomes typically ignored in the applicant reactions literature (Ford et al., 2009; Truxillo & Bauer, 2011) such as job attitudes (e.g., organizational satisfaction, organizational commitment), and behaviors (e.g., organizational citizenship behaviors, withdrawal), and occupational health outcomes, resulting in detrimental consequences for the organization. To compound matters, the likelihood of litigation may be stronger among job incumbents than among applicants, because current employees are likely to be more invested in the company and are more aware of selection processes (Anderson, 2011; Giumetti & Sinar, 2012).

To date, the limited research that compares the reactions of internal and external candidates has yielded mixed findings. For example, there is evidence that external applicants generally have more positive perceptions of selection procedures than do job incumbents (e.g., Arvey et al., 1990; Brutus & Ryan, 1998; Giumetti & Sinar, 2012). On the other hand, Truxillo and Bauer (1999) found that applicants' reactions to banding were far stronger (and for some white applicants, more negative) in the promotional context than in entry-level selection, and Ambrose and Cropanzano (2003) found that the effects of internal candidates' perceptions of distributive justice can last for a year. Thus, additional work that directly compares internal and external candidates is needed, particularly with respect to different outcome variables.

A handful of studies have also examined the reactions of employees who are rejected for promotion, but remain with the organization. In general, findings indicate that promotional rejectees have higher levels of absenteeism than their promoted counterparts (Lam & Schaubroeck, 2000; Schwarzwald, Koslowsky, & Shalit, 1992). Promotional "rejectees" have also been found to have invidious reactions to promoted employees. Specifically, Schaubroeck and Lam (2004) found that feelings of envy toward promoted employees are highest when promotional rejectees had high promotion expectations and viewed the promoted employee as similar to themselves. In turn, envy resulted in higher levels of perceived injustice. Thus, it would be particularly valuable for future work to consider the effects of providing explanations and giving feedback to *promotional rejectees*. In doing so, companies may wish to incorporate the likelihood of future advancement, as well as provide concrete steps for career progression.

FURTHER RESEARCH REGARDING WHICH EXPLANATIONS WORK BEST

In addition, research has examined the effects of fairness explanations on applicant outcomes. In their meta-analysis of 26 studies, Truxillo, Bodner, et al. (2009) found that such fairness explanations affected fairness perceptions, perceptions of the organization, test-taking motivation, and cognitive-ability test performance, but not self-perceptions. Further, they found that the effects of explanations on cognitive test performance were mediated through test-taking motivation. In addition to justifications and excuses, these authors also identified a range of explanation types such as social fairness explanations and those focused on very specific justice rules. The relative effects of different types of explanations on applicant reactions seems to be a fruitful line of research to help employers improve applicant reactions.

CONSIDER ORGANIZATIONAL SIZE

We propose that applicant reactions may have stronger effects in small to medium-sized enterprises (SMEs) than in larger organizations. SMEs are generally defined as organizations that have fewer than 200 employees (Sutton, 1989), or those that have between 10 and 249 employees (Wessel & Burcher, 2004) and account for 99.7% of businesses in North America (US Census, 2008). Importantly, the selection systems in small companies are markedly different from those of large firms in that they are less likely to hire large numbers of employees, less likely have a human resources department that is responsible for hiring, and less likely to develop and adopt standardized testing procedures (Cardon & Stevens, 2004; Mayson & Barrett, 2006). Further, in SMEs, applicants are more likely to have their future co-workers and/or supervisors conducting the selection tests and interviews. As a result, the hiring manager is more proximal to the actual job, and perceptions of fairness in the hiring process are likely to be more salient. In fact, in many large organizations, such as police services and multinational corporations, selected applicants do not interact with recruiters at all after they have been hired for the position. Given that most of the applicant fairness perceptions research takes place in large organizations, organizational size could be considered as a moderator of the effects of applicant reactions on important outcome variables.

CONSIDER CHANGES TO THE HIRING PROCESS

The world of personnel selection has witnessed profound changes in the intervening years since the development of the original applicant reactions models, particularly with respect to the use of Internet-based assessment (Tippins, 2009). Although some of the selection fairness research has addressed Internet-based assessment (e.g., Bauer et al., 2006), researchers are beginning to recognize that many other dimensions may be salient to today's applicants. These dimensions include the user-friendliness of hiring websites (Sylva & Moll, 2009), the use of social networking cites (Madera, 2012), privacy concerns (Celani, Deutsch-Salamon, & Singh, 2008), and sharing of data across employers (Bauer et al., 2006). We thus see a strong need for empirical work to augment original approaches to selection fairness, taking into account these new dimensions of applicant reactions.

Conclusion

There is theoretical and empirical support for the role of applicant fairness perceptions on subsequent attitudes. However, the link with actual behaviors is less clear, and has led some to question whether reactions actually "matter." In the current chapter, we provide evidence that applicant reactions are a critical concern from the perspective of both the organization and the individual applicant. Indeed, there is no doubt that they affect a wide range of important outcomes and need to be carefully managed by organizations. Future research that explores more nuanced questions in the field of applicant reactions, as discussed earlier, is likely to uncover additional boundary conditions and outcome variables. We expect that such research will continue to highlight the necessity of ensuring that job applicants and incumbents are treated fairly when faced with the challenge of a selection process.

References

Ababneh, K. I., Hackett, R. D., & Schat, A. C. H. (2014). The role of attributions and fairness in understanding job applicant reactions to selection procedures and decisions. *Journal of Business and Psychology, 29*(1), 111–129. doi: 10.1007/s10869-013-9304-y

Ajzen, I., & Fishbein, M. (1977). Attitude-behavior relations: A theoretical analysis and review of empirical research. *Psychological Bulletin, 84*, 888–918. doi: http://dx.doi.org/10.1037/0033-2909.84.5.888

Ambrose, M. L., & Cropanzano, R. (2003). A longitudinal analysis of organizational fairness: An examination of reactions to tenure and promotion decisions. *Journal of Applied Psychology, 88*, 266–275. doi: http://dx.doi.org/10.1037/0021-9010.88.2.266

Anderson, N. (2011). Perceived job discrimination: Toward a model of applicant propensity to case initiation in selection. *International Journal of Selection and Assessment, 19*, 229–244. doi: http://dx.doi.org/10.1111/j.1468-2389.2011.00551.x

Anderson, N., Ahmed, S., & Costa, A. C. (2012). Applicant reactions in Saudi Arabia: Organizational attractiveness and core-self evaluation. *International Journal of Selection and Assessment, 20*, 197–208. doi: http://dx.doi.org/10.1111/j.1468-2389.2012.00592.x

Anderson, N., Salgado, J. F., & Hülsheger, U. R. (2010). Applicant reactions in selection: Comprehensive meta-analysis into reaction generalization versus situational specificity. *International Journal of Selection and Assessment, 18*, 291–304. doi: http://dx.doi.org/10.1111/j.1468-2389.2010.00512.x

Anderson, N., & Witvliet, C. (2008). Fairness reactions to personnel selection methods: An international comparison between the Netherlands, the United States, France, Spain, Portugal, and Singapore. *International Journal of Selection and Assessment, 16*, 1–13. doi: http://dx.doi.org/10.1111/j.1468-2389.2008.00404.x

Anseel, F., & Lievens, F. (2009). The mediating role of feedback acceptance in the relationship between feedback and attitudinal and performance outcomes. *International Journal of Selection and Assessment, 17*, 362–376. doi: http://dx.doi.org/10.1111/j.1468-2389.2009.00479.x

Arvey, R. D., & Sackett, P. R. (1993). Fairness in selection: Current developments and perspectives. In N. Schmitt & W. C. Borman (Eds.), *Personnel Selection in Organizations* (pp. 171–202). San Francisco, CA: Jossey-Bass.

Arvey, R. D., Strickland, W., Drauden, G., & Martin, C. (1990). Motivational components of test taking. *Personnel Psychology, 43*, 695–716. doi: http://dx.doi.org/10.1111/j.1744-6570.1990.tb00679.x

Banki, S., & Latham, G. P. (2010). The criterion-related validities and perceived fairness of the situational interview and the situational judgment test in an Iranian organization. *Applied Psychology: An International Review, 59*, 124–142. doi: http://dx.doi.org/10.1111/j.1464-0597.2009.00418.x

Bauer, T. N., Maertz, C. P., Dolen, M. R., & Campion, M. A. (1998). Longitudinal assessment of applicant reactions to employment testing and test outcome feedback. *Journal of Applied Psychology, 83*, 892–903. doi: http://dx.doi.org/10.1037/0021-9010.83.6.892

Bauer, T. N., McCarthy, J., Anderson, N., Truxillo, D. M., & Salgado, J. (2012). What we know about applicant reactions: Research summary and best practices. *SHRM/SIOP White Paper series.*

Bauer, T. N., Truxillo, D. M., Paronto, M. E., Weekley, J. A., & Campion, M. A. (2004). Applicant reactions to different selection technology: Face-to-face, interactive voice response, and computer-assisted telephone screening interviews. *International Journal of Selection and Assessment, 12*, 135–148.

Bauer, T. N., Truxillo, D. M., Sanchez, R. J., Craig, J., Ferrara, P., Campion, M. A. (2001). Applicant reactions to selection: Development of the selection procedural justice scale. *Personnel Psychology, 54*, 387–419. doi: http://dx.doi.org/10.1111/j.1744-6570.2001.tb00097.x

Bauer, T. N., Truxillo, D. M., Tucker, J. S., Weathers, V., Bertolino, M., Erdogan, B., & Campion, M. A. (2006). Selection in the information age: The role of personal information privacy concerns and computer use in understanding applicant reactions. *Journal of Management, 32*, 601–621. doi: http://dx.doi.org/10.1177/0149206306289829

Becker, W. J., Connolly, T., & Slaughter, J. E. (2010). The effect of job offer timing on offer acceptance, performance, and turnover. *Personnel Psychology, 63*, 223–241. doi: http://dx.doi.org/10.1111/j.1744-6570.2009.01167.x

Bertolino, M., & Steiner, D. D. (2007). Fairness reactions to selection methods: An Italian study. *International Journal of Selection and Assessment, 15*, 197–205. doi: http://dx.doi.org/10.1111/j.1468-2389.2007.00381.x

Bilgiç, R., & Acarlar, G. (2010). Fairness perceptions of selection instruments used in turkey. *International Journal of Selection and Assessment, 18*, 208–214. doi: http://dx.doi.org/10.1111/j.1468-2389.2010.00502.x

Brutus, S., & Ryan, A. M. (1998). A new perspective on preferential treatment: The role of ambiguity and self-efficacy. *Journal of Business and Psychology, 13*, 157–178. doi: http://dx.doi.org/10.1023/A:1022950705299

Cardon, M. S., & Stevens, C. E. (2004). Managing human resources in small organizations: What do we know? *Human Resource Management Review, 14*, 295–323. doi: http://dx.doi.org/10.1016/j.hrmr.2004.06.001

Carless, S. A., & Imber, A. (2007). The influence of perceived interviewer and job and organizational characteristics on applicant attraction and job choice intentions: The role of applicant anxiety. *International Journal of Selection and Assessment, 15*, 359–371. doi: http://dx.doi.org/10.1111/j.1468-2389.2007.00395.x

Celani, A., Deutsch-Salamon, S., & Singh, P. (2008). In justice we trust: A model of the role of trust in the organization in applicant reactions to the selection process. *Human Resource Management Review, 18*(2), 63–76. doi: http://dx.doi.org/10.1016/j.hrmr.2008.04.002

Chan, D. (1997). Racial subgroup differences in predictive validity perceptions on personality and cognitive ability tests. *Journal of Applied Psychology, 82, 311–320.*

Chan, D., & Schmitt, N. (1997). Video-based versus paper-and-pencil method of assessment in situational judgment tests: Subgroup differences in test performance and face validity perceptions. *Journal of Applied Psychology, 82*, 143–159.

Chan, D., & Schmitt, N. (2004). An agenda for future research on applicant reactions to selection procedures: A construct-oriented approach. *International Journal of Selection and Assessment, 12*, 9–23. doi: http://dx.doi.org/10.1111/j.0965-075X.2004.00260.x

Chan, D., Schmitt, N., DeShon, R. P., Clause, C. S., & Delbridge, K. (1997). Reactions to cognitive ability tests: The relationships between race, test performance, face validity perceptions, and test-taking motivation. *Journal of Applied Psychology, 82*, 300–310.

Chapman, D. S., Uggerslev, K. L., Carroll, S. A., Piasentin, K. A., & Jones, D. A. (2005). Applicant attraction to organizations and job choice: A meta-analytic review of the correlates of recruiting outcomes. *Journal of Applied Psychology, 90*, 928–944. doi: http://dx.doi.org/10.1037/0021-9010.90.5.928

Cohen-Charash, Y., & Spector, P. E. (2001). The role of justice in organizations: A meta-analysis. *Organizational Behavior and Human Decision Processes, 86*, 278–321. doi: http://dx.doi.org/10.1006/obhd.2001.2958

Colquitt, J. A., Conlon, D. E., Wesson, M. J., Porter, C. O. L. H., & Ng, K. Y. (2001). Justice at the millennium: A meta-analytic review of 25 years of organizational justice research. *Journal of Applied Psychology, 86*, 425–445. doi: http://dx.doi.org/10.1037/0021-9010.86.3.425

Cropanzano, R., & Wright, T. A. (2003). Procedural justice and organizational staffing: A tale of two paradigms. *Human Resource Management Review, 13*, 7–39.

Derous, E., Born, M. P., & De Witte, K. (2004). How applicants want and expect to be treated: Applicants' selection treatment beliefs and the development of the social process questionnaire on selection. *International Journal of Selection and Assessment, 12*, 99–119. doi: http://dx.doi.org/10.1111/j.0965-075X.2004.00267.x

Fiske, S. T., & Taylor, S. E. (1991). *Social cognition*. New York, NY: McGraw-Hill.

Folger, R., & Cropanzano, R. (1998). *Organizational justice and human resource management*. Thousand Oaks, CA: Sage.

Folger, R., & Cropanzano, R. (2001). Fairness theory: Justice as accountability. In J. Greenberg & R. Cropanzano (Eds.), *Advances in Organizational Justice* (pp. 1–55). Stanford, CA: Stanford University Press.

Ford, D. K., Truxillo, D. M., & Bauer, T. N. (2009). Rejected but still there: Shifting the focus in applicant reactions to the promotional context: A new path for applicant reactions research. *Applicant Reactions to Selection* [special issue], *International Journal of Selection and Assessment, 22*, 402–416. doi: http://dx.doi.org/10.1111/j.1468-2389.2009.00482.x

Forsterling, F. (2001). *Attribution: An introduction to theories, research and applications*. Hove, UK: Psychology Press.

Garcia-Izquierdo, A. L., Moscoso, S., & Ramos-Villagrasa, P. J. (2012). Reactions to the fairness of promotion methods: Procedural justice and job satisfaction. *International Journal of Selection and Assessment, 20*, 394–403. doi: http://dx.doi.org/10.1111/ijsa.12002

Geenen, B., Proost, K., van Dijke, M., de Witte, K., & von Grumbkow, J. (2012). The role of affect in the relationship between distributive justice expectations and applicants' recommendation and litigation intentions. *International Journal of Selection and Assessment, 20*, 404–413. doi: http://10.1111/ijsa.12003

Gillespie, J. Z., & Ryan, A. M. (2012). Gender-based preferential selection: Influences of perceptions of procedurally unfair advantage on performance and self-evaluations. *Journal of Applied Social Psychology, 42*. doi: http://10.1111/j.1559-1816.2012.01016.x

Gilliland, S. W. (1993). The perceived fairness of selection systems: An organizational justice perspective. *Academy of Management Review, 18*, 694–734. doi: http://10.5465/AMR.1993.9402210155

Gilliland, S. W. (1994). Effects of procedural and distributive justice on reactions to a selection system. *Journal of Applied Psychology, 79*, 691–701. doi: http://dx.doi.org/10.1037/0021-9010.79.5.691

Gilliland, S. W., Groth, M., Baker, R. C., Dew, A. F., Polly, L. M., & Langdon, J. C. (2001). Improving applicants' reactions to rejection letters: An application of fairness theory. *Personnel Psychology, 54*, 669–703. doi: http://dx.doi.org/10.1111/j.1744-6570.2001.tb00227.x

Gilliland, S. W., & Steiner, D. D. (1999). Applicant reactions to interviews: Procedural and interactional justice of recent interview technology. In R. W. Eder & M. M. Harris (Eds.) *The Employment Interview Handbook*. (pp. 69–82). Los Angeles, CA: Sage.

Gilliland, S. W., & Steiner, D. D. (2012). Applicant reactions to testing and selection. In N. Schmitt (Ed.), *The Oxford handbook of personnel selection and sssessment* (pp. 629–666). New York, NY: Oxford University Press.

Giumetti, G. W., & Sinar, E. F. (2012). Don't you know me well enough yet? Comparing reactions of internal and external candidates to employment testing. *International Journal of Selection and Assessment, 20*, 139–148. doi: http://10.1111/j.1468-2389.2012.00587.x

Goffin, R. D., Rothstein, M. G., & Johnston, N. G. (1996). Personality testing and the assessment center: Incremental validity for managerial selection. *Journal of Applied Psychology, 81*(6), 746–756. doi: http://dx.doi.org/10.1037/0021-9010.81.6.746

Greenberg, J. (1993). The social side of fairness: Interpersonal and informational classes of organizational justice. In R. Cropanzano (Ed.), *Justice in the workplace* (pp. 79–106). Hillsdale, NJ: Erlbaum.

Hausknecht, J. P, Day, D. V., & Thomas, S. C. (2004). Applicant reactions to selection procedures: An updated model and meta-analysis. *Personnel Psychology, 57*, 639–683. doi: http://psycnet.apa.org/doi/10.1111/j.1744-6570.2004.00003.x

Hiemstra, A. M. F., Derous, E., Serlie, A. W., & Born, M. P. (2012). Fairness perceptions of video resumes among ethnically diverse applicants. *International Journal of Selection and Assessment, 20*, 423–433. doi: http://10.1111/ijsa.12005

Hoang, T. G., Truxillo, D. M., Erdogan, B., & Bauer, T. N. (2012). Cross-cultural examination of applicant reactions to selection methods: United States and Vietnam. *International Journal of Selection and Assessment, 20*, 209–219. doi: http://10.1111/j.1468-2389.2012.00593.x

Hofstede, G. (1980). *Culture's consequences: International differences in work-related values*. Beverly Hills, CA: Sage.

Holtz, B. C., Ployhart, R. E., & Dominguez, A. (2005). Testing the rules of justice: The effects of frame-of-reference and pre-test validity information on personality test responses and test perceptions. *International Journal of Selection and Assessment, 13*, 75–86. doi: http://dx.doi.org/10.1111/j.0965-075X.2005.00301.x

Honkaniemi, L., Feldt, T., Metsapelto, R., & Tolvanen, A. (2013). Personality types and applicant reactions in real-life selection. *International Journal of Selection and Assessment, 21*, 32–45. doi: 10.1111/ijsa.12015

Horvath, M., Ryan, A. M., & Stierwalt, S. L. (2000). The influence of explanations for selection test use, outcome favorability, and self-efficacy on test-taker perceptions. *Organizational Behavior and Human Decision Processes, 84*, 310–330. http://dx.doi.org/10.1006/obhd.2000.2911

Ispas, D., Ilie, A., Iliescu, D., Johnson, R. E., & Harris, M. M. (2010). Fairness reactions to selection methods: A Romanian study. *International Journal of Selection and Assessment, 18*, 102–110. doi: http://dx.doi.org/10.1111/j.1468-2389.2010.00492.x

Jelley, R. B., & McCarthy, J. M. (2013). Examining a strategy for improving candidate perceptions of test fairness.

Journal of Police and Criminal Psychology, doi: http://dx.doi.org/10.1007/s11896-013-9122-1

Kohn, L. S., & Dipboye, R. L. (1998). The effects of interview structure on recruiting outcomes. *Journal of Applied Social Psychology, 28*, 821–843. Retrieved from http://search.proquest.com/docview/619344272?accountid=14771

Kravitz, D. L., Stinson, V., & Chavez, T. L. (1996). Evaluations of tests used for making personnel selection decisions. *International Journal of Selection and Assessment, 4*, 24–34.

LaHuis, D. M., MacLane, C. N., & Schlessman, B. R. (2007). Do applicants' perceptions matter? Investigating reapplication behavior using fairness theory. *International Journal of Selection and Assessment, 15*, 383–393. doi: http://10.1111/j.1468-2389.2007.00397.x

Lam, S. S. K., & Schaubroeck, J. (2000). The role of locus of control in reactions to being promoted and to being passed over: A quasi experiment. *Academy of Management Journal, 43*, 66–78. doi: http://dx.doi.org/10.2307/1556386

Lemons, M. A., & Jones, C. A. (2001). Procedural justice in promotion decisions: Using perceptions of fairness to build employee commitment. *Journal of Managerial Psychology, 16*, 268–280. doi: http://dx.doi.org/10.1108/02683940110391517

Leventhal, G. S. (1980). What should be done with equity theory? New approaches to the study of fairness in social relationship. In K. J. Gergen, M. S. Greenberg, & R. H. Willis (Eds.), *Social exchange: Advances in theory and research* (pp. 27–55). New York, NY: Plenum.

Lievens, F., De Corte, W., & Brysse, K. (2003). Applicant perceptions of selection procedures: The role of selection information, belief in tests, and comparative anxiety. *International Journal of Selection and Assessment, 11*(1), 67–77. doi: http://dx.doi.org/10.1111/1468-2389.00227

Lind, E. A. (2001). Thinking critically about justice judgments. *Journal of Vocational Behavior, 58*, 220–226. doi: http://dx.doi.org/10.1006/jvbe.2001.1793

Macan, T. H., Avedon, M. J., Paese, M., & Smith, D. E. (1994). The effects of applicants' reactions to cognitive ability tests and an assessment center. *Personnel Psychology, 47*, 715–738. doi: http://10.1111/j.1744-6570.1994.tb01573.x

Madera, J.M. (2012). Using social networking websites as a selection tool: The role of selection process fairness and job pursuit intentions. *International Journal of Hospitality Management, 31*, 1276–1282. doi: http://10.1016/j.ijhm.2012.03.008

Madigan, J., & Macan, T. H. (2005). Improving applicant reactions by altering test administration. *Applied Human Research Management Research, 10*, 73–88.

Marcus, B. (2003). Attitudes towards personnel selection methods: A partial replication and extension in a German sample. *Applied Psychology: An International Review, 52*, 515–532. doi: http://10.1111/1464-0597.00149

Mayson, S., & Barrett, R. (2006). The 'science' and 'practice' of HRM in small firms. *Human Resource Management Review, 16*, 447–455. doi: http://dx.doi.org/10.1016/j.hrmr.2006.08.002

McCarthy, J. M., Hrabluik, C., & Jelley, R. B. (2009). Progression through the ranks: Assessing employee reactions to high-stakes employment testing. *Personnel Psychology, 62*, 793–832. doi: http://10.1111/j.1744-6570.2009.01158.x

McCarthy, J. M., Van Iddekinge, C. H., Lievens, F., Kung, M., Sinar, E. F., & Campion, M. A. (2013). Do candidate reactions relate to job performance or affect criterion-related validity? A multistudy investigation of relations among reactions, selection test scores, and job performance. *Journal of Applied Psychology, 98*, 701–719. doi: http://dx.doi.org/10.1037/a0034089

McHenry, J. J., Hough, L. M., Toquam, J. L., Hanson, M. A., & Ashworth, S. (1990). Project A validity results: The relationship between predictor and criterion domains. *Personnel Psychology, 43*, 335–354. Retrieved from http://search.proquest.com/docview/617779397?accountid=14771

Mount, M. K., Witt, L. A., & Barrick, M. R. (2000). Incremental validity of empirically keyed biodata scales over GMA and the five factor personality constructs. *Personnel Psychology, 53*, 299–323. doi: http://dx.doi.org/10.1111/j.1744-6570.2000.tb00203.x

Muchinsky, P. M. (2004). When the psychometrics of test development meets organizational realities: A conceptual framework for organizational change, examples, and recommendations. *Personnel Psychology, 57*, 175–209. doi: http://dx.doi.org/10.1111/j.1744-6570.2004.tb02488.x

Nikolaou, I., & Judge, T. A. (2007). Fairness reactions to personnel selection techniques in Greece: The role of core self-evaluations. *International Journal of Selection and Assessment, 15*, 206–219. doi: http://dx.doi.org/10.1111/j.1468-2389.2007.00382.x

Patterson, F., & Zibarras, L. D. (2011). Exploring the construct of perceived job discrimination in selection. *International Journal of Selection and Assessment, 19*, 251–257. doi: http://dx.doi.org/10.1111/j.1468-2389.2011.00553.x

Phillips, J. M., & Gully, S. M. (2002). Fairness reactions to personnel selection techniques in Singapore and the United States. *The International Journal of Human Resource Management, 13*, 1186–1205. doi: http://dx.doi.org/10.1080/09585190210149475

Ployhart, R. E., Ehrhart, K. H., & Hayes, S. C. (2005). Using attributions to understand the effects of explanations on applicant reactions: Are reactions consistent with the covariation principle? *Journal of Applied Social Psychology, 35*, 259–296.

Ployhart, R. E., & Harold, C. M. (2004). The applicant attribution-reaction theory (AART): An integrative theory of applicant attributional processing. *International Journal of Selection and Assessment, 12*, 84–98. doi: http://dx.doi.org/10.1111/j.0965-075X.2004.00266.x

Ployhart, R. E., & Ryan, A. M. (1997). Toward an explanation of applicant reactions: An examination of organizational justice and attribution frameworks. *Organizational Behavior and Human Decision Processes, 72*, 308–335.

Ployhart, R. E., & Ryan, A. M. (1998). Toward an explanation of applicant reactions: An examination of organizational justice and attribution frameworks. *Organizational Behavior and Human Decision Processes, 74*, 88–88. doi: http://dx.doi.org/10.1006/obhd.1997.2742

Ployhart, R. E., Ryan, A. M., & Bennett, M. (1999). Explanations for selection decisions: Applicants' reactions to informational and sensitivity features of explanations. *Journal of Applied Psychology, 84*, 87–106. doi: http://dx.doi.org/10.1037/0021-9010.84.1.8

Proost, K., Derous, E., Schreurs, B., Hagtvet, K. A., & De Witte, K. (2008). Selection test anxiety: Investigating applicants' self- vs other-referenced anxiety in a real selection setting. *International Journal of Selection and Assessment, 16*(1), 14–26. doi: http://dx.doi.org/10.1111/j.1468-2389.2008.00405.x

Ryan, A. M., Boyce, A. S., Ghumman, S., Jundt, D., Schmidt, G., & Gibby, R. (2009). Going global: Cultural values and perceptions of selection procedures. *Applied Psychology: An International Review, 58,* 520–556. doi: http://10.1111/j.1464-0597.2008.00363.x

Ryan, A. M., & Huth, M. (2008). Not much more than platitudes? A critical look at the utility of applicant reactions research. *Human Resource Management Review, 18,* 119–132. doi: http://dx.doi.org/10.1016/j.hrmr.2008.07.004.

Ryan, A. M., McFarland, L., Baron, H., & Page, R. (1999). An international look at selection practices: Nation and culture as explanations for variability in practice. *Personnel Psychology, 52,* 359–391. doi: http://dx.doi.org/10.1111/j.1744-6570.1999.tb00165.x

Ryan, A. M., & Ployhart, R. E. (2000). Applicants' perceptions of selection procedures and decisions: A critical review and agenda for the future. *Journal of Management, 26,* 565–606. doi:10.1177/014920630002600308

Rynes, S. L., Bretz, R. D., & Gerhart, B. (1991). The importance of recruitment in job choice: A different way of looking. *Personnel Psychology, 44,* 487–521. doi: http://10.1111/j.1744-6570.1991.tb02402.x

Sackett, P. R., & Lievens, F. (2008). Personnel Selection. *Annual Review of Psychology, 59,* 419–450. doi: http://10.1146/annurev.psych.59.103006.093716

Saks, A. M., & McCarthy, J. M. (2006). Effects of discriminatory interview questions and gender on applicant reactions. *Journal of Business and Psychology, 21,* 175–191. doi: http://dx.doi.org/10.1007/s10869-006-9024-7

Salgado, J., Anderson, N., & Hulsheger, U. R. (2010). Personnel selection in Europe: Psychotechnics and the forgotten history of modern scientific personnel selection. In J. L. Farr & N. T. Tippins (Eds.), *Handbook of personnel selection*, pp. 921–941. Mahwah, NJ: Erlbaum.

Salgado, J. F., Gorriti, M., & Moscoso, S. (2008). The structured behavioural interview and job performance in Spanish public administration: Psychometric properties and fairness reactions. *Psychology in Spain, 12,* 88–96.

Sanchez, R. J., Truxillo, D. M., & Bauer, T. N. (2000). Development and examination of an expectancy-based measure of test-taking motivation. *Journal of Applied Psychology, 85,* 739–750. doi: http://psycnet.apa.org/doi/10.1037/0021-9010.85.5.739

Schaubroeck, J., & Lam, S. S. K. (2004). Comparing lots before and after: Promotion rejectees' invidious reactions to promotees. *Organizational Behavior and Human Decision Processes, 94,* 33–47. doi: http://dx.doi.org/10.1016/j.obhdp.2004.01.001

Schinkel, S., van Dierendonck, D., & Anderson, N. (2004). The impact of selection encounters on applicants: An experimental study into feedback effects after a negative selection decision. *International Journal of Selection and Assessment, 12,* 197–205. doi: http://dx.doi.org/10.1111/j.0965-075X.2004.00274.x

Schinkel, S., van Dierendonck, D., van Vianen, A., & Ryan, A. M. (2011). Applicant Reactions to rejection: Feedback, fairness, and attributional style effects. *Journal of Personnel Psychology, 10,* 146–156. DOI: 10.1111/j.0965-075X.2004.00266.x

Schinkel, S., van Vianen, A., & van Dierendonck, D. (2013). Selection Fairness and Outcomes: A field study of interactive effects on applicant reactions. *International Journal of Selection and Assessment, 21,* 21–31. doi: http://10.1111/ijsa.12014

Schleicher, D. J., Venkataramani, V., Morgeson, F. P., & Campion, M. A. (2006). So you didn't get the job... now what do you think? Examining opportunity-to-perform fairness perceptions. *Personnel Psychology, 59,* 559–590. doi: http://dx.doi.org/10.1111/j.1744-6570.2006.00047.x

Schmidt, F. L., & Hunter, J. E. (1998). The validity and utility of selection methods in personnel psychology: Practical and theoretical implications of 85 years of research findings. *Psychological Bulletin, 124,* 262–274.

Schreurs, B., Derous, E., Proost, K., Notelaers, G., & De Witte, K. (2008). Applicant selection expectations: Validating a multidimensional measure in the military. *International Journal of Selection and Assessment, 16,* 170–176. doi: http://dx.doi.org/10.1111/j.1468-2389.2008.00421.x

Schuler, H. (1993). Social validity of selection situations: A concept and some empirical results. In H. Schuler, J. L. Farr, & M. Smith (Eds.), *Personnel selection and assessment: Individual and organizational perspectives*, pp. 11–26. Hillsdale, NJ: Erlbaum.

Schwarzwald, J., Koslowsky, M., & Shalit, B. (1992). A field study of employees' attitudes and behaviors after promotion decisions. *Journal of Applied Psychology, 77,* 511–514. doi: http://dx.doi.org/10.1037/0021-9010.77.4.511

Shao, R., Rupp, D. E., Skarlicki, D. P., & Jones, K. S. (2013). Employee justice across cultures: A meta-analytic review. *Journal of Management, 39,* 263–301. doi: http://dx.doi.org/10.1177/0149206311422447

Shaw, J. C., Wild, E., & Colquitt, J. A. (2003). To justify or excuse? A meta-analytic review of the effects of explanations. *Journal of Applied Psychology, 88,* 444–458. doi: http://10.1037/0021-9010.88.3.444

Singer, M. (1993). *Fairness in personnel selection*. Brookfield, VT: Avebury.

Slaughter, J. E., Zickar, M. J., Highhouse, S., & Mohr, D. C. (2004). Personality trait inferences about organizations: Development of a measure and assessment of construct validity. *Journal of Applied Psychology, 89,* 85–103. doi: http://10.1037/0021-9010.89.1.85

Smither, J. W., Reilly, R. R., Millsap, R. E., Pearlman, K., & Stoffey, R. W. (1993). Applicant reactions to selection procedures. *Personnel Psychology, 46,* 49–77. doi: http://10.1111/j. 1744-6570.1993.tb00867.x

Society for Industrial and Organizational Psychology. (2003). *Principles for the validation and use of personnel selection procedures* (4th ed). Bowling Green, OH: Author.

Steiner, D. D., & Gilliland, S. W. (1996). Fairness reactions to personnel selection techniques in France and the United States. *Journal of Applied Psychology, 81,* 134–141. doi: http://dx.doi.org/10.1037/0021-9010.81.2.134.

Stinglhamber, F., Vandenberghe, C., & Brancart, S. (1999). Les réactions des candidats envers les techniques de sélection du personnel: Une étude dans un contexte francophone. *Le Travail Humain: A Bilingual and Multi-Disciplinary Journal in Human Factors, 62,* 347–361.

Sutton, D. (1989). A not so happy medium? *Director, 42,* 59–62.

Sylva, H., & Moll, S. (2009). E-recruitment: A study into applicant perceptions of an online application system. *International Journal of Selection and Assessment, 17,* 311–323. doi: http://10.1111/j.1468-2389.2009.00473.x

Thibaut, J., & Walker, L. (1975). *Procedural justice: A psychological analysis.* Hillsdale, NJ: Erlbaum.

Tippins, N. T. (2009). Where is the unproctored Internet testing train headed now? *Industrial and Organizational Psychology, 2*, 69–76. doi: http://10.1111/j.1754-9434.2008.01111.x

Truxillo, D. M., & Bauer, T. N. (1999). Applicant reactions to test score banding in entry-level and promotional contexts. *Journal of Applied Psychology, 84*, 322–339. doi: http://dx.doi.org.myaccess.library.utoronto.ca/10.1037/0021-9010.84.3.322

Truxillo, D. M., & Bauer, T. N. (2011). *Applicant reactions to organizations and selection systems.* Washington, DC, US: American Psychological Association, Washington, DC. doi: http://dx.doi.org/10.1037/12170-012

Truxillo, D. M., Bauer, T. N., & Campion, M. A. (2009). Organizational justice interventions: Practicalities, concerns, and potential. *Industrial and Organizational Psychology: Perspectives on Science and Practice, 2*, 211–214. doi: http://dx.doi.org/10.1111/j.1754-9434.2009.01141.x

Truxillo, D. M., Bauer, T. N., Campion, M. A., & Paronto, M. E. (2002). Selection fairness information and applicant reactions: A longitudinal field study. *Journal of Applied Psychology, 87*, 1020–1031. doi: http://dx.doi.org/10.1037/0021-9010.87.6.1020

Truxillo, D. M., Bauer, T. N., Campion, M. A., & Paronto, M. E. (2006). A field study of the role of big five personality in applicant perceptions of selection fairness, self, and the hiring organization. *International Journal of Selection and Assessment, 14*, 269–277. doi: http://dx.doi.org/10.1111/j.1468-2389.2006.00351.x

Truxillo, D. M., Bodner, T. E., Bertolino, M., Bauer, T. N., & Yonce, C. A. (2009). Effects of explanations on applicant reactions: A meta-analytic review. *International Journal of Selection and Assessment, 17*, 346–361. doi: http://dx.doi.org/10.1111/j.1468-2389.2009.00478.x

Truxillo, D. T., & Fraccaroli, F. (2011). A person-centered work psychology: Changing paradigms by broadening horizons. *Industrial and Organizational Psychology: Perspectives on Science and Practice, 4*, 102–104. doi: http://10.1111/j.1754-9434.2010.01304.x

Truxillo, D. M., Steiner, D. D., & Gilliland, S. W. (2004). The importance of organizational justice in personnel selection: Defining when selection fairness really matters. *International Journal of Selection and Assessment, 12*, 39–53. doi: http://10.1111/j.0965-075X.2004.00262.x

Tyler, T. R., & Bies, R. J. (1990). Beyond formal procedures: The interpersonal context of pro-cedural justice. In J. S. Carroll (Ed.), *Applied social psychology and organizational settings* (pp. 77–98). Hillsdale, NJ: Erlbaum.

Uggerslev, K. L., Fassina, N. E., & Kraichy, D. (2012). Recruiting through the stages: A meta-analytic test of predictors of applicant attraction at different stages of the recruiting process. *Personnel Psychology, 65*, 597–660. doi: http://dx.doi.org/10.1111/j.1744-6570.2012.01254.x

US Census Statistics (2008). Retrieved March 4, 2013 from http://www.census.gov/econ/smallbus.html

van Vianen, A. E. M., Taris, R., Scholten, E., & Schinkel, S. (2004). Perceived fairness in personnel selection: Determinants and outcomes in different stages of the assessment procedure. *International Journal of Selection and Assessment, 12*, 149–159. doi: http://dx.doi.org/10.1111/j.0965-075X.2004.00270.x

Visser, D., & DeJong, A. (2001). Comparing fairness perceptions of personnel selection techniques of American, French, and South African job applicants. *Journal of Industrial Psychology, 27*, 62–68. doi: http://10.4102/sajip.v27i2.789

Viswesvaran, C., & Ones, D. S. (2006). Importance of perceived personnel selection system fairness determinants: Relations with demographic, personality, and job characteristics. *International Journal of Selection and Assessment, 12*(1-2), 172–186. doi: http://dx.doi.org/10.1111/j.0965-075X.2004.00272.x

Walker, H. J., Bauer, T. N., Cole, M. S., Bernerth, J. B., Feild, H. S., & Short, J. C. (2013). Is this how I will be treated? Reducing uncertainty through recruitment interactions. *Academy of Management Journal, 56*, 1325–1347. doi: http://10.5465/amj.2011.0196

Walsh, B. M., Tuller, M. D., Barnes-Farrell, J. L., & Matthews, R. A. (2010). Investigating the moderating role of cultural practices on the effect of selection fairness perceptions. *International Journal of Selection and Assessment, 18*, 365–379. doi: http://dx.doi.org/10.1111/j.1468-2389.2010.00519.x

Waung, M., & Brice, T. S. (2000). Communicating negative hire decisions to applicants: Fulfilling psychological contracts. *Journal of Business and Psychology, 15*, 247–263. doi: http://dx.doi.org//10.1023/A:1007739127638

Waung, M., & Brice, T. S. (2007). The effect of acceptance/rejection status, status notification, and organizational obligation fulfillment on applicant intentions. *Journal of Applied Social Psychology, 37*, 2048–2071. doi: http://dx.doi.org/10.1111/j.1559-1816.2007.00250.x

Wessel, G., & Burcher, P. (2004). Six sigma for small and medium-sized enterprises. *The TQM Magazine, 16*(4), 264–272.

Zapata-Phelan, C., Colquitt, J. A., Scott, B. A., & Livingston, B. (2009). Procedural justice, interactional justice, and task performance: The mediating role of intrinsic motivation. *Organizational Behavior and Human Decision Processes, 108*, 93–105. doi: http://dx.doi.org/10.1016/j.obhdp.2008.08.001

CHAPTER

31 Failure and Complaint Handling in Marketing: An Organizational Justice Perspective

Ronald L. Hess, Jr. *and* James Olver

Abstract

The purpose of this paper is to review the existing research on justice theory as applied to failures and complaint handling, the area in which this theory has been most applied within the marketing discipline. *Failures* are product or service performances that fall below customer expectations and produce losses for customers. These losses produce customer perceptions of inequity with the exchange, creating an appropriate context for the application of justice principles. Our goal for this paper is to define the types of justice examined in marketing, as well as review the key antecedents and outcomes of justice. Particular attention is given to the relative impact of justice on these outcomes, as well as the nomological network that has been established in the literature. Finally, we identify several areas that warrant further attention by researchers.

Key Words: service failure, complaint handling, failure types, distributive justice, procedural justice, interpersonal justice, informational justice, satisfaction, loyalty, trust

Product and service failures represent critical negative events that can seriously threaten the health and longevity of customer–organizational relationships. *Failures* are defined as product or service performances that fall below customer expectations (Hoffman & Bateson 1997). A predominant view in marketing is that failures produce economic (i.e., tangible) and noneconomic (i.e., intangible) losses for customers (Smith, Bolton, & Wagner 1999). For example, customers can experience economic losses when a meal at an upscale restaurant is poorly prepared, as well as noneconomic losses from the embarrassment and humiliation caused when expressing displeasure to the waiter.

These losses produce customer perceptions of inequity with the exchange, creating an appropriate context for the application of justice principles. In this chapter, we review the existing research on justice theory as applied to failures and complaint handling, the area in which this theory has been most applied within the marketing discipline. The scope of this review is summarized in Figure 31.1. We begin by defining justice within this context and reviewing the key antecedents of customers' perceptions of justice. Next, we consider the outcomes of justice that have been examined. We focus particular attention on the relative impact of justice on these outcomes, as well as the nomological network that has been established. Finally, we identify several areas that warrant further attention by researchers. We begin by defining the types of perceived justice that are commonly applied within a complaint handling context.

Justice and Complaint Handling

Complaint Handling in Organizations

Much research demonstrates that the success of complaint handling programs in restoring equity, satisfaction, and repurchase intentions depends on customers' perceptions that their complaint was handled fairly (Blodgett, Hill, & Tax 1997; Clemmer 1993; Smith, et al., 1999; Tax, Brown, & Chandrashekaran 1998). *Complaint handling* (also known as recovery) is defined as the activities (and

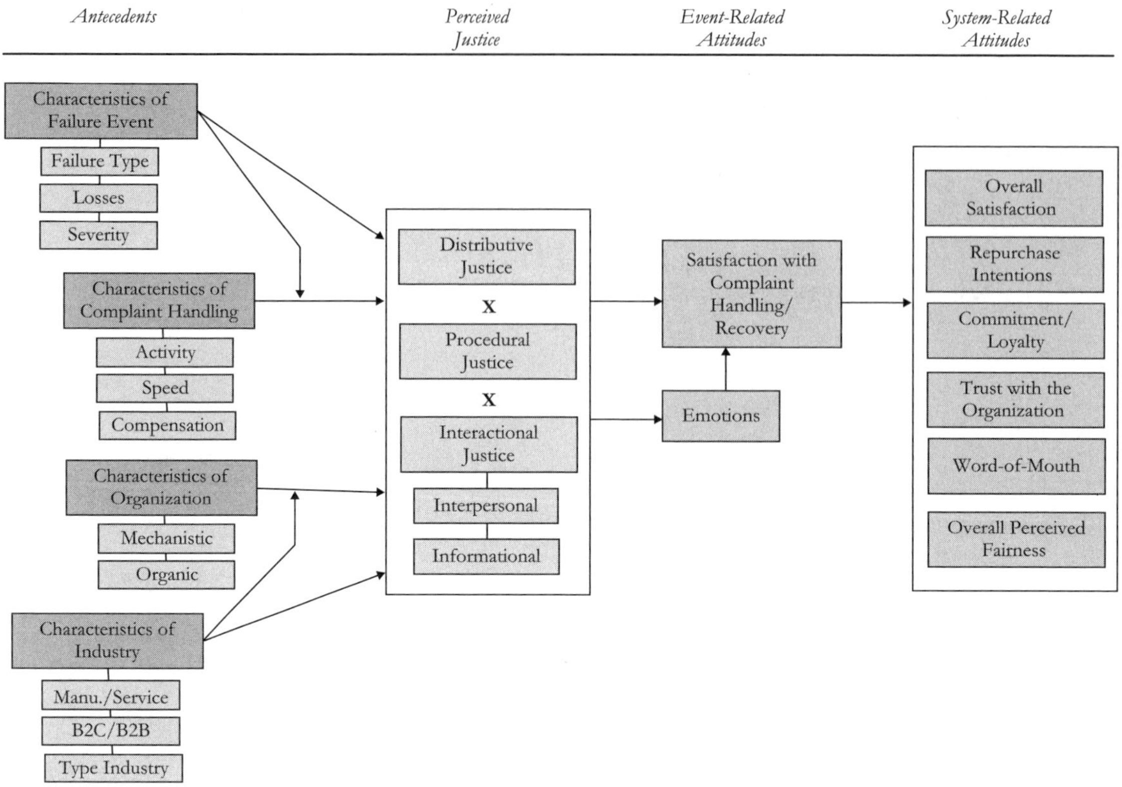

Fig. 31.1 Application of Perceived Justice in a Customer Complaint-Handling Context.

efforts) that organizations and employees use to correct the inequity caused by failures (Gronroos 1988). These activities may include compensation, discounts, free items, apologies, empathy, helpfulness, and an opportunity to voice, among others (Tax et al., 1998; Smith et al., 1999).

Unfortunately, few organizations can effectively handle customer complaints. For example, Fornell (2007) reports that the average complaint-handling satisfaction scores fall below 60 (100-point index) on the American Customer Satisfaction Index. Research indicates that approximately 50% of complaints are handled poorly, resulting in a "double deviation" and considerable customer dissatisfaction (Bitner, Booms, & Tetreault 1990). As a result, customers are frequently turning to social media, blogs, and other online sources to exact their revenge, reaching potentially millions with negative word-of-mouth and creating public relations nightmares for organizations.

Perceived Justice in a Complaint Handling Context

With few exceptions, research on complaint handling has adopted the three-factor model of justice (distributive, procedural, and interactional) to understand how customers respond and evaluate the fairness of organizational complaint handling efforts (Blodgett et al., 1997; Clemmer 1993; Smith et al., 1999; Tax et al., 1998). *Distributive justice* is the perceived fairness of outcome allocations, and is typically evaluated with respect to the equity of complaint handling distributions (Adams 1965; Deutsch 1985; Homans 1961). Next, *procedural justice* refers to the perceived fairness of the process(es) by which complaint handling allocation decisions are made. Finally, customers are also highly sensitive to *interactional justice*, the fairness of the treatment that one receives during the complaint handling process (i.e., enactment of procedures and distribution of outcomes) (Bies & Moag, 1986; Blodgett, et al., 1997; Smith et al., 1999; Tax et al., 1998).

Within the management discipline, several researchers have argued that interactional justice is better conceptualized as two distinct forms of justice: *interpersonal justice,* defined as the fairness of interpersonal treatment provided during the enactment of procedures and distributions of outcomes, and *informational justice,* defined as the fairness of explanations and information (Greenberg 1993).

Colquitt (2001) has provided support for this four factor model of justice. The distinction between interpersonal and informational justice is appealing given the importance of empathy/sensitivity and postrecovery follow-up in the execution of a high-quality complaint-handling effort. However, only a single study, to our knowledge, has adopted the four-factor model within a complaint-handling context (Ambrose, Hess & Ganesan 2007). These researchers found that the four factors of justice significantly influenced satisfaction with complaint handling, which, in turn, was related to customers' overall attitude toward the organization. We will explore the results of this study in more detail in a later section of this chapter.

Antecedents of Justice

Four general groups of antecedents of justice have been examined in the literature on complaint handling. These include characteristics of the complaint handling activities, failure event (failure type, customer losses, severity), organization factors related to complaint handling (mechanistic, organic), and industry type (manufacturing, service, business-to-business (B2B), business-to-consumer (B2C), industry type).

CHARACTERISTICS OF COMPLAINT HANDLING

Research in this area has primarily focused on the effectiveness of different complaint handling activities in improving perceptions of distributive, procedural, and interactional justice. Surprisingly, this issue has received only limited attention in the marketing literature, and it remains rather unclear which activities or combinations of activities provide the most optimal outcome for organizations when customers complain.

Early research on this issue attempted to identify those complaint-handling activities that were specifically related to distributive, procedural, and interactional justice (see Table 31.1). Much of our understanding about these relationships is based on the qualitative findings from Tax et al. (1998). As shown in Table 31.1, complaint handling activities that involve tangible compensation in the form of reimbursement, product/service replacement, credit, apology, repair, refund, correction, and additional tangible compensation are positively related to customer perceptions of *distributive justice* (Goodwin and Ross 1992; Smith et al., 1999; Tax et al., 1998). Smith et al. (1999) verified these findings through the use of a quasi-experimental design. They found that complaint handling that involved compensation was significantly related to customer perceptions of distributive justice in both restaurant and hotel contexts.

Early work on procedural justice in management identified several procedural rules that influence perceptions of fairness: consistency (across individuals and over time), accuracy of information, representativeness (voice), bias suppression, correctability (of incorrect decisions), decision control, and ethicality (Leventhal, Karuza, & Fry, 1980; Thibaut & Walker 1975; Colquitt 2001). The authors found that when individuals believed procedures were fair, they were more satisfied with the outcome they received, even when the decision outcome was unfavorable (Lind & Tyler 1988; Thibaut & Walker 1975).

Consistent with these views, researchers in marketing found that customer perceptions of *procedural justice* are based on complaint handling activities that include convenience, flexibility, speed of response, opportunity to voice, helpfulness, efficiency, assumption of responsibility, and follow-up (Conlon & Murray, 1996; Goodwin & Ross, 1992; Tax et al., 1998). Once again, Smith et al. (1999) demonstrated that the speed of complaint handling responses were an important antecedent of procedural justice.

It is interesting to note that the activities discussed earlier for complaint handling are quite different from those identified previously in the management literature. More recently, Hollensbe, Khazanchi, and Masterson (2008) posed a different set of antecedents for justice in the management literature. These authors examined entity-based (e.g., organization, co-worker, supervisor) rather than event-based rules of justice (e.g., performance appraisals, job applications). Surprisingly little research has reconsidered the factors that drive justice. Such a study could be quite interesting for complaint handling, which has considered only event-based rules of fairness.

Finally, researchers in marketing found that complaint handling activities such as empathy, perceived effort, politeness, friendliness, sensitivity, apologies, thorough explanations, justifications, lack of bias, honesty, candid communications, and postrecovery follow-up have an important influence on customers' perceptions of *interactional justice* (Conlon & Murray 1996; Goodwin & Ross 1992; Smith et al., 1999; Tax et al., 1998). Smith et al. (1999) verified these qualitative findings by showing that organizations that initiate complaint handling activities and apologize for customer

Table 31.1 Relative Strength of Justice Types on Satisfaction with Complaint Handling

Studies without Explicit Mediation Tests	Context	Relative Strength
Goodwin & Ross (1992)	Air, Auto Rep., Rest., Dental	DJ > PJ > IJ
Tax, Brown & Chandreshakan (1998)	Various Contexts	IJ > IJ/PJ
Smith, Bolton & Wagner (1999)	Restaurant Hotels	IJ > DJ/PJ
Matilla (2001)	Restaurants, Dry cleaning, Hair stylists	DJ > IJ > PJ (Restaurants) DJ > PJ/IJ (Cleaning) IJ > DJ > IJ (Hair)
Smith & Bolton (2002)	Restaurant Hotels	IJ > DJ/PJ
Homburg & Furst (2005)	Various Contexts	DJ > PJ/IJ
Maxham & Netemeyer (2002)	Banking New Home	DJ > IJ > PJ (Banks) DJ > IJ/PJ* (Home)
Vazquez-Casielles, Alvarez, & Martin (2010)	Cell Carriers	PJ > IJ > DJ
Studies with Explicit Mediation Tests		
Ambrose, Hess, & Ganesan (2007)	Various Contexts	DJ > InfoJ > PJ/InterJ
Orsingher, Valentini, & de Angelis (2010)	Various Contexts	DJ > IJ > PJ
Del Rio-Lanza, Vazquez-Casielles & Diaz-Martin (2009)	Cell Carriers	PJ > IJ/DJ

* Not significantly related to SATCH.

inconvenience have a significant impact on perceptions of interactional justice.

Although some research has identified some complaint handling activities that influence customers' perceptions of distributive, procedural, and interactional justice, little is understood about which set of activities are most appropriate and effective in restoring the equity lost by customers during the failure event. Similarly, we know little about which activities should be applied—and in what order and to what degree—to achieve the greatest gains for restoring customer perceptions of equity (see Hess 2010 for review).

CHARACTERISTICS OF FAILURE

Early research in marketing attempted to develop taxonomies of the failures that customers most frequently experience during exchanges with organizations (Bitner et al., 1990; Kelley, Hoffman & Davis, 1993; Keaveney, 1995). Although most of this research did not explicitly link failure types to justice, this research represents an important stepping stone to establishing such links.

Bitner et al. (1990) were first to develop a taxonomy of events that caused customer dissatisfaction (i.e., failure types) using the critical-incident technique. They identified three general classifications of failures: (1) unacceptable complaint-handling activities, (2) undesirable interpersonal employee treatment of customers, and (3) inadequate response to customer needs and requests. Most interesting, these authors discovered that unacceptable complaint handling was the most frequently occurring category of failure type in the airline and hotel industries.

Kelley et al. (1993) performed a failure categorization study within a retailing context using a similar technique. They found that product defects represented fully 70.5% of failures mentioned. Kelly et al. (1993) also categorized retailer complaint-handling activities and they were among the first to examine which complaint-handling activities retailers actually employ to respond to specific failure types. Their results, however, were generally inconclusive as considerable variation existed in how retailers addressed the same type of failures.

Finally, Keaveney (1995) focused on categorizing the reasons that customers switch to alternative service organizations. This was an important study because it examined why customers actually ended relationships with organizations. Not surprising, the reasons for customer switching were primarily failure related. Specifically, Keaveney (1995) discovered that core-service failures (44%); service-encounter failures (i.e., poor employee treatment, uncaring, impolite, unresponsive, unknowledgeable) (34%); unfair pricing practices (30%); inconvenient hours, locations, and waiting time (20%); and poor complaint handling responses (17%) were most frequently listed by customers as causing them to switch. Also striking, Keaveney (1995) indicated that 55% of switching occurred because customers experienced *multiple* failure events during a single encounter with an organization. The prevalence of multiple failure events is quite intriguing and will be addressed further in the later section on future research.

Although these studies were quite useful for understanding what produced dissatisfying encounters and customer switching behavior, this stream of research did little to advance a prescriptive approach to complaint handling. Such an approach required an understanding of how specific complaint handling activities may best address specific types of failures. Thus, the next stream of research focused on failures and the subsequent losses that customers experienced. This stream was motivated by a contingency approach to complaint handling. Specifically, these researchers argued that the optimal customer outcome occurred if the complaint handling activity (or set of activities) *matched* the specific type of loss experienced by the customer (Smith et al., 1999; Oliver, 1997).

Smith et al. (1999) specifically examined the effects of two types of failures—outcome (what is received from the service delivery) and process (how the service is delivered). The authors argue that customers experience different losses from outcome and process failures. They suggest that customers categorize the losses they experience during failures into economic (e.g., financial, product and service functionality) and noneconomic (e.g., social, esteem, emotional) accounts. For example, a poorly prepared restaurant meal may be considered economic by customers because of the financial and functionality losses involved, whereas the neglectful behavior of a waiter may be regarded as noneconomic due to the social and emotional losses experienced.

Smith et al. (1999) empirically tested for interactions among failure types (i.e., outcome versus process failures) and four complaint-handling activities (i.e., compensation, speed, apology, and organization-initiated) on distributive, procedural, and interactional justice. Although this prescriptive approach represented a novel view for understanding complaint handling, the results offered only limited support for this perspective. Specifically, the data supported the interaction between compensation and outcome failure type on distributive justice (compensation x failure type → distributive justice). The remaining three proposed interactions (speed x failure type → procedural justice; apology x failure type → procedural justice; and organization-initiated → interactional justice), however, were *only* supported within the hotel context. Support for these interactions were not confirmed for the restaurant context.

Hess (2010) acknowledged the lack of significant interactions among failure types and complaint handling activities on justice and argued that customers may experience many more losses following a failure than simply economic and noneconomic. Thus, based on established research on risk types, this author proposed a multidimensional categorization of 8 postfailure losses. These losses include: (1) performance (loss of product/service performance), (2) financial, (3) experiential (loss of life experiences), (4) physical (physical pain and suffering), (5) social (loss of self-esteem and self-confidence from perceptions of others), (6) psychological (harm incurred to ego), (7) collateral (indirect losses caused by focal failure), and (8) convenience (loss of time, effort, inconvenience).

Hess (2010) also argued that some of these eight losses can be experienced postfailure or when/if customers chose to file a complaint (prior to the complaint- handling process). For example, customers often feel uncomfortable when communicating their displeasure to an employee (social losses), and filing a complaint often requires considerable time and effort, adding to the convenience losses already produced by the failure. This author also proposed several theoretical models for complaint handling to address this more complete set of customer losses. Not all of these models dealt with the "matching approach." We will explore this issue in more detail in the future research section.

Beyond research on failure types and customer losses, one characteristic of failures that has received particular attention is failure severity. Kelley and Davis (1994) were among the first to suggest that customer perceptions of failures may vary in terms of severity. This characteristic suggests that a missed delivery date for wedding flower arrangements will be viewed as significantly more severe than a poorly prepared meal. It should also be noted that an *identical* failure type can impose significantly different severity responses from customers. For example, coffee spilled (failure type) on the table should be considered very different in terms of severity than coffee spilled on the customer.

Not surprisingly, early empirical evidence indicates that more severe failures lead to greater customer (dis)satisfaction than mild failures (Gilly & Gelb, 1982; Hess, Ganesan, & Klein 2003, 2007; Hess 2008). Few studies have established a direct relationship between failure severity and justice, however. Hess et al. (2003) showed that more severe failures led to higher customer expectations for recovery (i.e., complaint handling), which, in turn, necessitated a higher-quality recovery to restore equity and overall satisfaction with the organization.

Instead, most researchers in marketing have considered failure severity as a moderator of complaint-handling activities on justice. Matilla (2001) showed that failure severity moderated the relationship between recovery type (apology/20% discount versus no apology/no tangible compensation) on satisfaction with complaint handling and loyalty. Similarly, Smith et al. (1999) proposed that a complaint-handling activity would have a greater positive effect on perceived justice when mild (rather than severe) failures were experienced. Their findings were mixed. Failure severity positively moderated the effect of compensation on distributive justice within the hotel and restaurant contexts, as expected. Within a restaurant context, however, the sign of the regression coefficient was reversed, indicating that compensation had a *smaller* effect on distributive justice for less severe failures. Next, they found that severity significantly moderated the effect of speed on procedural justice across both hotel and restaurant contexts. As proposed, speed had less impact as perceptions of severity increased. Finally, the authors found no support for severity × apology or severity x organization-initiated complaint handling on interactional justice.

In sum, previous research has focused much attention on how the characteristics of failure events experienced by customers affect the complaint-handling activities that can be applied to optimize perceptions of justice. Much of this research has focused on failure types and failure severity. These failure characteristics have led researchers to develop a "contingency approach" to complaint handling. Although this approach is intuitively appealing, only partial empirical support has been found for this perspective. This lack of support has led other researchers to consider a more comprehensive set of customer losses to improve the effectiveness of complaint handling in restoring customer perceptions of justice (Hess, 2010). Complicating matters, however, is the reality that customer transcripts describing failure events clearly indicate that most involve multiple and different failures types within the same transaction, making the "contingency approach" inappropriate for most situations. Thus, additional research needs to address how the characteristics of the failure impacts the complaint-handling process and perceptions of justice.

CHARACTERISTICS OF THE ORGANIZATION

Observing the interpersonal interactions that occur between customers and employees during the complaint-handling process clearly exposes the complexities that are inherent in these situations. Undoubtedly, employee roles grow considerably more challenging and stressful during the complaint-handling process. Indeed, confronted by angry customers, employees must remain calm, be empathetic and apologetic, and make often hasty decisions based customers' vague and sometimes questionable accounts of their failure experiences. This is indeed a difficult role for employees. However, very little attention has been given to how internal organizational characteristics such as complaint-handling policies and procedures, training, management support, or climate influences the execution of complaint-handling processes on customer perceptions of justice.

One exception is a study by Homburg and Furst (2005), who examine two general approaches for influencing employee behavior during the complaint-handling process. The *mechanistic approach* involves establishing quality procedures and guidelines for specific activities that must be executed by employees during the complaint-handling process. In contrast, the *organic approach* deals with the influence that a supportive internal organizational environment has on employee behavior during the complaint-handling process. A supportive internal environment can be established through personnel-related activities (training, performance evaluations, rewards), strong service-related culture (shared values, norms, behaviors), and a positive organizational view of complaints and failures as an organizational learning opportunity (Tax & Brown 1998).

Homburg and Furst (2005) obtained strong support for the effects of both the mechanistic and organic approach on distributive, procedural, and interactional justice. Specifically, they found that the quality of process guidelines (e.g., established time standards, status updates, record/forward complaint information) to be significantly related to procedural justice. Likewise, the quality of behavioral guidelines (e.g., direct employees to be polite, helpful, understanding, show concern, and take responsibility for failures) influenced perceptions of interactional justice. Furthermore, the authors showed that quality behavioral guidelines (e.g., policies for providing compensation, decision authority, granting generous compensation, and matching form of compensation to customer needs) were significantly related to distributive justice. Finally, a supportive internal environment for complaint handling directly influenced all three types of justice.

Although these direct relationships are interesting, the researchers also tested for the moderating effects and relative importance of the mechanistic and organic approaches. Homburg and Furst (2005) found that a supportive internal environment for complaint handling moderated the relationship of quality behavioral (outcome) guidelines on interactional (distributive) justice. Similarly, the authors showed that internal supportiveness moderated the effect of the quality of outcome guidelines on distributive justice. The interaction between supportiveness and quality of process guidelines on procedural justice was not supported, however.

The authors also examined the relative strength of the mechanistic and organic approach on satisfaction with complaint handling. By calculating the total effects for each of these approaches using the estimated parameters from the results of structural equation modeling analysis, the authors concluded that the mechanistic approach (0.45) had a stronger total effect than the organic approach (0.27) on satisfaction with complaint handling. This finding supports a view that the most satisfying complaint handling customer outcomes are reached when employees are provided clearly communicated "hard" policies.

This is a very interesting and somewhat surprising finding for practitioners attempting to implement successful complaint-handling programs. In our experience, organizations often rely on a customer-centric and supportive service culture to motivate employees to "do the right thing" for customers during failure events. This finding indicates that, although a supportive culture is mandatory, optimal outcomes are reached when employees are also provided with a well-defined set of policies or directions for dealing with these very complicated situations.

Taken together, previous research on how the characteristics of the organization influences the delivery of an effective complaint-handling process is quite limited but provides some very interesting insights. This research indicates that both an organic and mechanistic approach is necessary to ensure that customers' complaints are properly addressed. Yet, more specific information and direction is needed for the successful introduction and implementation of complaint handling "hard" policies and procedures, training, management support, and culture.

CHARACTERISTICS OF THE PRODUCT/ INDUSTRY

There is plenty of evidence to suggest that the characteristics of the product/industry influence customer perceptions of justice. Table 31.1 provides a brief overview of several studies that were conducted across many contexts. Although this table includes only a subset of studies that reported the relative strength of justice, it illustrates that the findings vary considerably across studies. Only a limited set of studies, however, specifically tests for the effect of product or industry characteristics.

In an early study, Goodwin and Ross (1992) found that customer evaluations of perceived fairness varied across air travel, auto repair, restaurants, and dental services. Furthermore, Maxham and Netemeyer (2002) examined how justice (distributive, procedural, and interactional) influenced satisfaction (with complaint handling and overall), word-of-mouth, and repurchase intentions within the banking and new-home construction industries. Although distributive justice was significantly related to satisfaction with complaint handling for both contexts, interactional justice was only related to this outcome in the banking context. Likewise, the direct effect of satisfaction with complaint handling on overall satisfaction was only supported in the banking context.

The type of service has also been explored as a moderator of the effects of distributive, procedural, and interactional justice on satisfaction with complaint handling. Matilla (2001) uncovered many differences in the relative strength of the three types of justice. Specifically, for restaurants and dry-cleaning services, distributive justice explained the greatest variance in satisfaction with complaint handling, whereas interactional justice was most influential within the hair-stylist context.

Finally, Homburg and Furst (2005) examined whether the type of business (B2B versus B2C) and type of industry (service versus manufacturing) moderated the effects of aspects of the mechanistic approach (e.g., quality of process, behavioral, and outcome guidelines) on distributive, procedural, and interactional justice. They found support for the type of industry (service versus manufacturing) for quality of process, behavioral, and outcome guidelines on procedural, interactional, and distributive justice, respectively. This indicates that these guidelines have a stronger impact on justice in services than in manufacturing industries.

Homburg and Furst (2005) also found support for most of the interactions involving the type of business (B2B versus B2C). Specifically, the type of business (B2B versus B2C) significantly moderated the impact of quality of process guidelines on procedural justice, as well as quality of outcome guidelines on distributive justice. They failed to find support for type of business (B2B versus B2C) × behavioral guidelines on interactional justice. Overall, these results show that for businesses with more business-to-business characteristics, process and outcome guidelines have less impact on justice.

Taken together, some existing research provides reasonably strong evidence that product and industry characteristics have an impact on justice perceptions. These studies suggest some interesting insights that are worth mentioning. First, the results from the Matilla study indicate that distributive justice explained greater variance for dry-cleaning and restaurant services; whereas, interactional justice was most influential in the hair- stylist context. This suggests that for some services, a service outcome cannot be replaced or redone (e.g., poor haircut). Thus, interactional-type complaint-handling activities may be the only available actions at the employee's disposal for restitution. This also illustrates that contextual differences drive the application of different complaint handling activities.

Second, Homburg and Furst (2005) found that the type of industry (B2B versus B2C) moderated the relationships among process guidelines on procedural justice and outcome guidelines on distributive justice. Thus, the unique characteristics of B2B (e.g., small customer base, significant economic value per customer, deeper and long-term relationships, norms of reciprocity, etc.) may influence the complaint-handling process. In these situations, specific complaint-handling guidelines may not be necessary because the appropriate responses to failures are more the norm or convention in these contexts (i.e., "the right thing to do"). A better understanding about how this develops would be highly beneficial to B2C organizations. These finding strongly suggest that a contingency approach to complaint handling may be appropriate due to the unique characteristics of many contexts.

Outcomes of Justice

Relative Strength of Justice

Early marketing studies sought to understand the linkages among distributive, procedural, and interactional justice and important customer outcomes, including overall perceived fairness (Goodwin & Ross, 1992), service encounter satisfaction (Smith et al., 1999), overall satisfaction, word-of-mouth (Maxham & Netemeyer, 2002) repurchase intentions (Maxham & Netemeyer, 2002), and satisfaction with complaint handling (Goodwin & Ross, 1992; Maxham &Netemeyer, 2002; Tax et al., 1998). Thus, these early studies established that successfully handling customer complaints mattered to customers, as evidence showed that customer perceptions of distributive, procedural, and interactional justice were significantly related to several important outcomes.

Findings concerning the relative impact of distributive, procedural, and interactional justice on these consumer outcomes were inconsistent, however (see Table 31.1). Blodgett et al. (1997) found that interpersonal justice explained more variance for repurchase intentions and negative word-of-mouth than distributive or procedural justice. In sharp contrast, Goodwin and Ross (1992) found that distributive justice explained greater variance than procedural or interpersonal justice for satisfaction with complaint handling and perceived fairness. Meanwhile, Maxham and Netemeyer (2002) revealed inconsistent findings for distributive (DJ), procedural (PJ), and interactional (IJ) justice on satisfaction with complaint handling (DJ > IJ > PJ), overall satisfaction with the organization (PJ > IJ > DJ), word-of-mouth (PJ and IJ > DJ for banks; IJ > PJ > DJ for new-home construction) and repurchase intentions (IJ > PJ > DJ).

Up to this point, marketing studies had paid little attention to what became known as the "event mediation" approach explored by the management discipline to explain the inconsistencies observed earlier. This approach suggests that attitudes about a *specific event* fully mediate the effect of distributive, procedural, and interactional justice on overall attitudes about an organization (i.e., system-related attitudes) (Ambrose and Arnaud, 2005; Ambrose et al., 2007). Ambrose et al. (2007) were among the first to recognize that such a relationship may exist within a complaint-handling context—specifically, satisfaction with complaint handling (i.e., event-related attitude) may fully mediate the effects of distributive, procedural, interpersonal, and informational justice on overall attitude toward the organization (i.e., system-related attitudes).

Nomological Network and Mediation Tests

To our knowledge, three studies have attempted to validate the nomological properties of the "event-mediation" approach by explicitly testing whether satisfaction with complaint handling (SATCH) fully mediates the relationships among justice and system-related outcomes (Ambrose et al., 2007; Del Rio-Lanza, Vazquez-Casielles, & Diaz-Martin, 2009; Orsingher, Valentini, & Angelis, 2010). Ambrose et al. (2007) included four types of justice (e.g., distributive (DJ), procedural (PJ), interpersonal (InterJ), and informational (InfoJ)) and compared three nomological models of how these relate to event and system-related outcomes (i.e., a higher-order construct that included measures of trust, commitment and word of mouth). The three models include:

1) *Three-Factor Model*:
   DJ → SATCH
   InterJ, PJ, and InfoJ → Overall Attitude
2) *Four-Factor Model*:
   DJ, InterJ → SATCH
   PJ, InfoJ → Overall Attitude
3) *Event-Mediation Model*:
   DJ, InterJ, PJ, InfoJ → SATCH
   SATCH → Overall Attitude

Ambrose et al. (2007) found that the Event-Mediation Model was superior to the other two models in terms of the variance explained and fit of the model to the data. A test for mediation revealed that SATCH fully mediated the impact of distributive (DJ), procedural (PJ), and interpersonal (InterJ) justice on customers' overall attitude toward the organization, but only partially mediated the impact of informational justice (InfoJ). In addition, distributive justice (DJ) represented a stronger driver of SATCH than the other three types of justice.

Next, Orsingher et al. (2010) performed a meta-analysis to determine if SATCH mediated the effects of DJ, PJ, and IJ on three outcomes that included word of mouth, overall satisfaction, and return intentions. The researchers found that the relative impact of the three types of justice on SATCH varied significantly. Specifically, they discovered that DJ (sample-weighted reliability adjusted average r = 0.65; y_{11} = 0.45, path coefficients of the structural model) was most strongly related to this outcome, followed by IJ (r = 0.52; y_{12} = 0.25) and PJ (r = 0.45; y_{13} = 0.09). Also interesting, full mediation was supported for distributive (DJ) and procedural justice (PJ), but not for interactional justice (IJ). In addition, SATCH was significantly related to word of mouth; SATCH was not related to overall satisfaction or return intention.

Finally, del Rio-Lanza et al. (2009) examined whether negative emotions (i.e., considered an event-related response) mediated the effects of DJ, PJ, and IJ on SATCH. Consistent with cognitive appraisal theory, del Rio-Lanza et al. (2009) argued that negative emotions result from justice assessments which, in turn, impact customers' SATCH. Their results, however, failed to support this perspective because DJ and IJ were *not* significantly related to negative emotions, and PJ was only partially mediated by negative emotions. In terms of relative strength, del Rio-Lanza et al. (2009) found that PJ was more strongly related to SATCH than either IJ or DJ.

In sum, these three studies offer some very interesting insights about the relative strength of justice and the nomological relationships that exist among justice, SATCH, and various outcomes. First, these studies generally support the Event-Mediation Model but with some important exceptions. Both Ambrose et al. (2007) and Orsingher et al. (2010)

provided support for SATCH mediating the effects of justice on system-related attitudes. Orsingher et al. (2010), however, only found this to be the case for word of mouth. They also found that SATCH was *not* related to overall satisfaction or return intentions.

Second, although both Ambrose et al. (2007) and Orsingher et al. (2010) generally support the Event-Mediation Model, they also revealed that some types of justice directly impact outcomes (rather than only effect outcomes through SATCH). Specifically, Ambrose et al. (2007) found that informational justice had a direct and significant impact on system-related attitudes. Likewise, Orsingher et al. (2010) found that IJ directly influenced word of mouth. These results suggest that IJ and informational justice InfoJ may play an interesting and important role in system-level outcomes.

Finally, the findings involving relative strength of justice types on satisfaction with complaint handling were somewhat inconsistent. There was agreement that DJ was the most important driver of satisfaction with complaint handling from Ambrose et al. (2007) and Orsingher et al. (2010). In contrast, del Rio-Lanza et al. (2009) showed that PJ had a greater influence on this event-related outcome than IJ or PJ. This inconsistency suggests that some important moderators may exist that best explains these relationships.

Issues for Future Research

In this chapter we have reviewed the primary research involving justice within a complaint-handling context. This review has exposed several important gaps in the literature that require further attention.

Models to Optimize the Effectiveness of Complaint Handling

Although considerable research over the past several decades has examined the effectiveness of various complaint-handling activities on restoring equity and enhancing customer satisfaction, it is our belief that a better understanding is still required. Thus, we suggest that more research focus on developing a more thorough prescriptive model for complaint handling as a guide to organizations and employees trying to direct and execute an optimal complaint-handling program. Unfortunately, a comprehensive model of this type does not yet exist.

One study to our knowledge has made some progress along these lines. Recently, Hess (2010) proposed *three* theoretical complaint handling models in an attempt to provide some prescriptive direction for this process. First, he proposed a more complex *Matching Model,* whereby the most optimal customer outcomes may occur when the organization applies complaint-handling activities that restore the *eight* losses that he argued could be experienced. Next, he offered the *General-Specific Purpose Model,* which stipulated that some complaint-handling activities may be effective across many types of losses (i.e., general purpose activities), whereas others should only be applied for specific losses (specific-purpose activities).

Third, the *Sequential Model* suggests that fairness is optimized when the order in which different complaint-handling activities is carefully considered. Specifically, customers may have more positive perceptions if favorable (unfavorable) complaint-handling decisions are presented before (after) the process that is followed to make the decision is explained. This model is based on research by van den Bos, Vermunt, and Wilke (1997). In addition to these models, we recommend the *Multiplicative Model,* which suggests that activities related to each type of justice must be applied during the complaint-handling process in order to achieve an optimal outcome. Once again, it should be noted that the effectiveness of any of these models may be contingent on the multitude of contextual differences that have been identified by previous research on complaint handling.

The following set of research questions may help guide such efforts:

- Which specific complaint-handling activities (and levels) are most effective at maximizing customer perceptions of distributive, procedural, and interactional (interpersonal and informational) justice and satisfaction?
- Does a combination of activities provide the most optimal outcomes for customers?
- Does this prescriptive model depend on the type(s) of failures experienced?
- Does "matching" the complaint-handling activity to customer losses provide the most optimal outcome?
- Is "over-compensating" customers for failures advisable?
- What is the role and importance of follow-up communication during this process? Our understanding of informational justice is lacking,

yet Ambrose et al. (2007) found it to have a direct impact on system-related attitudes.

Employee Defensive Responses to Complaint Handling

The next research stream we propose involves developing a better understanding of the employee-specific attitudes that often hinders even a meticulous complaint- handling program. As we discussed previously, the employee role during the complaint-handling process is extremely complex, riddled with stress and uncertainty. These employees possibly have the only opportunity to save a dissatisfied customer from defecting to the competition. The potential lost income, especially when considered over the lifetime of the customer relationship, can be significant. Yet, despite the importance of the employee role during the complaint-handling process very little research has examined these issues in detail.

Our experience with teaching executive programs on complaint handling has uncovered many types of employee defensive responses, with two occurring with notable frequently. The first involves the "failure to take ownership" of the customer's complaint and involves deflecting responsibility to other employees or entities (e.g., organization, management). For example, employees may direct customers elsewhere through responses such as "it's not my fault" or "it's not my responsibility." Worse, employees often blame others for failure events. Statements such as, "they (the buyers) buy the wrong products," "they (management) will not listen," "they (headquarters) make the policy or are unwilling to fix this problem" are representative responses.

Diverting responsibility to others is particularly worrisome because this can alter the attributions that customers formulate about failures. Employees that blame others or "they (management and headquarters)" send a message to customers that company policies are flawed and will not be altered. We contend that flawed company policies are considered highly controllable (i.e., volitional versus non-volitional), and stable (e.g., consistent and likely to recur). These attributions are quite damaging to the overall reputation of the organization (Bitner, 1990; Folkes, 1984; Folkes, Koletsky, & Graham, 1987; Folger & Cropanzano, 1998, 2001).

The second defensive employee response we have uncovered involves "protecting the assets" of the organization. This occurs when the employee feels compelled to validate the customer's account of the failure. Account validation can be costly to both the customer relationship and organization. Fornell (2007) examined this issue financially and found that the cost of validation for 30,000 complaints exceeded addressing every complaint without question by $150,000. This cost differential exists even without considering the lost equity that occurs because the employee failed to be the customer's advocate (Eisenberger et al., 2010).

No research to our knowledge has examined how customer perceptions of justice are affected by employee defensive responses. Our belief is that such responses should significantly impact both *procedural* and *interactional* justice. As we described earlier, Table 31.2 lists the complaint-handling activities that are related to the three types of justice. Given that the assumption of responsibility is related to procedural justice, it is likely that the diversion of responsibility to others by employees may negatively impact customer perceptions of procedural justice. Furthermore, Table 31.2 also indicates that bias and empathy are related to interactional justice. Thus, employee validation of customers' accounts of failures is expected to enhance customer perceptions of bias and indifference and negatively impact interactional justice.

In addition, several moderators may influence the degree to which defensive employee responses affect justice perceptions. These include supervisor's organizational embodiment (SOE) and attributions of globality. In the management literature, supervisor's organizational embodiment (SOE) is the degree to which the employee believes that the supervisor's identity is consistent or shared with the organization (Eisenberger et al., 2010). Thus, within a complaint handling context, customers' perceptions that an employee's defensive responses are representative of the organization should negatively impact their perceptions of justice and attitude toward that organization.

Furthermore, Hess et al. (2007) examine a similar relationship using attributions of globality, which represent the degree to which causes of failures are considered event-specific versus global throughout the organization. They found that previous failures led to greater global attributions about poor employee service behavior, which enhanced dissatisfaction with the organization. In contrast, when no previous failures were experienced, the poorly behaving employee was considered employee-specific and thus had less negative impact on the organization.

Table 31.2 Relationship Among Complaint-Handling Activities and Types of Justice

Types of Justice	Complaint Handling Activities[1]
Distributive Justice[1]	• Tangible compensation in the form of reimbursement • Product/service replacement • Credit • Repair • Refund • Correction
Procedural Justice	• Convenience • Flexibility • Timeliness (of response) • Opportunity to voice • Process control • Process knowledge • Helpfulness • Efficiency • Assumption of responsibility • Follow-up
Interactional Justice	• Empathy • Effort • Politeness • Friendliness • Sensitivity • Apology • Justification • Lack of bias • Honesty • Feedback • Postrecovery follow-up • Candid communication • Thorough explanation about procedures followed • Timely communication about procedures • Tailor communications to specific needs

[1] Based on taxonomy by Tax, Brown, and Chandrashekaran (1998); interactional justice used in their study to represent a combination of interpersonal and informational justice.

Another area that requires additional attention involves the implementation of complaint-handling guidelines for front-line employees. As described earlier, Homburg and Furst (2005) verified the importance of mechanistic and organic guidelines, as well as a supportive organizational environment during the complaint-handling process. Very little research, however, has investigated employee willingness to embrace and follow these guidelines. One possible explanation for employees' reluctance to follow such guidelines is that mechanistic guidelines may be incomplete or impractical for some types of failures. Failures are often very complex and unique situations. Some do not follow typical conventions or fail to fit into one specific type. In these situations, employees must create unique complaint-handling solutions. This entails well-developed skills in creative problem solving. Yet, little research has examined this creative problem-solving exercise or what type of training can effectively improve these skills. The following research questions may help guide advancement of this research stream:

- What factors motivate employees to exhibit defensive responses in response to customer complaints?
- How can organizations reduce employee defensive responses?
- How are customer causal attributions and perceptions of justice influenced by employee defensive responses to complaints?

• How do employee defensive responses to complaints impact customer satisfaction, loyalty, and purchases over time?

• What are employee perceptions of complaint-handling guidelines?

• What factors (customer, employee, policy and organizational) influence employees' willingness to follow complaint-handling guidelines?

• How can organizations develop employee skills in creative problem solving to enhance the quality of complaint-handling solutions for customers?

Multiple Failures and System-Related Customer Perceptions

Another important research stream involves the impact of multiple failures and system-related perceptions on justice. As indicated by Keaveney (1995), many failures contain a number of failure events that contribute to customer perceptions of inequity and dissatisfaction. In our experience, very few failures involve only a single dissatisfying event. Indeed, evidence suggests that approximately 55% of customer switching behavior results from multiple failures (Keaveney 1995). Unfortunately, very little attention has been given to customer responses to multiple failures. We contend that multiple failures can occur during the *same encounter* or *across encounters (*i.e., over time).

Maxham and Netemeyer (2002) examined the impact of multiple failures across encounters. Although they do not specifically examine justice, these authors provide some evidence that multiple failures are linked to justice perceptions. First, they demonstrate that customers who experience two previous failures consider the current failure to be significantly more severe than those who did not have such experiences. This occurred even when those previous failures were handled to satisfaction. Next, the authors found that two failures, even when handled satisfactorily, led to higher expectations for complaint handling. Finally, they found that the increase in complaint- handling expectations was greater from the initial to second failure when customers received satisfactory versus unsatisfactory recovery of the initial failure. Taken together, these findings suggest that customer expectations of justice are influenced by multiple failures, and more research should examine these important and interesting relationships.

Also notable, previous research provides little direction about the effectiveness of complaint-handling activities when multiple failure events occur. Even when well executed, complaint-handling efforts may do little to restore the equity lost due to multiple failures. This suggests that multiple failures cause customers to believe that the organizational system is flawed. If customers do give the organization a chance to resolve the failure, very different complaint-handling activities may be necessary. We argue that restoring customer equity and trust in the organization may entail more personal communications that not only sincerely apologizes for the inconvenience but also provides details about how the organization intends to eliminate these failures in the future. Thus, informational and interpersonal justice may play critical roles under these circumstances. In addition, special and creative invitations for free products or services (i.e., distributive justice) may be needed to persuade the customer to give the organization a second chance and reestablish trust. A better understanding about the effectiveness of these and other unique complaint-handling activities on perceptions of justice is warranted.

Relatedly, customers may perceive some failures at different levels. For example, failures related to unhelpful employee behavior are likely to be viewed as event-specific, whereas failures related to organizational policies (e.g., return policies) or multiple failure events such as those discussed earlier, may be considered systematic of the organization. Little is understood about which failures are considered systematic or how failure events can escalate to systematic status. Systematic failures are likely to severely impact or even terminate customer-organization relationships. Future research should address these issues to better understand customer expectations when multiple failures and systematic failures are experienced.

Taken together, these issues suggest that a complex attribution-updating process may emerge, especially when multiple or systematic failures are experienced. There is little research in marketing that addresses the important relationships among causal attributions and justice. Such a gap is surprising given that attribution theory has been used frequently to explain how customers respond to product and service failures (Bitner 1990; Folkes 1984; Folkes, Koletsky, & Graham 1987). Much of the research listed earlier considers causal attributions as a postfailure response (prerecovery). In contrast, Wirtz and Matilla (2004) include causal attributions as a consequence of distributive, procedural and interactional justice (postrecovery response). Specifically, these authors found that distributive justice (i.e., compensation) and procedural justice (i.e., recovery speed) were significantly related to controllability attributions. Only procedural justice influenced stability attributions.

The management literature recognizes that attributions, especially counterfactual thinking, are an important component of justice perceptions (Folger and Cropanzano 1998, 2001). These authors contend that three components are necessary for fairness perceptions: (1) negative outcomes, (2) attributions of volitional actions (i.e., controllability), and (3) violations of established norms or ethical standards. Some empirical support for portions of this model exists. Nicklin (2013), Nicklin and Williams (2009), and Nicklin, Greenbaum, McNall, Folger, & Williams (2011), found that *would* (i.e., present situation compared to alternative scenario) and *should* (i.e., violation of norm or standard) counterfactual thinking influenced fairness perceptions. Meanwhile, Khan, Quratulain, and Bell (2014) examined the moderating roles of own/other's distributive and procedural justice on internal attributions for episodic envy.

Future research on complaint handling should integrate attributions of causality and justice perceptions to understand how these factors inter-relate to affect important organizational outcomes. The following research questions may help to advance this research stream:

- Can customer equity and satisfaction actually be restored when multiple failures or systematic failures occur?
- If so, what specific complaint-handling activities render the most positive outcomes?
- What failures are considered systematic events? What factors cause failures to escalate to systematic failures?
- What attribution process exists when multiple failures or systematic failures occur?
- How are attributions related to justice during the complaint handling process?

Conclusions

In this paper we have reviewed the existing literature on perceptions of justice in the context of complaint handling. Considerable progress has occurred over the past few decades to understand customers' responses to product and service failures, as well as organizational efforts to restore justice perceptions, satisfaction, and loyalty. Marketing has uncovered, in some detail, the types of failures that frequently occur to customers (Bitner et al., 1990; Keaveney 1995; Kelley et al., 1993). These failure typologies have provided us with some direction about the events that most frequently produce customer dissatisfaction and those that require the development of effective complaint-handling activities.

Research in this area has also made progress in identifying the specific complaint handling activities (see Table 31.2) that are most related to customer perceptions of distributive, procedural, and interactional justice (Tax et al., 1998). More work needs to consider which of these activities are most effective at handling specific types of complaints. Finally, researchers have also provided some support for the event mediation model of justice, demonstrating that justice perceptions are related to event-specific outcomes (e.g., satisfaction with complaint handling) which, in turn, impact system-related outcomes (Ambrose et al., 2007; Orsingher et al., 2010). Relatedly, there has also been limited agreement on the relative strength of distributive, procedural, and interactional justice on satisfaction with complaint handling. Several studies have found that distributive justice explains greater variance on procedural and interactional justice (Ambrose et al., 2007; Orsingher et al., 2010). Certainly these findings have been important advancements in developing strategies to effectively handle customer complaint.

Although considerable progress has been made in this area, it is our opinion that interest in complaint handling has waned to some degree over the past several years. This is quite unfortunate given the significant gaps that remain in our understanding of customer responses to complaints. We believe that there may be several explanations for this trend. First, there may be a general sense in the marketing domain that the gaps in our understanding of this issue are limited. We believe that this is unfounded as demonstrated in the previous section on future research. Next, anecdotal evidence suggests that customers are more frequently turning to social media to voice their dissatisfaction with organizations. As such, the marketing literature has focused much attention on how organizations should appropriately respond to negative word of mouth that appears on social media websites. Possibly customers consider social media to be the only outlet to resolving their service complaints.

In addition, there has been some reluctance from organizations to treat complaints as learning opportunities. Instead, organizations attempt to reduce the numbers of customer complaints and mistakenly believe that the current processes are improving. Instead of improvements in service, a reduction of customer complaints may indicate that issuing complaints is overly difficult, time-consuming, or useless. Relatedly, the marketing literature has recently focused much attention on innovation to improve service processes and thus reduce failure from occurring. In our experience, service innovations, although improving service delivery and processes to some degree, have not eradicated failures from occurring. We find this lack of attention to complaint-handling issues to be quite unfortunate. Despite progress in our understanding of this area, many issues remain relatively unclear or unknown at this point.

References

Adams S. J. (1965). Inequity in social exchanges. in L. Berkowitz (Ed.), Advances in experimental social psychology (pp. 267–299). New York, NY: Academic Press.

Ambrose, M. L., & Arnaud, A. (2005). Distributive and procedural justice: Construct distinctiveness, construct interdependence, and overall justice. In J. Greenberg & J. Colquitt (Eds.), *The handbook of organizational justice* (pp. 59–84). Mahwah, NJ: Erlbaum.

Ambrose, M., Hess, R. L., & Ganesan, S. (2007). The relationship between justice and attitudes: an examination of justice effects on event and system-related attitudes, *Organization Behavior and Human Decision Processes, 107* (1), 21–36.

Bies, R. J., & Moag, J. S. (1986). Interactional justice: Communication criteria for fairness. In B. Sheppard (Ed.), *Research on negotiation in organizations* (Vol. 1, pp. 43–55). Greenwich, CT: JAI Press.

Bitner, M. (1990). Evaluating service encounters: the effects of physical surroundings and employee responses. *Journal of Marketing, 54*(2), 69–82.

Bitner, M., Booms, B. M., & Tetreault, M. S. (1990). The service encounter: diagnosing favorable and unfavorable incidents. *Journal of Marketing, 54*, 71–85.

Blodgett, J. G., Hill, D. J. and Tax S. S. (1997). The effects of distributive, procedural, and interactional justice on post-complaint behavior. *Journal of Retailing, 73* (2), 185–210.

Clemmer, E. C. (1993). An investigation into the relationships of justice and customer satisfaction with services. In R. Cropanzano (Ed.), *Justice in the workplace: approaching fairness in human resource management* (pp. 193–207). Hillsdale, NJ: Erlbaum.

Colquitt J. A. (2001). On the dimensionality of organizational justice: a construct validation of a measure. *Journal of Applied Psychology, 86*, 386–400.

Conlon, D. E., & Murray N. M. (1996). Customer perceptions of corporate responses to product complaints: the role of explanations. *Academy of Management Journal, 39*, 1040–1056.

Del Rio-Lanza, A. B., Vazquez-Casielles, R., & Diaz-Martin, A. M. (2009). Satisfaction with service recovery: Perceived justice and emotional responses. *Journal of Business Research, 62*, 775–781.

Deutsch M. (1985). Distributive justice: A social-psychological perspective. New Haven, CT: Yale University Press.

Eisenberger, R., Karagonlar, G., Stinglhamber, F., Neves, P., Becker, T. E., Gonzalez-Morales, M. G., & Steiger-Mueller, M. (2010). Leader-member exchange and affective organizational commitment: The contribution of supervisor's organizational embodiment. *Journal of Applied Psychology, 95*(6), 1085. doi:10.1037/a0020858

Folger, R., & Cropanzano R. (1998). Organizational justice and human resource management. Thousand Oaks, CA: Sage.

Folger, R., & Cropanzano, R. (2001). Fairness theory: Justice as accountability. In Greenberg, J., & Cropanzano, R. (Eds.), *Advances in organizational justice* (pp. 1–55). Lexington, MA: New Lexington Press.

Folkes, V. (1984) Consumer reactions to product failure: an attributional approach. *Journal of Consumer Research, 10*(2), 398–409.

Folkes, V., Koletsky, S., & Graham, J. (1987). A field study of causal inferences and consumer reaction: The view from the airport. *Journal of Consumer Research, 13*(2), 534–539.

Fornell, C. (2007). *The satisfied customer: winners and losers in the battle for buyer preference.* New York, NY: Palgrave MacMillan.

Gilly, M., & Gelb, B. (1982). Post-purchase consumer processes and the complaining customer. *Journal of Consumer Research, 9*(3), 323–328.

Goodwin, C., & Ross, I. (1992). Consumer responses to service failures: influence of procedural and interactional fairness perceptions. *Journal of Business Research, 25*, 149–163.

Greenberg J. (1993). The social side of fairness: interpersonal and informational classes of organizational justice. In: Cropanzano R. (Ed.), *Justice in the workplace: approaching fairness in human resource management* (pp. 79–103). Hillsdale, NJ: Erlbaum.

Gronroos, C. (1988). Service quality: the six criteria of good perceived service quality. *Review of Business, 9*(Winter), 10–13.

Hess, R., Ganesan, S., & Klein, N. M. (2007). Interactional service failures in a pseudorelationship: the role of organizational attributions. *Journal of Retailing, 83*(1), 79–95.

Hess, R. L. (2010). Failures, losses, and fairness: the customer's perspective. In Schminke, M. (Ed.), *Managerial ethics: managing the psychology of morality* (pp. 155–177). New York, NY: Psychology Press/Routledge Taylor and Francis Group.

Hess, R. L. Jr. (2008). The impact of firm reputation and failure severity on customers' responses to service failures. *Journal of Services Marketing, 22*(5), 385–398.

Hess, R. L. Jr., Ganesan S., & Klein, N. M. (2003). Service failure and recovery: the impact of relationship factors on customer satisfaction. *Journal of the Academy of Marketing Science, 31*(Spring), 127–145.

Hoffman, K., & Bateson, J. (1997). *Essentials of services marketing.* Fort Worth, TX: Dryden Press.

Hollensbe, E. C., Khazanchi, S., & Masterson, S. S. (2008). How do I assess if my supervisor and organization are fair? Identifying the rules underlying entity-based justice perceptions. *Academy of Management Journal, 51* (6),1099–1116.

Homans, G. C. (1961). *Social behavior: Its elementary forms.* New York, NY: Harcourt, Brace & World.

Homburg, C., & Furst, A. (2005). How organizational complaint handling drives customer loyalty: an analysis of the mechanistic and the organic approach, *Journal of Marketing, 69*(3), 95–114.

Keaveney, S. (1995). Customer switching behavior in service industries: an exploratory study, *Journal of Marketing, 59*(2), 71–82.

Kelley, S., & Davis, M. (1994). Antecedents to customer expectations for service recovery, *Journal of the Academy of Marketing Science*, 22, 52–61.

Kelley, S., Hoffman, K. D., & Davis, M. A. (1993). A typology of retail failures and recoveries. *Journal of Retailing, 69*(4), 429–452.

Khan, A. K., Quratulain, S., & Bell, C. M. (2014). Episodic envy and counterproductive work behaviors: is more justice always good? *Journal of Organizational Behavior, 35*, 128–144.

Leventhal, G. S., Karuza, J., & Fry, W. R. (1980). Beyond fairness: a theory of allocation preferences. In Mikula G. (Ed.), *Justice and social interaction* (pp. 167–218). New York, NY: Springer-Verlag.

Lind, E., A., & Tyler, T. R. (1988). *The social psychology of procedural justice.* New York, NY: Plenum.

Matilla, A. S. (2001). The effectiveness of service recovery in a multi-industry setting. *Journal of Services Marketing, 15*(7), 583–596.

Maxham, J. G., & Netemeyer R. (2002). Modeling customer perceptions of complaint handling over time: the effects of perceived justice on satisfaction and intent. *Journal of Retailing, 78*, 239–252.

Nicklin, J. M. (2013). Expertise, counterfactual thinking, and fairness perceptions: a test of fairness theory. *Social Justice Research, 26*, 42–60.

Nicklin, J. M., Greenbaum, R., McNall, L. A., Folger, R., & Williams, K. J. (2011). The importance of contextual variables when judging fairness: an examination of counterfactual thoughts and fairness theory, *Organizational Behavior and Human Decision Processes, 114*(2), 127–141.

Nicklin, J. M., & Williams, K. J. (2009). Reactions to others' mistakes: an empirical test of fairness theory. *The Journal of Psychology: Interdisciplinary and Applied, 143*(5), 533–558.

Oliver, R. (1997). *Satisfaction: A behavioral perspective on the consumer.* New York, NY: McGraw-Hill.

Orsingher, C., Valentini, S., & de Angelis, M. (2010). A meta-analysis of satisfaction with complaint handling in services. *Journal of the Academy of Marketing Science, 38*, 169–186.

Smith, A. K., & Bolton R. N. (2002). The effects of customers' emotional responses to service failures on their recovery effort evaluations and satisfaction judgments. *Journal of the Academy of Marketing Science, 30*(1), 5–23.

Smith, A. K., Bolton, R. N., & Wagner J. (1999). A model of customer satisfaction with service encounters involving failure and recovery. *Journal of Marketing Research, 36*(August), 356–372.

Tax, S. S., & Brown S. (1998). Recovering and learning from service failure, *Sloan Management Review, 40*(1), 75–88.

Tax, S. S., Brown S. W., & Chandrashekaran M. (1998). Customer evaluations of service complaint experiences: implications for relationship marketing. *Journal of Marketing, 62*(April), 60–76.

Thibaut, J., & Walker, L. (1975). *Procedural justice: a psychological analysis.* Hillsdale, NJ: Erlbaum.

van den Bos, K., Vermunt, R., & Wilke, H. A. M. (1997). Procedural and distributive justice: what is fair depends more on what comes first than what comes next. *Journal of Personality and Social Psychology, 72*(1), 95–104.

Wirtz, J., & Matilla, A. S. (2004). Consumer responses to compensation, speed of recovery and apology after a service failure. *International Journal of Service Industry Management, 15*(2), 150–166.

INDEX

K

L

P

Q

R

S